The
AMERICAN NEGRO
Reference Book

The
AMERICAN NEGRO
Reference Book

Edited by John P. Davis

Prentice-Hall, Inc., Englewood Cliffs, New Jersey

The American Negro Reference Book
edited by John P. Davis

Second printing........May, 1966

Library of Congress Catalog Card Number: 65-12919

Printed in the United States of America

T 02816

PRENTICE-HALL INTERNATIONAL, INC., *London*
PRENTICE-HALL OF AUSTRALIA, PTY., LTD., *Sydney*
PRENTICE-HALL OF CANADA, LTD., *Toronto*
PRENTICE-HALL OF INDIA (PRIVATE) LTD., *New Delhi*
PRENTICE-HALL OF JAPAN, INC., *Tokyo*

Preface

The Editor

The purpose of *The American Negro Reference Book* is to bring together in a single volume a reliable summary of current information on the main aspects of Negro life in America, and to present this information in sufficient historical depth to provide the reader with a true perspective. In the footnotes to the text and following most of the chapters are bibliographical references to help the student go more deeply into subjects covered here. At the same time, a full index with numerous cross-references makes possible the use of this book as a convenient spot reference tool to specific questions about the American Negro.

It is hoped that *The American Negro Reference Book* will have many uses. The book as a whole is designed to give the persevering reader a fully-dimensioned picture of the Negro within the context of past and present American Society. Certain chapters read together furnish the student of social sciences or the humanities a rounded discussion of the Negro in these fields. For example, the chapters on "The Negro Population in the United States" (Taeuber and Taeuber), "Patterns of Employment of Negro Men and Women (Ginzberg and Hiestand), and, "The Negro in the National Economy" (Brimmer) form a unit which provides an analysis of the socioeconomic characteristics of the Negro. Or reading the chapters "The Negro and American Music" (George), "Blues, Jazz and the Negro" (Jones), "The Negro in Fine Arts" (Brown), "The Negro and American Entertainment" (Hughes), and, "The Negro Contribution to American Letters" (Bontemps) will give anyone interested in American culture fresh insights into the Negro contribution of this culture. A look at the Table of Contents will soon suggest other useful groupings of the material.

There are books within the book which hold special interest. Dr. John Hope Franklin's "Brief History of the Negro in the United States" is one example. New York State Senator Constance Baker Motley's "The Legal Status of the Negro in the United States" is almost by itself a handbook on civil rights. Other chapters cover in some depth many facets of the Negro experience in the United States.

Changes in the status of the Negro in the United States have occurred and are occurring with such rapidity and over so wide a range that it is impossible to speak with scientific finality about any significant feature of Negro life in America. All the reader may fairly hope to find here is an historical appraisal (brought up to date) of the directions in which Negroes are moving in American society; with possibly here and there a reasoned prediction as to future trends. Rather than weakness, this is, perhaps the book's greatest strength. For in charting the trend of advantages and disadvantages facing the Negro in his search for full citizenship rights, it may well be providing the reader with the most meaningful benchmark that can be found to measure social progress.

Twenty-four scholars have contributed twenty-two articles which make up the main body of material in this book. A list of these contributors and their scholarly interests will be found on page ix. Each of the contributions has been read by one or more review consultants who, while not responsible for the final text presented here, have made valuable criticisms of the material. In listing their names below we make public acknowledgment of our sincere thanks:

Dr. Morroe Berger, professor of sociology, Princeton University; Mr. Arna Bontemps, head librarian, Fisk University; Dr. Lewis A. Coser, professor of sociology, Brandeis University; Dr. W. Allison Davis, professor of education, University of Chicago; Mrs. Dina Epstein, scholar in the field of musical Americana; Mr. James C. Evans, counselor, Office of the Assistant Secretary of Defense; Judge William H. Hastie, United States Circuit Court of Appeals; Dr. Dale Hiestand, assistant professor of economics, Graduate School of Business, Columbia University; Dr. Hylan G. Lewis, director of the Child-Rearing Study, Health and Welfare Council of the District of Columbia; Dr. Vernon McKay, professor of African Studies, Advanced School of International Studies, Johns Hopkins University; Professor Charles Page, Head of the Department of Sociology and Anthropology, Princeton University; Dr. Ira DeA Reid, professor of sociology, Haverford College; Dr. Gregory P. Stone, associate professor of psychology, University of Minnesota; Mr. Robert L. Teague, correspondent on the news staff of the National Broadcasting Company, formerly sports writer on *The New York Times*; Dr. Charles H. Thompson, professor of education, Howard University; Dr. Glenn W. Trimble, Home Missions Research Department, National Council of the Churches of Christ in the USA; Dr. Caroline F. Ware, member of the President's Commission on the Status of Women; Dr. Lauris B. Whitman, executive director, Bureau of Research and Survey, National Council of the Churches of Christ in the USA; Dr. Vincent H. Whitney, chairman, Department of Sociology, University of Pennsylvania, and, representative for Asia, Demographic Division, The Population Council; and, Mr. Hale Woodruff, professor of art education, New York University.

Since this book is sponsored by the Phelps-Stokes Fund it will not be amiss to add a brief word about the sponsor. The Fund was created in 1911 through a bequest in the will of Miss Caroline Phelps Stokes. From its beginning it has sought to stimulate objective study of the American Negro, to aid and encourage the publications which will be of value to an understanding of the Negro at home and abroad. The Fund gave financial assistance to the late Dr. Monroe N. Work for the publication of his monumental *Bibliography of the Negro* (1928). It sponsored exploratory work of the late Dr. W. E. B. DuBois and Dr. Guy B. Johnson of the University of North Carolina which led to the publication of *Encyclopedia of the Negro—Preparatory Volume* (1945). The Fund has sought—especially in this period of profound social change in the life of the Negro in the United States—to encourage a broad program of American Negro studies. The present volume is evidence of the Fund's continued commitment to this goal. We hope to see *The American Negro Reference Book* become the first volume in *The American Negro Reference Shelf*, containing a whole array of timely books by scholars of proven merit. We hope—in time—to see evolve from these monographs an *Encyclopedia of the American Negro.*

The Phelps-Stokes Fund is deeply indebted to a foundation for a generous grant which has made possible its work in this field. The Fund for the Advancement of Education made monies available to "explore the need for and feasibility of a handbook/or encyclopedia on the American Negro." With this help a survey was made of the need of public libraries for current materials on the Negro; and conferences were held at which a number of experts gave wise counsel in the development of the project. To The Fund for the Advancement of Education the Phelps-Stokes Fund wishes publicly to express its thanks.

Finally, the editor would exercise his prerogative of acknowledging his own debts. Sincere thanks are most certainly due the Trustees and Officers of the Fund for their confidence in the project; and warm appreciation must be extended to the entire staff of the Fund for the day-to-day encouragement and cooperation it has given the editor during the preparation of this book. A special debt of gratitude is owing to the Chairman of the Board of Trustees, Mr. I. N. P. Stokes; to the President of the Fund, Dr. Frederick D. Patterson; and, to Trustees, Dr. Ralph J. Bunche and Dr. Carroll V. Newsom. From the beginning they have seen the great need for and high purpose of this book and have unstintingly shared their time and wisdom to see it through.

Contributors

Gordon W. Allport. Professor of Psychology, Harvard University, Cambridge, Massachusetts. Past President of the American Psychological Association and recipient of the Gold Medal from the American Psychological Foundation (1963). Author of *The Nature of Prejudice, Personality and Social Encounter* and many other books in his field.

Calvin L. Beale. Head, Farm Population Analysis Section, Economic Research Service, U.S. Department of Agriculture; formerly statistician with the Population Division, Bureau of the Census. Winner of the Superior Service Award of the Department of Agriculture for writings on the farm population. Co-author [with Donald J. Bogue], *Economic Areas of the United States* [Glencoe, Ill. The Free Press, 1961]; contributor to numerous government and social science bulletins and magazines.

Horace Mann Bond. Dean of the School of Education, Atlanta University, Atlanta, Georgia. Author of *Education of the Negro in American Society; The Search for Talent*; Contributor to *Encyclopaedia Britannica, Dictionary of American History, Encyclopedia of Modern Education* and to leading professional journals and anthologies.

Arna Bontemps. Head Librarian, Fisk University, Nashville, Tennessee. Author of *American Negro Poetry; The Story of the Negro, Black Thunder, God Sends Sunday;* coauthor (with Langston Hughes) *The Poetry of the Negro;* (with Countée Cullen) *St. Louis Woman* (a musical play); (with W. C. Handy) *Father of the Blues;* (with Jack Conroy) *They Seek a City;* and numerous other books, collaborations, poems and magazine articles.

Andrew F. Brimmer. Assistant Secretary for Economic Affairs, United States Department of Commerce, Washington, D. C. Formerly Assistant Professor of Finance, Wharton School of Finance, University of Pennsylvania. Author of *Life Insurance Companies in the Capital Market.*

Marion Brown. Young freelance writer currently devoting his attention to the fine arts and avant garde music, educated at Morehouse College and Howard University.

Virgil A. Clift. Professor of Education, New York University, New York, New York. Formerly Member of U. S. State Department Mission to Pakistan. Editor of the Sixteenth Yearbook of the John Dewey Society, *Negro Education in America.*

John P. Davis. Editor of Special Publications, Phelps-Stokes Fund, New York, New York.

Joseph H. Douglass. Chief, Program Analysis and Scientific Communications Staff, Office of the Director, National Institutes of Health, Public Health Service, United States Department of Health, Education and Welfare. Formerly Fulbright Lecturer, Cairo, Egypt. Author of *The Negro Family's Search for Economic Security* (monograph of U. S. Department of Health, Education and Welfare); "Aspects of Marriage and Family Relations Among the Fellaheen," *Journal of Marriage and Family Relations* (April 1954).

St. Clair Drake. Professor of Sociology and Director of the African Studies Program, Roosevelt University, Chicago, Illinois. Formerly Professor and Head of the Department of Sociology, University College of Ghana; visiting Professor of Sociology, Stanford University, Palo Alto, California. Author of (with Horace R. Cayton) *Black Metropolis;* contributor of numerous articles on Africa to leading magazines and anthologies.

G. James Fleming. Professor of Political Science and Director of Institute for Political Education, Morgan State College, Baltimore, Maryland. Author of *An All-Negro Ticket in Baltimore* and other studies of the Negro in politics.

John Hope Franklin. Professor of American History, University of Chicago, Chicago, Illinois. Formerly Chairman of the Department of History, Brooklyn College, Brooklyn, New York; and William Pitt Professor of American History and Institutions, Cambridge University, England. Author of *From Slavery to Freedom, The Militant South, Reconstruction After the Civil War, Emancipation Proclamation* and other books.

Dr. Zelma George. Lecturer. Formerly Opera Singer. Sang title role in *The Medium* by Gian-Carlo Menotti on Broadway. Member of the U. S.

Delegation to the 15th General Assembly of the United Nations. Author of *A Guide to Negro Music: Toward a Sociology of Negro Music*, a doctoral dissertation submitted in fulfillment of requirements for a doctorate at New York University.

Eli Ginzberg. Professor of Economics, Graduate School of Business, Columbia University, New York, New York. Director, Conservation of Human Resources Project, Columbia University. Author of *The Uneducated, The Negro Potential, The Nation's Children* and other books.

Dale L. Hiestand. Assistant Professor of Business Economics, Graduate School of Business, Columbia University, New York, New York. Research Associate, Conservation of Human Resources Project, Columbia University. Author of *Economic Growth and Employment Opportunities for Minorities*.

Langston Hughes. Poet, playwright, author, lecturer. Author of *Selected Poems, The Big Sea* (an autobiography), *Pictorial History of the Negro, The Best of Simple, Troubled Island* (an opera with William Grant Still), *Mulatto* (a play) and a wide assortment of volumes of poetry, biography, essays, as well as a large number of recordings from his writings and songs.

Le Roi Jones. Poet and playwright. Instructor of Creative Writing at The New School for Social Research, New York City. Author of *Blues People, The Dutchman* (a play), *The Black Bohemians*. He is a frequent writer on jazz in such magazines as *Downbeat, Metronome* and *Jazz Review*.

C. Eric Lincoln. Professor of Social Relations and Director of Institute for Social Relations, Clark College, Atlanta, Georgia. Formerly Visiting Professor, Social Relations and Public Affairs, Dartmouth College. Author of *The Black Muslims in America*.

Constance Baker Motley. President of the Borough of Manhattan, City of New York. Formerly Associate Counsel, Legal Defense and Educational Fund of the National Association for the Advancement of Colored People; and member of the Senate of the State of New York. Member of the New York Bar and admitted to practice before the United States Supreme Court. Author of *The Constitution—Key to Freedom*.

Dr. Jeanne L. Noble. Associate Professor of Education, Center for Human Relations and Community Studies, New York University, New York, New York. Consultant, President's Task Force in War Against Poverty. Past

President Delta Sigma Theta Sorority. Assistant National Secretary, Girl Scouts, U.S.A. Author of *The Negro Woman's College Education.*

Thomas Fraser Pettigrew.   Associate Professor of Social Psychology, Harvard University, Cambridge, Massachusetts. Author of *A Profile of the Negro American;* (with E. Q. Campbell) *Christians in Racial Crisis.*

Harry V. Richardson.   President of The Interdenominational Theological Center, Atlanta, Georgia; President of Georgia Council of Churches. Author of *Dark Glory.*

Alma F. Taeuber.   Research Associate, Department of Sociology, University of Wisconsin, Madison, Wisconsin. Coauthor (with Karl E. Taeuber) of *Negroes in Cities: Residential Segregation and Neighborhood Change* (Aldine Press, 1965).

Karl E. Taeuber.   Professor of Sociology, University of Wisconsin, Madison, Wisconsin. Coauthor (with Alma F. Taeuber) of "The Negro as an Immigrant Group" and "The Changing Character of Negro Migration" (*American Journal of Sociology,* January 1964 and January 1965); author of "Negro Residential Segregation: Trends and Measurements" (*Social Problems,* Summer 1964).

Robin M. Williams, Jr.   Professor of Sociology, Cornell University, Ithaca, New York. Past President of the American Sociological Association and Fellow at the Center for Behavioral Sciences. Author of *Strangers Next Door, American Society.* Coauthor (with Samuel A. Stouffer and others) of *The American Soldier.*

James Q. Wilson.   Associate Professor of Government, Harvard University, Cambridge, Massachusetts. Director of the Joint Center for Urban Studies of Massachusetts Institute of Technology and Harvard University. Author of *Negro Politics.* Coauthor (with E. C. Banfield) of *City Politics.*

Contents

List of Tables

Chapter 3
The Negro in American Agriculture

Chapter 4
Employment Patterns of Negro Men and Women

Chapter 5
The Negro in the National Economy

Chapter 6
The Urban Negro Family

Chapter 7
Educating the American Negro

Chapter 14
The Negro Scholar and Professional in America

Chapter 15
The Negro in the Armed Forces of America

Chapter 23
The Negro in American Sports

chapter 1

A Brief History of the Negro in the United States

John Hope Franklin

NEW WORLD ADVENTURE

Negro Pioneers in the New World

It is significant that the first Negroes in the New World were not from Africa but from Europe. Their involvement in the European exploration of the New World in the fifteenth and sixteenth centuries is an important commentary on the connections that had developed between Europe and Africa by that time. As early as the fourteenth century, if not earlier, Europeans had begun to bring Africans into Europe. As the Spanish and Portuguese made contacts with the coast of Africa, going as far as the Gulf of Guinea, they began to appreciate the possibility of using Africans as an important source of labor for European ports, businesses and homes. Thus, they took Africans to Europe and made servants of them, justifying this invasion of human rights by declaring that Africans would have the opportunity to cast off their heathenism and become Christians.

It was not long before Europeans were selling Negro servants in their home markets, as well as other African imports. Soon the slave trade came to be accepted as an important part of European commerce. Spanish and Portuguese traders appreciated the economic advantages afforded by the African slave trade; and by the time Portugal's remarkable Prince Henry died in 1460 the trade in black men had become more than a passing fancy. Europeans were becoming accustomed to having Negroes do their work; and already they were looking into the possibility of using them in other ways. It was only natural, therefore, that as Europeans turned their eyes toward the New World they would enlist the services of the Africans to help further the cause of Christianity as well as to aid in their plans for domination of the New World.

There was never a time in the Europeans' exploration and exploitation of the New World when they were without the services of some black Europeans. The claim that Pedro Alonso Niño of Columbus' crew was a Negro has never been disproved; and if he was indeed a Negro he performed more than yeoman service for the Admiral of the Ocean Sea. In 1501 Spain lifted her ban on the taking of Negroes to the New World,

1

and after that time Negroes almost invariably accompanied Spanish explorers and settlers. There were at least thirty Negroes with Balboa when he discovered the Pacific Ocean in 1513. When Hernando Cortes conquered Mexico in 1519 he had several Negroes with him, one of whom planted and harvested the first wheat crop in the New World. Alvarado, the intrepid explorer of Equatorial South America, had two hundred Negroes with him when he arrived at Quito; and in his Peruvian expedition Pizarro took several Negroes along. Indeed, they were the ones who took their leader into the cathedral after he was murdered.

When the Spanish and Portuguese explorers moved into what is now the United States, Negroes were with them. They accompanied Narváez on his expedition in 1527 and were with Cabeza de Vaca in the exploration of the Southwest. Perhaps the outstanding Negro explorer was Estevanico, Little Stephen, who went deep into the interior of the Southwest. When he encountered hostile Indians, he insisted that he was the emissary of white men; but they killed him, believing him to be an imposter. Even so, he had paved the way for the conquest of the Southwest by the Spaniards.

The French also had their Negro servants when they undertook their explorations of the New World. In the Canadian expeditions, Negroes were with the Jesuit missionaries. As the French opened up the Mississippi Valley in the seventeenth century, Negroes assisted in the settlement of the region. At the places that were later to be known as St. Louis and New Orleans, French Negroes helped plant the flag of France and establish the culture that was to make an indelible mark on the interior of the United States.

Exploitation of the rich natural resources of the New World was the primary aim of the Europeans. For this they needed an abundance of labor. Soon it became obvious that Indians would not do. The great susceptibility of Indians to the diseases of the Europeans, their firm commitment to a much simpler economic system, and their determination to escape the wrath and inhumanity of the Europeans ruled them out as a permanent and satisfactory source of labor. Europeans not only wanted more tractable servants, but they also wanted them in greater quantities than the Indians could provide. They used Indians to the extent possible, but they soon turned to other possible sources.

Europeans did not at first regard Negroes as the solution. They first considered the poorer Europeans. In the first half of the seventeenth century, these landless, penniless whites were brought over in considerable numbers. Some were voluntary indentured servants, others were prisoners working out their fines, and still other powerless Europeans, especially the English, were kidnaped and sold into servitude. As Eric Williams has indicated in his *Capitalism and Slavery,* the horrors that the poor whites of Europe experiencd were as great as any experienced by any group in the later years of the African slave trade.

The English gradually came to realize that white servants would not do, either. Whites tended to become restive, and when they ran away it was extremely difficult to identify them as servants bound to a particular master. Some of them, conscious of their rights as Englishmen, began to sue their masters for illegal detention. Even if these white servants worked well, their terms of service were not indefinite; and the task of recruiting new white workers was at best irksome. Englishmen soon came to realize that Negroes presented few of the difficulties they were encountering with whites. Negroes could be purchased outright, and their years of servitude would be for life, making them cheaper in the long run. Since they came from a pagan land, moreover, with no exposure to the principles of Christian brotherhood, they could be subjected to the most rigid discipline with impunity. And the masters could rationalize that they were giving Negroes advantages of Christianity to which they would not be exposed otherwise. More and more, this appeared to Europeans to be the solution; and finally they embraced it with enthusiasm.

The Beginnings of the Slave Trade

In 1517 the great Spanish bishop, Bartolomé de Las Casas, took a step that greatly encouraged the establishment of slavery in the New World. He had noticed with apparent horror the wholesale destruction of the Indians by the Spaniards in the effort to force them to work. Convinced that the Indians could never become good slaves and hoping, at any rate, to make good Christians out of them, he persuaded Charles V to encourage immigration to the New World by permitting Spaniards to import twelve slaves each. This step may be regarded as the formal opening of the slave trade to the New World. In subsequent years an increasing number of Africans was imported into the Spanish colonies, at times by Dutch traders, at other times by Portuguese, French or English. Soon the trade had become a huge, profitable enterprise. By 1540 the annual importation of Negro slaves into the West Indies had reached ten thousand.

The trade continued, and by the seventeenth and eighteenth centuries it was largely in the hands of Dutch, French and English companies. In 1621 the Dutch West India Company was organized with a monopoly both of the African trade and of trade with the Dutch colonies in the New World. This company then challenged the right of the Portuguese to trade on the coast of Africa, and by the middle of the century it had gained a substantial foothold there. Perhaps the English would have challenged the Dutch, but they were preoccupied with civil wars at home. Soon the Dutch slavers were visiting the ports of almost all the American colonies, and were even engaged in trade with the French and Spanish colonies.

The trade was so profitable that the English were not content to see the Dutch reap all the benefits. The Dutch wars with France and England, moreover, generally weakened the position of the leading slave trading power, giving the English an opportunity to make a bid for at least a portion of the rich trade. Although the French would make a rather feeble effort to enter the picture, they were never a match for the English who seemed to be in the ascendancy in this area as well as in others.

English interest in Africa and the slave trade was by no means new when she made a bid for leadership in the second half of the seventeenth century. Before the end of the reign of Henry VII in 1509 traders from Britain were establishing connections along the Guinea coast and at other important points in Africa. England contented herself by trading in gold, ivory and spices until 1562, when Captain John Hawkins broke the Portuguese monopoly in Africa and the Spanish monopoly in the New World by taking slaves from Portuguese Africa to Spanish America. It thus became easy for James I in 1618 to grant a charter to the Company of Adventurers of London, trading into parts of Africa which had control over the West Coast trade. In 1631 Charles I granted a group of traders a 31-year monopoly of the trade in Guinea, Benin and Angola. This became the pattern by which the English claimed a large share of the African trade in human flesh.

Competition for the slave trade was keen not only among nations but also among trading companies within countries. In England, for example, many individuals and organizations, including the powerful East India Company, were interested in the African slave trade. As the demand for slaves in the New World increased and as conditions in Europe remained unsettled, it seemed that any group might have a chance to reap some benefits from the slave trade. The restoration in England brought with it a semblance of stability as well as renewed activity in Africa. In 1672 the King chartered the Royal African Company, which held a monopoly for a decade, and which dominated the slave trade for another fifty years. It assumed the responsibility for driving the Dutch and the French out of West Africa, and its efforts were crowned with considerable success. It held sway until 1731 when, with its margin of profits in the slave trade dwindling, it began to devote its attention to ivory and gold dust.

What the Royal African Company failed to do in driving the other European powers from Africa, the English succeeded in doing in the eighteenth century. In a series of wars the English had defeated the

Dutch, thus dealing a powerful blow to Dutch prestige in Africa. Then the English defeated the French, thereby securing in 1713 the exclusive right to carry slaves to the Spanish colonies. With a strengthened navy and almost unlimited resources England could now undertake to provide not only her own colonies with slaves but those of the other European nations as well. As English hegemony in the New World became secure, the slave trade provided an important source of strength and wealth.

Slave Trading as Big Business

In the eighteenth century the African slave trade became an important economic institution; and since the English dominated it, their slave-trading practices became standard. Slavers left European ports laden with goods to be used in the trade: cotton textiles, brass, pewter, beads, gunpowder, whiskey, brandy and rum. They proceeded to the trading posts maintained by the company or the country, where the factors in charge maintained contacts with key Africans. The factors secured permission from the chief who was plied with gifts, to trade on his domain. From this point on it was not too difficult to round up some Africans—slaves of the chiefs or captives in war —to be sold. The price varied, of course, depending on the age and condition of the slave, the period of trading and the location of the post.

It was not at all unusual for a slaver to make calls at a number of posts before a full complement of slaves was secured for the voyage to the New World. On occasion it was necessary for a slaver to call at four or five posts before securing a sufficient number of slaves. Once that was done, the captain of the slaver had to make certain that he had sufficient provisions to make the crossing to America. Foodstuffs, water and medicines were indispensable to a successful voyage. If any room was left, spices and ivory were regarded as certain to bring revenue which the captain might not even have to report to the company that had engaged him.

Perhaps the most poignant aspect of the transaction was the resistance that the slaves put up to their forced sale and incarceration on the floating prison. Fierce wars broke out between tribes when the members of one sought to capture members of another for the purpose of selling them to traders. Even after the slaves were sold and chained, it was necessary to guard them heavily lest they make a futile attempt to escape and injure or kill themselves in the process. One trader remarked that the Negroes were "so wilful and loth to leave their own country that they have often leap'd out of the canoes, boat and ship, into the sea, and kept under water till they were drowned." They preferred a watery grave or to be devoured by sharks to enslavement in some faraway land.

Mankind has experienced few tortures as ghoulish and uncivilized as the transportation of slaves from Africa to the New World, known as the "Middle Passage." The men were chained two by two, the right wrist and ankle of one to the left wrist and ankle of another. They were then sent to the hold or to the "house" that the sailors had built on deck. On some ships the women and children were allowed to wander about almost anywhere by day, the women being regarded as fair prey for the sailors; but at night they were sent to rooms other than those occupied by the men. There were two schools of thought among captains of slavers regarding the loading of slaves. The "loose packers" believed that by giving the slaves a bit more room and better food, they reduced the mortality and could get a better price for healthier slaves in the New World. The "tight packers" argued that although the loss of life might be greater if they started out with larger numbers, they were likely to arrive with more and thereby get a larger profit from the cargo.

Regardless of the point of view of the captains, most ships transported many more Negroes than could be adequately accommodated; and this is undoubtedly responsible for the high incidence of disease and death during the Middle Passage. Usually they were packed in so close that they had no room even to sit upright during the entire voyage. In some instances they were packed close together like books on a shelf. Remarking on a situation such as this, one contemporary said, "The poor creatures, thus cramped, are likewise in irons for the most part which makes it difficult for them to turn or move or attempt to rise or to lie down without hurting themselves or each other. Every morning, perhaps, more instances than one are found of the living and the dead fastened together."

Because of the enormous profits made by some slavers the "tight loaders" gained the ascendancy. Despite the death from a variety of maladies, it was not unusual for a ship carrying 250 slaves to net as much as £7,000 on one voyage. Profits of 100 percent were not uncommon for Liverpool merchants. As a result there emerged in England and, to a lesser extent, on the Continent a class of wealthy men whose new position was firmly based on the trade in men. They gained not only economic power but also political influence and were in a position to resist for many years the efforts of the humanitarians to control the slave trade and, ultimately, to put a stop to it.

There is no way of knowing how many Negroes were taken in Africa and sent on to slavery in the New World. In the period between 1783 and 1793 Liverpool traders alone were responsible for sending out some 300,000 slaves, while in the following decade they were certainly responsible for as many if not more. It has been estimated that 2,750,000 were sent in the seventeenth century, 7 million in the eighteenth, and 4 million in the nineteenth. Millions died en route, and millions who arrived were permanently disabled. Millions arrived and were sold into slavery. Whatever the total number, whether ten or fifteen millions or more, it is a remarkable commentary on the profitableness of the trade as well as on the brutality and ruthlessness of the Europeans who were willing to enjoy the luxury and wealth afforded by such an operation.

Early Slave Practices

African slavery thus solved the labor problem for Europeans in the New World. The seventeenth century, which witnessed the coming of age of the slave trade, also witnessed the rapid growth of colonial enterprise in the New World. In the Caribbean, where the European foothold was strongest, one sees the evolution of the institution of slavery as the vehicle for the development of the earliest major economic enterprise on this side of the Atlantic.

Negroes were first used on the tobacco plantations of the Caribbean islands. As the European tobacco market became glutted, the Caribbean planters turned to sugar and other staples for their money crops. As sugar became a major crop, the importation of Negroes into the Caribbean began in earnest. In 1640 there were only a few hundred Negroes in Barbados. By 1645, after the new sugar plantations had proved themselves, there were six thousand slaves there. By the middle of the century the Negro population had increased to twenty thousand. A similar growth in the slave population could be seen on the other Caribbean islands. Indeed, the importation of slaves accelerated to such a degree that by the end of the century, when the demand for slaves on the islands was declining, the importation not only continued but, in some cases, increased.

There were few humanizing influences on the institution of slavery in the West Indies in the seventeenth century. The slaves were "black gold," as their labor produced the profits that made the islands the favorite colonies of the European powers. Many of the landlords were in London or some other European city; and their only interest was in the profits that were increasing annually. The islands were not places of residence, but merely sources of wealth; and the slaves were not human beings, but merely factors in production. Overseers and plantation managers were expected to perform any tasks that increased profits, and this included getting work out of slaves by whatever method seemed necessary. Slaves who offered resistance were to be "broken in," and this meant flogging or any other form of torture that would get results.

Since the Negro population tended to exceed that of the whites, the laws governing the conduct of Negroes were designed to provide a maximum of security for the whites as well as to make the Negroes effective workers. Slaves had few if any rights in the English colonies, while in the French colonies, though they were recognized as persons with souls, conditions were scarcely better. But the laws did not succeed in creating a tractable, docile slave population. There were uprisings in Jamaica, Barbados, Saint Domingue and elsewhere. Groups of Negroes organized themselves into Maroons and defied the whites to attempt to subjugate them. On occasion, therefore, it became necessary for the whites in the Caribbean to resort to the force of arms to keep the Negro slaves in line.

By the end of the seventeenth century the Caribbean was no longer the principal source of wealth of Europe in the New World. Already the Portuguese had Brazil as their main New World colony, while the Spaniards had numerous important colonies in North and South America. The British were turning their attention more and more to their colonies that extended from the Carolinas to Massachusetts; and they were concentrating their attention on the mainland. They began to import slaves from Africa to the mainland and to send many of them from the islands to the mainland. Soon the European powers expected to increase their profits many times over by utilizing the experience they gained in the island colonies to establish a much more elaborate system of plantation slavery in Virginia, the Carolinas and similar mainland colonies than had ever existed in the islands. If there was disappointment over the decline in Jamaica, there was hope for unlimited expansion in Maryland. More and better slaves would make the difference.

COLONIAL SLAVERY

Virginia's Leadership

The twenty Negroes who were put ashore at Jamestown in 1619 by the captain of a Dutch frigate were not slaves in a legal sense. And, at the time, the Virginians seemed not to appreciate the far-reaching significance of the introduction of Negroes into the fledgling colony. These were simply more of the indentured servants; they happened to have been black. They were listed as servants in the census counts of 1623 and 1624; and as late as 1651 some Negroes whose period of service had expired were being assigned land in much the same way as it was being done for whites who had completed their indenture. During its first half-century of existence Virginia had many Negro indentured servants; and the records reveal increasing numbers of free Negroes.

Only after Virginia had failed to satisfy her labor needs with Indians and indentured servants did she give serious thought to the "perpetual servitude" of Negroes. She began to see what her neighbors in the Caribbean had already seen, that Negroes could not easily escape without being identified, that they could be disciplined, even punished, with impunity since they were not Christians, and that the supply seemed inexhaustible. Black labor was precisely what Virginia needed in order to speed up the clearing of the forests and the cultivation of larger and better tobacco crops. All that was missing was the legislative approval of a practice in which many Virginians were already involved.

The actual statutory recognition of slavery in Virginia came in 1661. The status of Negroes already there was not affected if they had completed their indenture and were free. Indeed, the recognition was almost casual and was first indicated in a law directed at white servants: "That in case any English servant shall run away in company with any negroes who are incapable of making satisfaction by addition of time . . . that the English so running away . . . shall serve for the time of said negroes absence as they are to do for their owne. . . ." In the following year Virginia took another step toward slavery by indicating in her laws that children born in the colony would be held bond or free according to the condition of the mother. Some mitigation to the recognition of slavery was intended by the law of 1667 that provided that slaves could be baptized as Christians. In order to protect the institution of slavery, however, the law continued, "the conferring of baptisme doth not alter the condition of the person as to his bondage or freedome." Thus, "diverse masters, freed from this doubt, may more carefully endeavour the propagation of christianity."

At first the Negro population of the colony grew quite slowly. In 1625 there were only twenty-three Negroes there; and as late as the middle of the century scarcely three hundred could be counted. With the chartering of the Royal African Company in 1672 the shipment of slaves into the colony was accelerated. By the end of the century they were being brought in at the rate of more than one thousand per year. It was in the eighteenth century that the Negro population grew at what some Virginians began to view as an alarming rate. In 1708 there were 12,000 Negroes and 18,000 whites. By 1756 there were 120,156 Negroes and 173,316 whites. By that time Negroes outnumbered the whites in many Virginia communities.

Although Virginians greatly appreciated the importance of Negro slave labor in the development of the colony, they soon became apprehensive about such large numbers of Negroes living among the whites. Already whites and Negroes were mixing, and a mulatto population was emerging.

There were, moreover, the persistent rumors of conspiracies of rebellion; and many whites feared for their lives. Those who were apprehensive took the lead in attempting to control the importation of slaves, but the commercial interests fought off these attempts with all the resources at their command. For the time being they were successful.

But the fears of insurrection were not groundless. Within two years after the first statutory recognition of slavery, the Negroes of Virginia were showing clear signs of dissatisfaction and had begun to plot rebellion against their masters. In 1687 a group of slaves in the Northern Neck planned an uprising during a funeral, but it was discovered before it could be carried out. Rumors continued, and plots of varying sizes were uncovered. Where there were no plots there was general disobedience and lawlessness. By 1694 the Virginia slaves had become so ungovernable that Governor Andros complained that there was insufficient enforcement of the code which, by that time, had become elaborate enough to cover most activities and relationships of slaves.

The Virginia slave code, borrowing heavily from practices in the Caribbean and serving as a model for other mainland codes, was comprehensive. No slave was permitted to leave the plantation without the written permission of his master. Slaves wandering about without such permits were to be taken up and returned to their masters. Slaves found guilty of murder or rape were to be hanged. For major offenses, such as robbing a house or a store, a slave was to receive sixty lashes and be placed in the pillory where his ears were to be severed from his head. For petty offenses, such as insolence and associating with whites or free Negroes, they were to be whipped, maimed or branded. The docility of which masters boasted was thus achieved through the enactment of an all-inclusive code containing provisions for punishment designed to "break" the most irascible "blacks" in the colony. With the sheriffs, the courts and even the slaveless whites on their side, the masters should have experienced no difficulty in maintaining peace among their slaves.

Slavery in Maryland

While slavery in Maryland was not recognized by law until 1663, the first Negroes introduced into the colony were sold into slavery immediately. As early as 1638 there was reference to slavery in some discussions in the legislature; and in 1641 the governor himself owned a number of slaves. The colonists had no difficulty, therefore, in turning their attention to the problem of the status of Negroes and concluding that legislation was necessary to fix their status as slaves. The law of 1663 was rather drastic. It undertook to reduce all Negroes in the colony to slavery even though some were already free, and it sought to impose the status of slaves on all Negroes to be born in the colony regardless of the status of their mothers. It was not until 1681 that the law was brought in line with established practices by declaring that Negro children of white mothers and children born of free Negro mothers would be free.

The slave population of Maryland was slow to increase, not because of any disinclination on the part of the colonists to own slaves, but because they were not in ample supply during the early years of the colony. This is the principal reason why, during the restoration period, laws were enacted to encourage and facilitate the importation of slaves. In 1671 the legislature declared that the conversion of slaves to Christianity would not affect their status. Masters now felt that they could import African heathens, convert them to Christianity and thus justify the act of holding them in slavery. By the end of the century the importation of slaves was increasing steadily. In 1708 the governor reported that six or seven hundred had been imported during the preceding ten months. By 1750 there were 40,000 Negroes as compared with 100,000 whites.

As in Virginia, the Negroes of Maryland early showed resentment against their status as slaves. In several instances white masters died at the hands of their slaves; and there was more than one case of a Negro cook poisoning her owner. In 1742 seven Negroes were executed for the murder of their master. Others were convicted for committing acts of sabotage such as arson, stealing of property and the brutal treatment of livestock.

The increase in the Negro population and the whites' fear for their own safety led to the enactment of stringent laws covering the conduct and activities of Negroes. In 1659 came the laws relating to the return and treatment of fugitive slaves. Soon there were laws forbidding slaves to deal in stolen goods and liquor, and laws providing for the punishment of free Negroes and slaves found guilty of murder, arson, larceny, association with whites, insolence and going about without permission. Punishment ranged from death to branding and whipping. Enforcement was rigorous, but clemency was not rare. There were numerous examples of intervention on the behalf of accused slaves by masters who, while approving the strict enforcement of the law, would want "on just this occasion" a bit of leniency.

The Carolinas and Georgia

It was a foregone conclusion that slaves would be introduced into the Carolinas as soon as was feasible. After all, four of the proprietors of the colony were members of the Royal Africa Company and fully appreciated the profits that could come from the slave trade. By 1680, moreover, the example of Virginia and Maryland led them to believe that Carolina could become a prosperous colony with plantation slavery as one of the important foundations. Perhaps John Locke had these things in mind when, in his *Fundamental Constitutions,* he wrote, "every freeman of Carolina shall have absolute power and authority over his negro slaves, of what opinion or religion soever." This sanctioned slavery and protected it against any possible destruction that might have come through the conversion of slaves to Christianity.

Negroes were in the Carolina colony virtually from the beginning. This was undoubtedly the result of the deliberate encouragement of the importation of slaves by the proprietors themselves. In 1663 they offered to the original settlers twenty acres for every Negro man slave and ten acres for every Negro woman slave brought into the colony in the first year. Somewhat smaller incentives were offered for the importation of slaves in subsequent years. Perhaps such legislation had the desired results, for twenty years after the original settlements, the Negro population in the Carolinas was equal to that of the white. By 1715 the Negroes led the whites with 10,500 to 6,250. In 1724 there were three times as many Negroes as whites, and the growth of the Negro population was to continue for decades to come.

As in the other colonies the growth of the Negro population led to the enactment of legislation looking to its control. As early as 1686 the Carolina colony forbade Negroes to engage in any kind of trade; and it enjoined them from leaving their masters' plantation without written authorization. In 1722 white justices were authorized to search Negroes for guns, swords "and other offensive weapons" and to take them unless the Negro could produce a permit less than one month old authorizing him to carry such a weapon. Patrols were given authority to search Negroes and to whip those deemed to be dangerous to peace and good order. Punishments for offenses by slaves were summary and severe.

The Carolinians had not established their controls too soon; for as early as 1711 there were rumors that the Negroes were getting out of hand. In 1720 several slaves were burned alive and others were banished because of implication in a revolt near Charleston. In subsequent years there were other revolts or rumors of revolts. In 1739 the well-known Cato conspiracy twenty miles west of Charleston threw the countryside into a state of terror. After slaves killed two guards in a warehouse and secured arms, they went on a full-scale drive to destroy slavery in that area. Soon, the uprising was put down, but not before thirty whites and forty-four Negroes had lost their lives. Later in the century there were other uprisings, and the general state of affairs led to a full-scale revision of the slave code. Before the Revolution, South Carolina, then divided from North Carolina, had enacted one of the most stringent sets of laws governing slaves to be found in the New World.

Georgia was the only important New World colony established by England in the eighteenth century. In several significant ways it was different from the others: it was to grant no free land titles, permit the use of no alcoholic beverages and to allow no slavery. From the time of its establishment in 1733, however, each of these proscriptions was subjected to enormous pressure on the part of the settlers themselves. One by one they fell. It was in 1750 that the third petition of the colonists brought about the repeal of the hated prohibition against Negroes. From that point on the Negro population grew, and slavery flourished. By 1760 there were six thousand whites and three thousand Negroes. In the last estimate before the War for Independence, in 1773, the white population had increased to eighteen thousand, while the Negro population numbered some fifteen thousand.

Georgia adopted her slave code in 1755, and much of it was taken from the South Carolina code. It reflected South Carolina's experience rather than Georgia's. For example, the interdiction against more than seven Negroes being out together without a white chaperon was taken from the general fear of South Carolina against Negro uprisings. Between Saturday evening and Monday morning, not even those slaves who were authorized to possess firearms were permitted to carry them on their person. Under no conditions were Negroes to be taught to read and write.

If the slaves of colonial Georgia did not erupt into rebellion, they resisted their enslavement by running away into Florida as well as by sabotage. Strangely enough, Georgia displayed a relative indifference to insurrection by subjecting her slaves to service in the militia. Perhaps the service which Spanish Florida rendered as a place of escape for the more discontented Negroes made possible the paradoxical practice of using Negroes as Georgia militiamen in the colonial period.

The Middle Colonies

Although the Dutch were primarily interested in the slave trade and made great profits from transporting them to various colonies, they did not neglect their own New World settlements. There were large plantations in New Netherland, particularly in the valley of the Hudson River, and by 1638 many of them were cultivated largely with the labor of Negro slaves. The institution of slavery as practiced by the Dutch in the New World was relatively mild, with slaves receiving fairly human treatment and many considerations as to their personal rights. The Dutch slave code was not elaborate, and manumission was not an uncommon reward for long or meritorious service. Although the demand for slaves always exceeded the supply, the number imported by the Dutch never reached such proportions as to cause serious apprehension or difficulty during the period of their domination.

The character of the institution of slavery changed the moment the English took over New Netherland in 1664. The Royal African Company promoted slavery in New York as it did in other colonies. In the year following the takeover, the colonial assembly recognized the existence of slavery where persons had willingly sold themselves into bondage; and in the statute of 1684 slavery was recognized as a legitimate institution in the province of New York. As a result the Negro population of New York grew. In 1698 there were only 2,170 Negroes in a total population of 18,067, while in 1723 the census listed 6,171 slaves. By 1771 the Negro population had increased to 19,883 in a total population of 168,007.

The slave code of New York became refined early in the eighteenth century. In 1706 a law was enacted stating that baptism of a slave did not provide grounds for the slave's claim to freedom. A further significant provision was that a slave was at no time a competent witness in a case involving a freeman. In 1715 the legislature enacted a law providing that any slaves caught traveling forty miles above Albany, presumably bound for Canada, were to be executed upon the oath of two credible witnesses. Meanwhile, New York City was enacting ordinances for the better control of slaves. In 1710 the city forbade Negroes from appearing "in the streets after nightfall without a lantern with a lighted candle in it."

The concentration of an increasing number of slaves in the city of New York brought with it increased dangers to the white population. Negroes defied authority and disobeyed the laws. In 1712 the ungovernable temper of New York Negroes flared up into a fully organized insurrection, in which twenty-three slaves armed with guns and knives met in an orchard and set fire to a slaveholder's house. In the melee that followed nine whites were killed and six were injured. In the ensuing trial of the accused Negroes twenty-one were found guilty and executed. Later, in 1741, rumor of an even larger insurrection occurred. After a series of fires, the rumor spread that Negroes and poor whites were conspiring to destroy law and order in the city and seize control. After the city offered generous rewards for the apprehension of the conspirators, almost two hundred whites and Negroes were arrested and prosecuted. At least one hundred Negroes were convicted, of whom eighteen were hanged, thirteen burned alive, and seventy banished. Four white people, including two women, were hanged. There were no more serious outbursts during the colonial period, and by the time of the Revolution New York had begun to recognize the moral and economic undesirability of holding men in bondage.

South of New York, the colonies of New Jersey, Pennsylvania and Delaware each in their own ways subscribed to the institution of slavery. After the English came to dominate New Jersey, they encouraged slavery in every way. Soon, the Negro population there was growing steadily: 2,581 in 1726, 3,981 in 1738, and 4,606 in 1745 out of a population of 61,000. In Pennsylvania the growth was not so rapid, due largely to the opposition to slavery by the members of the Society of Friends. In 1688 the Germantown Quakers issued their celebrated protest, and in 1693 George Keith remonstrated Pennsylvanians for holding men in perpetual bondage. But in 1685 no less a person than William Penn himself had expressed the view that Negro slaves were better than white servants; and this had the effect of greatly encouraging slavery in some quarters. In 1721 the Negro population of Pennsylvania was estimated as being between 2,500 and 5,000. Thirty years later there were about 11,000 in the colony. In 1790 there were 10,274 Negroes, of whom 3,737 were slaves and 6,537 were free. Meanwhile, as early as 1636 slavery existed on the right bank of the Delaware. Since Delaware was a part of Pennsylvania down to 1703 the laws of the latter colony applied to Delaware. After that date Delaware was on its own, and the slave population increased at a somewhat more rapid rate than that of Pennsylvania. As this occurred, Delaware drifted away from her mother colony and became more and more identified in interests with her Southern neighbors.

Slavery was never really successful in the Middle Colonies. Their predominantly commercial economy, supplemented by subsistence agriculture, did not encourage any large-scale employment of slave labor; and many of the slaves that cleared through the New York and Pennsylvania ports were later sent into the Southern colonies. Even where there were extensive agricultural enterprises, there was no desire for slaves; for the Dutch, Swedes and Germans cultivated their farms with such meticulous care that they were not inclined to use slaves. Many of them, moreover, had moral scruples against using slaves at all. The Quakers, with their respect for Negroes as human beings, and others like them contributed as much to the failure of slavery as the economic practices that were antithetical to the institution. Thus, many in the Middle Colonies welcomed the arguments against slavery that became more pronounced during the Revolutionary period.

The Negro in Colonial New England

Although New England's primary interest in slavery was in the trade, Negroes were early introduced into Massachusetts and Connecticut. In 1638 a Salem ship unloaded several Negroes in Boston, and in the following year there were Negroes in Hartford. Before a decade had passed Negroes were used in the construction of houses and forts in New Haven and New Hampshire. By the middle of the century the refugees who founded Rhode Island were employing Negroes to help establish that colony. While the status of these early New England Negroes was rather uncertain, it gradually became clear in all New England colonies that slavery was a legitimate institution. In 1641, for example, Massachusetts cautioned that only those slaves could be brought in who were taken in wars or had willingly sold themselves or were sold to the traders by someone else.

Whether slaves landing in New England were to be settled there or shipped to other colonies, they became important to the commercial life of the New England colonies. New England slave traders competed in the trade, although they were at a serious disadvantage with the powerful European trading companies. After England secured a monopoly of the slave trade to the New World in 1713 she welcomed New England merchants into the trade, for there was enough for more traders than England could herself provide. In the first half of the eighteenth century the New England traders thrived. Boston, Salem, Providence and New London bustled with activity as outgoing ships were loaded with rum, fish and dairy products, and as Negroes, molasses and sugar were unloaded from the incoming ships. Down to the War for Independence the slave trade was vital to the economic life of New England and, indeed, the very heart of the highly profitable triangular trade.

The Negro population in New England grew slowly. In 1700, when the total population of the entire region was approximately 90,000, there were only 1,000 Negroes there. In the eighteenth century the growth was more rapid. Massachusetts led with 2,000 Negroes in 1715 and 5,249 by 1776. Connecticut was second, with 1,500 Negroes in 1715 and 3,587 by 1756. The largest percentage of Negroes was to be found in Rhode Island where in 1774 there were 3,761 Negroes to 54,435 whites. The number in New Hampshire remained negligible all during the colonial period.

New England slavery needed little legal recognition for its growth and development. When the codes emerged late in the seventeenth century slavery had already become well established. In 1670 Massachusetts enacted a law providing that the children of slaves could be sold into bondage, and ten years later it began to enact measures restricting the movement of Negroes. In 1660 Connecticut barred Negroes from military service, and thirty years later it restrained Negroes from going beyond the limits of the town without a pass. The restrictions against the education of slaves were not as great as in other regions, and frequently Negroes learned to read and write with no difficulty.

Since the number of slaves remained relatively small throughout the colonial period, there was no great fear of insurrections in New England as in some other colonies. Nevertheless, many slaves indicated their dislike of the institution by running away. Others attacked their masters and even murdered them. Still others plotted to rebel. In 1658 some Negroes and Indians in Hartford decided to make a bid for their freedom by destroying several houses of their masters. In the eighteenth century there were several conspiracies to rebel in Boston and other Massachusetts towns. The situation became so serious in Boston in 1723 that the selectmen found it necessary to take precautionary measures by forbidding slaves to be on the streets at night and refrain from "idling or lurking together."

The Negro in New England was rather unique in colonial America. He was not subjected to the harsh codes or the severe treatment that his fellows received in the colonies to the south. But it is possible to exaggerate the humanitarian aspects of their treatment. Masters in New England held a firm hand on the institution and gave little consideration to the small minority that argued for the freedom of the slaves. Although the New Englander took his religion seriously, he did not permit it to interfere with his appreciation of the profits of slavery and the slave trade. At the same time, he did not glut his home market with slaves and increase the number to the point where he would be fearful for the safety of himself and his family. There seemed to be the characteristic Yankee shrewdness in the New Englander's assessment of the importance of slavery to his economic and social life.

NEGROES AND THE RIGHTS OF MAN

Slavery and the American Revolution

By the middle of the eighteenth century slavery had become a very important part of the evolving economic order in colonial America. There had been some reservations registered by certain individuals and groups, of course. The Quakers had questioned the right of one man to hold another in perpetual bondage. Some colonists greatly objected to the indefinite expansion of the slave system lest the slaves themselves engulf the whites in a blood bath of resentment and revenge. Some Christians persisted, moreover, in their belief that there was a fundamental contradiction between the principles of Christian brotherhood, on the one hand, and the enslavement of one's brother—whether he be Christian or heathen—on the other. None of these reservations prevailed, however; and the colonists, preoccupied with critical problems of a social and economic nature, either tolerated slavery as unavoidable or embraced it with enthusiasm as indispensable.

When England revised her colonial policy at the end of the French and Indian War in 1763, she ushered in a new approach on the part of the colonists to the problem of slavery. If the colonists were to object to the new, stringent policies imposed by England, they felt also compelled—for the sake of consistency—to say something against the holding of slaves, which was, after all, a similar form of oppression. John Woolman, the New Jersey Quaker, and Anthony Benezet, the Philadelphia Huguenot, had already begun their antislavery activities even before the controversy between England and her colonies flared into the open. But when England imposed new laws on the colonists, such as the Sugar Act of 1764 and the Stamp Act of the following year, the colonists began to think of their dual roles as oppressed and oppressor. Soon the leaders were denouncing not only England's new imperial policy but slavery and the slave trade as well.

It was almost natural for the colonists to see a connection between the problem of slavery and what they regarded as their oppression by England. When James Otis penned his eloquent protest on the *Rights of the British Colonies* he affirmed the Negro's inalienable right to freedom. "Does it follow that it is right to enslave a man because he is black?" Otis asked. He and a respectable number of colonists began to insist on freedom for all as well as political independence from England. Negroes themselves sensed the dilemma of their masters and began to press for their own freedom. Addressing the Massachusetts General Court in 1774, several of them said, "we have in common with all other men a natural right to our freedoms without Being depriv'd of them by our fellow men as we are a freeborn Pepel and have never forfeited this Blessing by any compact or agreement whatever."

For the time being the General Court could not be moved to act. But neither the members of the General Court nor the other citizens of Massachusetts could soon forget the incident a few years earlier in which, according to the Negro historian, George Washington Williams, a Negro became the "first to pour out his blood as a precious libation on the altar of a people's rights." The presence of British soldiers in Boston in 1770 excited the indignation of the people, and many wondered what could be done about it. On the fifth of March, a crowd of colonists began to taunt a group of British soldiers under the command of Captain Thomas Preston. When one of the soldiers received a blow from the unruly mob, the soldiers began to fire. One of the patriots, a mulatto named Crispus Attucks, "whose looks was enough to terrify any person . . . had hardiness enough to fall in upon them, and with one hand took hold of a bayonet, and with the other knocked the man down." But Attucks had been fatally struck, and with his fall the first blood of the struggle against England had been shed. The colonists were shaken by the realization that their fight for freedom had been waged by one who was not as free as they.

In the years that followed the Boston Massacre, as the incident was called, the colonists almost always spoke out against slavery and British colonial policy at the same time. In 1774 Abigail Adams wrote to her husband John, "It always appeared a most iniquitous scheme to me to fight ourselves for what we are daily robbing and plundering from those who have as good a right to freedom as we have." Their feeling of inconsistency was reflected in the act of the Continental Congress that provided that after December 1, 1775, no slaves would be imported into the colonies. One would have assumed that the colonists' stand against slavery and the slave trade would become unequivocal and irrevocable.

The real test of the colonists' regard for slavery came in their reaction to the Declaration of Independence submitted to the Continental Congress by Thomas Jefferson. Most of the draft was acceptable, but one of the arraignments against the King was not. In part it declared that the King had "waged cruel war against human nature itself, violating the most sacred rights of life and liberty in the persons of a distant people who never offended him, captivating and carrying them into slavery in another hemisphere, or to incur miserable death in their transportation thither." Such acts were described as piratical warfare, and they were vigorously denounced by the Declaration. This charge was described by John Adams as the "vehement phillipic against Negro slavery." But it was unacceptable to the Southern delegation at the Continental Congress, and it was stricken from the final draft of the Declaration. In thus declining to accuse the King of perpetuating slavery and the slave trade and making certain that these practices would survive independence, the colonists contented themselves with engaging in what one critic called "glittering generalities." Thus, the status of the Negro was connected all too vaguely with the philosophy of freedom for all men.

There was no uniform policy among the several colonies on the use of Negroes as soldiers when hostilities broke out in April, 1775. In Massachusetts slaves as well as free Negroes fought in the battle of Bunker Hill. Peter Salem, who had been a slave in Framingham, won the plaudits of his fellows when he shot down the British Major Pitcairn. Another, Salem Poor, a soldier in a largely white company, distinguished himself by behaving "like an experienced officer as well as an excellent soldier." There were other Negroes who, like Poor and Salem, fought bravely at Bunker Hill: Caesar Brown of Westford, who was killed in action; Titus Coburn and Alexander Ames of Andover; and Prince Hall, later an abolitionist and leader of the Masons.

The performance of Negroes at this early stage of the revolutionary struggle did not settle their status as soldiers in the War for Independence. Shortly after George Washington took command of the Continental Army in 1775 an order was issued to recruiting officers instructing them not to enlist "any deserted from the ministerial army, nor any stroller, negro or vagabond, or person suspected of being an enemy of the liberty of America nor any under eighteen years of age." In October of that year Washington's council of war agreed unanimously to reject all slaves and, by a large majority, to reject Negroes altogether. This remained the policy until the end of the year.

It was British policy that forced the Americans to change their position with regard to enlisting Negroes in the Continental Army. When Lord Dunmore, the governor of Virginia, invited Negroes into the British army in November, 1775, General Washington seemed to begin to realize that he had made an error in turning down Negro volunteers. Later in the year he learned that Negroes, slave and free, were rallying to the British flag. Wherever the British armies went they attracted many Negroes with their promise of freedom to those who would serve. On December 31 Washington reversed his policy and, with the approval of Congress, ordered the enlistment of free Negroes. In the ensuing months the policy was liberalized further, so that before the end of the war Negroes, slave and free, were being permitted to enlist in all states with the exception of Georgia and South Carolina.

Of the 300,000 men who saw service in the cause of American independence, some 5,000 were Negroes. They served in the Navy as well as the Army; some volunteered, while others were substituted for whites. Most of them served in outfits that were predominantly white, but there were a few predominantly Negro fighting units, such as the two companies in Massachusetts, one in Connecticut, and one in Rhode Island. They saw action all over the country: at Lexington, Concord, Ticonderoga, Bunker Hill, Trenton, Princeton, Brandywine, Saratoga, Savannah, Eutaw Springs and Yorktown. Most of them remain anonymous, as far as military exploits are concerned. Indeed, Benjamin Quarles points out in his *The Negro in the American Revolution* that many Negroes who enlisted were enrolled without specific names. They were "A Negro Man," or "Negro by Name" or "A Negro name not known."

Some Negroes distinguished themselves by the service that they rendered. Two of them, Prince Whipple and Oliver Cromwell, were with Washington when he crossed the Delaware on Christmas Day, 1776. Lemuel Haynes, who was later to have a career as a minister to white congregations, joined the expedition to Ticonderoga to stop the inroads of Burgoyne's northern army. The victory of Anthony Wayne at Stony Point in 1779 was made possible by the spying of a Negro soldier named Pompey. At the siege of Savannah in 1779 more than five-hundred Negroes from Haiti were with the French forces that helped save the day. Among them and perhaps the youngest was Henri Christophe, "who one day would become King of Haiti, but was then a bootblack and messboy, not yet out of his teens."

The First Antislavery Movement

Early in the seventeenth century colonists here and there began to speak out against slavery. It was not until the revolutionary period, however, that a full-scale, organized opposition to the institution of slavery emerged. In a sense it was nurtured by the same sentiments that fostered the movement for independence. In Rhode Island the Reverend Samuel Hopkins made a house-to-house canvass urging masters to liberate their slaves. In Pennsylvania Anthony Benezet, who has been called "the foremost antislavery propagandist of his day," was writing and speaking against the practice that was "repugnant to humanity" and "inconsistent with the Bible." He joined with others, like Benjamin Rush, in organizing The Society for the Relief of Free Negroes Unlawfully Held in Bondage. This and other organizations with similar purposes reflected the social implications of the revolutionary philosophy. In 1785 the New York Society for Promoting the Manumission of Slaves was organized with John Jay as president. In Delaware a similar society was set up in 1788; and by 1792 there were antislavery societies in every state from Massachusetts to Virginia.

Negroes themselves took heart from the efforts of the whites as well as from the congenial climate produced by arguments for the rights of man. In 1777 a group of Massachusetts Negroes asked for a law against slavery, declaring that a life of slavery was "far worse than Nonexistence." Two years later a group of nineteen Negroes in New Hampshire asked the state to enact a law whereby they might regain their liberty, "and that the name of slave may not more be heard in a land gloriously contending for the sweets of freedom." Throughout the country individual Negroes and groups of Negroes were seeking legislation that would bring an end to slavery.

States soon began to respond to the pressure. As early as 1777 the Massachusetts legislature considered a bill for "preventing the practice of holding persons in Slavery"; but it postponed action. In 1780, however, the new Massachusetts constitution stated that "all men are born free and equal," and this was the beginning of the end of slavery in that state. New Hampshire legislators debated the question of abolishing slavery in 1780, but postponed action to a "more convenient opportunity." While some states equivocated Pennsylvania took decisive action. On March 1, 1780, it passed a law providing that when children of slaves reached twenty-eight years of age, they would be free. Manumission acts were passed in New York in 1785 and in New Jersey in 1786, although effective legislation was not achieved in those states until 1799 and 1804 respectively. Finally, Congress indicated its interest in the antislavery movement by enacting a law providing that in the Northwest Territory neither slavery nor involuntary servitude should exist.

Slavery and the Constitution

The antislavery leaders experienced only limited success during and after the War for Independence. Resistance to the abolition of slavery hardened in the Southern states, where much capital was invested in slaves and where, during the postwar years, a new economic importance was being attached to slavery. Nowhere was the resistance to abolition reflected better than in the convention that wrote a new Constitution for the United States in 1787. In the debates over representation in Congress, the question arose as to how the slaves should be counted. Most of the Northern delegates regarded slaves as property and therefore not deserving of representation. Southerners were loud in their demands that slaves be counted as people, in which case the slave states would gain in the number of members they would have in Congress. Despite the objection on the part of some antislavery delegates to recognizing slavery in the Constitution, the compromise finally agreed upon permitted states to count slaves as three-fifths of other persons.

By 1787 several states, including such slave states as Virginia, North Carolina and Georgia, had taken action to prevent the importation of slaves. The opponents to the slave trade hoped that the convention would put an end to the trade in all parts of the United States. When the matter came before the convention, it was debated with such vehemence that some feared a disruption of the entire proceedings. One Southerner said that his own state, South Carolina, could never accept a constitution that prohibited the slave trade. After much acrimonious debate the members agreed on a compromise that provided that the slave trade "shall not be prohibited by the Congress prior to the Year one thousand eight hundred and eight, but a Tax or duty may be imposed on such importation, not exceeding ten dollars for each Person."

Runaway slaves had always been a problem in the colonies; and it is significant, but not surprising, that there was almost no opposition to the proposal that states give up fugitive slaves to their owners. When Roger Sherman of Connecticut declared that he saw "no more propriety in the public seizing and surrendering a slave or servant, than a horse," he found little support, even among his New England colleagues. Thus, the provision was written into the Constitution calling for the rendition of fugitive slaves "upon Claim of the Party to whom such Service or Labour may be due." In these several ways the new Constitution not only recognized the institution of slavery but offered the resources of the government of the United States in its protection and support. To the extent that it did it made it more difficult to carry out the sentiments regarding the rights of man that had been set forth in the Declaration of Independence.

Negroes in the New Nation

When the new Constitution went into effect, there were approximately three-quarters of a million Negroes in the United States. Almost 90 percent of them were slaves in the South Atlantic states, while some 60,000 free Negroes were scattered all over the country. The Negro population was essentially rural. Here and there one found a slight concentration in the cities: New York City with 3,252, Philadelphia with 1,630 and Baltimore with 1,578. Nowhere was the Negro population dying out; indeed, there were signs of significant increase, especially in the slave states. In the North the only significant development was the increase in the number of free Negroes. By 1790 all of Boston's 761 Negroes were free.

Nor was the American Negro altogether anonymous, even at this early date. There was, for example, Phillis, the personal maid of Mrs. Susannah Wheatley of Boston. She early displayed an interest in writing poetry; and in 1770 her first poem, "On the Death of Reverend George Whitefield," appeared. Three years later she published a collection of her verse, *Poems on Various Subjects, Religious and Moral.* During the war she composed a tribute to "His Excellency General Washington," which the general acknowledged by declaring that the poem was "striking proof of your great poetical talents." Then there was Paul Cuffee, the Massachusetts Negro who built and sailed his own ships. He owned a 69-ton schooner, the *Ranger*, two brigs and several smaller vessels. When settlers refused to do so, he built a school in Westport, Massachusetts, and gave it to the community. He also helped build a meeting house for the Society of Friends, to which he belonged. In 1780 he presented a petition to the Massachusetts legislature asking to be relieved from paying taxes since he and the Negroes who joined him in signing the petition had "no voice or influence in the election of those who tax us." As businessman, philanthropist and petitioner he won recognition among his fellow citizens in Massachusetts.

Perhaps the most significant of the Negroes in the new nation was Benjamin Banneker, mathematician, astronomer and political philosopher. In 1791 this Maryland free Negro published his first almanac, a worthy yearly undertaking that lasted until 1802. Thomas Jefferson, to whom Banneker sent a copy of his first almanac, was greatly impressed and told Banneker that it was a work that justified the Negro's resentment against the claims that he was intellectually inferior. At the suggestion of his friends, George Ellicott and Thomas Jefferson, Banneker was appointed by Washington to serve with the commission to define the boundary and lay out the new Capital—the District of Columbia.

There were also several Negro religious leaders who became well known for their initiative and courage in the early days of the new nation. George Liele founded a Baptist church in Savannah in 1779 before quitting the United States and settling in Jamaica. In Philadelphia Richard Allen founded the African Methodist Episcopal Church after he was thrown out of the St. George Church because he refused to accept segregation. Soon branches of Allen's church sprang up in Baltimore, Wilmington and various Pennsylvania and New Jersey towns. Able colleagues such as Absolom Jones, Daniel Coker and Morris Brown helped to promote this branch of Methodism among Negroes in the South as well as the North. In New York in 1796 Negroes, under the leadership of Peter Williams, James Varick and Christopher Rush withdrew from the John Street Methodist Church and organized the African Methodist Episcopal Zion Church. Before the beginning of the nineteenth century Negro Baptist and Methodist churches had been established in all the states of the Union.

If there were no outstanding Negro leaders in the field of education, it did not prevent a movement for the education of Negroes from getting under way. In 1798 a separate school for Negro children was established by a white teacher in the home of Primus Hall, a prominent Boston Negro. In 1800 the Negroes of Boston asked the city to establish a school for Negroes, but the request was not granted. Not until 1820 did the city open the first school for Negro children. The first school for Negroes in New York City was established in 1787 by the Manumission Society. By 1820 the school had more than five hundred children. New Jersey began educating her Negro children in 1777. Soon there were schools in several New Jersey towns. Philadelphia, which began Negro education in 1787, had seven schools for Negroes before the end of the century. In the other states the beginnings were not as auspicious and the task was more difficult, but even in Virginia and the Carolinas schools for Negroes were founded. The insurrection of 1800 in Richmond frightened many slaveholders who feared that Negroes were reading incendiary literature. From that point on it became increasingly difficult to establish and maintain schools for Negroes in the slave states.

AMERICAN NEGRO SLAVERY

Growth of an Institution

By the beginning of the nineteenth century there were unmistakable signs of profound economic and social change taking place in the United States. The commercial activities of the new nation were expanding; and there were those who already were beginning to think in terms of promoting industrial development similar to that which was occurring in England and on the Continent. Beyond the areas of settlement, rich new land was beckoning settlers who could plant staple crops and enjoy the freedom offered on the frontier. In 1803 the United States purchased the vast Louisiana Territory, and although it would be many years before the entire area would be settled, Americans and European immigrants were rapidly moving beyond the mountains. The greater portion of the people who moved from the Atlantic seaboard were committed to the institution of slavery, and if they had any slaves they took them along. Not even the War of 1812, in which several thousand Negroes fought, halted the march of Americans and slavery into the new West.

When peace came in 1815 the movement to the West accelerated. The men of the South and West, the most enthusiastic supporters of the war, now felt that they had a right to move on to better lands. Into the Gulf region went large numbers of settlers to clear the rich lands and cultivate extensive crops of cotton and sugar. Louisiana had already become a state in 1812; Mississippi and Alabama became states in 1817 and 1819 respectively. By 1820 the Gulf region had about 200,000 inhabitants, and twenty years later there were almost a million people there. The increase of the white population, coupled with the tremendous growth of the Negro population, largely slaves, is essentially the story of the emergence of the cotton kingdom.

The rise of the cotton kingdom was America's response to the growing demand for cotton brought on by the industrial revolution in England. The system of producing cotton textiles was undergoing revolutionary changes; and with the invention of spinning and weaving machinery the manufacturing process was so cheapened that the demand for cotton goods was greatly stimulated. The demand for cotton fiber to feed the newly developed machinery seemed insatiable, and the cotton farmers of the United States undertook to satisfy this demand. Already, they had made two significant steps in that direction. First, they put into use a type of cotton, the short-staple variety, that could be grown almost anywhere in the South. Secondly, they made greater use of the cotton gin that had been developed by the Connecticut schoolteacher, Eli Whitney. Within a few years the South was on its way toward making the economic transition that these new developments induced.

As the planters expanded their operations, the need for additional labor became urgent. By now they were committed to Negro slavery, but the supply of slaves was not abundant. The African slave trade had officially closed in 1808, but even after that date American capital, American ships, and American sailors were carrying on an extensive slave trade between Africa and the New World. The long, unprotected coast, a sure market for their wares, and the prospect of huge profits were enough to tempt many Americans. W. E. B. Du Bois, in his *The Suppression of the African Slave Trade,* asserts that thousands of slaves were smuggled into the country each year from the time of the closing of the trade down to the outbreak of the Civil War. It was the domestic slave trade, however, that constituted the principal means by which farmers of the cotton kingdom secured the slaves that they needed.

Even before 1800 the domestic slave trade in Maryland and Virginia was well developed. As tobacco cultivation tended to decline and as the farmers of the upper South proceeded to diversify their economic activity, they discovered that there was a ready market for the surplus of slaves they had on hand. Slave-trading firms like Woolfolk, Saunders and Overly of Maryland and Franklin and Armfield of Virginia did a lively business in purchasing slaves in the upper South and selling them "down the river" to planters in Mississippi and Louisiana who desperately needed them. Traders made individual deals with planters or attended auctions of estates and sales by the sheriff of bankrupt estates. At times planters sold incorrigible slaves—habitual runaways or those who refused to work—and the traders in turn sold them to unsuspecting planters in some faraway community. Baltimore, Washington,

Richmond, Norfolk and Charleston were principal trading centers in the older states; while Montgomery, Memphis, and New Orleans were the outstanding markets in the newer areas.

The domestic slave trade involved some of the most sordid practices that were developed in the sordid business of slavery. Slave families were ruthlessly divided, with mothers being frequently sold away from their children or vice versa. In his journal William Reynolds, an itinerant merchant, recorded this account of the sale of twenty-three slaves at auction in Memphis: "One yellow woman was sold who had two children. She begged and implored her new master . . . to buy her children, but it had no effect. . . . She then begged him to buy her little girl, about five years old, but all to no purpose." In the states of the upper South owners encouraged the breeding of slaves in order to increase profits. As early as 1796 a South Carolina slaveholder declared that the fifty slaves he was offering for sale were purchased for stock and breeding. In 1832 Thomas R. Dew admitted that Virginia was a "Negro-raising state" and that she was able to export six thousand slaves per year because of breeding. Moncure Conway of Fredericksburg, Virginia, boldly asserted that the "chief pecuniary resource in the border states is the breeding of slaves. . . ."

Because of the foreign slave trade, the illicit foreign slave trade after 1808, slave breeding, the normal excess of births over deaths among slaves, and a booming domestic slave trade, the Negro population grew steadily in the first half of the nineteenth century. In 1790 there were 604,000 slaves. By 1808, when the foreign slave trade officially closed, there were about one million. In 1830 there were 2,156,900; and by 1860 the number had increased to 3,953,760. In 1860 Virginia continued to lead in numbers with 549,000, followed by Georgia with 465,000 and Alabama and Mississippi with approximately 435,000 each. The most significant increase was in the states of the cotton kingdom—Georgia, Alabama, Tennessee, Mississippi, Arkansas, Louisiana and Texas—where by 1860 there were approximately two million slaves, more than half the Negro population.

There were 384,000 owners of slaves in 1860; and this means that since the white population of the South numbered around eight million, fully three-fourths of the whites had neither slaves nor any immediate economic interest in the institution of slavery. Most of the slaveowners had only a few slaves: 200,000 owners had five slaves or less, while 338,000 owners, or 88 percent, held less than twenty. Nevertheless, the institution came to dominate the political and economic thinking of the entire South. The vast majority of the staple crops was produced on those relatively few plantations employing large numbers of slaves (2,000 planters had more than 100 slaves each in 1860), thus giving such owners an influence all out of proportion to their numbers. Even those who had no slaves hoped that some day they would; and they took on the habits and patterns of thought of the slaveholders. Too, in the context of a slave society in which all slaves were black people, the color of the whites became a badge of superiority in which *all* whites took pride.

The Slave Codes

Slaves were a special kind of property, not quite like houses or beasts of burden, but not quite like people, within the meaning of the law. They required, therefore, a special set of laws designed to protect the owners of such property and to protect the whites against any dangers that might arise from the presence of so much slave property. These codes began to develop in the seventeenth century, and long before the Civil War they were fully refined. From time to time it was necessary to modify them and they differed from state to state; but in important particulars they were quite similar. Since they were designed to achieve due subordination of the slaves, they were frankly repressive; and the white planters and legislators made no apologies for them.

A slave had no standing in the courts. He could not be a party to a suit at law; and he could not offer legal testimony except against another slave or a free Negro. Since he had no legal responsibility, his oath was not binding. Thus, he could not make a contract, and his marriage was therefore not legal. His children were not legitimate. The ownership of property by slaves was generally forbidden, although some states permitted them to possess certain types of property. There was no legal basis for even this concession. A slave could not strike a white person, even in self-defense; but the killing of a slave, however malicious, was rarely regarded as murder. The rape of a female slave was a misdemeanor because it involved trespassing on the property of another person. Slaves could not leave the plantation without the permission of their master; and any white person encountering a slave who was away from the plantation without permission could take him up and turn him over to the public officials. Slaves could not possess firearms and, in Mississippi, they could not beat drums or blow horns. Laws generally forbade the hiring out of slaves by themselves, but many owners ignored this proscription.

Slaves could not purchase or sell goods or visit the homes of whites or free Negroes. They were never to assemble unless a white person was present; and they were never to receive, possess or transmit any incendiary literature calculated to incite insurrections. They were not to be taught to read or write or cipher; and any white person or free Negro found guilty of violating this law was to be subjected to severe punishment of fine or imprisonment or both. Slaves guilty of petty offenses were to be punished by whipping, but the more serious offenses drew severe punishments, such as branding, imprisonment or death. Arson, rape of a white woman and conspiracy to rebel, for example, were capital crimes in all the slaveholding states. Since slaves were always regarded with suspicion and since they could not testify against a white person who accused them, many of them were found guilty of crimes they did not commit and against which they were unable to defend themselves.

Despite the elaborateness of the slave codes and the machinery of enforcement. there were numerous infractions that went unpunished altogether. When times were quiet the laws were disregarded; the slaves could get away with a great deal. But when there were rumors of revolts among the slaves, the white community became apprehensive and tended to enforce the codes with unusual zeal. Slave owners, moreover, were not inclined under ordinary circumstances to give much attention to the slave codes where their own slaves were concerned. The planter conceived of himself as the source of law and justice, and he preferred to take all matters involving his own slaves into his own hands and mete out justice in his own way. He was certain that he could handle his own slaves, if only something could be done about those on the neighboring plantation! Such an attitude was not conducive to the uniform, effective enforcement of the slave codes.

Slaves at Work

A great deal has been written about the institution of slavery as "a matrimonial bureau," and "a chapel of ease" and the like. All too often the planter is described as a patrician who, as a great humanitarian and Christian, maintained his establishment largely as a civilizing institution. Such descriptions hardly square with the facts. Slavery was essentially an economic institution; the primary concern of the slaveowner was to get work out of his slaves. And the work was largely agricultural. In his study of urban slavery Richard Wade has pointed out that only some 400,000 slaves lived in towns and cities in 1850 and that slavery in the urban areas was largely unsuccessful. Of the 3,200,000 slaves in the United States in 1850 approximately 2,800,000 worked on farms and plantations. Some 1,800,000 of these were on cotton plantations, while the remainder worked in tobacco, sugar and rice fields. Where there were few slaves on the agricultural unit, as was the case in a vast majority of instances, the slaves and their owners worked together in the fields and were compelled to engage in a variety of tasks. On the larger plantations, where organization and the division of labor were elaborate, there was extensive supervision by the owner or his overseer or both. In such instances there might be two distinct groups of slaves, the field hands and the house servants.

The cultivation of a crop was a most demanding activity; and the entire future of both slaves and owners depended on the success with which this was carried out. It was generally believed that one Negro was required for the successful cultivation of three acres of cotton. The planting, cultivation and picking of the cotton required little skill, but a great deal of time. Men, women and children could be used and, indeed, they all were used. Other duties included clearing new land, burning underbrush, rolling logs, splitting rails, carrying water, mending fences, spreading fertilizer and breaking the soil. Small wonder that many slaves worked not merely from sunrise to sunset, but frequently long after dark.

On some plantations slaves were assigned tasks for each day, and when they had completed their tasks they were through for the day. Much more common was the gang system, in which gangs of slaves were taken to the field and put to work under supervision. Where there was not watchful supervision little was likely to be accomplished. Negro slaves felt no compulsion to extend themselves, since their benefits were more or less the same, regardless of effort, except on the few plantations where systems of bounties and rewards were developed. Masters complained much about the idleness and laziness of slaves. If slaves felt overworked they frequently feigned illness or simply walked off for a day or two, or perhaps forever. The constant evasion of work was one reason why planters always felt the need for more slaves in order to increase productivity.

In order to get work out of slaves the lash was frequently used. There was the general belief, born of a naïve defense of the institution of slavery, that Negroes were a childlike race and should be punished just as children were punished. The excessive use of the lash was one of the most flagrant abuses of the institution of slavery. As Thomas Jefferson pointed out in his *Notes on Virginia,* the whole master-slave relationship was "a perpetual exercise of the most boisterous passions, the most unremitting despotism on the one part; and degrading submission on the other. . . ." The dominion over the slave that the master enjoyed all too frequently brought out the worst in the master and stimulated a brutality in treatment that seemed to be inherent in the relationship. Excessively cruel treatment at the hands of the planter or the overseer, together with his natural aversion to enslavement, explain the tendency of slaves to run away or, worse still, to revolt against their masters.

An Ignoble Existence

Except for the house servants who had special advantages and opportunities, it may be said that slaves generally merely subsisted. Many planters were so preoccupied with growing staple crops that they gave little attention to growing foodstuffs for their slaves. Many plantations were compelled to purchase food and other supplies for the slaves and for the planting family. Few Mississippi planters raised enough food for their needs and were compelled to purchase large quantities from the outside. The meal and meat, infrequently supplemented by potatoes, peas and syrup, was not a particularly exciting fare. Some slaves had their own gardens and chickens, but there was always the possibility of incurring the disfavor of the owner by spending too much time in this pursuit. It would be too much to suppose that slaves always resisted the temptation to take food from the owner's larder if the opportunity presented itself. As far as clothing was concerned, no more was provided than was absolutely necessary. Housing was especially poor and uncomfortable. When Frederick L. Olmsted toured the South he was shocked to see such small, dilapidated cabins on some of the plantations he visited.

Generally, slaves had no time that they could call their own. They might expect, however, to be free from work on Saturday afternoons and Sundays. But there was little in the way of enjoyment or satisfaction during the moments or hours they were off the job. Plantations were isolated, and slaves were not free to go and come at will. There was not much to do, even during the free periods, unless the plantation were large enough to have enough slaves to provide some social diversions of their own. At Christmastime and on a few other holidays, the rules of the plantation were relaxed, additional food was provided and slaves were permitted to dance and sing. Some were permitted to hunt and fish on special occasions. But there was little to relieve their existence of the depressed drabness that seemed to be inevitable.

As long as the proper precautions were taken there was little opposition to some form of religious activity among the slaves. After the Nat Turner revolt of 1831, some states banned Negro preachers and required slaves to attend the churches of their masters. Generally, however, Negro congregations flourished in the towns and on certain plantations, supported by several neighboring planters. Toward the end of the slave period Negro churches were generally frowned upon; and planters were encouraged to permit religious services for slaves only when some responsible white person was present. If this was not possible, slaves were expected to worship in white churches. The earliest examples of the segregation of Negroes are to be found in the practices of the white churches. In one instance the white congregation constructed a partition several feet high to separate the masters from the slaves.

Even if the slave had some social life and even if he was permitted to attend church regularly, he could never escape the fact that he was a slave and that his movements as well as his other activities were almost always under careful surveillance. This created a restiveness among some and a sense of despair among others. If a slave found it possible to be indifferent to the ignoble existence to which fate consigned him, it was because he possessed a remarkable capacity for accommodation or he was totally ignorant of the depth of his degraded position.

The prevailing notion a century ago was that the slave was docile, tractable and happy; and this view is held in some quarters even today. Advocates of the institution of slavery defended it on these grounds, and they pointed to the conduct of many slaves to support their contention. Slaves developed many techniques to mislead the owner regarding their real feeling. In the process of adjustment they learned how to escape work as well as punishment, and they were not above obsequiousness and meekness when it served their purposes. These actions do not reveal the real feelings of the slaves about the institution of which they were the unwilling victims. For, as old as the institution of slavery was, human beings had not, even by the nineteenth century, brought themselves to the point where they could be subjected to it without resistance and protest. Resistance to slavery has been found wherever slavery has existed, and Negro slavery in the United States was no exception. There are numerous examples of kindness and understanding on the part of the owner as well as docility and tractability on the part of the slave; but this can hardly be regarded as typical of a system based on the exploitation of one group by another.

Slaves reacted to their status in various ways. Some sang songs and expressed the hope that their burdens would be relieved in the next world. As long as they were in this world, they attempted to make the most of an unwelcome situation by loafing on the job, feigning illness in the fields and on the auction block and engaging in sabotage. Slaves would destroy farming tools, drive animals with a cruelty that suggested revenge, and when possible damage the crops, burn forests and homes and destroy their master's property in other ways. Self-mutilation and suicide were popular forms of resistance to slavery. Slaves would cut off their toes and hands in order to render themselves ineffective as workers. Or they would do violence to the master class. Poisoning was always feared, and with reason. As early as 1761 the *Charleston Gazette* remarked that the Negroes had "begun the hellish act of poisoning." On occasion slaves murdered their masters by stabbing, shooting and choking.

Running away began the first year that slavery was established in the New World and continued down to emancipation. There was Federal and state legislation to assist in the recovery of runaway slaves, but many of them escaped forever. Long before the Underground Railroad became an efficient operation under the abolitionists, slaves were running away: men, women and children, singly, in pairs, in groups. Some disguised themselves; others, armed with counterfeit passes, claimed that they were free. If they were apprehended, they would do it again. One woman in North Carolina fled from her master's plantation no less than sixteen times. While there is no way of even approximating the number of runaways, it is obvious that it was one of the most effective means of resisting slavery. Neither the Fugitive Act of 1793 nor that of 1850 could put an end to it.

Revolting against the whites was the most desperate form of resistance to slavery. To Negroes, it was "carrying the fight to the enemy." To the whites, it was a mad, sinister act of desperate savages, who had no appreciation for the benign influences of slavery. There were numerous revolts, large and small. And there were numerous rumors of revolts. Whether they were real or fancied, any suggestion of them threw the white community into a paroxysm of fear and led it to adopt desperate measures to prevent a blood bath. In 1800 a thousand slaves, led by Gabriel Prosser, attempted to march on Richmond and destroy the town and their masters. A violent storm and betrayal by two slave informers brought a tragic end to the attempt. In 1822 the slaves and free Negroes of Charleston planned a revolt, under the leadership of Denmark Vesy. The word leaked out, and it was aborted. In 1831 the Negroes of Southampton County, Virginia, under Nat Turner, were almost successful in their bid for freedom through revolt. They began by killing Turner's master and his family and several other white families. Within the first day some sixty whites had been killed, and the revolt was spreading rapidly when the main body of Negro revolutionaries were met and overpowered by state and Federal troops. More than a hundred slaves were killed immediately, and within a few weeks Turner himself was captured and executed. Right down to the Civil War slaves demonstrated their violent antipathy to slavery by attempting to rise against it, but their successes were few indeed.

Free Negroes, South and North

In 1790 there were some 59,000 Negroes in the United States who were not slaves, a considerable increase over the twenty black indentured servants who landed in Jamestown in 1619. By 1830 there were 319,000; and by 1860 there were 488,000, of whom 44 percent lived in the South and 46 percent in the North. Some had been set free by their masters. Others had purchased their freedom. Some were born of free mothers, white and

Negro. Others had run away and made good their bid for freedom. In the South the existence of a large number of free Negroes proved to be a source of constant embarrassment to the slaveholders, since their existence undermined the very foundation on which slavery was built. Southerners carried on a campaign of vilification against free Negroes and undertook a program of legislation designed to keep the free Negro in his place.

A free Negro's existence, even in the North, was precarious. A white person could claim, however fraudulently, that the free Negro was his slave; and the heavy burden of proof that he was not rested on the accused. There was the danger, moreover, of his being kidnaped, as often happened. In the South the chances of being reduced to servitude or slavery by court decree was also great. All Southern states required free Negroes to have passes and certificates of freedom. Some states, such as Virginia, Tennessee, Georgia and Florida, required registration; some others compelled free Negroes to have white guardians.

The controls which the state and community exercised over free Negroes increased year by year. In no Southern state could a free Negro move about as he wished, and in some Northern communities it was dangerous to try. Some states forbade free Negroes to possess or carry firearms without a license. By 1835 the right of assembly had been taken away from almost all Negroes in the South, and their contact with others was, by law, kept to a minimum. Many proscriptions interfered with their making a living. In 1805 Maryland prohibited free Negroes from selling corn, wheat or tobacco without a license. In 1831 North Carolina required all Negro traders and peddlers to be licensed, while most states required free Negroes to work and their means of support had to be visible.

In the nineteenth century Negroes steadily lost their various citizenship rights. In 1800 they voted almost everywhere. By 1835 they could vote in no Southern state, while Pennsylvania and Indiana confined the franchise to whites in 1838 and 1851 respectively. Seldom did they enjoy protection at the hands of the state or local government. In cities such as Pittsburgh, Philadelphia and New York they were attacked with impunity by mobs, their homes and churches destroyed, and they were run out of the community. It was this kind of treatment, North and South, that caused Fanny Kemble to say, "They are not slaves indeed, but they are pariahs, debarred from every fellowship save with their own despised race. . . . All hands are extended to thrust them out, all fingers point at their dusky skin, all tongues have learned to turn the very name of their race into an insult and a reproach."

In the face of all this, however, there were free Negroes who not only survived but did rather well. They were engaged in numerous occupations, and some of them accumulated considerable wealth. Individual cases of affluence are numerous. They extend from the wealthy Thomy Lafon, who accumulated an estate in New Orleans of more than a half-million dollars, to James Forten, the Philadelphia sailmaker who had a fortune of more than one hundred thousand dollars. Schools for Negro children increased in the North during the nineteenth century; and in some communities, such as Boston and New Bedford after 1855, they were permitted to attend school with the whites. In the South, where teaching of free Negroes was generally outlawed after 1830, many of them received private instruction. There are examples, moreover, of free Negroes going to the North, to Canada and to Europe for an education during the antebellum period. Some Northern free Negroes were attending colleges and universities. Bowdoin was the first college to graduate a Negro when John Russwurm received his degree there in 1826. After that time Oberlin, Harvard and other institutions received free Negroes.

Negroes were becoming articulate and expressed their views in a variety of media. They held conventions, beginning in 1831, and in their resolutions and petitions they indicated their feelings and aspirations. They published newspapers, *Freedom's Journal,* the *North Star* and the *Anglo-African.* They wrote books: Frederick Douglass and a host of former slaves wrote autobiographies; J. W. C. Pennington wrote a history of the Negro people; George Moses Horton published a book of verse, and William Wells Brown published numerous works, including a novel.

Perhaps the most important work performed by free Negroes was the general assistance they gave to the antislavery movement as it increased in intensity after 1830. Negroes were among the most enthusiastic supporters of William Lloyd Garrison when he began to publish his *Liberator* in 1831. Many joined the American Antislavery Society and the regional and state societies when they were organized. Frederick Douglass was merely the best known of a larger number of writers and speakers in the antislavery cause. Others were Charles Remond, Charles B. Ray, Henry Highland Garnet, David Ruggles, Sarah Remond, Frances Harper, Sojourner Truth and Harriet Tubman. In their militant bitterness the Negro abolitionists equaled and sometimes surpassed their white colleagues. Perhaps not even Garrison reached the intensity of feeling against slavery that David Walker, a Boston Negro, reached in his *Appeal in Four Articles.* Many Negro leaders, moreover, counseled violence if no other approach against slavery was successful. In 1854 the Negro convention adopted a resolution that represented the views of an increasing number of Negroes. In part it declared that "those who, without crime, are outlawed by any government can owe no allegiance to its enactments. . . . We advise all oppressed to adopt the motto, 'Liberty or Death.'" This was five years before John Brown attacked Harper's Ferry.

CIVIL WAR AND RECONSTRUCTION

The Evolution of Federal Policy

The unequivocal stand that white and Negro abolitionists took against slavery in the 1850's made compromise difficult, if not impossible, from their point of view. The vigorous defense of slavery by white Southerners as best for the country and best for the Negro, ruled out any possibility of concessions on their part. The impasse was not relieved by the position of the leading political parties: the Southern Democrats held that the election to the Presidency of a "Black Republican" such as Abraham Lincoln was wholly unacceptable to them and they would prefer secession to abolitionist rule. The Republicans would not concede that slavery should be permitted in the territories, and while they would permit slavery to continue where it existed, they were determined to pursue a policy of containment. When Lincoln was elected the Southern leaders concluded that secession was their only recourse. When Lincoln decided that the secessionists were not entitled to all the Federal forts, post offices and other properties in the South, the war broke out.

When Lincoln issued a call for 75,000 volunteers in April, 1861, Negroes rushed forward to offer their services. Frederick Douglass expressed the sentiments of many Negroes when he said, "Standing outside the pale of American humanity, denied citizenship, unable to call the land of my birth my country . . . and longing for the end of the bondage of my people, I was ready for any political upheaval which should bring about a change in the existing condition of things." Indeed, as the Negro historian, Joseph T. Wilson, recalled, "at the sound of the tocsin at the North, Negro waiter, cook, barber, bootblack, groom, porter and laborer stood ready at the enlisting office." In many parts of the country—Boston, Providence, Philadelphia, Cleveland, Battle Creek—Negroes organized themselves into military corps and offered their services. In every instance their services were declined. The Secretary of War was curt and firm: "this Department has no intention to call into the service of the Government any colored soldiers."

Negroes were critical of the Government for rejecting them, and so were many whites. Horace Greeley, after the fiasco at Bull Run in the summer of 1861, was bitter in his denunciation as were some other anti-slavery editors. But the Lincoln government wanted to be careful not to convey the impression that the war was one for freedom. There were many Northerners, including some soldiers, who feared that it would become one. "We don't want to fight side and side with the nigger," said a young soldier from New York; "We think we are too superior a race for that." But if Negroes could not fight, they would help in other ways. Many Southern Negroes offered to help the Confederacy, which also rejected their services as soldiers. Northern Negroes offered money, goods and their support of the Union in other ways. They served as cooks, teamsters, hospital attendants and body servants.

At some point early in the war, perhaps in the first year, Negroes even in the South began to believe that their freedom was connected with the war. As they did, they not only took a greater interest in the war but also did whatever they could to promote a Union victory. Slaves, who had vowed to help their masters in any way that they could, now began to leave the plantations and join the Union lines, if they were close enough. Loyalty, about which masters boasted, became the exception rather than the rule, according to Bell Irvin Wiley in his *Southern Negroes, 1861–1865*. When the slaves of Georgetown, South Carolina, sang "We'll fight for liberty" in 1861 they were thrown in jail. By the second year of the war, slaves were leaving the plantations in such large numbers that the whites became apprehensive not only because of the loss of labor but also because they feared uprisings and acts of revenge.

President Lincoln was under severe pressure from a powerful sector in Congress not only to permit Negroes to enlist as soldiers but also to issue a proclamation setting all Negroes free. Charles Sumner, United States Senator from Massachusetts, was one of the leaders urging such a policy upon the President. But the President was adamant. He feared, he said, that if Negroes were set free and given arms, thousands of white soldiers from the border states would lay down their arms. In his newspaper Frederick Douglass urged a policy of emancipation, declaring that the "Union cause would never prosper till the war assumed an Antislavery attitude, and the Negro was enlisted on the loyal side." But the President would not be moved.

Union generals were moving, however, much to the embarrassment of the President. In May, 1861, the daring, flamboyant Benjamin Butler, in command at Fort Monroe, refused to give up three slaves and, in effect, had set them free as contrabands of war to be employed by the Union forces there. In August, 1861, General John C. Frémont proclaimed martial law in Missouri and declared as free the slaves who had been confiscated from persons resisting the authority of the United States. Lincoln ordered Fremont to show leniency as to martial law and to modify the emancipation order to conform to existing law. In March, 1862, General David Hunter, in command of the Department of the South, began to issue certificates of emancipation to all slaves who had been employed by the Confederacy. In the following month he declared slaves free throughout the Department of the South. This was too much for Lincoln. On May 19 he countermanded the Hunter proclamation, making it clear that neither Hunter nor any other commander had been authorized to emancipate the slaves.

Even the Congress was moving. In August, 1861, it passed the first Confiscation Act, providing that when slaves were engaged in hostile military service, the owners' claims to the labor of such slaves were forfeited. In April, 1862, Congress abolished slavery in the District of Columbia, and in the following June it abolished slavery in the territories. Congress took its boldest step toward emancipation when it passed the Second Confiscation Act in July, 1862. The act provided that if anyone committed treason, his slaves were free. It further provided that the slaves of all persons supporting rebellion should be "forever free of their servitude, and not again held as slaves." Perhaps now it was time for the President to act.

While Lincoln was unequivocally opposed to slavery, he firmly believed that Negroes and whites could not live together side by side once Negroes were free. He therefore looked toward the colonization of Negroes outside the United States—in Africa or in the Caribbean area. He attempted to enlist the support of Negroes as well as influential members of Congress in his colonization schemes, but he was totally unsuccessful. The President also believed that there would be less controversy over emancipation if the owners of slaves were compensated for their losses. It was at his insistence that Congress wrote into the act setting slaves free in the District of Columbia a provision for the compensation of their owners. But he was unable to persuade any considerable number of the wisdom of such a policy.

Early in the second year of his administration Lincoln decided that he should emancipate the slaves. It was not only just and right, he was later to say; it was also good policy that would hasten the end of the war. In the late spring of 1862 he began to draft a proclamation setting the slaves free. After the Second Confiscation Act was passed, he rewrote his draft and read it to a meeting of the Cabinet on July 22, 1862. Some members did not like it at all, while others thought that he should wait until a propitious moment to issue it. He decided to wait. Meanwhile, he was attacked by numerous persons for not issuing such a proclamation. Five days after the Battle of Antietam, he issued the preliminary Emancipation Proclamation, declaring that slaves in states still in rebellion on January 1, 1863, would be set free.

Reaction to the Proclamation was mixed. The President's critics said that it was an act of desperation calculated to incite the slaves against their masters. His supporters greeted the Proclamation with enthusiasm. Even the abolitionists, while not entirely satisfied, regarded it as a good beginning. When the President issued the final Emancipation Proclamation on January 1, 1863, he named the states and portions of states where it was applicable. He also invited Negroes to enlist in the armed service of the United States "to garrison forts, positions, stations, and other places, and to man vessels of all sorts in said service." As he put his signature to the Proclamation, the President said, "I never, in my life, felt more certain that I was doing right than I do in signing this paper." There was rejoicing throughout the Union. Union policy had evolved.

Negroes Fighting for Freedom and Union

Even before Lincoln issued the Emancipation Proclamation, the War Department had authorized the enlistment of Negroes in the Department of the South, "not exceeding five thousand"; and Ben Butler in Louisiana and Jim Lane in Kansas were receiving Negroes in the Army. Early in 1863 the enlistment of Negroes accelerated. In the North leading Negroes like Frederick Douglass acted as recruiting agents, while in the South white soldiers were assigned to the task of enlisting slaves. Rallies were held at which speakers urged Negroes to enlist; and in Boston, New York, and Philadelphia they went to the recruiting stations in large numbers. By the end of the war more than 186,000 Negroes had enrolled in the Union Army. From the seceded states came 93,000; from the border slave states, 40,000; and from the free states, approximately 53,000. It is possible that the total figure was larger, for some contemporaries insisted that many mulattoes served in white outfits without being designated as Negroes.

While some whites declined to command the men serving in the group designated as "United States Colored Troops," others were pleased to do so. Among them were outstanding leaders such as Colonel Thomas Wentworth Higginson, of the First South Carolina Volunteers; Colonel Robert Gould Shaw, of the Fifty-Fourth Massachusetts Regiment, and General N. P. Banks, of the First and Third Louisiana Native Guards. There were several outstanding Negro officers: Captain P. B. S. Pinchback and Major F. E. Dumas of Louisiana; Major Martin Delany and Captain O. S. B. Wall of the One Hundred and Fourth Regiment; hospital surgeons such as Charles B. Purvis and John Rapier, and chaplains such as Henry M. Turner and James Underdue. At the beginning there was discrimination in pay, and the Negro soldiers were bitter in their denunciation of the practice. Finally, in 1864 they were successful in their drive to secure equal pay.

Negroes saw action in every theater of operation. They were at Milliken's Bend in Louisiana, Olustee in Florida, Vicksburg in Mississippi and at the siege of Savannah. They took part in the reduction of Petersburg and were at the surrender at Appomattox Court House. Many of them were cited for gallantry. Four men of the Massachusetts Fifty-Fourth earned the Gilmore Medal for their heroism in the assault on Fort Wagner, in which their commanding officer, Colonel Shaw, lost his life. George Washington Williams, in his *History of the Negro Troops in the Rebellion,* says that Negroes saw action in more than 250 skirmishes and that the "roll of honor is luminous with the names of Negro soldiers who, by deeds of personal valor, won the applause of the commanding general and the Congress of the United States."

Negroes served in other ways. They organized raiding parties, went through Confederate lines to destroy fortifications and supplies, built fortifications and supplies, built fortifications along the coasts and up the rivers, and served as spies and scouts. Some women, such as Harriet Tubman, spied for the Union army.

More than 38,000 Negroes lost their lives in the war, their rate of mortality being about 40 percent greater than that of the white soldiers. It would be difficult for later critics to say that Negroes did not fight for their freedom but had it handed to them, just as it was unrealistic for white soldiers to object to fighting on the grounds that they were not anxious to risk their lives to set idle Negroes free.

If the end of the war marked a victory for the theory of the indestructibility of the Union, it was a signal victory for the cause of freedom. The end of the war brought to a close a period of enslavement that had lasted for some two hundred and fifty years. The desire for freedom had been kept alive through the centuries by those Negroes who demonstrated by their conduct that freedom and the right to it transcended racial lines. The victory was won, in part, by their struggles through the centuries as well as by their services in the final battles.

An Uncertain Peace

As the war progressed Lincoln made many plans. One of them had to do with the settlement of the problems of war once the hostilities ceased.

In his Proclamation of Amnesty and Reconstruction, in December, 1863, he spelled out these plans. The spirit was one of leniency. Only a few of the leaders of the Confederacy were not to be restored to the full enjoyment of their rights as citizens, and when 10 percent of the 1860 electorate had taken the oath of allegiance, the government of a given state would be restored. This meant, of course, that the government would be exclusively white. But Lincoln also had plans for Negroes. He hoped that they would be given the franchise; and in 1864 he suggested to the governor of Louisiana that at least Negroes of education and property should be permitted to vote. He also hoped, through the Freedmen's Bureau and otherwise, that adequate educational opportunities for Negroes would be provided. On more than one occasion toward the end of the war, he indicated that Negroes should receive the same treatment as other citizens.

The former Confederate states that were restored by Lincoln and, after April, 1865, by Johnson were dominated by former Confederate leaders. They had no intention of extending any semblance of equality to their former slaves. Indeed, they had little enthusiasm for the Thirteenth Amendment that was being ratified during the summer and fall of 1865. It is not surprising, therefore, that as these governments formulated new policies they were controlled by the view that the Negro was inferior and should be kept subordinate. The new black codes, passed by the Southern legislatures in 1865 and 1866, gave expression to this view. Negroes could now own and dispose of property, could make contracts and enter into marriage and were competent witnesses in cases involving Negroes. The vagrancy laws, authorizing the arrest of Negroes with no visible means of support, were a thinly disguised plan to exploit the services of the Negro working force. Some states forbade Negroes to purchase farm land, while others enacted curfew laws for Negroes, forbade the possession of liquor and firearms by Negroes and outlawed acts of insolence by Negroes. No Southern state made any provision for the education of Negroes at the time that schools for whites were being established.

When Congress met in December, 1865, it was greeted with the news of the black codes and of the domination of the Southern state legislatures by former Confederates. Congress refused to seat members from those states, and many members began to talk openly of the necessity of punishing traitors. Early in the following year the Joint Committee that had been set up by Congress recommended the continuation of the policy of keeping Southern members out and the enactment of legislation designed to protect freedmen.

One piece of legislation growing out of these recommendations was the Civil Rights Act of 1866 that guaranteed the rights of all citizens regardless of race. Another was the extension of the Freedmen's Bureau, which was vetoed by the President but finally passed over his veto. A third was the passage of a resolution that incorporated in it the provisions of the Civil Rights Act and that became in 1868 the Fourteenth Amendment. News from the South put Congress in an even more uncompromising mood. The Freedmen's Bureau was helping destitute whites as well as Negroes and was making provisions for schools for Negroes where the whites had neglected them; but it was being bitterly opposed in virtually every Southern community. White Northern teachers who had been engaged by the Bureau or by religious groups to teach Negroes were not only ostracized by the whites but were, in some cases, run out of the community. Negroes, moreover, were being subjected to numerous forms of intimidation and terror. In their conventions in 1865 and 1866 the Negroes passed resolutions asking the President and Congress for protection. In the spring and summer of 1866 race riots in Memphis and New Orleans confirmed the worst fears of the Northerners. A reign of terror was sweeping the South. Something would have to be done.

It was in March, 1867, that Congress took over from the President the task of Reconstruction. It reimposed military rule on the South, disfranchised all former Confederates who had voluntarily taken up arms against the United States, called for new governments based on the suffrage of all loyal men, regardless of race, and required the ratification of the Fourteenth Amendment as a condition for readmission to the Union. No provisions were made for the economic rehabilitation of the former slaves, no "forty acres and a mule" that some had believed they would receive. Political power was in the hands of the Northern whites who had taken up residence in the South, Southern whites who could take the oath that they had not voluntarily fought against the United States, and the Negroes. Economic power, however, remained in the hands of the former Confederates who, now, were sitting on the sidelines, ready to attack and oppose everything that the new political leaders sought to establish.

In the constitutional conventions called to write new organic laws for the former Confederate states, Negroes were in the majority in only one of them, South Carolina. In Louisiana the forty-nine Negro delegates were equal in number to the whites. In some states, such as Georgia, Alabama and North Carolina, the native whites outnumbered the Negroes. In states such as Texas and Arkansas, the number of Negroes in the conventions was small. Even so, the conventions were ridiculed as "Ethiopian minstrelsy" and "Ham radicalism." Much more was said about how the delegates looked than about what the delegates did.

The conventions gave the South the best constitutions it had ever had.

The new documents forbade any race or color distinctions in their suffrage provisions. They provided for free common school systems; but only in South Carolina and Louisiana were integrated schools attempted. The right to travel, to a proper trial and to the fair administration of justice were provided for. They eased the burdens of the debtors, but did not provide for the confiscation and redistribution of the land. In each state the black codes were either repealed outright or superseded by new laws. By the summer of 1868 all states, except Virginia, Texas and Mississippi, had been readmitted to the Union and their representatives in Congress seated. By 1870 all states were back in the Union.

The period that followed has been described as one of Negro rule. But Negroes were not in control of the state governments at any time anywhere in the South. They held public office and, at times, played important parts in public life. Only in South Carolina did they ever have a numerical majority in the lower house of the legislature. From the outset, whites controlled the upper house. At all times the governor was white. There were other leaders: Negroes were lieutenant governors in 1870 and 1872. From 1868 to 1872 Francis Cardozo was secretary of state and from 1872 to 1876 he was state treasurer. The situation was not so favorable for Negroes anywhere else in the South. In Mississippi of seven state officers, only one, that of secretary of state, was filled by a colored man, until 1873 when colored men were elected to three of the seven offices. In some states, very few Negroes held positions of prominence.

The Negroes who stood out were those of education and experience. Cardozo of South Carolina had been educated at the University of Glasgow and in London. Hiram Revels, elected to the United States Senate from Mississippi, had been educated in a seminary in Ohio and at Knox College in Illinois. James T. Rapier, Negro member of Congress from Alabama, had been sent by his white father to school in Canada. Jonathan J. Wright had been educated in Pennsylvania and was a member of the Pennsylvania bar before he migrated to South Carolina, where he became a member of the state supreme court. Some, however, were self-made, like Robert Smalls who had won fame during the Civil War by piloting the Confederate ship, the *Planter,* out of Charleston harbor and delivering it to Union officials. He was later to sit in Congress. Or, like John R. Lynch, speaker of the house in Mississippi and later a member of Congress, who sat outside the window of a white school and learned everything the white students were being taught.

Sixteen Negroes served in Congress between 1869 and 1880. Two of them, Hiram Revels and Blanche K. Bruce, represented Mississippi in the Senate. South Carolina sent six Negroes to the House of Representatives, the largest number from a single state; but they were not all in the House at the same time. Alabama sent three, while Georgia, Florida, Mississippi, North Carolina and Louisiana sent one each. Their responsible conduct moved James G. Blaine, their contemporary, to observe, "The colored men who took their seats in both Senate and House did not appear ignorant or helpless. They were as a rule studious, earnest, ambitious men, whose public conduct . . . would be honorable to any race."

It cannot be said that the Reconstruction governments or that the Negro leaders were more corrupt than their contemporaries in other parts of the country. There was graft in connection with railroad construction, printing contracts, public works and the like. Wherever there was corruption, it was marked by the participation of all segments of society: former Confederates as well as Northern Whites and Negroes. Corruption was bisectional, bipartisan and biracial.

If no race or party had a monopoly on public immorality, it can be said that no group was the sole keeper of the public conscience. In the South, however, the groups that opposed Reconstruction insisted that they were. They insisted that "Negro rule" had brought on evils and sufferings and must be destroyed. This view is what stimulated the growth of the Ku Klux Klan and similar groups after 1867. Rumor had it that the Union League, which had been organized during the war, was teaching Negroes not only to be faithful to the Republican Party but also to regard themselves as the equals of whites in every respect. The Klan began to assail the league as the enemy of the South. It began to attack white and Negro members, destroy their property, and whip and sometimes murder them. Politically minded Negroes and so-called Negro militia units were the special objects of attack by Klansmen. Despite the fact that very few troops had ever been in the South after the Civil War, the Klan used any and all armed Negroes as an excuse to attack Negroes generally. Murders, lynchings and drownings were the hazards facing Negroes and whites who played any part in the reconstruction of the South.

Reconstruction had no chance in the South because it did not provide for even a semblance of economic security and independence on the part of the Negroes. Negro voters were still at the mercy, for a livelihood, of those who were bitterly opposed to their exercising the franchise. It is remarkable that Negroes were able to gain any economic security, but some of them did. By 1866 the freedmen in Florida had secured homesteads covering 160,000 acres of land; and by 1874 the Negroes of Georgia owned more than 350,000 acres. Those with some skills, moreover, such as tailors, caulkers, blacksmiths and cabinetmakers, were able to secure employment. But the vast majority of Negroes had neither the means nor the skills to achieve economic stability. Most of them were employed by their former masters who could merely threaten them with starvation if they persisted in exercising the franchise. Meanwhile, Northern financiers and industrialists were gradually moving in to establish economic control over the South. Negroes were excluded altogether from the new opportunities; and they could hold their old jobs only if they obeyed the command of their employers to stay out of politics. The economic stranglehold that the whites held over Negroes was enough to put an end to Reconstruction.

Indeed, Reconstruction was over in some places almost before it began. If one measures the time from the readmission of the reconstructed states to the time of Democratic victories, one is impressed with how short the period was. While these periods varied from state to state, they were less than a decade, except in Florida, South Carolina and Louisiana. Even during the time it existed, Reconstruction was not very radical. Segregated schools and laws against intermarriage persisted. There was no confiscation and redistribution of the land. The military occupation was brief and ineffective, and Negroes did not dominate any governments. The Fourteenth Amendment was, on the whole, a dead letter; and the Fifteenth Amendment was not enforced by the Federal Government. In the end, the Negro was only slightly better off than he had been when the war came in 1861.

EARLY STRUGGLES FOR CITIZENSHIP

Loss of Civil Rights

When chattel slavery was abolished in 1865, some interested observers made the direst predictions about the future of the freedmen. They entertained serious doubts about the Negro's capacity to survive as a free man. Ignoring the incredible suffering that made little distinction among the races at the end of the war, these observers saw in the destitution and disease among Negroes a portent of their complete extinction. An eminent white Southerner, Dr. C. K. Marshall of Mississippi, was quite certain about this when he said in 1866, "In all probability New Year's Day, on the morning of the first of January, 1920, the colored population in the South will scarcely be counted." While most Americans were uncertain about the future of the Negro in the United States, they were not nearly as pessimistic regarding numbers as Dr. Marshall. Most of them seemed to agree that the

American Negro would at least survive; and many entertained the hope that he could be utilized, if not exploited, in the advancement of American civilization. The Negro not only survived, but demonstrated a remarkable capacity to thrive even in an atmosphere where his freedom was continually compromised. When the war came in 1861 there were approximately 4,441,830 Negroes in the United States, of whom 3,953,000 were slaves. By 1900 the Negro population had virtually doubled.

While the problem of survival was early solved once and for all, the problem of the status of the Negro was a continuing one, long after the end of Reconstruction. Toward the end of Reconstruction, as the collapse of the enforcement of Federal laws deprived Negroes of their opportunity to vote, their enjoyment of other rights was also being challenged. Congress made one last effort to protect them. In May, 1870, Senator Charles Sumner introduced the most far-reaching civil rights bill that was to be considered by Congress until 1964. The bill provided for equal rights in railroads, steamboats, public conveyances, hotels, licensed theaters, houses of public entertainment, common schools, all institutions of learning authorized by law, churches, cemetery associations and juries in Federal and state courts. For a time the bill had a rocky and uncertain fate. When it finally became law in 1875, it declared that the United States should "mete out equal and exact justice to all, of whatever nativity, race, color, or persuasion, religious or political." From the beginning the climate in the country was not favorable to the enforcement of the act, which had already been "watered down" by the deletion of the provision to desegregate the schools. During its eight years of life the act provided little protection for Negroes because of the rather general failure to enforce it.

That the act would ultimately be tested in the courts was a foregone conclusion; and its unhappy fate was almost as certain. Of the incidents involved in the cases that came to the Supreme Court under the Civil Rights Act, one involved the use of a parlor car by a Negro in Tennessee; another involved the denial of hotel accommodations for Negroes in one Northern state; others involved the use of public facilities in Missouri, California, Kentucky and New York. In the decision of the Court, Mr. Justice Bradley, speaking for the majority, held the relevant provisions of the act unconstitutional. Congress could enact legislation to meet the exigency of state action adverse to the rights of citizens as secured by the Fourteenth Amendment, he said. But Congress could not properly "cover the whole domain of rights appertaining to life, liberty, and property, defining them and providing for their vindication."

Under the Fourteenth Amendment, as interpreted by the Court, there could be no significant advancement of the Negro toward full citizenship.

Negroes were generally discouraged by the decision, and they recalled that the Court had not been a source of strength, as far as they were concerned. The Dred Scott decision in 1857 had declared that Negroes were not citizens. The decisions in the Reese and Cruikshank cases in 1876 indicated that the Congress could not enact legislation to protect the rights guaranteed in the Fifteenth Amendment. Now, in the Civil Rights Cases the Fourteenth Amendment was rendered ineffective. Small wonder that Negroes saw it as reversing the trend and moving the Negroes back toward slavery. T. T. Allain, a Negro leader in Louisiana, said that the decision showed that whites of the North and South had allied "to leave the Negro to fend for himself." T. Thomas Fortune, the Negro editor and essayist, said that Negroes felt that they had been "baptized in ice water." John Mercer Langston who, in 1889, would become the only Negro ever elected to Congress from Virginia, called the decision "a stab in the back."

The attitudes of vast numbers of the country's influential white people had as much to do with defining the status of the Negro as anything that the Supreme Court or any other branch of the Federal Government was doing. The dark cloud of assumed racial differences became more ominous than ever; and it bespoke a new, more frightening conclusion that many Americans had reached: that racial differences were normal and natural and the American Negro was a classic example of the hopeless inferiority of a whole race of people. It was the Darwinian mood that sustained the belief in Anglo-Saxon superiority and obsessed many American thinkers in the last quarter of the nineteenth century. Whites were in a dominant position because they were the superior race; they were the fittest. Primitives such as Negroes were in an arrested stage of childhood or adolescence and could never gain the full stature of manhood. Distinguished white scholars argued that it was absurd to attempt to change the natural order of things. As early as 1876 William G. Sumner advocated the restoration of "home rule" in the South because Reconstruction had attempted the impossible in trying to reverse the natural course of things in which superior whites ruled over inferior blacks.

The leading and most respected literary journals of the country reflected the view that the Negro was inferior and did not possess rights which should be protected by government. In the last two decades of the nineteenth century such journals as *Harper's, Scribners,* and the *Atlantic Monthly* strained their own ample ingenuity by portraying the Negro in the most unfavorable light. In an exhaustive study of the period, *The Negro in American Life and Thought,* Rayford W. Logan has shown that every possible insulting term was used by these journals in reference to Negroes. They were made to appear ludicrous by the bestowal of absurd titles on them. Invariably they were described as ugly. In articles, stories, anecdotes, poems and cartoons, Negroes were made to appear superstitious, dull, stupid, imitative, ignorant, happy-go-lucky, improvident, lazy, immoral and criminal. Southern writers were doing the same thing. In his *The Leopard's Spots: A Romance of the White Man's Burden* and in other works, Thomas Dixon, Jr., described in vivid terms the "base" character of the Negro. This, he argued, justified almost any degradation the Negro received at the hands of his white superiors.

It followed that if Negroes were as undesirable and unfit for civilization as the writers, North and South, claimed, they were not fit associates for white people and should be segregated. There had been some segregation, both in law and in practice before and during Reconstruction. But, as C. Vann Woodward has pointed out in *The Strange Career of Jim Crow*, it was not nearly so extensive as was once believed. There were many instances of unsegregated relations between Negroes and whites. The major Protestant churches were divided as between North and South even before the war; but within the South there were few if any separate white and Negro Protestant churches. From their beginnings after the Civil War, the public schools of the South were, with few exceptions, segregated. The armed services were segregated during the Civil War and remained so during the following years. The first state segregation statutes were those of Mississippi and Florida in 1865. The Tennessee law of 1881, sometimes referred to as the first jim crow law, directed railroad companies to provide separate cars or portions of cars for first-class Negro passengers, instead of relegating them to second-class accommodations, as had been the custom.

In the ensuing twenty years, the separation of Negroes and whites on public carriers and almost everywhere else became a favorite preoccupation of some Southern legislators, although opposition on the part of some articulate whites, such as George W. Cable, continued until the end of the century. By 1892 six southern states had joined Tennessee in segregating Negroes on public carriers—Texas, Louisiana, Alabama, Arkansas, Georgia, and Kentucky. In some states there was substantial opposition on the part of Negroes and their white supporters. In Louisiana a Negro representative declared that the segregation law would humiliate Negroes and "make them appear before the world as a treacherous and dangerous class of people." In Arkansas a Negro member of the House sought to ridicule the segregation bill's supporters by insisting that if whites did not want to associate with Negroes, there should be laws to divide the streets and sidewalks so that Negroes could go on one side and white people on the other. He would like "to see an end put to all intercourse between white and colored people by day, and especially by night."

As the pattern of segregation took shape in some states, pressure for various forms of segregation mounted in other states. South Carolina passed a law segregating Negroes and whites on railroads in 1898. North Carolina and Virginia enacted similar legislation in 1899 and 1900 respectively. When Oklahoma entered the union in 1907 every conceivable form of segregation had already been provided for. Segregation was spreading to other activities related to transportation. In 1888 the railroad commission of Mississippi was authorized to designate separate waiting rooms for Negroes and whites. By 1893 the railroad companies, on their own initiative, were doing the same thing in South Carolina. By 1907 segregation had been enacted into law in all Southern states on street cars, penitentiaries, county jails, convict camps, institutions for the blind and deaf, hospitals for the insane and other institutions.

While the Southern states were in the process of enacting laws to separate the races, the Supreme Court, in the decision of *Plessy* v *Ferguson,* gave them all the encouragement they needed. In 1890 Louisiana had enacted a law providing that "all railway companies carrying passengers in their coaches in this state, shall provide separate but equal accommodations for the white and colored races." When Plessy, who was as white as any person in New Orleans but who was known to have Negro blood, boarded a coach reserved for whites, he was ordered to the colored coach. When he refused to do so, he was arrested and charged with violating the law. Plessy argued that the Louisiana statute was in conflict with the Thirteenth Amendment abolishing slavery and the Fourteenth Amendment, which prohibits certain restrictive legislation on the part of the states. The Supreme Court did not agree. Speaking for the Court, Mr. Justice Bradley interpreted the statute as intending to enforce "absolute equality of the two races before the law" while recognizing fundamental distinctions between them. Thus, the doctrine of "separate but equal" became the law of the land and gave moral as well as legal support to those who were busily engaged in enacting segregation statutes.

Meanwhile, the Southern states had undertaken to disfranchise Negroes in order to make certain that they would not have the political strength to resist the move to make permanent their status as second-class citizens. Advocates of disfranchisement had to be certain that they did not contravene the Fifteenth Amendment or offend illiterate poor whites. As early as 1886 sentiment in Mississippi, where a majority of the population were Negroes, was strong for constitutional revision. A convention met in 1890 for the primary purpose of disfranchising the Negro. A suffrage amendment was written which imposed a poll tax of two dollars, excluded voters convicted of bribery, burglary, theft, arson, perjury, murder and bigamy, and also barred all who could not read any section of the state constitution, or understand it when read, or give a reasonable interpretation of it. Before the convention Negroes from forty counties met and protested to President Harrison their impending disfranchisement. The President did nothing; and since the new constitution was never submitted for ratification but simply put into effect, its opponents had no change of working to defeat it.

South Carolina followed Mississippi by disfranchising Negroes in 1895. Ben Tillman, who had initiated the campaign for disfranchisement, left the United States Senate and returned to the convention in South Carolina to push through the desired revision of the constitution. The new clause called for two years' residence, a poll tax of one dollar, the ability to read and write the constitution or own property worth three hundred dollars, and the disqualification of convicts. Negro delegates bitterly denounced the move. In answer to Tillman's charge that Negroes had done nothing to demonstrate their capacity for government, Thomas E. Miller, a leading Negro in the state, replied that Negroes were largely responsible for the "laws relative to finance, the building of penal and charitable institutions and, greatest of all, the establishment of the public school system." The story was essentially the same in Louisiana where, in 1898, a new device, the "Grandfather Clause," was written into the constitution. This called for an addition to the permanent registration list the names of all males whose fathers or grandfathers were qualified to vote on January 1, 1867. At that time, of course, no Negroes in Louisiana were qualified to vote. Negroes, but not whites, therefore had to comply with the educational and property requirements. By 1910 the Negro had also been effectively disfranchised in Virginia, Georgia, North Carolina, Alabama and Oklahoma.

By the end of the nineteenth century the Negro had lost most of the civil rights that he had ever enjoyed, however fleetingly. He had been denied the use of public accommodations; he had been disfranchised; and the concept of "separate but equal" had given the whites an opportunity to reduce Negro schools to the lowest level of inadequacy. In South Carolina, where Negroes constituted 61 percent of the school population, they received 21 percent of the school funds. Already, separation seemed to be a guarantee not only of inequality in education but also of a permanently inferior status in American life.

Out of the Mainstream

The end of Reconstruction brought little improvement in the social and economic status of the Negro. While Southern whites were not willing to appropriate very much for the education of Negroes, they seemed less opposed than formerly to the support of Negro education by northern philanthropic and religious organizations. Meanwhile, many Negroes viewed education as their greatest single opportunity to escape the indignities and proscriptions of an oppressive white South. Negro parents sent their children to school in increasing numbers at great sacrifice to themselves; and while the schools were not excellent, they did provide the rudiments of an education. Religious groups such as the American Missionary Association and the Freedmen's Aid Society of the Methodist Church continued the work of the defunct Freedmen's Bureau. Philanthropic agencies such as the George Peabody Fund, the Anna T. Jeanes Fund and Rockefeller's General Education Board gave attention to special problems of Negro education such as teacher training and vocational education. Since many of the grants made by philanthropists were on the condition that local school boards and agencies would match their gift, they had the effect of stimulating a limited amount of local support for Negro education.

Negroes themselves were contributing substantially to the support of their own schools and colleges. At the Sixth Atlanta Conference for the Study of Negro Problems in 1901 it was reported that between 1870 and 1899 Negroes paid a total of $25 million in direct school taxes; while the indirect taxes they paid amounted to more than $45 million. Negroes had paid more than $15 million in tuition and fees to private institutions. The report concluded, "It is a conservative statement to say . . . that American Negroes have in a generation paid directly forty millions of dollars in hard-earned cash for educating their children." The institutions, meanwhile, had done much to sustain themselves. The Fisk Jubilee Singers had gone out in 1875 and had raised more than enough money to construct the first important building at the young university. Other institutions had sent out speakers, demonstrators, and others in the effort to gain support. Self-help became an important principle in the early days of Negro schools and colleges.

The results of the efforts of Negroes to secure an education were gratifying. In 1900 there were 28,560 Negro teachers and more than 1,500,000 Negro children in school. Thirty-four institutions for Negroes were giving collegiate training; and more Negroes were entering the institutions of higher education in the North. There were four state colleges for Negroes —in Virginia, Arkansas, Georgia and Delaware. By 1900 more than two thousand Negroes had graduated from institutions of higher learning, while more than seven hundred were in college at the time. As Negroes manifested an avid interest in education, there were some whites who questioned the wisdom of their securing an education to live in a society in which they were not in the main stream.

Even among Negroes there was no agreement as to the amount and type of education that Negroes should seek. Booker T. Washington, who founded the Tuskegee Institute in 1881, thought that Negroes could be most effective and would be acceptable in the Southern communities if they sought to provide many of the services and much of the produce that the white community needed. He emphasized the intelligent management of farms, ownership of land, proficiency in mechanics, domestic service and the professions. On numerous occasions, and especially in his celebrated speech at Atlanta in 1895, he assured the whites that the Negroes were their friends, that they did not seek social equality but merely an opportunity to serve. His advocacy of vocational education for Negroes was hailed by whites in the North and in the South. They came to regard him as the wisest and most reliable spokesman of his race.

Some Negroes, however, rejected him as their spokesman. Among them was W. E. B. Du Bois, a young Negro trained at Fisk, Harvard (where he received the degree of doctor of philosophy) and Berlin. In books, essays and addresses Du Bois criticized what he viewed as the narrow educational program of Washington which was too predominantly economic in its objectives. He accused Washington of preaching "a gospel of Work and Money to such an extent as apparently almost completely to overshadow the higher aims of life." Du Bois also criticized the manner in which Washington ignored or winked at the white South's denial of the Negro's civil rights. A policy of conciliation had resulted, he insisted, in the disfranchisement of the Negro and the enactment of discriminatory legislation of many kinds. Despite these criticisms of Washington, he remained the most important and, indeed, the most powerful Negro in the United States down to his death in 1915. It was during his ascendancy, however, that lynchings of Negroes reached a new high, Negroes were effectively disfranchised, and Negroes were systematically excluded from American industry and from American labor unions.

In 1880 some 75 percent of the Negroes in the United States were still in the former Confederate states and were primarily engaged in agricultural work. Most of them were without capital with which to purchase land and were compelled to engage in various forms of tenancy and sharecropping. As farm workers their incomes were meager. In 1902 farm laborers in South Carolina were receiving ten dollars per month, while those of New York were receiving twenty-six dollars per month. Some, however, accumulated enough capital to purchase farms. In 1890 Negroes owned 120,738 farms, while in 1910 they owned 218,972 farms, with the average size less than ten acres. Booker Washington, through the farmers' conferences at Tuskegee, sought to eliminate "the evils of the mortgage system, the one-room cabin, buying on credit" and the like; but it was a difficult task in the face of persistent hostility on the part of the white community.

As industry came to the South, the Negro, for the most part, was left out. The iron industry was growing in Tennessee and Alabama, cloth was being manufactured in the Carolinas, and the business of transporting manufactured goods to the Southern consumer was becoming a major economic activity. In 1891 some 196 industrial employers of the South were using only 7,395 Negroes, largely as menials. Ten years later the number had increased substantially, and some Negroes were employed in cotton seed oil mills, saw mills and furniture factories. By 1910 the Negro factory workers had increased to more than 350,000. Prejudice against the Negro worker and the refusal of numbers of whites, North and South, to work with Negroes served to exclude many Negroes from labor unions. Manufacturers thus had two excuses to justify their exclusion of Negroes from greater employment: they were temperamentally unfit, according to no less an authority than *The Manufacturer's Record,* and whites would not work with them.

But Negroes were, in some instances, contributing to the growing industrialization of the United States. Jan E. Matzeliger, a Negro from Dutch Guiana, invented the shoe-lasting machine, which was purchased by the United Shoe Machinery Company of Boston. In 1884 John P. Parker invented a "screw for tobacco presses" and through his own company made many presses. Elijah McCoy patented fifty different inventions relating principally to the automatic lubrication of machines. Granville Woods made significant contributions in the fields of electricity, steam boilers and automatic air brakes. Several of his inventions were assigned to the General Electric Company, the Westinghouse Air Brake Company and the American Bell Telephone Company.

Many Negroes concluded that since they were not in the mainstream of American economic life, they should organize and promote their own businesses. It was with this in mind that Booker Washington called a group of Negro businessmen together in 1900 in Boston and organized the National Negro Business League. Washington urged Negroes to enter a wide variety of business fields. Either in response to Washington's urging or because they already realized the importance of such moves, many Negroes organized their own businesses. They operated grocery and merchandise stores; they were restaurant operators, caterers, bakers, tailors, builders, and contractors. Some operated shirt factories, cotton mills, rubber stamp goods shops, lumber mills and carpet factories. They were also engaged in cooperative enterprises. Most of these businesses were not profitable and lasted only a short time. There were exceptions, however. Madam C. J. Walker founded a hair and skin preparation business and made a fortune. Negro banking and insurance companies in Richmond, Atlanta, Washington, Birmingham and Montgomery achieved both stability and respect.

These signs of progress and prosperity were not enough for many Negroes who remained dissatisfied with their lot in their communities. Their political and social degradation was not relieved by their economic condition; and some of them decided to leave the South for some other part of the country. In 1879 and 1880 thousands of Negroes left the lower South and took up residence in the North and West, and the movement continued for the next several decades. While they met hostile labor unions and rejection by industrialists in the North, they continued to believe that their opportunities were greater elsewhere than in the South. Neither a Congressional investigation nor promises by Southern whites of good treatment and high wages could dissuade them. They were in search of the mainstream of American life that seemed more and more like a will-o'-the-wisp.

The Negro World

Whites in the South and in the North maintained a discreet distance from Negroes and welcomed them into no area of their social activities. Negroes were compelled to work out their own means of survival in a hostile world, and this involved creating institutions and activities that, in turn, created a Negro world. One of the mainstays in the process of providing group cohesion and rendering self-help was the Negro church. Seeing that they were not welcome among the white Baptists, Negroes in 1880 organized the National Baptist Convention. Soon the National Baptist Publishing House began to circulate Sunday School and other religious literature among Negroes. The older denominations among Negroes, African Methodists and Colored Methodists, continued their activities; and in the cities the churches did many things to assist Negroes to adjust to their new environment. In New York, Detroit, Chicago, St. Louis and other cities the Negro churches established employment bureaus, maintained schools of domestic training, and organized various clubs for boys and girls. In Atlanta, Dr. H. H. Proctor's Congregational church organized a day nursery, kindergarten, gymnasium, and school of music; while in Springfield, Massachusetts, Dr. W. N. DeBerry led his Congregational members in the establishment of a home for working girls and a welfare league for women.

Fraternal organizations, with auxiliary activities such as insurance and burial societies, became numerous during the period. The Knights of Pythias and the Knights of Tabor competed for membership among Negro men. Others, such as the Independent Order of St. Luke and the Order of True

Reformers, were open to men and women. Out of some of these organizations came the founders of important insurance companies. S. W. Rutherford left the True Reformers and organized the National Benefit Life Insurance Company of Washington, D.C. In Durham, North Carolina, John Merrick, who had been a True Reformer, joined several others to establish the North Carolina Mutual Life Insurance Company. These and similar businesses grew into important social and economic institutions, providing a variety of benefits for the Negro community.

As Negroes became better educated and more articulate they began to write extensively; and most of their writings dealt with their being Negroes in a white world. Frederick Douglass and Booker Washington wrote their autobiographies. Henry O. Flipper wrote of his experiences as a Negro cadet at West Point. In the effort to refute the arguments of some whites that Negroes had contributed nothing to American civilization, several writers published histories of the Negro in the United States. In 1883 George Washington Williams published his *History of the Negro Race in America* in two volumes. Soon there were histories by E. A. Johnson, W. H. Crogman, and Booker Washington. In 1896 W. E. B. Du Bois brought out his *Suppression of the African Slave Trade,* which became the first work in the Harvard Historical Studies. Negroes were also writing about "the Negro problem" as is evidenced in T. T. Fortune's *Black and White* in 1884 and *The Negro in Politics* in 1885. Meanwhile, Charles W. Chesnutt rose to prominence as a novelist with such works as *The House Behind the Cedars, The Marrow of Tradition* and *The Conjure Woman.* Perhaps no Negro writer of the period had a greater impact than Paul Laurence Dunbar, whose poems won the critical acclaim of such a person as William Dean Howells. Dunbar's *Lyrics of a Lowly Life* and *Oak and Ivy* were widely read at the turn of the century.

Negro newspaper editors remained preoccupied in this period, as they had earlier, with the problem of fighting for a larger place for Negroes in American life. Magazines like the *Southern Workman,* published at Hampton Institute, and the *A.M.E. Review* begun in 1884 were concerned primarily with educational, literary and religious matters. In 1900 there were three daily newspapers—in Norfolk, Kansas City and Washington—and 150 weekly newspapers. Some were widely read and provoked considerable discussion. In Boston, George Forbes and Monroe Trotter were publishing the *Guardian,* which led the fight against Booker Washington. In the nation's capital, the *Washington Bee* was vigorous and outspoken and the *New York Age,* edited by T. Thomas Fortune, was outstanding.

Nothing suggests the extent to which the Negro was still out of the mainstream of American life more than the attention given to the Negro problem by conferences and conventions by whites and by Negroes. At the Lake Mohonk Conference on the Negro Question white citizens in 1890 discussed the educational and economic problems affecting Negroes. The Hampton Conference, conducted in part by Negroes, dealt with similar problems, as did the Capon Springs Conference. There were, moreover, the Tuskegee Conferences conducted by Booker Washington and the Atlanta University Conferences on the Negro Problem conducted by W. E. B. Du Bois. Out of some of them, such as the Atlanta Conferences, came significant published studies. Out of all of them came much talk. Out of none of them came any effective solutions of the many problems that beset American Negroes at the turn of the century.

NEW PATTERNS OF RACIAL ADJUSTMENT

Urban Problems

Writing shortly after the beginning of the twentieth century, W. E. B. Du Bois said that the problem of that century would be the problem of the color line. It was the experience of the closing years of the nineteenth century that prompted Du Bois to make the observation. It was not merely the Supreme Court decision in the Plessy case, or the riot in Wilmington, North Carolina, or the increase in the number of lynchings each year. It was also the employment of the total political and legal apparatus of many of the states for the purpose of making full citizenship for Negroes impossible. It was the meek acquiescence of the Federal Government in the South's so-called "legal" disfranchisement of Negroes through state constitutional amendments that were as transparent as they were specious. It was the use of law enforcement officers to sanction the denial of the rights of Negroes. It was the perfection of the machinery of segregation and discrimination in many parts of the country. It was the determination to frustrate those Negroes, who, like so many other Americans, believed that their major problems could be solved in the cities to which they flocked in ever increasing numbers.

The trickle of Negroes northward, that began in the late eighteen seventies, was almost a steady stream by 1900. The stimulus was not only the depressing conditions of the South but also the opportunities that Negroes thought they would have in the North. Agents of Northern employment offices or Northern factory owners went to Southern farms as well as Southern towns to lure Negro workers to the North. As long as the agents could evade hostile local police or other authorities their task was not very difficult. Thousands of Carolina and Georgia Negroes migrated to the industrial Northeast. Similar groups from the South Central states—Alabama, Mississippi, Louisiana—went to Ohio, Indiana, Michigan and Illinois cities. Those who did not dare venture so far went to Atlanta, New Orleans, Louisville, and other thriving Southern cities.

By 1900 only 27.7 percent of the Negro population was urban, but this represented a significant increase over the figure in 1860, when approximately 16 percent of the nation's Negroes were living in cities. In 1900 there were seventy-two cities with more than five thousand Negroes, while six cities—Philadelphia, New York, Baltimore, Washington, Memphis and New Orleans—each had more than fifty thousand. There were several cities of moderate size, all in the South, where Negroes outnumbered the whites. Among them were Charleston, Savannah, Jacksonville, Montgomery, Shreveport, Baton Rouge and Vicksburg.

As the Negro urban population grew, its problems multiplied. There was no longer the stultifying control by the Southern plantation owner, and the opportunities for education were somewhat improved. But labor unions were as hostile to Negroes as they were to other newly arrived groups. Most of them excluded Negroes from membership; and when Negroes accepted employment to break a strike, labor leaders accused Negroes of betraying the principles of trade unionism. Likewise, Negroes arriving in the city fresh from the country discovered that all but a few sections of the city were closed to them for housing. And when they crowded into the few areas that were open to them, where housing was frequently already substandard and falling apart, they were accused of destroying property values and running down the neighborhood. It was this attitude that led to the passing of the first housing segregation law in Louisville, Kentucky, in 1912. The law provided that city blocks containing a majority of whites were designated as white blocks; and those with a majority of Negroes were Negro blocks. No Negroes could move into the white blocks, and vice versa. Other cities, including Baltimore, Richmond and Atlanta, followed Louisville's lead; and Negro ghettoes, sanctioned by law, became well established in many parts of the country.

One of the most characteristic manifestations of the problem of Negro assimilation in the urban community at the beginning of the century was the race riot. Lynchings and burnings were rural fare; but rioting, on an even larger scale than occurred in Philadelphia and New York before the Civil War, became the typical expression of resentment of the urban Negro in the twentieth century. While there were outbreaks in numerous small Southern towns in the first decade of the century, the Atlanta riot of 1906 was the largest Southern disturbance of the period. For months the city had been lashed into a fury of race hatred by loose talk and by the movement to disfranchise Negroes. In September Atlanta newspapers told of four successive but entirely unsubstantiated assaults on white women by Negroes. The country people, in town on the last Saturday of the month, joined the urban element in creating an outraged, panic-stricken mob. Whites began to attack every Negro they saw. Many innocent persons were beaten, others were dragged from vehicles. For several days rioting continued; factories were closed and all transportation stopped. Many Negroes were killed, and there was a general destruction of Negro property. When it was all over, the whites confessed their shame and condemned the rioters. But a scar remained on Negro-white relationships in the fastest-growing city of the South.

Rioting in Northern cities was about as prevalent as in the South. Springfield, Ohio, had two riots within a few years—in 1904 and 1906. The Northern riot that shook the entire country occurred in Springfield, Illinois, in August, 1908. A white woman claimed that she had been dragged from her bed and raped by a Negro, who was then arrested and jailed. Before a special grand jury the woman admitted that she had been severely beaten by a white man whose identity she refused to disclose and that the Negro had no connection whatever with the incident. By this time, however, feeling was running high. Mobs gathered, raided stores, secured guns and other weapons, and began to destroy Negro businesses and drive Negroes from their homes. Before order was restored by more than five thousand militiamen, two Negroes had been lynched, four white men killed and more than seventy persons injured.

Thus, in the early decades of the twentieth century Negroes found scant acceptance in the American urban community. They were unable to make good their claim to equal treatment in the labor market; and in the laissez-faire atmosphere that prevailed, the Government declined to come to their rescue. Indeed, in 1894 Congress had repealed much of the Civil Rights Act of 1866 that could have been invoked for the protection of Negroes. Theodore Roosevelt, who had become President in 1901 and on whom many Negroes had pinned their hopes, had proved a great disappointment. He talked a great deal about justice, but did little for the Negro aside from inviting Booker T. Washington to dine at the White House. Negroes had already come to the conclusion that Harold Laski was to reach much later: that Roosevelt had great "verbal audacity" but this was accompanied "by a relative caution in action." Negroes were suffering numerous political disabilities and enormous personal indignities, including living in ghettoes; and they were lucky to escape with their lives from the violent attacks of white mobs. What little relief Negroes got came from organized groups of whites and Negroes who could no longer tolerate the conditions that prevailed.

The tragic events of the early years of the century caused many Negroes to lose faith in government at every level. They no longer felt that any whites could be trusted to act in their behalf. As one Negro put it, "In the degree that the southern people stand by in silence and see the Negro stripped of his civil and political rights by a band of unscrupulous men . . . they compromise their own civil and political freedom. . . . If by a mere technicality one class of citizens can be deprived of their rights and immunities . . . what is to prevent any other class from sharing the same fate?" It was at this point that some Negroes began to think in terms of an action program capable of formulating specific plans to secure full citizenship for all Americans, black and white. Soon, groups as far apart as the New England Suffrage League and the Georgia Equal Rights League had resolved to press for equal rights for Negroes.

New Organizational Efforts

The most articulate spokesman in this new drive for full citizenship was W. E. B. Du Bois who in 1905 called a conference of Negro leaders to meet in Niagara Falls, Canada, to formulate a program. After discussing their numerous problems, they drew up a "Declaration of Principles," which stated, among other things, that "We believe that Negroes should protest emphatically and continually against the curtailment of their political rights. We believe in manhood suffrage; we believe that no man is so good, intelligent or wealthy as to be entrusted wholly with the welfare of his neighbor." The group demanded equal economic opportunity, equal education, a fair administration of justice, and an end to segregation. For the next three years members of the group, now calling itself "The Niagara Movement," met and renewed its protests against injustice. By 1908 the group had won the respect and support of large numbers of Negroes, including the Equal Suffrage League, the National Association of Colored Women's Clubs and college and high school students. And it had begun litigation to knock out some of the jim crow laws of the Southern states. By that time, however, several of its leading members had become involved in another movement which was soon to eclipse the Niagara Movement.

The Springfield riot of 1908 plunged Negroes to the bottom of despair and shocked the sensibilities of many whites. In a widely read article, "Race War in the North," William English Walling deplored the conduct of the white people of Springfield and called on the responsible whites of the country to make amends. In 1909, in response to Walling's call, a small group met and formulated plans for an organization to fight for the rights of Negroes. In May, 1910, there came into existence the National Association for the Advancement of Colored People. It was composed of prominent whites as well as distinguished Negroes; and it pledged itself to work for the abolition of all forced segregation, equal education for Negro and white children and the enforcement of the Fourteenth and Fifteenth Amendments. Moorefield Storey of Boston was the first president, and Du Bois became the director of publicity and research and editor of the house organ, *The Crisis*.

In its first year of existence the NAACP launched a program to widen industrial opportunities for Negroes, to seek greater police protection for Negroes in the South, and to carry on a crusade against lynching and lawlessness. Instrumental in carrying out this program were *The Crisis* and the Legal Redress Committee, of which a New York lawyer, Arthur B. Spingarn, was chairman. White and Negro attorneys worked closely with Spingarn, and within a short time plans were made to test the constitutionality of state laws and state constitutions discriminating against Negroes. Spingarn's committee reasoned that if the Supreme Court was hostile of efforts of Congress to implement civil rights—as was inferred from the decision in the Civil Rights cases of 1883—perhaps it could be persuaded to frown upon the efforts of states to eliminate the Negro from consideration as a citizen.

The NAACP contended that the Negro's best opportunity to protect his rights lay in his exercise of the franchise. It was fitting, therefore, that the organization's first efforts would be against franchise restrictions. In 1910 it began its attack on the Grandfather Clause of the Oklahoma state constitution. It assailed that provision which stated that "no person who was, on January 1, 1866, or who was at any time prior thereto, entitled to vote under any form of government . . . and no lineal descendant of such person shall be denied the right to register and vote because of his inability to read and write" any section of the state constitution. In 1915 the United States Supreme Court, in its decision in *Guinn* vs. *United States*, pronounced as unconstitutional the suffrage provision of the Oklahoma constitution. "We seek in vain" Chief Justice White declared, "for any ground which would sustain any other interpretation but that the provision . . . adopted . . . to make [those conditions] the basis of the right to suffrage conferred in direct and positive disregard of the Fifteenth Amendment." In another NAACP case two years later, *Buchanan* vs. *Warley*, the

Supreme Court outlawed the city ordinances requiring Negroes and whites to live in separate blocks in the city.

Fair administration of justice was one of the most serious obstacles to the Negro's enjoyment of full citizenship. The NAACP was determined to put an end to the abuse of the Negroes' rights in the courts; and it found ample opportunity to launch its crusade in Elaine, Arkansas. During a riot that followed, when a group of white men fired on an assemblage of Negroes in a church, one white man was killed. For several days after, Negroes were hunted down and killed like animals. In the melee, another white man was killed, for which crime several Negroes were arrested and charged with murder. The Negroes were tried in the midst of a surging, unruly mob. Thy had no opportunity to consult with counsel, and witnesses were not called. The trial lasted forty-five minutes; the jury deliberated less than five. The verdict was murder in the first degree. When the NAACP took the case to the Supreme Court on the ground that the defendants had been denied due process of law, the Court agreed. Justice Holmes was appalled by the flagrant denial of the rights of the five defendants; and the decision of the state court was reversed and a new trial ordered.

The NAACP also sought to meet, head on, the violence against Negroes that was increasing almost everywhere. It organized a parade in New York City to protest the terror against the Negro community that characterized the riot of East St. Louis, Illinois, in 1917. Two years later it held a national conference on lynching, at which the chief speaker was Charles Evans Hughes. Shortly thereafter, it was engrossed in a campaign to secure the passage of a Federal law against lynching. In 1921 a Missouri representative, L. C. Dyer, introduced such a bill in the lower house of Congress, and it passed by a vote of 230–119. When it reached the floor of the Senate the Southern senators succeeded in organizing a filibuster that ultimately prevented a vote on the measure.

Economic opportunities for Negroes were even less certain, if such was possible, than their enjoyment of their civil rights. Their situation as farm employees and sharecroppers was deteriorating; and in the new Southern industries exclusion or discrimination continued. Even as they migrated to the cities, their problems were, in some instances, aggravated. Employment opportunities were fewer than the number of people moving to urban areas; and Negroes found great difficulty in securing anything except the more onerous and less attractive jobs, if they were lucky enough to secure anything at all. They continued to live around the "ragged edge of industry" with organized labor evincing a pronounced feeling of hostility. Only the Cigarmakers' International Union and the United Mine Workers of America seemed to welcome Negroes, although some other unions had Negro members. Negro women more easily found employment than men, as maids and household servants; and the more certain employment of women had the effect of attracting a larger number of women than men to the cities. The implications of this for family disorganization, juvenile delinquency and other problems were considerable.

Although the NAACP included in its program a plan to widen industrial opportunities of Negroes, it had neither the time nor the resources to do much in this area. More and more it concentrated on securing civil rights for Negroes. The need for organized effort in the economic and social spheres was especially urgent. In 1905 two organizations were established in New York looking toward the solution of the major economic and housing problems among Negroes. They were the Committee for Improving Industrial Conditions of Negroes in New York City and the National League for the Protection of Colored Women. Soon, they began to work together; and in 1911 they organized the National League on Urban Conditions, commonly known as the National Urban League. The new organization undertook to open new opportunities for Negroes in industry and to assist newly arrived Negroes in their problems of adjustment in the cities. Branches were opened in many of the larger cities, with programs for meeting the migrants, directing them to jobs and lodgings and offering information on how to live in the city. It did an effective job in bringing the employer and employee together and easing the difficulties of mutual adjustment.

There were numerous other efforts on the national and local levels to assist Negroes with their problems. The Young Men's Christian Association and the Young Women's Christian Association began to organize Negro branches and provide recreational as well as religious opportunities in the Negro community. Civic clubs among Negro men and women took on special projects designed to raise the level of aspiration among Negroes. Some of them fostered civic pride by encouraging home improvement, while others grappled with the more serious problems of crime and juvenile delinquency. In some Northern communities Negro political groups were already attempting to capitalize on the concentration of Negroes and elect Negroes to local offices.

Making the World Safe for Democracy

Negroes had never been wholly politically inactive, despite the concerted efforts of the Southern whites and some of their Northern white friends to make them so. During the Roosevelt and Taft administrations, they made themselves felt in some sectors of the Republican Party; but their disillusionment deepened when neither Roosevelt nor Taft did much to help them secure their civil rights. In 1912 they were willing to turn to any group that promised some hope. To some Negroes, Woodrow Wilson seemed to provide some hope when he said, during his campaign, that he wished to see "justice done to the colored people in every matter; and not mere grudging justice, but justice executed with liberality and cordial good feeling." Shortly after Wilson's inauguration, it became clear to most Negroes that they could not rely on Wilson or his party for support in their efforts. Soon, segregation was reintroduced in the nation's capital and in the offices of the Federal government.

The experience of Negroes during World War I pointed up the painful fact that nowhere, not even in the armed services of the United States, did Negroes enjoy full citizenship. Under the Selective Service legislation 2,290,525 Negroes registered and 367,000 of them were called into the service. But everywhere there was discrimination. In the newly organized Air Force, Negroes were rejected altogether. In the United States Navy they were used only as menials; and in all other branches of the service they were segregated. The war was well under way before the War Department begrudgingly made some arrangements for the training of Negro officers at Fort Des Moines, Iowa. Few if any communities were pleased to have Negroes in training camps near them, and there were numerous incidents of clashes between Negro soldiers and white civilians. Negro soldiers complained, moreover, that they were constantly subjected to insults at the hands of their white officers.

Overseas, the situation was not much better. Negro combat troops were placed in various divisions of the French Army, and they were naturally faced with numerous problems of adjustment. They were taunted by the Germans who reminded them that they were fighting for the benefit of "Wall Street robbers" and others and not for their own freedom. Meanwhile, the French soldiers and citizens were warned by white Army officials from the United States not to treat Negro soldiers as equals. Despite all this, Negroes fought loyally and gallantly. Hundreds of them received the Croix de Guerre and other citations by the French Army, but none of them received the Medal of Honor from the United States.

During the war Negroes rushed to Northern industrial communities in the hope of finding employment in war-time industries. Upwards of 300,000 Negroes left the South and settled in the North and West in the war decade. Consequently, the urban problems became more acute than ever. In 1916 the National Urban League held a Conference on Migration and issued recommendations and advice to employers and migrants. But the hostility directed against Negroes was a clear indication that they were not welcome. The riot in East St. Louis, Illinois, in which forty Negroes lost their lives in 1917, was merely the worst of a series of racial clashes arising from the resentment of whites to the presence of Negro workers. Even so, many Negroes secured the best jobs they ever had. They were engaged in the manufacture of ammunition and iron and steel products. They were in the meat packing industries, and large numbers found employment in the new automobile industry. They were in the coal mines, on the railroads, and in the shipbuilding yards.

Some articulate Negroes despaired over the treatment that Negroes were receiving. For their article, "Pro-Germanism among Negroes," in which they severely criticized the policy of the United States, the editors of *The Messenger*, A. Phillip Randolph and Chandler Owen, were sentenced to jail for two and a half years and their second-class mailing privileges revoked. They did not serve their sentences, however. More influential among Negroes, however, was the editorial in July, 1918, by W. E. B. Du Bois, entitled "Close Ranks." In it, he said, "Let us not hesitate. Let us, while this war lasts, forget our special grievances and close our ranks shoulder to shoulder with our white citizens and the allied nations that are fighting for democracy."

The Reaction

Talk of democracy during the war had raised the hopes of most Negroes, and they were optimistic about the future. But their hopes were soon dashed by the events that followed the war. Already, the Ku Klux Klan had been revived and had adopted a broad program "for uniting native-born white Christians for concerted action in the preservation of American institutions and the supremacy of the white race." Within ten months, shortly after the close of the war, the Klan made more than two hundred public appearances in twenty-seven states. Soon, the Klan and other anti-Negro groups were terrorizing the Negro population in a variety of ways. Returning Negro soldiers discovered that neither they nor their fellows had won a semblance of equality or decent treatment for themselves. More than seventy Negroes were lynched during the first year of the post-war period. Ten Negro soldiers, several still in their uniforms, were lynched. Mississippi and Georgia mobs murdered three returned Negro soldiers each. Fourteen Negroes were burned publicly; and eleven of them were burned alive. In despair a Negro editor in South Carolina cried out, "There is scarcely a day passes that newspapers don't tell about a Negro soldier lynched in his uniform. Why do they lynch Negroes anyhow? With a white judge, a white jury, white public sentiment, white officers of the law, it is just as impossible for a Negro accused of crime or even suspected of crime to escape the white man's vengeance or his justice as it would be for a fawn to escape that wanders accidentally into a den of hungry lions."

With the summer of 1919 came the riots, twenty-five of them, North and South. In Longview, Texas, a Negro school principal was flogged on the streets, and several leading Negro citizens were run out of town. In Washington, D.C., mobs, consisting primarily of white sailors, soldiers and marines, ran amuck through the streets for three days, killing several Negroes and injuring scores of others. In Chicago, when a Negro attempted to swim in a part of Lake Michigan that whites had reserved for themselves, a riot began that lasted for thirteen days. Thirty-eight persons were killed —fifteen whites and twenty-three Negroes—and more than five hundred were injured. More than a thousand families, largely Negroes, were homeless due to the burnings and general destruction of property.

The racial strife of the post-war years indicated that the Negro was willing to fight and die for himself as well as for democracy in Europe. It was no longer a case of one race intimidating another into submission. Now it was war in the full sense of the word, and Negroes were as determined to win at home as they had been in Europe. And even if they could not win in an obviously one-sided struggle, they sought to make a good showing. They loudly protested against what they termed injustices and oppressions. But soon, they realized that protests were not enough; not even fighting back was enough. Intelligent planning and action were needed. The following years would be characterized by their efforts to do precisely that.

THE RESTORATION OF SELF-RESPECT

The New Negro

The migration of Negroes from their ancestral homes on the plantations to urban America that began during the war placed the destiny of the Negro into his own hands more than ever before. And the forces that touched off this wave of migration gave way to other factors in the years following the war that continued to stimulate the migration of Negroes down to the present day. The urban North was becoming increasingly attractive, while the South, even as it became industrialized, gave every indication that it had no intention of revising its views regarding the inferior position in which the Negro should be kept. In 1910 no city in the United States had as many as 100,000 Negroes. By 1920 there were six such cities; and by 1940 there were eleven: New York, Chicago, Philadelphia, Detroit, Washington, Baltimore, New Orleans, Memphis, Birmingham, St. Louis, and Atlanta. Meanwhile, scores of thousands of Negroes were moving into urban communities where, up to that time, the Negro population had been negligible if, indeed, it existed at all.

This extensive urbanization of the Negro had a profound effect upon his status and, especially, on the way he viewed himself. He developed a sense of responsibility and a self-confidence that he had not previously known. During the war he learned from no less a person than his President of the promise of freedom, and on the battlefield he served his country. He began to see the discrepancies between the promise of freedom and his experiences in his own country. He became defiant, bitter and impatient. In company with his fellows, who were congregating in the cities in large numbers, he was no longer afraid as he had been on the Southern plantation. And he was more than willing to speak out against his injustices. It was not the timorous, docile Negro of the past who said, "The next time white folks pick on colored folks, something's going to drop—dead white folks."

The Negro was achieving, moreover, a degree and kind of articulation that made it possible for him to state his feelings clearly and forthrightly. Despite his intense feelings of hate and hurt, he possessed sufficient restraint, if not objectivity, to use his materials artistically, but no less effectively. He was sufficiently in touch with the main currents of American literary development to adapt the accepted forms to his own materials and, therefore, gain a wider acceptance. The result was the emergence of a remarkable crop of Negro writers who made up what was later called the "Harlem Renaissance." Through poetry, prose and song they cried out against social and economic injustices. They protested against segregation and lynching; and they demanded better conditions of work. And in their demands they were almost unanimous in their efforts to secure justice in the framework of the existing economic and political structure.

There was a sense of satisfaction among Negroes as they insisted that they were on the right side of the country's professed ideals. As Alain Locke said in his volume, *The New Negro*, published in 1925, "The Negro mind reaches out as yet to nothing but American wants, American ideas. But this forced attempt to build his Americanism on race values is a unique social experiment, and its ultimate success is impossible except through the fullest sharing of American culture and institutions. . . . We realize that we cannot be undone without America's undoing. It is within the gamut of this attitude that the thinking Negro faces America, but with variations of mood that are, if anything, more significant than the attitude itself." Articulate Negroes sensed the moral advantage that they possessed, and they used it in every way possible.

The number of Negroes who now came forth in the nineteen-twenties to write about the plight of their race was itself an indication of the intellectual achievement so many of them had made. Du Bois continued his creative writings, bringing out several novels, two volumes of poems and essays, and other works. James Weldon Johnson, who had published his *Autobiography of an Ex-Colored Man* in 1912 and in the following year his poem "Fifty Years," commemorating the anniversary of the Emancipation Proclamation, was even more prolific in the years following the war. His Book of *American Negro Poetry* and his own volume of folk poems, *God's Trombones,* placed him in the mainstream of American writers. Claude McKay, regarded by many as the leading poet of the Harlem Renaissance, was also one of the most caustic in his strictures of American life. His *Harlem Shadows* and *Home to Harlem* intensively examined the Negro ghetto in poem and prose. Countée Cullen published his first volume of poems, *Color,* in 1925, when he was only twenty-two years old. In succeeding works such as *The Ballad of the Brown Girl* and *Copper Sun* he demonstrated his capacity for imagination as well as critical insight into the problems that beset the American Negro. There were others: Jean Toomer, whose *Cane* displayed a rare talent; Langston Hughes, whose most significant work belonged to a later period; Jessie Fauset, who captured the problems of the middle-class Negro to a remarkable degree, and Walter White, whose studies of lynching did much to dramatize American mob violence. These and a dozen others gave ample evidence that the new Negro was not only deeply sensitive but extremely articulate.

There were other even more dramatic manifestations of the New Negro, orthodox and unorthodox. The NAACP was not only carrying on its campaign against lynching, under the leadership of James Weldon Johnson and Walter White, but it was also attempting to break the practice of Southern states of excluding Negroes from Democratic primaries. It succeeded, in the case of *Nixon* vs. *Herndon* (1927), in having the Supreme Court of the United States declare null and void a Texas statute which excluded Negroes from the Democratic primaries in the state. When the Texas legislature enacted a law giving the executive committee of the party the authority to fix the qualifications for party membership, the association, in *Nixon* vs. *Condon* (1932), succeeded in having the law nullified by arguing that the statute had set up a party committee and made it a state agency with certain powers and duties. It suffered a setback, however, in 1935, when, in *Grovey* vs. *Townsend,* the Court refused to interfere with the exclusion of Negroes from the Democratic primaries when such an exclusion had been effected by a resolution of the state convention of the party. It was not until 1944 that the NAACP recovered its lost ground when, in *Smith* vs. *Allwright*, the Court decided that the exclusion of Negroes from the Democratic primary was a clear violation of the Fifteenth Amendment. Although these decisions were to prove insufficient to destroy the resistance to Negroes voting in the South, they were important steps toward the enjoyment of political participation.

The concentration of Negroes in urban centers in the North had much to do with another manifestation of the New Negro, namely, political regeneration. As early as 1915 a Negro, Oscar DePriest, was elected alderman from the densely populated South Side of Chicago. In 1917 the Negroes of New York sent E. A. Johnson to the state assembly. In the years following they became more aware of their political strength and took advantage of it. By 1928 some Negroes began to turn from the Republican Party to support Alfred E. Smith, a Democrat, for the Presidency because they thought he would do more for them than Herbert Hoover, the Republican candidate. In the same year they sent Oscar DePriest to Congress, the first Negro to serve there since 1901. And in 1930 they used their political influence to block the confirmation of John J. Parker for the Supreme Court, because they regarded him as an enemy of Negroes. By the time that Franklin D. Roosevelt ran for President in 1932 on the Democratic ticket, Negroes were in a position to use their political strength to force greater consideration on the part of the major parties.

The New Negro became more militant in the economic sphere. In 1929 the National Negro Business League, more certain than ever that white businesses and labor unions were passing the Negro by, organized the Colored Merchants Association, which undertook to establish stores and to purchase their wares cooperatively. Shortly thereafter a "Jobs-for-Negroes" movement began in earnest in St. Louis, where the Urban League led a boycott against a white-owned chain store whose trade was almost exclusively Negro but employed no Negroes. The movement spread to Pittsburgh, Chicago, Cleveland and other midwestern cities, and many Negroes found employment because of the pressure brought on white employers in Negro sections. Even during the depression such movements continued. In New York City the Reverend John H. Johnson organized in 1933 the Citizens' League for Fair Play and attempted to persuade white merchants to employ Negro clerks. When their first efforts failed they resorted to picketing the stores and appealing to Negroes with the motto, "Don't Buy Where You Can't Work." The campaign resulted in the employment of hundreds of Negroes in the white stores of Harlem and in such public utilities as the telephone, electric and bus companies.

There were some Negroes, bitter, defiant and frustrated, who believed that practical programs to achieve equality were impossible. The strain and stress of living in hostile urban communities left them completely disillusioned and willing to accept more drastic solutions to their problems. That is why so many of them embraced the Universal Negro Improvement Association, organized by Marcus Garvey during the war. Garvey insisted that the Negro had no future in the United States, and he declared that the only hope for American Negroes was to flee America and return to Africa to build up a country of their own. "Wake up Ethiopia!" he cried out; "Wake up Africa! Let us work toward one glorious end of a free, redeemed and mighty nation. Let Africa be a bright star among the constellation of nations." To inculcate a sense of self-esteem among Negroes Garvey exalted everything black. He insisted that black stood for strength and beauty, not inferiority.

The Garvey Movement grew rapidly. He claimed that he had six million followers in 1923. That was a wild exaggeration, of course; but even his severest critics conceded that he had perhaps a half-million members, which was more than the NAACP had at any time during this period. His Universal African Legion, Black Eagle Flying Corps, Black Star Steamship Line, and his numerous orders of African nobility captured the imagination of many American Negroes. His many projects came to naught, but not before they had given many frustrated Negroes a sense of hope and dignity that had long been denied them. It was the first and only real mass movement that Negroes had embraced; and its momentary success is a testimony of the extent to which Negroes entertained doubts about ever gaining first-class citizenship in the country of their birth.

Perhaps even more bizarre was the movement led by George Baker, commonly known as "Father Divine," who promised his followers a veritable heaven on earth. Beginning with a small group on Long Island in 1919, this remarkable leader built up a following within the next two decades that amused some observers and perplexed others. Although his followers deserted their churches and began to call their leader "God," it was as much a social movement as a religious development. By 1930 Father Divine was holding open house and feeding thousands in buildings that came to be known as "heavens." In many Eastern cities and in some Midwestern communities Father Divine had large followings. It became interracial as early as 1926, and within a few years it had attracted a considerable number of white members, some of whom were wealthy. That such a movement flourished at all suggests a variety of social ills as well as a great deal of frustration among whites as well as Negroes.

The New Deal

Despite the growing political sophistication of the American Negro, it is doubtful that a majority of them turned away from the Republican Party and supported Franklin D. Roosevelt, when he was elected to the Presidency in 1932. But he was not long in office before he gained a large following among Negroes and other minority groups. He was the first President to appoint Italo-Americans and Negroes to the Federal bench. He frequently received Negro visitors, and it was widely reported that he listened to suggestions and advice from certain powerful Negro politicians. Mrs. Roosevelt, moreover, was active in a variety of social programs that involved the improvement of disadvantaged groups, including Negroes. On several occasions, during his first year in office, the President denounced lynching and mob violence. His Secretary of the Interior, Harold L. Ickes, had been president of the Chicago branch of the NAACP, thus becoming the first Cabinet officer to have been so intimately associated with the struggle for Negro rights. The President appointed Negroes as "advisers" in several executive departments; and it was assumed that they were in a position to state the case for the economic and political equality of Negroes. In some sectors of the Federal government the racial segregation that had been established by the last Democratic President was abolished by Roosevelt.

While there was no civil rights legislation during the period of the New Deal, the relief and recovery legislation helped to improve, to a limited extent, conditions among Negroes as well as the rest of the population. Under such agencies as the Agricultural Adjustment Administration, the Rural Electrification Administration and local production credit associations, Negroes received benefits, though not in proportion to their numbers and needs. They were substantially aided by the Farm Security Administration, which insisted that there be no discrimination between white and Negro farmers. The Civilian Conservation Corps and the National Youth Administration provided employment for thousands of young Negroes. By 1939 more than one million Negroes owed their living to employment under the Works Progress Administration. Even some of the writers, actors and musicians who got their start during the period of the Harlem Renaissance found an opportunity to continue their creative work under the WPA. There was much discrimination against Negroes, particularly in the local administration of New Deal agencies in the South and in some places in the North. However, the old patterns of discrimination that had existed for decades were weakened to some extent during the New Deal period.

The New Deal was particularly favorable to labor, but not necessarily to Negro labor. The Wagner Act of 1935 gave permanency and strength to the National Labor Relations Board, which enjoyed wide powers in handling labor disputes and in settling strikes. It was labor's "bill of rights," but it did not break the barriers by which Negroes were excluded from the unions. The Fair Labor Standards Act of 1938 established the principle of a minimum and a maximum work week. Better than a million Negroes were affected by the act, but several millions were not. The act meant little to Negroes if they were unable to secure employment in those industries covered by it. There were few unions like the United Mine Workers which brought together in one union all the workers of the industry and which, since its organization in 1890, had encouraged the organization and participation of Negro workers. Most of the principal unions in the American Federation of Labor either barred Negroes or accepted their membership only on a segregated basis.

It was the so-called industrial bloc in the American Federation of Labor that gave the Negro his first real opportonity in organized labor. Led by John L. Lewis of the United Mine Workers, the bloc organized the Congress of Industrial Organizations and left the Federation. Soon, the C.I.O. was organizing the mass production industries; and the Amalgamated Clothing Workers, the International Ladies Garment Workers and the Steel Workers gave Negro members something resembling equal opportunity to participate in the affairs of the unions. The C.I.O. became active in the political sphere and sought equal opportunities for Negroes through its Committee to Abolish Racial Discrimination and its Political Action Committee. Meanwhile, the Brotherhood of Sleeping Car Porters, under the leadership of A. Philip Randolph, successfully pressed for better working conditions for its members and proved that Negroes, when given the opportunity, could adhere to the principles of organized labor.

The Negroes' patience, in waiting for justice through the courts and for equity at the hands of government leaders—including those of the New Deal—was wearing thin. They had to fight for their rights, many began to insist. As one Negro wrote to President Roosevelt's Attorney General, "It strikes us that the time is just about at hand when we must cast aside our Bible, stop offering so many solemn addresses to the Supreme Being and fight for our rights. . . . We would prefer death in lieu of remaining here on earth and have our manhood trampled upon." Such views were provoked by the persistence of the denial of the rights of Negroes, even when so much was being said about the protection and support of the disadvantaged elements of the American population. Consequently, Negroes sought to mobilize their intellectual and political resources for the purpose of pressing for their rights. Even as they supported Roosevelt in 1936 and 1940 they made it clear that they reserved the right to give their support to the political organizations that were most sensitive to their needs. In organizations such as the Joint Committee on National Recovery, the National Negro Congress and the Southern Negro Youth Congress they came together and formulated plans for pressing ever more vigorously for full citizenship. Even if these groups accomplished little, they developed approaches and techniques that were to be most valuable in the decades ahead.

The New Negro Community

The inability of the Negro to become a part of the mainstream of American life in the urban community did much to disillusion him further as well as make more permanent his separate institutions. The almost universal difficulty in securing adequate housing, discrimination in employment, and the absence of equity in the administration of justice contributed significantly to family disorganization among Negroes. At the same time, as E. Franklin Frazier pointed out in his *The Negro in the United States*, there has been an improvement in the stability of the Negro urban family in recent years. With the growth of the Negro middle class and the improvement of educational opportunities the Negro family as well as other institutions reflected a capacity to provide some strength and stability for the Negro community.

The practice of forcing Negroes into ghettoes and of barring them from participation in the life of the white community helped to create new forces for the perpetuation of the Negro's world. In a nation dedicated to the idea of the essential equality of mankind and in which there is a general commitment to the fusion of races and cultures, the existence of a separate Negro community constitutes one of the truly remarkable social anomalies of the twentieth century. This situation has created innumerable problems of a political, social and economic nature that have confounded both Negroes and whites who have sought solutions to them.

The most powerful institution in the Negro's world is the church. More and more, as he found himself rejected by the white churches and by the white community generally, the Negro turned to the church for self-expression, recognition and leadership. Nothing in his world was so completely his own as the church, whether it was one of the more common branches like the Baptists or Methodists or one of the more exotic institutions like the Apostolic Overcoming Holy Church of God or the Kodesh Church of Immanuel. The Negro church stimulated pride and preserved the self-respect of many who had been humiliated in their efforts to adjust themselves in American life. By the middle of the twentieth century thirty-four all-Negro denominations claimed a membership of more than five million Negroes, more than 35,000 churches, and property valued at $200 million. By that time one could see the first signs indicating a move to reintegrate American religious institutions. Roman Catholics insisted that they could never countenance segregation in the churches, while even the Methodists began to take steps to unite the Negro and white branches.

In the new Negro community the press played an increasingly important part. The white press of the South ignored the Negro community except to publicize crimes allegedly committed by Negroes, while the white press of the North paid scant attention to the activities of Negroes. The Negro press became the medium for the dissemination of information among Negroes and a powerful voice in expressing the aspirations of Negroes. It was during World War I that the Negro press became powerful and prosperous. It encouraged Negroes to move to industrial centers in search for work; it urged support of the war; but it also led the fight for the complete integration of Negroes in American life. Newspapers such as the *Baltimore Afro-American*, the *Chicago Defender*, the *Norfolk Journal and Guide* and the *Pittsburgh Courier* made rapid strides both in circulation and influence. In later decades the number of Negro newspapers, primarily weeklies, increased enormously, while weekly and monthly periodicals such as *Jet* and *Ebony* provided brief, pictorial summaries of Negro life in modern America.

The free, separate Negro community provided a great stimulation for the rise of Negroes in the professions. The Negro world needed teachers, clergy, physicians, dentists, pharmacists, nurses, attorneys, social workers, recreation leaders, morticians and many others to minister to its needs. They constitute the most highly trained group in the Negro community and are the basis for the rise of the Negro middle class. Preoccupied as they necessarily have been with their own training and service and the maintenance of high standards, they have not always been as aggressive in the advocacy of full citizenship for all. They have been compelled to organize their own associations for their protection and mutual assistance, but it would not be accurate to suggest that they have altogether neglected the important role of leadership in the Negro community. There are numerous examples of Negro attorneys and physicians and members of the clergy serving as officials in civil rights organizations, for they would be the first to realize that segregation and discrimination are, in the last analysis, as oppressive to them as to the least advantaged member of their race.

The education of Negroes remained a separate enterprise, for the most part. Almost nowhere did Negroes enjoy equal educational opportunities, although the white community was scrupulously careful in seeing to it that such opportunities remain separate. In the South separate schools were maintained by law. In the North they were maintained by the Negro ghetto. In the South the disparity between the money spent on the education of white children and that spent for the education of Negro children prevailed throughout the first half of the twentieth century. As late as 1935–36 the current expenditures per Negro pupil in ten Southern states averaged $13.09, while such expenditures per white pupil averaged $37.87. While precise figures for ghetto schools in the North cannot be obtained, even a most cursory observation of buildings, equipment and facilities indicate considerable disparity.

It is not possible to measure precisely the effects that separate and unequal education have had on both white and Negro populations in the areas where it has been maintained. Separate schools have been one of the strongest supports of the concept of white supremacy in the South. They have, moreover, contributed to the perpetuation of a leadership devoted not only to separate education but to the maintenance of economic and political inequalities between the white and Negro populations of the South. In the face of these difficulties, however, the number of Negro schools, colleges and universities increased, while the Negro student population virtually exploded in the years following World War I.

Even out of the confused pattern of education for Negroes there emerged a body of highly trained men and women who may be regarded as scholars by any criteria. While almost all of them, until quite recent years, received their graduate and professional training in Northern and European universities, many of them were products of separate schools on the lower levels and even of Negro colleges. There was, of course, the usual complement of Negro clergy, teachers, physicians and attorneys; but to these were added, in more recent years, an increasing number of scholars in various scientific fields, history, sociology, political science and the humanities. Negro scholars became increasingly articulate, contributing articles to learned journals and publishing numerous books. Many of them devoted much of their talents and energies to studying and describing the place of the Negro in American life. The Association for the Study of Negro Life and History, founded in 1916 by Carter G. Woodson, went so far as to promote the works of Negro scholars and, indeed, of white scholars who were concerned with reassessing the role of the Negro in American history. Its *Journal of Negro History* soon became a respected periodical in the most scholarly circles, while the *Journal of Negro Education,* published at Howard University, and *Phylon, A Journal of Race and Culture,* published at Atlanta University, joined in the vigorous efforts of Negro scholars and their friends to restore the American Negro to a place of respect in the larger community.

GLOBAL WAR AND THE AFTERMATH

Fighting for the Four Freedoms

Negroes were among the first Americans to advocate intervention against the aggression of the fascist powers. As early as 1935 they were bitterly protesting the invasion of Ethiopia by Italy. In many communities funds were raised for the defense of the African kingdom. In New York the International Council of Friends of Ethiopia was organized, and one of its founders, Willis N. Huggins, pleaded before the League of Nations for support of Ethiopia. The *Pittsburgh Courier* sent a reporter, J. A. Rogers, to cover the war; and upon his return he published *The Real Facts About Ethiopia* and lectured to many Negro and white groups. As they witnessed the rape of Ethiopia by Italian fascists and the slaughter of Jews by German Nazis, Negroes reached the conclusion that racism in Europe was inimical to their best interests.

When Europe was plunged into war in September, 1939, the armed services of the United States were in a low state of preparedness. The Army in 1940 contained some 230,000 enlisted men and officers, of whom less than 5,000 were Negroes. Only the four Negro units in the standing army, the 24th and 25th Infantries and the 9th and 10th Cavalries, were up to their full strength. Some other Negro units were activated: quartermaster regiments, antiaircraft battalions, corps of engineers and some others. But Negroes generally had had little interest in the armed services in the years between the wars; and few were, therefore, ready to participate in the first stages of building up a large fighting force.

Under the Selective Service Act of 1940 more than three million Negro men registered for service in the armed forces of their country. In the first year of the operation of the act, while hope remained that the United States could stay out of the war, only 2,069 Negroes were drafted. In the following year more than 100,000 entered the service, while in 1942 approximately 370,000 Negroes joined the armed forces. In September, 1944, when the Army was at its peak, there were 700,000 Negroes in that branch of the service alone. Approximately 165,000 served in the Navy, 5,000 in the Coast Guard, and 17,000 in the Marine Corps. The total number of Negroes in the several branches of the armed services during World War II was in the neighborhood of one million men and women.

At the beginning of the war the armed services were generally segregated, and there was considerable discrimination. But the Negro had a much greater opportunity to serve his country than in any previous war. Negroes were in the infantry, coast and field artillery, cavalry, tank battalions, transportation units, signal corps, engineer corps, medical corps and many other branches where they had previously served. When the Women's Auxiliary Corps was organized, Negroes were received; and before the end of the war more than four thousand Negro women had enlisted. In 1940 the War Department announced that Negroes would be trained as aviation pilots at Tuskegee, Alabama. Some Negroes violently objected to the segregation of Negroes in the Air Force, but others looked upon the acceptance of Negroes as candidates as officer-pilots as a step forward. Late in 1941 the 99th Pursuit Squadron was ready for organization into a fighting unit, and other groups of Negro fighter pilots were undergoing training. Approximately six hundred Negro pilots had received their wings before the end of the war.

In June, 1940, there were four thousand Negroes in the Navy, and most of them served as messmen. Since World War I Negroes had no opportunity either to learn the many trades provided in naval training or to become combat seamen. In April, 1942, the Secretary of the Navy announced that the Navy would accept the enlistment of Negroes for general service and as noncommissioned officers. Soon, a program for the training of Negroes as officers was launched, and Negro women were permitted to enlist in the Waves. At the same time it was announced that Negroes would be received in the Marine Corps, a break with tradition that was as old as the Corps itself. In the Army, meanwhile, a policy had been laid down of training Negro and white officer candidates in the same schools. Despite considerable resistance on the part of some white officers of the regular Army, Negroes received their commissions and through pressures brought by William H. Hastie, the Civilian Aide to the Secretary of War, and others, they received advanced training that made them eligible for promotion.

Approximately a half-million Negroes saw service overseas during World War II. Most of them were in separate outfits, more frequently than not, commanded by white officers. They served in port battalions, truck companies and other units of the transportation corps. After D-Day in 1944, more than fifty thousand Negro engineers erected camps, tents, and buildings, cleared debris, rebuilt cities and performed other important services. Twenty-two Negro combat units participated in the ground operations in the European theater. Negro fighter squadrons participated in the air operations over Italy, Rumania and Austria. In January, 1945, the War Department announced that Negro troops would be integrated with white troops in an experimental unit to fight on German soil. Negroes everywhere were elated over the news of the experiment and were delighted to learn that the mixed units were a success. Meanwhile, Negro troops were becoming more active in the war in the Pacific and the Orient. Negro combat units saw action against the Japanese in the New Georgia Islands, the Solomons, the Philippines and elsewhere, while Negro engineers worked on the building of the Ledo Road and various military installations.

The problem of maintaining high morale among Negroes in the service was a most difficult one. White officers and white civilians subjected Negroes to numerous indignities and humiliations. In Durham, North Carolina, a white bus driver was found not guilty of murder after he left his bus in July, 1944, and killed a Negro soldier with whom he had argued on the bus. In the South Negro soldiers were refused food in places where German prisoners of war were eating and enjoying American hospitality. In Kentucky three Negro WACS were beaten by civilian police when the women did not move promptly from the white waiting room in a railroad station, when asked to do so. In South Carolina a white policeman gouged out a Negro soldier's eyes in an altercation. On military posts the situation was scarcely better. At many camps Negro soldiers were forced to wait until white soldiers had boarded the buses and, if any room was left, they could ride. When the War Department issued an order in 1944 forbidding racial segregation in recreational and transportation facilities at all Army stations, the *Montgomery Advertiser* said, "Army orders, even armies, even bayonets cannot force impossible and unnatural social relations upon us."

If whites were resisting moves toward the equal treatment of Negro soldiers, Negro newspapers and Negro leaders were constantly protesting against all forms of segregation and discrimination. They protested the practice of the Red Cross of separating Negro and white blood in the banks that had been established for the relief of wounded servicemen. They were quick to point out that there would, perhaps, have been no blood banks without the work of a Negro, Dr. Charles Drew. They also criticized the USO when that organization banned Ruth Benedict's *The Races of Mankind* in its clubs. While Negroes were willing to serve their country in war as well as in peace, most of them insisted that the Four Freedoms and the other noble sentiments expressed in the war aims should be practiced at home as well as abroad. The *Pittsburgh Courier* launched a vigorous Double V campaign: Victory at home as well as abroad.

Problems of Employment

As the United States began to put itself on a war footing, Negroes wondered where they would fit in as far as defense and war industries were concerned. They found untold difficulties in securing employment. The first benefits they derived from the boom in defense industries were in securing the jobs deserted by whites who were attracted by higher wages to plants making weapons of war. The Federal Government made several gestures to discourage discrimination. The Office of Education declared that in the expenditure of funds in the defense training program there should be no discrimination based on race, creed or color. In August, 1940, the National Defense Advisory Committee issued a statement against the refusal to hire Negroes in defense plants. These actions brought few satisfactory results, and discrimination continued. Negroes saw wages skyrocket in plants holding huge defense contracts, and they saw few signs that the rigid anti-Negro policy in industry was undergoing any change. All too typical of industry was the statement by a West Coast aviation factory which said, "We will receive applications from both white and colored workers. However, the Negro will be considered only as janitors and in other similar capacities. Regardless of their training as aircraft workers, we will not employ them."

Such positions as these were indications to Negro leaders that they should develop a program for drastic action. In January, 1941, A. Philip Randolph, president of the Brotherhood of Sleeping Car Porters, advanced the idea of fifty to one hundred thousand Negroes marching on Washington and demanding that their government do something to insure the employment of Negroes in defense industry. The idea was received with enthusiasm by many Negroes, while Federal officials viewed the prospect as most regrettable. Soon, a full-scale March on Washington Movement had developed; and it was supported by the heads of all the major Negro organizations. The President sought to head off the movement by speaking out against discrimination; but Negroes felt that he was not doing enough. Mrs. Roosevelt and Mayor LaGuardia of New York attempted to persuade the Negro leaders to abandon the idea of the march, insisting that it would do more harm than good. The President himself appealed to Randolph and his colleagues to call off the March, but Randolph remained adamant.

In late June, 1941, Negroes all over the United States—thousands, if not a hundred thousand—were making preparations to entrain for Washington to be ready to march to the Capitol and White House on July First. Governmental officials became more desperate. Finally, after several conferences, the President said that if Randolph would call off the march, he would issue an order prohibiting discrimination in employment in defense industries. Randolph agreed, and on June 25, 1941, the President issued his famous Executive Order 8802, saying, "There shall be no discrimination in the employment of workers in defense industries or Government because of race, creed, color, or national origin. . . . And it is the duty of employers and labor organizations . . . to provide for the full and equitable participation of all workers in defense industries, without discrimination because of race, creed, color, or national origin. . . ." Later a Fair Employment Practices

Committee was established; and this was the beginning of the involvement of the Federal Government in programs to improve the economic status of Negroes. Undoubtedly, many employers persisted in their discriminatory practices, but the even lukewarm commitment of the Federal Government to fair employment created a generally improved climate in which Negroes could seek employment.

In another way, however, the climate was deteriorating. The migration of large numbers of Negroes to the North and West raised anew the difficult question of how Negroes and whites could live together peacefully in communities where the patterns of race relations were not clearly defined. Within the five-year period between 1940 and 1945 the Negro population of Los Angeles County increased from 75,000 to 150,000. Negroes were also moving in large numbers to Oakland, Detroit, Cleveland, Chicago and other industrial centers. The lack of housing, the presence of race-baiters and demagogues, the problem of organizing the newly arrived workers and the impotence of the local government created an ideal atmosphere in which racial violence could break out.

Consequently, as Negroes and whites were fighting the Germans, Italians and Japanese abroad, they were fighting each other at home. In June, 1943, the most serious race riot of the war period broke out in Detroit. Months of race tension were climaxed on June 20 when a fist fight occurred between a Negro and a white man. Soon, several hundred persons were involved, and Negroes and whites were fighting in various parts of the city. Nothing effective was done to bring order out of chaos until President Roosevelt declared a state of emergency and sent six thousand troops to patrol the city. After thirty hours of rioting, twenty-five Negroes and nine whites had been killed, and property valued at several hundred thousand dollars had been destroyed. There were other racial clashes on a smaller scale, in New York, Los Angeles, Chicago and several Southern cities. No city wanted to become another Detroit, however, and numerous efforts were made after the summer of 1954 to prevent the recurrence of such a tragedy.

Post-War Breakthrough

Shortly after Harry S. Truman took office, upon the death of President Roosevelt in April, 1945, it became clear that the new President would be an active exponent of a greater enjoyment of equality for Negroes. In an address to the annual meeting of NAACP in 1947, he said, "As Americans we believe that every man should be free to live his life as he wishes. He should be limited only by his responsibility to his fellow countrymen. If this freedom is to be more than a dream, each man must be guaranteed equality of opportunity. The only limit to an American's achievement should be his ability, his industry and his character." Already, the President had taken steps to provide this equality of opportunity. Late in 1946 he created the President's Committee on Civil Rights "to inquire into and determine whether and in what respect current law enforcement measures and the authority and means possessed by federal, state, and local governments may be strengthened and improved to safeguard the civil rights of the people." After surveying every aspect of American life involved in the problem of civil rights, the committee published its report under the title, *To Secure These Rights*. It made comprehensive and far-reaching recommendations calling for concrete measures to improve the administration of justice, protect the exercise of the franchise and the elimination of segregation in American life. In the same year the President appointed another interracial committee to look into the problem of higher education. In their report the committee recommended not only the elimination of inequalities in educational opportunities but the abandonment of all forms of discrimination in higher education.

The integration in the armed services that had been inaugurated in the closing years of World War II was accelerated by President Truman. In 1948 he appointed a committee to study the problem, and its report, *Freedom to Serve*, was a blueprint of the steps by which integration was to be achieved. In Korea, in 1950, there were new opportunities to test military integration under battlefield conditions. Between May and August, 1951, integration in the Korean forces jumped from 9 percent to 30 percent of troops in the field. A special Army report declared that the integration of Negroes had resulted in an overall gain for the army. At long last American Negroes had become a vital and integral part of the manpower pool of the nation.

In February, 1948, President Truman sent to Congress a special message on civil rights, the first such message that any President had ever sent. He called for the establishment of a permanent Commission on Civil Rights, Federal legislation against lynching, the establishment of a permanent Fair Employment Practices Committee, the prohibition of discrimination in interstate transportation facilities and the strengthening of existing civil rights statutes. Congress did nothing to implement the demands of the President or the recommendations of his several commissions. But the stand taken by the President was a new one for American Presidents. After Truman, no President could turn his back on this important problem.

While Congress paid little attention to the matter of civil rights, the Supreme Court was willing to take cognizance of them in a variety of cases. Indeed, there was scarcely an area of American life in which the rights of citizens were jeopardized that escaped the Court's attention in the years following World War II. In 1946, in a case coming up from Virginia,

Morgan vs. *Virginia,* the Court held unconstitutional a Virginia law that segregated passengers traveling across state lines. In 1948 the Court held that racially restrictive covenants in the conveyance of real property could not be enforced in the courts. The decision in this case, *Shelley* vs. *Kraemer,* was the first significant assault on segregation and discrimination in housing since the ordinance requiring whites and Negroes to live in separate blocks was outlawed in 1917. In 1950 the Court, which in 1938 had already required states to provide Negroes with professional training if it was provided for whites, held that such facilities not only must be equal but must, indeed, be the same facilities. To many white Southerners, this was a frightening departure from the "separate but equal" doctrine laid down in the Plessy case in 1896. It seemed clear that in time the Court would open all public institutions of higher education to Negroes. Many whites hoped that the Court would not desegregate primary and secondary schools.

In the hope that the Court would not disturb separate schools at the lower levels, the Southern states made a desperate effort to equalize Negro primary and secondary schools. In the late Forties and early Fifties, they spent millions of dollars for the improvement of segregated Negro schools. The more they spent the more they seemed to convince themselves that this was the best, indeed, the only solution to the problem of segregated education in the South.

The assault on segregated schools was the part of a larger drive to eliminate segregation in the United States. It could be seen in the emergence of new groups that joined with the older ones to challenge segregation laws and practices. In the midwest the American Council on Race Relations was active. In the North the Anti-Defamation League, the American Jewish Congress, the CIO Committee to Abolish Racial Discrimination, the National Lawyers Guild, the American Veterans' Committee, the Workers Defense League represented a wide variety of interests working for the elimination of segregation. In the South the Southern Conference for Human Welfare and the Southern Regional Council began to take action. In Washington the National Committee on Segregation in the Nation's Capital was working. In 1948 it described Washington, D.C., as the "capital of white supremacy," and called for the elimination of all practices of segregation and discrimination. Early in 1949 the Washington hotels began to accept Negro guests. Soon, some theaters and motion picture houses took steps to desegregate. In 1953 the Supreme Court, invoking a law that had been passed in 1873, declared that restaurants in Washington could not refuse to serve "well-behaved and respectable persons."

The move to desegregate Washington schools was a part of the move to desegregate schools in other parts of the country. Taking cognizance of the efforts of many Southern states to make their segregated schools equal as far as facilities were concerned, the NAACP and its supporters began to argue that segregated education, regardless of equal facilities, was *per se* unconstitutional. They set forth this position in the five cases arising in Kansas, South Carolina, Virginia, Delaware and the District of Columbia. Numerous organizations entered briefs in behalf of the position of the Negroes. The Attorney General of the United States asked the Court to strike down the doctrine of "separate but equal." Racial discrimination, he said, furnishes "grist for the communist propaganda mills, and it raises doubt even among friendly nations as to the intensity of our devotion to the democratic faith." The decision of the Court on May 17, 1954, was the most significant breakthrough of the twentieth century. It was unequivocal in outlawing segregation in public schools. Speaking for a unanimous court, Chief Justice Warren said, "Separate educational facilities are inherently unequal." There was no doubt, therefore, that Negro children who were segregated in public schools had been deprived of the equal protection of the laws guaranteed by the Fourteenth Amendment. The implications of the decision were highly significant and they would not be fully appreciated for many years to come.

There were those, however, who understood, from their own vantage point, what the decision meant. A Richmond editor denounced the Court as "that inept fraternity of politicians and professors" who had "repudiated the Constitution and spat upon the Tenth Amendment." More than a hundred Southern members of Congress issued a manifesto saying, "The unwarranted decision of the Supreme Court . . . is now bearing the fruit always produced when men substitute naked power for established law. We regard the decision as a clear abuse of judicial power." But one white editor in Knoxville, Tennessee, said, "No citizen, fitted by character and intelligence to sit as a justice of the Supreme Court, and sworn to uphold the Constitution . . . could have decided this question other than the way it was decided." A group of leading Negro educators said simply, "It was the right and moral thing to do."

TOWARD ONE AMERICA

An Improved Climate

Many factors and forces were operating to create a better climate for Negroes in the years following World War II. The assumption by the United States of a position of leadership in world affairs made the country particularly vulnerable regarding the position of the Negro in the United States. As one of the chief builders of the United Nations and as the host country to the new international organization, it became increasingly embarrassing to speak out against the denial of human rights in far away lands and be forced to admit that there were flagrant denials of those same rights in many parts of the United States. Other nations, including Russia, India, France and the Philippines, entertained serious doubts about the sincerity of America's professions regarding the rights of all peoples. The United States became sensitive to the discrepancies in its own human relations and sought to make amends by appointing Negroes to the delegations to the United Nations and to commissions dealing with international problems. Such moves, however, did not cover up the housing and employment problems that Negroes experienced and that even the casual visitor could see; nor did it obscure the numerous practices of segregation and discrimination that were mentioned all too frequently in the Russian press.

The emergence of independent states in Africa added to America's distress, in a sense. Beginning with Ghana in 1957, one African state after another gained its independence, and as they did so they inadvertently contributed toward the changing of the racial climate in the United States. Psychologically, the Negroes of the United States immediately identified with the new African nations and pointed with pride to the accomplishments of their brothers. They also reminded white Americans that Negro states in Africa were "living proof" of the Negro's ability to assume responsibilities at the highest level; and this "living proof" stimulated the Negroes of the United States to press a bit harder for their own rights. Equally important was the presence in the United States of an increasing number of African representatives to the United States and ambassadors to the United States and their staffs. In the "cold war" competition with Russia, it was most important that the African nations be won by the United States; and it was most difficult for the United States to accomplish this feat in the face of insults and indignities heaped upon African diplomats by white Americans. It became a major concern of the United States, therefore, not only to treat the Africans with dignity and respect but also to assure them that such treatment should be accorded Americans of dark skins. As this problem came to be a major concern of the President of the United States and the Secretary of State, they used their power and prestige to seek to correct some of the racial practices in the United States. And in so doing, they contributed to the improvement of the racial climate.

The extensive urbanization of the American Negro during and after World War II greatly contributed to the improvement of the political climate as far as the Negro was concerned. Between 1940 and 1960 the Negro population outside the old Confederacy increased two and one-fourth times, from nearly four million to more than nine million, representing 48 percent of the total Negro population. Most of this growth outside the South has been in the central cities of the twelve largest metropolitan areas of the United States: New York, Los Angeles, Chicago, Philadelphia, Detroit, San Francisco-Oakland, Boston, Pittsburgh, St. Louis, Washington, Cleveland and Baltimore. These twelve areas now hold 31 percent of all the Negroes in the United States; and these areas and other areas where the Negro population is concentrated are where the Negro wields the greatest amount of political influence.

Ironically, one of the very significant results of herding Negroes into urban ghettoes in the North has been the ernomous increase in their political power. Negroes sit in law-making bodies in every Northern state where the Negro population is concentrated in the large cities. They serve as state and municipal judges, city commissioners, corporation counsels and in a variety of other important elective and appointive public offices. Negroes have been elected to the school boards of Atlanta and Houston, to the state senate in Georgia, and to the councils of several Southern cities. They have won state-wide elections, as, for example, the election of Edward Brooke to be attorney general of Massachusetts, Otis Smith to be auditor general of Michigan and Gerald Lamb to be state treasurer in Connecticut. Five of the great metropolitan areas of the North—New York, Chicago, Philadelphia, Detroit, and Los Angeles—have Negroes in Congress: Adam C. Powell, William L. Dawson, Robert N. C. Nix, Charles C. Diggs, Jr., John L. Conyers, Jr. and Augustus F. Hawkins.

The growing political strength of the Negro and the improved climate are reflected in a notable way in the appointment of Negroes to important positions by the Chief Executive of the Federal Government. It began with the appointment of William H. Hastie to the United States Court of Appeal for the Third Circuit. It was continued by President Eisenhower in his appointment of J. Ernest Wilkins as Assistant Secretary of Labor, Scovel Richardson as Chairman of the United States Parole Board and later to the United States Customs Court, E. Frederic Morrow to the White House Staff and Clifton Wharton as Ambassador to Rumania. President Kennedy made numerous appointments of Negroes to important posts: Robert Weaver as Administrator of the Housing and Home Finance Agency, Clifton Wharton as Ambassador to Norway, Carl Rowan as Ambassador to Finland, Thurgood Marshall to the United States Circuit Court, James B. Parsons, Wade McCree and A. Leon Higginbotham to the United States District Court, Merl McCurdy and Cecil F. Poole as United States Attorneys and John B. Duncan as a member of the District of Columbia Board of Commissioners. In his first year in office President Johnson appointed Carl Rowan to be Director of the United States Information Agency Andrew F. Brimmer, Assistant

Secretary of Commerce and Mrs. Frankie Freeman as a member of the United States Commission on Civil Rights.

There were numerous other manifestations of an improved racial climate in the United States. Both political parties, for example, came out for strong civil rights planks in their platforms in 1960. In 1964 the Republican Party was equivocal on the issue, but the Democrats strengthened their pro-Civil Rights position. In every section of the country, even in the South, white citizens are becoming active in the civil rights struggle; and religious bodies —Protestant, Catholic, and Jewish—have become more active in behalf of equality than they ever have been before. Numerous local and national groups that heretofore had excluded Negroes from membership have, in the last decade, opened their doors to all qualified persons. In most litigations involving civil rights in recent years, numerous groups—law school professors, religious organizations, civic groups, and educational societies— have presented briefs as friends of the court asking that segregation laws and discrimination practices be outlawed.

The manner in which Negroes entered areas of American life that had always been closed to them was a measure of the improved climate in the years following World War II. When Jackie Robinson entered organized baseball in 1947 as a member of the Brooklyn Dodgers, it created a sensation. Within a few years virtually all the baseball teams in the two major leagues had Negroes, and the signing of an additional Negro team member was no longer even newsworthy. Despite the long tradition of Negro singers performing creditably on the concert stage, the announcement that Marian Anderson, one of the world's greatest contraltos, would have a small part in a production at the Metropolitan Opera Association was sensational news. Within five years Negroes were singing leading roles, and in 1961 Leontyne Price sang the title role on opening night. For many years Negroes played only stereotype roles as clowns and servants in motion pictures and on the legitimate stage. In recent years actors and actresses such as Sidney Poitier, Ossie Davis, Ruby Dee and Diahann Carroll were accepted on the basis of their skills and talents rather than their color. When Negro professors are appointed to predominantly white colleges and universities, it no longer surprises anyone. Thus, the air was clearing; and the climate was much improved by 1965.

The Involvement of Government

The involvement of government at every level in the movement to improve the condition and status of Negroes in the United States has been one of the most significant developments of the post-war period. Many of the states of the North and West had civil rights statutes dating back to the period before World War I, but many of them were universally disregarded. In the nineteen-fifties, there was a significant move to revive and enforce such statutes and, in many cases, to strengthen them. By 1964 twenty-one states had enacted enforceable fair employment practice laws. New York took the lead in 1945, and the number of such states had increased to eight by 1950. In 1955 three states— Michigan, Minnesota and Pennsylvania—enacted fair employment practice laws; and in each succeeding year new states passed such legislation. By 1965 nineteen states and fifty-five cities had barred discrimination in some aspect of housing. Eleven states, the Virgin Islands and three cities adopted fair housing laws which apply to privately financed as well as governmentally aided housing. Meanwhile, many volunteer fair housing groups have been organized in many sections of the country.

The courts, especially the Federal judiciary, continued to support the general principle of equality. In 1955, one year following the Supreme Court's decision in the school segregation cases, the Court remanded the cases to the courts of origin and indicated that it expected the courts to require that the states make a prompt and reasonable start toward full compliance with the decision of May, 1954. From that point on, the district and circuit courts have had the responsibility of examining the compliance measures of the several states. In numerous cases the judges of the lower Federal courts have carried out the decision of the Supreme Court by refusing to countenance techniques and devices developed by the several states to render ineffective the historic Supreme Court decision. The decision, moreover, sped up action in other areas. Even after the Morgan decision in 1946, there had been numerous efforts to segregate Negroes in interstate transportation as well as travel within the state. After hearing a variety of cases on the subject over the years, the Supreme Court seemed exasperated in 1962 when it stated in *Bailey* vs. *Patterson*, "We have settled beyond question that no state may require segregation of interstate or intrastate transportation facilities. . . . The question is no longer open; it is foreclosed as a litigable issue." The Court also upheld the argument advanced by Negro litigants that tax-supported public institutions, including parks, golf links and swimming pools, could not be segregated. In 1964 it ruled unconstitutional the separate but equal provision of the Hill-Burton Act which provides federal funds for hospital construction.

Even the Congress reacted favorably to the winds of change that were sweeping over the United States in midcentury. In 1957 it passed a civil rights act, the first such legislation since 1875. Among other things the act created a Civil Rights Commission as a continuing agency concerned with the enforcement of civil rights and enlarged and strengthened the Civil Rights Section of the Department of Justice. Furthermore, it authorized the Department of Justice to institute injunction proceedings against persons conspiring to deprive citizens of their rights. The act was certainly not revolutionary as many Southern members of Congress claimed; nor was it merely a sham, as Senator Wayne Morse of Oregon claimed. It focused attention on the Government's responsibility in the area of civil rights in a way never done before. The Negroes of Tuskegee now had a national agency to which they could relate the manner in which they had been gerrymandered out of the city limits and denied the right to vote. Negroes in Louisiana could now tell of acts of violence and intimidation against them if they attempted to vote. And the reports of the Civil Rights Commission would constitute a significant body of information to be used in the protection of civil rights in the future.

Having broken its silence in 1957 after so many years, Congress in 1960 took another step by enacting additional civil rights legislation. Opposition had not been stilled; and only after one of the longest and bitterest debates in the nation's history did the rather mild bill become law. The law singled out for punishment any person or persons defacing or damaging synagogues, churches or other buildings. All election officials were required to keep registration and other records for twenty-two months and make them available, upon request, to the Attorney General or his representatives. If a court found a pattern or practice of denial of the right to vote by reason of race or color, any Negro within the affected area would be entitled to vote upon proof of qualification. Court-appointed referees could receive applications, take evidence and report the findings to the court. The Attorney General hailed the new law as having "historic significance" by making it clear "that all branches of the Federal Government firmly support the proposition that the Fourteenth and Fifteenth Amendments to the Constitution are not to be considered mere promises but must become realities for all citizens in all areas of the country." No dramatic changes stemmed from the laws of 1957 and 1960, but the Civil Rights Commission gathered very important information on the status of the rights of citizens and there was soon a groundswell of interest in and support for a strong Civil Rights Act.

The executive branch of the Federal Government was, in recent years, even more active than the other branches in promoting equality in American life. The work begun by Truman and continued by Eisenhower was carried forward with vigor by Presidents Kennedy and Johnson. During the campaign, candidate Kennedy indicated that he fully appreciated the significance of the civil rights struggle. When the civil rights leader, Dr. Martin Luther King, was in jail in Georgia, Kennedy called Mrs. King, expressed his sympathy, and offered to do whatever he could to help. Although many factors contributed to the Kennedy victory in the closest Presidential contest in years, there can be no doubt that one telephone call swung thousands of votes to Kennedy in states that otherwise would have been in doubt. Once in office he would have every opportunity to demonstrate what he contended during the campaign, that the office of the President of the United States was "a place of moral leadership."

It appeared for a time that the new President would not provide the kind of leadership in this area that many hoped for and others expected and still others feared. He took the position that no additional legislation was needed except, perhaps, to protect voting rights. At the same time, however, he and his brother, the Attorney General, worked quietly with Southern railroads and Southern municipal governments in a largely successful effort to eliminate segregation in interstate transportation facilities. In September, 1961, he issued a personal plea for the ending of segregation and discrimination in restaurants and other places of public service. President Kennedy took the initiative in promoting fair employment by creating the President's Committee on Equal Employment Opportunity, with Vice President Lyndon B. Johnson as Chairman. At that time he said, "I have dedicated my Administration to the cause of equal opportunity in employment by the government or its contractors. The Vice President, the Secretary of Labor and the other members of this committee share my dedication." For the next three years the committee took steps to eliminate discrimination in employment in government and private enterprise.

Meanwhile, the Kennedy administration, through the Department of Justice, the Federal Bureau of Investigation, and the several Executive Offices sought to implement the stated commitment of the administration to equality. The Department of Justice participated in numerous litigations for the protection of civil rights. The Federal Bureau of Investigation not only looked into numerous complaints regarding discrimination and the denial of civil rights, but in the interest of a better administration of justice conducted numerous schools and institutes for law-enforcement officers. In November, 1962, the President signed the long-awaited order prohibiting discrimination in federally assisted housing. During the campaign, two years earlier, he had taunted President Eisenhower by saying that he could have done that "with the stroke of a pen." When asked why he waited so long, he replied that he had always intended to issue the order at the right time, and the right time had come.

The President was not slow to act in emergencies, however. In September, 1962, when the state of Mississippi, in defiance of a court order, attempted to prevent the enrollment of James Meredith at the University of Mississippi, the President acted promptly by sending Federal troops as President Eisenhower had done in Little Rock, to protect Meredith in the exercise of his rights. When the Birmingham demonstrations were at their height in April, 1963, he sent three thousand Federal troops to protect the rights of Negroes. When it appeared that the governor of Alabama, in June, 1963, would prevent the enrollment of three Negroes at the University of Alabama, the President ordered Federal officials to the University to assist in enforcing the court order to admit the Negro students. He then addressed the American people and warned them that there was "a rising tide of discontent that threatens the public safety"; and he declared that "the events in Birmingham and elsewhere have so increased the cries for equality that no city or state or legislative body can prudently choose to ignore them."

The Civil Rights Revolution

One of the most significant chapters in the recent history of American Negroes has been the development of new techniques to achieve old goals. Within the past decade, many people—white and Negro—began to consider the possibility of taking matters into their own hands by direct action. They had seen violent direct action in the emergence of the white citizens councils and the revival of the Ku Klux Klan to fight, with every means at their disposal, the enforcement of desegregation decisions. Perhaps, some Negroes began to believe, that they might accelerate the rights through nonviolent direct action. In 1956, a year before the passage of the Civil Rights Act, the Negroes of Montgomery, Alabama, began to boycott the bus lines of the city to protest white driver's abuse of Mrs. Rosa Parks, who had refused to move to the back of the bus with other Negro passengers. They now wanted to obtain a more satisfactory seating practice on the buses and to secure the employment of Negro drivers on buses serving predominantly Negro sections of the city.

As Negroes proceeded with their boycott, the white community was outraged. Some ninety Negroes were indicted under a 1921 antiunion law forbidding conspiracy to obstruct the operation of a business. Their leader, the Reverend Dr. Martin Luther King, Jr., was the first to be tried. He was found guilty. Immediately he served notice of appeal, while the bus company frantically sought to settle the problem before it became bankrupt. The Montgomery Negroes finally won their battle; and the effective weapon of boycott gained in popularity as Negroes of Tallahassee, Atlanta and Nashville successfully tested the practice of picketing and boycotting as civil rights weapons.

Soon, other organizations committed themselves to direct, nonviolent action. Within the next few years numerous groups, most of them inter-racial, became active. Among them were the Congress of Racial Equality, the Southern Christian Leadership Conference, and the Student Non-Violent Coordinating Committee. In addition, there were other groups giving aid and comfort to those involved in direct action. Among them were the NAACP, the National Urban League, the Southern Regional Council, numerous religious groups and labor and civic organizations.

On February 1, 1960, four students from the Negro Agricultural and Technical College of Greensboro, North Carolina, entered a variety store, made several purchases, and sat down at the lunch counter and ordered coffee. They were refused service because they were Negroes; and they remained in their seats until the store closed. This was the beginning of the sit-in movement, the second phase of the civil rights revolution, which spread rapidly through the South and to some places in the North. In the spring and summer of 1960 thousands of young people, white and Negro, participated in similar peaceful forms of protest against segregation and discrimination. They sat in white libraries, waded into white beaches and slept in the lobbies of white motels. Many of them were arrested for trespassing, disorderly conduct and disobeying officers who ordered them off the premises.

A Southern journalist labeled the sit-ins "the South's new time bomb," and observed that young Negroes were infused with a new determination to risk violence to acquire some of the rights they believed were due them. When Negro students were criticized for their actions, they placed a full-page advertisement in the white *Atlanta Constitution,* in which they said, "We do not intend to wait placidly for those rights which are already legally and morally ours to be meted out to us one at a time." Negro students and their white colleagues were on the march to secure their rights. As a result, literally hundreds of lunch counters across the South began to serve Negroes, and other facilities began to open up. When their efforts were not successful, they boycotted white businesses or en-gaged in "selective purchasing," thus bringing to bear another effective weapon to secure their rights.

In May, 1961, an even more dramatic attack on segregation and discrimi-nation than sit-ins was undertaken by the Congress of Racial Equality. It sent "Freedom Riders" through the South to test segregation laws and practices in interstate transportation. In Alabama the interracial team was attacked at Anniston and Birmingham. Although the Attorney General was obviously a bit annoyed by the aggressiveness of these unorthodox fighters for civil rights, he ordered the Federal Bureau of Investigation to look into the matter and made it clear that the Freedom Riders would be protected. In the summer of 1961 the jails of Jackson, Mississippi, and other Southern communities were virtually filled with Freedom Riders who had been arrested for the alleged violation of some law. The Federal Government maintained an active interest in these proceedings, sent some four hundred United States marshals to Alabama to restore order and secured an injunction to prohibit any attempt to stop, by force, the Freedom Riders from continuing their test of bus station segregation.

At about the same time the Negroes of Albany, Georgia, began to demonstrate their plight by marching through the streets and holding large mass meetings. Hundreds were arrested, and the officials of the city were adamant in their refusal to discuss the situation with Negro leaders. In the two years that followed, marching, picketing and public demonstrations were taken up by Negroes in Atlanta, Danville, Virginia, Cambridge, Maryland, and many other communities. In March, 1963, for example, the Negroes of Leflore County, Mississippi, began to march in order to dramatize a voter registration drive sponsored by the Student Non-Violent Coordinating Committee. In April, 1963, Dr. King inaugurated the forty days of marching in Birmingham, Alabama, during which time more than 2,500 Negroes were arrested. The Birmingham marches inspired scores of others, North and South; and some were attended by violence and rioting. They were the occasion, moreover, for the focusing of attention on the Black Muslims, who used the marches to point out one of the basic tenets of their position: that the United States will never grant equality to Negroes. Negroes, therefore, should reject any semblance of cooperation and turn their attention to the development of their own culture as well as their own political and economic institutions. While the movement is not large in numbers, its popularity is considerable, even among those who reject its program.

In the year of the centennial of the Emancipation Proclamation the civil rights revolution reached its peak. The numerous successful demonstrations and marches suggested to the leadership that one massive march on Washington might dramatize to the nation and to the world the importance of solving the problem of the status of the Negro in the United States once and for all. Soon, plans were made to carry out the march on August 28, 1963. All of the major Negro organizations joined in formulating the plans, and they were joined by scores of other organizations, white and Negro. A wide-eyed world watched as a quarter of a million Negroes and whites converged on Washington from all over the United States, by every conceivable mode of transportation and under every conceivable auspice.

Washington had never seen such a day as this. The businesses in the downtown area closed, not out of respect to the marchers but because of the fear of rioting and looting. Most of the Federal employees took the day off, some to participate in the march, others to get as far from the center of things as possible. Before the impressive memorial to Abraham Lincoln the civil rights leaders spoke: Whitney Young, Roy Wilkins, Martin Luther King. From his jail cell in Louisiana, James Farmer, Director of the Congress of Racial Equality, sent a message. Mahalia Jackson sang. Ministers, movie stars, radio commentators, college students, thousands of organizations and ordinary citizens participated. The President of the United States cordially received the leaders, while others called on their Representatives and Senators. The nation looked on via television, and the entire world would later see in the newspapers and on the newsreels the most remarkable testimony in behalf of the equality of mankind ever made in this or any other country. One important figure was absent. Fifty-odd years earlier he had assumed the leadership in the fight for equality. On the eve of the march, W. E. B. Du Bois, now a citizen of Ghana, had passed away in Accra.

In June, before the march, President Kennedy had asked Congress to enact laws that would provide a legal guarantee to all citizens of equal access to the services and facilities of hotels, restaurants, places of amusement and other public establishments in interstate commerce; authorize the Attorney General to start school desegregation suits when he is requested by someone unable to do so; broad Federal action to stop discrimination in Federal jobs and activities financed wholly or in part with Federal funds; create a Community Relations Service to act as a mediation agency in communities with racial tensions; make it clear "that the Federal Government is not required to furnish any kind of financial assistance to any program or activity in which racial discrimination occurs."

The President's message of June 19, 1963, is not only a historic document, a veritable landmark in the history of the drive for equality. It is also the best summary available of the unfinished business of democracy. He deplored the fact that Negroes did not have equal access to public accommodations and facilities. "No one has been barred on account of his race from fighting or dying for America—there are no 'white' and 'colored' signs on the foxholes and graveyards of battle. Surely, in 1963, one hundred years after emancipation, it should not be necessary for any American citizen to demonstrate in the streets for the opportunity to stop at a hotel, or to eat at a lunch counter in the very department store in which he is shopping, or to enter a motion picture house, on the same terms as any other customer." With regard to segregated schools, he said, "Many Negro children entering segregated grade schools at the time of the Supreme Court decision in 1954 will enter segregated high schools this year, having suffered a loss which can never be regained. Indeed, discrimination in education is one basic cause of the other inequities and hardships inflicted upon our Negro citizens."

Those who marched on Washington in August, 1963, were doing what they could to emphasize the importance of enacting the legislation the President had called for. More than that, they were expressing their continuing faith in the efficacy of democratic institutions in righting the wrong of centuries and of giving themselves a new lease on life through a process of self-purification. But those who marched were under no illusions and were not blindly optimistic. As soon as they returned to their respective homes, they continued their fight. In Chicago they urged the end of *de facto* segregation in the schools in a boycott which kept 250,000 Negro children out of classes. In New York they did the same. In Birmingham they called for some tangible indication of good faith on the part of the city administration. In Placquemine Parish, Louisiana, they called for obedience of the law regarding the rights of citizens to register and vote.

The Civil Rights Act of 1964

When President Kennedy was assassinated on November 22, 1963, many civil rights leaders as well as ordinary citizens thought that the cause of civil rights had suffered a permanent setback; and many were disconsolate. The manner, however, in which the new President, Lyndon B. Johnson, counseled with Negro leaders, the numerous instances during his early days in office in which he pledged himself to fight for equality, and his unequivocal stand in favor of a strong civil rights bill without crippling amendments were a source of some considerable satisfaction. With the Senate Majority Whip, Hubert H. Humphrey, in charge of the bill and with strong bipartisan support, Congress proceeded to enact the strongest civil rights bill that had ever been passed. The very process of enactment was historic, in that a majority of the members of both parties supported the bill, thereby making it possible for the Senate to invoke cloture and cut off the bitter-end marathon filibuster conducted by a bloc of Southern Senators.

It was a great day of rejoicing, therefore, when President Johnson signed the new civil rights bill, on July 2, 1964, in the presence of Congressional and civil rights leaders. The chances for the enforcement of the bill were substantially increased when several prominent Southern Senators who had fought its passage called for Southerners to obey the new law. The appointment of Leroy Collins, former governor of Florida, as the first director of the Community Relations Service, was widely hailed as an auspicious beginning in the effort to gain acceptance of the law, despite the fact that one prominent Southerner called him a "renegade Confederate." There was vigorous opposition in some quarters, of course, but the prompt declaration by a Federal district court that the bill was constitutional and the refusal of Supreme Court Justice Black to suspend its enforcement contributed to the decrease of opposition. Consequently, Negroes began to eat in restaurants and register in hotels in many parts of the South where hitherto they had not found it possible to secure service.

Perhaps it was the general improvement of the climate of race relations that brought about other desegregation steps in the months following the enactment of the civil rights bill of 1964. The summer had witnessed some ugly manifestations of racial unrest, as rioting erupted in New York City, Philadelphia, Chicago and several New Jersey cities. But civil rights leaders were quick to point out that these were not civil rights riots but the angry outbursts of poverty-stricken, jobless people living under intolerable conditions in the city slums. There had also been numerous incidents of violence in the South—the mysterious murder of three civil rights workers in Mississippi and the brutal slaying in Georgia of a Negro educator returning from reserve officer training to his home in Washington. But the process of desegregation continued. Segregated public facilities in many parts of the country bowed to the new law, and the pace of school desegregation increased noticeably. In Orangeburg, South Carolina, Negro children attended desegregated schools for the first time in September, 1964. In the same month, other Southern schools were desegregated, notably some for the first time anywhere in Mississippi as well as in Americus, Georgia, and St. Helena Parish, Louisiana.

The issue of civil rights became an important matter in the presidential campaign of 1964. While the bill had received generous bipartisan support in Congress, the man who became the Republican nominee for the Presidency, Senator Barry Goldwater, had voted against the bill on the ground that he regarded certain parts of it as unconstitutional. This gained for him strong support in many parts of the South, but it alienated virtually all Negroes—even those who had been lifelong Republicans—from the Republican nominee. If the votes of the so-called white backlash—those opposed to the Negro's vigorous drive for equality—drifted to the Republican party, there were those of what President Johnson and his supporters called the frontlash—supporters of civil rights—who joined the Democratic ranks. Nearly six million Negro voters gave their overwhelming support to the election of the Johnson-Humphrey ticket in November 1964.

The Civil Rights movement was greatly strengthened when, in an early test case, the Supreme Court upheld the Act of 1964. The world spotlight was again thrown on the movement when Martin Luther King was awarded the 1964 Nobel peace prize for his leadership. Shortly thereafter, King and other leaders stepped up their voter registration campaign in Marion and Selma, Alabama. The coordination of all federal civil rights activities by the new Vice President, Hubert H. Humphrey, was a source of some encouragement to Negroes.

Thus, Negroes faced their second century of emancipation not only with a new President whose stand on civil rights, housing, and poverty they generally supported, but also with a new civil rights law that many regarded as an indication that at long last the government of the United States was on their side. Perhaps the second century, some of them thought, would not be as difficult as the first.

BIBLIOGRAPHY

Bennett, Lerone, *Before the May-flower*, Chicago, Johnson Publishing Company, 1964.

Butcher, Margaret J., *The Negro in American Culture*, New York: Alfred A. Knopf, Inc., 1956.

Franklin, John Hope, *From Slavery to Freedom, A History of American Negroes*, New York, Alfred A. Knopf, Inc., 1956.

Frazier, E. Franklin, *The Negro in the United States*, New York, The Macmillan Co., 1957.

Hill, Herbert, *Soon One Morning, New Writing of American Negroes*, New York, Alfred A. Knopf, Inc., 1963.

Logan, Rayford W., *The Negro in American Life and Thought*, New York, Dial, 1954.

Meier, August, *Negro Thought in America*, Ann Arbor, University of Michigan, 1963.

Myrdal, Gunnar, *American Dilemma*, New York, Harper & Row, 1963.

Rose, Arnold, *Assuring Freedom to the Free*, Wayne State University, 1964.

Redding, Saunders, *Lonesome Road*, New York, Doubleday & Co., Inc., 1958.

U.S. Commission on Civil Rights, *Freedom to the Free*, Washington, D.C., Government Printing Office, 1963.

Woodson, Carter G. and Wesley, Charles H., *The Negro in Our History*, Washington, D.C., Associated publishers, 1961.

chapter 2

The Negro Population
in the United States

Karl E. Taeuber and Alma F. Taeuber

Both Negroes and whites originally came to North America as immigrants, and the history of their settlement is only a few hundred years old. Most of the white immigrants came in search of an increased measure of freedom and enlarged opportunity. Most of the Negro immigrants came after losing their freedom, in the bondage of others. As the years went by, both groups expanded in number, and participated in the settling of a continent and the creation of a gigantic urban and industrial nation out of a small number of agricultural colonies. In this chapter, many of the ensuing social transformations are traced with the aid of population statistics from a long series of national censuses.

Data from the censuses tell a story of increasing numbers of Negroes and whites, of expanding Negro settlement in the South, and then in the cities of the North and West. Other data tell of the characteristics of Negroes today, their social and economic status, their housing, the rates at which they give birth and the rates at which they die. The charts and tables that tell this story are, like pictures, worth thousands of words. The reader who examines the charts and tables will find far more information than can be conveyed in the text, and will be able to form his own conclusions.

A few words of introduction to census data may help the reader of this chapter and several later chapters. The category "Negro" as used in census publications is a peculiar one. It is arbitrarily designed for simple application and does not convey any biological, anthropological or legal meanings. A person who appears to be or claims to be white is so listed. Everyone else is regarded as nonwhite and classified according to "race" as Negro, Indian, Japanese, Chinese, etc. Taking a census is a massive operation, and it is not possible to make finer distinctions. The color-race classification used by the census is merely a rough estimate of the person's social identity in his local community.

In this volume, attention is centered on the Negro population. Sometimes, however, data will be presented for nonwhites. In 1960, Negroes made up 92 percent of all nonwhites in the country. Except for a few areas (mainly in the West) containing large numbers of Indians, Orientals or other non-

FIGURE 1—Regions and Geographic Divisions of the United States

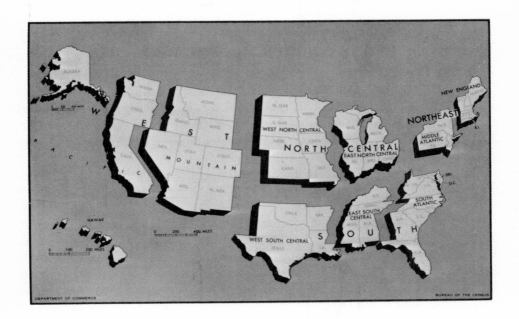

whites, figures for nonwhites may be regarded for practical purposes as referring to Negroes.

Many people attribute too much accuracy to statistical data. It is important to realize that a census is taken by tens of thousands of enumerators, administrators and other personnel, and many errors are possible. Although the 1960 census reported a total Negro population of 18,871,831, nobody would claim that the last few digits are precise. Furthermore, it is not important whether they are, since to know that there were in 1960 about 19 million Negroes is quite accurate enough for almost any purpose. The data presented are not perfectly accurate, but they are more accurate than anybody's guess.

There are many ways of dividing the country into North, South and West. Census data are usually presented for four geographic regions, or nine geographic divisions, portrayed in Figure 1. In this chapter, "the South" refers to all those states in the three southern divisions; the "West" refers to those states in the Mountain and Pacific divisions; and "the North" refers to all other states. The term "conterminous United States" refers to the first forty-eight states, excluding Alaska and Hawaii.

GROWTH AND DISTRIBUTION OF NEGRO POPULATION

The history of Negro population is one of gradual obliteration of the slave heritage of southern rural residence and depressed social and economic status. In the decades since Emancipation, the Negro population has been approaching a pattern of distribution and of social characteristics increasingly like that of the white population. At the time of our first national census in 1790, the total population of the new nation was about four million, 3.2 million whites and 757,000 Negroes. Nearly all of the Negroes were slaves, and nearly all lived in the South. On the eve of the Civil War the situation of the Negro population was not greatly different. In 1860, there were about 4.4 million Negroes in the United States—more than the total national population at the time of the first census. Nearly 90 percent were slaves and more than 90 percent still lived in the South. In the one hundred years since Emancipation, however, there have been dramatic changes. The Negro population increased to 19 million in 1960, of whom 7.5 million lived outside the South and 14 million lived in cities.

The Spread of Slavery

Many of the current features of Negro population distribution are the product of patterns laid down before the Revolutionary War and the formation of the United States. The southern colonies developed as suppliers of agricultural commodities to Britain, and plantation agriculture proved to be an efficient means of exploiting some of the rich resources of the region.

The first ship bringing Negroes to the colonies reportedly arrived in Virginia in 1619. From this beginning, an agricultural system utilizing slave labor was gradually developed and expanded. Slaves were used in the raising of tobacco in Virginia and Maryland before 1700, and spread into South Carolina and Georgia with rice cultivation after 1700. Cotton was not a big crop until later, but once under way in South Carolina and Georgia, it spread rapidly. The invention of the cotton gin in 1793 led to an increase in the efficiency of slave labor. With the depletion of much of the land in the eastern portions of the South, there was a westward expansion of cotton and tobacco cultivation, and of slavery. The maps in Figure 2 reveal very clearly this westward movement as well as the heavy concen-

FIGURE 2—Geographic Distribution of Slave Population, 1790, 1800, 1830 and 1860

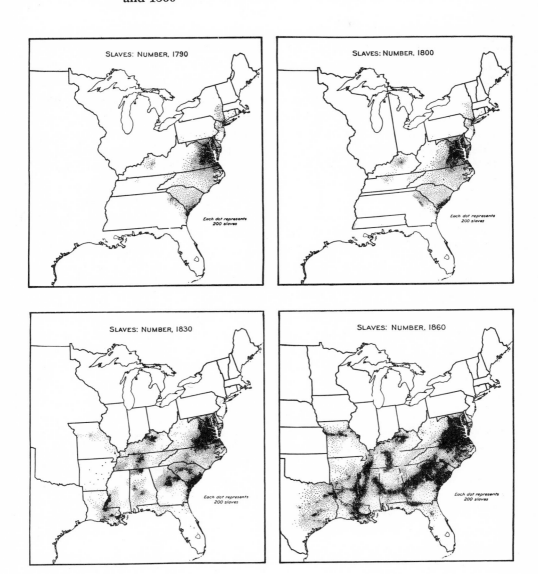

SOURCE: E. Franklin Frazier, *The Negro in the United States* (New York: The Macmillan Company, 1957), Maps II, III, IV, and V.

trations of Negro slaves in selected agricultural areas of the South, and their virtual absence from other areas—particularly the Appalachians and the Ozarks.

The slave trade flourished well into the nineteenth century, despite its legal abolition in 1808. It is estimated that about 400,000 slaves were imported between 1619 and 1808, and another 270,000 entered illegally after 1808 to meet the continuing demand for agricultural labor.

For Negro slaves, there was always some possibility, however slight, for a change in status from slave to free. Because of the constitutional provision that slaves counted only three-fifths as much as free persons in determining congressional representation, the 1790 census and subsequent censuses to 1860 counted the number of Negroes who were slave and the number who were free. Although manumission became increasingly difficult as various Southern states enacted legislation discouraging it, the free Negro population grew, being added to by births occurring to free Negroes, by legal abolition of slavery in Northern states and by the escape of slaves into freedom. In 1790, about 8 percent of Negroes were free and the other 92 percent were slaves. In 1830, about 14 percent of all Negroes were free, but during the decades before the Civil War the growth of the free Negro population slowed and by 1860 this percentage had slipped back to 11.

The slave population was very heavily concentrated in the South. In fact, slavery outside the South after 1830 was found almost exclusively in Missouri. Free Negroes, on the other hand, were more equally divided between North and South, with about 40 percent living in the North. At a time when only a small portion of the white population and an even smaller portion of the slave population lived in cities, many free Negroes found that large cities offered greater freedom and wider opportunities for earning a living. Sizable free Negro colonies appeared in several cities of the South —Baltimore, Washington, New Orleans, Charleston, Richmond and Petersburg. In the North, Negro population (virtually all free) was concentrated in Boston, New York, Chicago, Cincinnati and Philadelphia. Despite discrimination and restrictive legislation, free Negroes in cities held a variety of skilled jobs and in many cases owned property and voted. In general, however, the economic circumstances of free Negroes were precarious, whether in large cities or rural areas.

Growth of White and Negro Population

The population of the colonies in 1650 included an estimated 1,600 Negroes and 48,768 whites. During the next three centuries, both groups grew rapidly, although their periods of rapid and slow growth did not

FIGURE 3—Population of the United States by Race, 1650–1960

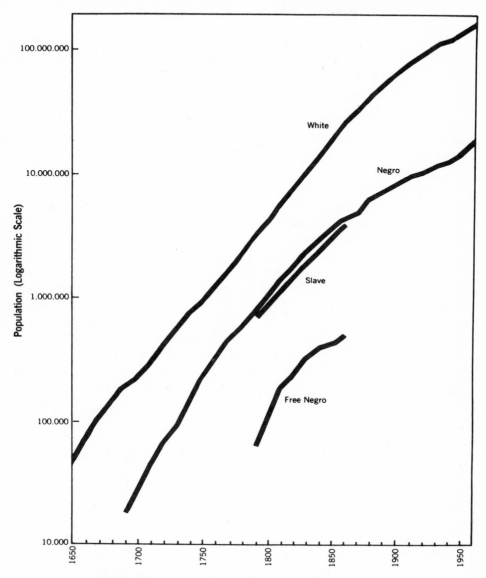

SOURCE: 1650–1950 from U. S. Bureau of the Census, *Historical Statistics of the United States, Colonial Times to 1957* (Washington, D.C.: U.S. Government Printing Office, 1963), Series Z 1–19 and Series A 95–122; 1960 from U.S. Bureau of the Census, *U.S. Census of Population: 1960, General Population Characteristics, U.S. Summary,* Final Report PC (1)–1B (Washington, D.C.: U.S. Government Printing Office, 1961), Table 44.

always coincide. By 1960, there were in the United States 18.9 million Negroes and 158.8 million whites. The patterns of growth from 1650 to 1960 are portrayed in Figure 3.

The relative proportions of Negroes and whites in the population have varied considerably throughout our history. This is shown in Figure 4. During the colonial period, there was little new immigration of Europeans, but continued importation of slaves. Negro population grew at a faster rate than white population, and the percentage of Negroes in the total rose from 1.3 percent in 1630 to a peak of 21.4 percent in 1770. During the next fifty years, both Negroes and whites gained population mainly by natural increase, the excess of births over deaths, and the percentage of Negroes remained close to 20.

Since the Civil War, the Negro population has increased very little due to immigration. The white population, however, embarked upon a period of very rapid growth as the great period of migration from Europe began. Millions of immigrants were added to a high rate of natural increase. The percentage of Negroes declined, reaching a low point of 9.7 in 1930. With restrictive legislation choking off the flow of immigrants from Europe in the early 1920's, both white and Negro populations in recent decades have grown mainly by natural increase. During these decades, Negroes have been increasing at a slightly faster rate, and their share in the population has been increasing slowly. By 1960, Negroes constituted 10.6 percent of the United States population, and this figure may increase slowly in the years to come. Nonetheless, Negroes will continue to comprise a smaller percentage of the population than at the time of the founding of the country.

Regional Distribution

Although many free Negroes and a small share of the slave population lived in the North, the overwhelming bulk of Negro population until recently was concentrated in the South. At every census from 1790 to 1900, at least 90 percent of the Negro population of the United States lived in the South (Figure 5). In 1910, 89 percent of Negroes still lived in the South, but the percentage fell in succeeding decades, to 85 percent in 1920, 77 percent in 1940 and 60 percent in 1960. The reverse pattern, of course, is apparent for Northern and Western states. Prior to 1900, states outside the South never contained more than 10 percent of the Negro population, but by 1920 they contained 15 percent, by 1940, 23 percent, and by 1960, 40 percent.

It is clear that the last few decades have been a time of great migrations for Negroes. Millions of Negroes made the long journey from South to

FIGURE 4—Percent Negro of Total Population in the United States, 1630–1960

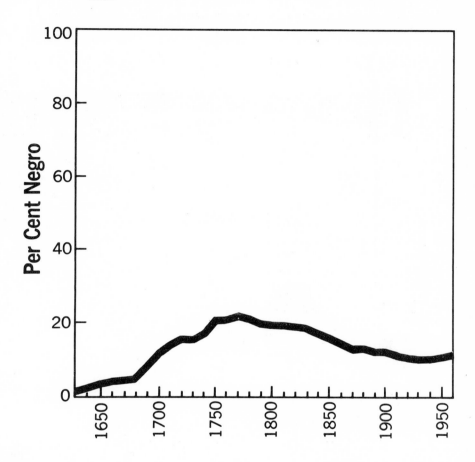

SOURCE: Donald J. Bogue, *The Population of the United States* (New York: The Free Press of Glencoe, 1959), Table 7–2; U.S. Bureau of the Census, *Historical Statistics of the United States, Colonial Times to 1957* (Washington, D.C.: U.S. Government Printing Office, 1963), Series Z 1–19; and U.S. Bureau of the Census, *U.S. Census of Population: 1960, General Population Characteristics, U.S. Summary,* Final Report PC(1)–1B (Washington, D.C.: U.S. Government Printing Office, 1961), Table 44.

North or West. After a century of relative stability in the regional distribution of Negro population, amazingly rapid and profound changes have taken place within the last fifty years.

For nearly fifty years before 1910, however, Negroes had the freedom to move. The freedom to move was granted with Emancipation, and there are many reports of newly freed slaves testing their freedom by moving to another farm, village, county or state. During the decades following the Civil War, there was a continued westward settlement within the South

FIGURE 5—Percent Distribution by Region for Negroes, 1790–1960

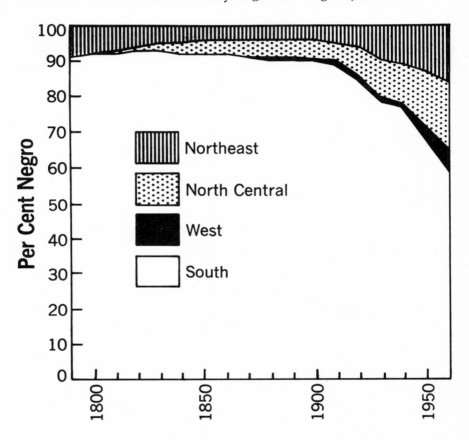

SOURCE: 1960 from U.S. Bureau of the Census, *U.S. Census of Population: 1960, General Population Characteristics, U.S. Summary,* Final Report PC(1)–1B (Washington, D.C.: U.S. Government Printing Office, 1961), Table 57; 1790–1950 from U.S. Bureau of the Census, *Historical Statistics of the United States, Colonial Times to 1957* (Washington, D.C.: U.S. Government Printing Office, 1963), Series A 95–122.

carrying increasing numbers of Negroes as well as whites into new agricultural lands in Louisiana and Texas. Within the North there was also westward movement into Ohio, Michigan, and Illinois, with a few Negroes accompanying the many whites settling these states. Yet there was very little movement of Negroes from South to North for fifty years after Emancipation. During the war and its aftermath, thousands of Negroes migrated to Washington, D.C. and even further north, but hundreds of thousands of Negroes remained near where they had lived as slaves.

The explanation for the stability of Negro population in the decades following Emancipation must lie in the failure of Emancipation to bring with it any organized programs to provide Negroes with new means of earning a livelihood. Many plans were considered, and some tried on a small scale, but for a variety of reasons the Reconstruction programs never included any major effort to alter the economic circumstances of Negroes. Colonization abroad was discussed then as in later times, but never undertaken on a large scale. Utilization of Negroes in the expanding industrial cities of the North was ruled out by prejudice, lack of effort and the continuing availability of millions of European immigrants. Major governmental programs would have been necessary to provide large quantities of land for Negro agricultural settlement either on new farm lands in the North and West or by facilitating Negro land ownership in the South. Neither did the newly freed Negroes find many new economic opportunities in Southern cities, where they had to eke out an existence earning wages in competition with whites and with skilled and experienced Negroes who had been free before Emancipation. Furthermore, after the war, the high price of cotton eased the process of Southern economic recovery and encouraged the continued use of Negro labor on white-owned farms and plantations, under new forms of tenancy. One result was a high degree of stability in Negro population distribution.

No one of the major regions of the country is homogeneous, and there are wide differences within each region in the distribution of Negro population. During the last century, for example, the movement of Negroes from South to North has meant a decline in the percentage of Negroes in the population of the South. Whereas in 1860 Negroes comprised 37 percent of the total, in 1960 they comprised 21 percent. In Kentucky, however, the change was from 20 to 7 percent, while in Mississippi it was from 55 to 42 percent. Full data on the Negro population in each state in 1860, 1910 and 1960, and the percentage of Negroes at each date, are given in Table I. Differences between states in their response to school desegregation and many other aspects of race relations can be traced in part to differences in population such as those found between Kentucky and Mississippi.

Similar arguments about variation in Negro population distribution can be applied to states. Southern states with high percentages of Negroes may have some counties where Negroes form a vast majority of the population,

TABLE I—Negro Population and Percent Negro by States, 1860, 1910 and 1960

State	Negro Population			Percent Negro		
	1860	1910	1960	1860	1910	1960
NORTH	**340,240**	**1,027,674**	**6,474,536**	**1.7**	**1.8**	**6.7**
New England	**24,711**	**66,306**	**243,363**	**0.8**	**1.0**	**2.3**
Maine	1,327	1,363	3,318	0.2	0.2	0.3
New Hampshire	494	564	1,903	0.2	0.1	0.3
Vermont	709	1,621	519	0.2	0.5	0.1
Massachusetts	9,602	38,055	111,842	0.8	1.1	2.2
Rhode Island	3,952	9,529	18,332	2.3	1.8	2.1
Connecticut	8,627	15,174	107,449	1.9	1.4	4.2
Middle Atlantic	**131,290**	**417,870**	**2,785,136**	**1.8**	**2.2**	**8.2**
New York	49,005	134,191	1,417,511	1.3	1.5	8.4
New Jersey	25,336	89,760	514,875	3.8	3.5	8.5
Pennsylvania	56,949	193,919	852,750	2.0	2.5	7.5
East North Central	**63,699**	**300,836**	**2,884,969**	**0.9**	**1.6**	**8.0**
Ohio	36,673	111,452	786,097	1.6	2.3	8.1
Indiana	11,428	60,320	269,275	0.9	2.2	5.8
Illinois	7,628	109,049	1,037,470	0.5	1.9	10.3
Michigan	6,799	17,115	717,581	0.9	0.6	9.2
Wisconsin	1,171	2,900	74,546	0.2	0.1	1.9
West North Central	**120,540**	**242,662**	**561,068**	**5.6**	**2.1**	**3.6**
Minnesota	259	7,084	22,263	0.2	0.3	0.7
Iowa	1,069	14,973	25,354	0.2	0.7	0.9
Missouri	118,503	157,452	390,853	10.0	4.8	9.0
North Dakota	—a	617	777	—a	0.1	0.1
South Dakota	—a	817	1,114	—a	0.1	0.2
Nebraska	82	7,689	29,262	0.3	0.6	2.1
Kansas	627	54,030	91,445	0.6	3.2	4.2
SOUTH	**4,097,111**	**8,749,427**	**11,311,607**	**36.8**	**29.8**	**20.6**
South Atlantic	**2,058,198**	**4,112,488**	**5,844,565**	**38.4**	**33.7**	**22.5**
Delaware	21,627	31,181	60,688	19.3	15.4	13.6
Maryland	171,131	232,250	518,410	24.9	17.9	16.7
District of Columbia	14,316	94,446	411,737	19.1	28.5	53.9
Virginia	548,907	671,096	816,258	34.4	32.6	20.6
West Virginia	—	64,173	89,378	—	5.3	4.8
North Carolina	361,522	697,843	1,116,021	36.4	31.6	24.5
South Carolina	412,320	835,843	829,291	58.6	55.2	34.8
Georgia	465,698	1,176,987	1,122,596	44.1	45.1	28.5
Florida	62,677	308,669	880,186	44.6	41.0	17.8
East South Central	**1,394,360**	**2,652,513**	**2,698,839**	**34.7**	**31.5**	**22.4**
Kentucky	236,167	261,656	215,949	20.4	11.4	7.1
Tennessee	283,019	473,088	586,876	25.5	21.7	16.5
Alabama	437,770	908,282	980,271	45.4	42.5	30.0
Mississippi	437,404	1,009,487	915,743	55.3	56.2	42.0

| | Negro Population | | | Percent Negro | | |
State	1860	1910	1960	1860	1910	1960
West South Central	**644,553**	**1,984,426**	**2,768,203**	**36.9**	**22.6**	**16.3**
Arkansas	111,259	442,891	388,787	25.6	28.1	21.8
Louisiana	350,373	713,874	1,039,207	49.5	43.1	31.9
Oklahoma	—	137,612	153,084	—	8.3	6.6
Texas	182,921	690,049	1,187,125	30.3	17.7	12.4
WEST	**4,479**	**50,662**	**1,085,688**	**0.7**	**0.7**	**3.9**
Mountain	**235**	**21,467**	**123,242**	**0.1**	**0.8**	**1.8**
Montana	—	1,834	1,467	—	0.5	0.2
Idaho	—	651	1,502	—	0.2	0.2
Wyoming	—	2,235	2,183	—	1.5	0.7
Colorado	46	11,453	39,992	0.1	1.4	2.3
New Mexico	85	1,628	17,063	0.1	0.5	1.8
Arizona	—	2,009	43,403	—	1.0	3.3
Utah	59	1,144	4,148	0.2	0.3	0.5
Nevada	45	513	13,484	0.7	0.6	4.7
Pacific	**4,244**	**29,195**	**962,446**	**1.0**	**0.7**	**4.5**
Washington	30	6,058	48,738	0.3	0.5	1.7
Oregon	128	1,492	18,133	0.2	0.2	1.0
California	4,086	21,645	883,861	1.1	0.9	5.6
Alaska	—	—	6,771	—	—	3.0
Hawaii	—	—	4,943	—	—	0.8
U.S. TOTAL	**4,441,830**	**9,827,763**	**18,871,831**	**14.1**	**10.7**	**10.5**

a Dakota Territory.

SOURCE: 1860 and 1910 from U.S. Bureau of the Census, *Negroes in the United States, 1920–32* (Washington, D.C.: U.S. Government Printing Office, 1935), Chapter II, Table 12 and Chapter III, Table 4; 1960 from U.S. Bureau of the Census, *U.S. Census of Population: 1960, General Population Characteristics, U.S. Summary,* Final Report PC(1)–1B (Washington, D.C.: U.S. Government Printing Office, 1961), Table 56.

and others where they make up only a small percentage. Similarly, those states with small percentages of Negroes may nonetheless have some counties with large concentrations of Negro population. In 1880, there was a belt of about 300 mainly contiguous counties in the rich argricultural area of the central South in which Negroes constituted more than half of the population. The number of "black belt" counties has been steadily declining, numbering 264 counties in 1910 and 138 in 1960. Several Southern states (Delaware, Kentucky, Maryland, Oklahoma and West Virginia) have no counties in which Negroes are in the majority. Such counties are still found in the remaining Southern states, particularly Georgia (34), Mississippi (29), Virginia (15), and South Carolina (15). Washington, D.C., is the only large city in the country in which Negroes outnumber whites; in 1960 Negroes comprised 53.9 percent of the population of the capital city. Space does not permit a full presentation of data for small areas. Readers are urged to consult the census volumes for their states to obtain specific information on such local variations.

PATTERNS OF MIGRATION, 1870–1960

If the early history of Negro population is linked with the development of southern agriculture, its current history is part and parcel of the history of the entire nation. Millions of Negroes have left the South to seek new opportunities in the cities of the North, and to join with whites in the ever-increasing migrations to the West. The volume of these movements during some decades has been nearly unbelievable, especially when it is recognized that the movement often involves radical transformations in the way of life of the Negro migrant.

The Evidence of Migration

A population in a given area can grow through an excess of births over deaths (natural increase) or by an excess of in-migrants over out-migrants (net migration). In the absence of migration, population growth occurs within a fairly narrow set of biological limits. The Negro population of the U.S. has rarely increased by more than 25 percent in a single decade. Thus, the extremely rapid increases in Northern Negro population in the last fifty years are the product of large-scale population movement. Had these migrations not occurred, the Negro population would still be 90 percent Southern.

During the first fifty years after Emancipation, the relative stability in residential distribution was broken only by some movement to new agricultural areas in the western portion of the South. Although the movement of whites to cities in North and South was already gaining momentum, the rural Southern character of the Negro population remained substantially intact. In the decades since 1910, Negro migrations, rural-to-urban and North-to-South, have been proceeding at a rapid pace, at times at an incredible pace, completely altering the patterns of distribution which would have resulted in the absence of migration.

From 1870 to 1910 the Negro rural population of Georgia increased steadily from 500,000 to 952,000, but despite a continuing excess of births over deaths, this population diminished to 478,000 in 1960. The same pattern is true of Negro rural population in many other states. At the same time, the Negro urban population of New York State, which numbered 118,000 in 1910, has multiplied tenfold in the past fifty years, numbering more than one million in 1960. In fact, in 1960 for the first time, a Northern state, New York, had a larger Negro population than any southern state.

That continuing massive migrations of Negroes have been taking place in the past half-century is obvious from these facts of population redistribution. Unfortunately, direct information is lacking on the numbers involved, the characteristics of migrants, the paths they follow and the forces that impel them to leave their homes for new places and opportunities. In the United States, anyone can move from one part of the country to another without notifying the government and without any records being kept. Data on migration come indirectly. The fact of out-migration, for instance, becomes apparent when the census counts fewer Negroes in Mississippi in 1960 than in 1950, and records a doubling of the Negro population of California in the same period.

Immigration from abroad is evident from the decennial census questions on place of birth. Negroes, however, are overwhelmingly a native population. Since the days of the slave trade, there has been only a tiny stream of Negro immigration. At no time during this century have foreign-born Negroes comprised as much as one percent of the total Negro population. In 1900, the census recorded only 20,000 Negroes as born abroad. During the next fifty years, this number increased, primarily as a result of immigration from the West Indies. In 1950, of a total of 114,000 foreign-born Negroes, 67,000 or three-fifths were from the West Indies. Over half of all foreign-born Negroes lived in the New York metropolitan area. Similarly detailed data are not available for 1960, but the total number of foreign-born Negroes was up only slightly, to 125,000.

Migration from South to North, 1910 to 1960

The general patterns of Negro migration during each decade from 1910 to 1960 can be seen from the data in Table 2. This table presents, for geographic divisions and selected states, the estimated net population gain or loss from migration. Northward movement of Negroes was large between 1910 and 1920, and increased to even larger numbers in the next decade. During the depression decade, migration into the North continued at a much diminished pace. The volume of migration picked up during the war decade of 1940–50, and reached the highest levels ever recorded during 1950–60. The movement of Negroes to the West, which has been gaining momentum since 1940, has been mainly to California.

Negro migration out of the South was greater during 1920–30 than 1910–20, but fell off during the depression decade. During the 1940's and 1950's, net out-migration of Negroes from the South assumed record proportions. Between 1950 and 1960, the South lost nearly 1.5 million Negroes by migration, while the North gained more than one million and the West nearly 400,000.

TABLE II—Estimated Net Intercensal Migration of Negroes, for Geographic Divisions and Selected States, by Decade, 1910–1960

Area	1950–60 [a]	1940–50	1930–40	1920–30	1910–20
Geographic Division					
New England	70,000	24,900	5,200	7,400	12,000
Middle Atlantic	472,000	386,800	165,700	341,500	170,100
East North Central	521,000	493,800	107,700	323,700	200,400
West North Central	37,000	35,000	20,100	40,300	43,700
Mountain and Pacific	385,000	304,300	49,000	36,100	28,400
South Atlantic	−542,000	−424,100	−175,200	−508,700	−161,900
East South Central	−620,000	−484,600	−122,500	−180,100	−246,300
West South Central	−295,000	−336,000	− 49,800	− 60,200	− 46,200
Selected States					
Pennsylvania	77,000	89,600	20,300	101,700	82,500
New York	282,000	243,600	135,900	172,800	63,100
Illinois	189,000	179,800	49,400	119,300	69,800
Michigan	127,000	163,300	28,000	86,100	38,700
Ohio	133,000	106,700	20,700	90,700	69,400
California	354,000	258,900	41,200	36,400	16,100
District of Columbia	54,000	61,200	47,500	16,000	18,300
Florida	101,000	7,200	49,900	54,200	3,200
Virginia	− 70,000	− 30,600	− 36,900	−117,200	− 27,200
North Carolina	−207,000	−127,300	− 60,000	− 15,700	− 28,900
South Carolina	−218,000	−159,000	− 94,400	−204,300	− 74,500
Georgia	−204,000	−191,200	− 90,300	−260,000	− 74,700
Alabama	−224,000	−165,400	− 63,800	− 80,700	− 70,800
Mississippi	−323,000	−258,200	− 58,200	− 68,800	−129,600
Arkansas	−150,000	−116,100	− 33,300	− 46,300	− 1,000
Louisiana	− 92,000	−113,800	− 8,400	− 25,500	− 51,200
Texas	− 27,000	− 67,200	4,900	9,700	5,200

Note: A minus sign indicates net out-migration; no sign indicates net in-migration.

[a] Figures for 1950–60 refer to non-whites and were estimated by a different procedure from that used for the 1910–50 estimates.

SOURCE: U.S. Bureau of the Census, *Historical Statistics of the United States, Colonial Times to 1957* (Washington, D.C.: U.S. Government Printing Office, 1963), Series C 25–73; and U.S. Bureau of the Census, *Current Population Reports,* Series P-25, No. 247, Table 4.

Causes of Migration

There is still no scholarly agreement on the precise causes of these massive movements of population. Their timing, however, provides some insight into the factors involved. The major northward migration of Southern Negroes appears to have started about 1915 and to have continued at a high rate during most of the next ten years. In discussing causes of migration, it is helpful to distinguish between those causes of dissatisfaction in the local community which "push" people out, and those attractions at the place of destination which "pull" people in.

Among the push factors it might be thought that discrimination, segregation and injustice would be the most important. However much these factors contributed to a general willingness to move, there is no evidence that they were any worse during 1915–25 than in preceding years. This is not to deny that many of the Negroes leaving the South before 1915 as well as later did so out of a sense of personal mistreatment. But the causes of the change in volume of out-migration must include certain precipitating factors not present in earlier periods, such as the severe devastation of Southern agriculture caused by the combination of the boll weevil and a series of bad crop years. Conditions had often been depressed, but the devastation and depth of the agricultural depression in many counties were greater than ever before. Out-migration increased greatly from many of the hardest hit counties.

A change in pull factors inducing migration is also clearly evident about the time of the rapid increase in Negro northward migration. With the onset of war in Europe, immigration of Europeans to the United States, which had been bringing more than a million persons a year to Northern industrial cities, was cut off. The war, even before direct U.S. involvement, brought new demands upon Northern manufacturing industries. Industry, which had been providing hundreds of thousands of jobs each year for new immigrants, now had this labor supply cut off during a period of great demand for labor. Despite widespread prejudice and concern about the "suitability" of Negroes as industrial laborers, many firms not only found that Negroes were suitable, but sent out labor recruiters to the South to encourage Negroes to come North. Many Negroes who made the move encouraged friends and relatives to join them, and the move became easier for those with someone at the other end to help them find a place to live and a job. After the First World War, immigration from Europe resumed, only to be cut back permanently by restrictive legislation in the early 1920's. The Negro then retained a position in the Northern industrial scheme.

Migration Rates and Their Social Impact

The impact of migration on both the community where the migrants originate and the community which is their destination can be better appreciated if the number of migrants is related to the number of people left behind or the number already at the destination. When expressed in this way, the Negro migrations imply tremendous upheavals in both Northern and Southern communities. For instance, between 1910 and 1920, the state of Alabama lost one-tenth of its Negro population by out-migration. Between 1940 and 1950, Mississippi lost over one-fourth of its Negroes by out-migration. Without the continual replenishment of population by natural increase, these states would by now have few Negroes left.

Migration is a highly selective process. Young adults are usually much more eager to give up the old for the new than are those with families, homes, and secure attachments to customary ways of earning a living. The Negro migrations are no exception to this rule, for they have always drawn most heavily from those in the young adult ages. Some of the migration rates shown in Table III for young Negro males are almost beyond belief. Consider Negro males in Georgia who were between the ages of fifteen and thirty-four in 1920. Out-migrants among this group during the 1920–30 decade numbered forty-five out of every one hundred average population in Georgia. Similarly, between 1940 and 1950, Mississippi lost nearly one-half of its young Negro adults by out-migration, principally to Northern states. The impact of migration on the Negro population in some Northern states was also large. In 1920, 1930 and 1950, from one-third to one-half or more of the young adult Negroes in such states as Michigan, Illinois and New York were persons who moved there within the preceding ten years.

Dramatic as some of these figures are, they are understatements. They refer to net migration, the balance of in- over out-migration or out- over in-migration. Not all Negroes who move from one state to another go from South to North. Many who have been in the North move back to the South. Many others move from one Southern state to another or from one Northern state to another. Thus, in-migration and out-migration are both heavy, and the figures shown in the tables indicate the extent to which one movement predominates over the other. But gross movement is always higher, usually much higher, than net movement.

The impact of migration is also understated by using states as units. During the First World War, there are stories of special trains taking away virtually the entire young adult population of a small Southern community at one time, and many entire families. Similarly, the dramatic impact of

TABLE III—Net Intercensal Migration for Negro Males Age 15–34 at Beginning of Decade, by Decades for Selected States, 1870–1950

Intercensal Period	Southern States			Northern States		
	Alabama	Georgia	Mississippi	Illinois	Michigan	New York
1870–80	−20.9	−4.6	4.0	37.1	12.5	23.9
1880–90	−8.8	2.9	−4.1	28.7	—	32.1
1890–00	−12.5	−7.6	−2.6	53.9	10.5	55.2
1900–10	−10.1	−5.0	−5.5	33.3	25.0	44.4
1910–20	−22.1	−16.7	−23.3	67.4	138.4	53.6
1920–30	−21.3	−44.7	−14.2	65.5	88.4	79.3
1930–40	−11.7	−13.5	−9.8	14.5	19.0	29.8
1940–50	−32.3	−30.9	−47.0	59.0	81.5	54.3

Note: A minus sign indicates net out-migration; no sign indicates net in-migration.

SOURCE: Everett S. Lee, Ann Ratner Miller, Carol P. Brainerd, and Richard A. Easterlin, *Population Redistribution and Economic Growth, United States, 1870–1950, I. Methodological Considerations and Reference Tables* (Philadelphia: The American Philosophical Society, 1957), Table P–1.

Negro migration on New York City's Harlem or Chicago's South Side is somewhat obscured when data are presented for entire states.

The social costs of these migrations are extraordinarily difficult to calculate. High rates of natural increase among rural Southern Negroes have not led to a piling up of Negro population in depressed agricultural areas. Rather, the continuing migrations sketched above have transferred much of the increase in Negro population from the South to the North. To an extent, this out-migration helps alleviate economic problems, for in its absence the South would have been confronted with the need to provide jobs and housing for a great many additional Negroes. Out-migration, however, is not an unmitigated blessing. The South's investment in food, clothing, housing and schooling required to raise children from birth to an age when they are ready to begin productive employment is lost when these youths migrate. Hundreds of thousands go North to add to the productive labor force there rather than in the region which raised and educated them. The remaining Southern rural Negroes are a population with many dependent children and old folks, but with depleted numbers of young and middle-aged adults to support them. The effects of these migrations on Northern cities are similarly complex. A rapid rate of in-migration not only permits a rapid expansion in the productive labor force, but also augments housing shortages, accelerates overcrowding, complicates the task of providing suitable jobs for all those seeking work, and adds to the need for city social and welfare services.

As economic opportunities outside of agriculture increase in the South, and as the number of rural and village Negroes decreases, it seems unlikely that the volume of net out-migration from the South will continue at the same high levels as in the recent past. Whether it does or not, the impact of Negro in-migration on Northern cities cannot again attain its former dimensions. As the Negro population increases in the North, a given number of new in-migrants forms a smaller percentage of the population already there. In the past, migration has accounted for a high proportion of Negro population increase in most Northern and Western cities. The share of population growth attributable to natural increase, however, has been moving rapidly upward and is already the major source of growth in many cities.

Despite the high rates of Negro migration from South to North during the past half-century, just under one-half of the nonwhite residents of the North and West were born in the South. There were even 146,000 Northern-born nonwhites living in the South in 1960. Many Northern Negroes have never been in the South. Currently a high proportion of these Northern-born Negroes are children, but there are already many in the adult ages, and this number is increasing rapidly. If these children are inadequately trained and educated, the North and not the South must bear the responsibility.

Residential Mobility and Short-Distance Moving

Mobility is a prominent feature of an urban industrial society. People in the United States are frequent movers, and Negroes are no exception. They move from one community to another or from one house or apartment to another with high frequency. In March, 1961, the Bureau of the Census asked a large sample of the population where they were living one year earlier. Of nonwhites, 23 percent were in a different house, compared to 20 percent for whites. Every year, about one of every five families, white and Negro, shifts residence. No wonder that the 1960 census reported that only 11 percent of nonwhites and 14 percent of whites had lived in their present housing unit since 1940.

Sociologists sometimes split residential mobility into "migration," referring to moves involving a change of community, and "local movement," referring to moves within a single community. The Bureau of the Census makes a similar distinction by referring to persons moving from one county to another as "migrants," and to persons whose move is entirely within a county as "local movers." Most of the one-fifth of people who move each year are "local movers" rather than "migrants." In 1960–61, for nonwhites, 18.4 percent of the mobile population were local movers and 4.3 percent were intercounty migrants. Of the migrants, roughly one-half moved to a different county within the same state, and one-half moved to a different state. The Bureau of the Census has been collecting similar data each year since 1948, and although the specific percentages vary from year to year, the general pattern has been remarkably constant for both whites and non-whites. Each year about one in five persons moves, with about two-thirds of movers shifting residence within a county and the remaining one-third migrating to a different county.

It is misleading to view "local moving" as being without social consequences. A move from one neighborhood to another can entail as many changes in the lives of a family as a move from one city to another. The consequences for urban planning are likewise just as important for the short move as for the long. When one-fourth, one-third, or even more (as is true of many apartment areas) of the population has lived for less than a year in a neighborhood, how much sense of community identification can there be? Under such circumstances, can there be effective local participation in planning, as envisioned by many planners and written into Federal urban renewal law? An urban industrial society, however, is a changing one, and it could not function in the absence of residential mobility. Not only is the freedom to move necessary for the adjustment of people to changing situations and changing opportunities, but it is a basic liberty of Negroes and whites alike.

URBANIZATION OF THE NEGRO POPULATION, 1910–1960

One simple piece of information from the 1960 census summarizes the profound change in the status of the Negro population that has been taking place during the past half-century. In 1960, Negroes were more urbanized than whites. Of the nonwhite population, 73 percent lived in cities, as compared to 70 percent of the white population. Not only has the movement of Negroes from South to North been a movement to cities, but within the South itself Negroes have been moving from rural areas to cities. Civil rights struggles in Birmingham and Little Rock, Atlanta and Norfolk share headlines with those in Chicago, Detroit and New York. Although there are still hundreds of thousands of Negroes living in poverty in the rural South, the picture of the typical American Negro as a Southern sharecropper is a long outdated stereotype.

Urbanization before 1910

The United States began as a rural nation, with most of its people dependent on agriculture for their livelihood. Her rise to world power, however, depended not only on her bountiful agriculture, but also on her becoming an urbanized industrialized nation. Cities have always played an important part in national life. Boston, New York, Philadelphia, Charleston and other cities were already centers of commerce, trade, politics and culture in the eighteenth century. Even the largest cities of those days, however, would be considered small by today's standards. It was not until the nineteenth century that American cities, paced by New York, increased by leaps and bounds to truly large size. The urbanization of America was accelerated after the Civil War by rapid industrial growth and the laying out of the nationwide rail transportation network. Already by 1910 most of the large cities of today had reached large size. Yet in 1910 fewer than 50 percent of Americans lived in cities. The movement of people to cities has continued at a rapid pace ever since.

Negro participation in the urbanization of America was slight during the early stages. The concentration of free Negroes in cities has been discussed above, but their numbers were never large relative to the total population of the cities in which they lived. Within the South, Negro slaves were utilized in greatest numbers in agriculture, and they lived in rural areas and villages. Rural settlement, however, was also characteristic of the white population. The small Southern urban population included its proportionate share of Negro population.

From 1860 to 1910 the movement of Negroes from the South to Northern cities was very slight. Within the South, what Negro migration occurred was primarily in response to changing opportunities in agriculture, particularly the westward movement of cotton. As of 1910, just over one-fourth of Negroes and just under one-half of whites in the United States lived in cities. These national figures mask considerable regional variation. Within the South, Negroes and whites were equally urbanized, with about one-fifth living in cities. Within the North and West, Negroes, with 77 percent in cities, were much more urbanized than whites. These patterns are portrayed in Figure 6. In 1910, nearly all Negroes lived in the South. Despite the high percentages shown as "urban" among Northern Negroes, the numbers involved were small and the national average reflected primarily the pattern in the South. For whites, however, the national percentage urban was an average of the high figure in the North and West, and the low figure in the South.

FIGURE 6—Percent Urban by Race and Region, 1900–1960

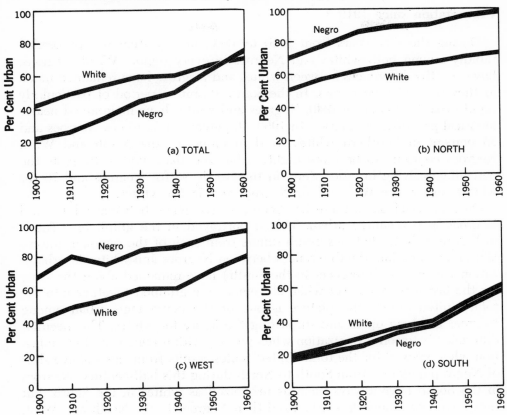

Note: Definition of "urban" not fully comparable throughout this period.

SOURCE: 1960 from U.S. Bureau of the Census, *U.S. Census of Population: 1960, General Population Characteristics, U.S. Summary*, Final Report PC(1)–1B (Washington, D.C.: U.S. Government Printing Office, 1961), Table 51; 1950 from U.S. Bureau of the Census, *U.S. Census of Population: 1950*, Vol. II, *Characteristics of the Population*, Part 1, U.S. Summary (Washington, D.C.: U.S. Government Printing Office, 1953) Table 145; 1940 from U.S. Bureau of the Census, *Sixteenth Census of the U.S.: 1940, Population*, Vol. II, *Characteristics of the Population*, Part 1, Table 21 and *Characteristics of the Nonwhite Population by Race*, Table 3 (Washington, D.C.: U.S. Government Printing Office, 1943); 1930 from U.S. Bureau of the Census, *Sixteenth Census of the U.S.: 1940, Population*, Vol. II, *Characteristics of the Population*, Parts 1-7 (Washington, D.C.: U.S. Government Printing Office, 1943), Table 5 for each state; and 1900–1920 from U.S. Bureau of the Census, *Fourteenth Census of the U.S. Taken in the Year 1920*, Vol. II, *Population* (Washington, D.C.: Government Printing Office, 1922), Table 20, p. 79.

Urbanization since 1910

During the fifty years from 1910 to 1960, urbanization has proceeded rapidly among both whites and Negroes in every region. Within regions, however, the differences between whites and Negroes have remained much as they were fifty years ago. In the South, despite a period of particularly rapid urbanization since 1940, Negroes and whites have maintained nearly identical proportions in cities. In 1960, 58 percent of Southern Negroes and 59 percent of Southern whites lived in cities. In the North and West, Negroes continue to be more highly urbanized than whites. In 1960, the percentages living in cities were, in the North, 96 for Negroes and 73 for whites, and in the West, 93 for Negroes and 78 for whites.

On a national basis, there has been a convergence between whites and Negroes in percentage urban. This is portrayed in the graph for "Total" in Figure 6. Note that this graph differs from each of the regional graphs. Within each region, the differences between Negroes and whites in urbanization (or lack of differences in the South) have remained about the same for the last fifty years. Yet when all regions are grouped together into the total United States, the picture is one of the percentage urban among Negroes catching up to and surpassing the figure for whites. This peculiar difference between urbanization when viewed within regions and urbanization when viewed for the total United States results from the massive shift of Negro population from South to North during this half-century. Negroes in the South have always been as urbanized as whites in the South, but they have been much less urbanized than Negroes in the North and West. As hundreds of thousands of Negroes have moved from the South to the North and West, they have taken on the urban residential distribution of Negroes in the North and West. In 1910, the percentage urban for Negroes for the total United States was very close to the percentage for the South alone, since 89 percent of Negroes in the United States lived in the South. In 1960, 60 percent of Negroes lived in the South and the percentage urban for the total United States is in between the figure for the South and the figure for the North and West.

Cities with Large Numbers of Negroes

In 1910, there were fewer than one million Negroes living in cities in the North and West. In 1960, there were more than one million Negroes in New York City alone, and more than seven million in cities throughout the North and West. Fifty years ago, there were a few Northern cities with large Negro populations, but most urban Negroes lived in Southern cities. The

TABLE IV—The Twenty-Five Leading Cities in Negro Population, 1910 and 1960

City	1910 Negro Population (000)	Percent Negro	City	1960 Negro Population (000)	Percent Negro
Washington	94	28.5	New York	1,088	14.0
New York	92	1.9	Chicago	813	22.9
New Orleans	89	26.3	Philadelphia	529	26.4
Baltimore	85	15.2	Detroit	482	28.9
Philadelphia	84	5.5	Washington	412	53.9
Memphis	52	40.0	Los Angeles	335	13.5
Birmingham	52	39.4	Baltimore	326	34.7
Atlanta	52	33.5	Cleveland	251	28.6
Richmond	47	36.6	New Orleans	236	37.2
Chicago	44	2.0	Houston	215	22.9
St. Louis	44	6.4	St. Louis	214	28.6
Louisville	41	18.1	Atlanta	186	38.3
Nashville	37	33.1	Memphis	184	37.0
Savannah	33	51.1	Newark	138	34.1
Charleston	31	52.8	Birmingham	135	39.6
Jacksonville	29	50.8	Dallas	129	19.0
Pittsburgh	26	4.8	Cincinnati	109	21.6
Norfolk	25	37.1	Pittsburgh	101	16.7
Houston	24	30.4	Indianapolis	94	20.6
Kansas City	24	9.5	Richmond	92	41.8
Mobile	23	44.2	Oakland	84	22.8
Indianapolis	22	9.3	Kansas City	83	17.5
Cincinnati	20	5.4	Jacksonville	83	41.1
Montgomery	19	50.7	Norfolk	79	25.8
Augusta	18	44.7	Columbus	77	16.4

SOURCE: 1910 data: U.S. Bureau of the Census, *Negro Population 1790–1915* (Washington: Government Printing Office, 1918), p. 93; 1960 data: U.S. Bureau of the Census, *U.S. Census of Population: 1960, General Population Characteristics* (Washington, D.C.: U.S. Government Printing Office, 1961), Table 21 for states.

twenty-five cities with the largest Negro populations in 1910 and 1960 are listed in Table IV.

In 1910, no single city had as many as 100,000 Negro residents, as compared with a 1960 total of eighteen cities with more than 100,000 Negro residents. In 1910, there were eight Northern and no Western cities on the list. In none of these Northern cities did Negroes comprise as much as 10 percent of the population because the cities were so large. There were few large cities in the South, and even though Negroes often comprised 30,

40 or 50 percent of the population, few southern cities had as many as 20,000 Negro residents.

The rapid urbanization of the Negro population since 1910, and particularly the pronounced movement to Northern and Western cities, is evident in the changes in the list of the twenty-five leading cities in Negro population between 1910 and 1960. New York, Chicago, Philadelphia, and Detroit lead the 1960 list, and Los Angeles and Cleveland also appear in the top ten. Fourteen of the twenty-five cities are in the North or West. In all of these cities, Negroes comprised more than 10 percent of the population. In contrast to fifty years earlier when Negroes were but a very small segment of most Northern and Western cities, in several cities Negroes now comprise one-fourth to one-third of the population.

Sources of Urban Population Growth

Migration from the South to Northern cities and within the South from rural areas to cities has been taking place at a rapid rate during much of the last fifty years. Migration, however, is not the only source of growth of urban Negro population. The excess of births over deaths contributes to population growth even in the absence of migration. In the previous section it was demonstrated that migrants tend to be young adults of both sexes. Migration thus brings to cities large numbers of young couples and young persons about to form families. As compared to a population with a larger share of older persons, a city population heavily augmented by migration contains many couples in the childbearing ages. Birth rates are therefore high, and in the absence of a large older population, death rates are low. The difference between high birth rates and low death rates is a high rate of natural increase. Urban Negro populations, therefore, are increasing rapidly not only because of in-migration, but also because of natural increase.

The large volume of natural increase augmenting the growth of urban Negro populations is undercutting still another aspect of the old stereotypical picture of Negroes as Southern sharecroppers. In a more up-to-date version of this stereotype, Northern urban Negroes are pictured as recent migrants from the rural South, lacking in knowledge of the manners and niceties of city living. However, more than half of Northern Negroes are Northern-born. Of the migrants from the South, many come from Southern cities rather than rural areas. For instance, of nonwhite males aged 45–64 living in large metropolitan areas, nearly two-thirds have lived in the same city for at least twenty years. While there undoubtedly are some Negro migrants to Northern cities who have difficulties adjusting to urban living, their share in the total northern Negro population must be small.

NEGROES IN METROPOLITAN AREAS

As the urbanization of the United States has progressed, the society has increasingly come to be organized around the large cities. The sphere of influence of a large city extends far beyond its boundaries. A very large city such as New York has economic and cultural ties with every part of the country and with much of the world. Other cities do not have such an extensive range of influence, but there is at least a high degree of interdependence between each large city and its surrounding area. The political boundaries of large cities have not expanded to encompass the entire population that is socially and economically integrated with the city. The entire suburban area of a large city, together with much of the close-in rural area, can be considered together with the central city as comprising a single metropolitan area.

Consideration of the changing distribution of Negro population, thus, is incomplete without an indication of the position of Negroes in the metropolitan system of the country. To permit analysis of metropolitanization, the Federal Government has recognized, for statistical purposes, a number of "Standard Metropolitan Statistical Areas" (SMSA's). Each SMSA consists of at least one city of fifty thousand inhabitants or more, together with the county (or counties) in which the city is located, and as many contiguous counties as are essentially metropolitan in character and socially and economically integrated with the central city. The metropolitan area concept is quite distinct from the concept of urban population. Cities are politically incorporated units. A metropolitan area includes at least one large city, a number of nearby large and small cities, and considerable rural population, both farm and nonfarm.

Both Negro and white population movement has been largely to the cities and suburbs of metropolitan areas. Cities outside of metropolitan areas have not participated to the same degree in the urbanization of the population. The increasing concentration of Negroes and whites in metropolitan areas over the period 1900 to 1960 is shown in Table V. In

1900, 44 percent of whites and 27 percent of Negroes lived in metropolitan areas, whereas by 1960 the figure was 63 percent for whites and 65 percent for Negroes. (In this section, all data for metropolitan areas refer to the 212 SMSA's as delineated for the 1960 census.)

TABLE V—Percent Residing in SMSA's by Race and Region, 1900–1960*

Race and Year	Conterminous United States	Region		
		North	West	South
NEGRO				
1960	64.7	92.8	92.8	45.9
1950	55.6	91.5	91.1	38.7
1940	45.4	88.7	86.0	32.5
1930	42.0	87.1	83.3	29.8
1920	33.9	81.7	68.4	25.7
1910	28.7	72.5	72.5	23.3
1900	26.6	66.1	66.7	22.1
WHITE				
1960	62.8	67.1	71.6	48.7
1950	59.5	65.8	67.1	41.9
1940	56.2	64.2	62.4	35.2
1930	55.7	63.9	61.4	33.2
1920	51.4	60.0	52.2	29.1
1910	47.7	55.5	50.6	26.0
1900	44.0	50.9	47.0	23.9

* SMSA's as defined in 1960.

SOURCE: Compiled from data in U.S. Bureau of the Census, *Historical Statistics of the United States, Colonial Times to 1957* (Washington, D.C.: U.S. Government Printing Office, 1960), Table A 95–122; U.S. Bureau of the Census, *U.S. Census of Population: 1960, General Population Characteristics, United States Summary,* Final Report PC(1)–1B (Washington, D.C.: U.S. Government Printing Office, 1961), Table 56; and U.S. Bureau of the Census, *U.S. Census of Population: 1960, Selected Area Reports, Standard Metropolitan Statistical Areas,* Final Report PC(3)–1D (Washington, D.C.: U.S. Government Printing Office, 1963), Table 1.

Regional Trends in Metropolitanization

Because the population movements to urban areas have been principally to urban places within metropolitan areas, regional differences in the patterns for Negroes and whites resemble those already noted for urbanization. In the South, both Negroes and whites have participated about equally in metropolitan concentration, with just under one-fourth of each group in metropolitan areas in 1900 and just under one-half in 1960. In the North and West, Negroes have always been more concentrated than whites in metropolitan areas. In 1960, over 90 percent of Negroes in these regions were metropolitan, as compared to about 70 percent of whites.

A large proportion of metropolitan population lives in the very large metropolitan areas—in 1960, 54 percent of metropolitan whites and 58 percent of metropolitan Negroes were in areas of over 1,000,000 total population (Table VI). Regional differences are again evident. Large metropolitan areas are principally located in the North and West, and Negroes moving North have been particularly attracted to these centers. In 1960, 80 percent of metropolitan Negroes in the North lived in areas of this size. In the South, however, metropolitan Negroes and whites are similarly distributed among areas of each size.

The concentration of Negro population in a few locations, particularly in the North and West, is even greater than indicated by the figures for all metropolitan areas combined. One of every fifteen Negroes in the coun-

TABLE VI—Percent Distribution of Population by Size of SMSA, Race, and Region, 1960

| Size of SMSA | Region and Race | | | | | | | |
| | Conterminous United States | | North | | West | | South | |
	White	Negro	White	Negro	White	Negro	White	Negro
3,000,000 or more	27.8	31.3	35.9	24.5	24.5	46.7	—	—
1,000,000–3,000,000	26.5	26.8	27.1	55.6	33.7	30.7	26.2	28.9
500,000–1,000,000	16.7	16.5	11.4	9.4	22.9	12.7	26.3	25.4
250,000–500,000	14.5	11.3	12.8	5.6	11.4	6.2	21.8	18.9
100,000–250,000	12.9	13.1	11.6	4.7	6.2	3.5	22.5	24.6
Less than 100,000	1.6	1.0	1.2	0.2	1.3	0.2	3.2	2.2
TOTAL	100.0	100.0	100.0	100.0	100.0	100.0	100.0	100.0

SOURCE: Compiled from U.S. Bureau of the Census, *U.S. Census of Population: 1960*, Vol. I, *Characteristics of the Population* (Washington, D.C.: U.S. Government Printing Office, 1963), Table 21 for each state.

try lives in the New York metropolitan area. Ten metropolitan areas in the North, each with more than 100,000 Negro residents, together contain 70 percent of all Northern Negroes (Table VII). Two metropolitan areas in the West contain 65 percent of that region's Negro population. There are thirteen metropolitan areas in the South with more than 100,000 Negro residents, and together they contain one-fourth of the region's Negro population.

Regional differences in the course of metropolitanization of Negroes have many causes. In the South, Negroes were an integral part of the initial

TABLE VII—List of SMSA's with 100,000 or More Negroes in 1960, by Region

Region and SMSA	Negro Population	Region and SMSA	Negro Population
NORTH	**4,525,234**	**SOUTH**	**2,811,082**
Chicago	889,961	Atlanta	230,737
Cincinnati	127,713	Baltimore	378,333
Cleveland	257,258	Birmingham	219,482
Detroit	558,792	Dallas	155,081
Kansas City	117,210	Houston	246,118
Newark	223,210	Jacksonville	105,624
New York	1,224,590	Memphis	227,180
Philadelphia	670,939	Miami	137,492
Pittsburgh	160,845	Mobile	100,933
St. Louis	294,716	New Orleans	267,303
		Norfolk-Portsmouth	150,442
WEST	**701,540**	Richmond	107,240
		Washington	485,117
Los Angeles-Long Beach	464,112		
San Francisco-Oakland	237,428		

settlement of the region and have always been distributed similarly to the white population. Both races are now responding in similar fashion to the social and economic forces which are producing a metropolitan society. In the South, both races started as predominantly rural and the process of urbanization since 1900 has been gradually erasing their common rural heritage. In the North and West, on the other hand, Negroes represent a new group, similar in this respect to the immigrants of the past, being superimposed upon established settlement patterns.

Negro Migration to Metropolitan Areas, 1955–60

The large Negro population in metropolitan areas has been achieved by the migration of thousands of Negroes in search of a share in the economic benefits accruing from industrialization. Lack of data, however, has prohibited careful documentation of the character of these migrations. The best detailed migration data for the United States refer to the two periods 1935–40 and 1955–60, and are based upon responses to a census question on place of residence five years earlier.

Much of what we know about the early movement is based upon fragmentary sources and the reports of observers. Most of this literature is in agreement that Negro in-migrants to cities were of lower social and economic status than the resident Negro population and, as a result, considerable friction was generated between the two groups and between them and whites. Increased racial tensions were blamed upon the heavy influx of Negroes of low socio-economic status. Considerable evidence also exists that the newcomers were a higher status segment of the Southern Negro population from which they were drawn. Several studies have shown with regard to educational levels that the better-educated Negroes in the South were the ones who tended to migrate, but because their educational level was below that of Negroes already residing in cities, the net effect of the movement was to dampen the educational level of the Negro population both at place of origin and place of destination.

As the Negro population in metropolitan areas has grown, movement of Negroes between metropolitan areas has been added to the earlier rural-to-urban movement. This intermetropolitan movement is an increasingly important component of total Negro migration. Among nonwhite in-migrants to Northern metropolitan areas between 1955 and 1960, about one-half, on the average, came from other metropolitan areas (Table VIII). The figure is about one-third among nonwhite migrants to Southern metropolitan areas. Once resident in a metropolitan area, Negroes are much more likely to move to other metropolitan areas than back to the rural areas and small towns of the South. Clearly, in a society which is overwhelmingly metropolitan, the predominant movement is intermetropolitan rather than rural-to-urban. Most Negro newcomers, particularly to Northern metropolitan areas, have had considerable experience with metropolitan living.

It is possible to trace the origins of in-migrants and the destinations of out-migrants in somewhat more detail. Table IX presents the distribution by region of origin of nonwhite in-migrants to twenty-five metropolitan areas with large Negro populations. Nonwhite migrants to metropolitan areas in the Northeast (Newark, New York, Philadelphia and Pittsburgh) are drawn primarily from the Atlantic Seaboard states. Metropolitan areas in the North Central region (St. Louis, Detroit, Cleveland, Cincinnati and Chicago) receive substantial shares of their nonwhite in-migrants from the states of the middle South (the East South Central division). Los Angeles-Long Beach and San Francisco-Oakland draw from the states along the western edge of the South (the West South Central division) and the North Central region. For metropolitan areas of the South, the major source of in-migration is the nonmetropolitan areas of their own or neighboring states.

Corresponding information on the destinations of out-migrants is presented in Table X. Less than one-third of the nonwhites leaving Northern metropolitan areas moved to the South, while one-third to one-half of those leaving most Southern areas moved to the North or West. Most of the nonwhites leaving Southern SMSA's stayed within the South, the overwhelming majority of them going to nonmetropolitan areas of the same or nearby states.

TABLE VIII—Metropolitan Origin of Nonwhite In-Migrants and Metropolitan Destination of Nonwhite Out-Migrants for Selected SMSA's, 1955–60

SMSA	Percent of In-Migrants from Other SMSA's	Percent of Out-Migrants Going to Other SMSA's
NORTH		
Chicago	44.0	66.3
Cincinnati	58.9	71.1
Cleveland	56.2	70.5
Detroit	56.6	73.7
Kansas City	45.2	72.6
Newark	48.0	61.5
New York	48.8	65.6
Philadelphia	53.7	69.8
Pittsburgh	57.9	72.7
St. Louis	41.1	71.6
WEST		
Los Angeles-Long Beach	71.6	77.7
San Francisco-Oakland	68.3	75.4
SOUTH		
Atlanta	29.4	57.7
Baltimore	43.7	64.0
Birmingham	34.4	75.4
Dallas	34.1	67.8
Houston	34.2	61.9
Jacksonville	37.8	56.5
Memphis	19.5	71.9
Miami	32.4	57.1
Mobile	30.4	59.7
New Orleans	28.5	65.4
Norfolk-Portsmouth	45.4	64.1
Richmond	33.2	58.2
Washington	47.2	67.2

SOURCE: U.S. Bureau of the Census, *U.S. Census of Population: 1960, Subject Reports, Mobility for Metropolitan Areas,* Final Report PC(2)–2C (Washington, D.C.: U.S. Government Printing Office, 1963), Tables 1 and 5.

TABLE IX—Percent Distribution of Nonwhite In-Migrants to Selected SMSA's by Region of Origin, 1955–60

SMSA	Total	Same State	North-east	North Central	West	South Atlantic	East South Central	West South Central
				Region or Division of Origin				
NORTH								
Chicago	100.0	5.3	3.5	18.1	4.4	8.2	46.2	14.3
Cincinnati	100.0	17.2*	7.0	17.9	3.5	20.4	32.4	1.6
Cleveland	100.0	11.1	10.8	14.6	2.6	22.6	34.2	4.1
Detroit	100.0	8.3	6.5	16.9	3.9	21.0	33.8	9.6
Kansas City	100.0	13.3*	4.5	18.9	8.3	3.3	15.4	36.3
Newark	100.0	17.0	16.7	3.8	1.4	55.9	4.3	0.9
New York	100.0	2.5	11.4	6.6	2.9	67.0	7.3	2.3
Philadelphia	100.0	7.8*	17.2	6.0	2.7	59.9	4.0	2.4
Pittsburgh	100.0	17.0	10.1	20.4	3.4	34.3	11.1	2.7
St. Louis	100.0	10.2*	3.1	21.4	5.0	4.3	36.5	19.5
WEST								
Los Angeles-Long Beach	100.0	13.9	6.5	19.7	15.5	5.3	11.5	27.6
San Francisco-Oakland	100.0	23.4	5.1	14.0	16.2	7.1	7.6	26.6
SOUTH								
Atlanta	100.0	62.2	5.4	6.9	1.8	9.1	12.4	2.2
Baltimore	100.0	8.8	13.1	4.2	2.6	66.5	3.1	1.7
Birmingham	100.0	65.7	4.7	13.9	1.8	7.5	5.5	0.9
Dallas	100.0	68.1	0.6	4.2	6.4	1.3	2.5	16.9
Houston	100.0	58.7	1.5	2.8	5.8	2.2	3.3	25.7
Jacksonville	100.0	27.3	8.5	4.1	2.8	49.7	5.1	2.5
Memphis	100.0	18.4	1.7	11.8	1.7	2.6	51.6	12.2
Miami	100.0	21.5	7.5	4.2	0.9	50.8	13.5	1.6
Mobile	100.0	64.0	4.7	6.5	3.2	4.5	14.2	2.9
New Orleans	100.0	39.7	2.8	4.6	4.5	4.8	37.4	6.2
Norfolk-Portsmouth	100.0	20.5	15.1	7.1	2.7	47.3	3.9	3.4
Richmond	100.0	58.6	8.6	0.9	0.7	29.2	1.7	0.3
Washington	100.0	6.8*	13.6	7.6	3.5	60.8	4.6	3.1

* Since SMSA crosses state boundaries, "same state" refers to in-migrants to that portion of the SMSA lying in a given state from the remainder of that state.

SOURCE: U.S. Bureau of the Census, *Mobility for Metropolitan Areas, op. cit.*, and U.S. Bureau of the Census, *U.S. Census of Population: 1960, Subject Reports, Mobility for States and State Economic Areas,* Final Report PC(2)–2B (Washington, D.C.: U.S. Government Printing Office, 1963), Table 34.

TABLE X—Percent Distribution of Nonwhite Out-Migrants from Selected SMSA's by Region of Destination, 1955–60

SMSA	Total	Region or Division of Destination						
		Same State	North-east	North Central	West	South Atlantic	East South Central	West South Central
NORTH								
Chicago	100.0	10.4	7.0	29.7	24.0	8.1	12.2	8.6
Cincinnati	100.0	30.3*	11.5	15.5	14.9	11.7	12.6	3.5
Cleveland	100.0	26.2	13.7	15.2	16.2	12.8	11.9	4.0
Detroit	100.0	16.5	10.0	25.8	17.6	13.9	10.0	6.2
Kansas City	100.0	12.1*	3.4	23.8	39.0	5.1	2.8	13.8
Newark	100.0	33.9	22.6	5.1	7.5	26.8	1.7	2.4
New York	100.0	13.2	29.0	8.1	12.0	30.9	3.2	3.6
Philadelphia	100.0	14.3*	27.0	7.2	10.0	34.3	3.4	3.8
Pittsburgh	100.0	18.4	18.1	25.6	10.4	19.8	4.4	3.3
St. Louis	100.0	16.9*	6.6	30.2	25.2	5.0	8.9	7.2
WEST								
Los Angeles-Long Beach	100.0	45.3	5.0	11.2	16.4	5.1	2.3	14.7
San Francisco-Oakland	100.0	56.0	5.6	6.9	14.9	4.2	1.4	11.0
SOUTH								
Atlanta	100.0	34.2	14.7	16.9	7.3	16.1	8.1	2.7
Baltimore	100.0	18.6	28.8	5.8	7.1	34.3	2.7	2.7
Birmingham	100.0	24.7	13.3	30.9	12.5	11.6	4.6	2.4
Dallas	100.0	47.7	2.5	7.2	33.6	2.5	1.1	5.4
Houston	100.0	45.1	2.3	5.1	30.3	3.5	2.2	11.5
Jacksonville	100.0	38.4	22.3	4.2	7.3	22.0	3.7	2.1
Memphis	100.0	9.5	6.7	41.7	17.5	4.9	11.2	8.5
Miami	100.0	40.9	19.3	6.3	4.4	21.1	5.5	2.5
Mobile	100.0	32.6	9.9	14.5	16.1	12.7	8.4	5.8
New Orleans	100.0	29.9	5.5	12.8	31.2	5.4	9.1	6.1
Norfolk-Portsmouth	100.0	22.4	30.3	4.7	8.0	30.8	2.1	1.7
Richmond	100.0	36.8	27.8	3.3	4.6	23.8	2.2	1.5
Washington	100.0	5.9*	25.3	10.1	12.2	39.0	3.4	4.1

* Since SMSA crosses state boundaries, "same state" refers to out-migrants from that portion of the SMSA lying in a given state to remainder of that state.

SOURCE: U.S. Bureau of the Census, *U.S. Census of Population: 1960, Subject Reports, Mobility for States and State Economic Areas,* Final Report PC(2)–2B (Washington, D.C.: U.S. Government Printing Office, 1963), Table 36.

These data reveal the existence of a large circulation of nonwhite population between metropolitan areas within each region, from Southern to

Northern and Western areas, and a smaller movement in the reverse direction. The movement from nonmetropolitan to metropolitan areas occurs principally in the South, and is accompanied by a sizable reverse movement. Each of these "streams" of nonwhite migrants tends to consist of persons with different socio-economic characteristics.

Data on the relative frequency of high school graduates and white collar workers in the several migrant groups are presented in Tables XI and XII for a few of the largest metropolitan areas. The intermetropolitan migrants, those moving from one metropolitan area to another, are of unusually high educational and occupational status. By contrast, in-migrants from nonmetropolitan areas as well as out-migrants to nonmetropolitan areas are of much lower socio-economic status.

The net effect of migration on the educational and occupational status of the resident nonwhite population during 1955 to 1960 was, in most areas, to retard improvement slightly. This effect is the product of both the number and characteristics of the movers during the 1955–60 period. Very likely a high status intermetropolitan stream of migration always existed, but its relative importance has increased substantially in recent years owing to the rapid urbanization of the Negro population. It is only the in-migrants of nonmetropolitan origin who even partially resemble the stereotype of the poorly educated and economically depressed migrant. With continuing metropolitanization, it seems reasonable that this component will decline and the intermetropolitan component increase in relative importance. The general educational and occupational levels of migrants should continue to improve.

As the character of the Negro population has changed from a disadvantaged rural population to a largely metropolitan population of rising socioeconomic position, its patterns of migration have begun to manifest the same responses to economic pushes and pulls as are found in the white population. Although Negro in-migrants in the past generally were of somewhat lower socioeconomic status than the resident Negro population, this is no longer an adequate description of current patterns of Negro migration. There is a large and increasingly important high status intermetropolitan movement in the over-all migration of the Negro population.

The redistribution of Negro population from the rural South to northern cities appears to be an indirect process. Few Negroes move directly from southern farms to Chicago or New York. Negro farmers, croppers, or farm laborers are more likely to move to a nearby southern city. Later they or their children may move to one of the northern cities. Such "stage migration" may encompass a number of moves, from farm to village to town to city to metropolis. Some migrants, indeed, do skip all or most of the intervening stages. Others move only one or two stages, and still others, few in number, move in the reverse direction, from North back to South, or from large place to small. The exchange of migrants between regions and types of place is an incredibly complex process. If the data presented here help demolish old stereotypes of migrants, they should show also that there is no such thing as the "typical" migrant.

TABLE XI—Percent of Nonwhites Over 25 Completing Four or More Years of High School, by Migration Status 1955–1960, for Selected SMSA's

SMSA	Total Population	In-Migrants			Out-Migrants		
		Total	From Other SMSA	From Non-met Area	Total	To Other SMSA	To Non-met Area
NORTH							
Chicago	29.0	32.2	39.5	24.5	41.3	47.8	27.5
Cleveland	28.1	37.5	40.1	33.0	34.4	38.2	23.3
Detroit	26.5	37.3	41.4	30.3	31.8	33.3	26.6
New York	31.2	37.4	42.0	31.2	40.6	45.7	28.5
Philadelphia	23.6	36.1	41.0	29.0	39.4	43.0	29.9
St. Louis	23.7	31.2	42.0	21.3	36.2	40.7	24.3
SOUTH							
Atlanta	21.0	25.4	33.5	20.7	31.4	37.6	23.3
Baltimore	19.7	32.2	39.7	25.7	35.8	39.2	28.7
Birmingham	19.1	20.4	29.4	14.4	30.4	33.6	21.4
Memphis	14.6	16.0	32.9	10.9	23.3	27.6	13.6
New Orleans	15.0	22.0	35.0	14.9	30.6	35.7	21.3
Washington	33.5	45.7	54.3	36.6	45.5	50.0	34.8

SOURCE: U.S. Bureau of the Census, *U.S. Census of Population: 1960, Subject Reports, Mobility for Metropolitan Areas*, Final Report PC(2)–2C (Washington, D.C.: U.S. Government Printing Office, 1963), Tables 4 and 5.

Negroes in Suburbs

A metropolitan area can conveniently be divided into two parts—the central city (or cities) which gives it its name, and the surrounding suburban "ring." The extent of suburbanization can then be measured by the percentage of a metropolitan area's population which resides in the suburban ring. Using this measure, it is easy to document that Negroes and

TABLE XII—Percent of Nonwhite Employed Males Engaged in White
Collar Occupations, by Migration Status 1955–60, for Selected
SMSA's

SMSA	Total Population	In-Migrants			Out-Migrants		
		Total	From Other SMSA	From Non-met Area	Total	To Other SMSA	To Non-met Area
NORTH							
Chicago	14.8	21.2	28.7	15.1	30.2	34.2	17.0
Cleveland	16.4	17.9	22.0	13.2	24.2	24.4	23.4
Detroit	14.9	24.7	31.3	15.1	18.4	19.0	15.8
New York	27.1	25.5	32.3	18.6	31.7	32.5	28.7
Philadelphia	18.4	21.3	28.6	14.0	26.6	27.6	23.0
St. Louis	17.1	21.0	28.4	14.7	25.8	28.2	17.3
SOUTH							
Atlanta	12.3	14.7	25.1	11.1	25.7	28.5	21.2
Baltimore	16.3	22.7	36.1	13.9	21.5	24.4	14.4
Birmingham	8.6	9.7	14.1	7.4	17.6	17.9	16.3
Memphis	11.3	14.0	24.3	11.6	18.0	18.3	17.1
New Orleans	12.8	10.9	20.7	7.1	24.9	24.9	25.0
Washington	28.2	29.3	40.0	21.1	37.6	42.2	24.3

Note: "White collar" includes professional, manager, clerical and sales occupations.

SOURCE: U.S. Bureau of the Census, *U.S. Census of Population: 1960, Subject Reports, Mobility for Metropolitan Areas,* Final Report PC(2)–2C (Washington, D.C.: U.S. Government Printing Office, 1963), Tables 4 and 6.

whites have not shared equally in the movement to the suburbs. Although whites and Negroes are about equally concentrated in metropolitan areas, within metropolitan areas Negroes are confined to the central cities to a much greater extent than are whites (Table XIII). In all metropolitan areas combined, about half of the whites live in the suburban ring as compared to only 20 percent of Negroes. This underrepresentation of Negroes in suburban areas obtains within each region.

From 1900 to 1960, the concentration of metropolitan Negroes in central cities increased, in contrast to the suburbanization trend among the white population (Table XIV). As a result, the racial composition of cities and suburban rings has been altered. If the Negro and white populations of cities (or rings) changed at the same rate, then Negroes would remain a constant percentage of the total city or ring population. To the extent that

TABLE XIII—Metropolitan Distribution by Race and Region, 1960

Metropolitan Residence	Population (000)		Percent Distribution	
	White	Negro	White	Negro
CONTERMINOUS U.S.	**158,455**	**18,860**	**100.0**	**100.0**
Inside SMSA's	99,509	12,202	62.8	64.7
In Central City	47,575	9,704	30.0	51.5
In Ring	51,934	2,498	32.8	13.2
Outside SMSA's	58,946	6,658	37.2	35.3
NORTH	**89,525**	**6,475**	**100.0**	**100.0**
Inside SMSA's	60,102	6,010	67.1	92.8
In Central City	28,617	5,105	32.0	78.8
In Ring	31,485	905	35.2	14.0
Outside SMSA's	29,423	465	32.9	7.2
WEST	**25,453**	**1,074**	**100.0**	**100.0**
Inside SMSA's	18,220	997	71.6	92.8
In Central City	7,841	723	30.8	67.3
In Ring	10,379	274	40.8	25.5
Outside SMSA's	7,233	77	28.4	7.2
SOUTH	**43,477**	**11,312**	**100.0**	**100.0**
Inside SMSA's	21,187	5,194	48.7	45.9
In Central City	11,116	3,875	25.6	34.3
In Ring	10,071	1,319	23.2	11.7
Outside SMSA's	22,290	6,118	51.3	54.1

SOURCE: U.S. Bureau of the Census, *Historical Statistics of the United States, Colonial Times to 1957* (Washington, D.C.: U.S. Government Printing Office, 1960), Table A 95–122; U.S. Bureau of the Census, *U.S. Census of Population: 1960, General Population Characteristics, United States Summary,* Final Report PC(1)–1B (Washington, D.C.: U.S. Government Printing Office, 1961), Table 56; and U.S. Bureau of the Census, *U.S. Census of Population: 1960, Selected Area Reports, Standard Metropolitan Statistical Areas,* Final Report PC(3)–1D (Washington, D.C.: U.S. Government Printing Office, 1963), Table 1.

the percent Negro in the city or ring increases, this indicates that the Negro population is growing at a faster rate than the white population. Similarly, a decline in the percent Negro in an area indicates that the white population is growing at a faster rate than the Negro population. In the North and West, both suburban rings and central cities have increased in percent Negro during 1900–60, indicating that the Negro population in both components of metropolitan areas was increasing more rapidly than the corresponding white population (Table XV). The percent

TABLE XIV—Percent of SMSA Population Residing in Central City by Race and Region, 1900–1960*

Race and Year	Conterminous United States	Region		
		North	West	South
NEGRO				
1960	79.5	84.9	72.5	74.6
1950	77.2	83.5	69.9	72.0
1940	74.6	81.1	78.3	69.5
1930	72.8	79.8	79.8	67.3
1920	67.2	78.0	83.8	61.1
1910	60.4	72.1	81.7	55.7
1900	54.5	68.6	80.3	49.5
WHITE				
1960	47.8	47.6	43.0	52.5
1950	56.6	58.1	49.6	57.3
1940	61.6	62.5	57.7	60.6
1930	63.9	64.4	61.5	63.6
1920	65.9	66.8	66.8	61.0
1910	64.9	66.4	65.3	56.0
1900	62.8	64.7	62.3	51.8

* SMSA's as defined in 1960.

SOURCE: U.S. Bureau of the Census, *U.S. Census of Population: 1960, Selected Area Reports, Standard Metropolitan Statistical Areas,* Final Report PC(3)–1D (Washington, D.C.: U.S. Government Printing Office, 1963), Table 1.

Negro in cities, however, rose to much higher levels than in rings. In Southern metropolitan areas, on the other hand, the percent Negro in the rings has declined rapidly, while the color composition of the cities has remained about the same.

Recent gains in the Negro population residing in some suburban rings, although small, have been hailed by some as the beginnings of large-scale suburbanward movement of Negroes. Such a forecast may well be correct, but a closer look at actual trends to date prompts a more cautious view. Not all parts of the suburban ring conform to the suburbia of the Sunday supplements. For illustrative purposes, consider the Chicago metropolitan area. The Negro population outside Chicago city increased from 44,000 to 78,000 between 1950 and 1960. More than half of the 34,000 increase went to neighborhoods in such industrial suburbs as Evanston, Joliet, North

Chicago, and similar places listed in Table XVI. These suburbs already had Negro communities in residentially segregated neighborhoods in 1950, and the addition of Negro population to these areas did not represent an opening up of suburbs in general to Negro residents. An additional one-fourth of the increased Negro population in Chicago's suburban ring is accounted for by the addition of Negro population to existing or newly created "Negro suburbs," entire communities or separate sections of communities developed expressly for the purpose of providing new suburban housing for Negroes. There are several such developments in Cook County just southwest of Chicago. The net gain of Negro population in all the rest of the suburban area surrounding Chicago was less than 6,000 in the entire decade.

Moderate increases in the number of Negroes have produced large percentage increases in Negro suburban population elsewhere than in Chicago. There is little evidence, as yet, that much of this suburbanization is different from the expansion of Negro residential areas within the central cities, except that it is taking place outside the city limits. Clearly little of it represents the development of integrated residential patterns.

Urban Residential Segregation

Within the central cities of our large metropolitan areas dwell a high proportion of the nation's Negroes. Not only are these Negroes virtually absent from most of suburbia, but they are virtually absent from many residential neighborhoods within these cities. Individual city neighborhoods throughout the country tend to be occupied either by Negroes or by whites, with few areas of sustained racial intermixture on a residential basis. Civil rights struggles for open occupancy, against *de facto* school segregation and against a variety of other forms of segregation in parks, libraries and other public facilities have called attention to the prevalence of racial residential segregation in many cities. A recent study has documented the prevalence of residential segregation by examining data for individual city blocks from the 1940, 1950 and 1960 censuses. If race were not a factor in where a person lives, and whites and nonwhites had similar socio-economic characteristics, then every city block might be expected to have the same proportion of white and nonwhite residents as every other block. In fact, the data reveal very clearly that blocks tend to be occupied by whites or by nonwhites, with relatively few blocks having a high degree of intermixture. With these data it was possible to demonstrate that residential segregation is not characteristic only of Northern cities or only of

TABLE XV—Percent Negro in Central City and Suburban Ring by Region, 1900–1960*

Residence and Year	Conterminous United States	Region		
		North	West	South
TOTAL SMSA				
1960	10.8	9.1	5.1	19.6
1950	9.4	6.9	3.9	20.4
1940	8.0	5.0	1.7	22.4
1930	7.5	4.4	1.4	22.9
1920	6.8	3.1	1.1	24.6
1910	6.7	2.4	1.1	27.4
1900	7.4	2.4	1.0	30.7
CENTRAL CITY				
1960	16.8	15.1	8.2	25.8
1950	12.4	9.6	5.4	24.3
1940	9.6	6.4	2.3	24.8
1930	8.4	5.5	1.8	23.9
1920	6.9	3.6	1.5	24.6
1910	6.3	2.6	1.3	27.5
1900	6.5	2.5	1.3	29.6
RING				
1960	4.6	2.8	2.5	11.6
1950	5.2	2.8	2.4	14.3
1940	5.5	2.6	0.9	18.2
1930	5.7	2.6	0.7	21.0
1920	6.5	2.1	0.5	24.5
1910	7.5	2.0	0.5	27.4
1900	8.9	2.1	0.5	31.7

* SMSA's as defined in 1960.

SOURCE: U.S. Bureau of the Census, *U.S. Census of Population: 1960, Selected Area Reports, Standard Metropolitan Statistical Areas,* Final Report PC(3)–1D (Washington, D.C.: U.S. Government Printing Office, 1963), Table 1.

Southern cities. Every city with a sizable Negro population displays a high degree of residential segregation, regardless of region or size, regardless of whether it is a manufacturing center, a trade center or a suburb. Sometimes groups protesting housing discrimination in a city contend that their city

TABLE XVI—Negro Population in 1950 and 1960 of Selected Chicago Suburbs

| Suburb | Negro Population | | | Percent Negro, 1960 |
	1960	1950	Change 1950–60	
INDUSTRIAL SUBURBS				
Aurora	2,227	1,151	1,076	3.5
Chicago Heights	6,529	4,109	2,420	19.0
Elgin	1,595	768	827	3.2
Evanston	9,126	6,994	2,132	11.5
Harvey	1,986	1,010	976	6.8
Joliet	4,638	1,950	2,688	6.9
Maywood	5,229	2,500	2,729	19.1
North Chicago	4,577	832	3,745	23.4
Waukegan	4,485	2,313	2,172	8.0
TOTAL			**18,765**	
"NEGRO SUBURBS"				
Dixmoor	1,855	554	1,301	60.3
East Chicago Heights	2,794	1,190	1,604	85.4
Markham	2,505	66	2,439	21.4
Phoenix	2,744	1,461	1,283	65.3
Robbins	7,410	4,729	2,681	98.7
TOTAL			**9,308**	
Total Ring of Chicago SMSA	**77,517**	**43,640**	**33,877**	**2.9**

Note: The designation of a suburb as "industrial" is based upon data for manufacturing establishments and employment and amount of commuting to Chicago to work, as described in the suburban histories of the Kitagawa and Taeuber volume cited below.

SOURCE: Evelyn M. Kitagawa and Karl E. Taeuber, *Local Community Fact Book Chicago Metropolitan Area 1960* (Chicago: Chicago Community Inventory, University of Chicago, 1963); U.S. Bureau of the Census, *U.S. Census of Population: 1960*, Vol. I, *Characteristics of the Population*, Part 15, Illinois (Washington, D.C.: U.S. Government Printing Office, 1963), Tables 21 and 22; and U.S. Bureau of the Census, *U.S. Census of Population: 1950*, Vol. II, *Characteristics of the Population*, Part 13, Illinois (Washington, D.C.: U.S. Government Printing Office, 1952), Tables 34 and 38.

is the most segregated in the country. Examination of the census data indicates that this type of segregation is found in all American cities, and that no city can lay claim to being much more or much less segregated than any other.

HOUSING OF THE NEGRO POPULATION

Trends in Homeownership

Today more than 1.5 million Negro families are homeowners, and owners make up nearly 40 percent of Negro households. Despite this impressive achievement, Negroes still lag behind whites in homeownership, and in a variety of indicators of housing quality and amenities.

Trends in homeownership in the United States, pictured in Figure 7, tell a surprising story. From the earliest period for which reliable statistics are available, in 1890, until sometime after World War II, a minority of Americans were homeowners. For whites, the homeownership rate varied

FIGURE 7—Percent Owner-Occupied by Color: Conterminous United States 1890–1960

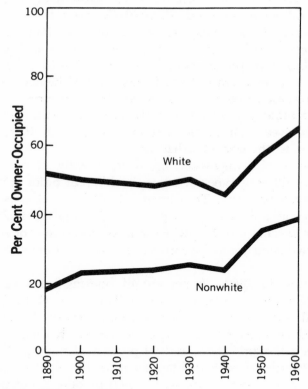

Note: Data for 1910 not available.

SOURCE: U.S. Bureau of the Census, *U.S. Census of Housing: 1960*, Vol. I, *States and Small Areas, United States Summary*, Final Report HC(1)–1 (Washington, D.C.: U.S. Government Printing Office, 1963), Table H.

around 50 percent until 1940. It was only during the post-war period of economic prosperity, accompanied by high levels of accumulated savings, high rates of marriage and household formation and extensive governmental programs to facilitate homeownership, that the balance was finally tilted strongly in favor of ownership. In the two decades from 1940 to 1960 (and mainly in the fifteen years from 1945 to 1960) homeownership among whites climbed from 45 percent of households to 64 percent. The levels of homeownership among nonwhites have always been much lower than among whites, but the trend has been rather similar. From 1900 to 1940, the percent owners among nonwhites remained steady at 24–25, and then increased sharply to 38 percent in 1960.

For both Negroes and whites, the first thirty years of this century were a period of increasing income and wealth, which should have augmented homeownership. These years were also a time of rapid urbanization, however, and the move to cities inhibited the growth of ownership which otherwise would have occurred. Particularly prior to the days of mass automobile ownership and easy transportation over long distances, cities tended of necessity to be settled very densely. Under such circumstances, multiple-dwelling units predominated over single-family dwellings. In addition, millions of the immigrants from Europe and white and Negro migrants from rural America came to cities in search of economic opportunities. Despite considerable improvement in the economic well-being of many of these migrants over their former circumstances, their incomes were not high in relation to the cost of urban housing.

The prevalence of homeownership varies greatly in different parts of the country, in different types of areas, in different cities and even in different parts of a single city. To a great extent these differences are determined when an area is first built up, for single-family detached dwellings are usually for purchase, and multiple-unit dwellings are for rent. Old units which were once owned may be converted into rental units, but the reverse seldom happens.

For nonwhites, in 1960, 30 percent of housing units in metropolitan areas of the North were owner-occupied. These nonwhites live chiefly in the old central portions of cities that were built up in the dense tenement pattern prevailing many decades ago. In the South this type of housing has always been less prevalent, and 39 percent of metropolitan nonwhites are owners. Outside of metropolitan areas in the South, the majority of nonwhites are also tenants in housing owned by others, but building codes are not as strict, inexpensive units are more common and 44 percent of the units are owner-occupied. For whites, the levels of ownership are much higher, but the variations tend to be similar. In Northern metropolitan areas, ownership is 60 percent, in Southern metropolitan areas 66 percent, and in the small towns and rural areas of the South 67 percent.

Housing Characteristics of Whites and Nonwhites

Whether they are renters or owners, the housing obtained by nonwhites is less adequate or less desirable in many respects when compared to housing obtained by whites. Evidence for this statement is presented in Table XVII. Nonwhite households are more likely to live in substandard housing, more likely to be overcrowded, less likely to be in new housing and less likely to have amenities such as air-conditioning or an automobile. Nonwhite households are even less likely to own television sets. Television is lacking in 28 percent of nonwhite units as compared to only 11 percent of white units.

The reported value of housing occupied by nonwhites tends to be less than that for housing occupied by whites. This pattern is particularly clear for owner-occupied housing. Within Northern metropolitan areas, half of the units owned by whites are valued at more than $14,200, and half for less. The corresponding median value for nonwhites is $9,400. Similar differences obtain in the South. In the South, rents paid by nonwhites are also lower than those paid by whites—the median rent is $53 monthly for nonwhites in metropolitan areas of the South, as compared to $73 for whites. In the Northern metropolitan areas, however, the difference is small—$73 for nonwhites and $77 for whites.

There is considerable controversy over the question of whether nonwhite housing is inferior because nonwhites pay less, or whether because of segregation and discrimination nonwhites get even less quality than they should for what they pay. One careful study of the situation in Chicago in 1956 came to the conclusion that for roughly equivalent housing, nonwhites had to pay about fifteen dollars a month more than whites.[1] To the extent that Negroes, by virtue of residential segregation, have access to only a limited amount of housing, despite rapidly increasing numbers, then the laws of supply and demand operate in Negro residential areas to raise housing prices in relation to housing quality. However, this is a controversial topic, and it is difficult to determine what conditions would be like in the absence of discrimination.

Regardless of the source of white-Negro housing differences—whether due to segregation and discrimination in housing, or whether it is traced back to segregation and discrimination in the means of earning a livelihood

---

[1] Beverly Duncan and Philip M. Hauser, *Housing a Metropolis—Chicago* (New York: The Free Press of Glencoe, 1960).

TABLE XVII—Selected Characteristics of Housing Units by Color, Tenure, Region and Inside or Outside SMSA's, 1960

Color and Characteristic	Inside SMSA's				Outside SMSA's	
	North		South		South	
	Owner	Renter	Owner	Renter	Owner	Renter
Number of housing units (000)						
White	11,060.5	7,285.5	4,165.5	2,160.5	4,301.6	2,119.3
Nonwhite	510.8	1,182.8	517.5	813.6	628.2	796.3
Percent substandard						
White	3.6	13.5	5.5	14.7	26.4	41.1
Nonwhite	10.4	28.0	29.8	46.8	71.7	89.4
Percent overcrowded						
White	7.1	13.4	8.5	19.1	12.1	24.8
Nonwhite	14.6	31.8	22.8	42.4	29.4	52.3
Percent built 1950–60						
White	33.5	11.0	49.9	25.1	33.2	20.1
Nonwhite	10.6	8.2	26.7	18.8	23.2	12.9
Percent air-conditioned						
White	14.1	9.7	32.5	20.2	16.6	9.8
Nonwhite	7.1	2.9	9.2	3.3	3.1	1.3
Percent with automobile						
White	87.4	61.1	90.6	73.8	83.9	74.9
Nonwhite	68.3	35.8	64.0	36.4	53.7	39.8
Median value, gross rent						
White	$14,200	$77	$11,800	$73	$7,400	$53
Nonwhite	$ 9,400	$73	$ 6,900	$53	$5,000—	$30
Percent with gross rent 35% or more of income						
White	—	18.6	—	20.0	—	18.6
Nonwhite	—	32.6	—	33.5	—	29.6

Note: Substandard units include dilapidated units and all other units lacking some or all plumbing facilities. The measure of overcrowding relates the number of units with 1.01 or more persons per room to the number of multiple-person households.

SOURCE: U.S. Bureau of the Census, *U.S. Census of Housing: 1960, Metropolitan Housing*, Final Report HC(2)–1 through 10 (Washington, D.C.: U.S. Government Printing Office, 1963), Tables B–3, B–7, B–13, C–3, C–7, and C–13.

—Negroes usually pay a high proportion of their low incomes for their housing, whether good or bad. Nearly one-third of nonwhite renters, as compared to one-fifth of white renters, spends more than 35 percent of their annual income on rent (Table XVII). Interpretation of these figures can lead to very tricky problems in economic theory, but it is clear that the gap between Negroes and whites is much greater in income than in amounts actually spent on housing, and that the housing obtained by Negroes is much inferior to that obtained by whites.

Sources of the Housing Supply

The number of nonwhite households has been increasing quite rapidly in recent decades, particularly within metropolitan areas. Yet only a small proportion of housing occupied by nonwhites is new. Obviously much of the additional housing required by increasing Negro population is obtained "hand-me-down" from whites. In connection with the 1960 census, a special investigation was made of these processes of change in the housing inventory. Understanding of the housing circumstances of Negroes and of the processes of neighborhood change occurring in cities throughout the country can be facilitated by studying the rather complex reports of this investigation.

What are the types of change which can affect the stock of housing and its racial composition? First, of course, is the addition of units by new construction. Additional units can also be obtained by converting one unit into two or more units by adding partitions and plumbing facilities. Garages, lofts and other nonresidential structures can be converted to residential use. Housing units may be lost through deliberate demolition for highways, urban renewal or other purposes, and through accidental demolition as by fire. Units can be merged together to create a single larger unit, and units can be converted to nonresidential use. During the 1950–59 period, the available stock of housing was affected by all of these types of change. Most of the housing inventory in 1959, however, had existed in 1950 and was retained through the decade. An additional complication arises when race of the occupant is considered, for although a housing unit may be the same in 1959 as in 1950, it may have been transferred from white to Negro occupancy or from Negro to white occupancy.

This scheme for accounting for what happens to housing during a decade is put to use in Table XVIII, where data from the 1959 National Housing Inventory are assembled to show the source of housing occupied by whites and nonwhites in 1959. To simplify the discussion, reference will be made mainly to the figures for all metropolitan housing in the United States.

TABLE XVIII—Sources of 1959 Housing Inventory, by Color, Region and Inside or Outside SMSA's

Color and Source of 1959 Housing Inventory	U.S. Total		North	South	
	Inside SMSA's	Outside SMSA's	Inside SMSA's	Inside SMSA's	Outside SMSA's
Nonwhite-occupied dwelling units, 1959					
Total, in thousands	3,249.0	1,527.0	1,618.6	1,136.5	1,309.0
Percent	100.0	100.0	100.0	100.0	100.0
Same units, 1950–59	75.3	78.3	81.2	68.7	80.0
White-occupied, 1950	30.1	9.6	40.5	14.6	7.8
Nonwhite-occupied, 1950	36.7	52.7	32.9	44.8	56.1
New construction	13.4	15.7	6.4	19.7	14.4
Conversion	5.5	2.0	6.9	5.1	1.3
Other	5.8	4.0	5.5	6.5	4.3
White-occupied dwelling units, 1959					
Total, in thousands	29,711.4	18,468.0	18,138.8	5,946.3	7,060.4
Percent	100.0	100.0	100.0	100.0	100.0
Same units, 1950–59	66.1	71.6	71.0	58.0	68.8
White-occupied, 1950	58.7	60.3	64.2	49.1	56.0
Nonwhite-occupied, 1950	0.3	0.3	0.3	0.1	0.5
New construction	29.0	22.5	23.8	37.1	26.1
Conversion	2.6	2.2	3.0	2.5	1.7
Other	2.3	3.7	2.2	2.4	3.4

SOURCE: U.S. Bureau of the Census, *U.S. Census of Housing: 1960*, Vol. IV, *Components of Inventory Change*, Final Report HC(4), Part 1A, No. 1 (Washington, D.C.: U.S. Government Printing Office, 1962), Tables 1, 2, and 4.

In late 1959, there were about 3,249,000 dwelling units occupied by nonwhites in metropolitan areas. Three-fourths of these were "same units," units that existed in 1950, and were retained in use through 1959. Of same units, somewhat under one-half had been occupied by whites in 1950, and somewhat over half had then, as now, been occupied by nonwhites. (Some units which were vacant in 1950 or for which the color of the 1950 occupant could not be determined are not shown separately in the table.) One-fourth of nonwhite housing in 1959 remains to be accounted for. About 13 percent came from housing built during the decade, 5.5 percent came from conversion of one or more large units into two or more smaller ones, and 6 percent came from miscellaneous other sources.

Sources of metropolitan housing for white occupancy display a different pattern. New construction was much more important for whites, accounting for 29 percent of their housing in 1959. Only 5 percent came from conversion or miscellaneous sources combined. Two-thirds of the housing occupied by whites had existed in essentially the same form in 1950. In contrast to nonwhites, who obtained one-third of their housing from units formerly occupied by whites, only one out of every three hundred units occupied by whites was obtained from nonwhites.

The major regional variations in these patterns can be specified briefly for metropolitan housing. In the North, nonwhites obtained only 6 percent of their housing from new construction, and another 7 percent from conversion. More than 40 percent of their housing came from units occupied by whites ten years before. In the South, nonwhites obtained much more new housing (20 per cent) and there was much less transfer of dwellings from white to nonwhite occupancy.

One other piece of information from the National Housing Inventory may be noted. Nonwhites occupied a far higher proportion of units which were demolished during the decade than their share in the population would indicate. These demolitions included many due to highway construction and private redevelopment in addition to those undertaken for slum clearance and urban renewal. In their abstract technical way, these statistics help tell the story of thousands of urban Negroes forced to relocate, despite the difficulties encountered by Negroes in locating suitable housing.

SOCIAL, ECONOMIC AND HEALTH CHARACTERISTICS OF NEGROES

Negroes today are confronted with a wide variety of social problems, some of them the heritage of slavery, all of them a reflection of their current position in American society. At Emancipation, most Negroes were illiterate, lived in the rural South, worked in agriculture (primarily as laborers) and received little cash income. Marriage was not a stable institution; large proportions of children were illegitimate and lived in families where a woman was the effective head. Sanitary conditions were often bad, medical and hygienic knowledge slight and death rates high. The history of the Negro since Emancipation has been one of absorption into a changing industrial society. For many of the characteristics which distinguished the position of the Negro from that of the white, the century since Emancipation has been one of gradual but not yet completed convergence of the races.

The topics touched upon in this section are especially difficult to discuss briefly. Several of them are subject to more extensive analysis in later chapters. Here the attempt is to emphasize the mutual interrelations, omitting some of the technical complexities and regional variations.

Educational Attainment

In 1870, about 80 percent of nonwhites were illiterate, and fifty years later the figure was down to 23 percent. Not until 1959 was illiteracy down to 7.5 percent, a level attained by whites seventy years earlier. Although Negroes have to a considerable degree caught up with whites in ensuring that their children receive at least a primary education, there is still a large lag at the higher educational levels.

Virtually all children between the ages of seven and thirteen, white and Negro, are enrolled in school. The percentage enrolled, however, falls off faster for nonwhites than for whites. At ages 14–17, the enrollment in the fall of 1962 was 87 percent for nonwhites, 93 per cent for whites. At ages 18–19, beyond the ages of compulsory attendance, the percentages dropped to 33 and 43 percent, respectively, and at ages 20–24, to 10 and 16 percent.

School attendance, of course, is not a valid measure of education actually received. There are substantial differences in the extent of age-grade retardation. For example, of 18–19 year-olds enrolled in school, 78 percent of the whites as compared to 50 percent of the nonwhites in 1962 were enrolled in college. Quality of education is more difficult to measure. If it is related to the educational attainment of teachers and the per capita expenditure on schooling, then nearly all Southern Negroes and the great bulk of Northern Negroes who attend predominantly Negro schools receive inferior education.

By age twenty-five most persons have completed their schooling. Examination of trends in the median years of school completed for whites and nonwhites in the 25–29 age group suggests convergence between the two groups during the last twenty-two years (Table XIX). While the figure for white males advanced from 10.5 school years in 1940 to 12.5 in 1962, the figure for nonwhites increased from 6.5 to 11.0. Nonwhites in the North and West report higher levels of education than do those in the South, while levels in the urban South greatly exceed those in the rural South. As Negroes have moved in large numbers from the rural South to the cities of all regions, they have improved their educational opportunities and attainment.

TABLE XIX—Median Years of School Completed by Persons 25–29 Years
Old, by Color and Sex, 1940–1962

Date	Male			Female		
	White	Nonwhite	Percentage, Nonwhite of White	White	Nonwhite	Percentage, Nonwhite of White
April, 1940	10.5	6.5	61.9	10.9	7.5	68.8
March, 1957	12.3	9.4	76.4	12.3	10.3	83.7
March, 1959	12.5	10.9	87.2	12.4	11.0	88.7
March, 1962	12.5	11.0	88.0	12.4	11.4	91.9
Increase, 1940–62	2.0	4.5		1.5	3.9	

SOURCE: 1962 from U.S. Bureau of the Census, "Educational Attainment: March 1962," *Current Population Reports*, Series P–20, No. 121, Tables 2 and 3; all other years from U.S. Department of Labor, *The Economic Status of Negroes in the United States*, Bulletin S–3, Revised 1962, Table 17.

Educators have long recognized that a person's family background, even in a society which provides free public education, affects whether the child attends school and how far he progresses in school. A recent special survey by the Bureau of the Census revealed that college attendance is much more frequent among children of high school and college graduates than among children of parents with only a grade school education. Because of past differences between Negroes and whites, however, Negro children are much more likely than white children to come from those families which send few children on to college. Among families at each educational level, however, nonwhites were less likely to have children enrolled in college than whites. If a high percentage of Negro children fail to surmount this handicap, then they will become yet another generation of parents who are poorly educated, and whose children in turn are handicapped by lack of a family background encouraging educational attainment.

This vicious circle in educational attainment is difficult to break. Education takes place early in life, and is seldom continued after a person first leaves school. By the time a person reaches age twenty-five, therefore, he has reached the educational level which he will retain throughout the rest of his life. Persons who reach adulthood with low educational attainment must live out their life span before they can be replaced by persons with higher levels. Even if Negroes reaching ages 25–29 matched the educational achievements of whites, it would be more than a generation before educational levels in the total adult Negro population caught up with those in the white population.

TABLE XX—Percent Distribution of Major Occupation of Experienced Civilian Labor Force by Educational Attainment and Color for Males Aged 35–44 in Central Cities of Urbanized Areas, 1960

Years of School Completed and Color	Total *	Professional, Technical	Managers, Officials	Clerical	Sales Workers	Craftsmen, Foremen	Operatives	Service Workers	Laborers
Total									
White	100.0	13.3	13.9	8.7	8.4	23.5	21.0	6.2	5.0
Nonwhite	100.0	4.8	3.5	8.5	1.7	13.9	30.9	15.4	21.3
None									
White	100.0	1.2	4.0	2.3	2.1	18.9	29.7	13.2	28.6
Nonwhite	100.0	—	2.8	2.6	—	8.1	30.3	17.7	38.5
Elementary, 1–4 years									
White	100.0	0.8	3.5	2.6	2.6	23.0	36.2	11.5	19.8
Nonwhite	100.0	0.3	1.4	2.4	0.7	11.4	32.8	14.0	37.0
Elementary, 5–7 years									
White	100.0	1.0	4.9	3.9	2.8	28.3	37.7	8.4	13.0
Nonwhite	100.0	0.4	1.8	2.5	0.7	13.8	35.1	15.2	30.5
Elementary, 8 years									
White	100.0	1.2	6.3	5.5	3.9	29.0	36.7	7.8	9.6
Nonwhite	100.0	0.8	2.3	4.2	1.1	15.1	35.7	16.9	23.9
High School, 1–3 years									
White	100.0	2.8	9.6	8.1	6.2	30.3	29.6	7.5	5.9
Nonwhite	100.0	1.0	3.0	8.3	1.4	14.7	35.6	17.0	19.0
High School, 4 years									
White	100.0	7.6	16.0	12.2	10.7	26.8	17.2	6.7	2.8
Nonwhite	100.0	3.1	5.0	16.2	3.2	16.2	27.2	16.1	13.0
College, 1–3 years									
White	100.0	19.4	24.7	12.2	16.1	14.7	7.6	4.1	1.2
Nonwhite	100.0	11.1	7.7	21.9	3.3	14.5	19.4	14.3	7.8
College, 4+ years									
White	100.0	57.5	20.8	5.9	8.8	4.2	1.3	1.1	0.4
Nonwhite	100.0	58.4	9.4	13.9	2.6	3.9	4.5	5.4	1.9

* Occupation not reported excluded.

SOURCE: U.S. Bureau of the Census, *U.S. Census of Population: 1960, Subject Reports, Educational Attainment,* Final Report PC(2)–5B (Washington, D.C.: U.S. Government Printing Office, 1963), Table 8.

Occupation and Income

The legacy of lower educational levels among the Negro population would be expected to be reflected in a concentration in the lower occupational levels. At each level of educational attainment, however, Negroes obtain a smaller proportion of upper level jobs than do whites with the same amount of education. Illustrative data are presented in Table XX for males aged 35–44 in 1960. For these men, the disparity between whites and nonwhites in occupational levels is greatest at the intermediate levels of education (where most of the population is found) and least at the lowest and highest levels of education. Apparently for persons with little formal education, few occupations are open, whether the person is white or nonwhite. At the college graduate level, nonwhites do fairly well in terms of broad occupational categories—perhaps because of the many outlets for professional employment within the Negro community as teachers, clergymen, doctors and lawyers serving a Negro clientele.

Some of the advancement in occupational status which has occurred for Negroes derives from an increase from 214,000 to over one million Negroes employed in Federal, state and local governments between 1940 and 1962. Much of the advancement in occupational levels, like that in educational levels, results from the migration of Negroes from areas with few economic opportunities to the rapidly growing metropolitan focal points of the expanding national economy.

The chief source of income for most Negro families is the wages received for their labor. With the twin disadvantages of lower educational attainment and lower occupational levels at each educational level, Negroes must be expected to fare much worse than whites in the amount of income they receive. Median family income for white families rose from $3,157 in 1947 to $6,237 in 1962, and for nonwhite families from $1,614 to $3,330. Throughout this post-war period the nonwhite figure remained about one-half of the figure for whites, and there was no discernible trend in the relationship. During the Second World War, the income of nonwhites increased faster than the income of whites, but changes in the post-war period have mainly been due to the regional migration of nonwhites from low-wage areas to high-wage areas. Nonwhite incomes are particularly low in the South, whereas in the North and West they receive as much as Southern whites, though still less than Northern and Western whites (Table XXI).

Basic to an individual's ability to get along in an industrial society is his training and education, which fit him for an occupation. A job, in turn, provides his principal source of income and largely determines the style of life he will be able to maintain for himself and his children. The preceding discussion shows that at several critical junctures in the life history of Negroes they are unable to keep pace with whites. In comparison with whites, Negroes complete less formal schooling, obtain poorer jobs than do whites with comparable levels of education, and apparently are rewarded by receiving lower earnings than do whites with similar educations and occupations. It was recently estimated that the average nonwhite with four years of college can expect to earn less over his lifetime than the average white who did not go beyond the eighth grade. The close relationships between education, occupation and income, however, suggest that reduction in discrimination might have a cumulative impact on the economic welfare of Negroes.

Family and Fertility

The Negro family under slavery was an unstable arrangement, for there was little security in the bond of marriage or parenthood. Fertility must have been high, for death rates were high and yet the Negro population increased by more than the number of slaves imported. There is evidence that at least since 1850, birth rates among Negroes have been higher than among whites. The historical trends, however, are difficult to document, and the statistical picture begins about 1920. Higher birth rates among Negroes since 1920 are apparent in Figure 8.

TABLE XXI—Median Total Money Income of Males 14 Years Old and Over, by Region and Color, 1960

Region	White	Nonwhite	Percentage, Nonwhite of White
U.S. Total	$4,297	$2,258	52.5
Northeast	$4,605	$3,513	76.3
North Central	$4,429	$3,359	75.8
South	$3,361	$1,255	37.3
West	$5,043	$3,692	73.2

SOURCE: U.S. Bureau of the Census, "Income of Families and Persons in the United States: 1960," *Current Population Reports*, Series P–60, No. 37, Table 34.

Various aspects of population distribution and social structure are related to fertility patterns. Farm families and other rural families, for instance, tend to have more children than city families. Part of the high fertility among Negroes, then, can be attributed to their population concentration in the rural South. Since 1910, of course, Negroes have been leaving the rural South in great numbers and moving to cities where they have tended to display a lower rate of child-bearing. Whites were also moving from high fertility areas to low fertility areas, however, and the Negro-white difference persisted. In fact, during the 1920's and the first half of the 1930's, birth rates among both Negroes and whites fell rapidly, and both races rose sharply during World War II and the postwar "baby boom."

Since 1947, birth rates among Negroes and whites have followed divergent paths. White fertility diminished a bit after the peak during the baby boom, rose during the early 1950's, and has since entered a period of gradual decline. Negro fertility, by contrast, continued increasing after 1947

FIGURE 8—Births per 1,000 Females Aged 15–44 Years,[a] by Color, 1920–1961

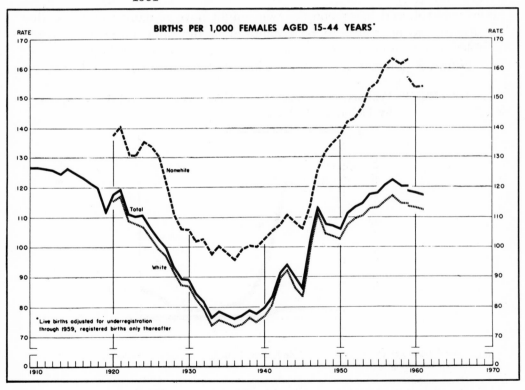

Note: Live births adjusted for underregistration through 1959; registered births, 1959-1961.

SOURCE: U.S. Department of Health, Education, and Welfare, *Health, Education, and Welfare Indicators,* March, 1963 (Washington, D.C.: U.S. Government Printing Office, 1963), p. xxvi.

for another ten years. Only in the last few years have Negro birth rates reached a plateau, with some signs of a slight decline. Birth rates among Negroes are now far higher than among whites. Continuation of current rates of births and deaths for a generation would result in an increase in population of 60 percent for whites and 100 percent for Negroes. The dramatic fluctuations which have occurred in birth rates in recent decades, however, suggest how hazardous it would be to assume that birth rates among Negroes or whites will continue unchanged, and it would be equally hazardous to predict just what changes will take place.

Historically, Negroes in comparison with whites have had more childlessness among married couples, as well as a higher proportion of couples with large numbers of children. The net balance has been an average number of children per couple only slightly above the figure for whites. The childlessness among Negro couples, however, may often have been involuntary—venereal disease may well have placed a prominent role in Negro infertility. Since 1940, venereal disease has been largely brought under control, and many couples who might have remained childless due to disease are now able to bear children in the same numbers as other couples. The incidence of venereal disease is not known with high accuracy, but Figure 9 portrays the rapid decline in the rate of reported cases of

FIGURE 9—Primary and Secondary Syphilis Cases per 100,000 Population, by Color, 1941–1962.

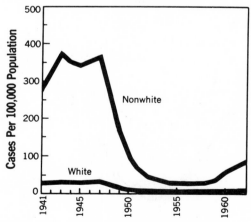

Note: Data not available for 1942 and 1946. Data include Alaska beginning with 1959 and Hawaii beginning with 1960.

SOURCE: U.S. Department of Health, Education, and Welfare, *Health, Education, and Welfare Trends,* 1963 Edition (Washington, D.C.: U.S. Government Printing Office, 1963), p. 18.

syphilis during the post-war years. The figure also shows the resurgence in syphilis cases in the last few years which has alarmed public health personnel, although the rates are still far below levels obtaining in past decades.

In the post-war period, for both Negroes and whites, the proportion of women never marrying has declined, as has the proportion of married women remaining childless. Childbearing in the teens and early twenties has become much more prevalent. Both whites and Negroes appear to have developed a pattern of youthful marriage and early childbearing. These patterns probably reflect a high level of economic welfare and readily obtainable credit for home-buying and the purchase of other durable goods, as well as more permanent social changes. A better assessment can be made a few years from now, when it should be apparent whether the current plateaus in birth rates are the beginnings of a significant downturn, or whether fertility will continue at the high levels maintained throughout the post-war period.

Not all babies are born to mothers who are married. Illegitimacy is not uncommon in the United States, and has been increasing in recent years among both Negroes and whites. More than half of the nation's illegitimate births occur to white mothers, but rates of illegitimacy are far higher among Negroes (Figure 10). Many sociologists think Negro illegitimacy is historically connected to conditions under slavery, when marriage was unstable. The persistence of mother-centered families is facilitated by social conditions which consign many Negro males to failure in their task as breadwinners. Whatever the reasons, for both whites and Negroes, illegitimacy is particularly prevalent among young girls, with just under one-half of illegitimate births occurring to mothers under twenty years of age.

Crude birth rates are sometimes poor measures of fertility. For instance, in 1960 in Chicago birth rates among nonwhites were 37 per thousand population, as compared to 21 per thousand among whites. These rates are highly misleading. Nonwhites in Chicago include many who migrated to the city in the past twenty years, and who are still young. Many young white families, however, have moved to the suburbs, and white birth rates in the city are low in part because of the high proportion of older persons who are beyond the childbearing ages. If adjustments are made for age differences and for the greater proportion of single women among whites, the differences between the groups are considerably reduced. In fact, there is very little difference between whites and nonwhites in Chicago in patterns of marital fertility. There is about a 25 percent excess fertility of nonwhites, due to their high rates of illegiti-

FIGURE 10—Percent of Total Live Births Illegitimate, by Color, 1944–1961

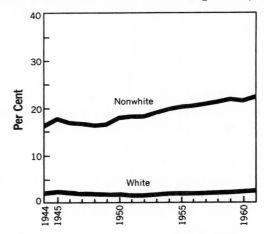

SOURCE: U.S. Department of Health, Education, and Welfare, *Health, Education, and Welfare Trends,* 1963 Edition (Washington, D.C.: U.S. Government Printing Office, 1963), p. 7.

macy.[2] Crude birth rates sometimes underlie assertions that Negroes are breeding at extreme rates, or that there is a population problem among U.S. Negroes comparable to that in many underdeveloped countries. Such claims cannot be sustained if the facts are examined with due care.

Of the many factors affecting marriage and fertility, urban and rural residence, levels of economic welfare and social status have traditionally been important. During the period of rapidly declining fertility in the 1920's, fertility tended to be lower among those higher in economic and social status, while those with lower status bore children at higher rates. Now that knowledge of family planning has spread throughout society, and some degree of family limitation characterizes couples in all social and economic groups, the former differentials in fertility seem to have diminished, and even to have been partially reversed. A detailed analysis cannot be undertaken here but some of the recent patterns among Negroes can be indicated, if only to illustrate the complexity of reproductive behavior.

The illustrative data here refer to women who were aged 35–44 and living in urbanized areas at the time of the 1960 census. These women had largely completed their childbearing, much of which occurred during the late 1930's and the 1940's. Women of different ages in 1960 bore their

[2] Evelyn M. Kitagawa and Philip M. Hauser, "Trends in Differential Fertility and Mortality in a Metropolis—Chicago," in Ernest W. Burgess and Donald J. Bogue (eds.), *Contributions to Urban Sociology* (Chicago: University of Chicago Press, 1964).

children during different time periods, and the patterns for them might differ. In Table XXII, there are three columns of data for each race: percent ever married; percent childless of those ever married; and children per 1,000 ever-married women. In this group of women, nearly all were married at least once, 93 percent among both whites and nonwhites. Of those ever married, about 13 percent of white women, but 25 percent of nonwhite women, never bore any children. This high proportion of childlessness among nonwhite women reduces the fertility of the total group. Despite this, the number of children per 1,000 ever-married women was 2,515 for nonwhites, as compared to 2,352 for whites.

TABLE XXII—Percent Ever Married, Percent Childless of Ever Married, and Number of Children Ever Born per 1,000 Ever-Married Women, for Women 35–44 Years Old, by Color and Educational Attainment, Urbanized Areas, 1960

Years of School Completed	Percent Ever Married		Percent Childless of Ever Married		Children Ever Born per 1,000 Ever-Married Women	
	White	Nonwhite	White	Nonwhite	White	Nonwhite
Total	92.8	92.8	13.0	24.5	2,352	2,515
Less than 8 years	92.0	92.1	13.6	25.1	2,869	2,807
8 years	93.9	93.5	13.6	25.6	2,444	2,621
High school, 1–3 years	95.1	93.8	11.5	23.0	2,417	2,663
High school, 4 years	93.4	93.2	13.2	23.8	2,244	2,219
College, 1–3 years	91.9	92.4	13.7	27.2	2,259	2,029
College, 4+ years	83.5	87.9	14.7	27.1	2,235	1,649

SOURCE: U.S. Bureau of the Census, *U.S. Census of Population: 1960, Subject Reports, Women by Number of Children Ever Born,* Final Report PC(2)–3A (Washington, D.C.: U.S. Government Printing Office, 1964), Tables 28 and 29.

If women are classified according to their education, there is a distinct pattern among both whites and nonwhites of higher fertility among those with least education. Particularly striking is the low level of fertility among nonwhite women who are college graduates. About 12 percent of these women never married, and 27 percent of those who married remained childless (among this group it is obvious that disease was not the major cause). Among these nonwhite college graduates, children per 1,000 ever-married women numbered 1,649, as compared to 2,807 among nonwhite women with less than eight grades of school, and 2,235 among white women who are college graduates. At the highest educational levels, nonwhite fertility is less than white fertility.

Social scientists have been rather unsuccessful in their attempts to explain reproductive behavior. It is clear that among nonwhites, just as among

FIGURE 11—Expectation of Life at Birth, by Color and Sex, 1900–1961

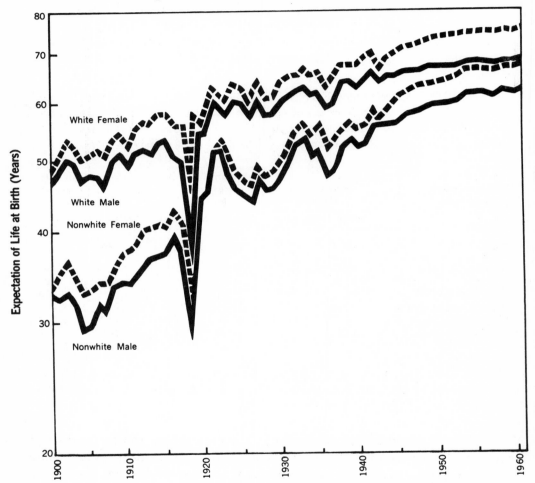

Note: Data include Alaska beginning with 1959 and Hawaii beginning with 1960. Data refer to the death registration area, which did not include the total United States, until 1933.

SOURCE: U.S. Bureau of the Census, *Historical Statistics of the United States, Colonial Times to 1957* (Washington, D.C.: U.S. Government Printing Office, 1950), Series B 92–100; and National Vital Statistics Division, *Vital Statistics of the United States, 1961,* Vol. II, Sec. 2, *Life Tables* Washington, D.C.: U.S. Government Printing Office, 1963).

whites, there are many different individuals, with many different characteristics. Their behavior in childbearing depends on their background, their education, their family status, the current occupation of husband and wife and similar social factors. Race is significant only as it involves the concentration of individuals with particular characteristics which are associated with high or low fertility.

Mortality and Health

Poverty and illness are intertwined in complicated ways. Sustained periods of illness may hamper a man in his efforts to earn a livelihood, and place a limit on his income. Sustained periods of low income, on the other hand, can lead to overcrowding, inadequate nutrition, a low level of preventive medical care and an increased incidence of ill health. That many Negroes in the United States are economically less well off than most whites has been demonstrated above. Nonwhites see physicians less often than do whites, make less use of hospitals, and have fewer of their hospital bills paid by insurance. That Negroes suffer from higher death rates should therefore not be surprising.

Perhaps the best single measure of the general level of health among a population is the expectation of life at birth. This figure summarizes the death rates prevailing among people of all ages during a given year. It indicates the average length of life a newborn child can expect, given the current patterns of mortality. In 1900, white males in the United States had an expectation of life of 47 years, nonwhite males 32 years. In industrial societies the figures for women tend to be higher than those for men. Among females the white figure, 49 years, was nearly half again as large as the nonwhite figure, 34 years.

Death rates in the white population had already been falling for many decades prior to 1900, and continued to fall in succeeding years. The trend in expectation of life has been upward, with much annual fluctuation and a large interruption during the influenza epidemic of 1917–18 (Figure 11). The figures for nonwhites have followed somewhat the same path, but have shown an even sharper rate of increase. With improvements in levels of living, in hygienic knowledge and nutrition, in public health and general medical care, the gap between whites and nonwhites was considerably narrowed. In fact, by 1961 nonwhite females had nearly caught up with white males in expectation of life, 67.0 *vs.* 67.8 years.

Despite the remarkable trend toward convergence of white and nonwhite death rates, a gap still exists. In 1961, white babies had about seven more years of life to look forward to than did nonwhite babies. Many of

FIGURE 12—Infant Mortality Rate Per 1,000 Live Births, by Color, 1915–1960

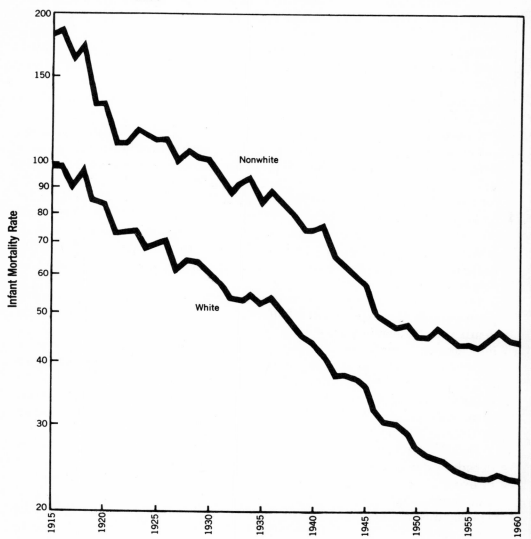

Note: Data refer to the death registration area, which did not include the total United States until 1933.

SOURCE: U.S. Bureau of the Census, *Historical Statistics of the United States, Colonial Times to 1957* (Washington, D.C.: U.S. Government Printing Office, 1960), Series B 101–112; and National Vital Statistics Division, *Vital Statistics of the United States, 1960*, Vol. II, Sec. 3, *Infant Mortality* (Washington, D.C.: U.S. Government Printing Office, 1963), Table 3–A.

the missing years of life for nonwhites are lost within the first year after birth. About 23 of every 1,000 white babies do not survive their first year. The figure is nearly twice as high for nonwhite babies, 43 per 1,000. Infant mortality rates, shown in Figure 12, have declined tremendously during this century, but during the last decade there has been a halt in the downward trend particularly for nonwhites and a widening of the differences between whites and nonwhites.

A recent study utilizing special tabulations for Chicago has assessed the impact of economic differentials between whites and nonwhites on their mortality differentials.[3] Using data for 1950, it was shown that virtually all of the differences between whites and nonwhites in death rates were attributable to their economic status differences. Within each color group,

TABLE XXIII—Age-Adjusted Death Rates per 100,000 Population for Selected Causes, by Color and Sex, United States, 1960

Cause of Death	White		Nonwhite		Percentage, Nonwhite of White	
	Male	Female	Male	Female	Male	Female
All Causes	917.7	555.0	1211.0	893.3	132.0	161.0
Major cardiovascular renal diseases	493.2	291.5	564.0	467.1	114.4	160.2
Malignant neoplasms	141.6	109.5	154.8	125.0	109.3	114.2
Accidents	70.6	25.4	101.1	36.1	143.2	142.1
Influenza and pneumonia	31.0	19.0	68.0	43.3	219.4	227.9
Diabetes mellitus	11.6	13.7	16.1	26.8	138.8	195.6
Cirrhosis of the liver	14.4	6.6	14.9	9.1	103.5	137.9
Tuberculosis, all forms	6.8	2.2	21.4	9.3	314.7	422.7

SOURCE: National Vital Statistics Division, *Vital Statistics of the United States, 1960*, Vol. II, Sec. 1, *Mortality Analysis and Summary* (Washington, D.C.: U.S. Government Printing Office, 1963), Table 1–J.

death rates were higher for those of lower status. If the death rates of the highest status group of whites are taken as a standard which could be achieved by the rest of the population, then one-fifth of the deaths among whites and one-half of the deaths among nonwhites were "excess" deaths that could have been avoided.

The Chicago study demonstrated that economic differentials in mortality were particularly large for the infectious diseases, and much less for the principal degenerative diseases, heart disease and cancer. The death rates for selected specific causes of death, presented in Table XXIII, indicate

[3] *Ibid.*

that white-nonwhite differences follow the same pattern. Nonwhite death rates from tuberculosis, influenza and pneumonia are more than double those for whites, while the excess of the nonwhite rates is less for the other principal disease categories.

THE FUTURE NEGRO POPULATION

Forecasting the future is at best a tricky business, and the latest projections published by the U.S. Bureau of the Census show not one but four different estimates. According to these figures, the total population of the nation may increase from 192 million in mid-1964 to 248–276 million in 1985. If a major depression or war occurs, or some other factor produces radical changes in rates of birth, death or immigration, the actual figure in 1985 might well fall outside these limits.

The official projections do not include separate estimates for whites and Negroes. In 1960, Negroes constituted 10.6 percent of the total population. Since the rate of increase of Negro population has been greater than that of white population, it is likely that this percentage will slowly rise, to about 12 percent by 1985. The Negro population would then be about 30–33 million, as compared with 21 million in mid-1964. By extrapolation of recent trends in the distribution and composition of population, some reasonable guesses can be made about what changes to expect in where Negroes will be living and what their characteristics will be.

Changes in population distribution during past decades have already moved us beyond the position where problems of race relations can be regarded as regional, and the future will see a further spread of Negro population throughout the nation. The Negro population increase will probably accrue mainly to cities, and to cities in the North and West more than in the South. Well before 1985 a majority of the nation's Negro population may be living in Northern cities. Negroes may then comprise a majority or near-majority of the population in several large cities other than Washington, D.C., where they already outnumber whites. The Southern rural Negro population may continue to decrease in size, despite high fertility. Out-migrants from this population may be numerous, but they will be a diminishing share of all Negro migrants.

Large-scale migrations produce unusual age distributions in both the place of origin and of destination. Age distributions are further distorted by fluctuations in fertility rates. For example, many of the Negroes who moved to cities in the early 1940's were young adults in the childbearing ages. There would have been sharp increases in the number of Negro babies in these cities even without the post-war "baby boom." Barring major catastrophes, it is obvious that if more babies were born from 1946 to 1951 than from 1940 to 1945, more children will be reaching age 18 from 1964 to 1969 than from 1958 to 1963. In many cities, problems such as those of school dropouts and the provision of jobs for new entrants to the labor force are rapidly becoming more difficult, in large part because the number of people in the relevant ages is growing.

Anticipating changes in the age distribution of a population is relatively easy. Anticipating changes in socio-economic characteristics is more difficult. Educational advancement seems fairly certain to continue at a rapid pace, with high school graduation becoming increasingly common and college graduation more frequent. Just how rapidly improvements in educational background can be translated into rising occupational and income levels depends on the business cycle, actions of the Federal Government, and other quite unpredictable factors.

Social change is continuous, and with change comes a diminution in the importance of old social problems and a rise in the importance of new ones. For example, although the problems of the illiterate Negro sharecropper newly arrived in a Northern industrial city are perhaps more acute than ever, the number of such migrants is small and diminishing. In contrast, continued growth of urban Negro populations if combined with maintenance of a high degree of residential segregation can only aggravate the many problems already attributable to *de facto* segregation. How well these problems will be met we cannot predict. They can certainly be better met if the social transformations of the past fifty years are recognized, and continuing rapid changes during the coming years are anticipated.

BIBLIOGRAPHY

Bogue, Donald J., *The Population of the United States,* New York: The Press of Glencoe, 1959.

Davie, Maurice R., *Negroes in American Society,* New York: McGraw-Hill Book Co., 1949.

Frazier, E. Franklin, *The Negro in the United States,* rev. ed., New York: The Macmillan Co., 1957.

Hare, Nathaniel, "Changes in the Occupational Status of Negroes, 1930–1960: An Intracohort Analysis."

Paper read before the annual meetings of the American Sociological Association, Los Angeles, 1963.

Journal of Negro Education, XXXII, No. 4 (Fall, 1963).

Kiser, Clyde V., "Fertility Trends and Differentials Among Nonwhites in the United States," *The Milbank Memorial Fund Quarterly,* XXXVI, No. 2 (April, 1958), 149–97.

Taeuber, Conrad and Taeuber, Irene B., *The Changing Population of the United States,* New York: John Wiley & Sons, 1958.

Taeuber, Irene B., "Migration, Mobility, and The Assimilation of the Negro," Population Reference Bureau, *Population Bulletin,* XIV, No. 7 (November, 1958), 125–51.

Taeuber, Karl E., "Negro Residential Segregation: Trends and Measurement," *Social Problems,* 12, No. 1 (Summer, 1964), 42–50.

U.S. Bureau of the Census, *Historical Statistics of the United States, Colonial Times to 1957,* Washington: U.S. Government Printing Office, 1960.

———. *Negroes in the United States 1920–32,* Washington: U.S. Government Printing Office, 1935.

———. *Negro Population 1790–1915,* Washington: Government Printing Office, 1918.

U.S. Department of Labor, "A Century of Change: Negroes in the U.S. Economy, 1860–1960," *Monthly Labor Review* (December, 1962), 1359–65.

———. *The Economic Situation of Negroes in the United States,* Bulletin S–3, revised, 1962.

———. "Economic Status of Nonwhite Workers, 1955–62," *Monthly Labor Review* (July, 1963), 1–9.

chapter 3

The Negro
in American Agriculture

Calvin L. Beale

"Not one single book, monograph, or article has been found which . . . adequately orients the current status of the Negro in American agriculture." This statement seems as true today as it was in 1946 when made by the compilers of a bibliography on the Negro in the United States.[1] In the reams of material written about the American Negro in the last few years there is little concerning the Negro farmer and farm hand.

Perhaps this should not be surprising, for the dominant trend in Negro affairs since the beginning of the Second World War has been the wholesale flight of people to the cities—the big cities—and the rising concern over the problems that face them there. In the tempo of urbanization, rural life is for many *declassé,* an unpleasant reminder of the miseries of the past that have been shaken off and exchanged for the hope of the metropolis. Nor is the study of a society in decline an attractive subject for most research workers. Yet for all that the Negro rural population has dwindled and lost its place in the order of things, it still comprises nearly three-tenths of the total Negro population. Many of the problems that beset the Negro everywhere occur in their most severe, undiluted and least hopeful settings in the countryside, and to the extent that rural areas continue to be a seedbed for the cities, the problems of the rural minority continue to be the problems of all.

Former Concentration of Negroes in Agriculture

Agriculture was the basic purpose of the importation of Negroes into the American colonies as slaves. Some were used as domestic servants and to a limited extent others were employed in industry in the South. But only in agriculture did their large-scale use develop. Free Negroes who moved North often settled in the cities, but their numbers were few compared with the farm workers still held as slaves.

[1] Paul B. Foreman and Mozell C. Hill, *The Negro in the United States: A Bibliography,* Bulletin of the Oklahoma A & M College, 44, No. 5 (February, 1947), 4.

Emancipation did not radically alter the dependence on agriculture. Comparatively few Negroes moved to the North, except from the border states, and these did not usually find themselves welcome. In the South, there was some initial rush to the towns, but urban work was scarce and cotton was still king.

An entirely new system of relations had to be worked out between the freed Negroes and their former owners. With rather rare exceptions, the freedmen were not provided land by the Federal Government and the land ownership of the planters was not broken. At first, efforts were made to hire the former slaves for wages. The result was not very successful. Cash was scarce for the average planter, the freedom-sensitive Negroes did not respond well to the demands of gang work any longer, and hiring made for an unreliable supply of workers. Soon a predominant system of renting developed in which a family was assigned to work a particular piece of land and receive a share of the crop as wages. This proved to be a more stable arrangement for all and guaranteed that a family would remain until the crop was in.

To finance this arrangement, a system of credit was created in which the tenants were "furnished" with supplies on which to live during the year by a merchant or by the planter (who was himself usually operating on credit). As security for the credit, the tenant mortgaged his share of the crop he was making and repaid his debts after the harvest.

In the absence of land reform and a program of Federal intervention, the system was probably the most practical available for getting the agriculture of the South on its feet again. But it provided many opportunities for abuse. The rates of interest charged the tenants were usually very high and the goods they received were often overpriced. Most of the Negroes were illiterate, and they were unable to detect sharp practices. At the end of a season they were essentially lucky if any cash were left after the bills were paid. Some of the most diligent and fortunate earned enough to buy a small farm of their own or to obtain tools and work animals and rent a farm for cash. For the majority, the share-tenant system seemed to encourage improvidence. The once-a-year payday led to unrealistic debts during the year and to quick dissipation of earnings in the fall. Share tenancy was not limited to Negroes. In the course of time, many small white farmers entered into similar arrangements. Their lot was not enviable either, but they were somewhat less likely to be victimized by the system.

In the same period when tenancy was becoming the prevailing way of life, the seeds of agricultural education for Negroes were first sown. There was much to do. Although many Negroes aspired for knowledge, it was professional training and classical subjects that attracted many. After years of servitude in the cotton fields, there was little incentive or felt need to learn to farm.

The beginning in the training of agricultural leaders came with the opening of Hampton Normal and Agricultural Institute at Hampton, Virginia, in 1868, under the auspices of the American Missionary Society.

A decade later Hampton had trained Booker T. Washington, whose ideas dominated Negro agricultural thinking for at least two generations thereafter. Washington established Tuskegee Institute in Alabama in 1881. Here in the years that followed he saw the need for demonstration work in the field, for scientific research at the Institute and for the organization of farmers. Tuskegee hired the man who was to become the foremost Negro scientist, George Washington Carver, in 1896, and sponsored the first Negro demonstration specialist, T.M. Campbell, in 1906. In the 1890's the Tuskegee Farmers Conference was created. This annual event had a South-wide influence in the shaping of programs and thought for Negro farm families, and similar conferences were developed by other states. Unfortunately it never became what perhaps was Washington's ultimate aim, an organized, economically effective organization of Negro farmers, and in time it lost its vitality.

The beginning of change

Twenty-five years after the Civil War, the census of 1890 showed that over 60 percent of all employed Negroes were farmers or farm laborers. In the south the figure was about 65 percent.

During the late nineteenth and early twentieth centuries, the position of the Negro in farming was not static, although the rapidity of chance in later years may make it appear so. A considerable westward movement took place as new lands were drained in the Mississippi Valley or cleared farther west. In certain older areas, the role of Negroes in farming declined, as final ruin came to rice farming along the South Atlantic States or as most Negro farmers gave up agriculture in the border ex-slave states, such as Kentucky and Missouri. By and large, however, the increase in farmers in growing areas offset the losses elsewhere.

With the opening of the First World War, Negroes had a golden opportunity to enter industrial work in the North, first as foreign immigration was cut off and then as many white workers went into military service. This period is discussed elsewhere,* but suffice it to say that thousands of farm people moved out despite opposition from landlords and creditors.

* See "The Negro Population in the United States" by Karl E. and Alma F. Taeuber in the preceding chapter.

The lines of family communication with the North were soon established for the millions who have since followed.

In the same era, the menace of the boll weevil was reaching its climax. This beetle, which lays its eggs in cotton bolls and whose larvae consume the cotton, had entered southern Texas from Mexico in the 1890's. It gradually penetrated northeastward into the areas heavily settled by Negro farmers, and by 1921 had spread over the entire Cotton Belt. For a few years the boll weevil caused great panic as millions of acres of cotton were heavily damaged and production fell. Some of the sections most susceptible to damage were those with heavy slow-warming soils, such as in the Black Belt of Alabama, where the majority of farmers were Negroes. In these sections, cotton never regained its prominence, and thousands of Negroes emigrated as the landlords turned to livestock and dairying.

In the rolling Piedmont country of Georgia and South Carolina, severe erosion and soil depletion added to the problem and impelled other thousands to leave or look for industrial work. Thus, in general, the time between World War I and the depression was a time of troubles and receding activity in farming for Negroes in the old Cotton Belt. In less severely affected areas, means of limiting the damage by weevils were devised after a few years, and cotton expanded northward into safer areas. But the old pattern of Negro farming was never the same. Particularly affected were Negro owners, a number of whom lost their land or gave up farming. The developing opportunities in the fertile Delta country were mostly for tenants. Hundreds flocked in to work the large plantations on shares.

The Depression and the New Deal

It is difficult to say whether the great economic depression of the 1930's affected Negro farmers any worse than white farmers. It was nightmarish enough for both. With his already precarious financial position and limited possessions, perhaps the typical Negro had less room to fall.

The bottom dropped out of the cotton market. In many states the number of Negro farmers declined and the number of white tenants rose rapidly. In 1934 and later years the coming of the New Deal introduced an entirely new level of Federal Government activity in agriculture. In addition to widespread relief and welfare measures, the Government developed programs to provide cheap credit for farmers and to help them become land owners. Plantations heavily in debt were acquired by the Government, then subdivided and sold in family-farm sizes to former tenants. Writing of a Black Belt county in Alabama, Morton Rubin has said, "The number of Negroes who have become operators [owners] without the help of the federal government and its agencies is a small proportion of the total." [2]

At this time, too, the idea of farmers agreeing by majority vote to institute programs such as limitations of crop acreage in return for certain Federal price and other benefits was put into practice. It can be argued that these programs often worked to the ultimate disadvantage of the small farmer who found himself restricted to a very small allotment of acreage. But for many Negro farmers such programs offered an opportunity to do something that they had never been able to do before—vote.

WORLD WAR II TO THE PRESENT

Mechanization of Cotton

In the years just before Pearl Harbor the future character of cotton farming in the United States became discernible. In the northern part of the Mississippi Delta country instances occurred of scores of tenant people being "tractored off" the cotton plantations. Mules were replaced by tractors and families were displaced, to camp along the roadside until publicity and aroused public opinion induced some efforts to help them. But the tractor alone did not permit fully mechanized methods of cotton production. Indeed, in many respects the availability of tractor power created a frustrating situation for both landlord and tenant. The tractor was clearly preferable to the mule in preparation of land and planting. But no way had been found to mechanize the hand "chopping" operation (thinning and weeding) or the picking of cotton. Thus the planter continued to need large amounts of hand labor at certain times of the year but was not able to provide regular work for such laborers throughout the crop season.

In the same period the mechanical cotton picker was being developed and it was obviously only a matter of time before it would be perfected. The coming of the war rather effectively delayed the practical introduction of the picker, although in the drier cotton areas of Oklahoma and West Texas, where relatively few Negro farmers lived, efforts were made to harvest cotton during the war without hand picking.

After the war the mechanical harvesters began slowly but surely to replace hand picking and snapping, beginning first on the drier, flatter and larger

[2] Morton Rubin, *Plantation County* (Chapel Hill: University of North Carolina Press, 1951), p. 64.

farmlands in the western part of the Cotton Belt and working their way eastward as they were perfected. The machines can do the work of many hands, but they are rather expensive and require the creation of larger but fewer farms and fields to make their use economical. Thus they typically add one more competitive burden to the small-scale farm owner.

In the 1950's the final technical hurdle to complete elimination of hand field labor became possible through several developments in planting and weed control, especially the use of chemical and oil herbicides applied mechanically both before and after the cotton plants emerged from the ground. These methods are not perfect under all conditions, but under conditions of very heavy weed infestation they are even cheaper than laborers paid less than fifty cents an hour.

As a result of the triple triumph of tractors, pickers and weed control, thousands of tenants—the majority of them Negroes—have been released who could not have been spared until all aspects of cotton cultivation were mechanized or chemicalized. Mechanical picking has advanced into the southeastern states, where much of the acreage once grown in the rolling Piedmont sections has been transferred with Government permission into the level Coastal Plain where more suitable field conditions can be created. The following table shows the progress of mechanical harvesting. From 8 percent of the crop in 1950, the proportion picked or snapped by machine rose to 32 percent in 1957 and 70 per cent in 1962 (see Table I). Further gains are continuing.

TABLE I—Percentage of cotton harvested by machine and by hand

Area	1962	1957	1950
United States			
Machine	70	32	8
Hand	30	68	92
California			
Machine	94	70	34
Hand	6	30	66
Texas and Oklahoma			
Machine	78	38	11
Hand	22	62	89
South, except Texas and Oklahoma			
Machine	55	11	1
Hand	45	89	99

SOURCE: Economic Research Service and Agricultural Marketing Service, U.S. Department of Agriculture.

Another trend of equal importance for the Negro cotton farmer in the last generation has been the growth of cotton cultivation under irrigated conditions in the West. Until after World War I comparatively little cotton was grown in areas where there were few Negro farmers. However, it was found that with irrigation, bumper yields of cotton could be had in the High Plains of Texas, and in parts of California, Arizona and New Mexico. These Western farms did not inherit the Southern tenant system and often were developed by people with capital and zeal to operate under conditions of high labor productivity. The dry climate also gave certain advantages in harvesting. The Western cotton areas produced cotton at a lower price per bale than all but the most productive sections of the old Cotton Belt. Especially since World War II, the competition produced by the Western areas—in which few Negroes work except as hired hands—has helped to force many small independent Southern farms out of cotton and has hastened the tenant-displacing changes made by the plantations. The proportion of all cotton raised in Arizona, California and New Mexico and West Texas rose from 2 percent in 1919 to 34 percent in 1959.

The changes in methods and location of cotton cultivation, combined with the poverty of most Negro farmers, worked both to push Negroes out of farming and to make the attractions of city life irresistible. As a result the 482,000 nonwhite farmers growing cotton in the South in 1945 plummetted to 181,000 in 1959, a decline of 63 percent in slightly less than fifteen years. As noted in the discussion of the Negro as a hired farm worker, some of this loss was converted into an increase in hired hands, but most of it was not. The change was particularly acute in the Mississippi Delta lands where the large plantations were concentrated. Although the decline was greatest for tenants, it also affected the Negro owners.

Adding to the problem has been the steady erosion of the market for cotton, caused by competition from other fibers and increased production abroad. Marketing problems coupled with increased yields per acre have caused farmers to vote every year since 1954 to restrict the acreage planted. When a cut in acreage allotments occurred, as in 1955 and 1956, it was the Negro farmer with his predominantly tenant position who was most likely to find himself forced out altogether because there was simply not enough acreage to support as many tenants per landlord as before.

Diversification

As the cotton acreage in the South has declined since the mid-1920's, some of the land has been put to other agricultural uses and some has been taken out of farming altogether. Naturally the least productive and suitable lands have been the most likely to go out of cultivation. Many hundreds of thousands of acres of rolling land in the Piedmont country from North Carolina to Alabama have been put into timber. Vast acreages here and elsewhere have been turned into pastures or used to grow feed crops for cattle. Even in the fertile Delta sections a diversification into soybeans, grain and cattle has occurred.

The theme of diversification has been preached to Negro farmers just as it has been to white farmers. But the forms of agriculture resulting from diversification typically do not use a system of tenant operation and usually require more land than the average Negro owner-operator has or can obtain. In addition, in areas of the South where he has historically been concentrated in a few traditional field crops—cotton, tobacco, peanuts—the Negro farmer often finds himself unwelcome in other enterprises which might have been rather exclusively the white man's province. Such pressures vary widely from area to area and may range from completely prohibitive to nonexistent. But in many cases they are all too real. For example, the only feasible way to market some specialty crops may be through cooperatives and the Negro may find that the co-op will not handle his crops. In other instances the Negro farmer may be unable to obtain credit for any but his traditional enterprises, in some cases through nothing more malicious than a lack of confidence by lenders that he can succeed in other enterprises.[3]

The greatest single source of diversification for Southern farmers has been cattle raising. Since 1945 the number of Negro owner-operators who raise cattle for sale has been stable, despite the general decline in the total number of Negro-owned farms. But the average number of cattle and calves sold by Negro owners was only four animals per farm in 1959, representing the merest increase from three per farm in 1945. Thus, although there has been some gain in cattle raising, it has not been of a generally significant nature. Furthermore, in 1959 the average value of cattle sold by Negro farmers was less than a hundred dollars per animal. Either because of a higher proportion of calves or lower quality of animals, this was one-fifth below the average for white farmers.

In crop production, an easy means of diversification has been to grow soybeans. The crop has had several advantages. It can be produced in many states under a wide range of conditions. The market for the beans in oleo-

[3] For an example of the expression of such an attitude, see J. Sullivan Gibson, "Alabama Black Belt: Its Geographic Status." *Economic Geography*, January 1941. Gibson declares, "The negro (sic) farmer of this section, by nature and experience, is a cotton grower." "Lacking good judgment, a sense of thrift, and a feeling of responsibility, the average Black Belt negro is decidedly incompetent as a stock farmer" (pp. 21 and 22).

margarine, cooking oils and other uses has expanded rapidly, and the price has remained good. Furthermore, there are no restrictions on the acreage that a farmer may plant.

With these incentives the number of farmers growing the crop has increased in the South as elsewhere. Generally, soybeans are well adapted to those sections of the South where Negro farmers are located—in the Coastal Plain and the Mississippi Delta. Many Negro farmers grow soybeans as a supplement to their other crops, although the full number is not known.

The Increased Importance of Tobacco

During and after the First World War a trend developed in the habits of Western civilization that unquestionably intensified and prolonged the role of Negroes in American agriculture. This was the rise of cigarette smoking. Cigarettes were not new, but for whatever reasons—urbanization, the growing number of women smokers, a rise in personal income or the invention of cigarette-making machinery—the consumption of cigarettes soared. Much of the tobacco used was grown only in the South. The result was a steady expansion of tobacco farming throughout the Coastal Plain from North Carolina to northern Florida—predominantly in sections where many Negro farmers were already present.

The Negro farmer was well-suited to tobacco, which was grown strictly by hand and animal labor, making good use of the plentiful labor of large families. And tobacco was well-suited to the Negro farm owner, for it did not require much land. Between 1910 and 1945 the number of nonwhite Southern farmers who grew tobacco—both owners and tenants—rose from 42,000 to 91,000, in a period when the net change in cotton farmers was down. The increase in economic importance of tobacco was much greater than the mere change in number of farmers raising it. In 1910 hundreds of farmers in the Deep South were raising only small patches for home use, whereas almost all of the farms in the latter period were producing for sale.

The growth of the cigarette tobacco industry continued with little slackening until the middle 1950's. At that time, bumper yields, new methods of using less tobacco per cigarette, and a near halt in the growth of per capita consumption produced conditions that led to severe cutbacks in acreage allotments per farmer. A decline in number of farms raising tobacco has now set in, but not nearly so rapidly as with cotton. Thus tobacco has continued to increase in its relative importance to the Negro farmer.

The proportion of all Southern nonwhite farmers who grew any tobacco was less than 5 percent in 1910, but 14 percent in 1945 and 24 percent in 1959. In relation to cotton there was just one Negro farmer growing tobacco in 1910 for every sixteen growing cotton. Today there are fewer than three Negro farmers producing cotton for every one growing tobacco.

In general, the Negro-operated farms growing tobacco (1) have been somewhat more likely to produce on a commercial scale than farms producing cotton; (2) have tended to yield a higher value of products sold; and (3) are somewhat more likely to be operated by owners than the cotton farms. Negroes have achieved a more important role in cigarette tobacco production than in any other commodity. They grow one-sixth of all cigarette tobacco, compared with one-tenth of cotton (1959). Of the principal cigarette type—flue-cured tobacco—Negro farmers account for one-fourth of the crop.

The greater persistence of tobacco than cotton is shifting the principal centers of Negro farming away from the Deep South over toward the Atlantic Coastal Plain. North Carolina, the leading tobacco state, is now second only to Mississippi in number of Negro farmers, and the total value of its Negro-operated farms—both owner and tenant—exceeds all other states.

THE POSITION OF NEGRO FARMERS TODAY

Number of Farms

At their peak in 1920, Negro farm operators numbered 926,000 (Table II) and comprised one-seventh of all farmers in the Nation. This number includes all tenant farmers, even though many of them exercised little or no managerial functions and were essentially laborers paid with share of the crop. As a result of all the influences that have combined to lower the number of farms, only 273,000 Negro farmers were counted in the 1959 Census of Agriculture, a drop of 70 percent since 1920 and of 50 percent in less than ten years since 1950. In 1964, the number was not more than 180,000.

Currently (1965) about 3 percent of all employed Negro men work solely or primarily as farm operators. The comparable percentage for white men is 5 percent. An additional number of both races do some farming but spend most of their time at other jobs. About 8 percent of Negro men work as farm laborers. Thus direct work in agriculture is the sole or primary employment of about 11 percent, or one-ninth of the employed Negro male labor force. Including women, about 9 percent of all Negro workers are principally in agriculture compared with 6 percent of white workers.

Location of Farms

The great majority of Negro farmers are located in a huge sickle-shaped stretch of land that begins on the northeast in southern Maryland, sweeping southward through Virginia, the Carolinas and Georgia east of the Blue Ridge Mountains (Figures 1 and 2). The area curves through Georgia below the southern end of the mountains, across central Alabama, and in a northwestward direction through Mississippi, with the end in western Tennessee and eastern Arkansas. A handle can be thought of as extending across northern Louisiana, curving down into eastern Texas. There are very few Negro farmers in the mountain and plateau parts of the South, in the Florida peninsula or in the plains portions of Texas.

TABLE II—Negro farm operators in the United States, 1900–1959

Area	1959	1950	1940	1930	1920	1900
United States	272,541	559,980	681,790	882,850	925,708	746,715
Northeast	596	1,002	1,432	1,021	1,469	1,761
North Central	4,259	6,700	7,466	10,083	7,911	12,255
South	267,008	551,469	672,214	870,936	915,595	732,362
West	678	809	678	812	735	337
Selected States						
Missouri	1,684	3,214	3,686	5,844	2,824	4,950
Maryland	2,132	3,595	4,049	5,264	6,208	5,842
Virginia	15,629	28,527	35,062	39,598	47,690	44,795
North Carolina	41,023	69,029	57,428	74,636	74,849	53,996
South Carolina	30,953	61,255	61,204	77,331	109,005	85,381
Georgia	20,163	50,352	59,127	86,787	130,176	82,822
Florida	3,664	7,473	9,731	11,010	12,954	13,521
Kentucky	3,327	4,882	5,546	9,104	12,624	11,227
Tennessee	15,018	24,044	27,972	35,123	38,181	33,883
Alabama	29,206	57,205	73,338	93,795	95,200	94,069
Mississippi	55,174	122,709	159,256	182,578	161,001	128,351
Arkansas	14,654	40,810	57,011	79,556	72,275	46,978
Louisiana	17,686	40,599	59,556	73,734	62,036	58,096
Oklahoma	2,633	5,910	8,987	15,172	13,403	6,353
Texas	15,432	34,389	52,648	85,940	78,597	65,472

SOURCE: 1959 Census of Agriculture, Volume II.

The densest concentrations are in the tobacco and cotton country of eastern North and South Carolina, and in the Cotton Belt for a distance roughly fifty miles north and seventy-five miles south of Memphis, Tennessee. In these areas, together with central Alabama, there are eighty-seven counties in which Negro farmers are still in the majority. Mississippi has had more Negro farmers than any other throughout this century—one-fifth of the national total in 1959. However, as a result of the rapid loss of cotton tenants now taking place in Mississippi, this distinction will probably go to North Carolina in the future.

Negro Farmers Outside the South

Little more than one percent of all Negro farmers live outside of the states where slavery existed at the time of the Civil War. It is the remarkable concentration in one region of the nation—the South—that so distinguishes the Negro's role in farming from his participation in other industries and that has such great influence on his prospects in farming.

In the post-revolutionary period of our history there was a scattering of Negro farmers in the Hudson Valley, in New Jersey and in southeastern Pennsylvania. These settlements were relics of the use of Negroes as slaves once attempted in the North or of the attraction of Negroes to Quaker communities, which usually had an active interest in the welfare of former slaves.

As the land north of the Ohio River was settled, where slavery was forbidden, some free Negroes and escaped slaves gradually moved in. Many were persons of mixed ancestry, some so much so that they formed distinct communities aloof from the general Negro population. A majority of the Negro settlers went to the hilly wooded country of southern Ohio and Indiana where farming was largely of a small-scale nature. Others, however, obtained better lands in the Corn Belt parts of these states and of southern Michigan and engaged in a more commercial type of agriculture.

Often the free Negro farmer was resented, and repressive laws were passed in some states that forbade any more to enter the state. The Civil War brought a number of refugees north, but after the war the Negro rural settlements began to decline despite ownership of land and an improved social climate. The farms were usually small, the land was often of below average quality and developing opportunities in the cities drained off the younger people.

West of the Mississippi, Negroes took very little part in the great homesteading movement after the Civil War. The one notable exception was in Kansas, where a number of communities of Negro farmers were founded

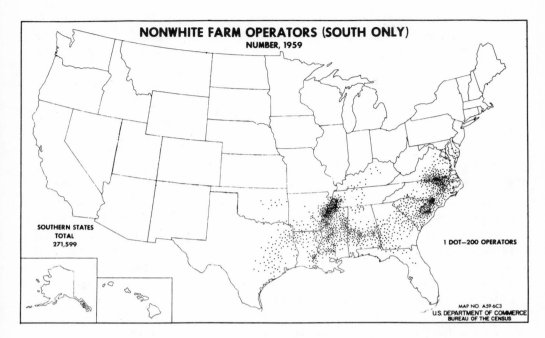

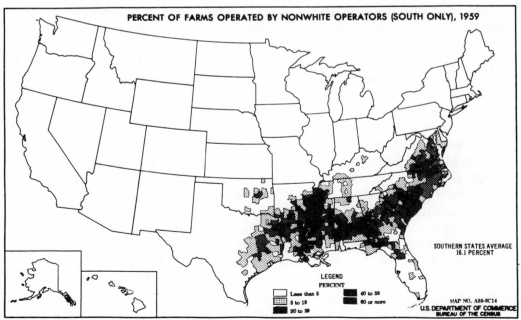

in the so-called exoduster movement. But here again, almost no sooner had the settlements been founded than they began to decline. People accustomed to cotton farming with almost no managerial experience or capital found it very difficult to succeed as independent farmers in the plains.

In 1900, the North and West had 9,400 Negro-operated farms, with more than 1,000 each in Ohio, Indiana, Illinois and Kansas. By 1959, there were only 3,850 left. When the millions of rural Negroes who left the South in the twentieth century went North, they avoided like the plague the farm work they had been used to back home.

Today the largest number of Negro farmers in the North and West is in Michigan. The largest settlement is in Cass and Berrien Counties, Michigan, not far from South Bend, Indiana. This is perhaps the most persistent of the Northern areas developed by free Negroes in the generation before the Civil War. After a period of some decline as a commercial farming area, it has begun to grow again as a part-time farming and residential area. South of Chicago near Kankakee, Illinois, is another much more recent rural settlement. It consists largely of middle-aged and older families who combine a rural residence with off-farm sources of income.

In California, some Negroes worked in farming as hired hands many years ago. During the 1930's and early 1940's their number was greatly swelled by migrants fleeing the depression or, later, seeking defense work. A few have gone into agriculture on their own, so that by 1959 California with 443 farms operated by Negroes had become the third largest site of Negro farmers outside the South (after Michigan and Ohio). The farm families are somewhat scattered in California and no longer increasing, but the Negro farm community achieved a distinction recently when one of its young men was elected to head the state chapter of the Future Farmers of America.

The history of Negro farm communities outside of the South is often of great interest. But with few exceptions these communities have been disintegrating in modern times. The people who have grown up in them have usually assimilated well the characteristics and aspirations of the local culture. But they are not staying in agriculture. Their stable Northern background and higher than average education have made it easier for them to succeed in the cities than for their Southern cousins, and it is to the cities that they are going. If those born to the land in the North and West seldom wish to make their future in farming, the reluctance of the Southern Negro to attempt to enter agriculture outside the South is understandable.

Tenure of Farming

In the twentieth century, the traditional image of the Negro farmer has been that of the sharecropper. It is not surprising that this has been so, for from about World War I until 1950, half or more of all Negro farmers were landless tenants working for a share of the crops they produced. Others rented for cash, but until the end of World War II not more than one-fourth of Negro farmers owned their property (mortgaged or unmortgaged). Many white farmers were tenants also, but not in the same proportions as the Negroes. Even during the worst years of the 1930's, more than half of the Southern white farmers were owners. This difference has had a far-reaching effect on the ability of Negroes to survive and prosper in agriculture. Lacking land, the tenant has no defense against mechanization and may find himself displaced if the landlord decides to operate with more machinery and fewer men. He is usually the loser, too, when crop allotments are cut and there is less acreage to be divided among the tenants.

The number and proportion of Negro tenants has been greatly reduced in the last twenty years because of these and other reasons. Relatively few of them have become owners. From 1945 to 1959, a 70 percent loss of Negro tenants took place. Owners declined by 33 percent—a heavy loss in itself, but much less than that of tenants.

The most viable and progressive element among farmers in the post World War II period has been the part owners. These are men who own some land and rent additional land. The system has the advantage of enabling a man to expand his operations without tying up additional money in land. Instead, he may use his capital for machinery and then rent enough extra land to keep himself and his machines fully and profitably employed. Although the traditional view of the hierarchy of farmers has had the full owner at the top, the part owners as a class have larger operations and earn more money. Negro part owners were increasing in number as late as 1950, but have declined somewhat since then. Their relative importance has continued to grow, however, and they now account for a seventh of all Negro farmers.

Negro owners (full and part) numbered 127,000 and operated 8.7 million acres of land in 1959 (Table III). That is a little more than 13,000 square miles, an area about the size of Connecticut, Massachusetts and Rhode Island.

There are some counties (twenty in 1959) in which Negro farm owners outnumber white owners. About two-thirds of these counties are concentrated in the Black Belt of Alabama and the Coastal Plain of South Carolina.

In no case, however, do Negro farmers own the majority of the farmland in a county. The maximum relative land ownership occurs in Jefferson Davis County in southern Mississippi, where Negro owners operate 26 percent of all farmland.

Type of Farming

The peculiar concentration of Negro farmers in a few kinds of activities can be easily seen from census figures on the types of commercial farms (Table IV). In the fall of 1959, 56 percent of the commercial-size farms run by nonwhite farmers in the South were cotton farms (meaning that over half of their gross income came from the sale of cotton). Considering that Negroes were historically concentrated in the Cotton Belt, this per-

TABLE III—Number, Acreage and Value of Farms Operated by Nonwhites in the South 1959, 1950 and 1920

Tenor of operator	Number of farms			Land in farms (Thou. acres)		
	1959	1950	1920	1959	1950	1920
Total	265,621	559,090	922,914	13,901	26,275	41,318
Full owners	89,749	141,482	178,558	5,577	8,391	11,950
Part owners	37,534	51,864	39,031	3,104	3,723	2,126
Managers	290	239	1,770	351	347	368
All tenants	138,048	365,505	703,555	4,869	13,815	26,874
Cash	14,855	39,562	100,275	784	2,097	4,011
Share cash	2,406	5,656	8,207	144	271	272
Crop share	31,714	95,461 }	176,711	1,410	4,424 }	7,815
Livestock share	946	1,736 }		73	136 }	
Croppers	73,387	198,057	333,713	1,880	5,540	10,141
Others and unknown	14,740	25,033	84,649	576	1,346	4,636

Average acres per farm			Average value of farms ($)		
1959	1950	1920	1959	1950	1920
52.3	47.0	44.8	6,240	2,792	2,414
62.1	59.3	66.9	6,255	3,062	2,561
82.7	71.8	54.5	9,436	4,165	2,421
1211.0	1451.1	207.9	107,072	43,661	12,166
35.3	37.8	38.2	5,284	2,464	2,352
52.8	53.0	40.0	4,299	2,021	2,016
60.0	47.9	33.1	8,297	3,532	3,668
44.5	46.3 }	44.2	6,880	2,906 }	2,765
77.1	78.5 }		11,587	4,908 }	
25.6	28.0	30.4	4,809	2,311	2,190
39.1	53.8	54.8	4,166	2,266	2,397

SOURCE: 1959 Census of Agriculture, Volume II.

TABLE IV—Type of Commercial Farm by Value of Products sold in 1959, for Nonwhite-Operated Farms in the South

Type of farm	Total commercial	Value of products sold, 1959					
		$40,000 and over	$20,000 – $40,000	$10,000 – $20,000	$5,000 – $10,000	$2,500 – $5,000	Under $2,500
All types	154,298	197	520	2,663	20,230	51,862	78,826
Cash grain*	2,286	17	47	96	228	487	1,360
Tobacco*	40,670	—	80	891	9,831	17,942	11,921
Cotton*	87,074	66	193	839	6,828	26,839	52,139
Other field crops*	4,867	5	20	215	736	1,405	2,201
Poultry	448	52	36	85	80	80	115
Dairy	1,131	1	15	65	145	310	595
Livestock	6,618	9	36	72	319	970	5,222
General	9,596	11	48	339	1,868	3,498	3,832
Vegetable, fruit, nut and miscellaneous**	1,608	36	45	61	195	331	1,441

* Value of products sold not known for some farms.
** Distribution includes value of products sold for 501 grain, tobacco, cotton and other field crop farms.

SOURCE: 1959 Census of Agriculture, Volume I.

centage might not seem particularly high were it not for the much lower emphasis on cotton by Southern white farmers. The heavier Negro reliance on cotton was true throughout the South. In its most extreme form in Arkansas, 94 percent of all nonwhite commercial farmers were cotton specialists in 1959.

After cotton, tobacco culture is by far the most common type of farming for Negroes, being the principal product of 26 percent of nonwhite Southern commercial enterprises. Tobacco is especially important in North Carolina, where more than half of the nonwhite tobacco specialists operate.

The third most common commercial type for Negroes (6 percent of the total) is the general farm, on which no one product accounts for half of the total sales. Such a type sounds like the acme of stability and diversification—and often is larger than the cotton or tobacco specialty farms. In many cases, however, it simply represents farms on which small amounts of the traditional crops—cotton and tobacco—are of about equal importance or on which one or the other is supplemented with peanuts. A group which in the official statistics is called "other field crop" farms accounts for an additional 3 percent of the commercial farms and consists principally of peanut specialty farms in North Carolina and Georgia.

The four types cited—cotton, tobacco, general and other field crops—amount to 92 percent of all Southern nonwhite farms operated at the commercial level, as compared with 49 percent for Southern white farmers. The major significance of this fact is that the crops involved are allotted crops for which the acreage is restricted by law, that more often than not they are in surplus supply, and they are either stationary or contracting in acreage.

In contrast the nonwhite farmer has only minor representation in the sectors of agriculture that have been expanding in the South, such as livestock, dairy or poultry farming and truck crops. Throughout the South the agricultural colleges and other shapers of farming trends have long been preaching the theme of a "green revolution" to Southern farmers— that is, a conversion of lands to hay crops and improved pastures and the raising of more livestock. This movement clearly came of age in the 1950's, for the 1959 census revealed that the South as a region for the first time had more livestock farms than cotton farms. But for the Negro farmer it is almost as though such a change had never occurred. Only 4 percent of the nonwhite Southern farmers were livestock specialists (cattle, hogs, and sheep), and only an additional one percent were dairymen or poultrymen.

Nothing more sharply distinguishes white from nonwhite farmers in the South than the different degree of reliance on livestock. Ninety percent of the total value of products sold by nonwhite farmers in 1959 consisted of crops and only 10 percent of livestock and livestock products. On Southern white-operated farms, 52 percent of the total product value was from crops and 48 percent from livestock—almost an even balance.

Size of Farms

Perhaps the most widespread trend in American agriculture since the end of the depression has been the increase in the physical size of farms— in the number of acres of land per farm. The acreage needed to farm successfully differs widely from one part of the country to another— depending on the climate and the quality of land—and from one type of farming to another. In general, the greater the amount of labor per acre required to produce a commodity, the smaller the average amount of land in a family farm will be or need be. And the labor used per acre is roughly proportional to the money yielded. For example, tobacco requires heavy inputs of labor per acre and the average amount of land planted in tobacco per farm is small—only about three acres per farm in the South. However, the value of the crop may be more than a thousand dollars per acre. With cotton or peanuts typical production per acre might be one to two hundred dollars, depending on the region. But, with soybeans the best areas of the South would yield less than sixty dollars per acre on the average. Thus, the need for land varies with the crop. In livestock production, the acreage needed for pasture and to raise feeds is usually much larger for each dollar of product yielded than is true for cash crop farming.

The farms operated by Negroes have historically been small. With their limited capital, Negroes were lucky to acquire land at all, let alone buy a large place. If they were tenants, the usual rental included only as much cotton land as a family could work by hand and mule, plus a few acres to grow corn for the mule.

In 1935, at the time the modern trend toward larger farms was beginning, the average size of a Negro-operated farm in the South was 44 acres; white farmers averaged 131 acres. As the ability and necessity to have larger units grew, the size of white farms grew. This was not a result just of landlords displacing tenants and operating their land in fewer units without an overall increase in land holdings. All classes of white-operated farms became steadily larger, including tenant farms, and by 1959 the white average had nearly doubled, rising to 249 acres.

Among Negro farmers little of this trend is evident. Although hundreds of thousands of small tenant units have disappeared, the average size of all farms has gone up to only fifty-two acres, an increase of just eight acres since 1935. Nonwhite full owners average sixty-two acres and part owners eighty-three (Table III).

The limited size of land resources has been one of the factors retarding the ability or willingness of Negro farmers to diversify into more extensive types of farming such as grain and livestock. Typically the pasture land alone on a white livestock farm is larger than the entire acreage of a Negro-operated farm.

Economic Scale of Farming

Farms vary widely in the amount of business they do and it is necessary to consider this factor in judging the position of a group of farmers. The best available way to rank them is by the value of products sold from the farm. The Bureau of the Census classes as "commercial" farms those selling over $2,500 worth of products in a year, plus those selling a lower amount whose operators are not elderly and have little off-farm work. Under these rules 154,298 farms in the South operated by nonwhite farmers were termed commercial in 1959, amounting to about three-fifths of all nonwhite-operated farms. Of the others, 67,065 were classed as part-time, 43,973 as part-retirement farms whose operators were sixty-five years old or over (Table V).

The Department of Agriculture figures as a rule of thumb that a farmer must sell at least $10,000 of products annually if he expects to make a minimum net income of $2,500, and that he needs $2,500 of net income to maintain a minimum decent level of living. The gross sales needed for a net of $2,500 vary from one type of farming to another. For example, dairy and poultry farms typically have a high volume of sales and a low profit margin, whereas crop farms that are not turning over their capital as often usually have a higher profit margin. Because profit margins in agriculture have narrowed in recent years, the value of sales needed to return a given net income has risen steadily and will probably continue to do so. If $10,000 of sales is accepted as the minimum adequate scale of farming, then only 1.3 percent of all nonwhite farms in the South were of adequate size in 1959 (see Table V). By contrast, 14.1 of Southern white farmers had adequate sized units. If because of their concentration in annual cash crops it is suggested that nonwhite farmers might get by if they sell a minimum of $5,000, the proportion with adequate sized units is still only 9.0 percent,

TABLE V—Economic Class of Nonwhite-Operated Farms in the South, by Tenure, 1959

Economic class*	Number of farms				Percentage distribution			
	Total**	Full owners	Part owners	All tenants	Total	Full owners	Part owners	All tenants
TOTAL	265,336	89,754	37,534	138,048	100.0	100.0	100.0	100.
Commercial	154,298	28,556	22,446	103,296	58.2	31.8	59.8	74.8
$40,000 plus	197	50	105	42	.1	.1	.3	.
$20,000–$40,000	520	109	197	214	.2	.1	.5	.
$10,000–$20,000	2,663	294	921	1,448	1.0	.3	2.5	1.
$ 2,500–$ 5,000	20,230	1,672	3,458	15,100	7.6	1.9	9.2	10.
$ 5,000–$10,000	51,862	6,350	7,284	38,228	19.5	7.1	19.4	27.
Under $2,500	78,826	20,081	10,481	48,264	29.7	22.4	27.9	35.
Noncommercial	111,038	61,198	15,088	34,752	41.8	68.2	40.2	25.
Part time †	67,065	32,475	10,091	24,499	25.3	36.2	26.9	17.
Part retirement	43,973	28,723	4,997	10,253	16.6	32.0	13.3	7.

* Dollar values refer to value of farm products sold from the farm in 1959. Part-time farms are those selling less than $2,500 of products a year whose operators are under age 65 and depend heavily on off-farm jobs or income. Part-retirement farms are those selling less than $2,500 of products a year whose operators are 65 years old or over.
** Total excludes 290 managers.
† Includes 1,000 noncommercial farmers of unknown age.

SOURCE: 1959 Census of Agriculture, Volume I.

compared with 26.6 for white farmers. Since a majority of nonwhite farmers are still tenant farmers, it must be remembered that the landlord's share of the crop has to come out of the value sold.

The number of nonwhite farmers in the South who sold $10,000 or more of products in 1959 was 3,380. An additional 20,230 sold between $5,000 and $10,000 worth. At the lower extreme there were 130,688 commercial farmers whose gross receipts were less than $5,000. These figures indicate

TABLE VI—Selected Characteristics of Southern Farms and Farmers, 1959

Characteristic	Nonwhite operators								White operators	
	Grand Total	Commercial			Tenants			Noncommercial	Grand Total	Commercial Totals
		Total	Full owners	Part owners	Cash	Crop share	Croppers			
Average farm size (acres)	52	56	82	104	64	47	27	47	249	382
Value of farm ($)	6,240	7,328	8,382	11,667	5,412	7,798	5,295	4,778	25,370	37,816
Value per acre ($)	122	134	107	115	85	166	192	104	111	107
Cropland harvested (acres)	20	26	23	41	28	28	21	10	51	85
Pasture, excl. woods (acres)	9	8	15	18	11	4	1	11	116	187
Have tractor (%)	22	26	37	51	26	27	11	16	61	75
Have hogs (%)	76	76	84	89	85	79	64	76	52	55
Have cattle (%)	50	45	68	66	67	47	22	58	75	75
Sold hogs (%)	25	24	36	43	29	23	12	27	29	35
Sold cattle (%)	23	18	35	33	26	14	6	30	61	64
Plant cotton (%)	68	—	—	—	—	—	—	—	24	—
Plant tobacco (%)	24	—	—	—	—	—	—	—	24	—
Corn per acre (bu.)	24	26	23	25	17	26	30	19	35	36
Value of products sold per farm ($):										
All products	2,055	3,029	2,130	3,725	1,916	3,281	3,196	700	6,068	10,396
Crops	1,840	2,777	1,652	3,168	1,711	3,168	3,123	537	3,272	5,688
Livestock (including dairy and poultry)	214	252	478	557	205	113	73	163	2,796	4,707
Average value sales per acre ($)	40	54	26	36	30	70	118	15	24	27
Operators having 100+ days off farm work (%)	21	4	4	7	3	3	4	55	35	17

SOURCE: 1959 Census of Agriculture, Volume II.

more clearly than any others how very small the number of Negroes is who have a real toehold in agriculture, and how large the proportion is who have little chance of making a decent living from farming alone without a radical change in their scale of operation. Among commercial farmers, the average value of products sold by all Southern nonwhite farmers was $3,029; the average for white commercial farmers was $10,396 (Table VI).

One of the most serious ultimate problems for the future of the Negro in agriculture is the low state of production by Negro farmers who own all or part of their land. With the steady decline of the tenant system of farming, the future of Negro farmers will be increasingly determined by the level of activity of the owner-operator. At present fully 60 percent of the Negro owners (full and part owners combined) are not even producing enough to be classed as commercial farmers. The part owners—who are the less numerous of the two owner groups—are usually commercial, but more than two-thirds of the full owners are not. In part the low production of the full owners is the result of age—many of them are too old to be active. But even among those under fifty-five years old, a majority fail to sell $2,500 worth of products.

In the light of the small size of most farms run by Negroes, one might logically expect that the farms would be fully utilized. However, the proportion of crop land that is idle or had crop failure is high. In 1959, one-fourth of all the crop land on the farms of Negro full owners was idle or had crop failure, compared with one-ninth on farms of white full owners, indicating the lower intensity of land use.

In addition, the proportion of land remaining in woods is high, amounting to about three-eighths of the total land acreage of commercial Negro owners. These woodlands are usually of low economic value in their present state, except for hunting and as a source of firewood to feed the archaic stoves that still serve as the means of cooking or heating on many farms.

In short, it is not surprising that with such small farms the Negro farmers remained concentrated in the production of intensive crops in which labor can be substituted for land. It is contrary to expectation, however, that their limited land resources are not used more fully. Generally the Negro farmer comes closer to operating his place in the old-time manner, using older methods and equipment and producing much for home use.

A generation ago the emphasis on food for home use would have gladdened the hearts of extension agents and others concerned for the rural Negro's welfare, for it was commonly observed that much of the debt of Negro tenants was for purchase of food that they would not or were not permitted to raise on their farms. But today the trend in agriculture is for farmers not to produce their own meat or milk or eggs, although the vegetable garden shows no sign of demise. Specialized production and marketing have commonly made it cheaper or safer or more convenient for the farmer to purchase most foods. The following figures clearly show that even commercial Negro farmers put much more emphasis on subsistence than do their white neighbors.

	Nonwhite	White
Percent of Southern commercial farmers who sold cattle, 1959	18	64
Percent who kept cattle but sold none	26	11
Percent who sold hogs, 1959	24	35
Percent who kept hogs but sold none	52	20

The majority of white Southern commercial farmers who keep cattle or hogs keep them for sale; the majority of Negro commercial farmers who have them keep them for home-produced meat. A similar pattern shows up for chickens and milk, although less pronounced. The additional emphasis that the Negro farmer puts on subsistence farming certainly offsets to some extent the money income difference between himself and white farmers, but it is unmistakably associated with a less advanced attitude toward farming as a business.

Productivity

In the last fifteen years, as profit margins have narrowed, farmers have attempted to maintain their income level by increasing the size of operation and raising the yields per acre. Production has been the key to survival.

The patterns of productivity per acre in the three crops that form the backbone of Negro agriculture—cotton, tobacco and peanuts—give some interesting insights into the competitive position of Negro farmers. The table below has been compiled for North Carolina where Negro farmers have been the most successful on the average and where all three crops are important. It shows the yields per acre for white and nonwhite commercial farmers in 1959—the latest and only year for which all data are available (Table VII).

Notice that the yields obtained by white full and part owners are substantially superior to those of nonwhite farmers for tobacco and peanuts and moderately so for cotton. On the other hand, among tenant farmers the yields of white farmers are only slightly higher than those of nonwhites.

Among the white farmers, owners (full or part) generally obtain some-what better yields than do tenants. Applying conventional logic, this seems fitting, considering the higher ability and greater experience that one associates with those who have acquired farms compared with those who are landless.

TABLE VII—Yields per Acre of Specified Crops on Commercial Farms in North Carolina, by Color and Tenure of the Operator, 1959

Crop and color of operator	Total commercial	Full owners	Part owners	Tenants		
				Total	Cash tenants	Croppers
Cotton (lbs.)						
White	440	450	443	433	435	434
Nonwhite	410	395	392	415	371	425
Peanuts (lbs.)						
White	1,578	1,566	1,632	1,529	1,180	1,535
Nonwhite	1,466	1,252	1,339	1,513	1,184	1,536
Tobacco (lbs.)						
White	1,490	1,543	1,489	1,466	1,410	1,468
Nonwhite	1,378	1,269	1,276	1,411	1,134	1,432
Soybeans (bu.)						
White	21.0	21.0	21.0	21.0	18.4	22.7
Nonwhite	20.2	17.5	18.2	22.0	17.3	22.2

SOURCE: 1959 Census of Agriculture, Volume I.

But the conventional picture of the relationship between the tenure classes does not apply to nonwhite farmers. Among these men it is the tenants who show considerably greater yields of all three crops than do the owners. Furthermore within the tenant class, the croppers—who have been least successful in advancing towards farming independence, who have the least managerial ability, and bring nothing to their work except their labor—produce higher yields than the tenant groups who operate their own equipment.

The answer to the riddle is at least two-fold. First, Negro croppers typically occupy much of the best land owned by white landlords, compared with the poorer average quality of land that Negroes have been able to buy or to rent on a fixed rent or semi-independent basis. Secondly, the croppers' land is managed by the landlord, whereas the Negro owner or cash renter is his own boss.

The implication of the riddle is that the Negro owner-farmers—from whom most future Negro farmers will be drawn—do not compete well with white farmers in the same type of farming. To some extent economies of scale may operate. The Negro farm with its small typical size may be analogus to small family-run businesses in other industries competing with larger firms. But poorer land and smaller size considered, there seems also to be a residual factor of poorer average farming know-how and managerial performance.

The author recalls an interview with a Negro county extension agent in the best part of the North Carolina Coastal Plain. When the agent was asked about the farming practices of Negro owner-operators, he smiled a little wryly and said, "Sadly enough, the tenants are often the best farmers, and if I were going to take you to see a good Negro farmer I would probably show you a tenant." He attributed much of the difficulty to the fear of Negro owners of going into debt and to a lack of understanding on their part of the role of credit in modern farming. Many of the good tenant farmers might fail, he believed, if they assumed the burdens—real and psychological—of ownership.

As indicated under the discussion of diversification, many Southern farmers have added soybeans to their cash crops. In North Carolina, a leading producer, the proportion of farmers harvesting soybeans was the same for nonwhite commercial owners as for white (19 percent) in 1959. This equality of adoption of a profitable crop is superficial, however. The white owner-operators harvested twice as many acres of beans per farm and were obtaining about 15 percent more bushels per acre. Thus in newer crops as with the old, Negro farmers are handicapped by their smaller farms and by their lower productivity.

Facilities

Negro farmers, like all others, have moved into a completely different era from the days before the First World War when most power was supplied by hand or by animals, when it took all day to get to the county seat and back and when electrical or engine-driven equipment was unknown. The extension of electricity to farms is now so nearly complete that the census of agriculture no longer bothers to inquire about it. True, Negro farmers were typically the last to obtain it, but today it is standard even in sub-standard houses.

The majority of Negro farmers (about two-thirds) also have acquired either an automobile or truck, giving them much more freedom of movement and choice in purchasing or selling. Still, the one-third with no automotive transportation is a much greater proportion than is common among farmers in general, and there are other facilities now conventional elsewhere that most Negro farmers do without.

For instance, only one out of every eight nonwhite operated farms has a telephone, compared with over half of the white farms. This is not just the result of so many Negro farmers being tenants. Even among commercial nonwhite farmers who own their places, just one-sixth have installed phones. Why should this be so? The statistics do not explain themselves. The answer seems to be a combination of lack of access to the telephone lines, lack of steady income to afford a phone and lack of strong desire for one—the persistence of older ways of doing business or communicating in which a phone does not figure.

Another facility of importance to a farmer is the paved or improved road. It improves his marketing ability and reduces his degree of isolation. But here as with other facilities, it is the Negro farmer who is more likely to find himself at a comparative disadvantage. The hard-surface or gravel road has come to the farms of a majority of Negro farmers, but not to the same degree as other farmers. In the South as a whole, 43 percent of all commercial scale nonwhite farmers were still located on a dirt or unimproved road in 1959, compared with 28 percent for commercial white farmers. The disparity was even greater for the noncommercial group.

Ironically enough, it is the least independent of the Negro farmers who are most likely to be on a good road. The croppers with minor exceptions work the farms of white landlords. Three-fifths of their farms are on improved roads, whereas only half of the full or part owners are so located. The least fortunate group in this respect is the cash tenant, nearly three-fifths of whom have to contend with dirt roads.

Again we wish the cold figures would tell us why, as well as whether. There certainly would seem to a correlation with the often repeated observation that as the last claimants to land Negro owners more often obtained poorer land away from the main-traveled roads. In the case of rented land, a landlord is more likely to rent poorer farms for a fixed rent (cash) than on a share basis. To these explanations, we must add the fact that Negro districts in the South have seldom received standard levels of public roads from the governing authorities. For thousands of Negro farmers a poor road is one more handicap they must carry in competition with other farmers. In a majority of instances the farmer whose place fronts on a dirt road is more than one mile from an improved road.

With few exceptions, modern types of farming require the use of a tractor for efficient operations. Particularly for farmers as heavily committed to field crops as Negro farmers are, the lack of a tractor connotes either a lack of capital or lack of incentive to advance beyond a low-income operation.

In examining the extent to which Negro farmers have acquired tractors, it would be somewhat misleading to focus on the overall frequency of tractors, for so many of the farmers are croppers. Although croppers by definition do not have their own machinery, they usually have the use of a tractor through the landlord. Limiting the comparison to commercial owners shows unmistakably, however, that even the elite group of Negro farmers is far behind the white in possession of tractors. Among full owners 38 percent of nonwhites had one or more tractors compared with 70 percent of the white farmers, and among part owners the percentages were 50 for nonwhites and 87 for white. Noncommercial Southern white farmers are more likely to have tractors than are commercial Negro full owners.

The corollary of these figures is the fact that the Negro farmer is more likely than the white farmer to be using a horse or mule. Nearly two-thirds of the nonwhite farmers, excluding croppers, had a horse or mule in 1959 as against 40 percent of white farmers. On tobacco farms the mule still has a useful place where rows are closely spaced, but the proportion of white farmers in the South who grow tobacco is the same as the proportion of Negro farmers who do, so tobacco farming is not the explanation for the overall differences.

CHARACTERISTICS OF FARMERS

Age

In each major tenure class—full owners, part owners and tenants—the average age of nonwhite southern farmers is older than that of white farmers. Yet the average age of all nonwhite southern farmers is younger than that of all white farmers. These two statements may appear to be contradictory, but the explanation is rather simple. Many young men who eventually own farms begin as tenants because they lack the money to buy land at an early stage of life. Thus, the average tenant farmer is younger than the average owner. Unless one inherits at an early date, ownership usually takes time. Since Negro farmers are abnormally concentrated in the tenant class, their overall average age (51.1 years) is a little lower than that of Southern white farmers (51.6). But the rapid decline in Negro operated farms has lowered the rate at which young Negro men enter farming, so that within each tenure group the Negro farmers tend to be older.

How much older? Not a great deal among commercial farmers—an average of a year older or less. But among noncommercial farmers, the average Negro owner or tenant is four to five years older than white farmers in the same tenure group. For example, noncommercial Negro full owners averaged 59.7 years of age in 1959; their white counterparts averaged 55.5. With many tenant farmers now being displaced or converted to hired workers, the average age of Negro operators is rising rapidly.

The most numerous group of farmers is that between the ages of 45 and 54. But among full owners the largest group consists of those 65 years old and over—more than one-third of all full owners. This high age level of owners explains in part the rather low level of productivity of Negro owned farms in general.

Education

The position and prospect of the Negro as a farmer cannot be discussed without reference to the educational situation in the farm population. Even in the most progressive agricultural areas of the country the notion that a grade school training was sufficient for a farmer lingered for many years after it ceased to be valid.

For the Southern Negro farmer, several factors added to the traditionally conservative rural view of education to produce the lowest levels of schooling in the United States, outside of certain Indian tribes. These factors included the extended neglect of rural Negro school facilities, the closing of schools during peak farm work seasons for use of child labor, and the lack of educational incentive inherent in the sharecropper mode of life.

In 1960, the average years of schooling completed by the nonwhite farm population 25 years old and over was 5.7 years, compared with 8.9 years for the white farm population and 11.1 years for the total urban population. Only 7 percent of adult Negro farm residents have completed high school. Some gradual improvement is taking place, but the pace is so slow. The increase in high school graduates has gone only from 2 percent to 7 percent in 20 years. In this respect the Negro farm population is more than one generation behind white farm people, 14 percent of whom had a high school diploma in 1940.

More than 40 percent of the nonwhite farm people 25 years old and over did not complete as many as five years of school (compared with 8 percent of the white farm population). The situation is not much better for nonwhites among the rural-nonfarm population, but is far better in the cities. Some of the problem in the Negro farm population is due to the siphoning off to the cities of those young people who do go through high school. Negro county extension agents are almost unanimous in saying that it is very difficult to interest rural high school students in farming. The good student usually associates the widespread poverty of the population from which he comes with agriculture, and sees the city as the avenue of opportunity.

But even among the young, the academic performance of children from Negro farm families is in a class totally apart from that of the general population. For example, in 1960 more than half (57 percent) of all Southern nonwhite farm boys aged fourteen and fifteen years old were retarded in school. That is to say, they had not reached the grades that are normal for persons of their age. The corresponding proportion for white farm boys that age was 26 percent in the South and only 11 percent in the North and West. Even more astonishing is the fact that of the nonwhite farm boys who were behind in school a substantial majority had fallen two or more years behind. In most instances retardation becomes a prelude to quitting school altogether—and three-fourths of all Negro farm boys do drop out before completing high school.

With such a small fraction of the Negro farm people having received a modern education, it is easy to understand how difficult it is to develop group leadership in that population, and how frequently it is possible for a semiliterate farmer to fail to understand the complexities of Government programs that affect his heavily controlled crops or to take full advantage of the services that the Government and the experiment stations can provide him.

Housing

Housing has been as much a perennial problem for the Negro population in the countryside as it is considered to be in the city. Rural housing has typically had two advantages over that in the city—it has often been provided "free" as part of a tenant farm or as part of a man's pay, and although families have often been very crowded in their own quarters, they have not usually had to share the same building with other families. On the other hand, the flush toilets, bathtubs, running water and central heating of most city slum housing were and still are amenities which the typical rural Negro has never had.

Farm housing for Negroes is often of inadequate original construction, frequently consisting of only one thickness of boards, without insulation, glassed windows or screens. Rooms are often small and usually number only from two to four for tenant families. Gradually much of the poorest housing has been abandoned as the number of farm people has decreased. In the 1940's and 1950's almost complete electrification occurred, even in the rudest shacks.

Today, aside from quality of the home, the greatest discrepancy in white and Negro rural housing or between rural and urban Negro housing is in water supply. Most rural homes have a well or spring, but it is not as easy to provide running water for the scattered population of the country-side as it is in the city. As a result, modern water facilities have lagged behind electricity. In 1950, only one-fifth of the white farm families in the South and two-fifths of the nonfarm white rural families had homes with hot and cold running water. During the 1950's the white population made great strides in modernizing its water supply, either through community systems or individual pumps, so that by 1960 the majority of both the farm and nonfarm white rural houses (over 60 percent) had installed heated running water. On the other hand, only 2 percent of the Southern farm Negro homes and 5 percent of other rural Negro homes had a modern water supply in 1950. During the 1950's, a little progress was made as the proportion with piped hot and cold water rose to 10 percent of the farm homes and 16 percent of the nonfarm rural homes (Table VIII). However, the improvement is so small compared to that of the white rural population that the relative disparity between the adequacy of water supply of white and Negro rural people actually widened in the decade.

TABLE VIII—Selected Family and Housing Characteristics, by Color and Residence for the South, 1950 and 1960

Characteristic	Urban		Rural nonfarm		Rural farm	
	1960	1950	1960	1950	1960	1950
Average number of persons per household						
White	3.19	3.30	3.49	3.67	3.62	4.06
Nonwhite	3.70	3.55	4.26	3.93	5.10	4.87
Percent 5–9 year old children in household not headed by parent						
White	4	7	5	6	7	8
Nonwhite	18	23	20	20	21	20
Percent of housing units not in sound condition						
White	2	6	7	15	7	19
Nonwhite	19	34	33	44	31	44
Percent of housing units having hot and cold piped water						
White	94	82	64	41	60	20
Nonwhite	58	27	16	5	10	2

SOURCE: 1950 and 1960 U.S. Censuses of Population and Housing.

The importance of hot and cold running water can hardly be overestimated. It is the indispensable basis for adequate bathing facilities, for sanitary indoor toilets and for modern kitchen equipment. There is no other measure of level of living that continues to show such a disparity between white and Negro rural people as water supply.

TABLE IX—Days Worked and Wages Earned by Persons Doing 25 or More Days of Farm Wage Work in 1962, by Color

Area, color and sex of worker	Number of workers	Farm work		
		Days worked	Wages earned	
			Per year	Per day
	Thou.	No.	Dol.	Dol.
United States				
Total	2,067	134	913	6.80
White	1,398	145	1,083	7.45
Male	1,162	159	1,232	7.75
Female	237	78	351	4.50
Nonwhite	669	111	556	5.00
Male	414	138	748	5.45
Female	255	68	243	3.60
South				
Total	1,127	122	689	5.65
White	574	136	917	6.75
Nonwhite	553	107	451	4.20

SOURCE: Advance Report on the Hired Farm Working Force of 1962, U.S. Department of Agriculture, Table 5.

Despite the wholesale abandonment of much of the worst rural housing in the South in recent years, the condition of the majority of homes of rural Negroes remains "deteriorating" or "dilapidated," in Bureau of Census terms. In 1960, 71 percent of all nonwhite farm homes were so described. These terms imply much more than mere shabbiness. A deteriorating house is one with defects of a nature that require more than a regular amount of repair, and that must be corrected if the house is to continue to provide safe and adequate shelter. A dilapidated house is one in such a poor state that it presently endangers the health, safety or well-being of the occupants. Thus, the great majority of all Negro farm housing is still far substandard. Rural nonfarm homes are in little better average condition. The problem is thus of a general rural character. Deterioration and dilapidation were characteristic of only 27 percent of all white farm homes—a serious enough condition in itself, but far better than the situation for Negroes.

Another useful measure of the adequacy of housing is the ratio of persons per room. In general, a dwelling unit is regarded as definitely overcrowded if there are more than 1.5 persons per room. In the case of nonwhite farm households, 30 percent had more than 1.5 persons per room in 1960. This was 10 times the relative frequency in white farm households (3 percent). Crowding has become somewhat worse in recent years.

One helpful approach to better rural housing has been developed in South Carolina, where a demonstration house for Negroes was built with the assistance of the General Education Board. Groups of women come to the house and live for a week, where they have the chance to enjoy and have training in the use of modern housing facilities. Such experience is often the stimulation to improvements in their own homes.

Two comparative aspects of Negro farm housing need emphasis. One is the fact that rural Negro housing is far inferior in quality to urban Negro housing. This can easily be lost sight of in the public and political attention being given to urban Negro housing problems. For example, although crowding in the homes and apartments of densely settled Negro districts in major cities is often stressed, only 11 percent of all urban dwellings inhabited by nonwhites contained more than 1.5 persons per room in 1960, compared with the 30 percent incidence of this condition in nonwhite farm homes. The proportion of urban nonwhite homes that were in sound condition (not deteriorating or dilapidated) was more than double that of nonwhite farm homes (62 percent vs. 29 percent).

The second point to be noted is that the adequacy and condition of farm tenant housing is usually much poorer than that of owner-occupied housing. Nonwhite farm tenant homes average one room less than owned homes, but typically have one more person per house. Thus the tenant families are much more likely to be overcrowded; 37 percent have more than 1.5 persons per room. (Half of all persons living in nonwhite farm tenant households live in households that have eight or more members.) Only 20 percent of nonwhite farm tenant homes are in sound condition; only 3 percent have bathrooms. Inasmuch as most tenant-occupied farm homes of nonwhites are received as a part of farm rental or as payment in kind for hired work, it is clear that this aspect of the total income of farm Negroes is just as low as the money income component.

There is a circular cause and effect to tenant housing that is difficult to break. It might be very costly in cash outlay for farm landlords to provide minimally decent housing of sound construction, ample space, and modern water, toilet and heating equipment. Yet the continued occupancy of present rural tenant housing undoubtedly has a severely limiting and conditioning effect on the lives of the children who grow up in it and of the adults who remain in it. Landlords, on the other hand, often complain that the tenants will not take care of the improvements that are made;

that screens are soon broken out, etc. Probably the problems of rural Negro housing cannot successfully be attacked piecemeal and will not be solved until the whole structure of low education and underemployment of rural people is modified.

Hired Farm Workers

In one aspect of American agriculture the role of the Negro has increased somewhat rather than diminished. That aspect is doing farm work for cash wages. In many respects the sharecropper has been little different from a hired worker, because he usually contributes nothing to his operation except his labor. But technically the cropper has been an operator, for he is paid with a share of the crop rather than with money and is clearly attached to a particular farm for the season.

The hired farm wage laborer—black or white—is usually society's low man on the totem pole. He is typically at the bottom in income and in the respect accorded to him. Some of the reasons for the low standing of the occupation are not hard to find. The average wages paid to farm workers in the South were only seventy-eight cents an hour in 1963 without room and board. The frequency of unemployment is high, the average education of hired farm workers is lower than that of any other major occupation group, and except for inclusion in the Social Security system they are excluded from the basic protections that people in most other jobs take for granted. With few exceptions, farm workers are not covered by minimum wage and hour laws, not included in unemployment compensation insurance, not protected by workmen's disability compensation, and not guaranteed the right to bargain collectively with their employers. As a group they are the closest approximation that the United States has to a pariah occupational caste. Under these conditions it is extremely difficult to develop a career attitude towards hired farm work and to raise the status of the work.

Where does the Negro worker fit into this picture? Because of the low status of the job and the low degree of education expected, Negroes have always been heavily used in hired farm work wherever they have lived and have been a logical group to supply migratory workers to other parts of the Nation for seasonal farm work.

In 1961, one-fourth of all days of farm wage work in the United States was performed by Negroes. Today the hired Negro farm worker makes a greater labor contribution to supplying the nation's agricultural needs than does the Negro farmer. In the South, where Negro farmers comprise one-sixth of all farmers, Negro workers do fully half of all farm wage work.

In the North and West, the use of regular hired workers on farms has been declining almost everywhere. This is not true of Negroes in the South.

The South has had mechanization just as the rest of the nation has, but landowners have often adjusted to it by abandoning the tenant method of working their land and substituting hired workers for tenants.

In April 1950 the South had 392,000 white hired farm workers and 298,000 nonwhite. Ten years later, in April, 1960, the white workers had declined to 308,000, while the nonwhites had increased to 311,000. For the first time nonwhites made up over half of the South's farm wage workers.

The switch from tenants to hired hands is nowhere more evident than in the Mississippi Delta country. Here in just five years' time, from the fall of 1954 to the fall of 1959, the number of tenant farmers (white and non-white) dropped by 60 percent (from 83,000 to 33,000). At the same time the number of regular hired workers on farms rose by 62 percent (from 24,000 to 39,000). The Delta is mostly cotton country. As the farm owners switched from hand chopping and hand picking by tenants to machine methods by wage hands, they have had to hire only about three new regular hands for each ten tenants displaced. Of course, many of the new wage hands are selected from former tenants—those who are good at mechanical work. The same type of trend has occurred at a slower rate in other cotton areas and in the tobacco and peanut belts.

When this type of mechanization arrives, the problems created are often severe for many people. Some men lose their work and many women and youths who worked in the fields at harvest time and other peak seasons find a much-needed source of income cut off. Yet the trend is inevitable. Hand methods of farming simply do not produce enough income to warrant continuing them when other ways are developed.

In the traditional "tenure ladder" the landless laborer was regarded as a more pitiable creature than the sharecropper. But interestingly enough this does not usually seem to be the case with the new Negro wage hand. Generally these former tenants who have survived the changeover seem to feel that they are better off. For one thing, there is a regular payday and less likelihood that a man will find himself badly in debt at season's end as tenants often do. Regular wage work is covered by Social Security, which gives some assurance for the future. And if a man can save some money and find off-farm work in slack farm seasons, he may even aspire to buy a house of his own, which as a furnished tenant he would not have done. To an increasing extent the hired workers are living away from the farm on which they work.

In 1962 there were 623,000 nonwhite households from which one or more persons did farm work for wages at some time during the year. More than 3,050,000 people lived in these households, indicating the large number of nonwhite people who have some financial dependence on farm wage work.

In about half the cases the dependence was rather minor (less than twenty-five days of work by the household head and less than 150 days by all other family members).

A distinctive feature of nonwhite farm worker households is the abnormally high number of them that are headed by women. More than a fourth (26.5 percent) do not have a male head, compared with only 8.5 percent among white farm worker families. The occurrence of many families with a woman head is common in the urban and nonagricultural Negro population as well, but seldom is the difference between the white and nonwhite populations in this respect as great as it is among farm workers. Generally the women heads do not have farm work for as much as 150 days per year, and the income position of such families is often very low.

Several factors serve to concentrate the Negro hired farm worker in hand or stoop labor. Two-thirds of all nonwhite workers who did more than twenty-five days of farm wage work in 1961 worked only as hand or stoop laborers; only one-fourth operated or repaired trucks and machinery. Among white workers the situation is different, with the more skilled workers outnumbering the unskilled hand and stoop laborers. In part the nonwhite disadvantage results from their location in the South where hand work is more needed, and from the greater role of women, almost none of whom are used in machine jobs. Low education and lack of technical training are also factors.

The low average skill level of work performed seriously affects the income that nonwhite workers receive from farm wage work. This is not because hand laborers earn much less per day, but because they have fewer days of work. Male hand laborers actually earned as much per day ($6.40) as operators of self-propelled farm machines in 1961, but the hand workers averaged only ninety-three days of farm work in the year compared with two hundred for the machine operators. (See Table IX for selected statistics on hired farm workers.)

THE PROSPECT

Land—a Key Factor

In a preceding section the anomaly was mentioned that the Negro farmers who are landowners have poorer land on the average and work it less intensively than the Negro tenant farmers who do not control the land they work. Despite the apparent underuse of farms by many Negroes who have become owners, the possession of land is nevertheless a key to future participation by Negroes in American agriculture as operators.

Outright tenancy as a form of land occupancy is in full retreat, especially in the South. Until the end of World War II, Southern farmers who rented all the land they worked outnumbered the part owners by more than six to one. Since the war, full tenancy has declined so rapidly and part owner-ship has become so attractive and necessary that in the 1964 census part owners will outnumber full tenants in the South for the first time, as they have in the North and West since 1954.

Some instances of full tenancy will always exist, but the practice is becoming a minor factor in Southern farming. The principal use of tenancy in the South was for cotton farming. With the near total elimination of hand and animal labor in this crop, it becomes logical for landlords to operate their places as complete units, using hired labor if necessary. Although the end result in tobacco is less clear at the moment, the tendency seems to be the same. The majority of Negro tenant farmers have already vacated, been displaced, or converted to hired work, and a majority of those tenants remaining will follow the same path.

The farmer who does not control the land he works does not control nis own destiny in the far-reaching changes now affecting agriculture. This puts the typical Negro farmer with his limited capital and lack of ownership experience at a disadvantage.

There is also the legacy of racial discrimination and distrust to combat. With most land in the hands of white owners, Negroes have often found it difficult to be considered as potential buyers, unless the market was poor. For example, in the heart of the tobacco country in eastern North Carolina it was not uncommon in the 1950's for auctions of farmland to begin with a statement that bids would be received from white persons only.

In addition distrust by Negroes of white officials and of the white-con-trolled credit structures seems to be widespread. Conditions vary greatly from county to county, but all too many Negroes are apprehensive of at-tempting to purchase land or to encumber the land they may already have.

Since 1910 the amount of land owned by Negro farmers has gone steadily downward, with the exception of the period from 1940 to 1950. During that one decade, under the prosperous conditions of the war and immediate post-war period, there was a growth in both the number of Negro farmers who owned land and in the amount of land owned. Since that time, the gains of the 1940's have disappeared as far as agriculture is concerned. Some of the families who obtained land may continue to own it but no longer use it for farming.

Technological Changes Affecting Negro Farmers

Technological innovations are man-made, but the effects of technological change operate on most men in a very impersonal and neutral way. The effect of the rapid and continuing technological advance in agriculture is usually no different for Negro farmers as such than for any other farmers. But Negroes often are concentrated in those classes and types of farming that are most affected by technology.

The case of cotton, discussed earlier, is a prime example. The successful mechanization of this crop probably has had a more fundamental effect on the Negro farm population than any other event. Within the Southern states, where most Negro farmers live (excluding Texas and Oklahoma), the percentage of cotton mechanically harvested accelerated from 11 percent in 1957 to 55 percent in 1962. Experts of the Department of Agriculture expect that by the end of the 1960's only a very small percentage of Southern cotton will be hand harvested. Thus many more cotton tenants will be displaced, and certain adjustments will become logical for owners —such as larger and more consolidated fields—that lead toward fewer but larger farms.

The changes in tobacco farming have been much less than those affecting cotton, as yet. In the complicated process of harvesting, curing and marketing cigarette tobacco, a variety of time-consuming hand operations have been necessary. For example, in producing the flue-cured type of the South Atlantic States, the leaves are actually pulled from the stalk by hand. Furthermore, since the leaves ripen at different times the field has to be gone over ("primed") several times. Then the leaves have to be individually handled in preparing them for the curing barn and rearranged by hand in preparing them for auction. Tobacco requires 486 man hours of labor per acre, compared with seven for corn and forty-nine for all cotton (1960–62 averages). Naturally this tremendous labor requirement in tobacco farming stands as a challenge to agricultural engineers, and they are succeeding in ways to reduce it.

In the last few years machines have come into use which permit workers to ride through the fields while priming and preparing the leaves for the curing barn. In addition, new types of curing barns have been invented which reduce the handling of the crop. The major breakthrough is dependent upon the invention of a machine that will mechanically sever the ripe leaves from the plant and prepare them for curing—a so-called combine. Models of such machines are now in operation, and it appears only a matter of time before they are perfected for commercial use.

The mechanization of tobacco will not come overnight. The crop is geared much more to family sized farms and less to plantations than cotton was. But the initial effects have been evident since the mid-1950's, and the incentive for the larger operatives to procure reliable mechanical methods and free themselves from dependence on a labor pool is great. It seems inevitable that the direct and indirect pressures on Negro tobacco farmers to get larger or give up will become greater as this decade progresses.

In addition to the technological changes in their production, both cotton and tobacco are affected by recurring surplus supplies. Cotton is under pressure from competition of synthetic fibers. The price of synthetics such as rayon and nylon has been greatly reduced and there are many uses for which manufacturers can switch between cotton and synthetics, depending on prices. If the Government price support should be cut further, many of the higher-cost farmers concentrated in the Southeast could not grow cotton at a profit. There is almost no prospect of an increase in acreage allotments—most of which are now very small among Negroes—and always the threat of a loss of Government support if the public and the Congress become impatient with the subsidy burden.

In the case of tobacco, the finding by the Public Health Service that cigarette smoking is a health hazard has raised questions about the long-term future of the tobacco production. Per capita consumption has fallen, at least temporarily, and it seems likely that educational programs discouraging smoking will be directed at the public until such time as (and if) research can devise a benign cigarette. In addition, the quality of American cigarette tobacco has fallen in recent years from several reasons and the vital export market has been endangered. Owing to a build-up in supplies, the acreage farmers were permitted to raise of the principal cigarette tobaccos was cut by over 20 percent from 1963 to 1965.

Such are the effects of technological and related changes on the two crops that Negro farmers are most reliant on. Similar comments could be made about peanut farming.

The Effect of Rural Traditionalism in Racial Matters

As is evident from many sections of this chapter, the position and prospects of the Negro farmer cannot be divorced from the fact that he is almost entirely located in the South—and the inner part of the South at that. Within the South, the rural areas are for the most part more traditional and conservative in race relations than are the medium and large cities. The progress of the Negro in exercise of his civil rights, in desegregation or equalization of education, in the extension of social courtesies (the handshake, forms of address), in occupational opportunities, in interracial participation in civic life, and in public accommodations has been very limited in rural areas as compared with the cities.

Cowhig and Beale of the Department of Agriculture have shown that in most available measures of socio-economic status the already wide gaps between the white and nonwhite rural populations in the South have widened in recent years. This is true of income, proportion of young adults without a high school diploma, unemployment rate, proportion of workers in blue collar jobs, number of children born per women, proportion of young children living in households where the head is not their parent, proportion of people living in crowded housing and proportion living without hot and cold running water in the home. By contrast, in urban areas of the South there was some narrowing of the white-nonwhite gap in five of the measures mentioned.[4]

In rural communities it is easier for the white population to exercise informal and personal controls over the Negro population. The anonymity of large city populations is missing, as is the ease of organizing effective protest movements in the settled urban community. The low level of education and income in most rural areas is also a handicap. In addition, it is in rural counties that the Negro population most often constitutes a large segment of the population and thus poses a greater ultimate threat to the traditional structure of southern society. In such situations the white community feels less leeway in granting concessions and promoting change than is true tionin areas where Negroes are a smaller minority. The general racial conservatism of rural areas makes it difficult for Federal authorities—or even state authorities, if so inclined—to secure the impartial operation of Government-financed agricultural programs or economic development projects. By the nature of his occupation the farmer must carry on his business in the rural countryside, and in most instances live there as well. This is a basic handicap that the Southern Negro farmer seems destined to have to carry in comparison with his industrial or professionally-employed brother who can readily perform his occupation in the cities or in the North if he chooses.

The Status of Farming and Rural Life among Young People

Is it an exaggeration to suggest that the young Negro who goes into farming or farm work today is either a person with a great interest in agriculture and some resources to give promise of success, or else a person who

[4] James D. Cowhig and Calvin L. Beale, "Relative Socio-economic Status of Southern Whites and Nonwhites, 1950 and 1960." *Southwestern Social Science Quarterly*, 45 (September 1964), p. 113–24.

is essentially indifferent in aspirations and social sensitivity? Undoubtedly
the characterzation is oversimplified, but it would seem to have some truth.
Observers in the South, both white and Negro, express the opinion that the
propect of farming in the rural South has become emotionally unattractive
to most rural Negro youth. It is urban and especially metropolitan life that
has status. This attitude is not confined to Negroes. It is common among rural
white youth as well. The image of agrarian life as the ideal and inherently
best form of society, inherited from the Jeffersonian period, died a slow
death, but research indicates that a large proportion of rural youth prefer
to seek an urban life even without economic motivation. In the case of
rural Negro youth in the South both the economic and social disadvantages
of rural life are magnified, and the majority have been migrating away
before they are twenty-five years old. This pattern has helped raise
the average age of Negro farmers until the presently oncoming youth may,
in turn, think of farm operation as an old man's job and a relic of an unpleasant past.

The Future Role of Negroes in American Agriculture

To be optimistic about the future of Negro farmers would be to disregard almost every facet of their past and present status and of the factors
that impinge upon them. But then, the odds have always been against them
even in the period when they reached their greatest number. The dissolution of their former concentration in farming was probably a precondition
to the general advance of the race, so limiting were the semifeudal conditions of the rural South to social progress for the Negro.

The loss of one-half of all Negro farm operators in less than ten years
(1950–59) impels the question of whether there is any future at all for
them. Is the discussion in this chapter really an epilogue for a role that in
fact has nearly vanished? To an extent—to a great extent—yes.

Of the 266,000 nonwhite farmers in the South in 1959, 44,000 (a sixth)
were sixty-five years old and over and producing less than $2,500 of products
for sale. They are essentially in retirement. Most of their farms have less
than twenty acres of cropland and thus are not suitable as complete farms,
although they might be useful as additions to other farms.

Another 130,000 farmers were classed as commercial but selling less
than $5,000 of products a year. Few economists would give many of these
much hope of becoming units capable of providing a decent income from
farming alone, especially since two-thirds of them are tenant farms. About
three thousand had one hundred or more days of off-farm work.

One-fourth of Southern nonwhite farmers (67,000) are small-scale operators who depend primarily on off-farm work (the "part-time" census class).

Only half of them, however, have two hundred or more days of off-farm work per year and are thus employed on a relatively full-time basis.

Finally, there were somewhat less than 24,000 nonwhite southern farmers who produced and sold more than $5,000 of products. These men and their families would seem to be the core of the future potential of Negro farmers in commercial agriculture. But here again, less than one-third (7,000) own their land, and some of them who were tenants have undoubtedly already lost their lease or share arrangements since 1959.

In sum, there were in 1959 about 7,000 nonwhite owner operators with an adequate or marginally-adequate level of production, 3,000 owners with inadequate commercial production, but a fair amount of off-farm work, and 34,000 owners and renters who did not produce very much but had rather steady farm work. The sum of these groups (44,000) appears to be the total of the Negro farmers with a tangible expectation of obtaining a minimum adequate income from farming or a combination of farm and nonfarm work. They represent only 17 percent of the total number of Negro operators in 1959.

Perhaps others could successfully remain in farming or part-time farming if the land in the hands of small-scale owners could be combined through lease or purchase into larger units, or if Federal programs of assistance in land purchase could be made effective on a widespread basis for low-income landless farmers, or if additional nonfarm employment opportunities became available for rural Negroes.

Negro farm owners have about 4.7 million acres of land, but 2.0 million acres of it is in the hands of elderly and part-time noncommercial farmers, who are cultivating only half of their crop land. If more of this decidedly underused 2.0 million acres were channeled into the hands of aspiring tenants or commercial owners, as many as 10,000 additional commercial Negro farmers might have a reasonable chance for survival. But the trend has been for a decline in Negro-owned farm land, while the total of land in white-owned farms has been stable.

In addition to the groups mentioned, who in our judgment probably represent the maximum future potential number of Negro farm operators earning an acceptable income from all sources, there are other families who will remain in farming at the poverty level. Their numbers are diminishing rapidly, however.

A major effort by the Department of Agriculture to provide access to its programs impartially by all is basic to any successful future for Negro farmers as a class. Beyond impartial access it is necessary to schedule particular attention to the situation of Negro farmers to help offset the all too obvious effects of years of indifference to their problems.

Fortunately the passage of the Civil Rights Act of 1964 gives the Government the leverage as well as the obligation to act to remedy many of the prevailing conditions of Negro farmers' inadequate access to Federal programs. Shortly after the passage of the act, Secretary of Agriculture Orville Freeman called some 250 administrative officials of the Department of Agriculture to Washington to discuss those sections of the act affecting the department's work. In an uncompromisingly firm statement, Freeman said that ". . . there will be no delays in eliminating discrimination where it exists within the agencies of the Department; and . . . in the operation of any program carried out by the Department." "The time to put this legislation in effect is now," he said, "not tomorrow—or next week—or soon—but today."

Simultaneously, the U.S. Commission on Civil Rights was engaged in a long investigation of discrimination in the programs of the Department of Agriculture. Its report, issued in February 1965, was very critical of many conditions. The Commission concluded that ". . . the Department has generally failed to assume responsibility for assuring equal opportunity and equal treatment to all those entitled to benefit from its programs. Instead, the prevailing practice has been to follow local patterns of racial segregation and discrimination in providing assistance paid for by Federal funds."[5] The Commission recommended to the President an end to discriminatory practices, encouragement of full participation by Negroes in agricultural programs, and equal employment opportunities in programs.

The potential benefits for Negro farmers of the Civil Rights Act and the investigative report of the Commission on Civil Rights are great. But if the widespread and long entrenched disadvantages under which Negro farmers operate are not very soon corrected, Negro farmers may well disappear as a significant group in American agriculture before the end of the twentieth century. Here and there a number of fortunate and persistent operators would undoubtedly remain, but the presently high emigration rate of Negro farm people indicates that a continuation of present conditions is inimical to their general survival as farmers.

Paradoxically, the prospects for the future continuance of Negroes in hired farm work are high. Whereas in operation of a farm the race is being won by the strong who have the capital and organization to survive in modern agriculture, in hired farm work the race is being left to the weak. Because of the relatively unattractive conditions of much farm work, hired farm workers are being drawn from an increasingly atypical section of society. Except for a minority of well-paid supervisory or technical jobs, regular farm wage work has largely become a residual occupation hiring those who from poor education, lack of vocational training, or other limita-

[5] *Equal Opportunity in Farm Programs—An Appraisal of Services Rendered by Agencies of the United States Department of Agriculture*, United States Commission on Civil Rights, Washington, 1965, p. 100.

tions cannot succeed as farmers or do better in nonagricultural jobs. In the South and in migratory farm work the Negro worker best fits this description.

Although the chances for the continued existence of a large number of Negro farm operators in the United States are problematical, the persistence of several million Negroes in rural areas seems certain in the foreseeable future, in part because of their continuance in farm wage work. The rural nonfarm Negro population has increased in every decade since 1920 when first counted. In 1960 there were an estimated 2,655,000 rural nonfarm Negroes [6] up more than 6 percent from 1950 (Table X). Well over 90 percent are in the South. In addition to those who are in agriculture as hired workers, many work in agriculturally related industries such as food

TABLE X—Rural Negro Population in the United States, by Farm-Nonfarm Residence, 1920–1963

Year	Population		
	Total rural	Rural nonfarm	Rural farm
	Thou.	Thou.	Thou.
1920	6,903.7	1,803.7	5,100.0
1930	6,697.2	2,016.7	4,680.5
1940	6,611.9	2,109.6	4,502.3
1950*	5,649.7	2,491.4	3,158.3
1960**			
Census	5,056.7	3,574.7	1.482.0
Revised	5,056.7	2,666.7	2,390.0
1963**	—	—	1,730.0

    * The definition of rural was made more restrictive in 1950 than formerly, accounting for about 500,000 of the total rural decline from 1940–50.
    ** The definition of farm residence was made more restrictive in 1960, and the 1960 census obtained a distinct undercount of the Negro farm population. The revised figure shown is a more accurate estimate based on the Current Population Survey of the Bureau of the Census. The estimate for 1963 is also based on the Current Population Survey.

SOURCE: U.S. Censuses of Population, 1930, 1940, 1950, 1960, and *Farm Population,* Series Census-ERS (P–27), No. 34, Bureau of the Census and Economic Research Service, April 1964.

processing, woodcutting, and the making of lumber and other wood products. Other thousands engage in a variety of manufacturing, construction or service jobs.

The total Negro rural population—farm and nonfarm—declined from 1950 to 1960 by nearly 600,000 because of the heavy loss of farm people. But because the declining farm population is now smaller than the rural-nonfarm population, relatively heavy farm losses are no longer large enough to greatly offset rural nonfarm gains. It is quite possible that the Negro rural

[6] Revision of 1960 census figures of 3,575,000, to accord with a more accurate estimate of farm population from the Current Population Survey.

population will not drop below 4,500,000 and could begin an increase after about 1970–75.

Thus, whatever the fate of Negro farm operators, the total rural Negro population is expected to remain a numerous element. Its current rate of social and economic progress is far behind that of the urban Negro population or of the white rural population. Its problems are somewhat peculiar to their setting, as many rural problems are. They merit the continued attention not only of the Federal Government but also of the predominantly urban Negro leadership.

BIBLIOGRAPHY

A Study of Negro Farmers in South Carolina. Atlanta: Southern Regional Council, 1962.

Beale, Calvin L., Negro Farm Operators: Number, Location, and Recent Trends. Washington: Agricultural Marketing Service, U.S. Department of Agriculture, 1958.

"Color, Race and Tenure of Farm Operator," U.S. Census of Agriculture: 1959. Washington: U.S. Bureau of the Census, 1962, Vol. II, Chap. X.

Cowhig, James D., and Beale, Calvin L., "Socioeconomic Differences Between White and Nonwhite Farm Populations in the South." Social Forces, 42 (March 1964), 354–62.

—— "Relative Socio-economic Status of Southern Whites and Nonwhites, 1950 and 1960." The Southwestern Social Science Quarterly, 45 (September 1964), 113–24.

Equal Opportunity in Farm Programs —An Appraisal of Services Rendered by Agencies of the United States Department of Agriculture, Washington: United States Commission on Civil Rights, 1965.

Jones, Lewis W., ed., The Changing Status of the Negro in Southern Agriculture, Rural Life Information Series, Bulletin No. 3 (Alabama: Tuskegee Institute, 1950).

Land Tenure in the Southern Region —Proceedings of Professional Agricultural Workers Tenth Annual Conference. Alabama: Tuskegee Institute, 1951.

Neal, Ernest E., and Jones, Lewis W., "The Place of the Negro Farmer in the Changing Economy of the Cotton South." Rural Sociology, 15 (March 1950), 30–41.

Rubin, Morton, Plantation County. Chapel Hill: University of North Carolina Press, 1951.

Schuler, Edgar A., Social Status and Farm Tenure—Attitudes and Social Conditions of Corn Belt and Cotton Belt Farmers. (Social Research Report, No. IV.) Washington: Bureau of Agricultural Economics, U.S. Department of Agriculture, 1938.

"The American Farmer." Population Bulletin. Washington: Population Reference Bureau, May 1963.

Woodson, Carter G., The Rural Negro. Washington: The Association for the Study of Negro Life, 1930.

chapter 4

Employment Patterns
of Negro Men and Women

Eli Ginzberg and Dale L. Hiestand

In a democratic society, based primarily on private enterprise, the work that an individual does largely determines his income, his status and his way of life. Hence, a major dimension of the role of Negro men and women in American society and more particularly the changes in their position can best be obtained by studying their experiences in the realm of work. Among the key factors are the proportion of adults who are in the labor force; the proportions of those in the labor force who are employed or, alternatively, unemployed; their occupational status; and the wages or salaries which they earn. A group may be better or worse off depending on the proportion that are employed; the types of occupational skills and opportunities which they possess; and the wages which they are able to earn.

Minorities in the Labor Force

Negroes are only one of several minority groups in the labor force. Women, both white and nonwhite, are often viewed as a minority group in the labor force, both because they account for less than one-third of all persons in paid employment, and because they are subject to discrimination in employment. But the term *minority* is usually restricted to persons identified on the basis of race, religion, color, national origin, or other ethnic or cultural distinction. Formerly, Catholics were a minority group in certain regions and localities, but they are now so widespread and economically well off that they can no longer be so classified.

Negroes comprise the largest single minority group in the United States. As Table I shows, in 1960 there were 6.8 million Negroes in the total American labor force, compared with 4.2 million foreign-born whites, 1.1 million whites of Spanish descent in the Southwest, 326,000 of Puerto Rican birth or parentage and lesser numbers of Japanese, American Indian, Chinese, Filipino and other nonwhites. Exactly comparable data are not available for Jews but that which is available suggests that their number in the labor force reached nearly 2.5 million in 1960. Of course, many of the above groups overlap one another.

TABLE I—Various Minority Groups in the Labor Force, by Sex, 1960

	Total	Male	Female
Negro	6,806,968	4,116,194	2,690,774
Foreign-born white	4,159,006	2,869,060	1,289,946
Spanish-surname white *	1,114,688	819,271	295,417
Puerto Rican birth or parentage**	325,523	222,883	102,640
Japanese	202,405	125,239	77,166
American Indian	138,692	97,197	41,495
Chinese	104,368	75,805	28,563
Filipino	83,955	69,800	14,155

* In five Southwestern states.
** Includes less than 4 percent nonwhites; also includes some Spanish-surname whites in five Southwestern states, probably less than 5 percent.

SOURCE: U.S. Bureau of the Census, U.S. Census of Population, 1960: *Nonwhite Population by Race*, Tables 32–36; *Persons of Spanish Surname*, Table 6; *Puerto Ricans in the United States*, Table 5; *Employment Status and Work Experience*, Table 3.

The Negro Labor Force

The labor force includes all who work for pay or profit, and all who are seeking paid work. It includes the self-employed and those who work in family businesses or family farms. It includes the employees of profit-seeking firms, nonprofit enterprises such as hospitals, unions and civic associations, and Federal, state and local governments. It also includes members of the Armed Forces. It includes those who work full time or part time. Finally, it includes the unemployed.

The best way to introduce the reader to a consideration of the employment status of the Negro is to trace the growth which has occurred in the numbers of Negroes in the labor force; and to follow this with an evaluation of the occupational fields in which they are concentrated. Later stages of the analysis can then center around the income which Negroes are able to earn and the extent to which they are able to find employment, particularly on a year-round basis.

There are two closely related concepts of the labor force: one refers to the civilian labor force and the other refers to the total labor force which includes, in addition to civilians, the approximately 3 million persons who are currently in the Armed Forces. In 1960 the total labor force amounted to 69.9 million, of which 6.8 million or just under 10 percent were Negroes. However, if the male and female components of the total labor force are differentiated, one finds that Negro men accounted for only 8.7 percent of the men, while Negro women accounted for 12.0 percent of all women workers.

The growth of the labor force is conditioned by a great many different factors, including the number of adults in the population; the conventions governing the ages at which they enter upon or withdraw from employment; the job opportunities that prevail; social attitudes toward the employment of special groups such as young people, married women, and old persons, and still other factors.

TABLE II—Percentage Change in Labor Force, by Decades, by Sex and Race, 1890–1960

	1890 to 1900	1900 to 1910	1910 to 1920	1920 to 1930	1930 to 1940	1940 to 1950	1950 to 1960
Total labor force	25	29	14	15	7	14	16
White	24	30	15	16	8	14	15
Negro	30	19	6	9	−3	9	18
Male labor force	23	26	13	13	4	9	8
White	22	27	13	13	4	9	8
Negro	27	17	9	7	−4	7	10
Female labor force	33	40	16	24	17	29	35
White	32	46	20	27	21	31	35
Negro	36	22	1	13	−3	13	37

SOURCE: Based on data in U.S. Bureau of the Census, Census of Population: 1910, Vol 1V, *Occupation Statistics,* Table 15; *Negro Population, 1790–1915,* Table 3; *A Social-Economic Grouping of the Gainful Workers of the United States,* Tables 3 and 4; U.S. Census of Population: 1950, *U.S. Summary, Detailed Characteristics,* Table 195.

Since the beginning of the century (Table II) the white labor force has been growing more rapidly than the Negro labor force. Different forces in different decades can help to explain this trend. Up to the outbreak of World War I, the white labor force grew very rapidly, among other reasons because of the very heavy immigration which characterized those years. For twenty years more, the white labor force continued to have significant incremental gains because the offspring of these earlier immigrants were reaching working age. During most of these decades the proportion of Negroes shifting from rural to urban areas was greater than for whites, and incident to such a shift was later entrance into the labor force and earlier retirement in urban areas than on the farm. Also, more and more white women tended, especially after 1940, to return to work in middle age. Although the Negro birth rate was rising more rapidly and the Negro death rate was falling more rapidly than the corresponding white rates, the above factors operating to accelerate the growth of the white labor force overbalanced the population factors that were increasing the size of the Negro labor force. Since 1950, however, the Negro labor force has been growing slightly more rapidly than white, primarily because during the 1930's and 1940's the reproduction rate was higher and increased more rapidly among Negroes than whites.

The regional distribution of the Negro labor force has followed the population distribution set out in Chapter 2. As late as 1910 almost 90 percent of the Negro labor force continued to be concentrated in the South. World War I gave a substantial impetus to the northward migration of the Negro which had been underway since even before the Civil War. The 1920's saw a continuation of this trend, though at a reduced rate, and the same was true for the depressed 1930's. While there were no great numbers of jobs opening up for Negroes in the North between 1920 and 1940, the depressed status of Southern agriculture pushed many Negroes off the farm and many felt they were better off in the North, even if they had no more to look forward to than menial employment or a job on work relief. World War II ushered in an accelerated shift of the Negro labor force out of the South, both to the North and to the West. This continued after hostilities came to an end. By 1960 more than four out of every ten Negroes were employed outside of the South.

These gross movements mask some important additional shifts that took place. Many Negroes who left the South for the North and West did so as a result of a two-staged move. First they moved off a Southern farm into a Southern city; and only later, after they had become somewhat acclimated to urban ways, did they relocate outside of the South, again in urban centers. In fact, the Negro has tended both in the South and outside of the South to be disproportionately heavily represented in a selected number of large cities.

By 1960 the Negro population was more urbanized than the white population, more than three of every four Negroes being an urbanite (Table III).

TABLE III—Negro and White Labor Forces, Urban and Rural, by Sex, 1960

	Percent Distribution	
	Negro	White
Urban total	78.4	72.2
Male	75.6	69.9
Female	82.8	77.2
Rural total	21.6	27.8
Male	24.4	30.1
Female	17.2	22.8
Total U.S.	100.0	100.0
Male	100.0	100.0
Female	100.0	100.0

SOURCE: U.S. Bureau of the Census, Census of Population: 1960, *United States Summary, Detailed Characteristics*, Table 194; *Nonwhite Population by Race*, Table 32.

While a few Negroes joined the white rush to the suburbs during the 1950's, most of them remained locked in the central city, where they found it somewhat easier to secure, in the face of serious privation, at least the minimum housing which they required. Today the Negro labor force is more heavily concentrated than the white labor force in the larger cities of the South and the North.

The occupations that individuals pursue are determined by a variety of forces, including in particular the education and training which they have undergone, the job openings that exist in the communities where they grow up or to which they relocate and the extent to which their access to better jobs is facilitated or retarded by special forces, including such matters as segregation practices and discrimination. Conventionally, the occupational structure is viewed as a 10-stage hierarchy, from professional and related occupations at the top to laborers and farm workers at the bottom. Although some farmers do quite well, most have relatively low incomes, and they therefore may be classified at the bottom with farm laborers. It is also conventional to distinguish between white collar workers, including professional, managerial, clerical and sales workers, and blue collar workers, including craftsmen, operatives, laborers and service workers. Although there are a great many exceptions, the higher the proportion of a group in the white collar occupations at the top of the scale, the better their jobs, incomes, and status. The reverse is true for concentrations at the bottom of the hierarchy.

The Occupational Structure of the Negro Labor Force

The Negro labor force is substantially concentrated in the semiskilled, unskilled, service and farm occupations. This is true for both men and women. As Table IV indicates, over 70 percent of both Negro men and women are in these occupations. Among Negro men, one in four is an operative—typically a semiskilled worker in manufacturing or a truck driver—one in five a laborer, one in seven a service worker, one in ten a craftsman or foreman and another in ten a farm operator or worker. As Table V shows, one quarter of a million Negro men are employed as janitors and porters and another quarter million are truck drivers and deliverymen. Of the eleven largest occupations for Negro males, only one, automobile mechanics and repairmen, is above the semiskilled level.

Although Negroes comprise only 8.4 percent of total male employment, they comprise a far higher proportion in many occupations at the lower end of the scale, where skill, income and prestige are low. As Table VI shows, Negroes comprise one fourth or more of all male employees among janitors, longshoremen, laundry and dry cleaning operatives, and laborers in many industries. Other fields in which Negro men comprise a relatively high share of the male employees include various foundry occupations such as furnacemen and metal molders, plaster and cement finishers, elevator operators, taxicab drivers and chauffeurs, and operatives in sawmills, motor vehicle manufacturing and diverse other industries.

TABLE IV—Occupations of Employed Negroes by Sex, 1960

	Number			Percent distribution		
	Total	Male	Female	Total	Male	Female
Total employed Negroes	6,099,089	3,643,949	2,455,140	100.0	100.0	100.0
Professional, technical, etc.	287,969	112,661	175,308	4.7	3.0	7.1
Managers, officers and proprietors, exc. farm	87,950	63,193	24,757	1.4	1.7	1.0
Clerical	360,598	178,920	181,678	5.9	4.9	7.4
Sales	82,768	46,685	36,083	1.4	1.3	1.5
Craftsmen, foremen, etc.	372,463	356,586	15,877	6.1	9.8	0.6
Operatives	1,197,667	887,434	310,233	19.6	24.4	12.6
Private household workers	915,494	27,288	888,206	15.0	0.7	36.2
Service, exc. pvt. hshld.	1,027,765	507,942	519,823	16.9	13.9	21.2
Laborers, exc. farm and mine	768,621	744,994	23,627	12.6	20.4	1.0
Farmers and farm managers	168,776	154,240	14,536	2.8	3.0	0.7
Farm laborers and foremen	326,193	256,698	69,495	5.3	7.0	2.8
Occupation not reported	502,825	307,308	195,517	8.2	8.4	8.0

SOURCE: U.S. Bureau of the Census, Census of Population: 1960, *United States Summary, Detailed Characteristics*, Table 205.

TABLE V—Occupations Employing Large Numbers of Negro Men, 1960

	Number	Percent of all employed Negro men
Janitors and porters	265,339	7.3
Truck drivers and deliverymen	248,276	6.8
Farm laborers, except unpaid, and farm foremen	237,108	6.5
Laborers (n.e.c.), construction	157,724	4.3
Lumbermen, raftsmen and wood choppers	111,603	3.0
Laborers (n.e.c.), wholesale and retail trade	56,881	1.6
Operatives (n.e.c.), food and kindred products mfg.	44,369	1.2
Automobile mechanics and repairmen	44,272	1.2
Laborers (n.e.c.), primary metal industries	44,113	1.2
Cooks, except pvt. household	42,998	1.2
Waiters, bartenders and counter workers	37,527	1.0

SOURCE: Same as for Table IV

TABLE VI—Occupations in Which a Large Percentage of the Male Employees Were Negro, 1960

Occupation	Negro men as a percent of all men
Private household workers	44.7
Janitors and porters	37.2
Laborers (n.e.c.), not specified mfg. industries	35.1
Longshoremen and stevedores	34.5
Laundry and dry cleaning operatives	33.3
Laborers (n.e.c.), misc. nonmanufacturing industries	31.2
Lumbermen, raftsmen and woodchoppers	30.8
Laborers (n.e.c.), communications, and utility and sanitary service	30.7
Laborers (n.e.c.), chemicals and allied products	30.2
Laborers, furniture, saw and planing mills, and misc. wood products	30.0
Laborers (n.e.c.) transportation equipment mfg.	27.9
Laborers (n.e.c.) railroads and railway express	27.8
Laborers (n.e.c.), primary metal mfg.	26.4
Laborers (n.e.c.), construction	25.9
Misc. specified laborers	23.7
Furnacemen, smeltermen and pourers	22.8
Laborers (n.e.c.) textile mill products and apparel mfg.	22.7
Farm laborers, exc. unpaid, and farm foremen	22.7
Molders, metal	22.3
Misc. service workers, exc. private household	22.1
Laborers (n.e.c.), food and kindred products mfg.	21.8
Plasterers and cement finishers	21.7
Cooks, except private household	21.5
Elevator operators	21.4
Laborers (n.e.c.), transportation, except railroad	21.0
Laborers (n.e.c.), stone, clay, and glass products	19.7
Operatives (n.e.c.), saw and planing mills and misc. wood products	18.8
Taxicab drivers and chauffeurs	18.3
Laborers (n.e.c.), fabricated metal industries	18.0
Laborers (n.e.c.), wholesale and retail trade	17.9
Sawyers	17.8
Operatives (n.e.c.), wholesale and retail trade	17.2
Packers and wrappers (n.e.c.)	15.4
Operatives (n.e.c.), primary metal mfg.	15.0
Operatives (n.e.c.), food and kindred products mfg.	14.7
Operatives (n.e.c.), misc. nonmfg. industries	14.7
Operatives (n.e.c.), motor vehicles and motor vehicles equipment mfg.	14.0
Laborers (n.e.c.), machinery mfg., including electrical	13.4
Truck drivers and deliverymen	12.7
Farm laborers, unpaid family workers	12.6
Stationary firemen	12.3
Waiters, bartenders, and counter workers	12.2
Shoemakers and repairmen, exc. factory	12.1
Operatives (n.e.c.), transport, commun., and other public utility	11.5
Masons, tile setters, and stone cutters	11.4
Sailors and deck hands	10.5
Mail carriers	10.4
Painters, exc. construction and maintenance	10.3
Operatives (n.e.c.), stone, clay and glass products mfg.	10.2
Bus drivers	10.1

SOURCE: Same as for Table IV

TABLE VII—Occupations Employing 10 Percent or more of the Negro Men within each Occupational Group, 1960

Occupation	Number	Percent distribution within group
Professional, technical and kindred	**112,661**	**100.0**
Teachers		
secondary	14,823	13.1
elementary	13,451	11.9
Clergymen	13,955	12.4
Managers, officials, & prop. exc. farm	**63,193**	**100.0**
Wholesale and retail trade		
Self-employed	17,791	28.2
Salaried	6,373	10.0
Clerical and kindred workers	**178,920**	**100.0**
Postal clerks	*	16.5
Shipping and receiving clerks		
Stock clerks and storekeepers	*	14.4
Mail carriers	20,050	11.2
Salesworkers	**46,685**	**100.0**
Retail trade—food and dairy products	*	20.2
Newsboys		
Insurance agents, brokers, underwriters	4,901	10.5
Hucksters and peddlers	*	10.3
Craftsmen, foremen and kindred	**356,586**	**100.0**
Carpenters	35,830	10.0
Automobile mechanics and repairmen	44,272	12.4
Operatives and kindred	**887,434**	**100.0**
Truck drivers and deliverymen	248,276	28.0
Service workers, exc. pvt. hshld.	**507,942**	**100.0**
Janitors and porters	265,339	52.2
Laborers, except farm & mine	**744,994**	**100.0**
Laborers (n.e.c.), construction	157,724	21.2
Lumbermen, raftsmen, and woodchoppers	35,870	4.8

* Actual count not available; percentage estimated from sample data.

SOURCE: U.S. Bureau of the Census, Census of Population: 1960, *United States Summary, Detailed Characteristics,* Table 205; *Occupational Characteristics,* Table 3.

Among the higher ranking occupations, one third of all Negro men in the professional and technical occupations are teachers or clergymen (Table VII). Since many clergymen are not graduates of theological institutions and many lead very small congregations, their occupational status does not carry with it the usual prerequisites of such employment. Nearly four out of ten Negro male managers and proprietors are in wholesale and retail trade, primarily in eating and drinking places and food and dairy products stores. The latter stores also employ one in five Negro male sales workers. Clearly these are small establishments where the sales volume permits at best a relatively small net profit and correspondingly relatively small salaries. Over half of all Negro male clerical workers are postal clerks, shipping and receiving clerks, stock clerks, storekeepers, and mailmen.

TABLE VIII—Occupations Employing Large Numbers of Negro Women, 1960

Occupation	Number	As percent of all employed Negro women
Private household workers, living out	848,334	34.6
Laundry and dry cleaning operatives	99,494	4.0
Cooks, except private household	80,980	3.3
Teachers: elementary school	75,695	3.1
Attendants, hospital and other institutions	66,997	2.7
Farm laborers, exc. unpaid and farm foremen	57,647	2.3
Waitresses, counter workers, etc.	54,123	2.2
Charwomen, janitors and porters	50,655	2.1
Operatives (n.e.c.), apparel and other fabricated textile products mfg.	34,550	1.4
Practical nurses and midwives	32,192	1.3
Nurses, professional	32,034	1.3
Hairdressers and cosmotologists	31,918	1.3
Saleswomen and sales clerks (n.e.c.), retail trade	28,691	1.2
Typists	27,142	1.1

SOURCE: Same as for Table IV

Negro women are even more strongly concentrated in a few lower level jobs than are Negro men (Table IV). Seventy percent are in the two fields of service workers and operatives. Fully one third of all employed Negro women, or 848,000, were employed as private household workers in 1960 (Table VIII). Other leading occupations at the semiskilled and service level include laundry and dry cleaning operatives, cooks, hospital attendants, waitresses, and charwomen. In contrast to the men, however, a substantially larger proportion of Negro women are in more desirable jobs, such as elementary school teacher, nurse, hairdresser or cosmetologist, sales clerk and typist.

Among all female workers, Negro women thus comprise half or more of the domestics and paid farm workers, one fourth or more of the laundry and dry cleaning operatives and charwomen, and one fifth of the cooks and institutional attendants (Table IX). Fully half of the Negro women in the professional and technical occupations are school teachers, and half of those who are managers and proprietors are in wholesale and retail trade (Table X). Negro women in managerial and sales positions are primarily in food and dairy products stores, as are Negro men. These white collar jobs do not necessarily carry high earnings or high prestige. Substantial numbers of Negro women clerical workers, whether typists, secretaries or in miscellaneous other fields, are governmental employees.

TABLE IX—Occupations in which a Large Percentage of the Female Employees Were Negro, 1960

Occupation	Negro women as a percent of all women
Private household workers	53.4
Farm laborers, exc. unpaid, and farm foremen	48.1
Laundry and dry cleaning operatives	35.9
Charwomen, janitors, and porters	25.0
Attendants, hospital and other institutions	23.2
Cooks, except private household	22.4
Operatives (n.e.c.), nonmanufacturing	17.9
Practical nurses and midwives	16.3
Operatives (n.e.c.), food and kindred products mfg.	16.0

SOURCE: Same as for Table IV

If the occupational distribution of the Negro male population is studied on a regional basis one does not find any striking variations from one region to another (Tables XI and XII). The major difference is that in the South about 17 percent of the men are still in farming compared to less than three percent in the Northeast, North Central and Western regions. Also, 24 percent of all Negro male workers in the South are laborers, compared with 15 to 18 percent in the three other regions. The South does not differ strikingly from the other regions in terms of the proportion of Negro men employed in the operative, professional, proprietary or sales categories. The South does employ relatively fewer Negroes than all the other regions in service, skilled and clerical occupations. However, only in the clerical field

TABLE X—Occupations Employing 10 percent or More of the Negro
Women within each Occupational Group, 1960

Occupation	Number	Percent distribution within group
Professional, technical and kindred	**175,308**	**100.0**
Teachers		
elementary school	75,695	43.1
secondary school	18,194	10.4
Mgrs., officials and prop., exc. farm	**24,757**	**100.0**
Wholesale and retail trade		
self-employed	10,023	40.5
salaried	2,831	11.4
Clerical and kindred	**181,678**	**100.0**
Typists	27,142	15.0
Clerical and kindred workers (n.e.c.),		
public administration	*	12.9
Secretaries	20,650	11.4
Sales workers	**36,083**	**100.0**
Retail trade	28,691	79.5
Food and dairy prod. stores	*	22.7
General mdse.	*	19.4
Apparel and accessories	*	11.1
Operatives	**310,233**	**100.0**
Laundry and dry cleaning	99,494	32.0
Apparel and other fabricated textile products	34,550	11.1
Service, exc. pvt. household	**519,823**	**100.0**
Cooks, except pvt. hshld.	80,980	15.6
Chambermaids and maids, exc. pvt. hshld.	*	19.1
Attendants, hospital and other institutions	66,997	12.9
Waitresses, bartenders and counter workers	54,123	10.4

* Actual count not available; percentage estimated from sample data.

SOURCE: Same as for Table VII

is the discrepancy relatively marked. There are fewer Negro men employed in the South in this field than in other regions.

The differences among the regions are more marked in the case of the employment patterns for Negro women. Although nearly 5 percent of employed Negro women in the South are in farming, compared to almost none in the other regions, this is but one of the sharp contrasts that exist between the South and the rest of the country. Marked discrepancies occur in the area of clerical work, in which only 4 percent of the Negro women in the South, but 13 percent in the other regions, are employed; in the operatives category, in which less than 9 percent are employed in the South, but from 13 to 22 percent in the other regions; and in private household service, which accounts for roughly 25 percent of the Negro women in the Northeast, North Central and West, but as much as 45 percent in the South.

TABLE XI—Occupations of Employed Negroes, by Sex, for Regions, 1960

	Northeast	North Central	South	West
Total males	**638,866**	**678,393**	**2,118,185**	**208,505**
Professional, technical, etc.	23,256	20,595	59,429	9.381
Managers, offs. & prop. except farm	17,035	12,144	29,155	4,859
Clerical	56,946	45,913	61,062	14,999
Sales	12,456	10,568	20,176	3,485
Craftsmen, foremen, etc.	73,272	74,954	181,516	26,844
Operatives	174,359	196,646	472,752	43,677
Private household workers	5,347	3,515	17,184	1,242
Service, exc. pvt. hshld.	99,847	101,757	269,288	37,050
Laborers, exc. farm & mine	97,206	119,689	490,102	37,997
Farmers and farm mgrs.	698	1,580	151,014	948
Farm laborers & foremen	4,982	4,596	242,309	4,811
Occupation not reported	73,462	86,436	124,198	23,212
Total females	**486,506**	**414,098**	**1,414,932**	**139,604**
Professional, technical, etc.	31,192	28,147	105,458	10,511
Managers, offs. & prop. except farm	4,377	4,623	13,967	1,790
Clerical	61,222	51,797	50,110	18,549
Sales	10,526	8,900	14,344	2,313
Craftsmen, foremen, etc.	4,684	3,795	6,082	1,316
Operatives	108,146	62,460	120,943	18,684
Private household workers	120,524	91,370	637,273	39,039
Service, exc. pvt. hshld.	87,323	106,078	295,094	31,328
Laborers, exc. farm & mine	3,670	5,658	12,865	1,434
Farmers and farm mgrs.	65	118	14,312	41
Farm laborers & foremen	738	653	67,536	568
Occupation not reported	54,039	50,499	76,948	14,031

SOURCE: U.S. Bureau of the Census, Census of Population: 1960, *United States Summary, Detailed Characteristics*, Table 257.

TABLE XII—Percentage Distribution of Employed Negroes by Sex and Occupation, for Regions, 1960

	Northeast	North Central	South	West
Total males	100.0	100.0	100.0	100.0
Professional, technical, etc.	3.6	3.0	2.8	4.5
Managers, offs. & prop. exc. farm	2.7	1.8	1.4	2.3
Clerical	8.9	6.8	2.9	7.2
Sales	1.9	1.6	1.0	1.7
Craftsmen, foremen, etc.	11.5	11.0	8.6	12.9
Operatives	27.3	29.0	22.3	20.9
Private household workers	0.8	0.5	0.8	0.6
Service, exc. pvt. hshld.	15.6	15.0	12.7	17.8
Laborers, exc. farm & mine	15.2	17.6	23.1	18.2
Farmers and farm mgrs.	0.1	0.2	7.1	0.5
Farm laborers & foremen	0.8	0.7	11.4	2.3
Occupation not reported	11.5	12.7	5.9	11.1
Total females	100.0	100.0	100.0	100.0
Professional, technical, etc.	6.4	6.8	7.5	7.5
Managers, offs. & props. exc. farm	0.9	1.1	1.0	1.3
Clerical	12.6	12.5	3.5	13.3
Sales	2.2	2.1	1.0	1.7
Craftsmen, foremen, etc.	1.0	0.9	0.4	0.9
Operatives	22.2	15.0	8.5	13.4
Private household workers	24.8	22.0	45.0	28.0
Service, exc. pvt. hshld.	17.9	25.6	21.0	22.4
Laborers, exc. farm & mine	0.8	1.4	0.9	1.0
Farmers and farm mgrs.	0.0	0.0	1.0	0.0
Farm laborers & foremen	0.2	0.2	4.8	0.4
Occupation not reported	11.1	12.2	5.4	10.0

SOURCE: Same as for Table XI

On the other hand, the South is in some regards much like the other regions. For instance, relatively few Negro women in the South, as elsewhere, are sales workers, business managers and proprietors, craftsmen and foremen, and unskilled laborers. Both in the South and elsewhere a substantial proportion are employed in nonhousehold service work (18 to 26 percent) and in the professions (6 to 8 percent).

There is a widespread but erroneous notion that there are deeply ingrained patterns of Negro employment which prevail for long periods of time in different regions of the country. Even in the South, however, study after study has revealed that while a general pattern could be discerned, significant exceptions existed in almost every community. Moreover, the

TABLE XIII—Occupational Distribution of Negro Workers, by Region, 1940, 1950, and 1960

	South			Other Regions		
	1940	1950	1960	1940	1950	1960
Total Negro male employment *	100.0	100.0	100.0	100.0	100.0	100.0
Professional, technical and kindred	1.6	2.0	3.0	3.1	2.6	4.0
Managers, officials and proprietors	0.9	1.4	1.5	2.8	3.0	2.5
Clerical and sales	1.2	2.4	4.1	5.6	7.8	11.0
Craftsmen and foremen	3.6	6.4	9.1	7.7	10.8	13.0
Operatives	10.9	18.6	23.7	19.6	27.4	30.8
Service	11.2	11.2	14.4	32.6	21.4	18.5
Nonfarm laborers	20.6	23.6	24.6	24.5	24.9	18.9
Total nonfarm	50.0	65.6	80.3	95.9	97.9	98.8
Farmers and farm workers	50.0	34.4	19.7	4.1	2.1	1.2
Total Negro female employment *	100.0	100.0	100.0	100.0	100.0	100.0
Professional, technical and kindred	4.4	6.3	7.9	3.7	4.6	7.6
Managers, officials and proprietors	0.6	1.3	1.0	1.1	1.4	1.2
Clerical and sales	0.9	3.5	4.8	3.0	9.0	16.7
Craftsmen and foremen	0.1	0.4	0.4	0.3	1.1	1.0
Operatives	5.0	9.5	9.0	10.6	24.7	20.5
Service workers, private household	58.8	45.4	47.6	64.4	35.8	27.2
Other service workers	8.9	18.2	22.0	15.9	20.9	24.4
Nonfarm laborers	0.9	1.2	1.0	0.8	2.1	1.2
Total nonfarm	79.6	85.8	93.9	99.8	99.6	99.8
Farmers and farm workers	20.4	14.2	6.1	0.2	0.4	0.2

* Those for whom no occupation was reported are distributed proportionately among the occupational groups.

SOURCE: Eli Ginzberg, *The Negro Potential*, New York, Columbia University Press, 1956, pp. 23 and 28.

general patterns can best be described in terms of the gross proportions of Negroes in the major occupational fields and industries, for considerable variability within the general patterns can be discerned. For instance, while it is true that the proportion of Negro women among operatives in the South is relatively small, there are localities where their proportion is very large. Moreover, while certain industries may have very few such operatives, other industries may have a substantial number.

Occupational Trends

There is a tendency for occupational trends to shift relatively slowly. This reflects the fact that the technological and economic factors in the several sectors of the economy, the geographical distribution of various population groups and the educational, political and social factors that affect their access to various occupations are all likely to change relatively slowly. In reviewing the occupational trends of the Negro population since the outbreak of World War II, one finds both relative stability and substantial changes. For instance, in 1940 as in 1960 the major difference between the South and the North lay in the heavier concentration of Negro males in farming in the South. At that time, as Table 13 shows, 50 percent of all Negro men in the South were in farming, 11 percent were in service occupations and another 11 percent were operatives, whereas in the rest of the country only 4 percent were in farming, but 20 percent were operatives, and 33 percent were in service occupations. However, in the years intervening, the Southern Negro male labor force has been shifting out of farming primarily in the direction of semiskilled and skilled work. In the North, the more important trends have been the decline in the relative importance of service and unskilled labor and the increased importance of semiskilled, skilled and clerical work. On the other hand the relative importance of the professions and management has changed very little, although such changes as have occurred have been more pronounced in the South than in the rest of the country.

Over the last two decades, there have not been striking changes in the occupational distribution of Negro women in the South. During the 1940's, there was a substantial reduction in the proportions employed as private household workers and to a lesser extent on farms. The major growth areas were among nonhousehold service occupations and semiskilled operatives. In the 1950's, a major decline occurred in farm occupations, with minor growth in service employment. Over both decades, there were also significant although not large increases in the proportion of Negro women in the South employed in professional, clerical and sales occupations.

The shifts in the occupational distribution of Negro women in the rest of the country were somewhat more dramatic. The proportion employed as domestics declined from 64 to 36 percent between 1940 and 1950, and declined further, down to 27 percent, by 1960. The major increase was a growth from 3 to 17 percent in clerical and sales work. The proportion employed as operatives first increased dramatically from 11 to 25 percent, but then declined to 17 percent. There were more sustained increases in the proportion employed as service workers other than in households and in professional and related fields.

The continuing shift of the Negro population from the Southern farm to

TABLE XIV—Percent Distribution of White and Negro Employed by Occupational Fields, 1910–1960

	1910 White	1910 Negro	1920 White	1920 Negro	1930 White	1930 Negro	1940 White	1940 Negro	1950 White	1950 Negro	1960 White	1960 Negro
All sectors	100.0	100.0	100.0	100.0	100.0	100.0	100.0*	100.0*	100.0*	100.0*	100.0*	100.0*
Nonfarm, total	72.0	49.6	76.0	53.4	80.6	63.9	82.3	66.6	81.6	79.5	89.6	83.6
White collar sector, total	23.8	3.0	27.8	3.6	33.0	4.6	35.7	6.0	39.9	10.2	44.1	13.4
Professional & tech.	4.8	1.4	5.3	1.5	6.5	2.1	8.0	2.7	8.6	3.4	11.9	4.7
Props., mgrs. & offcls.	7.4	0.8	7.4	0.8	8.3	1.0	9.0	1.3	9.8	2.0	9.1	1.4
Clerical & sales	11.6	0.8	15.1	1.3	18.2	1.5	18.7	2.0	21.5	4.8	23.1	7.3
Manual & service sector	48.2	46.6	48.2	49.8	47.6	59.3	46.6	60.6	47.7	69.3	45.5	70.3
Skilled	13.0	2.5	14.5	3.0	14.2	3.2	12.2	3.0	14.4	5.5	14.3	6.1
Semiskilled & operative	16.1	5.4	16.8	7.3	17.2	9.4	19.0	10.3	20.3	18.3	18.3	19.6
Laborers	14.3	17.4	13.4	20.8	11.7	21.6	6.1	14.3	5.0	15.7	4.0	12.6
Service	4.8	21.3	3.5	18.7	4.5	25.1	9.3	33.0	8.0	29.8	8.9	31.9
Farm, total	28.0	50.4	24.1	46.6	19.4	36.1	16.7	32.8	11.1	19.0	5.9	8.1

* Sum of items does not equal 100.0 because of those for whom no occupation was reported.

SOURCE: Dale L. Hiestand, *Economic Growth and Employment Opportunities for Minorities*, New York, Columbia University Press, 1964, p. 42 and U.S. Bureau of the Census, *Census of Population: 1960, U. S. Summary, Detailed Characteristics*, Table 205.

the Southern city and to the urban centers in the North and West, as well as the continuing improvement of their occupational position within each region, has profoundly altered their overall occupational distribution. Each improvement in the position of the Negro lays the basis for further gains. As the incomes of Negroes have grown, opportunities in Negro owned businesses have increased. Improvements in the political and economic position of the Negro in both the South and the North have facilitated his increased employment in government. The result has been a fairly steady and long-run upgrading in the total Negro labor force.

As Table XIV shows, in 1910 half of the Negro labor force was in farming, as compared to only 28 percent of the white labor force. This discrepancy no longer prevails, for only 7 percent of the white labor force and 11 percent of the Negro labor force were in farming in 1960. As the white labor force transferred out of farming, its major growth area was in white collar work. The proportion of the white labor force in manual and service work has remained remarkably stable since 1910 at almost 50 percent. In contrast, as the Negro labor force shifted out of farming, it went until 1940 almost wholly into manual and service work. Since then, the shift has been evenly divided, with white collar work being as important as manual and service. Over the decades, the proportion of the Negro labor force in manual and service work has increased from 47 to 73 percent, while the proportion in white collar work has increased from 3 to 15 percent.

Each decade is more or less unique in terms of the major occupational opportunities which open up to Negroes. Between 1910 and 1920, for instance, Negroes found substantial opportunities in unskilled labor but also made a sizeable breakthrough into semiskilled work. The 1920's were noted chiefly for substantial withdrawals from Southern agriculture to service work, but also saw a significant expansion in semiskilled employment. The depression of the 1930's hit Negroes severely as job opportunities declined severely even in such traditional fields as service and unskilled labor. As a result not only did total Negro employment decline between 1930 and 1940, but the total number of Negroes in the labor force also declined. During the 1940's their major improvements occurred at the operative level. These fields accounted for 10 percent of all Negro employment in 1940 but over 18 percent in 1950. The 1940's also marked the beginning of significant employment at the clerical and skilled level. The 1950's saw continued improvement at the semiskilled and higher levels, particularly at the clerical level. There has been a slow but steady growth in the relative importance of the professional and related occupations for Negroes, but no significant increase has occurred as yet at the managerial level.

Trends Toward Occupational Equality

Throughout all earlier generations, there were striking differences in the occupational patterns of Negro and white workers, not only on the basis of national comparisons, but also even when comparisons were made in the same region. Originally these differences reflected such overriding institutions as slavery and later racial segregation, particularly in the farming communities of the South, where most Negroes lived and worked. In recent decades, Negroes have relocated to areas where the labor market has been less sharply differentiated on a racial basis. Moreover, there is much greater concern and efforts are now being made to open employment opportunities to the Negro from which he had previously been barred. These developments bring into focus the question of the trends towards occupational equality between whites and Negroes.

While Negroes have moved increasingly into high-level occupations, whites have also been shifting from farming and the lesser skilled fields into these higher level occupations. The question whether Negroes have achieved a greater measure of occupational equality must consider not only their gains, but also the gains that the whites have been able to make. The data in Table XV provide one way of looking at this. This table traces out the changes in the relative number of white and Negro workers in the various fields, account having been taken of relative size of each group.

This table shows that throughout the past half-century, white men have been and continue to be present in white collar occupations in relatively greater numbers than Negro men. In 1910, white men were seven times more numerous in white collar work than Negro men, and they were still relatively three times more numerous in 1960. The position of white men in clerical and sales work has declined from ten times to two times the proportion of Negro men. On the other hand, there has been little change over the long run in the relative position of white men in the professions, for they have had a threefold lead over Negroes throughout the half-century, a lead that increased slightly during the last decade. The relative position of white men in the managerial fields decreased from eightfold to fivefold between 1910 and 1950 but increased to sevenfold by 1960.

In the manual and service sector, quite diverse patterns can be found. Among operatives, Negro men are now overrepresented, where they were formerly underrepresented. The relatively greater number of white men among skilled workers and foremen has declined, from fourfold to twofold. Among laborers and service workers, Negro men continued to be over-represented, although the extent thereof has increased among laborers and

TABLE XV—Ratio of White to Negro Workers* by Occupational Field and Sex, 1910–1960

	Male						Female					
	1910	1920	1930	1940	1950	1960	1910	1920	1930	1940	1950	1960
All sectors	1.0	1.0	1.0	1.0	1.0	1.0	1.0	1.0	1.0	1.0	1.0	1.0
Nonfarm, total	1.5	1.4	1.3	1.3	1.1	1.1	1.3	1.6	1.3	1.2	1.1	1.0
White collar sector, total	6.8	6.6	6.3	3.4	3.8	2.9	12.7	12.7	10.5	7.8	4.5	3.5
Professional & technical	2.9	2.9	2.8	3.2	3.1	3.7	6.6	5.9	4.8	3.4	2.3	2.4
Props., mgrs., & officials	8.1	8.7	7.8	6.4	5.1	6.8	4.9	4.6	4.7	5.7	3.4	2.9
Clerical & sales workers	10.1	8.1	8.3	6.4	3.4	2.0	43.2	34.2	30.5	21.3	6.9	4.7
Manual & service sector, total	1.1	1.0	0.9	0.9	0.8	0.7	1.0	0.8	0.6	0.6	0.5	0.5
Skilled workers & foremen	4.3	4.0	3.7	3.6	2.4	2.1	30.5	13.9	12.1	7.1	2.5	1.6
Operatives & semiskilled	2.5	2.0	1.7	1.5	1.0	0.8	5.2	3.5	2.6	2.1	1.3	1.0
Laborers	0.7	0.5	0.5	0.4	0.3	0.3	1.5	0.9	0.8	1.1	0.5	1.4
Service workers	0.2	0.2	0.2	0.4	0.4	0.4	0.4	0.3	0.3	0.3	0.3	0.3
Farm, total	0.6	0.6	0.6	0.5	0.6	0.6	0.2	0.2	0.2	0.1	0.3	0.4

* Relative to their number in total work force.

SOURCE: Same as for Table XIV, Hiestand, p. 48.

decreased among service workers. The relative underrepresentation of white men in farming continued at approximately the same level throughout the half-century.

In comparing Negro and white women, the trend toward equality in the white collar sector has been even stronger than among men, particularly in the professional and in the clerical and sales categories. Among women in manual and service categories, a position of relative equality prevailed in 1910. Negro women are now relatively more prominent in this sector, although the degree to which this is true has changed little since 1930. Among operatives, white women were once relatively five times as numerous, but now a position of "equality" prevails. The underrepresentation of white women in the service occupations, as well as in farming, has changed little over the past half-century.

Despite, or perhaps because of these differing trends in the several occupational groups the search for a clear answer to the question of whether the Negro has been improving his position relative to the white continues. The data in Table XVI provide one answer to this question. This provides an index of relative occupational position, which takes into consideration the respective distribution of whites and Negroes at various occupational levels, but does not reflect changes in earnings in these several fields. The index reflects the shifts in the distribution noted in Table XIV.

TABLE XVI—Index of Occupational Position of Negroes Relative to Whites, by Sex, 1910–1960

	Men	Women
1910	78.0	78.0
1920	78.1	71.3
1930	78.2	74.8
1940	77.5	76.8
1950	81.4	81.6
1960	82.1	84.3

SOURCE: Dale L. Hiestand, *Economic Growth and Employment Opportunities for Minorities*, New York, Columbia University Press, 1964, p. 53.

As Table XVI shows, the occupational position of Negroes relative to whites has improved very slightly over the long run. The index for men hardly changed between 1910 and 1930. Between 1930 and 1940, the position of Negro men relative to whites actually deteriorated. The major improvement in the position of Negro men relative to whites has occurred since 1940 and nearly all of it during the 1940–50 decade.

A different pattern is found among women. The occupational position of Negro women relative to whites deteriorated greatly between 1910 and

1920, but has improved significantly in each decade since then. As a result, a smaller gap between the races now prevails among women than among men.

Regional Differences in Relative Occupational Status

While these national comparisons are illuminating and useful for certain purposes, there is the question of whether important regional and state differences lurk back of the national figures. Are there areas in the United States where the Negro has moved toward occupational equality with the white population, or did the trend toward equality found in the national data fail to appear in some regions and states? The data in Table XVII, computed in a slightly different way from those in Table XVI, provide an answer.

These data confirm the finding that Negro men made significant progress in closing the occupational gap during the 1940's, but their rate of progress relative to white men slowed down considerably during the 1950's. More importantly, the data in Table XVII show that in not a single state was the improvement in relative occupational position as great as in the nation as a whole. The improvement was particularly marked in Louisiana, South Carolina, Massachusetts and Maryland. In some cases, this reflects a relatively rapid growth in employment opportunities in higher level occupations; in others it reflects a rapid reduction of employment in farming and other low paying occupations as a result of outmigration.

The relative occupational position of Negro men improved in most states. In a number of states—notably in all of the North Central states—their relative occupational position declined slightly between 1940 and 1960. During this period, these states experienced substantial inflows of Negro manpower.

This points up the fact that the rapid improvement of the Negro position reflects two trends: their relative improvement within specific states, and their migration from states in the South where they have done relatively poorly to states in the North where they do relatively better, even though they remain at a disadvantage.

Negroes in the Armed Forces

The analysis up to this point has been concerned almost exclusively with the position of the Negro in the civilian labor force. However, as was pointed out at the beginning of this chapter, nearly three million white and Negro men and women are in the Armed Forces. For many, such service is the equivalent of a career in the civilian sector of the economy.

But the Armed Forces have a significance that transcends the fact that they offer employment for considerable numbers of white and Negro workers. Even those who remain for only one or two tours of duty and then return to civilian life will have a better or worse opportunity to find a desirable job, depending on the training, skills and experiences that they had while on active duty.

The experience of Negroes in the Armed Forces has therefore a twofold significance: as an area of employment while they are in service, and as a factor in facilitating or retarding the type of employment which they can secure when they return to civilian life.

TABLE XVII—Index of Occupational Position of Negro Relative to White Males, by States,* 1940–1960

	1940	1950	1960
United States, total	70	77	81
Northeast			
Massachusetts	81	84	88
Connecticut	82	84	83
New York	85	86	87
New Jersey	78	80	83
Pennsylvania	85	85	86
North Central			
Ohio	87	86	86
Indiana	92	90	89
Illinois	89	88	88
Michigan	91	90	88
Missouri	87	88	86
South			
Maryland	71	75	78
District of Columbia	75	77	79
Virginia	73	76	76
North Carolina	71	72	73
South Carolina	62	65	69
Georgia	71	73	73
Florida	68	67	69
Kentucky	93	89	83
Tennessee	84	83	79
Alabama	75	77	74
Mississippi	63	66	64
Arkansas	73	74	77
Louisiana	66	70	74
Oklahoma	77	78	82
Texas	73	77	79

* Actually index of nonwhite to white; includes all states with 100,000 or more Negroes in 1960 except California where such a ratio may not be representative of Negroes.

SOURCE: U.S. Senate, Subcommittee on Employment and Manpower, Hearings on *Equal Employment Opportunity*, 1963, p. 323.

TABLE XVIII—Total and Negro Personnel by Grade, and Negro Personnel as a Percent of Total Personnel in Each Grade, for Each Service (1962)

Pay grade	Army			Air Force*		
	Total personnel	Negro personnel	Percent Negro	Total personnel	Negro pesonnel	Percent Negro
Officers						
General	15			6		
Lieutenant general	35			27		
Major general	197			142	1	0.7
Brigadier general	248			172		
Colonel	5,127	6	0.1	4,066	6	0.1
Lieutenant colonel	12,309	117	1.0	12,337	67	0.5
Major	17,100	424	2.5	20,395	124	0.6
Captain	29,397	1,532	5.2	35,180	615	1.7
1st lieutenant	14,978	650	4.3	20,292	317	1.6
2nd lieutenant	18,559	421	2.3	11,664	170	1.5
Total	97,965	3,150	3.2	104,281	1,300	1.2
Warrant officers						
Chief (W-4)	1,140	28	2.5	383		
Chief (W-3)	2,674	102	3.8	969	15	1.6
Chief (W-2)	4,383	158	3.6	1,058	13	1.2
Warrant officer	1,523	33	2.2	1		
Total	9,720	321	3.3	2,411	28	1.2
Enlisted personnel						
Sergeant major	2,549	76	3.0	3,813	32	0.8
Master or 1st sergeant	10,239	586	5.7	8,358	140	1.7
Platoon sergeant or sergeant 1st class	41,107	3,143	7.6	24,629	616	2.5
Staff sergeant	82,951	10,496	12.7	50,374	2,115	4.2
Sergeant	134,457	21,892	16.3	110,152	10,287	9.3
Corporal	173,188	21,133	12.2	114,768	14,321	12.5
Private first class	286,597	26,985	11.9	124,158	11,505	9.2
Private	102,332	10,836	10.6	67,921	6,951	10.2
Recruit	75,778	8,456	11.2	3,476	597	17.1
Total	849,198	103,603	12.2	507,549	46,564	9.2
Grand total	956,883	107,074	11.2	614,241	47,892	7.8

* Represents 75 percent of total strength

SOURCE: U.S. Commission on Civil Rights, *1963 Report*, Washington, 1963, p. 219.

In many respects, the Armed Forces have made greater progress than any other sector in providing more equal employment opportunities for Negroes. This advance has been most conspicuous with respect to enlisted men and noncommissioned officers, although opportunities for Negroes at officer levels have also expanded rapidly. The major improvement in the position of Negroes in the Armed Forces has occurred in the Army and Air Force, with the Navy particularly, and the Marines to a less extent, lagging. As Table XVIII shows, in 1962 Negroes accounted for more than 11 percent of all Army personnel, 8 percent in the Air Force, 7 percent in the Marines, and less than 5 percent in the Navy. The most striking differences occur at the officer level, with Negroes comprising 3 percent of all Army officers, one percent in the Air Force and only 0.3 and 0.2 percent respectively in the Navy and Marines.

Significant numbers of Negroes had achieved relatively high positions. One was a major general in the Air Force, six were colonels in the Army and an additional six were at this level in the Air Force, while those at lieutenant colonel or equivalent level numbered 117 in the Army, 67 in the Air Force and 3 in the Navy.

Over the past several decades, the Army has consistently had a higher proportion of Negro personnel than the other services, while the Air Force, since it became independent in 1948, has ranked second. The Navy has changed little over the years, while the Marines, who formerly trailed, now utilize Negroes relatively more than the Navy (Table XIX).

TABLE XIX—Negroes as a Percent of Officers and Enlisted Personnel for Each Service, for Selected Dates (1945, 1949, 1954, and 1962)

	1945	1949	1954	1962
Officers				
Army	0.7	1.7	2.9	3.2
Air Force		0.6	1.1	1.2
Navy	(1)	(1)	0.1	0.3
Marines	N.A.	(1)	0.1	0.2
Enlisted personnel				
Army	10.3	9.6	12.3	12.2
Air Force		5.1	8.6	9.2
Navy	4.8	4.5	3.6	5.2
Marines	N.A.	2.1	6.5	7.6

1 Less than 0.5 percent.
N.A.—Not available.

SOURCE: U.S. Commission on Civil Rights, *1963 Report*, Washington, 1963, p. 221.

Both Negro enlisted men and officers enjoy relatively better occupational opportunities than do Negroes in civilian employment. As Table XX shows, Negroes comprise a higher percentage of the enlisted men than they do of the civilians in every clerical, technical and skilled field for which a comparison is possible. These include such occupations as electronic, medical and dental, drafting and other kinds of technicians; aircraft and automotive mechanics; electricians and communications linemen, construction and related craftsmen and printing craftsmen. Negroes comprise 9 percent of those who might be considered as craftsmen and foremen, compared to only 5 percent in civilian life.

A slightly different pattern emerges among officers, Negroes comprise a smaller proportion of military than civilian personnel in such fields as law, medicine, dentistry, nursing and the clergy—traditionally the major fields of professional employment because those so employed serve the Negro community. However, in a number of fields Negroes represent a larger proportion in the Armed Forces than in civilian life. This is true in engineering, the applied sciences, finance and accounting, aviation and navigation and a wide variety of management fields.

TABLE XX—Part 1—Negroes as a Percent of Total in Selected Fields, for Civilian Employment Compared to Armed Forces

		Male[1] civilian employment, 1960	Armed Forces, 1962				
			Total	Army	Air Force	Navy	Marines
			Professional and managerial versus military officers				
1	Legal	1.0	0.7	1.0	0.8	..	N.A.
2	Chemical and scientific	2.0	2.8	5.1	1.7	..	..
3	Electrical engineers, signal, electronics, etc.	0.7	2.2	3.1	1.8	0.1	0.2
4	Civil, aeronautical and other engineers	0.6	1.4	2.6	1.0	0.0	..
5	Finance, accountants, auditors, etc.	0.9	1.5	1.8	1.4	N.A.	0.5
6	Supply, transportation and misc. managers	0.9	2.2	3.8	1.6	0.1	0.4
7	Physicians, medical corps	2.0	1.2	1.7	1.2	0.6	N.A.
8	Dentists	2.5	1.6	1.9	2.4	0.4	N.A.
9	Nurses	[1]5.4	3.4	3.8	4.5	1.3	N.A.
10	Clergymen, chaplains	7.1	1.9	3.2	1.6	0.4	N.A.
11	Air pilots and navigators	0.4	0.7	N.A.	0.4	0.2	0.2
12	Policemen, etc.; officers in military police, etc.	[2]3.4	3.2	3.7	1.8	N.A.	..

TABLE XX—Part 2—Negroes as a Percent of Total in Selected Fields, for Civilian Employment Compared to Armed Forces

	Male[1] civilian employment, 1960	Armed Forces, 1962				
		Total	Army	Air Force	Navy	Marines
		Technicians, craftsmen, clerical, and service versus enlisted men				
1 Electronic technicians including television repair	2.9	4.7	8.8	4.8	2.0	1.9
2 Other technical	[1]3.1	8.5	12.1	6.5	4.7	3.4
a. Medical and dental	[1]7.1	11.0	16.0	8.6	5.2	N.A.
b. Draftsmen and related	1.1	5.4	4.4	7.1	2.9	6.6
3 Clerical and related	[1]3.9	10.6	10.0	14.2	4.6	6.3
4 Mechanics and repairmen	4.4	5.8	9.6	5.3	3.7	4.8
a. Aircraft and engine	2.9	4.6	4.6	4.9	3.8	3.9
b. Electricians, linemen, etc.	1.4	9.9	12.4	7.2	1.5	7.9
c. Automotive	6.5	8.4	11.5	10.7	4.8	6.3
5 Miscellaneous craftsmen	5.7	8.4	11.5	10.7	4.8	6.3
a. Construction and related	6.2	10.1	12.1	13.5	3.9	7.0
b. Printing	2.2	9.6	6.0	11.1	3.3	5.3
6 Service occupations	[1]18.9	16.6	15.6	15.4	22.9	15.6
a. Food service	[1]11.5	19.9	17.7	18.4	23.9	20.3

[1] Most figures for civilian occupations include males only; noted figures include females on the assumption that a significant number of the Armed Forces personnel in the field are female.

[2] The civilian figure includes all policemen, sheriffs, and marshals and would undoubtedly be much smaller if it included only those in grades of lieutenant or above, or equivalent, as do the military figures.

N.A.—Not available or not applicable.
Blanks indicate no Negroes in these occupational fields.

SOURCE: U.S. Commission on Civil Rights, *1963 Report*, Washington, 1963, p. 223

There are marked differences among the services in the occupational levels of their Negro personnel. The better opportunities in military life primarily reflect Army and Air Force practice. In nearly all of the clerical, technical and skilled fields, the Army's proportion of Negroes is at least two and sometimes four times higher than in comparable civilian jobs. The Army also has a higher proportion of Negroes in most professional, scientific and managerial fields than does the civilian economy. The Air Force presents substantially better patterns than the civilian labor market in most occupational categories.

The Navy is the only service that does not utilize Negroes as heavily as the civilian economy in almost every occupational category, from the professional, scientific and managerial to medical and dental technicians, general mechanics and repairmen, administrative and clerical personnel and construction and utility craftsmen. Negroes in the Navy are heavily concentrated in the service occupations, although it is said the Navy is trying to change this traditional pattern. As yet, however, little success has been achieved, among other reasons because the Navy has accepted a smaller proportion of Negroes than the other services.

Incomes of Negro Workers

The preceding analysis of occupational status has been important not only in its own right but also because the type of work that an individual performs largely determines what he is able to earn, which in turn determines how he can live and maintain his family. However, an occupational analysis by itself can at best shed only indirect light on the question of income. More direct information on incomes is presented in Tables XXI and XXII.

TABLE XXI—Median Income of Experienced Civilian Labor Force, by Occupation, Sex and Color, 1960

Occupational group	Men		Women	
	Total	Nonwhite	Total	Nonwhite
Total	4,621	$2,703	$2,257	$1,219
Professional, technical, etc.	6,619	4,563	3,625	3,571
Farmers and farm managers	2,169	778	836	589
Mgrs., offs. and prop., exc. farm	6,664	3,869	3,355	1,927
Clerical	4,785	4,072	3,017	2,993
Sales	4,987	2,809	1,498	1,562
Craftsmen	5,240	3,480	2,927	2,314
Operatives	4,299	3,040	2,319	1,829
Private hshld. worker	1,078	1,216	684	704
Service workers exc. pvt. hshld.	3,310	2,529	1,385	1,365
Farm laborers and foremen	1,066	816	602	553
Laborers exc. farm and mine	2,948	2,394	1,872	1,444

SOURCE: U.S. Bureau of the Census, Census of Population: 1960, *United States Summary, Detailed Characteristics,* Table 208.

The improvement of the occupational position of the Negro in the American economy has been matched only partially by an improvement in their income position. The occupational indexes previously developed treated all workers within a given occupational group as equal. But Table 21 emphasizes that Negroes tend to be concentrated in the lower-paying positions within each occupational field. In almost every field Negroes tended to earn less than whites. This was particularly true among men. Nonwhite women

TABLE XXII—Median Income of White and Nonwhite Wage and Salary Workers, by Sex, 1939 and 1947–1962

	Male			Female		
	White, in dollars	Nonwhite		White, in dollars	Nonwhite	
		In dollars	As percent of white		In dollars	As percent of white
1939	$1,112	$ 460	41.4	$ 676	$ 246	36.4
1947	2,357	1,279	54.3	1,269	432	34.0
1948	2,711	1,615	59.6	1,615	701	43.4
1949	2,735	1,367	50.0	1,615	654	40.5
1950	2,982	1,828	61.3	1,698	626	36.9
1951	3,345	2,060	61.6	1,855	781	42.1
1952	3,507	2,038	58.1	1,976	814	41.2
1953	3,760	2,233	59.4	2,049	994	48.5
1954	3,754	2,131	56.8	2,046	914	44.7
1955	3,986	2,342	58.8	2,065	894	43.3
1956	4,260	2,396	56.2	2,179	970	44.5
1957	4,396	2,436	55.4	2,240	1,019	45.5
1958	4,569	2,652	58.0	2,364	1,055	44.6
1959	4,902	2,844	58.0	2,422	1,289	53.2
1960	5,137	3,075	59.8	2,537	1,276	50.2
1961	5,287	3,015	57.0	2,538	1,302	51.3
1962	5,642[a]	3,023[a]	53.6[a]	b	b	b

[a] Preliminary.   [b] Not available.

SOURCE: *Manpower Report of the President*, March, 1964, Table H-10; U.S. Bureau of the Census, *Current Population Reports*, Series P-60, annual issues.

earned more than white women in sales and private household work, and almost as much in professional, clerical and service employment. Among men this occurred only in the relatively small field of private household work.

Relative incomes provide a better index of the changing economic position of Negroes in relation to white workers than do relative occupational positions. As Table XXII indicates, the average income of Negro male workers was only 41 percent of that of white male workers in 1939. Between 1939 and 1947, there was a substantial improvement in the relative income position of Negro men to 54 percent. Since then, however, the ratio of Negro to white male income has fluctuated between 54 and 62 percent. The low points have been somewhat associated with years of high unemployment, although there has been no clear-cut pattern. Neither has there been any consistent trend in these ratios over time.

For Negro women, the pattern has been somewhat different. The pre-war ratio of the average incomes of Negro to white women workers amounted to 36 percent. From 1939 to the immediate post-war period, there was little change. Since then, the ratio has increased to over 50 percent.

TABLE XXIII—Percent of employed persons with two or more jobs, May, 1962

	Both sexes	Male	Female
Total	4.9	6.4	2.0
White	4.9	6.5	1.8
Nonwhite	4.6	5.6	3.1

SOURCE: U.S. Department of Labor, "Multiple Job Holders in May 1962." *Special Labor Force Report,* No. 29, Table A.

These shifts in relative income positions reflect a great many different forces that have been interacting upon one another. They reflect shifts in occupational patterns previously noted, but they also reflect shifts in prevailing incomes in various occupations, in unemployment rates, in multiple job-holding rates and in the importance of part-time versus full-time work. As the nation moved from the depressed economic conditions of the 1930's to higher price and wage levels after World War II, wage rates in low paying jobs increased more rapidly than those in high paying jobs. Since Negroes were concentrated more heavily in the lower paying jobs, their incomes tended to increase more rapidly than those of whites. Indeed, there is evidence that there was a long-run tendency extending over the period from before World War I to after World War II for relative income differentials to decline; that is, for incomes to increase more rapidly in the occupations and regions (i.e., the South) where they were relatively low. However, this decline in relative income differentials has not continued in the last decade. In this connection one should recall the shift of the Negro out of the South to regions where he has found greater opportunities to work at a higher occupational level. This internal migration probably accounted for much more of his total gains than a move towards equality within particular regions.

Employment, Unemployment and Labor Force Participation Rates

One aspect of the lower income position of Negroes than whites is that they are employed to a lesser extent than whites. This can be shown in a variety of ways. Among employed men, Negroes are less likely than whites to hold two or more jobs (Table XXIII). On the other hand, Negro women are more likely than white women to hold two or more jobs, which helps to explain the large number of occupational fields in which Negro women earned approximately as much per year as white women.

The lesser degree of employment among Negroes is attested in another way in Table XXIV. In recent years, unemployment rates for Negroes have tended to run slightly more than twice as high as whites. This is, in fact, a slightly higher differential than prevailed prior to about 1955. In earlier years, the Negro rate tended to be slightly less than twice as great as the white rate. Since 1957, the unemployment rate for the entire labor force has tended to be higher than formerly. Thus, as unemployment rates have increased, those among Negroes have increased even more rapidly than those among whites.

Higher unemployment rates among Negroes are in part a reflection of the fact that they tend to be concentrated in the low paying, low skilled jobs in which employment is more unstable. This is not the only factor, however, for, as Table XXV shows, Negroes tend to suffer higher unemployment rates than whites at each occupational level.

The unemployment statistics do not provide an adequate picture of the extent of joblessness among Negroes. In terms of their relationship to paid employment, the population may be divided into three groups. First are the employed. Second are the unemployed who are defined as those without a job who are looking for work. The employed and the unemployed comprise the labor force. There is a third group—those who neither work nor look for work. They are not counted as part of the labor force. Many who do not look for work may do so as a matter of choice, because they have no need or desire for a job.

Some who do not look for work may fail to do so because they know or believe that no job opportunities are available to them. Such persons are

TABLE XXIV—Unemployment Rates, by Color and Sex: Annual Averages, 1948-62

	White			Nonwhite		
	Both Sexes	Male	Female	Both Sexes	Male	Female
1948	3.2	3.1	3.4	5.2	5.1	5.2
1949	5.2	5.2	5.2	8.2	8.8	7.2
1950	4.6	4.5	4.9	8.5	8.9	7.8
1951	2.8	2.4	3.7	4.8	4.4	5.4
1952	2.4	2.2	2.9	4.6	4.5	4.8
1953	2.3	2.2	2.6	4.1	4.4	3.7
1954	4.5	4.4	4.9	8.9	9.2	8.2
1955	4.6	4.8	4.3	10.1	11.3	8.1
1956	3.3	3.1	3.8	7.5	7.3	8.0
1957	3.9	3.7	4.3	8.0	8.4	7.4
1958	6.1	6.1	6.2	12.6	13.7	10.8
1959	4.9	4.6	5.3	10.7	11.5	9.5
1960	5.0	4.8	5.3	10.2	10.7	9.5
1961	6.0	5.7	6.5	12.5	12.9	11.9
1962	4.9	4.6	5.5	11.0	11.0	11.1

SOURCE: *Manpower Report of the President*, March 1964, Table A-10.

TABLE XXV—Unemployment Rates by Occupational Group, Sex, and Color, 1960

Occupational group	Male		Female	
	White	Nonwhite	White	Nonwhite
Total	4.5	8.4	4.7	7.9
Professional and technical	1.4	2.3	1.4	2.2
Managers, officials, and proprietors, exc. farm	1.4	2.9	1.8	2.5
Clerical	3.2	5.6	3.1	5.8
Sales	2.5	5.6	4.8	8.0
Craftsmen and foremen	5.2	8.3	5.6	9.2
Operatives	6.2	8.2	9.6	12.3
Private household workers	5.8	6.4	4.6	6.0
Service, exc. pvt. hshld.	4.9	7.1	5.3	7.9
Laborers, exc. farm and mine	11.8	12.5	10.9	16.6
Farmers and farm mgrs.	0.7	1.7	0.8	5.2
Farm laborers and foremen	6.6	7.4	6.1	17.4

SOURCE: Same as for Table IV

clearly unemployed, but there is reason to believe that many, and perhaps an increasing number, are not counted as being in the labor force. This is suggested by Table XXVI, which presents labor force participation rates for men and women at different age levels in 1940, 1950 and 1960. These describe the percentage of persons in the respective groups who are employed or looking for work. The reciprocal of these figures would be the percentages of those in the respective groups who neither worked nor looked for work.

TABLE XXVI—Percent in the labor force by age group, sex, and color, 1940–1960

	Nonwhite			White		
	1940	1950	1960	1940	1950	1960
Age in years			Men			
14 and 15 years	19.3	20.2	12.5	6.7	14.9	16.5
16 and 17 years	46.1	43.0	28.8	27.4	34.9	37.8
18 and 19 years	73.1	68.7	58.8	65.0	66.5	67.2
20 to 24 years	88.5	80.3	82.0	88.0	82.1	86.7
25 to 29 years	92.1	84.5	87.6	95.1	91.0	94.7
30 to 34 years	92.7	88.2	89.1	95.7	94.5	96.6
35 to 39 years	92.9	90.4	89.7	95.4	95.1	96.5
40 to 44 years	91.7	90.7	89.6	94.3	94.7	95.0
50 to 54 years	88.9	86.9	85.9	91.1	91.0	92.8
55 to 59 years	87.7	82.9	80.6	87.9	87.0	88.5
60 to 64 years	80.5	76.0	68.7	78.9	79.7	78.4
65 to 69 years	64.3	56.1	40.8	59.0	60.0	44.1
70 to 74 years	43.7	40.2	27.4	38.0	38.6	28.8
75 years and over	23.5	21.9	15.7	17.8	18.4	15.5
Age in years			Women			
14 and 15 years	7.8	7.2	5.4	1.6	4.8	7.1
16 and 17 years	20.3	16.5	14.0	12.4	17.9	21.8
18 and 19 years	36.7	30.9	34.8	40.6	45.6	47.9
20 to 24 years	44.9	39.6	45.4	45.7	43.6	44.8
25 to 29 years	46.1	42.9	46.9	34.2	31.3	33.5
30 to 34 years	46.2	46.3	50.2	29.1	29.1	33.5
35 to 39 years	45.7	48.6	54.7	26.1	32.1	38.5
40 to 44 years	44.3	48.1	57.0	24.0	34.9	43.9
45 to 49 years	41.8	45.3	56.5	21.9	33.6	46.4
50 to 54 years	37.6	40.9	52.6	19.8	29.8	45.1
55 to 59 years	33.6	34.9	44.8	17.4	25.2	39.1
60 to 64 years	27.8	27.6	34.2	13.9	20.0	29.0
65 to 69 years	18.5	16.4	19.6	8.8	12.5	16.3
70 to 74 years	9.5	8.4	11.5	4.8	6.5	9.4
75 years and over	4.9	3.8	5.5	2.1	2.5	4.1

SOURCE: U.S. Bureau of the Census, Census of Population: 1960, United States Summary, Detailed Characteristics, Table 195.

Several quite striking points arise in comparing labor force participation rates of Negro and white men and women over the last several decades. In the first place, the labor force participation rates have tended to be higher among white than Negro men throughout the age range from twenty-five to sixty years. These differences, moreover, have tended to widen with time. The rates for Negro men have declined slightly since 1940, while those for whites have tended to increase slightly. This pattern was even sharper among teenage Negro boys, who once were more likely than white boys to be in the labor force, but now are less likely. The tendency toward a higher proportion of white boys to be in the labor force has occurred despite the fact that more of them attend school.

Among older men, the reduction in labor force participation rates has also been sharper among Negroes than whites. As a result, while formerly relatively more Negro than white men worked throughout the range from sixty to seventy-four years of age, now labor force participation rates are higher for whites than for Negroes. The fact that there has been a tendency for relatively fewer Negroes to be in the labor force at the same time that their unemployment rates have increased substantially faster than whites, suggests that many are not in the labor force because there is no work for them. To the extent this is true, they represent unemployed manpower and the unemployment rates referred to earlier really understate the true figure.

Somewhat comparable tendencies can be found among women workers. The proportion of Negro women who work has always tended to be higher than among white women. There has been an increase in the proportion of Negro women above the age of thirty-five who are employed. This has been particularly so since 1950. The proportion of white women in the middle and higher age brackets who are in the labor force increased even more rapidly during the 1940's and the 1950's. As a result, the current differences between the labor force participation rates of white and Negro women in these higher age ranges, while sizeable, are not really distinctive.

Among women of childbearing age, from twenty to thirty-five among white women and eighteen to thirty-five among Negro women, there has been very little change in their labor force participation rates in recent years. In the still younger age group, among teenagers, one finds that relatively more white girls and fewer Negro girls have entered the labor force than in the past. As a result, teenage white girls are now more likely to be employed than are teenage Negro girls.

A substantial part, but by no means all, of the differences in labor force participation rates is related to differences in the marital status of the Negro and white population. Among men of both races, labor force participation rates are higher among those who are married and whose spouse

TABLE XXVII—Labor Force Participation Rates by Age, Sex, Marital Status and Color, 1960

Age group	Single		Married spouse present		Other marital status	
(in years)	Total	Nonwhite	Total	Nonwhite	Total	Nonwhite
Males						
14 to 17	26.2	20.2	81.1	69.8	35.6	37.0
18 to 19	63.9	56.2	95.4	92.4	77.8	69.6
20 to 24	78.3	74.7	96.3	95.1	83.6	76.6
25 to 29	83.8	75.6	97.8	96.4	82.1	75.5
30 to 34	84.0	74.0	98.6	96.3	82.1	74.7
35 to 44	80.3	72.1	98.2	95.8	81.7	76.4
45 to 64	75.8	69.6	96.2	92.8	79.8	76.9
55 to 64	65.2	61.7	87.3	82.0	68.2	64.2
65 to 74	28.9	28.3	41.1	40.3	27.5	28.8
75 and over	14.2	15.2	19.0	19.1	11.1	12.7
Females						
14 to 17	13.9	8.8	16.4	18.1	22.0	22.6
18 to 19	53.6	37.4	29.2	25.7	43.6	34.8
20 to 24	73.2	59.4	31.1	34.0	53.9	48.7
25 to 29	79.1	66.8	26.8	38.2	58.2	56.3
30 to 34	79.4	68.1	29.0	43.0	62.2	62.4
35 to 44	78.2	68.1	36.5	48.7	68.2	67.7
45 to 54	76.1	66.0	39.3	47.2	67.3	65.3
55 to 64	64.8	49.5	25.2	33.6	47.6	46.2
65 to 74	30.5	27.9	7.7	12.7	15.8	17.3
75 and over	10.2	14.5	3.0	6.5	3.9	5.0

SOURCE: U.S. Bureau of the Census, Census of Population: 1960, *Employment Status and Work Experience*, Table 6.

is present than among those who are single or who are divorced, widowed, or separated. Among women, those who are single are more likely to be in the labor force than those who are divorced, widowed or separated, while those who are married are the least likely to work.

Negroes are more likely than whites to be divorced, widowed or separated. This is associated with higher labor force participation rates in general among Negro than white women, but lower labor force participation rates in general among Negro men than white men.

Differences in marital status do not, however, account for all of the differences in labor force rates. As Table XXVII shows, in all three types of marital status, Negro men are almost consistently less likely than white men in the same age range to be in the labor force. The same is true in comparing Negro and white women who were single or divorced, widowed or separated. The exception is women with spouse present, among whom Negroes are more likely than whites to work.

The cause and effect between work and marital status is difficult to unravel. On the one hand, men who are single or not with their spouse may have less pressure on them to seek or find work. On the other hand, those who are unable to find work, for whatever reason, may be less likely to marry or, if they marry, to maintain a stable family relationship. Thus, the high proportion of Negro men who are unemployed or out of the labor force may cause or it may reflect the fact that many of them have a broken marital status. The fact that many more Negro than white women work is undoubtedly due to their broken marital status, although even here some may be able to leave unhappy situations because they have jobs. Higher labor force participation rates among Negro than white women even when their spouse is present undoubtedly reflect their greater need for income because their husband is more likely to be unemployed or in a low paying job.

The previous data on unemployment and labor force participation refer to data collected at a particular point in time. There are also data available that show that a higher proportion of Negroes than white men tend to be unemployed or out of the labor force during longer periods of time. As Table XXVIII shows, at every age level, Negro men were less likely than whites to have held a job during 1962. Among men in the prime working ages of twenty-five to sixty-four years, over 7 percent of the Negroes but less than 4 percent of the whites did not hold any job during 1962. Among those who did hold a job during the year, 78 percent of the white men worked full time the year round, while only 62 percent of the Negroes were able to do so.

Among girls and young women under twenty-four years of age, relatively more Negroes did not hold a job during the year. Among older women, however, Negro women were more likely than whites to have worked. Indeed, two out of every three Negro women in the age range twenty-five to sixty-four worked at some time during the year, compared to only half the white women. Regardless of their age, Negro women workers were less likely, however, than whites to have held a full time job the year round.

Another evidence of the instability in the employment of Negroes is that they tend to have, on the average, a shorter period of tenure on their jobs. There are in fact few differences between Negro and white women on this score. As Table XXIX shows, however, the average white male worker in 1963 had been on his current job for nearly six years, while the average Negro male worker had been on his job little more than four years, or a difference of nearly two years. As workers grow older, there is obviously a greater opportunity for this difference to be larger, and it

TABLE XXVIII—Two Indexes of Work Experience in 1962 for Whites and Nonwhites, by Age and Sex.

	Percent of population with no work experience in year		Percent of workers with full-time full year jobs	
	Male	Female	Male	Female
Age group				
14–19 years				
White	41.9	56.0	6.6	8.3
Nonwhite	55.1	65.0	11.0	4.8
20–24 years				
White	7.4	36.0	45.1	34.6
Nonwhite	10.0	41.7	46.8	30.7
25–64 years				
White	3.7	49.5	77.7	44.0
Nonwhite	7.2	35.5	61.7	37.3
65 years and over				
White	61.4	86.1	38.6	26.7
Nonwhite	63.9	81.3	27.9	12.9

SOURCE: U.S. Department of Labor, "Work Experience of the Population in 1962," *Special Labor Force Report*, No. 38, Table A-9.

TABLE XXIX—White and Nonwhite Workers: Median Years on Current Job, by Age and Sex, January 1963

Age	Both sexes			Male			Female		
	Total	White	Non-white	Total	White	Non-white	Total	White	Non-white
Total, 14 years and over	4.6	4.7	3.6	5.7	5.9	4.1	3.0	3.0	2.9
14 to 24 years	0.8	0.8	0.6	0.8	0.9	0.7	0.8	0.8	0.5
25 to 34 years	3.0	3.1	2.4	3.5	3.6	2.6	2.0	2.0	2.1
35 to 44 years	6.0	6.1	5.0	7.6	7.7	6.5	3.6	3.6	3.7
45 to 54 years	9.0	9.3	7.3	11.4	11.6	9.6	6.1	6.1	5.7
55 to 64 years	11.8	12.1	8.8	14.7	15.1	11.2	7.8	7.9	6.4
65 years and over	13.8	13.6	17.3	16.6	16.3	19.7	8.8	8.4	(1)

[1] Median not shown where base is less than 100,000.

SOURCE: U.S. Department of Labor, "Job Tenure of American Workers, January 1963," *Special Labor Force Report*, No. 36, Table 2.

reached nearly four years among white and Negro men aged fifty-five to sixty-four. In addition to unemployment, the fact that relatively more Negroes than whites migrated in the last few decades tends to shorten the average job tenure of the Negro worker.

The Causes of Negro Disadvantage

The simplest and most obvious reason for the inferior economic and occupational position of Negroes is, of course, discrimination. But discrimination takes many forms, both direct and indirect. In addition, the Negro is handicapped by additional factors that cannot be labeled as discriminatory.

In the first place, the job opportunities available to Negroes have been profoundly affected by their geographic distribution. Negroes at the end of the Civil War were heavily concentrated in the rural South. The fact that the South was agricultural, that it industrialized slowly and that education and other public services have lagged in that region has affected Southern whites and Negroes alike. Much of the gap between the economic position of the Negro and white populations stems from this historical circumstance.

The impact of geography on the occupational structure of Negroes in recent years has been much moderated. True, Negroes are still relatively heavily concentrated in the South. And in the North they are found predominantly in the central city rather than in the suburb. The fact that they did not follow the whites to the suburbs has had a twofold impact on their position in the labor market. It has kept them closer to certain jobs, but it has put a gulf between them and the many service jobs that have developed in the white suburbs.

The fact that Negroes have received less education than whites, and that it has been of inferior quality (see Chapter 7) has obvious occupational implications. In both the North and the South, Negroes receive poorer education than whites. In addition, even among Negroes living in the North, many were originally educated in the South, which means that they carry with them a serious educational deficiency.

In addition, Negroes generally secure less desirable employment than whites with comparable education and background, even after some allowance is made for the poorer quality of Negro education. Table XXX shows that among male college graduates, 20 percent of the nonwhites were skilled, semiskilled, service or unskilled workers, compared to 9 percent of the whites. At the other extreme, 24 percent of the whites but only 8 percent of the nonwhites were managers, officials and proprietors. A

TABLE XXX—Occupational Distribution of White and Nonwhite College, High School and Elementary School Graduates,[a] by Sex, 1960

Years of School Completed	Male		Female	
	Nonwhite	White	Nonwhite	White
College—4 years				
Total	100.0	100.0	100.0	100.0
Professional and technical	47.4	42.5	73.6	68.9
Mgrs., officials, and props. exc. farm	7.9	24.4	1.7	4.5
Clerical	12.7	6.7	11.2	16.1
Sales	3.6	12.5	0.9	2.9
Craftsmen and foremen	5.2	5.5	0.2	0.5
Operatives	5.1	1.7	2.1	0.8
Service workers	6.7	1.0	4.9	1.9
Laborers, exc. farm and mine	2.7	0.4	0.1	0.0
Farmers	0.9	1.8	0.0	0.3
Farm laborers and foremen	0.4	0.2	0.1	0.1
Occupation not reported	7.3	3.2	5.1	3.8
High School—4 years				
Total	100.0	100.0	100.0	100.0
Professional and technical	3.2	7.1	5.8	7.5
Mgrs., officials and props., exc. farm	3.8	15.1	1.7	5.3
Clerical	11.6	9.8	19.7	47.9
Sales	2.5	8.8	3.0	9.9
Craftsmen and foremen	14.1	24.8	1.1	1.3
Operatives	23.9	16.8	16.0	10.8
Service workers	15.7	4.7	42.7	11.5
Laborers, exc. farm and mine	12.1	3.0	0.8	0.3
Farmers	1.7	5.2	0.2	0.4
Farm laborers and foremen	1.4	0.7	0.7	0.7
Occupation not reported	9.8	4.0	8.1	4.4
Elementary—8 years				
Total	100.0	100.0	100.0	100.0
Professional and technical	0.9	1.4	0.8	1.8
Mgrs., officials, and props., exc. farm	2.2	7.9	1.1	3.7
Clerical	3.1	4.3	1.7	12.5
Sales	1.0	4.0	1.5	10.0
Craftsmen and foremen	12.7	26.2	0.6	2.0
Operatives	27.6	25.8	15.8	31.6
Service workers	16.1	6.6	65.6	28.6
Laborers exc. farm and mine	20.5	7.3	0.9	0.8
Farmers	3.2	10.5	0.6	1.1
Farm laborers and foremen	3.7	2.0	2.4	1.7
Occupation not reported	9.0	3.8	8.9	6.2

[a] Employed persons aged 25 years or more.

SOURCE: U.S. Bureau of the Census, Census of Population: 1960, *Educational Attainment*, Table 8.

slightly higher proportion of nonwhites than whites were in professional and technical occupations, but closer examination reveals that the whites are more likely to be in such higher paying professions as medicine, law, engineering and the sciences, while the nonwhites are concentrated in teaching and the clergy. Most of the remaining Negro men who are college graduates are in low paying clerical jobs, while the remaining white men who finished college are in sales work where they may earn quite large salaries.

Among male high school graduates, nearly 40 percent of the whites were in white collar jobs, including nearly 15 percent who were salaried or self-employed managers, compared to only 21 percent among the non-whites, almost none of whom were managers. In addition, 25 percent of the white men but only 14 percent of the Negro men were employed as craftsmen and foremen. Negro high school graduates were far more likely than whites to become operatives, service workers or laborers. Over 60 percent of the nonwhites, but only 25 percent of the whites entered these positions.

The discrepancy remains even among those who complete only grade school. Nonwhite men were far more likely to become service or unskilled workers, while the whites had far greater than proportionate concentrations among craftsmen, foremen and managers.

Among women college graduates, there was little difference between the occupational distributions of whites and nonwhites. Among high school graduates, white women tended strongly to become clerical workers, while Negro women tended to enter service jobs. Among those who finished only elementary school, nearly two-thirds of the Negro women but little more than one-fourth of the white women entered service occupations. Over 30 percent of the white women but only half that many Negro women entered semiskilled jobs. In addition, 28 percent of the white women but only 5 percent of the Negro women were employed as clerical, sales and other white collar workers.

From these figures it is reasonable to conclude that discrimination in employment represents the major reason for the less favorable employment patterns of Negroes. The varieties of employment discrimination are too many and complicated to be set forth here. They exist at every turn. They may be overt or covert; they may be unconscious or simply a matter of indifference. They may reflect the fact that Negroes have great difficulty in learning about job opportunities. They may also reflect the fact that standards of selection or practices used in hiring, placement, promotion and admission to training opportunities may work to the disadvantage of Negroes. The policies of trade unions, employment agencies and the other private or public organizations may have adverse effects on Negro employment, which may also be true for the behavior of workers, customers or others who affect the course of business.

These economic realities, by affecting the attitudes and actions of Negroes, set up a reinforcement mechanism that helps to compound the situation. There is, in fact, no way to disentangle the role of any individual factors, for they are linked together in a vicious circle. Lack of opportunities discourages favorable work attitudes, while poor work attitudes help to provide a rationalization or justification for discrimination. The vocational value of additional education is not as clear for a Negro, particularly in the case of men, as it is for whites. Apparently for this reason, Negroes do not aspire to as much education as do whites, and this is particularly true of Negro men. Their relative lack of education thus helps to explain their lower occupational levels. Many Negro families are broken as a result of low income and high geographical mobility, and for other reasons. In many broken families youngsters may not receive the emotional and economic support necessary for the development of work attitudes and skills essential for proper performance on the job.

Programs and Policies for Greater Opportunity

Just as this analysis cannot deal with all the causes and ramifications of the limited opportunities of Negroes, so it cannot deal with all of the ways in which disadvantage and discrimination may be successfully attacked.[1] The following will suggest some of the programs and policies which may have a direct effect on expanding the employment opportunities of Negroes. In the first place, broadened employment opportunities for Negroes depend on the establishment and maintenance of full or nearly full employment. Given the rapid growth in the labor force and the continued displacement of labor through changes in technology, a high level of employment requires rapid economic growth. The policies best able to promote full employment and economic growth fall beyond the confines of this analysis, but there can be no doubt whatever that if it were achieved it would greatly reduce the heavy burden of unemployment on Negroes.

Rapid economic growth which would involve the emergence and expansion of newer occupations would help to open up job opportunities for Negroes. In the past, the pattern has been for employment to expand more rapidly for Negroes than whites in rapidly growing fields. Such opportunities, while not numerically great, have been significant in develop-

[1] For one view on approaches to improving the situation, see Ginzberg, *et al., The Negro Potential*. (New York: Columbia University Press, 1956).

ing beachheads for future expansion. At the same time, the past pattern has been for large numbers of whites to move up to higher level occupations, leaving opportunities for more Negroes to enter occupations in the intermediate range of the job hierarchy. This is necessary if Negroes, who are displaced more rapidly than whites from any declining fields, are to find reemployment.[2]

But economic growth alone is not enough to assure equal employment opportunities for Negroes. What is also required are changes in the whole range of policies that affect the employment process.

Much has been happening on this front. More and more employers have been moving in the direction of providing greater opportunities for Negroes. Sometimes this is a policy which management initiates on its own. For several decades, a number of nationally known companies, such as the International Harvester Company, Pitney-Bowes, Inc., and the Radio Corporation of America have actively worked toward this end, sometimes in hostile environments. This has also been true of a number of trade unions.

Increasingly, governments have become directly involved in programs to improve employment opportunities for minorities. This has proceeded on two fronts. In the first place, governments as large employers can themselves unilaterally improve Negro employment opportunities. Governments can also influence employment opportunities in private employment, either through persuasion or compulsion. Compulsion, moreover, has many facets, for in addition to forcing the recalcitrant to change, it may also provide the stimulus to help those who want to change.

The Federal Government's efforts to improve opportunities within its own operations have proceeded along two lines. The strong push toward more equal opportunity in the Armed Forces and its substantial success has been previously noted and dealt with at length in Chapter 15. In addition, the Federal Government, through the Civil Service Commission, the President's Committee on Equal Employment Opportunity and the operating agencies, has sought to improve opportunities in its employment of civilians. There are no precisely comparable data over any long period which would reveal exactly how much progress has been made. Such evidence as is available indicates that the opportunities for Negroes have improved substantially over the last three decades, after declining materially during the preceding twenty-five years or so. The most recent distribution of Negro employment in the Federal Government is presented in Table XXXI.

---

[2] This pattern is set out more fully in Hiestand, *Economic Growth and Employment Opportunities for Minorities.* (New York: Columbia University Press, 1964).

TABLE XXXI—Employment in the Federal Government, by Pay Category, Grade and Salary groups, and Race, June 1961 and June 1962[a]

	June 1961			June 1962		
	Total	Negro		Total	Negro	
Pay Category	Employees	Number	%	Employees	Number	%
Total	2,197,360	282,616	12.9	2,259,993	293,353	13.0
Total Class. Act or Similar	1,012,447	89,784	8.9	1,065,420	96,711	9.1
GS-1 thru 4	355,446	64,242	18.1	363,970	66,101	18.2
GS-5 thru 11	503,058	24,505	4.9	532,888	29,204	5.5
GS-12 thru 18	153,943	1,037	0.7	168,562	1,406	0.8
Total Wage Board	568,835	106,853	18.8	569,116	105,784	18.6
Up to $4,499	N.A.	N.A.	N.A.	104,210	44,680	42.9
$4,500 to $7,999	N.A.	N.A.	N.A.	441,198	60,953	13.8
$8,000 and over	N.A.	N.A.	N.A.	23,708	151	0.6
Total Postal Field Service	566,151	83,187	14.7	576,047	86,842	15.1
PFS-1 thru 4[b]	487,407	78,981	16.2	497,396	81,887	16.5
PFS-5 thru 11	74,980	4,195	5.6	75,016	4,939	6.6
PFS-12 thru 18	3,764	11	0.3	3,635	16	0.4
Total Other Pay Categories	49,927	2,792	5.6	49,410	4,016	8.1
Up to $4,499	N.A.	N.A.	N.A.	12,635	2,691	21.3
$4,500 to $7,999	N.A.	N.A.	N.A.	20,825	1,104	5.3
$8,000 and over	N.A.	N.A.	N.A.	15,950	221	1.4

[a] 1961 data covers all employment worldwide. 1962 data excludes employment in Alaska, Hawaii, and Puerto Rico. Overseas data is as of July 31, 1962 and covers U.S. citizens only in Department of State (including Agency for International Development and Peace Corps), Department of Defense, U.S. information Agency, Panama Canal Co. and Canal Zone Government.
[b] Includes 4th Class Postmasters and Rural Carriers.
N.A.—Not available.

SOURCE: President's Committee on Equal Employment Opportunity, unpublished data.

Many state and local governments have also made strides in opening up opportunities in their own work force. Again little in the way of data is available. Overall, however, governments can be seen to be major areas of expansion for Negro employment between 1950 and 1960 (Table XXXII). The employment of Negroes in Federal, state and local governments increased by over 400,000 between 1950 and 1960, an amount equal to 40 percent of the net increase in total employment of Negroes. In so doing, Negroes increased from 8.7 percent to 11.2 percent of all governmental workers. They also markedly increased their relative importance among all governmental employees in every occupational group.

TABLE XXXII—Nonwhite Governmental Employees by Occupational
Groups, 1950 and 1960

| | 1950 | | 1960 | |
Occupational group	Number	As percent of total in group	Number	As percent of total in group
Total	479,190	8.7	879,704	11.2
Professional and technical	105,780	6.2	210,987	8.0
Managers and officials	5,280	1.6	12,282	2.8
Clerical	94,200	6.9	191,948	10.3
Craftsmen and foremen	23,070	4.7	49,754	7.3
Operatives	49,950	13.6	80,463	17.9
Service workers exc. pvt. household	118,740	14.2	224,287	17.3
Laborers exc. farm and mine	75,660	22.4	88,583	25.5
Other and not reported	6,540	a	21,400	a

a Not relevant.

SOURCE: U.S Bureau of the Census, Census of Population: 1960, *Occupational Characteristics*, Table 21, Census of Population: 1950, Table 13.

The impact of government on private employment policy has been through requiring contractors selling goods and services to government to follow nondiscriminatory policies and through regulatory activities directed toward other employers to do likewise.

The most far-reaching effort is the Federal executive order that nearly all contracts entered into by the Federal Government must contain a provision that the contractor and his subcontractors follow fair employment practises. The enforcement of this clause has been left primarily to the contract agency. Enforcement has not been very successful. A succession of five Presidential committees have also had a measure of responsibility for enforcement. In the only comprehensive review of this program, Norgren and Hill conclude "that the earlier committees did not effect any significant abatement of employment discrimination. The currently functioning committee [the President's Committee on Equal Employment Opportunity], however, has a somewhat better record of accomplishment." [3]

There are, in addition, fully enforceable fair employment practices laws in twenty-one states and many municipalities. In ten of these states, laws have been in effect for more than a decade. Norgren and Hill conclude, however, that very few of the administering commissions are supplied with adequate funds to deal effectively with the problem. In New York

[3] Norgren and Hill, *Toward Fair Employment*, Columbia Univ. Press, p. 10.

and several other states, the commissions' efforts in dealing with selective employers were viewed as successful. The effort to deal with employment agencies and labor unions was deemed considerably less successful.[4]

Conclusion

It is not easy to summarize what has emerged from the critical review of the multiple dimensions of the work status of the Negro in the United States as of the 1960's. There is much that provides ground for optimism, if only guarded optimism. Negroes have succeeded during the past half-century in flowing from the major declining industry to which they were overwhelmingly attached—agriculture—and latching on to jobs in the expanding industrial sectors. What is more, they have relocated in large numbers from the South, where their opportunities were more constricted, to the North and West, where they were broader. Finally, they have benefited from certain wage trends which have helped to narrow the differentials that previously existed between the higher paying jobs where they were underrepresented, and the lower paying jobs, where they were overrepresented. All these were favorable developments and have helped the Negro to improve his occupational status and his earnings, and further to narrow the gap between himself and his white fellow citizens.

But there are other signs that are less favorable. The Negro was so far behind at the start of this century that despite his progress he remains today still very far behind. In fact the relatively slow pace at which the occupational gap is being closed reflects increasingly the educational gap between Negroes and whites, for increasingly education has come to determine what one can accomplish in the job market. Moreover, being the most vulnerable group in the labor market Negroes have been particularly hard hit by the general easing in the employment situation during the past decade. And the future is even more ominous because of the much larger numbers of better educated whites who will be competing for the available jobs. Hence the continuance of a slack labor market is a major danger to the Negroes' occupational future.

Aside from these favorable and unfavorable forces playing on the Negro community as a whole, it is important not to lose sight of the individual Negro and his preparation for and access to employment. The United States is moving with varying degrees of speed to remove overt and covert discrimination in education and employment and in housing, which is directly related to both. The faster the progress which it makes on these crucial fronts to eliminate discrimination, the faster the opportunity for the

---

[4] *Ibid*, Ch. 5, passim.

individual Negro to prepare himself adequately for work and to secure the full benefits of work preparation. This is the challenge that faces the nation as a whole, as well as every individual Negro.

BIBLIOGRAPHY

Becker, Gary S., *The Economics of Discrimination.* Chicago: University of Chicago Press, 1957.

Dewey, Donald, "Negro Employment in Southern Industry." *Journal of Political Economy,* LX (August, 1952), pp. 279–293.

Edwards, G. Franklin, *The Negro Professional Class.* Glencoe, Illinois: The Free Press of Glencoe, 1959.

Feldman, Herman, *Racial Factors in American Industry.* New York: Harper & Brothers, 1931.

Frazier, E. Franklin. *The Negro in the United States,* rev. ed. New York: Macmillan, 1957.

Ginzberg, Eli, *et al., The Negro Potential.* New York: Columbia University Press. 1956.

Henderson, Vivian, "The Economic Imbalance. An Inquiry into the Economic Status of Negroes in the United States, 1935–1960, with Implications for Negro Education." *Quarterly Review of Higher Education Among Negroes,* XXVIII (April, 1960), pp. 84–98.

———. *The Economic Status of Negroes: In the Nation and in the South.* Atlanta: Southern Regional Council, c. 1963.

Hiestand, Dale L., *Economic Growth and Employment Opportunities for Minorities.* New York: Columbia University Press, 1964.

Hope, John, II, "The Employment of Negroes in the United States by Major Occupation and Industry." *The Journal of Negro Education,* XXII Summer Issue, 1953, pp. 307–21.

Myrdal, Gunnar, *An American Dilemma.* New York: Harper & Co., 1944.

National Manpower Council, *Womanpower.* New York: Columbia University Press, 1957.

National Planning Association, Committee of the South, *Selected Studies of Negro Employment in the South* (Report No. 6). Washington, National Planning Association, 1955.

Norgren, Paul H., and Samuel E. Hill, *Toward Fair Employment.* New York: Columbia University Press, 1964.

U.S. Bureau of the Census, *Sixteenth Census of the United States, 1940, Population,* "Comparative Occupation Statistics for the United States, 1870 to 1940" (by Alba M. Edwards). Washington: Government Printing Office, 1943.

———. *Negroes in the United States, 1920–32.* Washington: Government Printing Office, 1935.

U.S. Commission on Civil Rights, *Civil Rights '63,* 1963 Report of the Commission, "The Negro in the Armed Forces." Washington: Government

Printing Office, 1963, pp. 169–83, 214–24.

U.S. Department of Labor, *The Economic Situation of the Negro in the United States* (Bulletin S3). Washington: Government Printing Office, October, 1960.

——, *Negroes in the United States: Their Employment and Economic Status* (Bulletin No. 1119). Washington: Government Printing Office, 1952.

U.S. Senate, Committee on Labor and Public Welfare, Subcommittee on Employment and Manpower, *Hearings: Equal Employment Opportunity*. 88th Congress, First Session, 1963, Washington: Government Printing Office, 1963.

Vance, Rupert B., and Nicholas J. Demerath, eds., *The Urban South*. Chapel Hill: University of North Carolina Press, 1954.

Wagley, Charles, and Marvin Harris, *Minorities in the New World*. New York; Columbia University Press, 1958.

Weaver, Robert C., *Negro Labor, A National Problem*. New York: Harcourt, Brace, 1946.

chapter 5

The Negro
in the National Economy

Andrew F. Brimmer

INTRODUCTION

The Negro lives and works in the backwaters and eddies of the national economy in the United States. This has been true since he arrived on these shores long before the colonies became a nation. In recent years, Negroes have made a number of vigorous advances in their efforts to enter the mainstream of economic activity. However, they remain at best a marginal factor in virtually every field, except those protected by the legacy of racial segregation and discrimination. Yet, the winds of change are blowing across the land, shaking old arrangements and creating new opportunities for men with imagination and enterprise. The objectives in this chapter are to identify and explain the forces which are re-making the economic world of the American Negro.

An appraisal of the Negro's role in the national economy can be approached in a number of ways. One alternative is to chronicle the progress the Negro has made within the long-term development of the economy as a whole. This approach would be primarily historical and descriptive. Since the record of the Negro's progress is impressive, the result might be both a colorful document and a monument to perserverance against great obstacles.

Another alternative is to highlight the strategic factors influencing the conditions under which Negroes participate in the economy and share the benefits of national production. This approach, which is basically analytic and statistical, emphasizes the Negro's adaptation to the malfunctioning of the market place. In general, both resource allocation and income shares are determined by the price system in an economy such as that found in the United States. But the existence of racial discrimination and the mosaic of social disorganization associated with segregation have severely restricted the Negro's opportunities to acquire skills and property and to offer them in exchange for income. Partly because of the resulting limited ability to earn—but also because of additional barriers—the Negro in turn has a restricted access to the market for consumer goods and services.

251

The effect of these constraints has been essentially the same as that produced by a protective tariff in international trade: two markets have emerged. One is open to the white public virtually without limitations, and whites are free to purchase both goods and services with complete freedom of choice. However, for Negroes entry into this market is extremely circumscribed. While they enjoy considerable freedom of choice in the purchase of goods (except housing), a wide range of services (especially personal services) offered to the general market is unavailable to them. Consequently, a second market has arisen. This is basically a Negro market, and the provision of personal services lies at its core. Thus, the Negro market is entirely derivative; it has evolved behind the walls of segregation to meet a demand left unfilled by business firms operating in the general market.

As background for the rest of the Chapter, it would be helpful to begin with a brief introduction to the general market economy in the United States, with special reference to the way it affects the Negro. Chart I, presenting a schematic view of the circular flow of economic activity, makes it clear that the Negro's role is both critical and marginal: he is a critical factor in the labor market and in the market for goods and services. On the other hand, the Negro makes little impact on the national economy in his role as an entrepreneur.

In general, the economy can be visualized as consisting of the four sectors described in Chart I: (I) the household sector; (II) the market for productive resources; (III) the business sector and (IV) the market for consumer goods and services.[1] The schema rests on two principal assumptions: (1) that the dominant motivating forces in the economy are the attempts of households to maximize consumer satisfaction and the attempts of business firms to maximize profits; (2) the primary way to obtain income is to work for it. These assumptions lead to the first link traced in Chart I between the household sector (I) and the market for productive factors (II). (In tracing the flows, it should be noted that the movement of money is marked by $). To obtain income, households offer their resources in the market to those willing to employ them. For convenience, we can group these productive factors into four classes according to the types of income they receive. The most important factor of production is *labor,* and its income consists of *wages* (including salaries). Owners of *land* (including

---

[1] The actual structure of the economy is clearly more complicated. The present description neglects a number of strategic roles, of which that of government, trade unions and nonprofit institutions are perhaps the most important. Moreover, the business sector could be broken down to show the market for capital goods and the financial system. But for the present summary analysis, greater detail appears not to be necessary.

Chart I

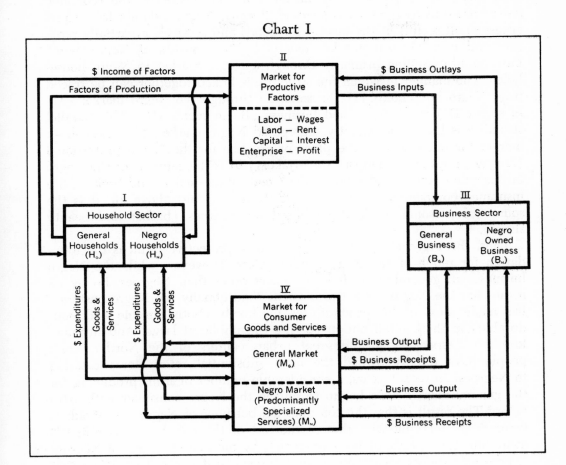

buildings and other improvements) receive *rent*. Owners of *capital* (defined broadly as loanable funds) receive *interest*. Finally, persons who take the risk of operating an *enterprise* (including common stockholders) receive *profits* (or bear *losses*). In our economy, the private business sector employs the vast proportion of the labor force; it rents or owns most of the land and structures, and it borrows most of the loanable funds. Thus, as labor and other resources flow from the market for factors into the business sector (III), they account for the bulk of business outlays. These business inputs are required to produce the output of goods and services demanded by, and sold to, consumers in the retail market (IV).

At this stage, however, a significant branching occurs in the economic stream as far as Negroes are concerned. Because Negroes do not have equal access to all sectors of the market for goods and services, a partially separate and parallel structure has emerged. This consists of Negro-owned business firms selling primarily through a Negro market to Negro households. The manner in which the structure is linked together can be traced from Negro households (H_N in sector I) through the Negro market (M_N in sector IV) to Negro-owned business (B_N in sector III). This parallel structure is the predominantly segregated Negro market. It is basically a market for services. It is the place of practice for the Negro professional (lawyers, physicians, dentists, undertakers). It is the counter for the Negro businessmen (owners of retail outlets, real estate dealers and brokers, life insurance companies, cosmetics manufacturers). And above all, it is the source of personal services purchased by Negroes (barber and beauty shops).

Thus, this segregated market, serving as a protective tariff, is the foundation for much of the Negro middle class. However, while the Negro businessman generally has few customers other than Negroes, he by no means has the Negro market to himself. Traditionally the Negro customer has made most of his expenditures for goods (both durable and nondurable) in those retail outlets serving the public at large. And in many localities (especially in the great urban centers of the North) white people have usually owned the more substantial retail stores catering to Negroes. In recent years, a considerable number of firms producing for the general market have begun to pursue the Negro consumer with extra vigor.[2] The result is that the consumption behavior of Negro households is increasingly merging with that of the rest of the population. But in the meantime, the historic dichotomy created by the limited access of Negroes to personal services persists and imparts a peculiar flavor to the participation of the Negro in the Nation's economy.

In Chapter 4, dealing with the Employment Patterns of Negro men and women, the changing occupational structure among Negroes has already been discussed. However, that chapter, designed with a different orientation, contains little discussion of the size, composition, trends and determinants of the income of the Negro community. Consequently, a look at the income picture is the point of departure in this chapter. The next task is the explanation of the changing pattern of expenditures by Negro consumers. A principal objective of the analysis is to weigh the implications

[2] In fact, an entire fraternity of marketing specialists, the National Association of Market Developers, has grown up, and its members are employed in helping many leading corporations to penetrate the Negro market.

of these emerging trends of consumer behavior for the future of the Negro market.

The remainder of the chapter is given to an examination of the changing environment in which Negro-owned businesses must operate and the prospects for careers as corporate officials. In the final section, the results are summarized and the principal conclusions are restated briefly.

Income of the Negro Community

Trends and Cycles in Income

In a price-directed, free-market economy, the size and distribution of income are prime indicators of economic progress and the well-being of citizens. Measured by either of these indicators, American Negroes, since World War II, have made mixed progress: as a group their incomes have grown both in absolute terms and as a share of the nation's aggregate income. However, because of the rapid strides made by white families, taken as a group, little actual improvement in the Negro's relative position was registered.

This experience is clearly evident from Table I, which shows the estimated aggregate income of families and individuals, by color, for the United States from 1947 through 1963. The personal income of nonwhites (about 92 percent of whom are Negroes) amounted to $23.6 billion in 1963, or 6.4 percent of total personal income. This was a record by both measurements. However, the most striking feature of Table I is the stagnation in the relative position of nonwhites between 1953 and 1960, during which years their share of personal income was frozen at approximately 5.8 percent of the total. This retardation is partly explained by the sluggishness of the economy as a whole from the end of the Korean War to the end of the decade.

This slow rate of economic growth had a particularly adverse effect on nonwhites. The dimensions of this impact are compared in Chart II; panels (a) and (b) trace the level and trend of total and nonwhite personal income from 1947 through 1963. As the trend lines indicate, total personal income increased by an average of $14.3 billion each year, and the income of nonwhites rose by an average of $1.0 billion. This represented an annual average rate of growth of 6.0 percent for the total and 7.7 percent for

Chart II

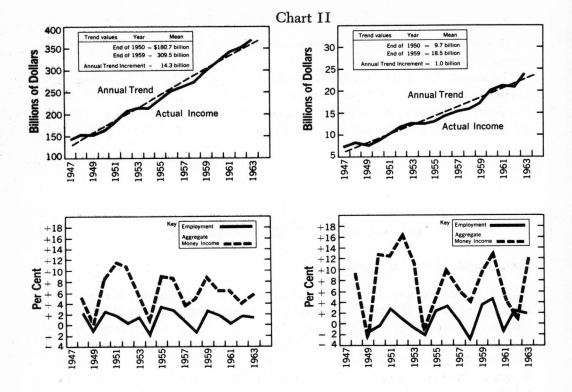

SOURCE: U.S. Department of Labor, *Manpower Report of the President,* March, 1964.

nonwhites. However, for the years of relative stagnation (1954–59 inclusively), the annual average growth rate of total income eased off to about 5.9 percent. In sharp contrast, during this same period, the growth rate in the income of nonwhites dropped to 5.4 percent. The result was a much greater gap between potential and actual level of income for nonwhites than for the nation as a whole. The size of this gap is roughly indicated by the spread between actual income and the trend lines. By this benchmark, the accumulated shortfall in total personal income during these six years amounted to about $86 billion, or about 5.8 percent less than the higher growth rate would have produced. For nonwhites, the accumulated shortfall in income was around $6.9 billion, representing a difference of 7.8 percent. Put differently, the sluggish behavior of the economy in the last half of the 1950's cost nonwhites the equivalent of 3.5 months' income at the 1963 rate, compared with just over 2.8 months' income for the entire economy.

The much greater impact of postwar business cycles on the employment and incomes of nonwhites also is graphically marked in Chart II. Panel (c)

TABLE I—Estimated Aggregate Income of Families and Unrelated Individuals, by Color, for the United States, 1947–1963

Year	Aggregate Money Income (Billions)				Percent		
	Total	White	Nonwhite		Total	White	Nonwhite
1947	$147.0	$139.8	$7.2		100.0	95.1	4.9
1948	154.4	146.5	7.9		100.0	94.9	5.1
1949	153.9	146.2	7.7		100.0	95.0	5.0
1950	167.3	158.6	8.7		100.0	94.8	5.2
1951	186.2	176.4	9.8		100.0	94.7	5.3
1952	205.5	194.1	11.4		100.0	94.5	5.5
1953	215.4	202.7	12.7		100.0	94.1	5.9
1954	216.1	203.6	12.5		100.0	94.2	5.8
1955	235.1	222.0	13.1		100.0	94.4	5.6
1956	254.4	240.0	14.4		100.0	94.3	5.7
1957	263.3	248.0	15.3		100.0	94.2	5.8
1958	276.2	260.3	15.9		100.0	94.2	5.8
1959	301.2	283.8	17.4		100.0	94.2	5.8
1960	319.5	299.8	19.7		100.0	93.8	6.2
1961	339.1	318.3	20.8		100.0	93.9	6.1
1962	351.5	330.4	21.1		100.0	94.0	6.0
1963	371.1	347.5	23.6		100.0	93.6	6.4

SOURCE: U.S. Department of Commerce, Bureau of the Census, *Current Population Reports*, series P–60, annual issues. (Washington, D.C., Government Printing Office)

shows the annual percentage changes in total employment and total personal income over the years 1948–63; panel (d) shows the same information for nonwhites (except that estimates of changes in nonwhite employment are not available for 1949).[3] The effects of the four postwar recessions are clearly visible. The lowest levels in employment were reached in 1949, 1954, 1958 and 1961, respectively. During the first three recessions, the level of total employment declined by one-two percent; but no actual decrease in the level of total employment occurred in 1961. In contrast, the level of nonwhite employment dropped by approximately 2 percent in each of the recessions, and the decline was close to 3 percent in 1958. On the other hand, the return of better conditions also benefited nonwhites relatively more than the country as a whole. For instance, while total employment advanced by an average of 2.4 percent in the first year following each recession (excluding the 1949 setback), the corresponding increase in nonwhite employment was 2.7 percent. Moreover, for nonwhites, the largest percentage gains in employment were registered in

[3] See Technical Note 1 on p. 336.

the second year of recovery, rather than in the first year as was the case for total employment. This tendency for nonwhite employment to lag may well be further evidence of the apparent habit for nonwhites to be "the last hired."

The more volatile behavior of nonwhite income is also traceable. The first thing to note, however, is that total personal income and the incomes of nonwhites are considerably more stable than the level of employment. This undoubtedly reflects the short duration of postwar recessions, as well as the influence of unemployment compensation, welfare payments and other sources which prevent incomes from falling in tandem with employment during recessions. In fact, total personal income declined absolutely only during 1949, and it actually rose by 5–7 percent in 1958 and 1961. Moreover, in the first year following each recession, total personal income climbed by an average of 7.6 percent. Nonwhite incomes displayed significantly more instability. A decline of about 2 percent was registered in both 1949 and 1954. While nonwhite incomes also showed advances in 1958 and 1961, the gains were substantially less than for the total. Increases during the first year of recovery after each recession were also less— averaging about 7 percent.

In summary, we can conclude that both business cycles and the relatively slow growth of the economy in the decade of the 1950's affected nonwhites considerably more adversely than all citizens combined. Since the evidence in Chapter 4 (Patterns of Employment of Negro Men and Women) suggests that little fundamental improvement is occurring in the relative position of the Negro in industry, we can expect nonwhites to continue to bear a disproportionate share of the burden of economic instability in the future.

We must now look behind these aggregate figures to the behavior of family and individual incomes, for it is at this more personal level that the welfare of the Negro community must be judged. Table II presents the median income [4] of families and individuals, by color, for the years 1947 through 1963. The general advance of family income is striking. Between 1947 and 1963, median family income, for both total and nonwhite families, just about doubled. For all families, the median rose from $3,031 in 1947 to $6,249 in 1963. The advance for nonwhites was from $1,614 in 1947 to $3,465 in 1963. Equally striking, however, is the evidence that nonwhite families made virtually no net improvement in their income position relative to white families. In fact, the slight closing of the income gap which occurred between 1947 and 1952 was actually reversed over the

[4] "Median income" is that figure which divides the number of income recipients into two equal groups.

TABLE II—Median Income of Families and Unrelated Individuals, by Color, for the United States, 1947–1963

| | Families | | | | Unrelated Individuals | | | |
Year	Total	White	Nonwhite	Ratio of Nonwhite to white	Total	White	Nonwhite	Ratio of Nonwhite to white
1947	$3,031	$3,157	$1,614	0.51	$ 980	$1,035	$ 746	0.72
1948	3,187	3,310	1,768	.53	996	1,053	789	.75
1949	3,107	3,232	1,650	.51	1,050	1,134	819	.72
1950	3,319	3,445	1,869	.54	1,045	1,115	817	.73
1951	3,709	3,859	2,032	.53	1,195	1,258	929	.74
1952	3,890	4,114	2,338	.57	1,409	1,519	1,051	.69
1953	4,233	4,392	2,461	.56	1,394	1,473	1,161	.79
1954	4,173	4,339	2,410	.56	1,224	1,317	875	.66
1955	4,421	4,605	2,549	.55	1,316	1,402	935	.67
1956	4,783	4,993	2,628	.53	1,426	1,466	1,087	.74
1957	4,971	5,166	2,764	.54	1,496	1,592	1,013	.64
1958	5,087	5,300	2,711	.51	1,486	1,592	1,080	.68
1959	5,417	5,643	2,917	.52	1,556	1,663	1,075	.65
1960	5,620	5,835	3,233	.55	1,720	1,860	1,064	.57
1961	5,737	5,981	3,191	.53	1,755	1,885	1,160	.62
1962	5,956	6,237	3,330	.53	1,753	1,876	1,251	.67
1963	6,249	6,548	3,465	.53	1,800	1,887	1,294	.69

SOURCE: U.S. Department of Commerce, Bureau of the Census, "Current Population Reports", series P–60, annual issues. (Washington, D.C., U.S. Government Printing Office)

next decade. Thus, by 1963, the median income of nonwhite families was 53 percent of that for white families—compared with 51 percent in 1947. The ratio had climbed to 57 percent in 1952, but it had also shrunk to a low of 51 percent in 1958. This deterioration further reflects the erosion of the Negro's position during the years of slack economic growth beginning in the mid-1950's. The more burdensome consequences of this slow-down on nonwhite families is also reflected in Table II. For instance, during the post-war period as a whole, the annual average rate of growth in median income was about the same for white and nonwhite families—4.7 percent and 4.8 percent, respectively. But during the years when nonwhites registered their largest relative gains (1947–52), the annual growth rate in their incomes was 7.7 percent, compared with 5.4 percent for white families. In contrast, during 1953–63, the order was reversed: the growth rate was 4.4 percent for whites and 3.6 percent for nonwhites. Again, the explanation for this weakness in the Negro's income position is to be found in the host of factors (including automation in industry and the continued ravages of racial discrimination) discussed in Chapter 4.

Education and Income

For the average American, education is undoubtedly the most promising escalator for advancement from low to high income status. For Negroes,
education has been virtually the only escalator. However, the financial advantage for Negroes of an additional year of educational attainment is
just over half that of whites. The general relationship between education
and expected lifetime earnings of men, by color, is shown in Table III.
Perhaps the most striking feature of these statistics is the fact that a nonwhite man must have between one and three years of college before he can
expect to earn as much as a white man with less than eight years of
schooling, over the course of their respective working lives. Moreover, even
after completing college and spending at least one year in graduate school,
a nonwhite man can expect to do about as well as a white person who only
completed high school.

A number of considerations may account for the observed differentials.
In the first place, whites and nonwhites reporting the same years of

TABLE III—Education and Differential Lifetime Earnings of Men, by Color *

(Thousands of Dollars)

Level of Education	White	Nonwhite	Nonwhite as Percent of white
Elementary School:			
Less than 8 years	$157	$ 95	61
8 years	191	123	64
High School:			
1 to 3 years	221	132	60
4 years	253	151	60
College:			
1 to 3 years	301	162	54
4 years	395	185	47
5 years or more	466	246	53

* For men aged 18 to 64. Derived from 1960 Census data. See U.S. Senate, 88th Congress, 1st
Session, *Hearings Before the Committee on Labor and Public Welfare on Bills Relating to Equal
Employment Opportunities,* July and August, 1963.

schooling undoubtedly have received educations differing vastly in quality.
The historical pattern of legal and *de facto* school segregation, plus the
cultural deprivation associated with it, have generally meant inherently
unequal educational opportunities for nonwhites. The result has been a
serious deficiency in the level of qualifications which nonwhites have been

able to achieve in a wide range of occupations. Nevertheless, the corrosive effects of racial discrimination on earnings differentials for white and nonwhite men are also evident—even after one allows for differences in the quality of education. This is clearly illustrated by data relating to carpenters, truck drivers and semiskilled factory workers with less than eight years of schooling. Among these workers, the influence of differential quality in education is probably minimized. The expected lifetime earnings of nonwhite carpenters amount to 60 percent of that of white carpenters, or $91,000 versus $152,000. For truck drivers, the ratio was the same— $97,000 to $162,000. For factory workers, white and nonwhite lifetime earnings were $167,000 and $120,000, respectively, or a ratio of 72 percent. Within this structure, there was considerable variation, but the ratios of nonwhite to white earnings were generally lowest in the South and highest in the North and West. Moreover, U.S. Census Bureau figures relating to about twenty-seven other occupations reveal essentially the same pattern of variation. Thus, it seems that, even given about the same educational attainments, the money value of a nonwhite man is about two-fifths less than that of a white man when weighed in the general market for skills.

Poverty and Prosperity Among American Negroes

For a large number of Negro families, poverty is the normal state of existence. However, contrary to popular belief, the entire Negro community is certainly not poverty stricken—no matter what standard of measurement is applied. In fact, a substantial proportion of such families enjoys a standard of living thoroughly comparable to that enjoyed by the white middle class, and a fairly sizable number can afford the luxuries which cushion the lives of some of the nation's most well-off households.

But taken as a group, Negroes are about two and one-half times more likely than white families to be found among the poor (see Table IV). Of course, it is virtually impossible to define precisely the boundaries of poverty, and it is almost as difficult to obtain general agreement on any definition adopted. For the purpose of this brief analysis, it is useful to follow the rough benchmark set by the Council of Economic Advisers.[5] Thus, a family of four with $3,000 or less per year can be considered "poor." Unattached individuals with incomes of $1,500 or less also can be considered "poor." These are obviously arbitrary cut-off figures, and they could be refined in a variety of ways to permit income variations according

[5] Council of Economic Advisers, *Economic Report of the President,* January 1964, p. 58.

TABLE IV—Selected Characteristics of Families with Incomes Under $3,000 in 1959 for the United States, 1960
(Numbers in Thousands)

Selected Characteristics	All Families		White Families		Nonwhite Families	
	Number	Percent	Number	Percent	Number	Percent
All families	9,650	100.0	7,616	100.0	2,034	100.0
Male head	**7,573**	**78.5**	**6,190**	**81.3**	**1,383**	**68.0**
Head under 65 years	5,073	52.6	3,948	51.8	1,125	55.3
Husband-wife families	4,846	50.2	3,784	49.7	1,062	52.2
No earners	541	5.6	461	6.1	80	3.9
1 earner or more; head not earner	287	3.0	224	2.9	62	3.1
Head worked 50 to 52 weeks	1,945	20.2	1,544	20.3	401	19.7
Farmers and farm managers	570	5.9	525	6.9	46	2.2
Craftsmen, operatives, and kindred workers	479	5.0	357	4.7	122	6.0
Service workers, including private household	129	1.3	69	0.9	60	2.9
Laborers, except mine	290	3.0	170	2.2	121	5.9
All other occupation groups	476	4.9	423	5.6	53	2.6
Head worked less than 50 weeks	2,073	21.5	1,555	20.4	519	25.5
Farmers and farm managers	184	1.9	138	1.8	46	2.2
Craftsmen, operatives and kindred workers	867	9.0	705	9.3	162	8.0
Service workers, including private household	128	1.3	82	1.1	46	2.3
Laborers, except mine	549	5.7	329	4.3	220	10.8
All other occupation groups	345	3.6	300	3.9	45	2.2
Other male head families	226	2.3	164	2.2	62	3.1
No earners	44	0.5	34	0.4	10	0.5
1 earner or more	182	1.9	130	1.7	52	2.6
Head 65 years and over	2,500	25.9	2,242	29.4	258	12.7
No earners	1,545	16.0	1,434	18.8	111	5.5
1 earner or more	955	9.9	808	10.6	147	7.2
Female Head	**2,077**	**21.5**	**1,426**	**18.7**	**651**	**32.0**
Head under 65 years	1,625	16.8	1,066	14.0	559	27.5
No earners	584	6.1	409	5.4	175	8.6
1 earner or more	1,041	10.8	658	8.6	383	18.8
Head 65 years and over	452	4.7	360	4.7	92	4.5
No earners	229	2.4	195	2.6	34	1.7
1 earner or more	223	2.3	165	2.2	58	2.8

source: U.S. Department of Commerce, Bureau of the Census. *U.S. Census of Population, 1960*, PC(2)–4C, "Sources and Structure of Family Income", Tables 1, 2A, and 2B. (Washington, D.C., U.S. Government Printing Office).

to size of family, location, age and other factors influencing household needs and living costs. But the $3,000 income figure for families does provide a crude yardstick for measuring the incidence of poverty among different groups in the population. Translated another way, an annual income of $3,000 means a weekly pay of about $60, compared with an average factory pay of around $100 per week in 1963. It means only $15 per week per person for a family of four. In the case of unattached individuals, an annual income of $1,500 implies a weekly income of less than $30. Clearly, these criteria are by no means generous, and if anything they probably understate the real incidence of poverty in the United States.

By the $3,000-income criterion, there were about 8.8 million poor families in 1963 (see Table V). This represented about 19 percent of the 47.4 million families in the country in that year. There were also about 3.9 million poor individuals in 1963, when the $1,500 income limit is used. The proportion of nonwhite families and individuals in the poverty group was considerably higher. For example, in 1963, there were 4.8 million nonwhite families; yet 2.1 million (or 43 percent) were poor. In fact, nonwhite families constituted just over 10 percent of all families in the country, but they represented about 23 percent of all the poor families. In 1963, there were 1,457 thousand nonwhite individuals, and they accounted for an even larger share (56 percent) of all poor and unattached individuals.

Poverty among Negroes is about three times more prevalent in the South than in the rest of the country. For example, of the 2,060 thousand Negro families with incomes under $3,000 in 1959, almost three-fourths lived in the South; less than one-fourth lived in the North; and only 4 percent lived in the West.[6] Within the South, well over half of the poor Negro families resided in urban areas; about one-third were rural families not on farms, and 15 percent lived on farms. The situation was sharply reversed in the North and West. Virtually all (95 percent) of the poor Negro families in these regions lived in cities. Among cities, however, the incidence of poverty among Negroes also varied widely. As Table VI shows, in generally poor areas of the country, the economic gap between nonwhites and the population at large is likely to be particularly wide. Thus, in New Orleans, where just over one-fourth of all families had incomes of $3,000 or less in 1959, about half of the nonwhite families were in that category. Moreover, nonwhites represented one-third of all families in New Orleans, but they accounted for three-fifths of all poor families in the city. Of

[6] See Deborah P. Wolfe and Andrew F. Brimmer, Editors, *Poverty in the United States*, Committee on Education and Labor, House of Representatives, 88th Congress, 2nd Session, April 1964, Tables C, D, and E, p. 29.

TABLE V—Color and Farm-Nonfarm Residence: Families and Unrelated Individuals by Total Money Income in 1963, for the United States: 1964

| | Families | | | | | Unrelated Individuals | | | | |
| | United States | | | | | United States | | | | |
Total Money Income	Total	White	Nonwhite	Nonfarm	Farm	Total	White	Nonwhite	Nonfarm	Farm
Total										
Number—thousands	47,436	42,663	4,773	44,343	3,093	11,182	9,725	1,457	10,817	365
Percent	100.0	100.0	100.0	100.0	100.0	100.0	100.0	100.0	100.0	100.0
Under $1,000	3.8	3.2	9.2	3.3	11.1	28.2	26.2	41.1	27.7	44.4
$1,000 to $1,499	3.2	2.6	8.3	2.9	8.1	15.9	16.0	15.2	15.7	22.6
$1,500 to $1,999	3.6	3.2	8.0	3.3	8.9	9.8	10.0	8.9	9.8	9.3
$2,000 to $2,499	4.2	3.6	9.6	4.0	8.5	7.2	7.2	7.3	7.3	5.2
$2,500 to $2,999	3.7	3.3	8.0	3.5	6.8	4.7	4.5	6.1	4.8	3.3
$3,000 to $3,499	4.6	4.3	7.4	4.4	7.7	4.0	3.9	4.2	4.0	4.4
$3,500 to $3,999	4.1	3.9	6.1	4.1	5.4	4.2	4.3	3.6	4.2	3.7
$4,000 to $4,999	9.0	8.8	10.9	8.9	10.3	7.8	8.0	6.1	7.9	3.7
$5,000 to $5,999	11.1	11.3	8.7	11.2	8.9	6.2	6.6	3.7	6.4	1.1
$6,000 to $6,999	10.2	10.5	7.3	10.5	5.5	4.0	4.3	1.6	4.1	0.7
$7,000 to $7,999	9.1	9.6	4.7	9.4	4.7	2.8	3.0	1.6	2.9	—
$8,000 to $9,999	13.4	14.2	6.1	13.9	6.2	2.6	2.9	0.6	2.7	0.7
$10,000 to $14,999	14.5	15.6	4.1	15.0	5.9	1.8	2.1	—	1.9	0.7
$15,000 and over	5.4	5.9	1.6	5.7	2.1	0.7	0.8	0.2	0.7	—
Median income	$6,249	$6,548	$3,465	$6,427	$3,435	$1,800	$1,887	$1,294	$1,839	$1,123
Head Year-Round Full-Time Worker										
Percent of total	64.7	66.1	51.6	64.5	66.4	33.1	33.8	28.2	33.3	28.2
Median income	$7,458	$7,664	$4,847	$7,644	$4,107	$4,343	$4,486	$2,840	$4,411	(B)

— Entry rounds to zero.
(B) Median not shown where base is less than 200,000.

SOURCE: U.S. Department of Commerce, Bureau of the Census, "Consumer Income", *Current Population Reports*, Series P-60, No. 42, (Washington, D.C., Government Printing Office June 1964.)

the cities shown, the smallest gap between nonwhite and whites existed in Los Angeles, with Washington, D.C., second.

It is not possible here to offer a full explanation of the much greater incidence of poverty among Negroes. However, it seems evident that Negroes—far more than any other ethnic group (with the possible exception of American Indians)—suffer from the vicious circle of hereditary poverty. Because of the legacy of slavery, racial discrimination and the historical alienation of Negroes from the economic mainstream, the typical Negro family has long suffered from low and unstable incomes and the inadequate living standards made possible by such meager earnings. These circumstances have also meant that generation after generation of Negro children have been reared in an environment which heretofore has placed a low premium on education and the acquisition of technical skills which in turn

TABLE VI—Relative Poverty Among White and Nonwhite Families in Selected Cities

A. All Families and Families with Income of $3,000 or less, 1959

| | Total | | | Nonwhite | | |
| | | Poor Families | | | Poor Families | |
City	Total Families	Number	Percent of Total	Total Nonwhite	Number	Percent of Total
Chicago	909,204	123,214	13.6	184,682	52,341	28.3
Los Angeles	636,522	91,513	14.4	98,653	23,778	24.1
Baltimore	229,069	42,493	18.6	68,229	21,719	31.8
Washington	173,695	30,077	17.3	91,058	21,614	23.7
New Orleans	152,518	42,381	27.8	50,678	25,471	50.3

B. Relative Position of Total and Nonwhite Families, 1959

	All Nonwhite Families As Percent of Total Families	Poor Nonwhite Families As Percent of Total Poor Families
Chicago	20.3	42.5
Los Angeles	15.5	26.0
Baltimore	29.8	51.1
Washington	52.4	71.9
New Orleans	33.2	60.1

SOURCE: U.S. Census of Population, 1960.

form the basis of higher earning capacity. Numerous other elements help define and explain this mosaic of social disorganization and economic dependence which characterize poverty among Negroes, but the aim here is to present only a panoramic view within a general discussion of the income of the Negro community.

Although the Negro community can claim only a handful of millionaires, it can boast of a fairly large number of prosperous families and individuals. For example, as shown in Table V, in 1963, 274,000 nonwhite families had incomes of $10,000 or over, and more than one quarter of these earned in excess of $15,000. Between 1959 and 1963, the number of nonwhite families in the $10,000-and-over group rose by about 93,000, or about 50 percent. In contrast, the corresponding rise for all families was about 2,700,000, or 40 percent. In 1963, these relatively high income nonwhite families represented just under 3 percent of all families with incomes over $10,000, compared with about 2.5 percent in 1959. Yet these figures clearly demonstrate that a sizable number of Negroes dwell well beyond the margin of subsistence. With incomes of this level, such families not only can afford comfortable housing (when they can manage to purchase it in an essentially segregated market), but they can also provide a college education for their children. They can entertain graciously and participate in a variety of cultural activities. They can travel widely at home and abroad. In fact, a number of travel agencies have grown up (and prospered) through serving predominantly Negro middle class customers. As a matter of fact, a substantial portion of the advertising in *Ebony* Magazine reflects the tastes and aspirations of a rising Negro middle class—and their increasing ability to purchase the goods and services which support a middle class existence.

But this relatively broad carpet of prosperity among middle class non-whites rests heavily on the labor of multiple earners. For instance, of the 181,000 nonwhite families earning $10,000 or over in 1959, 161,000—or almost 90 percent—had two or more earners.[7] Among all families in that income bracket, multiple-earner families accounted for just under two-thirds of the total. Thus, it seems evident that a nonwhite family head has a slim chance to attain a middle class plane of living if he is the only breadwinner. In fact, an extra worker in a nonwhite household makes a contribution to the family budget which is worth approximately one and one half times as much as that contributed by an extra earner in households in general. In 1959, the median income of nonwhite families with only one earner was $2,903; in nonwhite families with two or more earners, the figure was $4,370 or 50 percent greater. For all families in the country, the respective median incomes were $5,326 and $7,009—suggesting only a

---

[7] U.S. Department of Commerce, Bureau of the Census, *U.S. Census of Population, 1960*, PC (2)-4C "Sources and Structure of Family Income", (Washington, D.C., Government Printing Office 1964), Table 1.

one-third gain attributable to the presence of one or more additional earners.

Income Distribution

A particularly distressing trend is evident in the distribution of income within the Negro community: the middle and upper income groups are getting richer, while the lowest income group is getting poorer. The basis for this conclusion can be readily seen in Table VII and Chart III. Table VII shows the percentage distribution of families and aggregate money income, by color, in 1947 and 1960. It will be observed that in both the white and nonwhite communities, the middle income groups made sizable gains in their share of total income. While such gains were made at the expense of both extremes of the income spectrum, the shrinkage in the relative share of the lowest fifth of nonwhite families is especially noticeable.

Chart III provides a visual perspective on the changing pattern of income distribution among white and nonwhite families since World War II. Panels (a) and (b) of the chart give a graphic picture (known technically as a "Lorenz Curve") of the distribution of total money income among the white and nonwhite families in 1947 and 1960. These are the same figures shown in Columns (4) and (8) of Table VII. For example, reading along the bottom of panel (a), one can see that in 1947 the lowest fifth (or 20 percent) of white families received about 5.5 percent of the income (shown along the vertical axis of the chart). The corresponding figures were about 4.8 percent for the lowest 20 percent of nonwhite families. The second fifth of white families in 1947 received 12.2 percent of aggregate income, making a total of 17.7 percent for the lowest 40 percent of the white families combined. For the lowest two-fifths of nonwhite families, the proportion was 13.5 percent in 1947. Thus, by plotting successive fifths of the families along the horizontal axis and indicating the relative share of total income received along the vertical axis, one completes the Lorenz Curve.

This curve is a handy tool with which to examine the extent of income equality within any specified group. For instance, if incomes were equally distributed, the Lorenz Curve would be the diagonal line rising from the lower left of each panel. It would mean that 20 percent of the families received 20 percent of the income; 60 percent of the families received 60 percent of the income—and so on. Consequently, the deviation of the actual pattern of income distribution from this diagonal line is a measure of the degree of income inequality within a particular community. In fact, this

Chart III

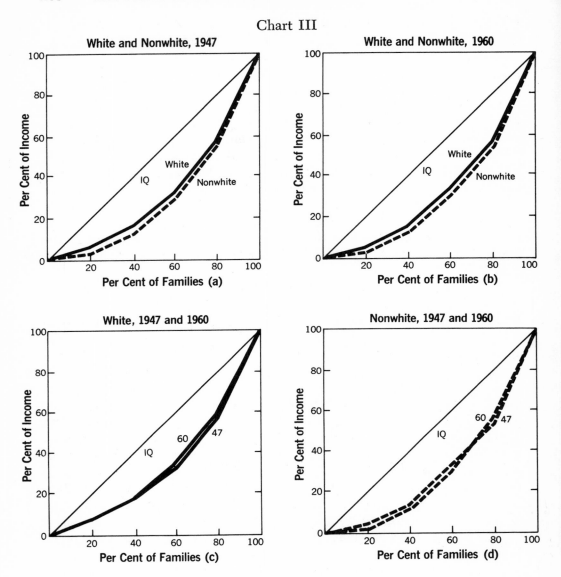

degree of inequality can be stated with considerable precision. It is the ratio of the area between the diagonal line and the actual Lorenz Curve [marked by IE in panel (a)] to the area of the triangle X, Y, Z. This ratio is known technically as the "Gini Index" of income concentration.[8] As

[8] The technique of computing the Index is explained in Herman Miller's *Trends in the Income of Families and Persons in the United States: 1947 to 1960*, United States Department of Commerce, Bureau of the Census, Washington, D.C. 1963), p. 26.

TABLE VII—Percentage Distribution of Families and Aggregate Money Income, by Color, 1947 and 1960

Distribution of Families	Percentage of Aggregate Income							
	White				Nonwhite			
	1947		1960		1947		1960	
	Share (1)	Cumulative (2)	Share (3)	Cumulative (4)	Share (5)	Cumulative (6)	Share (7)	Cumulative (8)
Lowest Fifth	5.5	5.5	5.3	5.3	4.8	4.8	3.9	3.9
Second Fifth	12.2	17.7	12.4	17.4	10.2	15.0	9.6	13.5
Middle Fifth	16.9	34.6	17.5	35.2	15.7	30.7	16.4	29.9
Fourth Fifth	22.8	57.4	23.3	58.5	23.6	54.3	25.4	55.3
Highest Fifth	42.6	100.0	41.4	100.0	45.7	100.0	44.7	100.0
Top 5 percent	17.4	—	16.7	—	17.0	—	16.2	—

SOURCE: Herman P. Miller, *Trends in the Income of Families and Persons in the United States: 1947 to 1960.* (U.S. Department of Commerce, Bureau of the Census, Technical Paper No. 8, Washington, D.C. 1963, pp. 168–189.

income inequality increases, the deviation of the Lorenz Curve widens, the IE area is enlarged, and the Gini Index rises. The Index varies between 0 and 1.00, indicating respectively, complete equality and complete inequality of income distribution.

In Table VIII, the Gini Index is shown for white and nonwhite families in the United States for each year 1947 through 1960, and for the South for each year 1953 through 1960. It will be noted that in every year income was distributed considerably more unequally among nonwhite than among white families [see also panel (b) of Chart III]. This was particularly true of the South, although income was distributed less equally among southern white families than among white families in the nation as a whole. Moreover, income inequality among nonwhites has been intensified over the years, a fact indicated by the steady upward creep of the Gini Index. In contrast, the trend was toward greater equality among white families as witnessed by the slight downward drift of the Gini Index. These trends are also shown graphically in panels (c) and (d) of Chart III. The Lorenz Curves in panel (c) for white families indicate a moderate shift to greater equality, because the 1960 curve lies on the 1947 curve, or slightly to its left toward the upper end of the distribution. The picture for nonwhite families, shown in panel (d) is quite different: over most of the distribution, the 1960 Lorenz Curve lies to the right of the 1947 curve, signifying increased inequality in income distribution. Only in the upper income range, where the 1960 curve is closer to the diagonal line, was there evidence of a tendency toward greater income equality.

This drift toward further income inequality among nonwhite families is exhibited even more clearly in Table IX, showing the percentage distribution of families and mean family income, by color, for 1947 and 1960. First, it will be observed that nonwhite families as a whole made moderate gains relative to white families, reflected in the rise in the income ratio from 54.2 percent in 1947 to 58.8 percent in 1960. Even larger percentage advances were registered by those in the middle-through-highest fifth of families. The top 5 percent of nonwhite families also did moderately well in relation to their white counterparts. However, the story was far different for those nonwhite families at the bottom of the income ladder. For them, the income ratio actually dropped, falling from 47.4 percent of white family incomes in 1947 to 43.2 percent in 1960. Although the mean income of the lowest group of nonwhite families more than doubled between 1947 and 1960, it still amounted to only $764 in the latter year. In fact, the relative gap between the lowest and highest nonwhite income groups widened appreciably, while the relative income spread between the lowest and highest white families remained virtually unchanged.

While it is comparatively easy to describe the deterioration in the relative position of the nonwhite families at the bottom of the income distribution it is far more difficult to explain it. Initially, however, it seems to reflect the same complex of factors described in Chapter 4. The handi-

TABLE VIII—GINI Index of Income Concentration, by Color, for the United States and the South, 1947–1960

	White Families		Nonwhite Families	
Year	U.S.	South	U.S.	South
1947	.363		.406	
1948	.361		.406	
1949	.367		.415	
1950	.372		.402	
1951	.352		.405	
1952	.359		.365	
1953	.353	.380	.393	.400
1954	.359	.415	.402	.418
1955	.358	.394	.388	.400
1956	.347	.367	.396	.401
1957	.345	.364	.405	.433
1958	.340	.364	.412	.425
1959	.349	.377	.414	.422
1960	.357	.394	.414	.437

SOURCE: Herman P. Miller, *Trends in the Income of Families and Persons in the United States: 1947 to 1960.* (United States Department of Commerce, Bureau of the Census, Technical Paper No. 8, Washington, D.C. 1963), pp. 168–189.

TABLE IX—Percentage Distribution of Families and Mean Family Income, by Color, 1947 and 1960

Distribution of Families	1947			1960		
	White	Nonwhite	Nonwhite as Percent of White	White	Nonwhite	Nonwhite as Percent of White
All Families	$3,718	$2,016	54.2	$6,674	$3,921	58.8
Lowest Fifth	1,022	484	47.4	1,769	764	43.2
Second Fifth	2,268	1,029	45.4	4,138	1,882	45.5
Middle Fifth	3,142	1,583	50.4	5,840	3,216	55.1
Fourth Fifth	4,238	2,380	56.2	7,775	4,980	64.1
Highest Fifth	7,919	4,619	58.3	13,815	8,766	63.5
Top 5 Percent	12,938	6,858	53.0	22,293	12,677	56.9
Total Number of Families (thousands)	34,158	3,121	—	41,104	4,331	—
Aggregate Income (millions)	$126,999	$6,292	—	$274,328	$16,982	—

SOURCE: Herman P. Miller, *Trends in the Income of Families and Persons in the United States: 1947 to 1960.* (United States Department of Commerce, Bureau of the Census, Technical Paper No. 8, Washington, D.C. 1963), pp. 168–189.

caps of limited education, the changing demand for skills, and the effects of racial discrimination—all seem to interact to trap a vast number of nonwhite families in the dismal poverty so characteristic of the backwaters of the nation's economic life. And there they seem to remain, while others move ahead, including an increasing number of better-equipped nonwhites. Clearly, some large-scale, national economic and community development effort is required to break the cycle of poverty in the United States— especially among nonwhites.

The Economic Cost of Racial Discrimination

It is appropriate to conclude this discussion of the income of the Negro community by an assessment of the overall economic cost of racial discrimination. In 1962, the Council of Economic Advisers [9] estimated this cost at about $17.3 billion, or roughly 3.2 percent of a gross national product (GNP) which totaled $554.9 billion in that year. Using a different estimating procedure, the U.S. Bureau of the Census has prepared a similar

[9] See Press Release, September 25, 1962.

estimate for each year 1949 through 1963. The results are shown in Table X. Before examining these figures, it should be pointed out that these estimates are tentative, because it is not possible to measure with any degree of certainty the full effects of non-discriminatory employment practices on the relative distribution of jobs, occupations, and earnings among whites and nonwhites. Moreover, the estimates approximate only the economic cost of racial discrimination, which is but a minor part of the damage done to the entire community—Negro and white—by the ravages of racial discrimination.

The estimates attempt to account for the economic losses arising from two sources: (1) inefficiencies in the use of the labor force resulting from failure to utilize fully the *existing* experience and skills of our population; (2) failure to develop *potential* experience and skills fully. The losses are described in terms of the gains that might accrue to GNP if discrimination were eliminated—or had been eliminated in the past. However, because the legacy of past discrimination affects today's occupational, geographic and capital structure, and the skills, training and education of the nonwhite labor force, the gains would accrue only over time as the economy adjusts and the labor force is upgraded.

As Table X shows, the economy has been losing between 1.9 percent and 2.4 percent in GNP simply because racial discrimination prevents the full use of the *present* educational attainment of nonwhites. In 1963, this loss amounted to 1.9 percent of GNP or $11.1 billion. However, this source of loss in GNP has declined compared with the six years 1949–54, when it amounted to 2.4 percent of the value of total output of goods and services. Behind this loss in GNP is a number of interrelated factors. In the first place, discrimination limits nonwhites primarily to job categories in which they cannot fully use their qualifications. If discrimination were lessened, nonwhites could migrate more readily from low to high productivity positions. The result would be an increase in the total output of goods and services. Moreover, a more rational utilization of the labor force probably would also require greater additions to the capital stock; plant and equipment expenditures would rise—further boosting the gain in output. Thus, capital as well as labor income would be enhanced, and the larger earnings of capital would also expand GNP. Self-employed entrepreneurs (especially nonwhites) would have more open access to markets, and thus become more efficient, in the absence of racial discrimination; and their incomes would reflect their higher productivity. This is another source of the improvement in GNP resulting from a decline in racial discriminaton.

TABLE X—Estimated Gains in Gross National Product from the Elimination of Racial Discrimination
(Amounts in Billions of Dollars)

Year	Actual GNP	Gains in GNP from Full Use of Present Educational Attainment of Nonwhites		Gains in GNP from Raising the Educational Level of Nonwhites		Gains in GNP from Raising and Fully Using the Educational Level of Nonwhites	
		Amount	Percent	Amount	Percent	Amount	Percent
1949	$258.1	6.2	2.4	3.2	1.2	9.4	3.6
1950	284.6	6.8	2.4	3.1	1.1	10.1	3.5
1951	329.0	7.9	2.4	3.5	1.1	11.4	3.5
1952	347.0	8.4	2.4	3.5	1.0	11.9	3.4
1953	365.4	8.9	2.4	2.9	0.8	11.8	3.2
1954	363.1	8.8	2.4	3.4	1.0	12.2	3.4
1955	397.5	7.5	1.9	5.8	1.4	13.3	3.3
1956	419.2	7.9	1.9	6.3	1.5	14.2	3.4
1957	442.8	8.3	1.9	6.7	1.5	15.0	3.4
1958	444.5	8.4	1.9	6.3	1.4	14.7	3.3
1959	482.7	9.2	1.9	7.9	1.6	17.1	3.5
1960	502.6	9.5	1.9	6.2	1.4	16.7	3.3
1961	518.2	9.9	1.9	7.7	1.5	17.6	3.4
1962	554.9	10.6	1.9	9.1	1.7	19.7	3.6
1963	583.9	11.1	1.9	9.0	1.6	20.1	3.5

SOURCE: See Technical Note 2, p. 335.

We can express in other ways the magnitude of the loss in GNP attributable to the failure to use efficiently the present educational achievements of the nonwhite labor force. For example, nonwhites account for about 10 percent of the country's total civilian population aged fourteen and over and for approximately 11 percent of the labor force. Consequently, the country is wasting about one-fifth of the potential productivity and contribution of nonwhites to the national economy. Put still another way, the $11.1 billion lost to the nation in 1963 because of racial discrimination—ironically—is almost identical to the amount which the Council of Economic Advisers estimated would be required for the conquest of poverty in the United States.[10] Using an annual income of $3,000 or less as a poverty benchmark, it would require about $11 billion to lift all poor families to a minimum standard of well-being.

If Negroes and other nonwhites could also achieve the same educational levels obtained by the white population—and if discrimination did not hamper their full participation in the economy—GNP might be expanded by about 3.5 percent. In 1963, this was equivalent to $20.1 billion. This figure includes the previous gain of $11.1 billion which might accrue from the eradication of discrimination. Thus, equal education for nonwhites in a nondiscriminatory economy could be valued roughly at $9 billion in terms of 1963 GNP. Moreover, the proportion of the total loss in GNP accounted for by the differences in the level of education of whites and nonwhites has risen sharply. It was around one-third in the years 1949–52, and it dropped to about one-fourth in 1953–54. However, since 1956, it has remained well above two-fifths.

Finally, one could aggregate the loss in GNP accruing from racial discrimination over the years. During the period 1946–1963, the failure to use fully present skills of nonwhites cost the nation approximately $129.4 billion; the persistence of educational differences (which itself reflects the legacy of discrimination) added a further loss of $85.8 billion. These two sources combined were responsible for aggregate losses in GNP of $215.2 billion, or 3.4 percent of the total output of goods and services during these years. Everyone can visualize easily the improvements in the general welfare which could have resulted from such a windfall gain in the nation's output of goods and services.

---

[10] *Economic Report of the President*, January, 1964, p. 77.

CONSUMER EXPENDITURES AND THE NEGRO MARKET

Historical Divergence in Negro-White Consumption Patterns

In the past, the pattern of expenditures among Negroes has diverged sharply from that of the general population. This divergence has resulted from a number of circumstances, but low incomes and the restrictions of racial discrimination have been principally responsible. Because of low incomes, the typical Negro family has had to spend a somewhat larger proportion of its paycheck for basic necessities, such as food, clothing and housing, than have white families. Because of limited access to public accommodations, Negroes have tended to entertain more at home than white families in the same income group. Moreover, Negroes seem to be particularly brand conscious; and (when they can afford them) they appear to lean toward higher priced items in any specific line. Finally, expenditures in personal care (including the costs of cosmetics and patronage at beauty and barber shops) normally run much higher for Negroes than for whites in the same income category.

In some cases it is possible to obtain a reasonably good quantitative estimate of the effects of racial discrimination on Negro consumption expenditures. The effects are particularly noticeable in the pattern of spending for the services of the amusement, restaurant, hotel and motel industries. Here the availability or nonavailability of desegregated facilities seems to outweigh any special kinds of taste or conspicuous consumption in shaping the behavior of Negro consumers. The differential effects of the segregated market are clearly discernible in Table XI, showing average Negro and white family expenditures for "admissions," which is a good proxy for patronage of theaters and recreational facilities; "food eaten away from home," which covers restaurants, diners and other eating places; and "automobile operations," that is, the cost of driving and maintaining a car—a key to travel, including the use of hotels and motels. From these data it is clear that Negroes in large Northern cities spend considerably more than Southern Negroes of the same income bracket for each of the services listed in Table XI; on the other hand Northern city white families spend less than Southern city families. Within the same income class, Negroes in the North spend more than whites in the North for "admissions." But Southern Negroes spend less than either Southern whites or Northern

TABLE XI–Average Family Expenditures for Admissions, Food Eaten Away from Home, and Automobile Operations, for 3 Income Classes, Large Northern and Southern Cities, by Race, 1950.

Income Class and Region	Admissions			Food Eaten Away From Home			Automobile Operation		
	Negro	White	Negroes Percent of Whites	Negro	White	Negroes Percent of Whites	Negro	White	Negroes Percent of Whites
$2,000 to $3,000:									
Large Northern Cities	$31	$29	107	$148	$184	80	$52	$86	60
Large Southern Cities	$23	$36	64	$113	$194	58	$52	$95	55
Northern Expenditures as Percent of Southern	135	81	—	131	95	—	100	91	—
$3,000 to $4,000:									
Large Northern Cities	$45	$37	122	$138	$170	81	$67	$158	42
Large Southern Cities	$37	$39	95	$117	$180	65	$86	$170	51
Northern Expenditures as Percent of Southern	122	95	—	118	94	—	78	93	—
$4,000 to $5,000:									
Large Northern Cities	$57	$48	119	$182	$234	78	$148	$220	67
Large Southern Cities	$39	$45	87	$166	$257	65	$136	$225	60
Northern Expenditures as Percent of Southern	146	107	—	110	91	—	109	98	—

SOURCE: "Study of Consumer Expenditure Income and Saving," tabulated by Bureau of Labor Statistics, U.S. Department of Labor, for Wharton School of Finance and Commerce, University of Pennsylvania, Philadelphia, Pa., 1956–57.

Negroes. In both the North and South, Negroes spend less on "food eaten away from home" than white people in the same income categories. However, the differential is much greater in the South. The table also indicates that both Northern and Southern Negroes spend much less than whites of the same income class on "automobile operations"—40 to 60 percent less.

These summary statistics certainly suggest that Negroes are less likely than whites to be patrons of cultural events, customers of restaurants or tourists along the open road. Since Negroes spend close to the same amount, on the average, for the purchase of automobiles as did whites of the same income level (and proportionately more for food) it seems evident that their limited access to adequate facilities historically has distorted their overall pattern of consumption.

Recent Trends in Negro Consumption Behavior

In recent years, however, Negro consumers have displayed a marked tendency to behave like other consumers with similar incomes and education. In Tables XII and XIII, one can observe the broad trends in Negro-white expenditure patterns in the last decade and a half. For example, between 1950 and 1960–61, the average urban Negro family increased its spending for current consumption by 42 percent. In the process, the distinguishing characteristics of the Negro market were blurred substantially. While the overall pattern of expenditures by Negro families continues to be typical of that generally found among low income groups, there is also evidence of rapidly emerging middle class spending habits.

In 1960–61, the average urban Negro family spent about $3,707 for annual living expenses (see Table XII). This amount was just over two-thirds that spent by the average family in the Nation as a whole—a ratio which was virtually unchanged from 1950. Also in 1960–61, the average Negro family paid $293 in income and other personal taxes; channeled about $203 into life insurance and retirement funds and made gifts and contributions of approximately $150. Finally, such families typically increased both their assets and liabilities. But on balance, they registered net savings of $23 compared with an increase of $116 in net indebtedness in 1950.

The income of average urban Negro families, both before and after taxes, registered a sizable gain. Before taxes, their income in 1960–61 was $4,133, a rise of about 53 percent. However, increases in taxes held their after-tax income to $3,840, representing an advance of 47 percent. For all urban families in 1960–61, average before tax income was $6,691, and after taxes the figure was $5,906. However, after adjusting for the increase in

TABLE XII—Summary of Family Expenditures, Income, and Savings, by Race, All Urban Families and Single Consumers, United States, 1950 and 1960—61

	1950		1960–61	
	Total	Negro	Total	Negro
Family Characteristics:				
Number of families ('000)	31,539	2,965	40,132	4,398
Percent of families	100.0	9.4	100.0	11.0
Average				
Family size	3.0	3.1	3.1	3.2
Money income before taxes	$4,237	$2,709	$6,691	$4,133
Net change in assets and liabilities	—74	—116	$ 177	$ 23
Number of full-time earners	0.9	0.8	0.8	0.7
Age of head	47	45	47	46
Education of head	10	9	11	8
Number of children under 18 years			1.2	1.4
Percent				
Homeowners, all year	48	32	53	31
Auto owners, end of year			73	43
Reporting savings increase			52	43
" " decrease			41	43
" " no change			7	14
With children under 18 years			50	50
With persons 65 years and over			23	19
Average income, expenditures and savings:				
Total receipts	$5,237	$3,125	$7,747	$4,512
Money income after taxes	3,910	2,605	5,906	3,840
Other money receipts	49	15	82	33
Decrease in assets	753	153	897	128
Increase in liabilities	525	352	862	511
Account balancing difference	—117	—64	—207	—210
Total disbursements	$5,354	$3,189	$7,954	$4,722
Increase in assets	955	291	1,423	346
Decrease in liabilities	249	98	514	316
Personal insurance	177	106	324	203
Gifts and contributions	165	81	303	150
Expenditures for current consumption	$3,808	$2,614	$5,390	$3,707

SOURCE: Data for 1950 are from *Study of Consumer Expenditures, Incomes and Savings,* Statistical Tables, Urban—1950 (University of Pennsylvania, 1956–57.) Data for 1960–61 are from *Consumer Expenditures and Income, Urban United States, 1960–61* (U.S. Department of Labor, Bureau of Labor Statistics), Supplement 1 to BLS Report No. 237–38, Washington, D.C. April, 1964.)

consumer prices during the 1950's, the gain in aftertax income for urban families as a whole was 22 percent and in expenditures 14 percent.

Negro families, along with other families in the Nation, increased their total outlay for consumption between 1950 and 1960–61. But there were notable shifts in the proportion of their expenditures devoted to different purposes. (See Table XIII.) The share spent for food dropped from 32 percent to 25 percent—with the biggest decline occurring in spending on food consumed at home. By 1960–61, there was little difference on the average between the share of expenditures devoted to home consumption of food by Negro families and those in the society at large. Another sizable shift occurred in the pattern of spending on housing. Total housing outlays absorbed about 31 percent of the current consumption expenditures for Negro families in 1960–61, compared with 28 percent in 1950. The sharp advance in the proportion spent by the home-owning group was parallel to that of all families. But among Negro families, spending on rented dwellings also expanded relatively, while the trend was slightly downward for all renters combined. Part of this changing pattern of housing expenditures undoubtedly reflects inflation in rents and construction costs during the last decade, but even after adjusting for price increases the overall tendency to spend relatively more on housing would probably remain.

There is other evidence of up-grading in the consumption behavior of Negro families. Their purchase and operation of automobiles rose from 7.0 percent to 9.5 percent of their total expenditures for current consumption. Although this proportion is still substantially below that for white families (13.3 percent), the relative gain for Negro families was considerably larger than for white families in urban areas. Spending by Negro families on personal care remains comparatively higher than for families in general, but for the former such outlays are growing less rapidly than for the latter. In contrast, the spread between the percentage of expenditures for medical care made by Negro and white families narrowed somewhat, because Negro families increased the proportion devoted to medical care at a greater rate.

Alcoholic beverages and tobacco have traditionally accounted for a larger share of expenditures by Negro families than of expenditures by white families. Between 1950 and 1960–61, this pattern of spending was modified. Negro families' relative outlays on alcoholic beverages eased off, but those for tobacco edged up slightly. For white families, both categories registered modest losses on a relative basis.

Expenditures by both white and Negro families for recreation lost a bit of ground relatively, but the loss for white families was moderately large.

TABLE XIII–Distribution of Expenditures for Current Consumption, Negro and White Families, Urban United States, 1950 and 1960–61

	Negro Families				White Families			
	Amount		Percentage Distribution		Amount		Percentage Distribution	
	1950	1960–61	1950	1960–61	1950	1960–61	1950	1960–61
Expenditures for Current Consumption:								
Total	$2,614	$3,707	100.0	100.0	$3,938	$5,610	100.0	100.0
Food, total	834	929	31.9	25.1	1,162	1,357	29.5	24.2
Food prepared at home	720	760	27.5	20.5	936	1,070	23.7	19.1
Food away from home	114	169	4.4	4.6	227	287	5.8	5.1
Clothing, materials, services	356	464	13.6	12.5	446	571	11.3	10.2
Housing: total	723	1,163	27.7	31.4	1,069	1,647	27.1	29.3
Shelter	296	554	11.3	14.9	453	775	11.5	13.8
Rented dwelling	213	389	8.1	10.5	230	316	5.8	5.6
Owned dwelling	77	159	2.9	4.3	198	416	5.0	7.4
Other shelter	6	6	0.2	0.2	26	43	0.7	0.8
Fuel, light, refrigeration, water	132	178	5.0	4.8	161	253	4.1	4.5
Household operations	107	228	4.1	6.1	186	332	4.7	5.9
Household furnishings and equipment	188	203	7.2	5.5	269	287	6.8	5.1
Transportation	253	435	9.7	11.7	538	839	13.7	15.0
Automobile purchase and operation	184	352	7.0	9.5	470	745	11.9	13.3
Other travel and transportation	69	83	2.6	2.2	67	94	1.7	1.7
Medical and personal care	175	319	6.7	8.6	294	537	7.5	9.5
Medical care	96	178	3.7	4.8	208	378	5.3	6.7
Personal care	79	141	3.0	3.8	86	157	2.2	2.8
Alcoholic beverages and tobacco	117	155	4.4	4.2	135	189	3.5	3.3
Alcoholic beverages	61	75	2.3	2.0	66	92	1.7	1.6
Tobacco	56	80	2.1	2.2	69	97	1.8	1.7
Recreation	95	130	3.6	3.5	176	228	4.5	4.1
Reading and Education	29	55	1.1	1.4	61	117	1.5	2.1
Reading	21	31	0.8	0.8	36	52	0.9	0.9
Education	8	24	0.3	0.6	25	65	0.6	1.2
Other Expenditures	30	57	1.1	1.5	58	127	1.5	2.3

SOURCE: Data for 1950 are from *Study of Consumer Expenditures, Incomes and Savings*, Statistical Tables, Urban–1950 (University of Pennsylvania, 1956–57.) Data for 1960–61 are from *Consumer Expenditures and Income, Urban United States, 1960–61* (U.S. Department of Labor, Bureau of Labor Statistics, Supplement 1 to BLS Report No. 237–38 Washington, D.C. April, 1964.

Recreation includes purchases of TV sets, as well as the cost of admission to theaters, sports events, concerts, etc. The share of spending represented by admissions to motion pictures undoubtedly declined over the decade, while the share of TV sets rose sharply. Spending for reading matter accounted for about the same percentage of expenditures for current consumption in both Negro and white families, and its relative position in both sets of family budgets remained unchanged between 1950 and 1960–61. However, both Negro and white families just about doubled the percentage of expenditures devoted to education.

TABLE XIV—Percentage Change in Selected Consumption Expenditures in Response to Percentage Change in After-Tax Income for Negro and White Families, 1950 and 1960–61

Expenditure Item		Negro Families	White Families
1.	Education	4.22	3.06
2.	Household Operation	2.39	1.50
3.	Housing: Owned Dwelling	2.25	2.11
4.	Automobile	1.93	1.12
5.	Medical care	1.80	1.56
6.	Housing: Rented Dwelling	1.74	0.72
7.	Personal care	1.66	1.58
8.	Food away from home	1.02	0.51
9.	Reading	1.00	0.85
10.	Tobacco	0.91	0.78
11.	Recreation	0.78	0.56
12.	Fuel, light, etc.	0.73	1.09
13.	Clothing	0.64	0.54
14.	Alcoholic beverages	0.49	0.75
15.	Transportation (exc. auto)	0.43	0.77
16.	House furnishings	0.17	0.13
17.	Food (at home)	0.12	0.27
18.	Total Consumption	0.80	0.81

SOURCE: Computed from TABLES XII and XIII.

In general, this shifting pattern of outlays by Negro families represents a gradual conversion toward the consuming behavior of white families. The implications of these changing preferences may be quite serious from the point of view of the future composition of the Negro market. Table XIV highlights the main tendencies which will basically shape the Negro market in the years ahead. This table shows the percentage increase between 1950 and 1960–61 in consumer expenditures for selective categories of goods and services in response to the percentage increase in family incomes after taxes. (In economists' language, this is a rough measure of the income elasticity of consumption. A ratio greater than 1.00 indicates a stronger than average preference for a particular item.) The expenditure categories have been ranked according to the strength of the response of consumption for Negro families to the rise in their income. The corresponding measure for white families is also shown. It will be noted that for both Negro and white families, the percentage increase in total consumption was about four-fifths that of the percentage increase in income. Spending for education by Negro families had the strongest response—a gain of 4.22 percent for each 1.00 percent increase in income. Spending for food consumed at home by Negro families had the lowest response at 0.12 percent.

In general, the figures in Table XIV suggest that, in the future, Negro families will register the strongest demand in those areas associated with overall upgrading in their standard of living. There should be a strong market for housing and household operation, automobiles and medical and personal care. Those areas which have traditionally received a good share of the Negro's patronage—tobacco, clothing, alcoholic beverages and food —will probably be characterized by relatively slow growth.

Potential Expansion of the Negro Market

Another perspective on the Negro market can be provided by linking the potential gains in income from eliminating racial discrimination shown in Table X with the pattern of consumer expenditures shown in Table XII.

On the basis of calculations discussed above, it was estimated that the nation lost about $11 billion in gross national product in 1963 because racial discrimination prevented the efficient use of the present educational attainment of nonwhites. If we included the gains which would result from raising the educational levels of nonwhites to that of the rest of the population, GNP could have been further increased by $9 billion. Thus, an additional $20 billion could have been added to a GNP of $584 billion in 1963, raising the total by almost 3.5 percent. These global gains in the output of the nation's goods and services can be translated into rather striking implications for the Negro market. For example, if racial discrimination were removed, by how much would the income of the nonwhite population increase? What would be the effect of the increase in income on the level of consumer spending? What would this increased spending mean in terms of the market for food, clothing, housing and automobiles? What would be the effect on the level of savings? The answers are roughly as follows:

Personal income of nonwhites after taxes, which amounted to about $21.9

billion in 1963, would increase by $14.7 billion to a new level of approximately $36.6 billion. This is a gain of two-thirds.

The level of consumer expenditures by nonwhites would increase by roughly $11.8 billion, rising from $21.1 billion to $32.9 billion. This is an advance of 56 percent.

Outlays on food would rise by $3.0 billion, from $5.3 billion to $8.3 billion. This is an increase of 57 percent.

Clothing expenditures would rise by $1.5 billion, raising the level from $2.6 billion to $4.1 billion. This also represents an increase of about 57 percent.

Money spent on household operations, which amounted to $6.6 billion in 1963, would increase by $3.7 billion to a new level of $10.3 billion. This represents a gain of 56 percent.

In 1963, nonwhites spent about $2 billion in the operation of automobiles. Another $1.1 billion would be added, raising the total to $3.1 billion. This represents a gain of 55 percent.

The level of current savings by nonwhites was roughly $800 million in 1963. This would make a spectacular jump of $2.9 billion to a new level of $3.7 billion. Thus, savings would advance by a remarkable 364 percent.

We could go on describing the beneficial economic effects of the elimination of racial discrimination. However, enough has been said to demonstrate that the economy as a whole—and not Negroes alone—would reap immense advantages if the legacy of racial discrimination could be erased from the face of the land.

Economic Consequences of the Changing Negro Market

The shifting pattern of consumer expenditures described above has had a significant impact on the fortunes of those professionally involved in developing the Negro market. Expressed succinctly, it appears that non-whites depending directly on the Negro market made only spotty progress during the last decade. In contrast, those who have found new opportunities in the marketing channels for the economy as a whole made substantial progress. This impression is sustained by the evidence relating to the structure of employment and income in marketing.

Table XV shows the number and distribution of sales workers by major fields of activity in 1950 and 1960. It will be observed that a substantial number of opportunities were opened in marketing during the 1950's. However, such jobs for nonwhite workers grew at a much faster rate than for all employees as a group. The bulk of the new sales opportunities as far as nonwhites are concerned was concentrated in the semiskilled category consisting of counter salesmen and clerks. These were employed

TABLE XV—Number of Sales Workers, All Professional and Employed Workers, Experienced Civilian Labor Force by Color, 1950–1960

| | 1950 | | 1960 | | Percentage Distribution | | | | Rate of Growth, 1950–1960 | | | |
| | | | | | 1950 | | 1960 | | Percentage Change | | Annl. Average Rate of Growth | |
	Total	Nonwhite	Total	Nonwhite	Total	Non-white	Total	Non-white	Total	Non-white	Total	Non-white
Sales Workers	4,014,210	77,400	4,807,637	116,907	100.0	100.0	100.0	100.0	+ 19.8	+ 51.0	+ 1.8	+4.2
Advertising Agents & Salesmen	35,370	480	33,785	208	0.9	0.6	0.7	0.2	− 4.5	− 56.7	− 0.5	−8.0
Auctioneers	5,430	120	4,267	—	0.1	0.2	0.1	—	− 21.4		− 2.4	
Demonstrators	14,130	480	25,909	262	0.4	0.6	0.5	0.2	+ 83.3	− 45.4	+ 6.2	−5.9
Hucksters and Peddlers	23,370	3,580	54,290	3,116	0.6	4.6	1.1	2.7	+132.3	− 13.0	+ 8.8	−1.3
Insurance Agents, Brokers and Underwriters	305,130	7,860	370,982	8,933	7.6	10.2	7.7	7.6	+ 21.6	+ 13.7	+ 2.0	+1.3
Newsboys	180,270	4,020	200,032	9,568	2.7	5.2	4.2	8.2	+ 11.0	+138.0	+ 1.1	+9.1
Real Estate Agents & Brokers	141,030	3,480	200,070	4,365	3.5	4.5	4.2	3.7	+ 41.9	+ 25.4	+ 3.6	+2.3
Stock and Bond Salesmen	11,100	240	30,796	388	0.3	0.3	0.6	0.3	+177.4	+ 61.7	+10.7	+4.9
Salesmen and Clerks (nec)	3,370,380	58,140	3,887,506	90,067	84.0	75.1	80.9	77.0	+ 15.3	+ 54.9	+ 1.4	+4.5
Manufacturing	321,090	1,860	474,865	4,134	8.0	2.4	9.9	3.5	+ 47.9	+122.3	+ 4.0	+8.3
Wholesale Trade	406,050	2,370	506,377	5,574	10.1	3.1	10.5	4.8	+ 24.7	+135.2	+ 1.5	+8.9
Food & Related Prods.			86,861	937			1.8	0.8				
Other Wholesale Trade			419,516	4,637			8.7	4.0				
Retail Trade	2,510,730	51,060	2,719,796	76,540	62.5	66.0	56.6	65.5	+ 8.3	+ 49.9	+ 0.8	+4.1
Food & Dairy Product Stores			519,859	26,667			10.8	22.8				
Genl. Mdse Retailing			595,195	12,789			12.4	10.9				
Ltd. Price Variety Stores			185,210	4,292			3.9	3.7				
Apparel & Accessories Stores			340,830	7,647			7.1	6.5				
Motor Vehicles & Access. Retailing			228,250	3,213			4.7	2.7				
Other Retail Trade			850,452	21,932			17.7	18.8				
Other Industries (incl. not reporting)	132,510	2,850	186,468	3,819	3.3	3.7	3.9	3.3	+ 40.7	+ 34.0	+ 3.5	+3.0
Total Employed Persons	58,550,700	6,083,340	68,006,553	7,216,836					+ 16.1	+ 18.6	+ 1.5	+1.7
All Professional Workers	4,937,790	191,970	7,324,906	360,070					+ 48.3	+ 87.6	+ 4.0	+6.5

SOURCE: U.S. Census of Population, 1950, Special Reports, "Occupational Characteristics," 1956, p. IB–29–36. U.S. Census of Population, 1960, "Occupational Characteristics," pp. 21–30.

TABLE XVI—Median Income of Sales Workers, All Professional Workers, and All Employed Persons, by Color, 1949 and 1959 (Amounts in Dollars)

	1949				1959				Percentage Change, 1949–1959			
	Total		Nonwhite		Total		Nonwhite		Total		Nonwhite	
	Male	Female	Male	Female	Male	Female	Male	Female	Male	Female	Male	Female
Sales Workers	3,026	1,243	1,659	1,923	5,119	1,619	2,845	1,582	69.2	30.2	71.5	70.8
Advertising Agents and Salesmen	3,750	2,060	—	—	6,417	3,572	—	—	71.1	73.4	—	—
Auctioneers	3,266	—	—	—	5,398	—	—	—	65.3	—	—	—
Demonstrators	—	845	—	—	4,333	853	—	—	—	0.9	—	—
Hucksters and Peddlers	1,404	—	—	—	2,826	758	1,815	769	101.3	—	—	—
Insurance Agents, Brokers and Underwriters	3,711	2,168	2,300	—	6,331	3,367	3,947	2,021	70.6	55.3	71.6	—
Newsboys	320	478	—	—	567	709	556	—	77.2	48.3	—	—
Real Estate Agents and Brokers	3,712	2,000	—	—	6,508	3,188	5,037	2,555	75.3	59.4	—	—
Stock and Bond Salesmen	4,386	—	—	—	7,730	4,096	—	—	76.2	—	—	—
Salesmen and Clerks (nec)	2,974	1,227	1,692	920	5,101	1,597	3,052	1,577	71.5	30.2	80.4	71.4
Manufacturing	3,868	1,485	—	—	6,835	1,768	4,008	1,953	76.7	19.1	—	—
Wholesale Trade	3,635	1,722	—	—	6,146	2,451	4,431	—	69.1	42.3	—	—
Food & related prods.	—	—	—	—	5,545	1,773	—	—	—	—	—	—
Other Wholesale Trade	—	—	—	—	6,329	2,553	4,370	—	—	—	—	—
Retail Trade	2,543	1,221	1,629	921	4,027	1,585	2,874	1,575	58.4	29.8	76.4	71.0
Food & Dairy Products Stores	—	—	—	—	2,955	1,459	2,599	1,294	—	—	—	—
General Merchandise Retailing	—	—	—	—	3,977	1,710	2,862	1,895	—	—	—	—
Limited Price Variety Stores	—	—	—	—	2,114	1,106	—	1,263	—	—	—	—
Apparel and Accessories	—	—	—	—	3,829	1,740	2,969	1,924	—	—	—	—
Motor Vehicles and Accessories Retailing	—	—	—	—	4,947	2,193	3,730	—	—	—	—	—
Other Retail Trade	—	—	—	—	4,256	1,661	2,950	1,453	—	—	—	—
Other Industries (including not reporting)	3,152	1,157	—	—	5,590	1,503	2,897	1,083	77.3	29.9	—	—
Total Employment	2,668	1,575	1,483	786	4,720	2,333	2,750	1,320	76.9	48.1	85.4	67.9
Professional	3,949	2,265	2,269	1,923	6,778	3,711	4,640	3,587	71.6	63.0	104.5	86.5

SOURCE: U.S. Census of Population: 1950, Special Reports, "Occupational Characteristics" 1956, IB–183–198 and IB–215–230. U.S. Census of Population: 1960, "Occupational Characteristics," pp. 296–335.

primarily by department stores and other retail outlets serving the general market. In contrast, among nonwhite professional salesmen who work almost exclusively in the Negro market, the growth rate lagged considerably behind that for professional sales workers in the rest of the economy.

For example, the number of nonwhite sales workers grew by 50 percent, while the number of total sales workers expanded by one-fifth. In the professional category, the total number of stock and bond salesmen rose by 177 percent, but the number of nonwhites in this occupation increased by 62 percent. The corresponding figures for insurance agents, brokers and underwriters were: total up 22 percent, nonwhite up 14 percent; real estate agents and brokers: total up 42 percent, nonwhite up 25 percent. While the number of advertising agents and salesmen declined for both groups, the percentage decrease was greater for nonwhites than for whites: down 57 and 5 percent, respectively.

The growth profile for the clerical group was exactly opposite to that for the professional category. The total number of salesmen and clerks grew by 15 percent, compared with 55 percent for nonwhites. Clerks employed in manufacturing industry expanded by 48 percent, as against 122 percent for nonwhites. In wholesale trade, the corresponding figures were 25 percent for the total and 135 percent for nonwhite. Total clerical employment in retail stores grew by 8 percent, while the number of nonwhites employed in such stores rose by one-half.

This slower improvement in the position of nonwhite professionals in the marketing field is also documented in the income figures. Table XVI shows the median income of sales workers, of professional workers and of employed persons by color in 1949 and 1959. The first thing to note is that over the decade a substantial improvement occurred in all types of incomes. However, the largest increase was registered by nonwhite male professional workers taken as a group; for them, the increase was 105 percent compared with 72 percent for all male professional jobholders. But in the marketing group, the percentage gains for nonwhite men holding professional positions was about the same as the total. This is typified by the 72 percent increase for those in the insurance area. In contrast, the increase in median income of nonwhite male clerical workers exceeded that for the total—80 percent versus 72 percent. Among female clerical workers (virtually none of whom were in the professional class in 1949), the percentage increase was 71 percent compared with only 30 percent for all female sales workers.

Moreover, the greatest relative gains were made by nonwhite female workers. In 1949, their median income was about 75 percent of that of all female sales workers. By 1959, the ratio had climbed to 98 percent. On the other hand, nonwhite female insurance agents in 1959 had a median income only 60 percent of that of all females employed as insurance agents. The relative income position of nonwhite males in the marketing field registered only a modest improvement over the decade. For all sales workers, the median income rose from 55 percent to 56 percent of the median income for all males. Among male clerical workers, the ratio rose from 57 percent to 60 percent. On the other hand, for nonwhite male insurance agents, the figure was virtually unchanged—62 percent in 1949 and 63 percent in 1959.

Taken together, the above statistics on employment and income trends in the marketing field appear to lead to an inescapable conclusion: nonwhite professional salesmen, concentrating on the development of the Negro market, have made new gains, but they have been relatively modest.

Within this framework, it may be interesting to examine the employment and income position of public relations men and publicity writers. The experience of this group is probably typical of the professional workers engaged in marketing. Table XVII shows the number of public relations men and publicity writers by color and industry of employment in 1960. It will be noted that the nonwhite workers in this category were concentrated in only a few industries. Manufacturing accounted for 28 percent —divided equally between food and miscellaneous durable goods. Communications (especially radio and TV), wholesale trade, business services, personal services and educational services—each accounted for about 14 percent. Aside from communications and educational services, neither of these industries is currently experiencing a particularly rapid rate of growth. In contrast, public relations men and publicity writers in the economy as a whole were widely distributed among industries. There was a good scattering in the rapidly growing areas of finance, communications, real estate and the newer types of manufacturing industries.

The distribution of public relations men and advertising agents and salesmen by income class in 1959 is shown in Table XVIII. The first point to observe is that public relations men seem to do much better than advertising agents and salesmen. This is true for nonwhites, as well as for the total. The median income of all PR men in 1959 was about $8,000. For nonwhites, the figure was between $6,000 and $7,000. The corresponding figures for advertising agents were $6,400 for the total and between $3,000 and $4,000 for nonwhites. Moreover, the gap between the median income of nonwhites and all PR men taken as a group seems to be much smaller than that for advertising agents. In 1959, the median income for nonwhite PR men was equal to about 80 percent of the median income for all PR men combined. Among advertising agents, the corresponding figure was approximately 54 percent.

TABLE XVII—Number of Public Relations Men and Publicity Writers, by Color and Industry of Employment, 1960

Industry	Nonwhite		Total Employment	
	Number	Percent of total	Number	Percent of total
All Industry	**142**	**100.0**	**21,434**	**100.0**
Agriculture, forestry and fisheries	none	—	20	0.1
Mining	none	—	183	0.9
Construction	none	—	241	1.1
Manufacturing: total	40	28.2	5,097	23.8
Food and kindred products	20	14.1	785	3.7
Misc. durable goods	20	14.1	402	1.9
All other manufacturing	none	—	3,910	18.2
Railroads and RR express	none	—	299	1.4
Other transportation	none	—	703	3.3
Communications	21	14.7	1,304	6.1
Utilities	none	—	688	3.2
Wholesale trade	20	14.1	851	4.0
Retail trade	none	—	567	2.6
Finance, insurance and real estate	none	—	2,477	11.6
Business services	21	14.7	2,078	9.7
Personal services	20	14.1	141	0.7
Other services	none	—	204	1.0
Education services, government	20	14.1	551	2.6
All other industries	none	—	5,980	27.9

Source: *U. S. Census of Population: 1960,* "Occupational Characteristics," Table 37, pp. 519–530. Bureau of the Census, U. S. Department of Commerce.

TABLE XVIII—Median Income of Public Relations Men and Advertising Agents, by Color, 1960

Income Class	Public Relations Men and Publicity Writers		Advertising Agents and Salesmen	
	Total	Nonwhite	Total	Nonwhite
Total Persons with Income	23,855	203	28,487	166
$1–999	285	20	775	41
1,000–1,999	710	—	1,304	22
2,000–2,999	627	—	1,237	—
3,000–3,999	733	63	2,136	20
4,000–4,999	1,456	—	3,268	21
5,000–5,999	2,395	—	4,061	20
6,000–6,999	2,699	20	3,509	—
7,000–7,999	2,793	60	2,737	21
8,000–9,999	3,679	—	3,504	—
10,000–14,999	5,352	40	3,548	21
15,000 and Over	3,126	—	2,408	—
Median	**$8,125**	**$6,000–6,999**	**$6,417**	**$3,000–3,999**

SOURCE: *U.S. Census of Population: 1960,* "Occupational Characteristics," U.S. Department of Commerce, Bureau of the Census, pp. 296–335.

A Profile of the Professional Negro Market Developer

Against this background, it may be interesting to look more closely at those professionals engaged principally in the Negro market. A substantial number of these hold membership in the National Association of Market Developers. Thus, a profile of NAMD members provides considerable insight into their perception of the Negro market. In Table XIX, a rough estimate is made of the distribution of NAMD membership by industry and type of employment, ownership of firm and the market focus of members. (However, no lists were available for NAMD chapters in Atlanta, Baltimore and New York.)

Several features of the table are striking. Of the 400-odd members represented, over four-fifths were salaried employees and the remainder were self-employed. More than one-third of the total (and over two-fifths of the salaried members) were concentrated in the distribution of food and kindred products. Here, the heaviest concentration was in alcoholic beverages, and soft drinks also accounted for a sizable proportion. There was only modest representation in the rapidly growing field of automobiles, other forms of travel and petroleum products.

Approximately 10 percent were associated with communications media, with newspapers having the largest representation. About 4 percent of the total list was employed in public relations firms. The self-employed members were almost exclusively concentrated in public relations and newspaper work.

It comes as no surprise to observe that the vast majority of the NAMD membership is employed by large corporations serving the economy as a whole. Where a member was employed in a Negro-owned firm, there is a good chance that the business was a bank, newspaper, magazine or public relations firm. Yet according to our estimate, about 80 percent of the NAMD membership was active almost exclusively in the development of the Negro market, as opposed to the general market. Virtually all of those employed in the food industry were concentrating on the Negro market. In fact, only those active in marketing automobiles, petroleum products, and banking and financial services, appear to be primarily active in the market catering to consumers as a whole. About one-third of the members active in the newspaper field were associated with newspapers with a readership substantially wider than the Negro community.

Of course, one must be extremely cautious in attempting to draw any overall conclusions about the activities of all Negro professional marketeers on the basis of data presented in Table XIX. As mentioned earlier, the NAMD membership list is incomplete, and the classifications were made

TABLE XIX—Estimated Distribution of NAMD Membership, by Industry and Type of Employment, Ownership of Firm and Market Focus of Member

Industry and Type of Employment	Total List		Market Focus of Member		Ownership of Firm	
	Number	Percent of Total	Negro Market	General Market	Negro	Other
Salaried	**343**	**84.3**	**278**	**65**	**67**	**276**
Food and kindred products	148	36.4	147	1		148
Beer and whiskey	120	29.5	119	1		120
Soft drinks	28	6.9	28			28
Tobacco	12	2.9	12			12
Automobiles	10	2.5		10		10
Petroleum Products	9	2.2		9		9
Travel	3	0.7	2	1	1	2
Banks and Savings and Loan Assns.	11	2.7	3	8	10	1
Government and Nonprofit	11	2.7		1		11
Other industry	76	18.7	61	15	16	60
Media	46	11.3	38	8	26	20
Newspapers	22	5.4	15	7	17	5
Magazines	8	2.0	8		8	
Radio-TV	16	3.9	15	1	1	15
Agency	17	4.2	15	2	14	3
Advertising	2	0.5		2		2
Public Relations	15	3.7	15		14	1
Self-Employed	**64**	**15.7**	**52**	**12**		
Public Relations	27	6.6	27			
Newspapers	30	7.4	18	12		
Other	7	1.7	7			
Totals	**407**	**100.0**	**330**	**77**		

SOURCE: National Association of Market Developers Membership Roster, 1964. Lists of members were unavailable for Chapters in Atlanta, Baltimore, and New York.

on the basis of the business affiliations identified in the membership roster. Moreover, NAMD itself does not represent all Negro professionals engaged in the Negro market.

But on this broad canvas, a rough profile begins to emerge. Tentatively, we can conclude that Negro professionals seem to be concentrating primarily in those sectors of the market for consumer goods and services which are not spearheading the growth of the economy as a whole. We might also conclude that the most promising marketing careers in the future will be found in rapidly growing fields such as housing, automobiles, travel and other services indicative of an evolving middle class mode of living.

Negroes as Entrepreneurs

Trends in General Business

As mentioned above, segregation has served the Negro businessman in the same way a tariff protects an infant industry. With the removal or reduction of a tariff wall, major adjustments must be made by those who have benefited from its existence. The Negro businessman is faced with such an adjustment. As the process of desegregation permeates the marketplace, Negro-owned businesses (the vast majority of which concentrate on providing personal services in a segregated market) are faced with increased competition from firms catering to buyers with a decreasing reference to race.

The consequences of this process are already evident. Because we have only fragmentary statistics on Negro-owned business, it is difficult to chart these trends with precision. However, since the vast majority of Negro businesses are single proprietorships—rather than partnerships or corporations—Bureau of the Census statistics on self-employed managers, proprietors and officials give a fair indication of the scope of Negro business. These statistics are summarized in Table XX.

Even a cursory analysis of the evidence clearly demonstrates the heavy dependence of Negro businessmen on the segregated Negro market. Where Negro customers have relatively free access to goods and services sold in the general marketplace, Negro businessmen have made little headway against the strong competition of white firms. In 1960, Negroes constituted about 2.5 percent of all self-employed businessmen, but this ratio varied

TABLE XX—Self-Employed Businessmen, by Race and Industry, 1950 and 1960

Industry	1950 Total¹	1950 Negro	1950 Negro as % of Total	1960 Total	1960 Negro	1960 Negro as % of Total	Annual Average Percentage Rate of Growth 1950–1960 Total	Annual Average Percentage Rate of Growth 1950–1960 Negro	Median Income 1949 White Males	Median Income 1949 Non-white Males	Median Income 1959 White Males	Median Income 1959 Non-white Males
Construction	191,820	3,390	1.7	222,601	3,978	1.8	1.7	1.6	$3,873	$1,922	$6,756	$3,239
Manufacturing	231,210	1,050	0.4	168,395	1,376	0.8	-3.1	2.7	4,700	2,250*	7,998	3,503
Transportation	50,940	2,430	4.7	38,223	1,241	3.2	-2.9	-6.5	3,535	2,250*	6,638	2,792
Communications, utilities & sanitary serv.	4,260	270	6.3	4,812	82	1.7	1.2	-11.2	3,310	2,500	7,138	3,500*
Wholesale trade	174,240	2,640	1.5	133,607	2,610	1.9	-2.6	-0.1	4,336	1,250*	7,813	2,693
Retail trade	1,349,190	38,730	2.8	994,425	26,303	2.6	-3.0	-3.8	3,277	1,838	5,332	3,511
Food & dairy prods.	376,350	14,520	3.9	214,758	8,740	4.1	-5.5	-4.9	2,875	1,819	4,464	3,487
Eating & drinking places	270,720	15,030	5.5	203,830	11,344	5.6	-2.9	-2.9	3,114	1,870	4,990	3,170
Genl. mdse. & ltd. price variety	63,690	750	1.2	46,406	640	1.3	-3.1	-1.6	3,211	2,000	5,416	2,500*
Apparel & accessories	82,140	600	0.7	56,722	321	0.6	-3.6	-5.9	4,725	1,250*	7,292	4,500*
Furniture & homefurn.	66,210	360	0.5	49,946	182	0.4	-2.9	-6.1	3,931	2,250*	6,923	5,500*
Motor vehicles & access.	58,590	180	0.3	55,476	163	0.3	-0.5	-0.9	6,367	2,000	7,460	3,500*
Gasoline service stations	143,010	1,290	0.9	152,294	2,153	1.4	0.6	5.3	2,906	2,250*	4,657	4,030
Hardware, bldg. materials	79,020	120	0.2	67,002	80	0.1	-1.6	-3.9	4,427	1,750*	6,552	2,500*
Other retail trade	209,460	5,880	2.8	147,991	2,680	1.8	-3.3	-7.5	3,330	1,717	5,794	3,737
Banking and finance	20,910	90	0.4	22,076	41	0.2	0.6	-7.5	8,277	n.r.	14,527	12,500*
Insurance & real estate	44,910	600	1.3	49,232	794	1.6	1.0	2.8	5,727	2,250*	10,393	5,500*
Business services	33,390	570	1.7	37,020	890	2.4	1.1	4.6	4,250	2,250*	7,626	4,500*
Automotive repair & garages	59,610	870	1.5	38,528	1,083	2.8	-4.2	2.2	3,183	2,000	5,237	3,564
Misc. repair services	29,070	450	1.5	19,317	414	2.1	-4.1	-0.8	2,713	1,750*	4,851	3,500*
Personal services	135,720	5,970	4.4	127,356	4,349	3.4	-0.7	-3.1	3,114	2,174	5,060	3,296
Other industries	97,080	2,760	2.8	95,311	3,239	3.4	-0.2	1.6	3,433	1,250*	5,777	2,508
Total	**2,422,350**	**59,820**	**2.5**	**1,954,903**	**46,400**	**2.4**	**-2.1**	**-2.4**	**3,502**	**1,860**	**5,932**	**3,368**

¹ White and Negro only.
* Estimated at mid-point of income class interval.
n.r. not reported

SOURCE: U.S. Census of Population, 1950, Special Reports, "Occupational Characteristics," 1956, IB Table 13. U.S. Census of Population, 1960, "Occupational Characteristics," 1963, Table 3.

greatly among different industries. Their largest share of a major industry was personal services (3.4 percent); at the bottom of the spectrum was banking and finance, where Negroes represented less than two-tenths of one percent of the total. But behind the array of ratios is an interesting and significant story. If we divide the retail trade sector according to the principal types of stores, we see immediately the importance of segregation in providing opportunities for Negro entrepreneurs. For example, in 1960, Negroes operated 2.6 percent of all retail outlets—but 5.6 percent of the eating and drinking establishments. They also had 4.1 percent of the food stores; this is a reflection of the fact that such stores (especially smaller ones) are typically located in or near segregated residential areas.

In sharp contrast, Negroes owned much less than one percent of the retail establishments selling apparel, furniture, hardware or motor vehicles. In these categories, the meager ownership role played by Negroes can be attributed partly to the fact that few of them can obtain the relatively large amount of capital required for successful operation. Another factor appears to be the sizable volume of sales necessary to sustain such a business. However, the most basic explanation seems to be the freedom Negro customers have to shop for these items in stores catering to the general market. The slightly stronger position of Negroes as operators of gasoline stations is due primarily to the vigorous and competitive efforts of the leading petroleum companies to establish franchise outlets in or near the geographical areas occupied by Negroes in the key population centers. Outside of retail trade, the provision of personal services to Negro customers has been a mainstay of Negro businessmen. The most outstanding examples are owners of barbershops and beauty salons. In fact, this area alone has generated a complex of interrelated activities by Negro businessmen shown under other headings in Table XX. For instance, the majority of the 1,300 Negroes who owned manufacturing firms in 1960 were probably producing cosmetics and barber and beauty shop supplies especially for the Negro trade. Undoubtedly, a fairly large proportion of the 2,600 Negro businessmen engaged in wholesale trade were distributing these items to local shops. Still other businessmen (e.g., insurance and real estate brokers, and those providing a variety of business services) were probably only slightly less dependent on the segregated Negro market. On the other hand, Negroes owning automotive repair facilities, running transportation (such as taxis and local haulage), and doing construction jobs normally would find their customers in the community at large— although Negro customers may provide their ultimate base of support.

But this configuration of Negro-owned businesses is changing drastically as Negro consumers are increasingly attracted to the general market.

Between 1950 and 1960, the total number of Negro businessmen shrank by more than one-fifth. While there was a similar decrease in the total number of self-employed businessmen during the decade, the proportion was smaller. Moreover, much of the decline in the overall number was accounted for by the change to the corporate form of organization. This was much less true for Negroes.

Furthermore, with few exceptions, the incidence of decline was greater for Negroes, compared with the total, in those fields where segregation and discrimination imposed the least constraints on Negro customers. For instance, the annual average percentage changes between 1950 and 1960 in several key areas for Negroes and the total self-employed, respectively, were: communications, utilities and sanitary services, -11.2 vs. $+1.2$; transportation, -6.5 vs. -2.9; furniture and housefurnishings, -6.1 vs. -2.9; apparel and accessories, -5.9 vs. -3.6; hardware and building materials, -3.9 vs. -1.6. It is difficult to account for the causes underlying these specific decreases, but several considerations can be cited. The sharp drop in the number of Negroes in the private sanitary services (and the growth in the total number of businessmen engaged in this activity) probably reflects the increased competition from large firms which move trash for restaurants, department stores and similar establishments on a contract basis. A similar explanation probably applies in the case of transportation. In the past, numerous small Negro businesses were formed around one or two trucks, with the owner and a few helpers providing local moving and job-by-job transportation services. However, with the growing unionization of the trucking industry, even extending into purely local transportation, the rising wage levels have made such opportunities increasingly attractive to white men. The trend toward the use of more sophisticated equipment (such as refrigerator trucks and other speciality vehicles) has also necessitated the accumulation of considerably more capital than most Negro truckers could raise. In addition, the number of Negro taxi owners in the major cities (with the possible exception of Washington, D.C.) has shrunk as gigantic corporations have acquired franchises to operate fleets of several thousand vehicles. The decline in the retail outlets undoubtedly reflects the diffusion of mass marketing throughout the economy; this has made it exceedingly difficult for the small Negro retailer (along with similarly situated white merchants) to compete with the super market, large department stores and discount houses.

Several other types of traditional Negro businesses, although not shown explicitly in Table XX, also experienced absolute decline or a severe slackening in the rate of growth. For example, the number of funeral directors dropped by 6 percent between 1950 and 1960, and the number of barbers decreased by over 16 percent. While the number of Negro-owned hotels and motels has continued to expand, they have lost a sizable proportion of their most desirable clientele—a loss only partly made up by the growth of luxury and semiluxury resort and vacation sites.

On the other hand, Negro businessmen made significant strides in several new or revitalized fields. The number of self-employed in construction climbed by more than 17 percent, about the same rate achieved by this category as a whole. Substantial gains were also registered in the ownership of gasoline service stations, automotive repair shops and garages. In manufacturing, modest expansion occurred. This gain was made despite the capture by large corporations of a fairly sizable share of the cosmetics market among Negro customers, which traditionally accounted for virtually all of the output of Negro manufacturing firms. Many of the more recent ventures in manufacturing include plastics, apparel, food processing and other relatively new areas.

In analyzing these general trends in Negro-owned businesses during the last decade or so, the intention is not to paint a bleak picture of total stagnation and decline. On the contrary, a great number of individual Negro businesses have been launched and have achieved considerable success. Moreover, many established firms have made substantial progress. Indeed, without much difficulty, one can find exceptionally prosperous businessmen whose enterprises stand out against the general trend in any of the areas described here. Nevertheless, when the basic trends are viewed against the panorama of the overall business landscape, one cannot escape concluding that Negro businessmen taken as a group have lost considerable ground and are facing an uncertain future.

Trends in the earnings of Negro businessmen also support this general conclusion. Again the historical paradox of segregation as a protective shield is evident: nonwhite businessmen concentrating in the segregated market tend to earn relatively more, compared with all self-employed entrepreneurs, than their colleagues competing in the open market. For example, in 1949, the median income of nonwhite professional workers taken as a group was $2,269, about 58 percent of the median income of all professionals ($3,949). Among salaried managerial personnel, total and nonwhite median incomes were $4,403 and $2,134, respectively, yielding a ratio of 49 percent. Among self-employed businessmen, the income figures were: total, $3,502 and nonwhite, $1,860, for a ratio of 53 percent. But nonwhites providing personal services to a segregated market (barbers, beauticians, etc.) had a median income of $2,174 in 1949, equal to 70 percent of that earned by all those offering personal services. For operators of retail food stores in predominantly Negro neighborhoods, the ratio was 63 percent, and for nonwhite restaurant owners it was 60 percent. By 1959, virtually all of these proportions had risen. However, the extra advantage derived by Negro businessmen from the segregated market was still visible. The ratio of nonwhite to total median income of self-employed owners was 56 percent; it was 78 percent for food outlets and about 65 percent for personal services and eating and drinking places. In contrast, in the more open manufacturing and transportation sectors, the proportions were much smaller—44 percent and 42 percent, respectively.

In interpreting the above figures, however, the reader should not conclude that self-employment is an easy way for Negroes to become rich. In fact, one can infer that the financial return to Negro risk-takers in general is probably substantially less than for the total population when appraised in terms of alternative opportunities. Yet, the gap appears to be smaller for nonwhite businessmen than for professionals. For instance, in 1959 self-employed nonwhites had a median income of 73 percent of that for all nonwhite professional workers. Comparable figure for all self-employed was 87 percent. Expressed differently, the typical nonwhite businessman in 1959 earned about $65 per week, while the average non-white professional worker earned approximately $90 per week. Among the total population the corresponding figures were $114 and $130, respectively. Once these figures are adjusted to reflect what Negro businessmen typically bring to their enterprises, the discrepancy seems to disappear. Of course, nothing is known about the amount of capital invested by either group of businessmen or professionals. Consequently, it is impossible to estimate the profitability of either type of activity; to do this figures on rate of return would be needed. However, the information available on educational attainment suggests that Negro businessmen do seem to enjoy a higher income per year of schooling than do Negro professionals. Self-employed nonwhite businessmen (with an average of 9.0 years of school completed) have just over half as much education as nonwhite professionals (with 16.3 years of schooling). In contrast, the comparable educational attainment for all self-employed businessmen was nearly three-quarters of that for all professionals—12.1 years and 16.3 years. Nevertheless, the median income of the nonwhite business group in 1959 was in the neighborhood of three-quarters of that for nonwhite professionals. Thus, there is a strong suggestion that part of the income of Negro businessmen is a reflection—not exclusively of their investment in capital and education—but also is a reflection of the partial protection afforded by a segregated market.

Banking and Finance

Even a cursory look makes it evident that Negroes cast a pale shadow on the financial landscape. At the end of 1963, Negroes owned or controlled thirteen banks and about fifty life insurance companies. They also had thirty-four Federally-insured savings and loan associations, of which twenty had charters granted by the Federal Government. The combined assets of these three groups of financial institutions amounted to $764 million, or only 0.12 percent of the total assets held by similar financial enterprises in the country as a whole. While a number of the individual businesses have been strikingly successful, their collective impact has been insignificant.

This indifferent progress cannot be attributed to the reluctance of Negroes to venture onto the financial terrain. Indeed, even before the Civil War, Negroes made numerous attempts to launch banks. The Freedmen's Savings Bank and Trust Company, sponsored by the Freedmen's Bureau, was the most ambitious effort. In its heyday, it had a network of branches in thirty-six cities, and its deposits reached a peak of $57 million. While the bulk of its deposits was backed by United States Government bonds, its reserve funds apparently were not managed well. In any case, the failure of the bank in the depression of 1874 greatly damaged the confidence of Negro depositors in Negro-owned institutions.[11] Yet, during each subsequent period of sustained prosperity, a new crop of Negro banks appeared. But again and again, the end of prosperity brought another epidemic of bank failures and widespread losses to depositors. While this pattern was also typical of the behavior of the banking system as a whole, the legacy in the poverty-stricken Negro community was particularly discouraging.

Among Negro-owned insurance companies, the record is somewhat better. The primary explanation, of course, is the protection provided by the discriminatory practices of the principal insurance companies serving the community at large.

In this section, recent trends in the Negro's participation in banking and finance are appraised. Because of the greater availability of data, the primary emphasis is on banking and insurance.

Negro-Owned Banks

As shown in Table XXI, the combined resources of the thirteen Negro banks amounted to about $77 million at the end of 1963, compared with $364 billion of total assets held by the 14,079 banks in the country as a whole. Thus, Negro banks represented only 0.021 percent of the nation's banking business. But even this small figure reflected an improvement, because in 1957, their share was 0.018 percent. In the intervening years, the Negro banks as a group experienced an annual average rate of growth of

[11] Gunnar Myrdal, *An American Dilemma,* (New York: Harper & Bros., 1944), Vol. I, p. 314.

TABLE XXI—Assets and Rate of Growth of Negro-owned Banks, 1957–1963

Name of Bank	Total Assets		Annual Average Rate of Growth 1957–1960
	1957	1963	(Percent)
Carver State Bank, Savannah, Ga.	$ 928,809	$ 1,643,904	10.0
Citizens and Southern, Phila., Pa.	3,541,965	5,823,293	8.4
Citizens Savings Bank and Trust Co., Nashville, Tenn.	2,494,140	3,313,879	4.9
Citizens Trust Co., Atlanta, Ga.	8,128,457	12,443,533	7.4
Consolidated Bank and Trust Co., Richmond, Va.	4,915,286	6,319,428	4.2
Crown Savings Bank, Newport News, Va.	3,188,498	6,221,454	11.8
Douglas State Bank, Kansas City, Kansas	2,501,053	4,754,632	11.3
First State Bank, Danville, Va.	2,064,146	3,016,630	6.6
Industrial Bank of Washington, D. C.	7,780,327	12,573,741	8.4
Mechanics and Farmers Bank, Durham, N. C.	7,144,257	13,112,958	10.7
Tri-State Bank, Memphis, Tenn.	3,056,718	4,717,471	7.5
Victory Savings Bank, Columbia, S. C.	916,203	1,421,368	7.6
Farmers' State Bank, Boley, Oklahoma	129,748	—	—
Riverside National Bank, Houston, Texas	—	1,502,077	—
All Negro-Owned Banks	46,789,607	76,864,368	8.6
All Banks in the United States (amounts in millions)	257,864	363,678	5.9

SOURCE: "All Banks," U.S. Bureau of the Census, *Statistical Abstract*, 1960, p. 436; 1964, p. 449. Emmer M. Lancaster, *Negro-owned Banks, Annual Report of Banking Institutions Owned and Operated by Negroes*, (Washington, D.C., 1957 and 1963 National Bankers Association.)

8.6 percent, compared with 5.9 percent for all banks in the nation. While the Negro banks' faster expansion partly reflected their small size (thus permitting even a modest absolute gain to be registered as a large percentage), much of their progress was genuine. Moreover, in 1964 six Negro banks received charters or actually opened for business, and three others were seeking charters. All except two of these new institutions were national banks, reflecting a substantial liberalization of policy by Federal banking officials. Nevertheless, Negro banks remain modest institutions.

The distribution of their assets and liabilities, as Table XXII shows, is essentially the same as that for all banks. Yet, a few significant variations are evident. In relation to total assets, Negro banks tend to hold a slightly smaller proportion of loans and a slightly larger proportion of securities and real estate. The lighter emphasis on loans may well reflect the higher risk

TABLE XXII–Distribution of Bank Assets and Liabilities, 1956 and 1963

Category	All Banks (Mill. of Dollars)		Negro-owned Banks (Thous. of Dollars)		Percentage Distribution — All Banks		Percentage Distribution — Negro-owned Banks	
	1956	1963	1956	1963	1956	1963	1956	1963
Assets								
Cash	49,836	51,677	7,355	11,087	19.8	14.2	16.4	14.4
U.S. Government securities	66,795	69,223	12,526	14,905	26.5	19.0	27.8	19.4
State and local government sec.	13,637	30,289	3,865	7,172	5.4	8.3	8.6	9.3
Corporate securities	6,920	10,291	1,264	3,116	2.8	2.7	2.8	4.1
Loans and discounts	110,632	193,442	19,314	38,531	43.9	53.2	42.9	50.1
Bank premises	2,111	4,300	504	1,492	0.8	1.2	1.1	1.9
Other real estate	195	491	30	126	0.1	—	0.1	0.2
Other assets	1,839	3,965	143	436	0.7	1.4	0.3	0.6
Total assets	**251,965**	**363,678**	**45,001**	**76,865**	**100.0**	**100.0**	**100.0**	**100.0**
Liabilities								
Deposits	228,579	320,746	40,613	69,035	90.7	88.2	90.3	89.8
Capital stock	5,007	7,616	1,750	2,551	2.0	2.1	3.9	3.3
Undivided profits and reserves	4,367	7,192	844	1,215	1.7	2.0	1.9	1.6
Surplus	9,976	15,155	1,441	2,949	4.0	4.1	3.2	3.8
Other liabilities	4,036	12,969	353	1,115	1.6	3.6	0.7	1.5
Total liabilities	**251,965**	**363,678**	**45,001**	**76,865**	**100.0**	**100.0**	**100.0**	**100.0**

SOURCE: "All Banks," U.S. Bureau of the Census, *Statistical Abstract*, 1960, p. 436; 1964, p. 449. Emmer M. Lancaster, op. cit. as shown in Table XXI ante.

inherent in a small bank lending to small borrowers. The average Negro bank, with $5.6 million, was only one-fifth as large as the average bank in the country as a whole, which had about $25.8 million in assets at the end of 1963. While we do not know the size of typical borrowers at Negro banks, they are obviously small. Moreover, as mentioned above, Negro businesses are highly concentrated in a narrow range of retail activities focused on the segregated Negro market. Thus, the Negro banker has little opportunity to reduce his risk through loan diversification. Consequently, he would naturally turn to securities for added diversification—although the net rate of return may be less than on loans. The higher percentage of real estate owned by Negro banks may reflect a similar effort to diversify their holdings. But it may also reflect a higher incident of mortgage foreclosures among Negro homebuyers.

The liabilities of Negro banks also exhibit a few distinguishing features compared with all banks combined. While the ratio of deposits to total liabilities is about the same for both groups, Negro banks seem to be somewhat more heavily capitalized. On the other hand, Negro banks in the past appear to have retained a smaller proportion of their profits to build up reserves and surplus.

The combined balance sheet summarized in Table XXII provides a fair description of the overall features of Negro banks, but it is basically a static picture. It would be particularly helpful to have an insight into their dynamic role of mobilizing savings and channeling them into various sectors of the economy. This role can be highlighted by the application of the "Sources and Uses of Funds" accounting system. Conceptionally, this method of accounting is derived by calculating changes between two or more dates in the combined balance sheets of the institutions. Table XXIII shows the sources and uses of funds of Negro-owned banks and all banks in the country over the period 1956–63. Basically, two questions are posed: First, how did the banks expand their resources during the years indicated, or what were the *sources* of the increase in their loanable funds? Second, what was the composition of the increase in the banks, assets, or what *use* did they make of their greater resources? To answer the first question, one must look at changes in the banks' liabilities; to answer the second, one must examine changes in their assets. As in the case of the traditional balance sheet in which liabilities must equal assets, sources of funds must equal uses of funds.

Table XXIII again puts into sharp focus the similarities and differences between Negro-owned banks as a group and those in the nation at large. The sources of funds for the two sets of institutions are virtually the same. During the period 1956–63, both types of banks relied on sales of new equity securities for roughly the same proportion (about 2.5 percent) of their total sources. However, since capital stock accounted for a larger proportion of Negro banks' assets in 1956, this implies that they sold new stock issues at a slower rate (in relation to their earlier position) than did banks as a group. Increased deposits were, of course, the principal source of funds for banks in general, but they were of more importance for Negro institutions. Because deposits are the primary means used by banks to mobilize financial resources which they lend to borrowers, it would be helpful to examine this source in greater detail. This is done in Table XXIV listing the type and ownership of bank deposits in 1963. As one would expect, demand deposits represent a smaller proportion of total deposits in Negro banks than in all banks combined. This is a reflection of the lesser use of checks by Negroes in day-to-day transactions and in paying bills, a mode of behavior typical of low-income status. On the other hand, time deposits constitute a larger share of Negro-owned banks' total deposits. For Negro banks, these

TABLE XXIII—Sources and Uses of Bank Funds, 1956–1963

Category	All Banks		Negro-owned Banks	
	Amount (Millions of Dollars)	Percent of total	Amount (Thousands of Dollars)	Percent of total
Sources of Funds				
New Capital	2,609	2.3	801	2.5
Deposits	92,167	82.5	28,422	89.2
Undistributed Profits	2,825	2.5	371	1.2
Surplus	5,179	4.6	1,508	4.7
Other sources	8,933	8.1	761	2.4
Total sources	**111,713**	**100.0**	**31,863**	**100.0**
Use of Funds				
Cash	1,841	1.6	3,732	11.7
U. S. Government Securities	2,428	2.2	2,380	7.5
State and local Govt. Sec.	16,652	14.9	3,307	10.4
Corporate securities	3,371	3.0	1,852	5.8
Loans	82,810	74.1	19,217	60.3
Real estate	2,485	2.2	1,085	3.4
Bank Premises	2,189	2.0	988	3.1
Other real estate	296	0.2	97	0.3
Other uses	2,126	1.9	291	0.9
Total uses	**111,713**	**100.0**	**31,863**	**100.0**

SOURCE: Calculated from Table XXI

TABLE XXIV—Type and Ownership of Bank Deposits, 1963

Type and Ownership of Deposits	All Banks		Negro Banks	
	Amount (Billions of of Dollars)	Percent of total	Amount (millions of Dollars)	Percent of total
Demand deposits of individuals, partnerships and corporations	125.4	39.1	25.7	37.3
Time deposits of individuals, partnerships and corporations	147.6	46.1	35.1	51.0
U.S. Government deposits	7.0	2.2	1.5	2.2
State and local government deposits	20.3	6.3	4.4	6.3
Interbank deposits	15.8	4.9	1.7	2.4
Other deposits	4.5	1.4	0.6	0.8
Total deposits	**320.7**	**100.0**	**69.0**	**100.0**

SOURCE: Same as Table XXI.

are primarily savings deposits of individuals, mirroring the normal way in which most resources of small savers are held. Individuals' savings accounts also make up the bulk of total time deposits. However, a fairly large component is owned by partnerships and corporations as a temporary means of holding funds accumulated as working capital or to pay income taxes.

Negro-owned banks and banks in general are about equally dependent on government deposits as a source of funds. Deposits of state and local governments are more important than those of the Federal Government. The U. S. Treasury Department tries to keep its cash holdings to a minimum and also holds its immediate working balances in Federal Reserve Banks. This ability to attract government deposits is a mark of considerable financial maturity, because such deposits are nearly always restricted to those institutions which have demonstrated a high level of stability. At the end of 1963, all except one of the thirteen Negro-owned banks held Federal Government deposits, and only three of them held none for state and local governments.

Finally, Negro-owned banks held a relatively smaller amount of interbank deposits, compared with banks as a whole. Such deposits are usually the basis of a rather sophisticated correspondence system in which big-city banks perform services for institutions in outlying areas. Among such services are purchases and sales of securities, foreign exchange and other international transactions, and marketing research. So far, because of the restricted nature of their customers' requirements, Negro banks have shown little need for interbank deposits. Where such deposits are held, they are typically owned by savings and loan associations which use them to cover unusual cash withdrawals.

If we look back to Table XXIII, it is again evident that Negro banks, during the period under review, retained a smaller proportion of their profits to strengthen the institution. This tendency may be attributable to the greater necessity to pay dividends in order to attract capital. The increment in surplus was relatively the same for both sets of banks.

When we examine the uses of bank funds between 1956 and 1963, the differences between Negro-owned and other banks are far more marked. The Negro institutions put a much larger percentage of their increased resources in liquid assets. Cash and U. S. Government securities combined represented almost one-fifth of their total uses of funds, compared with only 4 percent for all banks. While the banking industry in general channeled three-fourths of its new funds into loans, the proportion for Negro banks was about three-fifths. Again, this distribution of loanable funds is consistent with the differential risks of lending faced by Negro banks which was described above.

Negroes, of course, are attracted to the banking business by the same objectives which attract other investors: to make a profit. But here, as with many other pursuits in the field of business, the Negro appears to be less successful than his white counterpart in achieving his goal. Negro banks, taken as a group, seem to have higher operating expenses, lower rates of return on their resources—and thus lower rates of profit. However, what may come as a surprise to many readers, actual losses suffered by Negro banks on bad loans appear to be smaller, in relation to the volume of loans outstanding, than for banks in the economy as a whole.

Operating Ratios for Negro Banks

These general conclusions are amply supported by the evidence in Table XXV showing operating ratios for Negro-owned and member banks of the Federal Reserve system.[12] Because these ratios in many instances vary by size of bank, the Negro institutions are also compared with the smaller units in the Federal Reserve System. Operating ratios provide a convenient tool with which to appraise the performance of banks classified by type and size. Given the ratios for any particular class of bank, an individual banker (or his stockholders) has a standard to measure his own achievement. Some of the ratios are calculated by expressing various items from a bank's profit and loss statement as percentages of key components of the bank's

[12] These data are available in sufficient detail only for those banks which are members of the Federal Reserve System. The ratios were used only as rough benchmarks. Two Negro banks were members of the Federal Reserve System at the end of 1963.

TABLE XXV—Operating Ratios of Negro-Owned and Federal Reserve Member Banks,* 1963 (Percentages)

Item	Federal Reserve Member Banks		Negro-owned Banks
	All Member Banks	Banks with Total Deposits of $1 mill. to $25 million	
Number of Banks	1	2	3
1 Summary ratios:			
Percentage of total capital accounts:			
Net current earnings before income taxes	13.6	12.1	9.91
Net income before related taxes	11.9	10.5	7.96
Net income	8.2	7.4	6.22
Cash dividends declared	3.1	2.8	1.97
Percentage of total assets:			
Total operating revenue	4.69	4.72	5.31
Net current earnings before income taxes	1.18	1.15	.86
Net income	.71	.71	.54
2 Sources and disposition of income:			
Percentage of total operating revenue:			
Interest and dividends on:			
U.S. Government securities	22.0	22.8	13.1
Other securities	6.8	5.9	6.3
Revenue on loans	61.7	62.2	58.7
Service charges on deposit accounts	5.9	5.7	6.7
All other revenue	3.6	3.4	15.2
Total revenue	**100.0**	**100.0**	**100.0**
Salaries and wages	29.0	29.1	33.0
Interest on time deposits	25.4	22.5	25.9
Other current expenses	20.1	16.7	24.8
Total expenses	**74.5**	**75.3**	**83.7**
Net current earnings before income taxes	**25.5**	**24.7**	**16.3**
Net losses (or recoveries and profits +)	1.4	1.6	1.2
Net increase in valuation reserves	1.6	1.2	1.9
Taxes on net income	7.0	6.4	2.8
Net income after taxes	15.5	15.4	10.2
3 Rates of return on securities and loans:			
Return on securities:			
Interest on U.S. Government securities	3.48	3.50	3.53
Interest and dividends on other securities	3.23	3.45	1.39
(Net losses or recoveries and profits +)	+ .07	0.05	.01
Return on loans:			
Revenue on loans	6.71	6.92	6.55
Net losses	.17	.18	.11

* For Federal Reserve Member banks, averages of individual ratios expressed as percentages. For Negro-owned banks, ratios are for all banks combined.

SOURCE: For Negro-owned banks, same as Table XXI; for Federal Reserve Member banks, Federal Reserve Bulletin, April, 1964.

balance sheet. For example, income may be divided by the total capital account to indicate the rate of return on stockholders' investment. Other ratios may be calculated to show the sources and disposition of the bank's income.

The summary operating ratios shown at the top of Table XXV clearly suggest that a dollar invested in Negro banks earns only about three-quarters as much as it would in a typical bank serving the community at large. For Negro banks, net current earnings before income taxes in 1963 were 9.9 percent of invested capital, compared with 13.6 percent for all Federal Reserve member banks. Even when compared with the smaller institutions in the Federal Reserve System, the Negro banks' performance was not greatly improved. After paying income taxes, Negro banks earned about 6.2 percent on their employed capital, against 8.2 percent for all Federal Reserve member banks and 7.4 percent for banks of comparable size. However, Negro owners received proportionately less in cash dividends than did other investors in bank stocks. When total assets are used as a benchmark, the less vigorous performance of Negro banks is also evident.

This squeeze on the profits of Negro banks can be explained by the second group of operating ratios in Table XXV describing the sources and disposition of income. First, it will be noted that Negro banks receive a smaller share of their revenue from loans and securities than do other banks. On the other hand, they depend more heavily on receipts from service charges; this means that customers of these institutions pay relatively more for what is likely to be a less complete range of services. Moreover, revenue from other sources (such as the rental of real estate) is particularly important for the Negro banks. But the most significant figure bearing on the profits squeeze is the expense ratio. In Negro-owned banks, total expenses absorbed about eighty-four cents of each dollar of revenue; in other institutions the comparable figure was only seventy-five cents. In every expense category, Negro banks had higher operating costs than other banks. The extra pressure of salaries and wages on their operating revenue was especially noticeable. Of course, this does not mean that officers and employees of Negro banks are exceptionally well-paid. (In fact, the median income of salaried Negro bank officials in 1959 was less than 90 percent of that for all such officials.) Rather, it indicates that their small size and generally poor marketing area severely limit the cash inflow of Negro-owned banks. On this meager revenue stream, it is difficult to sustain even the modest salaries they pay their employees. The higher ratio of interest on time deposits to total revenue is due primarily to the fact that most Negro banks are located in the South where interest rates generally exceed those in the rest of the nation (with the exception of the far West). Finally, other current operating expenses of Negro banks (such as local taxes, stationery, building maintenance, etc.) appear to be much higher proportionally, even after allowing for the relatively small size of their enterprises. No explanation for this divergence is readily apparent. But, in any case, the impact of these differential operating expenses in 1963 left Negro banks with about sixteen cents of net earnings per dollar of revenue, compared with twenty-five cents for banks in general. After adjustment for taxes, additions to security reserves and losses on loans and investments, these figures were reduced to about ten cents and fifteen cents, respectively.

Finally, the third set of operating ratios reveal that, despite the fact that Negro banks primarily with customers whose economic position is particularly weak, their losses are proportionally smaller than banks in general. In 1963, losses on securities were 0.01 percent for Negro banks; they were 0.07 percent for all Federal Reserve members and 0.05 percent for the smaller members of the system. While losses due to bad loans were somewhat larger than on securities for both Negro-owned and other banks, the Negro banks still had a smaller loss ratio. This differential loss experience seems to pose a paradox: in view of their small size and the more economically unstable environment in which they operate, one might conclude that the loans made by Negro banks are inherently more risky. Yet, their loss experience seems to suggest the opposite. Actually, this apparent paradox may not exist at all. Exactly because of the inherently greater risk of lending to small business borrowers with an uncertain future, Negro banks seem to take extra precautions in extending loans. They generally accept a smaller percentage of applications and require proportionately more (and more easily marketable) collateral as security for loans. By thus restricting their loans to the best of the prospective borrowers, they may maintain a loan portfolio whose average quality actually exceeds that achieved by banks in the economy as a whole.

The Significance of Negroes in Banking

Against the above analysis of the role of Negroes in banking, one might still ask just how crucial is the entire effort. The reply, of course, must be that these institutions represent a vital link in the process of economic development in the Negro community. One can trace very briefly the basic features of this link. As is widely known, Negro businessmen have typically found it especially difficult to obtain sufficient credit to finance their operations. While other obstacles (such as insufficient management know-how, small markets and the inability to attract and hold enough capable employees) have also existed, the lack of credit certainly has posed one of the most difficult limitations. Furthermore, although these difficulties are typically faced by all small businessmen, white as well as Negro, they seem to be particularly distressing for Negroes.

Thus, the most vital function a strong bank can perform is to help finance the growth and expansion of those Negro businessmen who possess an idea and who can combine it with the knowledge and imagination to develop a market. Needless to say, the author by no means is advocating a segregated banking system to support a segregated Negro business sector. On the contrary, Negroes along with other businessmen will continue to look for financial accommodation at banks serving the general community. What is being stressed is that competition from strong Negro-owned banks can make just that margin of difference which will encourage leading institutions serving the general market to be somewhat more sympathetic and sensitive to the financial needs of potential Negro customers. In numerous cities (especially in Atlanta, Georgia, and Durham, North Carolina) there appears to be evidence that white bankers have become more liberal in both the size and terms of loans to Negro customers with the growth and expansion of Negro-owned institutions.

This beneficial influence stemming from the presence of Negro banks has not always been recognized. In fact, a definitive book on the Negro in America, which appeared in the early 1940's, not only failed to foresee this possibility—it actually concluded that the best course for Negroes in the field of banking was to seek fuller employment opportunities and the greater availability of credit at white-owned institutions.[13] Needless to say, the author does not share this pessimistic view. Instead it is vitally important for Negroes to be owners and risk-takers in banking as well as for them to seek a greater number of positions of dignity as employees of white-owned institutions.

As far as expanding banking employment is concerned, it is clear that the bulk of such opportunities must be sought primarily in white-controlled institutions. For example, between 1950 and 1960, the number of self-employed Negro bankers shrank from ninety to forty-one. The number in insurance and real estate climbed from 600 to 794. Over the same decade, the number of salaried Negro officials in all three fields rose from 183 to 293. However, only a handful of these Negro officials have found senior staff positions in white-owned banks. While the number is growing daily, this is still clearly an area where considerable strides can and should be made.

[13] G. Myrdal, *An American Dilemma* (New York: Harper & Brothers, 1944), Vol. I, p. 318.

TABLE XXVI—Selected Characteristics of all Life Insurance Companies and Negro-Owned Life Insurance Companies, 1962

Selected Characteristics	All Companies		Negro Companies	
	Amount (Millions of Dollars)	Percent of Total	Amount (Millions of Dollars)	Percent of Total
Assets				
Cash	1,457	1.1	8,595	2.8
Bonds	63,722	47.8	165,349	53.2
Stocks	6,302	4.7	15,887	5.1
Mortgages	46,902	35.2	86,718	27.9
Policy Loans	6,234	4.7	11,743	3.8
Other Assets	8,674	6.5	22,553	7.2
Total Assets	**133,291**	**100.0**	**310,845**	**100.0**
Obligations				
Policy Reserves	108,384	81.3	237,287	76.3
Capital	978	0.7	9,503	3.1
Special Surplus Funds	2,352	1.8	6,765	2.2
Unassigned Surplus	7,926	6.0	27,806	8.9
Other Obligations	13,651	10.2	29,484	9.5
Total Obligations	**133,291**	**100.0**	**310,845**	**100.0**
Life Insurance in Force Dec. 31, 1962				
Ordinary	389,150	57.5	614,891	37.4
Industrial	39,638	5.9	1,029,055	62.6
Other	247,189	36.6	6	
Group	209,178	31.0		
Credit	38,011	5.6		
Total	**675,977**	**100.0**	**1,643,952**	**100.0**
Life Insurance Purchases 1962	79,577		592,359	
Death Benefits Paid 1962	3,878		8,520	
Ratio of Death Benefits to Purchases (Percent)		4.9		1.4
Income Received				
Premium Income	19,373	74.5	74,221	83.5
Investment and Other Income	6,627	25.5	14,619	16.5
Total	**26,000**	**100.0**	**88,840**	**100.0**

SOURCE: All Companies, *Life Insurance Fact Book, 1964.* Negro-Owned Companies, based on a preliminary data compiled by Emmer M. Lancaster, supplemented with statistics from *Best's Life Insurance Reports.*

Negro-Owned Life Insurance Companies

The field of life insurance provides a classic illustration of the origins and rationale of Negro business: the exclusive and discriminating practices of the companies serving the national market created a protected environment in which the Negro institutions could develop. Beginning in the 1880's, most of the leading insurance firms began to employ a separate mortality table to estimate risks of insuring Negro lives; this separate table resulted in substantially higher premiums for Negroes for the same amount of coverage.[14] Still other companies refused to insure Negroes under any circumstances. Since many Negroes, along with other citizens, foresaw the desirability of insurance coverage, the conditions were set for the growth of Negro life insurance companies. While the record is replete with numerous failures (which is also true of white-owned and controlled companies), the life insurance field remains the outstanding example of Negro enterprise.

At the end of 1963, Negroes owned some fifty-odd legal reserve life insurance companies. They also maintained more than thirty burial and mutual aid societies. All of the latter are small, localized ventures, with a total of only $1 million of assets in 1962. Moreover, accurate statistics are available for only the twenty or so largest companies which hold virtually all of the assets owned by Negro institutions. Consequently, the following analysis is based on these companies. A detailed description of these companies is given in Tables XXVII, XXVIII and XXXI. But for the purpose of examining their structure and performance, a general summary is sufficient. This summary is provided in Table XXVI.

As the Table shows, the twenty leading Negro companies had total assets of $311 million in 1962. This represented about 0.23 percent of the $133 billion of total assets owned by all life insurance companies. Thus, compared with Negro-owned banks (which held only 0.021 percent of total banking assets at the end of 1963), the relative position of the Negro insurance companies in the financial community is considerably stronger. However, the table also suggests some basic differences in the life insurance business operated by Negroes and the industry as a whole.

Life Insurance in Force in Negro Companies

Perhaps the most striking difference between Negro and other companies is the type of life insurance coverage. Industrial life insurance represented more than three-fifths of the total life insurance in force with Negro companies. Among all companies in the nation, industrial policies accounted for

[14] Myrdal, *op. cit.*, Vol. I, p. 316.

only 6 percent of total life insurance in force. Industrial life insurance is issued in small amounts, usually not over $500, with premiums payable on a weekly or monthly basis. The premiums, which may be as low as twenty-five cents per week, are generally collected at the policyholders' home by an agent of the company. In 1962, industrial life insurance outstanding with Negro companies amounted to $1,029 million. This represented 2.5 percent of the industry total, by far the largest share which Negroes controlled of any part of the insurance business.

Ordinary insurance constituted 37 percent of the face value of all policies outstanding with the Negro companies, compared with 58 percent for the industry. Ordinary insurance (which is also called whole or straight life insurance) forms the backbone of the life insurance business. It is usually issued in amounts of $1,000 or more. Premiums are payable on an annual, semiannual, quarterly or monthly basis. The premiums, in turn, are calculated on the "level premium" basis. This means the cost of the coverage is distributed evenly over the period during which premiums are paid. Because the premium remains the same from year to year, it is more than the actual cost of protection in the earlier years of the policy and less than the actual cost in the later years. The excess paid in the early years builds up the reserve. This reserve, of course, is a fund of policyholders' savings. This latter feature makes ordinary life insurance the key to the role of life insurance companies as leading sources of funds to finance residential construction and the acquisition of plant and equipment by the business sector. Yet, because ordinary insurance with its large savings component occupies such a minor position in the affairs of Negro life insurance companies, the latter also can play only a minor role in the financing of long-term capital formation in the Negro community.

Negro life insurance companies have made virtually no headway in the relatively new fields such as group and credit life insurance. Group coverage is issued, usually without medical examination, on a group of persons under a single master policy. It is normally issued to an employer for the benefit of employees, and individual members of the group hold certificates stating their coverage. Group insurance has been one of the fastest-growing segments of the industry; by the end of 1963, there were $228.5 billion of group life insurance outstanding, accounting for 31 percent of all life insurance in force in the United States. Negro companies provided none of this group protection. The explanation is simple: group contracts are typically issued to relatively large employers (although some are also written for trade unions and professional associations), and their size is generally well beyond the financial and managerial capacity of all except the two or three largest Negro companies. For example, at the end of 1963,

TABLE XXVII–Selected aspects of Negro Life Insurance Companies' operation, 1962

Company	Type of Company	Life Insurance in Force, December 31, 1962				Life Insurance Purchases 1962	Death Benefits Paid, 1962	Income Received	
		Total	Ordinary	Industrial	Other			Total	Premium
North Carolina Mutual Life Insurance Co., Durham, N.C.	Mutual	337,013,000	158,993,000	178,020,000	None	133,310,000	1,212,765	21,981,281	16,028,184
Atlanta Life Insurance Co., Atlanta, Ga.	Stock	182,126,000	59,795,000	122,331,000	None	46,768,000	1,189,630	12,307,242	10,458,800
Supreme Life Insurance Co. of America, Chicago, Ill.	Stock	195,175,000	68,045,000	127,130,000	None	57,730,000	1,134,019	8,663,976	7,396,907
Universal Life Insurance Co., Memphis, Tenn.	Stock	140,226,000	27,573,000	112,653,000	None	77,903,000	830,798	7,605,042	6,740,561
Golden State Mutual Life Insurance Co., Los Angeles, Calif.	Mutual	161,060,178	110,982,000	50,078,000	178	43,613,000	553,015	8,198,131	7,378,388
Chicago Metropolitan Mutual Assurance Co., Chicago, Ill.	Mutual	126,073,000	20,425,000	105,643,000	5,000	42,550,000	683,339	5,179,383	4,493,343
Mammoth Life and Accident Insurance Co., Louisville, Ky.	Stock	116,082,000	34,129,000	81,953,000	None	62,606,000	678,829	5,980,436	5,470,851
Pilgrim Health Life Insurance Co., Augusta, Ga.	Stock	55,961,000	17,740,000	38,221,000	None	17,788,000	383,094	3,122,542	2,703,432
Afro-American Life Insurance Co., Jacksonville, Fla.	Stock	52,753,000	11,840,000	40,913,000	None	25,899,000	417,878	3,366,983	2,971,440
Great Lakes Mutual Life Insurance Co., Detroit, Mich.	Mutual	71,960,000	24,818,000	47,142,000	None	19,788,000	247,953	2,440,763	2,123,175
Victory Mutual Life Insurance Co., Chicago, Ill.	Mutual	34,559,000	34,559,000	None	None	N.A.	185,493	1,217,381	982,968

TABLE XXVII (cont.)

Company	Type of Company	Life Insurance in Force, December 31, 1962				Life Insurance Purchases 1962	Death Benefits Paid, 1962	Income Received	
		Total	Ordinary	Industrial	Other			Total	Premium
United Mutual Life Insurance Co., New York, N.Y.	Mutual	31,014,000	18,701,000	12,313,000	None	4,503,000	222,617	1,148,795	923,675
Booker T. Washington Life Insurance Co., Birmingham, Ala.	Stock	61,720,932	8,684,000	53,036,000	932	23,105,000	261,833	2,180,951	2,040,808
Mutual Benefit Society of Maryland, Baltimore, Md.	Mutual	13,348,000	1,366,000	11,982,000	None	3,843,000	126,390	839,371	704,781
Southern Aid Insurance Co., Richmond, Va.	Stock	15,726,000	4,622,000	11,104,000	None	4,764,000	121,139	1,062,985	904,856
Virginia Mutual Benefit Life Insurance Co., Richmond, Va.	Mutual	16,054,000	3,483,000	12,571,000	None	8,854,000	76,062	1,684,966	1,210,630
Union Protective Life Insurance Co., Memphis, Tenn.	Stock	15,588,000	1,025,000	14,563,000	None	10,976,000	112,651	1,055,591	988,820
Guaranty Life Insurance Co., Savannah, Ga.	Stock	7,492,234	1,033,000	6,459,000	234	3,352,000	49,148	486,480	423,721
Southern Life Insurance Co., Baltimore, Md.	Stock	2,943,000	None	2,943,000	None	1,154,000	27,273	156,383	137,000
Crusaders Life Insurance Co., Kansas City. Kans.	Stock	7,078,000	7,078,000	None	None	3,863,000	6,263	161,315	139,147
Total		1,643,952,344	614,891,000	1,029,055,000	6,344	592,359,000	8,520,189	88,839,997	74,221,487

SOURCE: All Companies, *Life Insurance Fact Book*, 1964.

TABLE XXVIII—Assets of Negro Life Insurance Companies

	Total Assets	Cash	Bonds	Stocks	Mortgages	Policy Loans	Other Assets
North Carolina Mutual Life Insurance Co., Durham, N.C.	76,762,500	2,054,398	41,317,359	5,531,834	20,843,094	2,905,174	4,110,641
Atlanta Life Insurance Co., Atlanta, Ga.	58,778,286	1,451,066	43,341,421	5,755,433	6,565,879	1,851,957	1,812,530
Supreme Life Insurance Co. of America, Chicago, Ill.	31,718,921	854,954	13,200,367	311,182	13,057,926	1,659,040	2,635,452
Universal Life Insurance Co., Memphis, Tenn.	23,803,449	468,873	9,797,113	764,631	10,248,262	808,758	1,715,812
Golden State Mutual Life Insurance Co., Los Angeles, Calif.	20,449,143	534,272	6,739,719	826,580	8,665,302	1,564,856	2,118,414
Chicago Metropolitan Mutual Assurance Co., Chicago, Ill.	16,497,977	283,831	8,379,252	100,000	6,702,076	157,950	874,868
Mammoth Life and Accident Insurance Co., Louisville, Ky.	16,114,327	301,120	9,270,214	239,877	4,520,020	156,785	1,626,311
Pilgrim Health Life Insurance Co., Augusta, Georgia	12,094,479	378,674	8,013,326	1,174,986	1,626,266	456,874	444,353
Afro-American Life Insurance Co., Jacksonville, Florida	11,177,673	201,249	6,142,300	812,712	2,384,178	272,577	1,364,657
Great Lakes Mutual Life Insurance Co., Detroit, Michigan	9,379,146	465,632	6,124,156	150,476	760,538	341,110	1,537,234
Victory Mutual Life Insurance Co., Chicago, Ill.	7,520,049	180,389	2,703,972	74,836	2,770,981	1,119,447	670,424
United Mutual Life Insurance Co., New York, New York	6,112,608	258,112	3,714,676	10,500	1,613,712	248,481	267,127

TABLE XXVIII (Cont'd)

	Total Assets	Cash	Bonds	Stocks	Mortgages	Policy Loans	Other Assets
Booker T. Washington Life Insurance Co., Birmingham, Ala.	4,446,784	231,369	540,370	662,788	1,287,322	41,379	1,683,556
Mutual Benefit Society of Maryland, Baltimore, Maryland	4,173,811	174,971	702,130	1,110,520	1,504,775	18,120	662,185
Southern Aid Insurance Co., Richmond, Virginia	4,040,120	142,131	1,841,696	148,610	1,647,535	45,882	214,266
Virginia Mutual Benefit Life Insurance Co., Richmond, Va.	3,095,037	378,917	1,648,775	None	761,351	52,043	253,951
Union Protective Life Insurance Co., Memphis, Tenn.	2,061,070	97,879	523,013	115,844	1,154,202	466	169,666
Guaranty Life Insurance Co., Savannah, Ga.	1,668,710	69,991	1,068,456	75,964	363,179	27,390	63,730
Southern Life Insurance Co., Baltimore, Maryland	587,644	17,980	177,651	None	111,878	4,407	275,728
Crusaders Life Insurance Co., Kansas City, Kansas	362,969	49,309	102,221	20,000	129,748	9,990	51,701
Total	**310,844,703**	**8,595,117**	**165,349,297**	**15,886,773**	**86,718,224**	**11,742,686**	**22,552,606**

SOURCE: All Companies, *Life Insurance Fact Book, 1964*. Negro-Owned Companies, based on a preliminary data compiled by Emmer M. Lancaster, supplemented with statistics from *Best's Life Insurance Reports*.

TABLE XXIX–Obligations of Negro Life Insurance Companies

	Total Obligations	Policy Reserves	Capital	Special Surplus Funds	Unassigned Surplus	Other Obligations
North Carolina Mutual life Insurance Co., Durham, N. C.	76,762,500	60,146,961	None	4,136,342	5,550,000	6,929,197
Atlanta Life Insurance Co., Atlanta, Ga.	58,778,286	36,103,703	4,000,000	1,000,000	10,080,452	7,594,131
Supreme Life Insurance Co. of America, Chicago, Ill.	31,718,921	26,996,676	1,665,000	200,000	1,001,486	1,855,759
Universal Life Insurance Co., Memphis, Tenn.	23,803,449	19,905,604	1,565,650	None	1,481,819	850,376
Golden State Mutual Life Insurance Co., Los Angeles, Calif.	20,449,143	16,359,533	None	98,949	1,350,000	2,640,661
Chicago Metropolitan Mutual Assurance Co., Chicago, Ill.	16,497,977	12,685,055	None	None	2,053,865	1,759,057
Mammoth Life and Accident Insurance Co., Louisville, Ky.	16,114,327	11,467,259	600,000	488,943	844,222	2,713,903
Pilgrim Health Life Insurance Co., Augusta, Ga.	12,094,479	9,789,942	200,000	300,000	1,244,980	559,557
Afro-American Life Insurance Co., Jacksonville, Fla.	11,177,673	9,462,161	500,000	None	438,217	777,295
Great Lakes Mutual Life Insurance Co., Detroit, Mich.	9,379,146	7,835,296	None	200,000	458,271	885,579
Victory Mutual Life Insurance Co., Chicago, Ill.	7,520,049	6,818,664	None	1,233	325,600	374,552
United Mutual Life Insurance Co., New York, N. Y.	6,112,608	5,514,679	None	None	240,277	357,652
Booker T. Washington Life Insurance Co., Birmingham, Ala.	4,446,784	3,513,621	100,000	None	607,685	225,478
Mutual Benefit Society of Maryland, Baltimore, Md.	4,173,811	2,609,619	None	None	568,793	995,399
Southern Aid Insurance Co., Richmond, Va.	4,040,120	2,697,186	300,000	150,000	636,476	256,458
Virginia Mutual Benefit Life Insurance Co., Richmond, Va.	3,095,037	2,335,498	None	None	351,421	408,118
Union Protective Life Insurance Co., Memphis, Tenn.	2,061,070	1,294,024	200,000	100,000	308,706	158,340
Guaranty Life Insurance Co., Savannah, Ga.	1,668,710	1,105,568	200,000	89,404	200,000	73,738
Southern Life Insurance Co., Baltimore, Md.	587,644	479,959	10,000	None	38,078	59,607
Crusaders Life Insurance Co., Kansas City, Kans.	362,969	166,274	162,271	None	25,068	9,356
TOTAL	310,844,703	237,287,282	9,502,921	6,764,871	27,805,416	29,484,213

the $228.5 billion of group life insurance outstanding had been written under 203,000 master contracts. These master contracts represented 50.9 million individual certificates, or an average of $4,490 per certificate. Thus, these figures imply that the average group consisted of about 250 individuals, with a group coverage of over $1 million. Since Negro companies write policies almost exclusively on Negro lives—and since there are only a handful of Negro firms employing even close to 250 workers—the group insurance market is extremely limited for these institutions. While Negro churches, fraternities and similar organizations do offer some potential for group insurance, little progress has been made in developing it.

Credit life insurance, designed to repay debt in case borrower should die, is the fastest-growing of all forms of life insurance, with the amount outstanding doubling every three years. But Negro companies have not even entered the field. By the end of 1963, about $43.6 billion of credit insurance were outstanding. This type of coverage has greatly reduced the risk of borrowing. By guaranteeing repayment of installment-plan debt or a personal loan in case the borrower should die, credit life insurance protects the borrower and his family as well as the bank, finance company, credit union or retailer that lent the money. However, because credit insurance is issued by life insurance companies through lending agencies, it is understandable that Negro insurance companies have not been able to penetrate this part of the life insurance market.

The reader should keep in mind, however, that the above discussion is focused on life insurance outstanding with Negro companies—and not on the ownership of life insurance by Negroes. While we have no firm estimates of the amount of protection purchased by Negroes, we do know that the great bulk of such coverage is provided by the leading insurance companies serving the general community. In fact, any one of the largest companies (such as Metropolitan or Prudential) probably has on its books far more coverage on Negro lives than the amount outstanding with all Negro-owned companies combined. In addition, we know that the proportion of Negro families covered by life insurance of any kind is still considerably below that for all families in the nation—although the gap has been closing in recent years. In 1963, about 67 percent of all heads of families owned individual life insurance, and the proportion rose to 85 percent with the inclusion of those holding group, veterans, fraternal and other types of insurance. For those with individual policies, the mean amount owned was $7,604; and the figure for all types of insurance was $10,600. Taking all families in the country, the average protection in 1963 was approximately $12,200, or roughly equivalent to 22 months of the average family's disposable personal income.

We do not have similar statistics for Negroes alone. However, among families with incomes below $3,000 (and about two-fifths of all Negro families had incomes below this figure in 1963), only 71 percent had insurance coverage of any kind, compared with 89 percent for the nation's families taken together. The proportions among Negroes were undoubtedly much smaller. We can get a slightly better feeling for the probable size of individual policies held by Negro families. In Table XII, it was shown that Negro families spent about $203 for personal insurance in 1960–61, compared with $324 spent by all families combined. These amounts represented 5.3 percent and 5.5 percent, respectively, of the after-tax personal incomes of Negro and all families. If a dollar of premiums purchased the same amount of protection for both groups, the average value of individual policies held by Negroes would have been about $5,150 in 1963, against $8,178 for all families. However, because a large proportion of coverage owned by Negroes consists of industrial insurance (where costs are much higher per dollar of coverage compared with ordinary insurance), the actual size of the average Negro-owned policy is probably much smaller than $5,000.

Operation of Negro Life Insurance Companies

The operations of Negro-owned companies are sketched in Table XXVI. In 1962, the 20 largest Negro institutions sold $592.3 million of new life insurance coverage. In the same year, industry sales amounted to $79.6 billion. Expressed another way, the average Negro company sold about $30 million of new life insurance coverage in 1962, compared with $54.1 million sold by the average company in the industry. So Negro companies accounted for 0.75 percent of total industry sales, a proportion more than three times their share of industry assets. Thus, while Negro companies remain small, collectively they are expanding their operations somewhat more rapidly than the industry as a whole. However, this is due partly to their small size, because the smaller units in the industry in general have made larger percentage gains in recent years than have the bigger institutions. But part of the growth undoubtedly reflects the expanding demand for insurance by Negro families as their incomes rise.

Negro companies paid about $8.5 million in death benefits in 1962. This represented about $425,000 per company. For the industry as a whole, death benefits amounted to $3.9 billion, or $2,620,000 per company. These figures indicate that for Negro companies, death benefits constituted 1.4 percent of new sales; for all companies combined the corresponding figure was 4.9 percent. The small ratio for Negro companies apparently reflects the mechanics in which industrial insurance plays a dominant role. When such policies are sold, their full face value is added to life insurance in force. The lapse rate for such policies is exceptionally high, and the proceeds paid on those which actually mature are relatively small. Death benefits are the primary form of payment made by Negro-owned companies to bene- ficiaries. This is far less true for the industry generally. For instance, in 1963 total life insurance benefit payments in the United States amounted to $10,028 million. Death benefits were only $4,209 million, or 42 percent. The remaining $5,819 million, or 58 percent, went to living policyholders. About $809 million were paid in matured endowments, $155 million in disability payments and $902 million in annuity payments. Dividends paid to policy- holders amounted to $2,165 million, and policies surrendered for cash had a value of $1,789 million.

Negro life insurance companies had an income of about $89 million in 1962. Premium income provided $74 million, or 83.5 percent of the total. Investments and other sources provided $14.6 million, making up the re- maining 16.5 percent. For the entire industry, total income amounted to $26.0 billion, of which $19.4 billion, or 74.5 percent, arose from premiums; investment and other income came to $6.6 billion, or 25.5 percent of the total. These income figures reveal a number of distinctions between Negro companies and the rest of the industry. The lesser importance of invest- ments as a source of income is a further reflection of their modest status as financial intermediaries. The factors underlying this situation are explored more fully below. Another feature accounting for the difference in premiums as a source of income for Negro companies is their lack of partici- pation in the market for group insurance. Group policies, which have been expanding rapidly, usually carry relatively low reserves, low premiums and no cash surrender values. Another factor has been the rise in family plan and family income policies, which with their term insurance features, also have relatively low premiums and no cash values on their term elements. All of these factors have combined to dampen the growth of premium income for industry as a whole. But since Negro companies for the most part have not joined in these innovations, premiums remain for them a far more im- portant source of income.

The obligations of Negro-owned companies also exhibit a few differ- entiating features. (See Table XXIX) Their policy reserves amounted to $237 million at the end of 1962, representing 76.3 percent of their total obligations. For the industry as a whole, policy reserves totaled $108.4 bil- lion and accounted for 81.3 percent of total obligations. These reserves have been set aside to meet the life insurance companies' future obligations to policyholders and their beneficiaries. State laws require each company to maintain its policy reserves at a level sufficient to ensure payment of all policy obligations as they become due. The amount of reserves required for this purpose is calculated actuarially, taking into account the additional funds forthcoming from future premium payments and investment earnings. In 1962, the $1,644 million of life insurance in force with Negro companies were backed by policy reserves amounting to 14 percent. For all companies combined, the ratio of policy reserves to life insurance in force was 16 percent. Again the smaller ratio for Negro companies can be attributed partly to their concentration on industrial policies.

Capital stock constitutes a much larger share of the obligations of the combined Negro companies than is true for the industry as a whole. The ratios were 3.1 percent and 0.7 percent, respectively, in 1962. This clearly reflects the fact that the 12 Negro institutions which are stock companies are a far more important segment of the Negro insurance sector than is true of stock companies in the industry generally. For example, in mid-1963, there were 1,347 companies owned by stockholders, and 156 were mutual companies owned by their policyholders. However, the 156 units (only one-tenth of the total) were generally older and larger. They accounted for about 60 percent of the life insurance in force, and for about 70 percent of the assets of all life insurance companies in the United States. Among the twenty Negro companies in 1962, the twelve owned by stockholders accounted for about 51 percent of insurance in force with the group as a whole, and for around 54 percent of the assets.

Investment Behavior of Negro Life Insurance Companies

Negro life insurance companies tend to be much more conservative in their investment policies than the industry as a whole. They tend to hold relatively more cash and government bonds and a relatively smaller proportion of common stocks. The net result is that the Negro companies, as mentioned above, play a somewhat less important role (even after allowing for their small size) as sources of funds to finance long-term capital formation by private borrowers.

At the end of 1962, Negro life insurance companies held 2.8 percent of their total assets in cash, or two and one-half times the proportion for all companies. As was true of Negro banks, their cash and bond holdings made them much more liquid than other institutions. Again, as with banks, their higher liquidity ratios reflect a limited range of investment opportunities in the private business sector—especially if the company attempts to strengthen its life insurance market by lending in the Negro community. But the extra risk inherent in lending to Negro borrowers (an extra risk associated with the instability of family incomes and the uncertain conditions under which

TABLE XXX–A comparative analysis of investment portfolios of
selected life insurance companies

Rank	Name and State	Total Assets Dec. 1961 (Thousands of $)	Selected Assets as Percentage of Total Admitted Assets								Annual Growth Rate	
			Cash	Bonds		Stocks			Mortgages	Period	%
				Total	U.S. Govt.	Total	Pref'd	Common				
1	North Carolina Mutual, North Carolina	$ 71,134	1.6	58.1	3.0	6.4	0.2	6.2	24.3	1951–61	7.8
2	Atlanta Life, Georgia	56,837	1.9	73.9	20.7	6.2	1.2	5.0	11.6	1951–61	7.9
3	Supreme Life, Illinois	30,688	1.2	32.5	1.7	0.5	0.4	0.1	36.2	1951–61	9.9
	Old Republic, Illinois	30,433	35.2	46.3	21.5	4.3	None	4.3	0.5	"	17.9
4	Universal Life, Tennessee	22,496	1.8	42.5	7.3	1.3	0.9	0.4	42.6	1951–61	9.3
5	Golden State Mutual, California	18,873	3.4	28.9	1.4	3.0	0.4	2.6	45.4	1951–61	12.5
	Pierce Insurance Co., California	18,078	4.3	43.8	39.2	3.1	1.1	2.0	38.6	"	17.6
6	Chicago Metro, Illinois	15,461	1.2	52.0	5.9	None	None	None	41.1	1951–61	10.9
	Globe Life, Illinois	15,047	1.6	49.2	11.7	2.9	1.7	1.2	38.9	"	8.6
7	Mammoth Life, Kentucky	15,234	1.9	57.0	12.4	0.6	0.3	0.3	29.7	1951–61	15.7
8	Pilgrim Health, Georgia	11,790	3.5	66.9	4.3	9.2	N.A.	N.A.	12.7	1951–61	6.8
	General Fidelity, Georgia	10,316	81.7	8.8	3.0	0.1	None	0.1	None	1955–61	25.0
9	Afro-American, Florida	10,915	1.8	55.7	11.0	5.4	1.9	3.5	20.4	1951–61	6.2
	American Bankers, Florida	12,702	9.2	26.6	6.7	8.1	8.0	0.1	29.4	1952–61	40.0
10	American Woodman, Colorado	9,350	1.3	77.1	33.9	None	None	None	13.9	1951–61	3.3
	National Farmers Union, Colorado	9,920	4.0	31.6	2.1	0.1	None	0.1	27.2	"	17.0
11	Great Lakes Mutual, Michigan	8,892	4.3	67.4	10.9	1.3	1.3	None	10.8	1951–61	13.0
12	Victory Mutual, Illinois	7,408	2.8	33.8	3.3	0.9	0.8	0.1	38.0	1951–61	7.0
	Horace Mann, Illinois	7,465	7.0	46.9	14.2	6.4	3.0	3.3	23.3	"	44.0
13	United Mutual, New York	5,802	3.1	63.0	2.6	None	None	None	25.1	1951–61	9.0
14	Southern Aid, Virginia	4,005	4.1	43.7	8.0	3.6	3.6	None	42.1	1951–61	3.5
15	Booker T. Washington, Alabama	3,969	5.8	13.3	2.2	15.9	0.2	15.7	30.5	1952–61	12.9
	Loyal American, Alabama	3,486	3.8	23.6	5.0	15.4	0.8	14.7	22.1	1956–61	27.0
16	Unity Mutual, Illinois	3,000	11.1	42.1	3.0	None	None	None	39.0	1951–61	16.1
17	Virginia Mutual, Virginia	2,984	9.2	54.5	6.9	0.7	N.A.	N.A.	26.3	1954–61	7.9
	North American Assurance, Virginia	2,861	6.7	69.3	6.9	12.4	1.7	10.7	5.6	1951–61	10.4
18	Union Protective, Tennessee	1,935	10.0	25.5	13.2	None	None	None	51.7	1952–61	9.0
	American Old Line, Tennessee	1,982	48.5	35.4	35.4	None	None	None	15.1	1960–61	27.1
19	Guaranty Life, Georgia	1,631	1.1	65.3	12.0	4.4	4.0	0.4	21.4	1951–61	4.0
	Farmers National, Georgia	1,729	15.6	51.3	43.3	1.0	0.5	0.5	8.6	1959–61	55.0
20	Southern Life, Maryland	584	3.4	27.6	25.2	3.3	None	3.3	36.1	1960–61	2.1
	Industry Totals1 (Amounts in Millions of Dollars)	126,816	1.1	48.0	4.9	4.9	1.6	3.3	34.9	1951–61	6.4

1 Life Insurance Fact Book, 1963
N.A. Not Available
SOURCE: Best's Life Insurance Reports, 1962.

Negro entrepreneurs operate) is a major factor restraining the acquisition of mortgages by Negro life insurance companies.

The investments of Negro life insurance companies in 1962, grouped by broad category, are shown in Table XXVIII. These assets, as in other companies, are held primarily to meet future obligations to policyholders. But the distribution of life insurance assets also provides a fairly clear insight into the role of life insurance companies as financial intermediaries. By tracing changes in this distribution over time, it is possible to gauge their impact on the market for long-term funds.[15]

To go behind the broad contours of portfolio management in Negro-owned life insurance companies, statistics were collected for 1961, the latest year for which detailed figures were available from reliable industry sources. These statistics are shown in Table XXX. The Negro companies shown in the table are essentially the same ones included in earlier tables. However, because of differences in state investment laws, where possible each Negro company has been compared with another company of similar size in the same state.

Several broad features stand out in Table XXX. As mentioned above, the Negro-owned companies appear to be somewhat more conservative in their ownership of common stock than other companies of similar size. This is less true of other assets. Having adjusted for size of company, it appears that their cash holdings, while still high relative to the industry, are slightly lower than for other companies with comparable total assets. While Negro companies' bond holdings tend to be relatively smaller than for other companies in the same size group, the composition of their holdings varies significantly. United States Government bonds make up a somewhat smaller proportion of the portfolios of Negro companies. Instead, considerable emphasis is placed on other types of debt obligations, especially bonds sold by state and local governments. The tax-exemption of the income from these securities makes them particularly attractive to some institutions. In addition, compared with other small companies, the Negro institutions also seem to have above average commitments in mortgages—just the opposite of the situation when they were contrasted with the industry as a whole.

The conservatism of Negro-owned companies with respect to equity securities is clearly evident in their holdings of common stocks. As a rule, the ratio of common stocks to total assets in Negro-owned companies is well below the average for both the industry and other institutions of comparable size. This pattern may be related to the fact that the management of a portfolio of common stocks requires the command of an expertise

[15] See Andrew F. Brimmer, *Life Insurance Companies in the Capital Market*. East Lansing: Michigan State University, Bureau of Business and Economic Research, 1962.

which most small companies (Negro-owned companies among them) find it difficult to employ. Furthermore, the required diversification of a common stock portfolio is hard to achieve in the typical small company.

However, many small companies rely on the expert guidance of outside investment advisers to assist them in portfolio planning. A number of Negro-owned companies are among them. If more companies were to employ such advisers, common stocks could be acquired by a greater number of institutions. In limited amounts, and provided seasoned and amply diversified stocks (although not necessarily blue chip stocks) are selected, common stocks are an advantageous investment outlet for these institutions. Because of the long-term nature of their liabilities and steady cash inflow, they are seldom—if ever—forced to liquidate assets to meet claims. Thus, they are free to hold common stocks primarily as a source of income. Over a period of time, and after allowing for occasional small capital losses, common stocks can make a major contribution to building up the net earnings of life insurance companies.

It will also be noted from Table XXX that, as a rule, the rate of growth of Negro-owned companies in the decade of the 1950's was somewhat below that for other companies of comparable size. Of course, this was not universally true, because the rate of growth in several Negro-owned companies was well ahead of that for the industry as a whole.

THE FUTURE OF NEGROES IN BUSINESS

If the fields in which Negro businessmen have traditionally concentrated are less promising than in the past, what alternative opportunities are likely to appear in the future? For Negroes, as for other citizens in the business world, such opportunities are likely to be found primarily as managers and officials employed by our medium and large corporations and public enterprises. That Negroes have made little progress in this field is common knowledge. For example, in 1960, about 8 percent of the total civilian labor force of 68 million was engaged as non-farm managers, officials and proprietors. Less than 1.5 percent of the 6.6 million Negroes in the labor force were so engaged. If the percentages had been approximately equal, there would have been about 525 thousand—rather than the actual 191 thousand—Negroes in the managerial class. Furthermore, over half of the Negro managerial group was self-employed, compared with just over one-third of all managers in the country.

Thus, from these data a clear inference can be drawn: with a change in aspirations among potential Negro businessmen, better preparation on their part and a genuine commitment to equal opportunity by leaders in the corporate business community, the future could be promising for a number of Negro businessmen.

Some progress is already being made in this direction, although few corporate executives would claim that the pace has been rapid. A rough indication of the current trends is given by the experience of those companies which participate in "Plans for Progress." This is a voluntary program to expand access to jobs, operated in conjunction with the President's Committee on Equal Opportunity. In a report covering the period when the companies joined Plans for Progress through mid-July, 1964, 103 of these firms reported that their total employment increased by 300,796 or 7.6 percent. Just over two-fifths of this gain represented an expansion in white collar employment. During the same period, these companies added 40,938 employees from minority groups. This represented about 13.6 percent of the expansion in total employment. On the other hand, nonwhites filled about 11.0 percent of the increase in white collar jobs.

When these companies joined Plans for Progress, nonwhites constituted about 5 percent of their total labor force, and they represented approximately 1.2 percent of those in the managerial group. In the subsequent expansion in employment, nonwhites obtained about 3,000 (or 2 percent) of the new jobs in the management category. While this gain is obviously very small, it does represent about 1,000 more managerial and technical positions for nonwhites than might have been expected on the basis of the companies' traditional employment practice.

Simultaneously, many corporations are making a special effort to recruit and train Negroes and other minority group citizens for corporate positions. Some of this effort undoubtedly can be written off as "image-making" by some firms, who would like to point to their recruiting efforts which have —unfortunately—failed to produce "qualified" candidates. On the whole, however, the vast majority of corporate recruiters seem to be making a genuine effort to identify and to enroll promising minority group candidates. On the other hand, given the criteria which the typical corporation uses in selecting its managerial personnel, most corporate recruiters are undoubtedly finding it difficult to locate qualified personnel. The sources of these difficulties are widely known. They spring from the vicious circle created by a history of discriminatory employment practices; poor undergraduate training provided by the archaic curricula of basically segregated institutions attended by many Negro college students; a resulting peculiar pattern of occupational preferences stressing medicine, law, teaching and the ministry; a reluctance to venture into the expanding fields of business administration and related social sciences, engineering and other technical areas—which result in only marginal preparation for management careers in business.

Pattern of Corporate Demand for Nonwhite Professional Personnel

In the meantime, it may be helpful to provide a profile of the types of skills for which corporations are searching among Negroes and other minority group members. A rough outline can be sketched by an analysis of the recruiting visits which corporations are currently making on predominantly Negro college campuses. For this purpose, the experience of Howard University may be taken as a prototype. (Of course, the Howard University experience is undoubtedly biased because its curricula are most varied and its program in engineering and the physical sciences probably far surpasses that of all other predominantly Negro schools; its program in business administration also ranks high among the three or four genuine programs to be found on Negro college campuses. But, if we keep in mind these limitations of the Howard data, we can gain an insight into the types of professions demanded by corporations.)

Table XXXI summarizes the Howard University experience for the academic year 1963–64. During that period, Howard's placement office received visitors from about 160 corporations and about 20 government departments and independent agencies. These companies represented a variety of industries, but the heaviest concentration was in chemicals, transportation equipment, and communications and utilities. Among government agencies, the Defense Department was the most frequent visitor.

Together, these potential employers made more than seven hundred requests about some forty-odd occupational categories. The engineering field accounted for about two-fifths of the total, with electrical and mechanical engineering being most frequently specified. Somewhat over one-fifth of the inquiries sought graduates in the physical sciences, with chemists and physicists taking the lead. Thus, more than three-fifths of all of the requests were concentrated in the engineering and technical fields. If the closely related field of mathematics is added, about 70 percent of the total inquiries were for candidates with highly technical undergraduate training.

In contrast, requests for personnel in the field of business administration represented only 15 percent of the total. General business administration and accounting each attracted 5 percent, and marketing about 4 percent. If we add inquiries for graduates in the social sciences—which frequently serve as a pool of skills that can be reshaped for business administration purposes—the share accounted for by the business area would rise to only one-sixth of the total.

A number of inferences can be drawn from these data, but one implication seems clear: if we can generalize the Howard experience, corporations (and to some extent government agencies) have directed their recruitment efforts on Negro campuses more to the technical and scientific fields and less to those which lead directly into key managerial functions in corporate enterprise. While engineers, chemists and other technicians (with years of experience) do frequently move into positions of general management responsibility, the more likely routes through the corporate hierarchy typically begin in the nontechnical fields, such as financial administration, accounting and marketing.

Future Opportunities for Ownership

Of course, the chance to go into business for themselves is an option which will remain open to Negroes along with other citizens. However, before this option is taken up in the future, potential Negro business should give careful consideration to several factors that are rapidly reshaping the environment in which they will have to operate. While the majority of Negro businessmen are correct in assuming that (within the foreseeable future) they will have to rely primarily on Negro customers for their patronage, they apparently do not realize that in the future they will have to compete in a wholly different type of market. As mentioned above, the desegregation of places of public accommodation, such as restaurants, theaters, hotels and similar establishments, will have a serious impact on many of the sheltered businesses which most Negro businesmen have operated behind the barriers induced by segregation. With greater access to facilities provided for the public in general, Negro customers will increasingly demand that Negro businesses compete in terms of quality of services provided at competitive prices.

Further, there is a prime need to shift from the single proprietorship form of organization, which is so dominant among Negro businessmen, to the corporate form which is the key to financing business expansion. The superiority of the corporation over unincorporated enterprises as a medium for expanding business has been clearly demonstrated, and growth as opposed to stagnation has always been a measure of business health. Recent data on the distribution of firms by type of organization and the relative share of receipts and profits show that relatively few companies account for the major share of the nation's business, and these are the

TABLE XXXI–Structure of Corporate Demand for Nonwhite Professional Personnel (Illustrated by Placement Inquiries at Howard University, 1963-1964)

INDUSTRY DISTRIBUTION OF REQUESTS

Professions	TOTAL INQUIRIES		Manufacturing	Research and Development	Communications	Wholesale and Retail Trade	Financial	Business Services	Education and Social Services	Government
	Number	Percent of Total								
Engineering:	**284**	**40.4**	**165**	**17**	**5**	**2**	—	—	—	**66**
Engineer, General	99	14.1	58	5	2	2	—	—	—	24
Electrical Engineer	77	11.0	41	7	3	—	—	—	—	18
Mechanical Engineer	82	11.7	48	5	—	—	—	—	—	17
Civil Engineer	16	2.3	8	—	—	—	—	—	—	7
Chemical Engineer	6	0.9	6	—	—	—	—	—	—	—
Industrial Engineer	4	0.6	4	—	—	—	—	—	—	—
Physical Sciences:	**157**	**22.3**	**94**	**9**	**34**	**1**	—	—	—	**52**
Scientist, General	21	3.0	18	2	10	1	—	—	—	14
Chemist	50	7.1	33	2	11	—	—	—	—	18
Physicist	57	8.1	34	5	12	—	—	—	—	17
Biologist	22	3.1	5	—	1	—	—	—	—	2
Pharmacist	6	0.9	4	—	—	—	—	—	—	1
Geologist	1	0.1	—	—	—	—	—	—	—	—
Mathematician	**51**	**7.3**	**20**	**3**	**1**	—	—	—	—	**27**
Business Professions:	**106**	**15.1**	**49**	—	**1**	**20**	**9**	—	—	**17**
Business Administration, General	36	5.1	16	—	—	3	5	1	—	9
Accountants	38	5.4	21	—	—	5	5	1	—	8
Management trainees	6	0.9	—	—	—	4	2	—	—	—
Marketing, General	14	2.0	7	—	—	4	2	—	—	—
Buyers	1	0.1	—	—	—	1	—	—	—	—
Sales and Advertising	11	1.6	5	—	1	3	—	1	—	—

	Number	Percent								
Social Sciences:	19	2.7	3	—	1	2	—	—	—	13
Social Scientist, General	2	0.3	—	—	—	—	—	—	—	2
Economist	8	1.1	1	—	1	1	—	—	—	5
Statistician	7	1.0	2	—	—	1	—	—	—	4
Sociologist	1	0.1	—	—	—	—	—	—	—	1
Psychologist	1	0.1	—	—	—	—	—	—	—	1
Other Professions:	60	8.5	19	11	16	—	—	—	8	6
Liberal Arts, General	33	4.7	12	—	12	—	—	—	6	3
Lawyer	4	0.6	3	—	1	—	—	—	—	—
Home Economist	5	0.7	2	—	—	—	—	—	2	1
Religious Worker	2	0.3	—	—	2	—	—	—	—	—
Architect	2	0.3	—	—	—	—	—	—	—	2
Education—University Professor	3	0.4	—	3	—	—	—	—	—	—
Primary and Secondary Teachers	6	0.9	—	6	—	—	—	—	—	—
Social Worker	2	0.3	—	2	—	—	—	—	—	—
Medical Personnel (premed.)	3	0.4	2	—	1	—	—	—	—	—
Humanities:	6	0.9	—	—	—	—	—	1	2	3
Art	4	0.6	—	—	—	—	—	1	2	1
Music	1	0.1	—	—	—	—	—	—	—	1
Drama	1	0.1	—	—	—	—	—	—	—	1
Miscellaneous:	20	2.8	2	—	—	—	2	—	8	8
Men (unspecified)	11	1.6	1	—	—	—	—	—	4	6
Women (unspecified)	6	0.9	—	—	—	—	2	—	4	—
Recreation Workers	3	0.4	1	—	—	—	—	—	—	2
GRAND TOTAL	703	100.0	352	30	47	29	16	7	30	192
Percent of Grand Total	100.0	—	50.1	4.3	6.7	4.1	2.3	1.0	4.3	27.3
Memo: Number of Companies and Government Agencies	179	—	90	11	19	11	8	5	15	20

large and ever-growing corporations. For example, in 1960, corporations constituted about 10 percent of the total number of businesses in existence. However, the total receipts of corporations were $803 billion, representing over three-quarters of the total. Their net profits, after allowing for losses, amounted to $44 billion, or three-fifths of the total net profits of business enterprises.

But whatever form of organization a businessman chooses for his operation, several conditions must be met if success is to be realized. In the first instance, a businessman must perceive a market for a product or service. Next, steps must be taken to translate this idea into a practical production process. Thirdly, technical and managerial know-how must be sufficient to establish and conduct an enterprise. Financial resources, especially equity capital, must be available or acquired. A skilled labor force must exist or must be trained. Finally, the businessman must possess enough marketing know-how to find and maintain customers in the face of competition from other products and services. As we all know, the typical Negro-owned firm is deficient in all or most of these vital requirements.

While there is no shortage of potential Negro businessmen, there is a severe shortage of technical know-how outside the traditional areas of trade and personal services. This lack of mastery over technical requirements may well be an obstacle as great as the lack of equity capital. To help fill this gap, a number of economic development and business service centers (including centers at Atlanta University and Howard University) were established in 1964. The objectives of these projects include:

—The provision of technical and management assistance to establish or expand businesses, particularly those that are Negro-owned or managed and have a preponderance of Negro employees.

—The provision of technical training and services to groups and communities, particularly Negro, in the field of economic development which will enable them to take a more active role in the creation of new enterprises and new job opportunities.

Such centers could become the locus of the kind of economic and technical research and guidance so necessary for economic development and successful business enterprise. Finally, they would provide for both students and faculty exposure to the variety and complexity of managerial problems with which virtually every future businessman must deal.

The above observations focus on only a few of the growing opportunities for Negro businessmen to participate in the future growth of the country. Above all, there will undoubtedly be a variety of ventures engaged in the production and distribution of goods and services for the community as a whole. Moreover, there will undoubtedly be growing opportunities for Negroes to participate in the management activities of large corporations which are also oriented to the general market. It should be emphasized again that desegregation of the marketplace which is already well under way will require desegregation in the ownership and management of business enterprises as well. While the future of a segregated Negro-owned business, existing in a segregated market, appears not to be bright, the future of Negroes in the business life of the country in general does appear to be more promising than ever before.

SUMMARY AND CONCLUSIONS

The principal conclusions reached in this chapter have been stated at the end of each section. However, the highlights can be summarized here. The basic theme is this:

General Position of the Negro in the Economy

Segregation has created a dual market for personal services in the United States. This in turn has created a Negro subsector of the national economy. This is the foundation of Negro business and of the Negro middle class.

Income of the Negro Community

Trends in personal income, the best overall indicator of economic well-being, suggest that Negroes as a group have shared in the long period of post-war prosperity along with the rest of the economy. However, both business cycles and the relative slowdown of the economy in the decade of the 1950's affected nonwhites considerably more adversely than the country at large. The net result was that Negroes made little progress in closing the income gap between themselves and the rest of the population. In 1947 the median income of nonwhite families was 51 percent of that of white families; in 1963 the ratio was still only 53 percent.

Within the Negro community, unlike the country at large, the distribution of income has become more unequal in the post-war period. Middle class Negroes have greatly improved their relative position during the last one and a half decades. But those at the bottom of the income ladder experienced some deterioration. In 1947, the lowest fifth of the nonwhite population received 4.8 percent of the aggregate family income; by 1960 their share had dropped to 3.9 percent. Among white families, the lowest fifth received 5.5 percent and 5.3 percent in 1947 and 1960, respectively.

Thus, the relative deterioration was much sharper for nonwhite families.

This deterioration in the position of the lowest nonwhite income group both reflects and contributes to the lingering poverty among Negroes in America. By almost any standard, poverty is the normal state of existence of most Negroes. Using the rough benchmark of $3,000 as a rough poverty line, Negroes are about two and one-half times more likely than white families to be found among the poor. While about one-fifth of the nation's 47.4 million families are poor, 43 percent (or 2.1 million) of the 4.8 million nonwhite families are poor.

At the opposite end of the income scale, the Negro community can claim only a handful of millionaires. But it can boast of a fairly large and growing number of prosperous families and individuals. For example, in 1963 approximately 274,000 nonwhite families had incomes of $10,000 or more. Between 1959 and 1963 the number of nonwhite families in the $10,000-and-over group rose by about 50 percent compared with 40 percent for all families. However, a much larger proportion of the nonwhite families than of white families in the higher income brackets depend on the earnings of two or more workers.

While racial discrimination clearly imposes a severe burden on the nation's economy, its economic costs have been difficult to assess. However, using the differential in education and occupation distribution between the whites and nonwhite, a rough estimate was made of this cost in terms of lost gross national product (GNP). The general findings are: if the present educational achievement of nonwhites were fully utilized, GNP would rise by 1.9 percent. If educational levels were equalized, GNP would rise further by 1.6 percent. Translated into the value of output, these percentage gains imply an increase of $11 billion and $9 billion, respectively, or a total increase of $20 billion, based on a GNP of $585 billion in 1963.

Consumer Expenditures and the Negro Market

An examination of trends in consumer expenditures shows a rapid conversion of Negro and white consumption patterns. With rising incomes, Negro families are spending proportionately more on goods and services typically purchased by middle-class consumers and proportionately less on the basic necessities to which low-income groups are restricted. Similarly, the erosion of segregation and discrimination is providing Negroes with greater access to places of public accommodation, and their expenditure pattern reflects this change.

But these shifting consumption patterns are also effecting drastic changes in the Negro market. Salesmen and other middle men who have earned their livelihood through developing the traditional Negro market are progressing more slowly than those who have detected the emerging trends and have moved into new channels of distribution.

Negroes as Entrepreneurs

Under the same set of dynamic forces, the Negro business sector is also changing rapidly. Since racial segregation has served Negro businessmen as a protective tariff, the decline of segregation is affecting them in the same way a reduction in a tariff affects domestic industry. In general, Negro businessmen have concentrated on providing a variety of personal services which were unavailable to Negroes from establishments catering to the public at large. In those areas in which Negro consumers have relatively free access to retail establishments (such as department stores, hardware, furnishings and similar outlets), Negro businessmen have not found fertile soil. On the other hand, in those areas where segregation has provided a shield (such as restaurants, barber shops, hotels, undertaker establishments, etc.), Negro businessmen in the past have made their greatest gains. They have made little headway in construction, transportation, public utilities, and similar fields. In manufacturing, which typically requires large investments of capital and a wide market, few Negro-owned enterprises exist. The few exceptions are principally cosmetic firms which produce for the segregated market provided by Negro barber and beauty shops. However, even these firms are beginning to feel the impact of competition from large nation-wide manufacturing enterprises who recognize the expanding market based on rising Negro incomes. In recent years, however, the number of Negro businessmen has been expanding in relatively new fields, such as automobile repair and service stations and automotive distribution. Gains have also been registered in a variety of business services.

The field of banking and finance has not been a growth area for Negroes. While they own or control about twenty banks, fifty-odd insurance companies, and thirty-odd federally insured savings and loan associations, these institutions combined hold only about 0.12 percent of the total assets held by these financial intermediaries in the nation at large. However, the Negro banks do serve two useful purposes: their presence and the potential competition this implies induce the large white-controlled banks to be more liberal in considering the credit needs of the Negro borrower. They also provide a marginal amount of funds to meet the requirements of Negro businessmen and home buyers. In general, the Negro banks appear to hold a higher percent of liquid assets than do other banks of the same size. While their operations seem to be basically similar to those conducted by other institutions, there are differences derived from lending to borrowers

exposed to inherently greater risks. But by modifying their lending practices, Negro banks have been able to achieve loss ratios which are actually
below those of other banks of comparable size. Nevertheless, Negro banks
tend to have lower rates of profit than banks in general.

Life insurance companies represent the classic example of Negro businesses which have grown up behind the walls of segregation. Beginning in
the 1880's, most leading life insurance companies either refused to sell
coverage to Negroes or did so on the basis of separate mortality tables
which meant higher costs. These discriminatory practices provided Negroes
with the opportunity and incentive to meet the insurance demands of
Negro citizens. The growth of Negro life insurance companies has been
based primarily on sales of industrial insurance which accounts for about
two-thirds of their business. In contrast, ordinary insurance is the backbone
of the nation's life insurance industry, representing about three-fifths of the
total amount of life insurance in force. Because of the high incidence of
poverty among Negroes, industrial insurance (sold in small amounts by
door-to-door salesmen who collect premiums on even a weekly basis) was
virtually the only type of insurance which the typical Negro family could
afford. With the rise in income, Negro families are becoming attractive
prospects for the large national insurance companies. In fact, they are
increasingly employing Negro salesmen to facilitate penetration of the
Negro market.

As financial institutions, Negro life insurance companies tend to be
quite conservative, and they hold relatively more liquid assets than other
companies. Partly because of the inherently greater risks of lending to low-
income Negro borrowers seeking to purchase homes or to small Negro
businessmen, Negro life insurance companies hold a lower percentage of
mortgages than do companies in the industry at large. Instead, they concentrate more heavily on bonds—especially on state and local government
issues, the income from which is exempt from Federal income taxes. But
with some liberalization in portfolio management (particularly the acquisition of more common stocks), life insurance companies could greatly
improve their investment position. While Negro insurance companies will
undoubtedly continue to exist, their future prospects will be dampened by
the continued competition from the large companies. This clearly suggests
that the Negro institutions may have to turn increasingly to the larger
market beyond the Negro community.

The Future of Negroes in Business

Since the fields in which Negro businessmen have traditionally served
are less promising than in the past, they must look for other opportunities.

For Negroes as for other citizens in the business world, such opportunities are likely to be found primarily as managers and officials employed by our medium and large corporations and public enterprises. While Negroes have made some progress in the executive suite, the gains are exceptionally modest compared with their progress in other areas of the economy. In an effort to remedy this situation, a number of corporations are attempting to recruit promising Negro college graduates. However, it appears that so far the main focus has been on technical fields (such as engineering, chemistry, physics, mathematics and other hard sciences) in which the number of Negro graduates remains relatively small. In contrast, the typical white entrant into corporations at the management level is employed as a management trainee. Moreover, he is recruited from a variety of fields which are predominantly nontechnical. These include business administration, economics and the other social sciences. It is precisely in these latter fields that the majority of Negro college graduates are found. Thus it appears evident that the future opportunities for Negroes in the corporation will depend heavily on the willingness of corporations to modify their recruitment practices. Simultaneously, however, these opportunities will also depend on substantial upgrading in the quality of training received by Negro college graduates—a predominant number of which still attend largely segregated Negro institutions.

Of course, the chances to go into business for themselves is an option which will remain open to Negroes along with other citizens. But in electing this option, Negroes will have to give careful consideration to the changing environment in which they must operate in the future if they wish to succeed. No longer will segregation provide relative security for ventures into traditional types of business. With the desegregation of places of public accommodation, Negro businessmen in these traditional fields will have to weather the competition of firms serving the community as a whole. Secondly, there is a prime need for Negro businessmen to adopt the corporate form of organization. Traditionally, the typical Negro enterprise has been a single proprietorship or a partnership owned by members of the same family. This arrangement has imposed several limitations on the development of managerial talents and the mobilization of financial resources to underwrite expansion. The corporation is an excellent instrument to overcome these handicaps.

While there is no shortage of potential Negro businessmen, there is a severe shortage of technical know-how outside the traditional areas of retail trade and personal services. This lack of mastery over technical requirements may well be an obstacle as great as the lack of equity capital —which has long been recognized as a basic problem facing Negro businessmen along with all other small entrepreneurs. In 1964 a number of economic development and business service centers (including centers at Atlanta University and Howard University) were established to help fill this gap. With the acquisition of greater technical know-how, and with the increased availability of credit which is coming about, there will be growing opportunity for Negro businessmen to participate in the future growth of the country. But it should be emphasized again that desegregation of the marketplace which is already well under way will require desegregation in the ownership and management of business enterprises as well.

TECHNICAL NOTE 1.

Calculation of Nonwhite Labor Force Data, 1948–1953

The U.S. Bureau of Labor Statistics has not published nonwhite labor force figures for years prior to 1954. The estimates shown in this chapter were calculated in the following manner:

Multiply the total number [1] of nonwhite males and females over fourteen years of age, excluding military, by the labor force participation rates [2] for the individual years. The products, added together, will give an approximation of the total nonwhite, civilian noninstitutionalized labor force. The unemployment figures are derived by multiplying the estimated total labor force figure by the published unemployment rates.[3] Subtract this estimated number employed. The results are shown below:

Estimated Nonwhite Labor Force Data, 1948–53
(Thousands)

Year	Estimated Labor Force	Estimated Employment	Estimated Unemployment
1948	6,891	6,533	358
1949	7,011	6,436	575
1950	7,006	6,411	595
1951	6,936	6,603	333
1952	6,997	6,675	322
1953	6,921	6,637	284

[1] U.S. Department of Commerce, Bureau of the Census, *Current Population Reports,* Series P–25, No. 98, Table 2; *Current Population Reports,* Series P–25, No. 265, Table A–3 and Table 3; *Current Population Reports,* P–25, No. 276, Table 3.

[2] U.S. Department of Labor, *Manpower Report of the President,* March, 1964, Table A–3, p. 197.

[3] U.S. Department of Labor, *Manpower Report of the President,* March, 1964, Table A–10, p. 201.

TECHNICAL NOTE 2.

Estimation of the Economic Cost of Racial Discrimination

1. *Estimation of the gain in gross national product (GNP) resulting from using more fully the* present *educational achievement of nonwhites.*

In making this estimate, the U.S. Bureau of the Census used income data from the 1950 and 1960 Census of Population. For each age-sex group, the mean income of nonwhites was changed to equal the mean income of whites reporting the same number of years of school completed. These calculations provided the percentage increase in total money income shown in Column (1) of Table A. In the second step, the wage or salary component (including supplements) of GNP was raised by the percentage increase in total money income; the results are shown in columns (2) and (3). In the third step, the entrepreneurial component of GNP was raised by one half the percentage increase in wage or salary income. Columns (4) and (5) show the results. In the final step, columns (2) and (4) were combined to produce columns (6) and (7), showing, respectively, the total amount and percentage increase in GNP.

The 1950 Census relationships were applied to the GNP figures for the years 1949 through 1954; the 1960 Census relationships were applied to the GNP figures for the years 1955 through 1963.

TABLE A—Estimates of Gain in GNP Based on the Assumption that the Present Educational Achievement of Nonwhites is Fully Used: 1949 to 1963 (Absolute numbers in billions of dollars)

Year	Percent Increase in Total Money Income	Applied to Compensation of Employees (wages)		Applied to entrepreneurial Income (other than wages)		Total Increase in the Gross National Product	
		Added Amount	Percent Increase	Added Amount	Percent Increase	Added Amount	Percent Increase
1963	2.4	$8.2	2.4	$2.9	1.2	$11.1	1.9
1962	2.4	7.8	2.4	2.8	1.2	10.6	1.9
1961	2.4	7.3	2.4	2.6	1.2	9.9	1.9
1960	2.4	7.0	2.4	2.5	1.2	9.5	1.9
1959	2.4	6.7	2.4	2.5	1.2	9.2	1.9
1958	2.4	6.2	2.4	2.2	1.2	8.4	1.9
1957	2.4	6.1	2.4	2.2	1.2	8.3	1.9
1956	2.4	5.8	2.4	2.1	1.2	7.9	1.9
1955	2.4	5.4	2.4	2.1	1.2	7.5	1.9
1954	3.1	6.4	3.1	2.4	1.6	8.8	2.4
1953	3.1	6.5	3.1	2.4	1.6	8.9	2.4
1952	3.1	6.0	3.1	2.4	1.6	8.4	2.4
1951	3.1	5.6	3.1	2.3	1.6	7.9	2.4
1950	3.1	4.8	3.1	2.0	1.6	6.8	2.4
1949	3.1	4.4	3.1	1.8	1.6	6.2	2.4

2. *Estimation of the gain in gross national product from using the* potential *contributions of nonwhites by raising their educational level to that of whites.*

The calculation is based on the Census Bureau's "Current Population Survey" data for each year. First, the mean income of nonwhite families was changed to equal the mean income of white families, and the mean income of nonwhite unrelated individuals was changed to equal that of white unrelated individuals. Next, the increase in GNP was obtained in the same manner as described above. The results are shown in Table B.

TABLE B—Estimates of Gain in GNP Based on the Assumption that the Achievement of Nonwhites is the Same as That of Whites: 1949 to 1963 (Absolute numbers in billions of dollars)

Year	Percent Increase in Total Money Income	Applied to Compensation of Employees (wages)		Applied to entrepreneurial Income (other than wages)		Total Increase in the Gross National Product	
		Added Amount	Percent Increase	Added Amount	Percent Increase	Added Amount	Percent Increase
1963	4.4	$15.0	4.4	$5.4	2.2	$20.4	3.5
1962	4.5	14.5	4.5	5.2	2.3	19.7	3.6
1961	4.3	13.0	4.3	4.6	2.2	17.6	3.4
1960	4.2	12.3	4.2	4.4	2.1	16.7	3.3
1959	4.5	12.5	4.5	4.6	2.3	17.1	3.5
1958	4.2	10.8	4.2	3.9	2.1	14.7	3.3
1957	4.3	11.0	4.3	4.0	2.2	15.0	3.4
1956	4.3	10.4	4.3	3.8	2.2	14.2	3.4
1955	4.3	9.6	4.3	3.7	2.2	13.3	3.3
1954	4.3	8.9	4.3	3.3	2.2	12.2	3.4
1953	4.1	8.6	4.1	3.2	2.1	11.8	3.2
1952	4.4	8.6	4.4	3.3	2.2	11.9	3.4
1951	4.5	8.1	4.5	3.3	2.3	11.4	3.5
1950	4.6	7.1	4.6	3.0	2.3	10.1	3.5
1949	4.7	6.6	4.7	2.8	2.4	9.4	3.6

chapter 6

The Urban Negro Family

Joseph H. Douglass

Introduction *

Today, as a result of large-scale urbanization, the Negro family [1] in the United States is in the process of transition. In their earliest experiences in the United States, Negroes were concentrated in rural areas, placed in the lowest rungs of the socio-economic ladder, rendering service as slaves or indentured servants. Over the years, however, the Negro family has come increasingly to approximate general American family patterns, becoming more urban and less identified with agricultural pursuits or with non-urban jobs in sawmills, turpentine plants and the like.

Growth and mobility have been characteristic of the population of the United States in general and of the Negro group in particular. For the past two decades the Negro population has been increasing at a significantly faster rate than has the white. The 1960 census showed nearly 20.5 million nonwhites in the United States. As of 1962 Negroes constituted approximately 12 percent of the total population.[2] Six states now have a Negro population in excess of one million. Outside the Deep South, the Negro population has increased fivefold since 1910, nearly tripling since 1940. Part of this expansion has come from natural increase and part from the movement of Negroes from the South to other regions.

* The author wishes to acknowledge with grateful appreciation the assistance of his friend and colleague, Dr. Israel Light, in the preparation of this paper.

[1] The family, as such, hardly existed for Negroes during at least two-thirds of their history in this country; and matriarchal aspects of family organization, which are so prominent in Negro families, were largely an outgrowth of the institution of slavery. The slave had no property rights, no rights as a human being before the law, no legal recognition of marriage, no recognition of lineage. The only group tradition was that of bondage. Roots of the Negro family have been grounded in a strong maternal affiliation because it was the mother who provided such nurturing of the young as was possible in a slave society. Vestigial evidence of this matriarchal form continues to the present day.

[2] U.S. Department of Health, Education, and Welfare, *Trends*, (Washington, D.C.: Government Printing Office, 1963 edition) p. 27.

Fifty years ago approximately three-fourths of the Negro population lived in areas classified as rural; now the order is reversed.[3] Now three out of four Negro families live in the city.

Negroes have not only left the South; they have left the farms also. The heaviest movements between 1950 and 1960 were out of the states of Mississippi, Alabama and South Carolina and into the urban centers in California, New York, and Illinois.[4] Within the South itself Negroes have been moving to the cities; apparently the city, no matter where it is, is believed to hold greater opportunities.

In the decade 1950–60 there were dramatic shifts in the color composition of the population in metropolitan areas. In each of the fifty largest cities in conterminous United States there were higher proportions of Negroes in 1960 than ten years earlier.

Although all of the country's largest cities had a higher proportion of nonwhites in 1960 than in 1950, the reasons for this distribution varied. In each of the largest Northeastern cities, and in all but two of the largest sixteen cities in the North Central region, the changing balance between color groups was due to losses in the number of whites. The outward flow of whites and the influx of nonwhites to these cities represented a sharpening of a trend which had been in process for a considerable period. In thirteen of the fifty largest cities, however, both whites and nonwhites increased in absolute numbers; in these cities the rise in the proportion of nonwhites reflected both a more rapid natural increase as compared to whites as well as in-migration of nonwhites.[*]

The experience of the South is in sharp contrast to that of the other regions, as over six out of every ten Southern metropolitan areas showed lower proportions of nonwhites in 1960 than in the previous ten years. These Southern communities have become progressively more "white" during the last decade.

Central City Concentration of Negro Population

Negro families in urban areas have gravitated into the "core" or "central city." In 1960 some 10.3 million, or slightly more than half the nonwhite population, lived in central city—a gain of 63 percent over 1950. In the

[3] Tobia Bressler, "Some Population Trends Involving and Affecting the Negro—Implications." Address, Association of Social Science Teachers, Nashville, Tennessee, March 22, 1962.

[4] U.S. Housing and Home Finance Agency, *Our Nonwhite Population and its Housing: The Changes Between 1950 and 1960*, (Washington, D.C.: Government Printing Office, July, 1963).

[*] For an extended discussion of this point see Karl and Alma Taeuber, "The Negro Population in the United States," earlier in this volume.

nation's 212 Standard Metropolitan Statistical Areas 78 percent of non-whites lived in the central cities, with only 22 percent in the suburbs; 52 percent of whites lived outside of the central cities. Only in the South do more whites live in central cities than in the suburbs.

The increased urbanization of Negro families has not extended to the suburbs. Only one in five Negroes in the Standard Metropolitan Areas in the United States live in the suburbs. In contrast one half of the whites live in the suburbs.

White families as they have become affluent have looked to the suburbs as an area where they can achieve what to them represents the highest living standards America offers. Some Negro families with the same aspirations as the white suburban families have found a place in the suburbs. Their proportion to the total Negro population, however, is smaller than is the case for white families; even though they often have the means to buy better homes outside the heart of the city, they are unable to do so largely for reasons of racial prejudice. Thus more and more Negro families —poor and better off—have been squeezed together in central city ghettoes irrespective of the wide social distance between them.[5] More and more in the use of such public facilities as parks, hospitals, schools, etc., their geographical separation has led to *de facto* segregation of increasing intensity. One glaring example of this is Washington, D.C., where effective racial exclusion of Negroes from the suburbs has resulted in a city school system with a school population 83 percent Negro.

Family Characteristics

In the city the Negro family is retaining many of the primary group characteristics of rural families. Nonwhite households contained a larger proportion of children in 1960 than white households. The Negro households had more than three times as many grandchildren living with grandparents as white households in 1950; by 1960 this proportion had become five times as large. Although the percentage of lodgers in nonwhite households was sharply reduced in the 1950's, it was still twice as large in 1960 as that in white households.

Nonwhite women who married averaged more children per woman than white women of the same status, but the amount of the difference was affected by the large number of children born, the proportion of nonwhite

[5] U.S. Housing and Home Finance Agency, op. cit., p. 3. This report goes on to state, "As the examination into the housing condition of the nonwhites will demonstrate, the failure of many nonwhite families to move into suburban communities was not necessarily due to a preference for the central city environment. Rather it reflected a lack of housing available to them in most suburban areas."

women with five or more children being much larger than that of white women.

During the 1950's the marriage rate for nonwhites also showed a reverse pattern to that of the white population, with an increase in the percentage single, and a decrease in the percentage married, for the decade.

Nonwhite women become widows at an earlier age than white women. About 20 percent of all nonwhite females between fourteen and thirty-five years of age, as compared with 6.9 percent of white females of the same age group, were widows in 1960.[6]

The nonwhite population has substantially higher percentages of divorced persons; in the proportion of those separated the percentage of nonwhite separated males is more than five times, and of females more than six times, that of the corresponding white population. These figures, however, do not give a complete picture of the greater tendency of nonwhite marriages to break up, because death contributes in considerable measure to the difference between whites and nonwhites in the number of broken family units.

Thus, while nonwhite families were slightly less than 10 percent of all families in 1960, they were only 8 percent of families with both husband and wife present in the home. They represented 21.0 percent of all families with a female head.[7] While one in eleven white families was headed by a female, one in five nonwhite families had a female head.

Educational Attainment

Gains have been made during the past two decades in reducing the educational gap between Negroes and whites. By 1962 the average white person twenty-five to twenty-nine years of age had completed 12.5 years of schooling compared with 11.2 years by the average nonwhite person. For nonwhite men this represented a gain of some four and one-half years of school since 1940; for whites the average gain was two years.[8] The narrowing of the educational gap can be attributed largely to the increased number of Negro youth who have enrolled in school.[9]

At the elementary school level, the differential has been markedly re-

[6] G. Franklin Edwards, "Marriage and Family Life Among Negroes." *The Journal of Negro Education Yearbook*, XXXII (Fall, 1963). Washington, D.C.: The Howard University Press.) p. 451.

[7] Edwards, *ibid.*

[8] Robert G. Goodwin, *America Is For Everybody* (U.S. Department of Labor, Bureau of Employment Security, Washington, D.C.: Government Printing Office, 1963).

[9] Cognizance should be taken of the observation that despite the increasing rate of educational attainment by Negroes, there continues to be significant variance in the quality of education obtained in various sections of the United States.

duced as practically all children of elementary school age were in school in 1961.[10] At the high school level, however, the percentage of nonwhites attending school was appreciably below that of white students.[11]

Proportionately fewer Negroes than whites go to college, although by 1960, approximately 40 percent of the nonwhite population had acquired some high school or college education, compared to 62 percent of the white population.[12] The number of Negro college graduates is rising at a faster rate than the overall increase in the total nonwhite population.

Educating any child in a central city environment always presents difficult school problems. These problems are usually more acute for the Negro child. Holsey observes that "One has only to listen to children's tragic expressions on how they feel about belonging to a discriminated against minority group to know the bitterness it engenders." Repeated blows to self-esteem unquestionably interfere with the ability to learn.[13]

As a consequence of barriers to learning, school dropouts have become a serious problem for Negro families.[14] As an example, Negroes constituted 20 percent of the 350,000 youth, sixteen to twenty-four years old, who left school between January and mid-October of 1961. Many of these failed to get jobs; and 80 percent of Negroes who did find employment were working in unskilled laboring or service jobs, compared with 45 percent of the employed white dropouts.[15]

As Holsey points out, the parents of such children frequently are emotionally and materially deprived. In speaking of Negro parents she states:

> Many of them . . . have sunk into despair because they are cut off from the mainstream of opportunity in our society. Many had their origins in a very

[10] Marion Hayes, "A Century of Change—Negroes in U.S. Economy 1860–1960." *Monthly Labor Review*, U.S. Department of Labor (December, 1962).

[11] U.S. Department of Commerce, Bureau of Census, *Current Population Reports, Population Characteristics*, Series P–20, No. 115 (Washington, D.C.: Government Printing Office, February 7, 1962).

[12] Goodwin, *op. cit.*

[13] Eleanor Holsey, "Culturally Deprived Children in Day-Care Programs." *Children*, 10, No. 5 (September–October, 1963). Dr. Carl F. Hansen, Superintendent of Schools, Washington, D.C., writes in the *Washington Post*, October 27, 1963: "In the cultural Siberia in which many Negro children live, they acquire too little that is educationally helpful before they come to school, and as a result teachers must supply many of the experiences and learnings which children should get as a matter of course in home and family life. The wonder is, then, that so many of the Negro children who have had so little in their homes have gained so much in school. . . ."

[14] Added difficulties which school dropouts will face are discussed in recent studies by the Department of Labor's Bureau of Labor Statistics. See "Employment of High School Graduates and Dropouts in 1961." *Monthly Labor Review* (May, 1962), and "Out of School Youth" February 1963, Parts I and II reprinted from the *Monthly Labor Review* November and December, 1964 (Reprints 2448 and 2452).

[15] Goodwin, *op. cit.*

different kind of life than the life they are faced with in the crowded core of a great metropolis . . . a few apparently do not care what happens to their children or get their satisfactions from victimizing them.[16]

Labor Force Participation

In the beginning of the Negro shift to the city the principal job opportunities open to them as well as the kinds of jobs they were prepared to hold down were unskilled and low paid. This pattern was similar to that experienced by European migrants to the United States at the turn of the century. But unlike the white European, the Negro families did not, for a complex of reasons, escape in large numbers from their occupational ghetto.

It was not until the World War II period and after that there developed wider occupational distribution in the employment patterns for Negroes. Despite the gradual movement of nonwhite workers into higher skilled and better paying jobs, great differentials still persist between them and white workers. Although professional and clerical occupations have provided a major source of both white and nonwhite employment growth since the mid-1950's, Negroes continue to be overrepresented in such occupations as domestic servants, laborers, and semiskilled operatives. Nonwhites are still seven times as likely as white workers to be employed as private household workers (including maids, babysitters, housekeepers, chauffeurs, laundresses). Less than 5 percent of nonwhites were employed as managers, officials, proprietors and sales workers in 1962, whereas the proportion of white workers in these occupations in 1962 was almost 20 percent.[17]

The educational lag of Negroes is clearly reflected in the types of occupations most common to the two races in 1960. The U.S. Department of Labor continues to report that educational and training specifications for jobs in today's labor market underscore the poor education, inadequate training and low skills of many Negro workers. The gap is steadily widening between Negro worker qualifications and hiring requirements, particularly in those occupations with a growing demand for workers.

Goodwin, for example, writes:

Many Negro families are trapped in what can only be called a vicious circle: Job discrimination and lack of educational opportunity or educational quality limit their employment opportunities and result in low and unstable incomes. Low incomes, combined with discrimination, reduce attainable

---

[16] Holsey, *op. cit.*

[17] Matthew A. Kessler, "Economic Status of Nonwhite Workers 1955–62." *Monthly Labor Review*, Preprint No. 2419, U.S. Department of Labor, July, 1963.

levels of health and skills, and thus limit occupational choice and income in the future. And limited job opportunities result in limited availability of education and apprenticeship training, thus completing the circle.[18]

In the urban population where approximately 23 percent of the white workers are in professional, technical, or management positions, roughly only 8 percent of the nonwhites are similarly employed. Among the skilled craftsmen the ratio of whites employed—14 percent—is double that for nonwhites, 7 percent.

In addition, nonwhite workers of both sexes are less frequently employed at full-time jobs than white workers, are about twice as likely as whites to have reduced workweeks, and about five times as likely as the white worker to face under-employment.[19] Related to this is the fact that Negroes also tend to have a somewhat larger number of wage earners per family unit and higher rates of labor force participation than whites. Reflecting the heavy concentration of Negro women in household service occupations, about 30 percent of the nonwhite married women in the labor force in March, 1960, were part-time workers, compared with only about 20 percent of white married women.

Nonwhite workers are subject also to more frequent periods of unemployment. About three of every ten nonwhite men who had been unemployed sometime during the year were subject to three periods or more of unemployment in 1961, compared with two of every ten white men who had some employment. Moreover, nonwhite workers spend a considerably longer period of time on layoff or looking for work between jobs.

Nonwhite married women are more likely to be in the work force than white married women, regardless of the presence and age of children or income of husband. Approximately two-fifths of all white women twenty-

---

[18] Goodwin, *op. cit.*

[19] Robert L. Stein and Jane L. Meredith, "Growth and Characteristics of the Part-Time Work Force, No. 10." *Monthly Labor Review*, Reprint No. 2356, U.S. Department of Labor (November, 1960). Margaret L. Plunkett observes that "The proportion of Negro men with some college education who work in comparatively low-paying service and laborer jobs is almost five times greater than for whites. Among the least educated (no high school) 34 percent of nonwhite men work as nonfarm laborers compared with only 10 percent of whites with a similar educational level.

"The same general situation applied to Negro women who work. Ten percent of Negro women who have gone to college work as domestics compared with about one percent of other college women. About 44 percent of white women who have attended high school become office workers of various kinds compared with only 12 percent of nonwhite women. Almost two-thirds of the Negro high school group work as domestics or in other types of service jobs as against only 17 percent in the comparably educated white group." See U.S. Senate, 86th Congress, 2nd session, Special Committee on Unemployment Problems, *Studies in Unemployment* (Washington, D.C.: Government Printing Office, 1960), p. 89.

five to sixty-four were in the labor force in 1962, compared with nearly three-fifths of nonwhite women of the same ages.[20]

Nonwhite boys and girls fourteen to nineteen years of age evidence one of the highest jobless rates of any age-color group. In 1962 the unemployment rate of nonwhite teenagers remained near 25 percent, compared with about 12 percent for white youth. Since 1955, the jobless rate of nonwhite teenagers has increased faster than that of white youngsters—up to about 60 percent among nonwhites compared with a 30 percent rise for white youth.

Income

The nature of the labor force participation of Negro family members has a direct bearing on income. The great disparity in income distribution between Negroes and whites is indicated in the following table.[21]

TABLE I—Relative Income Groups: Nonwhite—White

Income	Percent families	
	Nonwhite	White
Less than $4,000	60	26
$6,000–$14,999	19	47
More than $15,000	1	5

SOURCE: U.S. Department of Commerce, Bureau of the Census, *Current Population Reports, Consumer Income,* Series P–60, No. 41, October 21, 1963. See especially Tables 1 and 16.

Housing

Negro families are concentrated in the low rent areas of the larger cities and housing is one of the most critical aspects of the socio-economic status of Negro families. More than any other variable it symbolizes for many Negroes their "have-not" status.

[20] Kessler, *op. cit.* John Hope states that "Although a greater share of nonwhite girls are participants at ages 14, 15, and 16 than are white girls, at ages 17 to 23 a larger proportion of white girls is in the labor force. This may be explained by the fact that white girls have more job opportunities at these ages, and because nonwhite girls marry earlier than white girls. At age 20 the rate for white women decreased while that of nonwhite women continued to rise, reaching a maximum of 48 to 49 percent at ages 35 to 44 years." See U.S. Senate, 86th Congress, 2nd session, Special Committee on Unemployment Problems, *Studies in Unemployment* (Washington, D.C.: Government Printing Office, 1960), p. 175.

[21] The relatively low nonwhite median income in 1962 reflects in part the fact that

Out of the 3.7 million nonwhite families who moved between 1950 and 1960, only 23 percent moved into units built during that decade. By contrast, out of 19 million white families, 58 percent moved into a house or apartment built between 1950 and 1960.[22]

Thus "Negro districts" commonly are in the slum areas adjacent to the central business and older sections of the city abandoned by the white population. This concentration of Negro families in central cities reflects not only economic necessity but also the lack of open occupancy in new suburban housing.

Crowding

Within urban areas nonwhite households have an average of 3.63 persons versus 3.13 for white households. The HHFA data indicate that (with some variations) between 1950 and 1960 a better matching of nonwhite families with housing units gave more of them increased space by 1960. Yet, the number of overcrowded units among nonwhite families increased by more than a quarter over the decade from nearly one million in 1950 to 1.3 million in 1960, while the number of overcrowded white families decreased by almost a quarter or about 0.2 million.

The contrast between white and nonwhite families is sharper in reference to seriously overcrowded units; among nonwhites these decreased from 18 to 13 percent, but among whites they fell from 4.3 to 2.4 percent.

While the rents paid by nonwhite tenants and the value of homes owned by nonwhites more than doubled between 1950 and 1960, they were still far below comparable figures for housing occupied by white families. The lower level of rents and values reflects the poorer quality of much of the housing available to Negro families. Because of limitations in the availability of housing, the rents and values of units occupied by Negroes often run well above the costs at which houses of comparable quality can be obtained by white families. Although Negroes have improved their home ownership position, increasing from 35 percent in 1950 to 38 percent in 1960, the improvement was not as great as that of white householders where the proportion of owners increased from 57 to 64 percent.

---

about one-half of nonwhite families still live in the South where average family income is relatively low for both the white and nonwhite populations. For regions outside the South, this ratio was about two-thirds in 1962, whereas for the South it was less than one-half.

[22] Unless otherwise noted, the data on housing are from U.S. Housing and Home Finance Agency (HHFA) materials, *op. cit.*

Mortality[23]

Since the turn of the century the mortality rate among nonwhites has been reduced more than half; but compared with mortality rates of the total population, those of the nonwhites continue to be excessive at nearly all age levels. In 1960 mortality rates of the nonwhites were 1.5 or more times as high as those of the total population during early childhood and the period twenty to sixty-four years of age. The Negro infant mortality rate in 1960 exceeded that in the total population by 66 percent (compared with an excess of 52 percent in 1950.)[24]

Today both Negroes and whites may expect to live longer than in previous years. Since 1900, life expectancy has increased by more than twenty years for the total population and by about thirty years for non-whites.[25] In 1960 the average expectation of life at birth in the United States was 63.6 years for the nonwhite group and 69.7 years for the total population, a difference of 6.1 years, in contrast to a differential of 7.4 years in 1950. The recent increase in the proportion to the total population is due to the drop in the Negro death rate as well as the increasing birth rate. Hayes [26] indicates that much of this is due to improved health measures, particularly those that led to the near eradication of tuberculosis and typhoid, and to large reductions in the deaths of mothers and children. A major cause of the continuing disparity in health between nonwhites and the rest of the population is the relatively low economic status of the nonwhite group.

Probably one-quarter of the Negro families continue to be subjected to marginal employment opportunities, accompanied by sporadic work experience and unemployment. With roughly half of the income of white families, the Negro family is placed in a severely disadvantaged competitive position for the attainment of the necessities of life.

Poverty and Dependency

A disproportionately large number of Negro families thus live at the poverty level. While Negroes constitute approximately 12 percent of the population, they comprise 22 percent of the poor families. A recent report describes the life of the urban poor:

[23] The data on mortality are derived mainly from Marcus S. Goldstein, "Longevity and Health Status of the Negro American." *Journal of Negro Education* (Washington, D.C. Howard University Press, Fall, 1963), pp. 337–48.

[24] For 1960 U.S. Department of Health, Education, and Welfare *Trends*, 1963, p. 27, indicate that the infant mortality rate was 40.7 for nonwhites, and 22.4 for whites.

[25] U.S. Department of Health, Education, and Welfare, *Trends, op. cit.*

[26] Hayes, *op. cit.*

There are poor people in Washington who get water by carrying a bucketful from a gas station, who obtain light by running extension cords across an alley to a neighbor's home, who live like rats in enclosures under porches. . . . In the heart of the city, some of the poor try to make a living by "picking"—picking up discarded papers and bottles to be sold to the junkman, picking over gutter debris to see if last night's drunk lost any coins, picking at the slots of vending machines for a stray dime.[27]

As compared with whites, some of the evidences of the poverty status of Negro families are their generally higher dependence upon public maintenance programs and disproportionate numbers of children born out of wedlock. Walker observes that "faulty parent-child relationships, instability of parents and a harmful social environment, crowded living conditions, inadequacy of food and clothing, lack of supervised recreational facilities, racial hostility, and segregation are all factors provocative of illegitimacy." [28] Available data appear to support these observations.[29] For example, in 1961 22 percent of all nonwhite babies were born out of wedlock as compared with 2.5 percent of all white babies, and 62 percent of all illegitimate births were nonwhite.

For both mothers and children the problems of illegitimacy and poverty are compounded by the fact that two out of five mothers of babies born out of wedlock are under twenty years of age, and about 2 percent are under fifteen years.

Aid to Families with Dependent Children [30]

In 1961 the Bureau of Family Services, in cooperation with state public welfare agencies, studied the characteristics and financial circumstances of

[27] Eve Edstrom, "They're All Scufflin'—Like Me," *Washington Post,* January 12, 1964.
[28] I. Walker, and Eugenia Sullivan, *New Directions in Health, Education, and Welfare,* 1st edition, U.S. Department of Health, Education, and Welfare, 1963, p. 46.
[29] Helen E. Martz, "Illegitimacy and Dependency," *Indicators,* U.S. Department of Health, Education, and Welfare, Reprint, September, 1963. Mrs. Martz indicates that, taken alone, these facts can be misleading. For example, since 1956, the annual rate of increase of white illegitimate babies has been greater than for nonwhite illegitimate babies. In 1961, an estimated 8,600 more white babies than in 1960 were born out of wedlock as compared to 7,300 more nonwhite babies. The 1960–61 nonwhite increase was 5 percent whereas the white increase was twice as great—over 10 percent. Also, there is a disproportionate number of nonwhites in the lower social and economic groups, where most reported illegitimacies occur. Another misleading factor may be that middle-class white women can get abortions done more readily under secret and safe circumstances.
[30] U.S. Department of Health, Education, and Welfare, Welfare Administration, Bureau of Family Services, *Dependent Children and their Families.* (Washington, D.C.: Government Printing Office, 1963.)

the 910,000 families then receiving Aid for Dependent Children. It found that most of the dependent families have limited educational opportunity, lack skills needed for available work and live in crowded housing. Often they have been cut off by poverty and discrimination from constructive influences and community life.

Among all white children, 23 of each 1,000, and among all nonwhite children, 136 of each 1,000, needed AFDC at the time of the study.

The AFDC payments made up the largest part of the income of most dependent families, and more than half of the families (55 percent) had no income from any other source. These families had an average income of roughly 408 dollars a year per person, which was less than one-fourth of the national per person income at the time.

In one-third of the families there were four or more children. Three-fourths of the AFDC homes were fatherless. Fathers were away from the home in two-thirds of the cases. The fathers were dead in 7.7 percent of the cases. Nearly one-fifth of the families were in need because fathers were disabled. In another one-fifth, parents were not married. Separation, divorce and desertion, therefore, figure in approximately two-fifths of the families.

Few AFDC fathers had held, or were able to hold, jobs with high status or income. Only 3 percent had white collar employment experience, compared with almost 35 percent in this category among all employed males. Only 7 percent had worked in industry in such jobs as craftsmen or foremen, compared with 20 percent of all working men. About 34 percent were unskilled laborers, compared with 7 percent of all employed males. Some 3 percent of AFDC fathers had never held any full-time job. Thus, disability and low level of education go hand in hand with unemployment and dependency. Two large groups of AFDC fathers are to be found living in the home with the children—the incapacitated and the unemployed.

In the central cities, 63 of every 1,000 children under eighteen received AFDC. Almost 70 percent of all the assisted families lived in rented quarters, and 51 percent were crowded; the crowding was serious for almost half of these.

Old Age Assistance

A study of old-age benefit recipients in 1958 showed that 45 out of every 100 nonwhite aged persons in the United States received old-age assistance as compared to 17 out of every 100 white aged persons. The lower rate of insurance beneficiaries among the nonwhites is an important reason for the higher old-age assistance recipient rates. Nonwhites are more likely than whites to reach age 65 without sufficient income or savings, and must rely to a greater degree on public assistance payments.[31]

How the Poor Negro Family Sees Itself [32]

Low income, poor housing, lack of education, broken homes, and discrimination and segregation all affect the Negro adversely. The central problem—to which all others are related—is that of racial discrimination, which, psychologically, produces a self-image of low self-esteem as a result of the behavior and attitudes of whites toward him from childhood and its consequences for certain aspects of the Negro's ability to live at ease with his white fellowman. Among many Negro families this low self-esteem apparently often displays itself in numerous apathetic reactions and the search for the material pleasures of the day without regard for the future.

The Negro family suffers also, especially the lower-class family, from early death, abandonment or divorce, as well as discrimination. Children are the prime target of such social disorganization, and their intrafamily relationships are warped. Sibling rivalry mounts with increasing material scarcity. Youngsters are "farmed out" to relatives for custody because of a broken home. The parent or "relative" is a member of a despised and discriminated-against group, and the child cannot identify with his parents because such identification carries with it a guarantee of external and reflected hatred.[33] The broken home often makes the mother the object and the children the victims of dependency. Therefore, the male child

[31] U.S. Department of Health, Education, and Welfare, Social Security Administration, *Social Security Program Statistics Relating to Nonwhite Families and Children,* Note No. 29 (September 8, 1958).

[32] For an excellent discussion of the psychodynamics of the Negro personality see Abram Kardiner, and Lionel Ovesey, *The Mark of Oppression: A Psychosocial Study of the American Negro* (New York: W. W. Norton & Company, Inc.), 1951.

[33] Claire Hancock states that, "The more frequent and less pathological forms of exploitation also adversely affect children. Children may be overworked, or expected to take unreasonable responsibility for household tasks and care of younger children. Children who are kept out of school or denied time for normal school recreational activities are deprived of important opportunities for intellectual and social development. It is important to recognize the difficult task faced by parents who must live in slum areas where children are exposed to many dangers. Overcrowded households force children into the streets and sometimes into places where they may become victims of juvenile delinquency or adult degradation. . . . In some isolated rural areas, there are groups who are so withdrawn from contact with the larger community that inbreeding and deteriorated family and social life may result." (*Children and Neglect,* U.S. Department of Health, Education, and Welfare, Washington, D.C.: Government Printing Office, 1963).

either has no father image or model to look to or otherwise sees this model condemned.

Lacking status in the social community, the Negro parent is inclined to overwhelming dominance within the family. If the mother should be alone to head the family, her need to make a living leaves her little time to indulge the children. In the eyes of the children she thus frequently becomes someone ambivalently to fear and to rely upon.

If the broken home is the setting, there are apt to be few useful and positive parental models with consequent injury to family life. As a result, the tough competitive and segregated world provides the main source of satisfactions and values. The mores of the street often make school attendance quite irrelevant and crime the desired path to success.

As child or adult, the Negro often cannot identify. If parents are the model, they are either not at home or are discredited and vilified by the white world. If whites are the ideal, acceptance often results in self-hatred, frustration and unrealistic goals.

The so-called white ideal is particularly oppressive to the middle and upper class Negro family where ambition is heightened, marriage is more stable, material comforts have been acquired and time and energy are available to be conventional and respectable. But white idealization must be linked with segregation and discrimination.

These Negro individuals and families are caught in the middle of the ladder of life. They will not move down to lower-class Negro standards, but they are blocked from moving up to the white ideal.

Historically, two sets of factors have affected the Negro urban family. One relates to the circumstances of migration; the other, to the continuing handicaps of the Negro group.

In emigrating, Negro families have had to give up old patterns of behavior and leave old associates behind. In their new environment they had to learn new ways of doing things. Problems had to be faced in breaking through limited and marginal employment, in upgrading low educational levels and in overcoming various forms of personal and social maladjustment.

Old and unproductive family members often became a burden in the cramped tenement houses of the city, in contrast with a more viable status in the more kinship-oriented environment of rural areas.

Vice, crime and asocial behavior are much more in evidence in the big cities than in the rural places. Births out of wedlock, for example, are more likely to become apparent in urban areas.

Thus, Negro families have had experiences typical of a folk or peasant people adjusting to an urban way of life. Historically, the cities have provided the loci for integrating immigrants into the American culture.

The experience has proved to be one in which each immigrant group has improved its socioeconomic status. A similar rise in social and economic status, however, has not yet been achieved in the case of a majority of Negro families. This is also true of other minorities in the United States, notably the Puerto Ricans.[34]

The slowness of the rate of progress of Negroes in urban society is due in large degree to the special handicap of race imposed upon them by the majority group.

Despite an unfavorable social environment great "social distance" exists among Negro urban families. The overall urban experience of Negro families is not uniform. Among urban Negroes there are, at one extreme, families which are third-generation urban residents. At the other extreme, many have come to urban centers only within the last decade. The success achieved by Negro families in the cities thus is related to (a) length of urban residence, (b) the particular urban areas to which they migrated, (c) their educational levels, skills or other "equipment" for competition, and (d) their particular experience with racial discrimination.

For some Negro families the migration and adaptation to urban living have been successful. They have achieved relatively high income status, high levels of education, family integrity and solidarity, and economic security. For these families the cities have provided opportunities for them to achieve middle- and upper-class status. Some Negro families have been urbanized for a period of fifty years preceding the World War I exodus of rural migrants to urban areas. In Washington, D.C., New York, Chicago, Philadelphia and Detroit, for example, many of these older Negro residents have well-established neighborhoods, stable families and moderate to high income levels. In this group are physicians, bankers, lawyers and teachers. Many appear to have no rural antecedents.

Sutherland observed that a sizeable proportion of Negro families have "shared in the American dream." As he stated several years ago:

> Some Negro youth have been so completely surrounded by middle-class patterns that their expectation of achieving advanced degrees, high professional standing, and an income which will enable them to live as well as, or better than their parents is taken for granted.[35]

The majority of Negro families, however, have not yet made a successful transition to urban life. A disproportionately large number of these families

[34] For an extended discussion of racial comparisons between whites and nonwhites, of income, economic status, working wives, etc., see Herman P. Miller, *Rich Man, Poor Man* (New York: Thomas Y. Crowell Company, 1964).

[35] Robert L. Sutherland, *Color, Class and Personality*, American Council on Education, Washington, D.C.

are of low socio-economic status and live in the cities at the poverty level.[36] Therefore, as families and as individuals, they continue to show high rates of personal and social disorganization.

It is the accumulation and circular effects of disadvantages that accentuate the problems faced by the Negro family in the city. As one observer has stated:

> Some of the problems of the transplanted migrants are inevitable, for movement across centuries of experience can not occur painlessly within a few years. Some are associated directly with conditions of living in the initial areas of settlement. And some are associated with the barriers to mobility that lead to increasing density and more intense personal and social problems in areas of concentrated Negro settlement.[37]

Summary and Conclusion

In its development of a middle-class orientation, the Negro family is beginning to approximate the major trend affecting all American families in its movement toward urban centers. The urban location is producing an increasing dependence upon money income and is changing the older familial model of three generation groups (that is grandparents, parents and children living in one household), to two- and one-generation groups. As a consequence, numerous intrafamilial expectations are changing.

Brimmer has observed that while the overall pattern of expenditures by Negro families continues to be typical of that generally found among low-income groups, there is also evidence of rapidly emerging middle-class spending habits. In 1960–61, the average urban Negro family spent about $3,707 for annual living expenses. This amount was just over two-thirds that spent by the average family in the Nation as a whole—a ratio which was virtually unchanged from 1950.[38]

---

[36] For an excellent analysis of the class structures within the Negro group, see John R. Rohrer and M. S. Edmonson, eds., articles by Harold Lief; Daniel Thompson; and William Thompson, *The Eighth Generation*, (New York: Harper and Brothers, 1960). There it is observed (p. 54) that "the social structure of the lower class is less organized, less stable, and less coordinated than that of the middle class. Its family life is predicated on unstable (frequently 'common law') marriage and frequent desertion. The mother is often the chief breadwinner, augmenting her own earnings with what she can wheedle or extort from her current husband, and the discipline exercised over the children is apt to be harsh and inconsistent, with both parents frequently out of the home."

[37] Irene B. Taeuber, "Migration, Mobility, and the Assimilation of the Negro." *Population Bulletin*, XIV, No. 7, U.S. Department of Commerce, (November, 1958), pp. 127–151.

[38] Andrew F. Brimmer, remarks before the 11th Annual Conference of the National Association of Market Developers. (Press release of May 15, 1964, U.S. Department of Commerce, Washington, D.C.)

In many respects the Negro family has moved from one disadvantaged circumstance into another in its striving for urban status. The "core" and "gray" areas of the larger metropolitan areas most often are the locus of obsolescence and social and economic deterioration. The pattern of location of new "urbanites" has produced racial ghettoes. Concomitant with a general movement of the white population from these central portions of the city to suburban areas, the result most often has been a feeling on the part of the Negro population of at least psychological discrimination even when community efforts have been made to desegregate schools, or to undertake urban renewal programs, or to effect improved placement of groups. For example, even after efforts at desegregation, school populations have become resegregated. Churches, recreational areas and even business establishments have become largely identified with use by a particular group.

The recent shifting of Negro families to urban areas is related to the groups' growing protest movements. Negroes have become increasingly dissatisfied with their socio-economic status, and they point to housing restrictions, segregated education, discriminatory policies in trade unions and apprenticeship opportunities and other circumstances, as prohibitive of their achieving equal status. While the urban life of metropolitan areas appeared to have promised the Negroes greater freedom, the facts of everyday living are such that discrimination on the basis of race continues. Increased tension between Negroes and whites is the result.

Like the white family, the Negro family is beset with dynamic influences for which it is difficult to make adequate psychosocial preparation. Major social forces, such as the impact of automation on the labor force, the increasing reliance of society upon technically or professionally trained personnel and the continuing high levels of unemployment (even within a full economy) make it very difficult for families to prepare their members for the future.[39]

Today, however, the environment in which the urban Negro family lives contains numerous elements which result in "cultural deprivation" and social impoverishment; possibly half of the Negro youth live in such a situation.

Economic deprivation is conducive to cultural deprivation. The training ground for good citizenship, such as college education, adequate health protection, adequate recreation, reading, travel and involvement in community affairs, is not readily available to those at the bottom of the economic ladder.

It is difficult to assess the hopes and expectations of Negro youth, but

[39] See Margaret Mead, "The Changing American Family," *Children,* 10, No. 5 (September–October, 1963).

it is reasonable to assume that the lack of opportunity open to them in American society results in considerable frustration. Their level of opportunity is far below their potential for personal and social achievement.

As families and as individuals Negroes have become dissatisfied with their traditional status in the United States and they are participating in large-scale protest led in the main by the group's younger elements.

As examples:

The "sit-in" movement had its genesis in the Negro population of college age.

The hopes, plans and demands of the Negro population are being sharpened and lifted with the expectations that the rewards of American society will be forthcoming on a basis of racial equality.

The Negro family can now point to success models within the group in many walks of life.

The parental generation expects for its children opportunities much greater than any they might realize.

Thus, one consequence of urbanization appears to be an increasing sophistication and articulation on the part of Negro families; they are using techniques such as political participation, involvement in community organization and community processes and "movements" of various types to express their discontent and to effect widespread social change. The *Washington Post* reports:

> The Negro demands an end to housing shortages, limited job opportunities, the problems of slums. He sees symbols of discrimination everywhere—the all-white suburbs, his hand-me-down churches that whites have fled, the overcrowded and overaged schools that are now resegregated. . . . The Negro concedes the door to full equality is ajar. He demands that it open wide.[40]

The many trends affecting the American family generally, such as rising levels of health, increasing levels of educational attainment, improved occupational distribution, improved housing conditions and increased security through participation in public programs, are all having their beneficial effects on the Negro family. In part as a result of their determination to eliminate racial discrimination and achieve equality on all fronts, it is to be expected that in the future fewer and fewer distinctions may be drawn between the great mass of Negro families and those of the general population.

[40] Robert E. Baker, "Covert Segregation Galls D.C. Negroes," *Summer of Discontent,* VII, *Washington Post,* August 16, 1963.

TABLE II—"Balance Sheet" on Selected Aspects of Whites and Nonwhites

Item	White	Nonwhite
Population		
Size—growth—gains		
1960 total national	88.5%	11.5%
1940–50 gains	14.1%	17.1%
1950–60 gains	17.5%	26.7%
Outside the South		tripled since 1940
Migration		
From South	steady	marked
Rural to urban	steady	marked
To suburbia	major	minor
Concentration		
North Central cities	less	gain
Central or core city	out of	into
Family characteristics		
Units (household)		
Number households, 1960	47.9 million	5.2 million
Increase, 1960 over 1950	16.4%	21%
Living in urban areas, 1960	72%	77%
Marital Status		
Divorced males	2.1%	2.4%
Divorced females	2.7%	3.6%
Proportion separated males		over 5 × the whites
Proportion separated females		over 6 × the whites
Widows, ages 14–35	6.9%	20%
Total—separation, death, divorce		
Males	6.8%	15.7%
Females	16.7%	31.2%
Family Composition		
Size of household	3.23 persons	3.85 persons
Headed by male	9 of 10	3 of 4
Headed by female	1 of 11	1 of 5
Fertility		
Rate, 1961, age 15–44	112.3	153.8
Women not given birth	16.0%	21.3%
Proportion with 5–6 children		much larger than white
Proportion with 7 plus children		3 × the white
Babies born out of wedlock, 1961	2.5%	22.0%
Life expectancy, 1960	69.7 years	63.6 years
Mortality, 1960, early childhood and 20–64		1.5 × the white

TABLE II—continued

Item	White	Nonwhite
Housing		
Home ownership		
Moved into new suburban housing 1950–60	58% of 19 million	23% of 3.7 million
Increase in 1950's	57%–64%	35%–38%
Standardized units occupied in 1950's	68%–87%	25%–50%
Overcrowded units in 1950's	decreased 0.2 million	increased 0.3 million
Education		
Years of school completed, 1962, 25–29 age group	12.5 years	11.2 years
Gain since 1940 in school years completed	2 years	4.5 years
Elementary School enrollment, 1961	99.5%	98.2%
High School enrollment, 1956–61, increase for ages 14–17	89% to 92%	81% to 87%
Some College, total population	62%	40%
Labor Force participation		
White collar		
Increase, 1955–62	47%	17%
Managers, officials and proprietors, 1962	20%	5%
Service industries, 1960	8%	23%
Skilled		
Clerical, professional, technical and managerial	6%	20%
Professional and technical, 1962	12.5%	5%
Manufacturing, 1962	28%	18%
Professional, technical, managerial, 1960, urban	23%	8%
Unskilled and semiskilled		
Male, nonfarm	33%	75%
Females, proportion of		
Age 25–64, 1962	40%	58.5%
Part-time, married, 1960	20%	30%
All domestic and service, 1960	20%	60%
Income		
Median		
National, 1962	$6,200	$3,300
Males	$4,700	$2,300
Under $4,000, family	26%	60%

TABLE II—continued

Item	White	Nonwhite
$6,000–$14,900, family	47%	19%
$15,000– , family	5%	Less than 1%
Unemployment		
Age 25–44, 1962	3%	9%
Dropouts in unskilled and services	45%	80%
Teenagers, 1962	12%	25%
Teenagers, since 1955	up 30%	up 60%
Old Age assistance, recipients		
per 100 in all ages	17	45

Baker, Robert E., "Housing Restrictions Top Grievance List of Washington Negroes," *Summer of Discontent,* II, *Washington Post* (August 12, 1963).

———, "Covert Segregation Galls D.C. Negroes," *Summer of Discontent,* VII, *Washington Post,* August 16, 1963.

Bressler, Tobia, "Some Population Trends Involving and Affecting the Negro—Implications." Address, Association of Social Science Teachers, Nashville, Tennessee, March 22, 1962.

Coe, Paul F., "Nonwhite Population Increases in Metropolitan Areas." *Journal of the American Statistical Association,* 50, No. 270 (June, 1955).

Conant, James B., "Social Dynamite in Our Large Cities." *Children,* 8, No. 5 (September–October, 1961).

Deutsch, Martin P., "The Disadvantaged Child and the Learning Process," in Passow, A. Harry (ed.), *Education in Depressed Areas.* New York: Teachers College, Columbia University Press, 1963.

Douglass, Joseph H., *The Negro Family's Search for Economic Security,* U.S. Department of Health, Education, and Welfare, Washington, D.C., July, 1956.

Edstrom, Eve, "They're All Scufflin' Like Me," *Washington Post,* January 12, 1964.

Edwards, G. Franklin, "Marriage and Family Life Among Negroes." *The Journal of Negro Education,* Yearbook No. XXXII, Washington, D.C.: The Howard University Press, 1963. p. 451.

Frazier, E. Franklin, *The Negro Family in the United States.* Chicago: University of Chicago Press, 1939.

Gist, Noel P. and Bennett, William S., Jr., "Aspirations of Negro and White Students." *Social Forces,* 41, No. 1 (October, 1963).

Goldberg, Miriam L., "Factors Affecting Educational Attainment in Depressed Urban Areas," in Passow, A. Harry (ed.), *Education in Depressed Areas.* New York: Teachers College, Columbia University Press, 1963.

Goldstein, Marcus S., "Longevity and Health Status of the Negro American." *Journal of Negro Education*, Fall, 1963.

Goodwin, Robert G., *America Is For Everybody*. U.S. Department of Labor, Washington, D.C.: Government Printing Office, 1963.

Hancock, Claire, *Children and Neglect—Hazardous Home Conditions*, U.S. Department of Health, Education, and Welfare, Washington, D.C., 1963.

Handlin, Oscar, *The Newcomers— Negroes and Puerto Ricans in a Changing Metropolis*. Cambridge: Harvard University Press, 1959.

Hayes, Marion, "A Century of Change —Negroes in the U.S. Economy 1860–1960." *Monthly Labor Review*, U.S. Department of Labor, December, 1962.

Holsey, Eleanor, "Culturally Deprived Children in Day-Care Programs." *Children*, 10, No. 5 (September– October, 1963).

Kardiner, Abram and Ovesey, Lionel, *The Mark of Oppression: A Psychosocial Study of the American Negro*. New York: W. W. Norton and Company, Inc., 1951.

Kessler, Matthew A., "Economic Status of Nonwhite Workers 1955–62." *Monthly Labor Review*, Preprint No. 2419, U.S. Department of Labor, July, 1963.

Lewis, Hylan, "The Changing Negro Family," *The Nation's Children*, Vol. 1. New York: Columbia University Press, 1960.

Lewis, Hylan and Hill, Mozell, "Desegregation, Integration, and the Negro Community." *The Annals of the American Academy of Political and Social Science*, 304, March, 1956.

John H. Rohrer and M. S. Edmonson, eds.; co-authors Lief, Harold; Thompson, Daniel; and Thompson, William, *The Eighth Generation*. New York: Harper and Brothers, 1960.

Mead, Margaret, "The Changing American Family." *Children*, 10, No. 5 (September–October, 1963).

Miller, Herman P., *Rich Man, Poor Man*. New York: Thomas Y. Crowell Company, 1964.

National Association of Intergroup Relations Officials, *Public School Segregation and Integration in the North*. Washington, D.C. (November, 1963).

Pollack, Otto, "Some Challenges to the American Family." *Children*, 11, No. 1 (January–February, 1964).

Schiffman, Jacob, "Marital and Family Characteristics of Workers, March, 1960." *Monthly Labor Review*, Reprint No. 2364, U.S. Department of Labor (April, 1961).

Schnore, Leo F. and Sharp, Harry, "Racial Changes in Metropolitan Areas, 1950–1960." *Social Forces*, 41, No. 3 (March, 1963).

Silberman, C. E., "The City and the Negro," *Fortune*, LXV, No. 3, 65:88– 91 (March, 1962).

Stein, Robert L. and Meredith, Jane L., "Growth and Characteristics of the Part-Time Work Force, No. 10." *Monthly Labor Review*, Reprint No. 2356, U.S. Department of Labor (November, 1960).

Sutherland, Robert L., *Color, Class and Personality*, American Council on Education, Washington, D.C., 1942.

Taeuber, Irene B., "Migration, Mobility, and the Assimilation of the

Negro." *Population Bulletin,* XIV, No. 7, U.S. Department of Commerce, November, 1958.

U.S. Department of Commerce, Bureau of Census, *Current Population Reports, Population Characteristics,* Series P–20, No. 115 (February 7, 1962).

U.S. Department of Commerce, Bureau of Census, *Current Population Reports, Population Characteristics,* Series P–20, No. 118 (August 9, 1962).

U.S. Department of Commerce, Bureau of Census, *Current Population Reports, Consumer Income,* Series P–60, No. 41 (October 21, 1963).

U.S. Department of Commerce, "Negro Population for Selected Standard Metropolitan Statistical Areas: 1960," *Appendix* (release of February 26, 1961).

U.S. Department of Commerce, "Negro Population of the 25 Largest Cities in United States: 1960" (release of March 14, 1961).

U.S. Department of Commerce, *Summary Population Characteristics,* Final Report PC (1)–1D, Washington, D.C.: Government Printing Office, 1963.

U.S. Department of Health, Education, and Welfare, Welfare Administration, Bureau of Family Services, *Dependent Children and Their Families.* Washington, D.C.: Government Printing Office, 1963.

U.S. Department of Health, Education, and Welfare, *Indicators.* February, 1964.

U.S. Department of Health, Education, and Welfare, Office of the Secretary, *New Directions in Health, Education, and Welfare,* 1963.

U.S. Department of Health, Education, and Welfare, Social Security Administration, *Social Security Program Statistics Relating to Nonwhite Families and Children,* Note No. 29, September 8, 1958.

U.S. Department of Health, Education, and Welfare, *Trends,* 1963 edition.

U.S. Department of Labor, Bureau of Labor Statistics, *Economic Status of Nonwhite Workers, 1955–62,* Special Labor Force Report No. 33, Preprint No. 2419.

U.S. Department of Labor, "Employment of High School Graduates and Dropouts in 1961." *Monthly Labor Review* (May, 1962).

U.S. Housing and Home Finance Agency, *Our Nonwhite Population and its Housing: The Changes Between 1950 and 1960,* July, 1963.

U.S. Senate, 86th Congress, 2nd Session, Special Committee on Unemployment Problems, *Studies in Unployment,* Washington, D.C.: Government Printing Office, 1960.

Wagner, Robert F., Remarks at the Annual Civil Rights Conference of the New York City Central Labor Council, March 9, 1963. From *Congressional Record Appendix,* March 14, 1963.

Walker, I. and Sullivan, Eugenia, *New Directions,* 1st edition, U.S. Department of Health, Education, and Welfare, 1963.

Washington Post, Editorial (January 27, 1964).

White, Theodore H., "Racial Collision in the Big Cities," *Life,* 55:100–2 (November 22, 1963).

chapter 7

Educating the American Negro

Virgil A. Clift

The story of the education of the American Negro has raised fundamental questions throughout our history as to the extent and quality of his cultural integration. The ordeal of slavery, followed by a century of segregation and discrimination, forced the Negro to live in a cultural no man's land. He was stripped of his African culture, language and religion; and, at the same time, by exclusion and denial was not permitted to enter the mainstream of American life. Yet, in spite of differential treatment, inequality before the law and often intense, harsh and brutal treatment, he developed a devotion, loyalty and attachment to America. Therefore, one must understand the historical paradox of the Negro's life in America in order to gain insight into his past and present education. Historically, the development of schools and programs of education for Negroes has represented largely the influences of social forces outside the Negro community and over which he had little or no control.

EDUCATION DURING THE COLONIAL PERIOD

Since the introduction of the first Negro slaves (c. 1619) into the Jamestown colony, the question of Negro education has been a subject of controversy in America. During the colonial period, the institution of slavery was recognized as being incompatible with education. If made available to slaves, education would be a factor in destroying slavery. There are reports of instances, however, where organizations sought to provide some education for slaves. After 1740, the Society for the Propagation of the Gospel in Foreign Parts sought to raise the level of living among both whites and Negroes in the South. The missionaries of this organization urged the masters to provide opportunity for their slaves to be converted. They suggested that slaves be given time to study the Scriptures and to learn to read and write. Occasionally, they taught the slaves themselves and, in one notable instance, they fostered the establishment of a school for Negroes in Charleston, South Carolina, in which the teachers themselves were slaves owned by the society.[1]

"The Christianization of the Negro proceeded as the first great step in his larger American education."[2] There is considerable evidence that the Puritans favored conversion. In a tract published in London in 1673, Richard Baxter favored Christian instruction of slaves. In 1674, John Eliot, who had done much to improve life among the Indians, turned his attention to instructing Negroes. Cotton Mather, busy with writing and teaching, took time to instruct Negroes and, in 1717, began his evening school for Indians and Negroes. Samuel Sewall, a judge in Massachusetts, not only favored instruction but also was quite outspoken against slavery, believing it to be a curse against God and humanity. In 1728, Nathaniel Pigott announced that he was opening a school for the "instruction of Negroes in reading, catechizing, and writing," but there is no record of its success or failure.

The most conscientious effort to improve conditions among slaves was made by the Quakers. They not only took steps to abolish slavery, but some leaders such as George Fox urged owners of slaves to give religious instruction to them. In 1700, William Penn was instrumental in getting a Monthly Meeting established for Negroes. During this time many colonists were teaching their slaves and free Negroes; indeed, Paul Cuffee, a prosperous Negro, set up a school in Massachusetts in the eighteenth century. John Woolman's influence was especially noteworthy among Quakers.

Important also was the influence of Anthony Benezet, who began an evening school in his home in Philadelphia in 1750 and continued instruction there for twenty years. Regarded among his contemporaries as a highly enlightened man of letters, his views had much significance when he spoke out against the idea of Negro inferiority.

> I can with truth and sincerity declare that I have found amongst the Negroes as great a variety of talents as amongst a like number of whites; and I am bold to assert, that the notion entertained by some, that the blacks are inferior in their capacities, is a vulgar prejudice, founded on the pride or ignorance of their lordly masters, who have kept their slaves at such a distance, as to be unable to form a right judgment of them.[3]

[1] John Hope Franklin, *From Slavery to Freedom* (New York: Alfred E. Knopf, 1947), p. 80.

[2] W. A. Low, "The Education of Negroes Viewed Historically," in V. A. Clift, *et al.* (eds.), *Negro Education in America* (New York: Harper & Row, 1962), p. 35.

[3] George S. Brookes, *Friend Anthony Benezet* (Philadelphia: University of Pennsylvania Press, 1937), pp. 46–47.

Many other Quakers saw the need not only to give Christian instruction to Negroes, but to abolish slavery as well. In 1776, the Philadelphia Quakers decided to put an end to slaveholding. They founded the Pennsylvania Abolition Society, whose members included Benjamin Franklin, William Pitt, Noah Webster and Thomas Paine. This society aimed to establish schools for Negroes whenever possible, in addition to the abolition of slavery.

Prior to the Revolution there were a few other notable examples of attempts to educate the Negro. An early catechizing school was founded in New York City at Trinity Church in 1704, with instruction being given by Elia Neau. Reverend Thomas Bray in Maryland encouraged conversion and instruction, and, at times, white and Negro children were taught together.

Because of their concern for indoctrinating them with Christianity the French and Spanish settlers were more active in trying to educate slaves than the English. The Catholics in New Orleans, under the leadership of the Ursuline Nuns, attempted to teach Negroes and Indians in 1727, and established and conducted a school for Negroes in 1734.

The English were much slower to follow a similar policy until the provincial statutes and the declarations of the Bishop of London established the principles that conversion did not lead to manumission.[4]

FROM THE REVOLUTION TO THE CIVIL WAR [5]

The doctrine of the "natural rights" of man, which was a part of the philosophy of the American Revolution, helped the opponents of slavery espouse the right of the Negro education. Benjamin Franklin favored and encouraged the full education of the Negro. Thomas Jefferson thought that they should be given industrial and agricultural education but did not believe in the intellectual equality of Negroes and whites.

Education in the South

Despite legal restrictions and despite contentions of Southerners like John C. Calhoun that Negroes could not absorb educative experiences, Negro

[4] E. Franklin Frazier, *The Negro in the United States* (New York: The Macmillan Co., 1957), p. 418.

[5] One of the best and most reliable references on the early education of the Negro is Carter G. Woodson, *The Education of the Negro Prior to 1861* (New York: G. P. Putnam's Sons, 1919). One of the best references for later years is Horace Mann Bond, *Education of the Negro in the American Social Order* (New York: Prentice-Hall, Inc., 1934.)

slaves did receive education in various parts of the South. According to John H. Franklin,[6] some masters themselves taught their slaves. The case of Frederick Douglass having been taught by his mistress is perhaps the best known instance of an owner teaching a slave. One planter in northern Mississippi boasted that all twenty of his slaves could read and that they purchased their own books. In some cases, even where masters were opposed to their slaves receiving instruction, the children of masters would teach slaves to read and write.

The instruction of one or two slaves, though a violation of the law, was not regarded as serious, and there was hardly any danger of prosecution. However, the insurrection of 1800 so frightened Southern planters that further expansion of education for Negroes was discouraged. In the nineteenth century, Negroes in Southern states had to content themselves, for the most part, with clandestine schools and private teachers.

In some isolated instances, Negroes attended mixed schools in the South. In 1840, Negroes were permitted to attend schools with white children in Wilmington, Delaware. Julius Mebourn was sent to a white academy near Raleigh, North Carolina, by his mistress and remained there until it was discovered he was a Negro. Franklin [7] concludes that "There is no way of knowing the extent to which Negroes attended the schools of whites." Nor is there any way of ascertaining with any degree of accuracy the number of slaves who were literate before the Civil War. Amos Dresser believed that one out of every fifty slaves in the southwest could read and write. C. G. Parsons estimated that about five thousand of Georgia's 400 thousand slaves were literate.[8]

Education in the North

During the post-revolutionary period, Negroes in the North benefited from the general trend to establish and improve schools in the new nation. Whites in Boston taught Negro children both privately and in public institutions. In 1798, a separate school for Negro children was established by a white teacher in the home of Primus Hall, a prominent Negro. Two years later, Negroes asked the city of Boston for a separate school, but the request was refused. Negroes established a school anyway and employed two Harvard men as instructors. This school continued for many years; and finally, in 1820, the city of Boston opened an elementary school for Negroes. One of the best known schools for Negroes during the period was the

---

[6] Franklin, *op. cit.*, p. 200.
[7] Franklin, *ibid.*, p. 201.
[8] Woodson, *op. cit.*, p. 340.

New York African Free School, established by the Manumission Society in 1787. It began with forty students and the number never exceeded sixty in its first decade of existence. At first, there was great opposition to the school, but in 1800 interest in it increased. New impetus for its continued growth came in 1810, when New York required masters to teach all slave children to read the Scriptures. By 1820, the institution had enrolled more than five hundred Negro children.

New Jersey began educating her Negro children in 1777. By 1801, there had been short-lived schools established in Burlington, Salem and Trenton. In addition, Quakers and other humanitarian groups were teaching Negro children privately. As early as 1774, the Quakers of Philadelphia established a school for Negro children, and after the war, thanks to funds provided by philanthropist Anthony Benezet, the program was enlarged. In 1787, a school was built in Philadelphia, and ten years later there were at least seven schools for Negroes in this city. This interest in the development of Negro education continued until the nineteenth century. In most places, however, separate schools were maintained. The separate schools established in Boston in 1820 was followed closely by other Massachusetts towns which organized schools for Negroes.

In 1849, Charles Sumner in the case *Roberts* vs. *The City of Boston,* appeared before the Massachusetts Supreme Court on behalf of a Negro girl who had been barred from a white school under the local ordinance providing for separate education of the races. The Massachusetts Supreme Court held against Sumner and the Negro plaintiff; however, by 1855, sufficient public opinion had been mobilized to persuade the Massachusetts legislature to repudiate the court. In that year, segregation in the public schools of the state was specifically prohibited by statute.[9]

Rhode Island and Connecticut maintained separate schools, and in the last decade before the Civil War larger funds were given to them. Not until 1824 did the New York Common Council begin to support African Free Schools. The city took them over altogether in 1834. Although some communities in the state permitted Negro children to attend white schools, the legislature made it clear in 1841 that any district could establish separate schools. New Jersey also maintained separate schools for Negro children. The citizens of Pennsylvania continued to give both public and private support to their Negro schools and they increased in number, particularly in the western part of the state.

As more and more Negroes migrated to the West, citizens were faced with the problem of education. Ohio excluded Negroes from public schools

[9] H. S. Ashmore, *The Negro and the Schools* (Chapel Hill: University of North Carolina Press, 1954), pp. 3–4.

by law in 1829, and twenty years later provided separate schools, but never appropriated enough funds to set up anything creditable. Citizens of Indiana and Illinois were equally indifferent. Michigan and Wisconsin adopted more democratic policies, but most Negroes in the West had to wait until after the Civil War before they were able to be educated in considerable numbers at public expense.

It was during this period that Negroes began to attend some institutions of higher education. John Russwurm graduated from Bowdoin College in 1826. Before the Civil War a few Negroes were attending Oberlin, Franklin and Rutland Colleges and the Harvard Medical and other schools.

During the pre-Civil War period a few Negroes were appointed to the faculties of white colleges. Charles L. Reason, William G. Allen, and George B. Vashon each held for a time the professorship of Belle Lettres at Central College in McGrawville, New York. It was said that these teachers wore "the professor's mantle gracefully, giving proof of good scholarship and manly character." In this period also the American Missionary Association continued its work, administering the interesting experiment for the coeducaton of the races at Berea College in Kentucky.[10]

DEVELOPMENTS AFTER THE CIVIL WAR

Even after the Civil War efforts to educate the Negro were met with strong opposition. Public education was frequently denounced in Southern publications because it was identified with the idea of equality. Resentment against the Negro school and church sometimes flared into violence, with Negroes being forcibly stopped from attending schools and teachers being physically prevented from teaching. Churches which housed schools were often burned. In spite of these conditions, it was at this time that the first organized program of education was developed for the freedmen.

West Virginia, which became a separate political unit in 1863, was the first Southern state to make provision in its constitution for the "equal though separate" education of the Negro. In sections of Florida and Louisiana under the jurisdiction of the Union military forces, and in the border states, there were efforts to set up public schools for Negroes. In 1865, Missouri included Negroes in her school system.[11] In the border states, support for Negro public schools came from the taxes paid by Negroes. This was true even in the District of Columbia, where, in 1862,

10 Franklin, *op. cit.*, pp. 383–84.
11 Report of the U.S. Commission on Education, McKee's Report to the House Committee on Education and Labor, 1870, p. 187.

Congress passed a bill setting aside 10 percent of the taxes paid by Negroes to support Negro schools.[12]

During Reconstruction, the attitude of the South toward the education of the freedman was determined not only by the traditional attitudes toward the status of the Negro, but also by the outlook and interests of the various groups that emerged with the collapse of the Confederacy. Three elements in Southern society arose: (1) The Conservatives, who attempted (through the Black Codes) to reinstate as far as possible the servile status of the Negro. This class was opposed to any form of education of the Negro. (2) The moderates, who realized that slavery was dead and that the new status of the Negro should be recognized in creating a new society in the South. In this moderate group where many large plantation owners who were willing to provide some education for Negroes in order to secure a stable and reliable labor supply. (3) The radicals, comprised of the unpropertied whites and small farmers, who had no real interest in the slave system and who because of their cooperation with Negroes in establishing public schools were called "renegades and scalawags."

The chief contribution of the Reconstruction government was to set a precedent for the democratic right of all the people to public tax-supported education. However, education of whites and Negroes in the same school was not attempted on a large scale; and in Louisiana and South Carolina, where such attempts were made, there was violence or the whites generally boycotted the schools. At the time Negro leaders generally accepted separate schools as an inevitable consequence of the traditional attitudes of the whites toward the association of the races.

During the Civil War and immediately following, the War Department provided care and some instruction to Negroes who were either refugees or "contraband." The Freedman's Bureau (1865–72) acted as an agency of the department and expanded these early efforts under the leadership of General Oliver Otis Howard, Commissioner; Edwin M. Stanton, Secretary of War, and John W. Alvord, Superintendent of Instruction for the bureau. The Freedman's Bureau was influential in giving central organization, protection and financial support to the efforts of philanthropists, freedmen and the states. This framework was essential for the establishment of a system of education.

After the war, the Freedman's Bureau and various Freedman's aid societies helped to establish higher institutions as well as elementary and secondary schools for Negroes. But in addition to these efforts the churches also made a valuable contribution. Among the most important of these was the

---

[12] W. E. B. Du Bois, *The Negro Common School* (Atlanta, Georgia: Atlanta University Press, 1901), p. 38.

American Missionary Association, which set up schools in Newport News, Portsmouth, Suffolk and Yorktown in Virginia and Washington, D.C., as well as in Columbus, Ohio, as early as 1863. Other important church groups which gave aid to the education of the recently emancipated Negroes were: The Friends Association for the Aid to Freedmen, the Board of Freedmen's Missions of the United Presbyterian Church, the Freedman's Aid Society of the Methodist Episcopal Church, the American Baptist Home Mission Society, the American Church Institute of the Episcopal Church, and the Conferences of the African Methodist Episcopal Church. Among the outstanding leaders associated with these organizations and religious movements were Levi Coffin, Salmon P. Chase, Henry Ward Beecher, John M. Walden, Richard S. Rust, Mathias W. Baldwin (locomotive industrialist), Edward T. Atkinson (textile manufacturer), and William Claflin (Governor of Massachusetts).

In the decade immediately following the close of the Civil War, leading church groups were active in the establishment of a number of schools which although in the beginning were hardly more than secondary schools, later became landmarks in the system of higher education in the South. The most important of these include Atlanta University (1865) in Atlanta, Georgia, Talladega, in Alabama, (1867), Fisk University (1866) in Nashville, Tennessee, and Tougaloo University (1869) in Mississippi—all established by the American Missionary Association. The Arkansas Agricultural, Mechanical, and Normal College began as Branch Normal in 1873 at Pine Bluff, Arkansas. Morehouse College of Atlanta, Georgia, was originally established in 1867 as the Augusta Institute in Augusta, Georgia. It was supported by the American Baptist Home Mission Society which was also instrumental in the founding and support of Virginia Union University in 1865, Shaw University in Raleigh, North Carolina, in 1865, and Benedict College in 1870 in South Carolina. The Methodist Episcopal Church established an institution at Holly Springs, Mississippi in 1867, a school which was later known as both Shaw University and Rust College. The Presbyterians in North Carolina established the Scotia Seminary, which today is known as Barber-Scotia College. Biddle University was founded the same year at Charlotte, North Carolina, and is known today as Johnson C. Smith University. The Methodist Episcopal Church founded the Centenary Biblical Institute in Baltimore in 1866, which later became Morgan College and is today Morgan State College. Howard University in Washington, D.C., was established in 1867. These represent a few of the institutions of higher education, significant in America today, which can trace their roots to the post Civil War period.

Philanthropy also aided materially in Negro education by providing buildings, endowments, scholarships, support for teacher training and industrial education. The Daniel Hand Fund and the Anna T. Jeanes Fund were established exclusively for Negroes.

Land-grant colleges for Negroes were established under the provisions of the Second Morrill Act (1890). This provided the framework for the state-supported institutions for higher education. The Second Morrill Act was one of the first means of assuring land-grant funds for Negro education where the dual system of education existed. On the other hand, it gave strength to the doctrine of "separate but equal," with the result that the seventeen Southern states maintained colleges which came to be known as the Negro land-grant colleges. It was at these institutions which received a minimum of Federal and state support that the public system of higher education for Negroes in the South was based.

Immediately following the end of the Reconstruction period, the South deprived the Negro not only of citizenship rights but also of educational privileges. During the period from 1876 to 1895, in the Southern states as a whole, the enrollment of whites increased markedly and that of the Negroes was moderate, the increase for whites being 106 percent as compared with 59 percent for Negroes. During the 1890's, Negroes were disfranchised by state constitutional provisions and their subordinate status was given legal basis in the South. As a result, education for Negroes became more segregated in those areas where mixed schools had existed, and inequalities developed in teachers' salaries and in other provisions for Negro education.

In 1890, the influence of Booker T. Washington had begun to be felt. His campaign to establish an educational program for Negroes that would be acceptable to the South was widely discussed. It was during this period also that philanthropy became an important factor in the support of Negro education in the South. Seizing upon these two factors, Southern states soon introduced inequality into their support of Negro and white education. Gains which had been made toward mixing the schools for the races were quickly stamped out.

A dictum from the famous case of *Plessy* vs. *Ferguson* (1896) was the basis of saddling the "separate but equal doctrine" on education in the South.[13] The United States Supreme Court actually went out of its way to recognize "that segregation in education was a general American practice, not an uniquely Southern one."

From 1896 to 1954, the dual system of education was developed and

[13] For full discussion of this case see Constance Baker Motley, "The Legal Status of the Negro," later in this volume, p. 484.

expanded in the South. Permissive segregation was maintained in the border states. Schools remained, in fact, *separate and unequal.*

DEVELOPMENTS DURING THE TWENTIETH CENTURY

In the early years of the twentieth century, public education for Negroes in the South received significant impetus from the outside through the contributions of such philanthropists as Rockefeller and Peabody. The Anna T. Jeanes Fund, in 1908, inaugurated the Jeanes Teacher program to improve the quality of instruction in rural Negro schools. Beginning in 1913, the Julius Rosenwald Fund provided grants for Negro school construction, and by 1932 more than 5,000 Negro school buildings in 883 counties of fifteen Southern and border states had been built with Rosenwald aid. Rosenwald grants provided an invaluable incentive and accounted for about 15 percent of the money spent on school construction for Negroes. In addition, 17 percent came from direct contributions made by Negroes themselves. At the end of the Rosenwald building program, the per-pupil value of Negro school property was still less than one-fifth as great as that of white schools. An even more telling index of the relative growth of the dual school system is provided by a comparison of teachers' salaries. Between 1900 and 1930, the average white teacher's salary rose from slightly less than two hundred dollars to nine hundred dollars, while the average Negro teacher's salary rose from one hundred dollars to four hundred dollars. And these figures reflect the peak of a national boom, both in national income and in school population.[14]

The effects of this disparate policy were evident in the concentration of Negro children in the lower grades during the first half of the twentieth century. As late as 1920, 85 percent of all Negro pupils in the South were enrolled in the first four grades. In 1916, there were only sixty-seven Negro public high schools with fewer than twenty thousand students.[15]

The two decades between World War I and World War II were marked by profound changes in Negro education. As noted by Low,[16] there was

[14] Ashmore, *op. cit.*, pp. 17–18.

[15] For further information on the inequality of the segregated school system in the South, see Fourteenth U.S. Census, vol. 11, p. 1043; *The Negro Year Book, 1925–26* (Tuskeegee, Alabama, Negro Yearbook Publishing Co.); Bulletin No. 39, Department of Interior, Bureau of Education ("Negro Education"); N. C. Newbold, *Annals of the American Academy of Political and Social Sciences,* November, 1928, p. 209; and V. A. Clift, *School and Society,* 72 (October 7, 1952).

[16] W. A. Low, *op. cit.*, pp. 53–54.

significant increase in public high schools for Negroes, North and South—especially in large urban areas. Capital outlays for schools increased in substantial amounts. The number of high school teachers employed, students enrolled and high school graduates grew markedly. And all of this growth was accompanied by programs of school consolidation, new curricula and other educational advances which reflected the general American patterns on elementary and secondary education.

Also during this period, Low points out, there was a large increase in the numbers of college graduates from Northern schools and Negro institutions in the South. Improvement in the quality of the Negro colleges led to more and more of them receiving accreditation from regional accrediting agencies.

The Negro land-grant colleges in this period surpassed the private colleges in financial support and in consequence attracted an enrollment larger than these privately financed institutions. One consequence of this was the establishment of the United Negro College Fund at the end of World War II to buttress the rising financial needs of the private colleges.

During this period Negro education came increasingly under the scrutiny of students of American education. The focus was on quality. Studies in Negro education appeared regularly in the *Journal of Negro Education,* first published in 1932. Federal, state and local research greatly augmented our knowledge of Negro education.

The more deeply scholars probed into Negro education and made comparisons with the education of white youth the more they became aware of the appalling gap between education for Negroes and whites. Many noted also the predominance of teacher training in Negro colleges and the lack of democracy in the administration of Negro schools and colleges. The toll of Negro education taken by the doctrine in the Plessy case became increasingly apparent.

LEGAL ATTACKS ON JIM CROW SCHOOLS

Between 1896, when the Plessy decision was handed down, and 1930, only three cases involving Negro education came before the Supreme Court. In none of these was school segregation directly challenged, nor did the Court find occasion to order relief of any kind for Negro plaintiffs. In 1899, the Supreme Court heard an appeal by a group of Negroes from Augusta, Georgia, who demanded an end to public support for two white high schools after the sole Negro high school had been discontinued. The majority opinion in *Cumming* vs. *Richmond County* held that the relief requested was improper. In 1908, the Court heard the case of *Berea College* vs. *Kentucky,* which involved the right of a privately chartered college to teach both races in defiance of the Kentucky law making segregation mandatory. The Court ruled against Berea on technical grounds. The case was generally accepted as a reflection of the Court's feeling that segregation was a matter better left to the states. *Gong Lum* vs. *Rice* came before the Court from Mississippi in 1927. The issue was whether Mississippi could properly classify a Chinese child as "colored" and therefore require her to attend a Negro school. The Court upheld the Mississippi law and Chief Justice Taft took the occasion to offer a reminder that the "separate but equal" doctrine was still in effect; "had the petition alleged specifically that there was no colored school in Martha Lum's neighborhood to which she could conveniently go, a different question would have been presented. . . ." None of these cases directly challenged the constitutionality of segregation in education.

In 1935, almost forty years after the Supreme Court handed down the Plessy decision permitting "separate but equal" public educational facilities, Donald Murray, a Negro, applied for admission to the law school of the University of Maryland at Baltimore and was refused in accordance with Maryland's segregation statutes. His complaint was that Maryland provided no law school for Negroes within its boundaries but had attempted to meet the Plessy doctrine by offering a limited number of scholarships for Negroes in institutions outside the state. The Maryland Court of Appeals upheld Murray's contention and accepted the argument that out of state scholarships, which covered only the cost of tuition, placed Negro students at an economic disadvantage.

The Gaines case in 1938 was the real forerunner of the decisions of the 1940's which opened graduate schools in the South to Negroes. Lloyd Gaines sued for admission to the law school of the University of Missouri on the grounds that no separate school of law for Negroes was provided in the state and that the out of state scholarships available to him did not satisfy the requirement of equal treatment. The Supreme Court reversed the courts of Missouri in an opinion which announced a new point of law.[17]

This set into motion in the South a feverish expansion of state-supported Negro graduate and professional schools, an expansion designed especially to deny Negroes admission to white state-supported colleges and universities.[18] The decade following the Murray and Gaines cases witnessed the most

[17] For fuller analysis of this and other education cases which came before the United States Supreme Court see Motley, *op. cit.* p. 484.

[18] For details on this new pattern of discrimination see V. A. Clift, *op. cit.,* p. 226.

revolutionary change to take place in the whole history of education in the South: the entire South began to spend an unprecedented proportion of its income for the education of Negro children in public schools.

It came as a suprise to Southern state officials and legislators that Negroes were not impressed with the makeshift graduate schools, the increased expenditure on capital improvements, the attempts to equalize salaries and the general increase in expenditures for Negro education. Educational opportunities for Negroes were greatly improved, to be sure, but Negro citizens viewed this as irrelevant because they did not judge their conditions in comparison with, say, the impoverished millions in Asia. Instead, Negroes viewed their conditions by the standards of their white fellow citizens and by the guarantees the American system made for them. They were keenly aware that they were at the very crux of the Great American Experiment and that their drive to secure full educational rights as human beings and citizens was the acid test of the American Way of Life.

Therefore, Negroes prepared to make an onslaught and frontal attack on the validity of segregation in higher education. In cases against the University of Oklahoma and the University of Texas [19] Negro plaintiffs carried to the United States Supreme Court between 1946 and 1949 issues sharply testing the right of the states to alter in any substantial particular the opportunities for graduate and professional study offered Negroes from that offered whites. Indeed in the Texas case (*Sweatt* vs. *The University of Texas*) the plaintiff's attorneys argued that no segregated Negro school actually could provide equal educational opportunities. They not only argued that the new Negro law school which had been established by Texas was materially inferior, but also offered the testimony of anthropologists, psychologists and educators to show that Negroes were as capable of learning as whites, that classification of students by race was arbitrary and unjust and that segregation was harmful to personality adjustment. The Court obviously gave weight to these contentions by ruling out segregation in specific instances and largely invalidating it in the field of graduate and professional training. Few if any state Negro colleges in the South could meet the requirements posed by the Court in its decision.

Meanwhile, the Southern states had pooled their resources to set up regional programs for higher education which would serve the students of both races from all participating states. This plan was denounced by Negro leaders as another device for preserving segregation at the university level. The Southern Regional Educational Board and the regional compact were immediately challenged in 1949 when a Negro applicant was denied admis-

---

[19] *Sipuel* vs. *The University of Oklahoma; McLaurin* vs. *The University of Oklahoma; Sweatt* vs. *The University of Texas.* See Motley, *op. cit.,* p. 484.

sion to the University of Maryland School of Nursing on the grounds that she was entitled to out of state training at Meharry Medical School (Negro) under the regional plan. The Maryland Court of Appeals ordered her admitted to the state university. Beginning with this decision, more public institutions admitted Negroes. Enrollment of Negroes was restricted, however, primarily to graduate and professional schools.

The relentless legal assault upon the upper ramparts of the segregated educational structure had been planned and executed with great care. Negro leaders now reasoned that the anachronistic system of segregation in public elementary and secondary schools perpetuated segregation and discrimination in all other phases of public life of the nation. They maintained that segregation in the lower schools was a divisive and antidemocratic device perpetuating an obsolete caste system which flatly controverted the basic ethical concepts of the American Judeo-Christian tradition.

By this time the Negro masses were demanding that the National Association for the Advancement of Colored People press harder and with greater speed for equal rights in all fields. The masses, in the North and South, were making such great demands on Negro leaders that the leaders were actually being pressured into action in many instances where otherwise they would have been reluctant.

Therefore, in 1952, the long course of litigation over separate education in America brought before the Supreme Court five separate cases which challenged head-on the Plessy doctrine of "separate but equal." [20]

Each of these cases raised the basic issues of segregation in education in a somewhat different way. The implications reached the whole of the nation's segregated pattern as well as the basic division of authority between the Federal Government and the sovereign states. The moral overtones had practical repercussions on America's efforts in international politics to keep black, brown and yellow peoples of the world from swinging into the communist orbit.

On May 17, 1954, the United States Supreme Court ruled unanimously that segregation of the races in public education was unconstitutional. The Court made its position clear in the following unequivocal statement:

> In approaching this problem, we cannot turn the clock back to 1868 when the Amendment was adopted or even to 1896 when *Plessy* v. *Ferguson* was written. We must consider public education in the light of its full development and its present place in American life throughout the Nation. Only in

[20] These cases were from: Claredon, South Carolina (*Briggs* vs. *Elliot*); Prince Edward County, Va. (*Davis* vs. *County School Board*); Topeka, Kansas (*Brown* vs. *Board of Education*); Wilmington, Delaware (*Belton* vs. *Gebhart*), and Washington, D.C. (*Bolling* vs. *Sharpe*).

this way can it be determined if segregation in public schools deprives these plaintiffs of the equal protection of the laws.

. . . We come back to the question presented: Does segregation of children in public schools solely on the basis of race, even though the physical facilities and other "tangible" factors may be equal, deprive the children of the minority group of equal educational opportunities? We believe that it does.

. . . Segregation of white and colored children in public schools has a detrimental effect upon the colored children. The impact is greater when it has the sanction of the law; for the policy of separating the races is usually interpreted as denoting the inferiority of the Negro group.

Desegregation was progressing slowly, even in the South, before this historic and far-reaching decision. In compliance with the decision, school desegregation began in the fall of 1954 in a few large cities, notably Wilmington, Delaware, Baltimore, Maryland, and Washington, D. C., and in some scattered counties in Missouri, Arkansas, and West Virginia. By the fourth anniversary of the Supreme Court's original decision, the desegregation process was at work in ten out of the seventeen states that previously had compulsory school segregation. In keeping with the Court-ordained "deliberate speed" clause, desegregation moved faster in Kentucky, Oklahoma and Texas than in Tennessee and North Carolina. But it did spread. Out of 2,889 Southern school districts with both white and colored pupils, desegregation had begun in 764 by the end of four years. Of these, fewer than forty were compelled to desegregate by specific court order.

Then, in the fall of 1958, desegregation appeared to have been brought almost to a standstill by deep Southern hostility. New desegregation moves were limited to thirteen school districts in the entire South; and in contrast to this modicum of progress toward compliance, schools were closed in Little Rock, Arkansas, and in sections of Virginia to avoid integration. Desegregation seemed to have been stopped short by seven states willing to dispense with public schools rather than to yield to racial mixing.

By the middle of the 1958–59 school year, the situation had taken a different turn. Negro pupils had entered white schools in Alexandria, Virginia, without incident, bringing a third new community into the desegregation column—and not in a border state but in Virginia, the former center of massive resistance. Desegregation was thus on the move again, having met the ultimate test of school closing and having proved, at least in Virginia, that parents placed sufficiently high value on public education for their children to endure a limited amount of integration. Georgia, Alabama and Mississippi seemed not to be ready to back away from the massive resistance. But the solid front had been broken, and desegregation was making some marked advances in its sixth year; once again it began slowly to approach inevitability.[21]

DESEGREGATION DEVELOPMENTS SINCE 1960

Public Schools in the South

During the fall term of 1963, a decade after the 1954 Supreme Court decision, only 9.2 percent of the Negro public school students in the Southern and border states were attending elementary and secondary schools with whites on a desegregated basis. According to a survey reported in *Southern School News* [22] (Table I), the region enrolled 10,918,793 white students and 3,403,925 Negro students, but only 314,571 of the Negroes were in school with whites. In the eleven former Confederate States (Alabama, Arkansas, Florida, Georgia, Louisiana, Mississippi, North Carolina, South Carolina, Tennessee, Texas and Virginia), 30,798 Negro children attend school in mixed classes, with 14,000 of these being in the state of Texas. The bulk of the desegregation had taken place in the border area (Delaware, District of Columbia, Kentucky, Maryland, Missouri, Oklahoma and West Virginia) where 283,773 Negro children were attending mixed classes. This, however, represented only 56.5 percent of the Negro children in this area.[23]

Alabama and South Carolina permitted a few students to attend white schools for the first time in 1963. Mississippi up to 1964 remained the only state with complete segregation in its public schools. The much publicized University of Mississippi, where James Meredith had managed to survive as the lone Negro student until graduation, had admitted another Negro and then expelled him for disciplinary reasons in the fall of 1963.

In 1961, there were 6,196 school districts in the seventeen Southern and border states. Of these, 3,052 had Negro and white students and 979 (32.1 percent) of these biracial districts had policies or practices permitting the admission of Negroes to formerly all-white schools.

In the fall of 1962, fifty-two districts desegregated by policy or practice for the first time, as compared with thirty-one the previous year. Thirteen of the newly desegregated districts acted under court order, although in many of the others legal action was pending or threatened.

A total of 114 school districts were reported to be desegregating for the

[21] Editorial, *Baltimore Sun*, March 8, 1959.
[22] *Southern School News* (Nashville, Tenn.), 10, No. 6 (December, 1963), p. 1.
[23] See Table I for detailed distribution and extent of desegregation.

TABLE I–Public School Desegregation In Southern and Border States— 1963–1964

	School Districts With Negroes			Enrollment		In Desegregated Districts		Negroes In Schools With Whites	
	Total	& Whites	Deseg.	White	Negro	White	Negro	No.	%†
Alabama	114	114	4	539,996**	287,414*	106,199**	70,896**	21	.007
Arkansas	415	228	13	328,023**	112,012**	66,752	18,643	366	.327
Florida	67	67	16	964,241*	237,871*	669,375	130,667	3,650	1.53
Georgia	197	181	4	689,323	337,534	95,731	77,599	177	.052
Louisiana	67	67	2	460,589**	301,433**	68,700	79,077	1,814	.602
Mississippi	150	150	0	304,226**	291,971**	0	0	0	0
North Carolina	171	171	40	820,900*	347,063*	367,764*	133,164*	1,865	.537
South Carolina	108	108	1	368,496*	258,955*	3,108	9,539	10	.004
Tennessee	154	143	45	687,902*	164,940*	380,321	120,447	4,486	2.72
Texas	1,421	899	263	2,045,499	326,409*	1,300,000*	200,000*	18,000*	5.52
Virginia	130	128	55	710,176	228,961	486,231	145,658	3,721	1.63
SOUTH	**2,994**	**2,256**	**443**	**7,919,371**	**2,894,563**	**3,544,181**	**985,690**	**34,110**	**1.18**
Delaware	86	86	86	78,730	18,066	68,321	13,976	10,209	56.5
District of Columbia	1	1	1	19,803	117,915	19,803	117,915	98,813	83.8
Kentucky	204	165	163	611,126*	54,874*	492,701*	54,874*	29,855	54.4
Maryland	24	23	23	540,667	160,946	535,691	160,946	76,906	47.8
Missouri	1,597	212*	203*	793,000*	95,000*	NA	90,000*	40,000*	42.1
Oklahoma	1,160	241	197	541,125*	43,875*	324,023*	35,596*	12,289*	28.0
West Virginia	55	44	44	417,595*	23,449*	417,595*	23,449*	13,659*	58.2
BORDER	**3,127**	**772**	**717**	**3,002,046**	**514,125**	**1,858,134††**	**496,756**	**281,731**	**54.8**
REGION	**6,121**	**3,028**	**1,160**	**10,921,417**	**3,408,688**	**5,402,315††**	**1,482,446**	**315,841**	**9.3**

* Estimated. ** 1962–63.   † No. of Negroes in schools with whites, compared to total Negro enrollment.
†† Missouri not included.

SOURCE: Table adapted by permission from *Southern School News*, Vol. 10, No. 11 (May 1, 1964), p. 1.

first time in the fall of 1963, sixty-one more than September, 1962; and an additional eighty-three public school districts in eleven Southern states were desegregated in the 1964–65 school year. By fall of 1964 a total of 527 districts in these states were desegregated—about one-fourth of the 2,256 districts with students of both races enrolled.[24]

Thus, the number of school districts in the Southern states which claimed to be desegregating their schools was increasing. It should be noted, though, that the trend has been for a district to declare a policy of desegregation and then to permit only a very small number of Negro children to attend mixed classes. This was the policy followed in Atlanta in 1962 when only nine Negro students went to white schools. At the beginning of the same term, thirteen were admitted to mixed classes in Memphis and eighteen in Dallas. Thus the actual number of Negro children attending desegregated schools in the South remains exceedingly low.

The new resistance to desegregation, which amounts always to minimal compliance to the Supreme Court decision striking down compulsory school segregation, should properly be labeled *token desegregation*. This new strategy has several distinctive elements. First, desegregation plans are adopted which are as limited as possible. For example, the Nashville plan spreads the desegregation process out over a twelve-year period at the rate on one grade per year. Nashville began its plan with nineteen Negro students involved in the first-grade desegregation in 1957. Five years later it had 270 Negro children in the first five grades at formerly white schools.

Another example of tokenism is the pupil placement system which won court approval in North Carolina and Virginia. Under this plan only individual, "qualified" Negro students who actively seek admission may attend mixed classes. Negro children can and have been denied admission to white schools for academic, psychological, physical, geographic and other reasons. Applicants usually have been subjected to a series of special tests and personal interviews. Atlanta and New Orleans, as well as many other Southern communities, combined the grade-a-year plan with the pupil placement plan.

A final element of tokenism is the massive resistance and open defiance of the law by elected officials, including the governors of Arkansas, Mississippi and Alabama. Thus, defiantly in his inaugural address of January 14, 1963, Alabama's Governor George C. Wallace declared:

> I draw the line in the dust and toss the gauntlet before the feet of tyranny; and I say segregation now, segregation tomorrow, segregation forever.

[24] *Southern School News* [(II, No. 2 (August, 1964 p. 1)] The eleven Southern states in the fall of 1964 had desegregated 127 colleges and universities, leaving eighty-three still segregated; all eighty colleges in the border area have desegregated.

It should be noted, however, that when confronted by determined Federal law officers he receded from this position and permitted the enrollment of Negro students in Alabama's public collegiate institutions.

REGIONAL VARIATION IN DESEGREGATION

From a wide spectrum of rapid changes in the desegregation picture these developments compiled largely by the United States Commission on Civil Rights [25] are instructive:

The Border States (Delaware, Kentucky, Maryland, Missouri, Oklahoma, West Virginia)

While the principle of desegregation seems well established, actual practice is spotty. All school districts in Delaware which had made no plans to eliminate separate Negro schools were ordered by the Federal Court in 1959 to desegregate; but five years later in 1963–64 40 percent of the Negro children attended all-Negro schools. In Kentucky 137 out of 169 school districts have integrated schools attended by 54,000 Negro students, or one-half of the Negro school children in the state. The other half attend segregated schools. In Maryland twenty of its twenty-four school districts are desegregated, but Baltimore City and five western Maryland counties account for 97 percent of all the state's desegregation. In Missouri only 213 of the state's 1,597 school districts enrolled students in mixed schools. About 40,000 Negro youth were in schools with whites. Oklahoma, too, runs the gamut from wholly desegregated to wholly segregated school districts. All school districts in West Virginia had some integration and it was estimated in 1963 that 60 percent of the Negro children attended integrated school. West Virginia State College—once all-Negro—now actually has a slight majority of white students enrolled. As an investigator of the United States Commission on Civil Rights stated: "All in all, West Virginia has reached the point where it no longer fits the southern school mold."

In the early stages of the integration process a number of Negro teachers in all the border states were displaced, notably in Oklahoma where a survey by the State Department of Education in 1961 revealed that 394 Negro teachers had been released. Placement of Negro teachers in that state seems to be limited to all-Negro schools; in the other border states some Negro teachers work in integrated schools.

[25] From unpublished material of the commission.

Generally, the developing climate in these schools is reflected by the following statement of the Kentucky State Department of Education:

> There is very definite evidence that changing positive attitudes are taking place. Both races are growing in maturity, in education and in human development and relations.

The Deep South (Alabama, Georgia, Louisiana, Mississippi, South Carolina)

These states contain 636 school districts, but only fourteen of them were desegregated by the end of 1964. A hard core resistance to desegregation characterizes the educational climate in them.

Public high school desegregation had its first test in Alabama when thirteen Negro students were enrolled in Tuskeegee High School, Macon County, Alabama. Thereafter the school's 250 white students walked out. Then the school was closed. Immediately the Negro students were sent by the Federal court to enroll in another high school. This, too, was closed. At the end of the 1963–64 school term, the issue of the integration of public schools in Macon County, Alabama, was still undecided. Undecided also was the issue in the major cities of Birmingham and Mobile, where the Fifth Circuit Court of Appeals had issued desegregation orders. Pending was litigation in which Negro plaintiffs, supported by the United States Department of Justice, have contended that the governor of the state and the state board of education control education in Alabama and that, therefore, the Court should order the organization of the schools of the state into "a unitary, non-racial system." The court has not yet made so sweeping a ruling, but it had, by fall of 1964, ordered desegregation in four other Alabama counties, all of which agreed to comply.

In Georgia the only school system which actually had a desegregation program in operation by June, 1964, was the city of Atlanta, but only fifty-three of its 46,400 Negro children had by then been placed in biracial schools. Muskogee County School Board in the state, which has jurisdiction over the city of Columbus, agreed unanimously to the desegregation of its public schools and library. By fall, 1964, four additional counties had undertaken to desegregate their schools.

In Louisiana the school districts of East Baton Rouge and St. Helena have been under court order to desegregate since 1960, but not a single Negro child had been placed in a biracial school up to June of 1964. The parish of New Orleans was the only school district in the state where desegregation had commenced. Here, of the 59,000 Negro students enrolled in New

Orleans public schools 107 were attending desegregated classes by mid-1964. Another 200 Negro children were attending biracial parochial schools.

The school systems of Mississippi and South Carolina remained completely segregated through 1963. All suits to force desegregation brought before the Federal District Judge in Mississippi had up to 1964 been dismissed and appeals were pending. By 1964 only ten of South Carolina's 235,000 Negro pupils were attending schools with whites.

For the school term 1963–64, desegregation accelerated in South Carolina, with six counties agreeing to admit Negroes to formerly white schools; and in Mississippi the first breach of lily-white policy was made when four counties complied with a court order to desegregate.

Other Southern States (Arkansas, Florida, North Carolina, Tennessee, Texas, Virginia)

Of 448,000 pupils enrolled in public schools in Arkansas in the 1962–63 school year 26.1 percent were Negro, but only 247 of the Negro pupils or two-tenths of one percent were then attending biracial schools. Despite the gigantic struggle for integration in Little Rock which brought Federal troops to the city to enforce Federal Court orders during the Eisenhower Administration [1957] there were by 1964 only seventy-eight Negro pupils in five grade levels in schools with whites. In the entire state 1,084 pupils were then attending biracial public schools.

Thirteen of Florida's sixty-seven county school systems had begun desegregation by 1964 and nearly four thousand Negro children were in biracial schools. In Dade County, the first school district to desegregate, a policy of nondiscrimination in the hiring and placement of teachers had been adopted. The Dade County school board declared:

> We do not believe we can teach democracy in our schools without demonstrating our belief in the way schools are operated. All employees are notified that they are expected to teach or work with other employees and to teach pupils and to supervise or to be supervised in their work by other employees without regard for the creed or color of any individual.[26]

North Carolina has a "pupil assignment law" which gives each of its 173 school districts the right to assign each pupil to a particular school. This device has been used effectively to slow down integration in the state to a snail's pace. Each Negro child complaining of discrimination in assignment has been compelled under rulings of the Federal District Court to exhaust every remedy of appeal in the state before coming into the Federal Court.

[26] From unpublished material of the Commission.

The result is a long, drawn-out, expensive and cumbersome procedure which serves as a brake on the actual integration of Negro pupils.

Fewer than two of every one hundred Negro public school students in Tennessee were attending biracial classes. However, concurrent desegregation of big city and county school systems is more widespread in Tennessee than any other Southern state. In the state by 1964–65, forty-seven districts had been desegregated with more than 4,600 Negro children attending schools with whites. Nashville by the 1964–65 school year had reached the fifth grade in its grade-a-year desegregation plan.

By the 1964–65 school year 257 of Texas' 919 school districts had some form of desegregation plan and over 14,000 Negro pupils were attending biracial schools. This is an increase of thirteen school districts over the number which had desegregated in the previous year. However, more than 97 percent of Texas' Negro public school pupils still attend segregated schools.

Only 1,230 of Virginia's 229,105 Negro students were attending schools with white students in 1963—just over one-half of one percent. Of these more than eight hunderd were enrolled in the Washington, D.C., suburbs of northern Virginia and in the cities of Norfolk, Richmond and Roanoke. Only token desegregation existed in other school districts which had announced plans.

Ninety-six of the state's 128 school districts remained segregated in 1963. Most notorious of these had been the Prince Edward County School District, which abolished its public schools in 1960 rather than comply with a court desegregation order. By the 1964–65 school year, however, twenty-four new school districts in the state were desegregated.

HIGHER EDUCATION FOR NEGROES

The best available estimate of the number of Negro students attending American colleges and universities is about 225,000.[27] Although today substantial numbers of Negro students are attending both public and private biracial institutions of higher education(mainly in the North and West), the main source of Negro college graduates was for many decades "the

[27] Reported 1963–64 enrollment from 105 colleges and universities attended predominantly by Negroes totalled 107,278. To these enrollees must be added Negro students attending colleges where white students predominate. Following an intensive study of the latter schools, Dr. Benjamin Fine has estimated an average enrollment of about 125,000 Negro students. See Benjamin Fine, "Reverse Integration Will Bring End of All-Colored Higher Learning." *North American Newspaper Alliance,* (November 3, 1963).

Negro College." The number of such institutions has changed very little since 1900. In 1900 there were 99, in 1950 there were 118, and in 1964 there were 116 four-year and two-year collegiate-rank institutions operated primarily for Negroes.[28]

Enrollment in institutions of higher education primarily for Negroes was 2,624 in 1900 and had increased to 74,526 by 1950. Figure 1 indicates the growth in enrollment over the last decade. Figure 2 shows the trend in the number of graduates produced by these schools. When it is realized that in 1900 only twenty-two women were graduated from these colleges, the increase in the number of women graduates is phenomenal.

Equally remarkable has been the increase of advanced degrees awarded by these colleges and universities. In 1920 the first record of the awarding of master's degrees by these schools showed that five had been granted. By 1950 the number had increased to 768, with women receiving about half of these. The growth has continued. Recently Howard University and Atlanta University has instituted programs leading to a doctoral degree in some fields, but these programs have not yet fully developed. Most doctoral degrees received by Negroes are granted by Northern white universities.

A study published in 1946 by Green[29] reported 381 Negroes known to have received Ph.D. degrees between 1876 and 1943. More than half of these had earned their first degree from a Negro college. A more recent study[30] records that between 1920 and 1962 there were awarded doctorates to 1,478 graduates of Negro colleges. There were 312 Ph.D. degrees awarded such graduates between 1960 and 1962 (about one percent of the total granted in the United States). If to this number we add degrees received by Negro graduates of white colleges for whom racial identification is impossible, it seems reasonable to estimate an annual production of Negro doctorates of between 160 and 175. By contrast the range in 1950 was between 30 and 50.

When one appraises the growth in enrollment, the increase in the number of graduates, the progress made in the number of its students seeking advanced degrees in graduate and professional schools which has been evidenced in Negro colleges, the conclusion is unmistakable that Negro institutions of higher education have played a unique role in advancing American democratic education. It is therefore important that some atten-

[28] This final number may not be absolutely accurate because of the rapid change in racial enrollment in some institutions in states where desegregation has taken place.

[29] Harry Washington Greene, *Holders of Doctorates Among American Negroes* (Boston: Meador Publishing Company, 1946), p. 74.

[30] Lindey R. Harmon and Herbert Soldz, compilers, *Doctorate Production of United States Universities, 1920–1962* (Washington, D.C., Publication No. 1142, National Research Council, National Academy of Science 1963), p. 963.

FIGURE 1—College Enrollment from 1953–1954 to 1963–1964 by Sex for
105 Predominantly Negro Institutions Contrasted with That of
All Predominantly White Institutions in the United States

Note: This figure does not reflect enrollment of Negro students in other than predominantly
Negro colleges and universities.

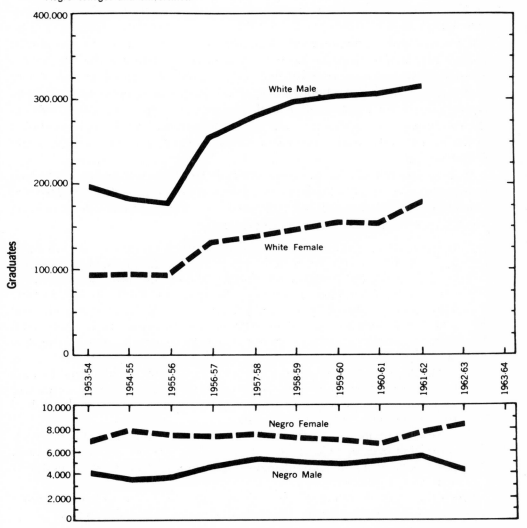

SOURCE: United States Office of Education, *Enrollment in Higher Education*
(for years shown in the figure). Responses to questionnaire of the
Phelps-Stokes Fund.

tion be given to the tremendous handicaps and disadvantages under which these institutions have been compelled to operate.

In 1950, there were 1,700 public and private colleges and universities in the United States. Of these, 118 were Negro institutions with 114 being located in the South and matriculating 85 percent of all the colored undergraduates from this section.[31] Approximately half of the Negro colleges of the United States were neither accredited nor approved by regional associations.[32]

Graduate and professional education for Negroes in the South was almost nonexistent as late as 1950. No work was offered leading to the doctorate. Two medical schools, Howard University Medical School and Meharry Medical School, supplied four-fifths of all Negro physicians and dentists. Opportunities for legal training and engineering were even more limited. By way of contrast, instruction was available for white students in medicine at thirty-one Southern institutions, in law at thirty-three, and in engineering at thirty-four.

In hearings before the Subcommittee of the Committee on Appropriations, 80th Congress, Mordecai W. Johnson, then president of Howard University, made the following summary on expenditures for education for Negroes in the seventeen Southern states:

> In states which maintain the segregated system of education there are about $137,000,000 annually spent on higher education. Of this sum $126,541,795 (including $86,000,000 of public funds) is spent on institutions for white youth only; from these institutions Negroes are rigidly excluded. Only $10,500,000 touches Negroes in any way; in fact, as far as state-supported schools are concerned, less than $5,000,000 touches Negroes. In these states there are about seventeen institutions undertaking to do higher education of college grade. . . .
>
> The amount of money spent on higher education by the states and Federal Government within these states is less than the budget of the University of Louisiana (in fact, only 65 per cent of the budget), which is maintained for a little over 1,000,000 in Louisiana. . . .
>
> This is one index, but the most serious index is this: that this money is spread out over so wide an area and in such a way that in no one of these states is there anything approaching a first-class state university opportunity available to Negroes.[33]

Since the 1954 decision of the United States Supreme Court outlawing segregation in public schools, important changes have taken place in the

---

[31] G. Myrdal, *American Dilemma* (New York: Harper & Brothers, 1944), p. 947.

[32] Martin D. Jenkins, *Journal of Negro Education*, XVII (Spring, 1948), p. 207.

[33] Hearings before Subcommittee of the Committee on Appropriations, House of Representatives, 80th Congress, February, 1947, p. 245.

FIGURE 2—College Graduates From 1953–1954 to 1963–1964, by Sex for
105 Predominantly Negro Institutions Contrasted with Those
of All Predominantly White Institutions in the United States

Note: This figure does not reflect degrees granted Negroes in other than predominantly Negro
colleges and universities.

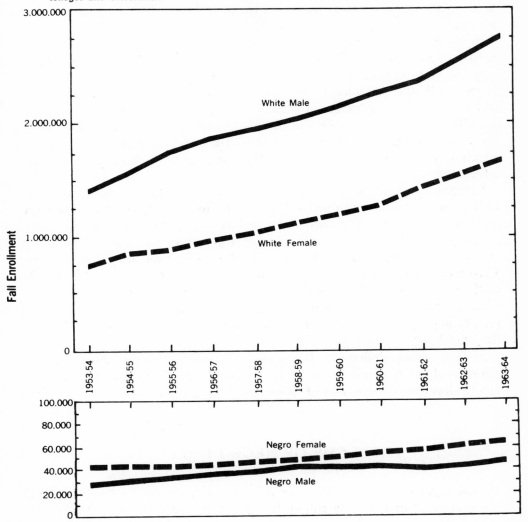

SOURCE: United States Office of Education, *Earned Degrees Conferred* (for years
shown in the figure). Responses to questionnaire of the Phelps-Stokes
Fund.

higher education of the Negro in the South. Negro students are now admitted to formerly white institutions, especially to the graduate and professional schools. Since records are no longer kept on the basis of race, we have no statistics on the number of Negroes attending these institutions. Integration has become a two-way street. Approximately two hundred white students have enrolled in all-Negro colleges of the South since 1954 and the number is increasing.

In the border area, especially in West Virginia, Missouri and the District of Columbia, formerly Negro colleges have become truly integrated. West Virginia State College at Institute, W. Va., was all Negro in 1954. Immediately with the Supreme Court decision white students began enrolling, and the number has increased steadily until white students now make up over 50 percent of the enrollment. Bluefield State College at Bluefield, West Virginia, was also an all-Negro college in 1954 and now has an enrollment which is nearly 50 percent white. The faculties at both institutions are integrated.

Lincoln University in Jefferson City, Missouri, was the Negro Land Grant College in that state with an all-Negro enrollment in 1954. It also became integrated soon after that date and now has a 50 percent white enrollment.

Lincoln University in Oxford, Pennsylvania, the first higher institution established for Negroes in America, has always had an integrated faculty. The faculty is now about evenly divided between Negro and white and the student body, which is all male, is about 20 percent white.

Howard University has become a truly international institution, drawing faculty and student body from all races and many nationalities throughout the world.

Morgan State College in Baltimore, Maryland, enrolled an increasing number of white students in both the regular and evening sessions. Its faculty has always consisted of members of both races.

PROBLEMS OF NEGRO COLLEGES

Although the faculties and student bodies of many of the Negro colleges are becoming increasingly integrated, these institutions seem destined to remain, for some decades to come, a major factor in the college education of Negro youth in the United States. In view of this fact it is important to consider hindrances which prevent these schools from providing high quality education. The four most pressing problems facing these colleges are discussed below:

Adequate Financial Support   Financial support of the predominantly Negro state-supported college in the South still remains woefully inadequate. Historically, segregation in education has always been used as a weapon for discrimination. The doctrine of separate but unequal is deeply imbedded in the culture of the South. Consequently, the budget for almost any land-grant university with an enrollment of twenty thousand or more has an annual budget that far exceeds the combined budgets of all of the Negro state colleges and the additional thirty-two private Negro liberal arts colleges being supported by the United Negro College Fund.

An Adequately Trained Faculty   Several forces operate in making it difficult to recruit and hold a highly competent faculty. Many other employment opportunities are now open to highly trained Negroes in industry and government. They therefore are attracted away from teaching. Formerly, teaching in a Negro college was almost the only employment open to them where they could use their advanced training. These new employment opportunities are more attractive than they might otherwise be because they are frequently more rewarding financially than the inadequately supported Negro college. Others leave teaching in these institutions because they prefer to bring their families to the North where they experience less hostility and discrimination because of race. Still others secure positions at "white" universities in the North because it is much easier to gain recognition and eminence as a scholar while attached to a "white" university.

A Student Body with an Academic Background for College Work   The problem of an inadequately prepared student body can be attributed to two factors. In the first place most of the schools attended by Negroes below college level are themselves inferior because of the lack of financial support, teachers with little training and experience, old and barely adequate buildings and deprivation of the neighborhood where located. Thus, many Negro youth who enter college are not prepared up to the required level. The other factor is that the most capable students whose parents are economically able and are of a higher social class tend to send their youngsters to the "white" prestige colleges and state universities. This amounts to skimming off the cream of the academic crop that once attended in larger numbers the all-Negro college.

Consequences of an Inferior Status Assigned the Negro College by White Culture   Another problem relating to the inferior status assigned to the Negro college is difficult to measure and assess in all its ramifications. The white majority seems never to hold the Negro college in as high esteem as institutions for whites. In the South, the Negro student is stigmatized as an individual because of the group to which he belongs. In reality he has a "double stigma" to overcome because the institution of higher education he attends, which is for the most part segregated, is also regarded as inferior. It has been subjected to a constant psychological attack in the press, on the screen and on the air. This "double stigma" has an adverse effect on personality, achievement, motivation and other factors contributing to success. This stigma of inferiority which is assigned to individuals and institutions in the segregated society was expressed in the Supreme Court's phrase, "separate educational facilities are inherently unequal."

FORCES FOR PROGRESS

One of the truly positive forces operating in the higher education of Negroes is the United Negro College Fund, which provides some of the financial support for thirty-two private Negro liberal arts colleges. The aim of the fund is to strengthen the curriculum and faculty of these institutions. Their "cash capital fund campaign" was launched in 1964 with a goal of $50 million. The Ford Foundation contributed $15 million to this drive and by the end of 1964 over $30 million had been raised.

Other sectors in education give assistance of one type or another to the Negro colleges and universities. The American Council on Education has appointed an eight member Committee on Equality of Educational Opportunity headed by President Elvis Stahr of Indiana University. The aims of the committee are: to formulate plans to strengthen the quality of education at Negro institutions, to bring Negro colleges into closer contact with the rest of higher education in America and to broaden opportunities for Negro students and faculty members to become integrated into universities.

Another significant movement is the "Big Brother" program, which attempts to pair a large integrated university of the North with one of the the predominantly Negro colleges. The faculties are brought together, attempts are made to raise the educational sights of Negro students who have had inferior schooling prior to college admission, and it aims to provide aspiration and incentive to Negro students.

Many institutions in the North and West are trying to attract qualified Negro college students, at both graduate and undergraduate level. In January, 1964, Dr. Robert F. Goheen, President of Princeton University, said that the competition among colleges and universities for able Negro students was much more intense than the traditional competition for football players. He pointed out also that it was clear that the number of able colored students who had had adequate educational opportunities was very small. He also called for more money and a staff to develop and expand such a program. He thought that cooperative programs between a number of institutions would be helpful in reducing competition for the same students and in making the effort more effective.

The University of California took a much more positive step toward solving this problem early in 1964. A $100,000 scholarship fund was established to assist students who come from the disadvantaged segments of the country. Scholarships are to be provided during the 1964–65 school year for certain students of minority status whose grades might otherwise bar their admission to college. Dr. Jerzy Neyman, Professor of Statistics emeritus, University of California, is one of the prime movers in this project. He has indicated that professors from other universities, including Stanford, Harvard and the University of Illinois, had agreed previously that a regular channel, similar to the fund and program in California, should be provided to enable exceptionally talented people from slum areas to be incorporated into the intellectual life of the country.

COLLEGE MOTIVATION FOR AMERICAN NEGRO STUDENTS

The need for the kinds of programs as described above was highlighted in a study of Negro enrollment in the colleges and universities in Indiana. Early in 1964 a report on a survey of all thirty-one colleges and universities in Indiana showed that only 2.9 percent of the total enrollment for the current year was Negro. In the state 6 percent of the high school graduating classes of the previous spring were Negro. *In the Indiana colleges and universities there were actually more African Negro students enrolled than American Negro.* In addition, the survey found that 60 percent of the 2,595 Negro students in Indiana institutions of higher learning were enrolled only part time. By contrast, only 16 percent of the white students are enrolled part time.

Director Harold Hatcher of the Indiana Civil Rights Commission said that this survey found no evidence of discrimination because of race. Rather, he felt that the cause for the low percentage of Negro students could be attributed to the median income of all Negro families in Indiana, which was $1,500 below that of white families.[34]

The evidence seems to indicate that Negro students attending interracial colleges and universities are far less likely to drop out before graduation than are white students or Negro students attending segregated colleges.

[34] Harold Hatcher, *Survey of Negro Enrollment at Indiana Colleges* (Indianapolis: Indiana Civil Rights Commission, 1964), pp. 10–61.

This was one of several very significant findings of a study entitled *The Negro Student at Integrated Colleges* by Kenneth B. Clark and Lawrence Plotkin under the sponsorship of the National Scholarship Service and Fund for Negro Students.[35] Some of the other important findings were: (1) The dropout rate was one-fourth the national one. Fewer than 10 percent of the Negro students studied failed to obtain a degree while approximately 40 percent of white students do not complete college. The authors advanced a motivational hypothesis to explain the very low dropout rate. These students feel motivated to complete college; "to drop out means that they will fall back into the ranks of the nonspecialized labor force where their race insures the permanence of low status." (2) Financial reasons for dropout lead all others. (3) The college grades received by these students were average with 31 percent earning an average "B" or better; less than 10 percent were graduated with honors; and a little more than one percent were elected to Phi Beta Kappa, the national scholastic honor society. (4) There was found no relationship between family income and academic success at college. (5) Academic success was found to be directly related to parents' occupational level. (6) The predictive value of intelligence tests administered in high school was not high.

PUBLIC SCHOOL EDUCATION FOR NEGROES IN THE NORTH

During the period since World War II, Negroes have migrated into the cities of the North at an unprecedented pace.[36] Housing is more segregated in the largest cities of the North than it was thirty years ago. Housing patterns have developed along social-class and caste lines and have therefore created *de facto* segregated neighborhoods and schools.

The first important fact about racial composition of public elementary schools in sixteen states in the North and West is that the percentage of nonwhite pupils greatly exceeds the proportion of nonwhites in the total population. Consider the nine largest cities. In Buffalo, Pittsburgh and St. Louis, the percentage of minority group children in the public elementary schools was more than double the proportion of the total population. In Chicago, New York and Philadelphia, it was almost exactly twice the total population percentage. Only in Baltimore, Detroit and Washington, D. C.,

[35] Kenneth B. Clark and Lawrence Plotkin, *The Negro Student at Integrated Colleges* (New York: National Scholarship Service and Fund for Negro Students, 1963), pp. 7–9.

[36] Karl E. and Alma F. Taeuber, "The Negro Population in the United States," earlier in this volume, p. 36.

was it proportionately less than twice the total population percentage. In the medium-sized cities, Camden, New Jersey, and Oakland, California, there were approximately more than twice as many Negroes in public elementary schools as in the general population. The small cities of Orange, New Jersey, had more than twice the proportion of Negroes in its elementary schools as in the total population.

The second important fact is that in five major cities, Baltimore, Newark, Philadelphia, St. Louis and Washington, the percentage of minority group children in the public elementary schools exceeded 50 percent of the total elementary school enrollment, the range being from 53 percent in Philadelphia to 86 percent in Washington. In six more the proportion was approaching 50 percent: 49.3 percent in Camden; 46 percent in Chicago; 46.2 percent in Detroit (that is, for all schools, high and elementary); 47.3 percent in Oakland, and 48.9 percent in Orange, New Jersey. In only four of the cities, Buffalo, Pittsburgh, Plainfield and Montclair, was the proportion below 40 percent, the range being from 32 percent in Montclair to 37 percent in Plainfield.

ACHIEVING RACIAL BALANCE IN SCHOOLS

It is well to note the significance of these concentrations of Negro population in terms of concepts of *de facto* segregation developed by social psychologists, educators and other experts.

School administrators have found Negro concentrations in schools in percentages ranging from 46 to 99 percent to be grounds for administrative action to reduce racial imbalance.

Pupil assignment to achieve desirable racial balance is not a simple process. Most Northern and Western cities have been operating public schools for seventy-five years or more. Many school buildings still in use were built fifty to seventy-five years ago. The size and location of these buildings were determined by the population density of the period in which they were built. New schools have been added and existing buildings enlarged to accommodate increased population. But change in population density has made many older schools in large cities inadequate for the present school population of the geographic area they serve.

St. Louis can be used as an example of this.[37] In the period between desegregation of the schools in September, 1955, and the school year

[37] The statistics presented here are taken from an unpublished report of the United States Commission on Civil Rights.

1961–62, the white elementary school population of St. Louis decreased from 44,779 to 37,669, and the Negro enrollment increased from 27,921 to 45,000.

The Negro-white inversion during this period was accompanied by an expanding of the Negro population from the central city line into the West End area in large numbers. The now crowded West End, a 98 percent white section in 1950, had become 64 percent Negro by 1960. Soldan High School, which serves this area as a general high school, was 74 percent white after desegregation in 1955 and 99 percent Negro in 1962. The eleven elementary schools in the West End district in 1955 ranged from 45 to 100 percent white in re-enrollment; six were over 90 percent or more white. In October, 1962, the school administration made a head count. At that date there was one more elementary school in the West End district than in 1955, making a total of twelve. All but two of the twelve schools were over 90 percent Negro.

Of greater importance, the enrollment in these schools had increased from 9,892 in 1955 to 19,527 in 1962. The classroom space which had been sufficient to accommodate the area's children in 1955 had become grossly inadequate because of the change in the density of the population. Enrollment in one elementary school in 1962 was almost three times its November, 1955, enrollment. Obviously, schools planned for some 10,000 pupils could not accommodate twice that number. St. Louis' partial answer has been to transfer about 5,000 of the pupils officially enrolled in these schools to distant and almost always predominantly white schools until the building program catches up with the increase in pupils.

New York City provides some interesting statistics and emerging patterns which are helpful in interpreting trends that are developing in other cities of the North. Three population trends stand out which have a direct bearing on what is happening to the public school system.

First, the population is more mobile; second, it is more segregated racially, and third, neighborhoods have become essentially of one social-class. Between 1950 and 1957, New York City lost a white population of about 750,000 and gained an ethnically identifiable Negro and Puerto Rican population of about 650,000.[38] During the period from 1956 to 1964 the number of predominantly Negro and Puerto Rican elementary and junior high schools in the city doubled.

In 1964, there were 264,616 Negro pupils in the New York City school system, an increase of 91,659, or 53 percent, over the 1957–58 total of

[38] Dan W. Dodson, *Interpreting the "Inner City,"* Human Relations Monograph No. 12 (New York: New York University, Center for Human Relations and Community Studies, 1961), p. 11.

172,957. For 1964 there were 177,544 Puerto Rican children in the system, an increase of 48,564, or 37.6 percent. There were 596,356 "others" (a term used by the New York City school system to refer to students not Negro or Puerto Rican) in the system, a decrease of 54,323, or 8.3 percent.

As a result of these population changes the number of elementary and junior high schools with a Negro or Puerto Rican enrollment of 85 to 90 percent had increased. Such elementary schools had increased from 64 in 1957–58 to 134 in 1964 and the number of junior high schools had increased during this period from 13 to 31. This change took place during a period when the board of education was trying to improve the ethnic distribution of children in schools.

CULTURAL DEPRIVATION AND LOW ACADEMIC ACHIEVEMENT

Much of the current thinking about the problems of the culturally deprived child in our urban areas has been focused on the Negro. The authorities in the behavioral sciences are agreed that cultural deprivation is not race-related. The ego development of individuals in each subculture (including the subcultures in the Negro minority) is directly influenced by the special nature and quality of multidimensional cultural factors which are operating in the culture. Therefore, cultural deprivation is not specific to racial groups, but to cultural factors. Ausubel sums up the position thus:

> Many of the ecological features of the segregated Negro subculture impinge on personality development in early childhood are not specific to Negroes as such, but are characteristic of most lower-class populations. This fact is not widely appreciated by white Americans and hence contributes to much anti-Negro sentiment: many characteristic facets of the Negro's value system and behavior pattern are falsely attributed to his racial membership, whereas they really reflect his predominant membership in the lower social class.[39]

Some of the cultural factors which will be described below contribute to deprivation which manifests itself in low levels of motivation, low achievement on standardized tests, negative self-evaluation, low levels of aspiration and behavior which deviates from accepted middle-class norms.

The urban population has grown and is growing increasingly homogeneous. Both the inner city and the suburbs have become a series of "one social

[39] David P. Ausubel and Pearl Ausubel, "Ego Development Among Segregated Negro Children," in *Education in Depressed Areas,* A. Harry Passow (ed.). (New York: Bureau of Publications, Teachers College, Columbia University, 1963), p. 113. By permission.

class" neighborhoods. People in these neighborhoods tend to be alike in income level, general employment classification, amount of schooling completed, racial identity and in ethnic background. The Negro migrant to the urban areas of the North must nearly always live in the worst and most crowded slum areas that are typically inhabited by his group. His economic resources, level of culture, sophistication and style of living all operate to force him to seek the "ghetto" as a place to live. Once in the "ghetto," he becomes even more isolated from the mainstream of American life than he was before moving to the city. His neighborhood, like other "one social class" neighborhoods, tends to be self-contained and an island unto itself. It is in this environment that children begin to take on a value system and patterns of behavior that are inconsistent with the demands and requirements for academic success in schools.

Typically, the neighborhood is more segregated racially than two or three decades ago; the school located there has ceased to represent a cross section of American life. The population in the neighborhood school is homogeneous. Therefore, the school no longer provides an opportunity for the cross-fertilization of ideas and cultures. It provides no opportunities for young people of different backgrounds to learn anything about each other. It provides no first-hand experiences which will help children to build understandings of and appreciations for people who are different.

The school has become the dominant institution in the control and socialization of youth because it is a major force in determining status transitions of youth. The child who is at the bottom of the socio-economic scale is isolated and completely apart from successful examples or models in the community and schools that can be emulated. Examples of success and of behavior that leads to high level attainment in the broader society are not a part of his environment at all. His world is void of abstract symbols, ideas, abstractions and a high level of verbal meanings. Therefore, it is not surprising that he has difficulty in making high scores on standardized intelligence and achievement tests.

The school tends to reflect the neighborhood in which it is located. Thus, schools in the higher social class neighborhoods tend to be of the "silk stocking" type with the better buildings and facilities, better and more enriched programs and better qualified teachers. At the bottom of this scale are typically found the all-Negro schools in the all-Negro residential areas of the inner city. These schools are nearly always inferior in quality. The larger society regards the people who attend these schools as being inferior and assigns to them a stigma and a negative evaluation. The teachers, the community, and the board in charge of operating the schools do not expect anything other than low-level performance. The curriculum is therefore accommodating and geared to a low level of ability and to shoddy academic performance. The consequence is that retardation begins for a large number of these children very soon after they enter school. By the time one-third of these children reach the fourth grade they are performing one grade behind their grade level. The longer they remain in school, the more retarded they become. It is a combination of these and other factors, thet most important of which is that of enforcing a negative self-evaluation on the Negro child that disarms him psychologically.

It is with these kinds of problems in our society that our educators are now working. Pioneer work of such scholars as Allison Davis [40] and Martin Jenkins [41] has provided us with a better understanding of the theoretical and practical significance of low scores that minority groups make on intelligence tests. As a result, psychologists now attribute the low average performance on intelligence tests of subcultures to cultural factors. Therefore, in the decade to come, the two most pressing and compelling factors related to the education of the Negro in America will be: (1) the desegregation of the schools, and (2) providing an adequate and meaningful education for the culturally deprived.

There now exist some notable examples of efforts to solve these problems in our major cities. The Higher Horizons Program in New York City, The Great Cities Project in fourteen major cities supported with Ford Foundation funds, the Banneker schools in St. Louis, and the Amidon School in Washington, all operate on the assumption that present problems of the culturally deprived youth in our schools can be solved by an expansion of services that have worked with middle-class white children. These are sometimes referred to as *saturation programs* which provide for more guidance, more remedial instruction, more emphasis on reading, more individual psychological testing, and more cultural programs. None of these programs has made extensive use of research in the behavioral sciences in designing programs and procedures. In the future more attention will have to be given to these areas for theoretical and empirical bases upon which to construct educational programs. Out of this search and effort may come answers which can be applied to the vital educational problems in America and in the emerging nations of the world.

[40] W. Allison Davis, with John Dollard, *Children of Bondage* (Washington, D.C.: American Council on Education, 1940); Kenneth W. Eells, under the chairmanship of Allison Davis, *Intelligence and Cultural Differences,* (Chicago: University of Chicago Press, 1951).

[41] Martin Jenkins, "Intelligence of Negro Children" in Paul A. Witty, ed. *Intelligence in a Changing Universe* (New York: Department of Supervisors and Directors of Instruction of the National Education Association of the United States, 1940).

chapter 8

The Negro
in American Religious Life

Harry V. Richardson

THE SLAVE ERA

The great majority of Negro slaves imported into the Western Hemispere came from the west coast of Central Africa. The region that is now the nation of Ghana was one of the focal points of the trade.

The natives of this region who were caught and sold into slavery came from tribes that had well-developed religions. Like most primitive peoples, religion played a large and fervent part in their lives. They were animistic, they believed in spirits, good and bad, and they practiced fetishism. In such religions with a multiplicity of spirits, there is usually one dominant or father spirit who is creator, ruler and protector. References to this dominant spirit, sometimes called Anyambe or Onyambe, are found in the language and practices of the people today, both Westernized and native.

Thus the fact that the African slaves already had a highly developed religious life when they arrived in America probably explains why many slaves, as they had the opportunity, took so readily to the Christian religion, and had so little trouble making the transition despite language and cultural barriers.

From the beginning, there was a serious effort to convert the slaves to Christianity. Indeed, this was one of the justifications for the slave trade. But for the first hundred years the question of converting slaves was highly controversial, and therefore was not as widespread or as effective as it might have been.

For example, at the time when the importation of Negro slaves began, it was commonly believed that one Christian should not hold another Christian in bondage. This meant that when a slave became a Christian he also should have been freed. This would have been ruinous to those who had invested in slaves, and it led to much of the opposition that missionaries faced in their efforts to convert the slaves.

To settle the issue in Virginia the legislature of that colony declared in 1667 that baptism did not alter the condition of a person as to his bondage or freedom. This started a process of enactments and rulings that removed the Christian religion as a legal barrier to slavery in the colonies. In 1729 the Crown Attorney and Solicitor General ruled that baptism in no way change a slave's legal status. Two years previously the Bishop of London had declared:

> . . . Christianity does not make the least alteration in civil property; that the freedom which Christianity gives, is a freedom from the bondage of sin and Satan, and from the dominion of their lusts and passions and inordinate desires; but as to their outward condition they remained as before, even after baptism.[1]

As the principle became established, that conversion did not alter slave status, ministers and missionaries were freer to work among the slaves. The religious body that most actively undertook this work in the seventeenth and early eighteenth centuries was the Church of England through its Society for the Propagation of the Gospel in Foreign Parts. Since the Anglican Church was the major religious body in the colonies, the responsibility of winning converts to Christianity fell mainly upon the ministers of this church. However, for many reasons they were not able to devote adequate effort to the task. To assist in evangelizing the growing colonial population the Society for the Propagation of the Gospel was organized in 1701. Its specific duties were: "the care and instruction of our people settled in the colonies; the conversion of the Indian savages, and the conversion of the Negroes."

Other bodies were active in the colonial period, but on a much smaller scale. Chief among them were the Moravian Brethren, the Presbyterians and the Society of Friends. The Friends took the most positive stand against slavery of any of the religious bodies during this period. They alone made the possession of slaves a cause for expulsion from the Society.

It is the opinion of Marcus W. Jernigan, a student of colonial history, that prior to the American Revolution, comparatively few slaves were converted to Christianity. His reasons as summarized from a published discussion of the subject are:

1.   Masters feared that conversion would interfere with slave labor. Slaves were required to work on Sundays, which conflicted with Christian teaching, and further, when converted, slaves would be equal in one respect to their masters, which would make them harder to control.

2.   The general interest in religion was low in colonial times. Masters

---

[1] W.E.B. Du Bois, *The Negro Church* (Atlanta, Georgia: The Atlanta University Press, 1903), p. 10.

were not much interested in their own spiritual welfare, and consequently were not deeply concerned about the welfare of their slaves.

3.   Many slaves were unable to understand religious teachings, due in large part to their lack of knowledge of the English language.

4.   The slave's environment was not conducive to the Christian life.

5.   The sparsely settled country and the difficulties of travel made it hard for ministers to serve their members, to say nothing of evangelizing the unchurched.[2]

It was not until the latter half of the eighteenth century, around the time of the American Revolution, that a number of significant developments took place that did much to spread Christianity among the slaves and to shape the course of Negro religion in America.

The Influence of Cotton

First of these developments was the increased production of cotton in response to a rapidly rising world demand. A series of remarkable inventions, beginning with the spinning and weaving machines in England and culminating in Whitney's cotton gin in America, greatly increased the output of cotton goods. The soil of the Southern colonies was admirably suited to grow the necessary cotton if an adequate supply of labor could be obtained. This labor was found in African Negro slaves, who first were legally imported into the country, then illegally smuggled, and all the while bred to meet the great demand. In 1790 there were approximately 700,000 slaves in the United States. In 1860 there were 4 million. Over 3 million were in twelve Southern states, engaged for the most part in producing the cotton and other crops that were rapidly building up the fortunes of the wealthier group among the Southern planters.

This concentration of Negroes on the farms and plantations of the South gave the busy evangelists of the time excellent opportunities to reach the Negroes and to win large numbers of them to Christianity.

The Evangelicals and the Slave

The second great development in Negro religion was the coming of the evangelical Christian bodies, particularly the Methodists, Baptists, and Presbyterians. These groups in their zeal to evangelize the young America, gave much attention to the growing body of slaves. In the early stage they

---

[2] Summary of statement from "Slavery and Conversion in the American Colonies," by Marcus W. Jernigan, in *American Historical Review*, XXI, No. 3 (April 1916), pp 504–527. Used by permission.

were strongly abolitionist. They felt that slavery was wrong, and they openly preached against it. Freeborn Garretson said in 1776:

> It was God, not man, that taught me the impropriety of holding slaves; and I shall never be able to praise him enough for it. My very heart has bled since that for slaveholders, especially those who make a profession of religion; for I believe it to be a crying sin.[3]

Bishop Asbury records in his Journal in 1780: "This I know. God will plead the cause of the oppressed though it gives offense to say so here. . . . I am grieved for slavery and the manner of keeping these poor people." [4]

Many preachers followed their words by freeing slaves they already held and by refusing to become slaveholders. In 1780 the Methodists required all traveling preachers to set their slaves free. The Baptists, because of their policy of local church government, were not as uniform or as effective in their attack on slavery as the Methodists. Yet in 1789 a Baptist Convention declared:

> Slavery is a violent depredation of the rights of nature and inconsistent with a republican government, and therefore, [we] recommend it to our brethren, to make use of their local missions to extirpate this horrid evil from the land; and pray Almighty God that our honorable legislature may have in their power to proclaim the great jubilee consistent with the principles of good policy.[5]

Although the evangelicals found it necessary to retreat considerably from the high ground they first had taken against slavery, they continued their efforts to convert the slaves, and to plead in the name of Christianity for amelioration of the more brutal aspects of slavery.

In seeking converts, the evangelicals had one great advantage over the Anglicans and other early missionaries. The evangelical religion was simple, personal and only slightly ritualistic. It was ideally suited to the unlettered masses of the colonial frontier both white and black. In order to become an Anglican it was necessary to know the creed, the catechism and other articles of faith, as well as to be able to follow the ritual of the service. To become a Methodist or Baptist it was only necessary to repent and accept Christ as personal Savior. This was a religion even the field-hand slave could understand. In the early evangelistic drives such as the Great Awakening and the Great Revival, large numbers of Negroes were

---

[3] Carter G. Woodson, *History of the Negro Church* (Washington, D.C.: The Associated Publishers, 1921), p. 28. Used by permission.

[4] *Journal of Reverend Francis Asbury*, I (New York: Lane and Scott, 1852), p. 306.

[5] Woodson, *op. cit.*, p. 32.

converted. But if the simplicity of the evangelical faith did much to determine the number of Negroes who became Christians, the emotionalism of the early evangelical faith did much to determine the nature of Negro worship. The religion that the Negro masses first received was characterized by such phenomena as laughing, weeping, shouting, dancing, barking, jerking, prostration and speaking in tongues. These were regarded as evidence of the Spirit at work in the heart of man, and they were also taken as evidence of the depth and sincerity of the conversion. It was inevitable, therefore, that early Negro worship should be filled with these emotional elements.

Although there is some tendency to regard high emotionalism as a phenomenon peculiar to the Negro church, in reality it is a hangover from the days of frontier religion. It should also be said that emotionalism of this type is to be found today chiefly among the less cultured rural and urban churches.[6]

The Negro Preacher

The third development that did much to shape the course of Negro religion was the rise of Negro preachers. These leaders began to appear in the latter part of the eighteenth century, the time when large numbers of Negroes were being converted to Christianity. Prominent among them were Black Harry (c. 1782), who traveled with Bishop Asbury and was a great attraction; David George (c. 1775), preacher of the first Negro Baptist church at Silver Bluff, South Carolina; George Liele, of Burke County, Georgia, an eloquent preacher to blacks and whites; Andrew Bryan of Georgia (1737–1812), founder of the First African Baptist Church of Savannah; John Chavis (c. 1801), who was made a missionary to slaves by the Presbyterians, and Henry Evans, organizer of the white Methodist church at Fayetteville, North Carolina, in 1790.[7] Most unusual among these early preachers was Lemuel Haynes, 1753–1833, a mulatto of learning and eloquence who through all of his ministry pastored only white Congregational churches in New England. He was quite a theologian, and debated with power the theological issues of his time.

The Negro preacher played a significant part in the social and religious development of Negro life. First, preaching was an outlet for leadership ability. It was the one position of leadership permitted Negroes, and the office carried considerable prestige. It did much to keep aspira-

[6] Gunnar Myrdal, *An American Dilemma*, II (New York: Harper and Brothers, 1944), pp. 937–38.
[7] Woodson, *op. cit.*, Chapter III.

tion alive among gifted Negro men. Secondly, the Negro preacher was able to communicate religion to the slave in a useful and intimate form. Being one of the people and suffering with them, he could make religion not only a discipline, but also a living ground of hope.

The preachers' task was hard, however. While preaching to slaves, they could not attack slavery, at least openly. The preacher himself was always suspected and closely watched as a potential source of rebellion. The controls over slave meetings even for worship were so rigid and severe that an attack on the slave system would have readily brought down terrible penalties upon both preacher and people.

Yet from the beginning the church served as the main outlet through which the slaves could express their sufferings and dissatisfaction. Although it was done covertly, the church rendered two great needed services to the slaves: first, it kept alive the consciousness that the slave system was wicked; and second, it kept alive the hope that in the plan of a good, just God, the wicked, brutal system under which they lived would have to pass away.

It should be said, however, that not all preachers were patient or un-resisting. Nat Turner, for instance, who led the bloody revolt of 1831, was a Baptist exhorter.

In the time of slavery there were three distinct types of slave churches: the "mixed" church with slaves as members of the congregation; the separate church under white leadership; and the separate church under Negro leadership. All three types existed simultaneously, but the gradual tendency was toward the separate, all-Negro church.

THE EMANCIPATION AND AFTER

On September 22, 1862, President Lincoln issued the Emancipation Proclamation that was to become effective January 1, 1863. Although it was not immediately enforceable in many parts of the South since un-occupied sections were outside the control of the national government, freedom became a reality for all Negroes with the close of the Civil War. Thenceforth they were free to move and to organize as they wished.

The great mass of undeveloped, unchristianized freemen in the South presented opportunity for many kinds of humanitarian service. Along with philanthropic whites who came into the South to render educational as well as religious aid to the freedmen, Negro missionaries also came as representatives of independent Negro denominations, seeking to win members for their particular churches from among the former slaves.

Partly because of their racial appeal, partly because of their greater activity, the Negro workers won far more members than the representatives of the white church bodies. In fact, the early days of the Reconstruction were marked by a strong tendency toward independent, all-Negro religious organizations. In the decade between 1860 and 1870 the African Methodist Episcopal Zion Church, one of the two principal Negro Methodist bodies, grew from 26,746 members to 200,000. The African Methodist Episcopal Church, the leading Negro Methodist group, in 1880 claimed a membership of 400,000. For both churches most of their members were the freedmen in the rural South.

Baptists quickly became the most numerous group among Negroes in the South. In this church, as in the Methodist, the tendency was toward independent, all-Negro units. Even in cases where Negroes had been members of white churches on amicable terms, there still was a desire for the separate all-colored church.

THE PRESENT CHURCH

Major Negro Denominations

Denomination	Number of Members	Number of Churches	Number of Pastors	Sunday School Members
National Baptist Convention, U.S.A.	5,000,000	26,000	27,500	2,407,000
National Baptist Convention of America	2,668,000	11,398	7,598	2,500,000
AME Church	1,166,000	5,878	5,878	363,432
AME Zion Church	770,000	4,083	2,400	199,250
CME Church	444,493	2,523	1,792	115,424

The Baptists

Prior to the Civil War, the Baptist Church among Negroes consisted almost entirely of local congregations. Organization into district, state or national bodies was difficult both for slaves and free Negroes. With the coming of freedom, the organization of larger bodies rapidly took place. The first state Convention was organized in North Carolina in 1866, just one year after the close of the war. Alabama and Virginia followed in 1867, and by 1870 all the Southern states had state conventions.

On the national level, the Negro groups at first were affiliated with white national bodies. In 1867, however, the Consolidated American Baptist Convention was organized and continued until 1880, when the National Baptist Convention was established at Montgomery, Alabama. Three smaller conventions grew out of this body: the Foreign Mission Baptist Convention of the U.S.A., 1880; the American National Baptist Convention, 1880, and the American National Educational Baptist Convention, 1893. All of these were united in 1895 at Atlanta, Georgia, into the National Baptist Convention of the U.S.A., which was incorporated in 1915. This convention when formed had three million members, and thereby became the largest single denomination of Negro Christians in the world. Such tremendous growth in the fifty years from 1865 to 1915 reveals the rapidity with which the church grew among Negroes after Emancipation.

With the passing years the National Baptist Convention of the U.S.A. [Incorporated] has suffered a number of splits. The largest of these separating groups is the National Baptist Convention of America.

The tendency toward division, so characteristic of Baptists, continues to the present time. Today there are three national conventions: the National Baptist Convention of the U.S.A., the National Baptist Convention of America and the Progressive Baptist Convention.

Although divided, Baptists are by far the largest single group of Negro Christians in the world. They have approximately 7,668,000 members, 37,300 churches, and 4,900,000 children in church schools. There are 35,000 preachers in the Baptist ministry.

There are no distinctive doctrines or patterns of policy in the Negro Baptist Churches. They adhere in all basic essentials to the beliefs and practices of the major Baptist bodies of the nation. The Baptists have played a great part in the progress of the Negro group in education, in civic leadership and in other ways. They also have an extensive foreign mission program.

The Methodist Churches

Methodists were early active among Negroes both in colonial and post-Revolutionary times. They won large numbers to Methodism and took them readily into church membership. They organized a number of Negro congregations, usually presided over by white preachers, and took a number of Negroes into the ministry.

The Negro members, both slave and free, were usually restricted, however, in their participation in church life. They sat in segregated seats during services, and communed after the others or in special services. Dissatisfaction with such arrangements steadily increased, so that by 1785 in several Northern cities Negro members had organized themselves into separate congregations. In 1787 a company of Negroes in Philadelphia withdrew from the white church, and under the leadership of Richard Allen, a free and well-to-do Negro, built a chapel where they held separate services under an ordained Negro Episcopal priest.

Despite opposition from the white Methodists in Philadelphia, in 1793 Bishop Asbury dedicated the chapel as Bethel Church, and in 1799 he ordained Richard Allen a deacon.

In 1814, out of litigation brought by the white Methodists, the Supreme Court of Pennsylvania ruled that Bethel Church was an independent body. In 1816 Richard Allen and others called together representatives of separate churches similar to Bethel that had been organized in Delaware, Maryland and New Jersey. This meeting resulted in the formation of the African Methodist Episcopal Church, the second separate Negro Methodist denomination. The first was the Union Church of Africans which had been incorporated in Wilmington, Delaware, in 1813. This church, however, has grown very little. About the same time a third separatist movement, much like the first, resulted in the formation of the African Methodist Episcopal Zion Church in 1820.

Prior to the Civil War, the Negro Methodist churches were not able to expand widely. The national pattern of church life characteristic of Methodism with its itinerant ministry and traveling officers, was not possible for Negroes, either slave or free. With the coming of freedom, permitting the movement and evangelism necessary for expansion, the Negro Methodist bodies grew very rapidly, but not as much as the Baptists. The Christian Methodist Episcopal Church, discussed below, illustrates the rise and growth of a church after the Emancipation.

The AME Church

The AME Church today is truly international in scope. It has churches in Africa, Canada and the Caribbean area. Figures on membership are only approximate because of the lack of reports. The last reported figure [1951] gave an inclusive membership of 1,166,301 and 5,878 churches. In the same year [1951] 6,472 Sunday Schools were reported, with 262,432 members. It seems that today this church has somewhere between a million and a million and a half members.

The AME Church is divided into eighteen episcopal districts. The governing bodies of the church are the General Conference, which meets quadrennially; the Council of Bishops and the General Board. The work of the church is under the supervision of ten Boards or Departments, such as the Board of Missions, the Board of Church Extension, the Department of

Education and the Department of Evangelism. There are five publications, the *Christian Recorder, The AME Review,* the *Voice of Missions,* the *Southwestern Christian Recorder,* and the *Woman's Missionary Recorder.* The church maintains a publishing house in Nashville, Tennessee.

The AMEZ Church

The origin of the AMEZ Church is much like that of the AME. In 1796 a group of colored members, led by James Varick and others, withdrew from the John Street Methodist Church in New York City to escape the problems of segregation in church life. In 1800 they built a church which they named Zion. They at first maintained cooperative relationships with the white Methodist Church, but in 1820 this cooperation failed. Joining with separate Negro congregations in other cities, in 1821 they held an annual conference, and elected James Varick their first bishop. Several elders had been ordained by sympathetic white Methodist ministers. This gave them a ministry.

This church, like all the others, experienced its great growth after the Civil War. By 1880 fifteen annual conferences had been organized in the South. Today this church performs missionary work in West Africa, South America and the West Indies.

The CME Church

The third major Negro Methodist body is the Christian Methodist Episcopal Church. Originally it was called the Colored ME Church, but in 1956 the word *Colored* was changed to *Christian.*

At the close of the Civil War there were over 250,000 Negro members in the Methodist Episcopal Church, South. They had long been dissatisfied with the segregation and restrictions imposed upon the colored members. Immediately after the war, in 1866, they appealed to the General Conference of the ME Church, South, to be set apart in a church of their own. The conference ruled that wherever there were sufficient numbers, they be set aside in separate annual conferences. It further appointed a commission to study the request for a separate church and to report to the next general conference. In 1870 the commission recommended that the Negro members be organized into a church of their own. Later that year, in December, the first General Conference of the CME Church was held at Jackson, Tennessee. Two Negro bishops were elected, Henry Miles and Richard H. Vanderhorst.

In the years since the separation the ME Church, South, has kept its interest in the CME Church, and has assisted it in many ways, especially in organizing and operating the educational program.

This church, like the others, has had substantial growth. It now has 444,493 members and 2,523 churches.

Negro Membership in White Churches

The great majority of Negro Christians are in five separate and predominantly Negro denominations. All major church bodies, however, have some Negro members, and sometimes this membership is large. When these memberships are added together, they constitute a significant segment of Negro Christendom.

The Methodist Church has the largest number of Negro members, 370,315. This membership at present constitutes a separate, nationwide "Central Jurisdiction," organized on racial grounds. Efforts are now underway in this church to remove this segregated arrangement of the Negro constituency.

Examples of churches with sizeable Negro membership are the Protestant Episcopal Church with 78,375, the Congregational Church with 38,000, and the Seventh Day Adventists with 49,489. Other churches which also have large Negro memberships are the Presbyterians, the American Baptist Convention and the Churches of God. Some churches keep figures on members by race, and some do not. This makes it difficult if not impossible to get an accurate total. A reasonable estimate would seem to be about 800,000.

In all of these bodies the membership of Negroes varies from a few individuals in white congregations to separate local churches composed wholly or almost wholly of Negroes. Some of these Negro churches may be quite large, such as St. Mark's Methodist Church in New York City, one of the largest churches in the denomination, or the First Congregational Church in Atlanta, the largest such church in the region.

In these denominations, Negroes often enjoy full participation in the life of the church, both as members and as officials. This is especially true of local congregations in Northern and Western regions, and in the regional and national boards of the churches. In the Methodist Church, for instance, the Negro bishops are equal in every respect to their white colleagues. Negroes serve on all national boards and agencies in the church. A Negro has served on the Judicial Council, one of the highest bodies in the church, and a Negro bishop has just been chosen president-elect of the Bishops' Council. Two Negro bishops have recently been appointed over predominantly white areas.

In addition to the established churches that have Negro members, there are also the sects, or smaller religious groups, some two hundred or more, nearly all of which have Negro members. Examples of such sects are various Churches of God, Holiness Churches, and Spiritualist Churches.

In the sects, as in the denominations, Negroes may be in separate congregations, or they may be full members of white congregations. Likewise, Negroes hold offices in the ministries and official life of these bodies. An estimate of this Negro membership is not possible.

Store Front Churches

For the past half-century an accelerating movement has been going on in America which is having a profound influence on Negro church life. That movement is the migration of Negroes from the rural areas of the South into the urban centers of the South, North and West. The movement began during the First World War, and it has grown continually ever since. It has been especially heavy in the past ten years because of the agricultural and technological changes in the South.

The present result of this migration is that large numbers of Negroes are crowded together in the decaying older sections of cities, living in poverty, without adequate employment or living necessities or hope. The more financially secure citizens, white and black, have fled to the suburbs, leaving the poorer masses piled in the inner city. The established church in many cases has followed its members, thus depriving the newly migrant masses in the city of effective service from the established church.

There are, however, certain churches that serve the inner city. These are the "store front" or "house front" churches. In depressed neighborhoods there are usually many vacant stores, which can easily be converted into meeting places. Or, where a store is not available, a residence may serve as well.

These churches are usually of the cult or sect type. Sometimes they are affiliated with national bodies, such as Holiness or Pentecostal groups. Sometimes they are single, separate churches arising out of the zeal of some interested evangelist. In most cases, these churches are marked by their emotionalism, by strict adherence to a biblical way of life and by severe injunctions to moral living. Their ministers are often poorly trained and have little concern with or ability to handle the social and economic conditions that depress the people.

There are four main reasons for the existence of the store front churches: (1) the lack of adequate follow-up by the established churches from which the migrants come; (2) lack of concern or programs by the established churches in the areas; (3) the evangelistic zeal of preachers and Christian workers who want to save the people from the sins of their environment, and (4) the continuing and genuine interest of the depressed people in religion as a source of help in their troubles.

A discussion of these reasons is not possible here. It is known, however, that many of the migrants were church members in their home towns, but because their churches have been derelict in keeping membership records, or in following members who move, there is no continuity of church life for the migrant. Also, studies have shown that membership in the established church is too often a matter of status; that is, membership declines as the people lose economic and social standing.

Yet, despite its obvious faults, the store front church does serve a great purpose among the depressed people who have urgent religious needs: ". . . it provides a reason for existence, a feeling of belonging, and a temporary escape from the dreariness of their lot. It also provides for the large number of rural Southern migrants a means of facilitating urbanization by becoming part of a closely knit 'we group' with which they can identify and emulate." [8]

The Church and Education

The Emancipation Proclamation of 1863 gave the Negro freedom, but it left the freedmen with little means for their education and cultural development. To provide these essentials, men and women from the established churches rushed into the South—often at great personal sacrifice—to establish schools, to teach and to render other needed services to the freedmen. In doing this they wrote one of the brightest pages in the history of Christian missions. Among the most active of these churches were the Methodists, Congregationalists, Presbyterians and Baptists. They opened schools, sometimes called "colleges" or "universities," which in the beginning were little more than high schools or academies. However, as educational levels have risen, many of these schools have developed into first-rate, fully accredited institutions of higher learning. These schools taught not only academic subjects, but also the basic elements of American culture. They helped the Negro to bridge the gap between slavery and citizenship, and they have provided much of the Negro leadership of the past century.

[8] Patricia M. Pettiford, "Harlem's Ministry," unpublished master's thesis, College of the City of New York, 1963.

The Negro Church and Education

The coming of freedom made it possible for the Negro church to work freely all over the nation, but especially in the South where most Negroes lived. The Negro churches were interested in gaining members, but they were also interested in the educational development of their people. They devoted a large share of their meager resources to setting up schools, colleges and seminaries. The AME Church, for instance, has seven colleges; the CME Church has three colleges plus several secondary schools, and a seminary.

The schools of the white and Negro denominations constitute the main source of private education among Negroes. At present these church schools train about 25,000 Negro students.

The Church and Civil Rights

It has already been seen that in the days of slavery the Negro's church was the main instrument for the expression of his sufferings on the one hand and of his hopes on the other. Similarly, in the contemporary struggle for civil rights the church is the main institution through which social dissatisfactions and civil aspirations can be expressed. In many communities, especially in the South, the Negro church is the only institution capable of working for civil rights at all. Because of its independent support and its relative freedom from governmental intimidation, the Negro church is often the center of protest meetings, voter registration projects and other mass efforts.

What is true of the church is also true of the Negro minister. He is playing a leading part in the struggle. In this social role he is perhaps best symbolized by Dr. Martin Luther King, Jr., a well-trained Negro pastor, who started with a revolt against segregated bus transportation in Montgomery, Alabama, and led that revolt into a great national demand for complete integration in the whole of American life. The Negro pastor and his church are still powerful influences in the social life and aspirations of Negroes in America.

The Catholic Church and the Negro

The Catholic Church has always been interested in the conversion of Negroes to that faith. In comparatively recent years, however, the work among Negroes has grown remarkably in scope and intensity. Negro membership has practically tripled in the past twenty-five years.

In 1963, the Catholic Church had 703,443 Negro members in 514 parishes, served by 775 priests. The church maintains 361 schools with an enrollment of 97,030 Catholic and non-Catholic students. In 1963 there were 12,638 adult baptisms (see Figure I).

In addition to these separate Negro churches, there are many Negroes who are members of "white" congregations, for whom separate figures are not kept. It thus can be seen that within a quarter-century the Catholic Church has grown to be one of the leading religious groups among Negroes, surpassing at least two, if not three of the major Negro denominations.

CHARACTERISTICS AND CONTRIBUTIONS

The question is often raised as to whether or not the Negro church possesses any distinct or unique features that would differentiate it from other church bodies. Does it differ significantly from other churches in theology or in polity or in patterns of church life?

The general conclusion is that the Negro church does not possess any significantly different features. In faith, in polity and in practice the Negro denominations all follow closely the parent white bodies from which they came. The Negro church was not born out of differences over theology or polity. It is simply a colored division of the general church.

Indeed, there is widespread objection to the very term "Negro church" on the ground that this is in itself a misnomer, and that there is no such thing as a "Negro" church. A more accurate term would seem to be the "Negro's church," or better still, "the church among Negroes."

But despite the lack of distinctive features, what we call the Negro church is well established as a separate institution or group of institutions, and bids well to remain so for a long time. The Negro church does participate fully, however, in cooperative activities with other churches. All major Negro denominations are members of the National Council of the Churches of Christ. They also share fully in state and local councils of churches. In a number of instances Negro churchmen hold prominent places in these bodies, even in the South. In Georgia a Negro was recently elected (1965) President of the Georgia Council of Churches.

The beginnings of interchurch cooperation among the Negro denominations themselves may be seen in the Fraternal Council of Churches, an organization that embraces all of the major groups. It is perhaps best seen in the Interdenominational Theological Center in Atlanta, Georgia, a new, well-equipped, fully accredited seminary, formed through the cooperation the Methodist, AME, CME and Baptist Churches.

FIGURE 1—Growth of Catholicism among Negroes

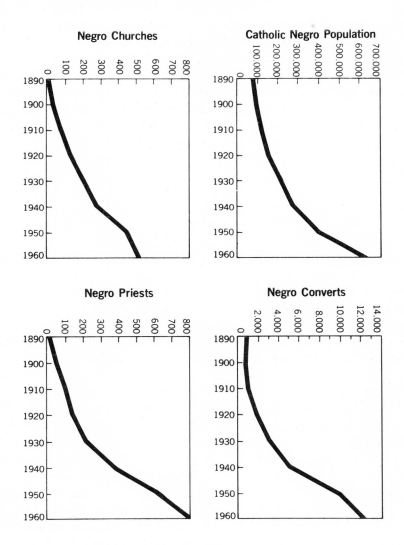

SOURCE: Rev. J. B. Tennelly, S.S. of the Commission for Catholic Missions among the Colored People and the Indians, Washington.

Perhaps the most distinguished contribution the Negro church has made
to general Christendom has not been in theology but in music—the Negro
"spirituals." These simple, rhythmic, harmonious songs, born in the hearts
of slaves and freedmen, have spoken to the hearts of people everywhere.
They have been accepted in established church music.

In their messages the spirituals reveal: (1) faith in God and in His ultimate
justice ("My Lord Is A-writin' All The Time"); (2) patience and suffering
("Nobody Knows the Trouble I've Seen"); (3) the desire for freedom ("Go
Down, Moses—Tell Ol' Pharaoh To Let My People Go"); (4) the passion
for progress ("We Are Climbin' Jacob's Ladder"), and (5) the deep rever-
ence of the Negro Christian ("Steal Away to Jesus" and "Were You There
When They Crucified My Lord?").

THE CHURCH: PRESENT AND FUTURE

The church has traditionally been a formative and controlling influence
in the life of the American Negro, not only in spiritual matters, but in other
areas as well. It is by far the largest institution the group has had, having
today better than twelve million members. It has served as an instrument of
expression and action in civic, cultural and educational concerns. It has
provided inspired leadership for the group in the struggle for fuller life. Will
this position of preëminence continue? The answer will depend upon several
facts.

First of all, life among Negroes is changing. From a predominantly rural
people, they are becoming a predominantly urban people. At present most
Negroes are a disadvantaged people, constituting pockets of poverty in inner
cities, suffering serious social and economic privations in the midst of an
affluent society. These conditions call for spiritual and cultural services of
the most intensive kind. Can the church render these services?

Studies conducted in a number of major cities show that the established
church is not serving the depressed urban masses as it should and as the
people need. In the first place, the church tends to follow its members to
the suburbs. It has not yet developed an effective program of serving the
indigent masses in inner cities. Unfortunately, church service declines as
economic status declines.

Secondly, the Negro church is handicapped by an inadequately trained
ministry. Recent figures show that only one out of fifteen men entering the
ministry has had seminary training. In other words, 92 percent of the men
entering the Negro ministry each year are professionally unprepared. Can

untrained leaders develop the intensive service programs necessary for the development of a handicapped people?

The answer, obviously, is that they cannot. As studies show, in Negro communities there are few church-sponsored programs for guidance of the young, for adult education, for health and cultural improvement or for help in occupational skills and placement. These are the kinds of services that will lead the people into a more abundant life.

At present the Negro church is a vast, influential, respected institution with between fifty and sixty thousand churches and forty to fifty thousand pastors. If this great body can develop the services that a growing and changing population needs, it will continue to grow and to hold its place in the life and esteem of the group. On the other hand, it is certain that people will not long respect or support an agency that plays no needed part in their lives.

chapter 9

The Negro in American Politics: The Past

G. James Fleming

It is a common belief that the Negro in America secured the first vestiges of citizenship only when Lincoln pronounced the Emancipation Proclamation. There are also those who see this citizenship made firm and universal with the passage of the Thirteenth, Fourteenth and Fifteenth Amendments. To these persons the American Negro first began to be a factor in politics only during the Reconstruction Period. Neither of these observations, however, is the fact, and neither singly nor together do they tell the whole story.

Negro Americans figured in political decisions long before they were citizens. Many laws and actions of the colonies and of the later Confederation governments were influenced by the presence of black men in the population. The Black Codes, the wording of the Articles of Confederation and of the Constitution, and court decisions, as in the Dred Scott Case, were all political acts and decisions which followed the patterns they did at least in part because of the presence of Negroes—although Negroes had no part in the making of any of these decisions. This was true for "free" Negroes and for slaves, for nowhere was the free Negro as free as the white man.

The exclusion of Negroes from politics and the privileges of citizenship was not monolithic and absolute. At least on paper, several of the constitutions of the new post-Revolution states extended the suffrage to free Negroes by not including any restrictions based on race. Accordingly, Negroes voted, but several states disfranchised them in later revisions of their constitutions.

Earliest Right to Vote

The New Jersey constitution of 1776 extended the suffrage to all residents of the colony, "of full age who were worth fifty pounds proclamation money." Not only were there no restrictions based on race or condition of servitude, but there was no restriction based on sex or place of birth; aliens could also vote. In 1807, however, New Jersey passed a "clarifying act" limiting the ballot to free, white, male citizens. There was protest, but this restrictive measure was reaffirmed in 1820.

In New York in the late 1700's, free Negroes could vote, if they owned land to the value of twenty pounds or showed financial substance in other ways. The first constitution, adopted in 1777, gave the right to vote for members of the State Assembly to "every male inhabitant of full age" who satisfied residence and property requirements, the latter being ownership of real property (a freehold) to the value of twenty pounds or the leasing of a tenement of forty shillings. To vote for the Senate the property requirement was a hundred pounds.[1] There was equality in the law as far as suffrage was concerned. These property requirements were nevertheless exorbitant for the rank and file of eighteenth-century Americans and more so for black men, who were the marginal workers.

Enough Negroes took to voting, however, to thereby irritate some politicians and their followers into devising ways and means of restricting or eliminating the Negro vote. This opposition first took the form of an act "to prevent frauds at elections." Section III of this act stated "that whenever any black person or person of color shall present himself to vote . . . , he shall produce to the inspectors or persons conducting such election a certificate of his freedom under the hand and seal of one of the clerks of the county of this state, or under the hand of any clerk with this state."[2]

Several objections were raised in the legislature to this bill, which set up prerequisites for voting that few Negroes could meet—prerequisites much more difficult of attainment than the property requirements. Wesley presents the objections that were sent to the Senate as follows:

> These were summarized as (1) the bill was "dangerous in precedent and against the public good"; (2) the description of a person of color was too vague; (3) many persons were born free and would find it difficult to secure freedom certificates; (4) the right to vote was subjected to the pleasure of others who in many cases would be interested in withholding the vote; (5) many Negroes lived and were far removed from their place of birth or manumission; (6) provisions necessary to qualify for the vote were impossible to secure before the election date of April 30, 1811; (7) there was no justification for the passing of an act which disfranchised a portion of the electors, even for a year; (8) there was no precedent for such a radical change in the election laws so close to an election.[3]

[1] After Leo H. Hirsch, "The Negro and New York, 1783–1865." *Journal of Negro Education,* XVI, No. 4 (October, 1931), 417.

[2] *Journal of the Senate of New York,* 1811, p. 143, as quoted by Charles H. Wesley in "Negro Suffrage in the Period of Constitution-Making, 1787–1865." *Journal of Negro History,* XXXII (April 1947, No. 2), 156.

[3] *Ibid.,* p. 156.

Nonetheless, this so-called antifraud act became law on April 9, 1811, shortly before a state election.

One of the reasons for the opposition to Negro voting was due to the contention that the Negroes tended to give their support to the Federalists, their aristocratic employers. This pro-Federalist alignment of Negroes is credited with providing the "balance of power" which kept the Federalists in power. The anti-Federalists and others were afraid that the growing Negro population would play an increasingly larger role in determining the outcome of New York's elections. Wesley notes that "In the election of 1800, it was extravagantly said that 'the political character of the national government was changed by the vote of a single Negro ward in the city of New York.'"[4] The opposition party to the Federalists, the Democratic-Republicans, also bellowed a campaign song whose theme was "Federalists with Blacks Unite."[5]

Despite the attempts to restrict Negro voting, black men could still vote if they met the stringent and discriminatory requirements of 1811. But they were to be restricted even more by the constitutional convention of 1821, in which Negro suffrage was a central argument. The convention was divided between those who urged equal suffrage for all citizens and those who were obsessed with the idea that the Negro vote was a bloc vote which could be manipulated against what these opponents considered the public good. In the legislature there were charges that the Negro was inferior, lacked intelligence and discretion, and was given to crime—and those who made these charges called on the Bible to help prove their points.

Negroes petitioned the New York legislature to protect their voting rights, and white men such as Peter Jay stressed that, although there were some 30,000 Negro voters in the state, they constituted only one-fortieth of the total vote and represented no threat to the body politic. Several other voices of non-Negroes were raised against restrictions on the Negro vote.

The proposal to limit the vote to white males only was lost, but a new plan was made into law which required of whites ownership of a 40-pound freehold, while setting a 250-pound freehold as the property requirement of Negroes. In addition, the law also set different residence requirements for whites and Negroes, with an unfavorable differential for Negroes. Whites could vote after a residence of only one year, while Negroes had to reside in the state three years. Furthermore, Negro voters had to have paid taxes,

[4] *Ibid.*, p. 155. Soon to be published is a new examination of the extent to which the Negro vote in New York might have provided a "balance of power" in New York politics. The author is Dr. Elsie M. Lewis, associate professor of history at Howard University.

[5] *New York Spectator*, April 29, 1809, as quoted by Wesley.

while whites could substitute highway or military service for money taxes.

In 1846 another constitutional convention retained all discriminatory differentials against Negroes, after most vituperative argument and after attempts both to strike out racial distinction and to deny the franchise to Negroes altogether were defeated.

While there were assertions that the Negro, voting as a bloc, could control New York City politics, Hirsch found that, according to the 1820 census, of 10,886 Negro voters registered in the city only 100 voted in 1819 and only 612 voted in 1820.[6] This was probably due to the restrictive law passed in 1811 and to the other obstacles raised by voting inspectors to keep Negroes from voting.

In addition to internal action by the state legislature, proposals to amend the New York constitution so as to strike down the discriminaion against Negro voters were also put before the people in referenda—in 1846, 1849, 1860 and 1869. In every instance the liberalizing proposal was lost. As late as 1869, the proposal was defeated, state-wide, by 249,802 to 282,403. The temper of the majority-group citizens (at least of their representatives) is also shown by the fact that the New York legislature, which had ratified the Fifteenth Amendment to the Federal constitution, rescinded its ratification in 1870, following the 1869 defeat of the local referendum. It took the ratification of the Fifteenth Amendment by three-fourths of the states to abolish racial discrimination in New York's suffrage laws.

New York furnishes the fullest example of the pattern of politics, especially to the right to vote, as far as Negroes were concerned, prior to the Emancipation Proclamation and the Reconstruction Period amendments to the U.S. Constitution. But there were other states in which Negroes enjoyed the suffrage, more or less, and for a shorter or longer period of time.

Vermont, Kentucky and Tennessee, in their constitutions of the 1790's, according to Wesley "made no provision in their constitutions concerning the exclusion of Negroes from the ballot." The Pennsylvania constitution of 1790 did not, on paper, exclude Negroes from the suffrage after the word "white" had been deleted in an earlier draft. The constitution adopted in Ohio in 1802 also granted the right of the ballot to Negroes, but intermittent objections to the inclusion of Negroes came to a head in the constitutional convention of 1850 and a resolution to limit the suffrage to white males was carried by a vote of 66 to 12.

In further reference to Pennsylvania, there is no evidence that Negroes voted in that state before 1790, although they could own property and were

---

[6] Hirsch, *op. cit.*, pp. 417–18.

taxed. From different arguments in the state legislature over several years, there are also indications that the state constitution, as to whether Negroes could vote or not, was observed differently in different parts of the state and at different times. One interesting example of this occurred nearly twenty years before the Dred Scott Decision (1857), when the Pennsylvania Supreme Court held that the Negro was not a freeman and therefore not entitled to vote. The case came before the highest court when "a candidate for office in Bucks County, who was defeated, claimed his opponent's seat because Negroes had been permitted to vote for him [the opponent] . . . contrary to law." [7] This case aroused the pent-up ill will of Negro voters but the Pennsylvania constitution was amended in 1838 to make it clear that the suffrage was limited to whites.

Tennessee, Kentucky and North Carolina permitted Negroes to vote at first, but after some years each amended its constitution to limit the suffrage to white males.

During the period between the Philadelphia conventions of 1787 and 1865, only Maine, New Hampshire, Vermont, Rhode Island and Massachusetts permitted Negroes to vote on equal terms with whites. All other states, at some time, have barred Negro Americans from the suffrage.[8]

Since citizen group activity is also political, it must be noted that free Negroes in New York, Ohio, Pennsylvania and the other states protested loudly against encroachment on their voting. They called *ad hoc* meetings, established numbers of organizations, filed petitions and made every effort to arouse sentiment favorable to the proposition that the ballot should be available to black men on the same terms as to whites. Some of the noted names of Negro history were in the forefront, including the Negro orator Joseph Sidney, of New York; Robert and James E. Forten, the inventors, of Philadelphia, and John M. Langston of Ohio, later member of Congress.

The Civil War and Reconstruction

Although Negroes enjoyed some right to vote before the Emancipation Proclamation and the related Fifteenth Amendment, no Negro was elected to any important office, although John M. Langston was elected a township clerk in Ohio. But with the Civil War over and the principal slave states brought under a Federal reconstruction plan, there was not only expansion of the suffrage, but Negroes also had an opportunity to fill both high elective and appointive office.

[7] Wesley, p. 162.
[8] *Ibid.,* p. 166.

The Reconstruction, as designed by the "Radical Republicans" in Congress (the Reconstruction Act of 1867), divided the rebel states, except Tennessee, into five military districts, and called for new state constitutions, promulgated by constitutional conventions elected by loyal male citizens "of whatever race, color or previous condition." Black men now could vote; and they helped to select delegates to the conventions and later, to ratify the resulting constitutions and to elect the first post-war legislatures. Although all the constitutional conventions had Negro delegates, only one (South Carolina's) had a majority of Negroes. Louisiana's convention was equally divided between whites and Negroes. The other conventions had only a small token number of Negroes. The racial composition of these conventions was as follows: [9]

State	Whites	Negroes
Alabama	83	17
Arkansas	68	7
Florida	29	17
Georgia	133	33
Louisiana	52	40
Mississippi	68	17
North Carolina	107	13
South Carolina	34	63
Texas	81	9
Virginia	80	25
Total	735	241

The Reconstruction Act of 1867 came two years after the ratification of the Thirteenth Amendment and while the Fourteenth Amendment was waiting for ratification. It preceded the Fifteenth Amendment (legalizing the right to vote regardless of race, color or previous condition of servitude) by three years. While aimed at the South, the post-Civil War actions by Congress affected, or were to affect, the entire nation politically for, in 1867, there were several Northern states which denied Negroes the right to vote.

According to whom one reads, the Reconstruction conventions were (1) composed of, and dominated by, illiterate ex-slaves who scarcely knew how to conduct themselves; or (2) not dominated by Negroes but only included some Negroes (among them former "freemen"), many of whom had some schooling and much worldly experience, and several of whom had returned from the North when slavery had been outlawed. The most

[9] *The Negro Year Book*, published by Tuskegee Institute, Tuskegee, Alabama (1921–22 edition), p. 176.

responsible commentators take the latter view. There is also much support for the position that the constitutions which were drafted by these conventions were "progressive," far-seeing, people-centered, aimed at improving the lot of whites as well as Negroes, and restrained in reference to former Confederates. Negroes, for instance, took the lead in giving constitutional authorization to publicly supported-education, perhaps because they knew so well the need for education.

By the time Reconstruction began, over 20 percent of the ex-slaves had had some schooling. At the Texas constitutional convention, it has been found that the delegates, "for the most part . . . were able to read and write. At least 30 percent of them had some college training.[10] North Carolina would make as good, or better, a showing in this area. Thus, the membership of the state conventions, the membership of the new state legislatures and the candidates for national office included Negroes of several levels of schooling and experience, the same as was the condition of white office-seekers. Woodson and Wesley note that, in some of the legislatures more than half of the Negro members could scarcely read or write," but the authors also hold that "the charge that all Negro officers were illiterate, ignorant of the science of government, cannot be sustained." [11]

Negroes filled many local elective and appointive offices during the Reconstruction years, but the total number of these offices and their incumbents are not as easy to ascertain as for the higher state and national offices. Two Negroes served for some time in the United States Senate: Hiram R. Revels, 1870–71 (an unexpired term), and B.K. Bruce, 1875–81 (a full term). Both were elected from Mississippi. Twenty-one Negroes served in the House of Representatives, from the 43rd through the 56th Congress, 1868–95. They were elected from eight states: Alabama, Florida, Georgia, Louisiana, Mississippi, North Carolina, South Carolina and Virginia. Eleven served a single full term (two years); six served two full terms each; two served three terms, and one, Joseph H. Rainey of South Carolina, served five terms. The largest number of Representatives, seven, came from South Carolina, followed by four from North Carolina; Georgia, Mississippi and Florida elected one each.

It should be noted that the Negroes elected to Congress were residents of states which were part of the military districts created by Congress in the Reconstruction Act of 1867. No Negro was elected from Tennessee, which was not subject to the Act and to post-war Federal "reconstruction." Similarly, during this same period no Negro was elected to the Congress

[10] John Mason Brewer, *Negro Legislators of Texas* (Dallas: Mathis Publishing Company, 1935), p. 217.

[11] Carter C. Woodson, and Charles H. Wesley, *Negro in Our History,* 10th ed. (Washington: Associated Publishers, 1962), p. 405.

from any northern congressional district. Prior to the establishment of Federal Reconstruction, the former Confederate states voted against extending the suffrage to the emancipated Negroes; so also (during 1865–68) did the states of Michigan, New York, Connecticut, Wisconsin, Minnesota, Kansas and Ohio. In 1866, however, the suffrage was extended by Congress to Negroes in all the territories and the District of Columbia.

Negroes were also elected to the state legislatures during the Reconstruction period; but they did not control the former Confederacy. Except in South Carolina, Negro legislators were always a minority. For example, during 1870–71, the racial distribution in the lower houses was as follows (all the senates were heavily white): [12]

State	Whites	Negroes
Alabama	73	27
Arkansas	71	9
Georgia	149	26
Mississippi	77	30
North Carolina	101	1
South Carolina	49	75
Texas	82	8
Virginia	116	21

In a review entitled *Race and Conscience in America,* prepared by the American Friends Service Committee for its Quaker and Quaker-minded clientele, it is observed of the Reconstruction Period:

> Bills to establish or improve the public school system, to counteract political corruption and extravagance, to establish a homestead law, and to provide relief for the needy were introduced by Negroes. Some former slave states, while condemning political participation by Negroes in the state governments, have continued to function under constitutions which Negroes helped to write.[13]

There was another area in which the Negro members of Reconstruction legislatures made a contribution. They were of one mind in working for the ratification of the post-Civil War amendments that came before them (the Fourteenth and Fifteenth), making the Constitution, even until today, protective of rights which might never have come under the purview of constitutional authority if, for instance, the Fourteenth Amendment had

[12] *Negro Year Book, op. cit.,* p. 176.
[13] By a "working party" of the American Friends Committee, including the present writer (Norman: University of Oklahoma Press, 1959), p. 13.

not been ratified by the necessary three-fourths majority of the states.

The Negroes who went to Congress and those who filled high administrative office in the state and national governments acquitted themselves as men usually do in a world where there are relatively few mental giants. That is not to say, however, that Senators Bruce and Revels would not be several cuts above most national lawmakers even in the 1960's; so would John M. Langston (Virginia), H.M. Cheatham (North Carolina), John R. Lynch (Mississippi), Joseph H. Rainey and Robert Smalls (South Carolina), all of whom served in the United States House of Representatives. Men, such as Francis L. Cardozo, who served South Carolina as secretary of state and later as treasurer; P.B.S. Pinchback, one of three Negro lieutenant governors of Louisiana; T.W. Cardozo, Mississippi's superintendent of education—all would stand muster well. Francis Cardozo was educated at the University of Glasgow; Langston was graduated from Oberlin College; Senator Revels had studied at Knox College.

One proof of the ability of Reconstruction period Negro leaders and office-holders is that when the period came to an end or when they left their offices, they went on to show competence as teachers, church leaders, lawyers, administrators, diplomats and the like.

When white Southerners could permit themselves to do so, there were those who did not see everything in Reconstruction government as undeserving of praise. Some publicly lauded the "dignity" and "behavior" of the Negro state legislators; some, because of their knowledge of some Negroes, protested against the passage of the first jim crow laws following the assumption of home rule.

Reconstruction Ends

While Negroes were enjoying their new political opportunities, year by year the former Confederates were showing that they knew practical politics and respected the doctrine of (to use the vernacular) "if you can't lick 'em, join 'em." The Confederates submitted to the side in power just enough to be politically able to recapture their state governments. This they did gradually, as their leaders were pardoned individually or amnesties were declared. This led, first, to border states being able to return Democratic majorities in county elections and to the resurrection of the Southern wing of the Democratic Party. By the mid-1870's the Confederate Democrats, officially purged, were on the march, with the blessings of their former enemies-in-war. They were taking over their South to reconvert it to lily-whitism, both by right of law and outside the law. What ballots could not do, or would not do fast enough, was done with the aid of the Ku Klux Klan and other groups of its kind.

The final blow to Reconstruction was the withdrawal of Federal troops and other Federal supports from the Reconstruction states, on orders of President Rutherford B. Hayes with the backing of both parties in Congress.

By 1902, there was not a single Negro in a state legislature and not a single Negro in the national Congress. In addition, the Southern states adopted numerous devices to prevent Negroes from voting: intimidation, laws setting up property and poll tax requirements, the famous "grandfather clause" (which denied suffrage to anyone whose grandfather could not vote prior to 1876), and the "lily-white" primary. These political measures were followed by the resegregation of those institutions which had been desegregated during Reconstruction, including state universities and other public facilities. All this happened, despite the Civil Rights Act of 1875.[14] Of all that was done and would be done to destroy Reconstruction, preventing Negroes from voting was considered the most fatal.[15]

It has taken nearly ninety years; countless lawsuits, carried from lower courts to the United States Supreme Court; the passage of four Federal Civil Rights Acts (1957, 1960, 1964, 1965), and ratification of the Anti-Poll Tax Amendment (1963), to correct the imbalance somewhat and establish equal treatment under law. This imbalance began when "home rule" was returned to the former rebel states. In the mid-1960's there are still Negroes who are not permitted to register and vote. There is no Negro representing a Southern state in the Congress; but there are Negroes in the legislatures of two former Confederate states—Georgia, with two state senators and five members in its lower house and Tennessee with one member in its state assembly.

Politics in the North

During the years that the defeated former Confederacy was represented by Negroes on the several levels of politics and government, there were

[14] This Act specifically provided to all citizens regardless of race, creed, color or previous condition of servitude "full and equal enjoyment of all accommodations at inns, conveyances on land or water, theaters, or other places of public amusement." It established a fine of up to $500 or imprisonment of from thirty days to one year for any persons excluding any one from these accommodations on account of race, etc. It further provided for equality in service on juries and set a penalty of up to a $5,000 fine levied against any person who excluded another from serving on a jury.

[15] V. O. Key, Jr., *Southern Politics* (New York: Alfred A. Knopf, 1950), p. 536; after an interpretation by S. S. Calhoun, president, the Mississippi Constitutional Convention of 1890.

almost no Negroes similarly situated in the North, with the exception of Massachusetts. In fact, Massachusetts was the first state to elect Negroes to its legislature. This it did in 1866; those elected were Edward G. Walker and Charles L. Mitchell.[16] Since that time the North has done better, but mostly in recent years.

When Oscar DePriest of Chicago entered the U.S. House of Representatives in 1929, it had been twenty-eight years since the last Negro sat as a member of Congress. Since then there have been seven other Negroes elected, all from the North. Together they are:

Oscar DePriest (R), Chicago, 1929–31
Arthur W. Mitchell (R), Chicago, 1934–43
William L. Dawson (D), Chicago, 1943–
A. Clayton Powell, Jr. (D), New York, 1945–
Charles C. Diggs, Jr. (D), Detroit, 1954–
Robert N. C. Nix (D), Philadelphia, 1958–
Augustus F. Hawkins (D), Los Angeles, 1962–
John L. Conyers (D), Detroit, 1964–

Some observers have said that the Negroes in Congress during Reconstruction made no notable contribution. This cannot be said of the more recent group. For instance, DePriest worked consistently to include in every bill possible a clause insuring no racial discrimination against Negroes. He held to this formula especially in reference to the emergency projects of the depression years. Representative Dawson, although not known as a "race fighter" in the open, has attained high office in his party, thus putting him in position to elevate the Negro because of his position as a vice president of the Democratic National Committee and chairman of the important House Committee on Government Operations. Representative Powell, a minister by profession, has been a racial protagonist, seldom being "polite" to those he suspects of doing or planning anything inimical to Negroes. He rubs many people the wrong way, but his constituents consider him "our man," and in the 88th Congress he demonstrated spectacular leadership in carrying President Johnson's welfare program through the House. He is chairman of the House Committee on Education and Labor. Representative Diggs has addressed himself especially to discrimination in the armed forces, at home and abroad. Representatives Nix and Hawkins are going through their learning years; Representative Conyers has just begun to serve.

Seniority has played an effective part in the kind of contribution present-

[16] *The Negro Year Book*, published by Tuskegee Institute, Tuskegee, Alabama (1918–19 edition), p. 208.

day Congressmen are and will be able to make; in addition, Negro candidates for higher office have increasingly had rather wide previous experience in other public or private responsibilities. For instance, Representative Hawkins was a member of the California legislature for twenty-eight years and both Diggs and Dawson served, respectively, in the Michigan legislature and on the Chicago Board of Aldermen.

It is not as easy to keep track of the membership in state legislatures and city councils. The best count shows twenty-four states having ninety-two Negro members in their legislatures. Some states, including little Nebraska and Vermont, are in the list, Nebraska having boasted a Negro legislator for many years. Illinois, New York, Pennsylvania and Missouri have had Negro lawmakers for years; New York since shortly after World War I.

Los Angeles elected its first city councilman in 1962, but many other cities have had councilmen over a much longer period, going back again to World War I. George W. Harris and Fred R. Moore of New York were among the earliest, in the 1920's. Oscar DePriest and others were members of the Chicago Board of Aldermen before they were elected to Congress. Some smaller cities, such as Evanston, Illinois, have had city councilmen from time to time. Since World War II a number of cities in the South have also elected Negroes to their city councils. These include Durham, Winston-Salem, Fayetteville and Greensboro, in North Carolina; Oak Ridge, Tennessee, which has joined Nashville; Louisville, Kentucky, and some others, from time to time. St. Louis and the Kansas Cities have had councilmen for some time. At present there are 84 Negroes in city councils in nineteen states. George D. Carroll was elected mayor of Richmond, California, by his fellow councilmen in 1964. Perhaps the apex of municipal city positions which has been regularly held by a Negro, since the 1950's is that of President of the Borough of Manhattan (in New York City). Partly administrative, this position is most important as political "plum." The highest purely political decision-making position held by a Negro is that of "leader of Tammany Hall," more formally chairman of the Democratic County Committee of New York County. J. Raymond Jones, a practicing politician for nearly forty years, was elected in 1965.

The only statewide elective offices are held by Gerald Lamb, treasurer of Connecticut and Edward Brooke, attorney-general of Massachusetts.

One historic city, Tuskegee, Ala., for the first time, in 1964, elected two Negroes to the Macon County Board (officially the "Board of Revenue") and a third to the County Board of Education.

Negro members on school boards, North and South, are no longer unusual, although there are still countless school boards that have never had a Negro member. One of the important cities that recently elected such a board member was Houston, Texas, where both Negroes and whites joined in sponsoring and supporting the Negro candidate, Mrs. Hattie Mae White. Increasingly, also, Northern cities are appointing or electing Negroes to the judiciary above the justice of the peace level. The Federal Government and the large urban areas take the lead in this category, with New York, Chicago, Pennsylvania, Michigan and California having had several such judges regularly for some time. On the Federal level, William H. Hastie and Thurgood Marshall, on the Circuit Courts of Appeal, hold the highest Federal judgeships. Presently there are Negroes on the Customs and District Courts on the mainland. Another district judge serves in the U. S. Virgin Islands.

As Negroes have been more active in politics, more of them have received higher appointments, so much so that President John F. Kennedy openly said that he planned to name Robert C. Weaver to a Cabinet post, if a Department of Urban Affairs had been established during his presidency. Since then, President Lyndon B. Johnson has named Carl T. Rowan director of the United States Information Agency, with the right to sit on the National Security Council.

It is not the recognition that comes to the individual Negro that counts heavily anymore, however; it is what political involvement does or brings to the masses of Negroes, economically, socially and psychologically, which is held most important. This means not only prestige benefits, but also those benefits which millions of marginal, working, job-seeking, home-making men and women need most.

Patronage and Party Recognition

Outside the South and in nonelective and party organization politics, the Emancipation meant that thousands of free Negroes came North, especially into the nation's Capital. In Washington they could find steady, nonmenial or semimenial employment or enjoy the fruits of patronage. It did not matter that most of them received the lowest paying jobs. Washington meant being out of the South and under the protection of the Federal Government. One price paid for employment in the Government was the frequent turnover as administrations changed. *The Tuskegee Year Book* of 1912 listed "colored officers, clerks and other employees in the service of the U. S. Government." The number included members of the diplomatic corps, enlistees in the Army, laborers employed by the District of Columbia, post office personnel, and miscellaneous department employees. The list shows:

Diplomatic and consular corps	11
Enlistees in Army	2,948
District laborers	2,824
Post Office personnel	2,997
Miscellaneous	14,386
Total	**23,166**

In addition, some prestige positions were given Negroes, such as Secretary of the Treasury, Recorder of Deeds of the District of Columbia, and minister to all-Negro nations. Some Negro consuls served in non-Negro countries. John Mercer Langston became U.S. Minister to Haiti; Frederick Douglass, ex-slave, greatest of the abolitionist orators and frequent advisor to Lincoln, became Minister to Haiti and also served at different times as assistant secretary of the San Domingo Commission, marshal of the District of Columbia and Recorder of Deeds. Fred R. Moore, New York political leader and editor (the *New York Age*) was one of a long line of Negro ministers and ambassadors to the American-sponsored Republic of Liberia. Some Negroes became collectors of internal revenue, one serving in Honolulu; others were customs collectors, paymasters for the Army, and receivers of public monies. John C. Napier was Register of the Treasury; Henry Lincoln Johnson, a national committeeman of the Republican National Committee, once served as Recorder of Deeds of the District of Columbia, a position that has been filled by other Negroes down the years.

When Woodrow Wilson ascended to the Presidency, there were 5,836 Negroes in the Federal service in Washington, according to the *New York Age*. The paper goes on to complain that since Wilson came into office, twenty-nine of those Negroes holding the highest office had been "turned out" and their places "filled by white Democrats." [17] This periodic turnover was regular procedure for political appointees, but it struck Negroes hardest of all because of their limited employment opportunities.

Another area of political opportunity for Negroes after emancipation, and for many years after, came through being elected as delegates to the Republican National Convention and as members of the Republican National Committee. But when the former Confederate states took over the state governments again and found ways to disfranchise Negroes, these national officers were leaders without an effective following. The last to serve was Perry W. Howard, a lawyer born in Ebeneezer, Mississippi, in 1877 and a graduate of Fisk University with an L.L.B. degree from DePauw University. He was once a special assistant to the Attorney General of the United States, and practiced law from 1905 to the late 1950's. Although national committeeman

[17] *New York Age*, October 26, 1916.

from Mississippi, he made Washington, D. C., his home for more than half of his adult years. But in his heyday he controlled the Federal patronage for Mississippi whenever the Republicans occupied the White House; he served on important committees at national conventions, and he led the Mississippi delegation (called "black and tan" by many in the state because it was racially mixed).

Howard and other Negro national committeemen were accused of representing "rotten boroughs," of preferring an all-Negro Republican Party in the South and, worst of all, of selling patronage. The latter accusation was made especially against Howard and became part of the U.S. Senate record when hearings were held in 1928 by the Presidental Special Committee Investigating Campaign Expenditures.[18]

Among other Republican national committeemen were Benjamin J. Davis and Henry L. Johnson, both from Georgia. Roscoe Conklin Simmons of Illinois, Robert R. Church of Tennessee, and William H. McDonald of Texas were also important Negro Republican leaders.

Benjamin Davis was the outspoken editor of the *Atlanta Independent*. He studied at Atlanta University and had been teacher and secretary of a national fraternal order, for which he arranged the building of a block of buildings. In addition to being a member of the Republican National Committee, he served as delegate-at-large to his party's convention for twenty-five years.

Simmons was journalist but became best known as a "silver-tongued" orator. Among Negroes he is remembered for standing under a White House window during the Hoover administration, when Negroes felt they had been forgotten by the Republican Party, and appealing: "Speak, Mr. President, speak. Tell us that Lincoln still lives." It is probably because Negroes felt they did not receive an answer that so many soon after turned to the Democratic party and Franklin Roosevelt. One writer says of Simmons that his "spell-binding oratory was the Negroes' answer to the fire-eating Vardaman, Bilbo and Heflin. . . ."[19]

Robert R. Church was a real estate operator and banker, born in Memphis in 1885 and educated at Oberlin College. He was a member of the Republican State Central Committee of Tennessee and Shelby County Executive and Congressional Committees. He was a delegate to the Republican National Conventions of 1912, 1916, 1920 and 1924. In 1922 he was appointed by Secretary of State Charles Evans Hughes on a special commission to study economic conditions in Haiti. Henry Lincoln Johnson was

[18] See Report of the committee, pp. 718–35.
[19] Richard Bardolph, *The Negro Vanguard* (New York: Rinehart and Company, 1959), pp. 149–50.

a noted fraternal leader, and William McDonald was reputedly a "Texas millionaire."

The foregoing is the typical experience of the Negro Republican leaders who figured largely as voices of the party and patronage dispensers between 1900 and 1932. They, like Frederick Douglass, believed "the Republican Party to be the ship, all else the sea." They were professionals.

There had been times when men such as Perry Howard have been called political bosses—bosses over certain groups of party followers in a given area; able to deliver promised or expected votes; having close relations with the greater powers that be in the party, and being in position to reward friends and punish enemies. But there have been other Negro bosses, both Republican and Democratic, not occupying offices as high as national committeemen. The bosses were usually allied with some white machine and were permitted to control certain territory, certain patronage or certain enterprises. Sometimes these enterprises were within the law, sometimes outside the law. The enterprises have included, at times, gambling or prostitution. Negro bossism has usually been a reflection of white bossism. At the present time, when old-fashioned bossism is no longer holding sway, Negro bosses as well as white have taken on a new image or disappeared.

Some Negro bosses, by supporting the "Big City" machines, have been able to increase their patronage and other gains for their districts. One reputed boss thereby secured Negro policemen in his Southern city decades before such employment was being made available to Negroes in the rest of the South. Other bosses were able to get new schools and other improvements for their people; still others controlled a share of the patronage jobs. Chicago, San Antonio, Baltimore, Memphis, New York, are cities often mentioned as having successful bosses. There have been many more sub-bosses and little bosses than top big bosses.

In Baltimore there were Marse Calloway, Republican, and Thomas Smith, Democrat, both of whom are credited with serving white overlords, sometimes even to the extent of "paying off" Negroes to prevent them from voting. Nevertheless, Marse Calloway is given credit for introducing one of the most popular and most highly esteemed men into politics—Theodore R. McKeldin, two-term Mayor of Baltimore and two-term Governor of Maryland.

Most Negroes in politics so far described have been Republicans because, over the long stretch of history and due to Reconstruction, most political activity by Negroes was in that party.

Since 1928, however, Negroes have increasingly supported the Democratic Party. Many Negroes were first attracted to the Democrats through New York's Governor Alfred E. Smith. Later, with the promise of the New

Deal, they allied themselves to the Democratic Party and the majority have remained there since. Negroes are given credit—election after election— for helping the party carry the fifteen urban industrial centers of the country. In nearly every urban district, Negro registered Democrats out-number Republicans by as much as 8 to 1. Some Republican candidates, in fact, have felt it is not worth the trouble to campaign in the Harlems of the country.

As a result of over thirty years of their support, the Democratic Party has rewarded Negroes with appointments to high-ranking responsible and pres-tige jobs. Under the Kennedy administration a Negro, Andrew Hatcher, was named associate White House press secretary, and President Johnson has named Hobart Taylor, a lawyer, an assistant special counsel on his White House staff.

In both the Kennedy and Johnson administrations, Presidential direc-tives have called on departments and agencies to do special recruiting to bring more Negroes into nontraditional positions in the government. What has been done on the national level has also been done on state and local levels; in fact, local Democrats were first in recognizing Negroes as long ago as 1917 when Ferdinand Q. Morton was appointed to the Civil Service Commission of New York City.

In the earlier Republican administration of President Eisenhower pioneer recognition was given Negro Republicans. Thus J. Ernest Wilkins of Illinois was named Assistant Secretary of Labor and became the first Negro to sit in a White House Cabinet meeting, and E. Frederic Morrow of New Jersey was named an administrative aid to President Eisenhower. Mrs. Robert L. Vann of Pennsylvania was named a member of the International Development Advisory Board, and Archibald J. Carey, Jr. of Illinois was made chairman of the President's Committee on Government Employment Policy. Scovel Richardson was appointed a member of the Federal Parole Board (of which he became chairman), and was later named a Judge of the United States Customs Court. Scores of other appointments at lower levels were also made during the Eisenhower administration.

Thus, increasingly both major political parties at Federal, state and local levels have sought to improve their image with Negro voters through the use of significant patronage appointments. This trend is likely to continue, with the Republican party making a special effort as part of its post-Goldwater reconstruction.

chapter 10

The Negro in American Politics: The Present

James Q. Wilson

Negro Political Participation

In 1960, there were in the United States about 11 million nonwhites twenty-one years of age or over; the great majority of these were Negroes, slightly more than half of whom lived in the South and slightly less than half in the North and West. The total *potential* Negro vote is thus well over 10 million, but of course the actual vote is—and for the foreseeable future will continue to be—much less. The number of Negroes voting at any given election is almost impossible to estimate with any accuracy, but was probably less than 4 million in the 1960 Presidential contest and rose to nearly 6 million in the 1964 national elections. In the North and West, where Negroes may register and vote freely, sample surveys suggest that between 60 and 70 percent actually do vote.[1] Applied to a Northern adult Negro population of about 5.5 million, this would produce an active electorate of 3.3 million. In the South, discriminatory practices as well as other factors kept the number of Negroes registered to vote in 1960 down to about 1.4 million, or 28 percent of those of voting age.[2] By 1964 this figure had risen to 1.9 million voters, or 38 percent of those eligible.

The political participation of the Negro in the North is significantly higher than in the South but even so is lower than that of most other Northern population groups. In Philadelphia, for example, there were four wards where, in 1960, less than 45 percent of the total population was registered to vote; in three of these (Wards 28, 32 and 47) Negroes were over 90 percent of the population. Further, these three wards were among the five which had a turnout of less than 60 percent of the registered voters in the 1959 mayoralty election. In the 1960 Presidential election, Negro voting

[1] Angus Campbell, et al., *The American Voter* (New York: John Wiley & Sons, 1960), p. 453.

[2] Donald R. Matthews and James W. Prothro, "Social and Economic Factors and Negro Voter Registration in the South," *American Political Science Review*, LVII (March, 1963), 27.

participation was much higher—over 80 percent of the registered voters in all wards—but still lower than that of almost all other wards.

The pattern varies from city to city, but the Philadelphia case—selected because it is one of the few Northern cities which keep registration figures by race—is a common one.[3] The reasons for relatively low participation are not hard to find. Social science surveys have repeatedly shown that persons who have little education, low incomes and blue-collar occupations vote less than persons with a higher socio-economic status.[4] Negroes, of course, rank low—in many cities, the lowest—in all these attributes, and thus their lower participation must be explained in part by considerations of class rather than race. In addition, persons who move a great deal are less likely to be able to meet residence requirements than those who stay in one home. On the average, almost one-fourth of all Negroes change residence each year, a proportion which is slightly higher than for whites.

The structure of government affects participation as well. In local elections where party labels do not appear on the ballot ("nonpartisan" elections), where the candidates for the city council run at large rather than from wards or districts, and where party organization is weak or nonexistent, the turnout of Negro voters (as well as of lower-income voters generally) is substantially lower than when the opposite of these conditions prevail.[5]

In sum, approximately one-third of adult Northern Negroes and five-sixths of adult Southern Negroes did not vote in recent Presidential elections;[6] a much larger—but unknown—proportion of these people did not vote in the most recent local elections.

The political strength of the Negro is affected by the political unit of which he is part as well as by his level of participation. The great internal migration of Negroes has not been simply from South to North but from farm to city and from small town to large. Seventy-five per cent of the Negro population in 1960 was "urban"—that is, living in communities with a population of 2,500 or more. In the North particularly, Negroes are not simply urban but "metropolitan"—that is, concentrated in the largest cities. In 1960 the twenty-one largest metropolitan areas (all but four of which were in the North) accounted for about one-third of all Negroes living in the United States. The electoral college method of choosing Presidents, by which the winner of a state's popular vote receives all the state's electoral

[3] See also comparable data in Oscar Glantz, "The Negro Voter in Northern Industrial Cities," *Western Political Quarterly*, XIII (December, 1960), 1004.

[4] Robert E. Lane, *Political Life* (Glencoe, Ill.: The Free Press, 1959) pp. 45–52.

[5] Edward C. Banfield and James Q. Wilson, *City Politics* (Cambridge: Harvard University Press, 1963), pp. 159–61.

[6] Campbell, et al., *op. cit.*, p. 453.

votes, gives, of course, great importance to the big cities and thus to population groups (including Negroes) in the big cities.

In Congress, it is another matter. The very concentration of the Negro vote in the big cities—and in only certain sections of the big cities at that—means that, even if all Negroes could and did vote freely, they would be under-represented in the House of Representatives. In the 88th Congress, which was elected in 1962 and took office in 1963, there were only five Congressional districts with a population more than half Negro and only twenty-one which were more than 40 percent Negro.[7] Since in most cases a Negro is not elected to a Congressional seat in the North until the population is over half Negro, the residential concentration of Northern Negroes lessens their representation.

Negroes do not, of course, have to have one of their kind in office to be represented; their presence in large numbers even in a district represented by a white man will constitute an influence on him and thus on public policy, provided the Negroes can and do vote. In the North and West only 7.5 percent of all Congressional districts are one-fifth Negro or more. By contrast, *over half* the Southern Congressional districts are one-fifth Negro or more. In short, because the Negro population (but not the number of Congressional districts) is equally divided between North and South and because the geographic dispersion of Negroes is much greater in the South than in the North, the greatest *potential* Negro influence on Congress is in the South. Figure 1 illustrates this by giving, for each of three regions in the country, the number of Congressional districts with various proportions of Negroes.

The reapportionment of Congress which followed the 1960 census hurt Negroes in some ways and helped them in others. Before reapportionment, there were seven districts that were half Negro; by 1963, after reapportionment in eighteen states, there were only five (states where Negroes lost were Illinois and North Carolina). On the other hand, the number of districts that were 40 percent Negro or more went from nineteen in 1960 to twenty-one in 1963 (about half were in the South).

The factors which reduce Negro political participation in the South are well known. Administrative practices and community attitudes often make Negro registration impossible or so difficult and perilous as to be a meaningless opportunity. The United States Civil Rights Commission estimates that there are about one hundred counties in eight Southern states in which "there is reason to believe that Negro citizens are prevented—by outright discrimination or by fear of physical violence or economic reprisal—from

---

[7] United States Department of Commerce, Bureau of the Census, *Congressional District Data Book* (88th Congress).

exercising the right to vote." [8] In 1956, about 5 percent of the voting-age Negroes in these counties could vote. In 1963, after passage of two civil rights laws (in 1957 and 1960), the institution of thirty-six voting rights suits by the United States Department of Justice, the operation of several privately sponsored registration drives (in 1962 there were an estimated 140 such drives in progress or in prospect), and the holding of hearings by the United States Civil Rights Commission, Negro registration in those counties had increased only to 8.3 percent of the adult Negroes. [9]

These one hundred problem counties are less than one-tenth of all the counties in the South, but they contain one-third of all the region's voting-age Negroes. Even if all discriminatory practices were ended, however, the low socioeconomic status of the Negro would result in relatively low registration and voter turnout figures. In 1959, urban Southern Negroes had a median income less than half that of urban Southern whites and less than two-thirds that of Negroes living in Northern and Western cities. [10] Professors Matthews and Prothro of the University of North Carolina, analyzing nearly one thousand Southern counties, estimate that socioeconomic factors are about as important as political ones in determining Negro registration levels; because of this, they caution that "reformers should not expect miracles in their efforts, through political and legal means, to increase the size and effectiveness of the Negro vote in the South. The Negro registration rate is low, in rather large part, because of the social and economic characteristics of southerners—both Negro and white. These factors are not easily and quickly changed by law or political actions." [11]

The two periods of greatest increase in Southern Negro voter registration were in the 1940's (registration rose from 5 percent of the voting-age Southern Negroes in 1940 to 28 percent in 1952) and again in 1963–64 (when registration rose to over 38 percent of the potential). [12] The first increase was the result, in great part, of the abolition by the Supreme Court in 1944 of the "white primary" laws and rules that had excluded Negroes from participation in Democratic party primaries. [13] The second increase was in part the result of intensive voter registration drives conducted, after the passage of the first two civil rights bills, by a variety of organizations,

[8] United States Commission on Civil Rights, *1961 Report,* "Voting," p. 5.
[9] United States Commission on Civil Rights, *1963 Report,* "Voting," pp. 14–15.
[10] United States Census of Population; 1960: General Social and Economic Characteristics, United States Summary: Final Report PC(1)–IC, Table 139.
[11] Matthews and Prothro, *op. cit.,* p. 43.
[12] *Ibid.,* p. 27.
[13] The early history of the white primary can be found in Paul Lewinson, *Race, Class and Party* (New York: Oxford University Press, 1932). It was declared unconstitutional in 1944 in *Smith* vs. *Allwright,* 321 U.S. 649 (1944).

FIGURE 1—Congressional Districts (1960) with 5 percent or more Negro population by North and West, South, and Border States.

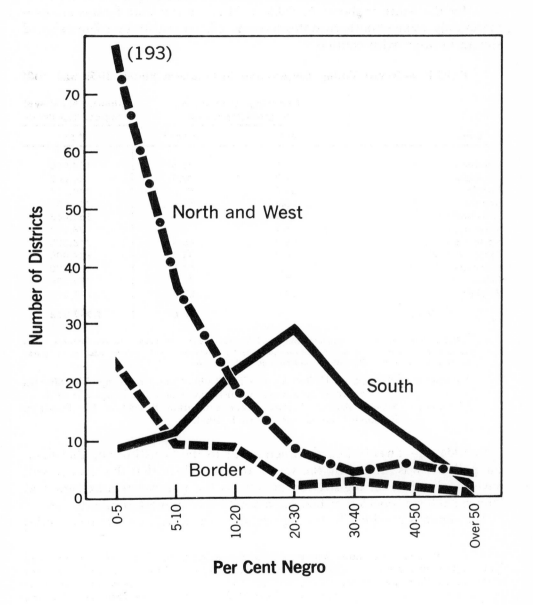

many under the auspices of the Voter Education Project of the Southern Regional Conference. These campaigns added more than half a million Negro voters to the rolls in eleven Southern states. Negro registration by state for the South is shown in Table 1. Many of the state figures are estimates only (some Southern states have no official registration figures) and should be used with caution.

TABLE I—Negro Voting Registration in Southern States, 1959 and 1964

State	Percentage of Voting-Age Negroes Registered		Estimated Number of Negroes Registered
	1959*	1964**	1964**
Alabama	13.7	21.6	104,000
Arkansas	37.7	43.5	80,000
Florida	39.0	51.1	240,616
Georgia	25.8	39.1	240,000
Louisiana	30.9	31.6	162,866
Mississippi	6.2	6.7	28,500
North Carolina	38.2	45.0	248,000
South Carolina	14.8	34.2	127,000
Tennessee	na	67.2	211,000
Texas	38.8	57.7	375,000
Virginia	23.0	27.7	121,000
Total	—	38.6	1,937,982

Note: These figures are estimates only and in many cases are subject to considerable error. Some states lack a formal registration procedure and as a result have no official registration figures for Negroes or whites. The data should be used with caution.

* SOURCE: 1959 *Report*, United States Civil Rights Commission, pp. 559–86, and 1961 *Report*, United States Civil Rights Commission, pp. 251–311.

** SOURCE: *Second Annual Report*, Voter Education Project of the Southern Regional Council, Inc., April 1, 1964.

In 1964, the Twenty-Fourth Amendment to the Constitution, abolishing the poll tax, was ratified by the states. It is not likely that this change will have much effect on registration figures, as the poll tax requirement had long since been repealed or become a dead letter in most Southern states.[14]

The counties in which Negro registration is the lowest tend to be counties

[14] Only five Southern states—Alabama, Arkansas, Mississippi, Texas and Virginia—still had the poll tax in 1963. Even at the end of its constitutional history, it no doubt deterred voter registration among both whites and Negroes, but more so (how much more so no one can say) among the latter. See Donald R. Matthews and James W. Prothro, "Political Factors and Negro Voter Registration in the South," *American Political Science Review*, LVII (June, 1963), 357 ff.

in which the Negro proportion of the total population is the largest: the more Negroes, the fewer are registered. Indeed, of all the socio-economic characteristics of Southern counties examined by Matthews and Prothro, a high Negro population percentage was most closely associated with a *low* Negro registration level.[15] Quite clearly, the larger the proportion of Negroes in a county, the greater the potential threat they represent to white voters and office holders and thus the greater the efforts made to prevent them from registering and voting. (There are some exceptions, of course; four of these exceptional counties will be discussed at the conclusion of this article.) There is some evidence that the size of the Negro population is even more important than the existence of restrictive suffrage laws in determining Negro voting participation. Professor Angus Campbell and associates present survey results suggesting—but not proving—that more Negroes vote in Southern counties with restrictive laws but a smaller proportion (under 30 percent) of Negroes than vote in counties with more liberal laws but a higher proportion of Negroes.[16] This indicates both the importance of informal as opposed to legal restrictions on voting and the possibility that, as Negroes continue to leave the South, their proportions in various counties may fall to the point where white fears—and hence white resistance—will begin to lessen.[17]

One apparent anomaly in the Southern Negro registration pattern is associated with religious differences. A careful study of registration by parish (*i.e.*, county) in Louisiana shows that, in general, the higher the proportion of Roman Catholics in a parish, the larger the proportion of adult Negroes who are registered to vote.[18] The twenty-five predominately French-Catholic parishes of southern Louisiana are also those in which Negro registration is highest (generally over 50 percent of the potential registration). In part this is no doubt the result of the economic structure of these areas. Unlike the Mississippi Delta region, most French-Catholic parishes have not had a plantation economy with its tenant farmers and tradition of master-slave relations. In part also these differences in registration are the consequence of differences in racial balance—on the whole,

[15] Matthews and Prothro, "Social and Economic Factors . . . ," *op. cit.*, p. 29. In some Southern communities, Negroes are allowed to vote in sizable numbers, despite the fact that they make up a large fraction of the population, because their vote can be manipulated by white politicians. See Alfred B. Clubok, et al., "The Manipulated Negro Vote: Some Pre-Conditions and Consequences," *Journal of Politics*, XXVI (1964), 112–29.

[16] Campbell, et al., *op. cit.*, p. 280.

[17] Matthews and Prothro, "Social and Economic Factors . . . ," *op. cit.*, p. 31.

[18] John H. Fenton and Kenneth H. Vines, "Negro Registration in Louisiana," *American Political Science Review*, LI (September, 1957), 704–713.

French-Catholic parishes have a lower proportion of Negroes than Protestant "Bible belt" areas. Nonetheless, cultural and religious factors are important even after allowance is made for the economy and the racial balance. In French-Catholic parishes which do have a plantation system, economic tenancy and high proportions of Negroes in the population, Negro registration is higher than in similar non-Catholic parishes.

Voting Behavior and Party Preference

Nationally, the Negro voter is a Democratic voter. He has not always been a Democrat and he has not invariably been a Democrat in all parts of the country, but since the 1940's his commitment to the Democratic Party, at least in the North, has been unswerving. There are no signs that this is about to change.

Table II shows the percentage of the two-party vote which was cast for the last four Democratic presidential candidates by voters in heavily Negro districts in the five largest Northern cities. The Negro in these big Northern cities has voted by large majorities for the Democratic presidential candidate; only President Eisenhower in 1956 was able to cause a significant drop in Democratic strength among Negroes, and even then not in all cities. President Kennedy more than recovered those temporary losses and President Johnson received an unparalleled majority.

Until the New Deal, the Negro voter was a Republican. He voted for the party of Abraham Lincoln when he could vote at all. It was not until Franklin Roosevelt persuaded Negroes that he was committed to welfare programs that would benefit low-income Negroes, and (at least in theory) to principles of equality that would benefit all Negroes that the massive shift from the Republican to the Democratic Party began. The speed of this shift varied from city to city and, within each city, from class to class. In 1932, Herbert Hoover captured a majority of Negro votes in Chicago, Baltimore, Philadelphia, Cleveland, New Haven, Wilmington (Delaware) and Columbus (Ohio). Indeed, in Chicago, the power of the Republican organization of William Hale ("Big Bill") Thompson was such that Negroes regularly gave him and his candidates over 80 percent of their votes. Where a Democratic machine was in power—as, for example, in Kansas City, Missouri—the Democrats did much better in the Negro precincts. (The heavily Negro Ward 4 in Kansas City voted over 70 percent for Roosevelt as early as 1932.)[19]

---

[19] Gunnar Myrdal, *An American Dilemma* (New York: Harper & Brothers, 1944), p. 496.

TABLE II—Democratic Vote as Percent of Two-Party Presidential Vote
Nationally and for Heavily Negro Wards of the Five Largest
Cities 1952–60

| City and Ward | Percent Democratic | | | |
(or District)	1952	1956	1960	1964
Chicago				
(Ward 2)	77	68	80	95
Detroit				
(Ward 3) *	90	84	90	
Los Angeles				
(62nd Assembly District) **	77	72	82	92 **
New York				
(11th Assembly District)	83	69	79	96
Philadelphia				
(Ward 32)	83	79	83	97
Nationally (estimate) ***	79	61	68	94

* Ward 3 abolished before 1964; no comparable figure available.
** Los Angeles redistricted; 1964 figure is for the new and comparable 53rd Assembly District.
*** Source of national estimate: Gallup Poll surveys as reported in *Congressional Quarterly*, Dec. 25, 1964.

By 1936, the swing to the Democrats had set in everywhere. In Cleveland, Philadelphia, Detroit, Kansas City, New Haven and Pittsburgh Negro voters gave Roosevelt large majorities (Chicago continued to lag behind this trend, the voters in Wards 2 and 3 giving a slight majority of their ballots to Landon.)[20] One study suggests that this transfer of allegiance began with the *least* disadvantaged Negroes; at first, it was a switch among middle-class Negroes who perhaps had greater information, were more sensitive to the ideological as distinguished from welfare aspects of the New Deal, and were less dependent upon the favors and friendships of precinct captains. Gosnell, for example, has shown for Chicago that the shift among Negroes in the 1930's occurred faster in those Negro areas with higher median rentals, lower unemployment rates and fewer relief cases.[21] Although somewhat slower to change originally (at least in Chicago), once committed to the Democratic party the lower-income Negroes have been the most steadfast. The defection to Eisenhower of some Negroes in 1956 was greater among middle-class than among lower-class Negroes.

In the South, some Negroes have been voting in a few large cities for

[20] *Ibid.*, and Henry Lee Moon, *Balance of Power: The Negro Vote* (Garden City, N.Y.: Doubleday & Co., 1948), pp. 18–19.
[21] Harold F. Gosnell, *Negro Politicians* (Chicago: University of Chicago Press, 1935), p. 34.

many years. The Negro vote in Atlanta was important in the success of a school bond issue as early as 1921. Negro voters were a significant part of the political machines of Edward Crump of Memphis and the Bellinger family in San Antonio.[22] Even in the days of the "white primary" there were a few Negroes who voted in general elections and in at least the nonpartisan city elections. In recent years there has been a substantial—though unmeasured—increase in this vote. Of all the cities of the Deep South, Atlanta has perhaps registered the most conspicuous gains. More than twenty thousand Negroes (over one-fourth of the total electorate) were eligible to vote in Atlanta as early as 1946 (this figure did not increase significantly during the next ten years owing to weak organization and an absence of dramatic contests).[23] After a massive voter registration campaign in 1961 and 1962, the number of registered Negroes rose to about 52,000. The Negro vote was greater than the margin of victory of the winning candidate for mayor in 1949; in 1953, a Negro college president was elected to the Atlanta Board of Education largely, though not entirely, with Negro votes; in 1957, the Negro vote in the mayoralty primary was estimated to be over 18,000, more than 93 percent of which went to the winning candidate, Hartsfield. Negroes still are not registered proportionally to their population. In 1960 38.8 percent of Atlanta's population but only 29.5 percent of the registered voters were Negro.[24]

In the 1952 Presidential election, Negroes in most Southern cities voted overwhelmingly for the Democrat, Adlai Stevenson. In 1956, however, there occurred a massive shift to Eisenhower. The results are shown in Table III. (Eisenhower increased his vote among Northern Negroes as well, but not as much; in no major Northern city did he win a majority of Negro votes.) The reasons for the shift have not been documented—national opinion polls usually have so few Negroes in the sample that the surveys are virtually useless for any analysis that requires one to separate Negro voters by region, class and party affiliation. It seems likely, however, that the appeal was less that of Eisenhower's personality than the events following the May, 1954, Supreme Court school desegregation decision. Republicans could point to the fact that the decision was written by a "Republican" Chief Justice (Earl Warren), that it occurred during a Republican administration, and that it was being bitterly resisted by many Southern Democratic politicians at the national as well as the local level.

[22] Moon, *op. cit.*, p. 176, and Myrdal, *op. cit.*, pp. 488–500.

[23] Clarence A. Bacote, "The Negro Voter in Georgia Politics, Today," *Journal of Negro Education*, XXVI (Summer, 1957), 307–318; Jack Walker, "Negro Voting in Atlanta: 1953–1961," *Phylon*, XXIV (Winter, 1963), p. 380.

[24] Walker, *op. cit.*, p. 381.

In 1960, of course, the Negro—North and South—was heavily Democratic. Again, no one can be certain of the reasons. Economic issues were probably important (there had been a serious recession); the Republican presidential candidate, Richard Nixon, seemed to be making a successful appeal for Southern white votes; Senator Kennedy placed a well-timed and well-publicized telephone call to the wife of Martin Luther King, Jr., then languishing in a Georgia jail.[25]

Whatever the reasons, the evidence of 1956 is strong enough to suggest that the Southern Negro voter is not as firmly committed as the Northern Negro voter to the Democratic Party. The former—perhaps because of his experience in nonpartisan local elections and Democratic Party primaries, where party labels are either absent or meaningless—is more sensitive to the positions of individuals and of factions and more susceptible to being organized by nonpartisan, all-Negro political associations.[26] The

TABLE III—Percent Voting for Eisenhower in Negro Wards and Precincts of Selected Southern Cities, 1952–56*

City	Percent for Eisenhower	
	1952	1956
Atlanta, Ga.	30.9%	85.3%
Charlotte, N.C.	16.3	38.5
Chattanooga, Tenn.	20.5	49.3
Houston, Texas	10.5	34.8
Jacksonville, Fla.	15.7	40.9
Knoxville, Tenn.	29.7	40.9
Memphis, Tenn.	34.4	54.0
New Orleans, La.	20.2	55.1
Richmond, Va.	21.9	73.0

* SOURCE: Henry Lee Moon, "The Negro Vote in the Presidential Election of 1956," *Journal of Negro Education*, XXVI (Summer, 1957), 224.

[25] Harold F. Gosnell and Robert E. Martin, "The Negro as a Voter and Officeholder," *Journal of Negro Education*, XXXII (Fall, 1963), 420–21.

[26] Cf. H. Douglas Price, *The Negro and Southern Politics: A Chapter of Florida History* (New York: New York University Press, 1957); Douglas S. Gatlin, "A Case Study of a Negro Voters' League," Political Studies Program: *Research Reports*, No. 2, March, 1960 (University of North Carolina Department of Political Science); Henry Holloway, "The Negro and the Vote: The Case of Texas," *Journal of Politics*, XXIII (August, 1961), 526–56. These Negro voters' leagues are only effective if they operate within the consensual framework of the Negro community. Price (at page 72) notes that a "league endorsement of a wrong candidate in a contest where a clear difference in attitude toward the Negro exists does not swing many Negro votes; rather it raises the question, 'who sold out?' " Holloway (at pages 539–40) observes that "Negro leaders don't have the power to deliver a bloc vote at will. . . . The Negro voter has his own fairly constant voting propensities which leaders disregard at risk to themselves."

great importance of race issues in the South gives a racial sensitivity to the Southern Negro vote that has been absent from the party-oriented Northern Negro vote. (In Atlanta, over 99 *percent* of the Negro voters are estimated to have voted for the winning mayoralty candidate in 1961.[27] It is inconceivable that such majorities could be obtained for a candidate in the North where *all* candidates profess to believe in equal rights and where party organization is much stronger.)

Negro voters are often described as holding the "balance of power." They are now 6 percent or more of the population of eight key states which have 210 electoral votes in presidential contests. In several of these states— California, Illinois, Michigan and New Jersey, among others—President Kennedy's margin among Negro voters in 1960 was greater than the margin by which he carried the state as a whole.[28] The same, however, could be said of any number of other groups—Catholics, for example, or Jews, or union members, or perhaps even college professors. Since all these groups— and more—could hold the "balance of power," then it is obviously incorrect to imply that any one of these groups holds it to the exclusion of the others. Furthermore, the Negro voter (particularly in the North) is *less* likely than other voters to change from one party to another (low-income voters are less likely than others to be "independent").[29] Negro votes are important, not because they are "swing" votes which reward friends and punish enemies, but because they are very numerous and strategically located; the object of a politician's strategy can only be to obtain a high turnout (if he is a Democrat) or a low turnout (if he is a Republican), not to change votes in wholesale numbers.

An illuminating case is that of Senator Jacob Javits of New York. A liberal Republican, Javits has been an outspoken proponent of vigorous civil rights measures. Nonetheless, he fared little better in the Negro areas of New York City when he ran, in 1962, against a conservative Democrat (James Donovan) whose position on civil rights was unclear than he did when he ran in 1956 against another outspoken liberal, Robert F. Wagner, Jr. Between 1956 and 1962, Javits' percentage of the two-party vote in certain Negro districts increased less than two percentage points—from 32.8 percent in 1956 to 34.5 percent in 1962.[30]

[27] Walker, *op. cit.*, pp. 383–84.

[28] Richard H. Scammon, "How the Negroes Voted," *New Republic*, November 21, 1960, pp. 8–9.

[29] Bernard Berelson, Paul F. Lazarsfeld, and William N. McPhee, *Voting* (Chicago: University of Chicago Press, 1954) and Robert Agger, "Independents and Party Identifiers: Characteristics and Behavior in 1952," in Eugene Burdick and Arthur G. Brodbeck, eds., *American Voting Behavior* (Glencoe, Ill.: The Free Press, 1959).

[30] Data courtesy of Professor Robert Peabody of Johns Hopkins University.

Negro Representation in Politics

There is an implicit tension between at least one conception of representation and the concept of integration. If all Negroes were fully assimilated into American society, distributed geographically and socially without regard to color, then Negroes might not occupy any elective offices —or they might occupy several, depending largely on chance. The greater the geographical concentration (*i.e.*, segregation, willing or unwilling) of Negroes, the greater the probability that Negroes will be elected to office, provided that elections are by districts.

Because of their dense concentration in relatively small political districts, Negroes in Chicago were able to elect an alderman as early as 1915, a ward committeeman (the key party official) in 1920, and a Congressman in 1928.[31] New York City, with somewhat larger districts, did not have a Negro district leader in the Democratic Party until 1935 or a Negro Congressman until 1944. Detroit, where council members are elected from the city at large rather than from districts, did not have a Negro council member until 1957. Los Angeles, with very large city council districts and relatively late Negro in-migration (mostly after World War II, rather than —as in the case of most Eastern cities—after World War I), did not have Negro council members until 1963.

The first Northern Negro Congressman—and the first Negro Congressman from any region since Reconstruction—was Oscar DePriest, a Chicago Republican who won office in 1928. The first Negro Congressman elected on the Democratic ticket was Arthur W. Mitchell, also of Chicago, who defeated DePriest in 1934. In each case, the Negro victory was made possible because the party's white nominee died before the election and had to be replaced; in each case, influential white politicians were persuaded to give the suddenly vacant nomination to a Negro.[32] Mitchell in turn was replaced by the present Negro Congressman from Chicago, William L. Dawson, in 1942.

In addition to Dawson, five other Negroes (all Democrats) serve in the United States House of Representatives: Adam Clayton Powell, Jr., of New York City (elected in 1944); Charles Diggs, Jr., of Detroit (elected in 1954); Robert N. C. Nix of Philadelphia (elected in 1958); Augustus F. Hawkins of Los Angeles (elected in 1962), and John L. Conyers of Detroit (elected in 1964).

[31] James Q. Wilson, *Negro Politics: The Search for Leadership* (Glencoe, Ill.: The Free Press, 1959), pp. 22–33, 50–51.
[32] Gosnell, *op. cit.*, pp. 90–91, 180–84.

In general, Negroes are elected to office when they constitute at least 50 percent of the electorate of the district or when a party organization seeks to offer the voters a "balanced ticket." Dawson, Powell and Nix were all elected from overwhelmingly Negro districts; all Negro city councilmen (or aldermen) in Chicago and New York are from Negro districts. In city-wide contests where a number of similar posts (such as county commissioner or municipal court judge) are to be filled, a strong party—as in Chicago or New York—will place one or more Negroes on the ticket in order to "recognize" that group within the party and, hopefully, secure a few additional votes from the group recognized without losing votes from other groups who are sufficiently loyal to the party label to refrain from "cutting" the ticket on the grounds that a Negro is on it. Hulan Jack was elected borough president of Manhattan even though Negroes were then only 21 percent of the population.

There are many exceptions, of course. Edward Brooke was elected attorney general of Massachusetts on the Republican ticket in 1962, even though Negroes are only about 2 percent of the population and party organization is particularly weak. Charles Diggs, Jr., became a Congressman in 1954 from a Detroit district which, as late as 1960, was less than half Negro.

TABLE IV—Negro Representation on City Councils in Selected Non-Southern Cities

City	Total Council Seats	Seats Held by Negroes (March, 1965)	Percent of Seats Held by Negroes	Negroes as Percent of 1960 Population
Detroit	9	0	0	28.9
Cleveland	33	10	30.3	28.6
St. Louis	29	6	20.7	28.6
Philadelphia	17	2	11.8	26.4
Chicago	50	7	14.0	22.9
Cincinnati	9	1	11.1	21.6
New York City	35	2	5.7	14.0
Los Angeles	15	3	20.0	13.5
Boston	9	0	0	9.1

SOURCE: Updated from table in Edward C. Banfield and James Q. Wilson, *City Politics* (Cambridge: Harvard University Press, 1963), p. 293.

There is no compilation of all the major elective offices held by Negroes. Table IV shows the number of Negroes on the legislative bodies of several large Northern cities. Negroes also sit in many state legislatures: as of 1962, Illinois and Michigan had nine each, Pennsylvania eleven, New York and Missouri six each, Maryland four and California three. For the first time in over ninety years, a Negro was elected in 1962 to the Georgia legislature as a state senator from Atlanta. Many other states have one or two Negro legislators.[33] After the 1964 elections, an estimated 280 Negroes held elective office.

The greatest formal political power held by Negroes is in the hands of two Congressmen, Dawson and Powell, each of whom has become— through the inexorable workings of the seniority system—chairman of an important committee in the House of Representatives (Dawson is chairman of the Government Operations Committee, Powell of the Education and Labor Committee).[34] At the local level, considerable influence—usually informal rather than formal—is wielded by Negroes who hold key party posts. Dawson is Democratic committeeman of Chicago's second ward, leader of the Negro bloc in the Cook County Democratic Committee, and vice chairman of the Democratic National Committee.

The prospects for increased Negro representation in Congress are fair in the North, slim in the South. There are (for the 88th Congress) twenty-one congressional districts that are 40 percent or more Negro; of these, five are over half Negro. Six districts, all in the North, are now held by Negroes; of the remaining fifteen, ten are rural Southern districts and five are Northern urban districts. Assuming that no Negro will win an election in a rural Southern district for many years to come, additional Negro Congressmen will not for the immediate future exceed five and they will come from these Northern cities: Baltimore, Chicago, Cleveland, Detroit and Philadelphia.

The number and kind of political offices held by Negroes are not necessarily a reflection of Negro electoral strength. Negroes in Chicago, for example, are far better organized politically than Negroes in New York. In 1959, however, a count showed four Negro judges holding office in Chicago, seventeen in New York City.[35]

No comprehensive survey exists of the number of Negroes holding political appointive offices. Both major political parties claim they have made a substantial number of Negro appointments while holding power in Washington. Lists compiled by the Democratic and Republican National Committees showed between ninety and one hundred such appointments; it is unlikely that either list is complete or entirely accurate. The vast majority of Federal administrative appointments given to Negroes by both

[33] Gosnell and Martin, op. cit., pp. 423–24.
[34] Cf. James Q. Wilson, "Two Negro Politicians: An Interpretation," Midwest Journal of Political Science (November, 1960), 346–69.
[35] Wilson, Negro Politics, op. cit., pp. 46, 320–21.

Democrats and Republicans have gone to Northerners rather than South-erners, despite the approximately equal division of the Negro population between North and South. Several factors are probably responsible: North-ern Negroes are politically more active and they include a substantially larger percentage of the educated, professionally qualified segment of the race. The extent to which political participation by Northern Negroes has led to appointment should not be exaggerated, however. It is unlikely that many Negro appointees were able to "demand" a job because of the votes they controlled or the influence they wielded. Few Negroes occupy a position in the political system that would give them such power (Con-gressmen Dawson and Powell may be exceptions).

Furthermore, Negroes in most cases are appointed by white officials; this undoubtedly introduces a certain selectivity into the appointment process and places a few constraints on the appointee. White liberals who select Negroes for appointive positions are likely to be just as sensitive (perhaps more sensitive) to the views of the NAACP, the Urban League and white liberal organizations as to the views of Negro elective officials. (It is, after all, the protest organizations, and only rarely the politicians, which make the headlines.)

Negro appointments have grown in number and stature in recent years. For example, President Eisenhower appointed Negroes to be Assistant Secretary of Labor, Chairman of the President's Committee on Government Employment Policy, a Special Assistant to the President, and member of the Civil Rights Commission; President Kennedy selected Negroes to be members of the Federal Circuit Court of Appeals and Federal District Courts, Ambassador to Finland (and later director of the United States Information Agency) and to Norway, Administrator of the Housing and Home Finance Agency, Associate White House Press Secretary, and United States Attorney for San Francisco.

Negroes have, of course, long been beneficiaries of the Federal civil service system. In most cases, appointments to positions in the classified civil service have no direct connection with politics (although the recent effort to increase the number of Negroes working for the Government un-doubtedly does in a general way). As of June, 1962, Negroes were slightly over-represented in the Federal service, holding about 13 percent of the jobs although they are only 10.3 percent of the work force.[36] Negro employment with the Federal Government has been growing faster than Federal employment generally (from June, 1962, to June, 1963, it increased

[36] John Hope II and Edward E. Shelton, "The Negro in the Federal Government," *Journal of Negro Education*, XXXII (Fall, 1963), 370.

3 percent)[37] and the gains have most recently been greatest in the higher grades of the civil service where Negroes are still, absolutely and in proportion to whites, very few in number.

In finding Negroes for both political and merit appointments, a seller's market prevails. The desire of Federal officials to demonstrate that their agencies are integrated and the desire of Federal political leaders to prove that they are "doing something" for the Negro has led, in many departments, for massive talent hunts in which the absence of qualified Negroes more than the absence of job opportunities accounts for much of the limited progress so far made.[38]

Negro Political Organization

American politics, it is often noted, is local in orientation, decentralized in structure and divided in leadership. It is at the local level that political parties exist on a day-to-day basis; it is in the cities, counties, and states that most party personnel are to be found, most party funds raised and spent and most party business conducted. Negro political organizations, to the extent they are organizations at all, are part and parcel of this system, suffering from its weaknesses and enjoying its benefits.

Some Negro politicians are, of course, national rather than local figures. Adam Clayton Powell is a familiar personality, his role in Congress and in various protest movements depending as much or more on the national following he has among some Negroes as it does on his political organization. Indeed, judged by the standards of Chicago, Philadelphia or even Detroit, Representative Powell can hardly be said to have an organization at all. He is clearly the exception, however.

Not only are Negroes part of a fragmented political system, they usually find it necessary to be politicians first and Negroes second. There is nothing unusual or discreditable about this; any politician (or, for that matter, anyone acting in his professional capacity) must either act as the organization or profession expects him to act or have his effectiveness curtailed and perhaps his membership revoked.

This means that, in most cases, Negro politicians are not likely to be the vanguard of civil rights protest movements. This is particularly the case if they are part of a strong, city- or county-wide party organization that

[37] *The New York Times,* March 4, 1964, p. 27.

[38] The search for qualified Negroes to fill appointive political posts in a state government is discussed in Daniel Patrick Moynihan and James Q. Wilson, "Patronage in New York State: 1955–1959," *American Political Science Review* LVIII (June, 1964), pp. 286–301.

insists on maintaining unity and following the leadership. It is also the case if the Negro is elected from a constituency that includes white as well as Negro voters—for example, if the Negro is elected to the city council from the city at large. Some Negro politicians, of course, are elected from all-Negro districts and are "lone wolves" who, because the party organization in the city is weak, do not find it to their advantage to follow its leadership. The utterly different political styles of William Dawson of Chicago and Adam Clayton Powell of New York can be explained by the great differences in the political systems and organizations of which they are part as well as by personality factors.

The forms of Negro political organizations are almost infinitely various; in all cases, they are strongly influenced—not to say determined—by the form of the white political organization, if any, of which they are a part.[39] The classical political machine continues to function in Chicago generally and in the Negro wards particularly. Precinct captains, relying on the exchange of favors and friendship and information, induce voters to support the organization's candidates—Negro and white—for office. Party loyalty is the governing principle and a concern for concrete, individual, often material interests is the motive force. The causes of the more militant civil rights advocates interest the party leaders but are not at the center of their concern.

The weak and divided remnants of a political machine struggle on in New York City; the Negro elements of this organization struggle with the white elements and with each other. Alliances are made and broken, party loyalty is an oft-proclaimed but rarely attained goal, and either ideology or tactical maneuver (or both) have replaced allegiance to a party hierarchy as the dominant political style. In Detroit, at-large nonpartisan elections have prevented the emergence of either a strong local party organization (the local Democratic party and its affiliated labor unions are powerful in Michigan politics but comparatively weak in city affairs) or of a stable Negro political leadership structure. Elective Negro officials must appeal to whites as well as to Negroes and have a political style consistent with the "good government" ethos that prevails in the community.

In the South, where Negro elective officials are few, Negro politics— as far as Negroes can participate in politics at all—tends to be in the hands, not of professional politicians, but of part-time amateurs whose standing in the community depends as much or more on their role as minister, businessman, lawyer or educator as it does on their political leadership.

---

[39] Banfield and Wilson, *op. cit.*, pp. 303–08, discusses the general relationship between urban political systems and Negro political organization and leadership.

In many Southern cities (such as Atlanta, Georgia, and Durham and Winston-Salem, North Carolina) the dominant Negro political organization is not an element of the regular party system but instead is a nonpartisan "voter's league" which endorses candidates, Negro and white, and mobilizes Negro votes for them.[40] The Atlanta Negro Voters' League, for example, was founded in 1949 to concentrate Negro voting strength behind those local candidates most advantageous (or least disadvantageous) to Negro interests while leaving members free to support candidates of their choice in national elections.[41] Since Atlanta has nonpartisan local elections, the endorsement of the Voters' League did not have to overcome traditional party loyalties in order to be effective. The Durham Committee on Negro Affairs has also proved to be an influential political force; like the Atlanta League, it has been able to muster large majorities in the Negro precincts (one observer estimates that 60 to 90 percent of the Negro voters will follow its endorsements).[42] Similar groups of varying effectiveness are found in other Southern cities. The polarization of public opinion on the race issue has made the Voters' League strategy far more effective in the South than the North: the policy of rewarding friends and punishing enemies is easier when one's enemies are openly and indisputably hostile.

Southern Negro political organizations differ in the extent to which they recruit and support, rather than simply endorse, candidates. Whatever the strategy, Negroes in the South as in the North tend to follow political patterns comparable to those of the whites. The weakness and factionalism of formal party organization in the one-party states of the South, coupled with widespread nonpartisan local elections (75 percent of all Southern cities over 25,000 population elect city council or commission members on ballots which do not reveal the party affiliation of candidates), has made it possible—even necessary—for white political leadership in many cities to be assumed by businessmen, civic associations, part-time political managers and a variety of individual political personalities and factions. Negro politics is often a mirror image of the white system with, in some cases, the additional advantage of a growing racial solidarity.

Not all Southern cities have organized Negro political movements. New Orleans, according to recent accounts, lacks—despite two decades of efforts—a city-wide Negro political organization; instead, a number of rival organi-

---

[40] Bradbury Seasholes and Frederic N. Cleveland, "Negro Political Participation in Two Piedmont Crescent Cities," in F. Stuart Chapin, Jr., and Shirley F. Weiss, eds., *Urban Growth Dynamics* (New York: John Wiley & Sons, 1962), pp. 265–70.

[41] Bacote, *op. cit.*, pp. 310–11.

[42] Seasholes and Cleveland, *op. cit.*, p. 266.

zations and factions—numbering as many as eight—have contended with each other for supremacy. Their efforts have never been united behind a single Negro candidate.[43]

In the North, Negro politicians have rarely been influential at the state level because Negroes are concentrated in the big cities and it is in the big-city organizations that Negroes wield influence, if they wield it at all. In the South, however, Negroes were once important state figures in the Republican Party. After Reconstruction, when the South became a one-party region, Republicans lost all hope of winning votes or office. Yet some nominal Republican organization was necessary in order for the South to be represented every four years in the Republican national nominating convention. After the new Southern state constitutions of 1890–1910 succeeded in disfranchising the Negro almost entirely, the Republican Party—which at one time drew on a sizable block of Southern Negro voters and elected numerous Negroes to state and local offices—almost ceased to exist. By 1920 it had virtually abandoned electoral politics, not bothering to hold primaries and often failing even to offer candidates in the general elections.

Many Southern Republican leaders at this time were Negro. In Mississippi, for example, Perry Howard, a Mississippi-born Negro lawyer resident in Washington, D.C., was Republican national committeeman; Dr. S. D. Redmond (a Negro) was, until his death in 1948, chairman of the Republican state executive committee; the Republican national committeewoman was for a number of years also a Negro.[44] A Republican organization such as this was of course not a vote-winning but a patronage-dispensing organization. Its only real function was to send delegates to the national convention; Northern Republican factions courted these votes and, if a Republican were elected President, rewarded the local officials.

These "black-and-tan" Republican organizations were from time to time challenged by so-called "lily-white" Southern Republican movements. White Republicans were in many cases eager to supplant the Negroes, in part to end the identification of the Republican party with "scalawags" and "nigger-lovers" and in part to get access to the perquisites of office. Several national Republican figures gave support to this effort, which in most states was successful. With the emerging prospect of a genuine Republican Party in the South, the assertion of white leadership has of course become even more pronounced. Perry Howard of Mississippi was the last Negro Republican national committeeman in the South.

[43] Daniel C. Thompson, *The Negro Leadership Class* (Englewood Cliffs, N.J.: Prentice-Hall, Inc., 1963), pp. 112–14.

[44] V. O. Key, Jr., *Southern Politics in State and Nation* (New York: Alfred A. Knopf, 1950), pp. 286–91.

Negro politics is not always the province of Negro politicians. Traditionally, the Negro minister has played a crucial role in the community as virtually the only leader with a mass following. Indeed, the early efforts of Negro political participation typically occur under clerical auspices, the ministers forming the organization, recruiting the members, and dealing with the white community. If Negroes succeed in politics—particularly if they elect a member of their race to office or persuade a white official to appoint one to office—Negro politics begins to become professionalized, control falling into the hands of persons who make political leadership their special responsibility. A division of labor occurs, the ministers being replaced (for example) by lawyers who have politically valuable skills, who are free of the constraints imposed by the need to maintain a church congregation, and who often have careers in which politics can be personally rewarding. Finally, if a stable party apparatus is created, or if Negro elective officials acquire fulltime political positions on a long-term basis, the leaders cease being lawyers dabbling in politics and become instead politicians dabbling in law.

This, of course, is an oversimplified account of a very complex phenomenon that has, in general, been insufficiently studied. In many places the critical roles may be played, not by lawyers, but by teachers, students or other members of the growing professional middle class. But in general the pattern is a familiar one: political leadership moves institutionally from one mass base (usually a church or neighborhood association) to a different mass base (a party organization) via an intermediary stage of half-amateur, half-professional political managers.

With the increased militancy of Negroes and the greater involvement of the Negro masses that has occurred since 1963, many wholly nonpolitical voluntary associations in Negro communities are acquiring, wittingly or unwittingly, political functions. The NAACP, for example, has traditionally been a legal defense and lobbying organization; in many communities today, however, its branches have become involved in voter registration drives. These drives are, of course, nonpartisan (the NAACP could not afford to become wholly identified with one political party), but in fact the Negro voters added to the registration lists by such drives are overwhelmingly Democratic. It is not because they are Democrats, however, that they are registered, but rather because they are voters needed in local, nonpartisan contests (in elections, for example, of city school board members) where racial issues are less obscured by party labels and loyalties.

Other civic groups, permanent and *ad hoc*, play a political role. Some sentiment is expressed from time to time in favor of a "Negro political party," distinct from the major parties. In the context of the American political system, where third parties have rarely had a significant impact on policy and almost never influence the outcome of important elections, such a strategy seems unpromising. One leader of the Negro "Nation of Islam" (the so-called Black Muslim movement), Malcolm X, announced in early 1964 his intention of forming a Negro nationalist movement with direct and immediate political objectives (in contrast to the long-range, separatist goals of the Muslims); what those objectives might be or how they might be attained was not clear. Until the split in leadership, Negro Muslims—notably Elijah Muhammed, founder of the movement—renounced political or civic action, both because it implied cooperation with rather than separation from white society and because it could not succeed.[45]

Effects of Negro Political Activity

The consequence of Negro participation in American politics are not as straightforward as they might at first seem. It is certainly true, of course, that the manner in which the President is chosen gives to him and his office almost regardless of party a particular sensitivity to the major population and interest groups—including the Negro which votes in the largest cities of the principal states. The first two civil rights bills were enacted under a Republican President; the third and fourth has been vigorously pressed by two Democratic Presidents, the last of whom—Johnson—is a Southerner.

The fact that American Presidents are proponents of civil rights should not lead us to assume that this response is solely the result of the strategic location of large numbers of voting Negroes. Presidents tend to be "liberal" on this and other matters because of the nature of their electorate as a whole and the key position in the national nominating conventions of liberal, urban forces (of which Negroes are only one part).

At the state level, the strengths and weaknesses of Negro political activity are clear. On the one hand, few governors of large Northern states would think of planning a campaign that did not include a reasonably clear defense of civil rights in general and Negro rights in particular. On the other hand, the Northern states with the earliest and strongest record of civil rights legislation are not necessarily the states with the most Negroes. For example (see Table V), the first four states to enact laws barring discrimination in the sale or rental of private housing (the so-called "open occupancy" laws) were Northern states with *few* Negroes (Colorado—2.3

[45] On the Black Muslims generally, see E. U. Essien-Udom, *Black Nationalism* (Chicago: University of Chicago Press, 1962). Malcolm X was assassinated in 1965; the remnants of his organization have not shown any significant potential for political activity.

percent Negro; Connecticut—4.2 percent Negro; Massachusetts—2.2 percent Negro; Oregon—1.0 percent Negro). By 1964, five years after these states had passed such laws, many of the Northern states with larger Negro populations had *not* acted. These included Delaware (13.6 percent Negro), Illinois (10.3 percent Negro), Maryland (16.7 percent Negro), and Ohio (8.1 percent Negro).[46]

The explanation for this anomaly may be (no one knows) that a large Negro population is politically both an asset and a liability. A large Negro populace may not only expect to influence the commitments and behavior of a governor, but it also may expect to arouse the fears of many

TABLE V—Non-Southern States with "Open Occupancy" Laws Barring Discrimination in Private Housing Market

State and Year	Percent Negro (1960)
1959	
Colorado	2.3%
Connecticut	4.2
Massachusetts	2.2
Oregon	1.0
1961	
Minnesota	0.7
New Hampshire	0.3
New Jersey	8.5
New York	8.4
Pennsylvania	7.5
1962	
Alaska	3.0
1963	
California	5.6
Michigan	9.2
Washington	1.7

whites. The larger the Negro population, the greater the perceived threat (in the eyes of whites) and thus the greater the resistance to broad civil rights laws.[47]

[46] Certain states with sizeable Negro populations were exceptions to this pattern. Michigan (9.2 percent Negro), New Jersey (8.5 percent Negro) and New York (8.4 percent Negro), have fairly strong civil rights laws and one of these—New York—was one of the first to act.

[47] White opinion is favorable to the granting of certain rights, hostile to the granting of others. The Louis Harris *Newsweek* poll, conducted in 1963, showed a majority (63 percent) of whites favoring the Kennedy civil rights bill but a majority (56 percent) opposing a Federal law forbidding discrimination in private housing. *Newsweek*, October 21, 1963, p. 45.

In securing the passage of civil rights laws, state and local officials have probably been as alert to the demands of white liberal groups as to those of Negroes. It has been suggested, for example, that the extensive civil rights enactments in New York (city and state) are the result as much of white liberal (chiefly Jewish) pressure as of Negro pressure.[48] The reason for this is not hard to find. White liberals interested in civil rights tend, on the whole, to be at or above the median in income, education and occupation and thus to have precisely those characteristics which are associated with the so-called "independent" voter. Particularly in local contests, it is the white liberal vote, more than the Negro vote, which may shift and which thus must be courted.

The effect of Negro political activity is potentially greater in primary than in general elections. In primaries, all candidates have the same party label, and thus voting for racial interests is not blunted by traditional party loyalties. The difficulty, obviously, is that relatively few voters participate in primaries (between 1926 and 1952, almost three-fourths of all gubernatorial primaries held in fifteen Northern states had the participation of one-third or less of the potential electorate).[49] Not only do few voters participate, those that do—except in communities where there are strong party organizations—tend to be highly motivated voters or those with a strong sense of duty. Negroes are under-represented in this group and thus their voting strength is diluted.

Where the primary contest offers a clear choice between candidates who differ greatly in their attitude toward race relations, Negro participation (assuming they are free to participate at all) is likely to be considerable. In the South, where the Democratic party primary has usually been more important than the general election, Negro voter registration is higher— other things, such as socio-economic characteristics, being equal—in those states where the primary is a contest between two easily identifiable factions and where the candidates or factions differ in their attitude toward Negroes.[50] (Tennessee and North Carolina are examples of such states.)

The long-heralded advent of a two-party South may or may not increase Negro political effectiveness. Southern counties with a competitive two-party system have slightly higher Negro voter registration rates, but most of the difference is apparently the result, not of the two-party system, but of socio-economic factors.[51] One would think that as the two parties com-

---

[48] Wilson, *Negro Politics, op. cit.*, pp. 150–55. In 1936 (the time of the last general religious census), the metropolitan portions of New York State were 28 percent Jewish.
[49] V. O. Key, Jr., *American State Politics* (New York: Alfred A. Knopf, 1956), p. 135.
[50] Matthews and Prothro, "Political Factors . . .", *op. cit.*, p. 362.
[51] *Ibid.*, pp. 360–61.

pete more evenly, each would bid for the vote of the major population
groups and thereby bring more Negroes into the electorate for reasons of
party advantage. This has not occurred to any significant extent, and the
reason seems to be that the growth in party competitiveness is largely
occurring in districts where relatively few Negroes live. Of the twenty-four
Southern congressional districts in which the Republican candidate polled
more than 35 percent of the vote in 1956, only two are more than one-fourth
Negro. Republicanism has long existed in a few Southern "mountain"
counties where relatively few Negroes live; it is now making inroads in
some middle-class urban districts where practically no Negroes live. In
seventeen of the nineteen most Negro districts in the South, the Republicans
did not even put up a congressional candidate in 1956.[52]

After all the qualifications have been made, however, it remains true
that the presence of Negroes in a political unit affects the behavior of the
politician who represents that unit. In the South, the presence of a large
proportion of Negroes in the district makes the congressman from that
district more hostile, not only to civil rights but to many other "liberal"
issues. In the North, where the presence of Negroes means the presence
of *voting* Negroes, the congressman is likely to be more sympathetic to
liberal and civil rights issues. (These generalizations are all matters of
degree, of course; no single factor—be it Negroes or anything else—can
"explain" the whole of any congressman's behavior.)

One student has analyzed the Democratic votes on labor legislation in
the United States House of Representatives since the Second World War
in terms of the frequency with which congressmen supported the party
leadership (*i.e.*, were "party regulars") and thus, generally, the more
liberal position. Southern congressmen with the smallest proportion of
Negroes in their district were most "regular" while those with the largest
proportions of Negroes were "least regular."[53] On race-relations votes,
another student has shown a similar general tendency for the Southern
states with the smallest proportion of Negroes to have congressmen with a
slightly higher level of support for civil rights legislation.[54]

In the North, it is hard to separate the influence of Negroes on congressmen from the influence of other factors. Northern congressmen from heav-

[52] Milton C. Cummings, "Congressman and the Electorate: A Study of House Elections in Presidential Years, 1920–1956," unpublished Ph.D. thesis, Department of
Government, Harvard University (1960), pp. 406–15.
[53] David R. Mayhew, "Democrats and Republicans in the U. S. House of Representatives: A Study of Intra-Party Coalition Patterns in the Postwar Period," unpublished
Ph. D. thesis, Department of Government, Harvard University (1964), pp. 161–71.
[54] Duncan MacRae, Jr., *Dimensions of Congressional Voting* (Berkeley and Los
Angeles: University of California Press, 1958), pp. 269–71.

ily urban districts are, in general, more "liberal" than ones from less urban areas; since Negroes are found most heavily in the big cities, the impact of the Negro voter is hard to distinguish from the impact of urban influences generally. However, there is some evidence that even among urban Northern Democratic congressmen, those with high proportions of Negroes in their districts are slightly more likely to follow the party leadership and thus, usually, the more "liberal" program.[55]

Viewed as a whole, Negro political activity must be judged as a strategy of limited objectives. Where Negroes can and do vote, they have it in their power to end the indifference or hostility of their elected representatives, but these representatives do not have it in their power to alter fundamentally the lot of the Negro. The vote is a legally important, morally essential weapon for the protection and advancement of individual and group interests but it cannot protect or advance all the relevant interests. It can force the passage of laws, the ending of obvious forms of state-sanctioned discrimination, and the removal from office of race-baiters and avowed segregationists. It can only marginally affect the income, housing, occupation, or life chances of Negro electorates.[56]

Even civil rights legislation is not simply the product of Negro voting. Although all five Negro congressmen voted for civil rights bills in 1964 none was prominently identified as a sponsor or legislative champion of these bills. Those who were such champions, like then Senator Hubert Humphrey, were not this simply (or even partly) because they had a "big Negro vote" at home to worry about (Minnesota in 1960 was less than one percent Negro). Between the casting of a Negro vote and the emergence of a civil rights bill, a vast and complicated institutional structure intervenes, including congressional committees, seniority system, party leadership, White House influence, the maneuvering of presidential candidates and the pressures of the mass media.

At the local level, political activity has a clear relationship to the incidence of at least certain kinds of abuses. The United States Commission on Civil Rights in its 1961 Report [57] examined twenty-one "black belt" counties (Southern counties in which the proportion of Negroes exceeded, in 1960, 50 percent), seventeen of which denied Negroes the right to vote

[55] Lewis A. Froman, Jr., Congressmen and their Constituencies (Chicago: Rand McNally, 1963), p. 93.

[56] James Q. Wilson, "The Changing Political Position of the Negro," in Arnold M. Rose, ed., Assuring Freedom to the Free (Detroit: Wayne State University Press, 1964), pp. 163–84.

[57] Book I, Part III. The Commission findings about these counties should be regarded as very tentative. It is not at all clear on what basis the counties were selected or how representative they are of all black belt counties.

almost entirely and four of which contained a substantial number (31 to 64 percent of the potential number) of registered Negroes.[58]

The commission compared these counties with respect to the civil rights status of Negroes in a variety of areas. Its conclusions were revealing. The principal differences between the two kinds of counties—the "nonvoting" and the "voting"—were in the administration of justice and education. In all the counties the schools were still firmly segregated, but those in the voting counties were of somewhat better quality (more were accredited by the state and fewer were in poor physical condition). In the voting counties, Negroes had served on juries and as justices of the peace (this was not true of most of the nonvoting counties); furthermore, the voting counties did not report any allegations of mob violence, police brutality or illegal police practices, while most of the nonvoting counties had a history of such abuses.[59]

In the other areas studied—housing, employment, public libraries, public accommodations and military establishments—"deprivations were found in all twenty-one counties, with little difference between the seventeen non-voting and the four voting counties," according to the commission. "Negro housing in all counties was found invariably inferior to white housing and always segregated, with Negro quarters often lacking the public services, paved streets, street lighting, sewage disposal, and garbage collection that white neighborhoods were accorded." [60]

These findings were presaged twenty years earlier by Gunnar Myrdal who, writing a section entitled "What the Negro Gets Out of Politics" for his book, *An American Dilemma,* observed that "unquestionably the most important thing that Negroes get out of politics where they vote is legal justice—justice in the courts; police protection and protection against the persecution of the police. . . ." [61] To this ought to be added, perhaps, the role of politics as an avenue of upward social mobility for Negroes.

To be sure, in some places politics will have an even broader effect (Negro voting in Atlanta, for example, probably has produced more gains than would such activity in a rural or small-town area), but in general it is easier to overestimate than to underestimate the effects of political participation. This is not a counsel of despair but only a sobering reminder that political activity can only produce political gains and that other—and far more difficult—remedies must be sought for most of the problems of race relations in America.

[58] The four were Hancock and Liberty counties, Georgia; St. James parish, Louisiana, and Charles City, Virginia.
[59] U.S. Commission on Civil Rights, *1961 Report, op. cit.,* p. 187.
[60] *Ibid.*
[61] Myrdal, *op. cit.,* p. 497.

chapter 11

The American Protest Movement
for Negro Rights

C. Eric Lincoln

Protest and Paradox

One of the great paradoxes of the democratic experiment in America has been the presence of racial segregation in the midst of a free society. Segregation, which in many cases was required or at least sanctioned by state laws, is a kind of unfreedom which is inconsistent with the principles basic to American political philosophy and the body of ideals and values which are understood as "the American way of life" or "the American Dream." America has championed the freedom of people all over the world, yet 22 million American Negroes are still struggling to be free at home. Their freedom to vote, to participate in government, to acquire an education, to move about without restriction, to marry whom they choose, to enjoy certain recreational facilities, to buy homes or eat in public restaurants is qualified severely by the issue of race.

For most of the century following their emancipation, most American Negroes accommodated themselves to the patterns of segregation, the fundamental institution of America's complex system of "race relations." Accommodation did not mean abject acceptance. There were always islands of protest rejecting the prevailing rapprochement. The hope and determination to be *completely* free has illustrated the entire history of the Negro's sojourn in America. The "protest movement" as we know it today is rooted in the activities of individuals and groups, who over a period almost as long as our national history established the beachheads which make possible today's civil rights offensive.

There is another paradox which reflects further the complex nature of the American society. It consists in the fact that although the problem of unfreedom in America is essentially a problem between the races, it is not one on which the races are absolutely divided. This fact is important for the success of the protest movement, which is trying to eliminate that unfreedom, and for the social and political health of the nation as a whole. The protest movement represents the combined efforts of thousands of Negroes and whites working together in the national interest and not merely

458

in the peculiar interests of Negroes. The matter of racial segregation is more than a social or a political issue. It is a moral issue as well. It is not just an issue between the races; it is also an issue among the people. The realization that America's racial problems could not be solved by "Negroes" or by "whites," but only by a concerted effort of the American people, was a long step toward the eventual resolution of the matter. The odds have been and are still quite formidable. Established mores and customs, taboos and habits of behavior are very difficult to change. The dramatic reality is that so many Americans were willing to involve themselves in the effort: clergymen, laborers, college students, creative artists, housewives, even high school boys and girls have given their time and energy, and sometimes their lives to help rid their country of the blight of a two-caste society.

A final paradox relating to the problem of discrimination in American life is that it is nationwide rather than regional. As long as discrimination was seen as a "Southern" phenomenon—as a problem deriving wholly from the issues of the slavery controversy a century ago—the tendency was to attack the region rather than the problem. Many Americans felt that segregation was no more than an expression of Southern prejudice aimed at keeping the Negro at a certain social distance from the white Southerner. Later the American public was to be made aware that there was segregation in the North, the East and West as well as in the South, and that the problem was considerably more complex than an adjustment between the descendants of white masters and black slaves.

New organizations and new techniques were developed to meet an enlightened concept of the depth and extensiveness of the problem. The American public had to be reeducated to grasp the gravity and the universality of racial segregation. Prejudice was not the only cause. The allies of prejudice were hidden in unemployment, economic insecurity, anxiety, fear and politics. In recent times there has been a proliferation of protest movements where previously one or two had carried the burden of the fight for first class citizenship. New leaders with a variety of strategies have gained temporary prominence, and sometimes faded from the scene to be forgotten. Still other leaders and organizations will come and go as new techniques are substituted for old ones which no longer work, or do not seem to work fast enough.

At its most elementary level, a protest movement is a symptom of a deep social conflict which has distorted the normal social relations between groups of people. It is an expression of the anxiety and discontent of one group reacting against what is perceived as the abuse of power by some other group. Protest is also a means of communication. Direct action protest has become a very important means of communication for Negroes in the South who, traditionally, have had no means available to them to let the white man know how much they resented segregation. In spite of persistent protest, however, the matter is far from being resolved. In 1963 thirty-five homes and churches were bombed in retaliation for racial protests, and at least ten people were killed. 930 demonstrations were held in the South alone. Twenty thousand demonstrators were arrested, most of them from the militant student organizations. Hundreds of others were shocked by cattle prods, pummeled by high pressure hoses, bitten by dogs and beaten by policemen. In 1964, at least twelve churches were burned and three civil rights workers killed in Mississippi alone. In 1965 the murders of the Reverend James Reeb and Mrs. Viola Liuzzo in the civil rights struggles in Alabama are other examples of the backlash of reactionary groups in America to the forward strides of the Civil Rights Movement. Yet the protests have continued. Why? They have an insistent message for America: Segregation is dead. The American Negro will no longer accommodate himself to so degrading and immoral a system; and a majority of American whites do not want him to.

PROTEST DURING THE SLAVE PERIOD

The Middle Passage

It is estimated that as many as eighteen to twenty million slaves were sent to the New World during the slave era. Perhaps half as many more perished during the so-called middle passage—the shipboard journey from Africa to the Americas. The conditions under which they were transported made for a high mortality rate aboard ship, for generally, slaves were chained between decks only forty-eight inches high. Crouching in their own filth with no sunlight and a minimum of fresh air, they expired in large numbers and were thrown overboard to the sharks which trailed the slave ships.

Many others died in individual protests against their abduction and enslavement. Some, for example, refused to eat and starved themselves to death. Others leaped overboard and drowned themselves in the sea. Some ripped their own throats and bled to death. Opportunities for concerted action were infrequent, but at least fifty slave revolts occurred at sea. Perhaps the best known revolves around Cinque, the son of a chief of the

Mendi people of Sierra Leone. In 1839 Cinque and his fellow prisoners captured the slave ship *Amistad,* and upon being recaptured and imprisoned in New Haven, they became the subjects of an important trial involving some of the fundamental issues of slavery and the slave trade. John Quincy Adams, who had served as sixth President of the United States (1824), successfully argued their appeal from an order of a lower court for their re-enslavement.[1]

Insurrections

The first slaves brought to America were landed at Jamestown, Virginia, in 1619, but slavery as an institution was not fully crystallized until the last quarter of the seventeenth century. This was a relatively late date in the history of black slavery in the West, for by this time the practice was already old in Europe and South America (and very ancient in Asia and Africa). Portugal was importing slaves from Africa as early as 1442 and continued to do so for the greater part of four centuries. In America, as in the Caribbean and elsewhere, the blacks mounted innumerable protests against their condition of servitude. One of the most successful slave revolts was that led by Toussaint L'Ouverture against the French on the island of Haiti. Toussaint's success in this uprising gave to the New World its first republic.

In the United States at least as many as two hundred uprisings took place during the two and one-half centuries of slavery. The uprisings or revolts differed widely in form, purpose and leadership, but they shared in common an insistent element of protest. Most of the revolts were led by slaves, and the fundamental purpose of such revolts was freedom, of course. It is worth noting, however, that free Negroes like Denmark Vesey, and even the slave leader Gabriel Prosser, were concerned with more than personal freedom: they sought the overthrow of the *system.* Indeed, it was Prosser's intent to establish a black state in Virginia, thus anticipating Elijah Muhammed by 150 years. In New York City in the year 1741, an alleged conspiracy between Negroes and poor whites to seize the city threw the townspeople into a panic. Although there was no substantial evidence to support the charges, eighteen Negroes were hanged, thirteen burned alive and seventy banished. Two white women and two white men were hanged also.

[1] John Quincy Adams, *Argument of John Quincy Adams* (New York: S. W. Benedict, 1841).

None of the black insurrections succeeded. The armed might of the state, the law, economic interest, religion and custom were all counter-forces to any possibility of success. During most of the period the Negro had no allies except an occasional white liberal who dared to face social disapproval, and frequently legal sanctions as well. The wonder is that against such odds and the certainty of swift and terrible reprisal, protest occurred at all. That it *did* occur, and consistently throughout the slave era, is indicative of the quality of the Negro's aspirations for freedom.

Individual Protest

The most frequent instances of protests against slavery were made by individuals, or were conspiracies between only two or three Negroes. Murder and arson were common protest forms, ground glass and poison being favorite murder weapons. Suicide, malingering, theft, the destruction of livestock and harvested crops, the sabotage of machinery, dikes and dams were also widely known. Infanticide was an extreme form of protest, but not infrequently practiced by Negro mothers. The commonest form of protest was running away. Tens of thousands of slaves worth millions of dollars escaped to the North or to Canada, and thousands of others lived in "maroons" in the swamps of the Old South or merged into nearby Indian tribes. Running away was so prevalent a phenomenon that the physicians of the period thought it to be a disease indigenous to Negroes and gave it the name "monomania." Lying, jokes about whites, and militant spirituals were other protest forms.

PROTEST AND SLAVERY

During the slave era the white man owned whatever there was in the slave that could be reduced to property values and protected by law. The slave had no rights that a white man was bound to respect. As a consequence, the quality and range of the slave's protest against his condition was conditioned severely by the fact that he was a chattel. The Emancipation Proclamation, and the Thirteenth, Fourteenth and Fifteenth Amendments to the Constitution purported to free the slave, make him a citizen and give him the franchise. In spite of the intent of the law, it was emasculated by the weight of custom and tradition, and by political collusion between the North and the South. In less than a generation after the Negro was made a "citizen" and given the right to vote, that right was challenged and abrogated severely throughout most of the South by one stratagem or another. In a democratic society the ballot is the most sophisticated instrument of protest or approbation. Since Negroes were largely disfranchised in most of the South, other means of protest were in need of development.

The Convention Movement

Even before the end of slavery, free Negroes of the North were concerned to make a corporate protest in behalf of their rights and against the bondage of their fellows. In 1830, the first National Negro Convention met in Philadelphia to discuss the "oppression of our brethren in a country whose republican constitution declares *that all men are born free and equal.*'" Among the leaders present were James Forten, Samuel Cornish, John B. Vashon and John T. Hilton. Among the measures considered were the establishment of a Negro college and the encouragement of Negroes to migrate to Canada. It is significant today that even in that first convention, leadership could not agree on "the best way" to solve the problem of racial oppression. Some leaders thought that migration to Canada was an evasion of the problem. Others thought that Negroes should seek admission to white colleges. Still others could not see the necessity of calling a convention.

The conventions met with some degree of regularity up to the Civil War. Some were joined by leading white liberals such as Arthur Tappan and William Lloyd Garrison. They convened in Rochester, Cleveland, New York and other cities. Among other things, the conventioners pledged themselves to resist all forms of oppression, to promote universal education and to encourage Negroes to improve their lot by learning skills and entering the professions. In 1849 a convention meeting in Ohio asserted its belief that Negroes were "entitled to all privileges—moral, mental, political and social—to which other men attain." It further resolved to aid escaped slaves and demanded educational rights in common with other citizens.

The conventions continued after the Civil War, although slavery was, of course, no longer an issue. There were other issues: lynching was widespread. There was gross intimidation at the polls. In parts of the South the Negro was all but re-enslaved under a system of quasi-peonage. The First California Negro Convention met in 1855; the Convention of the Colored Men of Texas in 1883; the Young Men's Progressive Association of New Orleans in 1878; the Macon, Georgia, Consultation Convention in 1888, and the National Afro-American League was founded at Chicago in 1890.

PROTEST AND SEGREGATION

The Niagara Movement

In 1896 a Supreme Court decision in the case of *Plessy* vs. *Ferguson* established the separate-but-equal doctrine upon which was built the legal institution of racial segregation, which was to circumscribe the activities and opportunities of Negroes in America for more than half a century. An important corollary to the doctrine of the Plessy case was the advent of Booker T. Washington to power and leadership. The philosophies of Mr. Washington were accommodative at a time when the white establishment South *and* North was anxiously seeking reassurance over the question of Negro intent in the political and economic spheres of American life. To the great dismay of the educated class of Negroes, Washington offered that reassurance in exchange for the South's tolerance and the North's philanthropy. To the bewildered Negro masses, he counseled "Let down your buckets where you are." To the anxious Southern whites, he promised that "In all things purely social, we can be as separate as the fingers, yet one as the hand in all things essential to mutual progress."

Professor Washington's Tuskegee Institute thrived, but the Negro's lot did not seem to improve in general despite his counsel of accommodation. Jim Crow became entrenched. Lynchings increased. Negroes began to leave the South in droves. The chief opponent of Washington's policies of accommodation and appeasement was W. E. B. Du Bois, a Negro militant in the tradition of Frederick Douglass, and a graduate of Harvard University. Du Bois wanted the immediate implementation of Negro rights, and contended that a people who voluntarily surrendered self-respect for "land and houses" could not be "worth civilizing." In a volume of essays called *The Souls of Black Folk*, Du Bois praised Washington for preaching "Thrift, Patience, and Industrial Training for the masses," but criticized him for "apologizing for injustices, North or South," and insofar as he did not "rightly value the privilege and duty of voting" or belittled "the emasculating effects of caste disinctions. . . ."

In 1905, Du Bois, then teaching at Atlanta University, issued a call for an organization of men of "determined and aggressive action . . . who believe in Negro freedom and growth." Some twenty-nine Negro intellectuals and professional men responded to Du Bois' call, and in a meeting at Niagara Falls in July of the same year they organized the Niagara Movement. At its second meeting a year later at Harper's Ferry, the objectives of the new movement were spelled out by Du Bois: "We want full manhood suffrage and we want it now. . . . We want discrimination in public accommodation to cease. . . . We want the Constitution of the country enforced. . . . We want our children educated. . . . We are men! We will be treated as men. And We shall win!" The third annual meeting of the Niagara Movement was held in Boston in 1907, and the following year public rallies were held in key cities across the country. In 1909 this movement of Negro militants merged with a nascent organization of white liberals to become the National Association for the Advancement of Colored People.

Booker T. Washington's leadership rested upon a kind of personal diplomacy which appealed ultimately to the white man's moral consciousness and his sense of fair play. The Du Bois philosophy represented an appeal to the abstract principles of law and order uniformly applied. The rights of citizenship must be the same for all Americans, and the historical context within which these rights were granted could not be held to justify any qualification.

THE NAACP

For more than fifty years the National Association for the Advancement of Colored People has been the chief instrument of protest on behalf of Negro rights. A broad-based organization with a membership of over 500,000 men and women of all races and creeds, the NAACP has 1,600 local chapters scattered through every region of the United States. Its annual budget is in excess of one million dollars, and it has a highly trained professional and legal staff. Roy Wilkins is its executive secretary; Arthur B. Spingarn is president. The large Board of Directors is multiracial, and the membership of the board, like the membership at large, represents every section of the country.

The NAACP was organized in 1909 in response to an obvious need of organized resistance to the steady erosion of the citizenship rights of Negroes. It is an interesting facet of the organization's history that the man who vocalized the need for "a large and powerful body of citizens" to come to the Negro's aid was a white Southerner, William English Walling. Walling, a journalist, shocked and dismayed at the gory race riot which took place in Springfield, Illinois, in 1908, wrote that unless "the spirit of the abolitionists, of Lincoln and Lovejoy" could be revived, the Southern racists would "soon have transferred the race war to the

North." Walling was joined in his concern by Mary White Ovington, a wealthy young humanitarian who had spent several years living and working among Negroes in New York city, and Dr. Henry Moskovitz, a New York social worker. Together they issued a call for a conference. The call, signed by some of the most prominent American men and women in public life, was released on the one hundredth anniversary of Abraham Lincoln's birth, February 12, 1909.

The conference met on May 30th and ended on June 1st. Four subsequent public meetings were held during that year, and the membership began to grow. The organization chose the name: The National Negro Committee. At the second annual meeting in 1910, the name was changed to the National Association for the Advancement of Colored People, and the fledgling movement was incorporated under the laws of the state of New York. It declared its purposes to be: "to promote equality of rights and eradicate caste or race prejudice. . . . to advance the interests of colored citizens; to secure for them impartial suffrage; and to increase their opportunities for securing justice in the courts, education for their children, employment according to their ability, and complete equality before the law." W. E. B. Du Bois was one of those signing the original papers of incorporation. The following year the Niagara Movement and the NAACP became one organization. By 1914 the association had fifty branches.

Historically the NAACP has sought to improve the Negro's lot through "litigation, legislation and education." Its legal specialists, in selecting key cases affecting the rights and status of Negroes in American society, have won important decisions in the Federal courts. These decisions over the period of a half-century have substantially broadened the Negro opportunity to more fully express the rights and privileges of full citizenship. Most notable of the organization's legal successes was the *Brown* v. *Board of Education* case decided by the Supreme Court in 1954. In that case the Court overturned the doctrine of the *Plessy* v. *Ferguson* case by holding that separate facilities in education are inherently unequal. The Brown case opened the door for the disestablishment of legal segregation throughout the South and in many areas of the North.

In the matter of legislation, the NAACP lobbies for the enactment of laws at the national, state and local levels which will "protect civil rights and bar racial discrimination." The association's Washington bureau represents the organization to the Congress, and maintains contact with key governmental agencies. There are regional offices in Atlanta, Dallas and San Franciso.

The association carries on an educational program aimed at creating a climate of opinion favorable for legal and social change. Under Du Bois' editorship from the early days of its founding, and for twenty-five years thereafter, the *Crisis* magazine achieved spectacular success as an organ of propaganda for the association. *Crisis* is still published, but most of the NAACP's educational endeavor is carried on through other channels.

More recently the NAACP has given some emphasis to various direct action programs. It has organized or participated in selective buying campaigns and the picketing of businesses refusing to serve or employ Negroes. Perhaps more importantly, the association has provided expert legal help and bail money for student groups with militant direct action programs.

In spite of its extensive membership, neither the NAACP nor its programs have succeeded in reaching the Negro masses, nor has it been able to perfect an alliance with labor which would be mutually strengthening to the association and the labor movement. It is essentially a middle-class organization, providing status and self-expression for middle-class Negroes and white liberals. Most of the country's Negro notables are members, and many of them work vigorously for the cause without pay. Its critics are many, but none deny its distinguished record of achievement.

Negro Mobility

At the beginning of the First World War 80 percent of America's Negro population still lived in the eleven states of the Old Confederacy. But the pattern of distribution was already changing. The hopelessness of sharecropping, boll weevil infestations, floods and the lynch mobs combined to push the Negro off the land and point him North. In addition, the jobs in the defense plants and shipyards, the packing industries and steel mills constituted a powerful lure to the millions of dejected blacks who had all but despaired of the American Dream. More than 100 Negroes were lynched the first year of the twentieth century. By 1915 the grand total had reached 1,100! The Ku Klux Klan had been revived. All over the South the Negro walked with economic and physical disaster.

White labor in the North was in short supply. The Armed Forces had taken their toll of available manpower, and the flow of European immigrants had been halted by the war. Agents for the hard-pressed war plants and collateral industries of the North scoured the South for labor without regard to color. Thousands of Negro families were advanced money for travel, and often under cover of darkness they escaped from the plantations and farms where they had been once again shackled to the land by a corrupt system of cotton tenancy. Beginning with the turn of the century, a great exodus of Negroes from the South to the North and

West got underway. It was greatly accelerated during and following both world wars, and is still in progress. The Negro, like the Jew, has become an urban dweller.

When the first census was taken in 1790, one of every five Americans was a Negro, and about nine-tenths of the Negro population was concentrated in the South, mostly in agriculture. Even as late as 1900, Negroes still made up one-third of the South's population. By 1940, 20 percent of all Negroes lived outside the South, and by 1960, nine million Negroes, or 48 percent of the total Negro population lived in the North and West. More than a half-million Negroes now live in Philadelphia. Negroes constitute at least 14 percent of the population of New York, 23 percent of that of Chicago, and 51 percent of the population of Washington, D.C. Nearly 500,000 Negroes live in metropolitan Los Angeles. The percentages are still rising.

The Urban League

Spatial mobility alone has not, and cannot, produce the new securities nor the enhanced opportunities for which the Negro has been searching. Employment opportunities in the South have not encouraged the acquisition of skills. The wide disparity of educational opportunities for whites and Negroes in the South left the Negro migrant unprepared to compete in the labor markets of the Northern cities. As a rule, the Negro who went North took nothing but his hands and a will to work. His work experience was limited to manual labor and domestic service. In the North he must compete with immigrant labor, migrating Southern whites and, ultimately, automation. Once the national emergencies were over, he found himself out of a job.

Prejudice and low skills prevented most Negroes from finding a place in the craft unions and the better paying industrial jobs. Negro leadership was powerless to help. Some unions, particularly in the CIO, were more liberal in their racial policies than others. Some railroad unions and some unions in the metal trades flatly refused to admit Negroes. There was little opportunity or incentive to acquire new skills.

The National Urban League, organized in 1911 as the National League on Urban Conditions Among Negroes, has been uniquely effective for almost fifty years in helping Negroes to adjust to the transition from rural to urban life. The league came into being as a result of the merger of three early social agencies which had been working to improve the health, housing and job opportunities of Negro migrants in New York City. The constituent organizations were the League for the Protection of Colored

Women, the Committee on Urban Conditions Among Negroes, and the Committee for Improving the Industrial Conditions of Negroes in New York. Like the NAACP, the Urban League has been interracial from its inception. Its executive board of fifteen members reflects its interracial constituency. The president and the executive secretary have traditionally been respectively white and black.

The Urban League is not strictly a protest organization. Rather, it is "a voluntary community service agency of civic, professional, business, labor and religious leaders . . . dedicated to the removal of all forms of segregation and discrimination based on creed or color." Nevertheless, under the aggressive leadership of Dr. Whitney Young, its executive secretary, it has done much in recent years to change its former image of lethargic conservatism. Young, who was formerly Dean of Atlanta University's School of Social Work, has a staff of five hundred paid professionals distributed among sixty-four affiliated local Urban Leagues in strategic industrial cities with large Negro populations. In addition some 61,000 volunteers assist in the work of the branches.

The Urban League and the NAACP are often linked together in the popular mind through a misconception of their respective roles in the Negro's pursuit of his full share of civil and economic opportunities. The Urban League is decidedly middle class, even more so than the NAACP. But the two organizations are quite different in almost every aspect except constituencies and goals. For example, the Urban League does not seek a mass membership. There are only fifty thousand members in its sixty-four affiliates, as compared to the NAACP membership of ten times that figure. Most of the Urban League's funds come from local Community Chests. It does not "go to court" on behalf of the Negroes it attempts to serve. Instead, the league relies rather heavily upon negotiation and conciliation to win new and better jobs for Negroes, better housing and schools, and improved family life. A well-trained research staff provides interested agencies and individuals with data on every aspect of Negro life, and the league frequently undertakes to screen (and sometimes train) Negro applicants for jobs they have not customarily held.

NONVIOLENCE, DIRECT ACTION AND MILITANCE

The technique of nonviolence has been widely used in Negro protest since the Montgomery bus boycotts of 1955. Martin Luther King, Jr., is the chief exponent and practitioner of this form of protest-resistance. King, who received his graduate training at the Boston University School of Theology, was acquainted with Gandhi's philosophy of nonviolence as well as the more demanding refinement of Christian morality that emphasizes love at the cost of the personal self. While King's followers are not necessarily oriented completely to the nonviolent philosophy as a total way of life, they have utilized nonviolence as a technique of protest with remarkable results. "Schools" or "institutes" are held by the King movement, and other groups espousing the nonviolent approach, to teach the rules and principles of nonviolence to those who are physically and psychologically prepared to participate in this form of protest. Basic to the idea are the concepts of "love force," "self-suffering," "adherence to truth" and the "spirit of reconciliation." Accommodation, or the acceptance of segregation, is considered an evil because it "cooperates" with evil. The objective is not to defeat or humiliate the opposition, but to overcome it with love and reconciliation. Practitioners must accept physical abuse without retaliation, for there is "redemptive power" in "unearned suffering." Justice will triumph ultimately, for the superior forces of the universe are on the side of justice.

The Montgomery Bus Boycott

The use of direct action techniques as a means of protest and communication in the racial struggles first caught the country's imagination during the Montgomery bus boycott. Direct action had been used before, of course, and some of the techniques of nonviolent protest popularized in the early 1960's had been used successfully by the Congress of Racial Equality (CORE) several years earlier in the large cities of the North and Midwest. The Montgomery incident, however, provided a dramatic opportunity for southern Negroes, historically divided in leadership and tactics, to demonstrate a solidarity which would give persuasive impetus to the protest movement. The issue which set off the boycott was the refusal of a Negro woman (Mrs. Rosa Parks) to relinquish her seat on a public bus to a white man. Throughout the South there were specific Jim Crow laws regulating the seating of passengers on public vehicles according to race. The usual requirement was that white passengers would seat from the front, while Negro passengers were required to fill all seats in the rear before they could occupy any forward seats. Mrs. Parks' impromptu defiance of the prevailing Jim Crow arrangement set off a chain of events which led to an organized effort to change the existing racial policies in Montgomery, and later, by extension, all over the South.

The local organization providing the leadership for the bus boycott in Montgomery was the Montgomery Improvement Association, of which Martin Luther King, Jr. was elected president. Specific demands for fairer treatment for Negroes as passengers and for the employment of Negroes as drivers were presented to the bus company. When the demands were ignored, the Negroes of Montgomery walked rather than ride the segregated buses, or they utilized a motor pool composed of the automobiles of private citizens. On December 13, 1956, in consequence of a suit brought by the NAACP, the United States Supreme Court ruled that state law requiring racial segregation on public buses was unconstitutional. A year had passed, and the Negroes of Montgomery through direct action combined with litigation had won an important victory. The spirit and techniques developed there would soon be increasingly employed elsewhere in the South and the North.

The Southern Christian Leadership Conference

The Southern Christian Leadership Conference (SCLC) is "a non-sectarian coordinating agency" of organizations and individuals. Its related aims and purposes include "full citizenship rights and total integration of the Negro into American life." It hopes to accomplish this through "non-violent direct mass action," operating under a philosophy espousing "the basic tenets of the Hebraic-Christian concept of satyagraha—truth force. . . ." The organization has headquarters in Atlanta, with affiliates in sixteen Southern and border states. Founded in 1957 as a logical extension and broadening of the Montgomery Improvement Association, the conference now has a full-time staff of more than sixty and an annual budget of about a million dollars.

SCLC is "interracial" and "nonsectarian," but its board of thirty-three is made up almost wholly of Negro ministers. Individuals hold membership through their affiliated organizations such as churches, fraternal orders and civic organizations. "Bona fide affiliates are restricted to the seventeen Southern states and the District of Columbia," although "supporting affiliates" are not geographically restricted. Conference funds come from fees and pledges of affiliated organizations, mass rallies, direct mailing appeals and personal appearances of Dr. King and other conference leaders. Benefits featuring nationally famous Negro and white entertainers such as Dick Gregory, Harry Belafonte, Jack Benny, Mahalia Jackson, Shelley Winters, Sammy Davis Jr. and others are important sources of financial support.

The Student Nonviolent Coordinating Committee

The Student Nonviolent Coordinating Committee, popularly known as "Snick," is as its name implies an "umbrella" organization for student groups engaged in civil rights protest. Organized in 1960, Snick has borne the brunt of direct action protest across the South, and has been effective in desegregating hundreds of lunch counters and other Jim Crow facilities in major Southern cities. The Student Nonviolent Coordinating Committee is widely associated with the "sit-in movement" which began in Greensboro, North Carolina, on February 1, 1960, when four freshmen from the local A & T College refused to leave a lunch counter in a Woolworth store. The sit-in technique was not new, for at least as early as 1875 a Negro staged a one-man sit-in at the New York City Metropolitan Opera House. Labor used the sit-in in the 1930's, and CORE adopted the technique in the early 1940's. However, the Woolworth incident fired the imagination of youth all over America, and within a year a mass movement built around this technique had developed.

The movement was widely endorsed by American liberals and received support from church groups and labor unions. Student groups on Northern campuses collected funds. White students from both North and South "sat in" and served on the picket lines. Within twelve months more than one hundred cities had desegregated some lunch counters or other facilities as a result of the sit-ins. Within two years the number had doubled. Hundreds of students went to jail for their activities, many refusing to accept bail. Hundreds of others paid fines or served sentences in jail or on the work gangs.

Snick has no stable membership, but draws upon almost all Negro colleges and a large number of predominantly white colleges and universities for its manpower. It has an interracial staff of around seventy-five working out of its Atlanta home office. Most of the staff workers draw only subsistence pay—fifteen to twenty-five dollars a week. Frequently less. James Forman, a former Chicago school teacher, is executive secretary. John Lewis is president.

A most ambitious undertaking was the 1964 Mississippi Summer Project, in which SNCC was able to move into Mississippi with more than five hundred volunteers (including 150 lawyers and law students) to run "Freedom Schools" and promote voter registration. Snick was joined in this effort by the National Council of Churches and the Council of Federated Organizations (made up of CORE, the NAACP, SCLC and SNCC). Other voter registration campaigns related to the Summer Project were carried out in southwest Georgia, eastern Arkansas and central Alabama.

The Congress of Racial Equality

Probably the oldest of the nonviolent direct action protest groups is CORE, the Congress of Racial Equality. CORE was founded as a local group to fight discrimination in Chicago but became a national organization in 1942. Its national director is James Farmer, a former NAACP official. James R. Robinson is executive secretary, and Floyd B. McKissick, an attorney of Durham, North Carolina, is national chairman. A National Advisory Committee is drawn from persons prominent in public life across the country. Headquarters are in New York City, and a staff of seventy carries on the program of the organization. Membership is placed at seventy thousand in ninety-six affiliated and fifty unaffiliated chapters in thirty-three states and the District of Columbia.

CORE believes its techniques of nonviolent direct action to be Gandhian traditions "adapted to American race relations." It conceives nonviolence as a most effective social force in the mobilization of wide public support, as well as in winning the respect and regard of the opposition. The organization is broadly interracial at every level, perhaps the most racially balanced of any of the major protest groups. "Membership involves no religious affiliation [and is] open to anybody who opposes racial discrimination . . . [except] 'those Americans whose loyalty is primarily to a foreign power.'" CORE is financed by contributions from individuals, churches, unions and other groups. Local CORE chapters support themselves through pledges and membership dues, and through local contributions. Most field directors work for subsistence.

CORE, like SNCC, has broad student appeal, and has effectively mobilized youth from all over the country. And like SNCC, it is commonly considered to be "more militant" than other civil rights organizations. On occasion, the national office has found it expedient to suspend some local chapters for deviation from national policy.

The most dramatic protest action initiated by CORE was the Freedom Rides of 1961. The rides were intended to test the desegregation of public waiting rooms and restaurants in interstate bus transportation in the South. The initial Freedom Ride was scheduled to begin in Washington, D. C., on April 28th and proceed southward across Virginia, the Carolinas, Georgia, Alabama and Mississippi to New Orleans where a CORE conference was to be held. A great amount of advance publicity preceded the ride, and President Kennedy was asked to provide Federal protection for the seven Negroes and six white volunteers who would make the test. In Anniston, Alabama, the riders were set upon by mobs and badly beaten. A bus was burned and the Greyhound drivers refused to take the group further. The initial group of riders went on to New Orleans by commercial airlines.

The savage treatment of the first group of Freedom Riders and the indecisive results of the test of desegregated facilities became a rallying point for subsequent groups of Negroes and whites determined to see the issue clarified. CORE, SNCC, SCLC and the Nashville Student Movement formed a Freedom Riders Coordinating Committee and sent more than one thousand volunteers on Freedom Rides through the South. Violence and tension in Alabama, particularly in the capital city of Montgomery, reached the point that six hundred Federal marshals were sent into that city to protect the riders and restore order. In Mississippi, the buses carrying the Freedom Riders were escorted to Jackson under heavy guard, whereupon more than three hundred riders, including at least fifteen priests, were arrested and jailed. Ultimately 120 interstate bus terminals were desegregated through the efforts of the Freedom Riders. Reacting to the militancy of the Freedom Riders the Interstate Commerce Commission on September 22nd ruled that passengers on interstate carriers would be seated without regard to race, and that such carriers could not use segregated terminals.

The Albany Movement

In the wake of the Montgomery protest, local protest movements have sprung up in cities and towns all over the South and in the North: Albany, Georgia, Tallahassee, Nashville, Memphis and Birmingham to name but a few. We cannot detail them all here. In most cases the issues were resolved in favor of desegregation and some changes took place. An important exception is Albany, where a unified segregation-oriented power structure, efficient police methods, the absence of sustained violence, a reluctance on the part of the Federal Government to intervene and a badly divided Negro leadership brought about a stalemate between Negro protest groups and entrenched segregation.

The Albany Movement, founded in 1961, was an unstable alliance of local clergymen, SNCC and the local NAACP, with some help from Martin Luther King, Jr. and his Southern Christian Leadership Conference. Seventy-five Protestant, Catholic and Jewish clergymen from the North came to help. Six percent of the Negroes in Albany were arrested at one time or another, as were King, Ralph Abernathy and the clergymen from the North. The stalemate in Albany continued until the passage of the 1964 Civil Rights Bill.

The Birmingham Movement

Birmingham, which has been called by some civil rights leaders "the American Johannesburg," was probably a decisive symbol of the true nature of the terror that stalks the South, and of the depth of the Negro's commitment to be free *everywhere* in America. The city of Birmingham, Alabama, was well known for its conservative views on the race problem, and as well known for its attraction and tolerance of the Ku Klux Klan and other racist elements. In most priorities of desegregative activities, Birmingham would probably rank logically near the bottom in terms of probable success.

In the spring of 1963, the Reverend Fred L. Shuttleworth, leader of the Alabama Christian Movement for Human Rights and a veteran of protest leadership in Birmingham, led local Negroes in a series of demonstrations aimed at the desegregation of lunch counters and other public facilities. With help from Martin Luther King, Jr. and Ralph Abernathy of the Southern Christian Leadership Conference, the demonstrations continued for five weeks, at which time a truce was arranged by Burke Marshall, Chief of the Federal Department of Justice, Civil Rights Division. The truce was broken and a period of uncontrolled rioting and lawlessness followed. Six Negro children were killed—four by a bomb planted in a church.

The spectacle of Birmingham—the vicious dogs, the high-pressure hoses, and police violence—drove home to America the seriousness of the Negro's plight, and his determination to alter it. Possibly it awakened President Kennedy and other Federal officials to the *immediate* need of new civil rights legislation. But more than anything else it catalyzed new protests in the South and in the North.

Protest in the North

A clear and unmistakable fact which emerges from the wide proliferation of protest movements is that prejudice and discrimination constitute a national phenomenon. No area of the country is free from bias or the consequences of bias. For years, the efforts of the NAACP were concentrated on improving conditions for Negroes living in the South. This was not because there was no discrimination in the North, but because it was less extreme and more insidious. With new national protest organizations in the field, and because new local groups usually win substantial support, the whole United States has become a potential arena of protest.

In the South protest has centered around schools, voting and public accommodations. In the North where public accommodations and voting are generally taken for granted (or protected by state law), protest emphasis has been on employment opportunities, housing and the elimination of *de facto* segregation (caused by housing patterns) in the schools. New York City, Chicago, Chester, Pennsylvania, Philadelphia and Englewood, New Jersey are among the Northern cities experiencing strong protest actions. Cambridge, Maryland, a small town in a border state, was under martial law for several months in 1963 because of the severity of racial clashes there.

The March on Washington

On August 28, 1963, 250,000 American citizens converged on Washington, D.C., and held a day-long protest before the Lincoln Memorial. Negroes and whites, Protestants, Jews, Catholics from all parts of the country took part. It was the largest single protest demonstration in the history of the United States. The march was a protest against unemployment, police brutality, discrimination in employment and all of the other civil inconveniences Negroes traditionally suffer. It was also a demonstration in favor of the passage of President Kennedy's Civil Rights Bill then before the Congress.

The march on Washington originated with A. Philip Randolph, militant head of the Brotherhood of Sleeping Car Porters. It was organized and programed by Bayard Rustin, former field secretary of CORE, who also organized the New York City school boycott. Every Negro protest organization working for integration was represented, as were a number of white or mixed supporting organizations representing labor, churches and civic and various liberal groups. Martin Luther King, Jr., James Farmer, Roy Wilkins, A. Philip Randolph and John Lewis were the principal speakers.

The march on Washington has been interpreted widely as physical evidence of solid American support for an open, desegregated society, and as an endorsement of nonviolent, direct action protest. Perhaps one-third of the marchers were white. Prominent clergymen, educators, labor leaders and other influential Americans were present in large numbers. However, critics of the march say that its chief effect was to dull the edge of the protest movement by dissipating its energies in a mass gathering of no final significance which impressed only the marchers themselves.

PROTEST AND SEPARATION:
THE BLACK NATIONALIST MOVEMENTS

The Universal Negro Improvement Association: Marcus Garvey

Marcus Garvey died in 1940, alone, poor and forgotten, but he left a philosophical legacy which continues to stir the minds of significant numbers of Negroes who live in the black ghettoes of America. Garvey, a West Indian by birth, was a hero of the black masses of the United States (and the Caribbean) during the early 1920's. The increase in lynchings, the decrease in employment, and the unconcern of the Federal Government left the Negro a "forgotten man" in America's impatience to return to normalcy after the war. Marcus Garvey organized The Universal Negro Improvement Association, the first Negro mass movement. It was not an integrationist movement, for Garvey, like his idol—Booker T. Washington—did not believe that the white man in America was willing to receive the black man into a common society on terms of equality, social or otherwise. Garvey's solution was a "return to Africa," there to prove the Negro genius in the establishment of a superior black civilization. To this dream he attracted perhaps three million Negroes who paid their dues and became members of his Universal Negro Improvement Association.

Neither the unrealistic nature of his goals nor the fact of his failures are the important features of the Garvey movement. What is important is that he left a legacy of attitudes and beliefs which continue to motivate, or at least to influence the behavior of a Negro protest segment which is decidedly outside the mainstream of Negro protest. Garvey taught his followers to distrust the white man and to rely solely upon their own efforts to better their condition. He taught them to reject the white man's standards of value and to dare create their own. He exalted what was black, rather than what was white, even going so far as to declare that since the white man's God was white, there could be no succor for black men in a white religion. The black people all over the world, he declared, had "One Aim! One God! One Destiny!" The Negro's salvation lay in racial solidarity and emigration rather than in waiting for the white man to share with him the good life in America. Today, the principal opposition raised by Negroes against integration comes from those elements among the Negro who, like Garvey, believe that ultimately the Negro must be his own salvation.

The Black Muslims: Elijah Muhammad

By far, the largest and best known of the black nationalist organizations is that headed by Elijah Muhammad and popularly known as The Black Muslim Movement. Muhammad claims 250,000 followers in his "Nation of Islam," but responsible elements place the number of dues-paying, card-carrying Muslims at no more than 100,000. Headquarters for the movement are in Chicago, and there are seventy to eighty "mosques" or "temples" scattered across the United States. Primary strength and membership is in the *black ghettoes* of the industrial cities of the North, but there are mosques as far south as Atlanta, Birmingham and Miami; and as far west as San Francisco, Los Angeles and San Diego.

The Black Muslim Movement was founded in Detroit in 1930. The founder was a certain Wali Farad, believed to have been an orthodox Moslem born in

Mecca around 1877. The Black Muslims believe Farad to have been an incarnation of Allah, or God, who came to America to rescue them (and all black men) from bondage to the "blue-eyed devils," or persons of the white race. Almost all of Farad's initial followers were illiterate or semiliterate Negro migrants from the South. They had come North during the boom times of the First World War, and by the 1930's were unemployed and destitute, as were many other Americans. As Negroes they were victims of the prevailing practices in employment and housing. They were "last hired and first fired," and they were confined to the shacks and tenements of their ghetto. Farad taught that the unfavorable condition of Negroes in America resulted from their dependence upon and fear of the white man, who kept them in economic and psychological bondage. Their only escape lay in withdrawing from the white man's society and establishing a "Black Nation" of their own.

The man who succeeded Farad in 1934, and in thirty years built the Muslim "nation" to its present extent, was Elijah Muhammed, born Elijah Poole in the town of Sandersville, Georgia. Muhammed developed Farad's philosophy to a categorical rejection of integration as a workable relationship between blacks and whites, and to a denunciation of Christianity as "the white man's slave-making" strategy for deceiving and subduing Negroes and other nonwhites. Muslims are taught to avoid contact with whites whenever possible; to treat them (and all others) with courtesy and respect when avoidance is not possible; and to require "an eye for an eye and a tooth for a tooth" in case of white aggression. They are also taught thrift, honesty, cleanliness and hard work. They believe themselves to be the "Original Man"—first to bring civilization to earth, and Allah's (God's) choice to survive the Armageddon—the final and conclusive struggle between the white and nonwhite races of the earth.

The Black Muslims are adamantly against integration, and against any Negroes who advocate it. They do not believe in nonviolent resistance, and they are required to retaliate in kind against any attacks made upon them, their families or any members of their organization. Their motto is "Never be the aggressor. Never look for trouble; but if any man molests you, may Allah bless you!" The Muslims appear prosperous. They own innumerable business enterprises and considerable real estate all over the country, and they "buy black" whenever possible. They maintain schools in Chicago and Detroit. The Muslim program calls for "full and complete freedom," "equal justice under the law," "equality of opportunity" and "a separate state or territory." They have frequently called for "a united front of black men" under the leadership of Elijah Muhammed, but cooperation with other protest groups is infrequent.

Organization of Afro-American Unity

Another black nationalist organization is the Organization of Afro-American Unity, founded by Malcolm X, a former follower of Elijah Muhammed. Malcolm, a fiery orator and a popular leader in Harlem, broke with Muhammed in 1963 and organized his own movement, the Muslim Mosque, Inc. His assassination in 1965 left the reins of leadership in the hands of his sister and other lesser known followers. The Organization of Afro-American Unity is a "broadly based non-sectarian movement designed to attract Negro intellectuals and others who do not necessarily subscribe to the religion of Islam, but who do not believe in racial integration." In a document presented to a meeting of delegates of thirty-four African nations requesting them to raise the issue of discrimination against American Negroes in the United Nations, Malcolm asserted the "right of maximum retaliation" against white racists. Both Malcolm X and Elijah Muhammed approach the status of folk heroes among the militant black youth of Harlem and other crowded ghettoes.

THE FEDERAL GOVERNMENT

The protest for Negro rights would be much less effective were it not for the fact that there has been increasing Federal intervention on the Negro's behalf during recent administrations. This is as it should be, of course, and the criticism that the Federal Government has not done enough and has not done it soon enough, is valid. The fundamental responsibility of any sovereign state is the equal protection of its own citizens under its own laws. Because of the traditional power of Southerners in the Congress, leadership in civil rights for Negroes has usually fallen to the executive branch. American presidents have not always cherished responsibility in this highly controversial area. The usual pattern has been to avoid disturbing established practices except in the face of crisis.

Franklin D. Roosevelt was the first modern president to give real leadership in race relations. He appointed Negroes to important Federal positions and gave free access to the White House to Negro leaders. In a move unprecedented for the times, Roosevelt in 1941 issued Executive Order 8802, establishing a Fair Employment Practices Commission designed to end discrimination in employment in defense industries. Congress killed the FEPC in 1945 by refusing to vote funds for it, but a precedent had been established. Many Northern states and cities wrote their own FEPC laws after the Federal law expired.

In 1946 President Truman through Executive Order 9808 created the President's Committee on Civil Rights to study minority rights and existing protection under Federal law, and to decide how existing Federal power could be improved or used more effectively. In a 1947 report entitled *To Secure These Rights* the committee recommended that the Civil Rights section of the Justice Department be expanded to a full division; that Congress establish a permanent FEPC, and that Federal laws be enacted prohibiting lynching, inequalities in law enforcement and in the administration of justice.

In 1948 Truman issued Executive Order 9981 which effected desegregation of the Armed Forces. He also created a Fair Practices Board within the Civil Rights Commission and assigned it the task of handling complaints of racial discrimination in the personnel policies of the Federal Government itself. The Truman Administration went even further to promote the Negro's civil rights by having the Justice Department enter antidiscrimination suits brought by private individuals. In *Shelly* vs. *Kramer* (1948) for example, the Government joined in a suit opposing the enforcement of restrictive covenants, and in *Henderson* vs. *United States* (1950), the Justice Department joined the plaintiff in seeking a ruling against segregation in interstate transportation. In 1951, President Truman established the Committee on Government Contract Compliance, aimed at preventing private companies doing business with the Government from discriminating against Negroes.

The Eisenhower Administration (1952–60) continued the program initiated by Mr. Truman to complete the integration of the Armed Forces. President Eisenhower also continued the fair employment practices program, designed to eliminate discrimination in Federal employment and among those contracting to do business with the Government. Further, the Eisenhower Administration sponsored legislation which culminated in the Civil Rights Acts of 1957 and 1960, the first such legislation since Reconstruction. Eisenhower made a further contribution to the cause of civil rights and to the dignity of the Federal Establishment when he called upon the Armed Forces to insure the rights of Negro children to attend a public school in Little Rock which had been desegregated under Federal Court order. However, the Eisenhower image as a champion of civil rights was compromised severely by his refusal to give public endorsement to the Supreme Court's decision outlawing segregated schools, and his tendency to avoid positive sanctions in other areas of discriminatory behavior.

President John F. Kennedy's strong backing of civil rights protest, and his personal leadership in trying to bring about a free society of citizens equal before the law, is unprecedented in modern times. Certainly no president other than Abraham Lincoln has committed himself so deeply on behalf of the Negro. Kennedy not only actively promoted the cause of civil rights by positive Federal action when such action was indicated, he also missed few opportunities to condemn bias and discrimination and to spell out his own philosophy for a equalitarian society. Mr. Kennedy proved himself a foe of "tokenism" by appointing more Negroes to high places in Government than any president in history. The President's Committee on Equal Opportunity under the directorship of Vice President Lyndon Johnson was set up to encourage firms holding Government contracts to eliminate discriminatory hiring practices, and the Justice Department under Attorney General Robert Kennedy took a direct interest in trying to protect the voting interest of Negroes in the South.

The chief civil rights legislation initiated by President Kennedy was an omnibus Civil Rights Bill of 1964, which was passed after his assassination with strong bipartisan support. The 1964 act, with eleven sections or titles, was somewhat stronger than the President himself had intended at first. It covered such matters as voting, public accommodations, education and equal employment, thus reflecting the emphasis of persistent protest by organized groups over the past several years.

Early in 1965 President Lyndon B. Johnson, now holding office by virtue of a national election, gave strong support to the struggle for voting rights for Negroes in the South. In an appearance before the Congress he pledged his administration to the fullest effort to end all manner of segregation and discrimination against Negro citizens, and ending his address in the historic words of the theme song of the Civil Rights Movement, "We shall overcome." In response Congress enacted "The Voting Rights Act, 1965."

NEGRO MILITANCE AND THE WHITE "BACKLASH"

The struggle for Negro rights increases in intensity as old barriers fall and new ones are recognized. America is still a long way from an equalitarian society, but real progress has been made since the courts and a majority of the American people changed their minds about the legality and the morality of the "separate but equal" doctrine. As the tempo of protest increases, there is an inevitable proliferation of leadership and techniques. The nearer we come to an equalitarian society, the further away it seems, and the more acute are the anxieties of those caught up in the struggle.

The older organizations like the NAACP and the Urban League are accused of being too soft and too conciliatory. Groups like CORE and SNCC are accused of being too militant. Everyone watches the Black Muslims as potentially dangerous to the whole civil rights effort. In many communities leadership is bitterly divided between militant youth and conservative age. In some communities the Negro middle class refuses to become involved. Nowhere has the seething mass of lower-class Negroes been tapped with leadership and direction. Without leadership, or with leadership of the most transient sort, they have taken their protest into the streets—in Harlem, Rochester, New Jersey, Chicago and Philadelphia.

"Too much militance" on the part of organized protest organizations and the uncontrolled rioting of the leaderless masses has produced a so-called backlash among whites who are willing to see Negroes make an "orderly" advance toward full citizenship, and who, in many cases, have supported them. There is some evidence of a falling away of white financial support, and some white moderates have become disillusioned about the possibility of solving the race problem within the foreseeable future. But not all the lashbacks are white moderates or erstwhile supporters of Negro protest. Many of them are, and have always been, white segregationists who capitalize on the excesses of the protest movement to justify their bias. Others are Northern whites who discovered their prejudices the first time when direct action protests appeared in their communities. All America is involved in the struggle in one way or another, and every home is touched by the success or failure of the protest for Negro rights.

BIBLIOGRAPHY

All About CORE. New York City: CORE.

Aptheker, Herbert, *American Negro Slave Revolts.* New York: Columbia University Press, 1943.

Bell, Howard, "Expressions of Negro Militancy in the North, 1840–1860." *The Journal of Negro History,* XLV (January, 1960), 11–20.

Burns, Haywood W., *The Voices of Negro Protest in America.* London: Oxford University Press, 1963.

Clark, Kenneth B., *The Negro Protest.* Boston: Beacon Press, 1962.

Elkins, Stanley M., *Slavery: A Problem in American Institutional and Intellectual Life.* Chicago: University of Chicago Press, 1959.

Franklin, John Hope, *From Slavery to Freedom.* New York: Alfred E. Knopf, Inc., 1956.

Hughes, Langston, *Fight for Freedom.* New York: W. W. Norton Company, 1962.

Jack, Robert, *The History of the NAACP*. Boston: Meador Publishing Company, 1943.

Killian, Lewis and Grigg, Charles, *Racial Crisis in America*. Englewood Cliffs: Prentice-Hall, Inc., 1964.

King, Martin Luther, Jr., *Stride Toward Freedom*. New York: Ballantine Books, 1958.

Lincoln, C. Eric, "The Black Muslims As A Protest Movement," in Rose Arnold (ed.), *Assuring Freedom to The Free: A Century of Emancipation in the U.S.A.* Detroit: Wayne State University Press, 1963.

—— *The Black Muslims in America*. Boston: Beacon Press, 1961.

—— *My Face Is Black*. Boston: Beacon Press, 1964.

—— "Patterns of Protest." *The Christian Century* (June 3, 1964).

—— "The Strategy of a Sit-In," in Sibley, Mulford Q., ed. *The Quiet Battle*. Garden City: Doubleday & Co., 1963.

Meier, August, "New Currents in the Civil Rights Movement." *New Politics* (Summer, 1963), 12–13.

—— *Mississippi Black Paper*. Affidavits 57. Negro and White Citizens on Police Brutality. (Random House, 1965.)

Myrdal, Gunnar, *An American Dilemma*. New York: Harper & Brothers, 1944.

The New York Times, "Organizations and Leaders Campaigning for Negro Goals in the United States." August 10, 1964.

St. James, Warren D., *The National Association for the Advancement of Colored People: A Case Study in Pressure Groups*. New York: The Exposition Press, 1956.

Southern Christian Leadership Conference *Newsletter* (March, 1964).

Southern Regional Council, "Direct Action in the South," *New South*, XVIII, No. 10–11 (October–November, 1963).

The SCLC Story in Words and Pictures. Southern Christian Leadership Conference, Atlanta, 1964.

Southern Regional Council, *Civil Rights: Year End Summary*. A Special Report. Atlanta: Southern Regional Council, Inc., September 29, 1961.

Zinn, Howard, *Albany: A Study in National Responsibility*. Atlanta: Southern Regional Council, 1962.

chapter 12

The Legal Status of the Negro in the United States

Constance Baker Motley

Introduction

In 1857 in the momentous *Dred Scott* case, nine members of the Supreme Court reviewed, at length, the prior and then current legal status of Negroes in the United States.[1] At that time, most Negroes were slaves. Some had been freed by their masters in accordance with the legal procedures established by the law of the slaveholding state; others had likewise purchased their freedom. Dred Scott had been a slave in Missouri. In 1834 he had been taken by his master, an army surgeon, into the free state of Illinois. Subsequently, he was taken to the territory which is now Minnesota. There slavery was prohibited by the Missouri Compromise of 1820. In 1838 Scott was returned to Missouri and later sold to another army surgeon. In 1853 Scott brought suit in a Federal court in Missouri claiming to be a free man. His claim was that he had become free upon being taken into free territory and consequently remained free upon his return to Missouri. The New York citizen who claimed to be his master defended on the ground, among others, that Scott could not bring suit in a Federal court because he was not a citizen of Missouri. Scott had just lost a suit on his claim to freedom in the Missouri courts. The New York master asserted the Federal court would have jurisdiction of the suit only if Scott could show diversity jurisdiction *i.e.*, a suit by a citizen of one state against a citizen of another. Thus two questions required resolution: first, whether Scott was a citizen of Missouri, and second, whether Scott had been freed by being taken into free territory. The latter question involved a determination whether Congress had the power under the Constitution to prohibit slavery in the territories, thus making Scott a free man in Minnesota. Chief Justice Taney's adverse conclusions on these questions were concurred in by the majority. He held Congress did not have power to prohibit slavery and consequently the Missouri Compromise was unconstitutional. He held Scott was still a slave because the highest court of the state of Missouri had held in

[1] *Dred Scott* v. *Sandford,* 19 Howard 393, 15 L. ed. 691.

Scott's case when it was before it that under the law of that state a master did not lose his property right in his slave by taking him to a free state like Illinois. Taney ruled the Supreme Court was bound by this decision of the highest court of a state involving a matter of state law. The former question necessitated a determination whether Negroes were citizens at the time of the adoption of the Federal Constitution. Taney's formulation of the issue was unequivocal:

> Can a negro [sic] whose ancestors were imported into this country, and sold as slaves, become a member of the political community formed and brought into existence by the Constitution of the United States, and as such become entitled to all rights, privileges, and immunities, guaranteed by that instrument to the citizens? One of which rights is the privilege of suing in a court of the United States in the cases specified in the Constitution. . . . The only matter in issue before the Court therefore, is, whether the descendants of such slaves, when they shall be emancipated, or who are born of parents who had become free before their birth, are citizens of a State, in the sense in which the word 'citizen' is used in the Constitution of the United States.[2]

Taney ruled that Negroes were not citizens within the contemplation of the Constitution. He based this on what he claimed to be the Negro's legal status throughout the civilized world at the time of the adoption of the Constitution. This status was a noncitizenship status and, he said, "so far inferior, that they [the Negroes] had no rights which the white man was bound to respect."[3] This view of the Negro's legal status at the time of the adoption of the Constitution was disputed by the dissenting justices.[4] One dissenting justice found that

> At the time of the ratification of the Articles of Confederation [which preceded the Constitution], all free native born inhabitants of the States of New Hampshire, Massachusetts, New York, New Jersey and North Carolina, though descended from African slaves, were not only citizens of those States, but such of them as had the other necessary qualifications possessed the franchise of electors on equal terms with other citizens.[5]

But the majority, holding that even free Negroes were not citizens of the United States within the meaning of the Constitution, became the law of the land in 1857. And as Chief Justice Taney points out, in 1857 Negroes

---

[2] *Ibid.*, 19 How. 403 and 15 L. ed. 700.
[3] *Ibid.*, 19 How. 407 and 15 L. ed. 701.
[4] See especially the dissenting opinion of Mr. Justice Curtis, 19 How. 564, 15 L. ed. 767.
[5] *Ibid.*, 19 How. 572–573, 15 L. ed. 770.

were still regarded in the United States as inferior beings unfit to associate with the white race. He noted, for example, that the 1855 laws of New Hampshire limited its militia to free white citizens and the 1844 Revised Code of Rhode Island forbade authorized persons to join Negroes and whites in marriage.[6]

The legal transition from slave—with no rights—to freedman—with equal rights—has spanned more than a century. It is not yet complete. In effecting this transition from slave status to equal status, three principal instruments for defining legal rights have been employed. These instruments are the Constitution of the United States, Federal statutes, and decisions of the Supreme Court of the United States.

Constitutional Amendments

In 1865 the Constitution was amended to prohibit slavery and involuntary servitude in the United States.[7] In 1868 the Constitution was further amended to confer national and state citizenship on the former slaves. This amendment also imposed three major prohibitions on the states. (1) It prohibited the states from abridging the privileges or immunities of citizens of the United States. (2) The states were also barred from depriving any person of life, liberty or property without due process of law. (3) The states were further restrained from denying to any person within their jurisdictions the equal protection of the laws.[8] In 1870 the Constitution was again amended. This time both the national government and the state governments were constrained. Neither could deny or abridge the right of citizens of the United States to vote on account of race, color or previous condition of servitude.[9] Congress was given the power to enforce each of these amendments by "appropriate" legislation. This power the Congress promptly exercised.

[6] *Ibid.*, 19 How. 415–416, 15 L. ed. 705.

[7] The first section of the Thirteenth Amendment provides:
   Neither slavery nor involuntary servitude, except as a punishment for crime whereof the party shall have been duly convicted, shall exist within the United States, or any place subject to their jurisdiction.

[8] The first section of the Fourteenth Amendment provides:
   All persons born or naturalized in the United States, and subject to the jurisdiction thereof, are citizens of the United States and of the state wherein they reside. No State shall make or enforce any law which shall abridge the privileges or immunities of citizens of the United States; nor shall any State deprive any person of life, liberty, or property, without due process of law; nor deny to any person within its jurisdiction the equal protection of the laws.

[9] The first section of the Fifteenth Amendment provides:
   The right of citizens of the United States to vote shall not be denied or abridged by the United States or by any State on account of race, color, or previous condition of servitude.

Civil Rights Statutes

Among the statutes originally enacted by the post Civil War Congress are those: (1) granting to all citizens of the United States the same right in every state and territory, as is enjoyed by white citizens, to inherit, purchase, lease, sell, hold and convey real and personal property (1866);[10] (2) abolishing and prohibiting peonage, a form of involuntary servitude (1867);[11] (3) securing the right to vote without distinction of race, color, or previous condition of servitude (1870);[12] (4) securing to Negroes the same right as white persons to make and enforce contracts, to sue, be parties, give evidence, and to the full and equal benefit of all laws and proceedings for the security of persons and property (1870),[13] and (5) prohibiting exclusion of Negroes from jury service (1875).[14] Congress made every state officer who deprived any person of these statutory rights, or any other right guaranteed by the Constitution, subject to suit in the Federal courts.[15]

The last civil rights statute enacted by the post Civil War Congress was the Civil Rights Act of 1875 which, in addition to prohibiting exclusion of Negroes from juries, prohibited their exclusion from common carriers, inns, theaters and other places of public amusement. These public accommodations provisions were subsequently held unconstitutional. The Congress did not enact any other major civil rights law directed against the states until 1957 and 1960 when the original voting law of 1870 was amended.

On July 2, 1964, Congress passed the first comprehensive civil rights bill since the post Civil War era. The Civil Rights Law of 1964 further strengthens the voting law of 1870 (Title I); reenacts and augments the public accommodations provisions of the Civil Rights Act of 1875 (Title II); authorizes suit by the Attorney General of the United States to desegregate public facilities (Title III) and public schools (Title IV) when an individual requests him to do so and that individual is otherwise unable to bring suit; establishes a four-year Commission on Civil Rights (Title V):

---

[10] Title 42, United States Code Annotated, §1982.

[11] Title 42, U.S.C.A., §1994. Peonage was a system whereby a person owing a debt was compelled by his creditor to work without pay to erase the debt. *Clyatt* v. *United States*, 197 U.S. 207 (1905); *Bailey* v. *Alabama*, 219 U.S. 219 (1911).

[12] *Ibid.*, §1971.

[13] *Ibid.*, §1981.

[14] Title 18, U.S.C.A., §243. See also Title 18, U.S.C.A., §§241 and 242 and Title 42, U.S.C.A., §§1984–1993 for other civil rights statutes.

[15] Title 42, U.S.C.A., §1983; Title 28, U.S.C.A., §1343(3).

prohibits discrimination in federally assisted programs and provides for withdrawing of Federal funds where discrimination persists (Title VI); prohibits discrimination in employment by employers, employment agencies and labor unions and establishes an Equal Employment Opportunity Commission (Title VII); requires compilation of registration and voting statistics by the Secretary of Commerce (Title VIII); provides for appeals where attempts are made to remove civil rights cases from state to Federal courts (Title IX); permits the Attorney General to intervene in any civil rights law suit of general public importance commenced in a Federal court (Title IX); establishes a Community Relations Service to assist communities or persons involved in civil rights disputes (Title X); and provides for jury trials and penalties for criminal contempts arising out of the enforcement of the act (Title XI).

Supreme Court Decisions

During the past century, the Supreme Court of the United States has been called upon to construe the post Civil War constitutional amendments and Federal laws. Two pre-twentieth-century landmark decisions sealed the Negroes' segregated fate. In 1883 the Court precluded Federal protection against discrimination in privately owned places of public accommodation. It held unconstitutional sections 1 and 2 of the Civil Rights Act of 1875.[16] The first section reads: "That all persons within the jurisdiction of the United States shall be entitled to the full equal enjoyment of the accommodations, advantages, facilities and privileges of inns, public conveyances on land or water, theaters and other places of public amusement; subject only to the conditions and limitations established by law, and applicable alike to citizens of every race and color, regardless of any previous condition of servitude." The second section provided civil and criminal penalties for violation of the first section. The Court held the sections constitutionally void on the ground that prohibitions of the Fourteenth Amendment applied only to the discriminatory actions of states, not the discriminatory actions of individuals such as owners of inns, carriers and theaters. The Court ruled the Thirteenth Amendment was not violated by such individual acts since refusing such accommodations could not be "justly regarded as imposing any badge of slavery or servitude upon the applicant."[17] It

---

[16] *Civil Rights Cases,* 109 U.S. 3. Mr. Justice Harlan dissented.
[17] *Ibid.,* p. 25.

ruled that whether the act might or might not be supportable under the commerce clause of the Constitution was not before it "as the sections in question [were not] conceived in any such view."[18] The Court assumed that the states would protect Negroes against discrimination.[19] In 1896 the Court sustained the infamous separate but equal doctrine. It held that a Louisiana law requiring separate railroad coaches for Negroes did not violate the equal protection clause of the Fourteenth Amendment.[20]

In 1880, prior to the rendition of these fateful decisions, the Court in construing the Fourteenth Amendment had decreed a different fate. It said: "The words of the amendment, it is true, are prohibitory, but they contain a necessary implication of a positive immunity, or right, most valuable to the colored race,—the right to exemption from unfriendly legislation against them distinctively as colored, exemptions from legal discriminations, implying inferiority in civil society, lessening the security of their enjoyment of the rights which others enjoy, and discriminations which are steps toward reducing them to the condition of a subject race."[21]

After almost a century of litigation, the Court has reverted and is thoroughly converted to this earlier view of the amendment. It has struck down virtually every state action discriminating against Negroes or segregating them or sanctioning racism.

The legal status of the Negro so nearly approximates equality with white persons that the Court has already begun to erase the last of the public indignities to which the Negro's former slave status has subjected him. On March 30, 1964, the Court reversed the conviction of Miss Mary Hamilton for contempt of an Alabama court. Miss Hamilton had been convicted of contempt by a white Alabama judge when she refused to answer questions of a white state prosecuting attorney who insisted on addressing her as "Mary." The attorney had addressed whites on the witness stand as "Mr." or "Mrs." The reversal of Miss Hamilton's conviction added common courtesy to the long list of rights the states could not deny.[22]

In the pages that follow, the major rights which have been the subject of litigation are described. Their present legal status is also explained.

[18] *Ibid.*, ftn. 16, pp. 19–20. The commerce clause gives Congress power to regulate commerce between the states. This clause is relied upon to support the Civil Rights Act of 1964, which contains a similar, modernized public accommodations provision.
[19] *Ibid.*, ftn. 16, pp. 19–20.
[20] *Plessy* v. *Ferguson*, 163 U.S. 537.
[21] *Strauder* v. *West Virginia*, 100 U.S. 303, 307–308.
[22] *Hamilton* v. *Alabama*, 376 U.S. 650.

PARTICIPATION IN GOVERNMENT

Negroes in the United States today vote and hold public office. Their right to vote may not be denied by the states or the national government because of race.[23] Racial designations of candidates may not appear on the ballot.[24] The right to vote is unimpeded on racial grounds in all Northern states. In the border states, this is also generally true. In the Deep South, there are still direct and indirect restrictions on Negro voting.

The Southern states in which there are still relatively few Negroes voting are those with disproportionately high Negro populations. These are the states with so-called Black Belt counties. In these counties Negroes greatly outnumber whites. United States Senator Allen J. Ellender of Louisiana admitted on the floor of the Senate in a debate on the Civil Rights Bill of 1964 that whites in these counties fear being outvoted by Negroes.[25] The states in this category are: Mississippi, Louisiana, Alabama, Georgia, parts of North and South Carolina and parts of Virginia.

After the Civil War, several of the Southern states were under control of the Reconstruction government in which Negroes participated. Negroes represented Southern states in both houses of Congress.[26]

Today there are no Negroes in Congress representing Southern states; however, there are representing congressional districts in Northern states. In the South there are a few Negroes holding state or local public office. Except for these few, Negroes, on the whole, are not participating in government as elected or appointed officials in the South. In the North the picture is relatively better.[27]

The right of former slaves to vote had been seriously threatened immediately after the Civil War. To secure this right the Congress proposed the Fifteenth Amendment to the Constitution. It was adopted in 1870. A law immediately was enacted to enforce the amendment.[28] This law was strengthened and augmented in 1957 and in 1960. It was amended to give

[23] 15th Amendment to the Constitution of the United States; Title 42, U.S.C.A., §1971.

[24] *Anderson* v. *Martin*, 375 U.S. 399 (1964).

[25] Cong. Rec. 88th Cong., 2d sess., p. 4828.

[26] John Roy Lynch, *The Facts of Reconstruction* (New York: Neale Publishing Co., 1913); W.E.B. Du Bois, *Black Reconstruction* (New York: Harcourt, Brace & Company, 1935); 3 Cong. Rec. 943 (remarks of Miss Rep. John R. Lynch); 3 Cong. Rec. 959 (remarks of S.C. Rep. Joseph Rainey).

[27] James Q. Wilson, *Negro Politics: The Search for Leadership* (Glencoe: The Free Press, 1960), and "The Negro in American Politics" in this volume, p. 414.

[28] Title 42, U.S.C.A., §1971.

voters protection against intimidation, threats or coercion and the Federal Government power to bring suits to enforce the right to vote. The Civil Rights Act of 1964 amends this law further. It forbids arbitrary disposition of applications by Negroes to register in Federal elections; makes a sixth grade education *prima facie* evidence of literacy in Federal elections, and expedites voting suits brought by the Federal Government.

After adoption of the Fifteenth Amendment, the South relied heavily upon intimidation of Negroes to reduce Negro voting. This led to additional Federal legislation protecting the right to vote.[29] Individuals and organized groups such as the Ku Klux Klan of those days engaged in such intimidation. In addition, the South employed many restrictive devices. The best known among these were the so-called grandfather clause, the white primary, the poll tax and the literacy test.

The grandfather clause typically provided for continued registration of old voters and their lineal descendants. Registration pursuant to more stringent criteria was required of new voters. The white primary was a whites-only party primary election to select candidates for the general elections. The poll tax made annual payment of a capitation tax a prerequisite to voting. The literacy test imposed a high standard of literacy to be judged by the registrar of voters. The registrar's judgment was largely uncontrolled. Generally, a voter applicant who could read, write, understand and/or interpret the Constitution to the satisfaction of the registrar qualified.

Oklahoma used the literacy test combined with the grandfather clause. After Oklahoma's admission to the union, its constitution was amended. The state's otherwise valid voting provisions were amended to require a literacy test. But those who were qualified to vote on January 1, 1866, or lineal descendants of such persons, were exempt from the test. Since few Negroes, if any, were qualified voters in 1866, most Negroes were required to take the test. In 1915 the Supreme Court invalidated this clause as a device discriminatory against Negroes.[30] Oklahoma then provided that persons who had voted in the general election of 1914 would remain qualified. All others who could qualify were required to register during a 12-day period, April 30, 1916, through May 11, 1916. The Court held this a continuation of the grandfather clause. It held the Fifteenth Amendment "nullifies sophisticated as well as simple-minded modes of discrimination." [31]

The white primary was challenged in Texas and South Carolina. First Texas passed a white primary law. It provided that "in no event shall a

29 Title 42 U.S.C.A., §1985.
30 *Guinn* v. *United States,* 238 U.S. 347 (1915).
31 *Lane* v. *Wilson,* 307 U.S. 268 (1939).

negro [sic] be eligible to participate in a Democratic party primary election held in the state of Texas." In Texas, as in most Southern states at that time, the Democratic Party was the only party of any significance. The Supreme Court held this enactment a direct violation of the Fourteenth Amendment. The Court then concluded it was unnecessary to consider the Fifteenth Amendment.[32] The Texas legislature immediately declared an emergency. It substituted another statute. This time the state executive committee of a party was given power to determine qualifications of voters in a party primary. The Democratic Party Executive Committee immediately adopted a resolution that only white Democrats could vote in its primary. This law was likewise held to violate the Fourteenth Amendment.[33] The Court said: "The 14th Amendment, adopted as it was with special solicitude for the equal protection of members of the Negro race, lays a duty upon the court to level by its judgment these barriers of color." Without any further statutory enactment, Texas then permitted the Democratic Party State Convention to determine the qualifications of voters in the party primary. The convention simply adopted the same resolution which the executive committee had adopted. The Supreme Court upheld this action in 1935.[34] It ruled that there was no state action involved in this decision and consequently no violation of the Federal Constitution.

Then the Supreme Court held in *United States* v. *Classic,* 313 U.S. 299 (1941), that Congress had the power to regulate primaries where the primary is made by law an integral part of the machinery of Federal elections. The *Classic* case provided a new legal basis for attacking the white primary in Texas. The primary was an important part of the Texas election process. Consequently, in *Smith* v. *Allwright,* 321 U.S. 649 (1944), the Court found that the Texas primary was by law a part of "the machinery for choosing officials, state and national." To this state function the Court applied the proscriptions of the Fifteenth Amendment.

South Carolina, another white-primary state, then repealed all its laws governing the primary but to no avail.[35] Another Texas white-primary device was struck down by the Supreme Court in 1953. In that case, the Jaybird Party in Texas, a purported private club, excluded Negroes. The club elected persons who then ran in the primaries and general election. These candidates were invariably elected. The Supreme Court held Negroes could not be excluded.[36] South Carolina's Democratic Party then tried to bar

---

[32] *Nixon* v. *Herndon,* 273 U.S. 536 (1927).
[33] *Nixon* v. *Condon,* 286 U.S. 73 (1932).
[34] *Grovey* v. *Townsend,* 295 U.S. 45 (1935).
[35] *Rice* v. *Elmore,* 165 F.2d 387 (4th Cir. 1947), cert. den., 333 U.S. 875 (1948).
[36] *Terry* v. *Adams,* 345 U.S. 461 (1953).

Negroes by requiring of party members an oath supporting segregation and opposing fair employment practices. This device for denying the franchise was also invalidated.[37]

The poll tax was eliminated as to Federal elections by Federal constitutional amendment in January, 1964.[38] Because of widespread poverty in the South, payment of a tax to vote had proved a major deterrent. It had been required in nine southern states. Alabama, Arkansas, Mississippi, Texas and Virginia still had such laws in 1960. Florida, Georgia, South Carolina and Tennessee had repealed their laws prior thereto.[39]

The literacy test is still employed as a device for restricting Negro voters. In Alabama the Boswell Amendment to the State Constitution in 1946 provided for such a test. It was held by the Federal courts to violate the Fourteenth Amendment to the Federal Constitution.[40] Its constitutional infirmity was clear. The registrar of voters had been given uncontrolled discretion to determine the literacy of prospective voters. Moreover, the racially discriminatory purpose of the amendment had been clearly stated by the author, an Alabama legislator. A similar law is presently in force in Mississippi.[41] Louisiana, Georgia, North Carolina, South Carolina and Virginia also have literacy tests.[42]

Under the Constitution of the United States, Congress has the power to regulate the conduct of Federal elections and to prevent racial discrimination in any election.[43] Power to determine in a nondiscriminatory way the qualification of voters is reserved to the states, as is also the regulation of state elections. The Civil Rights Act of 1964 and any subsequent Federal law would, therefore, seek to regulate Federal elections and to prevent racial discrimination in all elections.

Outright intimidation of Negroes seeking to vote in Southern communities is still employed.[44] The Selma to Montgomery, Alabama march which commenced on March 21, 1965 was designed to dramatize this pervasive fact in Black Belt counties of the Deep South. Requiring Negroes to wait in

[37] *Brown* v. *Baskin*, 80 F. Supp. 1017 (E.D.S.C. 1948), affirmed 174 F.2d 391 (4th Cir. 1949).

[38] *The New York Times*, January 24, 1964, pp. 1, 16.

[39] Jack Greenberg, *Race Relations and American Law* (New York: Columbia University Press, 1959), p. 145.

[40] *Davis* v. *Schnell*, 81 F. Supp. 872 (S.D. Ala. 1949), affirmed, 336 U.S. 933 (1949).

[41] Miss. Constitution, Section 244.

[42] Twelve non-Southern states also have literacy tests, but they are not used for racially discriminatory purposes. *Civil Rights Hearings, Subcommittee No. 5, House Judiciary Committee*, 88th Cong., 1st sess. (1963) pt. II, p. 909.

[43] Art. I., Sec. IV, Clause 1, Fifteenth Amendment to the Constitution, Section 2.

[44] *Voting, 1961*, United States Commission on Civil Rights Report, Vol. 1, pp. 67, 91; *Civil Rights, 1963*, United States Commission on Civil Rights Report, pp. 13–50, *passim. The New York Times*, Mar. 21, 1965, p. 1.

line for long periods of time in order to register has been used to halt recent registration drives.[45] However, these voter registration drives have registered 578,345 Negroes in eleven Southern states during 1962, 1963 and the first six months of 1964.[46]

ACCESS TO PUBLIC FACILITIES

The Supreme Court has divested "Jim Crow" of all legal status in the public domain by construing the equal protection clause of the Fourteenth Amendment as a prohibition against state-enforced racial exclusion or segregation in every facility owned or operated by the state.[47] In a case involving courthouse segregation, it held the issue no longer open to question.[48] This revolution in law occurred in the decade 1954–64. The Civil Rights Act of 1964 (Title III) authorizes the Attorney General of the United States to bring suits to desegregate state-owned or -operated facilities at the request of an individual otherwise unable to bring suit.

[45] *The New York Times,* March 2, 1964, p. 20.

[46] *Report of Results of Voter Education Programs* (Atlanta, Georgia: Southern Regional Council), prepared by Mrs. Barbara I. Whitaker, June 4, 1964. Reacting to widespread evidence of denial of the ballot to Negroes, the United States Congress enacted a Voting Rights Act. The act provides that the Federal Civil Service Commission may appoint examiners to register disenfranchised Negroes without regard to literacy tests in a state or county where [1] there was a literacy test on November 1, 1964; [2] less than 50 percent of the population of voting age was registered [3] more than 20 percent of the population was nonwhite. The Civil Service Commission would act upon certification of these facts by the U.S. Attorney General; he would act whenever in a political subdivision with the above characteristics, 20 or more persons complained that they had been denied the right to vote because of race or color.

The act further provides that the Attorney General may appoint poll watchers to see that persons registered by Federal examiners are permitted to vote and that their votes are counted. A three judge Federal court may impound ballots and hold up certification of an election until those registered by Federal examiners are permitted to vote and their ballots counted.

[47] *Johnson* v. *Virginia,* 373 U.S. 61 (1963) (court houses); *Watson* v. *City of Memphis,* 373 U.S. 526 (1963) (public parks, playgrounds, tennis courts, etc.). *Dawson* v. *City of Baltimore,* 220 F.2d 386 (4th Cir. 1955) aff'd 350 U.S. 877 (public beaches); *Holmes* v. *City of Atlanta,* 350 U.S. 879 (1954), vacating 223 F.2d 93 (5th Cir. 1953) (public golf courses). The Supreme Court let stand, by refusing to review, a Supreme Court of California decision holding racial segregation in public housing violative of the equal protection clause. *Banks* v. *Housing Authority of City and County of San Francisco,* 120 Cal. App. 2d 1, 260 P.2d 668 (1953), *certiorari* denied, 347 U.S. 974 (1954).

[48] *Johnson* v. *Virginia, supra.*

The Court has also applied the Fourteenth Amendment's proscription to state-owned facilities leased to private persons or corporations for operation for the benefit of the public,[49] and to private facilities, such as hospitals where there is significant state involvement.[50]

Where the state has required segregation in a privately owned place of public accommodation, the Court has interposed the amendment's prohibition as a bar to the owner's discriminatory acts. In such cases the state is significantly involved and the owner's wish is constitutionally indistinguishable from the state's command. This the Court held in 1963 in a group of "sit-in" cases involving convictions of Negro college students who sought food service at dime store lunch counters in several Southern communities.[51]

On June 22, 1964, the Supreme Court decided another significant group of "sit-in" cases without deciding by a majority vote the crucial constitutional issue raised.[52] These cases posed a question which, if decided in the affirmative, would have opened all privately owned places of public accommodations to Negroes. The question was whether the prohibitions of the Fourteenth Amendment or any other constitutional provisions preclude state court enforcement of state trespass laws against Negroes who, over the owner's objections, persist in peacefully seeking equal treatment in places of public accommodation. Three members of the court, Chief Justice Earl Warren, Mr. Justice Douglas and Mr. Justice Goldberg, answered this

[49] *Turner* v. *City of Memphis*, 369 U.S. 350 (1962) (municipally owned airport restaurant); *Burton* v. *Wilmington Parking Authority*, 365 U.S. 715 (1961) (municipally owned parking lot restaurant); *Muir* v. *Louisville Park Theatrical Ass'n*, 347 U.S. 971 (1954) vacating and remanding 202 F.2d 275 (6th Cir. 1953) (municipally owned amphitheater).

[50] *Burton* v. *Wilmington Parking Authority, supra.* See also *Simkins* v. *Moses H. Cone Memorial Hospital*, 323 F.2d 959 (4th Cir. 1963), *certiorari* denied, 376 U.S. 938 (1964).

[51] *Petersen* v. *City of Greenville*, 373 U.S. 244 (1963) (trespass conviction); *Lombard* v. *Louisiana*, 373 U.S. 267 (1963) (criminal mischief conviction); *Gober* v. *City of Birmingham*, 373 U.S. 374 (1963) (trespass). For an explanation of the charge in the *Gober* case, see *Shuttlesworth* v. *City of Birmingham*, 373 U.S. 262 (1963). In October, 1961, the first of the "sit-in" cases was argued in the United States Supreme Court. Baton Rouge, Louisiana, college students were arrested by a police officer who peered in a drug store window and saw them sitting unmolested at the lunch counter. They were charged with disturbing the peace. The Court reversed their convictions. It held there was no evidence to support the charge. In *McCain* v. *Davis*, 217 F. Supp. 661 (E. D. La. 1963), a Louisiana statute providing for hotel segregation was voided by a three-judge Federal court.

[52] These cases were: *Griffin* v. *State of Maryland*, 378 U.S. 130 (1964); *Barr, et al.* v. *City of Columbia* 378 U.S. 146 (1964); *Bouie* v. *City of Columbia*, 378 U.S. 347 (1964); *Bell, et al.* v. *Maryland*, 378 U.S. 226 (1964); *Robinson, et al.* v. *Florida*, 378 U.S. 153 (1964).

question in the affirmative. Three other justices, Black, Harlan and White, answered the question in the negative. Three other justices, Brennan, Clark and Stewart, avoided decision of the issue. They found other less farreaching constitutional grounds on which to reverse the trespass convictions in those cases.[53] The Chief Justice and the two who agreed with him on the major issue concurred in the reversal of the convictions on these lesser grounds, thus forming a six-member majority.

However, ten days after the court's decisions in these cases, the Congress, on July 2, enacted the Civil Rights Act of 1964. Title II of the act makes unlawful racial discrimination in a place of public accommodation "if its operations affect commerce, or if discrimination or segregation by it is supported by state action." The words "affects commerce" make most major places of public accommodation subject to the act.[54] The act was held constitutionally valid under the commerce clause of the Federal Constitution [Article I, Section 8] by a unanimous Supreme Court on December 14, 1964 in *Heart of Atlanta Motel* v. *United States,* 379 U.S. 241 [1964] and in *Katzenback* v. *McClung,* 379 U.S. 294 [1964]. On the same day, the high Court, in a five to four decision, barred further proceedings in thousands of prosecutions commenced in state courts against those who had peacefully sought service in segregated establishments through sit-in demonstrations. The Court held Title II also "prohibits the application of state laws in a way that would deprive any person of the rights granted under Act." *Hamm* v. *City of Rock Hill,* 379 U.S. 306 [1964].

[53] The Griffin case convictions were reversed on the ground that the arresting officer, a deputy sheriff, was simultaneously a private policeman and a state officer, thus making his action state action. The South Carolina cases were reversed on the ground that there was no evidence in the first case to sustain a conviction for breach of the peace and on the ground that the trespass statute upon which the second case convictions were based was too vague to have given the sit-ins notice that remaining in the drug store after being requested to leave would constitute a crime. The *Bell* case was sent back to the Supreme Court of Maryland for further proceedings on the ground that after the convictions Maryland enacted a public accommodations statute which might change the state court's result in that case. The Florida case was reversed on the ground that Florida has a state health regulation requiring restaurants to provide separate toilets for Negroes and whites, thus significantly involving the state in the private owner's decision to exclude Negroes.

[54] The act applies to: "(1) any inn, hotel, motel, or other establishment which provides lodging to transient guests, other than an establishment located with a building which contains not more than five rooms for rent or hire and which is actually occupied by the proprietor of such establishment as his residence; (2) any restaurant, cafeteria, lunchroom, lunch counter, soda fountain, or other facility principally engaged in selling food for consumption on the premises, including, but not limited to, any such facility located on the premises of any retail establishment; or any gasoline station; (3) any motion picture house, theater, concert hall, sports arena, stadium or other place of exhibition or entertainment; and (4) any establishment (A) (i) which

The attack upon public accommodations discrimination which resulted in Title II of the Civil Rights Act of 1964 commenced in 1960. Then, Negro college students in Greensboro, North Carolina, silently sat at a department store lunch counter reserved for white customers.[55] This was the birth of the "sit-in" movement. The movement mushroomed throughout the South.[56] The sit-in movement succeeded in desegregating many privately owned lunch counters without resort to the courts.[57] Violence ensued in several localities.[58] But in virtually every instance the sit-inners were arrested. They were charged with breach of the peace, disorderly conduct, refusing to obey an officer, trespass or some similar misdemeanor. Thousands of these cases were pending in Southern state courts at the end of 1963.[59]

The greatest achievement of the sit-in movement was the Civil Rights Act of 1964. The widespread public disorder created by sit-ins influenced President Kennedy in June, 1963, to propose to the Congress a bill prohibiting, among other things, public accommodations discrimination.

In the North, public accommodations discrimination has been prohibited by state law. Thirty-one states and the District of Columbia in 1964 had laws prohibiting discrimination against Negroes in privately owned places of public accommodation.[60] The number and types of facilities covered varies from state to state. The only Southern states with such laws were Delaware and Maryland.[61]

---

is physically located within the premises of any establishment otherwise covered by this subsection, or (ii) within the premises of which is physically located any such covered establishment, and (B) which holds itself out as serving patrons of such covered establishment."

[55] *Southern School News,* 6, No. 9 (March, 1960), p. 3.

[56] *Ibid.*

[57] *The New York Times,* April 10, 1964, pp. 1, 22.

[58] *Southern School News, Ibid.*

[59] NAACP Legal Defense and Educational Fund, *Annual Report,* 1963, p. 9. (New York, N.Y.).

[60] Alaska, Calif., Colo., Conn., Del., D.C., Idaho, Ill., Ind., Iowa, Kansas, Maine, Md., Mass., Mich., Minn., Mont., Neb., N.H., N.J., N.Mex., N.Y., N. Dak., Ohio, Ore., Pa., R.I., S. Dak., Vt., Wash., Wisc., Wyo. *Summary of 1962–1963 State Anti-Discrimination Laws,* prepared by American Jewish Congress (mimeograph booklet), December 31, 1963, p. 3.

[61] In some Southern states the law permits owners of places of public accommodation to exclude Negroes via broadly worded nonracial statutes. In Florida, for example, a group of Negroes and whites seeking to eat together were asked to leave the Shell City Restaurant in Miami. They refused. They were charged with a misdemeanor. The statute making their refusal to leave a misdemeanor is a new variety adopted by Southern states after the sit-in movement commenced. It provides that a place of public accommodation may exclude one who, "in the opinion of the management, is a person whom it would be detrimental for it any longer to entertain." Florida Statutes Annotated, Section 509.141. *Robinson, et al.* v. *Florida,* 378 U.S. 153 (1963).

The Civil Rights Act of 1964 (Title II) takes these state statutes into account and provides for suit by an aggrieved party in a Federal court thirty days after seeking relief as provided by state law. In such cases the Attorney General of the United States may intervene. The court, upon application of an aggrieved party, may appoint counsel; authorize commencement of the suit without payment of fees, costs or security; and may allow the prevailing party reasonable attorney fees.

When suit is commenced in a state having no protective legislation, the court may refer the matter to the Community Relations Service established by the Civil Rights Act of 1964 (Title X). This may be done where the court believes there exists a reasonable possibility of obtaining voluntary compliance but for a period not exceeding 120 days.

Suits may also be commenced by the Attorney General against any person or group of persons "engaged in a pattern or practice of resistance to the full enjoyment of any rights secured" by the public accommodations section of the law.

FREEDOM TO TRAVEL

Travel by common carrier is a notably important kind of use of public facilities which has a distinct history of its own. Travel is now free of all racial restrictions. By the end of 1961, the courts and the Interstate Commerce Commission had outlawed all segregation in transportation and racial restrictions in interstate transportation had virtually disappeared. The Jim Crow railroad car is no more. Segregation on intrastate carriers also has been outlawed. But some Negroes still ride in the back of local buses. Some still sit in the waiting rooms once marked "Colored." The habit carries with it the momentum of a century of segregation. Fear of local reprisals is also a deterrent.[62]

Segregation in transportation was first challenged in the Supreme Court by Homer Adolph Plessy. Mr. Plessy was a Negro because he had "one-eighth African blood," as defined by Louisiana law. He had been charged with refusing to occupy a seat in the colored coach of a local railroad. He tried to enjoin his prosecution for violating the Louisiana statute requiring such segregation. The Supreme Court in 1896 ruled against him. The case, *Plessy* v. *Ferguson,* 163 U.S. 537, was the Supreme Court's first

[62] For a compilation of state statutes which required transportation segregation, see Jack Greenberg, *Race Relations and American Law* (New York: Columbia University Press, 1959), pp. 116–17, Appendix A.1.

sanction of the "separate but equal" doctrine. The doctrine remained inviolate as to transportation for half a century.

In 1941, the Supreme Court construed the Interstate Commerce Act to require Pullman companies to provide equal accommodations for Negroes.[63] In 1946, the first successful and farreaching attack upon the doctrine of "separate but equal" as applied to transportation was made. The Supreme Court held a Virginia statute requiring segregation of Negroes on interstate buses an unreasonable burden on interstate commerce.[64] Then, in 1950, the Supreme Court forced an end to dining car segregation.[65] It required railroads to permit Negroes to occupy any empty seat on the diner. The custom had been to partition off a small part of the dining car for service of Negroes. When this small portion became filled, a Negro customer had to wait. The Court held this a violation of the Interstate Commerce Act.

The Interstate Commerce Commission in 1955 ordered an end to passenger segregation on eleven Southern interstate railroads. The suit had been filed by the National Association for the Advancement of Colored People on behalf of its members. Individual Negroes who had been segregated also joined in the suit.[66] On the same day the commission required an end to segregation on interstate buses.[67] Railroad terminals and bus depots remained segregated. The Montgomery, Alabama, bus boycott movement led to a Supreme Court decision barring segregation in intrastate travel in 1956.[68] In 1960, the Interstate Commerce Act was again construed by the Supreme Court. This time it required restaurants in depots utilized by interstate carriers to serve the carriers' Negro passengers.[69]

It was largely to test the extent of compliance with this decision that the Freedom Riders set out on their freedom journey in 1961. In the summer of that year, approximately three hundred persons from Northern communities traveled by bus to Jackson, Mississippi.[70] When these Freedom Riders arrived in Mississippi, each was arrested. They were charged with disorderly conduct. Most spent time in jail. Appeals were taken in most of the cases. Three years later the bulk of these cases were still making their way through the Mississippi courts. The wide publicity and an aroused public opinion caused the Attorney General of the United States

[63] *Mitchell* v. *United States,* 313 U.S. 80 (1941).
[64] *Morgan* v. *Virginia,* 328 U.S. 373 (1946).
[65] *Henderson* v. *United States,* 339 U.S. 816 (1950).
[66] *NAACP* v. *St. Louis and San Francisco Railroad Co.,* 297 I.C.C. 335 (1955).
[67] *Keys* v. *Carolina Coach Co.,* 64 M.C.C. 769 (1955).
[68] *Gayle* v. *Browder,* 142 F. Supp. 707 (M.D. Ala. 1956), aff'd, 352 U.S. 903 (1956).
[69] *Boynton* v. *Virginia,* 364 U.S. 454 (1960).
[70] *Southern School News,* 8, No. 2 (August, 1961), p. 15.

to request an order of the Interstate Commerce Commission banning segregation in train terminals and bus depots. The order issued and became effective November 1, 1961. It also took a Supreme Court decision and subsequent court action to desegregate transportation facilities in Jackson, Mississippi.[71] Shortly thereafter, the Supreme Court held racial segregation in an airport restaurant in Memphis, Tennessee, unconstitutional.[72] The restaurant had been leased to a private company. Memphis had previously removed signs designating separate restrooms for Negro and white passengers in the terminal. Air carriers were the only carriers which did not pursue a passenger segregation policy. Southern state laws did not require such segregation.

FREEDOM OF RESIDENCE

State-enforced residential segregation is constitutionally prohibited. It is barred by the Fourteenth Amendment to the Federal Constitution.[73] It is also precluded by a Federal statute first enacted in 1866.[74] Enforcement of residential segregation by the national government has been held to violate public policy.[75] It is clear, however, that such segregation would also violate the due process clause of the Fifth Amendment to the Federal Constitution.[76] In about twelve states and the District of Columbia racial discrimination in some portion of the private housing market is now banned.

Housing in urban centers in the United States is largely segregated. Segregated land areas involved in the major cities are now vast and well defined. They are in some instances tantamount to separate municipalities. Since World War II, many middle-class white families have vacated the decaying central cities as nonwhites have moved in. Many American cities

[71] *Bailey* v. *Patterson*, 369 U.S. 31 (1962), 323 F.2d 201 (5th Cir. 1963) certiorari denied, 376 U.S. 910 (1964). For the story of the first Freedom Rider see Allan F. Westin, "Ride In", *American Heritage*, 13, No. 5 (August, 1962), pp. 57–8.

[72] *Turner* v. *City of Memphis*, 369 U.S. 350 (1962).

[73] *Buchanan* v. *Warley*, 245 U.S. 60 (1917); *Shelley* v. *Kraemer*, 334 U.S. 1 (1948).

[74] Title 42 U.S.C.A. § 1982. This statute provides:
    All citizens of the United States shall have the same right, in every State and Territory, as is enjoyed by white citizens thereof to inherit, purchase, lease, sell, hold, and convey real and personal property.

[75] *Hurd* v. *Hodge*, 334 U.S. 24 (1948).

[76] In *Bolling* v. *Sharpe*, 347 U.S. 497 (1954), the Supreme Court held racial segregation in public schools by the Federal Government of the District of Columbia violates the due process clause of the Fifth Amendment to the Federal Constitution.

are now ringed by all-white suburbia.[77] Residential segregation in urban centers is the product of the interrelation of governmental power and private prejudice. These have often combined to contain the Negro population in ghettos. In Atlanta, Georgia, for example, in 1959, Negroes constituted 32 percent of the population. They occupied only 16 percent of the developed residential land areas.[78] This is the result of governmental zoning policies typical of most Southern cities. As late as 1963, Atlanta was still enforcing residential zoning segregation.[79] Segregation in housing is also the result of private discrimination against Negroes. The National Association of Real Estate Boards, for example, for many years advocated exclusion of Negroes from white areas.[80]

The role of government alone in initiating and sustaining residential segregation has been a pervasive one. Notwithstanding the Fourteenth Amendment and a Federal statutory bar, Southern cities enacted housing segregation ordinances. These were held unconstitutional by the Supreme Court. The first case arose in Louisville, Kentucky, in 1917.[81] The Court ruled the "separate but equal" doctrine inapplicable to property rights. The Court's exemption of property rights was predicated upon the express protection of property in the Fourteenth Amendment. It was also based on the Civil Rights Act of 1866. Although invalidated as early as 1917, a residential segregation ordinance was still being enforced in Birmingham, Alabama, in 1949. Its enforcement was enjoined the following year by a Federal appeals court.[82] A similar ordinance was being enforced in Palm Beach, Florida, as late as 1958.[83]

In both Northern and Southern cities, all-white residential communities were created by private builders. They were perpetuated through either voluntary adherence to, or court enforcement of, racially restrictive cove-

[77] Davis McEntire, *Residence and Race.* Final and Comprehensive Report to the Commission on Race and Housing (Berkeley: University of California Press, 1960), Chapter III. Charles Abrams, *Forbidden Neighbors* (New York: Harper & Brothers, 1955), *passim.* See "Negroes in Suburbs", in this volume, Chapter II, p. 131.

[78] Hearings Before United States Commission on Civil Rights—Housing, April 10, 1959, p. 480. (Washington, D.C.: U.S. Government Printing Office).

[79] *L. K. Googer, et al.* v. *City of Atlanta, et al.,* Case No. A97697, Fulton Superior Court, March 1, 1963. State court ordered wall erected by city to keep Negroes out of a residential area demolished.

[80] Charles Abrams, *op. cit., supra,* Chapter XIII.

[81] *Buchanan* v. *Warley,* 245 U.S. 60 (1917); *Richmond* v. *Deans,* 281 U.S. 704 (1930); *Harmon* v. *Tyler,* 273 U.S. 668 (1927).

[82] *City of Birmingham* v. *Monk,* 185 F.2d 859 (5th Cir. 1950), *certiorari* denied, 341 U.S. 940 (1951).

[83] *Holland* v. *Board of Public Instruction of Palm Beach County,* 258 F.2d 730, 731 (5th Cir. 1958).

nants. These agreements were contained in the deeds to individual lots. Racial prejudices of individual home owners have also played a significant role in keeping white housing areas white. However, court enforcement of agreements between white property owners not to sell to Negroes proved most effective. Other racial and ethnic groups were similarly barred. The Supreme Court, in 1948, held such agreements unenforceable by state courts.[84] At the same time, it held them unenforceable by Federal courts.[85] However, these decisions did not affect voluntary adherence to such agreements. The agreements, *per se*, were not held illegal. The Court held that state court enforcement of such agreements violated the equal protection clause of the Fourteenth Amendment to the Federal Constitution. Such enforcement was also declared to be contrary to the terms of the Civil Rights Act of 1866. Federal court enforcement of such covenants was held to violate the public policy of the United States, since the Fourteenth Amendment barred enforcement by the states.

In 1934, the Federal Housing Administration (FHA) was established by an act of Congress.[86] Its purpose was to stimulate the construction of new housing by insuring repayment of mortgages on housing meeting certain requirements. FHA's *Underwriting Manuals*, the 1935, 1936, 1938 and 1940 editions, advocated exclusion of Negroes and other minorities and mandated adoption of racially restrictive covenants for new construction.[87] The 1948 decision precluding governmental enforcement of such agreements forced deletion of these proposals from the 1949 edition. Thereafter, the agency announced it would refuse to insure mortgages where restrictive agreements were "recorded" after February 15, 1950.[88] FHA steadfastly refused to require builders involved to sell to Negroes. This alleged Government neutrality continued until 1962. Then, President Kennedy signed his promised Executive Order.[89] The order barred future Government insurance where builders refuse to affirm in writing a policy of nondiscrimination.[90]

Housing provided by public funds has been largely segregated, North and South. An easy legal target, numerous court decisions have held that the Fourteenth Amendment prohibits segregation in public housing projects.[91] The President's Executive Order permits the Attorney General

[84] *Shelley* v. *Kraemer*, 334 U.S. 1 (1948).
[85] *Hurd* v. *Hodge*, 334 U.S. 24 (1948).
[86] Title 12, U.S.C.A., §§1702, *et. seq.*
[87] Charles Abrams, *op. cit., supra*, pp. 229–33.
[88] Charles Abrams, *Ibid., supra*, p. 224; B. T. McGraw, "Desegregation and Open Occupancy Trends in Housing." *Journal of Human Relations* (Fall, 1954), pp. 59–61.
[89] Executive Order No. 11063, 27 Federal Register 11527.
[90] *Ibid.*, Section 302, p. 11528.
[91] These cases are collected in Jack Greenberg, *op. cit., supra*, p. 290, ftn. 71.

to sue to desegregate public housing aided financially by the Federal Government.[92] Prior to the order, the Federal Government's Public Housing Administration supported separate units for Negroes.[93]

The most difficult housing segregation areas to attack legally have been areas of mixed public and private involvement. The Federal urban renewal program exemplifies such a situation. The program involves Federal and city funds. Municipal planning, land clearance and use of the power of eminent domain are also involved. Private enterprise redevelops the area for residential or commercial use in accordance with a municipally approved plan. A Federal District Court recently held Negroes entitled to equal treatment in a Nashville, Tennessee, motel constructed under this program.

Nineteen states, the District of Columbia, Puerto Rico, and the Virgin Islands and twenty-six cities had laws in 1965 protecting against discrimination in some segment of the housing supply.[94] Legislative protection was first afforded in the area of public housing. Protection was then extended to publicly aided housing. Prohibited discrimination in 1965 now include private housing in fifteen states and the District of Columbia.[95] Recent Legislative attacks on private housing have been directed toward realtors and housing finance institutions.[96]

In those states in which there is protective legislation, change in existing patterns has been slowed by the shortage of housing. Delay in enforcement machinery has seriously affected confidence in the efficacy of such laws. In most states, these laws are enforced by an administrative agency. The agency's orders are generally subject to court review and the time between filing a complaint with the agency and its final court adjudication is apt to be too long for effective relief. Lacking the power to enjoin the sale of a house or the lease of an apartment, the agency's powers are usually inadequate to remedy denials of housing because of race. Without power of the injunction, the impact of these laws will remain largely educational.

Freedom of residence is not yet a reality in most of the United States. Nevertheless, that freedom too is in view. Recent increases in the housing

[92] *Ibid.*, ftn. 89, Section 303, p. 11529.

[93] *Heyward* v. *Public Housing Administration*, 238 F.2d 689 (5th Cir. 1956).

[94] *Fair Housing Laws*, Housing and Home Finance Agency, Washington, D.C., September, 1964, pp. 10, 234. These states are: Alaska, California, Colorado, Connecticut, Illinois, Indiana, Maine, Massachusetts, Michigan, Minnesota, Montana, New Hampshire, New Jersey, New York, Oregon, Pennsylvania, Rhode Island, Washington and Wisconsin.

[95] Alaska, California, Colorado, Connecticut, Indiana, Maine, Massachusetts, Minnesota, New Hampshire, New Jersey, New York, Oregon, Pennsylvania, Michigan (Constitution) Rhode Island and District of Columbia (Regulation).

[96] *E.g.,* New York has laws prohibiting discrimination by real estate brokers and lending institutions. McKinney's Executive Law, § 296–5(c)(4)(d) Fair Housing laws, *ibid.*

supply have permitted some Negro dispersion. Federal agencies no longer encourage housing segregation. Although it will require many years to undo the support once given, official attitudes are being tempered by the President's Executive Order, legislation and court decisions outlawing segregation. Private prejudices likewise are being neutralized by these recent developments.

EQUAL EDUCATION OPPORTUNITIES

Equal opportunity to obtain education afforded by the state without discrimination because of race is the right of every person in the United States. This right is guaranteed by the equal protection clause of the Fourteenth Amendment to the Constitution of the United States.

In *Brown* v. *Board of Education of Topeka, Kansas*, 347 U.S. 483 (1954), the Supreme Court held states cannot educate Negroes in separate educational institutions. This principle applies even where facilities afforded Negroes equal those afforded whites. Unanimously the Court ruled state-enforced racial segregation is psychologically harmful to Negro children. Such harm, inflicted by the state, deprives Negro children of equal educational opportunities. In so holding the Court relied upon a finding of fact made by a United States District Court in Kansas. The Kansas court had found as a fact that:

> Segregation of white and colored children in public schools has a detrimental effect upon the colored children. The impact is greater when it has the sanction of the law; for the policy of separating the races is usually interpreted as denoting the inferiority of the negro [sic] group.

The court also found that:

> A sense of inferiority affects the motivation of a child to learn. Segregation with the sanction of the law, therefore, has a tendency to [retard] the educational and mental development of Negro children and to deprive them of some of the benefits they would receive in a racial[ly] integrated school system.

Segregation of Negro children by the Federal Government was prohibited in a companion case. *Bolling* v. *Sharpe*, 347 U.S. 497 (1954). The Court held that although the Fourteenth Amendment did not apply to the Federal Government, the Fifth Amendment to the Federal Constitution does. That amendment contains a clause prohibiting Federal deprivation of "life, liberty or property without due process of law." The Court held that:

Liberty under law extends to the full range of conduct which the individual is free to pursue, and it cannot be restricted except for a proper governmental objective. Segregation in public education is not reasonably related to any proper governmental objective, and thus it imposes on Negro children of the District of Columbia a burden that constitutes an arbitrary deprivation of their liberty in violation of the Due Process Clause.

The Court's 1954 decisions in the *Brown* and *Bolling* cases were followed in 1955 by a supplemental *Brown* decision. *Brown* v. *Board of Education of Topeka*, 349 U.S. 294. This decision delegated to the Federal trial courts the task of deciding whether desegregation in a particular school district should occur immediately or "with all deliberate speed" predicated on the resolution of enumerated administrative problems. However, by the end of 1964 there had been largely only token compliance in the Deep South. A decade of official resistance, evasive schemes for avoiding compliance and gradual desegregation plans are described in the several volumes of *Southern School News*, a Southern Education Reporting Service publication published in Nashville, Tennessee.

The struggle to secure equal educational opportunities for Negroes preceded emancipation of the slaves. In 1831, Prudence Crandall, a Quaker school teacher, began operating a private school for girls in Canterbury, Connecticut.[97] She decided to admit a free Connecticut Negro girl in 1833. Enraged local residents first threatened to withdraw financial support. Miss Crandall then decided to dismiss all the white girls and recruit free Negro girls from other states. The townsfolk who had engaged Miss Crandall to conduct their school for young ladies vehemently opposed the idea of educating free Negroes to a status of equality with whites. A campaign of persuasion and harassment failed. The opposition then secured the enactment of a law by the Connecticut legislature. This law made it a crime to admit a nonresident Negro to a school in the state. Miss Crandall was convicted of violating the law. Instead of deciding the question whether free Negroes were citizens, the state's highest court voided the conviction on a technicality.[98] Nevertheless, the campaign of harassment continued. After the ground floor of the school was destroyed by a mob, Miss Crandall finally abandoned it and left the state.

The *Crandall* case was followed by a struggle against segregated public schools for Negroes in Boston. In 1849 in *Roberts* v. *City of Boston*, 5 Cush. (Mass.) 198 (1849), a separate school for colored children was unsuc-

[97] Eugene Rachlis, "The Magnificent Martyrdom of Prudence Crandall." *Coronet*, 50, No. 2 (June 1961), pp. 172–76.
[98] *Crandall* v. *State*, 10 Conn. 339 (1834).

cessfully challenged. In Boston, an abolitionist stronghold, Negroes were first excluded from public schools. In 1845, a state law conferred a right to recover damages to any person unlawfully excluded.[99] A separate school for Negroes was then established. One of the leading lawyers in Boston of that day, Charles Sumner, acted as one of the attorneys for the Negro children. A Negro lawyer, Robert Morris, was associated with him. Sumner argued that Negroes had a right under the Massachusetts Constitution not to be segregated in public schools. The Massachusetts courts disagreed with Sumner. The lost case resulted in a state law securing this right.[100]

After the Civil War, when Sumner was leading the fight in the United States Senate for equal rights, he remembered his defeat in the courts. He proposed, in 1871, an amendment to a bill which would have secured the right of Negroes in the public schools.[101] Equal treatment on common carriers, in inns, theaters, other places of public amusement and in cemeteries was also sought. This law was finally enacted. It became the Civil Rights Act of 1875.[102] However, before its passage, schools and cemeteries were stricken from the bill. The law was declared unconstitutional in 1883 by the Supreme Court in the *Civil Rights Cases,* 109 U.S. 1 (1883).

This early retreat from vigorous Federal enforcement of equality in the public domain was followed by a complete retreat in 1896. At that time, the Court in *Plessy* v. *Ferguson,* 163 U.S. 537, in an eight to one decision, sanctioned the "separate but equal" compromise of the Fourteenth Amendment. There the Court upheld a Louisiana statute requiring segregation on railroad cars. In short, "Jim Crow" acquired legal status. The lone dissenter in the Plessy case predicted: "the judgment this day rendered will, in time, prove to be quite as pernicious as the decision . . . in the *Dred Scott* case."[103]

A fatal legal assault upon the doctrine commenced in 1946 when a Negro, Herman Marion Sweatt, sought admission to the University of Texas Law School. He claimed it was impossible to secure an equal education in the law school hastily set up for Negroes in the basement of a building. He asserted the state's inability to duplicate intangible benefits accruing to those enrolled at the long-established University Law School. Four years later, in *Sweatt* v. *Painter,* 339 U.S. 629 (1950), the Supreme Court agreed with this contention. And for the first time in its history the Court ordered admission of a Negro to a previously all-white educational institution. In

[99] Massachusetts Acts 1845, §214.
[100] General Laws of Mass., c. 256, §1 (1855).
[101] Cong. Globe, 42nd Cong., 2nd sess., 244 (1871).
[102] 18 Stat. at L. 335.
[103] John Marshall Harlan dissenting, at p. 559.

retrospect, the end came quickly. After four years of litigation, the Court, in 1954, held "separate but equal" unconstitutional as applied to public education.[104]

In January, 1963, a law suit ended in the admission of Harvey Gantt to South Carolina's Clemson College.[105] The previous fall, Federal troops were required to enforce a Federal court order directing the admission of James Meredith to the University of Mississippi.[106] South Carolina was the

[104] Prior to the *Sweatt* decision, in 1948, a less determined attack had been made on the doctrine. This occurred in the case of a young Negro girl, Ada Lois Sipuel, who desired to attend the University of Oklahoma Law School. *Sipuel v. Board of Regents,* 332 U.S. 631 (1948). Oklahoma had failed to provide a separate law school for Negroes despite the Supreme Court's ruling in 1938 in *Missouri ex rel Gaines v. Canada,* 305 U.S. 337. There, Missouri had offered to pay the difference between what it would cost Lloyd Gaines to go to a law school outside the state that would accept him, and what it would cost at the state's University. The Court held this out of state scholarship plan a denial of the equal protection of the laws. It said that the state could only guarantee equal protection within its borders. Missouri then built a separate law school for Negroes at its previously established Negro college.

When the *Sipuel* case was before the Supreme Court, it ruled that Negroes were not required to first demand of the state the erection of separate facilities for them before they could claim a denial of equal protection. The Court put its first significant pressure on the doctrine of "separate but equal" by ruling that under the Fourteenth Amendment the state's duty was to provide "equal protection" for Negroes "at the same time" it provided such protection for other citizens. The practical result of this appeared to be that since the state had failed to set up a separate law school for Negroes, Miss Sipuel was entitled to immediate admission to the state's only law school. This conclusion was nourished by the fact that the Court ruled quickly after argument. Its ruling came shortly before a new semester at the University commenced.

Hope for such a result was also bolstered by the fact that in 1935, another Negro, Donald Murray, had been admitted to the University of Maryland Law School within the separate but equal context. There, Maryland had failed to provide a separate law school for the education of its Negro citizens. Consequently, the highest court of the state ruled that under the separate but equal doctrine Mr. Murray was entitled to admission in the state's only law school.

Prior to 1935, the Supreme Court had opportunities to strike down the doctrine as applied to education in several cases but failed to do so. One was *Gong Lum v. Rice,* 275 U.S. 78 (1927). Chinese children living in Mississippi objected to being classified as "colored" for school purposes. They did not attack the "separate but equal" concept. Their desire to be classified as "white" was denied. In the Berea, Kentucky, College case, in 1908, the Court upheld a state prohibition against corporations teaching white and Negro pupils in the same institution. *Berea College v. Kentucky,* 211 U.S. 45 (1908). It suggested such a prohibition might be invalid as to individuals. Negro children in a Georgia county sought to enjoin the maintenance of a white high school. None had been provided for Negroes. The Court denied this indirect assault on segregation in *Cumming v. Richmond County Board of Education,* 175 U.S. 528 (1899). It pointed to other remedies available to the complainants for securing a school facility for themselves.

[105] *Gantt v. The Clemson Agricultural College of South Carolina,* 320 F.2d 611 (4th Cir. 1963), *certiorari* denied, 375 U.S. 814.

[106] Fifteen thousand Federal soldiers, and six hundred United States marshals secured Meredith's admission. *Southern School News,* 9, No. 4 (October 1962), p. 1.

last state to maintain an all-white college and university system. In every other Southern state, except West Virginia and Arkansas, it had been necessary also to bring suit to secure the admission of the first Negro to a state college or graduate or professional school.[107]

One of the unexpected developments following the *Brown* decision was the attack upon segregated schools in the North. Such schools result largely from residential segregation. However, several cases have developed evidence of intentional segregation of Negro children in communities where no law required it.[108] In New Rochelle, New York, for example, the school authorities in 1963 finally tore down the Lincoln Elementary School. It was 94 percent Negro. For thirty-three years it had been the center of controversy. In 1961, a Federal court had ruled that the New Rochelle school board had segregated Negro pupils in the Lincoln School through its refusal to alter the school zone lines of the Lincoln School over the years.[109] It required the board to devise a plan of desegregation. The board's plan permitted the Lincoln School pupils desiring to do so to transfer to other schools in the city.[110] Continuing controversy led to the school's demise.[111] The New Rochelle case spurred a rash of similar legal action.

On June 17, 1963, the Commissioner of Education of the State of New York ruled that the school board in Malverne, Long Island, New York, should desegregate its three elementary schools.[112] One was 75 percent Negro. Each of the other two were 14 percent Negro. This resulted from residential segregation. The commissioner ordered the board to reorganize the attendance areas of the school districts so as to assign all pupils in grades kindergarten through grade three to the two schools with 14 percent Negro enrollment. The pupils in grades four and five were to attend the 75 percent Negro school. In short, pupils in the three elementary schools were to be redistributed to reduce the disproportionate number of Negroes

---

[107] Suit was also necessary in Florida, Georgia, Alabama, Virginia, North Carolina, Maryland, Texas, Tennessee, Kentucky, Delaware, Oklahoma, Missouri and Louisiana.

[108] *E.g., Walker* v. *Board of Education of City of Englewood, N.J.,* 1 Race Relations Law Reporter 255 (1956); *Clemmons* v. *Board of Education of Hillsboro, Ohio,* 228 F.2d 853 (6th Cir. 1956), *certiorari* denied 350 U.S. 1006; *Taylor* v. *Board of Education of City of New Rochelle,* 294 F.2d 36 (2nd Cir. 1961), affirming 191 F. Supp. 181 (S.D. N.Y. 1961), *certiorari* denied 368 U.S. 940; *Blocker* v. *Board of Education,* Manhasset, N.Y. 226 F. Supp. 208 (E.D. N.Y. 1964).

[109] *Taylor* v. *Board of Education of City School District,* (S.D. N.Y. 1961) 191 F. Supp. 181. There were Negroes in ten of the eleven other elementary schools in the District.

[110] *Taylor* v. *Board of Education of City School District,* 294 F.2d 36 (2nd Cir. 1961).

[111] *Standard Star,* New Rochelle, New York, November 16, 1963, p. 1.

[112] *Mitchell et al.* v. *Board of Education of Union Free School District No. 12 of Town of Hempstead, County of Nassau.* Commissioner's decisions No. 7240.

in one school. This decision was ultimately affirmed by the highest court of the State of New York.[13]

The United States Supreme Court declined on May 4, 1964, to review a northern school segregation case from Gary, Indiana. There a Federal district and appellate court had denied a claim that the *Brown* decision requires remedying the effects of residential segregation.[114] Similar suits asserting a constitutional duty to integrate *de facto* segregated schools have been filed in other Northern communities.[115] In a case filed in Pasadena, California, the state court ruled that the school authorities were under a duty to desegregate *de facto* segregated schools.[116] A ruling to the same effect was secured from a Federal District Court in Springfield, Massachusetts. In another development which appears to forecast the future of this controversy, the highest court of the state of New York upheld the voluntary action of the Board of Education of the City of New York in drawing school zone lines to promote integration against a challenge by white parents.[117] The United States Supreme Court likewise declined to review this decision. And it does appear there is nothing in the law which prevents a state from taking action to remedy the effects of housing segregation on public education.

EQUAL OPPORTUNITY FOR EMPLOYMENT

Government Employment

The Fifth Amendment to the Constitution of the United States would preclude the Federal Government from denying employment because of race or color. There are no Supreme Court cases specifically so holding. However, this is clear from a Supreme Court statement in a nonracial case as well as other Court decisions construing the amendment.[118] The Supreme Court has said: "Congress may not 'enact a regulation providing

---

[113] In the matter of application of Michael Vetere, et al.—N.Y. 2d, 21 A.D. 2d 561, 41 Misc. 2d 200.

[114] *Bell* v. *School City of Gary, Indiana*, (N.D. Ind. 1963), 213 F. Supp. 819, 324 F.2d 209 (7th Cir. 1963), *certiorari* denied, (1964).

[115] *Southern School News*, 8, No. 10 (April 1962) p. 10.

[116] *Jackson* v. *Pasadena School District*, 59 Cal. 2d 876, 382 P.2d 878 (1963). *Barksdale* v. *Springfield School Committee*, 237 F. Supp. 543 [D. Mass. 1965].

[117] *Balaban* v. *Rubin*, 250 N.Y. Supp. 2d 28, 20 A.D. 2d 438, aff'd 14 N.Y. 2d 193 *certiorari* denied, 379 U.S. 881.

[118] *Bolling* v. *Sharpe*, 347 U.S. 497 (1954), holds the Fifth Amendment bars Federal enforcement of racial segregation in public schools.

that no Republican, Jew or Negro should be appointed to federal office, or that no Federal employee shall attend Mass or take any active part in missionary work.' " [119] Nevertheless, all doubt as to national policy has been dispelled by a clear Federal statute barring discrimination in the Federal civil service. This law, adopted in 1949, prohibits racial discrimination "with respect to any person or with respect to the position held by any person." [120] Presidential executive orders aim to reduce discrimination in employment in Federal agencies and departments. The most recent order established, in 1961, the President's Committee on Equal Employment Opportunity.[121] However, this committee has no power to impose sanctions to enforce its own decisions or to resort to the courts for that purpose.[122] In short, executive orders to date have not afforded any additional legal protection. Their principal benefit has been to establish an administrative procedure for voluntary compliance.

There are no reported Supreme Court cases involving discrimination against Negroes seeking employment in state government. However, the Supreme Court has struck down state statutes which restricted private employment of aliens [123] and denied certain Orientals licenses to engage in the fishing industry.[124] In most of the Southern states, Negro teachers were paid less than white teachers in the segregated school systems. Invoking the Fourteenth Amendment to the Federal Constitution, Negro teachers, about a quarter of a century ago, won the right to equal pay.[125] They relied upon the amendment's equal protection clause. Fifteen states, like the Federal Government, bar by statute discrimination in public employment despite the applicability of the Fourteenth Amendment.[126]

---

[119] *United Public Workers* v. *Mitchell*, 330 U.S. 75, 100 (1947). This case involved the power of Congress to prohibit Federal employees from engaging in political activity.

[120] Title 5, United States Code Annotated, §1074.

[121] Executive Order No. 10925. 26 Fed. Reg. 1977 (1961).

[122] See, Jack Greenberg, *Race Relations and American Law* (New York: Columbia University Press, 1959), pp. 158–63, for more extensive discussion of a similar earlier order, Executive Order No. 10950 (1955).

[123] *Truax* v. *Raich*, 239 U.S. 33 (1915).

[124] *Takahashi* v. *Fish and Game Commission*, 334 U.S. 410 (1948).

[125] *Alston* v. *School Board of the City of Norfolk*, 112 F.2d 992 (4th Cir. 1940), *certiorari* denied, 311 U.S. 693 (1940).

[126] These states are: Arizona, California, Colorado, Connecticut, Illinois, Indiana, Massachuetts, Michigan, Minnesota, Missouri, Nevada, New Mexico, Ohio, Pennsylvania, Washington. *Equal Employment Opportunity*, Hearings Before The Subcommittee on Employment and Manpower of the Committee on Labor and Public Welfare, United States Senate, 88th Congress, First Session, 1963, Appendix.

Approximately fifteen states also prohibit discrimination in employment by contractors doing business with the state.[127]

Private Employment

Southern state segregation policies have included laws which curtailed equal opportunity to earn a living in one's chosen business or profession, solely because of race and color. These statutes have been struck down by the courts on Fourteenth Amendment grounds. In Louisiana there was a statute prohibiting mixed professional boxing matches between Negro and white boxers.[128] A similar statute was held constitutionally void by a Texas court.[129] A Georgia court invalidated an ordinance prohibiting colored barbers from serving white women or children.[130]

In 1965 thirty-three states and more than forty-five cities had fair employment practice laws, ordinances or policies.[131] In twenty states, the law was administered and enforced by a state agency with ultimate review by the courts available to an aggrieved party. [132] In two states, the law was applicable only to public contractors. [133] In one state it was applicable only

[127] These states are: Arizona, California, Colorado, Illinois, Indiana, Kansas, Michigan, Minnesota, Nevada, New Jersey, New Mexico, New York, Ohio, Pennsylvania, Vermont. *Equal Employment Opportunity, ibid.* Bureau of National Affairs, Inc., *Fair Employment Practices,* a looseleaf reference service published biweekly (Washington, D.C., March 15, 1965) Section 451.

[128] *Dorsey* v. *State Athletic Commission,* 168 F.Supp. 149 (E.D. La. 1958), affirmed, 359 U.S. 533 (1959).

[129] *Harvey* v. *Morgan,* 272 S.W. 2nd 621 (1954).

[130] *Chaires* v. *City of Atlanta,* 164 Ga. 755, 139 S.E. 559 (1927).

[131] *Equal Employment Opportunity.*

The states are: Alaska, California, Colorado, Connecticut, Delaware, Hawaii, Idaho, Illinois, Indiana, Iowa, Kansas, Massachusetts, Michigan, Minnesota, Missouri, Nebraska, Nevada, New Jersey, New Mexico, New York, Ohio, Oklahoma, Oregon, Pennsylvania, Rhode Island, op. cit. supra, ftn. 127 Vermont, Washington, West Virginia, Wisconsin.

Some of these cities are: Phoenix, Arizona; Bakersfield, Fresno, San Francisco, California; Boise, Idaho; Chicago, Illinois; East Chicago, Gary, Indiana; Des Moines, Iowa; Baltimore, Maryland; Ecorse, Hamtramck, Pontiac, River Rouge, Michigan; St. Louis, Missouri; Duluth, Minneapolis, St. Paul, Minnesota; Newark, Red Bank, New Jersey; Campbell, Canton, Cleveland, Girard, Hubbard, Lorain, Lowellville, Niles, Steubenville, Toledo, Warren, Youngstown, Ohio; Braddock, Clairton, Duquesne, Erie, Farrell, Johnstown, Monessen, Philadelphia, Pittsburgh, Sharon, Pennsylvania; Milwaukee, Wisconsin; District of Columbia.

[132] These states are: Alaska, California, Colorado, Connecticut, Delaware, Illinois, Kansas, Massachusetts, Michigan, Minnesota, Missouri, New Jersey, New Mexico, New York, Ohio, Oregon, Pennsylvania, Rhode Island, Washington, Wisconsin.

[133] Arizona, Nevada.

to those engaged in production of military or naval equipment.[134] Three of the state agencies have no enforcement powers.[135] A violation of the law in one state was a simple misdemeanor only.[136] In another, a fine up to five hundred dollars was the only sanction.[137]

An interstate air carrier sought to avoid compliance with the order of one state agency which directed the carrier to cease and desist discrimination against a Negro seeking employment as a pilot. The Supreme Court ruled the state's law applicable to the carrier.[138] The constitutionality of these laws has not been challenged in the Supreme Court. The effectiveness of such laws cannot be measured with any degree of precision.[139] Enforcement has seldom been vigorous. Complaints and court cases have been relatively few. However, their contribution to a climate of acceptance of equal opportunity in employment cannot be gainsaid.

On March 1, 1961, the President of the United States issued Executive Order No. 10925.[140] One objective of the order, noted above, is to promote and ensure equal opportunity for employment in the Federal Government. The second objective is to promote and ensure equal opportunity for all qualified persons employed or seeking employment on government contracts. Basically, the order requires all contracting Federal agencies to include in every contract certain prescribed nondiscrimination covenants. The contractor in turn is required to include same in every subcontract. The primary covenant is that the contractor and subcontractor will not discriminate in employment. The order provides sanctions and penalties for noncompliance. There are: (1) publication of names of contractors and subcontractors who have failed to comply, (2) recommending to the Department of Justice in serious cases of violation or threat of violation that appropriate proceedings be brought to enforce compliance, (3) recommending to Department of Justice criminal proceedings be brought for false information, (4) termination of contracts, (5) providing that contracting agencies refrain from further contracts. Efforts must be made by each contracting agency to secure compliance through conference, conciliation, mediation and persuasion before any of the foregoing sanctions may be invoked. The committee's view of the sanctions and penalties is that they are contained in

[134] Nebraska.

[135] Indiana, Nevada, West Virginia.

[136] Idaho. However, criminal sanctions are also available in other states. See *Equal Employment Opportunity, op. cit., supra*, pp. 552–553.

[137] Vermont.

[138] *Colorado Anti-Discrimination Commission, et al.* v. *Continental Air Lines, Inc.*, 372 U.S. 714 (1963).

[139] See, Jack Greenberg, *op. cit., supra*, pp. 192–206 for a discussion of these laws.

[140] 26 Fed. Reg. 1977.

the order but may never be employed. "The Committee seeks to accomplish its objectives primarily by alerting American businesses to the needs of the hour and seeking their voluntary cooperation. . . ." [141]

The Civil Rights Act of 1964 provides, for the first time, Federal remedies against discrimination in employment by employers, employment agencies and labor unions.[142] The first remedy provided is opportunity to file charges with the Equal Employment Opportunity Commission established by the law. This commission is empowered to redress the charge only by informal methods of conference, conciliation, and persuasion.

Charges arising in a state which already has a fair employment practices law may be filed with the Federal agency sixty days after the aggrieved party has sought relief at the state level. A charge may also be filed by a member of the Federal commission. Except where a complaint must first be filed at the state level, a Federal complaint must be filed within ninety days of the discriminatory act charged. Failure of the commission to eliminate the discriminatory practice complained of within thirty days may be followed by suit instituted by the aggrieved party in a Federal court within thirty days thereafter. The court, upon application by the aggrieved party, may appoint counsel and may authorize commencement of the action without payment of fees, costs or security. The court may also permit the Attorney General to intervene in such cases. If the court finds discrimination, it may enjoin the employer, employment agency or labor union from pursuing such action now declared by the statute to be unlawful. The court may also order reinstatement or hiring with or without back pay. Reasonable attorneys' fees may also be allowed by the court to the prevailing party's counsel. If an employer, employment agency or labor union fails to comply with a court order, the Federal agency may commence proceedings to compel compliance. The Attorney General may also institute suit whenever he "has reasonable cause to believe that any person or group of persons is engaged in a pattern or practice of resistance to the full enjoyment of any of the rights secured" by the fair employment practices provisions of the Civil Rights Act. The fair employment practices provisions of the act do not become effective until one year after enactment. During the first year after the effective date the law applies to employers of one hundred or more employees, during the second year seventy-five or more and during the third year fifty or more.

[141] Hobart Taylor, Jr., *The President's Committee on Equal Employment Opportunity,* 16 *Southwestern Law Journal* 101, 105. The 1961 Executive Order was amended in 1963 to include contractors performing under federally assisted construction contracts. Executive Order 11114. 28 Fed. Reg. 6485.

[142] Title VII.

Union Discrimination

Labor union discrimination has seriously complicated the private employment problem for the Negro worker. There are two basic discriminatory practices. Negroes are sometimes barred from union membership or segregated in powerless auxiliaries.[143] They also have been purposefully discriminated against by unions authorized by law to bargain for the nonunion Negro members of a bargaining unit as well as the white members of the unit who have been admitted to union membership.[144]

At common law, unions had the right to exclude Negroes from membership.[145] In most of the states with fair employment practices laws, discrimination by unions is also prohibited.[146] New York was the first state to prohibit discrimination in union membership in 1940. A union unsuccessfully challenged the law as unconstitutional in the Supreme Court.[147] The courts also have protected the right to work in a closed shop when union membership has been denied because of race or color.[148]

The Supreme Court has not yet ordered Negroes admitted to union membership on any theory. However, since 1944, it has required unions authorized by law to act as the exclusive bargaining agent for all members of a bargaining unit, whether union members or not, to represent nonunion Negro members fairly and "without hostile discrimination against them." [149] Applying this principle, the lower Federal courts have enjoined enforcement of contracts which discriminated against Negroes. And they have awarded damages against both the unions and the employers who were parties to such agreements.[150]

The National Labor Relations Board (NLRB) has only recently begun

[143] Clyde W. Summers, *The Right to Join a Union*, 47 *Columbia Law Review* 33, 34 (1947).

[144] *Steele* v. *Louisville and Nashville R.R.*, 323 U.S. 192 (1944).

[145] *Mayer* v. *Journeymen Stonecutters Association*, 47 N.J. Eq. 519, 20 Atl. 492 (Ch. 1890).

[146] *Equal Employment Opportunity, op. cit., supra,* ftn. 9, p. 550.

[147] *Railway Mail Association* v. *Corsi*, 326 U.S. 88 (1945).

[148] *James* v. *Marineship Corp.*, 25 Cal. (2d) 721, 155 Pac. (2d) 329 (1944). See Clyde W. Summers, *op. cit., supra* ftn. 143 pp. 44–45 for citation of other cases.

[149] *Steele* v. *Louisville and Nashville R.R., supra* at 203; *Syres* v. *Oil Workers International Union,* 223 F.2d 739 (5th Cir. 1955), reversed *per curiam,* 350 U.S. 892 (1955).

[150] *E.g., Central of Georgia Railway* v. *Jones,* 229 F.2d 648 (5th Cir. 1956), *certiorari* denied, 352 U.S. 848 (1956); *Rolax* v. *Atlantic Coast Line Railroad,* 186 F.2d 473 (4th Cir. 1950).

to enforce the duty of fair representation in its adjudications. Between 1944 and 1962 NLRB failed to construe a violation of the duty as a violation of the National Labor Relations Act.[151] (NLRA). On July 1, 1964, one day before the enactment of the Civil Rights Act of 1964 prohibiting discrimination in union membership and outlawing the segregated local (Title VII), the NLRB rendered a decision which so construes the duty and curbs union membership discrimination.[152] NLRB ruled that a union's failure to fairly represent Negro workers violates provisions of the National Labor Relations Act prohibiting prescribed unfair labor practices by labor unions. This ruling had been foreshadowed as the decision notes by a ruling in a nonracial 1962 case recognizing the NLRB's power to enforce the duty of fair representation in construing the NLRA. The duty, it further ruled, bars discrimination and segregation in union memberships. Unexpectedly NLRB ruled that when this duty is violated a defaulting union is subject to a revocation of its NLRB certification as the exclusive bargaining agent for the employee unit involved. For the first time the board said: "Where a union segregates members or excludes or denies full membership status to applicants, on racial grounds, it is violating its duty of fair representation to all members of the unit and should not be permitted to hold a certified status." In the case in which these rulings were made the segregated white local (Local No. 1) and the segregated Negro local (Local No. 2) of the Independent Metal Workers had been jointly certified as the exclusive bargaining agents of the employees of Hughes Tool Company of Houston, Texas. Local No. 1 entered into a contract with the employer which limited certain jobs to Negro employees and others to whites only. The better, higher paying jobs were limited to the latter. Apprenticeship training for the white jobs was open only to white employees by the contract. A Negro employee of Local No. 2 denied by the employer an opportunity for apprenticeship training filed a grievance with Local No. 1 which it refused to process. This refusal was also held to be an unfair labor practice and a violation of the duty of fair representation. If these rulings are affirmed by the courts, Negro workers will have available to them the more expeditious administrative remedy afforded of resort to NLRB proceedings to correct racial discrimination. Previously, the duty of fair representation had been enforced only in the Federal courts.

[151] Michael I. Sovern, *The National Labor Relations Act and Racial Discrimination*, 62 *Columbia Law Review* 563 (1962).

[152] *Independent Metal Workers Union, Local No. 1 and Local No. 2 and Hughes Tool Company,* 147 NLRB No. 166.

PROTECTION AGAINST MOB VIOLENCE AND
UNFAIR CRIMINAL PROCEDURES

The high-powered rifle killing of Mississippi's NAACP* Secretary, Medgar Evers, occurred on June 12, 1963.[153] This was during the height of antisegregation protest demonstrations in Jackson, Mississippi. On September 15, 1963, four Negro girls were blasted to death by dynamite hidden in the 16th Street Baptist Church in Birmingham, Alabama. The same day, a Negro boy was killed by two white boys as he rode down a street on a bicycle with his brother.[154] These killings followed desegregation of public elementary schools in Birmingham. All of these homicides bear witness to the fact that Civil Rights advances still subject Negroes to wanton acts of violence in the South.

The killer of Medgar Evers has not been convicted. A man charged with his murder is awaiting a third trial after a hung jury upon his first and second trials.[155] The killers of the four Sunday school children have not been apprehended at this writing. One of the white boys who killed the Negro boy on a bicycle has been convicted by an all-white jury of second degree manslaughter and sentenced to seven months in prison.[156]

There was a time when the lynching of Negro males was commonplace. This form of mob violence has virtually disappeared. To illustrate: in 1882, 49 Negroes were lynched; that number rose to 113 in 1891; in 1892, it was 161; but by 1902, the number of Negroes lynched decreased to 85; by 1912, it was 61; in 1922, it was 51; in 1932, it was 6.[157] Since 1952, the number has been no more than one per year.[158]

Specific Federal antilynching statutes have been proposed since the turn of the century. As the problem has receded, they have not been pushed actively.[159]

Federal protection of Negroes from bodily harm is sparse. There are

* National Association for the Advancement of Colored People.

[153] *Southern School News*, 10, No. 1 (July 1963), p. 2.

[154] *Ibid.*, No. 4 (October 1963), p. 1.

[155] *The New York Times*, April 18, 1964, pp. 1, 17.

[156] *Ibid.*, January 19, 1964, p. 46.

[157] Jessie Parkhurst Guzman, *Negro Yearbook* (New York: William H. Wise & Co., 1952), p. 278.

[158] Jack Greenberg, *op. cit., supra*, p. 320.

[159] See Maslow and Robison, *Civil Rights Legislation and the Fight for Equality (1862–1952)*, 20 *Chicago Law Review* 363, 380–85 (1953).

only four Federal statutes which bear directly upon the problem. Two of these are Federal criminal statutes.[160] One such statute, Section 242, condemns participation in lynchings by state officers. When read in connection with the general Federal conspiracy statute,[161] this Federal enactment applies to private citizens acting in concert with officers. There is a Federal statute which prohibits inducing or procuring the commission of a crime.[162] When read with Section 242, that statute outlaws private attempts to secure willful police cooperation with lynchings. The other federal Criminal statute, Section 241, has been held to cover a mob which seizes a prisoner from a Federal marshal. Such action deprives the victim of Federal protection.[163]

There are also two Federal civil statutes.[164] These allow suits for damages against state officers. Insofar as police brutality is concerned, the courts have placed generally the same construction on these civil statutes as on the criminal statutes.[165]

Many states have statutes condemning lynchings or mob violence. Some of these laws cover mob violence generally. Others merely govern seizing a prisoner who is in jail. They have resulted in few prosecutions, even fewer convictions. No convicted lyncher has ever been sentenced to death.[166] Those states which have statutes forbidding lynchings are: Alabama, California, Georgia, Illinois, Indiana, Kansas, Kentucky, Minnesota, Nebraska, New Jersey, New York, North Carolina, Ohio, Pennsylvania, South Carolina, Tennessee, Texas, Virginia and West Virginia—nineteen in all.[167] Some states, such as New York, allow civil suits against municipalities for police brutality.[168] However, most states, pursuant to theories of sovereign immunity, do not recognize the cause of action.

When a Negro comes before the bar of justice to be tried for the commission of a crime, his liberty is always in jeopardy. His life is likewise in jeopardy where the state law provides the death penalty for the offense charged.

Slaves were not permitted to serve on juries or to be witnesses in court

[160] Title, 18 U.S.C.A. §§241 and 242. For examples of the difficulty in securing convictions of police officers guilty of brutality against Negroes see *Screws* v. *United States*, 325 U.S. 91 (1945); *Williams* v. *United States*, 341 U.S. 97 (1951).
[161] Title 18, U.S.C.A., §371.
[162] Title 18 U.S.C.A. §2(a).
[163] *Logan* v. *United States*, 144 U.S. 263 (1892).
[164] Title 42 U.S.C.A. §1983 and §1985(3).
[165] See *Monroe* v. *Pape*, 365 U.S. 167 (1961); *Collins* v. *Hardyman*, 341 U.S. 651 (1951).
[166] Maslow and Robison, *op. cit.*, p. 383.
[167] For short descriptions of these statutes, see Jack Greenberg, *op. cit.*, *supra*.
[168] See, *e.g.*, *McCrink* v. *City of New York*, 296 N.Y. 99, 71 N.E. 2d 419 (1947).

against a white person.[169] Slaves were also subject to severer punishments for crimes.[170] Consequently, after adoption of the Fourteenth Amendment, Congress acted to enforce it by legislation removing these burdens and disabilities.[171] A law was enacted in 1870 securing the right of Negroes to be witnesses in court.[172] The same statute provided that all persons "shall be subject to like punishment, pains, penalties, taxes, licenses, and exactions of every kind, and to no other."

In 1875 Congress passed another civil rights law. One section made it a crime, punishable by a fine up to five thousand dollars, to exclude Negroes from service on either the grand or petit jury.[173] On March 1, 1880, the Supreme Court upheld a Federal indictment against a Virginia state court judge for violation of this section.[174] But it appears there have not been any Federal indictments sought or procured since that time. "That case has been allowed to stand as solitary and neglected authority for direct enforcement of the Negro's right to sit on juries." [175]

It also appears that a long neglected civil remedy is available.[176] Congress enacted a law in 1871 which permits Negroes to sue any state official who subjects any person to a deprivation of rights secured by the Federal Constitution and laws.[177] Relying upon this provision, and the one securing the right of Negroes to be witnesses, a Negro brought suit in a Federal district court in Kentucky. In 1956, the court agreed that Negroes were entitled to a Federal court injunction against such discrimination by the courts of a state.[178] Until recently, Negroes have not pursued this remedy. At the time of this writing, a similar suit was pending in the United States District Court for the Northern District of Alabama.[179]

Although the civil and criminal remedies have been neglected, Negro

[169] *Civil Rights Cases*, 109 U.S. 3, 22 (1883).

[170] *Ibid.*

[171] The Fourteenth Amendment to the Federal Constitution, among other things, conferred citizenship on the former slaves.

[172] Title 42, U.S.C.A., §1981.

[173] Title 18, United States Code, §243.

[174] *Ex parte Virginia*, 100 U.S. 339 (1880).

[175] *Cassell* v. *Texas*, 339 U.S. 282 (1950), Mr. Justice Jackson dissenting at p. 303. See also *Justice*, Report of the United States Commission on Civil Rights (1961) pp. 89–103.

[176] *Ibid.*

[177] Title 42, United States Code, §1983. This statute is invoked to enjoin school segregation and other forms of state discrimination based on race. See *e.g.*, *Brown* v. *Board of Education of Topeka*, 347 U.S. 483 (1954).

[178] *Brown* v. *Rutter*, 139 F. Supp. 679 (W. D. Ky. 1956).

[179] *Coleman* v. *Barton*, Civil Action No. 63-4-W, decided June 11, 1964 (jurisdiction retained).

criminal defendants have succeeded, on numerous occasions, in getting their convictions reversed because of jury discrimination. Reversals of convictions have been secured whenever Negroes have been systematically excluded from the grand jury which indicted or the petit jury which tried the case. The first Supreme Court reversal of such a conviction came on March 1, 1880, the same day on which the court upheld the indictment against the Virginia judge.[180]

Negro criminal defendants were responsible for establishment of the constitutional principle that no conviction may be predicated upon a coerced confession.[181] Convictions secured through the introduction into evidence of such forced confessions violate the due process clause of the Fourteenth Amendment to the Federal Constitution. This, of course, is a principle now relied upon not only by Negro criminal defendants but white criminal defendants as well.[182]

Constitutional protection against sham trials resulting from mob domination of the courtroom was also judicially affirmed as a result of an appeal to the nation's highest tribunal by Negro criminal defendants.[183]

The right to counsel in a capital case is another great precept of American constitutional law established by Negro criminal defendants. In the famous Scottsboro Case, *Powell* v. *Alabama,* 278 U.S. 45 (1932), the United States Supreme Court for the first time had occasion to rule that denial of counsel in a capital case violated the due process clause of the Fourteenth Amendment to the Federal Constitution. Conviction of a defendant in any felony case where he has been denied the right to counsel may now be reversed.[184]

FREEDOM TO CHOOSE ONE'S MATE

American racism was expressed most pointedly in state statutes prohibiting marriages between whites and Negroes. In 1964 nineteen states had such laws; two were non-Southern states. Seventeen states with a history of state-decreed racial segregation in several areas prohibited marriages be-

---

[180] *Strauder* v. *West Virginia,* 100 U.S. 303 (1880). For citation of a number of these cases see Jack Greenberg, *op. cit., supra,* pp. 323–29. See also *Justice, op. cit., supra,* ftn. 7.

[181] *Brown* v. *Mississippi,* 297 U.S. 278 (1936).

[182] *Ashcraft* v. *Tennessee,* 322 U.S. 143 (1944).

[183] *Moore* v. *Dempsey,* 261 U.S. 86 (1923).

[184] *Gideon* v. *Wainwright,* 372 U.S. 335 (1963).

tween the races.[185] The two non-Southern states with such laws were Indiana and Wyoming. At least eighteen other states had similar laws.[186] These statutes have been repealed.[187]

The Supreme Court has not ruled upon the validity of any antimiscegenation law. In 1954 and again in 1956 the Court declined to pass upon the issue when presented by two cases. One case arose in Alabama.[188] A request for review was denied. The other case came up from Virginia by way of appeal.[189] The appeal was ultimately dismissed without argument or decision on the merits.

In 1883, in *Pace* v. *Alabama,* 106 U.S. 583, the Supreme Court upheld a state statute imposing a greater penalty for adultery or fornication when committed by members of different races.[190] The Supreme Court, on appeal by a Negro man and a white woman, reversed convictions for violating a similar Florida statute in 1962.[191] The Florida statute of which the couple was convicted provided:

> Any negro (sic) man and white woman, or any white man and negro (sic) woman, who are not married to each other, who shall habitually live in and occupy in the nighttime the same room shall be punished by imprisonment not exceeding twelve months, or by fine not exceeding five hundred dollars.[192]

Florida did not also make criminal the same conduct when both parties were of the same race as was the case in Alabama. Florida also prohibited marriages between Negroes and whites. Its statute was typical of those still on the statute books in 1964. Florida law proclaimed:

> It is unlawful for any white male person residing or being in this state to intermarry with any negro (sic) female person; and it is in like manner unlawful for any white female person residing or being in this state to intermarry with any negro (sic) male person; and every marriage formed or

[185] These antimiscegenation states are: Alabama, Arkansas, Delaware, Florida, Georgia, Kentucky, Louisiana, Maryland, Mississippi, Missouri, North Carolina, Oklahoma, South Carolina, Tennessee, Texas, Virginia and West Virginia.

[186] Arizona, California, Colorado, Iowa, Kansas, Massachusetts, Michigan, Montana, Nebraska, Nevada, New Mexico, North Dakota, Ohio, Oregon, Rhode Island, South Dakota, Utah, Washington.

[187] Jack Greenberg, *op. cit., supra,* p. 344, 398.

[188] *Jackson* v. *State,* 37 Ala. App. 519, 72 So. 2d 114 (1954), *certiorari* denied 260 Ala. 698, 72 So. 2d 116 (1954), *certiorari* denied 348 U.S. (1954).

[189] *Naim* v. *Naim,* 197 Va. 80, 87 S.E. 2d 749 (1955), judgment vacated, 350 U.S. 891 (1955), judgment reinstated, 197 Va. 734, 90 S.E. 2d 849 (1956), appeal dismissed, 350 U.S. 985 (1956).

[190] See, Jack Greenberg, *op. cit, supra,* p. 396 for a collection of such statutes.

[191] *McLaughlin and Hoffman* v. *The State of Florida,* 379 U.S. 184 (1964)., No. 585 October Opinion of Supreme Court of Florida reported in 153 So. 2d 1 (1963).

[192] Florida Statutes Annotated §798.05.

solemnized in contravention of the provisions of this section shall be utterly null and void, and the issue, if any, of such surreptitious marriage shall be regarded as bastard and incapable of having or receiving an estate, real, personal or mixed, by inheritance.[193]

Also typical was Florida's statute defining who is a Negro. The state's definition was an essential element of the crime charged in the pending Florida appeal.

The words "negro," "colored," "colored person," "mulatto," or "persons of color," when applied to persons, include every person having one-eighth or more of African or negro blood.[194]

The Supreme Court of California in 1948 held that state's antimiscegenation law violative of the Fourteenth Amendment to the Federal Constitution.[195] It ruled such statutes unreasonably restrict the choice of one's mate.

The Supreme Court has struck down on constitutional grounds all other restrictive state statutes predicated wholly upon race. The constitutional demise of these antimiscegenation and cohabitation between the races laws is inevitable. The trend of American jurisprudence is inexorably in this direction.

[193] Florida Statutes Annotated §741.11.
[194] Florida Statutes Annotated §101. For a collection of similar laws see: Pauli Murray, *States' Laws on Race and Color,* (New York Woman's Division of Christian Service, Board of Missions and Church Extension, the Methodist Church 1950), *passim.*
[195] *Perez* v. *Lippold,* 32 Cal. 2d 711, 198 P. 2d 17 (1948).

chapter 13

The American Negro Woman

Jeanne L. Noble

When the late President Kennedy appointed a commission to study the situation of all American women, his action amounted to national recognition of women as a group needing special consideration if they are to develop fully their capacities as family members, workers and citizens. A detailed look at the conditions of women and the roles they play in our society is contained in the report of the President's Commission on the Status of Women, *American Women*.[1]

It is the purpose of this chapter to provide the reader with an assessment of the resources and appraisal of the obstacles faced by an important subgroup of American women—Negro women. Their historic role and current status deserve the fullest possible study and attention.

Sex and Age Distribution

In 1960, there were 18,871,831 Negro Americans of whom 9,758,423, or 52 percent, were women. These women constituted approximately 11 percent of the total female population of the United States. They outnumbered the Negro male population by 645,015. A preponderance of females held true for the white population as well, but to a lesser extent.[2]

Table I shows the number of females to each one hundred males by selected age groups and by color. There are presently in the population more Negro and white males than females below fifteen years of age; after fifteen years of age, however, there are more women at every age level. The excess of Negro females to Negro males exceeds that of white women to white men in every age group except sixty-five and over.

This excessive female population has implications for marriage, since it is precisely in the age groupings where most marriages occur that the greatest excess of Negro females over Negro males appears. As this writer

[1] *American Women,* Report of the President's Commission on the Status of Women, (Washington, D.C.: U.S. Government Printing Office, 1963.)

[2] U.S. Department of Commerce, Bureau of the Census: *General Population Characteristics, 1960.* PC (1) 1B (Washington, D.C.: U.S. Government Printing Office, 1961), Table 44.

TABLE I—Number of Females for Every 100 Males in the United States by Color and Selected Age Groups, 1960

Age	Negro	White
Under 15	99.7	96.1
15–24	106.7	100.3
25–34	116.4	102.7
35–64	113.6	105.0
65 and over	110.2	122.7

SOURCE: U.S. Department of Commerce, Bureau of the Census, *Detailed Characteristics of the Population, 1960*. PC (1) 1D (Washington, D.C.: U.S. Government Printing Office, 1963), Table 232.

has observed in an earlier study,[3] the marriage choice of the Negro woman may of necessity have to extend to males of other age groups (in some cases she must become the second wife of a widower or a divorced man), to other class stratifications and even to other ethnic groups.

Looking at these age distributions in each geographical region, we see striking dissimilarities: the marriage potential improves progressively as females move from the Northeast to the South, to the north central part of the country, and then to the West. In fact, there is almost an 8 percent excess of Negro females over males in the Northeast, while in the West both Negro and white men exceed Negro and white women in appreciable numbers.[4]

The distribution of Negro population by age (Table II) reflects the national population trend toward concentrations of numbers in the younger and older groupings. The median ages of Negro males and females is younger than the median ages of whites.

Over 40 percent of the Negro population is nineteen years of age and younger. This implies massive demands for economic and social stability among the adult population whose responsibility it is to rear children and prepare young people for adulthood. With the increasing complexity of our social and economic system these demands grow progressively greater. Yet, Negro women, on whom this responsibility falls most heavily, are themselves faced by overwhelming problems. Poverty, family disruption and marginal employment rule the lives of a substantial portion of Negro women; this cannot but have pernicious effects on children. It is hardly

[3] Jeanne L. Noble, *The Negro College Woman* (New York: Bureau of Publications, Teachers College, Columbia University, 1954).

[4] U.S. Department of Commerce, Bureau of the Census: *Detailed Characteristics of the Population, 1960*. PC (1) 1D (Washington, D.C.: U.S. Government Printing Office, 1963), Table 232.

TABLE II—Distribution of Persons in Designated Age Groups by Color and Sex in the U.S.A., 1960

Age	White Female Percent	Negro Female Percent	White Male Percent	Negro Male Percent
Under 5	11	14	11	15
5–19	26	30	28	31
20–49	37	38	38	35
50–64	15	12	15	12
65 and over	11	6	8	7
	Total 100	Total 100	Total 100	Total 100
	Median Age 31	Median Age 24	Median Age 29	Median Age 23

SOURCE: U.S. Department of Commerce, Bureau of the Census, *General Population Characteristics, 1960*. PC (1) 1B (Washington, D.C.: U.S. Government Printing Office, 1960), Table 46.

surprising that among the major problems of the Negro community are many relating directly to youth—unwed motherhood, drug addiction, juvenile delinquency and school failure. All of these reflect a lack of sturdy and wholesome family ties, and in many instances, that lack in turn relates back to poverty, family disruption and marginal employment.

The Aged

With increasing longevity, the aged, like the young, are of great public concern because they constitute a growing proportion of the population, frequently with special needs. The life expectancy of the Negro female now

TABLE III—Negro Females 65 Years Old and Over in 1960 by United States and South, Urban and Rural

	Total	Urban	Rural Nonfarm	Rural Farm
United States	627,357	442,050	142,463	42,844
South	417,283	243,238	132,273	41,772
Percentage of Total in South	79.1	54.9	92.8	97.5

SOURCE: U.S. Department of Commerce, Bureau of the Census, *Census of Population, 1960*, "Nonwhite Population by Race," PC (2) 1C (Washington, D.C.: U.S. Government Printing Office, 1963), Table 46.

averages sixty-seven years, and she, like the white female, can expect to live a longer life than her male counterpart.[5]

Table III shows that 627,357 Negro women are sixty-five years and over. These older women, whether urban or rural, are found mostly in the South, with nearly all of those living in rural areas concentrated there. Thus, it is in the South that the highest incidence of problems affecting Negro aged women occur.

Where the elderly Negro woman has been able to qualify for old-age benefits, she often finds her economic status improved.

> . . . thanks to old-age, survivors and disability insurance and other public programs that help support so many persons 65 or more, the Negro in his old age may find his income more closely approximating that of his white fellow American than often was the case during working years.[6]

Inadequate though this pension or stipend may be for the Negro, when judged by welfare standards, it approximates from two-thirds to three-fourths of the income of whites, depending upon marital status. Younger Negro families must get along on half as much income as whites.

Perhaps the income gap between white and Negro senior citizens, including Negro women narrows because such an overwhelming number of Negroes live in the South. Their earnings were low to begin with and often unavailable when the person was younger and had the greatest need. Thus, to Negro women, old age benefits may come as a welcome relief from a previous lifetime of poverty and deprivation. It may also have been a lifetime of participation in the labor market at the lowest possible income.

Negro Women in the Labor Force

Negro women were originally brought to this country as slaves. The word "slaves" automatically connotes bondage and hard labor, and the slave system put its highest value on Negro women as laborers. Any other roles they assumed—as wives or mothers—were considered secondary.

After the Civil War, Negro women continued to be predominantly unskilled farm workers, "washerwomen," and "domestics." Today, their successors are leaving the farm, abandoning it to the "old Negro," and migrating to rural nonfarm areas and to towns and cities. Yet, even in 1964, Negro women can most readily market the same skills as their

[5] National Vital Statistics Division, U.S. Public Health Service. *Vital Statistics of the United States, 1962*, Vol. II, Section 5, Life Tables (U.S. Government Printing Office, Washington, D.C., 1963.)—Table 5–2.

[6] Mollie Orshansky, "The Aged Negro and His Income." *Social Security Bulletin* (February 1964), p. 2.

ancestors did. Over 50 percent of them cook, launder clothes, clean homes or other establishments; and some still toil on the farms.

In 1960, women comprised one in three workers, or 24 million women. Of these, 12 percent (2,455,140) were Negro women.

Negro women are not as likely to be employed on farms (25.7 percent) as are white women (27 percent), but a much higher percentage of Negro women is employed in the cities (45 percent compared to 35 percent of white women). Unemployment is twice as high among Negro females as among whites; the unemployment rate of Negro farm women is three times as high as that of whites. Actually, about 30 percent of those who work on farms work part time, compared to 15 percent of white females who are part-time farm workers. The percentage of part-time work is generally higher among Negro women than whites.[7]

One speculates that part-time employment is not a preferred status for Negro women, as it may be for white women, but an indication of the *lack of job opportunities for Negroes who need to work*. Many domestic workers are employed "on call" from day to day; this accounts in part for the high proportion of part-time employment of Negro women.

At all ages, married Negro women are more likely to be in the work force than are single women. Negro women are less likely than white women to stop working after their children are born and to remain out of the labor force when their children are small. In 1960, one out of three Negro mothers with children under six was in the labor force, as compared with less than one out of five white mothers.[8]

The typical white woman follows a different work pattern from that of the Negro. She may work a few years, marry, and then stay home to raise her children, seeking part or full-time work when her children are older.

Labor and Income

Table IV shows the gap in income between Negro and white women. Actually, the income of whites is slightly higher than that of the entire population shown in this table, for incomes of Negroes tilt the whole scale downward. The median income of white women is nearly twice that of Negro women. This reflects, of course, the low status and low paying jobs widely held by Negro women.

---

[7] Jacob Schiffman, *Marital and Family Characteristics of Workers*, Special Labor Force Report No. 26, March 1962 (*reprint from Monthly Labor Review*, January, 1963), Table E., p. A–11.

[8] *American Women, op. cit.*, p. 7.

This table also shows the poverty level of Negro women as compared to white women. In fact, at every age and stage of life, Negro women are the poorest of the poor.

TABLE IV—Income in 1959 of the Female Experienced Labor Force, 14 Years Old and Over, Nonwhite and Total (in thousands)

| | LABOR FORCE | | | |
| | Nonwhite Female | | Total Female | |
Income	Number	Percent Dis.	Number	Percent Dis.
$1 to $999 or less	1,101	42	4,925	24
$1,000 to $1,999	640	25	3,939	19
$2,000 to $2,999	405	16	4,080	20
$3,000 to $3,999	251	10	3,515	17
$4,000 to $4,999	130	4	2,166	11
$5,000 to $5,999	49	2	967	5
$6,000 to $6,999	18	1	407	2
$7,000 to $7,999	7	—	187	1
$8,000 to $9,999	5	—	146	1
$10,000 to $14,999	2	—	79	—
$15,000 and over	1	—	38	—
Median Income (Dollars)	$1,320		$2,333	

SOURCE: U.S. Department of Commerce, Bureau of the Census, *U.S. Census of Population: 1960.* Subject Reports, "Occupational Characteristics, Final Report." PC (2)–7A, Tables 25 and 26. (Washington, D.C.: U.S. Government Printing Office, 1963).

Fourteen million women sixteen years old and over—more than a fifth of all women in the United States—are among the 35 million people living in poverty. An estimated 3 million nonwhite women, or two-fifths of all non-white women, are poor, in contrast to about one-fifth of all white women. (In the total population, about one in nine is nonwhite; among poor women, one in five is nonwhite). The number of poor women, including Negro, exceeds either the impoverished men (10.5 million) or the impover-ished children under sixteen (also 10.5 million). Women head 10 percent of all families, but they head 25 percent of all poor families and 75 *percent of nonwhite poor* families.[9]

[9] "The Women's Job Corp—An Attack on Persistent Poverty," President's Task Force on the War Against Poverty, unpublished Working Conference Paper, July, 1964.

TABLE V—Selected Occupations of Negro Women Employed in 1960 and 1950 (14 years of age and over)

Occupation	Number of employed Negro women		Per cent distribution		Per cent increase	Negro women as per cent of all employed women
	1960	1950	[1] 1960	1950	(1)	1960
Total employed Negro women	2,455,140	1,869,956	100.0	100.0	31	12
White collar workers:						
Professional, technical workers [2]	175,308	104,728	7.1	5.6	67	6
Accountants, auditors	1,342	372	0.1	(3)	261	2
Actresses, dancers, entertainers (n.e.c.)*	556	733	(3)	(3)	[4] 24	3
Artists, art teachers	729	394	(3)	(3)	85	2
College presidents, professors, instructors (n.e.c.)	1,897	1,517	0.1	0.1	25	5
Designers, draftsmen	465	319	(3)	(3)	46	2
Dietitians, nutritionists	3,507	1,733	0.1	0.1	102	14
Lawyers, judges	176	83	(3)	(3)	112	2
Librarians	3,144	1,469	0.1	0.1	114	4
Musicians, music teachers	3,566	2,947	0.1	0.2	21	3
Natural Scientists	552	300	(3)	(3)	84	4
Nurses (professional)	32,034	12,550	1.3	0.7	155	6
Nurses (student professional)	1,718	2,321	0.1	0.1	[4] 26	3
Physicians, surgeons	490	257	(3)	(3)	91	3
Social scientists	392	303	(3)	(3)	29	3
Social Welfare, recreation workers	8,683	4,454	0.4	0.2	95	11
Teachers (elementary school)	75,695		3.1			9
Teachers (secondary school)	18,194	67,857	0.7	3.6	47	7
Teachers (n.e.c.)	5,890		0.2			6
Technicians (medical, dental)	5,613	1,317	0.2	0.1	326	7
Therapists, healers (n.e.c.)	870	481	(3)	(3)	81	4
Managers, officials, proprietors [2]	24,757	24,557	1.0	1.3	1	3
Clerical workers [2]	[5] 181,678	74,255	[5] 7.4	4.0	[5] 145	3
Bookkeepers	6,887	2,993	0.3	0.2	130	1
Cashiers	10,265	3,897	0.4	0.2	163	3
Secretaries	20,650		0.8			2
Stenographers	4,630	21,593	0.2	0.2	143	2
Typists	27,142		1.1			5
Telephone operators	8,052	2,481	0.3	0.1	225	2
Sales workers	36,083	[5] 25,492	1.5	[5] 1.4	[5] 42	2
Blue collar workers:						
Operatives [2]	310,233	274,000	12.6	14.7	13	10
Dressmakers, seamstresses (except factory)	8,528	10,248	0.3	0.5	[4] 17	7
Laundry, drycleaning operatives	99,494	98,998	4.1	5.3	61	36
Spinners, weavers (textile)	264	413	(3)	(3)	[4] 36	(3)
Machinery (including electrical mfg.)	8,017	7,613	0.3	0.4	5	5
Food, kindred products (mfg.)	18,575	18,710	0.8	1.0	[4] 1	16
Textile mill products (mfg.)	5,004	6,063	0.2	0.3	[4] 17	3
Apparel, other fabricated textile products (mfg.)	34,550	52,910	1.4	2.8	[4] 35	12

TABLE V (Cont'd)

Occupation	Number of employed Negro women		Per cent distribution		Per cent increase	Negro women as per cent of all employed women
	1960	1950	[1] 1960	1950	([1])	1960
Craftsmen, foremen	15,877	11,629	0.6	0.6	37	6
Laborers (except farm and mine)	23,627	28,414	1.0	1.5	[4] 17	22
Service workers: Private-household workers	888,206	773,590	36.2	41.4	15	53
Service workers (except household) [2]	519,823	351,856	21.2	18.8	48	18
Attendants (hospitals, other institutions)	66,997	19,324	2.7	1.0	247	23
Service workers: Charwomen, janitors, porters	50,655	35,456	2.1	1.9	43	25
Cooks (except private-household)	80,980	60,385	3.3	3.2	34	22
Hairdressers, Cosmetologists	31,918	26,584	1.3	1.4	20	12
Housekeepers (except private household)	10,811	6,220	0.4	0.3	74	9
Practical nurses, midwives	32,192	16,141	1.3	0.9	99	16
Waitresses, bartenders, counter workers	54,123	42,139	3.2	2.3	28	6
Farm workers: Farmers, farm managers	14,536	30,949	0.6	1.7	[4] 53	12
Farm laborers, foremen	69,495	139,657	2.8	7.5	[4] 50	29
Occupation not reported	195,517	30,829	8.0	1.6	—	—

SOURCE: U.S. Department of Commerce, Bureau of the Census: *Detailed Characteristics of the Population, 1960.* PC (1) D, Table 205; and *Detailed Characteristics of the Population, 1950.* Vol. 2, Pt. 1, Table 128.

[1] Excludes Alaska and Hawaii, since detailed occupational data were not reported for the territories in 1950.

[2] Includes occupations not shown separately.

[3] Less than 0.05 per cent.

[4] A per cent decrease.

[5] Women employed as insurance adjustors, examiners, and investigators were included among sales workers in 1950 and among clerical workers in 1960.

* n.e.c: Not elsewhere classified.

Considering the fact that 45 percent of all Negroes are defined as poor by current standards (with annual incomes of below $3,000), the financial status of Negro women, with or without families, is indeed grim.

Many of the impoverished Negro women work, but their level of education and work skills is so low that their wages yield only bare subsistence. Others who need and want to work must stay home and care for their children. In poor families headed by women with children under eighteen,

23 percent of the white and 61 percent of the nonwhite mothers work full time.[10] And still others cannot find jobs because they are unskilled and untrained for those jobs that are available; or because they live in depressed areas where jobs are scarce and competition keen; or because the dual discriminations of race and sex combine to foreclose many employment opportunities.

Occupational Distribution

A comparison of the occupations of Negro women in 1950 and 1960 shows considerable increases among the numbers of clerical, professional and technical workers, and sales workers during that period (Table V).

Out of more than 175 thousand Negro women who are professional and technical workers, 60 percent are teachers, reflecting a traditional relationship of Negro women to teaching.

There has been some decline in the number of school administrative jobs held by Negro women. More men are moving into elementary teaching— and many aim at principalships. This is, of course, true of the educational field in general, but it represents quite a reversal in the Negro sex distribution in predominantly Negro schools, especially in the South.

Nurses account for nearly 20 percent of Negro professional women. Theirs is an exciting story of integration. They started with a separate Negro organization and separate schools; now they have integrated professional organizations and are moving toward the abolition of unaccredited Negro schools of nursing.[11]

It should be emphasized, however, that the percentage increase in these white collar occupations, though favorable, can be misleading; Negro women are still underrepresented in all of these categories. Furthermore, the median income for Negro women in almost all categories is lower than that of whites.

In other types of occupations, the picture is even less hopeful. Negro women do not appear to be doing well in business; the number of managers, officials and proprietors showed little improvement from 1950 to 1960, and there was little increase in the total figure for blue collar workers during this period.

The number of farm workers decreased by 50 percent, reflecting the substantial change in the Negro population from rural to urban.

[10] *Ibid.*
[11] Mary Elizabeth Carnegie, "Are Negro Schools of Nursing Needed Today?" *Nursing Outlook*, 12, No. 2 (February 1964).

When the number of women employed in the fields discussed above is contrasted with the data on service workers, whether in private households or elsewhere, the picture is illuminating.

In 1960 nearly 900,000 Negro women were service workers in households ("domestics"). This represents one-third of the Negro women workers and over half of all such workers in the United States. Paid low wages, frequently subject to part-time employment, and often at the mercy of her employer's whims, the domestic is on the very lowest rung of the economic ladder among female workers.

Only slightly above the household domestic are the half-million Negro women employed in service occupations outside of private homes. They held approximately one out of every five jobs in this category. In these service positions, too, the median income of the Negro workers is lower than that of the whites.

Because of the gross exploitation typical of the occupation of domestics in the past there has been an understandable rejection of this job by Negroes which envisions wide scale and systematic training of domestics in more sophisticated housekeeping skills so that they can demand and receive higher wages and improved conditions of work.

The economy is not likely to yield other jobs for these women in the immediate future; nor can many of them expect to acquire the requisite

TABLE VI—Occupational Distribution of Nonwhite and White Female Workers by Selected Occupation (Nonhousehold)

Category	Nonwhite			White		
	Number (in thousands)	Percent	Median Income (dollars)	Number (in thousands)	Percent	Median Income (dollars)
Total Employed Women	2,618	100	—	18,537	100	—
Private Household Workers	889	34	753	767	4.1	758
Service Workers (except household)	547	21	1,419	3,309	18.	1,487

Nonwhite women were 54 percent of all Private Household Workers; and 19 percent of all Service Workers (except Household).

SOURCE: U.S. Department of Commerce, Bureau of the Census, *U.S. Census of Population: 1960.* Subject Reports, "Occupational Characteristics, Final Reports." PC(2)–7A, Tables 25 and 26 (Washington, D.C., U.S. Government Printing Office, 1961).

skills and training for upgrading into other types of work. Then, too, census projections of estimated numbers of household workers required in the future suggests a steady demand for domestic workers.

Under the Manpower Training Act and certain other Government programs (such as the Job Corps for Women) a beginning is being made to plan a realistic training program for domestics. Such programs, to be effective, must not only give the trainees improved basic education and instruction in the use of modern appliances, but must also help trainees to fulfill their aspirations for better jobs when they reenter the labor market.

It should be pointed out, however, that training in homemaking skills is only one aspect of the Job Corps program. A variety of types and levels of occupational training are among the features of that program.

Jobs in Government

Even though the President's Commission on the Status of Women pointed out that inequalities exist among government workers, with women generally holding lower paying and less prestigious jobs, government is still the best employer Negro women have. Negro women enter government service because it offers them greater opportunity and job security than does private industry.

In 1960, census data [12] showed Federal, state or local government as the employer of:

70 percent of nonwhite women who are professional and technical workers;
42 percent who are clerical workers;
66 percent who are stenographers;
62 percent who are typists; and
20 percent who are service workers (outside of private households)

Education

Greater amounts of formal education as well as higher levels of occupational skill are becoming increasingly essential to the American worker. The accelerating pace of change caused by automation, industrial development and urbanization combine to make this so. For the Negro—frequently limited in both education and training in skills—the speed with which the occupational scene is changing makes for particularly critical and disturbing problems.

[12] Letter from Gertrude Bancroft, Special Assistant to the U.S. Commissioner of Education, dated January 29, 1964. (Statistics drawn from U.S. Bureau of the Census, *U.S. Census of Population: 1960,* Subject Reports. Occupational Characteristics. Final Report PC(2)–7A. U.S. Government Printing Office. Washington, D.C. 1963, Table 22.

Negro women are better off educationally than Negro males, but still have far from adequate education. As can be seen in Table VII, the Negro female stays in school slightly longer than the male. Fewer women are illiterate.

TABLE VII—Percent of Nonwhite Females and Males of Selected Ages by Year of School Completed for the United States, 1960

Age and Year of School Completed	Nonwhite Female	Nonwhite Male
14 and 15 years old		
No school completed	1	1
Finished elementary school	32	28
Finished high school	—	—
Median year of school completed	8.3	7.9
18 and 19 years old		
No school completed	1	1
Finished elementary school	8	10
Finished high school	28	21
Some college	6	4
Median year of school completed	11.0	10.4
20 and 21 years old		
No school completed	1	1
Finished elementary school	8	9
Finished high school	32	28
Some college	12	11
Finished college	1	—
Median year of school completed	11.6	11.0
55 to 64 years old		
No school completed	7	11
Finished elementary school	15	13
Finished high school	6	5
Some college	3	3
Finished college	1	1
Median year of school completed	6.7	5.8

SOURCE: U.S. Department of Commerce, Bureau of the Census: *U.S. Census of Population: 1960*. PC(2)–5B, "Educational Attainment," Table 2.

This does not mean, however, that there is not a problem of grave proportions concerning Negro female dropouts. In one school year (October 1962–October 1963), a third of a million girls dropped out of school, swelling to 1.7 million the total population of girls who had dropped out of high school before graduation. Of the 1.7 million girl dropouts one-fifth were nonwhite.[13] The low educational attainment pattern prevails at all age levels among Negro females. In fact, at no age level does one find as many as 50 percent of the Negro women equipped with the education needed to survive, let alone earn a decent living, in today's labor market.[14]

The College Educated Negro Woman

More Negro women than men have completed college; but even though the Negro woman fares better than the male, she does not do as well as her white counterpart. The percentage of college graduates is twice as high among white females. The gap between Negro men and women closes with five years or more of college. More Negro men obtain advanced degrees than Negro women. And here, again, Negro women lag behind white women. Sex and race evidently combine to discourage Negro women from pursuing Ph.D.'s, M.D.'s and other advanced degrees. This situation was commented on by Dorothy I. Height, National President, National Council of Negro Women:

> There is lack of opportunity for Negro women at the economic bottom and at the top. Too few Negro women push ahead of the B.A. degree and diversify their academic training beyond teaching. And, among those who do, too few are in top policymaking positions in any phase of American life.[15]

What, then, are the historic factors that have made for this disproportionate number of female college graduates?

Negro women were always educated either to teach or to do other kinds of work. Prior to emancipation, at least one school was founded for Negro girls. In 1858, Myrtilla Minor built a schoolhouse for the higher education of Negro girls in Washington, D.C., and clearly intended that her girls be equipped to participate in the world of work.[16]

Oberlin College, a leader in the education of Negroes and advocate of coeducation, graduated Mary Jane Patterson in 1862. She was the first

[13] "Who Are the Disadvantaged 16–21-Year-Old Girls?" Unpublished Report, Women's Bureau, U.S. Department of Labor, 1964.

[14] U.S. Bureau of the Census, *U.S. Census of Population: 1960,* Subject Report. Occupational Characteristics. Final Report PC(1)–1C, Table 76 and U.S. Census of Population: 1960, *Education Attainment,* Final Report PC(2)–5B. U.S. Government Printing Office. Washington, D.C. 1963, Table 2.

[15] Dorothy I. Height, Speech delivered at the NCNW Convention, Washington, D.C., November, 1963.

[16] Jeanne L. Noble, *The Negro Woman's College Education* (New York: Bureau of Publications, Teachers College, Columbia University, 1956), p. 18.

Negro woman to attain this distinction. Fletcher indicates that "at that time there were 13 Negro ladies and 13 gentlemen at Oberlin." [17]

Because Negroes were needed to educate other Negroes, colleges mushroomed all over the South in the late nineteenth and early twentieth centuries. Mary Church Terrell stated in 1898, ". . . of teachers engaged in the instruction of youth, 90 percent are women."

Between 1900 and 1910, the male graduates of Negro colleges increased from 134 to 233. For Negro women, the number grew from 22 to 277.[18] By 1910 there were a hundred colleges for Negroes, most of which admitted women. Since teaching was seen as a feminine occupation, it is not surprising that Negro women soon outnumbered Negro men in colleges,[19] *and that the trend continues* to the present day with more girls than boys completing high school and college. Educators state that Negro girls are not as prone to drop out of school as are Negro boys; and, existing data on year or school completed supports this conclusion (see Table VII).

The pursuit of higher education for Negro women has not proceeded easily. Indeed, much energy and "thought" have gone into debating the supposed natural inferiority of Negroes and women.[20] In addition, some Negro men preferred Negro women to follow a classical esthetic education resulting in gracious homemaking, while some thought a college education leading to a job most unbecoming to women. However, most Negro women were convinced that a college education should be utilitarian.

Then and now, this demand upon education has been consistent with the Negro woman's role as a working citizen. It is, apparently, a somewhat different demand upon education than that of white women,[21] who have been somewhat more likely to expect college to give them a cultural background for a well-rounded life and insurance against possible emergencies.

There is evidence that a drive toward utilitarian education begins before the Negro girl reaches college. In 1963, the Lotts reported in their study of girls in selected border states that more Negro girls (44 percent) than white (20 percent) were planning on vocational training rather than on college or a job; that fewer Negro girls desired glamorous jobs such as art, advertising, flying. And not one girl stated a desire to be a housewife ten years from the time of the Lott study. The Negro girls scored higher on

[17] Robert Samuel Fletcher, *A History of Oberlin College*, Vol. 2 (Oberlin: Oberlin College, 1943), p. 534.
[18] Jeanne L. Noble, *op. cit.*, Appendix D, Table 2.
[19] *Ibid.*, p. 22.
[20] Jeanne L. Noble, *op. cit.*, Chapter 2, p. 14.
[21] *Ibid.*, p. 117.

theoretical and political values than esthetic ones when compared to white girls. They seemed more occupied with pursuit of the concrete, while the white girls were more concerned with the abstract. Negro female leaders were moving in the direction of respectability, financial security and service; white female leaders, on the other hand, were concerned with the attainment of knowledge, religious satisfaction, psychological independence, creativity, family and happiness.[22]

MARRIAGE AND FAMILY LIFE

Even though there is an excess of females in the Negro population, there are more single Negro men than women. The Negro woman does not have difficulty getting married. The difficulty seems to be in staying married. The marriage rate of Negro women is the highest of any subgroup in the American population. In 1960 only 3 percent of Negro women who reached age sixty-five had never been married, compared to 7 percent of white women in the age group.[23]

According to 1960 census figures on those in the population fourteen years and older, the following are recorded as having been married at least once:

	White	Nonwhite
Male	76%	70%
Female	81%	79%

A study of marital status by urban and rural designations reveals that the Negro woman's chances for a stable marriage are better in urban centers than in rural farm areas. In all except rural farm areas, one-fourth of the married women had had multiple marriages.[24]

In 1960, 29 percent of nonwhite women, compared to 18 percent of white women, were married with husband absent because of separation, divorce or

[22] A. Lott, Bernice Lott, *Negro and White Youth* (New York: Holt, Rinehart & Winston, 1963), p. 162.

[23] U.S. Department of Commerce, Bureau of the Census, "Current Population Reports," Series P–20, No. 122, March 1963.

[24] U.S. Department of Commerce, U.S. Bureau of the Census: *Detailed Characteristics of the Population, 1960.* PS(1)–1D (Washington, D.C.: U.S. Government Printing Office, 1963), Table 176.

death.[25] More than half of all whites in the population live as married couples as compared to one-third of all Negroes. In both groups, a large percentage of these couples have their own household—but again Negroes are at a disadvantage, although a general decline over the last decade in the proportion of couples without their own households was experienced by both groups.

Thus, the general marriage picture among Negroes is a discouraging one. The path to the altar seems readily trod by the Negro female, but she does not stay on the road of lasting marriage as successfully as her white counterpart. Separation, divorce and widowhood are apt to be the lot of many Negro women.[26]

The economic, educational and marital factors discussed so far mesh and reinforce each other and not only affect women in their lives as wives, mothers, breadwinners and secondary wage-earners, but also influence the lives of their children. Deprivation—typified by low income, low educational attainment and minimal aspirations—can and does extend from one generation to another. An especially harsh consequence of these factors is to be found in Negro families where the mother is the head of the family.

MOTHER-CENTERED FAMILIES

Female heads of families among Negroes have received considerable publicity recently as the nation has turned its attention toward poverty and its characteristics. Out of 4,255,521 Negro families, 21 percent are headed by females. White women head 8 percent of their families.[27]

The image of the Negro women invoked by sociologists and community practitioners is most often that of "matriarch." This description applied to many women whose husbands are present, as well as to those who head families in the absence of husbands. In the former case the illness or in-

[25] *Ibid.*, Table 176.

[26] The student of Negro family life must look to the past for historical perspective. The slave system generally discouraged intact families. This concept had to be built out of the ruins of slavery; its development has been hindered by discrimination and lack of opportunity for Negro men to perform the key family role of "breadwinner." History and present circumstances both militate against a stable family life.

[27] U.S. Department of Commerce, Bureau of Census: Detailed Characteristics of the Population, 1960, PC(1)–1D (Washington, D.C.: U.S. Government Printing Office, 1963), Table 188.

capacity of the husband often reduces his role as breadwinner and his influence as family head. E. Franklin Frazier traced this "matriarchy" back to slavery and to the plantation system:

> As a rule, the Negro woman as a wife and mother was the mistress of her cabin, and save for the interference of master and overseer, her wishes in regard to mating and family matters were paramount. Neither economic necessity nor tradition had installed in her the spirit of subordination to masculine authority. Emancipation only tended to confirm in many cases the spirit of self-sufficiency which slavery had taught.[28]

Even today, the Negro woman is distinguished by a tradition of female independence and family dominance.[29]

Fortune, however, points out that the matriarchal concept may be rooted in "the African heritage" theory,[30] which holds that there is some survival of a matriarchal African culture in the Negro family today. The preoccupation with the dominant role of Negro woman is largely due to mounting concern over widespread social pathology among Negroes; this stems from psychological interpretations of ill effects on children, especially males, of mother-centered homes. Certainly it is true that a large number of Negro women are the mainstays of their families, and that this is related to the socio-economic situation which denies Negro males adequate opportunity to "win the bread." Very little is known, except by speculation, about the inner world of these "matriarchs" [31] and how it differs from that of white women, even of white matriarchs.

Some researchers believe that the popular stereotype of the matriarchal role of Negro women has been oversimplified and that tracing its descendency from slavery may be stretching a point. Herzog and Lewis express their views [32] thus:

[28] E. Franklin Frazier, *The Negro Family in the United States* (New York: The Dryden Press, 1948), p. 102.

[29] Hilda O. Fortune, "A Study of the Power Position of Mothers in Contemporary Negro Family Life in New York City" (Unpublished Ph.D Thesis, New York University, 1963), p. 11.

[30] In a matriarchal family, authority relating to the ordering and governing of the family—power over property, over inheritance, over marriage, over the house, is lodged in women rather than men. See: Margaret Mead, *Male and Female* (New York: W. Morrow, 1948), p. 301.

[31] How Negro women feel about their "feminine role" is an unresearched area. Not even the Kinsey report shared insight into their feelings about sex. Some interesting research is soon to be published by Dr. Anne Steinemann of New York, who has gathered psychological data from a sample of Negro women on their attitudes concerning femininity.

[32] Elizabeth Herzog and Hylan Lewis, *Priorities in Research about Unmarried Mothers,* presented at a symposium, "Research Perspectives on the Unmarried Mother," Eastern Regional Conference, Child Welfare League of America, New York, April, 1961.

One clue lies in the comparison between very low income Negroes and whites with regard to the elements of family structure usually assumed to be the Negroes' heritage from slavery. There are marked similarities between these two groups; and the whites did not get their characteristics from slavery. Leaning too much on the slavery crutch prevents us from moving more quickly toward sounder understanding and practice. Perhaps the most clearly cultural element in this connection is the belief of many that after one hundred years the heritage of slavery wields more influence than such intervening variables as urbanization and continuing social and economic deprivation.

Herzog and Lewis also question the common picture of the Negro woman as all-controlling.

> To what extent do the patterns of the dominant female and inadequate male correspond with reality? According to the testimony of some women on the lower socio-economic level, the men have the whip hand even if the women hold the purse strings.[33]

Lewis is inclined to give heavier weight, in accounting for mother-only families, to the economic facts of life. Quoting John Kenneth Galbraith's comment in *The Affluent Society,* "To some extent family life is itself a luxury of an adequate income," Lewis suggests that:

> A major point of pressure for the low income male appears to be an increase in family size with no possibility of a comparable increase in family income or earning power.[34]

He also notes that:

> It probably is significant that in roughly one-third of the instances of marital breakup for reasons other than death that we studied the wife was pregnant at the time of separation or desertion.[35]

Lewis comments:

> In a high proportion of marital breakups that occurred among study families, the wife either left or asked the husband to leave. One crucial difference between the middle and upper income husbands and the low income husbands is that the middle and upper income males have better chances of holding jobs and providing for their families. . . . There is much evidence that wives of all levels, and certainly many low income wives, will settle for husbands who provide financial support . . . even though it may be an empty shell family. . . . However, low income wives do not have the same

[33] *Ibid.*
[34] Hylan Lewis, *The Contemporary Urban Poverty Syndrome,* lecture delivered to Howard University Medical School students, April 28, 1964.
[35] *Ibid.*

chance to settle for basic material needs; therefore, the difference between the middle and upper income wife's staying and the low income wife's leaving—or asking the husband to leave—is often one of income and its management. We find few empty shell families among the poor. *The poor man cannot support them.*[36] [Italics added]

It is clear from this research that intensive study is needed of the dimensions and extent not only of the matriarchal role, but of the role of the impoverished Negro man, who, under intense economic pressure, may at last abandon his family.

The mother-centered Negro family is especially typical of the impoverished population. Within this population, 75 percent of nonwhite families are headed by women. The family life of the poor, particularly the poor in urban slums, is characterized by drifting movement. It is not unusual for a slum school's population to turn over almost completely in a semester. For thousands of young children in slums, every day is a grim, losing battle against all the grinding forces that harry and disintegrate family life.

The family experience of many children is stunted in mother-only families for one or several reasons. The absence of a father is harmful to all children in a family, but especially to boys. Poverty has historically degraded the male role to mere reproduction, causing him to take flight from family responsibility rather than encouraging him to enter into a marriage union.

Lacking male support the Negro mother carries a disproportionate family burden. Most often these families end up on Aid to Families of Dependent Children rolls. Table VIII shows the Negro caseload in thirteen states— the states with large concentrations of Negro population.

Among families receiving aid to families with dependent children (AFDC), about two out of every five are Negro, while among all families with children, about one in ten is Negro.[37] This table also shows the percentage of illegitimate children on the rolls in these states. Between 1958 and 1961, the AFDC rolls were increased 40 percent by illegitimate births.

The causes of mother-only families are multiple—widowhood, divorce, separation, illegitimacy—but the consequences differ only in degree. When the cause of family disruption is clothed in resentment and hostility on the

[36] *Ibid.*

[37] A sample of five hundred AFDC cases from fifty-one states or jurisdictions, or one percent of the caseload whichever was larger, was reported in a recent study. Out of 884,441 families, 40 percent were Negro. Out of 2,665,519 children, 43 percent were Negro children. ("Characteristics of Families Receiving Aid to Families with Dependent Children," November–December 1961), U.S. Department of Health, Education and Welfare, p. 17.

part of the mother against an alienated father, or accompanied by community stigma, as it is usually when illegitimacy is involved, the impact of the mother's feelings often blights the necessary process of sex-role identification and distorts the child's image of husband and wife relationship into the patterns that often prompt promiscuity, delinquency and asocial behavior.

TABLE VIII—States Claiming Negro AFDC Caseloads Above 50 Percent, November–December 1961 and Percentage of Negro Population

States	Percentage of AFDC Children	Father Absent from Home	Percentage of Illegitimate Children	Negro Percentage of State Population
Washington, D.C.	94	81	40	30
Mississippi	80	64	17	42
Delaware	73	74	36	14
Illinois	73	83	33	10
Louisiana	72	79	23	32
Maryland	69	80	31	17
Florida	68	80	24	18
South Carolina	68	47	10	35
Virginia	63	81	24	21
North Carolina	59	74	16	25
Michigan	55	92	16	9
Georgia	51	57	9	29
Ohio	51	91	29	8

SOURCE: "Characteristics of Families Receiving Aid to Families of Dependent Children," November–December 1961, U.S. Department of Health, Education and Welfare, April 1963, Tables 2, 12 and 34.

In many of these fatherless families (23 percent of white and 61 percent of nonwhite) mothers work full time and because of their meager incomes cannot provide satisfactory supervision and day care of children. Caring for the younger children frequently falls to the older daughters and further restricts their chances for educational advancement.

The mothers of children who drop out of school are often dropouts themselves. They neither understand the tie between education and work nor the demands of our society for continually rising educational sights. For girls this is particularly blighting—less than half the parents of girl dropouts in one state make any effort to convince them of the importance of schooling.[38]

[38] "President's Task Force on the War Against Poverty," *op. cit.*

Overcrowding, lack of privacy, noise, filth, disease—all these make for inadequate personal adjustment, lack of motivation and the development of self-images which are destructive rather than creative. All too often these are natural concomitants of a Negro family without a father.

One hopeful sign is that there is less family disorganization among Negro couples who have achieved a college education. Only 5 percent of these heads of families were college women—2 percent of them having four years or more of college. This picture is even more favorable than that of white college couples. Among these, 13 percent of families were headed by college women.

NEGRO WOMEN'S ORGANIZATIONS

An interesting and significant demonstration of how Negro women view themselves and their roles is provided by some of the major Negro women's organizations. The manner in which Negro women first organized owed its particular character to the racial and social inequalities they experienced. They did not concern themselves with labor unions, which began to grow enormously in strength and numbers in the latter part of the nineteenth century, because they were barred from membership in the unions and from most jobs. Only an educated few interested themselves in women's suffrage. The clubs which Negro women formed were usually connected with their churches, and the major focus of club activities was on caring for the sick and aged, helping the needy, and supporting the church and contributing to its growth.

The first national organization for Negro women was founded by Miss Hallie Q. Brown of Wilberforce University, Ohio, and the genesis of this organization was in the Columbian Exposition of 1893. Miss Brown was eager for the inclusion of Negroes in the planning of the exposition. When she requested that a Negro representative be appointed to the exposition's Board of Lady Managers, she was told that membership on the board only could be given to the representatives of a national organization. Thus, through her efforts to meet the need for a national organization, The Colored Women's League of Washington came into being, followed in 1895 by a national federation of clubs.[39]

[39] Mrs. Ida Wells Barnet was also in the forefront of this effort.

In 1895, representatives from over twenty Negro women's clubs responded to an invitation issued by Josephine Ruffin and formed the National Federation of Afro-American Women, with Mrs. Booker T. Washington as president. Within a few months, the federation had affiliates in sixteen states. The two national groups in existence merged to become the National Association of Colored Women, with Mary Church Terrell as its first president.[40]

Mary Church Terrell was active on picket lines and in sit-ins on behalf of civil rights as early as the 1940's. Largely through her leadership, Thompson's Restaurants were desegregated in the Capital, one of the landmarks in the desegregation of public accommodations. She was a strong advocate of women's rights and as a young woman spoke at several national suffrage conventions, where she was associated with Susan B. Anthony and other leading suffragettes.

Negro Sororities

While women were actively involved in developing community organizations on a national level, groups of young Negro girls on college campuses were influenced by the sorority movement on white campuses.

In 1908, at Howard University, the first Negro sorority, Alpha Kappa Alpha, was formed. In 1913, many of the girls in Alpha Kappa Alpha split away and formed the Delta Sigma Theta sorority.

Julia Quander, President of Alpha Kappa Alpha, then took an important legal step: incorporation. In doing so, she called upon members who had graduated and scattered across the country. She was responsible for a national federation of chapters, both college and alumna. Thus, in 1913, both Alpha Kappa Alpha and Delta Sigma Theta became national movements of collegiate women stretching across forty states and to Africa and Haiti.

By 1930, there were four national collegiate sororities, Zeta Phi Beta and Sigma Gamma Rho having been organized in the 1920's. The combined membership of all four is now over 80,000—a sizable proportion of all Negro college female graduates.

The history of these groups has often been marred by the "image" of snobbery which often characterizes sororities and fraternities.[41]

[40] Gladys Sheppard, *Mary Church Terrell, Respectable Person* (Baltimore: Human Relations Press, 1951), pp. 19–23. (This organization is known today as the National Association of Colored Women's Clubs, with a membership of more than 1500 state organizations and 100,000 members.)

[41] E. Franklin Frazier, *The Negro in the United States* (New York: The Macmillan Co., 1957), p. 383.

Nevertheless, Negro sororities have made significant contributions in the fields of public health, education, vocational guidance, civil rights and international understanding. Through the years, Negro sororities have become increasingly more public service-minded in recognition of the fact that they constitute the highest concentration of educated Negro women and of the current need for Negro volunteers to work on a multitude of pressing social problems. In most cities, these sororities today constitute the community's most visible and easily accessible reservoir of educated Negro women.

National Council of Negro Women

In 1935, Mary McCleod Bethune, one of the most effective and dynamic Negro women leaders the United States has produced, realized that the sororities were somewhat isolated from other organizations in the Negro community. There were by then several other large Negro women's groups with national memberships. Mrs. Bethune envisioned a council that would unite all the national groups under one aegis and with a common purpose— with the educated sorority woman working side by side with the domestic household worker or laundress.

Drawing upon those skills which had made her an adviser to President Roosevelt and upon the several Negro women's organizations of which she was an officer, Mrs. Bethune joined with thirty-five other Negro women leaders in forming the National Council of Negro Women. At that time, it represented eight national organizations. Today, the council is the clearing house for the activities of twenty-five national organizations with a combined membersip of over one million. Its farreaching program focuses on citizenship education, with particular emphasis on voter registration.

Negro Women in Other Women's Organizations

Over the years, Negro women have earned leadership in women's organizations whose membership is open to all groups. Negro women serve on the boards and as officers of a range of national organizations, from the Girl Scouts of the United States, whose membership is over three million, to the National Council of Women of the United States of America, whose membership is drawn from twenty-seven national affiliates. A review of the names of Negro men and women officers and board members in volunteer organizations suggests that Negro women have probably become more prominent in the volunteer power structure of America than Negro men.

Some few voluntary organizations, such as the Junior League of America, do not have Negro women members, but the majority of those that give voluntary service in the recreation, health and welfare area have helped Negro women to utilize their skills in the wider community. Negro women in these positions are able to articulate minority concerns and to influence power decisions affecting millions of citizens.

NEGRO WOMEN IN THE CIVIL RIGHTS STRUGGLE

The part played by the Negro woman in the Negro's fight for civil rights is legendary and significant. From Harriet Tubman to Gloria Richardson of Cambridge, Maryland, women have taken bold and decisive steps to further the cause of racial justice and equality.

Negro Women in the Negro Revolution of the Twentieth Century

Negro women have been playing an increasingly important role in the current civil rights fight, especially since the successful Montgomery, Alabama, bus boycott sparked by the arrest of Mrs. Rosa Parks, a seamstress who refused to give up her seat on a city bus to a white passenger. In September, 1957, Little Rock, Arkansas, became the focal point of the world's attention as six Negro girls and three Negro boys attempted to desegregate Central High. After the pupils finally were permitted to enter the school, they suffered continual physical and psychological harassment from their white schoolmates. The leading figure in the Little Rock crisis was Mrs. Daisy Bates, Arkansas State President of the NAACP. Her home was under constant attack from bombs, bricks and rifle shots; her house was twice set on fire; and despite the fact that city and state law enforcement officers did little to protect her or her home, she continued the fight to keep the "Little Rock Nine" in school. She served as advisor and protector to the pupils until they had all graduated in 1960.

Important roles have been played by such women as Gloria Richardson of Cambridge, Maryland, who is probably the only woman to lead a local desegregation movement; Diane Nash Bevel, who was chairman of the Student Protest Group in Nashville, Tennessee, and one of four Negro students chosen by Negro leaders to negotiate with Nashville merchants; Autherine Lucy, one of the pioneers in school desegregation; Mrs. Medgar Evers, wife of the slain Mississippi field secretary of the NAACP, who is carrying on her husband's work with courage and strength, and the hundreds of Negro girls who are active participants in SNCC and CORE activities all over the South.

One can walk into any church on "Movement Night" in the South and see hundreds of Negro women singing, exulting and putting hard-earned coins into the collection plates. They march, kneel-in, go to jail and do many of the chores necessary to keep a protest movement going.

Whatever their status may be in the future, the facts show that Negro women have performed unique roles in the nation. Imaginative social planning must begin with full knowledge of their efforts to shore up the ruins of what could very well have become a more disorganized family life than we are now witnessing, of their labor in jobs that are unrewarding and underpaid, and of their contributions as volunteers in the private sector of society and in the civil rights struggle. What Frederick Douglass said of Negro women in his day might well be repeated today:

> If judged by the depths from which they have come, rather than the heights to which those blessed with centuries of opportunities have attained, Negro women need not hang their heads in shame.

The civil rights movement has alerted most Americans to the fact that Negroes, too, are people with goals, dreams and aspirations. There remains to be explored, in much greater depth and detail than has been done so far, the inherent strengths and special characteristics of Negroes and their living patterns.

In particular, we need to give intensive study to Negro women, the specific qualities of their relationships with men, and their impact on their children. We need to develop programs which will help them not only to do more than barely subsist, but to nurture healthy, sturdy family relationships. As women learn the sensitive arts and skills of family life, as they develop insight into themselves and those around them, they can pass on to their children a heritage which is something more than the dead-end habit patterns of poverty, those stultifying patterns which in too many poor families—but especially poor Negro families—have ruled for generations.

We need to learn more about what Hylan Lewis calls the "urban poverty syndrome" and how to cope with it. This job will take an arsenal of tools, used not only by existing organizations but by new groups, public and private agencies as well. The challenge is one of almost frightening proportions: millions of Americans are impoverished; millions of boys and girls drop out of school every year; crime rates do not diminish; violence grows out of the tensions of our cities. But, because the dimensions of this challenge are so great, the efforts to meet it must be not only sizable, but also profound.

Perhaps, too, there is need to find new creative ways to develop opportunities for the gifted Negro girl in the arts (other Leontyne Prices), in the sciences (other Jane Wrights), in public life (other Constance Baker Motleys).

Women in the Negro community represent a great resource not only in numbers and economic power, but in the special qualities of empathy and sensitivity which distinguish all women. That there are many Negro women eager to contribute to such programs as civil rights and the war on poverty is self-evident. Hopefully, in the coming years and decades the work of Negro women as volunteers, employees, artists, scholars, scientists, civil servants and professionals will contribute uniquely and substantially to the solution of the grave social problems that exist.

chapter 14

The Negro Scholar and Professional in America

Horace Mann Bond

INTRODUCTION

In discussing the Negro scholar and professional, in describing the numbers of them in the population of the United States,[1] and in estimating future prospects for these classes among Negroes in generations to come, it is well to remember that the Negro population, for its first 250 years in America, was the victim of a way of life that denied to 90 percent of the group the very foundations of literacy and that, for the next century, refused to establish effective public educational agencies that might have endowed the entire population with a functional command of the language.

However small the numbers and proportions of the Negro scholar and professional in the United States, it is clear that a Negro who overcame the difficulties imposed on his race to become a qualified scholar and professional was likely to be an extraordinary person with an equally extraordinary family, and with personal endowments of sacrificial devotion, iron will and immeasurable persistence. American social science has only in the contemporary generation begun to understand the enormous importance of social and economic class differentials in their effect on the academic potential and achievement of children. With such new insights, and with more liberal opinion displacing prior racist and genetic explanations, the nature and development of a scholarly and professional class among Negroes can now be understood.

Limited access to educational institutions where the skills and knowledge of the scholar and professional could be learned, and beyond this, iron proscriptions excluding or severely limiting Negroes from an opportunity to practice their acquired skills and techniques: these make clear that the

---

[1] The United States Census occupational classification of "Professional, technical, and kindred workers" includes nearly all of those who might be designated scholar or professional. Of the 7,232,410 persons in the United States in this classification in 1960, 288,269, or 3.98 percent of the total, were Negroes. In contrast, 10.11 percent of the American population was reported to be Negro.

A scholar has come increasingly to mean "one who has actively engaged in the advancement of knowledge through research or, at some levels, through the constructive administration of research"; a "professional person" is "one engaged in one of the learned professions or in an occupation requiring a high level of training and proficiency." See Jacques Cattell, *Directory of American Scholars, A Biographical Directory* (Lancaster, Pa.: The Science Press, 1942), Introduction.

Negro scholar and professional has always been at a disadvantage compared to others not subjected to his initial handicaps of a frequently enforced illiteracy.

It is against this social setting in which, perforce, he had to be cradled, nurtured and succeed—or fail—that we shall look at the Negro scholar and professional.

THE NEGRO SCHOLAR

The Pioneers

Banneker and Rillieux   Two almost invariable necessities of the scholar are, first, that his early childhood provide opportunities for education; and, second, that he has a means of livelihood permitting time for scholarly reflection and study. Benjamin Banneker, born near Baltimore, Maryland, about 1731, had the twin advantages of early literacy and a family well above the subsistence level of the seaboard frontier. His grandmother, an Englishwoman who married and emancipated one of her slaves, taught Banneker to read and paid his tuition at school.

Banneker had high attainments in mathematics and in astronomy. He was widely recognized as a surveyor, and in 1789 Thomas Jefferson procured his appointment as a member of the engineering team of Major Pierre Charles L'Enfant, authorized to lay out the site of the proposed Capital City of Washington. Banneker in 1753 at the age of 22, constructed the first clock made in America. This clock was ingeniously carved out of hard wood and struck the hours. There is evidence that it was still functioning twenty years later in 1773. He published an *Almanac* that was highly regarded in Europe, as well as in this country.[2]

Banneker's career illustrated the inescapable preoccupation with racial problems that has beset the Negro scholar and professional in every generation, requiring him to divide his energies between advancing himself in his special field and advocating the claims of his racial fellows for equal opportunity. Banneker first displayed this obligatory compulsion in a 12-page letter addressed to Thomas Jefferson, published in 1792, in which he defended the mental capacities of the Negro.

Herbert Rillieux's invention of an evaporating pan for the refinement of sugar is regarded by technologists as a classic example of the great invention of marvelously simple design that transforms an industry and after

[2] Will W. Allen and Daniel Murray, *Banneker, the Afro-American Astronomer* (Washington: Published by the authors, 1921.)

eventually becomes basic to it. Born into the "free colored" community of Louisiana in 1806 and educated as an engineer in France, Rillieux enjoyed from his earliest childhood the advantages of a superior education, and lived and died in a cultural milieu far removed from the life of the typical American Negro.

The excellent early education of Banneker and Rillieux had few parallels among other Negroes of their time. But there were occasional cases, particularly in the cities, where superior education was provided for persons of African descent, either through private tuition or in private schools especially established for them. Anthony Benezet's school for Africans, established in Philadelphia in 1750, and the New York Free African School, founded in 1787, were two such institutions. Private instruction in these early schools slowly began the production of educated men, some of whom were later to attain distinction as scholars.

Early Negro College Graduates   Excellent secondary and advanced education, so essential to the progress of a scholar, was severely limited for Negroes in the period of the American Revolution and after. There were a few exceptions. Two Gold Coast-born Rhode Islanders, Bristol Yamma and John Quamine, privately tutored by the Newport antislavery pastor, Samuel Hopkins, were later sent by him to the College of New Jersey (Princeton) in 1774. The Revolutionary War ended their study there. By 1830 at least four Negroes had graduated from college. Edward A. Jones, privately tutored in Charleston, South Carolina, graduated from Amherst College in August, 1826, eleven days before John B. Russwurm (long thought the first Negro to graduate from an American college) took his degree at Bowdoin.[3] Theodore S. Wright, a product of the New York African Free School, graduated from the Princeton Theological Seminary in 1828, and Edward Mitchell, from Dartmouth in 1829.

Edward A. Jones became an Episcopal priest, migrated to Sierra Leone, West Africa, and won distinction as a cofounder and principal of the Fourah Bay College, the first higher educational institution in West Africa. Russwurm briefly edited the first Negro newspaper, *Freedom's Journal;* in 1828 he migrated to Liberia, finding the new colony a "promised land" compared to his native land. Theodore S. Wright pastored a Presbyterian church in New York, but later turned to the antislavery cause as a field worker and lecturer. When he returned to Princeton for the tenth anniversary of his seminary graduating class, he was attacked by the students of the adjoining College of New Jersey [Princeton College].

Smith and Delany   Two men professionally trained in medicine became notable scholars in the next generation. They were James McCune

[3] Hugh Hawkins, "Edward Jones: First American Negro College Graduate?" *School and Society* (November 4, 1961), 89:375–376.

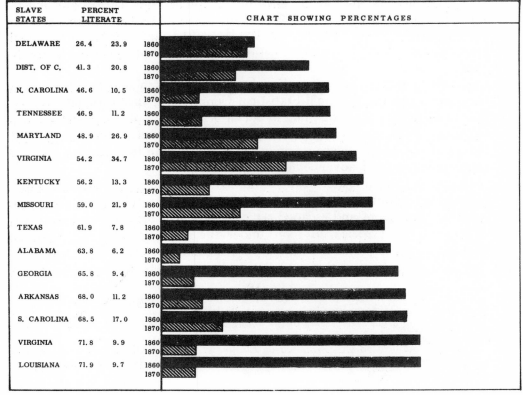

STATE	"FREE COLORED" Number	%	SLAVE Number	PERCENTAGE "FREE COLORED" WERE OF ALL. 1860
ARKANSAS	144	.01	111,115	
MISSISSIPPI	733	.10	437,404	
TEXAS	355	.20	182,566	
ALABAMA	2,690	.60	435,080	
GEORGIA	3,500	.70	462,198	
FLORIDA	932	1.40	61,745	
S. CAROLINA	9,914	2.40	402,406	
MISSOURI	3,572	3.0	114,931	
KENTUCKY	10,684	4.5	225,483	
LOUISIANA	18,647	5.3	331,726	
N. CAROLINA	30,463	8.4	331,059	
VIRGINIA	58,042	10.6	490,865	
MARYLAND	83,942	49.1	87,189	
D. OF COL.	11,131	77.8	3,185	
DELAWARE	19,329	91.7	1,978	
TOTAL SLAVE STATES	261,878		3,953,929	
TOTAL FREE STATES	226,066		60	
GRAND TOTAL	488,070		3,953,989	

LITERACY - "COLORED" - BEFORE (1860) AND AFTER (1870) EMANCIPATION

SLAVE STATES	PERCENT LITERATE			CHART SHOWING PERCENTAGES
DELAWARE	26.4	23.9	1860 / 1870	
DIST. OF C.	41.3	20.8	1860 / 1870	
N. CAROLINA	46.6	10.5	1860 / 1870	
TENNESSEE	46.9	11.2	1860 / 1870	
MARYLAND	48.9	26.9	1860 / 1870	
VIRGINIA	54.2	34.7	1860 / 1870	
KENTUCKY	56.2	13.3	1860 / 1870	
MISSOURI	59.0	21.9	1860 / 1870	
TEXAS	61.9	7.8	1860 / 1870	
ALABAMA	63.8	6.2	1860 / 1870	
GEORGIA	65.8	9.4	1860 / 1870	
ARKANSAS	68.0	11.2	1860 / 1870	
S. CAROLINA	68.5	17.0	1860 / 1870	
VIRGINIA	71.8	9.9	1860 / 1870	
LOUISIANA	71.9	9.7	1860 / 1870	

Smith and Martin R. Delany. Alexander Crummell, the ranking Negro scholar of the latter part of the nineteenth century, said that Dr. James McCune Smith "was undoubtedly the most learned Colored man in the United States" during Smith's lifetime. Educated first in the Free African School of New York City, Smith later enrolled in the University of Glasgow in Scotland, taking his M.D. degree in 1836. He returned to New York where he established a successful practice, gained a wide reputation as one of the first calculators of mortality rates for life insurance companies, and became a leading figure in the antislavery and "colored convention" movement.

He felt obliged to answer allegations of the physical and mental inferiority of his people then being made by such public figures as John C. Calhoun. He replied to Calhoun in such articles as "Comparative Anatomy of the Races" and "The Influence of Climate on Longevity, with Special Reference to Insurance." *

Martin R. Delany, a native of New York City, was educated, like Smith, in the African Free School of the city. He had a brief secondary school experience at the Canaan Academy in New Hampshire, which was destroyed by the townspeople when it admitted several Negro youth in 1831, and later at the Oneida Institute in upper New York State, where several distinguished Negroes received an education under the great schoolmaster Beriah Greene. Admitted to the Harvard University Medical School after several rebuffs from other institutions, he took his medical degree in 1852.

Delany acquired an international reputation as a scholar, became a member of the International Statistical Congress, of the National Association (British) for the Promotion of Social Science and of the Social Science Congress, Glasgow, Scotland. He practiced medicine in Pittsburgh, but the usual fate of the Negro made it necessary for him to enter the cause of racial polemics and advancement.[4]

Delany became a leader of the national convention movement of colored people. He immigrated to Canada, joining a large colony of expatriate free colored persons and escaped slaves. He helped organize an expedition to Nigeria, West Africa, in 1858, under the sponsorship of the National Emigration Society and the African Civilization Society. Delany's mission was successful; he negotiated treaties with the chiefs of Abeokuta, which

---

* See: (1) Kelly Miller, "Historic Background of the Negro Physician," p. 104; *Journal of Negro History*, Vol. 1, No. 2 (Apr., 1916); (2) Martin R. Delany, *Condition, education, emigration and destiny of the colored people in the United States* (Philadelphia; the author, 1852), p. 111.

[4] His last publication was *Principia of Ethnology, The Origin of Races and Colors, with an Archaeological Compendium of Ethiopian and Egyptian Civilization* (Philadelphia: Harper 1879).

granted land for prospective American Negro settlers; and began plans for the expanded production of cotton in the region, the importation of cotton gins and the development of a cotton export trade. His published *Report* has become one of the minor classics in the history and exploration of nineteenth-century Africa.[5]

During the Civil War, Delany was a medical officer in the Union Army with the rank of major; after the war he was commissioned justice of the peace in Charleston, South Carolina.

The Negro Teacher   Scholarship is one aspect of the culture that does not grow in isolation, and the Negro scholar's opportunity to teach and study in an institution of higher learning was long deferred. Prejudice against the employment of Negroes in scholarly communities has inhibited the growth and development of Negro scholars even up to the end of World War II and beyond; at this writing, none of the newly integrated Southern colleges or universities has employed a full-time Negro instructor on any level. Even in the colleges for Negroes created after the Civil War, the majority of governing boards held stubbornly to the idea that "the time was not ripe" to employ Negro teachers. Lincoln University in Pennsylvania, founded in 1854, elected its first Negro professor in 1932. Howard University and Wilberforce University in the North and a handful of colleges in the South provided the extremely limited market in which the Negro scholar found an opportunity to use and expand his scholarship.

But there were rare exceptions, North and South. Limited elementary and secondary educational opportunities slowly appeared in the North that employed Negro scholars. Peter Williams, the first well-trained Negro priest in the Protestant Episcopal Church, conducted a school in New York City as part of his parish duties (circa 1810). Among Charles C. Andrews' students at the African Free School were Ira Aldridge, the actor; Charles L. Reason, who became Professor of Belles Lettres and Mathematics in the New York Central College; Samuel Ringold N. Ward, an eloquent anti-slavery orator, and Alexander Crummell, who took a degree at Cambridge University in 1853. Dr. George F. Grant graduated from the Harvard University Dental School in 1870 and was made an instructor in the school in 1884. His reputation in his specialty—the treatment of the cleft palate and cognate malformations—was so widely established that he lectured by invitation in 1888 to the annual meeting of the British Dental Association. The serologist, William A. Hinton, became an instructor in the Harvard Medical School in 1915; but he did not attain professorial rank until 1949, the year before his retirement.

[5] Benjamin Brawley, *A Social History of the American Negro* (New York: The Macmillan Co., 1921), pp. 165–67. See also, Martin R. Delany, Chief Commissioner, Africa, *Official Report of the Niger Valley Exploring Party* (New York: T. Hamilton; 1861).

Berea College of Kentucky was an extraordinary institution founded in a slave state in 1856 on basic Christian principles, committing the college to a policy of integration. The institution was so conducted—board of trustees, faculty and student body—until 1907, when the United States Supreme Court upheld the Kentucky state law of 1904, requiring the segregation of the races. Atlanta University, after Wilberforce University, gave a home to the young scholar William E. B. Du Bois; the numerous scholarly studies he published during his stay there from 1898 to 1910 testify the opportunity was essential. Although the institution he founded boasted its vocational purpose, Booker T. Washington attracted to Tuskegee Institute the ablest minds he could; the development there of the distinguished bibliographer Monroe N. Work was one of the greatest contributions ever made by a Negro institution to scholarship.

As late as 1946, according to Dr. Robert Maynard Hutchins, there was opposition to the appointment of Negroes in the faculty of the University of Chicago; the head of the department of sociology, William F. Ogburn, a former president of the American Statistical Association and of the American Sociological Society, remonstrated because, he said, all of the white graduate students would withdraw. In a study made in 1961 of the employment of Negro teachers in colleges in New York City, Moss and Mercer state that it was not until after 1941 that Negroes began to be appointed in appreciable numbers to these institutions; their study lists fifty-two known to be so employed in 1961.[6] As there were reported to be 44,791 persons teaching in colleges and universities in New York State during the 1961 spring term, Negroes thus constituted slightly more than one-tenth of one percent of the total.

The Formative Years

Alexander Crummell and the American Negro Academy Alexander Crummell was born in New York City in 1819. He said that his father, Boston, had been a prince of the Timne tribe in Sierra Leone before being kidnapped and sold in America. As a boy, Crummell attended the New York African Free School. At the age of twelve, he was sent to an interracial school at New Canaan, New Hampshire, but was forced to leave when the townspeople burned the school building.

On learning of the New Canaan school's fate, the abolitionist headmaster of the Oneida Institute in New York State admitted Crummell and another Negro boy from New Canaan to his school. When he completed the course there, Crummell wished to study for the Episcopal ministry at the General

---

[6] James A. Moss, Ph.D., and Herman A. Mercer, Ph.D., *A Study of the Potential Supply of Negro Teachers for the Colleges of New York State,* mimeographed report (Schenectady: Union College, May, 1961), pp. 22f.

Theological Seminary in New York City, but his application was rejected because he was black. Persevering in his ambition to be a priest, he was aided by the young abolitionist John Jay; he studied in Boston, and was finally ordained to the Episcopalian priesthood in 1842.

He was not permitted to exercise his priestly functions in Philadelphia because Bishop Onderdonk demanded that Crummell accept a nonparticipating role for his parish in the affairs of the diocese. He finally found a parish in New York where he could be active and remained there until 1852. In that year he went to England where he enrolled at the Queens College, Cambridge University, and took a degree in 1853. Then Crummell went to Liberia where he found on the faculty of the College of Liberia some first-class minds that had been attracted to that outpost of freedom. The scholar Edward W. Blyden was among them.

Crummell returned to the United States after the American Civil War ended. He had the dream of organizing a group of younger Negroes who would apply scholarly methods to the task of elevating the Negro people. The result was the formation of the American Negro Academy, which held its inaugural meeting at Washington, D.C., on March 5, 1897.

Reviewing the circumstances of the organization of the academy, William H. Ferris wrote in 1920:

> He [Crummell] proposed to found and establish the American Negro Academy, an organization composed of Negro scholars, whose membership should be limited to forty and whose purpose should be to foster scholarship and culture in the Negro race and encourage building Negro genius. He communicated with colored scholars in America, England, Hayti and Africa. The result was that in March, 1897, when McKinley was inaugurated, the most celebrated scholars and writers in the Negro race for the first time assembled together in the Lincoln Memorial Church and formally organized into a brotherhood of scholars. Dunbar, the poet; Du Bois, the sociologist; Scarborough, the Greek scholar; Kelly Miller, the mathematician; Dr. Francis J. Grimke, the theologian; Prof. John W. Cromwell, the historian; President R. R. Wright [then President of the Georgia State College at Savannah], Principal Grisham [Principal of the Dunbar High School, Washington], Prof. Love and Prof. Walter B. Hayson, noted educators; Prof. G. C. Cook, the student of English Literature [and Professor in Howard University], and Bishop J. Albert Johnson, the brilliant preacher, were among those present. Bishop Tanner of the African Methodist Episcopal Church, and two or three other bishops were enrolled as members, and such distinguished foreign Negroes as Prof. Harper were added as members. The Academy seemed destined to do for the Negro race what the French Academy did for France.[7]

[7] William H. Ferris, *Alexander Crummell, An Apostle of Negro Culture,* (Washington, D.C.: American Negro Academy, 1920), pp. 1–2.

Officers in 1897 were: S. G. Atkins, Principal, Slater Normal School, Winston-Salem, North Carolina; L. B. Moore (A.B., Fisk, 1889, Ph.D., University of Pennsylvania, 1896), Professor of Latin and Dean, Howard University; and W. H. Crogman (A.B., M.A., Atlanta University), President, Clark University, Atlanta, Georgia.[8]

The objectives and purposes of the academy as formulated by Crummell were:

> For the promotion of Literature, Science, and Art.
> The culture of a form of Intellectual Taste.
> The Fostering of Higher Education.
> The Defense of the Negro Against Vicious Assaults.[9]

The Occasional Papers   The last objective proved to be the most important. The academy members continued to carry the old defensive burden of the Negro intellectual, from Benjamin Banneker's eighteenth-century letter to Thomas Jefferson, until well into the twentieth century. In a series of "Occasional Papers" they engaged in fierce scholarly polemics against race detractors.

The first paper published was Kelly Miller's *A Review of Hoffman's "Race Traits and Tendencies of the American Negro."* Hoffman, a statistician for the Prudential Insurance Company of America, had published an analysis of Negro birth and death rates, concluding with the prophecy that the American Negro was on the road to certain extinction in three decades due to inherent biological inferiority.[10]

W. E. Burghardt Du Bois' *The Conservation of the Races,* published in 1898, was the second "Occasional Paper." The young scholar had already made his mark with his *Suppression of the African Slave Trade;* he had be-

---

[8] Some of the other persons elected to membership in the academy were: J. E. Moorland (YMCA executive, bibliophile), Anna Julia Cooper (1859–1964; the only woman ever elected a member of the Academy; A. B. Oberlin, 1884, Ph.D., Sorbonne, 1925; teacher of the classics and Principal, M. Street High School); Edward C. Williams (Phi Beta Kappa, Western Reserve University; Principal, M. Street High School); L. Z. Johnson (A.B., A.M., S.T.B., Lincoln University, A.M., B.D., Princeton Theological Seminary, Professor, Howard University); Wendell P. Dabney (editor, bibliophile); Henry P. Slaughter (bibliophile); Monroe N. Work (Director, Department of Records and Research, Tuskegee Institute); Faduma Orishatukeh (writer, lecturer; from Sierra Leone; M.A., Yale, 1908); Arthur A. Schomburg (book collector, antiquarian); John E. Bruce (bibliophile); J. E. Kwegyir-Aggrey (then Professor, Livingstone College, later Vice Principal, Prince of Wales College, Achimota, Gold Coast); Carter G. Woodson (A.B., M.A., University of Chicago, Ph.D. Harvard University, Founder and Director, Association for the Study of Negro Life and History); George W. Cook (Professor, Dean, Howard University); and Bishop R. R. Wright, Jr. (Ph.D., University of Pennsylvania).

[9] This statement of purpose was printed in each of the twenty-two "Occasional Papers" published by the Academy from 1897 to 1920.

[10] The 113 percent growth of the Negro population from 1900, when it was 8,833,994, to 18,871,831 in 1960, is sufficient answer.

fore him another sixty-five years of active literary and scholarly production.

Illustrative of the intellectual thrust of these papers are their titles: *The Educated Negro and His Mission* (No. 8. William S. Scarborough); *Modern Industrialism and the Negro* (No. 11. Archibald H. Grimke); and *The Message of St. Domingo to the African Race* (Nos. 18–19, Theophilus G. Steward).

In this group of poets, pulpit orators, journalists and professors, there were at least three men whose work would find a place of highest distinction in their respective scholarly fields. They were: W. E. B. Du Bois, Monroe N. Work, the bibliographer, and William S. Scarborough, philologist. A fourth —Kelly Miller—showed promise in the field of mathematics, but was deterred by the urge to deal with pressing problems of Negro education. He became an outstanding educator and helped the American Negro Academy fulfill the dreams of its founder, Alexander Crummell.[11]

To the academy scholars, and to their thin and polemic pamphlets, must be credited a considerable influence on the intellectual life of the Negro during the first quarter of the twentieth century.

Social and Educational Background The American system has admired the man who rose from the bottom to the top, and it has had particular esteem for Negroes like Booker T. Washington, who came "up from slavery." An examination of the background of Negro intellectuals in any generation shows that such emergence is even more unlikely than among the whites.

Of the eighteen members of the American Negro Academy known to have been in attendance at the organization meeting in 1897, thirteen had been born before 1865. Eight of these thirteen had been born free—six in the United States, two in Canada. Five were born in a condition of slavery. But two of the five slave-born children were born into what might be called the "upper class" of the enslaved population and had extraordinarily special advantages over the ordinary slave child.

William S. Scarborough, one of the more privileged, was born at Macon, Georgia, in 1850. His father was a free artisan in Savannah, Georgia, who later moved to Macon to live. His mother was a literate slave, who enjoyed the extraordinary privilege of being paid a daily wage and of being permitted to live away from her master's house in her husband's home. Scarborough said of his mother that ". . . she lived in her own home and was able to give careful attention to her family, which never felt the harsh, restrictive features of the slave system." The father had progressed beyond the elementary school level; the mother was literate; an uncle taught the boy;

---

[11] W. E. B. Du Bois has paid a grateful tribute to the Scholar in his essay, "To Alexander Crummell," published in his *Souls of Black Folk* (Chicago: A. C. McClurg & Co., 1904), five years after Crummell's death.

his mother's master bought books for him, and a white neighbor gave him special tutoring. Before he was twelve, young Scarborough—nominally a slave—". . . had mastered Webster's blue-backed speller, and studied arithmetic, geography, and history." [12]

Francis J. Grimke, the second, came from an equally favored slave background. Quite without embarassment, this Presbyterian minister recounted in his autobiography that he was one of three sons of Henry Grimke, of an old aristocratic Charleston, South Carolina, family, and a beautiful slave, Nancy Weston. The claim was recognized by Grimke's famous abolitionist aunt, Angelina Grimke-Weld, who discovered her nephews enrolled at Lincoln University in Pennsylvania, assisted them through college, and sponsored Archibald through Harvard Law School and Francis through the Princeton Theological Seminary. Biographical information is lacking regarding the other three "slave-born" scholars of the American Negro Academy.

Racist Explanations of Negro Scholarship   Neither literacy nor skills are inherited, but this has not prevented racists from ascribing Negro scholarship to heredity. Noting that a number of Negroes who have attained distinction are of mixed racial extraction, the school of racists insists that the "white blood" is the cause. Carleton Putnam, one of this school of opinion, claims the scientist George Washington Carver as a representative of this group, stating that Carver's white blood "is proven by his blue eyes." While one person who knew Carver agrees that he did have blue eyes, others who knew him equally well deny it, and a physician who treated him in his declining years stated that Carver suffered from *arcis senilis,* an affliction arising from high blood pressure in the aged that accentuates the whitish-bluish color of the iris and creates the illusion of "blue eyes." The British racist, R. Ruggles Gates, widely quoted by American segregationists, even proposes the theory that there is a "sex-influenced gene for intelligence" as an explanation for a high number of high intelligence quotients reported for one Negro family.

A Social Environment Theory   George Washington Carver was reared by a German couple in Missouri that cared for him after his mother was kidnaped, and, says the social environment theory, he must have absorbed from these foster parents their habits and attitudes toward work and study; this environment was much more important to his future career as student and scientist than his alleged "white blood." These theorists believe that the "slave elite" circumstances of William S. Scarborough's mother and his free colored father were much more vital to his future than the curious

---

[12] Francis P. Weisenburger, "William Sanders Scarborough." *Ohio History,* 71, No. 3 (October, 1962), and p. 2 and 72, No. 1 (January, 1963).

mélange of racial "bloods" the scholar described in his autobiography. Social circumstances and education were far more significant in the emergence of Francis J. Grimke as a scholar than the fact that he was carrying the genes of his grandfather, Judge John Faucheraud Grimke, of the South Carolina Supreme Court. The social environment theory, as contrasted to the theory of "white blood," is the basic theme of this section.

Early Negro scholars, then, were derived overwhelmingly from what one can identify as a Negro "upper class"—even among slaves. The free colored population in the United States numbered 488,070 in 1860, or 10 percent of what came to be identified as the "Negro" population. The scholars were largely derived from this class and from the favored slaves. Such favored slaves were frequently related to the white master by kinship and by occupation, and thus more likely than the Negro field hand to receive elementary instruction, to observe and imitate and absorb the standard culture and to receive material assistance in obtaining both a sound economic base and an education from their masters before or their ex-masters after the Civil War.

Small as they were numerically and proportionately in the Negro mass, this small group of former "upper" class slaves—"upper" in relation only to the mass of enforced poverty and illiteracy most of the freedmen represented—provided the narrow apex of the flattened pyramid from which a middle class and emerging scholars could be built after the Civil War. Occupationally, the professions of school teaching and the ministry gave employment to the daughters and sons of the already literate, and increasingly to the new literates.

The children of the old upper class and the children of the impoverished freedmen alike were welcomed in the mission schools and colleges created in the South's various mission societies after the Civil War. In some of these institutions the large number of light-complexioned students was so noticeable as to arouse the curiosity of visitors. The phenomenon was not due, as many believed, to the "superiority" of the white blood; it was a social and economic, rather than a natural selection. Concubinage remained an openly sustained relationship between white men and Negro women in the South for fifty years after the Civil War; the children of such unions were more likely to have parents with the money, and the tradition, to send a child to school, than the former field hand slaves who were now sharecroppers and day laborers.

In addition the Federal Civil Service in all cities, especially in Washington, provided a steady employment for a growing class of literate Negroes, even though those so hired were frequently "underemployed" in terms of their actual abilities.

Role of the Mission Schools   The mission schools have been derided by many critics. The Yankee teachers, it has been said, were not realistic in their curricula, nor in their appraisal of the basic needs of the recently emancipated former slaves. The schools were frequently called "colleges" and "universities," when their enrollments were concentrated on the elementary and secondary school level. Instead of carrying on a practical education, designed to meet the illiterate and unskilled on their own level, they boasted courses of study taken directly from the programs of New England colleges, replete with Latin, Greek and the higher mathematics.[13]

These critics miss several important points necessary to the evaluation of an educational institution. One, that the process of education is a long-time one, requiring for final judgment on its outcome the entire life and career of the subject; further the effect of the educational process as transmitted to the entire community cannot be judged until it can be viewed from the perspective of generations. Another consideration is often omitted in the criticism of these institutions. For every "college" student actually graduated, these schools gave a thorough elementary and secondary education to scores of students who in their turn passed on, through family and friends, their knowledge of the fundamentals and their acquired habits and discipline. Their children and grandchidlren did not have to "start from scratch," or even behind it, in an illiterate home and a wretched school or in no school at all.

Based on the academic successes of first, second and even third generation descendants of the students of the early mission schools, available evidence suggests that these institutions provided for Southern Negroes some of the most effective educational institutions the world has ever known. The Negro scholars of today are, for the most part, the children and grandchildren of persons who received their education in these institutions.

In addition, one needs to consider the excellent schools located in many Northern communities; the Great Barrington High School in Massachusetts, of which Du Bois said:

> My high school principal was Frank Hosmer, afterward president of Oahu College, Hawaii. He suggested, quite as a matter of fact, that I ought to take the college preparatory course which involved algebra, geometry, Latin and Greek. . . . I did not then realize that Hosmer was quietly opening college doors to me, for in those days they were barred with ancient tongues.[14]

Two other examples are the Central High School in Philadelphia which helped start Alain Leroy Locke, the philosopher, on his scholarly way;

[13] Henry Lee Swint, *The Northern Teacher in the South, 1862–1870* (Nashville: Vanderbilt University Press, 1941).

[14] W. E. B. Du Bois, *Dusk of Dawn* (New York: Harcourt, Brace & Company, 1940), p. 15.

and Kimball Academy, in New Hampshire, where Ernest E. Just, the biologist, prepared for Dartmouth after his arrival from South Carolina (indeed, South Carolina gave him a good beginning in a missionary school).

Most instructive in the art of developing the Negro scholar is the example of M. Street High School and its successor, Paul Laurence Dunbar High School, in Washington, D.C.[15] M. Street began operation in 1870. From the first it followed the policy of employing the best-prepared teachers available. The salaries paid were on the Federal scale, and were far superior to those prevailing for teachers anywhere else in the country, even if positions had been available to Negro teachers, as they were not. M Street, and after it, Dunbar, took the pick of the crop of brilliant young Negroes who had graduated from the best colleges in the country.

Miss Mary Jane Patterson, whose graduation from Oberlin College in 1862 made her the first Negro woman college graduate in the United States, was principal from 1870–71 and from 1873–74. Richard T. Greener, who in 1870 became the first Negro to take an A.B. at Harvard, was principal from 1871–72. Francis L. Cardozo was principal from 1884–96; he had studied in the University of Glasgow and the London School of Theology. (As Secretary of State for South Carolina from 1868–72 and state treasurer from 1872–76, his bitterest enemies during the vicious struggles of the Reconstruction period acknowledged that he was the best-educated man in South Carolina.)

W. Scott Montgomery, of Dartmouth; Robert H. Terrell, of Harvard; Anna J. Cooper, of Oberlin; W. T. S. Jackson, of Amherst; E. C. Williams, Phi Beta Kappa from Western Reserve; and Garnet C. Wilkinson, of Oberlin, were other principals of M. Street, and Dunbar.

The Du Bois-Booker T. Washington controversy over "industrial education" came to a head during Mrs. Cooper's principalship (circa 1910). She aligned herself with the Du Bois group and succeeded in keeping M Street's curriculum that of the standard college preparatory school of the time.

The teachers joined the administration of the school in insisting upon the highest standards of achievement, in urging and assisting their students to emulate their own academic success. Tutorials were organized to help the most promising students with their college board examinations. The faculty solicited scholarships from their alma maters, the finest New England colleges and Oberlin; in Washington, they organized fund-raising campaigns to supplement the scholarships offered. Through these devices,

[15] Mrs. Mary G. Hundley, now retired from teaching in the Washington public schools and a former member of the Dunbar High School faculty, has kindly provided the writer with material she used in preparation of her book, *The Dunbar Book* (New York, Vantage Press, 1965).

several graduates of M Street, and later of Dunbar, were annually sent to such colleges as Amherst, Dartmouth, Harvard, Oberlin, Radcliffe, Wellesley, Williams, Vassar and Yale.

The results are now apparent. M Street and Dunbar have contributed to the ranks of Negro scholars in medicine, in law, in engineering, generally in the arts and sciences, to a truly extraordinary degree.

Data on the other high schools attended by Negro academic doctorates is available only for 609 who took their doctoral degrees from 1957 to 1962. This group completed their high school work at the latest in 1955, and for the most part, before 1952. Out of the 360 high schools from which these doctorates graduated, one—Dunbar produced sixteen or 2.62 percent. Two schools produced nine each—Frederick Douglass High School, Baltimore, Maryland, and McDonogh 35 High School, in New Orleans, Louisiana. Other high producers were Lincoln (Kansas City, Missouri) and Booker T. Washington (Atlanta, Georgia), with eight each; and Tuskegee Institute High School (Tuskegee, Alabama), with seven.

High mobility in urban populations since 1955 makes any effort to "rate" these and other predominantly Negro high schools on the basis of excellence as measured by later doctoral productivity meaningless. It is interesting to note, however, that 5.2 percent of these high schools produced 20.8 percent of the doctorates. It is significant also that each of the schools listed above has long had high academic tradition in its respective city and has been the principal college preparatory high school for Negroes, enrolling numbers of children of middle class, professional and semiprofessional occupations.

THE PIONEERS
NEGRO ACADEMIC DOCTORATES AND THEIR PROPORTION IN THE COMMUNITY OF SCHOLARS

Although the academic doctorate awarded by European universities had been the badge of scholarly attainment for centuries, it was not until 1866 that Yale became the first American University to offer the degree. The year of 1876 marking the organization of Johns Hopkins University, is generally accepted as the actual initiation in America of university studies on the graduate level.

Edward S. Bouchet, who received the doctor of philosophy degree at Yale, in Physics, in 1876, has been considered the first American Negro to receive a doctorate.[16] However, Father Patrick Francis Healy, S.J., born in 1834 near Macon, Georgia, of a white father and a Negro mother, received this degree from the University of Louvain, Belgium, in 1865. Patrick Healy attended Holy Cross College, in Worcester, Massachusetts, received a dispensation from the Vatican for his legally enforced illegitimacy, since the laws of Georgia did not permit his parents to marry, and entered the Jesuit order. He was an instructor in Holy Cross, studied for the priesthood in Rome, took his doctorate at Louvain and became an instructor at Georgetown University in 1867, a professor in 1868, and was inaugurated as president of the nation's oldest Catholic institution of higher learning in 1873. Ill-health forced his resignation in 1882; he is credited with having made the institution a true university, and is remembered as the "second founder" of Georgetown.[17]

The number of Negro academic doctorates grew slowly. Two of the first forty members of the American Negro Academy, founded in 1897, had earned the degree. Both were graduates of Fisk University: W. E. B. Du Bois, 1888 (Harvard Ph.D., 1896) and Lewis B. Moore, Ph.D., Pennsylvania, 1896. Harry Washington Greene's careful listing of Negro doctorates goes up to the year 1943. Data from a study of the American doctorate, made available to the writer by the National Academy of Sciences, National Research Council, reveals that approximately 1,500 graduates of predominantly Negro colleges received doctorates between 1920 and 1962. The elimination by law of racial designations in reporting race of graduates, as enacted since World War II in the major doctorate-producing states, makes it impossible to enumerate the total number of Negro academic doctorates since the time of Greene's report. Those who graduated from Negro colleges can be counted, but those who took their first degrees at integrated institutions cannot.

Major Fields of Study for Negro Doctorates   The percentage of Negro doctorates educated in Negro colleges exceeds 1.0 percent of the total number in only three major academic fields. These are: Education (2.19 percent), Religion and Theology (1.14 percent), and Agricultural Sciences (1.03 percent). The addition of those Negroes who earned undergraduate degrees in integrated colleges, and later academic doctorates, would perhaps double the numbers and percentages in all of the major fields listed with the exception of education; there would be, for example, twice as many persons in the physical and natural sciences, and larger numbers

---

[16] Harry Washington Greene, *Holders of Doctorates Among American Negroes* (Boston: Meador Publishing Company, 1946), p. 22.

[17] Albert S. Foley, S.J., *God's Men of Color* (New York: Farrar, Straus & Co., 1955) pp. 23–31.

TABLE I—Production of Negro Academic Doctorates Compared to All American Academic Doctorates

Five-Year Periods	All American Doctorates	Doctorates from Negro Colleges	Negro Doctorates, Integrated Colleges	Total, Negro Doctorates	Productivity Ratio, White to each Negro Doctorate
(1866–1879)	(Not known)	—	2	2	(Not known)
1880–1884	218	—	—	—	—
1885–1889	348	1	1	2	174 to 1
1890–1894	877	—	1	1	877 to 1
1895–1899	1,247	2	1	3	415 to 1
1900–1904	1,277	1	—	1	1,277 to 1
1905–1909	1,748	1	2	3	582 to 1
1910–1914	2,264	3	—	3	754 to 1
1915–1919	2,760	4	4	8	345 to 1
1920–1924	4,186	4	13	17	245 to 1
1925–1929	7,703	5	27	32	240 to 1
1930–1934	11,928	28	42	70	170 to 1
1935–1939	13,658	56	53	109	125 to 1
(1940–1943)	12,761	96	39	135	94 to 1
1940–1944	14,700	109	53 (est.)*	162 (est.)*	90 to 1
1945–1949	15,855	164	88 (est.)	252 (est.)	62 to 1
1950–1954	38,644	334	179 (est.)	513 (est.)	75 to 1
1955–1959	44,170	445	239 (est.)	684 (est.)	64 to 1
1960–1962	32,675	312	168 (est.)	480 (est.)	68 to 1

* The estimates are based on the assumption that 35 percent of the doctorates earned by Negroes since 1940 have been awarded to persons who earned undergraduate degrees at integrated institutions. While the Negro population in those states affording integrated higher education has greatly increased since 1940, the Negro enrollment in the major doctorate-producing undergraduate colleges has remained extremely small. While no statistics are available, largely because of Fair Educational Practices laws, testimony of teachers and administrators in the New York City colleges, that are among the Nation's largest undergraduate sources of doctoral degrees, is that Negroes probably constitute less than one percent of the enrollment of these institutions. A recent (1962) study of Negro enrollment in Pennsylvania colleges, made by William H. Gray, similarly indicates a very small enrollment of Negroes in those colleges.

SOURCE: Lindsey R. Harmon and Herbert Soldz, Compilers, *Doctorate Production in United States Universities, 1920–1962.* Publication No. 1142, National Academy of Sciences—National Research Council. Washington, D.C. Publishing Office, National Academy of Sciences—National Research Council, 1963, and Harry Washington Greene, *Negro Holders of Doctorates, op. cit.;* and unpublished materials provided this writer by the Office of Scientific Personnel.

and proportions in social sciences and in education. Of the ten physicists listed in Greene's early study, seven came from predominantly white Northern colleges; and in mathematics, five of seven. On the other hand, institutions with well-equipped physics laboratories and excellent faculties in the field, such as Fisk and Howard Universities, have good records in the producton of physicists. Howard University, Johnson C. Smith University, Fisk University, Morehouse College and Lincoln University have creditable records in chemistry and the biological sciences. Possible improvement in equipment and faculty and a change in the choice of careers may be indicated by the fact that twenty-five of the ninety-eight chemists reported to be graduates of Negro colleges, and fifty-three of the 184 persons in the biological sciences, received their doctorates in the brief period from 1960–62.

TABLE II—The Number of Negro College Graduates in the Major Fields Where They Earned Doctorates, 1920–1962, Compared to the Total Number of American Doctorates in These Fields

Major Fields of Study	Number		
	Total 1920–1962	Negro 1920–1962	Percent, Negroes
Mathematics	4,942	23	0.46
Physics and Astronomy	9,618	17	0.17
Chemistry	23,697	98	0.41
Earth Sciences	3,743	2	0.02
Engineering	10,209	3	0.03
Total, Physical Sciences	**52,209**	**143**	**0.27**
Agricultural Sciences	5,122	53	1.03
Medical Sciences	1,775	13	0.73
Biological Sciences	31,829	184	0.57
Total, Natural Sciences	**84,038**	**250**	**0.29**
Psychology	11,080	65	0.58
Social Sciences (Total, Including Psychology)	35,052	290	0.82
Humanities	(Not Available)	124	0.81
Business Administration	1,722	14	
Home Economics	(Not Available)	7	
Journalism	(Not Available)	3	
Law	(Not Available)	5	
Library and Archival	(Not Available)	3	
Religion and Theology	2,892	33	1.14
Education	26,363	579	2.19

SOURCE: Same as Table I.

The Scholar and Research   American Negro scholars in the physical sciences, in life sciences, in social sciences and in the humanities may be found today making respectable scholarly contributions to the broad spectrum of human knowledge. They will be found in our universities and medical centers, in laboratories of government and private industry, in the field, and both here and abroad. Their number is small; but in some instances their scholarship ranks with the best scholarly contributions in the world. It is all too true, as a great scientist, Charles Richard Drew, has pointed out, that many of these scientists are handicapped with the pittances paid them, heavy teaching loads they carry, and inadequate laboratory or library facilities. Yet among them, Drew observed, are "true scholars . . . the vast majority spend lives of diligent searching guided by rigid intellectual discipline, and led on much in the nature of the artist and dreamer toward new creative goals." [18]

A SUMMARY OF THE NEGRO AS SCHOLAR: ONE-TENTH OF THE NATION, PERHAPS ONE PERCENT OF THE SCHOLARS

The scarcity of Negro scholars in the American intellectual community throws into sharp relief not the deficiencies of the Negro intellect, but the imperfections of a system that now produces perhaps one percent of its greatest human asset from one-tenth of its population.

The scholar, in general, is likely to be that person whose early surroundings gave him—painlessly—the advantages of facility in the use of the written and spoken word and in other primary concepts basic to the learning process. Several generations of literacy are the usual endowment of the scholar, whether in Europe or in America.

By contrast, the Negro scholar had to emerge from a setting where, as short a time ago as two generations before, illiteracy was the rule enforced by savage laws proscribing the instruction of this part of the population. At Emancipation and up to the last two decades, the public school instruments designed to repair a state of almost universal illiteracy were of a disgracefully inadequate and ineffective kind. For a scholar to emerge from a social and educational system would be unlikely; Negro scholars did not. They have emerged where, almost fortuitously, an unusual social setting and unusual formal educational institutions—such as those provided by the "Yankee schoolmarm"—provided an educational foundation in earlier times to some few scholars themselves, or to the grandparents and parents of the prospective scholar.

The budding scholar also needs economic security, first to support him in his preparatory studies; and second, to sustain him during tedious and extended nonprofitable pursuit of the researches that attract him. Such support came infrequently to the prospective Negro scholar; poverty was

[18] Charles R. Drew, "Negro Scholars in Scientific Research." *Journal of Negro History*, XXXV, No. 2 (April, 1950), p. 140.

the order of his family and community life and of his racial group. Few could surmount this deficiency; those who did were likely to be men of the most indomitable purpose with a great capacity for hard work and tremendous self-sacrifice.

The gestating scholar requires the advantages of an excellent education all along the line: elementary school, secondary school, college and university. This advantage few Negroes have had; hence, few scholars.

Obviously, only the massive administration of fundamental remedial measures in each of these areas can be expected to affect the present rate of productivity of scholars from the Negro community. There are now (1965) some faint few signs that ameliorating circumstances are in sight. Scholarship, however, is a plant of long culture, measured by generations; profound changes in the present contribution made by American Negroes to the American and world communities of scholars are not soon to be expected.

THE NEGRO PROFESSIONAL IN 1960

An Overview

Statistical accounts of the numbers of Negro professionals have been suspect at least since 1934. Carter G. Woodson then demonstrated by actual count that the United States census reporting was extremely inaccurate in several cities where his workers had surveyed the field.[19] In addition trend projection from census figures suffers from frequent changes in the definitions used from decade to decade. In 1950, for example, the 18,150 male Negro clergymen reported were said to constitute 11.3 percent of all clergymen in the United States. The preliminary figures for 1960 give the total of male Negro clergymen as 13,955, constituting 7.10 percent of all United States clergymen. In fact, the substantial decrease shown is the result of the change in the form of the census occupational questionnaire; for in 1960, the number includes only those persons actively employed in the occupation and giving it as their "principal, full-time" job. A large number of persons who had been earlier classified as clergyman were excluded from the 1960 count.

The figures reported in Table II, which follows, do not include the unemployed, the retired or those who are not pursuing their avowed pro-

[19] Carter G. Woodson, *The Negro Professional Man and the Community, with Special Emphasis on the Physician and Lawyer* (Washington: The Associated Publishers, 1934).

fession for other reasons. Generally unemployment is lowest for all classes among the professionals, with Negro teachers reporting the highest percentage (7.3 percent). Even here the interruption of service for such causes as maternity leave, in a profession with a heavy female proportion, makes such high "unemployment" percentages misleading.

An examination of Table III reveals the fact that only in the category of "Social Welfare and Recreational Workers" do Negroes exceed their population proportion in any professional class. This fact speaks for three features characteristic of the Negro employment situation. The first, the general paucity of persons with the extensive education needed to qualify for professional positions. The second, equality of employment opportunity is more likely to prevail in functions largely governmental in support and control. The third, the high social pathology of the Negro community provides, in a segregated approach to social welfare operations, a larger than average "captive market" for the employment of skilled and semiskilled Negro professionals. The fairly large proportion of Negro teachers and clergymen likewise is testimony to the existence of segregated institutions.

A further breakdown of the data for selected occupations—using the broader "labor force" category of the 1950 census and the narrower "employed" of the preliminary 1960 figures—show gratifying increases for Negroes between 1950 and 1960, if percentage increases are accepted at face value. However, an examination of the actual numbers involved, as shown in Table IV, reveals the still microscopic proportions of Negroes employed in certain technological professions, which are the key to modern employment and economic problems. It is gratifying to be able to say that the Negroes employed as aeronautical engineers in 1960 represents a 68.0 percent increase over these in the labor force of that profession in 1950. But when it is noted that in 1960 there were only 312 such Negroes out of 50,778 persons employed and that they constituted only six-tenths of one percent of the class, the apparently spectacular "progress" is less impressive.

The decrease in the relative rate of growth for Negro physicians and surgeons was noted in 1958 by Reitzes.[20] An 11 percent differential between the increase of white and Negro physicians between 1940 and 1950 was then explained by the rapid broadening of other high-level opportunities for Negro youth, that diverted many who had previously found medicine one of few channels to higher social and economic status. The expansion of opportunity has continued at an accelerated rate during the 1960's; but the pool of young Negroes with the educated ability to enter either medicine

[20] Dietrich C. Reitzes, *Negroes and Medicine* (Published for the Commonwealth Fund. Cambridge: Harvard University Press, 1958).

TABLE III—Negroes Employed in Selected Professional and Technical Occupations by Sex in 1960

Occupation	Males No. in Occupation	%	Females No. in Occupation	%	Total No. in Occupation	%
Accountants and Auditors	2,320	0.59	1,342	1.69	3,662	0.77
		*		*	*	*
Architects	238	0.80	729	2.02	1,878	1.84
Artists and Art Teachers	1,149	1.72	410	0.92	1,161	0.90
Authors, Editors, and Reporters	751	0.89	*	*	*	*
Chemists	1,539	2.01	*	*	*	*
Clergymen	13,955	7.10	1,897	4.88	5,415	3.04
College Presidents, Professors, and Instructors	3,518	2.52	*	*	*	*
Dentists	1,998	2.46	*	*	*	*
Designers and Draftsmen	2,744	1.07	*	*	*	*
Engineers:						
Aeronautical	312	0.61	*	*	*	*
Civil	1,166	0.75	*	*	*	*
Electrical	1,216	0.66	*	*	*	*
Mechanical	684	0.46	*	*	*	*
Other Technical Engineers	1,000	0.32	*	*	*	*
Total, Engineers	3,374					
Lawyers and Judges	2,004	0.95	176	2.36	2,180	1.02
Musicians and Music Teachers	5,739	2.36	3,566	3.25	9,305	4.84
Natural Scientists	866	1.46	*	*	*	*
Pharmacists	1,462	1.71	*	*	*	*
Physicians and Surgeons	4,216	1.97	490	1.97	4,706	2.05
Social Scientists	1,667	1.96	392	2.74	2,059	2.07
Social Welfare and Recreation Workers	5,593	9.83	8,683	11.40	14,276	10.72
Teachers:						
Elementary School	13,451	9.46	75,695	8.79	89,146	8.88
Secondary School	14,823	5.39	18,194	7.42	33,017	6.36
Not elsewhere counted	2,606	4.51	5,889	6.34	8,495	5.65
Total, Teachers	30,880	6.49	99,778	8.33	130,658	7.81
Technicians:						
Medical and Dental	4,145	8.05	5,613	6.56	9,767	7.06
Electric and Electronics	1,613	1.84	*	*	*	*
Actors, Dancers, and Entertainers	*	*	556	2.85	*	*
Dietitians and Nutritionists	*	*	3,507	14.46	*	*
Librarians	*	*	3,144	4.37	*	*
Nurses, Professional	*	*	27,034	4.76	*	*
Nurses, Student	*	*	1,718	3.03	*	*
Therapists and Healers	*	*	870	4.40	*	*
Other Professional, Technical and Kindred Workers	22,902	2.41	9,385	3.77	32,287	2.69
All Prof., Tech., and Kindred Workers	112,931	2.52	175,338	6.36	288,697	3.98

* This table should be read: The 2,320 Male Negroes who were employed as Accountants and Auditors constituted 0.59% of all the employed Male Accountants and Auditors enumerated in 1960; the 1,342 Female Negroes who were employed as Accountants and Auditors constituted 1.69% of all the employed Female Accountants and Auditors enumerated in 1960; the total of 3,662 employed Negro Accountants and Auditors enumerated in 1960 constituted 0.77% of all employed Accountants and Auditors enumerated in 1960. The asterisk indicates occupations for which data were available for only one sex.

SOURCE: U.S. Bureau of the Census. *U.S. Census of Population: 1960. Detailed Characteristics. United States Summary.* Final Report P.C.(1)–1D. pp. 1–544–1–547 (Washington: U.S. Government Printing Office, 1963).

TABLE IV—Male Negroes in Selected Occupations in the Total Professional Labor Force in 1950 Compared with the Number and Percent of Negroes and Whites Employed in the Same Occupation in 1960

Titles of Occupations	Number White		Number Negro		Percent Negro		Percent Increases (1950–1960)	
	Labor Force (1950)	Employed (1960)	Labor Force (1950)	Employed (1960)	Labor Force (1950)	Employed (1960)	White	Negroes
Accountants and Auditors	319,503	390,904	900	2,320	0.3	0.6	22.3	159.7
Chemists	66,802	74,339	667	1,539	0.8	2.1	12.4	130.7
Engineers:								
Aeronautical	17,197	59,778	40	312	0.2	0.6	195.2	680.0
Civil	120,597	153,857	460	1,166	0.4	0.8	27.5	153.4
Electrical	104,742	180,539	337	1,216	0.3	0.7	72.3	260.8
Mechanical	109,068	150,734	326	684	0.3	0.7	38.2	100.9
Other Technical Engineers	164,679	309,348	351	1,000	0.2	0.3	87.8	184.0
Total—Engineers	516,276	845,274	1,514	4,378	0.2	0.5	65.6	189.1
Lawyers and Judges	172,719	202,940	1,367	2,004	0.9	0.9	11.1	46.6
Physicians and Surgeons	175,783	205,429	3,769	4,216	2.1	2.0	16.8	11.9

or other diversified professional fields has not had a corresponding expansion.

In all of these areas, the rate of relative increase would have to be maintained and multiplied for a number of decades if Negroes are to be represented in any approximate relation to their proportion in the population. In governmental circles and in private employment there is doubtless an additional pool of able and well-trained Negroes who have been underemployed in terms of their actual educational and ability attainments. The limits are easily reached on the professional level because of the long training period required. A shifting of aspirations in the Negro community—and in college, where formerly a career in schoolteaching was widely regarded as the only possibility for professional employment—may further enlarge the number of candidates for professional careers.

The basic problem of increasing the number of Negro professionals rests now on expanding the supply of prospective candidates. To do so will require so far unimagined applications of educational, economic and social remediation.

THE NEGRO PHYSICIAN AND DENTIST

Social Origins

Only towards the middle of the nineteenth century did medicine begin to emerge from being a craft that required apprenticeship as any craft, to a true profession requiring increasingly longer periods of sustained and arduous theoretical and practical education. The earliest Negro physicians were individuals who had unique opportunties from personal contact with their masters in what was then still a craft. Such a one was James Derham, born a slave in Philadelphia, and successively owned by three physicians who taught him to compound medicines and to administer treatment. His last master, a Dr. Robert Dove of New Orleans, allowed him to buy his own freedom. By 1800 Derham had an extensive practice in the city of New Orleans. Dr. Benjamin Rush, the Philadelphia physician renowned as the greatest medical man of his day, met Derham and commented favorably on his medical attainments.[21]

[21] Kelly Miller, "The Historical Background of the Negro Physician." *The Journal of Negro History*, 1, No. 2 (April, 1916), pp. 99–109. See also, Carter G. Woodson, *The Negro Professional and the Community*. (Washington, D.C.: The Association for the Study of Negro Life and History, 1934).

Negro graduates of the new medical schools were few; there was racial discrimination barring admission to many, and the free colored population that was the only possible source of candidates for a higher education was poor and with few opportunities for a premedical education. There were several exceptions, however. Dr. James McCune Smith, mentioned earlier as a scholar, after completing his medical education at the University of Glasgow in Scotland, returned to practice in New York in 1837. The child of literate free colored artisans, Smith received an excellent elementary education in the African Free School. Martin R. Delany, who has also been mentioned as a scholar, received a Harvard medical degree and became a physician, surgeon and specialist in women's and children's diseases with a successful practice in Pittsburgh.

Other early Negro physicians were from the free colored urban population, either native to Northern cities or sent North by free colored or white parents who could afford to educate their children. Several were given scholarships by the American Colonization Society, to prepare for medical service in Liberia, in West Africa. Kelly Miller has written:

> Dr. William Taylor and Dr. Fleet were thus educated in the District of Columbia. In the same way John V. DeGrasse, of New York, and Thomas J. White, of Brooklyn, were allowed to complete the medical course at Bowdoin in 1849. In 1854 Dr. DeGrasse was admitted as a member of the Massachusetts Medical Society. In 1858 the Berkshire Medical School graduated two colored doctors who were gratuitously educated by the American Educational Society. Dr. A. T. Augusta [member of a well-educated "free colored" family that took refuge in Canada] studied medicine at the University of Toronto. He qualified by competitive examination and obtained the position of surgeon in the United States Army, being the first Negro to hold such a position. After the War he became one of the leading colored physicians in the District of Columbia. Prior to 1861 Negroes had taken courses at the Medical School in Vermont; Berkshire Medical School in Pittsfield, Massachusetts; the Rush Medical School in Chicago; the Eclectic Medical School in Philadelphia; the Homeopathic College of Cleveland; and the Medical School of Harvard University.[22]

For reasons already mentoned, the Negro physician, especially those who attained greatest distinction, have continued to come from the most favored middle and upper classes of the Negro group. The famous surgeon Daniel Hale Williams, who won world renown for his celebrated "first" successful operation on the human heart, is described by one popularizing biographer as the conventional American folk-descended hero, who climbed from the depths of a deprived background to great heights: "From the age of

[22] Miller, *op. cit.*, p. 105.

twelve Daniel was on his own, working as an apprentice shoemaker, a roustabout on a lake steamer, and as a barber." [23]

In fact, on both his father's and mother's side, "Doctor Dan" came from at least three generations of freely and legally intermarrying whites, Indians and Negroes, who were well-educated for their times, and industrious and property-owning people of substance. His paternal grandfather had accumulated extensive property in the town of Holidaysburg, Pennsylvania, where Williams was born in 1856. His father was a highly articulate barber, who traveled widely as a lecturer for the abolitionist Equal Rights League.[24]

In view of his accumulated burdens, all rooted in slavery—of disorganized families, illiteracy, and poor education—any expectations that the Negro, by some strange alchemy, by now should have acquired a knowledge of the tools of his culture, equal to that of other portions of the population not so weighted down, is an absurdity. Yet such expectations are held and the deficiencies of the Negro are laid to an irreparable mental and emotional lack. An analysis of the occupational and educational background of the average, as well as of the distinguished Negro medical professional, yields information that should be a common-sense observation. These people come from families that have had the financial resources, the disciplined habits and the literacy that are required to pursue the arduous professions of medicine and dentistry. With admission to medical schools throughout the country increasingly open without regard to race, that there are not more Negro medical students is because there are not more Negro families to produce admissible students.

That this general rule of background factors is a fact is shown by a recent study of the educational and occupational status of the grandfathers and the fathers of a selected group of Negro physicians and dentists, located principally in the District of Columbia. In Table V, below, from Edwards, it will be seen that 31.1 percent of the fathers of physicians and 23.9 percent of the fathers of dentists, came in turn from fathers who had been occupied as professionals (principally clergymen, and teachers). This was a ratio of 27.71 times higher than the proportion of those classes in the general Negro population.

Note, also, that a number of the Negroes in Edwards' sample whose designated occupations place them in "lower" occupations were there in a period (1910) when the "underemployment" of Negroes in terms of their real abilities was chronic. There were hotel headwaiters who might as easily

[23] Russel L. Adams, Eugene Winslow, and David P. Ross, *Great Negroes, Past and Present* (Chicago: Afro-Am Publishing Co., 1963).

[24] Helen Buckler, *Doctor Dan, Pioneer in American Surgery* (Boston: Little, Brown & Company, 1954).

TABLE V—Occupation of Fathers of Physicians and Dentists

Classification of the Regular Occupation of the Father	Percentage, Physicians	Percentage, Dentists	Excess of Actual Ratio over expec- tation
Professional	31.1	23.9	27.71
Proprietor	13.3	8.7	10.0
Clerical	16.7	17.4	15.0
Skilled	10.0	6.5	3.11
Farm Owners	5.6	19.6	.28
Semi-Skilled	1.1	4.3	.99
Protective Service	—	—	1.11
Service Workers	16.7	15.2	2.02
Farm Laborers	4.4	4.3	.11

SOURCE: Franklin Edwards, *The Negro Professional Class* (Glencoe: The Free Press, 1959), p. 50.

have been hotel managers; pullman porters who could have easily operated as conductors, or even as division superintendents; bank porters who might well have been a cashier or even the bank president himself, had it not been for their color.

Education

The education of the Negro professional in medicine began in the home; most frequently, it was a middle-class home, and almost always a literate one; many of the fathers, with jobs classified as "lower" occupations had been sentenced by the caste system in which they lived to serve out their lives in capacities below their real skills and abilities. The very few Negro doctors from illiterate homes received uncommon instruction in good habits and were no doubt highly motivated, permitting them to override the handicaps of illiterate surroundings.

Up to the end of World War I, it was more than likely that the Negro doctor had received his elementary and high school education in one of the excellent mission schools sprinkled throughout the South; there were few publicly supported secondary schools and scarcely any excellent public schools of any description. Before 1915, he had occasionally attended a Northern medical school; more probably, he received his medical education in one of the five medical schools in the South: the Leonard Medical School of Shaw University, Raleigh, North Carolina; the Meharry Medical College of Walden University, Nashville, Tennessee; the West Tennessee Medical College at Memphis, Tennessee; the Flint-Goodridge Medical School of New Orleans University, New Orleans, Louisiana, and the Howard University Medical School, Washington, D.C. The schools at Raleigh, Memphis and New Orleans were among the numerous American medical schools obliged to go out of business following the publication in 1910 of Abraham Flexner's study of medical education.[25] Flexner had a good word for the Leonard School, commenting on the "aseptic cleanliness" of its laboratories and hospital, that he found unusual among the medical schools he studied; but he concluded that Leonard, and the other schools later discontinued, did not have the staff or resources necessary to give an adequate medical education.

For college study the prospective Negro medical or dental student favored such institutions as Howard University, Lincoln University, Morehouse College, and Fisk University. Up to 1930 these institutions furnished the undergraduate education of well over 70 percent of all Negro physicians and dentists. Together they still account for upwards of 20 percent of entering Negro medical students.

During and after World War I, the number of Negroes—never considerable—attending Northern medical schools was further reduced by the adoption of racial and religious quota systems. Howard and Meharry became the professional schools where the vast majority of Negro physicians and dentists were trained. This situation began to be altered after 1947, as private philanthropy and fair educational practices laws in Northern states combined to break down racially discriminatory admission practices. Litigation in the South opened most of the formerly all-white medical schools to Negro students. It is now (1965) reported that only six out of eighty medical schools in the United States refuse to accept Negroes; twenty-six of the open schools are in the South. By 1955–56 there were 236 Negro students attending forty-eight predominantly white medical schools, and 525 attending the two predominantly Negro medical schools.

But by 1961–62, only 154 Negro students were attending predominantly white medical schools, a 35 percent decrease since 1955–56. One result is that the proportion of Negroes in the medical and dental professions, 2.1 percent in 1960, is likely to show a continuing decrease.

The reasons for this decline vary. The opening up of other professions that require a much less arduous and extended course of preparation is one reason. At the same time, it is possible that medicine and dentistry no longer have their old prestige in the Negro community. The constantly increasing expense of medical studies is another factor, although scholarship and fellowship funds for medical aspirants are now substantial, in both size and number. The more rigid criteria for admission to medical schools

[25] Abraham Flexner, *Medical Education in the United States and Canada* (A Report to the Carnegie Foundation for the Advancement of Teaching. New York: Published by the Foundation, 1910).

reveals, it is said, decreasing numbers of Negro applicants able to meet highly competitive standards.

Increasingly, admission to medical and other professional studies is determined by the candidate's performance on standardized tests believed to measure "aptitude." In competition with white students, Negro applicants are likely to score poorly on such tests, whether the opportunity sought is a job on an assembly line, as a telephone operator, teacher, or for admission to a medical, law or graduate school. It is almost a rule of test-expectation that a given Negro population in a given locality will almost invariably test at a median point below that of the white population.

Scores in the medical college aptitude test made by 1,123 applicants enrolled in college who were applying for admission to medical schools in 1955–56 reveal a pattern that is characteristic of any Negro group compared to a similarly situated white group on any level. With five hundred considered the median score of a normal distribution, only 11.4 percent of the Negro students attained such a score in the verbal section of the test; only 7.6 percent in the quantitative section; only 9.2 percent in the modern society section; and only 10.9 percent in the science section (see Table VI.)

TABLE VI—The Percentage Distribution in Score Intervals of Students from Selected Negro Colleges in the Medical College Aptitude Test

Test Section	Score Intervals and Percentages					
	200–299	300–399	400–499	500–599	600–699	700–799
Verbal	12.5	45.1	31.0	9.5	1.9	0.0
Quantitative	16.4	46.5	29.5	7.2	0.4	0.0
Modern Society	12.9	48.6	29.2	7.6	1.6	0.1
Science	59.9	45.6	34.0	9.7	1.2	0.0
Normal Distribution of all applicants	2.0	14.0	34.0	34.0	14.0	2.0

SOURCE: Dietrich C. Reitzes, *Negros and Medicine*, (Cambridge, Mass. Harvard University Press, 1958), p. 16.

A number of persons have argued, and with determined passion, that these statistics incontestably establish the basic and unalterable inferiority of the Negro. A very zealot in the cause, Carleton Putnam, recently (June 4, 1964) published a full-page advertisement in the Baltimore *Sun*, "proving" Negro inferiority by recourse to such assorted bits of "evidence" in evolutionary appearance: smaller brain size in Negroes; less "relative fissuration (sulcification)" of the brain; "relative thickness of the supergranular

layer of the cortex in whites and Negroes"; "relative kinesthetic matura-
tion rates of White and Negro infants"; "differences in the electrical
physiology of White and Negro brains." Putnam's admired coadjutant in
establishing a scientific basis for Negro inferiority, Audrey Shuey, published
a book in which hundreds of studies of the comparative "intelligence" of
whites and Negroes gave unanimous testimony that Negroes make lower
scores than whites in the same locality.[26]

Such conclusions regarding "intelligence," based as they are on fossils
three hundred thousand years old; on the so-called interpretation of the
neurological examinations that have not advanced scientific knowledge
even to the threshold of understanding the complex mechanisms of the
human brain; and on studies of the "electrical physiology" of the brain,
may be left for what they are: pseudoscientific gibberish.

Test results, contrary to what a Putnam may believe, are a different
matter. Nothing is now better known to psychometrists than that test
results faithfully follow social and economic class, up and down, regardless
of race. We have long known, likewise, that test results follow geographical
patterns. In the World War I Alpha tests, racial explanations of difference
were popular until it was noted that white soldiers from the North made
much higher scores than white soldiers from the South; and indeed, that the
Negro soldiers in the North tended to score higher than white soldiers
from various Southern states. In the published lists of college test scores
from 1928–36, that appeared in the *Educational Record,* white Southern
collegians scored far below those whose scores were reported from Northern
colleges.

The Status of the Negro Medical Professional [27]

The physician and dentist have frequently been the most prestigious
members of the professional group in the Negro community. They enjoyed
the usual respect accorded to the skilled and wise miracle worker who
triumphs over pain, and frequently over death itself. Almost invariably the
best educated man in the community, tradition and current circumstance
required them to be leaders and spokesmen in local and national affairs.

[26] The Baltimore *Sun,* June 11, 1964. See also, Carleton Putnam, *Race and Reason:
A Yankee View* (Washington, D.C.: Public Affairs Press, 1961). See also, Audrey
Shuey, *The Testing of Negro Intelligence* (Lynchburg, Va.: Bell Publishing Co., 1958).

[27] A principal source of this section has been a "colloquy" among John P. Davis and
Dr. W. Montague Cobb, President of the National Medical Association, Professor of
anatomy at the Howard University Medical School, and a perceptive student of the
Negro in medicine; Dr. Thomas R. Payton, of Los Angeles; Dr. Kenneth W. Clement,
of Cleveland, President of the NMA; R. E. Stanley Grannum, of Newport News;
Dr. Arthur H. Coleman, of San Francisco; Dr. William H. Mile, of Staten Island; and
Dr. Arthur W. Pleasants, of Lexington, Virginia.

James McCune Smith and Martin R. Delany, who gave most of their effort to racial causes, were forerunners of a host that followed.

These professionals were also likely to be the most affluent in the community; their fine houses, automobiles and general way of life were as much a comment on the expectations of their public, as examples of conspicuous display. The overwhelmingly popular career choice of ambitious high school boys was to become a doctor. To attain his heart's desire required more than ordinary sacrifice and devotion. Sons though they might have been of a "professional" minister or teacher, few could count on family support for the long period of study required. The Negro medical graduate of a generation ago had worked as bellboy, waiter, pullman porter or day laborer, through college and professional school as well; he was a man acquainted with the problems of the man lowest down, for he had been one of them himself. He was admirably schooled to work for and with all manner of men; the ardors of his professional education made him almost certainly a well disciplined man, possessing the human experience helpful to form leaders as well as physicians.

Occasionally the Negro physician has shared criticism generally levelled at the professionals of the race, which implies that they are indifferent to the responsibilities they owe their people. Frazier, writing in a critical vein, has said:

> The standards which they (i.e., the criminal and underworld elements) set are emulated by Negroes in the professional classes—doctors, dentists, and lawyers, and even teachers as far as they are able to do so. . . . an expensive automobile, a "palatial" residence, and a yacht bring more recognition to a doctor than some achievement in medicine.[28]

This comment is scarcely fair. The mere affluence of a relatively high-income group in a generally depressed population has been enough to cause cries of extravagence, because the possession of ordinary middle-class status symbols is an extraordinary and highly visible exception to the general rule of life in the community. Few general practitioners—which most Negro physicians are—ever have the opportunity to record some spectacular "achievement in medicine"; the pride with which the Negro public acclaims the achievements of their medical heroes, even in small communities in response to the special skill of some otherwise unknown family doctor, is a part of the legend of the Negro physician.

Certainly this period of the "Negro revolution" has dissipated the picture of the Negro physician and dentist as an uncaring exploiter of his people;

[28] E. Franklin Frazier, The Black Bourgeoisie (New York: Collier Books paperback edition, 1962), p. 110.

these men have helped give leadership in their local communities during times of crisis in the long tradition of their profession. Emancipated from economic reprisal by the nature of their profession, they have, indeed, been able to lead and to initiate community civil rights activities in a degree impossible for other Negro professionals. They have themselves initiated action leading to the breaking down of bars of segregation in hospital and medical practices, restrictions that severely limited both their own practices and their provision of optimum medical care to the Negro community.

Although the Negro physician and dentist seem to be declining in both number and proportion as a part of the total American medical profession, and while the place they have long held at the prestige summit now appears threatened, they still occupy a favored status within the Negro group. After five years of practice, he may expect to be earning from twenty to thirty thousand dollars a year. His professional expenses are heavy; to earn his money, he must work extremely hard. His practice is with a low-income group; a common complaint of Negro practitioners is that white physicians, aided by superior access to hospital facilities, compete successfully with Negro physicians for the middle-class Negro patients who are able to pay substantial fees. There are Negro physicians and dentists who have done very well financially; but this success comes usually from using the small capital acquired in practice as investment in enterprises not associated with medicine.

The world in which the Negro physician must practice is changing so rapidly that any contemporary description is in danger of becoming outdated history between time of writing and time of publication. As noted above, restriction by race of admission to the great majority of American medical schools no longer constitutes a problem; the new problem is to find enough qualified Negro youth to present themselves as applicants for admission. The inability of Negro physicians to gain places on hospital staffs and the consequent "loss of their patients at the hospital door" promises to disappear, with the 1964 decision of the United States Supreme Court affecting federally aided hospitals in a case carried up from Greensboro, North Carolina. Not long ago Negro physicians could not be considered for certification as "specialists," because some of the accrediting boards had racially restrictive clauses in their constitutions. Now more than 10 percent of Negro physicians hold diplomas from various boards, and the number is growing rapidly.

Negro physicians and surgeons, who comprise only 2.0 percent of the profession in America, are outranked by Negro social welfare workers, with 10.7 percent of the total membership in their class; by teachers, with 7.8 percent, and college teachers, with 3.0 percent. The reason is that a system of segregation has created a "captive" group of the practitioners of the other professions. With his small numbers and proportions, it would be impossible for the limited number of Negro medical professionals to provide medical service for all Negroes. Yet there is justification in their noting with dismay that white practitioners have barred their Negro fellows from professionally stimulating and enriching associations and hospital facilities, while vigorously cultivating the patronage of Negroes. Lack of confidence in Negro physicians, especially when manifested by higher-income, middle-class Negroes, is a sore trial for the Negro practitioner. He knows his qualifications and experience are eminently satisfactory, and knows also that the services he is prepared to provide are offered with no taint of condescension or actual discrimination.

Opinion varies as to whether the status of the Negro physician and dentist is threatened by the growing provision of free clinical and hospital care for low-income people. Many doubt it; and, in fact, the National Medical Association is the only organized group of American physicians to adopt a resolution favoring the adoption of the Medicare program. A number of Negro physicians have taken advantage of the trend toward the practice of cooperative medicine; their handsome joint enterprises in a number of cities keep abreast of one of the major trends in medicine.

Reference has been made elsewhere to some of the genuinely noteworthy contributions made to the science of medicine by Negroes. Although limited now in number, and prospectively even more limited in the future, the current high standards of selection and education and the enlarged opportunities for growth and specialization insure a growing contribution by Negroes to the medical and dental professions.

THE NEGRO LAWYER [29]

Social Origins

As noted above, the Negro scholar and physician may have come from circumstances "humble" by comparison to the affluent in white American society; but he came from the upper ranks of his own Negro society. His greatest advantage was that he came from a more than ordinarily disciplined and stable family, and from one that was literate, as well.

[29] Among the distinguished panel of Negro lawyers who contributed data on the status of the Negro lawyer were: William R. Ming, of McCoy, Ming and Leighton, Chicago; Sidney R. Redmond, St. Louis; Arthur D. Shores, Birmingham, and U. Simpson Tate, Wewoka, Oklahoma.

So was it with the Negro lawyer. While Woodson did not group his lawyer's fathers by the conventional social or economic classifications used today, he reports that 6.8 percent of his sample were the children of lawyers, an extraordinary percentage considering how few Negro lawyers there were in the previous generation. In the sample, children of ministers comprised 9.9 percent of the lawyers; children of teachers, 3.1 percent; of government clerks, 2.5 percent; one-half of one percent were children of each of the following: clerks, accountants, insurance agents, undertakers, dentists, educators (in addition to teachers), physicians, Federal functionaries, grocers, livery-stable keepers, auditors, managers, mail carriers, authors, engravers, pharmacists and police officers. Thus a quarter of the Woodson sample in 1934 came from professional paternal occupations, and a large additional number were the children of proprietors, managers, other "white collar" occupations, and skilled trades requiring literacy for their execution.[30]

A more recent study by Edwards [31] indicates that Negro lawyers indeed are more likely to have a "white collar" grandparental and parental background than any other professional group among Negroes: 63.2 percent of the lawyers reported "white collar" fathers, as compared to 61.1 percent for physicians, 58.6 percent for teachers and 50.0 percent for dentists. If we add the percentages from backgrounds of skilled workers (8.8), farm owners (5.9), and the usually "underemployed" among the semiskilled (14.7) and service workers (2.9), it is clear that the Negro lawyer of the last two generations is the product of families with high literacy and relatively high occupational status.

The story of relatively advantaged homes among free Negroes prior to the Civil War was as true for the lawyer as for other early Negro professionals. Malcolm B. Allen, who was admitted to the Maine Bar in 1844 and as far as it is now known was the first Negro lawyer, actually came from South Carolina "free colored" background; during Reconstruction he returned to Charleston where he was admitted to the South Carolina bar; and in 1873 elected a judge of one of the lower courts in Charleston. John Mercer Langston graduated from Oberlin College in 1849, and after "reading law" in a lawyer's office, was admitted to the Ohio bar in 1850. Langston's father was a wealthy planter in Virginia who saw to it that each of his four children by a Negro woman, whom he emancipated and to whom he bequeathed a large estate, received a good education; the three sons all attended Oberlin College.

[30] Woodson, *op. cit.*, p. 185.
[31] Edwards, *op. cit.*, p. 50.

Education

Law was one of the last professions to emerge from the "apprenticeship" system of preparation; American Universities began to inaugurate special departments for the study of the profession only toward the middle of the nineteenth century. A number of the mission colleges established in the South immediately after the Civil War established law departments. One of these institutions was Howard University; its law school was established in 1871 and has had a distinguished history since. Lincoln University in Pennsylvania had a short-lived law school; established in 1869, it closed in 1874. The Central Tennessee College (later Walden University) in Nashville had a law school. Other law schools were located at Shaw University, Raleigh, North Carolina, and at Straight University, New Orleans, Louisiana. Straight's law school was unique in that it flourished with an interracial enrollment, principally white, until 1886, when the all-white Tulane University of Louisiana opened its law school. Straight University received its charter in 1869, sponsored by the Negro politicians Lieutenant Governor Oscar Dunn and P. B. S. Pinchback. Under that charter, Straight's law school had the rare right to qualify any graduate to whom its diploma was given for immediate admission to the Louisiana Bar.

No profession is as closely related to politics as the practice of the law; the disfranchisement of the Negro throughout the South and the subsequent denigration of the Negro's stature in public life sharply curtailed opportunities for the entry of Negroes into the legal profession in the section.

Negroes have been admitted to law schools in the North for generations. It is an irony that Donald A. Murray, whose successful 1935 case to gain admission to the University of Maryland Law School became a "landmark" court decision on the road to the 1954 school desegregation cases, was preceded as a student and graduate of the Maryland school by Harry S. Cummings, of the Lincoln University class of 1886. Cummings graduated from the Maryland Law School in 1889, and thereafter pursued a successful legal and political career in Baltimore.

The Status of the Negro Lawyer

The organization of Negro lawyers, the National Bar Association, states that it represents 4,000 lawyers. According to the 1960 United States Census, there were employed as lawyers and judges in that year, 2,004 Negro males, and 176 Negro females, for a total of 2,180. The nature of the profession is such that a considerable number of persons may be qualified to practice, but be employed and classified in other occupational categories. In his 1934 study, Woodson complained that the 1930 United States Census enumeration of Negro lawyers was a gross underestimation; there may well be even now as many, or more, Negroes practicing law, than medicine.

The disfranchisement of Negroes that followed upon the ending of the Reconstruction period, in the 1880's and 1890's, almost completely extinguished the prospects for a Negro lawyer in the South. In the North, there were occasional examples of highly successful Negro lawyers, such as Edward H. Morris in Chicago, who regularly represented both white and Negro clients in a wide range of litigation; and William H. Lewis of Boston —Harvard Law School graduate and former "All American" football player— who had an outstanding legal career in Massachusetts. The field for Negro lawyers has been extended by the migration of Negroes to the North, by the growing participation in politics of Southern Negroes, and by the spectacular broadening of Civil Rights litigation in Southern states in recent years.

The 2,004 Negro males reported by the 1960 Census as employed as lawyers represented only 0.95 percent of all males so employed in the United States in 1960; interestingly enough, the 176 Negro female lawyers and judges showed the higher percentage, of all female lawyers, of 2.36 percent. Negro lawyers and judges of both sexes were 1.02 percent of the total employed in this profession in 1960. It has been said, that in 1963, "of the Nation's 8,000 judges over 75 are Negro and are presently elected and appointed in the Federal and State courts." [32] According to this estimate, Negroes are about one percent of the judiciary, the same percentage they are of employed lawyers in the United States.

The status of the Negro lawyer can be appreciated only when he is viewed in the context of the organization of the profession in the United States. David Riesman has declared:

> Lawyers and how they act interest me. Lawyers bend the system they enter and are bent by it; some stay, and others leave, carrying their bent with them. Hopefully, one can begin to understand the law through the men, as well as vice versa.[33]

Jack Ladinsky separates lawyers into two major classes: [34] the "independents," who are 80 percent of all lawyers, and the "dependents." The

[32] Edward B. Toles, "The American Negro Lawyer, 1844–1963." the *Chicago Daily Defender*, August 5, 1963, as reprinted in the *Congressional Record*, October 2, 1963 pp. A. 6205–A–6206. Extension of remarks by Hon. Barrett O'Hara.

[33] David Riesman, "Law and Sociology: Recruitment, Training, and Colleagueship." *Stanford Law Review*, 9 (July, 1957), pp. 669–70.

[34] Jack Ladinsky, "Careers of Lawyers, Law Practice and Legal Institutions." *American Sociological Review*, 28 (February, 1963), pp. 47–54.

first class may be subdivided into the "solo" (individual practitioners) and the "firm" groups; it is estimated that the "solo" subgroup includes two-thirds of all lawyers. The "dependents" comprise "house counsel"—the salaried lawyer—and "Government counsel."

Ladinsky's research reveals wide divisions between the solo and firm lawyers by social origin, education and type of practice. The solo lawyer is likely to stem from some minority, ethnic or religious group; the firm lawyer, from the upper middle class possessing the dominant prestige attributes of his community.[35]

The education of the two groups differs. Only 14 percent of the solo lawyers come from such nationally known law schools as Chicago, Columbia, Harvard, Michigan and Yale, while 72.9 percent of the firm lawyers come from such schools. Large law firms are likely to seek new associates who have a high occupational family background; who have business and corporate contacts. They go to the national law schools to find such persons; the practice they are to engage in stresses business and corporate litigation. The solo lawyer, on the other hand, is likely to be confined to the "dirty work" of the legal profession: criminal work, collections, personal injury, divorce, and title searching.

The scanty evidence available would suggest that in terms of comparative social and educational background, the Negro lawyer may have come from a higher background level than the typical white American solo practitioner. Likewise, the ambition generated in a college-level family has apparently sent him more frequently to the national legal-training institutions than has been the case with his white solo contemporaries. An additional factor is the total lack of legal education available to Negroes in the South from 1887 to 1935. This lack led a number of Negroes to leave the South for their legal education and to choose the best schools available in the North.

Reports varied when the panel was asked to comment on the special difficulties in practice before the bar likely to be encountered by the Negro lawyer. A successful lawyer in Birmingham, Alabama, stated that there are few difficulties facing Negro practitioners; they have access to law libraries and court files; they frequently gain the confidence of Negro clients, whether lower class or middle class; the Negro firm gets a good share of any Negro corporate business. The principal difficulty "is the trial of jury cases, especially in negligence and damage suits," where the practice is to associate specialist [white] negligence lawyers with prosecution of the case.

One respondent reported a reasonable income from a practice voluntarily restricted in a small Oklahoma city, and enumerated a number of other Southwestern cities where he believed one or more Negro lawyers would

[35] Ladinsky, *loc. cit.*

do well. A member of a successful Chicago firm stated that there is a "deep-seated feeling on the part of both Negroes and whites that a white lawyer can obtain better consideration for them from courts, administrative agencies, and government than a Negro lawyer can."

Another commentator—from St. Louis—states that Negro lawyers get "the crumbs of litigation;" and this is due to the advance of what Ladinsky calls the increasing "bureaucratization" of the law, and what Riesman identifies as the growing fate of the "sole" lawyer of any race. Ladinsky says:

> Lay organizations in metropolitan areas have successfully taken over the title and abstract, collections and trust work. Accounting firms have taken over a great deal of tax work; automobile clubs, insurance and real estate companies, banks, and savings and loan associations have, each in their own way, made inroads upon spheres where solo practitioners customarily plied their trade.[36]

And David Riesman says: "The big firms are insulated from this 'intellectual slum.' "

The Negro lawyer is no exception; if his client has an automobile accident, the white insurance company's lawyer steps in; if he dies, leaving an estate, the white lawyer for the white bank steps in. The "crumbs of litigation, may provide him with an above average income; but, compared to the corporate business of his white "firm" fellow-professional, he is indeed the dweller in an intellectual slum, gazing from afar at the lush pastures of the affluent.

Yet the Negro lawyer makes progress. In the Civil Rights field, where the Southern white lawyer could not usually offend the sensibilities of his section by taking cases in this field, the Negro lawyer has developed in recent years an ingenuity and skill not hitherto known in the United States. And here it is appropriate to mention that brilliant mind, Charles Hamilton Houston—son of a Howard University Law School professor, graduate of Dunbar High School in Washington, D.C., Phi Beta Kappa graduate from Amherst College, and Harvard University Law School LL.B. and J.D. It was Houston who, as an instructor, vice dean and dean of the Howard University Law School, inaugurated those special educational procedures in legal training that produced the techniques on which the entire Civil Rights offensive has been waged; and the men, like Thurgood Marshall and Robert Carter, who had the ability and the knowledge to wage it.

The changing times promise much for Negro lawyers. Few lawyers may expect in the near future to attain the status of the firm of McCoy, Ming and Leighton in Chicago; among its other distinctions, the firm has one of

` [36] Ladinsky, *op. cit.*, p. 54.

its members on the faculty of the University of Chicago Law School, and a practice that includes such clients as Commonweath Edison Company. But the assimilation of the Negro into the total body public means peripheral benefits from the profession of the law; as St. Louis Attorney Sidney R. Redmond states, "he is getting numerous appointments in city and legal offices that were not dreamed of fifteen years ago. They are trying cases weekly if not daily and should develop into great trial lawyers." [37]

And, even in their "intellectual slum," along with other "solo" lawyers, they are on a firing-line the "firm" lawyers does not deign to occupy; that is, facing the plight of the poor Negro and white litigant in either civil or criminal cases, North or South. As recent legislation suggests, this may be the focus of the next great development in the practice of American law.

THE NEGRO IN ENGINEERING [38]

As is shown in the summary, Table III above, the 1960 Census reports 3,378 male Negro engineers—constituting four-tenths of one percent of all employed engineers in the United States.

Engineering is a relatively new profession among American Negroes; the principal training school for this professional group has been the School of Engineering of Howard University, that graduated its first baccalaureates in the field in 1910. Since that time, the school has granted 987 degrees as follows:

B. S. in Civil Engineering	218
B. S. in Electrical Engineering	367
B. S. in Mechanical Engineering	203
B. S. in Architecture	199
Total	987

Negroes have studied Engineering at some of the leading technological institutions in this country. Recently several predominantly Negro engineering schools have been initiated in the South; at the North Carolina Agricultural and Technical College at Greensboro, at the Tennessee State Agricultural and Mechanical University at Nashville, at the Tuskegee Institute in Alabama and at the Prairie View A & M College in Texas.

[37] In correspondence with the Phelps-Stokes Fund.
[38] Data for the Howard University School of Engineering was supplied by Colonel J. A. Robinson, Assistant to the Dean, Howard University School of Engineering and Architecture.

None of the predominantly Negro institutions has the facilities to conduct engineering education over the broad scope presented by modern technology. It is encouraging to note the admission, within the last three years, of Negroes to Southern engineering schools; notably, to the Georgia School of Technology; and to South Carolina's Clemson University.

In no profession is an excellent grounding in the fundamentals of science more requisite than in engineering. The provision of a larger supply of Negro candidates for engineering careers must depend on a revolutionary improvement of elementary and secondary educational facilities for Negroes all over the country.

BIBLIOGRAPHY

Books:

Bardolph, Richard, *The Negro Vanguard.* New York: Rinehart & Company, Inc., 1959. Thumbnail biographies of outstanding people arranged chronologically. The accounts are woven into a continuous fabric from the times of Jupiter Hammond and Phyllis Wheatley to the present.

Brawley, Benjamin, *The Negro Genius: A New Appraisal of the Achievements of the American Negro in Literature and the Fine Arts.* New York: Dodd, Mead & Company, 1937. Long out of print accounts of the lives of Negro leaders in literature and the fine arts. Some scholars are included.

—— *A Social History of the American Negro.* New York: The Macmillan Co., 1921. After more than forty years, this book yet contains one of the best available accounts of eighteenth- and nineteenth-century Negro affairs.

Brown, William Wells, *The Rising Son: Or, The Antecedents and Advancement of the Colored Race.* Boston: A. G. Brown & Co., 1874. Although long out of print, this is a valuable reference work for biographical sketches that convey the flavor of the times.

Edwards, G. Franklin, *The Negro Professional Class.* Glencoe: The Free Press, 1959. This is one of the few studies of the Negro of any class that applies statistical analysis to parental and grandparental backgrounds.

Haynes, Elizabeth Ross, *Unsung Heroes.* New York: Du Bois and Dill, 1921. Intended for a juvenile audience, this early example of Negro biography is useful.

Hughes, Langston, and Meltzer, Milton, *A Pictorial History of the Negro in America.* New York: Crown Publishers, 1956. Many of the early Negro professionals and scholars are to be found here, as well as those of more recent vintage.

Johnson, Charles S., *The Negro College Graduate*. Chapel Hill: The University of North Carolina Press, 1938. This study has separate sections to review the status of the college graduates who chose to enter professions. The historical accounts of the various professions are told well and briefly; the statistical material in the book is extremely useful.

Woodson, Carter G., *The Negro Professional Man and the Community, with Special Emphasis on the Physician and Lawyer*. Washington: The Associated Publishers, 1934. The book contains useful statistics and comments on the 1934 setting and the place of the Negro professional.

Woodson, Carter G., and Wesley, Charles H., *The Negro in Our History*. Revised and enlarged edition. Washington, D.C.: The Associated Publishers, Inc., 1962. This standard work is greatly improved by the additions supplied by the eminent historian, Dr. Charles H. Wesley.

Biographical Dictionaries:

American Men of Science. Cattell, Jacques, ed. 10th edition. Tempe, Arizona: Arizona State University Press, 1962. This dictionary has grown over the years to its present size, in which five volumes are needed to carry its 120,000 biographies. Preceding editions are of course indispensable in a historical study. The 1952 *Negro Year Book* carries a list of Negroes whose biographies appeared in the eighth edition.

Dictionary of American Biography. Johnson, Allen, and Malone, Dumas, eds. New York: Charles Scribner's Sons, 1930. The DAB gives some help to the student studying Negro scholars.

Simmons, William J., *Men of Mark, Eminent, Progressive, and Rising. With an Introductory Sketch of the Author* by Rev. H. M. Turner. Cleveland, Ohio: G. M. Rowell & Company, 1887. This is one of the places, where biographies of many of the early Negro scholars—including the members of the American Negro Academy—may be found.

Mather, Frank Lincoln, *Who's Who in the Colored Race; a General Biographical Dictionary of Men and Women of African Descent*. Chicago: By the author, 1912. Mather's book is the only source of specific biographical dates for Negro notables between Simmons' *Men of Mark* and the *Who's Who* volumes that began to appear in the 1920's.

Who's Who in Colored America. Fleming, G. James, and Burckel, Christian E., eds. Seven editions: 1927, 1928, 1930, 1933, 1938, 1941, 1950. Yonkers-on-Hudson: Christian E. Burckel and Associates, 10th ed., 1950. The successive volumes of this series are invaluable in studying the Negro professional and scholar.

Journals:

The Journal of Negro History. A quarterly journal. Washington: The Association for the Study of Negro Life and History. The files contain numerous articles on Negro professionals and scholars.

Negro History Bulletin. Published several times a year, by the Association for the Study of Negro Life and History. One continuing feature over the years has been a series of family histories that help illuminate the history of the Negro professional class.

General Works:

The Negro Year Book: Guzman, Jessie P., ed., Jones, Lewis Wade, assoc. ed. 11th Edition. Department of Records and Research, Tuskegee Institute, Alabama. New York: Wm. H. Wise & Co., Inc., 1952. This last published edition of the *Yearbook,* and its predecessors, contain useful data on the Negro scholar and professional.

chapter 15

The Negro in the Armed Forces of America

John P. Davis

THE COLONIAL PERIOD

Colonel Tyng's Negro

The entry read: "7th, 25th, 1689. A liste of the men that was slane in a fite at ffalmoth & all soe how many was wounded in said fight.

An Indian
An Naygro of Colo. Tyng." [1]

This is, perhaps, the earliest record of a Negro casualty on the North American continent. We do not know his name or whether he was killed or wounded. We know simply that he was a Negro and a slave.

Thirty-five years later another record of the Massachusetts Bay Colony provides a more complete bit of evidence:

An Account of the Dead, Dismist, killed and taken belonging to his Maj'ties Service from December ye 25th 1724, to April ye 24th, 1725.

Dead..Primus, Negroe.[2]

In the Colonial Militias

It is not surprising to find Negroes among those who served as defenders of early American settlements. Manpower was limited and dangers from the enemy in the newly settled wilderness were great. Each able-bodied male had to do his duty.

[1] Massachusetts Manuscript Archives. Volume 35 p. 15. Quoted in *The Negro in the Military Service of the United States* (A Compilation of Official Records, State Papers, Historical Extracts etc. relating to his military status and service from the date of his introduction into the British North American Colonies) Vol. I. p. 48. This compilation was prepared under the direction of Brigadier General Richard C. Drum, Adjutant General United States Army, by Elon A. Woodward, Chief of the Colored Troops Division, Adjutant General's Office, Washington, D.C. National Archives. 1888. 8 Volumes. Record Group 94. Available in microfilm: National Archives Microfilm T–823. Will be hereafter referred to as "Colored Troops Division."

[2] Massachusetts, *Ibid.* Vol. 72 p. 226. Colored Troops Division. *Ibid.* Vol. I p. 49.

The Dutch in New Amsterdam armed their Negro slaves with half-pikes and tomahawks to help them repel Indian attacks. Negro slaves were first landed in the Massachusetts Bay Colony in 1638. Five years later men called upon to bear arms and fight Indians included Abraham Pearse, described as "a blackamore." [3] In Massachusetts, in 1652, "Negroes, Indians and Scotchmen" were alike, by law, obliged to train for the militia. [4]

Colonial authorities vacillated in their position on permitting Negroes to serve in the militia. Some feared that to arm the slaves was to invite slave revolts. Others feared uprisings of hostile Indians more and felt the need for total mobilization of all available males against the enemy. Virginia, Rhode Island and Providence Plantation, New Hampshire and Connecticut exempted Negroes and Indians from militia training. South Carolina recognized that it might be "necessary for the safety of the Colony in case of actual invasion to have the assistance of our trusty slaves." [5] The general assembly of the province enacted a law that provided that if a slave "kill or take one or more of our enemies . . . he shall be free and his master paid fair value." Both Negroes and whites fought in the South Carolina militia under Governor Craven against Yamassee and Tuscarora Indians in the early eighteenth century.

In 1723, Virginia, while not rescinding its prohibition of the recruitment of Negroes into its colonial militia, provided that:

> . . . such free negroes, mulattoes, or Indians as are capable may be listed and employed as drummers or trumpeters: and that upon invasion, insurrection or rebellion all free negroes, mullatoes, or Indians shall be obliged to attend and march with the militia and to do the duty of pioneers or such other servile labor as they shall be directed to perform. [6]

Service in the French and Indian Wars

As the French and Indian Wars (1689–1763) drained away growing numbers of able-bodied white males, Negro free men and slaves became increasingly important to the defense of the colonies. Barzillai Lew, a six-foot tall Negro cooper from Chelmsford, Massachusetts, who was later to dis-

[3] Laura Wilkes, *Missing Pages in History* (Washington, D.C., Press of R. L. Pendleton, 1919), p. 1.

[4] Colored Troops Division, *op. cit.* Vol. I, p. 9. The Scotsmen were the captives of Oliver Cromwell, taken in the battle of Dunbar (1650) and transported across the ocean in punishment as indentured servants.

[5] Statutes at Large, December 23, 1703, General Assembly of the Province of South Carolina.

[6] Act of the Virginia General Assembly, May 9, 1723. Hennings, Statutes of Virginia, Vol. 4, pp. 118, 119.

tinguish himself at Bunker's Hill and Ticonderoga, appeared on the muster roll of Captain Thomas Farrington's company in 1760. There were others who enlisted as soldier-equals with white volunteers.

An act of the general assembly of the province of New Jersey, meeting at Perth Amboy in 1746, authorized John Hamilton, president of the general council and commander in chief of its militia, to raise a force of "five hundred Freemen or native well affected Indians" for service in Canada against the French and to offer each volunteer "six pounds proclamation money over and above his Majesty's pay." [7]

The following year the general assembly of South Carolina, acknowledging that in time of war the Negro slaves had "behaved themselves with great faithfulness and courage in repelling attacks of his Majesty's enemies," provided that slaves might be enlisted into the militia "up to one-third of the white men in a company" and not to exceed one-half of all the ablebodied slaves from sixteen to sixty. The slaves were to be incorporated into respective companies in which they were enlisted and "in time of general alarm and actual invasion of this Province *and not otherwise* [italics added] were to be armed with:

a] One sufficient gun
b] One hatchet
c] Powder horn and shot pouch with ammunition of powder and bullets for twenty rounds and six spare flints. [8]

THE WAR FOR AMERICAN INDEPENDENCE

The Revolutionary War

In Boston on March 8, 1770, to the solemn peal of church bells "a numerous train of persons of all ranks" followed slowly behind the coffins of four Americans who had been slain by British redcoats three days before

[7] Colored Troops Division, Vol. I, *op. cit.*, p. 35, quoting from Nevill's *Acts of New Jersey* Vol. I, page 314, 316.

[8] *Ibid.*, Vol. I, p. 36. Masters of slaves who were maimed or killed were to be reimbursed; and maimed slaves were promised a payment of twelve pounds a year if single, eighteen pounds if married. The slave who killed or captured an enemy went free. The slave who fought well but had not the good fortune to kill an enemy soldier was nevertheless to "receive from the public treasury every year a livery coat and a pair of breeches made of good red negro cloth [sic], turned up with blue, and a black hat and a pair of black shoes, and shall that day in every year during their lives . . . be freed and exempted from all personal service to their owner." Quoted from Statutes at Large. South Carolina. Published in 1841, Vol. 9, pp. 645, 658–663.

in an act of violence which was to lead to the American Revolution. One of these—and the first to die—was Crispus Attucks, a Negro runaway slave turned seaman.

From the death of Attucks to the end of the Revolutionary War, Negro free men and slaves were deeply committed to the struggle for American independence. Negro militiamen were among the group of Minutemen who responded to the alarm raised by Paul Revere and barred the march of the British Grenadiers on Lexington and Concord on April 19, 1775. Lemuel Haynes, Peter Salem, Barzillai Lew and Prince Estabrook are the names of some of these. Weeks later Haynes and Lew were—with other Negroes— members of a small group under the command of Ethan Allen which captured Fort Ticonderoga. In mid-June of that year Negro soldiers behaved with conspicuous bravery at the battle of Bunker's Hill. Salem Poor was commended by the General Court of Massachusetts as "a brave and gallant soldier" upon the petition of fourteen commissioned and noncommissioned officers who fought with him. Peter Salem's presence at Bunker's Hill was recorded in the famous painting of the battle by the contemporary painter, John Trumbull, a former aide-de-camp of General George Washington. The fact that Trumbull depicted Salem pointing his rifle straight at British Major Pitcairn has led many historians, whether erroneously or not, to credit Salem with Pitcairn's death.

No Stroller, Negro or Vagabond

Appointed by the Second Continental Congress in Philadelphia to command "all the continental forces," General Washington assumed command in Cambridge, Massachusetts, July 3, 1775. A week later his Adjutant General, Horatio Gates, issued the following order to recruiting officers: "You are not to enlist . . . any stroller, Negro [sic], or vagabond." [9] This was a sore trial for "Free Men of Color" who had been on the muster rolls of the army at Cambridge since its formation. The order reflected deep-seated fears of slaveholders among the colonists that the presence of Negro soldiers in the Continental Army might lead the British to arm the slaves.

The prohibition against Negro recruits, however, did not stop the British from trying to rally the slaves against their masters. Lord Dunmore, Royal Governor of Virginia, offered freedom to Negro slaves who would join the royal cause,[10] and many slaves flocked to his side. Truly alarmed, Virginia colonists made public threats against the "defenceless fathers, mothers, their

[9] Peter Force; *American Archives*, 4th series. Vol. 2, p. 1630.
[10] Henry Steele Commager and Richard B. Morris, *The Spirit of Seventy-Six* (Indianapolis: Bobbs-Merrill Co., 1958) Vol. I, p. 111.

wives, their women and children" of any slaves "wicked enough to provoke the fury of the Americans" by joining Lord Dunmore.[11]

By December, 1775, General Washington reversed himself and signed an order giving leave to recruiting officers to recruit free Negroes. Not long after the practice became common for masters to enlist slaves as substitutes for themselves or to get a bounty of land. An entry in the journal of a Hessian officer made October 23, 1777 read:

> The negro can take the field instead of his master; and, therefore no regiment is to be seen in which there are not negroes in abundance; and among them there are able-bodied and strong fellows.[12]

It is not likely that more than 5,000 Negroes were among the 300,000 men who made up the revolutionary forces.[13] Muster rolls of state militias did not distinguish Negro recruits. Only such forenames as "Liberty," "Freedom," "Freeman" told the double story of the race of volunteer and the cause for which he fought. There were an average of fifty-four Negro soldiers in each of the seven brigades of General Washington's army in 1778, and seven hundred are estimated to have fought at the battle of Monmouth in June of that year.[14] The historian, Luther Porter Jackson, authenticated the service of 179 Negro soldiers and seamen from Virginia and estimated the total number to be not fewer than five hundred.[15]

Some three hundred to four hundred free men and slaves formed the major part of a Rhode Island regiment which fought bravely at the battle of Fort Mercer. The slaves enlisted under a promise of freedom at the end of the war, their masters meanwhile being paid an average of 120 pounds for each of them. The regiment, under the command of Colonel Christopher Greene, met and withstood the assault of four Hessian regiments, mortally wounding the enemy commander, Count Carl von Donop. As one eyewitness described the encounter:

> Then it was that our black regiment, with their cocked hats and black plumes tipped with white, moving with charged bayonets as a single man, twice

[11] George Washington Williams, *The Negro In American History 1619–1880* (New York: G. P. Putnam's Sons, 1888) Vol. I., p. 340.

[12] George Livermore, *An Historical Research Respecting the Opinions of the Founders of the Republic on Negroes as Slaves, as Citizens, and as Soldiers* (Boston: J. Wilson & Son, 1862), p. 111.

[13] John Hope Franklin, "A Brief History of the Negro in the United States," Chapter I of this book p. 1.

[14] Army Service Forces Manual (M5) *Leadership and the Negro Soldier* (Headquarters, Army Service Forces, October, 1944) p. 78.

[15] Luther Porter Jackson, *Virginia Negro Soldiers and Seamen in the Revolutionary War* (Norfolk, Va.: Guide Quality Press, 1944) p iv.

or thrice rushed on the banded force of British and Hessians and as often drove them from the ground.[16]

In the Revolutionary Navy

Negroes served in substantial numbers in the Revoluntary Navy. At least seventy-five Negroes served on fifteen or more vessels in the Virginia Navy.[17] A single family of free Negroes (the Nickens family) had seven of its members serving on Virginia ships. Negro seamen were also aboard several fighting ships of the Connecticut Navy.[18] The 22-gun Pennsylvania privateer, *Royal Lewis,* commanded by Stephen Decatur, Sr., had a crew of two hundred of whom twenty were Negro. Among these was James Forten of Philadelphia, who at fifteen had enlisted as a powder boy. When the ship was captured by the British frigate *Amphyon,* Forten escaped the fate of his nineteen fellow Negro seamen of being sold into slavery in the West Indies because the British Admiral's son took a liking to him. He later distinguished himself as an abolitionist.[19]

The skill of Negro pilots on naval vessels in Virginia coastal waters was an important asset to the Revolutionary Navy in beating back the marauding expeditions of the British Navy in Chesapeake Bay and up the James River. Four Negro slave pilots, Caesar, Cuffey, Starlins and Minny fought in many naval skirmishes against the British throughout the war.

Spies and Guerrillas

Because their presence in the countryside was less conspicuous than that of white colonials, Negro slaves proved invaluable as spies for the Continental Army. In the guise of a vegetable huckster, the slave Pompey Lamb entered the enemy fort at Stony Point and brought back valuable information to General Anthony Wayne. The slave Saul Mathews was a spy for General Nathaniel Greene and Baron von Steuben. Quaco Honeyman was

[16] Quoted in Sidney S. Rider, *Historical Inquiry Concerning the Attempt to Raise a Regiment of Slaves by Rhode Island During the War of the Revolution* (Providence, Rhode Island historical tracts, 1st series, No. 10. 1880) p. 1. Rider, however, casts doubts on the exploits of these Negro troops and seeks to downgrade their accomplishments. Writing one hundred years after their battles, he is not in the best position to negate the accounts of eyewitnesses.

[17] Jackson, *op cit.,* p. 29 *et seq.;* effective use of Negroes was also made by the South Carolina Navy. See Benjamin Quarles, *The Negro in the American Revolution* (Chapel Hill, N.C. published for the Institute of Early American History and Culture, Williamsburg, Va. by the University of North Carolina Press, 1961) p. 90.

[18] Army Service Forces Manual (M5), *op. cit.,* p. 79.

[19] Ray Allen Billington, "James Forten: Forgotten Abolitionist." *Negro History Bulletin* (November, 1949 Vol. XIII, No. 1) p. 31.

a slave spy in Rhode Island who was later given his freedom for his service. James Amistad, a young slave of twenty-two, was a spy courier between the French general, Marquis de LaFayette, and American spies behind the enemy lines of Lord Cornwallis. Wrote LaFayette:

> His intelligences from the enemy's camp were industriously collected and more faithfully delivered. He properly acquitted himself with some important communications I gave him and appears to be entitled to every reward his situation can admit of.[20]

Negro slaves, too, were members of the guerrilla forces of General Francis Marion, "The Swamp Fox," which played the dangerous game of harassing the enemy behind its own lines.

At the Siege of Savannah

Negroes from the Island of St. Domingo (now Haiti) were in the troops of the French lieutenant general, Comte D'Estaing, at the seige of Savannah in 1779. Between six hundred and eight hundred of them as light infantrymen covered the retreat of the American column. On the same battlefield where the Polish patriot Count Pulaski fell, many of these black slaves also fell in the fight for "the rights of man." They well understood why they were fighting. One of these slaves, Jean Baptiste Chavennes, died leading a slave uprising in Haiti in 1790. Six of them (André, Beauvais, Christophe, Rigaud, Villette and Beauregard) later became generals and commanders in the Haitian revolution; of these, Henri Christophe—who served as a boy of twelve at Savannah—fought with Toussaint L'Ouverture to throw off the French yoke and became in turn president and king of Haiti.[21]

South Carolina Vetoes Use of Slaves

By the fifth year of the Revolutionary War the need for manpower became acute, especially in the South. Realizing that they had no army to dispatch to defend the region against the British, the Continental Congress on March 29, 1779 recommended to South Carolina and Georgia the formation of separate battalions of Negro slaves to the number of three thousand "if they shall think the same expedient."[22] In a letter to South Carolina's Governor Rutledge, Major General Nathaniel Greene, commander of revolutionary forces in the South, wrote:

[20] Jackson, *op. cit.*, p. 9.

[21] Jacques N. Leger, *Haiti, Her History and Detractors* (Neale Publishing Co., New York: 1907); Theophilus Gould Steward, "How the Black St. Domingo Legion Saved the Patriot Army in the Seige of Savannah, 1779." *American Negro Academy* (Occasional Paper No. 5, 1899).

[22] Secret Journals of Congress. Domestick Affairs, 1757–1778, p. 107.

The natural strength of the country, in point of numbers, appears to me to consist much more in the blacks than in the whites. Could they be incorporated and employed for its defence, it would afford you double security. That they would make good soldiers I have not the least doubt. . . .[23]

The nine members of the South Carolina Governor's Council of War unanimously rejected the proposal and voted 8 to 1 against raising even a force of a thousand slaves.[24] More than fear of a slave revolt was implicit in the state's continued refusal to enlist Negro slaves. Colonel John Laurens, a former aide-de-camp to General Washington and himself the son of a South Carolina slaveowner, worked arduously to secure agreement to slave enlistment. In a letter reporting his failure to Washington he attributed it to "the howlings of a triple-headed monster, in which prejudice, avarice, and pusilanimity were united." [25] Washington replied:

I am not at all surprised at the failure of your plan. The spirit of freedom, which, at the commencement of this contest, would have gladly sacrificed everything to the attainment of its object, has long since subsided, and every selfish passion has taken its place. It is not the public, but private interests which influence the generality of mankind; nor can Americans any longer boast of an exception.[26]

The refusal of South Carolina and Georgia to recruit Negro slaves did not, however, prevent frequent use of slaves for other war purposes. Slaves were impressed into service to repair roads so that supplies could follow the troops. On the expedition of the Continental Army against east Florida, the executive council of Georgia authorized the drafting of two hundred slaves into the Army to act as pioneers and another one hundred to do fatigue duty.[27]

As long as slaves were not private property they were expendable. Thus the Georgia council, to secure supplies for its troops, did not hesitate to adopt "a proposal of obtaining such supplies by exchanging Negroes belonging to state for same." [28]

The War of 1812

With the end of the American Revolutionary War there was virtual elimination of the Negro from the Armed Forces of the new nation. Some,

[23] William Johnson, *Sketches of the Life and Correspondence of General Nathaniel Greene* (Charleston, S.C., 1822) Vol. 2, p. 272.

[24] Colored Troops Division, *op. cit.*, Vol. I, p. 159.

[25] Jared Sparks, *Correspondence of the American Revolution* (Boston, 1853) Vol. 3, p. 505.

[26] *Ibid.*, Vol. 5, p. 322.

[27] Allen D. Caviller, *Revolutionary Records of Georgia* (Atlanta: Franklin-Turner Company, 1908), Vol. II, p. 78.

[28] *Ibid* and see Quarles, *op. cit.*, p. 156 for similar practices by the British.

like Joseph Ranger, ex-slave who had won freedom by active service aboard five ships of the Virginia Navy during the war, remained in service six years after its close.[29] However, most Negroes were prohibited from duty by an Act of Congress in 1792 which restricted service in the milita to "able-bodied white males." [30] Generally, the states adopted the pattern set by the Federal Congress, but there were exceptions. South Carolina included "free Negroes, Indians, Moors, mulattoes, and mestizoes." Georgia and North Carolina accepted free Negroes in the militia; and Louisiana, which became a state in 1812, permitted the governor to select "certain free men of color to be chosen from among the Creoles." [31] Many Negroes served aboard American ships, however, and when war with England broke out again, they became a valued reserve of seamen needed to defend the exposed American frontier along the Upper Lakes.

Across Lake Ontario and Lake Erie on the shores of Canada a well-armed British force threatened the sparsely settled American frontier outposts. Superior British armed vessels, under the command of seasoned naval Captain Barclay, who had fought under Lord Nelson, stood ready to sweep the lakes of American ships. Even more ominous, sixty-thousand Indians, under such ruthless chiefs as Tecumseh, were allied with the British and waited to lay waste with tomahawk and fire to the American settlements.

It was in the face of these odds that 27-year-old Master Commandant Oliver Hazard Perry asked his commanding officer, Commodore Chauncey, for reinforcements. Chauncey sent him a number of Negro seamen and when Perry complained of "this motley set of blacks, soldiers, and boys," the commodore tartly replied:

> I have yet to learn that the color of the skin or the cut and trimmings of the coat can effect a man's qualifications or usefulness. I have fifty blacks on board this ship and many of them are my best men; and those people you call soldiers have been to sea from two to seventeen years; and I presume you will find them as good and useful as any men on board your vessel.[32]

Chauncey's statement was soon confirmed for it was with this "motley crew" of 432 men, a tenth of them Negro, that Perry won a decisive battle of the war and was able to send the famous message:

> We have met the enemy and they are ours; two ships, two brigs, one schooner, and one sloop.[33]

[29] Jackson, *op. cit.* p. 13.
[30] U.S. Statutes At Large, Vol. I, p. 271.
[31] Colored Troops Division, *op. cit.* Vol. I, p. 314.
[32] George Washington Williams, *op. cit.*, Vol. II, p. 23.
[33] John R. Spears, *The History of Our Navy* (New York: Charles Scribner, 1899), Vol. II, p. 325.

The Negro seamen with Perry were only a few of several thousand Negroes who fought in the War of 1812 on both land and sea. They were part of an invading force which went into Canada. More than six hundred Negroes with Negro line officers in command fought under General Andrew Jackson in the decisive battle of New Orleans.

As the British had sought to strike terror among Americans on the shores of the upper lakes by the threat to arm the Indians, so in the South they hoped to follow the example of Lord Dunmore in Virginia in the earlier war, and to arm the Negroes. In New Orleans rumors ran far ahead of the deed, and despite the fact that free Negroes of the city had already formed a battalion to fight against England, there was wild talk of a British expedition on the way to New Orleans to "arm the Negroes."

General Jackson wrote Governor Clairborne of Louisiana of the Negro free men: "They must be either for us, or against us. Distrust them and you make them your enemies, place confidence in them, and you engage them by every dear and honorable tie to the interest of the country, who extends to them equal rights and privileges with white men." The Negro troops confirmed General Jackson's judgment and after his troops had routed the British and saved New Orleans, he singled out Negro units as having "manifested great bravery."[34]

The End of an Era

The Battle of New Orleans brought to a close the opportunities for Negroes to serve in their country's armed forces. On February 18, 1820, a general order from the Adjutant and Inspector General's Office of the United States Army read: "No Negro or Mulatto will be received as a recruit of the Army." [35] There were no new Negro recruits until the Civil War.

THE CIVIL WAR

An hour after midnight on April 12, 1861, batteries in the control of South Carolinian "Secessionists" fired upon the flag of the United States

[34] George Washington Williams, *op. cit.*, Vol. II, p. 27.

[35] Colored Troops Division, *op. cit.*, Vol. I, p. 348. A small number of Negroes remained in the service of the navy, however. In 1842 there was still extant a naval regulation restricting the number of Negroes to one-twentieth part of the crew of any vessel. (Document No. 282., U.S. House of Representatives, 27th Congress, 2nd Session.)

flying over Fort Sumter in the Charleston harbor. It was an act of treason and the Civil War had begun.

Eleven days later a free Negro of Washington, D.C., Jacob Dodson, offered his services to fight against the rebels and was turned down by Secretary of War Simon Cameron who told him "the Department has no intention to call into the service of the Government any colored soldiers." [36]

A White Man's War

It was to be a white man's war and a short one. The country was aroused, but President Abraham Lincoln issued a call for 75,000 volunteers to enlist for ninety days only. Regiments raised by Northwestern states were refused by the War Department on the ground that they would not be needed.

The Radical Abolitionists called for removing disabilities which prevented Negroes from enlisting. A mass meeting in Boston on April 24, 1861, heard Robert Morris, the Negro lawyer, declare that Negroes were "ready to raise an army of fifty-thousand." The Massachusetts legislature was petitioned to authorize the formation of a company of colored troops and it directed its Senators and Congressmen to work for Federal Government approval of this request.

Lincoln chose the course of moderation. He felt that arming the Negroes would destroy the last clear chance to save the border states of Tennessee, Kentucky and Missouri for the Union side; he reacted to the concern of some that slave insurrections would follow with savage violence and cruelty being visited upon civilized populations in the South. He vetoed a proclamation of emancipation issued by General John C. Frémont in Missouri in 1861 and countermanded a similar proclamation General David Hunter issued the following year in South Carolina.

Meanwhile from all over the North came offers of Negro regiments. Three regiments of colored men "armed, equipped, and ready for immediate service" were offered from New York. Michigan asked Secretary of War Cameron to accept a regiment "composed of colored men of the North"; and Cincinnati, Ohio proffered a regiment of one thousand colored men "three-fourths of whom are bright mulattoes. . . ." [37] These efforts to make the use of Negro troops more palatable by paying for their equipment, or restricting volunteers to free Negroes of the North or to Negroes who at a distance might look like white were all without result.

It was still a relaxed easy-going war, so much so that stragglers of (then Colonel) William Tecumseh Sherman's division stopped on the road to

---

[36] Colored Troops Division, *op. cit.*, Vol. II, p. 806.
[37] Colored Troops Division, *op. cit.*, Vol. II, pp. 813 and 816.

pick wild blackberries as they marched to Bull Run; [38] men who had enlisted for ninety days were thinking of going home. Even the defeat that came out of the hapless confusion at the First Battle of Bull Run did little to convince Lincoln or his Cabinet that Negro troops should be used.

Some Exceptions

There were exceptions to the rule of exclusion. As early as June 28 Colonel Charles P. Stone, commanding at Poolesville, Maryland, had Negro scouts in his employ.[39] At Hilton Head Island in South Carolina, General David Hunter, on his own, organized regiments of Negro troops but soon had to disband them for lack of money. And the Cincinnati regiment of "bright mullatoes"—a thousand strong—ended up as home guards defending the city in 1862 with all but three of its officers Negro.[40]

In July, while Union forces were being defeated at Bull Run, a Negro seaman, William Tillman, was engaged in a daring act against the Confederacy on the high seas. He had been a cook aboard the schooner S. J. Waring bound for Montevideo with a rich cargo when it had been captured by the Confederate privateer Jefferson Davis. The Davis put aboard a prize crew of a captain, two mates and two Confederate seamen with orders to sail the schooner to Charleston, South Carolina. Here Tillman knew he would be sold as a slave. Determined to resist enslavement, the cook took a hatchet from his galley and in the night killed the captain and his two mates and made the two Confederate seamen surrender to him. Then it developed that no one was left alive on the vessel who understood how to navigate. Tillman, however, knew enough to lay a course "that would bring the broadside of America in sight." After that he followed the coastline northward to New York.[41]

Fifty Thousand Pairs of Scarlet Pantaloons

While politicians in Washington looked on the recruitment of Negro troops against the background of political strategy, field commanders considered their use in the practical light of battle logic. The commanders knew that Negro slaves formed a great "army of the soil" that fed Confederate forces and provided the Confederacy with commodities it could exchange for war matériel in Europe. They saw through their field glasses Negroes engaged in throwing up fortifications, serving as teamsters and cooks for the enemy.

[38] William T. Sherman, Memoirs (Bloomington, Indiana: Indiana University Press, 1917), p. 181.

[39] Colored Troops Division, op. cit. Vol. II, p. 809.

[40] Ibid, p. 810.

[41] John R. Spears, op. cit., Vol. IV, p. 91 ff.

Indeed, there was one account of "a Richmond Howitzer Battery manned by Negroes."[42] Especially where Union armies had penetrated into the Deep South they were met by growing numbers of "contraband"—Negro slaves fleeing to hoped for freedom behind the Union lines.

From his Hilton Head headquarters Major General David Hunter wrote the newly appointed Secretary of War Edwin M. Stanton on April 2, 1862, proposing to arm fifty thousand Negroes and asking for fifty thousand muskets. "It is important," he wrote, "that I should be able to know and distinguish these men at once; and for this purpose I respectfully request that *fifty thousand* pairs of scarlet pantaloons may be sent me; and this is all the clothing I shall require for these people."[43]

At the end of April, 1862, white-bearded Gideon Welles, Secretary of the Navy, told flag officers of the Southern Squadron that they might enlist contrabands "freely in the Navy, with their consent, rating them as boys at eight, nine, or ten dollars a month and one ration."[44] By summer of 1862 a cautious change in Washington policy was apparent in the instruction Secretary Stanton gave to Brigadier General Rufus Saxton. Saxton was authorized to organize in squads, companies, and battalions up to fifty thousand Negro slaves for volunteer labor and to assign them to the Quartermaster Department of the Army. He was also to instruct up to five thousand of them in military drill and army discipline for use to guard plantations and settlements taken over by advancing Union forces.[45]

In May and June, Major General Benjamin F. Butler, in New Orleans, had mustered in the 1st, 2nd and 3rd Native Guards—later called *Corps D'Afrique*. These were the first Negro combat troops of the Civil War. In September he wrote Secretary Stanton: "I have succeeded wonderfully in my enlistment of volunteers here. . . . I shall also have within ten days a regiment 1000 strong of Nation [sic] Guards (Colored), the darkest of whom will be about the complexion of the late Mr. Webster."[46]

Fighting Men at Last

The change of policy in Washington had come after a summer of costly and indecisive fighting. Casualties in the Battle of Seven Days and the Second Battle of Bull Run had been severe. Everywhere victory raced just

[42] In a letter to the Acting Adjutant General at Fort Monroe, Virginia, from Colonel J. W. Phelps from Newport News, Va. on August 11, 1861. Colored Troop Division, *op. cit.* Vol. II, p. 819.

[43] April 3, 1862. Colored Troops Division, *op. cit.*, Vol. II, p. 837.

[44] April 30, 1862, *Ibid.*, Vol. II, p. 838.

[45] August 25, 1862, *Ibid.*, Vol. II, pp. 958–960.

[46] September 11, 1862, *Ibid.*, Vol. II, p. 963. Quotation (Letter Box No. 2, Department of the Gulf, p. 297).

beyond the grasp of Union generals. Lincoln had come to feel that decisive action must be taken to crush the rebellion. He promulgated a provisional emancipation proclamation. If those in rebellion had not ceased their resistance by year's end, then their slaves would be forever free.

Now the business of making Negroes into fighting men began in earnest. Almost simultaneously free Negroes in the North and slaves in the South began military training. The first Kansas Infantry Regiment began training at Fort Lincoln in October 1862. General Saxton ordered the organization of the First Regiment of South Carolina Volunteers the same month.

Of the Kansas Regiment one officer wrote:

> They exhibit a proficiency in manual and in company evolutions truly surprising, and the best company is one officered by black men.
>
> These men were recruited with the promise that they were to fight, not work as common laborers. . . . Many of them are intelligent free negroes.[47]

Of the South Carolina Regiment—in battle just two weeks or so after being mustered into the Army—their commander wrote General Saxton:

> The colored men fought with astonishing coolness and bravery. For alacrity in effecting landing, for determination and for bush fighting I found them all I could desire, more than I had hoped. They behaved bravely, gloriously, and deserve all praise.
>
> I started from St. Simons with 62 fighting colored men and returned to Beaufort with 156 fighting men [all colored]. As soon as we took a slave from his claimant we placed a musket in his hand and he began to fight for the freedom of others.[48]

The Character of the War has Changed

The shift of policy had both military and moral overtones. General in Chief of the Army H. W. Halleck articulated the military aspect when he wrote General Ulysses Grant at Vicksburg: "The character of the war has changed in the last year. There is now no possible hope of reconciliation with the rebels. We must conquer the rebels or be conquered by them. The North must either destroy the slave oligarchy, or become slaves themselves." [49]

Lincoln gave voice to the moral implications. He wrote James C. Conklin: "But Negroes, like other people, act upon motive. Why should they do anything for us, if we will do nothing for them. If they stake their lives for

[47] Letter of Colonel N. P. Chipman to Major General Samuel R. Curtis dated October 16, 1862. *Ibid.*, Vol. II, p. 977.

[48] Report of Oliver T. Beard, Lieutenant Colonel, 48th New York Volunteers to Brigadier General Saxton, November 10, 1862. *Ibid.*, Vol. II, p. 1056.

[49] Letter of March 31, 1863. *Ibid.*, Vol. III, p. 1148.

us, they must be prompted by the strongest motive, even the promise of freedom; and the promise being made must be kept." [50]

The pendulum had swung. The war had become a war against slavery and soon after January 1, 1863, when the Emancipation Proclamation became effective, Lorenzo Thomas, Adjutant General of the Army, was placed in charge of recruiting colored troops.

John Brown's Body Lies A Molderin' In The Grave

Frederick Douglass, ex-slave, and George Stearns, wealthy Boston businessman, were two of those chosen by Secretary of War Stanton to assist Thomas. Both were radical abolitionists. Both had been close friends of John Brown and supporters of Brown's antislavery activities and both had fled to Canada in 1859 after Brown's plan to arm the slaves by seizing the Government arsenal at Harper's Ferry, failed. Now, four years after Virginia had hung him, John Brown's soul was "marching on." His spiritual heirs were recruiting Negroes for service in a great army of liberation.

Stanton had authorized Governor John A. Andrews of Massachusetts to raise a regiment of colored troops and this was quickly done by Stearns. It was named the 54th Massachusetts Regiment and commanded by a 28-year-old son of a distinguished Boston family, Robert Gould Shaw. Proudly in its ranks marched Douglass' two sons.

Recruitment rapidly accelerated. Arkansas, Iowa, Kansas, Louisiana, Massachusetts, Mississippi, North Carolina and South Carolina had all contributed regiments of Negro troops. At the end of October, 1863, there were fifty-eight regiments under arms with a total strength of 37,482 men. There were other Negroes serving in the Navy. Rear Admiral David Porter commanding the Mississippi Squadron reported, "all our firemen and coal heavers are negroes." [51] Their number totaled 814.

There were still problems, however. Over-zealous recruiting agents were sometimes accused of impressing into service slaves of persons loyal to the Union as well as those of rebels. In the border states there was still uncertainty as to whether slavery was really at an end. To Andrew Johnson, Military Governor of Tennessee, President Lincoln had written in March:

> I am told you have at least thought of raising a negro military force. In my opinion the country now needs no specific thing so much as some man of your ability and position, to go to this work. When I speak of your position I mean that of an eminent citizen of a slave state, and himself a slave holder.

[50] Letter of August 26, 1863. *Ibid.*, Vol. III, Part I, p. 1534.
[51] *Ibid.*, Vol. III p. 1690.

The colored population is the great available, yet unavailed of force for restoring the union. The bare sight of 50,000 armed and drilled black soldiers upon the banks of the Mississippi would end the rebellion at once. And who doubts that we can present that sight if we but take hold in earnest. If you have been thinking of it please do not dismiss the thought.[52]

Johnson had been thinking of it, but he wanted to go slowly and he felt the immediate greater need was to use Negroes as laborers to support the rear of General Rosecrans' army in Tennessee. He suggested to Lincoln that to offer loyal slave owners three hundred dollars for each slave recruited would hasten recruitment and make emancipation easier to accomplish. He saw the inevitable end of slavery.

George Stearns had come to Tennessee and he assured Stanton that he had no difficulty in working harmoniously with Johnson. Together slave-owner and abolitionist laid the foundation for raising Negro troops in a slave state. In October, interestingly one week after the pro-Southern Governor Horatio Seymour of New York refused permission to raise a Negro regiment in his free state, recruiting stations for colored troops were set up in the slave state of Tennessee.

Meanwhile, Lincoln established ground rules for recruitment in a terse memorandum:

> To recruiting free negroes, no objection.
> To recruiting slaves of disloyal owners without their consent, no objection.
> To recruiting slaves of loyal owners with their consent, no objection.
> To recruiting slaves of loyal owners without their consent, objection, unless the necessity is urgent.
> To conducting oneself offensively, while recruiting and to carrying away slaves not suitable for recruits, objection.[53]

Emancipation had been instituted as a war measure and as a war measure it was still to be used.

"Nobody knows anything about these men. . . ."

Everywhere Negro free men and slaves had rushed to volunteer. Now the question was, would they fight? Between February and July of 1863 the answer was given on many fronts.

[52] March 26, 1863. *Ibid.*, Vol. II, p. 1144.
[53] October 11, 1863. *Ibid.*, Vol. III, Part I, p. 1644. Negroes—especially in the North —had ground rules, too. For an account of how many refused to enlist until given guarantees that they would be defended by the Union against threats of the confederacy to murder or reenslave them, if captured, see: James M. McPherson, *The Negro's Civil War* (New York. Pantheon Books, 1965) pp. 174 ff.

"Nobody knows anything about these men," wrote Colonel T. W. Higginson who had fought his way up the St. Mary's River in command of the First South Carolina Volunteers, "who has not seen them in battle. I find that I myself knew nothing. There is a fierce energy about them beyond anything of which I have ever read, except it be the French Zouaves. . . . No officer in this regiment now doubts that the key to the successful prosecution of the war lies in the unlimited employment of black troops." [54]

Before Port Hudson, the First and Third Regiment of U.S. Colored Troops held the right of the Union line with steadiness and bravery against sorties of Confederate troops from inside the fort. Major General Nathaniel Banks reported: "In many respects their conduct was heroic. No troops could be more determined or daring. They made during the day three charges upon batteries of the enemy, suffering very heavy losses and holding their position. . . ." [55]

On June 7, 1863, at Milliken's Bend, Louisiana, one thousand former slaves—many of whom had received their muskets only a few days before —fought against two thousand white Texans in fierce hand-to-hand combat. Their lines overrun by superior forces, they used the guns as clubs and bayonetted hundreds of their attackers. After the battle there lay as many dead with bayonet wounds and crushed skulls as from gunshot wounds. "It is impossible for men to show greater gallantry than the Negro troops in this fight," wrote Brigadier General E. S. Dennis.

At Fort Wagner, South Carolina, the 54th Massachusetts was placed in the front of the assault troops. At sunset, led by its colonel, Robert Gould Shaw, the regiment charged in the face of heavy fire and reached the parapets of the fort, where Shaw fell, mortally wounded. [56]

Appraising the first year's use of Negro troops, Secretary Stanton wrote: "the slave has proved his manhood . . . at Milliken's Bend, at the assault upon Port Hudson, and the storming of Fort Wagner." President Lincoln in his annual Message to Congress declared with obvious gratification:

> Of those who were slaves at the beginning of the rebellion, full one hundred thousand are now in the United States Military Service, about one half of which number actually bear arms in the ranks; thus giving double advantage of taking so much labor from the insurgent cause, and supplying the places which otherwise must be filled by so many white men. So far tested it is difficult to say they are not as good soldiers as any. No servile insurrection or

[54] *Ibid.*, Vol. III, Part 2, p. 2089.

[55] *Ibid.*, Vol. III, Part 2, p. 2124.

[56] For a detailed account of the 54th Massachusetts at Fort Wagner see Benjamin Quarles, *The Negro in the Civil War* (Boston, Little Brown and Company, 1953) pp. 3–21.

tendency to violence or cruelty, has marked the measures of emancipation and arming of the blacks. . . . The crisis which threatened to divide friends of the Union is past.[57]

For a Soldier's Duty . . . A Soldier's Pay

Corporal James Henry Gooding of Company C of the 54th Massachusetts Regiment sat in his camp on Morris Island, South Carolina, at the mouth of Charleston harbor and wrote President Lincoln a letter. He had fought at James Island and rushed the parapets of Fort Wagner in the face of "a living line of musket fire," his comrades dropping at his sides. Now he had a question to ask. He wrote the President:

> Now the main question is, are we soldiers, or are we laborers. We have done a soldier's duty. Why can't we have a soldier's pay?[58]

It was indeed, *the main question.* Prominent Bostonians—among them Oliver Wendell Holmes, Charles Eliot Norton and R. P. Hallowell—urged Secretary of War Stanton that "black troops . . . be treated as soliders and only called on for their fair share of fatigue duty." [59] Major General Butler could see no reason why Negro soldiers must fight for ten dollars a month, with three dollars deducted for clothing allowance, while white troops got clothing allowance extra. He could "see no reason why a colored soldier should be asked to fight upon less pay than any other. The colored man fills an equal space in the ranks while he lives, and an equal grave when he falls." [60]

Colonel M. S. Littlefield, commanding colored troops on Folly Island, South Carolina, explained to the Chairman of the U. S. Senate Military Committee:

"The First North Carolina enlisted also on the understanding that they were to have the same pay as white soldiers. They have seven months in service, and the average amount charged for clothing is $51, leaving $19 due each for the whole term of his enlistment—less than $3 a month." [61] The story was the same for the 55th Massachusetts; even worse for the 54th Massachusetts. The latter regiment by the end of January, 1864, lost fifty-

---

[57] December 7, 1863. *Ibid.*, Vol. III, Part 1, p. 1799.

[58] *Ibid.*, Vol. III, Part 1, p. 1809.

[59] *Ibid.* For full discussion of the "Rights of Colored Persons in the Army" see *Message of the President of the United States,* Executive Document 42, 38th Congress, First Session, May 7, 1864.

[60] General Order No. 46, 18th Army Corps, issued at Fort Monroe, Virginia, December 5, 1863.

[61] Letter to Senator Henry Wilson, January 25, 1864. Colored Troops Division, *op. cit.,* Vol. V, p. 2354.

nine of its members, killed in battle or died of disease; and there had been an additional 155 discharged because of battle wounds. "Every one of these," wrote Littlefield, "died actually in debt to the Government, having received no pay, and their families receiving no pension or bounty." A greater portion of the wounded had also been discharged with no pay.

Governor Andrews of Massachusetts, recalling that Stanton had promised him equal treatment for Negro troops, asked the legislature of his state to vote funds to equalize the pay of the two Massachusetts regiments. The legislature voted the funds, but the Negro soldiers would not accept pay from this source. Principle, not money was at issue. They wanted equality of treatment. Finally a ruling of the Attorney General of the United States opened the way for equal pay for Negro troops. This was in the summer of 1864.

The Black Army Grows

The historian Bruce Catton has described Major General Lorenzo Thomas as a "prim, paper-shuffling adjutant general." Thomas was, however, something more as far as Negro troops were concerned. He was busy weeding out inefficient white officers in command of Negro troops. The sanitary condition of camps for Negro soldiers was his concern and he insisted that none but graduates of approved medical colleges be commissioned as surgeons for these troops. He was everywhere inspecting Negro troops and would not tolerate unfair treatment of them.

On December 24, 1863, he wrote Secretary Stanton:

> I have now in course of organization two regiments of cavalry, both of which are advancing toward completion even more rapidly than I anticipated. Owing to the scarcity of horses these men have been mounted on mules. . . . The First Mississippi Cavalry of African Descent have already proved their efficiency in this branch of the service, one hundred and fifty having recently defeated three hundred of the rebels in a conflict near Vicksburg.[62]

On the 6th of February he wired his assistant, "Flags are much needed for recruiting rendezvous for Colored troops. Send immediately a dozen." Four days later from Nashville he wrote Stanton: "I have just ordered a regiment of Heavy Artillery of African Descent to be raised here for purpose of garrisoning forts around Nashville." By April 6, 1864, he was in New Orleans. He wrote headquarters in Washington:

> Ship Island I also inspected, garrisoned by a colored regiment of eight companies, the second one raised by General Butler from the New Orleans Home

[62] Adjutant General Lorenzo Thomas' Letterbook (National Archives, Checklist Entry No. 3), p. 87.

Guards. It is in capital order and fine drill. This regiment like the other colored troops is armed with old flint lock muskets altered to percussion, turned in by white volunteers, and some of them twice condemned. The Colored troops on every occasion of conflict, have shown themselves most worthy of confidence and I think the time has fully arrived for placing in their hands the best arms. The blacks will take the best care of them and use them with effect when the necessity arises. I desire to impress upon the Lieutenant General this important matter.[63]

The country welcomed the energetic recruitment of Negro troops. In New York, editor Horace Greeley in the *Tribune* thundered at the refusal of New York Governor Horatio Seymour to approve the raising of a regiment of Negro troops in the state; ". . . this Governor," he wrote sneeringly, "who loves white men so much that he is willing to send them to battle, danger and death. . . ." At long last the 20th United States Regiment was raised in the state under the auspices of the Union League and presented its colors by wealthy and socially prominent Mrs. John Jacob Astor.

By February 1864, more than 7,500 troops had been recruited in middle and east Tennessee. By October, 20,000 Negro troops had been recruited in Kentucky including a cavalry regiment and new recruits were volunteering at the rate of one hundred to two hundred a day.

There were gay martial bands and Brigadier General William Birney at Camp Stanton, Maryland, was directed "not to take Brigade Band Number One to South Carolina with your command, its services being considered indispensable to the recruiting service in Maryland." [64]

The question was no longer Shall we let the Negro fight? but How many, how soon? Miles O'Reilly expressed the popular sentiment in the statement:

> The right to be killed, I'll divide with the nayger,
> And give him the largest half.

Thus the black army grew. It added regiments of cavalry, light artillery, heavy artillery, and scores of infantry units. There was a scattering of chaplains, like Henry MacNeal Turner and Samuel Harrison of the 54th Massachusetts, who demanded and got the same pay and allowance as white chaplains: one hundred dollars a month and two rations.

There were army surgeons, Martin Delany of Harvard Medical School with the rank of major, Charles Purvis and A. T. Augusta of the University of Toronto Medical School. A group of white medical men wrote President Lincoln this note referring to Augusta:

---

[63] *Ibid.*

[64] Letter from Assistant Adjutant General C. W. Foster, February 26, 1864. Colored Troops Division, *op. cit.*, Vol. III, Part 2, p. 2380.

When we made application for positions in Colored Service, the understanding was universal that all commissioned officers were to be white men. Judge our surprise and disappointment when upon joining our respective regiments, we found that the Senior Surgeon of the Command was a Negro.[65]

Following the note Augusta was detached and assigned to the job of giving physical examinations to new recruits.

As a shortage of manpower developed in the Union Navy, Negroes were used to fill the ranks as gunners, loaders and other ratings. They served on the *Kearsarge* when she destroyed the *Alabama;* aboard the *Monitor* in its battle with the *Merrimac,* and aboard Rear Admiral David Farragut's flagship in the battle of Mobile Bay.

The Confederates

The Confederates were losing men, too—white soldiers and black slaves. Each hard-fought battle cost them the lives of soldiers. Each thrust of the Union Army into their rich farm territory meant not only loss of agricultural commodities for food and trade, but as well the loss of tens of thousands of slaves who were off and away at the sound of the Union guns.

Able-bodied male slaves were shipped, whenever possible, to the interior out of reach of the Union Army. To maintain fighting strength, Confederate President Jefferson Davis called for the impressment into service of twenty thousand slaves for duty as cooks, teamsters, hospital attendants.[66]

The Confederate Governor of Louisiana, Henry W. Allen, told Confederate Secretary of War James A. Seddon:

The time has come for us to put into the army every able-bodied negro man as a soldier . . . we have learned from dear bought experience the negroes can be taught to fight.[67]

Fort Pillow

From the time the first Negro Union soldier fired a gun in battle he was in double jeopardy: of being killed in the fighting or, if taken, of being killed, enslaved or beaten. The Confederate commanders recognized no right of Negro soldiers to be treated as prisoners of war. They claimed the Negroes were property and as such should be returned either to their rightful owners or sold for the benefit of the Confederacy. Against Negro troops the rebel battle yell was "No prisoners! No quarter."

One assault of Confederate troops upon Negro soldiers has gone down in

[65] *Ibid.,* Vol. III, Part 2, p. 2377.
[66] Message to the Confederate Congress, February, 1864.
[67] Colored Troops Division, *op. cit.,* Vol. IV, p. 2875.

history as "The Fort Pillow Massacre." On April 12, 1864, a cavalry force under command of Major General Nathan B. Forrest, who as a civilian had spent many years buying and selling slaves,[68] and General James R. Chalmers, overran Fort Pillow, Tennessee, which had been defended by four companies of Negro soldiers. Although later denied by General Forrest, evidence of Union survivors indicated a wholesale slaughter of combatants and noncombatants, even after all resistance had ceased.

At Mound City, Illinois, ten days after the battle, survivors testified before a congressional committee that hospital patients had been sabered to death in their beds, that Negro soldiers had been buried alive, Negro women and children slain, and that Major Bradford, white commander of the Negro troops, had been killed as a "Tennessee Traitor" while an unarmed prisoner of war.[69]

On May 3rd, President Lincoln wrote his Secretary of War:

> It is now quite certain that a large number of our colored soldiers, and their white officers, were by rebel forces, massacred after they had surrendered at the recent capture of Fort Pillow. . . . Give me in writing your opinion as to what course the Government should take. . . .[70]

Stanton was quick to suggest that Generals Forrest and Chalmers be excluded from any amnesty, that a certain number of Confederate officers be held as hostages for the delivery to the Union of these two officers, that certain rebel prisoners be exchangeable only for Negro prisoners. No final action on these proposals was taken, but as the wild rumors of Fort Pillow reached the ears of Negroes, black Union soldiers in Memphis sank to their knees and took a solemn oath never again to take a white prisoner.

Proving Themselves

Negro troops had few occasions in battle when they were not being called upon to prove themselves against fears and doubts of the white officers who led them and the white soldiers who fought beside them. The year 1864 placed new demands upon their courage. There was Olustee in Florida, Fort Pillow in Tennessee, Petersburg and Newmarket Heights in

[68] *The War of the Rebellion* (Washington, 1889) Series I, Vol. XXIII, Part 2, p. 955.
[69] United States House of Representatives, 38th Congress, 1st Session. Report Number 65.
[70] Colored Troops Division, *op. cit.*, Vol. VII, p. 4325; Lincoln, nearly a year before, on April 30, 1863, had issued an Executive Order of Retaliation designed to protect the Rights of Negroes as prisoners of war. See John Hope Franklin, *The Emancipation Proclamation*, (Garden City, New York: Doubleday & Co., 1963), p. 149. For extended discussion of this question see Dudley T. Cornish, *The Sable Arm* (New York: Longmans, Green and Co., 1956) pp. 157–180.

Virginia. In all of these battles they measured up to the high standards of a soldier, but perhaps nowhere better than at Petersburg.

The seige of Petersburg, or the "Battle of the Crater," got its name from a plan presented by Colonel Henry L. Pleasants for destroying Confederate batteries. He had observed that it would be possible to dig a tunnel unobserved directly under enemy fortifications, set a charge of dynamite (he estimated eight thousand pounds) and blow up the main batteries. Simultaneously assault troops were to charge up the hill to the enemy lines and attack while the enemy was still in panic. The tunnel was dug for over five hundred feet, and a division of Negro troops was chosen to lead the attack. Then began a series of events which led to disaster. Major General George Meade countermanded the order to use Negro troops in the first assault wave, assigning them instead to a support role. The line of the tunnel was not exactly true, the fuse to set off the charge did not explode and the explosion was delayed until the fuse could be repaired. When the explosion occurred it disrupted only momentarily the defending forces and they quickly rallied to repulse a wave of white troops now trapped in the crater made by the explosion. Now fully alerted the Confederates waited while Negro troops in two waves blindly leapfrogged over the white soldiers in a vain effort to reach the top. It was a failure, but several hundred black soldiers had proven they knew how to die, several thousand that they did not fear death. Around their campfires the night before they had sung a song with the line, "We looks like men-er-war." At Petersburg, they did indeed.

At Newmarket Heights in the fall of the year General Benjamin F. Butler, commanding the Army of the James River, had deliberately sent his Negro troops against the most difficult sector of the enemy line to prove, he was later to admit, to his white soldiers that a Negro regiment was the safest thing they could have on their flank. When he was relieved of command he said in a special farewell to his Negro soldiers:

> . . . With a bayonet you have unlocked the iron-barred gates of prejudice, opening new fields of freedom, liberty, equality, of right to yourselves and your race forever.[71]

"Inevitable Sambo"

In the ranks of Union generals there was one dissenter, Major General William Tecumseh Sherman. In his march to the sea he had brought release from Confederate control to countless thousands of slaves, among them many able-bodied men. However, he did not arm them as leaders like Charles Sumner of Massachusetts or Stanton in the War Department

[71] *Ibid.*

wished. His stubbornness brought resentment in Washington, about which General Halleck warned him in a personal confidential letter:

> While almost everyone is praising your great march through Georgia, there is a certain class, having now great influence with the President . . . who are decidedly disposed to make a point against you. I mean in regard to "inevitable Sambo."
>
> They say you have manifested an almost criminal dislike for the negro, and that you are not willing to carry out the wishes of the Government in regard to him, but repulse him with contempt.[72]

Sherman in his Memoirs denies this charge, claiming military necessity made it necessary for his army to be free from the tens of thousands of Negro contraband streaming for miles behind his lines. However, he could not hold back the stern determination of the Government to use Negro troops in ever greater striking force.

In January, 1865, Lorenzo Thomas was still recruiting Negro soldiers, still singing their praises. He wrote Stanton from Lexington, Kentucky:

> A battalion of the 6th Colored Cavalry commanded by Major General Burbridge, 300 strong, attacked and whipped Duke's Brigade of 350, the last remnant of Morgan's force.
>
> The rebels were driven half a mile with a loss . . . of 30 men killed and wounded. They were on the crest of a hill at Marion and the Negroes charged over open ground and did not fire a gun until within thirty yards of the rebels. This is the first time that any of these men were under fire.[73]

Recapitulation

Enlistment of colored troops was discontinued June 1, 1865. At that time there were 123,156 in the service of the United States, organized as follows:

120	Infantry Regiments	98,938
12	Heavy Artillery Regiments	15,662
10	Batteries of Light Artillery	1,311
7	Cavalry Regiments	7,245

This was the largest number in service at any one time during the war, although an overall total of 186,000 had been inducted. Nearly 3,000 were killed in battle or died of wounds received in battle. More than 26,000 died from disease, or one in every seven recruits, as compared with one in every seventeen white soldiers. The desertion rate for Negroes (though

[72] December 30, 1864. William T. Sherman, *op. cit.*, p. 247.
[73] Colored Troops Division, *op. cit.*

some may have been re-enslaved) was 67 per 1,000 as compared with the general volunteer ratio of 63 per 1,000.

That they had fought bravely was recognized by military leaders of the Union and the Confederacy alike. Proudly on their colors they bore the names of the battles where their blood was shed: "Port Hudson," "Olustee," "Honey Hill," "Deveaux Neck," "Pocatiglio," "Coosawatchie," "James Island," "Will Town Bluffs" . . . and many more.

SOLDIERS OF THE PLAINS

In the Regular Army

After the close of the Civil War many regiments of United States Colored Troops remained on active duty. Gradually they were demobilized, but Acts of Congress authorized the creation of two Negro regiments of cavalry and two of infantry to be part of the regular Army. About 12,500 veterans of the Civil War were recruited for the new units. On July 28, 1866, the 9th Cavalry was activated at New Orleans and that same day the 10th Cavalry was organized at Leavenworth, Kansas. In 1869, the 24th Infantry Regiment was constituted from volunteers out of the 38th and 41st Regiments of U.S. Colored Troops; and the 25th Infantry Regiment, from men of the 39th and 40th Regiments. As had been the case during the Civil War, nearly all officers of these regiments were white.

Until the Spanish-American War these troops had a lonely detail garrisoning isolated posts in sparsely settled regions of the country. They built roads and put up telegraph wires in Texas, served as escort to groups crossing the Indian Territory, scouted for hostile Indian bands on the Western Plains, in the high mountains of Montana and the Dakotas, and on the Rio Grande border.[74] On windswept plains in the winter the cavalrymen wore coats of buffalo skins and came to be called "Buffalo soldiers" by the Indians.

The Spanish-American War

During the Spanish-American War all four of the Negro units saw service in Cuba and were afterwards on duty in the Philippines. In the battle of Santiago de Cuba, dismounted companies of the 9th and 10th Cavalry flanked the First U.S. Volunteer Cavalry led by Colonel Theodore

[74] For a general account of the activities of these troops see: S. E. Whitman, *The Troopers* (New York: Hastings House, 1962); William G. Muller, *The Twenty-Fourth Infantry, Past and Present* (Privately Printed, 1922); John H. Nankivell, *History of the Twenty-Fifth Regiment United States Infantry, 1869–1926* (Privately Printed, 1927).

Roosevelt and shared the victory in the charge up San Juan Hill. Later Roosevelt wrote, "I want no better men beside me in battle than these colored troops showed themselves to be." [75] At El Caney the 25th Infantry won high praise for bravery when it stormed and took a stone fort from Spanish troops under a withering fire.

Displaying a different kind of bravery, members of the 24th Infantry, acting as guards in Siboney, Cuba, volunteered to serve as nurses during a yellow fever epidemic. Only 24 of 456 men in the regiment escaped illness from the fever and many died while nursing the sick.

All four regiments were in the Philippines where they fought against Filipino insurrection forces led by Aguinaldo, and later were used to garrison some of the island territory.

Brownsville and Houston

The 24th and 25th Infantries were returned from the Philippines to Texas. Around Texas towns there was white civilian resentment of the presence of uniformed Negro troops walking the streets. The soldiers did not conform to the stereotype of poorly clad subservient Negro males acceptable to the South. Friction between them and the civilians was frequent. When it occurred, the white commanders of the troops showed a tendency to support civilians against the soldiers of their command.

One such incident took place in Brownsville, Texas, which had national repercussions. In 1906, a Negro soldier of the First Battalion of the 25th Infantry had an altercation with a white Brownsville merchant. Following this occurrence Brownsville was placed off limits for the entire battalion and in retaliation a dozen or more Negro soldiers entered the town shooting wildly through the streets, killing one man and wounding several. Courts martial and special commissions of inquiry investigated the affair for three years. During this entire period, men of the three companies of the First battalion stood mute and would not testify against their fellow soldiers. For this refusal all enlisted men of the three companies were ordered discharged without honor by then President Theodore Roosevelt.

An even more serious racial disturbance occurred in Houston, Texas, in August of 1917. White hostility to Negro troops of the 24th Regiment in that city provoked an explosion on the part of some of the soldiers. Seventeen whites were killed and a score or more wounded. As an aftermath of the affair thirteen Negro soldiers were hanged after conviction for "murder and mutiny" and forty-one others were sentenced to life imprisonment.

[75] Herschel V. Cashin, *Under Fire* (New York: F. Tennyson Neeley, 1899), p. 147.

The bitterness engendered by these two events spilled over into both Negro and white communities nationally and was to have its repercussions during World War I.

WORLD WAR I

When the United States declared war on Germany, April 6, 1917, Negro participation in American Armed Forces consisted of the four Negro regiments of the regular Army and a number of National Guard units. In the course of the war 371,710 Negroes served in the Armed Forces. This was 10.7 percent of the total number of Americans who served. More than 200,000 Negroes saw service overseas, 150,000 in backbreaking work in labor and stevedore battalions.

Perhaps no segment of the American population at the beginning of the war stood more committed to the nation's war aims of making the world safe for democracy than did the American Negro. There were fourteen officer-training camps for whites, but War Department policy-makers claimed it would not be practical for Negroes to be trained at these camps. Still Negro enthusiasm could not be dampened. A Central Committee of Negro College Men to seek officer training opportunities was formed, with headquarters at Howard University in Washington, D.C.; more than three hundred Congressmen were visited by the committee members. One thousand Negro college students pledged themselves to enter an officer's training camp for Negroes when it was formed. Finally, on June 15, 1917, a Reserve Officer's Training Camp for Negroes, accommodating 1,250 men, was formally opened at Des Moines, Iowa.[76]

One of the Negro officers trained at this camp recalls the spirit that motivated the young Negro men who entered it. He writes:

> [italics his] We really believed that it was going to be a war to end oppression of all kinds and to make the world—of course the United States—safe for democracy. We felt that we were embarking upon a genuine crusade:
> > "Bliss was it in that dawn to be alive,
> > But to be young was very Heaven."
> I have a very vivid recollection of how my wife-to-be . . . *wept,* not because I was going to war but because for a while it seemed that *I wasn't going:* I was one of a number of young fellows [Campbell Johnson, as I

---

[76] Emmett J. Scott, *Scott's Official History of the American Negro in the World War* (Chicago: L. W. Walters Co., 1919), p. 82 *et seq.*

recall it, was another] who were first turned down for the Des Moines Camp because of underweight, youthfulness, or something; we were later accepted under a special dispensation of some sort. Rayford Logan, rather than miss the War, enlisted in the ranks.[77]

On October 14, 1917, commissions were given at Camp Des Moines to 639 young Negro men: 103 were commissioned captains; 329 first lieutenants; and 201 second lieutenants. Of the 1,353 Negro officers commissioned during World War I, most were trained at Des Moines.

Government Attitude on the Use of Negro Combat Troops

There were positive and negative aspects in Government policy on the use of Negro troops in World War I. When the British Government officially requested that Negro troops not be sent overseas, the Commander of the American Expeditionary Forces, General John J. Pershing, replied to the British War Minister, Lord Milner, and to the British Commander, Field Marshal Haig:

> You will, of course, appreciate my position in this matter, which is in brief that these Negroes are American citizens. My Government for reasons which concern itself alone, has decided to organize colored combat divisions and now desires the early dispatch of one of these to France. Naturally I cannot and will not discriminate against these men.[78]

Straightforward as this statement is, there are other facts which indicate that considerations other than military necessity actuated Government policy on Negro troops. It is significant that the four regular army units of seasoned Negro troops—the 9th and 10th Cavalry Regiments and the 24th and 25th Infantry Regiments—were literally quarantined from overseas combat duty throughout the war.

Two divisions of Negro combat troops—the 92nd and 93rd—were established, but they received treatment different from that accorded similar Army divisions. It is noticeable that the 92nd Division was one of two divisions which did not follow the training pattern of all other national Army divisions. It was never brought together as a division in the United States. Instead, elements of the division were separately trained at seven different camps from Kansas to Virginia and then shipped to France. The

---

[77] Letter of Lieutenant Colonel David A. Lane, U.S.A. Ret., April 1, 1964. Campbell C. Johnson is Colonel in the United States Army with the Selective Service Administration; Rayford Logan—too young for Des Moines, who rose from private to First Lieutenant through the ranks—is former Chairman of the Department of History at Howard University.

[78] John J. Pershing, *My Experiences in The World War* (New York: F. A. Stokes, 1931), Vol. II, p. 45.

93rd Division never existed as a division, except on paper. It was never assigned artillery or other necessary complements of transportation. Its four infantry regiments were split up in France and separately assigned to the French command.

Bulletin Number 35

This deviation from usual training patterns was motivated largely by the fear in War Department circles of another explosive Brownsville or Houston situation. They did not want to risk the congregation of 27,000 Negro soldiers in one camp coming in contact with surrounding white civilian communities. The sensitivity of top military leaders to this issue can be seen in Bulletin Number 35 issued by Brigadier General Charles C. Ballou, commander of the 92nd Division, at Camp Funston, Kansas, March 18, 1918.[79]

These were the facts which preceded the issuance of this bulletin: A Negro medical corps sergeant attempted to enter a movie theater near the camp and was barred by the white manager of the theater. Describing the occurrence, the bulletin went on to state:

> To avoid such conflicts the Division Commander has repeatedly urged all colored members of his command and especially officers and non-commissioned officers to refrain from going where his presence will be resented.

Admitting that the sergeant was within his legal rights in seeking admission to the theater, the bulletin continued:

> . . . nevertheless the sergeant is guilty of the greater wrong in doing anything, no matter how legally correct, that will provoke race animosity.

And it concluded with the veiled threat:

> . . . good will depends on the public. The public is nine-tenths white. White men made the Division and they can break it just as easy if it becomes a trouble maker. . . ."

The Ceiling on Negro Officers

Perhaps the most negative aspect of Government policy was the effective ceiling it placed upon the advance of Negro officers beyond junior grades. There were doubtless military leaders in positions of authority who honestly believed that the war would best be served by having Negro troops led by

---

[79] Scott, *op. cit.*, p. 97.

white officers. General Pershing in his book of reminiscences wrote after the war:

> It would have been much wiser to have followed the long experience of our Regular Army and provided these colored units with selected white officers.[80]

There were also some whose opinions were influenced by racial prejudice. In an environment where generally the capacities of Negro officers were clouded in doubt, it was easy for those with a perfervid hostility to the Negro officer class to materially affect War Department and Army policy.

Colonel Charles Young, highest ranking Negro officer, was one of the first to feel the sting of this hostility. A West Point Graduate and a former 10th Cavalry officer, he had served with distinction under General Pershing in the military actions on the Mexican border in 1916. He was the logical officer for command of a Negro division, but despite his futile effort to prove his fitness for command by a horseback ride from Ohio to Washington, he was retired from the Army as physically unfit. A black general was not wanted. Another Negro colonel, commanding the 370th Infantry (formerly the 8th Illinois National Guard Regiment) was also relieved for "physical fitness." Most of the other Negro field officers of National Guard units remained unassigned during the war.

The policy of holding the line against Negro field officers was clearly racial in origin. Thus, November 13, 1917, the Chief of Staff of the Army directed the Adjutant General:

> From surplus National Guard Officers now in federal service transfer white officers to fill all field and staff vacancies in the 372nd and colored officers from the National Guard or National Army to fill company vacancies.[81]

In the field, prejudice against Negro officers manifested itself in a variety of ways. The late Charles Houston, dean of Howard University Law School and a former First Lieutenant of the 368th Infantry, 92nd Division, wrote in the *Pittsburgh Courier*:

> The hate and scorn heaped upon us as Negro officers by our Americans, at Camp Mencou and Vannes, in France convinced me there was no sense of dying in a world ruled by them. . . . They boarded us off from our fellow white officers. They made us eat on benches in order to maintain segregation, and they destroyed our prestige in front of French officers.[82]

[80] Pershing, *op. cit.*, Vol. II, p. 228.
[81] National Archives, Historical Archives of the 93rd Division (Record Group No. 120), Box Number 1.
[82] *The Pittsburgh Courier*, March 19, 1960 (reprinted from previous edition).

A large body of evidence supports charges of prejudice against Negro officers—not as individuals, but as a class. It was precisely because the Negro officers were of superior educational attainment that they excited an even more furious hostility than was meted out to the plain Negro doughboy. For in the Negro officer the white racist saw a challenge to his claim to white supremacy. When—in France—French women drew no distinction between Negro officers and white officers, the cup of hostility was filled to overflowing. The following evidence supports these conclusions:

(1) December 8, 1918, in a letter to United States Senator from Tennessee Kenneth McKellar the Chief of Staff of the 92nd Division wrote:

The undoubted truth is that Colored officers neither control nor care to control the men. They themselves have been engaged very largely in the pursuit of French women, it being their first opportunity to meet white women who did not treat them as servants.[83]

(2) Five weeks after he assumed command of the 372nd Infantry Regiment, Colonel Herschel Tupes formally requested the Commanding General A.E.F., General Pershing, to permit the replacement of colored officers with white officers citing as his first reason for the request:

. . . The racial distinctions which are recognized in civilian life naturally continue to be recognized in military life and present a formidable barrier to the existence of that feeling of comradeship which is essential to mutual confidence and esprit de corp.[84]

The request was granted.
Both the 92nd Division and the infantry regiments of the 93rd Division were stripped of many of their Negro officers by hurried action of "efficiency boards" presided over by white officers. In a single week fifty white lieutenants replaced Negro officers in the 92nd Division.

The Grand Libel

Experience of French officers with Negro officers and soldiers led to mutual admiration and respect. The Negro members of the A.E.F. were greeted warmly by the French civilian population. However, instead of

[83] Documents of the War collected by W.E.B. Du Bois, *The Crisis*, XVIII (May, 1919), p. 19–20.
[84] *Ibid.*, p. 21.

welcoming this ease of relationships and seeking to extend it to all American troops, the effort was made in top circles of the American military command to destroy the fraternity between the French and American Negro soldiers. One famous libel exposed by *The Crisis* magazine in 1919 and never repudiated by the United States Government or the French Military Mission (from which it emanated) purported to give French officers "Secret Information Concerning Black American Troops."

The document asserted (1) that the Negro was regarded as an inferior human being by American whites; (2) that the vices of the Negro (the crime of rape was stressed) were a constant menace to the American who has to repress them sternly; (3) that French officers must not commend too highly the black American troops; (4) that the effort must be made to keep the French population from "spoiling" Negro troops and especially to prevent any expression of intimacy between white women and Negro soldiers. It was dated August 7, 1918, and signed "Linard." [85]

The evidence that an influential section of the American military command made libel of Negro troops a conscious policy does not rely upon the above evidence alone. There is the admission of General Robert Lee Bullard who commanded the 2nd Army to which the 92 Division was attached.

Immediately after the Armistice, November 11, 1918, the American commanders sought to have the 92nd Division sent back to the United States. Marshal Foch, the Allied Commander, refused this request, stating that he wanted no troops to leave the war zone until a treaty of peace had been signed. Wrote General Bullard:

> In answer I told the American headquarters to say to Marshal Foch that no man could be responsible for the acts of these Negroes toward French women, and that he had better send this division home at once.[86]

The Combat Record

Negro troops fought bravely and well. The first Negro soldiers under fire were members of the 369th Infantry. This regiment, upon landing at Brest, France, had been sent to a camp at St. Nazaire to perform noncombat work of service and supply. Describing the experience of soldiers of this regiment, their commander, Colonel William Hayward wrote:

> Here the regiment toiled for weeks building docks, erecting hospitals, laying railroad tracks, and constructing a great dam. The men never saw their

[85] *Ibid.*, pp. 16–17.
[86] Robert Lee Bullard, *Personalities and Reminiscenses of the War* (New York: Doubleday, Page & Co., 1925), p. 297.

rifles except by candlelight, but on March 10 was [sic] ordered to join a French combat unit at the battle line.[87]

The regiment held a sector in the Champagne region (Massiges, left of the Aisne river) until July and repulsed heavy German attacks in mid-July. It was relieved August 17 and sent to the rear, returning to the front line early in September, where it was constantly on the defensive against enemy raids. Between September 28 and October 2, it stormed Bellevue Signal Ridge, took the towns of Ripont and Sechault, and engaged in heavy fighting in the woods of Petit Rosière. It suffered 851 casualties in five days' fighting and its regimental colors were decorated by the French High Command with the Croix de Guerre with Silver Star for especially meritorious conduct in action. Two soldiers of the regiment, Henry Johnson and Needham Roberts, were the first American soldiers to receive the Croix de Guerre, for repelling a German raiding party of twelve to twenty men. When armistice was declared, the regiment could proudly boast that in 191 days in action on the front line it had never lost a trench or a foot of ground or had one of its soldiers taken prisoner.

The 370th Regiment, with all its company officers Negro, held a sector of the Allied front before St. Mihiel and later a sector in the Meuse-Argonne from June 22 to August 15, 1918. It was brigaded with the French 59th Division and with that unit drove the Germans north of the Oise-Aisne canal, advancing more than forty miles and reaching across into Belgium during the last week of the war. Company C of the 370th was singled out to receive the Croix de Guerre with Palm. The men of the regiment received sixteen Distinguished Service Crosses and seventy-five Croix de Guerre, besides company citations. In the Oise-Aisne Offensive the 370th suffered 665 casualties.

The 371st and 372nd Regiments fought as part of the French 157th Division in the Champagne region and later on the Meuse-Argonne front. In a few hours after midnight on June 12, 1918, German artillery concentrated on a narrow sector in the line east of Verdun where the 371st was defending and poured from three thousand to four thousand shells of its big guns on the trenches held by Negro troops. The regiment held firm and repulsed every attempt of German infantry to advance.[88]

In General Order No. 246, General Goybet who commanded the division wrote:

The 157th [French] Division will never forget the wonderful impetus irresist-

[87] National Archives, Historical Records of the 93rd Division, Record Group 120 Box Number 1. Report of Colonel Hayward.
[88] *The Crisis*, XVI (September, 1918), p. 238.

ible, the rush heroic of the colored American regiments on the "Observatories Crest" and in the Plain of Menthois. The most formidable defense, the nests of machine guns, the best organized positions, the artillery barrages most crushing, could not stop them. These best regiments have gone through all the disdain of death and thanks to their courage and devotedness, the "Red Hand" Division has during nine hard days of battle been ahead in the victorious advance of the Fourth [French] Army.[89]

Both regiments were awarded the Croix de Guerre with Palm and numerous individual citations for bravery in action. The 371st suffered 1,032 casualties and the 372nd, 616.

Still More Libel

Despite the Negro soldiers' record of bravery and heroism there were widespread rumors circulated in top military circles about the unreliability of Negro troops in combat. A principal source of these rumors was the Chief of Staff of the 92nd Division who in his letter to Senator McKellar of Tennessee wrote after the end of the war:

> Now that a reorganization of the army is in prospect . . . I think I ought to bring a matter to your attention not only from a military point of view *but from that which all Southerners have* [italics added]. I refer to the question of Negro officers and troops. . . .
> . . . From there we went to the Argonne and in the offensive starting there on September 26, had one regiment in the line attached to the 38th Corps. They failed there in all their missions, laid down and sneaked to the rear, until they were withdrawn.[90]

The charges were demonstrably false. Only one regiment of the 92nd Division was engaged in front line combat for any extended period, the 368th Regiment. Only one battalion of this regiment retreated and did so when its white commanding officer withdrew to the safety of the regimental command post after issuing a confusing order for retreat.

The noted historian W.E.B. Du Bois talked with Negro officers and men of this regiment in France in 1919. He wrote:

> The regiment as a whole was not equipped for battle in the front line. It had no artillery support until the sixth day of the battle; it had no grenades, no trench fires, trombones, or signal flares, no airplane panels for signalling and no shears for German wire. The wire-cutting shears given them were

[89] W.E.B. Du Bois, "An Essay Toward a History of the Black Man in the Great War," *The Crisis*, XVIII (June, 1919), p. 76.

[90] *Documents of the War, op. cit.*, p. 21.

absolutely useless with the heavy German barbed wire and they were able to borrow only sixteen large shears, which had to serve the whole attacking battalion. Finally they had no maps and were at no time given definite objectives.[91]

So virulent were the libels of white racists that a thorough investigation of the charges was ordered by Secretary of War Newton D. Baker, who after the completion of the inquiry made the following personal statement:

> The circumstances disclosed by a detailed study of the situation do not justify many of the highly colored accounts which have been given of the behavior of the troops in this action and they afford no basis at all for any of the general assumptions with regard to the action of colored troops in this battle and elsewhere in France. On the contrary it is to be noted that many colored officers and particularly three in the very battalion here under discussion, were decorated with Distinguished Service Crosses for extraordinary heroism under fire.[92]

Because of a difficult terrain in the Argonne forests the 368th Regiment suffered heavy casualties and was withdrawn, but not before it had attacked and captured the town of Binarville and five of its enlisted men had won the Distinguished Service Cross. Of the conduct of the whole regiment in this final action, Colonel Durand, its French commander, declared in a French General Order: "The honor of the prize of Binarville ought to go to 368th United States Infantry Regiment." [93]

Except for the 368th Regiment, other units of the 92nd Division had slight opportunity for combat. For about seven and a half weeks these units were stationed in a "quiet sector" on the Vosges front where there were no battles. During the last two days of the war, however, the 365th and 366th Regiments were in combat in the Marbache sector of the St. Mihiel region. Here in the face of poison gas, heavy artillery and machine-gun fire they advanced over two miles and occupied important positions in wooded areas of the region. Both regiments were cited for meritorious conduct in battle.

Negroes in the Navy

During World War I the United States Navy restricted Negro enlistments to its messman's branch, where approximately ten thousand Negroes served. No Negroes were permitted to enlist in the United States Marines.

[91] Du Bois (Essay), *op. cit.*, p. 80.
[92] Armed Service Forces Manual (M5), *op. cit.*, p. 93.
[93] "*L'Honneur de la prise de Binarville doit revenir au 368th R.I.U.S.*" Du Bois (Essay), *op. cit.*, p. 82.

BETWEEN TWO WARS

Striking Bottom

From the close of the war until 1932 the Navy halted all enlistments of Negroes for any purpose. Negro messmen were virtually eliminated from the Navy. Within half a dozen years after World War I, Negro strength in the Army had fallen below that of the year 1900. Many Negro National Guard units were deactivated, and the four Negro Regular Army regiments were greatly reduced in strength.

The decrease of the number of Negroes in service was part of an overall reduction in the size of the Armed Forces in peacetime, but while white youth found opportunities to leave the Army and enter the Army Air Force, the Marines or the Navy, no such alternatives were open to Negro youth. There were soon more Negro soldiers and more Negro noncommissioned officers than there were places for them in the Army. As a result the War Department officially prohibited the enlistment, reenlistment or promotion of Negroes in the Army.[94] Careers for Negroes in the Army were at an end, and Negro regiments, with a long and honorable record, began to "wither away."

There was sharp protest from Negro leaders and organizations over the disintegration of the Negro regiments. Typical was the letter of Major Robert Russa Moton, principal of Tuskegee Institute, to President Herbert Hoover. Major Moton wrote in part:

> It is more than unfortunate, it is an injustice, that regiments that have distinguished themselves in the way the 10th Cavalry and the 25th Infantry have done, should be reduced from combat service to be menials to white regiments, without chance for training and promotion and be excluded from other branches of the services. It is merely a pretense that Negroes are accorded the same treatment in the United States Army as is given white troops. It never has been the case and is not now so.[95]

Mobilization Plans

While there was no apparent change of policy affecting Negro troops, top military leaders in secret discussions had the question of the use of Negro manpower in time of war very much in mind. They were faced with a dilemma. On the one hand there was a widely held view among military

[94] Memorandum of the War Department (G-3) to the Adjutant General, June 17, 1931: Subject—Suspension of Recruiting in Colored Organizations.

[95] September 17, 1931. Quoted in Major Ulysses G. Lee, *U.S. Army in World War II—The Employment of Negro Troops,* an unpublished manuscript in the Office of the Chief of Military History. Hereafter will be referred to as "Lee."

planners that Negro troops were unreliable in combat.[96] On the other hand if losses in combat—estimated from previous experience at about 34 percent of the men in battle—were to be borne exclusively by white soldiers, there would be resentment from the families of white enlisted men. There had been evidence that this would result.

A study made for the Army Chief of Staff in November, 1922, undertook to solve this dilemma. It concluded that Negroes must be used in combat as well as in service units, that Negroes should be put into units smaller in size than a division, that Negro officers should be used, but no Negro officer should be put in a position where he could command white troops. The conclusions of this study became basic Army policy for the next fifteen years—at least on paper. There was little change in the actual status of the Negro in the Army, however. In 1937, the total strength of the Army and National Guard was 360,000. Negroes were only about 1.8 percent of this total, or 6,500.

The Selective Service Act

On September 14, 1940, President Franklin D. Roosevelt signed the Selective Service Act. War had broken out in Europe and the mobilization of American manpower had become essential to the security of the nation. Up to the time this Act became law the barriers to Negro participation in the Armed Forces were numerous. Negroes might volunteer for service in the Coast Guard and Navy only as menials. The Marine Corps admitted

[96] The stereotype of the Negro soldier in the minds of many military leaders derived from a number of sources: (1) The true fact that a high percentage of Negro draftees were either illiterate (40 percent of the 92nd Division in World War I) or were in disproportionate numbers among those with low scores on intelligence tests. This reflected only upon the educational systems that had denied Negroes equal educational opportunity. (2) The highly colored adverse reports on Negro troops by white commanders of proven anti-Negro bias such as General Robert Lee Bullard and Colonel Allan J. Geer, Chief of Staff of the 92nd Division. (3) Common racist views about Negroes. All of these currents of opinion are found reflected in studies and reports of officers of field grade made while they were students at the Army War College. This is significant because the students of the War College are the group from whom the nation's top military leaders are chosen. The following report of a group of War College students—all of them officers of field grade—on "Use of Negro Manpower in time of War"—made November 12, 1936, reveals the nature of the Negro stereotype in their minds. It read: "As an individual the negro is docile, tractable, light-hearted, care free [sic], and good natured. If unjustly treated he is likely to become surly and stubborn though this is a temporary phase. He is careless, shiftless, irresponsible and secretive. He resents censure and is best handled with praise and ridicule. He is unmoral, untruthful, and his sense of right doing is relatively inferior. Crimes and convictions involving moral turpitude are nearly five to one compared with convictions of whites on similar charges. . . ." And further: "Their emotions are unstable and their reactions uncertain. Bad leadership in particular is easily communicated to them."

whites only and this was true also of the Army Air Corps, the Army Artillery, Engineer, Signal and Tank Corps.

The Selective Service Act contained an amendment, which had been introduced by Representative Hamilton Fish, Republican of New York, that altered this situation. It read:

> ... providing that in the selection and training of men under [the] Act, and in the interpretation and execution of the provisions of this Act, there shall be no discrimination against any person on account of race or color.

Not only was there war in Europe, there was also a candidate in the White House running for an unprecedented third term as President of the United States. President Roosevelt and his advisers were keenly aware of pressures from Negro organizations for a "New Deal" for Negroes in the Armed Forces. In the month of October, 1940, before November elections, important steps were taken to meet the Negro demands.

Under the new Selective Service Act 400,000 Americans were to be drafted, 36,000 of them Negro. Roosevelt had told his Cabinet early in September that he was troubled by "representation of the Negroes that their race under the draft would be limited to labor battalions." A new policy prepared by the War Department and given the written approval of President Roosevelt was announced at the White House October 9, 1940. It declared in essence that (1) Negro strength in the Army would be in proportion to the Negro population's percentage of the total population; (2) that Negro organizations were to be formed in each major branch of the Service, combatant as well as noncombatant; (3) that Negroes would be given opportunity to serve as officers and to attend officer training schools; (4) that Negroes would be trained as pilots, mechanics and technical aviation specialists. The announcement went on to state, however, that it did not intend to mingle Negro and white enlisted men in the same regiments as this "would produce situations destructive to morale and detrimental to the preparation for national defense."

Elect and Elect

Negro leaders who had been at the White House in September were quick to point out that there was still to be a Jim Crow Army and this kind of repercussion set in motion other activity. Bishop R. R. Wright, chairman of the Colored Division of the National Democratic Headquarters, propounded to Stephen Early, White House Secretary, the leading question, "if it was a fact that under the present administration the Negro has gotten more recognition in the Army than ever before?" General George Marshall in an "immediate action letter" to a subordinate said "get for me today, for the White House, answers" to these (Bishop Wright's ed.) questions.[97] Promptly the War Department informed the White House of specific units of Negro troops to be formed and the date when this would be done.

Four days later (October 25, 1940), the simultaneous appointment of Colonel Benjamin O. Davis, ranking Negro officer in the Army, to be a Brigadier General—the first Negro general in American history—and of another Negro, William H. Hastie, to be civilian aide to the Secretary of War could hardly be overlooked by professional politicians. Although Oswald Garrison Villard termed it "a cheap political move," it was obvious that the "Third Term New Dealers" were carrying out the instructions of one of their main advisers, Harry Hopkins, "to spend and spend, tax and tax, elect and elect"—except that to the slogan they had added, "appoint and appoint." [98]

Jim Crow Logistics

On August 31, 1939, there were only 3,640 Negroes in the regular Army, but by November 30, 1941, the number had risen to 97,725. Every problem of selecting, quartering and training men under the Selective Service Act became much more complex when the drafted men were Negro. For many reasons it was virtually impossible to maintain a balance between Negro and white draftees as required by law. Negroes were between 9 and 10 percent of the population, but constituted 13 percent of those classified as I-A by the draft boards and hence eligible for immediate selection. Because Negroes were permitted to be housed only in segregated areas of Army camps, Negro selectees were frequently held back from induction for months until barrack space could be found for them. Meanwhile a disproportionate number of white youths were being rushed into training camps.

Even where there was housing, there was frequently objection from civilian circles to bringing any large number of Negroes into a camp. Inside and outside of the Army there was an inchoate fear of race riots, which made for a gingerly approach to the location of Negro trainees. Congressmen and Senators from the North and South voiced objection to Negro troops being placed in their states. The slightest sign of racial trouble led to relocation of Negro units. There were no large concentrations of

[97] Immediate Action Memorandum, Chief of Staff (signed G.C.M.) for General Bryden, October 21, 1940. Lee, op. cit.

[98] That the guiding hand of all this flurry of activity was Roosevelt's cannot be doubted. On that same October 25 he penciled on a note pinned to White House memorandum for the Secretary of War (Stimson) the following, for Undersecretary Robert Patterson: "Patterson—Colored Reserve Officers must be called just as white Reserves. Assign to new units and not just to National Guard units. F.D.R."

Negroes, and when 3,500 Negro soldiers went into training at Camp Lee, Virginia, their placement at the camp was approved by the general staff with the following stipulation:

> If the Commanding General, Third Corps Area, felt special precautions were necessary with this proportion, a detachment of a rifle company from the 12th Infantry Regiment could be made available to help prevent race riots.[99]

As larger numbers of Negro selectees were inducted into the Army, military necessity prevailed over civilian prejudices in the matter of the location of Negro troops. A new approach developed which called upon camp commanders to "forestall racial difficulties by firm discipline, just treatment, strenuous training, and wholesome recreation." [100]

Smaller Negro units—those less than division size—went into training at a number of camps, but only at Camp Huachuca, Arizona, was an entire Negro division (the 93rd) accommodated. Again, as had been the case in World War I, the effectiveness of the training program for the 92nd Division was weakened because units of the division were trained in widely separated camps in four states. The 2nd Cavalry Division, another Negro unit, was split up for training. While other Army divisions underwent training as an integrated whole, thus building an esprit de corps, Negro units, intended to fight together, were being trained as strangers to one another.

Bricks without Straw

One of the most serious deficiencies in the Army training program for its raw Negro recruits was the lack of adequate cadres around which new units could be built. Initially there were no Negro chemical, engineering or artillery units from which cadres could be drawn. Nor were the established Negro units in the Regular Army of much use in furnishing cadres. They had been greatly reduced in strength and were no longer combat-trained, having been assigned menial duties in service and supply. In some cases white noncommissioned officers were used as cadres for Negro troops, but only on a temporary basis. Thus many Negro combat units never had a hard core of seasoned veterans to serve as soldier-models for new recruits.

Studies of scores made by recruits in the Army General Classification Tests (AGCT scores) showed that in the early 1940's a much larger percentage of Negroes than whites fell into the lower test categories. Of

[99] Memorandum of General Staff (Organization and Training—G-3) to War Plans Division, October 5, 1940: Subject—Camp Lee, Virginia. Lee, *op. cit.*
[100] Memorandum of Lieutenant General Leslie J. McNair to Adjutant General, June 14, 1942.

4,129,000 white and 440,000 Negro men who entered the Army between March, 1941, and December, 1942, about 84 percent of the Negroes and 33 percent of the whites had test scores in the lowest categories (Army Grades IV and V), while only about 4 percent of the Negroes and 35 percent of the whites were in the two highest grades.

Lower scores for many of the Negroes reflected inferior educational opportunities as well as the repressive social environment in which they lived. A majority of those with lowest test scores came from nine Southern states where the per capita expenditure in public school education for Negro youth was $18.82 in 1939–40, while that for whites was $58.69—more than three times as large. Much lower scores for Negroes in mechanical aptitude tests reflected the lack of opportunity afforded Negroes for skilled work in American industry.

Negroes, irrespective of mental aptitudes or educational preparation, were bunched together in massive numbers. For example, in May, 1941, of 2,410 Negro selectees assigned to the 367th Infantry Regiment (of the Negro 92nd Division) 815 were completely illiterate and many others could barely read and write. In April, 1942, nearly 60 percent of the men in the 46th Field Artillery Brigade (a Negro unit) had scored in the lowest grade in the AGCT. Thus the rigid segregation policy of the Army General Staff operated as a major deterrent to the creation of Negro units where there was a balanced assortment of men with varying aptitudes and skills.

The Army Air Force

In 1942, the expansion of the Army Air Force to nearly one million men entailed the increase of its Negro strength by more than 50,000. Now with a total of 77,592 Negroes in the Air Force, the question was what to do with them.

A new type of organization—the air base security battalion—was created primarily to absorb the Negro additions. Of 296 authorized units of this type, 261 were to be Negro. The mission of the units was to be protection of air bases from riots, parachute raids, and aerial attacks. Since, however, there was an acute shortage of antiaircraft weapons these troops were in most instances not provided with nor trained in the use of such weapons. They were thus not equipped to provide effective defense against air attack.

By spring of 1943, fourteen Negro air base security battalions were overseas (6,000 men), another forty-nine battalions (20,000 men) were activated and ready for overseas shipment and fifty-five battalions (22,500 men) were waiting to be activated. Unwanted overseas because of race and because they were not equipped for effective use, these units soon began to clog existing training camps and caused a backup of training activity all along the line. They were clearly nonessential. As the Chief of the Air Force, Lieutenant General H. H. Arnold wrote:

> It is unlikely that theater commanders will require Negro Air Base Security Battalions or any other Negro units to the extent offering justification for their use.

In the months that followed many of these battalions were eventually deactivated and their personnel retrained and assigned to service units.

Negro Pilots

An even more nettlesome problem faced Air Force leaders as they began to implement the announced policy of training Negro pilots. Tuskegee Institute, which had previously begun a civilian pilot training program, was selected as the location of a school for Negroes as pilots of single-engine planes only.

This was the beginning in the breakdown of the barriers to Negro pilot training, but it was far from complete. Pilot training was limited to candidates who were five feet nine inches or under in height and who weighed 160 pounds or less. Nor did the school provide training facilities for essential auxiliary specialties needed to activate a squadron (aerial observers, weather, armament, engineer, aviation medical officers). Must there be a *separate Negro* school for each of these specialties? This was a problem which troubled General Arnold who wrote one of his aides (Brigadier General Davenport Johnson):

> General Johnson How should we go about training the colored mechanics for *1 squadron* with the least trouble and effort [Italics by General Arnold].[101]

Thus the airtight compartments of segregation in which Negroes were placed became less and less tenable as a means for effective utilization of Negro manpower in the Armed Forces. This point was forcefully made to Secretary of War Henry L. Stimson by his Civilian Aide, William H. Hastie, who declared:

> The traditional mores of the South have been widely accepted and adopted by the Army as a basis of policy and practice affecting the Negro soldier. . . . In tactical organization, in physical location, in human contacts, the Negro soldier is separated from white soldiers as completely as possible. . . .

[101] Marginal note penciled on memorandum of General Johnson and signed "H.H.A.," October 5, 1940.

The isolation of Negro combat troops, the failure to make any of them parts of large combat teams, the refusal to mingle Negro officers—many of whom have had little opportunity to command and train soldiers—in units with experienced officers of the Regular Army, all are retarding the training of Negro soldiers. . . .[102]

Through 1942 the Air Force experimented with the notion of completely separate facilities for training required by components of a Negro Pursuit Squadron. It did so in the face of mounting pressure from the Negro press and from Civilian Aide Hastie. Finally, Hastie resigned (January 6, 1943) in protest; and, as a probable consequence of this resignation, the Air Force announced (January 28, 1943—a day before Secretary Stimson accepted the Hastie resignation) a program for expansion of Negro pilot training. The new policy declared that Negroes would be accepted "throughout the entire Technical Training Command as well as at the Air Force's Officer Training School at Miami" (Florida). This marked a significant step toward integration.

WORLD WAR II

Fighting Mess Attendants

At the time of the Japanese attack on Pearl Harbor, December 7, 1941, Negroes in the Navy were restricted to service as mess attendants and stewards.[103] Even in these noncombatant ratings, many of them were among the first Americans to display conspicuous bravery in World War II. Under fire aboard the U.S.S. *Arizona* at Pearl Harbor, mess attendant second class Dorie Miller took the place of a dead gunner and turned a machine gun against enemy aircraft. For "distinguished devotion to duty, extreme courage, and disregard of his personal safety during attack" he was awarded the Navy Cross.

Miller was only one of scores of noncombatant Negro mess attendants who were decorated for heroism under fire. Mess attendant first class Leonard Roy Harmon, while serving aboard the U.S.S. *San Francisco* in

[102] Memorandum, September 22, 1941.

[103] The Navy declared officially: "the policy of not enlisting men of the colored race for any branch of the naval service but the messmen's branch was adopted to meet the best interests of general ship efficiency. . . . This policy not only serves the best interests of the Navy and the country, but serves as well the best interests of [Negroes] themselves." Quoted in *Freedom to Serve* (Washington, D.C.: Government Printing Office, 1950), p. 17.

the Solomon Islands area "deliberately exposed himself to hostile gunfire in order to protect a shipmate and as a result of this courageous deed was killed in action." William Pinckney, cook third class, when a bomb exploded aboard his ship, the U.S.S. *Enterprise,* "saved his comrade's life at great risk of his own." Harmon and Pinckney were awarded the Navy Cross. Six Negro steward's mates on the aircraft carrier U.S.S. *Intrepid* were awarded the Bronze Star Medal for manning an antiaircraft gun and bringing down an attacking dive bomber. Although wounded himself and bleeding profusely, Elbert H. Oliver, steward's mate first class, took over the station of a wounded gunner and maintained accurate fire against enemy torpedo planes. Oliver was awarded the Silver Star Medal. When his ship had been abandoned during the Battle of the Coral Sea, Charles Jackson French, mess attendant second class, tied a rope around his body, and, attaching it to a raft carrying fifteen men, swam for two hours without rest until the raft was beyond enemy fire. He was commended by Admiral William F. Halsey "for conduct in keeping with the highest traditions of naval service." Many others performed deeds of equal valor.

Policy Change

Not until the United States had been at war for more than six months were Negroes accepted for general service in the Navy—and then only for service ashore. Reacting to the steady drumfire of protest from the Negro press and Negro organizations, President Roosevelt in April, 1942, urged upon Secretary of the Navy Frank Knox the breaking of the deep-seated Navy tradition against the use of Negroes except as servants.[104] In June, 1942, some Negroes were placed in training for general ratings, but these were kept in segregated camps and schools.

It was more than two years later, August 9, 1944, before the restriction of Negroes to shore duty was lifted. Some five hundred Negro sailors were placed on seagoing auxiliary naval vessels stationed in the South Pacific with ratings as quartermasters, ship's carpenters, coxswains, gunner's mates, petty officers and the like. Between 1944 and 1945 a number of radical policy changes occurred in the Navy. Significant progress was made in eliminating segregation in most training activities, from mess and recreation facilities. The Navy declared its intention to assign Negroes in all ratings to auxiliary vessels up to 10 percent of the ship's complement and some Negro sailors were assigned to combat duties on warships. Negro exclusion from

---

[104] The President's Committee on Equality of Treatment and Opportunity in the Armed Services (The Fahy Committee), *Freedom to Serve* (Washington, D.C.: Government Printing Office, 1950), p. 18.

the Marine Corps and the Coast Guard (under Navy Control in wartime) was also abandoned.

By August, 1945, there were 165,000 Negro enlisted men in the Navy and 53 officers. There were nearly 17,000 Negro marines; while the Coast Guard had about 4,000 enlisted men and four officers. While these steps made for a much improved position of the Negro in the Navy, it was nevertheless a fact that 95 percent of all Negroes in the Navy were still in the messmen's branch at the end of 1945.

Developments in the Army

Induction of Negro draftees into most branches of the Army and on a massive scale occurred more rapidly than in the Navy. At the end of 1942 every arm and service of the Army except the Finance Department had Negro units. Nearly half a million Negroes were in Army uniforms (see Table I).

TABLE I—Racial Distribution in the Army by Types of Service as of December 31, 1942

Type of Service	White	Negro	Percentage of Negroes in Each Type of Service	Percentage of all Men in Army White	Negro
Combat Units	1,815,094	92,772	4.8	40.0	19.7
Service Units	616,851	161,707	20.7	13.6	34.6
AAF and ASWAF	1,190,363	109,637	8.4	26.4	23.5
Overheads*	303,820	65,880	15.3	8.0	14.1
RTC's	238,500	27,500	10.3	5.3	5.9
OCS	72,200	800	1.1	1.5	0.2
Unassigned	235,289	9,587	3.9	5.2	2.1

* Includes replacement depots and hospitals

SOURCE: Memorandum of War Department (G-3), January 25, 1943 showing use of manpower by race.

Dialogue on Negro Manpower

Momentous decisions affecting the use of Negro manpower were in process of being made in the midst of a world war. A dialogue of crucial significance was going on which involved both Negro civilian leaders and leading circles in the War Department and the Army.

One of the principal participants in the dialogue was the Negro Civilian Aide to the Secretary of War, Judge William H. Hastie. Since his appointment in October, 1940, he had made a ten months' survey of conditions affecting the use of Negro personnel. Hastie felt "a beginning should be made in the employment of soldiers without racial separation." He pointed out that this would stimulate the men in the Army and civilians at home to "believe in and work for democracy with . . . fever and determination." He declared his belief that "military authorities do not comprehend the amount of resentment among soldiers and civilians, white as well as black, over the rigid pattern of racial separation imposed by the Army." [105]

The dialogue was joined by the Army Chief of Staff, General George C. Marshall. "A solution of many of the issues presented by Judge Hastie," wrote General Marshall in a memorandum to Secretary of War Stimson, ". . . would be tantamount to solving a social problem which has perplexed the American people throughout the history of this nation. The Army cannot accomplish such a solution and should not be charged with such an undertaking. The settlement of vexing racial problems cannot be permitted to complicate the tremendous task of the War Department and thereby jeopardize discipline and morale." [106]

This reasoning became in time the oft-repeated refrain of lower echelons of Army leaders in answer to nearly every request for amelioration of the conditions under which Negro soldiers served in the Army. It was not an answer that satisfied Negroes. Papers like the *Pittsburgh Courier* called for a double victory: victory over fascism abroad and victory over segregation at home. Negro leaders pointed out that all Negro soldiers were forced to submit to humiliation from the segregation mores of the South even though many came from the North where such customs did not exist.

Walter White, national secretary of the NAACP, wrote General Marshall and suggested a conference to discuss the creation of a volunteer division composed of whites and Negroes. In a background memorandum which displayed no small amount of irritation and finality, Lieutenant Colonel J. W. Boyer advised his superior, Major General E. S. Adams:

> . . . I can see no useful purpose in any officer dissapating [*sic*] his time to discuss [the idea] with Mr. White or anyone else. There may be some super-tolerant people that would join a Negro outfit but their numbers would be few. Other whites that would join a Negro outfit would be of the same class of whites that would live in a Negro community. This Judge Hastie knows and admits and he does nothing to cut down useless and persistent correspondence on the subject.[107]

[105] Report of Judge William H. Hastie, Civilian Aide to the Secretary of War, September 22, 1941. Lee, *op. cit.*
[106] December 1, 1941.
[107] June 13, 1942.

The dialogue continued but it produced no significant change in the segregation policy announced by the War Department in 1940. The War Department was not convinced that the issue was important. John J. McCloy, the Assistant Secretary of War, wrote Judge Hastie:

> Frankly I do not think that the basic issues of this war are involved in the question of whether Colored troops serve in segregated units or in mixed units and I doubt whether you can convince the people of the United States that the basic issues of freedom are involved in such a question. If the United States does not win this war the lot of the Negro is going to be far, far worse than it is today.[108]

Use of Negro Troops Overseas

Although at the end of 1942 there were 467,000 Negroes in the Army, fewer than 54,000 were deployed overseas. Negroes constituted 9.35 percent of the Army, but only 5.61 percent of the American soldiers overseas. This fact reflected a condition reported upon by then Brigader General Dwight D. Eisenhower, chief of the War Plans Division, to the General Council on March 17, 1942. General Eisenhower had stated "that the problem was proving exceedingly difficult, for as yet, he had found no foreign country where Negro troops would be welcome."

The problem of Negro troops overseas became so acute that Generals Virgil Peterson and B. O. Davis of the Inspector General's Office questioned the wisdom of continuing to train and equip Negro troop units which could not be sent overseas while there was urgent need for combat troops. Planners in the War Department busied themselves with surveys of areas where it was felt Negro troops would be acceptable. Their wide-scale use in Liberia was contemplated, but abandoned when it became apparent that there was little liklihood of war action in that area. The Arctic area was advocated for Negro troops because there "[it] eliminates to a large extent the delicate social problems involved."[109]

Some, but not all theater commanders sought to avoid use of Negro troops in their areas. The commanding generals of several theaters requested that no Negro troops be sent to their areas. In the South Pacific Major General Millard F. Harmon in January, 1943, told General George C. Marshall that he would accept a Negro division under his command, but none but white officers should be sent with it. Since this requirement could not be met, the 93rd Division was not sent overseas at that time. One year later

[108] July 2, 1942.
[109] Memorandum of War Department (G-4), March 15, 1943: Subject—Negro Troops in Arctic Region.

(January 1, 1944) the 93rd Division was reluctantly accepted by General Harmon with its complement of Negro officers.

A notable exception to this position was General Douglas MacArthur, who wired General Marshall:

> I will do everything possible to prevent friction or resentment on the part of the Australian government and people at the presence of American colored troops. Please disabuse yourself of any idea that I might return these troops after your decision to dispatch them.[110]

The Growing Problem

Despite planning by the Army General Staff the problem of utilizing Negro manpower and especially of the use of Negro combat troops overseas did not abate. As the number of Negroes in the Army grew to more than 700,000 in 1943, the Army G-3 admitted that the War Department was in the unenviable position of:

> 1) Having a backlog of combat units in the United States;
> 2) Having to deplete or inactivate these units to provide personnel for service units to avoid wasting manpower;
> 3) Having to answer numerous queries from Negro organizations without having definite justification for failure to commit Negro personnel in combat units.[111]

The situation was fast becoming intolerable. Crack National Guard units, (the 366th and 372nd Regiments) had been placed on "home guard" duty in Massachusetts and New York in the spring of 1941 and three years later in 1944 lacked a definite combat mission. Elements of the proud 8th Illinois Infantry Regiment (National Guard) were inducted as field artillery in 1941, and reorganized as separate engineer combat battalions in 1943. The 2nd Cavalry Division (which included two Negro Regular Army units, the 9th and 10th Cavalry Regiments) was slated for conversion to noncombat status.

The Stimson Letter

On February 1, 1944, Representative Hamilton Fish, who had commanded Negro combat troops in World War I, queried Secretary Stimson about the report that the "fully trained and equipped 24th Infantry had been in the South Pacific for nearly two years performing only labor duties." The

[110] March 29, 1942.
[111] Memorandum of Colonel L. S. Partridge, January 6, 1944: Subject—Survey of Negro Units.

Stimson reply actually prepared by his military aides contained this paragraph:

> It so happens that a relatively large percentage of the Negroes inducted in the Army have fallen within lower educational qualifications, and many Negro units accordingly have been unable to master efficiently the techniques of modern weapons.[112]

The Stimson letter, when published, aroused criticism in the Negro press and among Negro leaders. The *Pittsburgh Courier* characterized the views expressed in the letter as "the Stimson-the-Negro-is-too-dumb-to-fight policy." In a sharp letter to the War Secretary, his former Civilian Aide Judge Hastie declared:

> The truth of the matter is that these original Negro combat units have been problem children of the Army for more than two years, not because they were incompetent, but because no one wanted them. Nurtured on the myth that Negro troops cannot be relied upon in combat and fearing to add a "racial problem" to other headaches in the theater of war, field commanders and the Operations Branch of the War Department turned thumbs down on the utilization of the great majority of the Negro combat units.[113]

Combat Under Klieg Lights

Army leaders felt the sting of public opinion. Within a month after the Stimson letter, Chief of Staff General Marshall (March 18, 1944) sent a highly confidential message "For Harmon's Eyes Only" to General Harmon. It read:

> War Department under constant pressure for alleged failure to use Negro troops in combat. . . . Anything warranting comment in conduct of 93rd under fire should be reported soon after their initial use. . . .[114]

News was not long in coming. Eleven days later, with war correspondents covering their engagement, the troops of the 25th Infantry landed on the island of Bougainville and were committed to combat.

The performance of these troops in their first engagement was such as might be expected of raw troops under fire for the first time. There were mistakes and unnecessary casualties, but as Assistant Secretary McCloy was to write Secretary Stimson:

> . . . On the whole I feel the report is not so bad as to discourage us. . . . The general tone of these reports reminds me of the first reports we got of the

[112] February 18, 1944.
[113] February 29, 1944.
[114] Memorandum of 1 June 1944. Lee, *op. cit.*

99th Squadron. You remember that they were not very good, but that squadron has now taken its place in line and performed very well. It will take more time and effort to make good combat units out of them.[115]

And Stimson endorsed the memorandum: "Noted—but I do not believe they can be turned into really effective combat troops without all officers being white."

The activities of the 92nd Division were given even closer attention. The first part of the division to be sent overseas was Regimental Combat Team 370, composed of the 370th Infantry Regiment, the 598th Field Artillery Battalion, and several small special units. The team left Fort Huachuca, Arizona, on June 15, 1944, and arrived in Naples, Italy, July 30. On August 26–28 it entered the battle zone at Pontedera on the Arno River facing the mountain slopes of the Northern Apennines, where German and Italian Divisions were defending their "Gothic Line."

The troops had scarcely taken their position when they were deluged by visits from high-ranking military and civilian personnel. Brigadier General B. O. Davis came, bringing with him a motion picture crew to make motion pictures of the troops "in action" for the propaganda film, *Teamwork*. Prime Minister Winston Churchill was another visitor. War correspondents came, eagerly seeking news that could be channeled to news media in the United States to prove to Negro Americans that their sons were to have an honorable combat role and not be used solely in labor battalions.

Most important visitor of all was the supreme commander of the Fifth Army, Lieutenant General Mark W. Clark, who inspected the troops on August 28th. General Clark asked the colonel commanding the troops if he had any problems. Upon being told that the only complaint was that promotions were too slow for some of the officers, Clark asked the colonel to point out an officer who was due for promotion; and, when a first lieutenant (Charles F. Gandy of Washington, D.C.) was presented to him, he borrowed a captain's bars from one of his aides and dramatically pinned them on the shoulders of the Negro officer. Immediately a news-hungry press heralded this act as a "battlefield promotion" although the unit had never been in combat.[116]

---

[115] *Ibid.* Above memorandum initialed and noted by Secretary Stimson, 5 June 1944.

[116] This is not to imply that Captain Gandy did not deserve promotion. Only two days later (August 30) he led a 22-man patrol across the Arno River behind enemy lines; there the patrol destroyed an enemy machine-gun position and captured two enemy soldiers: the first prisoners taken by Negro troops in Europe. Six weeks later (October 12–14) he led his troops up the steep cliffs of Mount Cauala, using scaling ladders; though mortally wounded he held a ridge on the mountain until ordered to withdraw by his regimental commander. He was posthumously awarded the Silver Star for conspicuous heroism.

Thus the division was well launched with all due publicity; but major problems were swept under a rug. More than 90 percent of the enlisted men in the division had AGCT scores placing them in the two lowest categories; many of them were illiterate. There was not and had never been an esprit de corps between white and Negro officers; white officers admitted a distaste for service with Negro troops and the enlisted men knew it; Negro noncommissioned officers felt so insecure in their rank (because they were so often peremptorily reduced in grade) that there was little incentive to maintain high discipline among the enlisted men; enlisted men disliked and distrusted many of their white officers, especially the large number from the South.[117] This was a canker that doses of ballyhoo were not going to cure.

What happened to the 92nd Division after those publicity-filled August days under sunny Italian skies is a mixture of frustration, unquestioned bravery and heroism, humiliation and sad confusion. As Lieutenant Colonel Marcus H. Ray, Negro commander of the 600th Field Artillery Battalion was to write when the fighting days of the division were over, "I do not believe the 92nd a complete failure as a combat unit but when I think what it might have been, I am heartsick. . . ."[118]

In the month of September the combat team advanced about twenty-one miles against light enemy resistance, penetrated the Gothic Line and sealed off Highway 12, a major enemy communications road; it had lost eight men killed in action and had 248 sick, wounded or injured. The weather had been good; the terrain presented few difficulties.

By October it found itself in the foothills of the Northern Apennines. Cold chilling rains made narrow, winding mountain roads literal seas of mud, impassable even for mules. Rock cliffs rose abruptly from the Arno plains to heights of from 1,500 to 3,000 feet. From concrete pillboxes, gun emplacements atop high ridges, defending German forces could engage in murderous enfilading fire upon the attackers.

"Melting Away"

Better led men, men with better motivation, might have overcome these hazards; indeed, many elements of the combat team did overcome them. Many soldiers, however, (on the basis of testimony of both Negro and white

---

[117] This assessment summarizes the comment of Captain Charles H. Welch of the Inspector General's Office, reporting on his investigation of the fatal shooting of a white officer of the division while he was asleep in his tent. Lee, *op. cit.*

[118] Letter to Truman K. Gibson, Civilian Aide to the Secretary of War, dated May 14, 1945.

officers) [119] wavered under fire, showed a tendency not to hold their positions, not to be aggressive in the advance, sometimes they "melted away."

This charge was soon blown up out of all proportion and was used as the basis for a generalization about the combat-readiness of all Negro soldiers. Truman K. Gibson, Civilian Aide to the Secretary of War, who had succeeded Judge Hastie in this post, went to Italy to visit the front. He listened to accounts of poor performance; and, in Rome, gave a "candid interview" to the press. In a story in *The New York Times*,[120] the charge that Negro troops "melted away" was attributed to Gibson. Other newspapers were quick to spread this account of the interview.

Gibson claimed his remarks were garbled. Later in a report to Major General O. L. Nelson, he pointed out:

> It is a fact that there have been many withdrawals by panic-stricken infantrymen. However it is equally evident that the underlying reasons are quite generally unknown in the division. The blanket generalizations expressed by so many, based on inherent racial difficulties, are contradicted by many acts of individual and group bravery.[121]

A dozen years after the 92nd Division's Italian campaign (1956) General Clark—whose grandstand "battlefield promotion" of Lieutenant Gandy had drawn such a favorable press—declared before an audience of Southern whites that the "92nd Division was the worst division I had." [122] His comment was soon endorsed by the wartime commander of the division, General Edward M. Almond.[123]

This invidious comment by General Clark—made, perhaps, to suit the prejudiced views of his auditors—need not be accepted as historical fact. There is convincing evidence that much of the ill luck of the 92nd may

[119] A variety of factors were cited to explain instances of poor combat performance of of some units of Combat Team 370: poor organization and control; insufficient information disseminated and understood by noncommissioned officers; feeling of the men that they were being made human targets; the contagion of panic spreading from one unit to another as one assault after another on the steep cliffs of Mount Cauala failed. Lee, *op. cit.*

[120] February 14, 1945; see also, "The Luckless 92nd, *Newsweek* Magazine, (February 20, 1945), pp. 24–35.

[121] March 12, 1945; quoted in Lee, *op. cit.*

[122] An "off the cuff" speech before the Southern Regional Conference of State Governments in Charleston, South Carolina, on April 27, 1956. Reported in *U.S. News & World Report*, Vol. XL, No. 19. May 11, 1956, pp. 54–58. General Clark in the same speech showed his attitude on racial matters when he said: "I do deplore court decisions which seek to force indiscriminate racial integration upon the South, contrary to its own laws and customs."

[123] *Ibid.*

have been due to the unimaginative military strategy of the commanding officers of the division. There is such evidence from staff officers of the German divisions which fought against the 92nd.[124] These German officers found the division to be "plan-bound." They criticized the divisional command as "irresolute" and as having made "poor use" of the terrain in its battle sector: fundamental weaknesses which influenced the combat efficiency of the troops.

Then, too, during its whole combat life command control, esprit and discipline were never developed in the division. Although the first elements of the 92nd arrived in Italy July 30, 1944, it was not until sixteen weeks later (November 22) that final segments of it arrived in Italy. Its regiments, battalions and even smaller units were shifted back and forth, shuffled and reshuffled from one command to another, creating a crazy quilt of command relationship.

The troops were never permitted to forget they were Negro, not even as they entered battle. For example, on April 5, 1945, Captain J. F. Runyon, white commander of Company C, of the 370th Regiment, began the "orientation" of his men by telling them that past rifle companies in the 92nd had not been satisfactory and that this time "the men of Company C were going to do their job and bring credit not discredit to Negroes in combat.[125]

Men of Company C moved against the enemy, cutting communications as they went, and in the face of heavy mortar and machine-gun fire stormed Castle Aghinolfi atop a steep hill. Sixty percent of the men of the company were casualties; the lone Negro officer of the company, Second Lieutenant Vernon J. Baker, personally destroyed with grenades a camouflaged machine-gun position, killing eight Germans, and volunteered to cover the withdrawal of casualties; he was awarded the Distinguished Service Cross, the nation's second highest decoration for combat.

That there were other men who fought bravely is evidenced by the fact that original elements of the 92nd Division had by July 10, 1945, received 542 Bronze Star decorations, 82 Silver Stars, 12 Legion of Merit awards, 2 Distinguished Service Crosses and one Distinguished Service Medal.[126]

---

[124] See the views of a group of captured German officers representing all staff sections of *OB Suedwest* and some subordinate commands. Headquarters Interrogation Center, 7769 Hq. & Hq. Co., Sp. Inv. and Int., Rpt.: Subject—Lightning. In Manuscript files of the Chief of the Office of Military History, Pentagon, Washington, D.C.

[125] Captain J. F. Runyon, report on combat operations of Company C on April 5 and 6, 1945, dated April 1945, cited in Lee, *op. cit.*

[126] Historical Committee, 92nd Infantry Division, *With the 92nd Infantry Division,* October 1942–June 1945 [privately published with approval of commanding General Edward M. Almond], p. 96.

By the April, 1945, offensive, the 92nd had been reorganized once again; this time the 370th Regiment had been coupled with a Japanese American Regiment, the 442nd, and an American white Regiment, the 473rd. Its organic artillery and services, however, remained Negro. On a divisional basis, at least, the troops had been integrated.

Thus reconstructed the division moved forward toward the mountain ridges of the Northern Apennines and across the heavily mined plain before the town of Massa. Strong attacks by the division along its whole front forced the enemy to commit its available reserves and thus weaken other parts of its defense line. By mid-April companies of the 371st Infantry (which had rejoined the division) crossed the Leo River and overran an enemy command post. Reported their commander to General Almond:

> For the first time our troops maneuvered on *level* ground. . . . While all companies had stragglers after the CO's were hit by artillery and mortar concentrations, each outfit came back with the idea that they are good and that the Tedeschi are not invincible. . . .[127]

By the end of the month—and for them the end of active combat—elements of the 92nd Division had fought their way successfully through La Spezia and on to Genoa.

Other Units

Good or bad, the combat career of the 92nd Division cannot be said to characterize all Negro soldiers. Men of the division were less than 2 percent of all Negroes under arms; the division was but one of four thousand Negro units which served in World War II.

In December, 1944, 71 percent of the 477,421 Negro troops overseas were in quartermaster (169,678), engineer (111,012) or transport (54,458) battalions. This did not mean that these troops were not under fire. Five hundred Negro soldiers landed at Omaha Beach on D-Day. At Anzio Beach on January 22, 1944, the 387th Separate Engineer Battalion went ashore to build roads and manage ammunition dumps. Its five hundred men unloaded 1940 tons of matériel a day for seven days. The battalion was under fire more than any other Negro unit in the Fifth Army; it remained at the Anzio-Nettuno beachhead for five months. It lost four officers and eleven men; three officers and 58 men wounded; and three of its men received Silver Stars for gallantry.

Negro antiaircraft units fought well in Burma, in the Ryukyus, on Normandy Beach, in Italy and North Africa. Negro engineer troops played a

---

[127] Letter of Colonel James Notestein, June 15, 1945.

THE NEGRO IN THE ARMED FORCES OF AMERICA

major role in building the Ledo Road in Burma, the Stilwell Road in China and the Alcan highway in the subzero weather of Alaska and Canada. Negro transport units operated supply lines to all battlefronts, delivering more than five hundred tons of aviation gasoline a day on the famous Red Lion Route from Bayeux to Brussels.

The 761st Tank Battalion—first Negro armored unit committed to combat —went into action on Omaha Beach October 10, 1944. It was attached to General Patton's Third Army. General Patton, speaking to men of the unit, said:

> Men, you're the first Negro tankers ever to fight in the American Army. I would never have asked for you, if you weren't good. I don't care what color you are, so long as you go up there and kill those Kraut sonsabitches.[128]

From November 7, 1944, the 761st spent 183 days in almost continuous action. Evaluating its record, Major General M. S. Eddy, Corps Commander, wrote:

> 1. I consider the 761st Tank Battalion to have entered combat with such conspicuous courage and success as to warrant special commendation.

Ten tanks of this outfit were chosen as part of the honor guard while German General Lothas von Rundulic signed the surrender of the German Army in Austria.

There were nine Negro field artillery battalions in combat in Europe. The 969th fought in the Battle of the Bulge. To the commander of the battalion, General Maxwell D. Taylor, the commander of the 101st Airborne Division wrote:

> The officers and men of the 101st Airborne Division wish to express to your command their appreciation of the gallant support rendered by the 969th Field Artillery Battalion in the recent defense of Bastogne, Belgium. . . . This Division is proud to have shared the battlefield with your command. A recommendation for a unit citation of the 969th Field Artillery Battalion is being forwarded by this Headquarters.[129]

On January 11, General Troy H. Middleton, in forwarding the Distinguished Unit Citation to the battalion, wrote: "Your contribution to the great success of our arms at Bastogne will take its place among the epic achievements of our Army."

---

[128] Trezzvant W. Anderson, *Come Out Fighting: The Epic Tale of the 761st Tank Battalion, 1942–1945* (Salzburger Druckerei und Verlag, 1945) pp. 15, 21 quoted in Lee, *op. cit.*
[129] Lee, *op. cit.* Letter of January 33, 1945.

Combat in the Air Force

The 99th Pursuit Squadron—the first Negro flying unit—on June 2, 1944, flew its 500th combat mission for a total of 3,277 sorties. The misgivings of top military leaders about their effectiveness had proved unwarranted. They had won a commendation from the Air Force Commanding General H. A. Arnold for especially effective air combat over the Anzio-Nettuno beach-head.

In June the squadron became a part of the newly activated 332nd Fighter Group—freshly equipped with P-47 long-range fighter-bombers and under the command of Colonel Benjamin O. Davis, Jr. The new unit began immediately to make a record for itself. On June 9th it downed five Messerschmitt 109's over Munich; on June 25th it sank an enemy destroyer off the shores of the Istrian Peninsula.

In March, 1945, the 332nd Fighter Group was decorated with the Distinguished Unit Citation (the highest unit decoration) for its 1600-mile roundtrip air attack on Berlin, Colonel Davis leading the attack. By that time the group had flown 1,578 combat missions for 15,553 sorties. It had destroyed 111 enemy aircraft in the air, 150 on the ground; had destroyed or damaged 619 railroad cars, 40 barges and boats, 87 motor transports, 2 oil and ammunition dumps, 23 buildings and factories.

Officers and men of the group had up to this time received 95 Distinguished Flying Crosses, one Silver Star, one Legion of Merit, 14 Bronze Stars, 744 Air Medals and Clusters, and 8 Purple Hearts.

Negro nonflying units in the Air Force also made generally satisfactory records. Notable among these was the 907th Air Base Security Battalion, commanded in North Africa by Lieutenant Colonel Charles M. Dewey. Wrote one brother officer in a personal letter:

> I don't know whether or not I told you this, but Dewey's outfit held down the right flank of a certain division at Faid Pass, when a white organization ran through his lines to the rear, losing a lot of their equipment in the process. This should have panicked Dewey's men but they held together without exception. . . . I thought you might be interested in knowing how some of your men held up under fire when according to most psychological standards they should have been unnerved.[130]

Integration

By the end of 1944 a shortage of infantry riflemen developed in the European Theater of Operations. It was a shortage that threatened to grind

[130] Letter of Lieutenant Colonel P. H. Dolman to Colonel L. B. Wyant, commanding the First Air Base Security Training Group at Camp Rucker, Alabama, May 16, 1943.

to a halt any effective attack upon the enemy. Faced with this critical need for fighting men, General John C. H. Lee, commanding Communications Zone units, proposed to General Eisenhower the retraining of twenty thousand men under his command for services as infantrymen; and he suggested that this recruitment and retraining program be extended to Negro soldiers under his command. Eisenhower approved the idea and a draft of a circular letter to the troops was approved by General Lee. This letter promised to assign volunteers "without regard to color or race to the units where assistance is most needed, and give you the opportunity of fighting shoulder to shoulder to bring about victory."

Before this letter could be issued, it met with the strong opposition from Chief of Staff, Lieutenant General Walter Bedell Smith, who wrote Eisenhower:

> Although I am somewhat out of touch with the War Department's negro [sic] policy, I did, as you know, handle this during the time I was with General Marshall. Unless there has been a radical change, the sentence which I have marked in the above circular [quoted earlier] will place the War Department in very grave difficulties. It is inevitable that this statement will get out, and equally inevitable that every negro organization, pressure group and newspaper will take the attitude that, while the War Department segregates colored troops into organizations of their own against the desires and pleas of all the negro race, the Army is perfectly willing to put them in units with white soldiers and have them do battle when an emergency arises. . . .
>
> I have talked with Lee about it and he can't see this at all. He believes that it is right that colored and white soldiers should be mixed in the same company. . . .[131]

The circular letter was never issued; General Eisenhower let himself be persuaded by General Smith; but the crisis of manpower caused military commanders to pledge the use of Negro volunteers (in excess of those needed for replacements in Negro units) in other organizations.[132]

Within one month of the issuance of the revised circular letter, 4,562 Negro troops had volunteered for combat service; many of them were non-commissioned officers who had to take a reduction in rank. The men were organized into platoons; after training until March first, there were thirty-seven platoons ready for combat.

Uniformly these Negro platoons attached to larger white units conducted themselves as good soldiers; often they found themselves moving almost

[131] Informal letter from SHAEF Office of Chief of Staff to General Eisenhower, January 3, 1945. Lee, op. cit.

[132] Letter from Headquarters of Communication Zone ETO to subordinate commanders, January 4, 1945.

immediately into heavy combat. The 60th Regiment's Negro platoon went into combat with other regimental platoons on April 5 at Lengenbach, Germany. Private First Class Jack Thomas led his squad on a mission to knock out an enemy tank; for heroism in carrying out his mission and saving the life of a wounded member of his squad he was awarded the Distinguished Service Cross. Staff Sergeant Edward A. Carter, with a Negro platoon attached to the 56th Armored Infantry Battalion, was awarded the Distinguished Service Cross for his single-handed destruction of an enemy bazooka emplacement, killing six Germans and capturing two others; wounded, and using his captives as a shield, he made his way back to his own lines. The Negro platoon with Company B of the 16th Infantry had nine of its men killed, thirty wounded and could muster only fifteen on V-E Day. Reported Colonel John R. Achor of the 99th Infantry Division:

> The Negro platoons performed in an excellent manner at all times while in combat. These men were courageous fighters and never once did they fail to accomplish their assigned mission. They were particularly good in town fighting and [were] often used as the assault platoon with good results. The platoon assigned to the 393rd Infantry is credited with killing approximately 100 Germans and capturing 500. During this action only three of their own men were killed, and fifteen wounded.[133]

A Company of Men

The use of Negro platoons with white troops—although only a token force of Negro troops was involved—represented a great wind of change. It was a profound experience for the Army from top to bottom; for many it provided a lesson of deepest significance. It was summed up best, perhaps, by Lieutenant Colonel Douglas P. Frazier, commander of the 2nd Battalion of the 309th Infantry:

> To date, there has never appeared the slightest sign of race prejudice, or discrimination in this organization. White men and colored men are welded together with a deep friendship and respect born of combat and matured by the realization that such an association is not an impossibility that many of us have been led to believe. Segregation has never been attempted in this unit, and is, in my mind, the deciding factor as to the success or failure of the experiment. When men undergo the same privations, face the same dangers before an impartial enemy, there can be no segregation. My men eat, play, work, and sleep together as a company of men, with no regard to color. . . .[134]

[133] Report on Negro troops to Commanding General of the XII Corps, June 21, 1945.
[134] Letter to Commanding Officer of the 309th Infantry Regiment, July 6, 1945. Quoted in Lee, *op. cit.*

KOREA

On June 25, 1950, troops of the Republic of North Korea invaded South Korea, crossing the Yalu River and the 38th Parallel. On July 12 the 24th Infantry Regiment, an all-Negro unit that had been part of the Regular United States Army for eighty-one years, landed in Korea from Japan. News from the battlefield had been grim: a story of the steady withdrawal of defending forces from one strategic military position after another.

Then came a break. *The New York Times* for July 22, 1950, announced the recapture of Yech'on, an important railhead city, after it had been lost by ROK (Republic of South Korea) troops. The victory had come, the newspaper story stated, after a 16-hour battle; and the victors were the 24th Infantry Regiment.

This heartening news was soon heralded in the House of Representatives of the United States Congress, where Congressman Lane of Massachusetts told his colleagues:

> Communist propaganda took it on the chin at Yech'on when the Korean Reds were blasted by American Negro troops who believed not only in the United States as it is, but in the better Nation it will become when intolerance is also defeated.

He continued:

> Let us pay tribute, then, to the men of the Twenty-Fourth, who have added battle honors to those they first started winning against the Comanche Indians over 70 years ago.[135]

On September 11, 1950, Lieutenant Colonel J. T. Corley became the new commanding officer of the 24th Infantry Regiment at Haman, Korea, and he issued the following memorandum to "The Fighting 24th Infantry Regimental Combat Team":

> 1. Upon assumption of command, I cannot help but express my opinion of the Fighting 24th United States Infantry. In sixty days of continuous combat, you have withstood a "roughness of battle" which I had not seen in five campaigns in Africa, Sicily and Europe with the First Infantry Division. You have held ground against superior odds. You have lived up to the regimental motto "Semper Paratus." The first United States victory in Korea was your action at Yech'on. It has been noted in Congress. The people back home cover in detail your efforts on "Battle Hill," West of Haman, Korea.

[135] *Congressional Record*, Volume 96, Part 8, p. 10866.

2. Other units have been unable to accomplish what depleted companies of the Fighting 24th have done. I am proud of the "Blockhousers."

The Phantom Battle

It would appear that at long last Negro soldiers were to be given a bright page in American military history. But this was not to be. A decade or more later, after seven years of research and interviewing survivors of the Korean Conflict a military historian, Lieutenant Colonel Roy E. Appleman (USAR, Ret.) wrote a book which challenged this estimate of the combat performance of the 24th Infantry. His book was sponsored, indeed, adopted officially by the Office of Military History, Department of the Army.

In his 700-odd page book, Appleman makes a dozen or more scathing attacks upon the fighting abilities of men of the 24th Infantry. In one curious passage he even musters up evidence that would seem to cast doubt not only upon the valor of the Negro troops, but also upon the fact that there was a "Battle of Yech'on." He writes:

> The first action between elements of the 25th Division [the 24th Infantry was attached to this Division—Ed.] and enemy forces, if indeed it was an action at all, appears to have occurred at Yech'on on 20 July. Company K, led by 1st Lt. Jasper R. Johnson, entered the town during the afternoon. When other units of the 3rd Battalion failed to take a ridge overlooking the town on the left, he requested and received permission to withdraw from the town for the night.
>
> At Hamch'ang next morning, Col. Henry G. Fisher, commanding the 35th Infantry, received message that the enemy had driven the 3rd Battalion, 24th Infantry from Yech'on. He started from the place at once. On the way there he found the battalion about five miles west of the town. He could get no information of value from the battalion commander. Fisher and a small party drove into Yech'on which was ablaze with fires started by American artillery shells. He encountered no enemy or civilians—the town was deserted. Whether there were North Koreans in the town on 20 July is something of a question. In any event, the 3rd Battalion, 24th Infantry, turned over on 21 July to the ROK Regiment of the Capital Division the task of holding Yech'on.[136]

It is hard to determine the implications of this curious bit of military history. Was there or wasn't there an enemy force in Yech'on? If there was, who drove them out? If there wasn't, who drove the 3rd Battalion out of Yech'on? If the town was ablaze when Colonel Fisher got to Yech'on, whom

---

[136] Roy E. Appleman, *The United States Army in the Korean War, South to Naktong, North to Yalu* (Washington, D.C., 1961. Office of Chief of Military History, Department of the Army), p 190, 191. By special permission of Chief of Military History, Department of the Army.

had the Army artillery been shooting at? Or were they shelling a ghost town? If Fisher could get "no information of value" from the battalion commander, is it likely that Appleman could years later (1957) get much information of value from Colonel Fisher who wasn't even there when the fighting took place? Military Historian Appleman leaves the paradoxical questions unresolved. Perhaps it is just as well.

Even more curious is the scientific documentation employed by Military Historian Appleman in piecing together his narrative. He uses, for example, an interview with Lieutenant Colonel Corley as his documentation for much of his description of the conduct of the troops in the bloody contest in August for control of "Battle Mountain"—events of which Corley could not have had first-hand knowledge since he didn't get to the battle zone until September 11; events to which he had already expressed written favorable opinion in his memorandum to the troops upon his assumption of command.

It is not difficult to find something less than objective reporting in the Appleman book. He follows each company and each battalion down to the smallest detail. He tells us that on August 20 all of the men of C Company, except for the commander and about twenty-five soldiers, abandoned their position on Battle Mountain and fled the scene of battle; but he does not find it necessary to report that from that same company came Sergeant Cornelius H. Charlton of The Bronx, New York. On June 2, 1951, Charlton led three attacks up an enemy-held hill after his platoon commander had been killed; though himself mortally wounded, he destroyed an enemy gun emplacement. He was awarded posthumously the Congressional Medal of Honor.

The author recounts a situation where the enemy was shelling the troops. He indicates that present were elements of the 27th Regiment, the 89th Tank Battalion, the 8th Field Artillery Division, and the 24th Infantry Regiment. Then, in a bantering tone he writes:

> The few mortar shells falling occasionally in the vicinity did no damage except to cause the troops of the 24th Infantry and intermingled South Koreans to scatter and increase their speed to the rear.[137]

Nobody ran, it seems, but black men and yellow men.

[137] Appleman, *op. cit.*, p. 479. Space does not permit the quoting of literally a dozen or more comments, generally unsupported by credible documentation. The pattern that runs through all of them is negative: "The tendency to panic continued in nearly all the 24th Infantry operations West of Sonju" (p. 269); "One officer in L Company stated he was knocked to the ground three times by his own stampeding men" (p. 270); "The 2nd Battalion of the 24th Infantry was still trying to clear this mountainous region" (p. 287); "E Company overrun and C Company routed" (p. 370); "E Company panicked under tank fire and ran off the hill" (p. 440).

It is doubtful if the 24th Infantry could have been as bad as Appleman would have his readers believe. Battle Mountain changed hands nineteen times; there were times when Communist troops retreated and times when American forces withdrew. There were times when Communists charged bravely up a hill and held a position against fearful odds. And times when black soldiers of the 24th behaved in like manner—such as when Pfc William Thompson manned a machine gun against a swarm of enemy soldiers to cover the withdrawal of men of Company M and was awarded the Medal of Honor, posthumously. There were doubtless times when black men fled; but as Lieutenant Colonel Corley was to testify, those who were stragglers were men who had fought for five days and "were dead on their feet." [138]

The bias of the Appleman book has been noted by one important reviewer of the work in *Armor* Magazine, Lieutenant Colonel Forrest K. Kleinman (USAR Ret.), himself a former officer in the 24th Infantry. In his review he called attention to Appleman's failure to discuss the valiant performance of Negro troops at Haman Notch where "not one of many stragglers was a Negro"; or of Negro replacements being brought into the all white 19th Infantry Regiment at Chinju while the unit was under fire; or how Pfc Arthur Dudley rose to command a white squad and killed "more of the enemy with an M-1 rifle than Sergeant Alvin York or Audie Murphy." [139] He might also have reminded Military Historian Appleman of the Distinguished Service Crosses awarded Second Lieutenant William M. Benefield of the 77th Combat Engineer Company, 25th Infantry Division, who was killed in July, 1950, while attempting to clear a minefield near Sonju; and to Lieutenant Ellison C. Wynn of B. Company, 9th Infantry Regiment, who covered the retreat of his men from an untenable position on the Yalu River in November, 1950, and had the side of his face blown off by an enemy grenade; or of the oak leaf cluster added in Korea to the Silver Star that Tank Battalion Lieutenant Theodore McClane had already won in battle in Italy; or of the numerous Bronze Star Medals awarded Negro officers and men for bravery under fire in the Korean conflict. On all this, the "Official History" of the United States Army in Korea is silent. Here, alone, these names must be recorded. Here, too, we record the death in combat of Major George Gray of Welch, West Virginia, who was killed while

---

[138] See Interview with Corley published in the *Pittsburgh Courier*, June 23, 30 and July 7, 1951, quoted in Lee Nichols, *Breakthrough on the Color Front* (New York: Random House, 1954), p. 21.

[139] *Armor* (May–June, 1961) p. 63. Sergeant Alvin C. York was awarded the Medal of Honor for bravery in action October 8, 1918. He killed 25 Germans; Audie Murphy also won the Medal of Honor for killing a large number of enemy soldiers in World War II.

flying a mission in Korea and was awarded the Distinguished Flying Cross; and of the first Negro Navy pilot, Jessie L. Brown, who died in the flaming pyre of his plane after being shot down over enemy lines. His death gave rise to an exceptional act of bravery on the part of one of his white fellow pilots, Lieutenant (j.g.) Thomas J. Hudner, who, seeing Brown in trouble, landed his own plane and tried to pull Brown from the cockpit. The effort was without success, but for his act Hudner was awarded the Medal of Honor.

EXECUTIVE ORDER 9981

"Whereas it is essential that there be maintained in the Armed Services of the United States the highest standards of democracy, with equality of treatment and opportunity for all those who serve in our country's defense:

"Now, therefore, by virtue of the authority vested in me as President of the United States, by the Constitution and the statutes of the United States, and as Commander-in-Chief of the Armed Services, it is hereby ordered as follows:

"1. It is the declared policy of the President that there shall be equality of treatment and opportunity for all persons in the Armed Services without regard to race, color, religion, or national origin. This policy shall be put into effect as rapidly as possible, having due regard to the time required to effectuate any necessary changes without impairing efficiency or morale.

2. There shall be created in the National Military Establishment an advisory committee to be known as the President's Committe on Equality of Treatment and Opportunity in the Armed Services, which shall be composed of seven members designated by the President. . . ."

The quotation above contains the essential parts of Executive Order 9981 signed by President Harry S. Truman on July 26, 1948. It was an historic order. For the first time an American President had openly placed the force of his high office on the side of the struggle of the Negro for equal rights.

It was a bold step and there were reasons for it. The date the order was signed is significant—two weeks before the Democratic National Nominating Convention had opened in Philadelphia in an atmosphere of sharp dissension between Southern Democrats on the one hand and Northern and Western Democrats on the other. A Negro minister (Marshall Shepard) had opened a session of the convention with prayer and a Senator from South Carolina ("Cotton Ed" Smith) had walked out on the prayer and the party. It was then that Truman crossed his political Rubicon: he decided that big city Bosses and the Negro vote offered his best road to an election victory. In a fighting speech made at convention hall long after mid-night, he announced he would call the Congress back into a special session to deal with civil rights legislation and would, himself, proceed to move vigorously for civil rights on all fronts. The Executive Order was one of his first steps.

The order, however, was not as precipitate as might appear. Not even President Truman could have been expected to move directly in the face of opposition from the Joint Chiefs of Staff. And, indeed, he did not. A large amount of ferment on the question of the best use of Negroes in the armed forces had already developed in the Armed Services themselves.

At the close of World War II frequent memoranda were circulated in top echelons of the Air Force, recommending that no one be restricted from any job on account of color.[140] Along the same line the Navy in a policy declaration stated "the Navy accepts no theories of racial differences in inborn ability, but expects that every man wearing its uniform be trained and used in accordance with his maximum individual capacity determined on the basis of individual performance." [141]

In the Army there had been an exhaustive reappraisal of manpower policies. In 1945 a 3-man board, under the chairmanship of Lieutenant-General Alvan C. Gillem, Jr., had spent three-and-a-half months in a staff and field study of racial policy in the Army. The report of the Gillem board, affecting as it did the largest numbers of Negro personnel in the Armed Services, was of particular significance. It reaffirmed the declaration of October 9, 1940, that Negroes are to be eligible for all types of Army jobs; it then called for a staff group in the Department of Defense and within every major command to be charged with implementation of this policy. Going a step farther, the board proposed experimentation with groupings of Negro and white units and the placement of some Negro soldiers (those with high AGCT scores and with satisfactory showing on mechanical aptitude tests) in overhead units with white troops.

Placement of Negroes in overhead units was termed "duty interspersal": Negro and white soldiers were to work together by day in common duty assignments; but at nightfall Negro troops went back to their own segregated messing, quartering and recreation area.

Not only the Army, but the Air Force and Navy as well were unable to break with the old tradition of keeping Negro and white servicemen apart in anything that might have suggested social equality.

However limited the earlier policies of the Service groups may have been,

---

[140] *Freedom To Serve, op. cit.,* p. 35.
[141] *Ibid.,* p. 19.

they formed a foundation upon which the Truman Executive Order might stand. They were a jump-off point from which the 7-man committee [142] appointed by the President could launch a campaign to democratize the Armed Services.

The President's Committee on Equality of Treatment and Opportunity in the Armed Services, or "the Fahy Committee," as it came to be called, worked on its problem nearly two years. It presented its report to the President on May 22, 1950.

The committee found a great gap between announced policy and actual practice in the Armed Services. Despite the Gillem board's proposals to open job specialties in the Army to Negroes, the committee found Negroes barred from 198 of the 490 specialties. It found Negro soldiers being trained in only 21 of the 106 training courses being offered enlisted men. It found a persistent practice in the Navy to identify menial jobs with Negro sailors.[143]

The Fahy Committee did not hesitate to hammer away at segregation as the root cause for the difficulties experienced in the training and utilization of Negro troops. Segregation, it charged, meant waste of potential skills and impairment of military effectiveness.

It would be idle speculation to attempt to assign any one cause as reason for drastic changes in Armed Services policies. Many social and political forces were at work during the period of change. However, in accomplishing an improved status for Negro servicemen the work of the Fahy Committee, its staff and others [144] played a useful role.

Just short of two years after its creation the Fahy Committee could report to the President (May 22, 1950):

    A. The Navy has:
        1 Opened all jobs and ratings to enlisted men without regard to race or color;

[142] Truman appointed the following to the Committee—Chairman: Charles Fahy, former Solicitor General of the United States and a native Georgian. Members: Alphonsus J. Donahue, prominent Catholic layman; Lester Granger, Executive Director of the National Urban League; John Sengstacke, publisher of the *Chicago Defender;* William E. Stevenson, President of Oberlin College; Dwight G. Palmer, Board Chairman of General Cable Corporation, and Charles Luckman of Lever Brothers. (Donahue died before the committee made its report; Luckman was inactive.)

[143] The report was called *Freedom To Serve.*

[144] Working closely with the committee and its staff was James C. Evans, who has served nearly thirty years in the Department of Defense; as assistant to Judge William H. Hastie, Truman Gibson, Lieutenant Colonel Marcus Ray, when they were Civilian Aides to the Secretary of War; succeeding Lieutenant Colonel Ray as Civilian Aide to the Secretary of War; and now Counsellor in the Office of the Assistant Secretary of Defense.

    2 Opened all courses in Navy technical schools on the same basis;

    3 Completely integrated Negroes with whites in basic training, technical schools, on the job, in messing and sleeping quarters, ashore and afloat;

    4 Abolished in the Marine Corps segregated training units.

B. The Air Force has:

    1 Integrated 74% of the 25,000 Negro airmen into mixed units;

    2 Opened all jobs and schools to all personnel, regardless of race or color; with Negro airmen constituting 6% of its enrollment in technical training schools.

C. The Army has:

    1 Abolished a 10% quota for Negro enlistment;

    2 Authorized assignment of all qualified Negro soldiers to any unit, including formerly white units, on a basis of qualifications alone;

    3 Authorized that Negro soldiers serving in mixed units be integrated on the job, in barracks, and in messing.

The changes were more than token in character. In the Army, with the largest number of Negro personnel, this was the reported progress as of September, 1955:

> In 1951 there were some 200,000 Negro soldiers serving in 385 all-Negro units. By September 1953 only 88 all-Negro units remained in the Army and they accounted for only 5% of the Negro enlisted men. Thirty-nine such units stationed in the United States had 3% of the Negro personnel; in the European Command 83% of all Negro troops overseas were integrated; the rest were in 49 all-Negro units.
>
> In Army commands in Alaska, Australia, Japan, and the Pacific integration was 100% complete.[145]

"Commanders at all echelons," said the report, "have indicated the absence of difficulties involved in the transition. They agree that efficiency has been increased, disciplinary problems reduced and morale improved."

Following the issuance of Executive Order 9981 the number of Negroes in the Armed Services increased, both officers and enlisted personnel. As of August 1, 1964, there were 115,646 Negro enlisted men in the Army out of a total strength of 867,618 (13.3%).[146] This compares with the figure of 103,603 (12.2%) for 1962. Similarly Negro enlisted men in the Navy rose from 30,408 (5.22%) in 1962 to 33,254 as of August 1, 1964. In 1962 there

---

[145] Summarization of report of Lieutenant Colonel Steve G. Davis, September, 1953. No similar analysis for other Services was available from official sources. However, a visit by the writer to more than a score of Army, Navy, Air Force and Marine Corps installations in continental United States in 1952 produced evidence of similar progress. See *Our World Magazine*, June, 1952.

[146] This total includes 1,209 enlisted women in the Women's Army Corps. There were at this date fifty-one Negro WAC officers.

were 46,564 Negro enlisted men in the Air Force (9.1%) and 13,351 in the Marine Corps (7.59%); later data was unavailable at this writing.

Officer strength of Negroes in the Services, so far as this information is presently available, is shown below:

Negro Officers All Grades*

Service	1962 Number and Percent	1964 Number
Army	3,150 (3.2%)	3,316
Navy	174 (0.24%)	188
Air Force	1,300 (1.24%)**	n.a.
Marine Corps	32 (0.21%)	n.a.

* 1962 figures from *Initial Report*, President's Committee on Equality of Opportunity in the Armed Forces, June 13, 1963, Table 1; 1964 figures supplied by Department of Defense.
** Air Force figure includes only officers assigned to duty in continental United States.

So far as can be seen from available data, enlargement of opportunity for Negroes as officers in the Armed Services has been slight. There are some evidences of progress. Some Negro officers command white troops. In the Air Force there is a Negro Lieutenant General (Benjamin O. Davis Jr.). In the Army there has been an increase in the number of Negro officers on active duty in the senior grades. Thus Negro Army majors had increased from 424 in 1962 to 482 in early 1964; Lieutenant colonels from 117 to 172 during the same period; and colonels, from 6 to 10. These gains, however, when viewed as a percentage of total officer strength, serve to accentuate the serious damage caused to the status of Negro Americans by nearly a century-long campaign of slander against Negro officers. With still only token representation in the Service Academies and with access to some Reserve Officer Training Courses and National Guard Units still barred to Negroes, the problem of repairing the damage remains largely unresolved.

The Armed Services and Social Change

Leading circles in the Armed Services had long answered demands for an end of segregation of Negroes on the part of the military by pointing to examples of discrimination against them in civilian life in parts of the United States, and by asserting that it was not in the high interest of national defense for the Armed Services to engage in "sociological experiments." By this reasoning they justified on-base segregation of Negro servicemen themselves; and obviously they could find no warrant whatsoever for meeting the demands of some civil rights groups that the Negro serviceman and his family be guaranteed full citizenship rights on and *off* base by affirmative action of their military commanders.

Indeed, no less an authority than Secretary of War Henry L. Stimson had declared during World War II:

> . . . I reiterate that the War Department is not an appropriate medium for affecting social readjustments. It has not been so employed nor will it be. . . .
>
> As stated in your letter, the War Department has no right to seek to effect changes in the life of the people of the Southland, or for that matter, in any other part of the country. This it has not attempted to do. The fact is, military personnel are carefully informed, in all sections of the United States, *that without the confines of the military establishment they are subject to State law. . . .*" [italics added] [147]

A drafted Negro soldier from the North assigned to a Southern camp was, under this line of reasoning, compelled to obey local Jim Crow laws; if he wanted to have his family with him would have to send his child to a segregated school of inferior quality and bring his wife into a substandard slum in a Negro ghetto. This was a set of circumstances that deadened the interest of Negro men in the Armed Services as a career even after Executive Order 9981.

In the 1950's dynamic developments in the social climate of the United States created a hard dilemma for the military. The United States Supreme Court (in *Brown* vs. *Topeka Board of Education*) outlawed racial segregation in public schools. Soon Army and National Guard troops, by order of their Commander in Chief, were using bayonetted rifles to uphold the mandate of the Federal Court, that nine Negro youth be admitted to an integrated high school in Little Rock, Arkansas. The nonviolent strikes of thousands of Negroes against a Montgomery, Alabama, bus company that enforced segregated seating, and the emergence of the leadership of the Reverend Martin Luther King, gave new emphasis to the century-old struggle of Negroes for equal rights. The presence back home of a million Negro veterans returned from World War II and the Korean conflict intensified the awareness of the Negro public concerning developments in the Armed Forces. The question had now become not whether the Armed Services would engage in "social experiments," but whether they would lag behind in the new push toward greater democracy for all citizens to which overwhelming numbers in the nation were now committed.

---

[147] Letter of the Secretary of War to United States Congressman A. Leonard Allen of Louisiana, September 20, 1944. Letters of similar nature were sent by such War Department spokesmen as General George C. Marshall and Undersecretary Robert Patterson to scores of Southern Senators and Congressmen who had protested the opening of certain on-base facilities to Negroes. Lee.

THE GESELL COMMITTEE

During the 8-year administration of President Dwight Eisenhower (1952–1960), nothing was done toward resolving the conflict of the military's accepting segregated schools and school busses for the children of its Negro servicemen, while the United States Supreme Court had declared that these practices were unconstitutional.

The next major advance in the status of Negro servicemen came during the administration of President John F. Kennedy. In June, 1962, he appointed the President's Committee on Equal Opportunity in the Armed Forces and named Gerhard A. Gesell, a lawyer, chairman.[148] The committee in the first instance limited its work to an intensive study of "problems of equal opportunity affecting Negro military personnel on and off base within the United States." After a year it sent the President its "Initial Report" covering this area. In his letter transmitting the report to his Secretary of Defense Robert S. McNamara, President Kennedy wrote:

> We have come a long way in the 15 years since President Truman ordered the desegregation of the Armed Forces. The military services lead almost every other segment of our society in establishing equality of opportunity for all Americans. Yet a great deal remains to be done.
>
> As the report emphasizes, a serious morale problem is created for Negro military personnel when various forms of segregation and discrimination exist in communities neighboring military bases. Discriminatory practices are morally wrong wherever they occur—they are especially inequitable and iniquitous when they inconvenience and embarrass those serving in the Armed Services and their families. Responsible citizens of all races in these communities should work together to open up public accommodations and housing for Negro military personnel and their dependents. This effort is required by the interests of our national defense, national policy and basic considerations of human decency.[149]

A new firm voice had spoken. Within a month Secretary McNamara made a strongly worded policy statement supporting the President, which was sent to commanders of every military installation:

> . . . Our military effectiveness is unquestionably reduced as a result of civilian racial discrimination against men in uniform. The Committee report has made this point with great clarity. With equal clarity it demonstrates that the Department of Defense has in the past only imperfectly recognized the

---

[148] Other members: Nathaniel S. Colley, Abe Fortas, Louis J. Hector, Benjamin Muse, John H. Sengstacke and Whitney M. Young, Jr.
[149] June 21, 1963.

harm flowing from off-base discrimination. That imperfect recognition has in turn meant the lack of a program giving rise to the conditions giving rise to the harm.[150]

The Secretary went on to announce preparation of "detailed directives" making clear leadership responsibility with respect to discrimination *on* and *off* the base. He implied the possibility of sanctions against local places of public accommodation which discriminated against clientele on the basis of race or color. He said:

> Certainly the damage to military effectiveness from off-base discrimination is not less than that caused by off-base vice, as to which the off-limits sanction is quite customary.

He concluded with the following statement of policy and assessment of responsibility:

I. POLICY

It is the policy of the Department of Defense to conduct all of its activities in a manner which is free from racial discrimination, and which provides equal opportunity to all civilian employees irrespective of their color.

Discriminatory practices directed against Armed Forces members, all of whom lack a civilian's freedom of choice in where to live, to work, to travel and to spend his off-duty hours, are harmful to military effectiveness. Therefore, all members of the Department of Defense should oppose such practices on every occasion, while fostering equal opportunity for servicemen and their families, on and off base.

II. RESPONSIBILITIES

. . . C. Military Commanders

Every military commander has the responsibility to oppose discriminatory practices affecting his men and their dependents and to foster equal opportunity for them, not only the areas under his immediate control, but also in nearby communities, where they may live or gather in off-duty hours.

In language hard as granite the policies of civilian and military leaders of the nation's Armed Services for the past one hundred years had now been categorically reversed.

Five months after the above statement President Kennedy had been assassinated and his successor, President Lyndon B. Johnson, had reaffirmed the Administration's intention to end discrimination. By July the Civil Rights Act of 1964 had been enacted into law and Secretary McNamara again placed the Department of Defense on record:

[150] Excerpts from Memorandum to the President which was relayed to all military commands and defense establishments, July 23, 1963.

The Civil Rights Act of 1964 is an immensely important and historic expression of this nation's commitment to freedom and justice. It has special meaning for the members of our Armed Forces, all of whom have already given a personal commitment to defend freedom and justice, and some of whom have not always been accorded full freedom and full justice in their own country.

The President has made it very clear that he expects each Department to move with dispatch within its areas of concern in developing programs and policies which will give full effect to the Civil Rights Act.

In the Department of Defense this means, primarily, the vigorous, determined, sensitive commitment by military commanders to a program of fostering and securing equal treatment for all their men, and their families, off base as well as on. This has been our policy for some time now, but the Civil Rights Act creates new opportunities to win equal treatment for all servicemen, and we cannot afford to lose any opportunity to gain a goal so simple, so just and so compelling.

I want to make it very clear that it is and will be a continuing responsibility for all commanders to foster equal treatment for every serviceman, and to support him in the lawful assertion of the rights guaranteed to him by the Constitution and the Civil Rights Act of 1964.

This Department was created to defend the freedom of the United States. The denial of the rights of members of the Armed Forces is harmful to the very purpose in which we are engaged, for discrimination against our people saps the military effectiveness we strive so to maintain. This last reason alone compels an affirmative commitment by all members of the Department of Defense to the cause of equal treatment and opportunity.[151]

CONCLUSION

There is still (1965) segregation in the Armed Services of the United States of America; still inequality of treatment and opportunity for Negro servicemen. Negroes still experience unequal treatment and segregation in the National Guard (especially in Alabama and Mississippi, where only token integration exists).[152] And in addition much larger opportunities

[151] Memorandum to Service Secretaries from Secretary of Defense, July 10, 1964, transmitted to all military commanders.

[152] In its final report to the President, November, 1964, The President's Committee On Equal Opportunity in the Armed Forces noted that 10 southern states (Alabama, Arkansas, Florida, Georgia, Louisiana, Mississippi, North Carolina, South Carolina, Tennessee and Virginia) which had no Negroes in any National Guard unit as of June 1962, had at the time of its report eliminated technical and legal barriers to Negro membership. Major General Winston P. Wilson, chief of the National Guard Bureau, while admitting that only token integration of Negroes had occurred in some of these States, hailed progress made as a "milestone in the history of the National Guard." *The New York Times.* December 30, 1964. p. 28.

for Negroes are needed in the Service Academies (West Point, Annapolis and the Air Force Academy) before they can claim to be free from racial bias; overseas Negro military personnel have problems in some areas.[153] These are not mere niggling criticisms; they go to the heart of the matter; have importance for future development of Negro officer cadres on an equitable basis.

Doubtless there are individual cases where a lower echelon military commander steeped in prejudice is using his influence to defeat the program. However, the compelling fact is that the letter of the law says that segregation and discrimination are illegal; and no matter how strong the backlash of reaction it cannot indefinitely withstand the new spirit of democracy abroad in the military establishment. Now it is clear that official policy stands on the side of Negro Americans.

[153] The Committee's report remained critical of the treatment of Negro servicemen overseas.

chapter 16

Negro Americans
and the Africa Interest

St. Clair Drake

During the first two hundred years of their existence as a racial and ethnic group in the North American lands which became the United States of America, there was a tendency for Negroes to refer to themselves as "Africans." In the early nineteenth century, however, free Negroes, of whom there were then over 100,000, sensed a danger in continued use of the term, for white friends and foes, alike, were supporting "colonization societies" and exerting pressure upon freedmen to leave the country for settlement in Africa.[1] The American Colonization Society had been founded in 1812 and the first settlers were landed in Liberia in 1815 from a U.S. naval ship.

Leaders among the freedmen felt that they might be told to "go back to Africa" if they continued to call themselves "African." But they could not call themselves "American," for they had no fixed legal or customary status yet in the land of their birth. The gradual change in nomenclature was one aspect of the freedmen's insistence that they had a right to remain in America and to be recognized, eventually, as citizens. It also emphasized their determination to fight for the emancipation of those still enslaved

---

[1] The shift away from the use of the word "African" to designate Negro organizations was associated with the rise of the Colored Men's Conventions which met annually between 1830 and 1953. See Howard H. Bell, *A Survey of the Negro Convention Movement, 1830–1861* (unpublished Ph.D. dissertation, Northwestern University, 1953). See also E. Franklin Frazier, *The Negro in the United States*, revised edition (New York: The Macmillan Company, 1957), pp. 79–81.

At the convention of 1835, it was reported that "William Whipper advocated that the word 'colored' be abandoned and the title, 'African' should be removed from the names of churches, lodges, societies and other institutions. . . ." (The extent to which the title "African" was used is evident from the list of churches given in Appendix I.) The quotation is from John W. Cromwell, *The Early Negro Convention Movement*, Occasional Paper No. 9 of the American Negro Academy, 1904, p. 10. Suggestions to drop the term, "colored," as well as "African" were a bit unusual. The term "Afro-American" came into vogue in some circles, but Negro (with a capital *N*) prevailed after Booker T. Washington threw his weight behind this particular form of group nomenclature.

rather than to become leaders, after emigration, in some black nation to be established overseas.[2]

The repudiation of the designation "African" was not necessarily a gesture of psychological rejection of Africa, nor did it imply lack of interest in the fate of the people of that continent who were still regarded as "kinsmen." However, an image was in the making throughout the nineteenth century which stressed the deadly character of Africa's climate, the menace of its fauna, and the "savagery" of its people. This image *did*, eventually, have a negative effect upon American Negro attitudes toward Africa, but it also spurred some Negroes to try to change the image to what they conceived of as the African reality.

All Negroes in the United States, whether they wished to or not, have been forced to react to the derogatory image of Africa and of Negroes fostered by some Europeans and white Americans, and to the fact of their own partial African descent.[3] Despite the virtual elimination of African cultural traits from the Negro American subculture, Negroes have never been allowed to forget their African origins (although the Negroid physical traits of many individuals have been greatly attenuated by miscegenation and some "Negroes" are indistinguishable from white persons).[4] The over-whelming majority of Africans, on the other hand, have never been aware, even, of the existence of people of African descent in the New World or

[2] No more than twelve thousand Negroes emigrated from the U.S.A. to Liberia between 1815 and the Civil War, but among them were some of the best prepared and most energetic leaders (such as John Russwurm, reputedly the first Negro graduate from an American University). See Gunnar Myrdal, *An American Dilemma* (New York: Harper & Brothers, 1944), pp. 186, 912; and Frazier, *op. cit.*, pp. 496–97. Pressure was put upon freedmen to emigrate and an agreement to do so was sometimes the price placed upon manumission. For an intimate human interest document dealing with such a situation see Jean E. Keith, "Joseph Rogers Underwood—Friend of American Colonization." *The Filson Club History Quarterly*, 22, No. 2 (April, 1948). Garrison headed a group of abolitionists which pleaded with freedmen "not to desert your slave brothers" (see Howard H. Bell, *op. cit.*, 1953).

[3] St. Clair Drake has discussed some of the implications of this "forced awareness" in an article, "Hide My Face? An Essay on Pan-Africanism and Negritude," in Herbert Hill, *Soon One Morning* (New York: Alfred A. Knopf, 1963), as has Harold Isaacs in *The New World of Negro Americans* (New York: John Day, 1963).

[4] There has been much lively controversy during the past forty years over the extent and significance of African cultural survivals in the U.S.A. There is general agreement, however, that African cultural survivals are relatively unimportant as compared with non-African elements in contemporary Negro subcultures in the United States. The case for a rather extensive persistence of such traits is made in Melville J. Herskovits, *The Myth of the Negro Past* (New York: Harper & Brothers, 1941), pp. 1 ff. E. Franklin Frazier supports the opposite position in *The Negro in the United States, op. cit.*, pp. 3–21. A recent statement in the controversy has been made by a student of Neo-African cultures, Janheinz Jahn in *Muntu* (New York: Grove Press Paperback, 1961), pp. 232–34.

of the facts of the slave trade and the fate of those "of African descent."
African consciousness of American Negroes is rapidly increasing, however,
due to more widespread school attendance and to the operation of the mass
media. Large numbers of Africans, too, are now acquiring an image of
America and of the Negroes who live there, and associated emotions
inevitably develop along with the image.

Despite the ever-present consciousness of Africa, very few American
Negroes since the Civil War have had any face-to-face contact with
Africans. From Emancipation until the close of World War II, the primary
type of contact between Africans and Negro Americans on American soil
was that which took place upon the campuses of Negro educational institutions between the few African students who happened to be in the
United States and Negro students and teachers. Significant extensions of
these contacts occurred when African students sought companionship,
financial aid or hospitality in Negro communities. Within Africa, itself, the
primary type of contact was that of a few Negro missionaries interacting
with varied categories of Africans, these, too, being relatively few in
number. The one significant exception was the Republic of Liberia, where
several waves of Negro Americans came as "settlers" and where there is a
long history of the utilization of Negro Americans in the diplomatic
service.[5]

Since World War II, Africans and Negro Americans have been thrown
into contact through a variety of new roles and types of relationships.
Within Africa itself, Negro Americans are functioning as resident businessmen and as technicians and teachers under Peace Corps auspices or sponsored by private or governmental organizations; as officials and members

[5] The first overseas appointment of a Negro in the diplomatic service was that of
Ebenezer D. Bassett as Minister Resident and Consul General to Haiti in 1869. Two
years later, James Milton Turner of Missouri was appointed to the equivalent post in
Liberia. Between 1882 and 1893, the Liberia post was held by Henry Highland Garnet
of New York, Moses A. Hopkins of North Carolina, and William D. McKay of Indiana,
all Negroes. After a period of over thirty years, the practice of sending Negro diplomats
to the highest post in Liberia was resumed when R. O'Hara Lanier was appointed
Ambassador Extraordinary and Plenipotentiary in 1946 to be followed by Edward R.
Dudley (1949–53); Jesse D. Locker (1953–55); and Richard L. Jones (1955–56).
Among other Negroes who have served, in what was referred to by Professor Rayford
Logan of Howard University in his 1964 Liberia Day speech as "a training ground" for
Negro diplomats, have been William C. George, who in 1931 was made Vice Consul in
Monrovia after serving in the Canary Islands, the Azores, Denmark and Canada. Clifton
K. Wharton, who subsequently became Minister to Rumania and Ambassador to
Norway, also spent a period of time in Liberia as did Rupert Lloyd, Principal Officer
of the United States Consulate in Tegucigalpa, Honduras (1963), and L. B. Polk of the
Bureau of African Affairs, Department of State in Washington (1963).

of such voluntary service groups as the YMCA, and the YWCA, the African-American Institute, Operation Crossroads Africa Inc., and various charitable organizations; as diplomats and employees of several government agencies, including the United States Information Agency; as members of the Armed Forces of the United States; as international civil servants under the United Nations; as wives of students returning home, and sometimes as voluntary exiles fleeing the pressure of race prejudice in America or seeking their fortunes in what they conceive of as "the land of the ancestors." They arrive, too, in increasing numbers, as tourists.[6]

In this post-war situation, Negroes in the United States have also had their contacts with Africans expanded. A greatly augmented student group now includes those who hold scholarships which release them from financial dependence upon the Negro community and who, if they wish to do so, can often find white friends to provide companionship and hospitality which a decade ago only Negro Americans were willing to supply. African heads of state and diplomats receive high honors and are sometimes accorded privileges denied Negro Americans. (Negroes occasionally even find themselves competing with white individuals and institutions for the honor of entertaining them.) Visitors under private and governmental auspices, the crews of new African shipping lines, buyers and salesmen—these are among new African social types which occasionally appear upon the American scene.

In addition to sustaining new kinds of face-to-face relations, both Negroes and Africans are having their images of one another reshaped by the mass media. Africans now appear on movie and television screens in situations ranging from U.N. conferences to terrorist camps in Angola; African political activities are becoming ingredients in the weekly diet of news. Sit-ins, Black Muslims, Freedom Riders—terms such as these are becoming familiar to Africans as radio and cinema reach ever-widening audiences. New personalities are joining Paul Robeson and Joe Louis as popular symbols of Negro achievement in the eyes of African schoolboys and schoolgirls.

Old stereotypes are in the process of dissolution, and attitudes are labile and uncrystallized. Both Africans and Negro Americans find themselves constantly "trying to make up their minds" about each other. To understand this dynamic, continuously changing, contact-situation, it is necessary always to ask the question: What type of Negro Americans are interacting

[6] Consult Appendix II for a list of Negroes who were serving in Africa under various governmental agencies in 1965 and Appendix III for a partial list of Negroes who have played prominent nongovernmental roles in Africa since 1951.

with what type of Africans, in what specific kind of situations, and for what ends? Any generalizations based upon data which have not been analyzed in this fashion will result in a distorted picture of relations between Negro Americans and Africans. This was evident, for instance, in 1961 and 1962 when several articles appeared which gave the general impression that "Africans don't like American Negroes," or "Africans and American Negroes do not get along well together." No statistically controlled research has been carried out on this problem except some superficial questioning of African students in America and a not too careful interpretation of the replies.[7]

In isolating critical problems for research and in providing background for interpretation, a consideration of the historic relationships between Negro Americans and Africans may be relevant. Some Negro Americans and some Africans have been continuously involved in intimate cooperative relations, under organizational auspices, for over 150 years. Throughout this period, too, various white groups as well as the United States Government, have utilized the services of Negroes in carrying out policies in Africa which Negroes had no share in formulating, while some Negroes have been constantly insisting (not without success) upon participation in the policy-making process when African affairs were concerned. Other

---

[7] The Institute of International Education released a study in November, 1961, entitled *The African Student, His Achievement and His Problems*, by James M. Davis, Russell G. Harrison, and Duane R. Burnor. The Preface expressed surprise over the fact that some African students reported problems in adjusting to Negro Americans. Wire service news items about the study played up a state of alleged "friction" between African students and Negroes in America. In fact, however, the proportion of African students who "made no friends" in Negro colleges was approximately the same as the proportion of African students generally in America who "made no friends"—about one in five. That there are areas of tension between African students and some Negro Americans is undeniable; that they are as important to the students as to the researchers is doubtful.

The New Yorker for May 13, 1961, carried an article by MIT researcher Harold Isaacs, "Back to Africa," which presented considerable case material to indicate that Negro Americans found it difficult to adjust to Africans when living in Africa. Russell Howe, a British journalist, took a very extreme position in an article, "Strangers in Africa," printed in the *Reporter*, June 22, 1961. He stated categorically that missions, business and government did not do themselves, the Africans, or Negro Americans "any good" by using Negro personnel in Africa. Horace Mann Bond, Negro scholar and educator of Atlanta University, replied to both articles in "Howe and Isaacs in the Bush," *Negro History Bulletin*, December, 1961. The February 1962 issue carried Russell Howe's "Reply to Horace Mann Bond." See also the text of a speech to the American Society for African Culture by St. Clair Drake in which he also discussed these issues, published in *Summary Report* of Fourth Annual Meeting of the society, Hotel Biltmore, New York City, June 23–24, 1961. See also J. C. Kennedy's articles in *The New York Times*, reader's letters, and his reply, February 25, 1962 and March 4, 1962, "Review of the Week."

Negro leaders have insisted that Negro Americans and Africans should define their relations with each other without "white interference." Thus, Negro Americans have had an historic "African Interest." [8]

Until the close of the Second World War, two "traditions" structured Negro American attitudes toward Africa and dominated the situations of contact: *The missionary tradition* and *racial Pan-Africanism.*[9] Both traditions have been diminishing in importance during the past decade, but are still viable, nevertheless. They are crucially relevant for an understanding of some of the complexities of contemporary relations.

The Missionary Tradition

From the close of the Civil War to the beginning of the depression, the major impact of Negro Americans upon Africa was through the presence of a small group of missionaries scattered about the continent. Some of them had been sent out by white missionary societies or the mission boards of white denominations, a practice which arose because of the belief that Negroes could withstand African climate and diseases better than whites, and the widespread conviction that Africans would respond more readily to the Gospel if it were preached by men who resembled them in color.[10]

---

[8] For a brief discussion of this "interest" see Vernon McKay, *Africa in World Politics* (New York: Harper & Row, 1963), "Interest Among American Negroes," pp. 263–64, and Rupert J. Emerson's article on this topic in Walter Goldschmidt (ed.), *The United States and Africa* (New York: Praeger, 1963), pp. 30–32. Cf. St. Clair Drake, *op. cit.*, and a memorandum by the same author prepared for the Arden House meeting of the American Negro Leadership Conference on Africa, November, 1962: *Negro Americans, "The Africa Interest" and Power Structures in Africa and America.* (Available in mimeograph form from Department of Sociology, Roosevelt University, Chicago.)

[9] For a brief, but comprehensive discussion of Pan-Africanism, see McKay, *op. cit.*, Chapter 6, "Concepts of Pan Africanism: 1900–1958" and "Pan-Africanism since 1958." For a longer and very perceptive analysis, cf. Colin Legum, *Pan-Africanism* (New York: Praeger, 1962). The concept of "Nègritude" as developed by some French-speaking Negroes is one variation upon the theme of *racial* Pan-Africanism, defined as the attempt to unite all Negroes everywhere. *Continental* Pan-Africanism stresses the unity of all people in Africa regardless of their race.

[10] Cf. *Ecumenical Missionary Conference, New York, April 2–May 1, 1900,* Volume I (New York: American Tract Society), which contains a section on "A Work For American Negroes," pp. 469–72. Both white and Negro speakers at the conference accepted the same basic beliefs about the role of the Negro in missionary work, but a Negro Baptist, Dr. C. S. Morris, castigated white people for hampering the work of the Gospel by transporting their prejudices to Africa, citing this as an additional reason why the use of Negro missionaries was imperative. See also Donald G. Fraser, *The New Africa* (New York: Missionary Education Movement of the U.S.A. and Canada, 1928), pp. 98–99, for a statement of the case for the use of Negro missionaries. He noted, however, that "they are not immune to African diseases."

It is likely that even larger numbers of New World Negroes would have been used by white mission boards had it not been for the objections of white settlers and some colonial administrators. By 1900, an image had arisen in their minds of Negro missionaries as "subversives," and they were actually barred from a number of territories. On the whole, it was the activity of Negro denominations such as the African Methodist Episcopal Church and the African Methodist Episcopal Zion Church which created the apprehension, but it was generalized to include all Negro missionaries, whether under Negro boards or not.[11]

The charges against Negro missionaries of organizing political action or stirring up revolt, with very few exceptions, were unfounded, but Negro missionaries did, wittingly or unwittingly, contribute toward the spreading of discontent by their very presence in Africa. They were living symbols of what Africans could be if education were made available to them, and of what Africans could do if their opportunities were not restricted. The African Methodist Episcopal Church also expressed willingness to affiliate to itself some separatist churches which broke away from white missions in southern Africa. And all denominations brought African students to

---

[11] There is some evidence to indicate that the first Negro missionary was sent out to Liberia in 1787 by the energetic Newport divine, Samuel Hopkins. The AME Church placed a missionary in the American Colonization Society's settlement which evolved into Liberia in the year 1820 and the white Baptists landed a Negro missionary the same year. No adequate history of the Negro missionary movement has been written, but C. S. Grove in *The Planting of Christianity in Africa* (London: Lutterworth Press), Vol. II, 1954, pp. 217–23; Vol. III, 1955, 120–21, mentions the work of a number of Negro missionaries and devotes a chapter to experiments in the use of West Indians in the African mission field. (See Chapter 2, Vol. II, "Contribution from the Caribbean.") Fraser (*loc. cit.*) discusses the fears of some white people that Negro missionaries might have an unsettling influence on the continent and describes the safeguards suggested by the Le Zoute Misionary Conference (1926), *viz.*, that they only be used under "responsible societies" and be carefully chosen. Interesting and informative material may also be found in the publications of the mission boards of the two major Negro Baptist conventions and of the African Methodist Episcopal Church and the African Methodist Episcopal Zion Church.

Dr. L. G. Jordan, Secretary of the Foreign Mission Board of the National Baptist Convention, reported in 1912 on work which the Negro Baptists had begun in 1880, involving forty-one men and women sent out since that year, the recruitment of 102 "native workers" and the bringing to the U.S.A. for study of twenty-six boys and girls. The African Methodist Episcopal Zion bishop, Alexander Walters, listed five mission stations run by his denomination in Liberia and eleven in the Gold Coast as well as three schools and colleges in West Africa. He noted that five AMEZ bishops had visited Africa. (See Booker T. Washington papers, Library of Congress, Manuscript Room, Washington, D.C.: hereafter referred to as B.T.W. with number following indicating box or container where found [No. 917] Cf. Note 34.)

America, often to Negro colleges and universities such as Hampton, Howard, Tuskegee, Lincoln, Wilberforce, Fisk and the schools in Atlanta. All of this activity had political repercussions.[12]

The missionary tradition had its roots in a still earlier one, that of the colonization movement during the first quarter of the nineteenth century. The supporters of the colonization movement elaborated the theory of "Providential design," *viz.*, that God has allowed a portion of the African population to be enslaved and brought to America where it had been "Christianized" and "civilized" for the purpose of raising up a group among them who would "return" and "redeem" Africa. While the doctrine served primarily as a rationalization for sending freedmen away from America to prevent them from stirring up trouble among the slaves and from raising embarrassing questions about their own right to citizenship, it also motivated idealistic white people and Negroes to found churches and schools in Africa and stimulated financial support of missions by Americans.

After the Civil War, the doctrine of "Providential design" became an important aspect of that home mission movement which led to the founding of schools in the South for freedmen and to the recruitment of volunteer teachers. Many of the educational institutions set up by Northern denominations were dedicated to a dual purpose: "the elevation of the Negro race in America" and "the redemption of Africa."[13] Hope was widespread that African students would flow to America for training in these schools and colleges and would return home to found similar institutions, and that Negro Americans would be inspired to go to Africa as teachers and evangelists. A small trickle of people did begin to flow in both directions,

[12] The most readily accessible analysis of the political repercussions of Negro missionaries on Africa is included in George E. Shepperson, "Notes on Negro American Influences on the Emergence of African Nationalism," AMSAC Newsletter Supplement No. 20, October 31, 1960, reprinted from *Journal of African History*, I, No. 2, 1960. Shepperson has also written a book-length account, with Thomas Price, of the life of the African preacher, John Chilembwe, who attended a Negro Baptist college in Virginia and then led the Nyasaland rising of 1915. (See George Shepperson and Thomas Price, *Independent African*, Edinburgh University Press, 1958). Grove, *op. cit.*, Vol. III, pp. 179–80, briefly discusses the impact of the AME Church on the African separatist churches and the Ethiopianist Movement of South Africa, a matter dealt with more thoroughly by Bengt G. M. Sundkler in *Bantu Prophets in South Africa* (London: Lutterworth Press, 1948), pp. 38–43.

[13] Dr. Horace Mann Bond, Dean of the Graduate School of Education of Atlanta University, has done extensive research on the ideologies behind the missionary movement and the founding of Negro educational institutions, the results of which will appear in a book sponsored by the United Negro College Fund.

and although the volume was small, the impact was great—far out of proportion to the numbers of people involved.[14]

By the 1880's, a secularized version of the missionary tradition was operating in close connection with the evangelizing thrust, an aspect which became institutionalized in what might be called "The Hampton-Tuskegee Approach." [15] This concern for Africa, as represented by Booker T. Washington and the influential white philanthropists who supported his work, emphasized Christian ethics, a highly practical form of education and accommodative race relations. The latter emphasis made it possible for Hampton and Tuskegee to secure a measure of trust and cooperation from the colonial powers which more militant Negroes and whites could never obtain. Supporters of The Hampton-Tuskegee Approach felt that it had been successful in dealing with problems which arose in the South in the wake of the Civil War; they were sure it could be equally useful (and successful in carrying out "the civilizing mission" in Africa.

The missionary tradition, prior to World War I, whether embodied in white or Negro institutions, and whether in its secular or religious version, carried overtones of condescension and implications of cultural inferiority. Also, except for a few Negro denominations with limited funds, missions in Africa were controlled by white people. However, an important post-World War I trend among missionary societies was the recognition of the fact that some African customs were well fitted to their specific milieu and that some aspects of African cultures were worth preserving. In fact, some mission-

[14] According to Bond, when the Congo Free State was organized, missionary hopes rose high. The American Methodists "conceived the idea of a vast chain of 'self-supporting' missions in Africa." They hoped that missionaries would come forward from Methodist schools for Negroes in the South, and one enthusiastic white Methodist donated over $200,000 to establish the Steward Foundation for Africa at Gammon Theological Seminary, which, in 1895, called the first important conference on Africa in the U.S. A number of American mission boards sent workers into the Congo, some of whom took an active part in the exposure of the atrocities which were eventually committed there in the interest of quick profits; the Rev. William H. Sheppard, a Negro Presbyterian missionary, spent eight months in prison for criticizing the Congo regime. (Cf. E. D. Morel, *Red Rubber,* Manchester: The National Labour Press, 1919.)

Several Spelman girls went to the Congo in the late 1880's and early 1890's. They promptly sent back some African girls who attended Spelman and, according to Bond, "had distinguished later careers in the teaching field in the Congo." He also says that Bishop Turner "sent literally dozens of young people from South Africa to AME colleges as well as to Tuskegee and other schools."

[15] For a study of "The Hampton-Tuskegee Approach," see August Meier, *Negro Thought in America, 1880–1915: Racial Ideologies in the Age of Booker T. Washington* (Ann Arbor: The University of Michigan Press, 1963). Note especially Chapter III, "Economics, Self-Help and Racial Solidarity," and Chapter VIII, "Agencies of Propaganda, Protest and Social Welfare."

ary societies made anthropological training a requirement. It is only since the Second World War, however, that serious consideration has been given to the relinquishment of the *control* of Christian activities in Asian and African countries to the indigenous people, as, for instance, in the case where the "Christian Church of India" has replaced "the mission field."

Negro missionaries of an earlier generation had the same attitudes toward African cultures as did their white colleagues, and it is not surprising that a Negro Baptist responsible for mission work should have made reference at the Ecumenical Missionary Conference in 1900 [16] to ". . . every bit of red paint that has been washed away and every blanket that has been cast away and every man that has been lifted up from degradation in Zululand. . . ." This attitude of "civilizing" while "Christianizing" was combined, in this case, with the concept of the "Providential design," the minister, Dr. C. S. Morris, expressing the belief that ". . . God is going to put it into the hearts of these black boys and girls in the schools of the South to go with the message to South Africa and to West Africa, and vindicate slavery as far as it can be vindicated by taking across the ocean the stream of life. . . ." The first and second generation of Africans who responded to "the message" also often saw themselves as "benighted heathens saved by grace." But most of those who become Christians today are not prepared to reject their cultural backgrounds in toto, nor to accept the belief in "Providential design," and they also expect the Negro American missionary to be as enlightened in his attitudes as is the liberal modern white missionary.

The condescending attitudes are less prevalent today among missionaries than in the past, but Negro missionaries like their white counterparts do not escape occasional criticism on other scores. For instance, throughout 1963 and 1964, a significant discussion went on in the AME mission press.[17] Adherents in Central Africa and West Africa raised the question of why their American "brothers" spent so little upon the physical facilities of their mission schools and churches and thus shamed them *vis-à-vis* African members of white denominations. This led one American Negro bishop in Central

---

[16] *Ecumenical Missionary Conference, New York, April 2–May 1, 1900* (New York: American Tract Society), Vol. I, p. 470.

[17] *Voice of Missions* (published by the Home and Foreign Missionary Department, Inc. of the African Methodist Episcopal Church); See Vol. LXV, No. 12, December, 1963, "Annual Report of Fourteenth Episcopal District," pp. 10–11; "Giving Credit Where Credit is Due," p. 12; "The Time Has Come," p. 12; Annual Conference Resolutions of the Fifteenth Episcopal District, p. 13; "How Much Do We Really Know About Our Missionary Investments Abroad," p. 14; and "The Silent African Student," p. 15. In Vol. LXVI, No. 1, January, 1964 see "President Tubman Dedicates," p. 10; "Report on A.M.E. School (Ghana)," p. 11; "Report of the Committee on the State of the Country, Ghana Annual Conference," p. 12.

Africa to react with some petulance in a section of an article captioned "Our Cause is Suffering by Comparison":

> We are fully aware of the fact that those who seek to compare our Church and its missionary efforts with other denominations . . . overlook very important and undenyable [sic] facts. In the first place they do not realize that the great African Methodist Episcopal Church is made up of people, many of whom are descents [sic], who are very limited economically. They do not take time to think that the forbares [sic] of these denominations with whom they seek to compare us [were] in bondage until a century ago, and still hold us in many aspects as such. They do not realize that these former slaves, turned loose a century ago with nothing much of this world's goods have collected their pennies, nickels and dimes and built up a fund out of which they are sharing with brothers and sisters here in Africa. If those who complain of our small financial efforts, and compare us with groups that are much stronger financially and numerically, would spend more of their time giving thanks instead of expressions of ingratitude for the little the home church is doing there may be an increase.

Then, speaking to the "home front," he called for more contributions and promised to streamline the work in the field rather than to expand it.

The AME bishop in West Africa was also faced with this type of complaint, but with others as well. For instance, an African divinity student from Ghana studying in the United States commended the bishop for his broadminded approach to the problems, but then wrote, "The time has come for a definite missionary program from the AME Church which will take the present spirit of Africa into consideration. . . ." He listed several complaints, stating at one point that:

> The AME Church does not seem to be sympathetic to the apparent aspirations of the Africans because while other churches are giving the Africans the role of leading their denominations in their countries and while other denominations are promoting Africans to great responsibilities and higher ecclesiastical honors, the AME Church is still sending American Bishops to supervise the work in Africa. A gesture which assumes that the Negro in America does not think the African is worthy to be trusted with leadership in the Church.

With the coming of independence, the Negro missionary can no longer function as he did in the colonial situation or still does in settler-dominated countries. He has lost his value as a symbol of protest. He may even become an impediment to African aspirations, as *national* solidarity and the desire for upward social mobility become paramount values.

None of these complaints, however, imply that missionaries from Negro denominations are not wanted—as long as they build schools and hospitals and give scholarships to deserving Africans. In fact, the same issue of *Voice of Missions* which carried "The Time Has Come" also carried an invitation from a chief in Nigeria to begin work in his area and a promise of land; as well as a reminder from an African student that "King Sobhuza II of Swaziland has given acres and acres of fertile land for use by the AME Church for building schools of high [*sic*] learning in Swaziland," and the lament that "so far the Mother Church has not taken an initiative on such a free offer." He then suggested that American AME members at least supply the Africans with tractors so that they could farm a large piece of land and support their churches and schools from the sale of cash crops.

Racial Pan-Africanism

Developing concurrently with the colonization movement and the missionary tradition, in both its religious and secular form, was the ideology of *racial Pan-Africanism* emphasizing *independent* activity on the part of Negro Americans designed to establish relations with Africans and people of African descent *everywhere* for the development of trade between dispersed groups of Negroes, for cooperation in the fight against color discrimination, for protesting against the derogation of the Negro race and for participation by Negroes returning to Africa in the nation-building process on that continent. The Negro missionary movement was always deeply influenced by *racial Pan-Africanism* as well as by its commitment to Christian beliefs and goals.[18] There is widespread awareness among older educated Africans of this fact.

Pan-African sentiments sometimes eventuate in "Back to Africa" movements espousing voluntary emigration. Three years before the white-controlled American Colonization Society landed its first group of settlers on the West African coast in 1815, a prosperous New England Negro ship owner, Paul Cuffee, had taken a group of freedmen to Africa at his own

[18] The Pan-African note was sounded by one Negro Baptist missionary to the Congo who, in a book on his work there, said, "So many have written and spoken concerning my people in Africa and have either attributed all of their ingenuity to the white man or discredited their capabilities altogether, that I am glad to be able to give a true testimony of what I really saw in the land of my fathers." He was particularly impressed by the skill exhibited in farming and the orderliness of family relations and public life. (C. C. Boone, *Congo as I Saw It*, New York: J. J. Little & Ives, 1927, p. 43.) The book was dedicated to his wife who died after a year of residence in the Congo. Rev. Boone had gone out under the auspices of the Lott Carey Baptist Foreign Missionary Convention and a white board, the American Baptist Foreign Missionary Society of Boston, from 1901 through 1906. The Negro Baptists who sponsored John Chilembwe (see ftn. 11) hoped for commercial relations with Nyasaland, and Shepperson presents data to indicate that a company to facilitate such relations was actually organized.

expense.[19] The dream of groups of Negro emigrants settling in Africa, helping to develop the natural resources of the continent and sustaining trade relations with the Negroes who remained in the New World, has been attractive to some Negro Americans ever since. The persisting idea, operating in conjunction with relevant socio-economic factors, has resulted in the rise of emigrationist movements from time to time.[20]

Emigrationist sentiment has sometimes been blended with the theory of "Providential design," as is evident in the following passage from an article by Bishop Henry M. Turner of the AME Church, written in 1901 when race relations were tense:

> The Negro race has as much chance in the United States . . . of being a man . . . as a frog has in a snake den. . . . Emigrate and gradually return to the land of our ancestors. . . . The Negro was brought here in the providence of God to learn obedience, to work, to sing, to pray, to preach, acquire education, deal with mathematical abstractions and imbibe the principles of civilization as a whole, and then to return to Africa, the land of his fathers, and bring her his millions. . . .[21]

[19] Note reference to Paul Cuffee in Howard H. Bell, "American Negro Interest in Africa, 1858–1861." *Journal of Social Science Teachers*, VI, No. 4 (November, 1960). Professor Bell has published detailed studies of Negro emigrationist movements including the following articles: "The Negro Emigration Movement, 1849–1854; A Phase of Negro Nationalism," *Phylon*, Second Quarter, 1959 and "Negro Nationalism: A Factor in Emigration Projects, 1858–1861." *The Journal of Negro History*, XLVII, No. 1 (January, 1962).

[20] Meier, *op. cit.*, Chapter IV, "Migration and Colonization," pp. 59–68, presents a comprehensive account of emigrationist ideology and action among Negro Americans with full documentation. One of the more interesting schemes for colonization was the plan of the Liberia Emigration Clubs of Oklahoma which grew up between 1897 and 1914. They created the atmosphere and provided the participants for the emigration project led by "Chief Sam," who claimed to be an African, organized the Akim Trading Company, and collected enough money to buy a ship which was to carry the emigrants to Africa to settle on his tribal lands. (See *New York Age*, January 22, 1914; *The New York Times*, February 11, 1914 and March 29, 1914; and *Crisis*, XVIII, June 1914, p. 115.) One study of West African history states that when Chief Sam's ship, the S.S. *Liberia* arrived in the Gold Coast in 1915, a newspaper, *The Gold Coast Nation*, said that "the scheme had a national object . . . of immense uplifting force to this country, and welcomed the 'Afro-Americans' to 'the home of their ancestors'; they were personally greeted by the ARPS (Aborigines Rights Protection Society) leaders. . . ." Due to British government hostility and other misfortunes they eventually left for Liberia. See David Kimble, *A Political History of Ghana: The Rise of Gold Coast Nationalism, 1850–1928* (London: Oxford Press, 1963), p. 542.

[21] Quoted from Bishop Turner's journal, *Voice of the People*, I, No. 4 (May, 1901), p. 4. (Rev. Josephus R. Coan, of Atlanta, Georgia, a student of Bishop Turner's life and works, made his files of *Voice of the People* available to the Phelps-Stokes Fund.) Meier (*op. cit.*, pp. 272–73) discusses the activities of Bishop Turner at some length and makes reference to his articles in favor of emigration and the Colored Emigration and Commercial Association, which he founded (see Meier, *op. cit.*, pp. 28, 65–67, 71, 82,

The dominant leadership within Negro American communities has always rejected the emigrationist variety of Pan-Africanism, but as one student of the subject has pointed out, "The persistence of emigrationist sentiment and the later mass appeal of the Garvey Movement suggest that perhaps the desire for colonization was more widespread among the masses than is generally ordinarily believed. . . ." [22]

Although emigrationist movements have been sporadic, involving complex motivations,[23] and the largest of such movements, Garvey's Universal Negro Improvement Association of the 1920's, seems to have had some important repercussions in Africa itself.[24] A number of scholars have pointed out that colonial governments and white settlers in Africa feared the Garvey movement and that one of the movement's slogans, "Africa for Africans," operated to increase racial consciousness and nationalism among Africans of all educational levels and varied degrees of sophistication. David Kimble, an

---

185, 218 and 272). Another AME leader, Bishop B. W. Arnett, favored the selective emigration of Negroes with capital who could ". . . build up a new Christian Nationality in the Fatherland . . . that would cause Negroes everywhere to be respected . . .." and he organized a company for trading with Africa in 1876. (See Meier, *op. cit.*, p. 61.) One group of Baptists named a missionary convention after Lott Carey who said, just before he emigrated to Liberia in 1815, "I am an African and in this country, however meritorious my conduct and respectable my character, I cannot receive the credit due either. I wish to go to a country where I shall be estimated by my merits not by my complexion." Lott Carey was born in 1780 in Virginia, purchased the freedom of self and family and emigrated. (Lucius E. Smith, ed., *Heroes and Martyrs of the Modern Missionary Enterprise,* Toronto: R. Dick, 1857.)

[22] Meier, *op. cit.*, p. 272.

[23] The most significant pre-Civil War project (discussed by Bell in "American Negro Interest in Africa") was that of a remarkable physician, Martin R. Delaney and an influential minister, Henry Highland Garnet. They founded the African Civilization Society, and given a mandate by the Emigration Convention of 1854, Delaney went to Africa and actually signed an agreement with several Yoruba rulers in what is now Nigeria to allocate land for settlement by Negro Americans. Delaney and Garnet had a bold and imaginative idea. They proposed to colonize a vast West African area with freedmen from the United States who would teach the Africans to grow cotton. They would then dump it on the world market at such a price as to break the back of the Southern plantation system. Cloth manufacturers would get cheaper raw goods, the slaves would be freed as the plantation system collapsed and Africans would learn new skills and become prosperous. The scheme won some support among British financiers. The Civil War ended it. (See M. R. Delaney, *Official Report of the Niger Valley Exploring Party,* New York; T. Hamilton, etc., etc. 1861, and William M. Brewer, "Henry Highland Garnet," *Journal of Negro History* XIII, January, 1928, pp. 36–52.

[24] The most comprehensive and serious study of Garvey and his movement has been made by E. D. Cronon, *Black Moses* (Madison: University of Wisconsin Press, 1955). The John E. Bruce Papers in the Schomburg Collection of the New York Public Library are a very valuable source of data on Garveyism and on Bruce's relation to the movement. For a description of Bruce, see Meier, *op. cit.*, pp. 130, 262–63, 267.

English scholar concerned with the "growth of national consciousness" in the Gold Coast, states that one of the leading West African nationalists, A. Casely Hayford, "considered that the UNIA had done more than any other agency to bring 'to the notice of world opinion the disabilities of the African race.' " [25]

The impact of emigrationist movements upon educated African leaders was weakened, however, by the assumptions always implicit in the ideology that the New World Negroes had a "mission" to "save," "redeem" or "regenerate" Africa.[26] As self-confident African leaders emerged they were not prepared to accept the doctrine that "salvation" must come from American or West Indian sources—white or black.[27]

The variety of racial Pan-Africanism which probably had the greatest impact upon Africa was that associated with New World intellectuals rather than the Pan-Africanism of mass leaders with an emigrationist orientation. By 1900, there were over two thousand Negro college gradu-

[25] A. Casely Hayford was a prominent West African intellectual. In his inaugural address delivered before the British West African Congress in 1920, he referred with approval of the Garvey movement and suggested that contact be established with its leaders so that they would accommodate themselves to some of the features of British West African political life which might be unfamiliar to them.

At the mass level, it has been reported that "probably the most important outside stimulus" to the formation of independent separatist African churches was knowledge of the existence of Garvey's African Orthodox Church and that "The impact of 'Garveyism' can be traced in British and French West Africa and the Cameroons, as well as in South Africa, particularly during the period of unrest and revolt that immediately followed the First World War." (Thomas Hodgkin, *Nationalism in Colonial Africa,* New York: New York University Press, 1957, pp. 101–02. See also Shepperson, *op. cit.,* p. 5.)

[26] There was an air of condescension and a patronizing tone even in Garvey's initial statement of objectives for his Universal Negro Improvement and Conservation Association and Communities League; written in 1914 (italics added):

"To establish a Universal Confraternity (among the race); to promote the spirit of race pride and love; to *reclaim the fallen of the race;* to administer to and assist the needy; *to assist in civilizing the backward tribes* of Africa; to strengthen the imperialism of independent African states; to establish Commissionaries or Agencies in the principal countries of the world for the protection of all Negroes, irrespective of nationality; to promote a conscientious (spiritual) *Christian worship* among the native tribes of Africa; to establish Universities, Colleges and Secondary Schools for the education and culture of the boys and girls of the race; to conduct a worldwide commercial and industrial intercourse." He later added "to establish a central nation for the race." (Quoted from E. D. Cronon, *Black Moses,* Madison: University of Wisconsin Press, 1955, p. 17.)

[27] Negotiations between John E. Bruce and Akinambe Agbebi drew a complaint from the latter, a Nigerian, that with respect to both the Black Star Line and some projected factories, the UNIA remained New York-centered and was not responsive to African sensitivities. (J. E. Bruce Manuscript Collection, Schomburg Collection of the New York Public Library, Agbebi to J.E.B., May 15, 1920; June 25th, 1920; and August 4, 1920.)

ates in the United States, and from within this group a small circle of scholars emerged who were deeply concerned about Africa and its image in America. They were devoted to correcting error and misinformation and to fostering appreciation for African cultures. They also called attention to neglected aspects of African history and sociology which were favorable to the continent and its people. They were concerned to "vindicate the race" by "setting the record straight." In defending Africa they were defending themselves against the charge of "a people without a past" and of being the descendants of savage and uncivilized people (as were those still living in Africa were reputed to be), people inferior in inborn ability and incapable of successful self-government. Most prominent of the scholars involved in such activity was Dr. W. E. B. Du Bois who, by 1900, had developed an interest in African affairs.[28]

By 1915 what has been called "The Negro History Movement" found institutional expression through the organization of the Association for the Study of Negro Life and History by a Harvard-trained Negro historian, Dr. Carter G. Woodson.[29] Books published by this organization, and its *Journal of Negro History,* include valuable material about African history and cultures.

The writings of these intellectuals were eventually read by Africans as well as by New World Negroes and made a major contribution to positive self-appraisal by some African leaders, as well as to the morale of Negro Americans.[30] It was from among this group of intellectuals that the drive toward participation in a Pan-African movement originated, and David

[28] His Ph.D. thesis at Harvard was concerned with the African slave trade. James Ivy reports that "Africa first appears in NAACP Board Minutes on January 3, 1916, when Du Bois reported on his 1915 researches into African history. In this report, Dr. Du Bois proposed an *Encyclopedia Africana,* to be published in 1919 to celebrate the tercentenary of the permanent landing of Negroes at Jamestown." (John A. Davis, ed., *Africa From the Point of View of American Negro Scholars,* New York: American Society for African Culture, 1958, p. 231.

[29] See Rayford Logan, "Carter G. Woodson." *Phylon,* VI, Fourth Quarter (1945), pp. 318–20 and L. D. Reddick, "As I Remember Woodson" *Crisis,* LX (February, 1950). Meier, *op. cit.,* who includes these items in his list of references, discusses the "Negro History Movement" in detail (pp. 51–53, 57, 67, 105, 167, 203, 257, 260–267, 275, 277).

[30] For example, Dr. Nkrumah has noted the influence of this group upon him as well as Garvey's influence in *Ghana, Autobiography of Kwame Nkrumah* (New York: Thomas Nelson, 1959 paperback edition). He honored Dr. Du Bois by inviting him to Ghana to direct the *Encyclopedia Africana* in 1960. Dr. Nnamdi Azikiwe suggested that the African studies department of the University of Nigeria be named for his Howard University history teacher, Dr. Leo Hansberry, and Dr. Hansberry retired there to teach. Mbiyu Koinange, Minister for Pan-American Affairs of the Kenya government, was very active in the Association for the Study of Negro Life and History when a student at Hampton between 1927 and 1931.

Kimble, in assessing the impact of Negro Americans on the Gold Coast during the decade after World War I, states that "Du Bois' leadership was destined to have a lasting influence. Gold Coast nationalists found that the Pan-African Movement helped them to become aware of problems in other parts of the continent and to acquire wider techniques of organization; and later they, themselves, were to take a prominent part. . . ." [31]

That Negroes in the New World pioneered in the effort to create a more favorable image of Africa and of Negroes, or that they initiated the early Pan-African protest gestures, was not due to any lack of ability upon the part of Africans, but rather to the fact that the few African intellectuals were so involved in the routines of preaching, practicing law, teaching and administering educational institutions, and were so isolated from the stimulation of sympathetic white scholars and adequate library collections, that research was unusually difficult. Also they were busy with the task of trying to prevent outright conquest or the alienation of their lands and, thus, had little time to theorize about distant goals and the world-wide solidarity of black men. Yet a few distinguished scholars resident in Africa do so, such as Casely Hayford of the Gold Coast with his *Ethiopa Unbound* (1911) and E. Wilmot Blyden of Liberia and Sierra Leone in a number of articles, speeches and books. [32]

During the first twenty years of the nineteenth century, African and New World Negro intellectuals began to share ideas more and more frequently. George Shepperson, an English historian, has summed up the significance of this aspect of racial Pan-Africanism in his statement that:

[31] David Kimble, *op. cit.*, p. 544, quoting from Casely Hayford, *"The Disabilities of Black Folk and Their Treatment With an Appeal to the Labour Party* (Accra: 1929). Kimble notes that Africans believed that *Philosophy and Opinions of Marcus Garvey* was "embargoed" by the Gold Coast Government. A full-page advertisement in the *Gold Coast Leader* called the book "A Second Uncle Tom's Cabin With the Appeal of a Bunyan's Pilgrim's Progress."

[32] See Ftn. 2 on p. 663; and Shepperson (1960), ftn. 12 on p. 669 for references to African intellectuals of this period. At least one such intellectual was active in America. In 1906, P. Ka Isaka Seme, a Zulu student at Columbia University, won first prize in the Curtis Medal Oration. His theme was "The Regeneration of Africa" and he argued that the continent had given the world its civilization, and then, "even as white empires rise and fall, it degenerated." But in his view, "The giant is awakening. From the four corners of the earth Africa's sons who have been proved through fire and sword, are marching to the future's golden door bearing the record of deeds of valor done." He called the roll of ". . . Africans who have shown marks of genius and high character sufficient to redeem their race from the charges . . ." of inferiority; and he spoke of the Congo where Africans "fight like men and die like martyrs." The Rev. James Morris Webb included the speech in his little book, *The Black Man: Father of Civilization,* along with biblical "proofs" of the African's civilizing mission and of the presence of Negro blood in the veins of Solomon and Jesus Christ!

The first British Empire owed much to the triangular trade between Africa, the West Indies and North America. The last British Empire has not been uninfluenced by another triangular trade not of pocatille, slaves and molasses, but a commerce of ideas and politics between the descendants of the slaves in the West Indies and North America and their ancestral continent. . . .[33]

This latter-day "commerce of ideas and politics" was one factor in the development of the African revolution in the second half of the twentieth century. But it had its roots in the nineteenth.

AFRICA, BOOKER T. WASHINGTON AND W. E. B. DU BOIS

The day-by-day activities of Negro missionaries carrying on their work in Africa and the routines of scholars and of students from Africa studying in America have been constants in the 100-year-old process of contact between Africans and New World Negroes. The activities of leaders, on the other hand, highlight unusual occurrences in the process and help to document shifts in trends. The two best-known Negro American leaders of the late nineteenth and early twentieth centuries, Booker T. Washington and W. E. B. Du Bois, were both involved in African affairs.[34] Each made an attempt to extend his philosophy of racial education and leadership to the African setting. Du Bois dreamed of a militant African "talented tenth" leading the masses to independence and "civilization." Booker T. Washington was sure that The Tuskegee Approach had the answer to Africa's basic problem.

[33] Shepperson (1960), p. 3. What Shepperson pointed out for the British Empire was equally true for the French Third and Fourth Republics. French-speaking Africans and West Indian Negroes and Malagasies shared a common intellectual life which gave rise to the founding of the Society for African Culture in Paris, the publication of *Presence Africaine* and the death of a man like Franz Fanon from Martinique in the cause of the Algerian Liberation Movement. The concept of "Négritude" is a joint product of Senegalese poet Leopold Senghor and Martinique poet, Aimé Césaire.

[34] That the more militant educated Negro Americans of the period looked to Dr. Du Bois for their lead in African matters as they did in domestic affairs is well known. That Dr. Washington was actively concerned with events in Africa is less well known, except for his interest in Liberia (see Basil Mathews, *Booker T. Washington,* Cambridge: Harvard University Press, 1948, p. 241 ff.). Professor Louis R. Harlan of the University of Cincinnati is currently doing preliminary source work for a future publication on Booker T. Washington and Africa. He has made available to the Phelps-Stokes Fund an index to African items in the Booker T. Washington papers of the Library of Congress which he has prepared. (Items from this collection are referred to in this article by "BTW" with the number of the Library of Congress container in parentheses.)

These two men represented a much wider circle of African interest among Negro Americans in the period between the Congress of Berlin and the turn of the century. This was a period when violence against Negroes was rising in the United States and a determined attempt was being made to institute a rigorous caste system in the South. These events sensitized literate Negro Americans to those events in Africa which seemed to have a similar aim of persecuting or degrading "black men."

The small but influential group of journalists, educators, doctors, lawyers and preachers who formed the leadership group among Negro Americans between 1885 and 1900 was alarmed by the growing deterioration of human relations in the Congo Free State, was aware of the problems facing the Republic of Liberia and admired the efforts of Ethiopia to defend itself against Italian aggression. They were also interested in the fight of the Zulus and other tribes in the Union of South Africa against conquest.[35]

At the same Cotton States and International Exposition in Atlanta where Booker T. Washingon proclaimed his famous "Atlanta Compromise" in September, 1895, Gammon Theological Seminary convened a "Congress on Africa," December 13–15, of which the *Atlanta Constitution* wrote that it was ". . . probably the most distiguished gathering of learned men of both colors that has ever assembled together in the history of the South. . . ." Scholarly papers were read, appeals for missionaries were made, and Bishop Henry Turner made a plea for emigration.[36]

In 1900, Dr. Du Bois, then a professor at Atlanta University, attended a conference of African and New World Negro intellectuals in London, which was convened by a West Indian, Sylvester Williams, who was practicing law in London and who had sent out a "call" to prominent Negroes all over the world. A few responded and came directly as delegates to the conference while others arranged to attend it while in Europe for pleasure or

---

[35] A sampling of two Negro newspapers during this period, the New York *Globe* and the Indianapolis *Freeman*, reveals discussion in the *Globe* of the Zulu warrior, Cetawayo (April 5, April 12, May 17, 1884); a critical letter on Liberia (January 27, 1883); and comments on Egypt and the Congo (April 2, 1884): in the *Freeman* denunciation of colonial exploitation (February 14, 1885); a letter from a "thoroughly disgusted" emigrant to Liberia (March 28, 1885); editorial on the death of the Baganda King Mutesa (April 4, 1885); and call for American intervention in the Congo, stating that "Africa is our fatherland . . . we must prepare to enter upon the elevation of Africa with other races . . . civilizing our brethren . . . as well as Christianizing them. . . . We must enter Africa with the Anglo-Saxons and help build it up" (January 23, 30, 1885). Note also such articles and publications as those listed in the notes and bibliography of Meier (*op. cit.*): J. W. E. Bowen (ed.,) *Africa and the American Negro* published in Atlanta in 1896; Bishop Arnett's article on "Africa and the Descendants of Africa." *AME Review*, XI, (October, 1894), or a symposium, "What Should be the Policy of the Colored American Toward Africa." *AME Review*, II (July, 1885).

[36] See J. W. E. Bowen (ed.), *Africa and the American Negro*, Addresses and Proceedings of the Congress on Africa (Atlanta: Gammon Theological Seminary, 1896).

business, including the Director of the Fisk Jubilee Singers. An American AMEZ bishop, Alexander Walters, was appointed chairman and Dr. Du Bois was made secretary.

The conference released an "Address to the Nations of the World" written by Dr. Du Bois. It contained the first recorded use of his famous dictum that "The Problem of the Twentieth Century is the Problem of the Color Line." Also, "A memorial setting forth . . . acts of injustice directed against Her Majesty's subjects in South Africa and other parts of Her dominions was prepared and sent to Queen Victoria." Mr. Secretary Chamberlain informed the members of the 1900 Pan-African Conference that ". . . in settling the lines on which the administration of the conquered territories is to be conducted, Her Majesty's Government will not overlook the interests and welfare of the native races. . . ."[37] During this same year in which Bishop Alexander Walters and Dr. Du Bois were participating in the framing of protests and appeals in London, Booker T. Washington was dispatching a team of Tuskegee graduates to Togoland in West Africa at the request of the German Government in order to teach the Africans there how to grow cotton. The project extended over a 6-year period.

During the next few years, Dr. Washington was actively associated with the Congo Reform Association of which his fellow educator, G. Stanley Hall, was president. (Dr. Washington's name appeared on the letterheads in 1905 and 1906 as a vice president along with that of Dr. Robert E. Park, the sociologist, as a recording secretary.) In October, 1904, Dr. Washington published an article in *Outlook* on "Cruelty in the Congo Country," and it was his hope, as it was that of many other Americans, that once the Congo was "reformed," Negro Americans could assume a constructive role in its development. Many felt that Tuskegee had a major role to play.[38]

During 1906, Tuskegee sent another team out to Africa, this time to the

[37] The quotation is from Bishop Alexander Walters, *My Life and Work* (New York: Fleming H. Revell Co., 1917), p. 257, which contains a full account of the conference activities and a list of persons who attended. Only four Africans were present, but one was listed as Aide-de-Camp to Emperor Menelik of Ethiopia.

[38] It is evident from correspondence between Dr. Robert E. Park (who later became one of Dr. Washington's secretary-advisers) and Booker T. Washington that members of the Congo Reform Association shared this hope. King Leopold had tried to interest Dr. Washington in the Congo also, and during 1905 and 1906 exerted a bit of pressure upon Dr. Washington to break with the Congo Reform Association. He offered Dr. Washington a free trip to the Congo, and his agents not only flattered Booker T. Washington highly but also tried to convince him that unscrupulous people were using him to attack a just and humane man, King Leopold. Dr. Park, on the other hand, tried to strengthen Dr. Washington's conviction in the righteousness of the cause. See Henry J. Kowalski to BTW, March 10, 1905 (No. 308); Robert H. Terrell to BTW, May 17, 1905 (No. 308) and correspondence with officials of the Congo Reform Association: Thomas S. Barbour to BTW, 1904 (No. 303) and February 13, 1906 (No. 2); Robert E. Park to BTW, 1904–1906 (No. 33).

Anglo-Egyptian Sudan, and Dr. Emmett J. Scott, secretary to Dr. Washington, prepared a memorandum on "Tuskegee in Africa and Africa in Tuskegee." [39] Dr. Washington himself had written an article indicating that Tuskegee should call a conference on Africa. In 1906 his secretary suggested that he now give serious consideration to implementing the idea, stating, "I believe that you can father this movement in a way to enlist worldwide attention." He expressed his confidence that "Such a conference would be productive of much good" and could set in motion ". . . a rational movement for the saving to the African of his dearest possession." Emmett Scott sent his letter to Dr. Washington along with one from the white U.S. Minister Resident in Liberia who said that ". . . Such a conference at this time would not only be interesting but would be helpful to Africans" since "The native problem is a great one" and "will be the most difficult to solve by the nations among whom the territory is parcelled out for colonial purposes." It was his view that if Dr. Washington would call a conference it would ". . . fill a unique place in the history of human events and must rebound in benefit to those for whom it was planned." [40] However, the idea of a conference was dropped during the next three years. The bitter struggle for leadership control on the domestic scene which went on between 1905 and 1909 absorbed much of the energy of the two leaders and resulted in that schism which led to the founding of the Niagara Movement in 1905 by Dr. Du Bois and the National Association for the Advancement of Colored People in 1909 by a group of Negro radicals and white liberals.[41]

In 1910, Dr. Washington made a tour of England and conferred with people there who were interested in African problems. During the same year, his secretary, Dr. Emmett J. Scott, went out to Liberia as Dr. Washington's choice for a Negro member of the 3-man commission appointed by the President of the United States to make recommendations concerning the financial plight of the country and threats to its sovereignty. Dr. Washington felt that Liberia was a testing ground of the Negro's ability to handle his own affairs, and believed that the country's history proved his point that political power without a firm economic base and a body of skilled artisans was detrimental to group welfare. He urged the American

[39] See Emmett Scott Memorandum in BTW (No. 335) (undated). For correspondence relative to Tuskegee teams in Africa see Baron Herman, German Embassy, Washington to BTW, December 30, 1900 (No. 174); S. L. Harris, Lome, Togo to BTW, May 15, 1900 (No. 199); John W. Robinson, Lome, Togo to BTW, May 26, 1901 (No. 215); J. N. Calloway, Lome, Togo to BTW, February 3, 1901 and November 3, 1901 (No. 213); Allen L. Burks, Lome, Togo to BTW, February 15, 1902 (No. 213); Cain W. Triplett, Zeidab, Sudan to BTW, March 12, 1905 (No. 308).

[40] Emmett J. Scott to BTW, June 29, 1906 (No. 326) with letter attached from Ernest Lyon to BTW, May 24, 1906.

[41] Meier, op. cit., pp. 100–18 summarizes the issues in this struggle.

Government to aid Liberia, and at one time felt so strongly about the matter that he considered accepting a post as Liberian Charge d'Affaires in the United States of America. American Government officials persuaded him that this was not the best way for him to help that country.[42] The advice of Dr. Washington and Dr. Scott played some part in saving Liberia from disaster.

In 1911 Dr. Du Bois went to England to address the Universal Races Congress [43] in London. Dr. Washington was back at home planning for a large-scale conference on the problems of Africa and peoples of African descent. The International Conference on the Negro met at Tuskegee on April 17, 18, and 19 in 1912. The delegates and the agenda expressed the close interplay between the missionary movement and Negro educational institutions, as well as the extent to which Pan-African thinking was also a force that could not be ignored. It was officially reported that people were present from eighteen foreign countries or colonies, and that they included representatives of twenty-five missionary societies and twelve religious denominations. The Negro mission boards were all represented, but less than a dozen Africans were present among over a hundred delegates. The African scholar Edward Blyden sent a letter and Rev. Mark Casely Hayford brought an address prepared by his famous brother, A. Casely Hayford.[44]

Dr. Washington, in his address, outlined the part which he thought Negro Americans could, and should, play as teachers and technical assistance experts in Africa. He cited the Tuskegee teams which had gone out to the Sudan and Togo, and emphasized the role which Negro educational institutions (especially Tuskegee) could assume in educating carefully selected African students in America.

The ideal of friendly interracial cooperation was implicit in the structure

[42] Booker T. Washington's interest in Liberia has been well-documented by Basil Mathews (loc. cit.). Dr. Scott reported on this trip in an address delivered for the Emancipation Association of Houston, Texas on June 20th, 1910, BTW Papers (No. 917). He referred to "Providential design" and actually called slavery the "first great missionary movement" because it rescued a portion of the African people from savagery! His trip to Africa had reinforced his belief in the Providential design. He conceived of the Americo-Liberians as involved in carrying out a civilizing mission. The United States Government should not let them down, and should give financial assistance and help to prevent colonial powers from menacing the country's sovereignty.

[43] Gustave Spiller (ed.), Universal Races Congress (London: P. S. King & Son, 1911), p. 348 ff.

[44] This discussion of the conference is based upon documents in BTW (No. 917) and the Negro Yearbook (Tuskegee: 1912). Among the conference notes in the Booker T. Washington papers is the printer's proof of the original list of invitees, over half of whom were representatives of missionary organizations and less than a dozen of whom were Africans. It is significant that representatives of the Ethiopianist Separatist Churches in South Africa were invited but none came.

of the conference and was made explicit by some of the speakers; but representatives of Negro mission boards with a Pan-African orientation also spoke and described their activities which were then over a quarter of a century old. It was reported that some of these ministers were among a group of "stormy Negro orators" who excited apprehensions among some of the white delegates. Those delegates were then led to raise questions as to what was really behind the interest of Negroes in Africa. A deputation waited upon Dr. Washington and urged him to attend a missionary conference in South Africa in order to reassure the white community there of ". . . the peaceful intentions of American Negroes." [45]

A permanent committee was set up to plan for a future conference, but World War I broke out two years later, and the year after that Dr. Washington died.[46] During the next two decades the Phelps-Stokes Fund, founded in 1911, was the major agency involved in trying to implement some of the ideas involved in the Hampton-Tuskegee Approach as applied to Africa, and to modify them in accord with changing political realities.[47]

Soon after the outbreak of World War I, the great migration of Negroes to

[45] Bishop Henry M. Turner was mentioned in a press release prepared at Tuskegee as one of the "stormy Negro orators, . . . the well-known apostle of the Back-to-Africa movement which is the lost cause of the Negro race. . . ." (See BTW Papers [No. 917].)

[46] In addition to Dr. Washington and Emmett Scott, his secretary, two Northern sociologists were on what was called "the permanent executive," Dr. Robert E. Park and Professor W. I. Thomas. The President of Hampton Institute, Hollis B. Frissell, was also on the committee. (Tuskegee, Alabama. Negro Yearbook Press, 1912.) p. 31.

Dr. Washington's death prevented a historic confrontation. Marcus Garvey wrote to Booker T. Washington from Jamaica in 1913, expressing admiration for the work of Tuskegee and telling Booker T. Washington that he was coming to America to explain his plans for worldwide organization of Negroes and to solicit his aid. Dr. Washington died before Marcus Garvey arrived in the country.

[47] The following reports of the Phelps-Stokes Fund give complete documentation and interpretation of the fund's work through 1948: *Educational Adaptations—Report of Ten Years Work of the Phelps-Stokes Fund, 1910–1920* (1920); *Twenty-Year Report of the Phelps-Stokes Fund, 1911–1931* (1932), and *Progress in Negro Status and Race Relations in the United States, 1911–1946: The Thirty-Five-Year Report of the Phelps-Stokes Fund* (1948).

The *Thirty-Five-Year Report* (q.v.) notes that while the fund's original terms of reference included Africa, it was not until the second twenty years of its existence that it came to ". . . include Negro education and race relations in Africa as almost equalling in importance, from the standpoint of the fund, to those in the United States. . . ." (p. 7) This intensification of interest took place during a period when the fund was associating Negroes more closely with the trustees in the decision-making process. When the *Thirty-Fifth-Year Report* was published, four of the eighteen members of the Board of Trustees were Negroes: Claude Barnett, founder of the Associated Negro Press; Dr. Ralph J. Bunche, Dr. Channing Tobias and Dr. Frederick D. Patterson. The latter two men have served in recent years as executive director and president of the fund, respectively.

the North began. Race riots and unemployment after the war provided a setting in which frustration and disillusionment formed the psychological base for the largest Negro emigrationist movement in American history, Marcus Garvey's Universal Negro Improvement Association and its affiliated organizations. Just before the Garveyite upsurge, Dr. W. E. B. Du Bois persuaded the board of the National Association for the Advancement of Colored People to sanction his journey to Paris for the purpose of calling a Pan-African Congress during the Versailles Peace Conference. Dr. Du Bois had to defy pressures from the United States Government, which disapproved of the idea, but he managed to get to Paris.

The Pan-African Congress was organized with the help of Blaise Diagne, the Senegalese Deputy, and met on February 19, 20, 21, 1919, with fifty-seven delegates in attendance, only twelve of whom were from Africa. The tempering hand of pro-French Diagne is apparent in the resolutions, which did not support Dr. Du Bois' plea for a demand to the Peace Conference that all colonies be "internationalized." (This conference is generally referred to in the literature as the *First* Pan-African Congress.) [48]

BETWEEN TWO WORLD WARS

A hundred and thirteen delegates attended the Second Pan-African Congress in 1923, forty-one from Africa, thirty-five from the United States and seven from the West Indies. Walter White and Dr. Du Bois represented the National Association for the Advancement of Colored People. A supplementary session was held in Brussels where the Pan-Africanists were accused of being Bolshevik agents. An editorial appeared some time later that year in the *Crisis* in which Dr. Du Bois rebuked Garvey for his Negro American "messianism."

> The editor [i.e., Dr. Du Bois] distinctly believes that Africa should be administered for the Africans and, as soon as may be, by the Africans. He does not mean by this that Africa should be administered by West Indians

[48] Dr. Du Bois has given his version of the Pan-African Congress movement in his autobiography, *Dusk of Dawn* (New York: Harcourt, Brace & Company, 1940) pp. 260–262. James Ivy, working from the NAACP files, has presented an objective analysis of the movement in John A. Davis (ed.) *op. cit.*, pp. 229–47. Some of the excitement and sense of dedication surrounding the First Pan-African Congress may be sensed from Dr. Du Bois' comments in *Crisis*, December 1, 1919 and January, 1920. See, for an evaluation of the congresses by the organizer of the Fifth Pan-African Congress, George Padmore, *Pan-Africanism or Communism?* (London: Dobson, 1956), p. 117.

or American Negroes. They have no more right to administer Africa for the native Africans than native Africans have to administer America.

By 1925, the excitement of the Garvey Movement had died down and two more Pan-African Congresses convened by Dr. Du Bois evoked only a moderate amount of attention, even among Africans and people of African descent. New voices were wooing Negroes, those of the Communists. Among the recruits was a young American-educated West Indian, George Padmore, who went on to Moscow for further training. The "Negro Renaissance" also burst forth among Harlem intellectuals, and although this talented group of writers and artists did not ignore Africa, there was no preoccupation with a search for "African roots." Near the end of the Twenties, intellectuals were becoming sensitized, however, to Marxian approaches to race and class, partly through the writings of Nancy Cunard and of George Padmore who began to publish a magazine, *The Negro Worker*, under the aegis of the International Trade Union Committee of Negro Workers.[49]

In 1924, Dr. Du Bois was appointed Envoy Extraordinary and Minister Plenipotentiary to the Republic of Liberia upon the inauguration of President Charles Dunbar King, and expressed the view that "in the great battle against color-caste in America, the ability of Negroes to rule in Africa has been and ever will be a great and encouraging reinforcement."[50] Before the decade ended, however, Liberia had become an embarrassment in this regard due to accusations that its leaders were involved in the "slave trade" and the subsequent censure of the Liberian Government by an international commission which included the Negro American sociologist, Dr. Charles S. Johnson.[51]

A second wave of African students began to come to the United States in the early Twenties—predominantly from West Africa. They were not

[49] The only accounts of George Padmore's activity during this period which are available in English are to be found in Wilson Record, *The Negro and the Communist Party* (Chapel Hill: University of North Carolina Press, 1951) and in Padmore's work previously cited, *Pan-Africanism or Communism?* where he states that "Had the Communists succeeded in capturing the Garvey movement and in gaining control of other black nationalist groups, especially selected Negro militants were to have been recruited and trained in Moscow as cadres for colonial work in Africa." (p. 318)

[50] DuBois, *op. cit.*, p. 125.

[51] It is significant that Dr. Johnson never published his critical though sympathetic report on Liberia, *Bitter Canaan*. (Dr. Johnson's widow very kindly gave permission for the author to examine the manuscript, which is in the Charles S. Johnson Papers at Fisk University.) The Negro journalist, George Schuyler, on the other hand, took the view that the Liberian officials should be criticized severely and castigated them in his *Slaves Today*. (New York: Brewer, Warren & Putnam, 1931).

sent by missionaries although they were often motivated to come through contact with Negro missionaries and teachers. Among this group were a number of Nigerians, including Nnamdi Azikiwe who attended Storer College, Lincoln and Howard, and subsequently became Governor-General of Nigeria and then President of the Republic.

By 1921, J. Kwegyir Aggrey had been "discovered" by Dr. Thomas Jesse Jones of the Phelps-Stokes Fund. This remarkable Gold Coast African had come to the United States before the First World War, along with two other converts to the African Methodist Episcopal Zion Church. After his graduation from that denomination's school, Livingstone College in North Carolina, he became associated with the Phelps-Stokes Fund and accompanied Dr. Jones on two highly successful journeys through Africa to study the problems of providing an adequate education for Africans. Aggrey always emphasized the piano keyboard analogy—that it takes both the white and the black keys to produce harmony—a welcome note then at a time when nationalist sentiment was rising. In 1928, Monroe Work's *Bibliography of the Negro in Africa and America* appeared under Phelps-Stokes sponsorship, and in 1929, the fund established the Booker T. Washington Institute in Liberia.[52]

The advent of the depression caused the Negro American leadership to "face inward," but the invasion of Ethiopia in 1935 stirred sections of the Negro community deeply.[53] With the rise of Hitler, the international Communists tended to moderate their anticolonialist pressures in the interest of Soviet military cooperation with Britain and France, leading George Padmore to decisively reject the Communist movement in 1936 and to found the Marxist, but non-Communist, Pan-African Federation in London.[54] A year later, Max Yergan (a former YMCA worker in South Africa) founded

[52] For use of the term "discovery" in referring to Dr. Aggrey, see Phelps-Stokes *Thirty-Five-Year Report*, p. 26. (Cf. other references to Aggrey, pp. 29, 30, 42, 65, 76, 78, 79, 83, 95, 96, 97, 99, 100, 173, 176, 204.) Aggrey was a member of two important educational missions sponsored jointly by the Phelps-Stokes Fund, the Colonial Office and various missionary groups (references to the missions on pp. 133–36. See *Education in Africa* (New York: Phelps-Stokes Fund, 1922), a study of western Africa in cooperation with the Foreign Missionary Society of North America and England; and *Education in Africa* (New York: Phelps-Stokes Fund, 1925), a study of eastern, central and south Africa. Condensations of these two reports have been republished. (Oxford University Press, 1961.)

[53] See Richard B. Moore "Africa-Conscious Harlem." *Freedomways,* 3, No. 3 (Summer, 1963), pp. 315–34.

[54] See Record, *op. cit.,* p. 138, and Roi Ottley, *No Green Pastures* (New York: Scribner's, 1951), p. 66. Some of the reasons for this break with the Communists are evident in Padmore, *op. cit.,* pp. 317–32.

the Council on African Affairs in New York with Paul Robeson as its chairman.

Dr. Du Bois' connection with the NAACP was severed during the mid-Thirties, due to his insistence upon the need for a tighter-knit organization of Negroes *as Negroes* in the United States to cope with problems arising from the depression. He returned to Atlanta University where he founded the journal, *Phylon*, in 1940. He also began work on an *Encyclopedia of the Negro*, sponsored by the Phelps-Stokes Fund, but he made no attempts to convene another Pan-African Congress between 1927 and the outbreak of World War II.

One of the more important activities of the Phelps-Stokes Fund during these years was the bringing to America of a number of Africans to view Negro life and to visit educational institutions for Negroes.[55]

Students who were destined to play a major role in post-war Africa were becoming acquainted with Negro institutions and Negro leaders and with the "Negro history movement" during the depression period. Paul Robeson, Alain Locke, W.E.B. Du Bois, Carter G. Woodson, W. Leo Hansberry were the object of particular respect from young Africans.[56] Many of them had found their way into the less eminent Negro schools as "ports of first entry" into American academia. Some, who needed them, there found friends who were tolerant of their idiosyncrasies and inadequate educational backgrounds. Some stayed in below-average Negro colleges. Others, better prepared and more independent, went on to better Negro institutions or "white" schools for their first degrees. Some took their first degrees at schools like Lincoln and Howard and then went to major universities for advanced work.[57]

---

[55] Among the visitors destined to become outstanding men was Robert K. Gardiner of the Gold Coast, who has had a distinguished academic career and record in government service in Ghana and Nigeria and who is now an international civil servant in the United Nations. See *Thirty-Five-Year Report*, p. 100.

[56] See Note 27 above. Mr. K. Jones-Quartey, in a forthcoming biography of Nnamdi Azikiwe (Penguin) notes that Professor Alain Locke of Howard University was greatly admired by Azikiwe and was both Azikiwe's teacher and confidant at one point in his career. Dr. Locke's influence extended beyond his students. Senghor distinguished poet-president of Senegal, writes:

> "Studying at the Sorbonne, I began to reflect upon the problem of a cultural renaissance in Black Africa, and I was searching—all of us were searching—for a 'sponsorship' which could guarantee the success of the enterprise. At the end of my quest it was inevitable that I would find Alain Locke and Jean Price Mars. . . ." (From Philippe Decraene, *Le Panafricanisme*, Paris: Presses Universilaires de France, 1959, p. 17.)

[57] Some students of the subject, among them Dr. Horace Mann Bond, feel that this personal attention to individuals represents a major contribution made by Negro educational leadership to the training of African leaders.

THE WAR YEARS

The only organization involving Negro leaders which was devoted solely to African issues during World War II was the Council on African Affairs. Paul Robeson, its chairman, made no attempt to conceal his left-wing leanings, but some of the country's most influential Negro churchmen and civic leaders were among the council members or sponsored specific activities.[58] Its position, that all colonies should receive full independence at the conclusion of the war, was attractive to African students as well as to many Negro Americans.

More moderate opinion on African issues tended to cohere around the Phelps-Stokes Fund whose leaders were inclined to favor large-scale, immediate expansion of educational and social services, followed by a transitional period after the war under either internationally supervised tutelage or enlightened and reformed colonial administration. The fund played a very important function in disbursing emergency aid to African students stranded in the country during the war, and some African students accepted the aid while disagreeing with the fund on the question of timing and priorities in the independence struggle.[59] Soon after the Atlantic Charter was proclaimed, the Phelps-Stokes Fund convened an important interracial

[58] This type of cooperation involving individuals from the extreme "left" and the "center" (and even of the "right") was general during the war after the Soviet Union was attacked by Germany in 1942, for the U.S.A. was in military alliance with the U.S.S.R. Little surprise or disapproval was expressed over "united front" activity of the type represented by the Council on African Affairs.

[59] Among the African students who received some financial aid during the depression and war periods were Kwame Nkrumah, now President of Ghana, and Nnamdi Azikiwe, President of the Republic of Nigeria. The *Thirty-Five-Year Report of the Phelps-Stokes Fund* (1948) noted that "There has been a marked development of African self-consciousness on the part of the native population in certain areas, especially Nigeria and some parts of South Africa. The leaders among educated Africans, especially in the former, are demanding self-government and speedy independence. They have developed some able leaders although at times extreme in their attitudes. In general there can be no question that the old era of unlimited imperialism is a thing of the past. . . ." But the Fund warned, "The goal of complete freedom, political and economic, must always be kept in mind and earnestly striven for, but historical facts cannot be transformed in a day, and progress, to endure, must be through accelerated evolution rather than by revolution in racial adjustments . . ." (pp. 41–44 and 61) It is relevant to note, and important, that as African nationalist movements developed, the Phelps-Stokes Fund adjusted its policies to the changing situation and has given various types of specialized aid to the new nations. The fund held its annual meeting in Ghana in 1961—which was attended by Ghana's President, Kwame Nkrumah.

conference to discuss the charter's implications for Africa. In 1942 the Fund published *The Atlantic Charter and Africa From an American Standpoint* as the official report of the committee on Africa and the war and peace aims which it had sponsored.[60]

In 1944, the NAACP board decided to appoint Dr. Du Bois to a special post as its adviser on African affairs during a period when it was being called upon to take a position on such matters as mandates and trusteeships and a United Nations Organization which was then being discussed. He accepted. The reconciliation was shortlived, however, and Dr. Du Bois was dropped again by the NAACP. This time he did not return to Atlanta, and eventually joined the Council on African Affairs. (He became a Ghanaian citizen in 1962 and died in Ghana in 1963.) The NAACP continued to devote a portion of its limited staff time and office space to aiding African political leaders on various missions to the U.S.A.[61]

A group of older students, mainly from Nigeria and led by D. O. Mbadiwe and M. Ojike, had formed an African Academy of Arts and Sciences in New York in the late 1940's. Then, after Ojike had returned home, Mbadiwe and A. A. N. Orizu founded the American Council on African Education in order to solicit scholarship aid for African students. It brought together a wide spectrum of Negro and white civic leaders, journalists, ministers and philanthropists on its interracial list of sponsors and its executive board.[62]

Another group of students, with Kwame Nkrumah of Lincoln and Penn as their leader, formed the African Students Association of America and Canada. They began to try to mobilize support for a firm stand against the continuation of colonialism in Africa. Two other Lincoln University students, E. Ako Adjei and K. Jones-Quartey, were active in the organization and assisted in the founding of a journal, *The African Interpreter*. As the war neared its end, Nkrumah and other members of this group left for London.[63]

In October of 1945, Kwame Nkrumah, George Padmore, Jomo Kenyatta

[60] For a full discussion of the committee and its report see *Thirty-Five-Year Report*, pp. 83, 95, 100–01, 105, 147–48.

[61] During this period, Dr. Du Bois wrote *Color and Democracy* (New York: Harcourt, Brace, 1945) and *The World and Africa* (New York: The Viking Press, 1947).

[62] Among the names of prominent Negroes appearing on the ACAE letterheads were: Roy Wilkins (NAACP); college presidents Mary M. Bethune, Mordecai Johnson, Charles H. Wesley, Benjamin E. Mays; publishers John H. Johnson and John Sengstacke; politician, A. Clayton Powell; college professor Alain Locke was vice president, journalist George Schuyler was secretary. Among the prominent whites were: John Gunther, Dorothy Parker, Bartley Crum, Frank Kingdon, John Hayes Holmes, Mrs. Herbert Agar, Vincent Sheean and philanthropist William J. Schieffelin.

[63] Kwame Nkrumah, *op. cit.*, pp. 35–36.

and other Africans and West Indians living in England convened the Fifth Pan-African Congress. Dr. Du Bois, at the age of seventy-eight, in his role as "Father of Pan-Africanism," accepted the invitation to serve as *Honorary* Chairman, but the leadership of the Pan-African Congress movement now passed out of the hands of New World Negroes into the hands of militant African leaders, preparing to place themselves at the head of mass movements already burgeoning in their homelands. Their goal was immediate independence, and many of them espoused some type of socialism although none of them were Communists.[64]

Throughout the war years, the Africans in the United States of America were racial Pan-Africanists in the sense that they identified psychologically with Negroes in America, took some part in Negro institutional activities and maintained close ties with individual Negro friends. But they also cultivated close relations with those who wielded power and had prestige in the general society, and they had their circle of white personal friends. Mrs. Franklin D. Roosevelt was highly regarded by this group of educated Africans and gave considerable aid and support to their various organizational ventures.

FIFTEEN POST-WAR YEARS

During the first decade of African protest and militant pressure after World War II, Ghana and Kenya tended to dominate the news about Africa in America. Nkrumah and Kenyatta took on some of the characteristics of "race heroes" to Negro Americans. Nkrumah visited the U.S.A. in 1951, soon after his release from prison, and Lincoln University conferred an honorary LL.D. upon him. Both Haile Selassie and President Tubman of Liberia visited the United States in 1954, the first of a long line of African heads of state to come, and both stressed their friendly attitudes toward the Negro population as well as toward the United States of America. Negro institutions vied with white ones to do them honor.

Ghana was the first African nation south of the Sahara to gain its independence. When it did so in 1957, Dr. Nkrumah invited a number of

[64] For versions of the Fifth Pan-African Congress written by participants, see Kwame Nkrumah, *op. cit.*, pp. 42–45 and Padmore, *Pan-Africanism or Communism* p. 152. Padmore notes that "For more than thirty years Dr. Du Bois watched over the gradual growth of the Pan-African Congress with the loving affection of a father until such time as his children had found a home on African soil. Today Pan-Africanism is becoming part and parcel of emergent African nationalism. . . ."

prominent American Negroes to attend the ceremonies as his guests. A few Negro Americans began to trickle into Ghana as teachers and businessmen. Dr. Nkrumah visited the United States as a state guest during the summer of 1958, a few months after he had been host to the First Conference of Independent African States in Ghana. At a large rally at the armory in Harlem he made an appeal for Negro Americans to come to Ghana as teachers and technicians. In response to the Pan-African overtones of the Nkrumah visit, the executive secretary of the National Association for the Advancement of Colored People took the occasion to clarify the position of Negro Americans during the epoch of African liberation:

> It is our hope that the devotion of Americans of all races and religions and colors to freedom and justice will be a source of strength and encouragement to Ghana and to other African peoples who seek and who deserve their independence. . . .
>
> Our great nation, the leader of free world democracy, will surely give ear and heart and help to the colonial people who would throw off the yoke of control from without. . . .
>
> We Negro members of the National Association for the Advancement of Colored People are American, for all the lapses and the shortcomings in our treatment, but we have felt the stirring of the blood tie between us and the land of our forefathers. As other loyal Americans look back upon their European homelands with affection and pride, so we look upon Ghana and the emerging nations of Africa. Your struggles and your successes have aided us in our trials and tribulations here as one among ten of our great population. . . .
>
> We pledge our encouragement and aid and our friendly interest in all possible ways to the end that our country, the United States of America, and your country, Ghana, may walk through history in mutual respect, mutual assistance and peace.[65]

In Africa, itself, the culminating event of this short period of the "breakthrough"—1957–60—was the Sixth Pan-African Congress called by George Padmore and Dr. Nkrumah in Accra in December, 1958, and named The All African Peoples Conference. (Dr. Du Bois could not attend, but his wife read his strongly anti-Western message.) The words with which Dr. Nkrumah opened the closing session of the conference were significant. He reciprocated the sentiments of Roy Wilkins in New York five months before, and after commenting upon the fact that some West Indians and Negro Americans were present and saying he was glad to see so many of them, he paid tribute to the New World Pan-African pioneers:

> We take their presence here as a manifestation of their keen interest in our struggle for a free Africa. We must never forget that they are part of us.

[65] *Crisis*, 65, No. 7 (August, 1958), pp. 410–11.

These sons and daughters of Africa were taken away from our shores and despite all centuries which have separated us they have not forgotten their ancestral links. . . . Many of them have made no small contribution to the cause of African freedom. Names which spring immediately to mind in this connection are those of Marcus Garvey and Dr. W.E.B. Du Bois. . . . Long before many of us were conscious of our own degradation these men fought for African national and racial equality. . . .[66]

In other parts of his speech, however, Dr. Nkrumah stressed the fact that a new concept of Pan-Africanism was emerging in which Africans, not New World Negroes, were leading and in which the primary goal was to secure the unity of all people *in Africa,* irrespective of race, creed, color or tribe, rather than unity around the Africa-West Indies-U.S.A. triangle. The implication was that at best now, New World Negroes were auxiliary forces in the struggle to "liberate Africa." *Continental* Pan-Africanism, not *racial* Pan-Africanism was emerging [67] as a significant force, and was the major interest of African leaders. At the same time, however, the interest of Negro Americans in the new Africa was increasing.

NEW INSTITUTIONAL INCREMENTS

The influence of the Council on African Affairs declined during the late Fifties and the organization disbanded. The intensification of the Cold War and the outbreak of the Korean War had destroyed the possibility of continued cooperation between Soviet-oriented leaders and other Negro leaders. Its place was taken on the national scene by a new interracial organization, originally pacifist in orientation, but equally vigorous in petition and protest, The American Committee on Africa (ACOA). A number of Negroes became active members of its board and of the staff of its publication, *Africa Today.* A distinguished Negro labor leader is co-chairman.[68]

A number of other specialized Africa-oriented organizations came into

---

[66] Quoted from a Radio Ghana broadcast of conference proceedings in St. Clair Drake, "What is Pan-Africanism?" *Africa Today* (January–February, 1959) p. 6.

[67] The shift in emphasis to continental Pan-Africanism became pronounced after the first Conference of Independent African States. The ideology behind the shift had been worked out by George Padmore some three years before. (Cf. his *Pan-Africanism or Communism?*)

[68] The American Committee on Africa was founded in 1953 by persons interested in promoting African-American understanding. The ACOA maintains offices at 211 East 43rd Street, New York 10017, New York. The Rev. Donald S. Harrington and Mr. A. Philip Randolph are co-chairmen of the committee. The committee places its major current emphasis upon the struggle for freedom in Southern Rhodesia, the Portuguese Territories and South and Southwest Africa.

being after World War II, among them the African-American Institute, founded originally by Dr. W. Leo Hansberry of Howard University, but destined to became a large-scale, foundation-supported effort with a scholarship and teacher placement program and a publication, *Africa Report*. Its board of trustees is interracial.[69] Rev. James Robinson, a New York Negro clergyman, founded Operations Crossroads Africa as a vehicle through which idealistic young college people could give a summer of service in Africa.[70] Negro scholars were among the Founding Fellows of the African Studies Association (ASA), organized in 1958, although only one Negro institution, Howard, had received foundation support for its African studies program.[71] The Foreign Area Fellowship Program, formerly administered by the Ford Foundation beginning in 1954 and now self-administered, offered new opportunities for African studies and this resulted in the emergence over a 10-year period of a dozen or so young Negro Africanists, highly trained and beginning to make valuable contributions to the scholarly literature.[72] Africa was no longer just the concern of the

[69] The African-American Institute, founded in 1953, is a private American agency in the field of African education and leadership training. AAI executives are Waldemar A. Nielson, President, John J. Mather, Secretary; and A. Francis Marchetti, Treasurer. AAI maintains offices at 345 East 46th Street, New York 10017, New York; 1340 Connecticut Avenue, N.W., Washington, D.C.; Lagos, Nigeria, and Dar es Salaam, Tanganyika.

[70] Operations Crossroads Africa, Inc. was founded in 1957 to establish person-to-person contact between American and African youth. Through the summer of 1964 a total of 1,342 American young people were sent by the organization on extended work visits to twenty-four African countries. Address: 150 Fifth Avenue, New York 10011, New York.

[71] For a discussion of difficulties in securing funds for African studies by Negro scholars and institutions, see St. Clair Drake's memorandum referred to in fn. 8 above.

[72] A partial list of Negro fellowship holders is given below with date of fellowship, area of research and present activity:

> Thomas Lucien Blair. September, 1960, 25 months study of the Hausa language and urbanization in northern Nigeria. Address (1964) c/o Mrs. L. Elliston, 95-28 160th Street, Jamaica 31, N.Y.
>
> James Lowell Gibbs, Jr. September, 1956, 23 months study of Kpelle language and native law of Kpelle tribe in Liberia. Address (1964) Department of Anthropology, University of Minnesota, Minneapolis 13, Minn.
>
> Martin Luther Kilson, Jr. September, 1959, 18 months study of the political development of Sierra Leone. Address (1964) Department of Government, Harvard University, Cambridge 38, Mass.
>
> Gloria Albertha Marshall. January, 1961, 27 months study of Yoruba language and the role of market women in Yoruba society. Address (1964) c/o Committee for the Comparative Study of New Nations, University of Chicago, Chicago 37, Ill.
>
> Albert James McQueen. September, 1961, 18 months African studies, Yoruba language training and problems of education and unemployment among Nigerian youth. Address (1964) Institute for Social Research, University of Michigan, Ann Arbor, Mich.

missionary tradition and racial Pan-Africanism; it had become a *national* concern in relation both to Cold War politics and humanitarian sentiment.

The one important new organization oriented toward Africa which arose among Negroes soon after the war was the American Society for African Culture (AMSAC), affiliated with the Society of African Culture in Paris (the *Présence Africaine* group). It has concentrated upon cultural exchanges, the provision of hospitality for prominent African visitors and some publication. It has never entered the field of exchange of personnel or of recruitment of Negroes for overseas service, however, although it has been of assistance to African students studying in the United States of America.[73]

In 1944, Gunnar Myrdal's *American Dilemma* predicted that the whole world would soon be involved in helping to bring a new Africa into being and that ". . . it would be natural that American Negroes would take both a great interest in the adventure and an active part in the staging. Many Negroes in America feel an emotional attachment to Africa and its population, and, because of their color they would with greater ease gain the confidence of the African Negroes. . . ."[74]

The same year, Fisk, in announcing its Inter-Departmental Curriculum

> Marian Ellen McReynolds. September, 1961, 39 months study of the Yoruba language and the history of the Yoruba and Nupe peoples. Address (1964) Department of History, University of California, Los Angeles 24, California.
>
> Elliott Percival Skinner. June, 1955, 18 months study of effects of European contact on the Mossi people in French West Africa. Address (1965) Department of Anthropology, Columbia University, New York, N.Y. 10017.
>
> Inez Virginia Smith. September, 1962, 12 months African Studies at UCLA. Address (1964) Ecole National de Droit et d'Administration, Leopoldville, Republic of the Congo.
>
> William Worthy, Jr. September, 1959, 9 months, African Studies at Boston University. Address: (1965) *The Baltimore Afro-American,* 628 North Eutaw Street, Baltimore, Md.

Two mature scholars who have received Ford area grants are:

> St. Clair Drake. July, 1954, 14 months study of African communications media in West Africa and London. Address (1965) Department of Sociology, Roosevelt University, Chicago, Ill.
>
> Hugh Heyne Smythe. September, 1957, 12 months study of the Nigerian elite in Nigeria. Address (1965) Department of Sociology, Brooklyn College, Brooklyn 10, N.Y.

[73] AMSAC publishes a monthly newsletter with occasional special supplements. One of its more significant publications is John A. Davis (ed.), *Africa From the Point of American Negro Scholars,* special number of *Présence Africaine,* Paris, 1958. It has also published a small volume of Leopold Senghor's statements on African socialism, translated by Dr. Mercer Cook. The proceedings of one of its important conferences was published by the Stanford University Press, *Pan-Africanism Reconsidered* (1959). AMSAC maintains a cultural center in Lagos, Nigeria.

[74] Myrdal, *op. cit.,* p. 807.

in African Studies, stated that in addition to general scientific and human-istic aims, a vocational aspect "must be emphasized," for "Opportunities will be increasingly offered for American Negroes to share with Africans in Africa those advantages which they have gained in the United States. Medical men and women, social workers, agriculturists, teachers, mission-aries—there is room for all these in Africa. . . ."

The English anthropologist, Edwin Smith, sometime-president of the Royal Anthropological Institute of Great Britain and Ireland, served as special consultant to the Fisk program in 1943–44 and reiterated the doc-trine of the special relationship of Negro Americans to Africa, even referring to "the call of blood" and "the ancestral home." He felt that "The great need for a long time will be trained leaders. . . . There is room for men and women who will share with Africans the advantages which they have reaped in the United States. Negro medical men and women, nurses, social workers, teachers, agriculturists, commercial men—there is scope for hun-dreds of them. . . . Negroes who wish to serve their African father-land. . . ."

(A few Negroes still clung to outmoded concepts of American Negro "messianism," such as those expressed in a book written in 1946, but they were a tiny minority:

> While we in America are confronted with the most serious problem any minority group anywhere in the civilized world faces and it will take all our efforts to work out our own salvation, still it seems to me *we are the most logical of the group anywhere to unite the foreign Negro in a world federation with headquarters in the United States. The American Negro owes a duty to Africa, our fatherland.* Not only does the American Negro owe a duty of serviceness and helpfulness to Africa, but likewise the pro-gressive and educated Negro throughout the North American Continent should be equally interested. [Italics added] [75])

Despite these predictions and hopes, and the expressed desire of Nkrumah and other leaders for Negro teachers and technicians, no Negro organization devoted to the recruitment of personnel came into being [76] (and very few

[75] Samuel Barrett, *The Need of Unity and Cooperation Among Colored Americans,* sixth edition (Oakland: Voice Publishing Co., 1946 available in Moorland Room, Founders Library, Howard University).
[76] Since 1961 Teachers College, Columbia University, has operated the Teachers for East Africa Project in cooperation with the Institute of Education of the University of London. It has been financed, in part, by the United States Agency for International Development. During the first three years of the program 370 teachers were recruited, selected and trained for teaching assignments in Uganda, Kenya and Tanganyika. At the end of 1964 the project hoped to have reached a total of five hundred teachers. A few of these have been Negro Americans.

Negroes have gone to Africa under Peace Corps or other auspices). The facts that the era of integration in the United States of America has co-incided with the epoch of African liberation and that there has been relatively full employment, may have been the major factors operating against an enthusiastic upsurge of sentiment for "service in Africa" by Negro Americans. Neo-Jarveyism did not fit the temper of the times.

Neither the missionary tradition nor the Pan-African movement has re-sulted in any large-scale expansion of relations between Negro Americans and Africans since World War II. Those few Negroes with a "service" orientation have tended to operate through *interracial* organizations, expressing general humanitarian values or ideals of national patriotism. Also, the use of Negroes in the diplomatic service in Africa and in a wide range of government technical assistance projects has added an important new dimension to the Negro-African contact situation. (See Appendix II.)

PROBLEMS AND PROSPECTS

The year 1960 marked the watershed in relations between Africans and Negro Americans just as it did in relations between the African states them-selves. The year began with only nine independent African states, it ended with twenty-three! The Congo crisis became a divisive element. One group of states formed a "radical bloc" composed of Ghana, Guinea, Mali, the U.A.R. and Morocco, pro-Lumumba and often critical of the actions of the West. All of these states except Morocco were militantly Pan-African, neutralist in foreign policy, and socialist (though not Communist). The other African states were, on the whole, more conservative in their orienta-tion. Ideological issues became more important to leaders of African states than racial Pan-Africanism. Negro Americans, as Americans, have also had to take ideology into consideration in their own relations with Africans. It is quite understandable why the "radical" states are sometimes suspicious of the actions and motivations of some Negro Americans, and why some Negro Americans tend to feel awkward and uncomfortable vis-à-vis "radical" Africans.[77]

[77] One area in which there is a division of opinion concerns trade union activities. Some Africans oppose the activities of the International Confederation of Free-Trade Unions and consider the very effective Negro American faculty member of the ICFTU Labor College in Kampala (Mr. George McCray of Chicago) a "neocolonialist tool." Unions friendly to ICFTU hold him in high regard. On the other hand, Maida Springer, representing the AFL-CIO in the implementation of a textile workers' training program

The fact that thirteen former French colonies became independent during 1960 posed difficult problems of communication between African states. Also, few leaders in these areas had had the extensive contacts with Negro Americans which Africans from English-speaking Africa had. It was inevitable that a period of "becoming acquainted" was necessary and AMSAC played an important part in this process. A number of African leaders from former French areas have expressed their interest in Negro Americans in the Pan-African idiom, especially in Senegal and Guinea.[78] But it is from these areas, too, that the most critical strictures arise from African Marxists against the orientation of Negro Americans.

Relations between Nigerians and Negro Americans tended to be strengthened with the coming of that country's independence in 1960.[79] The newly established University of Nigeria secured a president on loan from the staff of Howard University and it named its African studies program for Dr. William Leo Hansberry. (Simultaneously Ghana invited Dr. Du Bois to come to that country to direct the *Encyclopedia Africana;* he eventually became a citizen of Ghana, where he died in 1963 at the age of ninety-six.) AMSAC opened an office in Lagos, and the United States Government placed a number of prominent Negroes in important posts there. Negroes, like the United States Government, seemed to find working relations with Nigeria somewhat easier than with Ghana. It is likely that considerable diversity in the extent and quality of relations between Africans and Negro Americans will continue as new ideological orientations in Africa emerge.

The desire not to alienate a country whose financial and technical aid is needed, as well as a general recognition that the national Government has been trying to pursue a progressive policy, has softened the criticism of the

in Kenya, operates a noncontroversial activity and does not have to bear the ICFTU onus. The Ghana press occasionally prints quite caustic articles attacking what they call "American Negro rascals" and praising Negro "friends."

The first African edition of *Ebony* appeared in 1964 and had a mixed reception. Some of the more radical Africans criticized it as an attempt to weaken the African self-image by popularizing Amerian Negro "imitation of the white man."

[78] For instance Guinea's first purchasing mission to the United States was allegedly instructed to spend as much of its money as it could with Negro Americans to aid their economic development. AMSAC played an important role in trying to bring Africans of the French expression into contact with Negro Americans. It is significant that poet-president Leopold Senghor of Senegal paid tribute to Negro poets at a literary luncheon given by President Kennedy in the White House. The ambassador to the Republic of Senegal is a Negro, Dr. Mercer Cook, formerly active in AMSAC.

[79] A *Crisis* editorial written for the occasion said, ". . . many of our forefathers came from this section of Africa, from Bonny and Benin and Bornu and Kontagora. . . . The sympathy and support of Negro America go out to the newly independent state of Nigeria. . . ." (*Crisis,* 67, No. 9, November, 1960, p. 595)

United States of America's race relations policy. Individual African leaders do, however, occasionally make it very clear that they cannot fully trust the United States in its relations to them so long as segregation and discrimination are practiced on a wide scale against both Africans and peoples of African descent in the United States of America.

Despite the generally subdued nature of official comment on race relations in the United States of America by heads of African states, the Organization of African Unity, at its inaugural meeting in the spring of 1963, included the following in the list of "measures" decided upon at the conference:

> Expression of the deep concern aroused in all African peoples and governments by the measures of racial discrimination taken against *communities of African origin living outside the continent* and particularly in the United States of America. [Italics added]
>
> Expression of appreciation for the efforts of the Federal Government of the U.S.A. to put an end to these intolerable malpractices which are likely seriously to deteriorate relations between the African peoples and governments on the one hand and the people and government of the United States of America on the other.[80]
>
> The Congo crisis of 1964 which resulted, in part, from U.S. support of a Prime Minister (Moise Tshombe) who was unpopular with many Africans, sharpened the criticism of the U.S.A. After the use of American planes in the Stanleyville rescue mission the debate before the U.N. Security Council elicited charges by some Africans that the U.S. was "racist", and severe strictures were made against mistreatment of Negroes in the South.

Obviously feelings of racial Pan-Africanism are not dead.

Among some of the more militant Africans there is a tendency to feel that Africans should support the civil rights struggle in the United States and that Negro Americans should be vigorously active in trying to exert pressure upon South Africa, Southern Rhodesia and Portugal even to the extent of mass demonstrations. There is a general feeling among Africans that Africans and Negro Americans are involved in a common fight against racism and that this is the only enduring basis of racial Pan-Africanism.

During 1964 and 1965, some leaders in the more militant African states exhibited a tendency to support specific Negro activists. Leaders in the U.A.R. and Ghana entertained the late Malcolm X and advised him not to

---

[80] From conference resolutions as published in *Africa Report*, June, 1963. While official pronouncements have been restrained and "correct," the African press has frequently been quite sharp in its criticisms of the police handling of Negro demonstrators and of the slowness with which the Federal Government has sometimes reacted in specific cases. After the Birmingham disturbances, Dr. Azikiwe of Nigeria made a very critical statement.

isolate himself from other civil rights leaders and white allies. Officials of the student non-violent coordinating committee were semi-official guests of Guinea political groups.

A new organization was formed in 1962 to coordinate relations of Negro Americans with the New Africa, the American Negro Leadership Conference on Africa. Martin Luther King and A. Philip Randolph were co-chairmen and the organization had a full-time executive secretary. Its attempt to combine the functions of a pressure group for aid to Africans with objectives as they define them, with the functions of a pressure group for expanding the scope of Negro participation in the diplomatic corps and other Africa-oriented activities of the American Government, has probably weakened its influence with many Africans, however.[81]

The decline of racial Pan-Africanism as a focal point of orientation among both Africans and Negro Americans, the secularization of activities which were once the monopoly of the missionary movement, and the new roles being played by Negroes everywhere, have involved both Africans and Negro Americans in the process of groping for new fixed patterns of relationship with one another.

APPENDIX I
PRE-CIVIL WAR USE OF THE TERM "AFRICAN"
BY NEGRO AMERICANS

The practice of naming voluntary associations "African Societies" and of including the word "African" in the names of churches is illustrated by the "Free African Societies" which were organized in Newport, Rhode Island, Philadelphia, Boston and New York between 1787 and 1810, and in the names of the following churches and denominations: First African Baptist Church, Savannah, Georgia (1788); African Baptist Church of Lexington Kentucky (1790); Abyssinia Baptist Church, New York City (1800); Free African Meeting House, Boston (1805); First African Presbyterian Church, Philadelphia (1807); First African Baptist Church, Philadelphia (1809); Union Church of Africans, Inc., Wilmington (1813); African Methodist Episcopal Church, (national body, 1816); African Methodist Episcopal Zion Church (national body, 1821); St. James First African Church, Baltimore (1824); First African Baptist Church of New Orleans (1826); First African Baptist Church, Richmond, Virginia (1841); Second African Baptist Church of Richmond, Virginia (1846). (For a discussion of the processes leading to organization of these churches and societies, see

[81] A continuing committee of the conference known as the Call Committee was formed. It is composed of Roy Wilkins, chairman; James Farmer, Miss Dorothy Height, Martin Luther King, A. Philip Randolph, and Whitney M. Young, Jr. Mr. Theodore E. Brown is Director.

Frazier, *op. cit.*, pp. 345–47; 368–70; Benjamin E. Mays and J. W. Nicholson, *The Negro's Church* (New York: Institute of Social and Religious Research, 1933), pp. 20–28, and list of churches in *Negro Yearbook* for 1914–1915, pp. 177 et seq.).

Richard Allen, founder of the Afri-

can Methodist Episcopal Church, wrote of his journey to Philadelphia in 1786, "I preached at different places in the city. . . . I soon saw a large field open in seeking and instructing my African brethren." (He also referred to them, at times, as "our colored brethren.") *

APPENDIX II
NEGRO AMERICANS IN GOVERMENT SERVICE IN AFRICA

Foreign Service

A number of Negro Americans serve in the Department of State's Bureau of African Affairs. Special Assistant to the Bureau's chief, Assistant Secretary G. Mennen Williams, is David D. Bolen, a career foreign service officer who has served in Liberia and Ghana. An economist, Bolen was a member of the U.S. Observer Delegation to the Sixth Plenary Session of the U.N. Economic Commission for Africa in Addis Ababa, February 19 to March 2, 1964. Alvin Rucker is the bureau's Labor Adviser. Dr. William H. Martin is Education Adviser to the Bureau of African Affairs. He was formerly Dean of the Faculty at Hampton Institute.

Leslie D. Polk, whose overseas assignments include several Middle Eastern posts, has been appointed Assistant Officer-in-Charge of Tunisian Affairs.

Mercer Cook is serving as Ambas-

sador to Senegal, and has also been Alternate U.S. Representative to the United Nations' General Assembly. (He became Ambassador to Senegal in mid-1964.) Also in Niger is Cecil Richardson, who served previously in Nigeria. Other Negro American officers currently in Africa include:

Terence Todman, Tunisia
Alan Dean, Ghana
Lloyd Lee, Ivory Coast
James Frazier, Gabon

Public Health—Military

Negro Americans have also headed Public Health Service Missions in African countries. Now in Sierra Leone, Colonel Hildreth Poindexter served previously as USPHS Director in Liberia and in Libya. Colonel Theodore Gandy held a similar post in Egypt. Among other directors of the program in Liberia should be noted the late Colonel John West, who es-

* (Quoted in Benjamin Elijah May and Joseph William Nicholson, *The Negro's Church* (New York: Institute of Social and Religious Research, 1933), p. 21, from Bishop Richard Allen, *The Life, Experience and Gospel Labors* (Philadelphia: AME Book Concern, n.d.).

tablished the operation, and Colonel John Morehead, now in Ethiopia.

Negro officers have headed U.S. military missions in Liberia and served as military attachés in Ghana and in the Congo, Leopoldville.

Aid and Technical Assistance

Negro Americans have held a variety of responsible positions in the United States Government's economic aid and technical assistance programs in Africa. Dr. John W. Davis, former President of West Virginia State College, became the first mission director in 1952 when he was appointed to Liberia. He was succeeded as mission director in 1954 by Richard L. Jones, who was appointed ambassador a year later. Jones was succeeded by George Reed.

Robert W. Kitchen, former program officer in Liberia, became the second Negro American mission chief when he was appointed to the Sudan in 1958. Similar posts went to Dr. Ernest Neal in Sierra Leone in 1961; and to Dr. Samuel Adams in Mali that same year.

Today Negro Americans serve in nearly every African country where there are AID projects. Frank E. Pinder, who is a legend in Africa because of the work he accomplished as a food and agricultural officer in Liberia and Ghana, was appointed Director of the AID mission in Ghana in 1964.

Among others serving in Africa are:

Cameroun
Sheldon Cole—Trade Industrial Education Advisor

Dahomey
Sandy J. McCorvey—Agriculture Extension Advisor

Ghana
Lloyd C. Trawick—Extension Advisor Area
William T. Harris—Extension Advisor Area
William Mann, Jr.—Public Works Engineer
Edward A. Bolling—Farm Shop Specialist

Kenya
William R. Miner—Community Development Advisor Training

Liberia
Lawrence E. James—Business Education Advisor
Arthur D. Greene—Education Advisor Area

Malagasy
Ullmont L. James—Public Administration Advisor

Mali, Republic of
Herman Davis—Housing Advisor, Architect
Charles Sadler—Education Advisor, English Language

Nigeria
William E. Reed—Assistant Director, Western Area
John T. Bull—Extension Advisor Training
Samuel E. Fuhr—Deputy Chief Education Advisor
Charles L. Davis—Livestock Advisor Poultry
Patsy A. Graves—Home Economics Advisor
James W. Ford—Livestock Advisor Extension
Walter M. Austin—Agriculture Economic Advisor
Henry E. Van Blake—Livestock Advisor, Beef

Marshall Fields—Trade Industrial Education Advisor

Beverly Archer—Farm Machinery—Agricultural Engineer

Rhodesia/Nyasaland

J. Max Bond—Teacher Education Advisor

George Corinaldi—Teacher Education Advisor

Somali Republic

Timothy Edwards—Trade Industrial Education Advisor

Sudan

Arthur B. McCaw—End Use Officer

Madison Broadnax—Extension Advisor

Fenton B. Sands—Horticulture Advisor

Uganda

Thomas R. Stuman—Controller

United States Information Agency

Beginning with Wallace Van Jackson, who was named Public Affairs Officer at the American Embassy in Monrovia in 1948, Negro Americans have served with the United States Information Agency and its predecessor organizations in nearly every region of Africa.

In the past, Negro Americans have headed USIA missions in Liberia (Eugene Sawyer, Edward Brice and William C. Powell) and Ghana (Eugene Sawyer). Those who served as acting chiefs during substantial periods of time include Rudolph Aggrey, Nigeria; Lois Taylor, Congo (Brazzaville), and Wilbert Petty, Guinea.

Programs in Cameroun and Chad have been headed respectively by William C. Powell and John H. Russell. Deputy Public Affairs Officer in

Morocco is Dr. Francis M. Hammond, who served previously as Cultural Attaché at that post.

William Gordon is currently Chief Information Officer in Nigeria, Africa's most populous state, a post formerly held by Dr. Preston Valien. The Nigeria USIS staff also counts Dr. Elsie Austin, an Assistant Cultural Officer specializing in women's activities on a West African regional basis; William E. Jones, Assistant Branch Public Affairs Officer in Ibadan; Wendall Roye, Branch Cultural Affairs Officer in Kaduna; Katherine Wallace, Program Assistant in Enugu; Eugene Walton, Research Officer, John Thompson, Assistant Information Officer, and Bernard Coleman, Assistant Cultural Affairs Officer. The last three named are in Lagos.

Lindsey White, formerly Assistant Director of Operations, Crossroads Africa, is now Cultural Affairs Officer in Ghana. Similar positions are held in Liberia by Dr. Harold E. Brazil; Southern Rhodesia, by Dr. Warren Brown; Ethiopia, by William B. Davis; Uganda, by Dr. Horace G. Dawson; Tanganyika, by Norris Garnett; Guinea, by Thaddeous McDowell; in Senegal, by Wilbert Petty, and in Tunisia, by Lois Taylor, who until recently held the same position in the Congo (Brazzaville).

Fletcher Martin has served as Information Officer in Ethiopia. From his base in Lagos, Nigeria, John Twitty carries out an extensive space information program in English-speaking West Africa. Serving as Public Affairs Assistants are Yvonne Williams in Dahomey and Howard Hardy in Alberia.

In Egypt, a continental African nation which administratively falls under USIA's Near East bureau, Dr. Walter Simon is Assistant Cultural Attaché.

The Peace Corps

Mr. Joseph R. Harris, Associate Representative, Cameroun

Mr. Andrew Bell, Associate Representative, Ethiopia

Dr. Edward Cross, Peace Corps Doctor, Ethiopia

Mr. Hermon Davis, Deputy Representative, Gabon

Mr. Elton R. King, Associate Representative, Gabon

Miss Fran Carter, Secretary, Ghana

Mr. Henry Wheatley, Deputy Representative, Ivory Coast

Miss Dorothea Banks, Associate Representative, Ivory Coast

Mr. William Watson, Representative, Liberia

Mr. Linwood McDaniel, Asso-

ciate Representative, Liberia

Miss Hazel Clarke, Associate Representative, Liberia

Miss Hazel Fry, Administrative Assistant, Liberia

Mr. C. Payne Lucas, Representative, Niger

Mr. Jacques Wilmore, Deputy Representative, Nigeria

Mr. George Sealey, Associate Representative, Nigeria

Mr. James Jackson, Associate Representative, Nigeria

Miss Rosemary Fleming, Secretary, Nigeria

Mr. William T. Carter, Deputy, Senegal

Mr. Lenard Clarke, Associate Representative, Sierra Leone

Mr. George Dines, Associate Representative, Sierra Leone

Mr. James Blackwell, Deputy Representative, Tanganyika

Dr. Rodney Powell, Peace Corps Doctor, Tanganyika

APPENDIX III
A NOTE ON THE ACTIVITIES OF NEGRO AMERICANS NOT AFFILIATED WITH THE AMERICAN GOVERNMENT OR AMERICAN ORGANIZATIONS

In addition to Negro Americans who hold posts in Africa under the American Government or under the auspices of American organizations, there are a few who have held, or now hold, various posts under African governments or who are self-employed. Even before the Second World War, Ethiopia had attracted such personalities as "Colonel" Robinson of Chicago and "Colonel" Julian of New York

(known, respectively, as "The Brown Condor" and "The Black Eagle"). They received considerable publicity during the Italo-Ethiopian War and Colonel Robinson remained in the country until his death. Less well publicized were the activities of Dr. T. Thomas Fortune Fletcher who developed Medane Alem Secondary School into one of the best high schools in Addis Ababa during a decade of residence there. A Negro American anthropologist, Dr. William Schack, teaches at the University of Addis Ababa. After the war, Dr. J. Max Bond became the first president of the University of Liberia and was followed by Dr. Kermit King. (The university now has a Liberian president.) Dr. John West, after serving in the U.S. Public Health Service in West Africa during the war, organized and ran Liberia's first radio station, ELBC, while carrying on a medical practice and engaging in a number of business enterprises.

With the coming of internal self-government in the Gold Coast in 1951, a few Negro Americans assumed active roles in the country. William Sutherland of New Jersey served as personal secretary to the minister of finance for five years; Mr. James Moseley of Philadelphia entered the civil service and worked as engineer and teacher for a decade. Other Negroes have developed businesses, among them being three men from New York who set up a very successful insurance company which was eventually sold to the government. One of the partners then accepted a post as director of the government's national insurance scheme. Another Negro American is a partner in the plumbing firm of Tamakloe and Gardner, his associate being an African. Dr. Robert Lee and his wife Dr. Sarah Lee have operated a first-class dental office in Accra, Ghana, for a number of years. Dr. St. Clair Drake served as head of the Department of Sociology at the university in Ghana for two years and

some Negro Americans are still on the staff. Dr. Alphaeus Hunton (formerly of Howard University), after teaching in Guinea, came to Ghana to assist Dr. Du Bois in the secretariat of the *Encyclopedia Africana* and assumed major responsibility for the project after Dr. Du Bois' death. The novelist Julian Mayfield is in the secretariat of the organization set up to continue the work of the World Without the Bomb Conference of 1961.

A Negro American served as secretary of the planning board in the eastern region of Nigeria during the period just before independence, and Dr. Mozelle Hill organized the Department of Sociology at the University of Nigeria. Louis Martin, former editor of the *Chicago Defender*, spent some time in the western region of Nigeria with a project designed to improve the format and circulation of a group of newspapers.

With the attainment of independence in eastern Africa, Mr. Enoc P. Waters (also a former *Defender* editor) went to Uganda to organize the publication of the first African-owned daily newspaper in the English language and to train personnel. Mrs. Ruth Njeri, wife of a junior minister, serves as secretary to President Jomo Kenyatta in Kenya. Mr. Sutherland (formerly in Ghana) is working with the Tanzania Government on problems relating to political refugees.

The field of offering "specialist services" to governments and businesses in the new African states is, thus, one in which there has been some "pioneering" by Negro Americans.

chapter 17

Prejudice and the Individual

Gordon W. Allport

We here consider prejudice as a psychological condition lodged in single individual minds. To understand the total psychosocial complex of prejudice we need also to take into account situational and societal factors. The present article is one of a trilogy. The reader should consult also *Prejudice and the Situation* and *Prejudice and Society*, both in this volume.

DEFINITION AND EXTENT OF PREJUDICE

There are two ingredients in any prejudiced state of mind: (a) a feeling of favorableness or unfavorableness which in turn is (b) based on unsupported judgment. While some prejudice can be *pro*, or "love prejudice" (as when we think too well of our own group), the ethnic attitudes that cause most social concern are *con*, or "hate prejudice."

A scholastic definition states that hate prejudice is "thinking ill of others without sufficient warrant." An equivalent slang definition says "prejudice is being down on something you are not up on." Whatever wording we prefer, there is always an element of inadequate knowledge or false judgment in prejudice; if not, then we are dealing with a well-grounded dislike, not with prejudice. If a criminal gang threatens my safety my fear and hatred of it are not prejudice; but if I say that no ex-convict can be trusted, I am overgeneralizing and am therefore prejudiced. Examples are legion. An Oxford student said, "I despise all Americans, but I have never met one I didn't like." "Every Jew will cheat you if he gets a chance." "Negroes are a violent lot; they carry razors." "Puerto Ricans are ignorant." "I couldn't trust any white man."

It should be added that overgeneralized prejudgments of this sort are prejudices only if they are not reversible when exposed to new knowledge. A person (*e.g.*, a child) can start with a misconception about Jews, Negroes,

Puerto Ricans; but if he changes his mind when new evidence comes along he was not really prejudiced, only misinformed. Prejudices are inflexible, rigid and erroneous generalizations about groups of people.

DISCRIMINATION AND PREJUDICE

While discrimination ultimately rests on prejudice, the two processes are not identical. Discrimination denies people their natural or legal rights because of their membership in some unfavored group. Many people discriminate automatically (*e.g.*, in using a labeled waiting room) without being prejudiced; and others, the "gentle people of prejudice," feel irrational aversion, but are careful not to show it in discriminatory behavior. Yet in general, discrimination reinforces prejudices, and prejudices provide rationalizations for discrimination. The two concepts are most distinct when it comes to seeking remedies. The corrections for discrimination are legal, or lie in a direct change of social practices; whereas the remedy for prejudice lies in education and the conversion of attitudes. The best opinion today says that if we eliminate discrimination, then—as people become acquainted with one another on equal terms—attitudes are likely to change, perhaps more rapidly than through the continued preaching or teaching of tolerance.

Generality of Prejudice

While some people are prejudiced against one group only, it is more common to find that if a person is bigoted in regard to one nationality, race or religion, he is likely to be bigoted regarding all "out-groups." He feels safe only within the narrow confines of his own familiar circle. It is this finding that argues most cogently for regarding prejudice as rooted in personal character structure.

How Widespread Is Prejudice? Research suggests that perhaps 80 percent of the American people harbor ethnic prejudice of some type and in some appreciable degree. Only 20 percent of the people are, in Gandhi's terms, "equiminded" or completely democratic in all their attitudes.[1] Widespread though ethnic prejudice is, there is good reason to believe that in the U.S.A. it is declining year by year. One example may be given. A cross section of the population responded to the question, "Do you think Negroes are as

[1] Gordon W. Allport, *The Nature of Prejudice* (New York: Doubleday Anchor Books, 1958), p. 77.

intelligent as white people—that is, can they learn things just as well if they are given the same education and training?" In 1946, 60 percent of the Northern white population answered "yes," and the figure rose in 1956 to 82 percent. The rise among Southern whites for the same decade was from 33 percent to 59 percent.[2]

ORIGINS OF PREJUDICE

While some animals have an instinctive aversion to others, this is not true among species that are cross-fertile. Human beings of all races can (and do) mate and procreate. There is therefore no reason to assume that instinctive aversion exists between ethnic and racial groups. A young child may be frightened by a person of unfamiliar color or appearance, but ordinarily this fear lasts only a few moments. It is well known that young children will play contentedly together whatever their race or national origin. Thus since prejudice is not inborn but acquired, the question is: What are the chief factors in the complex process of learning?

Some prejudice is deliberately taught by parents. Children obediently learn the lesson, as in the case of the little girl who asked her mother, "What's the name of those children I am supposed to hate?" The parent may pass on prejudice by punishing a child for his friendliness to minority groups. A child thus punished may acquire a conditioned aversion to members of the out-group. Sometimes the teaching is subtler. Even to a four-year-old dark skin may suggest dirt; and since he is repeatedly warned to keep clean, he may develop an avoidance for dark-skinned people.

Tags are powerful factors in learning. Most children learn the emotional force of words long before they know the meanings of the words. An angry first-grader once called his white teacher a "nigger." She asked him what "nigger" meant. He replied, "I don't know, but you're supposed to say it when you're mad." Before the child has knowledge of the meaning of Jap, Jew, nigger, Pollak and similar labels, he senses the potency of the negative feeling-tone behind these labels. Derogatory chatter in the home may thus dispose a child of six or eight to "think ill of others without sufficient warrant."

Much prejudice is *caught* rather than directly *taught*. The whole atmosphere of child-training may be subtly decisive. Thus a child who is some-

---

[2] Bruno Bettelheim and Morris Janowitz, *Social Change and Prejudice* (New York: The Free Press of Glencoe, 1964) p. 11.

times rejected, sometimes loved, who is punished harshly or capriciously, who does not know unconditional trust at home—such a child grows up "on guard." Unable to depend emotionally upon his parents, he enters school with a suspicious, fearful attitude toward people in general, and especially toward those who have an unfamiliar appearance and (to him) odd and threatening ways of talking, or worshiping, or behaving. Although we cannot make the assertion with finality, it seems likely that the major factor in predisposing a child toward a lifetime of prejudice is this rejective, neglectful, harsh or inconsistent style of preschool training.[3]

As the child grows older additional factors may create or intensify prejudice. Around the age of eight or ten he goes through a period of fierce identification with his family. Whatever the family is, is "right" (whether it be Catholic, Jewish, white, Negro, Scotch-Irish or Hottentot). By comparison all other groups are of doubtful status and merit. At this point the church and the school have the opportunity of teaching the child the concept of reciprocity and basic equality among human groups. The lesson is difficult to learn, because as adolescence approaches the child seeks personal security and a new identity in his peer groups, which usually are of his own color, class and neighborhood. If adolescents are friendly with out-groups they risk a diffusion and loss of their own precarious identity.[4] To build up a sense of personal importance they often persecute out-groups. *The West Side Story* is an epic of this gang-age phenomenon.

Occasionally prejudice is formed on the basis of a single emotional trauma. A certain youngster who was chased by a Chinese laundryman felt ever after a terror of Orientals (a clear case of overgeneralizing from a single experience). Such traumatic origins are relatively rare. But we see that throughout childhood and youth there are many opportunities for irreversible and unfavorable belief-systems to become set.

PSYCHODYNAMICS

However prejudice is learned it takes root in a personality because it meets certain basic needs or cravings. It works for the person, and may be a pivotal factor in the economy of his life.

---

[3] Dale B. Harris, Harrison G. Gough, William E. Martin, "Children's Ethnic Attitudes: II, Relationship to Parental Beliefs Concerning Child Training," *Child Development*, 21, (1950), pp. 169–81. Also, David P. Ausubel, *Ego Development and the Personality Disorders* (New York: Grune and Stratton, 1962).

[4] Bettelheim and Janowitz, *op. cit.*, p. 57.

Need for Categorization

All mortals require simplified rubrics to live by. We think of school teachers, of physicians, of blind people, of Russians, or of ex-convicts, as homogeneous groups. All Orientals we perceive as mysterious (though many are not); we regard all weeds an inedible (though some are nutritious). Thus our thinking seems to be guided by a law of least effort. If I reject all foreigners (including the United Nations), I simplify my existence by ruling out the troublesome issues of international relations. If I say "all Negroes are ignorant," I dispose of 20 million more people. If I add "Catholics know only what the priest tells them," I eliminate 40 million more. With the conviction that Jews will skin me alive, I discard another 5 million. Labor unions I exclude by calling them "pirates." Intellectuals are simply "long-haired communists." And so it goes. My life is simplified when I invoke these stereotyped rejections. With the aid of aversive categories I avoid the painful task of dealing with individuals as individuals. Prejudice is thus an economical mode of thought, and is widely embraced for this very reason.

Anxiety and the Need for Security

A major source of prejudice is the sense that one's security and status are threatened. One fears for one's job, for one's home, especially for one's prestige. American culture is enormously competitive, and so we find ourselves keenly fearful of our rivals. Downwardly mobile people on the whole are more prejudiced than people who hold a stable social position.[5] Now in cold logic it is very seldom that any minority group actually threatens the well-being, safety or equity of our lives, but we nonetheless perceive them as the cause of our distress. Racist agitators play upon this anxiety. The easiest idea to sell anyone is that he is better than someone else, and that this someone else must be kept "in his place" so that we may enjoy our own position of superiority.

Scapegoating

When things go wrong we find it convenient to blame others. Since biblical times it has been known that a scapegoat relieves our own sense of failure or guilt. We say it is the Jews who are keeping us from a promotion, or the migration of Negroes that takes away available jobs. Or we may

[5] *Ibid,* pp. 29–34.

vaguely blame our failures or discomforts upon "the politicians." Few people take blame upon themselves. They are quick to adopt an extrapunitive ego-defense.

Sexual Conflict

A peculiarly deep complex is found in accusations that out-groups (especially Negroes) are immoral. Simply because they are "forbidden fruit" many white people find Negroes sexually attractive; much miscegenation has been the result. Since looseness of morals is condemned, the white person may exonerate himself from his web of desire, fantasy and guilt, by projecting it upon the Negro male, who, he says, is sexually aggressive—at heart a rapist. In Germany, Hitler accused the Jews of all manner of sexual irregularities; in the U.S.A., it is the Negro who is the projection screen (the "living inkblot") for one's own frightening id-impulses.

The Authoritarian Pattern

To summarize these, and other similar emotional needs, trends and twists that enter into the psychodynamics of prejudice, psychologists have formulated the concept of "authoritarianism." [6] It says that a person who is basically insecure, anxious, sexually repressed, suffering from unresolved Oedipal conflicts with his own parents, given to projection—such a person will develop a rigid, conventional, hostile style of life. Ethnic prejudice fits into this character syndrome. This formulation has been widely studied and debated. Just how to define it in detail is a matter of dispute, but most scholars believe that it contains an important truth. People having this syndrome are "functional bigots" whose whole style of life is hostile, fearful, rejective of out-groups. Such people need prejudice and are ready to follow a demagogue who focuses all this latent hate upon some ethnic target.

CONFORMITY

Although the authoritarian pattern clearly exists, we must not assume that it accounts for all prejudice. What we call "conformity prejudice" springs from the tendency of people to yield to local custom and to the

---

[6] T. G. W. Adorno, E. Frenkel-Brunswik, D. J. Levinson and R. N. Sanford, *The Authoritarian Personality* (New York: Harper & Brothers, 1952).

legends and ideology of their own class.[7] If bigotry is in the air, they are bigots; if tolerance is customary, they are tolerant. Perhaps half of our population can be considered to be in this middle range. Since prejudice is to some degree prevalent, especially in the Southern regions of the United States, this half of the population can be expected to go along with the existing biases.

What we have called the authoritarian syndrome accounts for about the same amount of prejudice in both Northern and Southern states, but there is much more conformity prejudice in the South.[8]

VICTIMIZATION

Those who are victims of prejudice cannot be indifferent to their plight; they must constantly defend themselves from discomfort or insult. One study states that 50 percent of Negroes say that when they are with a white person they expect him "to make a slip and say something wrong about Negroes." [9] Even when not expecting an insult, a minority group member must ordinarily plan his life within a racial or ethnic frame of reference.

Besides this chronic sensitization to the problem, additional psychological reactions to victimization may be noted; among them, withdrawal and apathy, slyness and cunning, clowning, rejection of one's own group—or quite the reverse, forming closer in-group ties—resignation, neuroticism, sympathy with other minorities and enhanced striving and militancy.[10] Of course not all members of a minority group will show all of these types of response.

REDUCING PREJUDICE

Someone has said that it is easier to smash an atom than a prejudice. In the case of deep-dyed functional bigots this verdict may be true. And yet change in prejudice does occur, and has clearly happened since World

[7] Gordon W. Allport, "Prejudice: Is It Societal or Personal?" *Journal of Social Issues*, 18, (1961), pp. 120–34.

[8] Thomas F. Pettigrew, "Regional Differences in Anti-Negro Prejudice," *Journal of Abnormal and Social Psychology*, 29, (1959), pp. 28–36.

[9] Robin M. Williams, Jr., *Strangers Next Door* (New York: Prentice-Hall, Inc., 1964), p. 47.

[10] Gordon W. Allport, *The Nature of Prejudice* (New York: Doubleday Anchor Books, 1958), Chapter 9.

War II in America. Prejudiced attitudes change when it makes sociological, economic and personal sense to change them. Not all people are incurably blind to their own illogical and harmful ways of thinking. Education combats easy overgeneralizations, and as the educational level rises we find reduction in stereotyped thinking.[11] Also we know that increased self-knowledge and personal insight reduce prejudice.[12] Education for mental health works in this direction. Furthermore, militant protests call attention to needed reforms and win the sympathy of potentially democratic citizens. Various measures of prejudice have been invented to help follow these trends, even the subtle factor of human-heartedness within the population.[13]

All progress toward the reduction of prejudice will be met by vociferous resistance from the functional bigots. And yet, even when violence flares up, the trend is unmistakable. Antidiscrimination laws, revised school curricula and effective desegregation, raising of educational levels, open discussion and enlightenment, nonviolent protests that focus attention and win sympathy—all these, and other forces, are working in a single direction. Let the reader also keep in mind the fact that the problem we are here discussing has had in the past twenty years more attention and intelligent study among people of goodwill than in all the millennia of human history previously. Recent research on ethnic prejudice has been remarkably rich and informative,[14] and shows clearly that the forces of social science are strongly arrayed in the battle against bigotry.

[11] Charles H. Stember, *Education and Attitude Change* (New York: Institute of Human Relations Press, 1961). Also, Henry G. Stetler, *Attitudes toward Racial Integration in Connecticut* (Hartford: Commission on Civil Rights, 1961).

[12] Richard M. Jones, *An Application of Psychoanalysis to Education* (Springfield, Ill.: Charles C. Thomas, 1960).

[13] Howard Schuman and John Harding, "Sympathetic Identification with the Underdog." *Public Opinion Quarterly*, 27 (1963), pp. 230–41.

[14] Bernard Berelson and Gary A. Steiner, *Human Behavior: an Inventory of Scientific Findings* (New York: Harcourt, Brace & World, 1964).

chapter 18

Prejudice and the Situation

Thomas F. Pettigrew

A white Little Rock garage mechanic stood patiently in line waiting to cast his ballot at his local voting precinct. Most of the other citizens standing with him were Negroes. A few months before he had enthusiastically participated in the white mobs protesting the city's school desegregation, yet the mechanic was not in the least disturbed over the interracial character of his surroundings. "It would be un-American," he later explained, "not to let 'em vote."

" 'Round here I support segregation," firmly announced a white veteran in south Georgia, " 'cause most folks want it and it's right. Of course, in the Army things were a little different. In fact my best friend in Korea was a colored guy from Alabama. You see, we were the only Southern boys in the whole platoon."

A white mother in New Orleans turned livid with anger over the prospect of educational desegregation. She joined the screaming, shouting women rallying near an embattled school. "I'll demonstrate as long as I have to," she asserted. And she was prepared for a long siege, for she had arranged with her Negro neighbor to look after her children each morning while she protested.

Such contradictions are the rule in American race relations today. Social change does not come in logical, even paces. Nor do people caught in a changing society necessarily alter their behavior and attitudes in rationally consistent ways. Racial prejudice may be elicited in one situation, tolerance in a related situation. Thus, the structure of the situation in which the two races meet face to face assumes critical importance; indeed, the *situation* provides the vital link between the *individual* and *societal* factors which determine racial prejudice and discrimination.

Social psychology has focused considerable attention upon the role of the situation in shaping intergroup attitudes and behavior. Answers can now be offered to the recurring questions: Will more contact between the races lead to improved relations? Can law change "the hearts and minds of men?"

714

CONTACT AND CHANGE

Many well-meaning Americans have expressed the opinion that if only Negroes and whites could experience more contact with each other the nation's racial difficulties would solve themselves. Unfortunately, the case is not so simple. Africans and Europeans have more contact in the Republic of South Africa than anywhere else on the African continent and Negro and white Americans have more contact in the South than in any other region of the nation, yet neither of these areas is conspicuous for its inter-racial harmony. It almost appears as if contact between two peoples exacerbates, rather than relieves, intergroup hostility; yet this conclusion would be just as hasty and fallacious as the naïve assumption that contact invariably lessens prejudice.

Increasing interaction, whether it be of groups or individuals, intensifies and magnifies the processes already underway. Hence, more interracial contact can lead either to greater prejudice and rejection or to greater respect and acceptance, depending upon the situation in which it occurs. The basic issues, then, concern the types of situations in which contact leads to distrust and those in which it leads to trust.

Gordon Allport, in his review of the relevant research, concludes that four characteristics of the contact situation are of utmost importance.[1] Prejudice is lessened when the two groups (1) possess equal status, (2) seek common goals, (3) are cooperatively dependent upon each other, and (4) interact with the positive support of authorities, law or custom.

Equal Status Between Groups

If groups are of widely different social status, contact between them may do little more than reinforce old and hostile stereotypes. In the typical Southern situation of interracial contact, the vast majority of Negroes encountered by white Southerners are servants and other low-status service workers. Many whites eventually conclude that these are the types of jobs best suited for Negroes, that somehow this is the Negro's "proper place." To be sure, there are professional Negro Southerners—doctors, ministers, teachers—but segregation forces them to stay deep within the Negro ghetto, where whites rarely meet them. The segregationist who boasts

[1] Gordon W. Allport, *The Nature of Prejudice* (Cambridge, Mass.: Addison-Wesley, 1954), Chapter 16.

that he "really knows Negroes" is usually referring to his casual encounters with Negroes of lower status. This is a principal reason why the plentiful Negro-white contact in the South has not led to interracial understanding.

The psychologically crucial aspects of equal-status situations are pointed up by recent research on the similarity of backgrounds, interests and values. This work suggests that such similarities are especially significant in prejudice. One study investigated the attitudes of a group of white teenagers in California toward four different types of peers: Negro and white youths with the same values as the respondents, and Negro and white youths with contrasting values.[2] The results were unequivocal. While race did affect "friendliness" and social distance ratings, similarity of values was by far the most important variable. Thus, the Negro teenager with consonant values was liked far better than the white teenager with different values.

The practical problem, however, is that many whites believe that Negroes do not share their interests and values; consequently, racial prejudice and assumed value conflict are often compounded. Equal-status contact attacks this problem in two ways. First, people of equal status are more likely than others to possess congruent outlooks and beliefs simply by virtue of their common positions in society. Second, equal-status situations provide the setting where this congruence can best be mutually perceived.

Common Goals of the Groups

When groups work together toward common goals, further opportunities are presented for developing and discovering similarities of interests and values. The reduction of prejudice through contact generally requires an active, focused effort, not simply a gathering together for the sheer sake of intermingling. Athletic teams furnish a pertinent example. In striving to win, interracial teams create a contact situation not only of equal status but also of shared dependence. Negro and white team members cannot achieve their common goal of winning without the assistance of each other. Under such conditions, race becomes irrelevant.

Cooperative Interdependence of the Groups

The shared dependence of athletic teams suggests a third condition. Not only must the groups seek common goals, but the attainment of these goals must be a mutually dependent effort involving no competition along strictly racial lines. For instance, if the San Francisco Giants were all white and the

---

[2] D. D. Stein, Jane A. Hardyck, and M. B. Smith, "Race and Belief: An Open and Shut Case." Unpublished paper, University of California at Berkeley.

Los Angeles Dodgers were all Negro, they could probably play indefinitely and not become more racially tolerant. Though equal-status and common-goal conditions would prevail, the lines of competition would make race relevant. Fortunately, professional athletic teams are interracial and provide a notable case of successful desegregation. But the lesson is clear. The contact situations which lead to interracial harmony must involve cooperative interdependence.

Positive Social Support by Authorities, Law or Custom

The final factor concerns the auspices of the contact. If the situation has explicit social sanction, interracial contact is more readily accepted and has more positive effects. Though the situation may be a bit awkward at first, recognized authority support helps make it "right." Failure of local authorities, law and custom to bolster even minimal desegregation in much of the South is a chief reason why many white Southerners have failed to support Federal court orders.

An interesting application of this social support principle occurs in situations where there are no established norms for interracial behavior. An ingenious project at Cornell University studied New York State facilities unaccustomed to Negro patronage.[3] Negro researchers would enter a tavern, seek service and later record their experiences, while white researchers would observe the same situation and record their impressions for comparison. Typically the first reaction of waitresses and bartenders was to turn to the owner or others in authority for guidance. When this was not possible, the slightest behavioral cue from anyone in the situation was utilized as a gauge of what was expected of them. And if there were not such cues, confusion often continued until somehow the threatening new situation was structured. Depending upon which way the delicate scales tipped, these interracial confrontations could either lead to increased animosity or increased acceptance.

Examples of Contact and Change

The research literature abounds with examples of these contact principles in operation. One study found that white merchant seamen tended to hold racial attitudes in direct relation to how many voyages they had taken with

---

[3] Melvin L. Kohn and Robin M. Williams, Jr., "Situational Patterning in Intergroup Relations." *American Sociological Review*, 21 (1956), pp. 164–174.

equal-status Negro seamen—the more desegregated voyages, the more posi-tive their attitudes.[4] Another investigation noted that white Philadelphia policemen who had personally worked with Negro colleagues were far more favorable toward the desegregation of their force than other white police-men.[5] A third study of white government workers, veterans and students found that those who had known Negro professionals were far less prejudiced toward Negroes than those who had known only unskilled Negroes.[6]

Evidence comes even during times of crisis. While Negro and white mobs raged during the Detroit race riot of 1943, integrated co-workers, university students, and neighbors of long standing peacefully carried on their lives side by side.[7] Mention of neighborhood integration introduces the integrated living in public housing developments that meet all four of Allport's contact criteria sharply reduces racial prejudice among both Negro and white neighbors.[8] And these same studies demonstrate that living in segregated, but otherwise identical housing developments structures inter-racial contact in such a way that, if anything, racial bitterness is enhanced. Additional data derived from the desegregation of the armed forces.[9] Once again, conditions involving equal status, cooperative striving toward com-mon goals and social support lead directly to the reduction of racial preju-dice among both Negro and white servicemen. As a Negro officer in Korea candidly phrased it: "After a while you start thinking of whites as people."

[4] I. N. Brophy, "The Luxury of Anti-Negro Prejudice." *Public Opinion Quarterly,* 9 (1946), pp. 456–66. One possible explanation for the results of this study and others cited below is that the people who were the least prejudiced to begin with sought out interracial contact. Most of these studies, however, rule out the operation of this self-selection factor.

[5] William M. Kephart, *Racial Factors and Urban Law Enforcement* (Philadelphia: University of Pennsylvania Press, 1957), pp. 188–89.

[6] Barbara MacKenzie, "The Importance of Contact in Determining Attitudes Toward Negroes." *Journal of Abnormal and Social Psychology,* 43, (1948), pp. 417–41.

[7] Alfred M. Lee and Norman D. Humphrey, *Race Riot* (New York: Dryden Press, 1943), pp. 97, 130, 140.

[8] Morton Deutsch and Mary Collins, *Interracial Housing: A Psychological Evaluation of a Social Experiment* (Minneapolis: University of Minnesota Press, 1951); Marie Jahoda and Patricia West, "Race Relations in Public Housing." *Journal of Social Issues,* 7, (1951), pp. 132–39; Daniel M. Wilner, Rosabelle Walkley, and Stuart W. Cook, *Human Relations in Interracial Housing: A Study of the Contact Hypothesis* (Minneapolis: University of Minnesota Press, 1955); and Ernest Works, "The Prejudice-Interaction Hypothesis from the Point of View of the Negro Minority Group." *American Journal of Sociology,* 67, (1961), pp. 47–52.

[9] Samuel A. Stouffer, Edward A. Suchman, Leland C. DeVinney, Shirley A. Star, and Robin M. Williams, Jr., *Studies in Social Psychology in World War II,* Vol. 1, *The American Soldier: Adjustment During Army Life* (Princeton, N.J.: Princeton Univer-sity Press, 1949), Chapter X.

One Qualification

One important qualification attends attitude change through interracial contact: at least in the early stages, the change is often limited to the specific situation involved. Recall the previously mentioned Little Rock garage mechanic, the Georgia veteran and the New Orleans mother; each of them had learned to accept Negroes fully in one context but not in another. This phenomenon is not peculiar to the South. Research on white Northern steel workers found that they often approved of the desegregation of their unions to the point of sharing all union facilities with Negroes and electing Negroes to high office, yet they sternly opposed the desegregation of their all-white neighborhoods.[10] Factors underlying this situational inconsistency are considered more fully in the next section by Professor Williams.

Two Summary Principles

These studies illustrate two related principles. First, attitudes and behavior need not always be congruent; particular situations can structure how most people behave in spite of what attitudes they may hold.[11] Second, prejudice and discrimination do not always coincide.[12] Many anti-Negro people do not racially discriminate, because they find themselves in situations where discriminatory behavior is not sanctioned (*e.g.*, professional baseball games). And many unprejudiced people discriminate every day of their lives, because they find themselves in situations which demand it (*e.g.*, certain public facilities in Jackson, Mississippi).

[10] Joseph D. Lohman and Dietrich C. Reitzes, "Note on Race Relations in Mass Society." *American Journal of Sociology*, 58 (1952), pp. 340–46; J. D. Lohman and R. C. Reitzes, "Deliberately Organized Groups and Racial Behavior." *American Sociological Review*, 19 (1954), pp. 342–44; and D. C. Reitzes, "The Role of Organizational Structures: Union Versus Neighborhood in a Tension Situation." *Journal of Social Issues*, 9(1), (1953), pp. 37–44.

[11] For research demonstration of this principle, see: Richard T. LaPiere, "Attitudes Versus Actions." *Social Forces*, 13, (1934), pp. 230–37; and Bernard Kutner, Caroll Wilkins, and Penny R. Yarrow, "Verbal Attitudes and Overt Behavior Involving Racial Prejudice." *Journal of Abnormal and Social Psychology*, 47, (1952), pp. 649–52.

[12] For research demonstrations of this principle, see: Henry A. Bullock, "Racial Attitudes and the Employment of Negroes." *American Journal of Sociology*, 56, (1951), pp. 448–57; and A. Kapos, *Some Individual and Group Determinants of Fraternity Attitudes Toward the Admission of Members of Certain Minority Groups*. Unpublished doctoral dissertation, University of Michigan, 1953.

LAW AND CHANGE

Within this situational perspective, a reappraisal can be made of the old saw—"laws cannot change the hearts and minds of men." A case in point is the 1945 antidiscrimination employment legislation enacted by New York State. This law led to the hiring of Negroes as salesclerks in New York City department stores for the first time. Two investigations conducted separate tests of the effects of this law-induced desegregation. One study of white sales personnel revealed that those who had experienced the new equal-status job contact with Negroes held more favorable attitudes toward interracial interaction in the work situation.[13] Once again, however, the initial effects of this contact did not extend beyond the immediate situation; equal-status clerks were not more accepting of Negroes in eating and residential situations.

The other investigation questioned customers.[14] Though reactions to later questioning varied, there was a widespread acceptance of this legally required racial change. Customers were largely concerned with shopping conveniently and efficiently; many hesitated to challenge the firm *fait accompli* established by the law; and for many the new situation was consistent with their belief in the American creed of equal opportunity for all.[15]

Law versus Exhortation

Law, then, *can* change the hearts and minds of men. It does so through a vital intermediate step. Law first acts to modify behavior, and this modified behavior in turn changes men's hearts and minds. Notice that this is precisely the opposite sequence commonly believed to be the most effective method of social change. Convince people to be less prejudiced through

[13] John Harding and Russell Hogrefe, "Attitudes of White Department Store Employees Toward Negro Co-workers." *Journal of Social Issues*, 8 (1952), pp. 18–28.

[14] Gerhart Saenger and Emily Gilbert, "Customer Reactions to the Integration of Negro Sales Personnel." *International Journal of Opinion and Attitude Research*, 4 (1950), pp. 57–76.

[15] Prohibition provides an interesting contrast at this point. Prohibition apparently failed largely because it was neither rigorously enforced nor, despite its moral overtones for some Protestants, did it articulate with national traditions or ease the consciences of many Americans.

informational and goodwill campaigns, goes the reasoning, and then they will discriminate less. To be sure, this sequence is sometimes effective, but the preponderance of social psychological evidence attests to the greater efficacy of the opposite approach. Behaving differently is more often the precursor to thinking differently.

The celebrated annual rituals of brotherhood week, brotherhood dinners and brotherhood awards illustrate the point. While they remind participants of their religious and national ideals and strengthen the already convinced, these events appear of limited value in convincing the unconvinced. The basic problem with such observances is that they do not require participants to change their behavior. The interracial contact is brief and artificial, and the emphasis is placed on exhortation and directly influencing attitudes. A vast body of psychological data indicates that prejudiced individuals in such situations will avoid the message altogether, deny the relevance of the message for themselves or find ways of twisting the meaning of the message.[16] In addition, ritualistic exhortations for brotherhood may often serve an unanticipated negative function. By attending the annual dinner and paying the tax-deductible fifty or one hundred dollars per plate, many individuals of considerable influence regularly relieve their guilt. Having gone through the motions of supporting "equality for all," participants are psychologically released to go on discriminating as before.

Antidiscrimination laws can also be tuned out by prejudiced individuals and used as conscience salves by the guilty. But, if properly enforced, such legislation has the potential for achieving behavioral change not possessed by exhortation. Several reasons for this are apparent. There is, of course, the threat of punishment and unfavorable publicity for recalcitrants. But more important is the "off the hook" function such laws provide. Thus, Macy's and Gimbel's stores in New York City may each have been afraid to hire Negro sales personnel as long as there were no assurances that their competitors would follow suit—but the law furnished this assurance. Finally, as noted in many of the studies cited, the legally established *fait accompli*, unlike exhortations for tolerance, generates its own acceptance.[17] The situational face-lifting it achieves is a 52-weeks-a-year process, not just a single week in celebration of brotherhood.

[16] Eunice Cooper and Marie Jahoda, "The Evasion of Propaganda: How Prejudiced People Respond to Anti-Prejudice Propaganda." *Journal of Psychology*, 23 (1947), pp. 15–25; and Herbert H. Hyman and Paul B. Sheatsley, "Some Reasons Why Information Campaigns Fail." *Public Opinion Quarterly*, 11 (1947), pp. 413–23.

[17] For an interesting political example of this phenomenon, see: Hadley Cantril (ed.), *Gauging Public Opinion*. (Princeton: Princeton Univerity Press, 1944), pp. 226–30.

A FINAL STUDY

The fundamental principles underlying situational factors in prejudice are dramatically highlighted by an ingenious field experiment conducted in Oklahoma.[18] Twenty young boys, of homogeneous backgrounds but previously unacquainted with one another, attended a summer camp set up for the investigation. From the start, the boys were divided into two groups —"the Rattlers" and "the Eagles." The first stage of the experiment was designed to develop high *esprit de corps* within each of the groups. Totally separated from each other, the Rattlers and Eagles engaged in a variety of satisfying experiences, and each group soon developed the pride and sense of "we-ness" characteristic of strong in-group solidarity.

The second stage brought the groups face to face in a series of grimly competitive tasks—tugs-of-war, baseball and football games and tent pitching. In all of these contact situations, only one group could win and the other had to lose. The inevitable intergroup animosity soon appeared. Derogatory songs and slogans were composed; destructive raids on "the enemy's cabin" began; negative stereotypes developed; and even preferences for group segregation were voiced. Competitive contact had wreaked its usual havoc.

The experiment's third stage tried to mend the damage. "The brotherhood dinner" approach came first. The boys met in such noncompetitive situations as eating good food in the same room, shooting off fireworks and attending a movie together. Note that all of these involve passive conduct without common goals or group interdependence. And, understandably, intergroup friction did not abate; in fact, the boys employed these unfocused events as opportunities for further vilification of their hated rivals. Next, the investigators introduced carefully contrived problems that required the cooperation of both groups for their solution. Fixing together the damaged water tank that supplied the entire camp, raising jointly the funds to show a favorite movie, and other functionally dependent behavior achieved a striking decrement in intergroup hostility. While at the close of the competitive second stage over half of the characteristics assigned by the boys to their group rivals were sharply unfavorable, over two-thirds of such judgments were favorable at the close of the interdependent third

---

[18] Muzafer Sherif, and others, *Intergroup Conflict and Cooperation: The Robbers Cave Experiment.* (Norman, Oklahoma: Institute of Group Relations, 1961).

stage. Moreover, the percentage of friendship choices across group lines multiplied fourfold.

One final result of this intriguing investigation replicates the limited nature of the attitude change initially induced even under optimal contact conditions. The first interdependent encounters of the two camp groups by no means removed all of the bad feeling between the Rattlers and the Eagles. But as these socially sanctioned confrontations continued, the prejudice-reducing power of this type of contact accumulated. This suggests that as the desegregation process proceeds, it may well receive increasingly greater support and have increasingly greater effects upon the participants, both Negro and white.

chapter 19

Prejudice and Society

Robin M. Williams, Jr.

Intergroup relations cannot be understood merely in terms of the "attitudes" of undifferentiated masses of individuals. Real societies and communities are highly differentiated systems, made up of networks of social relationships within and among subsystems. Groups, associations and other collectivities exist side by side; they overlap, interpenetrate and form complex sets of interrelations. In complex urban societies, intergroup relations necessarily transcend small groups and diffuse interpersonal relations; they necessarily come to be regulated in part by law and organized political and administrative action. Intergroup relations often are extensive, complex, persistent and highly structured. Often they are powerfully shaped by organized intergroupings. Much discrimination is not primarily an expression of prejudice but rather a byproduct of purposive striving to attain or hold economic, social and political advantages or privileges. And, indeed, research often shows that an individual's prejudiced or nonprejudiced initial attitudes are not closely related to intergroup behavior in the market or in the political arena.

The sheer fact of social differentiation means that there are individuals and collectivities that may differ in their interests and in their control of (and aspirations for), power, wealth, prestige and other scarce values. Whenever members of collectivities or social categories of persons engage in competition or rivalry for such values, the possibility arises for intergroup tension and conflict. This possibility would remain even in a world of psychologically stable and mature adults who always sought their goals in a rational manner.

Furthermore, conflicts often are not simply expressions of "prejudice" but arise from genuine injuries or threats. Real differences in values often lie back of the fears that so often lead to aggressive behavior and thence to conflict. Also, persons of similar interests and values tend to associate together and to distinguish themselves from others who differ. Besides, some preferential association would continue even in a homogeneous society. Time and effort are involved in social interaction. Functional proximity

724

alone, in the absence of any other factors, would result in selective inter-action. Group relations are embedded in an environing social structure.

Prejudice is a psychological condition, lodged in specific individuals. Discrimination is a particular quality of overt social behavior. The two sets of phenomena are interrelated, but neither one is a mere reflection or expression of the other. There may be prejudice without grossly detectible discrimination; there may be much clear discrimination with little or no prejudice. We cannot simply assume that the one always leads to or ac-companies the other. A white realtor may refuse to sell a listed house to a Negro buyer, not because he personally dislikes Negroes or accepts stereotypes about them, but because he will be expelled from the local real estate association if he does sell in violation of the enforced policy of the association. A prejudiced white person may accept Negro customers be-cause of antidiscriminatory legal provisions, or because his desire for profits outweighs his desires to express prejudice in overt acts.

It follows from these well-established conclusions that social patterns of exclusion, segregation, and differential treatment of whole social cate-gories of persons can not be fully or adequately "explained" solely by in-voking the prejudiced attitudes of individuals. Nor can we precisely infer from the sheer fact of conformity to discriminatory patterns how wide-spread, salient or intense prejudice may be. Prejudices are learned; they grow out of social experiences. The institutional structures and organiza-tion of a community or society shape and restrict the experiences particular individuals will have. Knowing that certain individuals have prejudices, we still want to ask what social conditions favored the establishment of such attitudes, and what shared social and cultural circumstances facilitate or hinder various modes of expressing prejudices in behavior.

By discrimination in the most general sense we mean, simply, any be-havior that represents differential treatment of persons solely because of their membership in a certain social category or collectivity, regardless of their personal qualities and achievements. Discrimination in this broad sense exists when there are systematic differences in conduct toward men in contrast to women, old persons and young persons, officers versus en-listed men, local residents and outsiders, Democrats or Republicans, Protestants and Catholics, Negroes and whites, Southerners and Northern-ers, farmers and bankers. Discrimination may be favorable or unfavorable toward the objects of discrimination. For our present purposes we are interested in the kind of discrimination that is disadvantageous to those discriminated against. The major kinds of negative discrimination in our society are so widespread and conspicuous as to be easy to identify: exclusion or inferior opportunity with regard to education, employment and promotion, housing, public accommodations and services, political rights, and civil liberties and protections.

Of course it is apparent that we all act toward other people partly in terms of the statuses or social positions they occupy. How we will behave differs as between men and women, young people and older people, between a policeman and a storekeeper, a judge and a longshoreman. Such differentiated behavior is found in every social system, and to some extent has a *functional* basis. That is, children are not adults and cannot be treated entirely as if they were; men and women do differ; different occupations serve different social functions. Ordinarily we would speak of discrimination in cases of this kind only if a person is denied rights otherwise available to all equally qualified persons. In American society all adult citizens with only a few stated exceptions, are suppose to have the right to vote and hold public office, but in some parts of our nation millions of Negro Americans are denied the exercise of these nominally universal rights. For the most part we are said to believe that "everyone" has the right to an education to the limits of his desires and abilities, to work in an occupation of his own choosing, to reside wherever he wishes within the limits of his economic resources, and in general to have access to all public facilities and services on equal terms with others. Very clearly, however, deep-seated and widespread patterns of discrimination often nullify these so-called rights for many members of minority groups— Negroes, Catholics, Jews, Mexican-Americans, Japanese- or Chinese-Americans and many others.

It is sometimes possible to reduce or eliminate discrimination in advance of any very great reduction in prejudice, as we have seen in the case of the elimination of official segregation in the armed services and in certain public housing developments. In general, however, prejudice and discrimination (including enforced segregation) mutually support one another. Discrimination reinforces people in the prejudices; prejudice furnishes the basis for and rationalizations of discriminatory conduct.

Now it is a very important fact that many people hold stereotypes and express prejudices without having any strong or active hostility toward the objects of their prejudicial attitudes. Those persons who have such attitudes and beliefs are the "gentle people of prejudice." They have learned their prejudices from their social environment in much the same way they learned table manners, how to speak English or tastes in music. They conform to the opinions of their associates, follow the local customs and voice the accepted stereotypes without much reflection, self-consciousness, or emotional involvement. For many such people their prejudices are, so to speak, out on the edges of the personality, not central to their self-conception or their basic emotional organization. On the other hand, we find people whose out-group stereotypes are saturated with active *hostility*. They feel and express attitudes of dislike, repugnance, or hate; they actively want to exclude, insult, deprive or hurt members of the groups toward which they are prejudiced. A basic question, accordingly, is: What are the social conditions most likely to lead to active hostility, to turn the mild prejudice of conformity into the hostility that leads to acts of aggression?

Back of prejudiced attitudes are massive economic and political arrangements and forces. Minority groups are formed, in the first instance, in these ways: by conquest, as with the American Indians; by shifts in national boundaries, as in Europe after World War I; by forced importation, as of Negro slaves into the United States; by forced transfers of populations, as in Europe and the Soviet Union; and by voluntary migration, as of the Chinese in Southeast Asia or the mass immigration of Europeans to America. Considerations of economic and political advantage—of group superordination and subordination—obviously bulk large in these massive historical events.

In every society, men are interested in and strive for the scarce values represented by power, wealth or income, and social prestige and deference. Whenever groups or categories of men who differ in visible physical and cultural characteristics are thrown into situations of competition or rivalry for these values, the likelihood of prejudice and discrimination is increased. When the Chinese first came to the West Coast as laborers, they were welcomed; although they were regarded as "exotic," they were received, for the most part, with friendly curiosity and were held to be industrious, sober, reliable and law-abiding. When the railroads were built and economic depression struck, the Chinese abruptly became the object of negative stereotypes and marked discrimination. Throughout our history, the waves of antiimmigrant agitation have been highest in periods of difficulty. For centuries in Europe, Jews were often welcomed when their economic services were wanted; often persecuted when it was to the economic or political advantage of ruling groups to do so. In the United States, the Southern defense of slavery became entrenched only after inventions and commercial developments made the system highly profitable. The disenfranchisement of Negroes and the growth of legalized segregation a generation after the end of Reconstruction was partly a result of political struggles within the dominant white groupings.

In a very basic sense, "race relations" are the direct outgrowth of the long wave of European expansion, beginning with the discovery of America. Because of their more highly developed technology and economic and political organization, the Europeans were able by military force or by economic and political penetration to secure control over colonies, territories, protectorates and other possessions and spheres of influence around the world. In a way, the resulting so-called race relations had very little to do with "race"—initially it was an historical accident that the peoples encountered in the European expansion differed in shared physical characteristics of an obvious kind. But once the racial ideologies had been formed and widely disseminated, they constituted a powerful means of justifying political hegemony and economic control.

In much the same way, present-day vested political, economic and social privileges and rights tend to be rationalized and defended by persons and groups who hold such prerogatives.

Perhaps this is the point at which to bring in the notion of "vested interests." Whenever a number of persons within a society have enjoyed for a considerable period of time certain opportunities for getting wealth, for exercising power and authority, and for successfully claiming prestige and social deference, there is a strong tendency for these people to feel that these benefits are theirs "by right." The advantages come to be thought of as normal, proper, customary, as sanctioned by time, precedent and social consensus. Proposals to change the existing situation arouse reactions of "moral indignation." Elaborate doctrines are developed to show the inevitability and rightness of the existing scheme of things.

An established system of vested interests is a powerful thing, perhaps especially when differences in power, wealth and prestige coincide with relatively indelible symbols of collective membership, such as shared hereditary physical traits, a distinctive religion, or a persistently held culture. The holders of an advantaged position see themselves as a group and reinforce one another in their attitudes; any qualms about the justice of the status quo seem to be diminished by the group character of the arrangements.

Economic competition tends to arouse prejudice, once given a visible group and a definition of its members as "different." Such prejudice is especially likely to appear when a racially or culturally recognized grouping is concentrated in highly visible occupations which involve direct contact with the public and in which economic conflicts of interest are already close to the surface—as for example, in money-lending and retail trade. Such vulnerable occupations are particularly likely to be entered upon by persons with little capital who risk a venture into marginal positions not already pre-empted by established groups. Prejudice is reinforced also by a concentration of members of a highly visible grouping in occupations of low prestige—the poorly paid, hot, heavy, dirty and otherwise disagreeable or morally rejected jobs and types of work.

In the realm of power, diffuse prejudices often are focused, intensified and sharpened by political processes. There is a notable and well-documented tendency for political candidates in some parts of the United States to appeal to the group prejudices of their constituents in the course of gaining and holding power. Once a tradition of prejudice has become well established, an appeal to voters on ethnic, religious or racial grounds constitutes a weapon that comes readily to hand in political maneuvers. It is, of course, a double-edged sword. It is of maximum effectiveness only when one element of the population is a definite political minority, as in the case with Negroes in many parts of the country. The larger the number of minority groups in the electorate and the more nearly equal they are in numbers of effective voters, the less likely it is that what we might call "ethnic politics" will be either effective or safe. In the United States the possibilities of serious social disruption from ethnic or racist politics are too obvious to require elaboration here.

Any careful study of the role of economic and political factors in intergroup relations quickly shows the importance of understanding the particular total situation in which they operate. Studies in Chicago showed that white union members who cooperated well with Negroes in their labor union, even electing Negroes to leadership positions, nevertheless could be brought, partly by the agitation of an organized neighborhood association, to intense opposition against Negroes moving into their residential area. A common device in real estate dealings is that of "block-busting"— in which Negroes (or other discriminated-against minority people) are induced or permitted to move into an area. The real estate dealers then seek to encourage "panic selling" by persuading the white residents that property values will drop. If the tactic is successful, the dealer acquires the properties at bargain basement prices, and then proceeds to raise the values above the original level by renting and selling at high prices to home-hungry members of minority groups. Thus, by reason of economic exploitation, preexisting prejudice is used in such a way as to reinforce and intensify prejudice.

Examples of such situational variation can be multiplied almost endlessly. The self-same proprietor of a restaurant will on one occasion cordially serve Negroes and on another occasion rudely refuse service, depending upon the anticipated reaction of white customers, the possibility of a court suit charging illegal discrimination and other similar factors. Quite often, the managers of business establishments claim to be more discriminatory than they really are when confronted with actual customers. This is partly because the businessman in these cases assumes that his majority-group customers are more prejudiced than they are in fact, and partly because his stereotype of Negroes or Chinese or Jews may not fit the tangible human being who requests a room or orders a meal.

Once prejudices are formed as a part of the basic social outlook of large numbers of like-minded persons within a society, the whole complex of beliefs, values and sentiments becomes a part of the social processes of socialization and conformity. The stereotypic images of ethnic, religious and racial groupings come to be embodied in literature, song and story. They impinge on us through newspapers and popular magazines, through movies, radio and television. They reach us through the nearly irresistible medium of jokes. And, perhaps above all, they may be so pervasive as to become almost a test of belonging to the in-group. In the family, the congeniality group, the local community lie the individual's most essential ties of social belonging. If these in-groups share stereotypes and prejudices, the lone individual finds that to question the assumptions of neighbors, friends and kinsmen is to risk ridicule, displeasure or even social rejection. In such circumstances, the forces of conformity are strong. It is through a process of interlocking demands and expectations of conformity that a cultural tradition of prejudice and discrimination gains much of its tenacity in influencing behavior. Under conditions of tight social conformity there often appears the phenomenon of *pluralistic ignorance*. Each person believes that the publicly accepted beliefs and attitudes are, in fact, the private attitudes of each of his fellows. No one dares to expose his own privately deviant attitudes to others, and hence remains in ignorance of the similarly deviant views of some of his associates.

BIBLIOGRAPHY

1. Gordon W. Allport, *The Nature of Prejudice*. Cambridge, Mass.: Addison-Wesley, 1954; Chapter 13.
2. Nathan Glazer and Daniel Patrick Moynihan, *Beyond the Melting Pot*. Cambridge, Mass.: The MIT Press and Harvard University Press, 1963; pp. 1–85, 288–315.
3. Raymond W. Mack, *Race, Class, and Power*. New York: American Book Co., 1963; Chapter V, X-XI.
4. Charles F. Marden and Gladys Meyer, *Minorities in American Society*. New York: American Book Co., 1962; Chapters 20-21.
5. Thomas F. Pettigrew, "Personality and Sociocultural Factors in Intergroup Attitudes: A Cross-National Comparison." *Conflict Resolution*, II, (1958), pp. 29–42.
6. Peter I. Rose, *They and We*. New York: Random House, 1964; Chapters 4–5.
7. George Eaton Simpson and J. Milton Yinger, *Racial and Cultural Minorities*. New York: Harper & Brothers, 1958; Chapters 4–5, 8–10.
8. James W. Vander Zanden, *American Minority Relations*. New York: The Ronald Press Co., 1963; Chapters 4–6.
9. Robin M. Williams, Jr., *Strangers Next Door*. Englewood Cliffs, N.J.: Prentice-Hall, Inc., 1964; Chapters 4–5, 9–10.

chapter 20

Negro Music in American Life

Zelma George

All art is a set of social facts as well as aesthetics, and knowledge of the role of the Negro in the development of America's music can help toward a better understanding of the total culture of America.

The militant, self-assertive Negro has always existed, even during slavery. In the struggle for recognition, a suppressed people develops group or "race" consciousness, and along with that, a body of attitudes, sentiments and beliefs which serve to unify its members. At the same time, it serves to isolate them from the larger society.

Isolation, in turn, breeds a community of interests, a sensitiveness and a group pride which must be fed with heroes, achievements and "collective representations" which will integrate and make for cohesion of the individuals in the group.

For the Negro, music has been the most socially permissive vehicle which he has used as a medium of social comment, criticism and protest, and to express his aggression. Negro music and musicians have provided a tradition of success, and until recent years they have often been the only source of a healthy self-esteem and self-confidence for the total group.

The Negro's music is a direct expression of his emotionalized thought, his consciousness of the world about him, his moods, concerns, aspirations and desperations. It reflects his concept of himself as a Negro and as a man, and his view of his role in society. This is true whether his music has been in the folk, popular or academic [1] tradition.

The Negro is a composite character in American culture. He is American, not African. His ideals, feelings, values, expressions, are products of the American culture, modified by a transmission of it through himself.

His music, then, is a result of reciprocal cultural interchange. The degree of its distinctiveness is determined by the amount and type of his exposure to, and participation in, the American culture, and by the extent to which

---

[1] The author avoids the term "classical music" and uses "academic" instead. She believes that there are "classics" in each of the three traditions.

he, as a member of the Negro community, has identified himself with it and maintained or developed a distinctive subculture.

The Negro has taken and has given culturally. There has been much mutual borrowing. His musical preferences, his affinities, even his celebrated sense of rhythm are not hereditary. They have been the result of environmental conditioning and have been culturally transmitted, by means of examples, attitudes and actual participation as a member of the Negro community.

Negro life has been a compelling force to composers around the world which they have tried to express musically. For example, Langston Hughes' poetry has been translated into nineteen languages and dialects;[2] and the *Bibliographical Index to Negro Music* [3] includes titles of songs by American, Russian, German, French, Spanish, Italian and Portuguese composers, using his lyrics, mostly in translated Negro dialect. W. C. Handy's "St. Louis Blues" has been translated into Japanese, Chinese, French, Italian, German, Portuguese, and Swedish.

WHAT IS NEGRO MUSIC?

Negro music is infinitely plural. It consists of three main currents—a folk music, sacred and secular; an academic music, and a popular music. Each has its own technique, its own idiom, its own repertoire and its own sociology. Each requires a different set of skills and must be judged by different criteria because each has a different function. There will be good and bad, and sometimes the vulgar, in each.

For purposes of this study, the term "Negro music" includes Negro folk music and all "art" music, whether popular or academic, which makes use of Negro thematic material. The repertoire, composer and performer techniques, idioms and sociological tradition of Negro folk music constitute the raw material which composers have used in many different ways. Whenever an attempt is made to define, describe or express, in terms of music, any part of this sociological tradition, or to make use of any part of the repertoire, techniques or idioms of the Negro folk music tradition, the composer is

---

[2] A letter from Langston Hughes to the author, April 8, 1953.

[3] Zelma George, *Bibliographical Index to Negro Music*, a card catalog of 9,592 titles of published Negro folk music, music by Negro composers, music by non-Negroes using Negro thematic material, and history and criticism of Negro music. The master catalog of 9,592 titles is located in the Moreland Collection of the Howard University Library, Washington, D.C.

using Negro thematic material. Limitless possibilities are open to the composer who consciously determines to use this material, and many such attempts have been made by both white and Negro composers.

The term "Negro music" also includes another body of music so far not specifically mentioned: all other music written by Negroes. The only connection this considerable portion of music has with the Negro is that the composer is Negro.

NEGRO FOLK MUSIC

Negro Folk Music Repertoire Defined

The great bulk of Negro folk music consists of songs. There are sacred songs, variously called "slave songs," [4] "jubilees," [5] "sorrow songs," [6] "plantation songs," [7] "mellows," [8] etc., but most often "Spirituals"; [9] there are also secular songs and dances, usually classified according to the social functions in connection with which they have appeared: work songs, dance songs, lullabies, children's game songs, love songs, social songs such as ballads, "badmen" songs, blues, folk minstrels and others.[10]

These constitute the Negro folk music repertoire, but the definition of

[4] This is the name given to them by the compilers of the first collection of spirituals in book form: William Francis Allen, Charles Pinkard Ware, and Lucy McKim Garrison (eds. and comp.), *Slave Songs of the United States* (New York: A. Simpson & Company, 1867), pp. XLII–115.

[5] This term was made famous by the Fisk Jubilee Singers from Fisk University, Nashville, Tennessee, who were the first to present them to the world at large in tours of the United States and Europe, 1871–78.

[6] See W. E. B. Du Bois, *The Souls of the Black Folk* (Chicago: A. C. McClurg, 1903), Chapter XIV, "The Sorrow Songs."

[7] See Thomas P. Fenner, *et al.* (*Cabin and Plantation Songs*, Institute Press, Hampton, Va. 1875).

[8] See Robert Emmet Kennedy, *Mellows, A Chronicle of Unknown Singers* (New York: Albert & Charles Boni, 1925), p. 183.

[9] See Alain Locke (ed.), *The New Negro; an Interpretation.* (New York: Albert & Charles Boni, 1925), "The Negro Spirituals," pp. 199–213.
Negro Spirituals spelled with a capital S are a specific body of musical literature produced by the slave during slavery and sung a certain way, much as German lieder is a specific body of song which, as every young singer learns, cannot be sung any way he personally might wish to sing it; tradition has much to say to that student. In the same way, much of the Negro Spiritual literature as sung by today's singers must be considered a new art form, for the performing artist, in taking "liberties," has been creating. It may be a spiritual song but it is not, in the author's opinion, a Spiritual.

[10] See Howard W. Odom and Guy B. Johnson, *Negro Workaday Songs* (Chapel Hill: The University of North Carolina Press, 1926), p. VII.

Negro folk music is incomplete without the addition of other aspects: Negro folk music techniques, idioms and content based on a sociological tradition; these add up to a distinctive style designated by many writers as "Negroid."

Negro Folk Music Techniques Defined

"Technique" as applied to the folk musician has to do with the skills necessary to the accomplishment of the function of that particular music. Given the whole gamut of tones and the degrees between them, what he creates with them is described in terms of rhythm, melody, harmony, tonality, texture, medium or instrumentation, form and style. We speak of the craft of the composition and refer to combinations of tones, ways of bending the melodic line, harmonic style, pitch range; and we use such terms as scales, intervals, harmonics.

But in creating a melody, the Negro folk knew nothing about auxiliary or returning tones, or passing tones, or about suspensions or anticipations. And yet, analyses of the great Negro folk music literature reveal the excellent craftsmanship of the Negro folk creators, the unconscious use of these skills. The textures, rhythms, forms and contents that have been employed by the Negro folk creators are the techniques of the Negro folk composers who were also the Negro folk performers.[11] There were no audiences in the Negro folk music experience. A distinctive characteristic of Negro folk music has been, and still is, the way in which it transforms listeners into participants, if in no other way than the unconscious patting of feet in response to the rhythm.

This composer-performer was almost without exception illiterate. This does not mean, however, that he was ignorant. The usual discussion of folk music employs such adjectives as "artless," "simple," "crude," "emotional," "primitive." A realistic evaluation of the Negro folk music demands a correction of this approach to it.

Negro folk music is also primarily folk poetry, but it is far from being primitive poetry. Indeed, it is rather the flower of an art which was formalized and developed among a people whose training was verbal

[11] *E.g.*, Richard Milburn, "Listen to the Mocking Bird" (1855). Milburn was an exceptionally skilled whistler. He spent his leisure time imitating the songs of birds and accompanying himself on the guitar. According to the Minutes of the Philadelphia Library Committee (a Negro literary organization), he was often engaged to exhibit his skill "to add interest to their meetings." He was induced to whistle his tune for Septimus Winner (pseudonym: Alice Hawthorne), a white composer and publisher who not only wrote down the bird-like notes but also published them. A first edition of this music is in the Schomburg Collection of the New York Public Library. The title page reads: "Music by Richard Milburn, words by Alice Hawthorne." Subsequent editions carried the name of Alice Hawthorne as composer and author.

instead of visual, and whose artists developed taste and skill with such ease and naturalness that the interaction of purpose and inspiration throughout the complex process of creation is not easily or often recognized. The Negro had been well trained in the music and poetry that he loved, lived and perpetuated. He used a technique within the capacity of the group; because of the homogeneity of the group, he expressed, for himself and many others, a feeling, a thought, a hope, a joy, a despair, a suffering and a philosophy shared by all.

What one does with his potential and ability largely depends upon his environment. The slave had much to say about his life and his environment, and his language was primarily music.

Here we can see the virtuoso craftsmanship of the individual slave's contribution to the creative process, revised and made to conform to the skills and needs of the folk who, by unconscious selection, developed a technique. These Negro folk technicians evolved certain musical forms as, for example, the antiphonal or call and response chant, the verse and chorus, the work song, the blues with its unique 12-measure, 3-line form, and dance music. These have been made distinctive by the particular melodic, harmonic and rhythmic treatments which the Negro folk have given them.

The Negro slave's music is a documentation of his attempt to redefine life for himself in a brand new world of relationships and functions, described in the term "chattel slavery." He used what he brought and what he needed for accommodation. How he achieved this involves his "technique."

Negro Folk Music Idioms Defined

The term "idiom" in music is frequently used in the discussions and controversies about African survivals in Negro folk music. Melville J. Herskovitz is the pioneer in a scholarly effort to describe the African survivals in Negro music which he contends have become the basis of what is now regarded as "Negroid." His *The Myth of the Negro Past* [12] was one of the important background studies which advanced this point of view. There have been many others, notably E. Franklin Frazier, who have disagreed.[13]

[12] New York: Harper & Bros., 1941, p. 374.

[13] Frazier contended that acceptance of the Herskovitz point of view would enable whites to lose whatever guilt they felt for oppression of the Negro because they could ascribe antisocial activities among Negroes to "Africanisms" rather than to their own repressive treatment of Negroes. Alain Locke criticized the Herskovitz theory as one which would lead white Americans to conclude that Negroes could not be assimilated. See Gunnar Myrdal, *The American Dilemma* (New York: Harper & Row), Twentieth Anniversary edition, Chapter 35, fn. 32, p. 1394.

Today there is a great deal more scientific data than the earlier writers had and this is lifting the entire subject out of the literature of polemics. Only recently a large body of recordings of African music and of folk music as sung by rural American Negroes has been made available. Several foundations and anthropological research organizations [14] have made this kind of collection, transcription and analysis possible; a high quality of scholarship by anthropologists, musicologists, sociologists, ethnologists and that new body of specialists called ethnomusicologists, is now being produced.[15] Notable as sources of these recordings are The Library of Congress Archives of Folk Song, Folkways Records, and the Ethical Folkways Library of Harold Courlander.[16]

Negro Folk Music Sociological Tradition and Content Defined

The fourth component in the definition of Negro folk music is the sociological tradition and content. It consists of that complex of (1) ancestry, the psychosocial, political and moral heritage and environment which is constituted by problems and conditions of slavery; (2) the status, the social goals and the organizational, moral, political, cultural and economic climate provided by non-Negroes; (3) the amount of intergroup interaction, and (4) the geography.

Today, a great deal is known about the institution of slavery and the relationships that existed between slaves and masters, the kinds of peoples

[14] Notable the John Simon Guggenheim Foundation and the Wenner-Gren Foundation for Anthropological Research.

[15] E.g., Alan P. Merriam, Introduction to *Tribal, Folk and Cafe Music of West Africa*, recorded by Arthur W. Alberts. Album notes for *South of the Sahara*, New York: Folkways Records and Service Corp., FE 4503, 1957, pp. 1–13. Album notes for Ekonda, *Tribal Music of the Belgian Congo*, New York: Riverside Records, LP RLP 4006, September, 1956. Harold Courlander, Album notes for *African and Afro-American Drums*, New York: Ethnic Folkways Library, FE 4502, 1954. *Negro Folk Music in Africa and America*, recorded and edited by Courlander, Foreword by Richard Alan Waterman and the compiler, New York: Ethnic Folkways Library, FE 4500, 1951. *Negro Folk Music of Alabama*, Recorded and edited by Courlander, Foreword by Ruby Pickens Tartt, New York: Ethnic Folkways Library, FE 4417, 4418, 4471, 4472, 4473, 4474, 1956.

[16] Harold Courlander, *Negro Folk Music, U.S.A.* (New York: Columbia University Press, 1963), pp x–324. This book deserves special mention. It is a fully documented survey of Negro folk music and provides the most up-to-date review of the thinking of modern scholars regarding the "distinctive elements and aspects" of Negro folk music and "how and where it may be *distinguished from* the mainstream." See Chapter II, pp. 13–34. This author would prefer to say that these "elements and aspects" help to *identify* Negro folk music *in* the mainstream. See also, Dena J. Epstein, "Slave Music in the United States Before 1860." *Music Library Association—Notes Second Series*. Vol. XX, Nos. 2 and 3 (1963), pp. 195–212; 377–390.

who furnished the nonslave culture contacts and the great variety of family life, religion, education, recreation, manners, morals, musical and other aesthetic interests and skills, and general behavior and attitudes which constituted these culture contacts.[17]

There is a great deal of new data available about the sources of the slaves and the role of music in their lives as Africans. Today's African scholars and performers are producing some extremely valuable insights into the role of music in the life of people of specific countries.[18]

One has but to see how almost every work on the development of jazz, for example, discusses the Negro's sociological tradition and content as necessary background, in order to appreciate its relevance in a discussion of Negro music.

As for the geographical locale of Negro music the climate, the nature of the soil and other similar factors did influence the music.

Negro Music of the Early 1900's

In the early 1900's, an establishment called The Marshall became important in the artistic life of New York. It was a beautifully appointed hotel, run by a Negro, which had become the center of a fashionable sort of life new to Negroes. For nearly ten years, beginning in 1900, The Marshall was headquarters for actors, musicians, composers, writers and the better-paid vaudevillians. An unsigned article in *The Cadenza* in 1902, quoted from the *New York Sun,* gives this account:

> The Negro composer is having an inning in the musical world just now, said a music publisher. You can count on your fingers the Negro composers who

[17] E.g., Dwight Lowell Drumond, *Antislavery The Crusade for Freedom in America* (Ann Arbor: The University of Michigan Press, 1961), p. 422. John Hope Franklin, *From Slavery to Freedom* (New York: Knopf, 1956), p. 639. Barnett Hollander, *Slavery in America: Its Legal History* (New York: Barnes & Noble, Inc., 1963), p. 212. William R. Bascom and Melville J. Herskovitz (eds.), *Continuity and Change in African Culture* (Chicago: University of Chicago Press, 1959). Alan P. Merriam, "Characteristics of African Music." *Journal of the International Folk Music Council,* XI (1959), pp. 13–19. Richard A. Waterman, "African Influences on the Music of the Americas," in Sol Tax, *Acculturation in the Americas* (Chicago: University of Chicago Press), Proceedings of the 29th International Congress of Americanists, II, 1952. A. M. Jones, *Studies in African Music* (London: Oxford University Press, 1959). Bernard Fagg, "The Discovery of Multiple Rock Gongs in Nigeria." *African Music,* III.

[18] E.g., J. H. Kwabena Nknetia, *African Music in Ghana,* African Studies Series No. 1 (Chicago: Northwestern University Press, 1963; London: Longman, 1962), Joseph Kyagambiddwa, *African Music from the Source of the Nile* (New York: Praeger, 2 vols., 1955), p. 225, inc. music; E. K. K. Sempebwa, "Baganda Folk Songs: A. Rough Classification." *The Uganda Journal;* "Comment on Nknetia: Possession Dances." *Journal of the International Folk Music Council,* IX (1957), p. 8.

have won fame in the past, but now it is a different story. The public is
beginning to recognize the talents of the colored man in song composition.
There is hardly a popular music publisher in the business at present who
does not employ at least one Negro musician who can compose music, write
songs or make himself useful as a singer. Some firms employ two or three,
for since the advent of the coon song, the Negro has become a factor in
producing popular ditties or evolving new ideas in musical composition.[19]

In the spring of 1905, the first modern jazz band was heard for the
first time on a New York stage and probably on any stage. Organized at
The Marshall, it was known as the "Memphis Students" [20]—a singing, playing, dancing orchestra which made dominant use of banjos, mandolins,
guitars, saxophones and drums, plus a violin, a couple of brass instruments
and a double bass. Among the twenty performers were Ernest Hogan,
comedian, Abbie Mitchell, soprano and Ida Forsyne, dancer. The band,
with its unusual features, became a hit; one of its innovations was the
introduction of a dancing conductor, Will Dixon.

One of the original members of this orchestra, Jim Europe, later organized
the Clef Club, a chartered group so organized that it could send out
bands of from three to thirty musicians at any time, day or night. Will
Marion Cook helped them to prepare for the opening. The crowning event
was in May, 1912, when they gave a concert at Carnegie Hall with 125
performers. There were a few strings proper, most cellos and double basses,
a few wind instruments—cornets, saxophones, clarinets and trombones, a
battery of drums with the banjos, mandolins and guitars as the main part,
and a background of ten upright pianos. Later this band, with Jim Europe
as Director, helped to make Vernon and Irene Castle famous. When World
War I came, Europe assembled the men for the band of the 369th Infantry,
a noted Negro regiment made up of members of the 15th National Guard
Regiment from New York.

For a long time, Negro bands had been playing jazz at dances and in
honky-tonks. Ford Dabney organized and directed a jazz orchestra which
for a number of years was a feature of Florenz Ziegfeld's roof garden shows.
The year 1912 also marked the publication of Handy's first blues, "The
Memphis Blues," followed by the even more popular "St. Louis Blues" in
1914.

Building on the folk tradition and making use of the talents of the day,
between 1905 and 1912, four gifted Negro musicians "organized Negro

19 "Chance for Colored Composers." *The Cadenza*, IX, No. 1 (September, 1902),
p. 14.
20 James Weldon Johnson, *Black Manhattan* (New York, Alfred A. Knopf, 1930),
pp. 120–22.

music out of a broken, musically-illiterate dialect and made it a national and international music with its own peculiar idioms of harmony, instrumentation and technical style of playing." [21] They were Ford Dabney, James Reese Europe, Will Marion Cook and W. C. Handy. Alain Locke calls the 1912 Carnegie Hall Concert of Negro Music "The formal coming-out party" and adds that "Perhaps the transformation was too sudden; many did not recognize this folk music in full dress." Without minimizing the significance of Paul Whiteman's famous 1924 concert of "Classical Jazz" when George Gershwin's celebrated *Rhapsody in Blue* was premiered or of a similar concert of the Vincent Lopez orchestra the same year, Alain Locke contends that it is important "to remember the historically more significant concert at Carnegie Hall, May, 1912. For that night the Cinderella of Negro folk music found royal favor and recognition and under the wand of Negro musicians put off her kitchen rags. At the time ragtime grew up to full musical rank and the golden age of jazz really began."[22]

ARE NEGROES STILL PRODUCING FOLK MUSIC?

Toward a New Definition of Folk and Folk Music

For two hundred years or more, students and collectors agreed on the general definition of folk music. Typical is the one of Marion Bauer:

> Folk music is the unconscious expression in melody of the racial feelings, character and interests of a people. It is music created without benefit of scientific training, by the common people or peasantry, which chronicles their lives in terms of design, melody, and rhythm, and has become traditional among them.[23]

There was agreement, also, that folk music is anonymous and is handed down orally from one generation to another.

This agreement has been brought to an end by several developments: the ever-increasing popularity of recordings and the ascendancy of popular (or "the people's") music in the last twenty years; the more recent revival of interest in "folk music" and the growth of the hootenannies; the new

---

[21] Alain Locke, *The Negro and His Music* (Washington, D.C., The Associates in Negro Folk Education, 1936), pp. 65–66.

[22] *Ibid.*, p. 68.

[23] Marion Bauer, "Folk Music—A General Survey," in Nicholas Slonimsky (ed.), *The International Cyclopedia of Music and Musicians*, 6th ed., revised, Dodd, Mead & Company, New York 1952, p. 559.

surge of "gospel music," and the vital and new body of songs of protest and freedom.

Furthermore, there is a new interest in the place of music in society and the influence of social forces on its development. Many new uses have been made of this music, and the academicians as well as the perfomers have attempted social analyses which have cast new light on its meanings and functions.

All of this literature has resulted in a reevaluation of what constitutes folklore and folk music. Indeed, there is a vigorous attempt to find a new definition of "folk" and to make distinctions between folk music which is rural and "ethnic" and the urban folk music of the city streets.

One school of thought believes that folk music is different for each generation and that "it would be as unthinkable for the folk music of today to sound like that of Elizabethan England or 19th-Century America as it would for Stravinsky, say, or Samuel Barber to sound like the 16th-Century composer, Giovanni Palestrina." [24] The entire first issue of *Hootenanny, The National Folk Singing Magazine*,[25] is devoted to an exploration of this point of view, and of a new definition for folk music. Some important insights into the role of the Negro and the "Negroid" in the development of today's folk music are also included.[26]

Typical and varying viewpoints have been expressed by:

Irwin Silber, editor of *Sing Out:* ". . . it is what these young people are singing, and not what we think they should be singing, that constitutes folk music." [27]

William Rhodes: "Evidently, this movement is satisfying or is filling a need of young people today. . . . The important thing to recognize is its functional aspect." [28]

Alan Lomax: contends there is no urban folk music unless you are talking about blues and gospel music. The others are "caricatures of folk music" and it is coming from people who are "singing folksongs for profit, prestige or learning." [29]

Performers and students of folklore have always been concerned with

[24] Mort J. Golding, "We Have Something to Say: Peter, Paul and Mary." *Hootenanny, The National Folk Singing Magazine*, I, No. 1 (December, 1963), p. 10

[25] *Ibid.*, p. 74.

[26] Two recent symposia on this subject are worthy of mention: Ben. A. Botkin, moderator, "The Folksong Revival," a Symposium. *New York Folklore Quarterly*, XIX, No. 2 (June, 1963), pp. 83–142; Sam Hinton, ed., "Folk Music Today." *Sing Out!* XII, No. 1 (February–March, 1961), pp. 16–25.

[27] Botkin, *op. cit.*, p. 111.

[28] *Ibid.*, p. 114.

[29] *Ibid.*, p. 121.

variants and versions of folk material and performance, viewing these as inevitable results of the process of change and growth. Recently there has been considerable question regarding the old assumption that these changes were always the result of faulty oral transmission. Instead there is strong support for the thesis that the crucial factor is the singer's desire and freedom to use his material in a creative manner, which permits him to make the song his song, to relate it to the lives of those about him. "Folk music is produced when people treat songs creatively, and when their creativity results in the development of a recognizable framework of musical and poetic expression." [30]

Whose Music?

It is generally agreed that the main roots of American folk music are in Negro blues, work songs and spirituals, and British ballads as handed down orally. Many of the singers of Negro folk music emulate the great Negro folk singers of the Twenties and Thirties. The recent emergence of a coterie of white city performers of Negro country blues has provided subject matter for spirited debates about the possibility of blues being sung meaningfully by those who have "never lived or suffered the blues." These singers are emulating, in the most painstaking detail, the vocal and instrumental language of the Southern rural blues of the Negro.

John Hammond, Jr., a powerful singer and excellent guitarist and harmonica player, is described by many as the strongest white interpreter of Negro blues, and an interview with this new young singer presents the crux of the controversy. He is said to have "identified himself with another musical idiom than the one he was born to," and such questions as these are asked: Can any white person know enough about what it means to be black, can he have suffered enough to sing the Negro's blues? Why shouldn't he create his own idiom to express the anguish he feels instead of borrowing one that is not really his?

Many young white singers answer that styles and idioms are languages and that one can become eloquent in a language not his at birth. In order to do this, the rural Negro tradition must be understood, assimilated, and re-created with empathy.[31]

Peter Seeger laments the fact that there are "no Negro traditional jazz fans or folk fans," and he predicts that "it will be a long time before there are many young Negro singers who will choose to emulate Blind Lemon,

[30] Hinton, op. cit., p. 17.
[31] For a typical discussion of the above, see: Bob Shelton, "John Hammond, Young Giant of the Blues." Hootenanny, I, No. 1 (December, 1963), pp. 50–51, 68–69.

Ledbetter or Robert Johnson. I'm not sure," he continues, "what that tells us about folk music, but as the fight for integration succeeds in making available other outlets to Negro genius, American popular music as a whole will be the poorer." [32] The names of several Negroes are among the top of the best-seller list of popular folk singers today [33] but most of them are not singers in the "rural, ethnic" folk tradition.

White performers are primarily responsible for the revival of the jugband, which uses Negro folk instruments [34] and plays ragtime, jazz, blues and stomp music.

Gospel

"Gospel" is the term used to designate the traditional religious music of the Negro church. In many Negro churches today, the music, in kind and quality of content and performance, is not unlike that of many white Protestant churches. On the other hand, more and more white churches are "borrowing" the music literature and performer techniques and are producing a comparable "gospel" music in their services. Usually such music is found in Holiness, Sanctified, Pentecostal, but often also Baptist and Methodist churches of both races—most often, in storefront meeting places, but also in large traditional church buildings.

The music literature of gospel may be Negro Spirituals or traditional hymns and revival songs, but most of it is a current, specific body of new music. It is very spirited with its own idioms and performer techniques, many of which are common property in all Negro folk music, used in a distinctive way. Antiphony is probably the most basic ingredient. Almost everything that takes place in this Negro church is antiphonal: the sermon, the prayer, the Scripture reading, the song. There are always "leaders and responses," much improvisation and no audience. Everybody present participates, even if only by patting a foot in response to the rhythm, and thereby contributing to the "beat." In the course of one song there may be several antiphonal cells, each built around a singer or "shouter" whose improvisation is an emotional response to the words or rhythm, but all of which are integrated as a response to the leader who may be the preacher

[32] Quoted in: Gottlieb, Lou, "Hootspeh! The Former Chief Limelighter Flexes His Ph.D. in Musicology and Belts out Some Frank Comments on 'Folk.'" *Hootenanny*, I, No. 1 (December, 1963), p. 67.

[33] *E.g.*, Harry Belafonte, Josh White, Sonny Terry, Odetta.

[34] For discussion: *in re* Negro Folk instruments, *see* Courlander, *Negro Folk Music, U.S.A.*, Chapter XI, pp. 204–220; *in re* African folk instruments, *see* Nkita, *op. cit.*; *in re* jugband revival, *see* Bob Shelton, "A New Trend in Folk Music," *Hootenanny*, I, No. 1 (December, 1963), pp. 12–14, 69.

or a soloist. This participation is not only vocal; it is also importantly instrumental: the piano and/or organ, and often also, drums, horns, guitars, bass fiddle. It is not uncommon to see a member of the congregation come up with a tambourine at some moment of emotional fervor. There is much handclapping, which can become very complex in its rhythm.

By the mid-Forties, this gospel tradition in Negro churches was known to the general public, mainly because of the growing popularity of the gospel singer, Mahalia Jackson.[35] Other individuals and groups have followed her.[36] Indeed, there are those who argue that some of them are better. At least one singer, Hattie Parker, recorded gospel much earlier, in the Twenties.

Gospel has become big business: publishing, recording, concert artists, managers, etc., and there has been much traffic between the blues and jazz field and the church, a traffic of personalities and of styles, even repertoire. The traditional blues came out of the slave church music. The influence of gospel today on popular music is very strong and the return to the church of many blues and rock-and-roll singers and the countermovement of gospel singers into the "pops" field have resulted in much cross-fertilization of styles and techniques.[37]

Sweet Chariot, a New York City night club, features gospel with all the wailing and shouting. Hostesses are clad in choir robes that reach to the thigh, where they meet opera length stockings, with small wings attached to the shoulders of their gowns and wire haloes topping their coiffures. Customers, predominantly white, are offered tambourines for use as participants in the music.

"By now," as Martin Williams says, "rhythm and blues, rock and roll, and jazz probably have achieved a kind of amalgamation in a certain urban blues style one hears more and more. . . . Such a style is becoming an established

[35] Her record "Move On Up a Little Higher" became the first (1945) big "Gospel" hit. It sold over a million copies. Born in New Orleans, Mahalia Jackson is one of the few gospel singers who will not take her music to night clubs. She has appeared often on radio, television and in concerts, with jazz orchestras and singers such as Duke Ellington and Dinah Shore. She has demonstrated that "gospel" has a universal appeal, not only in the United States but around the world.
[36] A few years ago the Pittsburgh Courier introduced gospel singers to its theatrical poll. The response was tremendous, and the list of nominations long. Among the top in the field are Mahalia Jackson, Rosetta Thorpe, the Ward Singers, the Boyer Brothers, Ernestine Washington, Georgia Peach, Lottie Peavy, The Five Blind Boys, Pilgrim Travelers, Sweet Chariots, Gospel Harmonettes, Spirit of Memphis Singers, the Statesmen, etc.
[37] For an excellent and detailed discussion of this interchange, see Martin Williams, "Free Flow." Down Beat, Music 64 (9th Yearbook), pp. 80–83. Also see Arna Bontemps, "Rock, Church, Rock." Common Ground, III, No. 1 (Autumn 1942), pp. 75–80, and Martin Williams, "Gospel at the Box Office." The Saturday Review, August, 1963, p. 41.

one, at least in urban Negro neighborhoods and spilling over into white ones as well." [38] He believes that jazz and rock-and-roll turned to gospel for renewed inspiration, and that its influence is clearly distinguishable.

Even in so sophisticated a spot as the theme melody for one of television's most popular programs, *What's My Line,* the influence of gospel music is evident. This melody was recently reorchestrated from "cool jazz" to "soul jazz" which, according to Martin Williams, means that "a few triplets, bent notes, and other devices borrowed from Gospel music have been introduced into the light, muted orchestration."

This event is one of the last links in a chain of popularization that began in the Fifties; by now devices of gospel pervade American popular music, top to bottom. "Hardly a rock-and-roll record, hardly a currently hip jazz performance, hardly a jazz-derived television or movie background score, indeed, hardly a sticky-string ballad arrangement appears these days without Gospel derivations of some kind." [39]

Freedom Songs

Music played an important role in the historic March on Washington of August 28, 1963. Not only the impassioned words of the Reverend Martin Luther King's—"I have a dream . . ."—but the songs, the chants, the spirituals, that resounded throughout the day made a total blend of "Freedom Now!"

The musical participants were as diverse as the crowd. Some of them were: Marion Anderson and Camilla Williams, of the concert world; Mahalia Jackson, queen of gospel singers; Joan Baez and Odetta, outstanding balladeers in authentic style; Peter, Paul and Mary, a popular and typically sophisticated trio of the urban folk school. In addition, there was the vigorous singing of the people within the integration movement itself: The Freedom Singers, four young field workers of SNCC [40] who began singing together specifically to spread the gospel of racial equality; the CORE [41] delegates from Mississippi and Alabama and other areas, who again and again broke into spontaneous song as they marched.

And finally there was the unforgettable sight of 200,000 marchers, many with arms linked and hands clasped, swaying in rhythm to the galvanic Spiritual, "We Shall Overcome." "These freedom songs have served and are serving with great effectiveness as common denominators of the Negro

[38] Martin Williams, *Ibid.,* p. 83.
[39] *Ibid.,* p. 80.
[40] SNCC—Student Nonviolent Coordinating Committee.
[41] CORE—Congress of Racial Equality.

people; they weld individuals with individual doubts and terrors and weaknesses—into a dynamic and inexorable striking force." [42]

There is no doubt about the importance of song in the freedom movement
today. In *Sing Out*, Sam Clark describes the folk process involved in the
making of these songs, which change almost every time they are sung. "Every
time a leader dies or a man is brave, or a group of students go to jail, or a
battle seems to go badly, these songs, born decades ago, become new songs.
A song will start as a shout and change to a chant, or a joke, a hymn, or
a prayer, as the mood of the moment changes." [43]

For example, in an integrated work camp sponsored by the Highlander
Center in the Smoky Mountains of Tennessee, Negro campers fresh from
Birmingham demonstrations had brought their music with them, but it soon
became the music of the camp with verses adapted to their concerns and
experiences. The leader would weave around the melody freely and bass
voices would improvise between the lines. "The sound was a composite of
blues, spirituals, and rock-and-roll that fitted perfectly with the songs we
sang and the things we sang about." [44]

Pete Seeger, in "The Integration Battle: [45] A 'Singing' Movement"
describes songs sung in Greenwood, Mississippi. The most popular one was:

> We got the Light of Freedom
> I'm gonna let it shine
> Let it shine, let it shine, let it shine.

Others, also adaptations of Negro Spirituals:

> We'll never turn back no more.
> Everybody wants freedom (The "Amen" Chorus).
> Ain't gonna let segregation turn me around.
> Keep your eyes on the prize, Hold on!
> I'm gonna walk the streets of Jackson, Some of these days.
> O Freedom!
> We shall not be moved.

The song "We Shall Overcome" has been called the theme song of the
movement. A song book by that title [46] is the first collection of freedom songs

[42] Sherman, *op. cit.*, p. 81.

[43] Sam Clark, "Freedom Songs and the Folk Process." *Sing Out!* XIV, No. 1
(February–March, 1964), p. 13.

[44] Sam Clark. *Loc. cit.*

[45] Pete Seeger, "The Integration Battle: A 'Singing' Movement." (Report from
Greenwood, Mississippi). *Broadside*, No. 30.

[46] Guy and Candic Carawan (eds.), *We Shall Overcome: Songs of the Southern
Freedom Movement*. (New York: Oak Publications, The Student Nonviolent Coordinating Committee, 1963), p. 112.

of the integration movement. It contains more than seventy songs and is profusely illustrated with photographs.

A publication "issued twice monthly to distribute typical songs and stimulate the writing of such songs" is *Broadside*,[47] containing songs with such titles as:

> The "Literacy Test" Song
> The Ballad of Oxford, Miss.
> Freedom Train
> Ballad of Medgar Evers
> I Can See a New Day
> Talking Birmingham Jam
> Talking Civil Rights
> Get on Board, Children, Let's Fight for Human Rights
> I Ain't a-Scared O' Your Jail, Cause I Want My Freedom Now

All these songs have sets of "zipper" words from Birmingham, such as Bull, hose, dogs, water; from Greenwood, such as dogs, Mayor Simpson, shooting, county farm, bombing, hose, etc. Many use old tunes; many have original tunes.

White composers have written many of these songs and some are directed to whites. An example is Bill Oliver's "Freedom Today"; it is subtitled "White Man's Song." The first lines of the two verses are:

> I've been waiting too long to meet my brother. . . .
> Time to walk out and stand up for my brother. . . .[48]

Leonard Feather has reported on how jazzmen responded to the crucial year 1963 in race relations. He states that "in 1963 every musician, Negro or white, was more aware than ever before of the struggle for equality . . ." and he reports in detail on three main forms of involvement: first, direct musical action through integration of one's own band or working toward integration in other bands; second, indirect action through participation in benefits for the National Association for the Advancement of Colored People, the Congress of Racial Equality, the Student Nonviolent Co-ordinating Committee, the Southern Christian Leadership Conference, the Urban League, etc.; third, direct extramusical action such as taking part in freedom marches or sit-ins, and working directly with the integration organizations. He goes on to list the ways in which musicians can participate more actively during 1964.

---

[47] Sis Cunningham, Editor; Gil Turner and Pete Seeger, Advisory, PO Box 193, New York 25, New York.

[48] Leonard Feather, "On the Racial Front." *Downbeat*, Music '64, 9th Yearbook, p. 20.

COMPOSERS USING NEGRO THEMATIC MATERIAL

Negro Composers

Negro thematic material was first used by minstrelsy, first by whites and later by Negroes who, in the period from the late 1880's to 1912, demeaned themselves to the popular taste. In the 1890's the "pickaninny" and the "coon" were discovered and the songs were "funny" at the expense of the Negro. Ernest Hogan, a Negro, wrote the song that created so many tense racial situations that the title—"All Coons Look Alike to Me"—became the byword and an epithet of derision. In later life he regretted having written it. The story of this era is best told by James Weldon Johnson in *Black Manhattan*.[49] Such names as Williams and Walker, Cole and Johnson can furnish important insights into some problems of Negro stereotypes even today.

Will Marion Cook, a very competent composer, was one of the first, if not the first, to take what was then known as ragtime and build a musically good show. *Clorindy—The Origin of the Cake Walk*, with lyrics by Paul Laurence Dunbar, opened in 1898. Others by Cook followed, featuring Abbie Mitchell, his wife, an artist of great musical ability and training. His work as a trained musician and composer gained for him his greatest acclaim. Cook studied violin under Joachim in Berlin.

In 1905, Samuel Coleridge-Taylor, an English Negro, used Negro thematic material in his *Twenty-Four Negro Melodies* for the piano. His interest in Negro music had begun when he heard Negro Spirituals sung by the Fisk Jubilee Singers during their first tour of England (1899). Later, visits to the United States sharpened his interest and added to his understanding. His first visit to this country in 1904 was of great importance. He had just been appointed conductor of the Handel Society of London, was professor at the Royal College of London and was recognized as one of England's foremost composers. He came to the leading music centers of the United States and conducted some of America's leading orchestras in his own compositions.

This was a new experience for the American Negro, the American white and for Coleridge-Taylor himself, whose discovery of prejudice and discrimination helped him toward a kinship with the American Negro he had not felt before. Many of his later works were based on Negro themes. He

[49] James Weldon Johnson, *Black Manhattan* (New York: Alfred A. Knopf, 1930), p. 284.

came to America again three times before his death in 1912. Each time he gave abundantly help, advice and sympathy, and he inspired new hope and a broader vision in musicians, young and old.[50]

Warner Lawson refers to the "Afro-American Five"; Harry T. Burleigh (1866–1949); Clarence Cameron White (1880–1960); R. Nathaniel Dett (1882–1943); William Grant Still (1895–   ) and William Levi Dawson (1899–   ). Lawson says, "Covering a total span of 97 years they bridge successfully the gap between raw folk music and concert music. They were well educated, cultured and refined in spirit, highly trained in their art and recognized for the quality of their creative work."[51] They all made use of Negro thematic material in different ways.

Harry T. Burleigh studied at the National Conservatory of Music while Anton Dvorák was the director. He studied harmony with Rubin Goldmark and counterpoint with Max Spicker. He had more than one hundred art songs published, but his greatest contribution was, perhaps, as the first composer to arrange Negro spirituals into art songs acceptable for use on the concert stage. There was a period when every concert artist included a group of Negro spirituals, usually his arrangements, on each program, even as many Negro artists do today.

R. Nathaniel Dett was born in a Canadian community consisting of former slaves who had escaped. There he heard them sing the old Spirituals, and the new spirituals they had created since their arrival in Canada. Although he never quoted these folk songs directly, all of his compositions were strongly influenced by them and by his experiences among the singers.

---

[50] The immediate results of his visits were: (1) Formation of music societies and clubs by Negroes in all large coast cities. (2) Emphasis on study and composition of academic music, demand for trained musicians as directors. (3) A turning away from Spirituals. (4) Promotion of study groups and music clubs of striving young musicians. Many, if not all, of the Negro singers or other musicians who achieved success during these years were first introduced to the white public as soloist for one or several of these clubs or societies. Roland Hayes and Marion Anderson are notable examples. (5) Establishment of music schools and conservatories among Negroes.

Some later developments from his visits: (1) The organization by Carl Diton of the National Association of Negro Musicians (1919) with stated objectives which fit well the above. (2) Music and art exhibits of the Negro musicians' accomplishments in the academic tradition. Notable was the one held in the Boston Public Library, October, 1922. For detailed description see: W.S.S., "They Compose as well," *Boston Evening Transcript*, October 25, 1922. (3) Establishment and maintenance of foreign scholarships for extended study of promising Negro musicians. Notable were those engineered by E. Azalia Hackley by which Carl Diton, pianist, and Clarence Cameron White, violinist, studied in Europe.

[51] Warner Lawson, "American Negro Music and the American Negro Composer, 1862–1962." A Voice of America broadcast, September, 1962, pp. 14 from text transcribed in nineteen typewritten pages.

Especially noteworthy are his smaller works for the piano such as "Juba Dance," "Magnolia Suite," "In the Bottoms," and "His Song." Dett's masterful setting in choral form of the Spiritual "Listen to the Lambs" represented, Lawson says, "the earliest effort by a Negro composer to use the folk idiom in an extended art form." [52]

Clarence Cameron White, the violinist and composer, made wide use of Negro thematic material. His arrangements of spirituals and his suite for violin, *From the Cotton Fields,* are "valued for real imagination and refined musicianship." [53] His opera, *Ouanga,* earned the David Bispham Medal.

William Grant Still is the first symphonic composer among Negro musicians. His larger works include the *Afro-American Symphony;* another symphony in G minor, subtitled *"Song of a New Race,"* and two operas, *Blue Steel* and *Troubled Island.* The most successful of his three ballets is *Lenox Avenue,* which depicts Negro life in Harlem.

Still's *Afro-American Symphony* has four movements. He makes use of a choice of instruments to produce a melody with a peculiar "whining effect"; this is his blues movement. In the third movement he adds the banjo to the score because of its association with the Negro in Southern United States. He invents his own melody and does not quote Negro folk song.

William Levi Dawson, director of the Tuskegee Choir for many years, used Negro themes exclusively. His one symphonic effort, *Negro Symphony,* was first presented by the Philadelphia Orchestra with Leopold Stokowski conducting. He is also known for his arrangements of spirituals for chorus.

White Composers

White composers have also made use of Negro thematic material in various ways. Academic works based on Negro thematic material appeared as early as 1886, the publication date of the first symphonic work using Negro folk song.[54] Forty years before that, Louis Gottschalk (1829–69), an American, had used Creole songs from Louisiana.[55]

While visiting America, the Bohemian composer, Anton Dvorák (with his Negro student, Harry T. Burleigh, as his interpreter of Negro music), became so well acquainted with Spirituals that he made use of Negro

[52] *Ibid.,* p. 16.
[53] *Ibid.,* p. 17.
[54] George W. Chadwick's *Second Symphony,* in which the Scherzo shows definite traces of a plantation melody.
[55] Louis Moreau Gottschalk's *Le Bananier* (1845) (subtitled "Negro Song"), *Bamboula* (1845) (subtitled "Negro Dance") and *Banjo* (1851).

thematic material in his major compositions.[56] Many other composers followed his lead.[57] Daniel Gregory Mason's *String Quartet on Negro Themes,* Opus 9, published in 1919, quotes for its theme the spiritual, "You may bury me in the East"; in the second movement, "Deep River"; in the third, "Shine, Shine, I'll Meet you in the Morning," "Deep River" again, and "Oh, Holy Lord."

Appalachia is a theme and variations on an old slave song with final chorus, for full orchestra, by Frederick Delius.

Sonata Virginianesque, for violin and piano, is a work by John Powell. Its first two movements use songs based on Negro themes: "Done poison my wife" and a Negro love song, "Lula My Darlin'."

This is a small sampling of the uses made of Negro thematic material. In the popular tradition the illustrations are myriad. "Song detectives" such as Sigmund Spaeth have found Negro melodies frequently used.

THE NEGRO AND "OTHER" MUSIC

The "Other" Music of the Slave

The slave's music was not confined to his folk repertoire. There is much evidence of the musical ability of the slave, and of the use made of it in the social and civic life of the total community. Eighteenth-century advertisements for runaway slaves contained descriptions of slaves who might be trying to get jobs playing for dances for whites, using European instruments.[58] Many travelers have described such occasions. Buckingham, describing a musical occasion in White Sulphur Springs, Virginia, 1839, says ". . . the orchestra was filled by negro [sic] musicians; the bands being almost always formed of coloured people." [59]

In Wiley's study of *Southern Negroes 1861–65,* he discusses the role of the Negro body servants of soldiers in the Union Army and states that "a

---

[56] E.g., Dvořák's *Symphony in E Minor,* Op. 95 ("From the New World"), *Quartet in F Major,* Op. 96, and *Quintet in E Major,* Op. 97.

[57] E.g., Schoenfield's *The Rural Symphony in G Minor* (1892), *In the Sunny South* (1899), *Sonata in G Minor for Violin and Piano;* Henry Gilbert used Negro thematic material. *The Americanesque* for orchestra (1903), *Comedy Overture on Negro Themes* (1910); Delius, *Appalachia,* a theme and variations on an old slave song for full chorus (1907).

[58] Anon., "18th Century Slave Advertisements." *Journal of Negro History,* I (April, 1916), pp. 163–216.

[59] James Silk Buckingham, *The Slave States of America,* Vol. II (London: Fisher, Son and Company, 1842), p. 336.

few of the body servants were sometimes called on to act as musicians for the units to which their masters were attached." Josephus Blake, servant of General John B. Gordon, said that he and two other servants provided the music to which Gordon's regiment marched. One played the fife and one beat the drum.[60] Strangely enough, Congress, by an early statute, provided for regular colored musicians to receive the same pay as regularly enlisted white musicians.[61]

The Music of the Free Negro

One of the greatest anomalies of social history is that while millions of Negroes were illiterate slaves many Negroes were free and often enjoyed the friendship and encouragement of the "best people" in their communities. Many of these Negroes were gifted, trained musicians, composers and performing artists, acclaimed by the press and persons of position in America and around the world.

Free Negroes were most active musically in the period from 1806–65. Negro minstrelsy as portrayed by white performers was very popular in this period and many of the free Negroes felt compelled to negate the characterization of the Negro popularized by these minstrels in both England and the United States.

Thomas J. Bowers, a tenor, born in Philadelphia in 1836, described as the "American Mario" by the critics of his day, illustrates the resentment of minstrelsy felt by the free Negro; he wrote, "What induced me more than anything else to appear in public was to give the lie to 'Negro serenaders' [minstrels] and to show to the world that colored men and women could sing classical music as well as the members of the other race by whom they have been so terribly vilified." [62]

In Hamilton, Canada, where a concert appearance had been arranged for him, the management had refused to admit a party of six Negroes to first-class seats, Bowers refused to perform if there were any discrimination.[63] He won his point and this was probably the first time a Negro artist used his artistic appeal to protest discrimination. His repertoire included arias from the standard operas and songs from the oratorios of the old masters.

---

[60] Bell Irvin Wiley, *Southern Negroes, 1861–1865* (New Haven: Yale University Press, 1938); Yale Historical Publications, XXXI, p. 136.

[61] See William Matthews (ed.), *Statutes at Large, First Congress*, 1862, 1st Session, Chapter 29.

[62] Quoted in Maud Cuney-Hare, *Negro Musicians and Their Music* (Washington, D.C.: The Associated Publishers, Inc., 1936), p. 201.

[63] *Ibid.*, p. 200.

Elizabeth Taylor Greenfield,[64] better known as the "Black Swan," was reared by a Quaker lady who early recognized her extraordinary voice and gave her training. After she sang for the Buffalo Musical Association (October, 1851) she was immediately compared to the greatest sopranos of her time: Jenny Lind, Parodi, Sontag, Malibran and Grisi. She had a sensational range of three and a quarter octaves (a few notes above Jenny Lind's highest). She toured the free states and then in 1853, left for Europe, after singing to a farewell audience in New York of four thousand persons. Laudatory press notices and testimonials tell of her career as singer, teacher and instrumentalist.

Frank Johnson from Philadelphia, an accomplished conductor, arranger and composer went to England, Scotland, and Ireland with his own band in 1843. After a command performance, Queen Victoria presented him with a silver trumpet in recognition of his artistry as a soloist.[65]

New Orleans, Virginia and Connecticut produced many other outstanding musicians, composers, pianists, directors of opera houses, violin cellists, organists, etc. The Luca Family—a singing family of six with each of them doubling on instruments—met and traveled with the famous Hutchinson Family, giving joint concerts.[66]

Among the earliest of Negro composers whose music made no use of Negro thematic material was James Hemmenway of Philadelphia, whose sentimental song entitled, "That Rest So Sweet Like Bliss Above" (1829) was published in the leading journal [67] of that day. John E. Bruce, a President of the Negro Historical Society of New York City, wrote an excellent article [68] about a number of these early musicians.

After Emancipation

Justin Holland's *Comprehensive Method for the Guitar* (1874) was standard for many years and his name appeared more often than any other in the music catalogs of that period under the heading of Guitar Music.

---

[64] The facts regarding her life are from *A Brief Memoir of the "Black Swan," Miss E. T. Greenfield, the American Vocalist* (London, 1853), p. 16. Includes testimonials regarding her appearances in various parts of the U.S. and Europe. Also see James Monroe Trotter, *Music and Some Highly Musical People* (Boston: Lee and Shepard; New York: C. T. Dillingham, 1878), pp. 202–204.

[65] See Trotter, *op. cit.*, pp. 306–08.

[66] For further details see Trotter, *op. cit.*, pp. 88–105; also Hare, *op. cit.*, pp. 204–05.

[67] *The Casket Flowers of Literature, Wit and Sentiment.* No. 10, October, 1829, p. 476.

[68] J. E. Bruce, "A History of Negro Musicians," *The Southern Workman*, XLV, No. 10 (October, 1916), pp. 569–573.

Gussie L. Davis wrote more than four hundred sentimental ballads which were "hits" at the turn of the century,[69] only two of which referred in any way to Negroes. Some of his most popular numbers were "In the Baggage Coach Ahead" (1896), "The Fatal Wedding (1893), "When Nellie was Raking the Hay" (1884) and "The Light House by the Sea" (1887). "Sob ballads" or "tear jerkers" were his specialty.

James Monroe Trotter, another Negro, published his *Music and Some Highly Musical People* (1878) just thirteen years after emancipation. It consists primarily of biographical sketches of Negro composers and musicians who specialized in the non-Negro academic repertoire of that day. The appendix of his book contains full scores of thirteen compositions by Negroes in which Negro thematic material is not used.[70]

Some of Harry T. Burleigh's best-known compositions not only are not "Negroid," but are about subjects distinctly white. His "Jean" has been a perennial favorite since 1903. Many songs which he dedicated to outstanding concert artists of that day became a part of their repertoire. Burleigh's "Little Mother of Mine" (1917) was made famous by Enrico Caruso.

Modern Negro Composers

The three most outstanding contemporary Negro composers who do not consciously write "Negro music," Howard Swanson, Julia Perry and Ulysses Kay, are thoroughly trained and securely grounded as composers. Each of the three "seeks an expression through music without the fetters of a 'school' or an 'ideology.' "[71]

Swanson, a former student of Nadia Boulanger, now lives and works in Paris, but received a large part of his training in the United States. His *Short Symphony* won the New York Critics Circle Award as the best new orchestral work during the 1950–51 season. In addition, his works include *Night Music*, for woodwinds, horns and strings; *Nocturne*, for violin and piano; *Suite*, for cello and piano; *Music for Strings*, and a number of songs.

Julia Perry's expert craftsmanship is evident in her *Stabat Mater*, a large work for contralto soloist and string orchestra. Miss Perry studied at the Westminster Choir College, with the Italian composer Luigi Dallapiccola and later with Nadia Boulanger in France. She has also written a *Short Piece for Orchestra* and has made choral arrangements of spirituals.

[69] See Edward B. Marks, *They All Sang* (New York: The Viking Press, 1934), pp. 34, 73, 81, 82. He is described by Marks as "the first prominent colored song writer" of ballads.

[70] Trotter, *loc. cit.*, 353 + 152 pages of music.

[71] Lawsons, *op. cit.*, p. 18.

Ulysses Kay has written in widely divergent fields. His works include the score for the documentary film, *The Quiet One; Of New Horizons;* an *Overture;* a *Cantata;* a *Suite for Strings,* and an opera, *The Juggler of Our Lady.* He has also written many works for choral groups. He has won two Prix de Rome prizes, the George Gershwin Prize, and a Fulbright scholarship. He was one of the American composers chosen to visit the Soviet Union in 1958 as part of the cultural exchange program.

Today there are many artists whose interests and skills are in the standard repertoire of our time. Although their repertoire usually includes a group of Negro spirituals, when they perform it is not as a Negro artist, but as an artist who happens also to be a Negro. However, it is probable that their inescapable identification with the Negro community furnishes them with additional incentive to do a good job.

Negro Shape-Note Singing

In the southeast corner of Alabama a unique musical organization involving large groups of Negroes has been in operation for more than seventy years.[72] It merits consideration in his article because of its sociological implication and its role in the life of these people.

These Negroes "have developed shape-note singing to such a degree that it claims the zealous participation of the larger portion of its population. Successful participation implies a complex reading skill which is acquired only with painstaking effort." [73] The organization and proceedings are well defined and the notes in the song books have different shapes. There is a leader who directs in an accepted fashion; no musical instrument of any kind is present. The pitch is given by the tuner who has absolute pitch. The singers produce a "shrill, hard, raspy and often strained" tone quality but with an "accuracy little short of phenomenal. . . . No one is a professional musician, none interviewed went beyond the fifth grade and some were never in school. There is no outside stimulation or sponsorship and no hope of profit." [74] It is a cultural creation unique in the Negro community. The literature consists of some well-known old hymns but the verse and melody of others are original. The songs are rendered first in *fa, sol, la, mi* syllables, and then the words are sung.

John Work muses that, "Regrettably to one whose interest in Negro folksongs has been lifetime, shape-note singing in southeast Alabama has

---

[72] John Wesley Work, "Plantation Meistersinger." *Musical Quarterly,* XXVII, No. 1 (January, 1941), pp. 97–106.

[73] Work, *Loc. cit.*

[74] *Ibid.,* p. 105.

stifled all other folk expressions. No spirituals or other folk-songs are sung. There is no opportunity afforded for their development. Time which might be given to camp meetings and church associations . . . is consumed in shape-note conventions." Then too, "the musical tastes of the people have developed an appreciation for the intellectual aspects of musicianship rather that an appreciation . . . for the sensuousness of a single strand of melody." [75] What the implications are here poses another interesting problem for Negro music research.

SOME OTHER CONTRIBUTIONS OF NEGRO MUSIC

The only true American instrument, the banjo,[75a] was invented during slavery. A free Negro, James Bland, added the fifth string and created a more versatile instrument which immediately became known as the "Bland Banjo." [76]

The Negro folk performer influenced the development of better instruments which have found their places not only in the jazz bands, but in the symphonic and other orchestras of the world. The folk performer had not learned from a traditional music teacher, or from the music itself which he could not read, that his instrument had limits, that one does not play above or below certain notes on a specific instrument; he often demanded much more from his instrument than it could give without damage to it. As a result, he often found it necessary to return the instrument for repair. When this happened frequently, the makers of these instruments made the improvements indicated. Through the years these demands have produced better and better instruments to fulfill the needs of these Negro folk performers.

R. Emmet Kennedy quotes Edmund Clarence Stedman as crediting Negro songs for the novel and artistic effects found in some of the poems of Edgar

[75] *Ibid.*, p. 106.

[75a] Thomas Jefferson, in his Notes on Virginia; written in the year 1781 . . . (n.i.) 1782, p. 257, is the reference usually quoted as the earliest written comment on the "banjar" as an invention of the slave. Dena J. Epstein, op. cit., p. 201, quotes a reference written seven years before Jefferson (journal of Nicolas Cresswell, 1774–1777. New York, L. MacVeagh, The Dial Press, 1924; pp. 17–19.) His journal entry was May 29, 1774.

[76] John Jay Daly, *A Song in His Heart* (Philadelphia, The John C. Winston Co., 1951), p. 63. Bland also composed at least three all-time favorites which many people think were written by Stephen Foster. They are: "Carry Me Back to Old Virginny," "Oh, Dem Golden Slippers," "In the Evening by the Moonlight."

Allen Poe (notably "The Raven") and of Charles Kingsley.[77] This, too, suggests that Negro music research has many fields as yet almost untouched which could further document the role of Negro music.[78]

From the days of minstrelsy to the latest Broadway hit, the Negro community has been the chief source of the styles, forms and much of the content, and spirit which have characterized each of the different periods of popular music.[79] In the diffusion of this music throughout the world there has been a revolution in musical taste.[80] Music has moved into cafés, beer halls, movies and, through television, into private homes, consistently projecting Negro music and/or performers. Jazz, and what some musicologists have labeled as "The Negroid"[81] in popular music, have played an important role in the democratization of taste, bands, and audiences.

Much of the literature about jazz is reduced to such practical matters as mixed bands, segregation, discrimination in hiring and such questions as: Why did the spread of jazz evoke such intense, emotional opposition? What is the actual process of diffusion of jazz from Negroes to whites? And of what significance is it that jazz brings together Negroes and whites in a relationship of social equality? As Monroe Berger says, "There is perhaps no other area of Negro-white contact . . . where the Negro is accepted so fully as an equal (and so often admired as a superior) without condescension."[82]

In Bertrand Russell's anthology, *The Impact of America on European Culture*, Cooper states that American Negro music has wrought a wholesome change in European music. "Music had become," he said, "too note-bound, too highly organized, with no scope left for the creative instincts of the individual performer. . . . American Negro bands, with their brilliant improvising trumpeters, clarinetists or saxophone players, reintroduced this element of creativeness. . . ."[83]

[77] R. Emmet Kennedy, "The Negro Spiritual," *Disque* II, No. 9 (November, 1931), pp. 382–88.

[78] See Zelma George, *Implications and Applications of the Bibliographical Index of Negro Music as a Tool* (unpublished doctoral dissertation, New York University), pp. 215–24 for suggested areas of needed research.

[79] There are many books which discuss this point. One of the best discussions is by Arnold Shaw, "Popular Music from Minstrel Songs to Rock 'n' Roll," in Paul Henry Lang (ed.), *One Hundred Years of Music in America* (New York: G. Schirmer, Inc., 1961), pp. 140–68.

[80] See Monroe Berger, "Jazz: Resistance to the Diffusion of a Culture-Pattern." *Journal of Negro History*, XXXII, No. 4 (October 1947), pp. 461–494.

[81] Notable in the use of this term is Wilder Hobson, in "Jazz," *The Encyclopedia Britannica* (1953), pp. 982–84.

[82] Berger, *op. cit.*, p. 494.

[83] Martin Cooper, "Revolution in Musical Taste," in Bertrand Russell (ed.), *The Impact of America on European Culture*. Boston: Beacon Press, 1951, p. 71.

WHERE DOES NEGRO MUSIC GO FROM HERE?

The Negro musical culture exists in several simultaneous active layers of which now one and now another is lifted into importance by a complexity of circumstances. The coexistence of these various layers makes possible the surprising situation that continuity and discontinuity are simultaneously present, that the ends and the beginnings of epochs overlap, that revolution and evolution coexist.

Where does Negro music go from here? It goes, of course, with the Negro because it is part of the structure and process of his life. Where does the Negro go from here? The reply is, "Which Negro?" Certainly the Negro is infinitely plural and he will continue to produce a music which is many sided.

As long as Negroes are denied the opportunity to become fully integrated into American life, and are subjected to isolation in the physical and/or psychological ghettos where communications and participation are more and more concentratedly Negro, they will have race consciousness and distinctive characteristics.

Negroes must live within the American culture, make their adaptations to the same culture, accept the same social goals, but with major limitations on their opportunities to develop the skills needed to achieve them.

In such a situation Negroes will continue to find their music a functionally effective bond. This will be true to a greater or lesser degree, whether or not the specific Negro has been able to move out of the physical ghetto; it will be modified, of course, by his attitude toward his Negroness, his reaction toward or away from it.

Certainly for all Negroes the achievement of Negroes becomes a psychological pattern of continuity with a recognizable past, present, and future. The experiences which come from creative and performing artists (with periodic performances or recitals and successes, hits, favorable critical notices, good press) provide acceptance of themselves and their music into the mainstream of universal music. This position of esteem which one Negro acquires in the community, nation, or world, is felt by all Negroes. Thus, in numerous direct and indirect ways, Negro life is strengthened by individual as well as collective experiences.

Negro music is a social function of the individual Negro. It has served as a refuge, an escape from the hard, competitive complex and often anonymous actions one may meet in the life about him, if not, indeed, an escape from the race itself on occasion.

And yet, Negro culture is breaking down on the fringes as more individuals move into the mainstream of American life, lose some of their race-consciousness, experience some of the cultural life of the total *community* and begin to relate themselves to the majority culture. The musical life of these Negroes will move away from the music of the Negro community, because it will no longer be functional for them.

But Negro music has had almost as profound an influence in the life of white people as it has had in that of the Negro. As a "collective representation" it has provided the American people with a documentary of social comment, criticism and protest from the Negro people, for it is an important body of literature. Its success is evidence of the potential of the Negro, if given an opportunity to develop. It has provided composers everywhere with raw materials of styles, forms, content, spirit.

Negro music has been a social process, conscious at times and unconscious at others, which has been effective in altering the functional relations between Negro and white individuals and groups, establishing communication, reducing conflict and promoting reciprocal adjustments, altering attitudes and behavior patterns to the end of a better accommodation of the races.

It has been a tremendous contribution to the diffusion of Western music throughout the world, making for the democratization of taste, of bands, theaters, audiences; it has been largely responsible for bringing the common man into the concert halls where he has often participated in a common enterprise of creation, as unmodified "folk."

Today, Negro music is providing an effective social device for channeling into nonviolent, creative action, the energy which legitimate discontent, impatience, and often anger, have created.

Is it not possible that the role which Negro music has played, and is continuing to play, in today's racial crises, has been the currency with which the Negro has bought some precious time in which all the people of this country are being given the opportunity to help America become what it purports to be—a Democracy of free men!

> There is no truer truth obtainable
> By man, than comes of music.
> —from *Parleying with Certain People: Charles Avison,*
> by Robert Browning

chapter 21

Blues, Jazz and the Negro

Le Roi Jones

When black men first came to this continent in the seventeenth century, they were Africans, and the music they made was quite naturally an African music. The first "work songs" were those that had been brought over from the old country. The African work songs served equally to help the Africans in the American white man's fields as they had served him in his own, since the impetus that creates a work song was still the same, i.e., the agricultural labor, even though the worker was now in bondage.

What developed next was the Afro-American work song, songs which were combinations of older African songs, and the stray words, phrases, ditties or songs the slaves picked up in the West. When the black man began to sing strictly in American, for instance, he had usually become an American.

The shouts, hollers, coon yells, arwhoolies, etc., of the early American Negro were the closest ancestors to both the latterly developed more formal music we have known as blues, as well as American Negro religious music. And it is in American Negro music (and of course religion) in most of its forms, that the most easily discernible African influences remain even to this day.

Blues as it became more formal utilized the call and response A-A-B form that seems to come directly from the type of song most common to West Africa, which Western musicologists call antiphonal. An easy analogy can be made between (1) a simple A-B, call and response song for leader and group (a type of song that was brought over to America in its exact form also, as a variety of work song), and (2) a kind of song to be sung by one person, where the first line of the song is sung twice (leader), and the third line, sometimes rhymed, always dissimilar and always a direct comment on the first two lines is the response.

Primitive blues differs from the older work songs, highly rhythmical shouts, yells and hollers, in one very important sense because it developed as a music that was sung in one's leisure, as music sung for pleasure. In this sense it is easy to see how the emancipation of the slaves contributed to an actual change of form in Negro music. But content changed as form does, and in some cases because it does. So even the lyrics of the more formal blues would change, since the people who were making these more formal blues were quite different from the older shouters and field hollerers, though the essential African/Afro-American emotional penchant for a "vocal tradition" was maintained in the newer forms.

What has been called classic blues (as well as the later city or urban blues) came into being in the period before World War I. The classic blues came about largely through the influence of the traveling minstrel and vaudeville shows. The blues then began to take on a degree of professionalism. It was suddenly an "entertainment"; that is, it could be used quite consciously to entertain others. And even though a great many of the social preoccupations extant in the primitive blues remained, it was no longer the group singing to ease their labors; the artisan had appeared, formally. Large groups of Negroes could sit quietly in a show and listen to a performer re-create certain serious areas of their lives. The classic singers appeared: Ma Rainey, Clara Smith, Chippie Hill, Ida Cox, Sara Martin, and perfection, Bessie Smith.

Whereas the shouts, hollers, etc., were, for obvious reasons, almost always unaccompanied, primitive blues did utilize guitars and banjos, and the addition of musical instruments was another factor that went into the shaping of basic blues form. Classic blues singers began to use not only these basic instruments, but fronted small and large theater bands with their diversity of instrumentation. The developing fluency Negroes were achieving with all manner of instruments was the main factor that led to the emergence of jazz, which is essentially a blues derived instrumental music. And the most expressive jazz music of any period has always made constant use of the vocal tradition of blues. Jazz is a music that could not have existed without blues and its various antecedents. However, jazz should not be thought of as a successor to blues, but as a very original music that developed out of, and was concomitant with, blues and moved off into its own path of development.

The marching bands started by Negroes around the turn of the century, often in imitation of the "Napoleonic" marching bands of the white Creoles were one beginning of jazz, especially around New Orleans. However, it is ridiculous to say, as has been said so often, that jazz "began in New Orleans." Jazz began any place in the South there were Negroes who learned to play and gained some fluency with the instruments first employed in making the new music. In New Orleans the untutored raw bands of the uptown Negroes—which were initially features at picnics, dances, boating trips and funerals—were the first primitive jazz bands. These musicians not only played the standard 4/4 of the marching band, but were also exposed to and influenced by the "exotic" rhythms of the French quadrilles (2/4 and 6/8), minuets, and music from the Caribbean which gave them ears for the music they called "Spanish tinge." All these rhythms were used by even the earliest jazz bands, as well as of course the deeply pervasive traditional African rhythms, which had persisted on plantations, in the form of log drums or even pans turned upside down in tubs full of water, well into the twentieth century. The most blatant "Africanism" in Negro music is to be found in its rhythms, and the emphasis which the Negro musician has always given to the rhythm of his music speaks openly of this elegant legacy.

One example of the way Negroes used "European" rhythms in conjunction with their own West African, now Afro-American, rhythms were the funeral processions. The march to the cemetery was played in slow, dirge-like 4/4 cadence. It was usually a spiritual that was played, but made into a kind of raw and bluesy Napoleonic military march. After the burial, the band, once removed some good distance from the cemetery, usually broke into the up tempo part of the march at some approximation of the 2/4 quadrille. "Didn't He Ramble" and "When The Saints Go Marching In" were two of the frequently played tunes—both transmuted religious songs. But even in this kind of march music the influence of the blues was very heavy.

By the time the first nonmarching, instrumental blues-oriented groups started to appear in numbers, i.e., the "jass" or "dirty" bands, the instrumentation was a pastiche of the brass bands and the lighter quadrille groups. In 1897, Buddy Bolden's group consisted of cornet, trombone, clarinet (the first reed instrument Negroes began to play with any frequency), violin, guitar, string bass (already an innovation over the tuba, the first timekeeping instrument in these bands), and drums.

Just before the First World War, the largest migration of Negroes ever to leave the South had begun, headed for the large Northern industrial centers. Cheap labor was needed in the North to keep up with the demands of the impending war, and many of the large industries even sent recruiters to enlist Negroes to work in Northern factories. A great many Southern musicians came North, bringing the blues impulse and fledgling Jazz and making this music available to even larger audiences.

The move by Negroes into the new black cities of the North (South Side Chicago, Harlem, Detroit, etc.) affected Negro music in a great many ways. Classic blues became popular in the larger Northern theaters and with singers, especially after the coming of radio and "Race records" (these were commercial recordings aimed strictly for the Negro market).

Once they discovered that there was a huge market for this music, record companies accelerated production of such records.

The larger Northern dance bands began to hire some of the Southern musicians because, at the time, the "dada strain" of the blues-oriented instrumentalists was thought to be an added novelty feature that could increase an orchestra's commercial value. But usually the Northern Negro musician came under the influence of these Southern musicians with their "hot" or bluesy intonation. The phonograph record spread this hot style to an even broader Northern audience, black and white alike. It was in the Northern cities that new forms like urban or city blues [1] and the piano music boogiewoogie began to thrive. In some ways boogie bears strong resemblance to ragtime piano style, although the repeated "rolling" (*ostinato*) figure used in boogie identifies it immediately. [2] Ragtime was the first appropriation of white pianistic techniques by Negro musicians, boogiewoogie was the second appropriation of a pianistic approach to the instrument, but in such a blatantly percussive and blues-like manner as to separate it immediately from any more Europeanized music. In keeping with the traditional styles of Negro music boogie also was predominantly a music of rhythmic contrasts, rather than melodic or harmonic variations.

The large dance bands of the Twenties became, with the addition of the Southern players, jazz bands. With the emergence of many good hot musicians from all over the country, the big jazz bands continued to develop. By the late Twenties there were quite a few very good jazz bands all over the country. "By 1930 every city outside the deep south with a Negro population [1920 census] above sixty thousand except Philadelphia had produced an important band; Washington, Duke Ellington; Baltimore, Chick Webb; Memphis, Jimmie Lunceford; St. Louis, the

---

[1] Urban blues resulted from the fusion of the older traditions of the blues (country and classic), which the Southern Negro migrants brought with them to the North, and the "new learning" (the adjustment to the conflicts and strangeness of the city). Urban blues music was harder, crueler and more stoical and hopeless than the country (folklore) and the classic (entertainment) blues. See LeRoi Jones, *Blues People* (New York: William Morrow & Company, 1963), pp. 105, 108.

[2] Ragtime is the most instrumental (more precisely, the most pianistic) or nonvocal music developed by Negroes. It developed from minstrelsy—it was a Negro imitation of white imitations of Negro music. Earlier Negro blues pianists used the piano in a percussive and vocal fashion—ragtime used a more florid, "hundred-finger'd" approach. A composed music, more formalized, less spontaneous.

Boogie is basically a piano music. Its origins were in the primitive blues of the Southern Negro. It seemed to be a fusion of vocal blues and the earlier guitar techniques of the country singers, adapted to the piano. Largely an improvised music. LeRoi Jones, *Ibid.*, pp. 114–15.

Missourians; Chicago, Luis Russell and Louis Armstrong; New York, Fletcher Henderson, Charlie Johnson, and a half dozen more." [3] The big colored dance bands of the Thirties were a national entertainment, even though their white imitators made more money, and the strongest influence on American popular music for twenty years. They were responsible for the whole swing era in jazz.

By the time the increasing popularity of the swing arrangements led to a general sameness and similarity of style in most of the big bands, Negro and white, a new development in the Forties served to pull Negro music abruptly back outside the mainstream. The music, onomatopoetically called bebop, was the new form of Negro music in the Forties that restored the excitement and beauty to jazz. Instead of the large jazz band playing arranged compositions, with only occasional solos, the bebop groups were small bands, quartets and quintets, thus restoring the burden of expression to the jazz soloist rather than the arranger. The boppers also began to abandon the traditional practice of improvising or providing variations on a melodic theme and instead began to play their variations on the chords on which the melody was based, creating new melodies. Sometimes they merely used the original melody as the bass notes for a new set of chords and improvised a countermelody. Young musicians like Charlie Parker, one of the most important soloists in all jazz, and Thelonius Monk, a major jazz composer and pianist, were among the most influential innovators of bebop.

Bebop, with its jagged rhythms and harsh timbres, seemed an extreme to a great many people, and two musical reactions to it seemed to be the music called Dixieland on the one hand, which was an attempt by young white musicians to revive the earlier "New Orleans" form of jazz, and another style called Progressive Jazz on the other hand, which sought to utilize the forms and attitudes of European classical music within a jazz context. Both of these were essentially "white styles" of jazz and figure only slightly in the most important history of blues and jazz.

Cool jazz became a ubiquitous jazz style during the late Forties into the Fifties, and while it was a style that many white jazz musicians found themselves at home with (especially because of the softened ensemble sound, rhythmic simplicity and heavy reliance on the popular song), a great many Negro musicians played music that could also be identified by the name *cool*. Tenor saxophonist Lester Young's playing in the Thirties with the Count Basie band and later with his own groups, was the most popular model for the cool saxophonists. Young's melodic approach was what many

[3] Hsio Wen Shih, "The Spread of Jazz and the Big Bands," in *Jazz*, p. 161.

young saxophonists of the Thirties and Forties were most struck by, as well as his completely relaxed antifrenetic approach and his languid, evanescent almost alto-like tone.

The stridently piercing timbre of the Parker horn, along with Young's completely antithetical approach, are the two most widely imitated styles of the post-bop era. Most of Young's disciples were involved with the cool school, which was also called West Coast jazz, while the Parker players and the men they eventually influenced became associated with what was called the hard bop school or East Coast jazz. Hard bop appeared during the early Fifties and was, in effect, an attempt to restore the broad "dramatic" bluesy sound to jazz, after the dilutions and softening of cool jazz. The jazz figures and contrapuntal jazz compositions which were two characteristic and ubiquitous examples of the cool tendency were replaced or at least grew less interesting for the hard boppers who reemphasized the hard harsh saxophone sound, and made use of a constant blues reference which they identified as "funk" or stemming from the influence of gospel and older blues forms.

By the mid-fifties, however, there were younger musicians who began taking the innovations of bebop quite literally, and who sought to reestablish the absolute hegemony of spontaneous improvisation in jazz and the ultimate freedom such an attack could provide. Hard bop, even though it did refocus the jazzman's attention toward traditional sources of Negro music, still maintained in many cases the formality and heavy reliance on arranged compositions that the cool people favored. (Though the most important musicians to emerge from hard bop, e.g., John Coltrane and Sonny Rollins, are glaring exceptions to this generalization.)

What has been called "free jazz" or "the new thing" or "the avant-garde" has in the last few years stripped jazz of most of the artificial conventions of Euro-American popular and classical music. The young musicians like Cecil Taylor and Ornette Coleman, who are the most important musical minds associated with this new style, have in one sense taken jazz back to its earliest aesthetic roots. That is, they have proposed that music and musician be brought face to face, without the strict and often grim hindrances of over-used Western musical concepts, and that is the overall musical intelligence of the musician which should be responsible for shaping the music. Their music, unlike most instrumental jazz that has preceded it, does not depend on constantly stated chords for its direction and shape. Nor does it pretend to accept the formal considerations of the bar or measure line. In a sense, the music depends for its form on the same references as primitive blues forms, i.e., it considers the total area of its existence as a means to evolve, to move, as an intelligently shaped musical concept, from its beginning to its end.

Negro music has undergone many changes in form. And even while it has been changing, the older forms continue to exist. The most expressive Negro music of any period will always be a reflection of what the Negro is at that particular time. The most gifted blues and jazz performers (one thinks immediately of Jelly Roll Morton, Louis Armstrong, Duke Ellington, Bessie Smith, Lester Young, Billie Holiday, Charlie Parker, Thelonius Monk, Ornette Coleman, but there have been so many more) have always been able to speak as profoundly about the world as any other artists, and in America, usually they have been able to speak more profoundly than most; certainly in terms of an American musical expression. Unfortunately, the enforced social suppliance that has been the Negro's traditional position in America has also almost automatically served to "invalidate" Negro music as a legitimate genre of artistic expression in the eyes of most Western men, black or white. But despite the artificial burden of "inferiority" that has always been attributed to blues and jazz, these musics have existed, usually at their most expressive when "separated" from the mainstream of American culture, as almost the most complete expression of the American experience available. But until most Americans are convinced that Charlie Parker, *et al.*, did, indeed, *know more* about the emotional life of American society than say Henry Wadsworth Longfellow, there will be no real understanding of just what Negro music is, or for that matter what the Negro himself is.

chapter 22

The Negro in the Fine Arts

Marion E. Brown

I

The Negro artist appeared in America at the handicraft stage. In colonial America, slave artisans produced many pieces of furniture, textiles and pottery which embellished pre-Civil War mansions. The skills which these artisans showed in woodcarving, weaving and carpentry are skills which for centuries have been evident among certain West African tribes.

Thomas Day was the most significant of these woodcarvers and cabinet-makers. He lived and worked in Charleston, South Carolina. James A. Porter reveals that "Day's talents as a cabinet artist were sought by the richest clientele in Charleston and in Virginia. His furniture, many pieces of which were created on the orders of numerous patrons, was of a pure and simple style, though founded on earlier adapted types of American and European styles." [1]

In eighteenth-century New Orleans there was a concentration of Negro master blacksmiths. These craftsmen forged iron grilles for balconies and for balustrades. Their works, often improvised as the situation dictated, without the use of precision tools, evince a delicate beauty often seen in Moorish ironwork.

Scipio Moorehead is thought the first formally trained Negro artist in colonial America. His known work was inspired by the classics. This inspiration resulted in two paintings. One of them was a work based on the legend of Damon and Pythias. The other, a painting entitled "Aurora," inspired the poetess Phillis Wheatley to write a poem to "S.M., a young African Painter on seeing his works."

In eighteenth-century Maryland the Negro artist Joshua Johnson painted portraits of many of the rich whites of the state. These paintings were characterized by a kind of decorativeness often seen in rococo and baroque painting. An oil, "Mrs. Andrew Beckford Bankson and Child," [2] done about

---

[1] James A. Porter, *Modern Negro Art* (New York: Dryden Press, 1943), pp. 19–20.
[2] *Ibid.*, p. 207.

1780, shows mother and daughter bedecked with jewels, sedately poised on what may have been a piece of Sheraton furniture studded with nails. Johnson's painting is considered in the finest tradition of American primitive art.

II

Near the beginning of the nineteenth century there were many free Negro artists who earned their livings at other jobs while painting in their spare time. Robert M. Douglas, Jr., in Philadelphia, painted signs for a living, but also became a recognized painter. His portrait style was reminiscent of Thomas Sully, the white Philadelphia painter. In 1833, Douglas made a lithographed likeness of William Lloyd Garrison. Because his works have been lost and what is known of them has been learned by hearsay, the aesthetic quality of his work is uncertain.

David Bustill Bowers, a cousin of Douglas, was also a sign painter who became an artist. Born January 16, 1820, in Philadelphia, his early work includes emblems and banners done for local firemen and fraternal organizations. In addition to these banners and insignia, he painted portraits and landscapes. He did a number of portraits of Abraham Lincoln, who may have himself sat for one of the originals. Supporting this claim, Bowers' relatives have mentioned a check made out to him in Lincoln's own hand. The unredeemed check is still reputedly in the possession of its Philadelphia owners.

Robert S. Duncanson, whose mural style recalls the panoramic effects of the Hudson River School, was obviously inspired by poetry. One of his mural landscapes was done for the Longworth Museum between 1843 and 1851; this museum later became the Charles P. Taft Museum. In 1843, he painted "The Trial of Shakespeare." It now hangs in Cleveland, the artist's home. "The Lotos-Eaters" brought him international fame, and when in England, Tennyson (whose poem had inspired the work) invited him to the Isle of Wight. He returned to America after a brief period of expatriation and later died while a patient in a Detroit hospital for the insane.

Edward M. Bannister, of Providence, was the first Negro painter to win wide recognition based on prizes won in exhibitions. He was born in Nova Scotia in 1828. He lived in Boston for a while, earning a living making prints. These prints sold fairly well and he was able to open a studio where he practiced as a professional artist. He showed regularly in Boston

Art Club exhibitions. His landscape "Under the Oaks" won a medal at the centennial exposition of 1876 in Philadelphia.

The period of Negro art until the emergence of Henry Ossawa Tanner may be styled "the apprentice period," and covered roughly from 1865 to 1890. From 1890 until near 1914, the Negro artist advanced from apprentice to journeyman.

Henry O. Tanner, the leading Negro artist of this later period, was born in Pittsburgh in 1859. His father, a bishop in the Methodist Church, desired a similar career for his son. Though Tanner did not enter the ministry, religious subjects did inspire many of his great works. He studied at the Pennsylvania Academy of Fine Arts, where Thomas Eakins was one of his first instructors. After graduation he went to Atlanta. Too poor to go abroad for further studies, he took a teaching job at Clark University and remained for several years. He found a friend and patron in a Bishop Hartzwell, who gave him some of the funds necessary for study abroad.

He went to Paris, and from there to Palestine, a sojourn which inspired the biblical series which brought him international acclaim. One of these religious paintings, "Resurrection of Lazarus," was purchased by the French Government for the Luxembourg Gallery collection. Tanner returned to Paris, where he remained committing himself to a kind of monastic isolation to his studio. His most important works, those which comprise the famous biblical series, are for the most part in European museums. In America his work is included in the Chicago Art Institute collection and at the Grand Central Art Galleries.

Pioneer Negro painters of the twentieth century were William A. Harper, Edouard Scott, Edward Harleston, Archibald Motley and Laura Wheeling Waring. These were among the first of the Negro painters and they painted largely in the tradition of other American artists. Some of them succeeded in having their work displayed at art exhibitions and in galleries with white American painters. These early Negroes were followed by other talented Negroes whose work has won wide acceptance. In this group are Charles Alston, Eldzier Cortor, Allen Freelon, Earnest Crichlow, Malvin Gray Johnson, William H. Johnson, Hale Woodruff, Georgette Seabrook, Norman Lewis, Romare Bearden, Horace Pippin and Jacob Lawrence.

For the Negro artists today (as is true for most white artists) the art world does not offer economic security from painting alone. Because of this, many Negro artists have become teachers, helping, where possible, to encourage talented young Negro students.

While some Negro painters accepted professorships, others chose the raw existence of the struggling artist. Henry Miller, in an essay, "The Amazing and Invariable Beauford DeLaney," describes cold winter nights when he and other white litterateurs visited Beauford's Green Street studio in New York's Greenwich Village. There they often found the artists swathed in rags, trying desperately to ward off the cold, but painting vehemently. Of Beauford at work, Miller says: "He paints today even more enthusiastically than when he began. He tackles each fresh canvas as though he knows not where the next tube will come from. He blesses himself when he begins and says amen when he is through." [3] There were other Negro painters who also subscribed to the artist's life. Many secluded themselves in local studios; others went abroad where the presence of sympathetic attitudes gave their lives more meaning, made it easier to create. William H. Johnson chose Norway, where he married a Norwegian girl. There he painted those beautiful Norwegian landscapes which suggest that he might have known, or have been inspired by, the work of Edvard Munch, the Norwegian expressionist.

Mural art afforded many Negro painters the opportunity to express themselves in epic scope. Most of the murals painted were evidence of an awakening interest in Negro life. These gigantic works were also evidence of a trend toward formal design. In the Thirties, certain prominent Americans had begun to show interest in materials relating to Negro life and folklore. Under grants from the Public Works Administration and certain philanthropic bodies, many Negro artists were commissioned to do murals for various institutions and public buildings. These murals show Negro life and history in America.

Several Negro artists distinguished themselves in this medium. Aaron Douglas, Hale Woodruff, Charles Alston and Charles White were the most significant. Douglas did "Evolution of the Negro Dance" for the Harmon Foundation. Charles Alston executed a work under a WPA grant from the Harlem Hospital, showing the progress of medicine from magic to modern science. Hale Woodruff painted the "Amistad" murals for Talladega College. He also painted a mural for the Trevor Arnette Library at Atlanta University; this work depicts the progress of the Negro in the arts. Charles White's mural, "Five Great American Negroes," done in 1941, is now the property of the Museum of Modern Art in New York.

Few Negro artists have been interested solely in the medium of church murals. One young Negro artist, Aaron Miller, has devoted himself entirely to painting in this genre. His work seems very much like the work of certain painters of the Renaissance, especially that of Piero della Francesca.

[3] Henry Miller, in *Remember to Remember*, "The Amazing and Invariable Beauford DeLaney" (New York: New Directions, 1947), p. 21.

III

It has probably been in the medium of sculpture that the Negro artist has achieved the highest level of creativity. The earliest manifestations of Negro American sculpture were certain tools and pieces of furniture which the Negro artist in colonial America fashioned for practical purposes. Slaves of the early part of the nineteenth century were also known to have pieces of pottery which they had made themselves. Some of these survived the Civil War and are now the property of the Museum of Modern Art and of the National Gallery of Art in Washington.

The first important Negro sculptor was a woman. Edmonia Lewis, born in 1745 near Albany, New York, attended some classes at Oberlin College before she went to Boston, where she took her first lessons in sculpture with Edmund Brackett. Shortly thereafter, she executed a bust of Colonel Robert Gould Shaw from a photograph. This work brought her a small degree of fame, and with the proceeds from sales, she managed to go to Europe. In Rome she studied and attempted original pieces of sculpture. Most of her work was done in marble. "Awake" and "Asleep" are two works which reveal her tendency toward a neoclassical approach. They are separate pieces, the first, showing two infants, half-asleep, but awakening; the other, showing the two infants going to sleep. Another of her works, "Forever Free," established her as a sculptress of fair distinction.

In the late Twenties, the sculpture of Sargent Johnson and Richmond Barthe attracted attention. The forms which Johnson and Barthe created were, in some cases, derived from African forms. Johnson seems to have been interested in Egyptian forms rather than those common to West African or to Sudanese sculpture. He is known as a sculptor who leans closely to ceramics, fashioning most of his work in glazed terra cotta. "Sammy" and "Chester," two studies of young Negro boys, are among his most important works. "Forever Free," a work done in porcelain showing a black madonna figure with two youths on either side, both of whom are protected by her outstretched arms, is particularly compelling.

For Richmond Barthe, the Negro physique was a source of great inspiration. His many pieces of dancers have a natural plastic quality. His bodies are usually elongated, but not distorted. He was deeply moved by the theater. This resulted in busts of John Gielgud and Katherine Cornell; and a frieze based on *Green Pastures* done by him for the Harlem River projects in New York City. His work has been shown in the major American galleries and is included in many important collections.

IV

Negro art reached a sizable public because of the activities of individuals who, while not interested in art directly, recognized the importance of Negro talent in the fine arts. Several officials of the African Methodist Episcopal Church had a great deal to do with furthering Negro art. This activity began toward the middle of the nineteenth century, when Bishop Daniel A. Payne initiated a program in Ohio for the encouragement of literature and the fine arts among interested Negroes of the day. Prizes were offered for the best work dealing with any historical subject or any theme taken from the Scriptures. His efforts brought about the discovery of A. B. Wilson, a promising painter who died before his art matured. A portrait of Bishop Payne's family done by William S. Duncanson still hangs at Wilberforce University.

In 1928 the Harmon Foundation began a series of exhibitions of the work of leading Negro artists of that time. A number of Negro painters who had not appeared in widely publicized shows were presented for the first time. Palmer Hayden's painting "The Schooners" was one of the pieces which won the William E. Harmon prize for distinguished achievement in the fine arts among Negroes in the first exhibition. Over the years the foundation has created a permanent general collection, which probably includes the largest single collection of Negro art in America.

While the Harmon Foundation was presenting annual art exhibitions, Altanta University was becoming an art center. Hale Woodruff, one of the leading American Negro artists, went to Atlanta in 1939 to become professor of art at Atlanta University. In 1941, under Woodruff's direction, the university began having annual art shows. He and other painters in Atlanta formed a small group which gave encouragement to one another. Some of Woodruff's best woodblock prints were made during this time, roughly from 1937 to 1939. Several members gained a reputation outside Atlanta. Wilmer Jennings, most widely known for his woodblock prints, and Fred Flemister were outstanding members of this group. Others in the group were Jewel Simon, Thomas Jefferson Flannagan, June Hector and John Biggers—all promising painters who have won prizes in the Atlanta University shows.

The work of Hale Woodruff, Wilmer Jennings and Dox Thrasher brought Negro woodblock printmakers great esteem in the late thirties. Woodruff and Jennings and their Atlanta contemporaries were members of the "outhouse" school. (This group, especially Woodruff, produced prints based on racial themes. They included lynchings, but at other times showed merely rustic scenes of Atlanta back streets, especially those near the university.)

Howard University has also played an important role in furthering Negro art. Dr. James Herring inaugurated the university art department and gallery. After his death, James A. Porter became head of the art department. Porter has written a definitive book on the Negro in modern art. Alain Locke, noted for his studies of the Negro's contributions to American culture and art, was also instrumental in Howard's fine arts program. James L. Wells, known as the dean of Negro woodblock printmakers, teaches graphic arts there. Lois Mailou Jones, David Driskell and Albert Carter make up the other faculty members in the art department. Lois Jones is well known as a deft water colorist who paints exotic Haitian scenes. David Driskell paints Georgia pines allegorically in a style reminiscent of Cézanne.

Another talented printmaker was James L. Wells of Howard University whose woodblock print "African Fantasy," an exotic print of a female head, is considered by many to be one of the best prints done during that time.

Howard University's efforts toward providing a comprehensive art education have resulted in some very talented young Negro painters, most of whom are yet developing. Mildred Thompson has studied in Germany. William White, an abstract expressionist, sold his prize-winning painting "African Metamorphosis" to the Nigerian government. Lloyd McNeil and Leo Robinson are two recent graduates of the Howard University art department who show considerable promise.

V

The most talented and original Negro painters have been known as primitives. This is most likely true because many of them were not formally trained, yet they have been recognized as having produced work which has equalled if not excelled some of what has been done by trained artists. The work of Jacob Lawrence, William H. Johnson, Ellis Wilson, and Horace Pippin is often termed primitive.

Jacob Lawrence, who works in a two-dimensional style using egg tempera, is the most widely shown of this group. His work, which is often episodic, always colorful and light, has dealt with historical themes relating to Negro life and history. William H. Johnson, after spending years in Scandinavia, returned to America in the middle 1940's. He abandoned the Norwegian countryside—which had produced an inspired "Kerteminde

Harbor, Denmark"—for a mystical approach to painting Negro life. "Jesus and the Three Marys," using Negro models, is evidence of return to familiar ground. In 1947 he was confined to a mental institution of Long Island, New York, where he is today.

Horace Pippin was certainly the greatest Negro primitive painter. Most of his paintings are of scenes remembered from World War I. He was wounded by a sniper's bullet which left him almost totally paralyzed, with only one good hand to paint with. His work is included in the most important American museum and gallery collections. "John Brown Going to His Hanging" is one of his most important paintings. He shows the abolitionist riding to his death aboard a wagon loaded with and surrounded by eager spectators. Critics agree that "among self-taught painters of the world, Pippin ranks close to Rousseau, and in the company of Bombois, Peyronnet, and Hippolite." [4]

Among the choices of Alain Locke as representative of the "New Negro" in art were Hughie Lee-Smith, Eldzier Cortor, Charles Seabree, Romare Bearden and Charles White. Cortor and Lee-Smith represent the furthest departure from the traditional Negro painters of the past. Cortor's work often depicts lonely females, usually nudes, in what seems an infinity of lonely mirrorlike harlequin patterns. Lee-Smith's subjects are forlorn people, either lost or abandoned on lonely deserted streets; "Festival's End" and "Impedimentia" are examples.

Certain Negro artists of the late 1940's were adopting an approach leaning toward abstraction. Among those pioneering in the new direction were Normal Lewis, Harper Phillips, Sam Middleton and Earnest Crichlow. In the late 1950's a host of young Negro artists appeared, most in painting, several in sculpture, but the trend seems to have reached a plateau with Barthe and Sargent Johnson. These new painters referred to themselves as "abstract" and/or "abstract expressionists." Each work of theirs can be identified only by its title, which implies an outlook broader than one based on social themes. Harvey Cropper, Virginia Cox, Gilbert Harris, James Weeks, Larry Compton, Walter Williams, Charles McGee and Paul Keene make up some of those who were moving further into abstract painting. James Week's painting "The Musician" won first prize at a recent Howard University show. Virginia Cox paints misty abstractions in pastel hues. Walter Williams's "Fighting Cox" is the best woodblock print done after the work of Wells and the "outhouse" group.

No doubt Bob Thompson is now the most striking and original young Negro painter to be shown widely since Hale Woodruff or Jacob Lawrence.

[4] Cedric Dover, *American Negro Art* (New York Graphic Society, 1960), p. 46. Quoted from Seldon Rodman, 1947.

He is both a primitive and a fine technician. In a recent review of his work, *Art News* says that "Thompson's creatures, winged bats of human features, loom and hover in a space that might be a spectacle, a performance, in which a naked figure (reclining, falling, upside down, stricken, leading) is a force of centrifugal attraction." [5]

Recent sculpture by Barbara Chase and Richard Hunt, like the painting of Negro artists of the late Forties and Fifties, evidences a departure from racial themes in favor of aesthetic principles that transcend the art of social commentary. Barbara Chase constructs profoundly, at times reminiscent of Giacometti, but always very personal. Richard Hunt, like Barbara Chase, chooses to work in metal. He uses tubular fittings to construct his pieces. As in "Hero Construction," these tubes and cylinders give an organic feeling to inorganic substance.

Today many young Negro artists are interested in a kind of painting based on interior action, which manifests itself in splashes of color, serving them as a kind of symbolic representation. This approach is expressionistic. Jack Whitten, Joe Overstreet, Sonny Hodge, William White and Larry Compton make up the New York group. These painters are all colorists of gigantic proportions who have no qualms about using nearly a full tube of color to express a fleeting emotion.

The future of the Negro artist in America is now almost solely limited only by his or her ability to create. Many Negro painters still go to Europe, but not so much for environmental freedom as for the benefits of seeing and feeling the cosmopolitan attitudes which Europe has always held for arts and the artists. Today Negro painters are painting and showing in the major cities of America and Europe.

[5] Jill Johnston in "Reviews and Previews," *Art News*, Vol. 61, No. 5 (September, 1962), p. 11.

chapter 23

The Negro in American Sports

John P. Davis

The first American prizefighter to earn an international reputation was Tom Molineaux, a Negro who boxed between 1810 and 1815. The jockey who rode Aristides, winner of the first Kentucky Derby (1875), was Oliver Lewis, a Negro. Back in 1884 the Toledo baseball team, champions of the Northwestern League, had a Negro catcher—Moses Fleetwood Walker— who was described as "something of a wonder" by the *Louisville Courier Journal.*[1] In 1889 two Negroes, William Tecumseh Sherman Jackson and William Henry Lewis, played on the varsity football team at Amherst College. Lewis later played center on the Harvard team and was chosen by Walter Camp as a member of his All-American team for 1892 and 1893. In 1900 Marshall W. "Major" Taylor, a Negro, was professional sprint champion of the United States in bicycle racing.

The examples above are important milestones in any chronology of Negro participation in American sports, but they do not mark the beginnings of that participation. These beginnings can only be gleaned—as is the case for American sports generally—from spotty, incomplete and inconclusive bits of historical evidence.

In the early seventeenth century there was little activity that could pass for sports. The colonists were too busy staying alive. Harsh colonial life left little time for pure leisure. If a man hunted or fished it was a businesslike enterprise performed to bring food to the household. Such few Negro slaves as there were had even less leisure than their masters. Even when frontier life became a little more regularized, strict Calvinistic religious concepts which dominated much of American thought looked upon idleness and play as the work of the devil. Nor were Quakers, Puritans or Anglicans less severe.

Despite the strictures of environment and religion, activity which passed for sport did occur and in the process the Negro slave was involved. Play was often concealed in work. Sometimes master and slaves went hunting and fishing together. In *Turf, Field and Farm,* Frederick Gustavas Skinner, a noted sportsman, has written of one such trip, when he took a dozen or more

[1] May 2, 1884, p. 12.

slaves with him from Maryland to Mississippi to hunt alligators.[2] He writes of an old Negro he found in the swamps, Cyrus (emancipated for age and infirmities), "a born angler [who] devoted himself night and day to fishing and trapping. He was a close student of fishing and trapping and familiar with the habits of all wild creatures of the district, whether land or water."

Master and slave shared the common excitement of field and stream. On larger plantations, where a division of labor was possible, some slaves became expert in the care and management of hunting dogs, horses or fighting cocks. Often slaves would accompany their masters to other plantations to share the thrill of cock fighting and horse racing. Frequently they were the trainers or the jockeys who actually took part in the contests.

At such meetings other contests of strength and skill were encouraged, sometimes between slave champions from different plantations. Foot racing, wrestling and "savage eye gouging fights in 'rough and tumble' or Yorkshire style" are mentioned as common pastimes in the South in the early nineteenth century.[3] It was in encounters such as this, legend has it, that Tom Molineux first tested his skill and gained experience as a professional boxer.

A CENTURY AND A HALF OF NEGRO PRIZEFIGHTERS

It seems fairly well-established that Tom Molineaux was a slave in Virginia, a dock hand in Baltimore, a porter at the Old Catherine Street Market in New York City. These jobs were such as to provide him with hard work and a rugged constitution. In a rough and tumble contest on a plantation, in a fight with other longshoremen on the docks, he could doubtless give a good account of himself. But it was on Catherine Street in the company of a fraternity of Negro fighters that he is most apt to have learned to exhibit his skill for money. That he shares this with a number of other unknown Negro boxers is obvious.[4]

[2] Harry Worcester Smith, "A Sporting Family of the Old South." Included in *Reminiscences of an Old Sportsman* by Frederick A. Skinner. (Albany, New York: J. B. Lyon Company, 1936), pp. 230–32.

[3] Russell Elaine Nye, *The Cultural Life of the New Nation* (New York: Harper and Row, 1960), p. 144.

[4] Not all of Molineaux's contemporaries are unknown. One of these was Bill Richmond, born a slave on Staten Island, New York, in 1765. As a boy of twelve he struck the fancy of a British officer, General Earl Perch, and was taken to England in 1777. There he learned the art of boxing. Richmond, known as the "Black Terror," fought Tom Crib for the championship of England in 1805 and lost after a fierce battle of one hour and a half. Later he was Molineaux's second and backer in both of the latter's fights against Crib. Because it is not likely that he had any training as a boxer in America, he is usually not considered an American sports figure.

It is possible that Negroes were prizefighting in America for well over a quarter of a century before whites. At least there are no early accounts of boxing contests between white boxers in America. Marquess of Queensbury rules were a long way off and Broughton's rules (1740) protected against little besides biting, kicking and eye-gouging. At least in the United States, prizefighting generally was looked upon as degrading, brutal and bestial. In 1817 when a group of English boxers arrived in New York, *Niles Register* warned against "these low wretches . . . (being) quietly permitted to beat, abuse and possibly kill one another as has frequently happened in the presence of Nobles and Divines in England." [5] There were laws against prize-fights in some states. Indeed on February 7, 1849, when Tom Higher met Yankee Sullivan in the first professional American prizefight, the contestants had to move from the originally announced site to Still Pond, Maryland, in order to escape law officers. Yet strange American ambivalence that established a different social conduct for Negroes than for whites, permitted Negro fighters to perform during customary holidays when dancing, drinking, and other letting-off-steam activities were engaged in by the slave and free Negro population alike.[6]

Thus it came about that the first American ready to be a logical contender for what may quite properly be described as the first contest for the heavyweight championship of the world was a Negro. The defending champion was Tom Crib, who had held the English prizefighting crown for several years and who had behind him more than a hundred years of British boxing tradition.

The first Crib-Molineaux fight took place out of doors in Capthall Common near East Grimstead south of London on Tuesday, December 18, 1810. Rain came down in torrents for several hours before the fight, but this did not prevent the contest from being witnessed by several thousand persons, from titled nobility down to light-fingered pickpockets.

The fight lasted fifty-five minutes during which forty-four rounds took place. It was a bloody fight and Molineaux lost. The London *Times* reported:

> Both of the combatants were badly beaten; and they were almost deprived of sight. They were so exhausted, that even the victor could not have stood five minutes longer. The Black gave in from weakness rather than from

[5] October 18, 1811.
[6] In Colonial New York where Molineaux began his fighting career, one popular holiday was Pinkster Day (a corruption of the Dutch word for Pentecost), which came in late spring seven weeks after Easter. The whole Negro population looked forward to this day as a festival. Slaves and free Negroes came from miles around to partake of homemade beer, dancing, as well as to witness contests of several sorts. Cf. Alice Morse Earle, *Colonial Days in Old New York* (New York: C. S. Scribner's Sons, 1899), p. 195.

want of courage. He is certainly one of the most promising pugilists that have appeared.[7]

Around the Molineaux defeat there has arisen in some books what is perhaps the first sports alibi on record. The claim is that Molineaux was robbed; that he was victim of the skulduggery of Crib's handlers. There is no evidence to bear this out. Molineaux himself, in his challenge to Crib for a return match, written three days after the fight, blames the weather, which was cold and blustery, for his defeat. The London *Times,* which carried a complete account of the fight, contains nothing to justify a claim that Crib did not win fairly. What the writers of the apocryphal commentaries missed was the subtle overtones of color prejudice which hovered over this contest; overtones which since have often attached themselves to other contests where black athletes and white athletes strive for physical supremacy.

Molineaux first raised the question of color when he publicly challenged Crib to a second fight. He wrote:

> As it is possible this letter may meet the public eye, I cannot omit the opportunity of expressing a confident hope that the circumstance of my being of a different colour to that of a people amongst whom I have sought protection will not in any way operate to my prejudice.[8]

The substance of Molineaux's suspicions was confirmed a few days before the second fight took place by the correspondent of the London *Times:*

> The prejudice against the black colour seems to exist as much in the country as in London; and whilst Molineaux remains unnoticed, the residence of Crib is continually filled with residents of the first consequence in the country.[9]

The reference to "the country" is to Thisselton Gap, a hundred miles north of London where the second fight occurred.

The fight took place under the noonday sun on September 28, 1811. Several thousand spectators drawn by the uniqueness of a Negro-white competition came—a fourth of them nobility and gentry. The night before every available bed within twenty miles had been rented. A 25-foot square ring had been raised on stubble ground. A purse of 600 guineas (worth about $10,000 today) was at stake.

The fighters came into the ring in peak condition. Captain Barclay, Crib's trainer, had brought Crib down from a weight of 16 stone (224 pounds) to 13 stone 6 pounds (188 pounds). Molineaux—not a large man—

[7] December 19, 1810, p. 3.
[8] Molineaux's letter to Crib dated December 21, 1810 and printed in the London *Times* December 25, 1810, p. 4.
[9] September 26, 1811, p. 3.

came into the ring at 13 stone (182 pounds), only a little heavier than a modern light-heavyweight. For eighteen minutes the fighters sat in the ring and glared at each other.

The fight began at a furious pace. Crib hit Molineaux on the throat and knocked him down in round one. Molineaux came back in the second with sharp lefts to the head. Crib's right eye was nearly closed; his mouth gushed blood. In round three Crib sent rights and lefts hard into Molineaux's body while Molineaux concentrated on Crib's head. Both of Crib's eyes were closed and he fell to the ring floor. In the fourth, Molineaux, according to the London *Times*, had "Crib bleeding from every organ." But the Negro fighter's seeming victory was short-lived. In the ninth round Crib struck him with a powerful blow that broke his jaw. He was unable to continue fighting after the eleventh round. The fight was lost—ending in nineteen minutes and ten seconds.

A challenge to white supremacy was ended. The anxious moments of the white spectators were over. For, as the London *Times* correspondent wrote:

> The Black's prowess was regarded by Crib's friends with a jealousy which excited considerable national prejudice against him; and although the task of a second combat was regarded with fearful anxiety by the fistic amateurs, inasmuch as the laurels of a British Champion were in danger of being wrested from him by a Baltimore man of colour, yet a challenge was sent Crib which he was bound to accept, although he had publickly declined fighting.[10]

The challenge was not to stay dead long. "Black" competition offered by such figures as Peter Jackson, George Dixon, Joe Gans, Joe Walcott, Jack Johnson, Battling Siki, Tiger Flowers, John Henry Lewis, Henry Armstrong, Sugar Ray Robinson, and Joe Louis was to emerge during the next 150 years to challenge white supremacy. Only John L. Sullivan, Jack Dempsey and Gene Tunney, among heavyweight champions, were wise enough "to hang their clothes on a hickory limb and not go near the water."

There were other fighters after Molineaux and before the Civil War. The names of many are now unknown, but there is the record of Bob Travers, born in 1831 who fought the Gypsy heavyweight Jem Mace, a 57-round bout and lost on a foul.

Prizefighting began to be popular after the Civil War, but not interracial fights. In 1882 John L. Sullivan, the reigning bare-knuckle champion, refereed a fight between two Negro boxers—George Godfrey (known as "Old Chocolate") and "Professor" Hadley—but Sullivan refused to match his own skill against any Negro fighter.

It was not until 1891 that a mixed bout of any significance took place:

[10] September 30, 1811, p. 3.

a fight between James J. Corbett and the champion of Australia, Peter Jackson, a Negro. Born in the Virgin Islands, Peter Jackson had been taken to live in Australia as a boy. There, in time, he rose to top ranks among that continent's boxers. He was a phenomenal fighter. Cool, skillful in the extreme, he was a master ring strategist. He had reach, strength and a lean, powerful physique. His left jabs were devastating.

In San Francisco, Corbett fought Jackson to a draw for sixty-one rounds. Corbett was later to write in his autobiography that Jackson was the most brilliant fighter he ever knew. He also tells a revealing anecdote: Corbett had given his father an expensive watch as a present. His father wore the gift to the fight and there had the misfortune of having a pickpocket steal it from him. After the fight Corbett, Sr. came into the dressing room and his son noticed and commented on the missing watch. "To hell with the watch," said his father, "you whupt the nigger."

This observation of the elder Corbett was not exactly true, but it serves to point up a process of identification between spectators and their chosen champions that goes as far back certainly as David and the Israelites against Goliath and the Philistines. The contest between a black man and a white man is, of course, only a test of superiority between these two men—that and nothing else. But by virtue of a strange mass hysteria, large numbers of supporters come to identify themselves with white champion or black champion on the basis of whether they be white or black. This phenomenon observed in the Molineaux-Crib fight became ever more persistent in the last decade of the nineteenth century when several Negro fighters showed true championship form.

As Charles A. Dana put it in an editorial in the *New York Sun* in 1895:

> We are in the midst of a growing menace. The black man is rapidly forging to the front in athletics, especially in the field of fisticuffs. We are in the midst of a black rise against white supremacy. Just at present we are safe from the humiliation of having a black man world's champion, but we had a pretty narrow escape. . . ."
>
> But the menace is still with us. There are two Negroes in the ring today who can thrash any white man breathing in their respective classes. Indeed, they can whip most men out of their class. . . . These ebony gladiators are George Dixon . . . and Joe Walcott.[11]

A clear enough statement, but even at that editor Dana left out one man: Joe Gans.

George Dixon (world's featherweight champion 1892–1900), Joe Walcott (world's welterweight champion 1901–04), and Joe Gans (world's light-

---

[11] Quoted in Nat Fleischer, *Black Dynamite* (New York: Ring Athletic Library, 1938) Vol. I, p. 6.

weight champion 1901–08) were, indeed, the menace editor Dana feared and they were not long in proving it.

Dixon began fighting in 1886 when he was sixteen years old and had his last match in the ring in 1906, twenty years later. He first held the world's bantamweight title (1890–92). He fought a 70-round draw with McCarthy, the American champion, and in a rematch won by a knockout in the twenty-fourth round. He followed this victory with others over Willis, the Australian champion, and Wallace, the British champion. The noted boxing authority Nat Fleischer tells how Dixon, in his fight against Johnny Murphy, had to do all his fighting in the center of the ring to stop white partisans of Murphy from hitting his legs with blackjacks and slug shots. Still he won the fight. In 1892 he refused to fight for a $17,500 winner-take-all purse in the New Orleans Olympia Club until the club set aside seven hundred seats for Negro spectators. For the first time in its history the Club's doors were open to Negroes.

Joe Walcott, stumpy (only five feet-one inch tall), bull-necked, 142-pound fighter was a power puncher, who enjoyed fighting men who were bigger and had longer reaches than he. He had an unorthodox way of fighting that took the form of a savage leaping attack in which he swarmed all over his opponent.

Joe Gans, who won a place in the Boxing Hall of Fame, defended his title against all comers for seven years, losing it at last—after two earlier vicious seesaw battles in which he won one and drew one—in his third fight with Battling Nelson.

There were, of course, other Negro fighters besides these three at the turn of the century. One of them was Andy Bowen, Louisiana lightweight, who fought what is still on record as the longest contest in the history of boxing: 110 rounds, lasting seven hours and nineteen minutes. It was called a draw.

The exploits of Dixon, Walcott and Gans, brilliant as they were, were only a curtain raiser to a far mightier drama: the advent of the heavyweight John Arthur Johnson.

Jack Johnson's fists rocked the world. Not just the hapless victims he conquered in the ring, but men of high and low degree everywhere. State legislatures, the Congress of the United States, the British Parliament, leaders of church, state and the press found themselves deeply involved. So were masses of black men and white men across the wide world. Jack Johnson's fists cast doubt upon one of the great dogmas of the nineteenth century: the claim of the supremacy of white men over black.

It is now ancient history how Johnson backers inveigled Tommy Burns, the Canadian fighter who claimed the world heavyweight title after the retirement of James J. Jeffries, into a contest by offering him the major share of the purse. The Negro fighter knocked out Burns in the fourteenth round in a championship match held the day after Christmas, 1908, in Sydney, New South Wales.

Almost instantly the hue and cry arose for a "White Hope." Others, to hide embarrassment, claimed publicly that Johnson, born in Galveston, Texas, was a "Numidian" and that Numidians were a lost tribe of a pure white race. The undefeated James J. Jeffries, who had held the title since the summer of 1899, stepped out of retirement to challenge Johnson.

Despite opposition, Governor Dickerson of Nevada permitted the fight to be held in Reno on July 4, 1910, after California's Governor had barred it. The contest was billed as the "Fight of the Century." It was in many ways. It drew the previously unprecedented gate of over $270,000. At ringside were John L. Sullivan and James J. Corbett, who had both drawn the color line as world champions; so was the great fighter Stanley Ketchel, whom Johnson had knocked out in the twelfth round in a fight held the previous year in Colma, California. Jack London, newspaperman later turned novelist, was there and wrote, with an obvious relish that betrayed his egalitarian background:

> Once again has Johnson sent down to defeat the chosen representative of the white race, and this time the greatest of them. . . . Johnson played as usual. . . . With his opponent not so strong in attack, Johnson, blocking in masterly fashion, could afford to play. And he played and fought a white man, in a white man's country, before a white man's audience.
>
> The greatest battle of the century was a monologue delivered to 20,000 spectators by a smiling negro (sic). . . .

The "White Hope" idea had failed. Among Negroes in the country there was great jubilation; in some cities, this led to riots. A Negro parade was broken up by the police in Columbus, Ohio. There was trouble in Kansas City, Missouri; Pittsburgh, Pennsylvania; New Orleans, Louisiana, and Roanoke, Virginia. In Washington, D.C., the dimension of the celebration can be measured by the number of arrests following the victory. One hundred and thirty-four persons faced the police court judge after the contest, while 102 others forfeited bail bonds. In her defense one Negro woman prisoner boldly told the judge she "had a right to hurrah for Arthur." [12]

Jeffries recognized the mistake also. He said after the fight:

---

[12] Sterling A. Brown, *The Negro in American Culture*. Section 1, "Sports." Unpublished typescript of Carnegie-Myrdal Study, *The Negro in America*. (New York: Schomburgh Collection), p. 41.

I would rather have been beaten three times over by a man of my own race. . . . It was to tear Johnson away from this honor that I consented to fight. . . . The color line should be drawn outside the ring. It cannot be done inside the ropes.

Great damage to the white supremacy legend had been done, but it was not too late to minimize the hurt. Quickly a number of state legislatures barred the showing of fight films, claiming that the picture of a white man flat on his back with a smiling Negro standing over him would be against public policy.

Negroes, of course, were not anxious to bind the wounds of the ruptured myth of white racial superiority. Not all of these sentiments were from the rank and file. Shortly after his Reno victory, Jack Johnson had lunch with Booker T. Washington, the outstanding Negro educator of that period. Johnson was quoted as saying:

Dr. Washington knows that my highest ambition after I get through with the pugilist game is to be a benefit and honor to my race.[13]

Both boxer and educator knew the size of the stakes.

There were those in the British Empire, too, who understood the social and political significance of a pair of lethal black fists. Perhaps nowhere can this better be seen than in the controversy that raged in 1911 over the staging of a fight in London between the Negro champion and Bombadier Wells, an English heavyweight.

For nearly two hundred years before the scheduled Johnson-Wells fight, Englishmen had been contesting against one another in the prize ring. The names of the champions in these contests are known as far back as 1719. Jim Figg, Jack Broughton, Daniel Mendoza, Jem Belcher, John Gully, Tom Crib (who fought Richmond and Molineaux) and Jem Mace (who fought the Negro pugilist, Bob Travers) are only the better known of a long line of bare-knuckle champions from whom Jack Johnson derived his world title. London, a fast growing urban center, was an ideal site for developing a mass spectator-base for the sport. It became the home of boxing, and here, for two centuries, English nobility and gentry, cleric and commoner witnessed prizefights. The sport gave employment to hundreds of boxers who had formed themselves into a boxers' union. It was against the tide of this strong tradition that a small voice of protest was raised in opposition to the Johnson-Wells fight in mid-September, 1911. It was the voice of the Reverend F. B. Meyer, Honorary Secretary of the National Free Church Council. Within two or three weeks this protest was to create a whirlwind.

[13] Brown, op. cit., p. 44.

The Reverend Mr. Meyer wrote a letter to the London *Times*. He wrote many letters to many people. He preached sermons denouncing the scheduled fight, even offering to raise a fund to reimburse the expectd losses to promoters if they would cancel the fight. Meyer won support in high places. From a vacation retreat on the shores of an Italian lake, the Archbishop of Canterbury, Primate of the Church of England, wrote to say that he shared the indigation at the prospect of such a fight, that he had asked the British Home Secretary (who was then Winston Churchill) to look into the matter.

Within two weeks the Meyer Memorial Petition to ban the fight had the further support of the Archbishop of York, the Lord Mayor of Bristol and Newcastle-on-Tyne, the Duke of Fife, Lord Avebury, Lord Roberts, Lord Hamilton, the Bishops of London, Manchester, Winchester, Rochester, Carlisle and Lichfield, the Dean of Wells, Canon Rawnsley, Sir Alfred Pearce Gould and Mr. Ramsey McDonald (who in later years was to become the British Labour Party's first Prime Minister). Tory and Laborite, the Nobility and great Divines—the most illustrious names in all England—made common cause against the Galveston Negro with a golden smile.

Not everyone in England shared the views of England's ruling class about the Johnson-Wells fight. James B. White, the fight promoter, who stood to profit several thousand English pounds by the match, was obviously opposed. Some rabid fight fans accused Meyer of meddling and humorously suggested that he himself step into the ring with Johnson. A meeting of members of the Boxers' Union stressed the obvious inconsistency of several decades of acquiescence to a steady series of bloody and brutal London prizefights by the very persons who now opposed the Johnson-Wells match.

Thus exposed, the Reverend Meyer took off his mask. A copy of his letter to Manager White was published in the London *Times* reiterating his opposition. As his main point he wrote:

> (1) The eyes of millions of the black and subject peoples are watching the issue of the contest (so widely advertised in the heart of London) as being in their judgement a decisive test in the matter of racial superiority, and, however you may guard it, you cannot alter its essential effect.[14]

Now the truth was out. It became even more explicit when the English magazine, *The Spectator*, summarized the arguments of the opposition:

> When a white policemen in the Fiji islands can say that since the Burns-Johnson fight he has had more trouble with colored people than in any similar period within his experience, we can readily believe that the result

[14] September 22, 1911, p. 6.

of the Johnson-Wells contest was being eagerly awaited by the black races wherever English newspapers, however indirectly, supply the matter for conversation. It is not merely that Johnson's past successes have taught the colored population to say "White man he no use; black man he knock him down every time." The correspondent who for some weeks past has been writing to the *Times* from Nigeria speaks quite truly of the harm that might be done to the native rulers of the interior by the to them astounding incident of thousands of Englishmen assisting at the public thrashing—if so it turned out—of an Englishman by a negro. (*sic*) [15]

It would have been easy to explain away Jack Johnson. One need simply accept the proposition that all races could produce men of superior physical endowments. However, as long as white men in England and America found themselves under the spell of a racist ideology which declared that it was the Anglo-Saxon's "manifest destiny" to rule over the darker, weaker peoples of the world, that long was such an admission impossible.

Jack Johnson did not fit into the mosaic of white supremacy. What is more, in his private life he showed his contempt for it. During his career he earned more than $600,000. This was in the years before income tax. Indeed, as Thorstein Veblen would have put it, Jack Johnson's wealth grew too fast for his spending habits to keep up. As other gentlemen of wealth and leisure of that day, he luxuriated himself in fine clothes, fast cars and three wives. There was one difference—he was black and his wives were white.

Just two days short of three years from the time he had knocked out Jim Jeffries, Jack Johnson was a fugitive from a prison term in the United States. He had been convicted of a morals charge under a law (the Mann Act) the United States Congress had enacted following lurid publicity about his escapades with women. Afterwards his path was all downhill. The Johnson-Wells match was halted in London, Johnson was barred from many hotels and public places, the stream of ready income dried up. A poor Jack Johnson agreed to meet a new "White Hope," Jess Willard, in Havana, Cuba, on April 6, 1915. His end of the purse was to be $30,000.

Whether Johnson "lay down" in a deal to escape going to prison or whether he was fairly beaten by an opponent ten years younger is of little importance. Both versions are extant. The old refrain that had dogged the footsteps of Negro boxers from the days of Tom Molineaux was present in Havana. Said the New York *World:*

> From the moment the two entered the ring it was more than a battle between prize fighters for those who saw the contest; to them it was a struggle between white and black races; an opportunity to reassert the superior-

[15] Vol. 107 (September 30, 1911), p. 483.

ity of Caucasians over Africans; and feeling so they groaned every time Johnson shot in a hard blow and cried with joy when their champion fought well.[16]

Willard was declared winner by a knockout in the twenty-sixth round and automobiles returning from the arena to Havana flew white flags to announce that the "White Hope" had won. The old champion was on his way to prison and oblivion; but his epitaph came from the Negro writer and poet, James Weldon Johnson, who wrote years later:

> It was easy to like Jack Johnson. . . . Frederick Douglass had a picture of Peter Jackson in his study and he used to point to it and say, "Peter is doing a great deal with his fists to solve the Negro question." I think Jack, even after the reckoning of his big and little failings has been made, may be said to have done his share.[17]

For the next two decades Negro heavyweight boxers were on a merry-go-round. They could get fights but not with white boxers—at least, not white champions. There was a color bar. They had to fight each other or not at all. Harry Wills fought Sam Langford twenty-two times; Same McVey, seven times, and Joe Jeannette, the "Hoboken Iron Man," six times.

The failure of these fighters to get a chance at the championship was a tragedy—they were all good fighters—but the tragedy was most grievous in the case of Sam Langford, the "Boston Tar Baby." Langford was one of the greatest fighters of all time. He was a small man (5'6½" tall) and never weighed in at more than 165 pounds. Yet he was fiercely aggressive. In 1906 he fought Jack Johnson before Johnson became heavyweight champion. Johnson was six feet tall and weighed 200 pounds. Langford weighed only 145. Yet he floored Johnson for a count of nine, and although the bigger man finally won, it took fifteen rounds. Johnson would never fight Langford again. Credited officially in *Nat Fleischer's Ring and Record Book* with 250 fights, 23 losses, 3 by knockouts, Langford is claimed by others [18] to have fought nearly 600 fights during his 22-year ring career— but not one of them for a title. In 1956, at long last, he was elected to the Boxing Hall of Fame, Old-Timers Division.

Tom Molineaux had to issue a public challenge in the London *Times* to win a second fight with Tom Crib. Jack Johnson had to chase Tommy Burns from England to Australia for more than two years and offer him the lion's share of the purse before he got his chance. Harry Wills tried a

[16] April 6, 1915, p. 8.
[17] James Weldon Johnson, *Along This Way* (New York: Viking Press, 1933), p. 208. By special permission.
[18] See, for example, Arthur Daley's column in *The New York Times*, January 13, 1956, p. 37.

similar tactic against Jack Dempsey (who took the title from Jess Willard by a technical knockout in the fourth round at Toledo, Ohio, in 1919), without success.

Seeing him fight second-rate boxers like Billy Miske and Bill Brennan, Negro sports writers contemptuously dubbed Dempsey "champion of the white folks." Indeed, Dempsey earned this title when he defeated the French pugilist Georges Carpentier at Boyle's Thirty Acres in Jersey City, New Jersey, in 1921. For after Jack Johnson became a fugitive from the United States and was barred from fighting in England, promoters ran an elimination series among white heavyweights which Carpentier won. By an ironic twist, a black man came within a hair's breadth of winning this title, too; for a French-African, "Battling Siki," in 1923 was to knock out this same Carpentier for the light heavyweight championship.

So obvious were the dodges Dempsey's managers used to avoid a fight with Wills, that when Tex Richard finally agreed to a match even white sports writers would not believe it. Wrote "Bugs" Baer in the *New York American,* July 15, 1922:

DEMPSEY-WILLS SOMETIMES MAYBE

Chicago Puts In Bid For Their Next World's Fair in 1992

Now that Dempsey and Wills have agreed to meet sometime before next Hailey's Comet, there ain't much to do but perch back and pick our false teeth with splinters from Weejee boards.

The promise of Dempsey to fight Wills was made in 1922. Four years later, when he lost his crown to Gene Tunney, Dempsey had still to make good on that promise. George Godfrey, who reputedly knocked out Dempsey in a training camp, was another Negro heavyweight never given a chance.

Although the lid was not as heavy on other divisions, Negro boxers made only slight gains. Battling Siki, having beaten Carpentier in 1923, was outpointed for the title by Mike McTigue the same year. Tiger Flowers, "The Deacon," held the middleweight championship in 1926, but only briefly; and in 1935 John Henry Lewis became undisputed light heavyweight champion. Waiting in the wings was a twenty-year-old Detroit fighter, born in Alabama, named Joseph Barrow. In the ring his name was Joe Louis.

It is doubtful if there is a sports figure in world history who is as great a legend as Joe Louis. Certainly there is not among Negroes. He was the Negro American Dream. After he flattened the Italian giant Primo Carnera in the sixth round at the Polo Grounds in Harlem on the night of June 25,

1935, Negro boys of ten and twelve raced in and out of the long line of the slow-moving cars of the wealthy white patrons of the fight, screaming at the top of their lungs the political slogan, "Let's get Mussolini next!" [19] If he, the son of Alabama sharecroppers (so legend had it), could in a few months use his fists to batter his way to a world's championship and a million dollars, what was to stop any Negro boy from doing anything?

Joe Louis became a race hero—the greatest! Of the ten persons receiving the most prominent front-page display in the *Chicago Defender* between 1933 and 1938, Joe Louis' name led all the rest, according to studies of the sociologists, Drake and Cayton.[20] He got more than three times as many mentions as Emperor Haile Selassie at a time when the Italian-Ethopian war was raging, and four times as many mentions as Oscar DePriest who, in 1928, became the first Negro to serve in the United States Congress in over a quarter of a century.

In and out of the ring Joe Louis' conduct was unerringly correct. He had been trained by a master boxer: Jack Blackburn, veteran of more than a hundred prize fights and never knocked out. To see the "Brown Bomber," as he was called, stalking his opponent in the ring, endlessly probing with power-packed left jabs, was like watching a jungle tiger paw a stricken antelope. To learn that he had said, "There's lots of things wrong with this country, but Hitler ain't gonna fix 'em," was to find in a single sentence the rationale of the Negro's loyalty to America for the past three hundred years.

Joe Louis had seventy-one professional fights. He defended his world title against twenty-five challengers. He won fifty-four fights by a knockout or a technical knockout, and fourteen by decision. He lost one fight by decision and two by knockout or technical knockout—once to Max Schmelling when Louis was on his way up; and once (a TKO) by Rocky Marciano when he was thirty-seven years old and had officially retired two years before. All in all he held the world's championship longer than any man before or since: from June 22, 1937, to March 1, 1949 when he retired undefeated (eleven years, eight months, seven days).

Then there was Pearl Harbor and the nation at war. Joe Louis went into the Army, fought two championship fights and donated his share of the purses to Army and Navy Relief. Louis became the pride of all America.

With deepest pride all Negro America hitched its wagon to Joe Louis' star. He created a milieu in which young Negro boxers could thrive. And they did. In 1948 nearly half of all boxers listed in *Ring* magazine were Negro,[21] replacing the ethnic groups which had produced the largest num-

[19] Mussolini's Italian Fascist armies were then invading Ethiopia.

[20] St. Clair Drake and Horace R. Cayton, *Black Metropolis* (New York: Harcourt, Brace & Company, 1945), p. 403.

[21] S. Kirson and Henry Arond, "The Occupational Culture of the Boxer." *The American Journal of Sociology*, LVII, No. 5 (March, 1952), 460.

bers in previous years: the Irish, the Jewish, the Italian fighters. A whole
crop of new champions were inspired by the Brown Bomber: Henry Armstrong, Sugar Ray Robinson, Sandy Saddler; and still other Negro fighters
profited from the high standards of sportsmanship Joe Louis brought to the
ring. The times had changed; the cry for a "White Hope" became fainter
and fainter.

Since 1937 Negros have held the world's heavyweight boxing championship for all but five years. Since Joe Louis there have been Ezzard Charles,
Jersey Joe Walcott, Floyd Patterson, Sonny Liston, and "Muhammad Ali"
(born Cassius Marcellus Clay). It is unlikely that any of them will join the
ranks of the "great men" in sports history as Joe Louis has done—unless,
indeed, it is the new convert to Islam, Cassius Marcellus Clay.

Why so many Negro champions? What brings so many to greatness, one
after another? Most Negro fighters have come from poor families, which
offered them little by way of educational or cultural advantage. To those
Negroes, a successful Negro fighter was a model. As youngsters they had
seen the great acclaim given Joe Louis; in Harlem they saw Sugar Ray
Robinson driving an orchid-colored Cadillac. Not only could fighting
quickly take them up the ladder of social and economic success; but
they scarcely needed anything except physical stamina and fighting skill
to do it. Or so they believed. Witness Joe Louis' broken English or Cassius
Clay's two-time failure to pass Army Intelligence Tests. Perhaps Clay has
explained what motivates these Negro fighters better than the sociologists.
On the eve of his championship with Sonny Liston he wrote:

> . . . A southern colored boy (Clay) has made $1 million just as he turns 22.
> I don't think it's bragging to say I'm something a little special.
>
> Where do you think I would be next week if I didn't know how to shout
> and holler and make the public sit up and take notice? I would be poor, for
> one thing, and I would probably be down in Louisville, Ky., my home town,
> washing windows or running an elevator and saying "yes suh" and "no suh"
> and knowing my place. Instead of that, I'm saying I'm one of the highest-
> paid athletes in the world, which is true, and that I'm the greatest fighter
> in the world, which I hope and pray is true.[22]

The road to success is not as easy as the young Negro fighter believes;
and the way is strewn with many a sad failure. There was Sam Langford.
In his day he made over $200,000 in the prize ring; gave away a fortune in
overcoats to the needy. But the time came when his own financial need

---

[22] From "I'm a Little Special" by Cassius Clay. *Sports Illustrated* (February 24,
1964), 14. © 1964 Time Inc., by special permission. There can be seen in this quotation hostility to the "yes suh-no suh" role of servility enforced upon the Negro poor.
Boxing is a way to give vent to aggressive feelings many young Negroes have against
white masters.

sent him into the ring in Mexico almost totally blind. He would let his opponent hit him and then flail away in the direction of the blow. He had to fight to eat. In 1935 he was a blind derelict living in Harlem when a sports writer discovered him and raised a fund to keep him from starvation. The trust established for him netted $1.65 a day for the rest of his life.

Even more tragic was the case of Beau Jack, for a brief time in 1943 lightweight champion. Born Sidney Walker in Albany, Georgia, Beau Jack was a shoeshine boy at the Augusta National Golf Club, playground of millionaires. He won the fancy of the club members and they sponsored his appearance in the ring. Arthur Daley of *The New York Times* described him as a "boundless and tireless youth." [23] On one occasion he went back into the ring to answer the bell with a broken kneecap. He had 108 fights in his career and earned over a million dollars in purses; but he could neither read nor write. Daley compared him to "a man who fell among thieves." All he ever got from his purses was weekly pocket change; the rest "being put away for him." At thirty he was broke. In 1951 he was pitifully beaten by Gil Turner. In 1952, because of his old knee injury, he was denied the boxing license he so badly needed to earn a living.

There is also Joe Louis' tax problem. In 1934 Louis' purse totalled $4,757. In 1935 his ring earnings were $429,655; in 1939 they were $901,995. Between 1934 and 1948 Louis earned purses amounting to $4,587,422. This did not include other earnings from a vast complex of other ventures which could have swelled his income to nearly $5 million.

Today Louis' tax liabilities to the Federal Government remain in excess of a million dollars. His earnings flew into many hands. His tax affairs were badly managed. A fighter, with no business training, he was at the mercy of advisers who were concerned more with immediate profit than with careful provision for the champion's future. Joe Louis is not broke; he still earns a living; but he is not a millionaire. And he might have been.

THE CURIOUS CASE OF THE DISAPPEARING
NEGRO JOCKEYS

In 1899 Tod Sloan from Kokomo, Indiana, earned nearly $75,000 from jockeying. He made that much more by betting on himself; and that year also he picked up $60,000 from Wall Street investments—all in all, four times as much as earned by the President of the United States, William

[23] *The New York Times*, May 25, 1951, p. 39.

McKinley. Sloan had twenty-five trunks of clothes from the best London tailors. He paid $300 a day for a suite in one of the finest London hotels. He was the first millionaire jockey and he was white.

Negro jockeys were riding steeplechase and flat races on American tracks thirty years before Sloan put his boot in a stirrup. They came from the ranks of a "considerable following of Negroes, usually found on race tracks in the capacity of exercise boys, trainers, rubbers, and stable attendants" [24] They were riding steeplechase races at such tracks as Jerome Park in New York in the early 1870's.[25] Their entrance in flat races probably came earlier. Writing about Isaac Murphy, who rode his first professional race in 1874, one authority describes him as the "greatest Negro jockey since the celebrated Abe." [26]

Abe's record has been lost to history, but if he deserved to be named in the same class with Ike Murphy, he was a great jockey indeed. Murphy is one of the immortals of American racing. For more than two decades he was outstanding among American jockeys. He began his career as a fourteen-year-old, weighing barely seventy pounds, riding for the stable of Williams and Owings. He won his first major race, The St. Leger Stakes, in 1877 at Churchill Downs on the famous colt Vera Cruz. In 1879 he won thirty-five out of seventy-five races to set a new record for jockeys. In Detroit on July 4 of that year he rode the entire card of four winners. In 1879 he also won the Travers Stakes at Saratoga on Falsetto, defeating the favorite, Spendthrift. Isaac Murphy's record as three-time winner of the Kentucky Derby (1884, 1890, 1891) remained intact for fifty-four years until matched by Eddie Arcaro in 1945. Murphy also won the American Derby three times, the Clark Stakes four times, the Latonia Derby five times. At the end of his twenty-one years of professional racing (1895), he had ridden in 1,412 races and won 628.

At peak form Murphy weighed 107 pounds and was a rider in the classic style. His mounts included such all-time greats as Leonatus, Emperor of Norfolk, Modesty, Checkmate, Kingston, Volants and others. "He was as graceful as Appolo," said one writer, "and sat on his horse like a Centaur." [27] Admirers called him "the Colored Archer."

Murphy was only one of a whole array of outstanding Negro jockeys. In 1888 "Pike" Barnes won the first running of the Futurity at Sheepshead

[24] F. W. Vosburgh, *Racing In America 1866–1921*. (New York: The Jockey Club, 1921. Private printing), p. 11.

[25] F. W. Vosburgh (under pen name Vigilante), *Steeplechasing in America*. (New York: Burke & See, 1895), p. 38.

[26] F. W. Vosburgh, *Famous American Jockeys*. (New York: R. A. Saalfield, 1884), p. 43.

[27] *Ibid.*

for a purse of $50,000. He was winner of the Champagne Stakes (1889), the Belmont Stakes and Alabama Stakes (1890). Willie Simms, a contemporary of Tod Sloan on race tracks in England, was twice winner of the Belmont Stakes (1893, 1894), the Kentucky Derby (1896, 1898), the Brighton Handicap (1897, 1898), and scored victories as well in the Champagne Stakes and the Annual Champion Stakes. James Winkfield was the second jockey to win two successive runnings of the Kentucky Derby (1901, 1902). The first was Isaac Murphy. No other jockeys have equalled their record. Winkfield went on to a notable career as a jockey in France. These are only three names from a list of probably as many as twenty to thirty top Negro jockeys who were mainstays of the sport of horse racing during the last third of the nineteenth century and the early years of the twentieth century.

The jockeys had their counterparts in Negro trainers. William Bird was an outstanding trainer for well over a quarter of a century. In the early 1850's he went to England as trainer for the noted owner, Richard TenBroeck. He trained a number of famous mounts, including Crickmore who twice beat the great Hindoo, and Buchanan, whom Ike Murphy rode in his first Kentucky Derby victory in 1884. Bill Perkins (brother of Jockey "Soup" Perkins, winner of the 1895 Kentucky Derby) was another among a number of Negro trianers who trained and handled some of the country's leading thoroughbreds. There were many more.

The glorious page in racing history written by the Isaac Murphys and William Birds is no more. Out of some 1,500 jockeys and 4,000 trainers in racing today, only a mere handful are Negro; and none of these has an outstanding record. This is the way it has been for fifty years or more. Bob McCurdy, a young jockey who competes in the East, is the first Negro rider to be rated highly in several decades.

No one can say for certain what caused this sudden famine of Negro jockeys and trainers on American race tracks. There are some facts, however, that should be considered. In the running of the first Kentucky Derby in 1875, fourteen of the fifteen jockeys in the race were Negro. However, the winner's fee for which they rode was insignificant when compared with those for which Tod Sloan was to compete a quarter of a century later. Fees for the winning jockey have been estimated at not more than five dollars.[28] Such rewards were hardly enough to tempt many white boys, who had more lucrative opportunities, to ride. On the other hand, for a Negro youth who grew up around the stables and who became expert in handling horses at an early age, the thrill of riding before a cheering

[28] By Marshall Cassidy, executive secretary of the Jockey Club, in interview with author.

crowd was a reward which helped compensate for unattractive cash wages. At any rate, although jockeys like Ike Murphy probably made a good living (he had enough money to buy his own race horse in 1886), none of the Negro riders ever closely approached the earnings of Tod Sloan.[29]

At the turn of the century things happened to racing. New York millionaires took over much of the horse breeding in Blue Grass Kentucky. A steady stream of the best yearlings went East in 1899, 1900 and 1901 to be crossed with the best blood lines among English thoroughbreds. Elaborate race tracks were built and horse racing became a rich man's game. A Board of Control made up of representatives of race track owners and stable owners was formed in 1891 to govern all racing. This body was replaced by the Jockey Club (1894), which ever since has been sole arbiter of which jockeys shall be licensed to ride on American tracks.

Each of these developments had its influence upon the future of the Negro jockey. Wealthy owners, racing for love of the sport, could and did afford to pay high riding fees to jockeys irrespective of the size of the purse. In 1899 millionaire William C. Whitney paid Tod Sloan $10,000 to ride Ballyhoo Bey in the Futurity. This kind of money had plenty of takers among white jockeys and made it more and more difficult for Negro jockeys to get mounts. This does not mean that some millionaire owners did not favor Negro riders. Favorite of the Dwyer brothers and of New York political boss Richard Croker (of the Croker-Dwyer Stables) was Willie Simms, the first American jockey to shorten his stirrup and ride his horse like "a monkey on a stick." But as riding became more lucrative, Negro jockeys became fewer.

The fact that the Jockey Club could control the licensing of jockeys did not help Negro jockeys either. Well-known Negro jockeys were not excluded from the tracks, but neither were younger Negro jockeys encouraged to enter the profession. Fewer Negroes got licenses, and without a license they could not ride.

In time the practice of giving the jockey 10 percent of the purse made riding even more profitable. The Kentucky Derby, which began with a purse of $2,850, now exceeds $110,000, with $11,000 of that for the winning jockeys. This is not the richest purse. A dozen more range from $150,000 to $250,000; over thirty carry purses from $50,000 to $85,000; and twenty more range betweeen $25,000 and $50,000. Ten percent of these amounts

[29] In 1904 O. E. Duncan in his column "The World of Sports" in the Indianapolis *Freeman* named eight Negro jockeys then active on the turf who were earning from $5,000 to $10,000 a year. They included J. Winkfield who was riding in Russia that year and had scored twenty-one firsts, eight seconds, and had failed to place only four times in his first forty mounts. Others were Willie Hicks, J. Hicks, J. Conley, C. Bonner, D. Austin and H. Crowhurst.

offers considerable inducement to the rider and there are literally hundreds of other races where the jockey can earn from $500 to $1,000 for a race of somewhere between two and three minutes. Then, too, he can—and often does—ride two to three winners a day.

Few jockeys riding today can match the record of Negro jockey "Monk" Overton, who on July 10, 1891 at Washington Park, Illinois, had six straight winners out of six mounts; or of Jimmie Lee, who, at Churchill Downs on June 5, 1907, was winning jockey of each of the six races scheduled at the track that day. These jockeys and scores of other nameless ones would, perhaps, agree with Isaac Murphy, who said shortly before he died in 1896:

> I am proud of my calling as I am of my record, and I believe my life will be recorded as a success, though the reputation I enjoy was earned in the stable and saddle. It is a great honor to be classed as one of America's greatest jockeys.[30]

THE SPORTS GHETTO

Almost from their beginnings boxing and horse racing were commercialized spectator sports; they conferred no particularly high status upon the fighters or jockeys. The participants in these sports were professionals who performed in hope of financial reward; to the spectators they were entertainers, but little higher than minstrels. It was, perhaps, this fact more than any other which explains the early entrance of the Negro into these two sports. No great social leap was involved in their participation; when affluence and prestige attached themselves to the role of a winning jockey, the Negro jockey disappeared.[31]

In other major sports there was a different situation. Baseball, football and basketball are of much later origin and were during much of their early history predominantly amateur, with baseball the earliest of the three to give way to commercialization, organization and exploitation as a mass spectator sport.[32] There was no significant social distance between player

[30] George B. "Brownie" Leach, *The Kentucky Derby Diamond Jubilee* (Louisville: Gibbs-Inman Co., 1949), p. 48.

[31] It is significant that the *Louisville Courier Journal's* account of the winning of the first Kentucky Derby in 1875 discusses the gowns the ladies wore to the race, the blood lines of Aristides, the winner, but barely mentions the Negro jockey who rode him.

[32] For the influence of the railroad, telegraph and news media in making baseball the national pastime in the 1850's, see: John Richard Betts, "The Technological Revolution and the Rise of Sports," *The Mississippi Valley Historical Review*, XL, No. 2 (September, 1953), p. 231 ff.

and spectator; the athletes came from the elite in the colleges and universities. Few Negroes were to be found with requisite ability and leisure to follow sport; these few made a name for themselves, but the mass of Negroes were for a variety of reasons forced to develop athletic skill in a kind of sports ghetto.

A good case can be made to show that the experience of the Negro in American sports is a microcosm of his experience in total American society. Privileges for American whites in sports has been paralleled by disadvantages for American Negroes; a pattern so clearly marked in such other areas as education, housing, jobs.

There have been few playing fields in the United States on which the Negro boy or girl could run, jump, swim or play, and develop athletic skills. In the South, where there was hardly any money for chalk and blackboard erasers in segregated Negro schools, there was less money for balls and bats for jim crow playgrounds. A study of recreational facilities for Negroes in seventeen Southern cities made in 1928 showed that:

> In the case of public parks, for instance, 4 out of 17 southern cities have facilities for whites only; one half of those cities which have recreation centers have none for Negroes; 3 have public bathing beaches for whites only, and 10 out of 17 have swimming pools for whites only.[33]

Even where facilities existed, they were inadequate. Thus, for example, in Nashville, Tennessee, in 1940, Negroes were 28 percent of the population and had access to only one percent of park and recreation space.[34]

Opportunity for recreation and sports had its limitations in the North, too. Up to 1900, Negro schoolboys were barred from taking part in athletic contests in the public schools of the city of New York. In the summer of 1919 in Chicago, clashes over the use of baseball diamonds, parks, swimming pools, public beaches exploded into a race riot in which 38 people were killed, 537 were injured, and more than 1,000 rendered homeless.

Negro youth often had to play their sports on unkempt vacant lots and learn to swim at unprotected beach and river bank sites. Even in the 1950's when Willie Mays would leave the Polo Grounds (the New York Giant's ball park) and come to Harlem to play stick ball with schoolboys, they had to play in the streets for lack of a playground.

It is doubtful that even the enactment of the Civil Rights Law of 1964 will soon change the asphalt-concrete environment of congested "central

[33] Forrester B. Washington, "Recreational Facilities for the Negro," in *The Annals of the American Academy of Political and Social Science*, November, 1928, p. 275.

[34] Charles S. Johnson, *Patterns of Negro Segregation* (New York: Harper & Brothers, 1943), p. 29.

city" in which large numbers of Negro youth must find their recreation and learn their sports. The lesser mobility of these youth caused by their low socioeconomic status will continue to hem them in and keep them out of the public recreation areas in the suburbs and the more distant state parks.[35] This is a serious challenge to officials of large cities; they must take positive and imaginative action to make it possible for masses of under-privileged youth to share equitably in public recreation.

Sports requiring playing areas of exact measurements and specific surfac-ing were even harder for Negroes to come by. The name of "Mother" Seames is legendary among those who have followed the Negro tennis player, because as early as 1910 she had her own tennis court in Chicago, where many a young Negro learned the game. Through the years Negro private clubs acquired their own golf courses, since they were barred from those owned by whites, but the expensive operation of such clubs and the thin layer of Negro middle-class persons available for their support have made it difficult to maintain most of them. A recent sports writer makes mention of two Negro clubs in North Carolina as "the only ones of their kind in the country." [36]

Still another factor contributing to the enforced sports ghetto for Negroes was the frequent taboo against playing teams that had Negro mem-bers. This often caused a coach to think twice before selecting a Negro player for his team. Such a taboo was more apt to rise at high school level than at college level, but it was frequent enough at both levels.

Often an outstanding Negro athlete would escape the ghetto during his college days only to sink back into it after college. Bill Mathews was as outstanding a shortstop on Harvard's baseball team as he was an end on her football eleven. And many "old grads" at Harvard still remember the day their star pitcher, Earl Brown, pitched a no-run, no-hit game to beat Yale 1-0. But neither of these Negro athletes stood a chance of winning an opportunity to play on professional baseball teams. The bars were up in basketball, too; and stellar players like George Gregory, captain of Colum-bia's basketball team, and William "Dolly" King of Long Island University in the Thirties, were not accepted into the then jim crow professional basketball leagues.[37] In football, beginning with Fritz Pollard (Brown) in

[35] For a discussion of the close correlation between low income and low personal mobility and of how segregated residential areas have led to perpetuation of recreational ghettoes, see: Outdoor Recreation Resources Review Commission, Report No. 21, *The Future of Outdoor Recreation in the Metropolitan Regions of the United States* (Washington, D.C.: Government Printing Office), 1962, Vol. 1, pp.9–10, 77–85, 240.

[36] Robert H. Boyle, *Sport—Mirror of American Life* (Boston: Little, Brown and Company, 1963), p. 206.

[37] King was later (1947) signed to play center on the Rochester Royals, a member of The National Basketball League, at a reported $9,000 a season.

1919, there were Negro players on professional teams, but only a few until recent years.

Barriers to the full and free participation in American sports forced the Negro to develop a sports world all his own behind the walls of his social ghetto. As early as 1878, a group of Negro waiters at the Argyle Hotel in Babylon, Long Island, in New York State, formed a baseball team. Frank Thompson, the headwaiter, was the organizer. Unlike many other Negro workers, the waiters had free time between serving meals in which to develop leisure-time activities. In 1887 Frank Peters in Chicago formed a semiprofessional baseball team in Chicago called the Union Giants.

In 1892, in New York City, the Calumet Wheelman, a Negro bicycle club, was formed and soon grew to 250 members. As years passed it fielded a base-ball team, a football team, and produced athletes in track, field, and cycling.

Clubs like this were the breeding ground of young Negro athletes in many cities. The Alpha Physical Culture and the Smart Set were begun in Brooklyn, New York, in 1903 and 1905 respectively. They, too, branched out into a variety of sports and, as late as 1922, were still represented by winning teams. The great University of Chicago Negro quarter-miler in 1915, Binga Dismond, who equalled the world's record at 440 yards, got his start with the Smart Set club. The St. Christopher's Club, founded in the early 1900's, a church group, also trained a number of Negro youths who were to make a creditable showing in sports. The Spartan A.C. also began in this period. In the Negro ghetto there was the first flowering of sports activity of Negro youth; perhaps nowhere in such lush growth as in the sport of baseball.

THE NEGRO IN BASEBALL

In addition to Moses Walker on the Toledo Baseball team, a few other Negroes (among them Walker's brother, Welday) had brief careers in major league baseball prior to 1900. There are several legendary accounts of white managers trying to palm off Negro players as Indians. But strong prejudices against Negroes soon brought an end even to this practice; it was not long, before they were completely eliminated from professional base-ball.

But raising the color bar did not thwart the desire of Negroes to play ball. The Cuban Giants, made up of Cuban and American Negroes and based in New York, was one of the first teams to achieve national promi-nence. In Chicago, Frank Leland, who had been scorekeeper on Frank

Peters' Union Giants, founded his own Leland Giants and brought the American Negro's "Mr. Baseball," Rube Foster, into the game as pitcher and later as manager. Soon many other teams were formed; in Pittsburgh, in Atlantic City, in Nashville, in Washington, D.C. and easily a dozen other cities. Sometimes they were semiprofessional, travelling around the the country and meeting all comers. Sometimes they were composed of regularly employed men who could play only on their days off. Or there was Rube Foster's Chicago American Giants (formed in 1912 after he left the Leland Giants), which rode between cities in special Pullman cars and played in major league ball parks just as the white major league teams did. For spring training Foster would take his team South to such Negro schools as Hampton, Tuskegee, Atlanta University and Claflin University to play a five-game series with each as a warm-up to the regular season.

Evidencing an obvious admiration for the baseball acumen of John J. McGraw, manager of the New York Giants, there developed a whole rash of Negro teams with the name "Giants" in their title. These are some of them: Cuban Giants, Bacharach Giants, Manhattan Giants, Harlem Colored Giants, Chicago Giants, Leland Giants, Philadelphia Giants, Lincoln Giants, Mohawk Giants, Brooklyn Giants, and Washington Elite Giants. There were also such teams as the Black Yankees, Baltimore Black Sox, Pittsburgh Crawfords, Kansas City Monarchs, Hilldales, Homestead Grays, and Louisville Cubs, the last considered in 1910 to be the best team in the South.

The officials annals of baseball in this country show nothing about these teams or their players. It is as though they did not exist. Yet they did exist and now and again there is a wisp of historical evidence to prove it. Thus one reads in the Indianapolis *Freeman* of August 11, 1888:

> The Cuban Giants, the famous baseball club, have defeated the New Yorks four games out of five and are now virtually champions of the world. The St. Louis Browns, Detroits, and Chicagos, afflicted with Negrophobia and unable to bear the odium of being beaten by colored men, refused to accept their challenge.

Nor was this an isolated instance. Year after year Negro teams contested with the best major league clubs and battered into defeat such baseball immortals as Christy Mathewson, Joseph "Iron Man" McGinnity, and Rube Marquard—not once, but many times. Indeed, victory of Negro teams became such a frequent occurrence that major league officials issued an edict banning such competition unless the white players played under a name other than that of the white major league team of which they were members.

It is hard to rate the Negro stars of teams of fifty years ago; none is in baseball's Hall of Fame; and there are few objective yardsticks for comparison with those who have been acclaimed baseball's all-time greats. But there are some comments made by sports writers who were contemporaries of these players which bear repeating.

For example, in answer to the question, "Who was the greatest player in baseball history?" an old-time St. Louis sports writer replied:

> If you mean the greatest in organized baseball, my answer would be Babe Ruth; but if you mean in all baseball, organized and unorganized, the answer would have to be a colored man named John Henry Lloyd.[38]

Lloyd, who played shortstop on Rube Foster's Chicago American Giants, was only one of many players the Texas-born player-manager developed. There were others such as Jimmy Lyons, claimed to be one of the fastest men ever to play baseball; George Harney, a great spitballer; William Sublett and Bruce Petway, a battery Foster brought up from Nashville; and many others.

One of the greatest players on his team was Foster himself; he was a master strategist, a superb pitcher. Wrote a Cleveland sportswriter after seeing Foster pitch:

> Cleveland fans have now seen two real pitchers: Addie Joss and Rube Foster.[39]

That was saying a lot, for Joss was the Bob Feller of his day. In 1908 in Chicago, Joss pitched a perfect game, allowing no runner to reach first base.

In 1920 Foster founded the Negro National League, which brought the best Negro clubs into organized competition and greatly improved their game. There was a High Commissioner of Negro Baseball, Ferdinand Q. Morton, Negro Tammany Hall Leader of New York City, a world series, and crowd-drawing stars. In the 1930's crowds of more than forty thousand Negro and white fans were frequent at games which featured pitchers like Leroy "Satchel" Paige and catchers like Josh Gibson. They outdrew many white major league teams.

Even in his twilight hour in the American League, Paige was a shrewd and exciting pitcher; in his heyday in the National Negro League he ranked with the best pitchers in baseball, bar none. The same thing can be said of Josh Gibson among the catchers. Gibson never got a chance to play baseball outside the ghetto (except in occasional unofficial exhibition games), but he was a consistent .400 hitter and led the league in home runs for a number of seasons. As a battery on Gus Greenlea's Pittsburgh Crawfords and later with the Homestead Grays, the playing of Paige and Gibson was sensational.

[38] Alvin F. Harlow, "Unrecognized Stars. *Esquire* Magazine Vol. X, No. 3 (September, 1938), p. 75.

[39] Quoted by Fay Young, *Chicago Defender*, August 7, 1948, p. 10.

It was the National Negro Baseball League which was a showcase for Negro stars, gave white fans exposure to an exciting and highly professional brand of baseball, and demonstrated to the astute manager of the Brooklyn Dodgers, Branch Rickey, that it was not only good statesmanship, but also good business to bring a Negro player into American organized baseball. Rickey planned carefully. He selected the outstanding Negro athlete of UCLA, sent him to the Montreal farm team for two years, and in 1947 brought him up to the majors. The player was Jack Roosevelt Robinson, shortstop of the Kansas City Monarchs.

The rest is history. After a few ugly moments of prejudice on the part of a rare white fan and a rarer white player, Robinson became the scrappy, colorful player that brought thousands of fans to see him wherever he played. Other Negro players broke into the National League: Larry Doby with Cleveland, Roy Campanella and Don Newcombe with the Dodgers, and Elston Howard with the New York Yankees.

Between 1947 when Jackie Robinson became the first Negro in major league baseball and 1964, eighteeen years, the Baseball Writers Association voted a Negro to be the National League's Most Valuable Player eleven times.[40] In 1963 Elston Howard, Negro catcher of the New York Yankees, received this award in the American League. Negro players have led the National League in batting seven out of eleven times [41] in the period from 1954 through 1964, in home runs eight out of eleven times.[42] The fleet-

[40] Most Valuable Player awards were made as follows: (1949) Jackie Robinson, Brooklyn; (1951, 1953, 1955) Roy Campanella, Brooklyn; (1954) Willie Mays, New York; (1956) Don Newcombe, Brooklyn; (1957) Hank Aaron, Milwaukee; (1958, 1959) Ernie Banks, Chicago; (1962) Maury Wills, Los Angeles. Newcombe also was National League pitching Champion in 1955 (W. 20—L. 5) and in 1956 (W. 27—L. 7); Wills, chosen by American sportswriters (Associated Press poll) "Athlete of the Year" in 1962.

[41] Jackie Robinson was National League batting champion in 1949 with an average of .342. Those Negro players who have held the National League title in the last decade are: (1954) Willie Mays, New York—.345; (1956, 1959) Hank Aaron, Milwaukee—.328 and .355; (1961) R. Clemente, Pittsburgh—.351; (1962, 1963) Tommy Davis, Los Angeles—.346 and .326; (1964) R. Clemente—.339.

[42] In the American League Larry Doby of the Cleveland Indians was leading home-run hitter in 1953 (32) and in 1954 (32). Negro National League home run champions follow:

1955	Willie Mays, New York	51
1957	Hank Aaron, Milwaukee	44
1958	Ernie Banks, Chicago	47
1960	Ernie Banks, Chicago	41
1961	Orlando Cepeda, San Francisco	46
1962	Willie Mays, San Francisco	49
1963	Willie McCovey, San Francisco	44
1963	Hank Aaron, Milwaukee	44
1964	Willie Mays, San Francisco	47

footed Negro shortstop, Maury Wills of the Los Angeles Dodgers, in 1963 shattered the stolen-base record of Ty Cobb, which had remained inviolate nearly half a century. Today nearly one out of every five major league baseball player is a Negro; their annual earnings exceed $2 million.

At least one superlative should be saved for Willie Mays, brought into the New York Giant farm team (the Minneapolis Millers) from Birmingham, Alabama. Mays played ball with his father on the Birmingham Black Barons and caught the eye of a Giant scout. He was signed for a bonus of $5,000, played thirty-five games with the Millers and had a batting average of .477. After that demonstration he was brought up to the Giants on May 25, 1951, and has been with the team (now the San Francisco Giants) ever since. In 1952 the St. Louis Cardinals are reported to have offered the Giant club $1 million for Mays and were turned down. He is captain of the team, earns one of the highest salaries in baseball—reputedly $107,000, and is the undoubted idol of millions of American youth. Perhaps the best superlative for Mays is one given him by the fans: Willie Mays—American.

Probably more than in any other aspect of American life, the Negro player has found, in baseball, freedom from color prejudice. He has gained wide acceptance by fan and player alike; he has seen baseball become a sport where race is almost irrelevant and where good sportsmanship is the dominant value. Indeed, even the "just average" Negro player (and there are some in the leagues) can now play in organized baseball.

It is significant that as Negro players near the end of the second decade of their free participation in American baseball, the first to break through the color barrier, Jackie Robinson, has entered Baseball's Hall of Fame.

THE NEGRO IN FOOTBALL

Jimmy Brown of the Cleveland Browns is the greatest running back professional football has ever known. In the opening game of the 1963 season, before 58,000 fans in Cleveland he scored 3 touchdowns, gained 102 yards in rushing and another 100 yards on pass reception, including an 82-yard touchdown pass. The next week at Dallas he ran through the Dallas Cowboys with a 71-yard and a 62-yard touchdown and gained overall 232 yards in the game.

Brown, chosen All-American when he played for Syracuse University in 1956, is a storybook player. How else can one explain the amazing record he has built up since he became a professional in 1957? In eight seasons he has achieved a lifetime rushing record of 10,768 yards in 2,070 attempts for an average gain of 5.2 yards for each carry. This is an all-time league record. Brown holds as well the all-time league record for the most touchdowns scored in a lifetime (82), and for the most yards gained in a single game (237 on November 24, 1957, against the Los Angeles Rams; he has rushed over 200 yards in a single game 4 times). In 1963 he broke his own 1958 record of most yards gained in a single season (1,527) with a new ground-gaining high of 1,823 yards: another all-time league record. He is the idol of millions who see him in person on the gridiron or over television, or read of his latest triumphs in the sports pages of Monday morning's metropolitan daily papers.

Jimmy Brown's football ancestors never had this public visibility, but theirs is a dazzling record that has shown the way to Brown and dozens of other Negro amateur and professional stars of today. Negro college athletes were playing football almost from the time it was decided to restrict sides to eleven men (1880). How much earlier they played, when football was a formless mass game with as many as twenty-five players to a team, is not known. It seems certain that the skills which qualified young William Jackson and William Lewis for the varsity team at Amherst in 1889 must have had their origin at a much earlier time.

At any rate most sportswriters have been content to date the beginning of Negro participation in American football with the advent of Jackson and Lewis on the Amherst team. From that day until this there have been Negro gridiron athletes of star-proportion almost every football season. Lewis led the way when he played center for Harvard in 1892 and 1893 and was named both years on Walter Camp's All-American team.

Bill Mathews at Harvard, Matt Bulloch at Dartmouth, and Bob Marshall at Minnesota followed Lewis by only a few years and kept up the tradition he had begun. Walter Camp selected Marshall for his Number 2 All-American in both 1905 and 1906. Of Bill Mathews, Harvard left end, a sports writer of the New York *World* wrote:

> Mathews, the colored player, came down the field like the cannon ball express and, with head down, hit the red-haired Yale man like a battering ram. The crash as they struck the ground fairly made the stands tremble and Rockwell dropped the ball.[43]

Rockwell's reputation and Yale's was saved that day when another Yale man recovered the fumble, and when shortly afterward Mathews had to leave the game because of injuries. Yale won 12–0.

But neither Harvard nor Yale was spared during the 1916 football season when Frederick Douglass (Fritz) Pollard played against them. Pollard

[43] November 20, 1904.

has been acclaimed as Brown University's greatest halfback of all time. This is what Eugene O'Connell wrote about him in the New York *Evening Globe:*

> Practically singlehanded the young colored boy has beaten Yale and Harvard on successive afternoons on their own fields. He's been the backbone of the hammering attacks which has brought Brown through a tough season with an unbroken string of victories. He plays football because he likes it, and his quiet deportment, grip and stamina, coupled with his remarkable abilities have forced crowds at both New Haven and Cambridge, sorrowful in defeat, to stand up and acclaim him as he left the field giving away to a substitute after the game was safely tucked away.[44]

Pollard was named on the 1916 All-American team. In the 1917 season, the name of another Negro star was in the spotlight, Paul Robeson of Rutgers. That season Robeson played every minute of every game, except one when he was barred from playing because of color. The greatest opportunity to display his skill came when Rutgers played the Newport Naval Reserves. It was a team of all-stars which included Charlie Barnett, All-American from Cornell, and Cupe Black, one of Yale's all-time greats, who had been chosen All-American in 1913. This veteran team had already beaten Brown and Harvard and it now came—brim full of confiidence—to face the undergraduate Rutgers team. In its account of the game, the New York *Herald Tribune,* under the headline DASHING ROBESON HUMBLES BLACK, wrote in part as follows:

> A tall tapering Negro in a faded crimson sweater, mole skins and a pair of worn maroon socks ranged hither, thither and yon on the wind-whipped Flatbush field yesterday afternoon. He rode on the wings of the frigid breezes, a grim, silent, compelling figure. Whether it was Charlie Barnett of old Cornell, an All-American glory, or Garish or Gardner who tried to hurl himself through a moiling gauntlet, he was met and stopped by this blaze of red and black. The Negro was Paul Robeson of Rutgers College and he is a minister's son. He is also nineteen years of age and weighs two hundred pounds. Of his football capacity you are referred to Cupe Black of Yale. He can tell you. It was Robeson, a veritable Othello of battle, who led the little Rutgers eleven to a 14 to 0 victory over the widely heralded Newport Naval Reserves.[45]

Robeson was Walter Camp's choice for All-American end in 1917.

Football began as a sport for the elite. Ivy League schools began the first intercollegiate competition. In 1877, when a Yale team played Princeton

[44] Quoted in the *New York Age,* November 23, 1916, p. 6.
[45] Quoted in Lester Walton's column in the *New York Age,* November 29, 1917, p. 6.

in Hoboken, New Jersey, there were fewer than a thousand spectators—quite a difference from the hundred thousand or more who witness a great Bowl game today. It was in this rarefied sports atmosphere that some of the few Negroes who entered Ivy League Colleges, rose to football fame. Their exploits gave the whole Negro race pride. Although football skill symbolized little beyond speed, endurance and physical strength, the achievement of the Negro gridiron heroes was seized upon as a symbol of the race's ability. Columnists like Lester Walton of the *New York Age,* bursting with enthusiasm, could write:

> Last fall it was Frederick Douglass Pollard of Brown who shone forth as the most brilliant of football stars. I now take pleasure in introducing you to Mr. Paul Robeson of Rutgers who has become a sensation of the present football season. For two successive years the Negro carried off the highest honors of the gridiron which in the vernacular of the turf is going some.[46]

At a time when equality of opportunity and citizenship was still a long way off for most Negroes, the Negro football star was a beacon of hope.

From the days of Paul Robeson to the days of Jimmy Brown is almost half a century. Year after year, in almost an unbroken line, Negro athletes have excelled in football. To mention only a few, there were: Joseph Trigg of Syracuse (who also was a stroke on the Syracuse crew); Fred "Duke" Slater at Iowa, who made the second All-American team in 1921; Charles West, who quarterbacked the Washington and Jefferson team in the Rose Bowl in 1922 to a scoreless tie against California; Jerome "Brud" Holland, Cornell's great All-American end; Homer Harris, who captained the Iowa Eleven in 1938; Kenny Washington and Jackie Robinson who led UCLA to an undefeated season in 1939; Bill Willis, Ohio State's All-American tackle, and Levi Jackson, captain of Yale's team in 1949.

One could go on. There were many more. But for many reasons the list should end with the name of Ernie Davis, the Syracuse halfback, who was twice named All-American (1960, 1961). Davis followed Jimmy Brown at Syracuse. Brown set new records at Syracuse, and Davis promptly broke them. In the Liberty Bowl game in Philadelphia in 1961, Davis gained 140 yards in thirty rushes. He was awarded the Heisman Memorial Trophy that year by the votes of sportswriters and sportscasters from every section of the country. Significantly the halfback Davis defeated for the honor was Bob Ferguson, Ohio State's All-American halfback, also a Negro. The standout draftee of professional football in 1961, Davis never lived to achieve new fame in professional ranks. He died of leukemia in 1963.

Not all Negro football achievement has been shown by stars on "white"

[46] November 29, 1917, p. 6.

college teams. For more than half a century Negro colleges and universities have fielded football teams. In earlier years when professional football teams barred Negro players, there was no common standard to evaluate the abilities of the teams or their players. In later years football stars from Negro colleges have been drafted by teams in the professional football leagues and have demonstrated their ability to equal the talents of the best players from white colleges and universities.[47]

In the 1920's homecoming games and "Thanksgiving classics" were the scenes of thrilling intercollegiate contests between Negro college teams. The traditional Thanksgiving Day Howard-Lincoln Game was for years the social event of the Eastern Seaboard.[48] Hardly less popular were the Hampton-Tuskegee contests. Perhaps the luster of these early sports events explains in part the high value which, according to the sociologist, E. Franklin Frazier, Negro professionals place upon sports. Wrote Frazier:

> Except when they [the Negro professionals] are talking within the narrow field of their profession, their conversations are generally limited to sports —baseball and football. They follow religiously the scores of the various teams and achievements of all the players. For hours they listen to radio accounts of sports and watch baseball and football games over television.[49]

It is doubtful if the emphasis noted by Professor Frazier remains as strong today. With the breakdown of many barriers to their attendance at concerts and theaters and with the favorable presentation of Negroes other than sports figures on radio and television, Negro cultural horizons have broadened. The Howard-Lincoln game is no longer a classic; in fact, Lincoln no longer has a football team.

In 1963, there were sixty-three Negro colleges that fielded football teams and that still engaged in intercollegiate contests among themselves. Four colleges that previously were predominantly attended by Negroes, but that since 1954 (as a result of the U.S. Supreme Court decision in *Brown* vs. *the Board of Education of Topeka*) have been integrated, play within their own integrated collegiate football conferences. Since 1951 these col-

---

[47] In 1964 a total of thirty-three Negro players were drafted by National League teams from seventeen Negro colleges; Texas Southern led the colleges in supplying football talent with five draftees; Florida A & M, Grambling, Johnson C. Smith and Virginia Union supplied three rookies each. The Pittsburgh Steelers led the league in drafting players from Negro Colleges with seven, while the Cleveland Browns, Chicago Bears and Dallas Cowboys each called up four. On the 1964 veterans roster of the professional teams were thirteen players who played football on Negro College teams.

[48] A total of 28,000 spectators saw the 1926 game in the then-new stadium at Howard.

[49] E. Franklin Frazier, *Black Bourgeoisie* (Glencoe, Ill.: The Free Press, 1957), p. 208.

leges have had the leading teams: Florida A & M, Prairie View, Southern, Texas Southern, Tennessee State and Grambling. The best of their former players have found places on professional football elevens.

The Negro colleges have not yet begun to schedule games with teams from white colleges, although it has been attempted.[50] Some post-season classics, such as the Sugar Bowl Game in New Orleans and the Blue-Gray contest in Montgomery, Alabama, continue to bar Negro players. Negro athletes have competed, however, in the Cotton Bowl and Orange Bowl games. Generally colleges in the Deep South refuse to play against Negroes or (where Negro students have been admitted) to let them play on their teams. Nor has the National Collegiate Athletic Association, which controls intercollegiate competition, taken a stand on integrated contests. Some Southern schools have revoked their policy against Negro players, however. There seems little reason to doubt that football will soon be a sport where only the test of ability, not skin color, will be used to determine player eligibility.

NEGROES IN BASKETBALL

Negroes were playing basketball as early as 1904 and by 1910 had teams of their own. Bob Douglass, manager of the Renaissance Casino, a dance hall in New York's Harlem, formed the New York Spartan basketball team. This team played in the Casino and proved a popular attraction for young people who came both to watch basketball and to dance. The Spartan name did not stick. Soon the team was called The Renaissance Big 5 or just The Rens, after the hall where they played. Soon, too, they began to be called the Colored Champions of the World. Stars of the team included its Captain, "Fats" Jenkins, "Pappy" Ricks, "Tarzan" Cooper, George Fiall and "Bruiser" Saitch—all fast and powerful players.

Competition for the Rens developed in New York and other cities. There were the Commonwealths, on which team Paul Robeson played briefly, and the St. Christophers from Brooklyn. From Pittsburgh came Cum Posey's Loendi Club, from Washington, D.C., the Crescent A.C., and from Chicago, the Chicago Defender 5. As in baseball, unofficial games were played with white professional teams.

Meanwhile Negro college stars were making enviable records only to find their way barred to most professional teams. George Gregory of Colum-

---

[50] One breakthrough was the post-season game between St. Johns and Prairie View in the Camelia Bowl in 1963.

bia was chosen in 1931 on the All-American team of the Helms Athletic Foundation. William "Dolly" King of Long Island was outstanding in 1937.[51] All-around athlete Jackie Robinson in 1939 was leading scorer in the Pacific Coast Conference with 148 points. Don Barksdale, All-American forward in 1947 from UCLA and USA Olympic team member in 1948, was named to the Helms Amateur Basketball Hall of Fame. These standout players are typical of the talent that was barred from professional basketball because of color.

The first Negro player signed to play professional basketball was Ed "Chuck" Cooper who was signed by the Boston Celtics to play in the 1950–51 season. That same season Nat "Sweetwater" Clifton was signed by the Knickerbockers. A year later Barksdale entered professional ranks.

Today, however, Negro players form an important part of professional basketball. Former All-American college stars like Oscar Robertson (Cincinnati), Wilt Chamberlain (Kansas), Bill Russell (San Francisco) and Elgin Baylor (Seattle) are mainstays of leading professional teams. Chamberlain (1960), Russell (1961, 1962, 1963), who also played on a U.S. Olympic team, and Robertson (1964) have held possession of the President's Trophy of the National Basketball Association for the last five years. This award is voted annually to the "most valuable player" in professional basketball.

The records of all these players are outstanding, but that of Wilt Chamberlain (7'1") with the San Francisco Warriors in the 1962–63 season is spectacular. He was that season the league's leading scorer with 3,586 points in eighty games for a scoring average of 44.8 points per game. He led the league in field goals (1,463), field goal percentage (.528), rebounds (1,946), rebounds per game (24.3), and in most points in one game (73). He was third in the free throws made (660) behind Bob Petitt of St. Louis (685) and Elgin Baylor of Los Angeles (661).

Sport or Spectacle

No story of the Negro in basketball would be complete without a discussion of the Harlem Globetrotters, although whether the Globetrotters are engaged in sport or spectacle is still an open question. The Globetrotters were formed by their owner Abe Saperstein in the 1927–28 basketball season. They have appeared before a million people in one season and, by the end of the 1963 season, had played over eight thousand games in eighty-seven countries on six continents. Indeed, the Globetrotters are no longer

[51] Clare Bee, LIU basketball coach, said: "King is the greatest athlete I ever coached. As a basketball player, no one can top him and as a footballer, I'd match him with any end in the country. If it wasn't for his color, he'd be a sure bet in pro football." Quoted by Jimmy Powers in "Powerhouse," New York *Daily News*, January 29, 1941, p. 50.

one team, but three teams playing under the name "Harlem Globetrotters" simultaneously in different parts of the world.

What is disturbing about the Globetrotters is that they never lose—or hardly ever. Gregory P. Stone, criticizing some aspects of the "massification" and commercialism of sports, states: "The spectacle is predictable and certain; the game, unpredictable, uncertain." [52] Judged by this standard there can be no doubt that the Globetrotters should be listed under the heading of spectacle and not sport. In 1962–63 they played 162 games in their regular season and won 162. Then in 99 games played against a team of Cherokee Indians on a four-months post-season tour of Europe, they won 99. You can always be sure of a Globetrotter victory and (in the words of the team's press agent) "of the finest show for its [the public's] entertainment dollar anywhere," as well.

Another more-spectacle-than-sport has been professional wrestling, which has seen the appearance of a few Negro performers. They attract little interest outside the smoke-filled arenas where hard-core wrestling fans watch them grunt and groan. Gone are the days of amateur wrestling, when Negro athletes like Eugene Davidson and Benner C. Turner distinguished themselves on the Harvard wrestling team.

THE "SOCIAL" SPORTS

In *Patterns of Negro Segregation,*[53] the late Charles S. Johnson described an incident in which a white principal refused to let his white students use a basketball after it had been handled by Negro youths. Such a taboo is, of course, extreme, but not so uncommon are taboos that have long operated to deprive Negroes of competitive opportunities in what might be called the "social" sports: bowling, swimming, golf and tennis.

Each of these sports has associated with it some form of social intercourse. There is frequent mixing of sexes in them. A cold beer after a bowling game, a shower after a tennis match or a swim, the nineteenth hole of the golf course—all spell a degree of social contact which invites the prejudiced white person to draw the color line.

Generally, too, these sports have required a fairly elaborate and expensive installation. Negroes have not been welcome to share these installations. The teenage son of Dr. Ralph Bunche, Undersecretary of the United Nations, was once barred from membership in the West Side Tennis Club, where

[52] Gregory P. Stone, "Play and Dis-Play." In Eric Larrabee and Rolf Meyersohn, editors, *Mass Leisure* (Glencoe, Ill.: The Free Press, 1958), p. 253.

[53] Charles S. Johnson, *Patterns of Negro Segregation* (New York: Harper & Brothers, 1943), p. 274.

American championship contests are held. Membership in most golf clubs is not open to Negroes and they are not welcome at many swimming pools. In Northern and Western cities they can and do use bowling alleys, but are often met with something less than enthusiasm.

Limited in the use of facilities in which to practice these sports, the Negro has rarely excelled in them. There is no tradition of great swimmers for a younger generation to emulate, although one Negro, sent to England by *Our World Magazine* in the 1950's, has attempted to swim the English Channel.

The lack of access of Negro youth in congested urban areas to water, a prime essential in any outdoor recreational environment, is one of the most serious sports handicaps they face. A measure of the extent of this recreational deprivation can be seen in the low rate of Negro participation in swimming, which is only 57 percent as great as the white rate.[54]

Golf

The picture is much the same in golf. As early as 1928 there were Negro-owned golf clubs in seven cities.[55] One in Los Angeles was located upon a 663-acre estate and had an 18-hole course for professionals and a 9-hole course for beginners. There was also a tennis court and a large swimming pool. This, however, was an exception and many golf clubs ceased to function because of financial difficulties. Negro players may play on municipal golf courses and there have been Negro qualifiers in such competitions as the Los Angeles Open. Tournaments of exclusively Negro players are held throughout the country.

The outstanding Negro golfer today is Charles Sifford, who in 1963 finished forty-ninth in golf earnings with over $16,000, even though he was unable to play in a number of Southern tournaments. Another promising Negro golfer is Peter Brown of Los Angeles, a 6'1", 200-pound player who won the $20,000 Waco Turner open golf tournament in May, 1964, with a 72-hole score of 280. He was the second Negro (Sifford was the first) to win a PGA-sponsored tournament and automatically became eligible for the 1965 Tournament of Champions at Las Vegas.

Tennis

The story of segregation would, in all likelihood, have persisted in tennis also if it had not been for a lanky and determined teenage Harlem schoolgirl named Althea Gibson. Miss Gibson is now rising swiftly in the ranks of women golf professionals. She twice became Women's Singles Lawn

---

[54] Outdoor Recreation Resources Review Commission, *op. cit.*, p. 79.
[55] Washington, *op. cit.*, p. 280.

Tennis Champion of the United States. Before this, however, there was a long tradition of all-Negro tennis.

An interstate tournament among Negroes was played in Philadelphia in 1900. The game caught on and by 1917 a tristate (New York, New Jersey, Pennsylvania) tennis association was formed by some twenty tennis clubs. Tournaments were held and Lucy Slowe, later Dean of Women at Howard University, was one of the earliest crowned champions (1917). At Wilberforce University (Ohio), at Morgan College (Maryland) and at Bordentown Institute (New Jersey), national tennis tournaments were held in the 1920's and 1930's and produced a number of creditable players. Tally Holmes, Edgar Brown, Ted Thompson and Eyre Saitch are the names of some of the championship titleholders of this period. Later players such as Dr. Reginald S. Weir, Douglas Turner, and Jimmie McDaniel were outstanding. McDaniel played the U.S. Men's Singles Champion, Don Budge, and lost 6–1, 6–2, but, as Budge pointed out, his weakness was lack of experience and lack of opportunity to play in steady competition. In 1948 Dr. Weir was admitted to competition in the United States Lawn Tennis Men's Singles Championships—the first Negro to gain admission.

Negro tennis from the 1920's to the 1940's was largely a social affair of the Negro middle class. There was money in boxing, which appealed to the young teenager. There was none in tennis. People with leisure who loved the sport as amateurs were the ones who played it and competition was not keen.

But there is every indication that Althea Gibson took up the game of tennis with the intention of becoming world's champion. She says in her autobiography that it offered her a chance "to be somebody." She continues:

> I really wasn't the tennis type. But the polite manners of the game that seemed so silly to me at first gradually began to appeal to me. So did the pretty white clothes. . . . After a while I began to understand that you could walk out on the court like a lady, all dressed up in immaculate white, be polite to everybody, and still play like a tiger and beat the liver and lights out of the ball.[56]

Thus a champion was born. In July, 1957, after an uphill fight of several years and many disappointments during which she several times planned to give up tennis, Miss Gibson won the Women's Singles Championship at Wimbledon, England, and then went on to team up with Darlene Hard to win the Women's Doubles crown. That same year and the next she won

[56] Althea Gibson, *I Want To Be Somebody*. (New York: Harper & Brothers, 1958), p. 29. By special permission.

the United States Women's Singles Championships as well as a number of lesser titles. Then she retired undefeated.

A new Negro tennis star came on the horizon in 1963: Arthur Ashe. He rose from eighteenth rank among men tennis players in 1962 to a place on the Davis Cup Team in 1963. Ashe, who began playing tennis on a playground in Richmond, Virginia, was ranked number six in 1964 when he was twenty-one years old. By the summer of 1964 he had beaten number four (Gene Scott) and number two (Dennis Ralston) to win the Eastern Grass Court Championship. By 1965 he was the mainstay of the Davis Cup team.

Other "Social" Sports

In addition to bowling, swimming, golf and tennis there are other "social" sports, or more properly middle-class outdoor sports that ought to be mentioned: hunting, fishing, camping and boating. Rural Negroes have always hunted and fished, but for food rather than for recreation; and it is when hunting and fishing are resorted to as a sport by urbanites that they become expensive and beyond the reach of a majority of Negroes. Only a few Negro professional men around large cities are able to avail themselves of these sports. There are some instances of Negro hunters maintaining a lodge or camp, but these are rare in the extreme. Until passage of the Civil Rights Act of 1964 access to public camping facilities has been severely restricted in most areas—enough at least to make camping a relatively infrequent activity among Negroes.

Boating is an even more exclusive pastime. One study of ethnic group participation in the sport showed that of persons interviewed in the South 23 percent of the whites and only 3 percent of the nonwhites had engaged in boating during June–August 1960. For the United States as a whole the corresponding percentages were 24 and 6 percent.[57]

TRACK AND FIELD

It used to be considered funny to point to the contradiction between the stereotyped notions people held of an ethnic group and an actual set of facts. One would contrast "the fighting Irish" with an Irishman who would not fight or the "stingy Scotch" with a generous Scotsman. It was thought

[57] *Boating 1959* (A statistical report jointly presented by the Outdoor Boating Club of America and the National Association of Engine and Boat Manufacturers, New York and Chicago, 1960), p. 7.

amusing, indeed, to point out that from the "lazy Negro" was derived "the world's fastest human."

Despite the stereotypes of laziness attached to Negroes by many racists in American society, the fact is that Negroes have been preëminent as sprinters and jumpers during over half a century of competition. Howard P. Drew, UCLA's Negro sprinter, held the AAU championship title in the 100-yard dash for 1912 and 1913; in 1914 he broke the world records for the 100-yard dash (9.6 seconds) and 220-yard dash (21.2 seconds), becoming in that year "the world's fastest human."

Speaking of Negro broad jumpers, one author has written:

> Besides monopolizing Olympic honours from 1932 to date [1964] they [Negroes] have so far accounted for fourteen of the twenty best performances of all time.[58]

Table I shows the record of American Negro track and field athletes who competed in the modern Olympic Games. Except for unusual cases, it mentions only those athletes who actually placed in competition. It is, perhaps, as good a barometer as any to register the achievement of Negro athletes in this sport.

Even before Drew set his world record, and, indeed, before Olympic competitions began in 1896, some Negro track and field men were outstanding. In 1891, William Tecumseh Sherman Jackson of Amherst College (also among the first Negro football stars) represented his school in the half-mile race at New England track meets. The first Negro Olympian was George C. Poag of Milwaukee, Wisconsin, a hurdler who placed third in both the 200-meter and 400-meter hurdle races at the 1904 Olympic Games in St. Louis. At St. Louis also, Joseph Stadler, a Negro athlete from Cleveland, Ohio, competed in the standing broad jump, but did not place. In 1904, 1907 and 1908 John B. Taylor of the University of Pennsylvania was intercollegiate champion in the 440-yard dash; he was a member of the United States Olympic team at the 1908 Olympic Games in London and ran on the United States 1600-meter relay team, which came in first.

Contemporaries of Drew were two Negro athletes at Harvard: Alexander Jackson, hurdler, and Theodore Cable, who held the intercollegiate championship in the hammer throw for 1912 and 1913. In 1916 Binga Dismond of the University of Chicago equalled the world record in the 440-yard dash (47.4 seconds); and in the 1920's the outstanding American broad jumper was Sol Butler of Dubuque.

Table I does not tell the story of many outstanding Negro track and field

58 R. L. Quercetani, A World History of Track and Field Athletics. (London: Oxford University Press, 1964), p. 256.

men who failed to make Olympic teams or to win a medal. First there was a whole group of stars who did not gain prominence in international competition because World War II brought about cancellation of the 1940 Olympic Games. In this category would be included two sprinters (Ben Johnson and Herbert Thompson) who equalled Jesse Owens' 1935 world record in the 60-meter dash (6.6 seconds)—which remains unbroken. Johnson, captain of the Columbia University track team, made his record in 1938; Thompson, in 1939. Mozelle Ellerbe of Tuskegee, the NCAA 100-yard dash champion of 1940, would also be included. Among the middle-distance runners of this period would be mentioned John Borican, who set a world's record in the 1000-yard run (2 min. 08.8 seconds); and James Herbert, whose 600-meter time (1 min. 20.3 seconds) is still the American record. Track captain Bill Watson and Willis Ward, both of Michigan, were outstanding all-around athletes who might have been strong contenders in the decathlon. Watson's 16-pound shot-put record was over a foot more than the winning distance for the event in the 1936 Olympics. He threw the discus within two feet of the 1936 Olympic record; and could make a distance of 25'5½" in running broad jump, which was a creditable distance until the world record jump of Jesse Owens. Ward, a high jumper, was also a sprinter who could do 9.6 seconds in the 100-yard dash and nearly 25' in the broad jump, also had Olympic potential.

Other Negro athletes who had proved themselves among the world's best were unable to compete because of injury. Howard Drew and Sol Butler were among the early members of the U.S. Olympic teams kept from the final competitions because of injuries. Charles Fonville of Michigan broke the world record in the 16-pound shot-put in 1948 with a heave of 58', only to sprain his back weeks later and become unable to compete in Olympic tryouts. Arthur Bragg of Morgan State in 1952 and Charles Tidwell in 1960 were both record-making sprinters kept from Olympic finals because of leg injuries.

Not in the record books—or at least not in the books where they belong—are several exceptional Negro athletes who had the hard luck not to win in a decisive competition, but who must be recognized among the best. Harrison Dillard, one of the best hurdlers of all time, who prior to the 1948 trials for the U.S. Olympic Team had won eighty-two hurdle races and had broken a world record, failed to qualify in this event for a place on the team; he barely made the team in the 100-meter run, coming in third in the trials. Then he went on to win the flat race over the world's fastest sprinters in Olympic record time. Later (at Helsinki in 1952) Dillard made up for his poor showing in 1948 by winning the 110-meter hurdles and establishing a new Olympic record.

TABLE I—Track and Field Athletics Records of Negro Athletes on United States Olympic Teams

Place and Date	Event	Athlete	Result and Record
St. Louis, 1904	200-Meter Hurdles	George C. Poag	Third
	400-Meter Hurdles	George C. Poag	Third
London, 1908	400-Meter Run	J. B. Taylor	Qualified to enter finals, but declined to compete.*
	1600-Meter Relay	United States [J. B. Taylor]	First—3 min. 29.4 secs.
Stockholm, 1912	100-Meter Run	Howard P. Drew	Qualified for finals but was unable to compete because of a tendon pulled in the semifinals.
Antwerp, 1920	Running Broad Jump	Sol Butler	Butler, who had jumped 24' 9½" in America, became lame on his first jump and could not continue competition. The event was won by a jump of 23' 5½".
Paris, 1924	Running Broad Jump	Dehart Hubbard	First—24' 5⅛".
		Edward Gourdin	Second—23' 10⅞"
Los Angeles, 1932	100-Meter Run	Eddie Tolan	First—10.3 secs. Olympic and World Record
		Ralph Metcalfe	Second—10.3 secs.
	200-Meter Run	Eddie Tolan	First—21.2 secs. Olympic Record
		Ralph Metcalfe	Third—21.5 secs.
	Running Broad Jump	Edward Gordon	First—25' ¾"
Berlin, 1936	100-Meter Run	Jesse Owens	First—10.3 secs. Olympic and World Record
		Ralph Metcalfe	Second—10.4 secs.
	200-Meter Run	Jesse Owens	First—20.7 secs. Olympic Record
		Mathew Robinson	Second—21.1 secs.
	400-Meter Run	Archie Williams	First—46.5 secs.
		James DuValle	Third—46.8 secs.

* Taylor, American intercollegiate champion who had been clocked at 49.2 in the 440-yard dash, ran in the Olympics with two other Americans against the British champion, W. Halswelle. In the race Carpenter, an American runner, crossed a lane and track officials ran onto the track crying "foul." They ran in front of Taylor who did not finish the race. The race was declared "no contest" and ordered run again, with Carpenter disqualified. Neither Taylor nor the other American runner would race because of the hassle over Carpenter. Haswelle was declared winner of the race in the only walkover in Olympic history.

Table **I**—*continued*

Place and Date	Event	Athlete	Result and Record
Berlin, 1936	800-Meter Run	John Woodruff	First—1 min. 52.9 secs.
	110-Meter Hurdles	Fritz Pollard Jr.	Third—14.4 secs.
	High Jump	Cornelius Johnson	First—6' 8" Olympic Record
		David Albritton	Second—6' 6¾"
	Running Broad Jump	Jesse Owens	First—26' 5 5/16" New Olympic and World Record; unbroken for 24 years
	400-Meter Relay	United States [Jesse Owens, Ralph Metcalfe]	First—39.8 secs. World Record
London, 1948	100-Meter Run	Harrison Dillard	First—10.3 secs.
		Norwood Ewell	Second—10.4 secs.
	200-Meter Run	Norwood Ewell	Second—21.1 secs.
	400-Meter Run	Mal Whitfield	Third—46.9 secs.
	Running Broad Jump	Willie Steele	First—25' 8 1/16"
		Herbert Douglass	Third—24' 9"
		Lorenzo Wright	Fourth—24' 9"
	400-Meter Relay	United States [Harrison Dillard, Norwood Ewell, Lorenzo Wright]	First—40.6 secs.
	1600-Meter Relay	United States [Mal Whitfield]	First—3 min. 10.4 secs.
	Women's 200-Meter Run	Audrey Patterson	Third—25.2 secs.
	Women's High Jump	Alice Coachman	First—5' 6¼"
Helsinki, 1952	200-Meter Run	Andrew Stanfield	First—20.7 secs.
		James Gathers	Third—20.8 secs.
	400-Meter Run	Ollie Matson	Third—46.8 secs.
		Mal Whitfield	Sixth—47.8 secs.
	800-Meter Run	Mal Whitfield	First—1 min. 49.2 sec Olympic Record
		Reginald Pearman	Sixth—No time
	100-Meter Hurdles	Harrison Dillard	First—13.7 secs. Olympic Record
	Running Broad Jump	Jerome Biffle	First—24' 10"
		Meredith Gourdine	Second—24' 8 7/16"

Table I—*continued*

Place and Date	Event	Athlete	Result and Record
	400-Meter Relay	United States [Harrison Dillard, Andrew Stanfield]	First—40.1 secs.
	1600-Meter Relay	United States [Ollie Matson, Mal Whitfield]	Second—3 min. 04.1 secs.
	Javelin	Bill Miller	Second—237' 8¾"
	Decathlon	Milton Campbell	Second—6,975 Points
	Women's 100-Meter Run	Mae Faggs	Sixth—
	Women's 400-Meter Relay	United States [Catherine Hardy, Mae Faggs, Barbara Jones]	First—45.9 secs. Olympic and World Record
Melbourne, 1956	200-Meter Run	Andrew Stanfield	Second—20.7 secs.
	400-Meter Run	Charles Jenkins	First—46.7 secs.
		Lou Jones	Fifth—48.1 secs.
	800-Meter Run	Arnold Sowell	Fourth—1 min. 48.3 secs.
	110-Meter Run	Lee Calhoun	First—13.5 secs.
	400-Meter Hurdles	Josh Culbreath	Third
	High Jump	Charles Dumas	First—6' 11¼" Olympic Record
	Running Broad Jump	Gregory Bell	First—25' 8¼"
	400-Meter Relay	United States [Ira Murchison]	First—39.5 secs. Olympic Record
	1600-Meter Relay	United States [Lou Jones, Charles Jenkins]	First—3 min. 4.8 secs.
	Decathlon	Milton Campbell	First—7,937 points
		Rafer Johnson	Second—7,587 points
	Women's High Jump	Mildred McDaniel	First—5' 9¼" Olympic and World Record
	Women's Running Broad Jump	Willye White	Second—19' 11¾"
	Women's 400-Meter Relay	United States [Mae Faggs, Margaret Matthews, Isabelle Daniels, Wilma Rudolph]	Third—45.4 secs.

Table I—*continued*

Place and Date	Event	Athlete	Result and Record
Rome, 1960	200-Meter Run	Les Carney	Second—20.6 secs.
	400-Meter Run	Lee Calhoun	First—13.8 secs. Olympic and World Record
	110-Meter Hurdles	Lee Calhoun	First—13.8 secs.
		Willie May	Second—13.8 secs.
		Hayes Jones	Third—14.0 secs.
	High Jump	John Thomas	Third—7' ¼"
	Running Broad Jump	Ralph Boston	First—26' 7¾" Olympic Record
		Irv. Roberson	Second—26' 7⅜"
	Run, Hop, Step, Jump	Ira Davis	Fourth—53' 11"
	1600-Meter Relay	United States [Otis Davis]	First—3:02.2 secs.
	Decathlon	Rafer Johnson	First—8,392 points Olympic Record
	Women's 100-Meter Run	Wilma Rudolph	First—.11 secs. Olympic Record; World Record disallowed because of helping wind.
	Women's 200-Meter Run	Wilma Rudolph	First—24 secs. Broke Olympic Record in qualifying heat with 23.2 secs.
	Women's Shot Put	Earlene Brown	Third—53' 10⅜"
	Women's 400-Meter Relay	United States [Martha Judson, Lucinda Williams, Barbara Jones, Wilma Rudolph]	First—44.5 secs. Olympic and World Record
Tokyo, 1964	100-Meter Run	Bob Hayes	First—9.9 secs.* * Beats World Record but not allowed because wind-aided.
		Mel Pender	Seventh—10.4 secs.
	200-Meter Run	Henry Carr	First—20.3 secs.
		Paul Drayton	Second—20.5 secs.
	400-Meter Run	Ulis Williams	Fifth—46 secs.
	100-Meter Hurdles	Hayes Jones	First—13.6 secs.
	400-Meter Relay	United States	

Table I—*continued*

Place and Date	Event	Athlete	Result and Record
Tokyo, 1964		[Paul Drayton, Bob Hayes]	First—39 secs. World and Olympic Record
	1600-Meter Relay	United States [Ulis Williams, Henry Carr]	First—3 min. 7/10th secs. World and Olympic Record
	High Jump	John Thomas	Second—7' 1¾"
		John Rambo	Third—7' 1"
	Running Broad Jump	Ralph Boston	Second—26' 4"
	Run, Hop, Step, Jump	Ira Davis	Fifth—52' 1¾"
	Women's 100-Meter Run	Wyomia Tyus	First—11.4 secs.
		Edith McGuire	Second—11.4 secs.
		Marilyn White	Fourth—11.6 secs.
	Women's 200-Meter Run	Edith McGuire	First—23.0 secs. Olympic Record
	Women's 80-Meter Hurdles	Rosie Bonds	Eighth—10.8 secs.
	Women's 400-Meter Relay	United States [Willye White, Wyomia Tyus, Marilyn White, Edith McGuire]	Second—43.9 secs.
	Women's High Jump	Eleanor Montgomery	Eighth—5' 7¾"
	Women's Running Broad Jump	Willye White	Twelfth—19' 8¾"
	Women's Shot Put	Earlene Brown	Twelfth—48' 6¾"

There have been other examples of Negro athletes who failed to live up to expectations held for them. Broad jumper George Brown, who jumped 26'3" to qualify for the 1952 U.S. Olympic team, fouled every jump attempt in competition and was disqualified; the event was won by a teammate with a jump of 25'8". This type of occurrence was repeated in 1956 when Lou Jones broke the world record in the 400-meter run (45.2 seconds) to qualify for the team and then was defeated in competition by his teammate, Charles Jenkins, in the comparably slower time of 46.7 seconds. There is the hard luck story of Ray Norton who had been clocked in United States competitions at 10.1 seconds in the 100-meter run and 20.1 seconds in the 200-meter run (a tenth of a second off the world mark); Norton ran dead last in both events.[59] He had the added hard luck of causing the U.S. 400-

[59] Winning time in the 100-meter run was 10.2 seconds; in the 200-meter run, 20.5 seconds.

meter relay team to be disqualified because he received the baton outside the passing lane. As a result, another Negro star (Stone Johnson), who had helped the team come in first in an unofficial time of 39.4 seconds, failed to receive a gold medal and make the record books. Finally there is the surprising showing of John Thomas, who had high jumped over 7' in competition thirty-seven times before the Rome Olympics. At Rome he could manage to come in only third behind the Russian jumpers Robert Shavlakadze and Valery Brumel.

The pace for recognition among Negro athletes has been so swift that many fine competitors have been overshadowed by even better ones. Eulace Peacock was a constant challenge to Jesse Owens and on several occasions beat Owens in sprint competitions; in the running broad jump he has a leap of 26'3" to his credit. However, Peacock had little chance to take the spotlight from a champion like Owens who, in a single day (May 25, 1935 at the Big Ten Championships), could break three world records (the 220-yard dash, 220-yard low hurdles, running broad jump) and equal a fourth (100-yard dash).

Since the first modern Olympic Games, track and field athletes have consistently improved upon performances at previous competitions; Negro athletes have been in the vanguard of this assault on world records. Edward Gourdin of Harvard was the first human to broad jump over 25', and Charles Dumas the first to high jump over 7'. Yet within a few years Jesse Owens had broad jumped over 26' and John Thomas was high jumping over 7'3" with clocklike regularity. The number of Negro track and field athletes is steadily growing; each new success encourages new young champions. In track meets there is the constant cry "the king is dead; long live the king." In the books the names of Jesse Owens, John Thomas and Ralph Boston no longer appear as holders of the world records. Among the male athletes, ten Negro stars at the end of the Tokyo Olympic Games were still among the track and field athletes who held world records. Table II lists them and their records; and, as well, the four Negro women in this class.

The prowess of American Negro women athletes in track and field sports is hardly less striking than that of the men. Since 1937 athletes from such schools as Tuskegee Institute and Tennessee A. & I. State College have increasingly dominated women's National A.A.U. meets. Sixteen of the twenty women athletes chosen to represent the United States in the 1964 Tokyo Olympic Games were Negro. Only American woman to win three gold medals in an Olympic (Rome) was Wilma Rudolph, holder of three world records (Table II). Table III shows American Negro Women who hold American Track and Field Records.

Today the impetus for much of the activity of Negro girls in track and

TABLE II—World Track and Field Records Held by American Negroes, 1964

Event	Record	Holder or Coholder	Date	Place
		Men		
100-Yard Dash	9.1 secs.	Robert Hayes	June, 1963	St. Louis, Mo.
220-Yard Dash	20.3 secs.	Henry Carr	May, 1963	Tempe, Ariz.
440-Yard Dash	44.9 secs.	Adolph Plummer	May, 1963	Tempe, Ariz.
400-Meter Run	44.9 secs.	Otis Davis	August, 1960	Rome, Italy
120-Yard Hurdles	13.2 secs.	Lee Calhoun	August, 1961	Berne, Switzerland
110-Meter Hurdles	13.2 secs.	Lee Calhoun	August, 1961	Berne, Switzerland
Decathlon	8,683 points	Rafer Johnson	July, 1960	Eugene, Ore.
400-Meter Relay [4 x 100 meters]	39 secs.	Hayes Jones Frank Budd Charles Frazier Paul Drayton	July, 1961	Moscow, U.S.S.R.
One-Mile Relay [4 x 440 yards]	3 min. 05.6 secs.	Otis Davis [member of team]	August, 1960	Walnut, Cal.
1600-Meter Relay [4 x 400 meters]	3 min. 02.2 secs.	Otis Davis [member of team]	September, 1960	Rome, Italy
		Women		
100-Meter Run	11.2 secs.	Wilma Rudolph	July, 1961	Stuttgart, West Germany
200-Meter Run	22.9 secs.	Wilma Rudolph	July, 1960	Corpus Christi, Texas
400-Meter Relay [4 x 100 meters]	44.3 secs.	Willye White Ernestine Pollards Vivian Brown Wilma Rudolph	July, 1961	Moscow, U.S.S.R.

TABLE III—Best American Citizen's Record Held by Negro Women Athletes, 1964

Event	Record	Holder	Date	Place
100-Meter Dash	11.2 secs.	Wilma Rudolph	July, 1961	Stuttgart, West Germany
200-Meter Dash	22.9 secs.	Wilma Rudolph	July, 1960	Corpus Christi, Texas
80-Meter Low Hurdles	10.8 secs.	Rosie Bonds	August, 1964	New York, N.Y.
Running High Jump	5' 9½"	Mildred McDaniel	December, 1956	Melbourne, Australia
Running Broad Jump	21' 6"	Willye White	July, 1964	Los Angeles, Cal.
4-Kilogram Shot Put	54' 9"	Earlene Brown	September, 1960	Frankfurt, West Germany
Discus Throw	176' 10½"	Earlene Brown	July, 1960	Los Angeles, Cal.

field sports is Tennessee A. & I. and its track coach, Edward S. Temple. As a sportswriter on *The New York Times* wrote:

> The cathedral of women's track in this country is Tennessee A. & I. and Temple is its high priest.[60]

Temple was coach of the United States Women's Olympic team in the Rome Olympics of 1960 and the Tokyo Olympics of 1964. Each year many of the most promising high school girl athletes are encouraged to come to the school and begin year-round training under him. The results have been remarkable. Not only have individual sprint stars like Wilma Rudolph, Wyomia Tyus and Edith McGuire been trained; relay teams of such swiftness have been developed that they have made up the full membership of the U.S. 400-meter relay teams in the last three Olympic games and in many dual international meets. Known as the Tigerbelles, successive Tennessee A. & I. women's relay teams have each broken the world record. Girls from this school have continually improved track and field performance, giving promise to produce the American women athletes who will be the first to broad jump over twenty-two feet and high jump over six feet.

The success of Tuskegee and Tennessee A. & I. track stars has been a spur to other sports clubs and groups to emulate them. Alumnae of the schools have often become members of such groups. Typical of organizations from which first-rank Negro women athletes have come are the Los Angeles Mercurettes, Mayor Daley Youth Foundation (Chicago), Compton (California) Athletic Club, Long Beach (California) Comets Track and Field, Cleveland Recreation Department, Pasadena (California) Athletic Club, and Frederick (Maryland) Track and Field. Each of these clubs produced one or more members of the U.S. Women's Olympic Team at the Tokyo Games.

Why do Negro athletes excel? Why have they not produced many distance runners, weight men, pole vaulters? These are frequently asked questions. To deal with the second question first: Actually there have been many Negro stars outside of sprints and jumps. Watson and Fonville of Michigan are examples. Bill Miller at Helsinki in 1952 represented the United States in the javelin throw and came in second. James Dupree is a leading American half-miler. In the decathlon, which includes such events as the 1500-meter run (.9 of a mile), javelin, pole vault, discus and shot put, Negro athletes have been Olympic champions in 1956 (Milton Campbell) and 1960 (Rafer Johnson). Johnson holds the world's record in this event.

The fact remains, however, that the greatest Negro track and field suc-

[60] September 9, 1960, p. 20.

cess has been in sprint and jump events; and racists—in America and abroad—have sought to bend their theories of supremacy of the white race to fit this set of facts. Never was this more apparent than at the Berlin Olympics in Germany at a time when Chancellor Hitler and his Nazi Party were conducting a strident campaign for Nordic supremacy.

Amidst the fanfare about purity of the white race and its consequent invincibility, Negro athletes from the United States dominated the meet. Jesse Owens won the 100- and 200-meter races and right behind him came another American Negro, Ralph Metcalfe. Archie Williams won the 400-meter run and John Woodruff was victorious in the 800-meter run. Jesse Owens won his third gold medal in the broad jump with a leap of 26′5⁄16″, setting a new world record that remained unbroken for more than a quarter of a century. Cornelius Johnson jumped 6′7¹⁵⁄₁₆″ to win the high jump, and Dave Albritton, another United States Negro, was second. Then Owens and Metcalfe ran on the team which won a first place in the 400-meter relay. Seven gold medals were too much for Aryan supremacy to bear. As Negro high jumpers Johnson and Albritton ascended the victory pedestal to receive their Olympic crowns, the German Fuehrer, Adolf Hitler, left the stadium.

A leading Nazi newspaper, *Die Angriff*, was furious. It derided the United States for relying upon its "black auxiliaries." It recited an alleged English claim that the feet of the Negro winners had been operated upon before coming to the Olympic Games. It claimed that the Negro was built anatomically different from other human species, that he had a longer heel bone and a stronger Achilles' tendon, which helped him run faster and jump farther.

There is, of course, not one scintilla of truth to the claim that Negroes are endowed with special anatomical characteristics. Scientists have exploded this myth thoroughly.[61] Both Negroes and whites have set or equalled world records in sprints and jumps and they have been short and tall, stocky and slender, long-footed and short-footed.

It is not an inherited physical endowment that accounts for the record made by American Negro athletes in track and field. Runners are made, not born. Wilma Rudolph, the "world's fastest woman," could not walk before she was eight years old. A gruelling training program, the constant effort to excel, led to her Olympic victories. But why did she make the effort?

There are no final answers to this question. The reasons are complex; many of them have yet to be unravelled. An approach to the answer,

[61] W. Montague Cobb, "Race and Runners." *Journal of Health and Physical Education*, VII (1936), 3.

however, is possible. For one thing, track and field is peculiarly well-fitted as a vehicle through which to achieve an acceptable status in American society. It is one of the few sports that is truly amateur, truly (thanks to the Olympic Games) international. Prominence in track and field partakes of none of the characteristics of entertainment that professional football, basketball, baseball—and even professional tennis—do. There is no social distance between athlete and performer. Excellence in the sport offers the reward of high self-esteem.

This esteem is enriched by the international arena in which it is experienced. Track and field is the only American sport in which the team in the fullest degree represents the nation. To win a gold medal at the Olympics is to be a national hero; to win three gold medals is to enter the Pantheon of American sports. This is the prize for which so many Negro athletes have striven and which a goodly number have achieved.

Has it anything to do with race? Yes. With opportunity for recognition so often barred in other fields in American society, the chances in this sport were the more earnestly reached for by Negro youth. Then, too—and here is where the mystery of why so many Negro sprinters and jumpers may find an answer—to see a Jesse Owens receive the cheers of millions of Americans was the charge of spirit many other Negro youth needed to try to be what Jesse Owens was: a sprinter and a jumper. Nor is it a coincidence that the best present-day women 100-meter and 200-meter sprinters, Wyomia Tyus and Edith McGuire, went to the same school (Tennessee A. & I.), as did Wilma Rudolph, holder of the world records in these events. The great stars of the past are models for the strivings of promising young athletes of today.

SPORTS AND THE AMERICAN DREAM

Perhaps in American sports to a larger degree than anywhere else in American society, does one see the emergence of the American dream of freedom and equality. Americans take their sports heroes to heart: Babe Ruth and Willie Mays, Joe Louis and Willie Pep, James Beatty and Rafer Johnson. Good sportsmanship transcends distinctions of race, class religion. American sports fans raise their voices loud for the ball well hit, the blow cleanly struck, the race well run.

And this trend is growing. As more and more international sports events have been staged, victory has become important to the nation's prestige, a symbol of the nation's vitality. Indeed, the "White Hope" has been replaced by the "American Hope" and all America cheered when a nineteen-year-old Negro boxer from Louisville, Kentucky named Cassus Clay defeated a champion from Poland named Zbigniew Pietrzykowski and won a medal for the United States; and America, black and white, wept when their finest champion, nineteen-year-old John Thomas, went down to defeat before the Russians.

In the face of international competition American ranks are closed; the American press is swift to spring to the defense of its own. When the German racist paper *Die Angriff* attacked American Negro members of the 1936 Olympic team, the *Richmond [Virginia] Times Dispatch* replied:

> Their press, which is about as free and uncensored as the average prison publication in this country, has been harping on the fact that if our "black auxiliaries," as they refer to Owens, Johnson, Woodruff et al. had been left at home, Germany would be ahead on points. . . . A German who runs second to one of the American Negroes in the race is given the front page spread as "the first white man to finish" while the American's feat of winning first place goes inside.[62]

The American press and other mass media have given generous recognition to American Negro sports personalities, thus spreading their fame. Wilma Rudolph was given the Helms World Trophy Award in 1960 as the foremost amateur athlete of the North American Continent. Jesse Owens has been declared the greatest American track athlete of the last half-century. Since 1954, the James E. Sullivan Memorial Trophy awarded annually by the AAU to the "athlete who by his or her performance, example, and influence as an amateur has done most during the year to advance the cause of sportsmanship" has four times been given to a Negro: Mal Whitfield (1954), Harrison Dillard (1955), Rafer Johnson (1960), and Wilma Rudolph (1961). This kind of widely acclaimed recognition has wiped out many stereotypes concerning the Negro; has been a powerful unifying force in the American community.

Negro Olympic champions have not only starred in athletic competition, they have been used as well to implement American foreign policy.[63] As part of a United States State Department program Americans Abroad, such athletes as Harrison Dillard, Mal Whitfield, Jesse Owens, Rafer Johnson and Wilma Rudolph have been sent to Latin America, Africa, Asia and the

---

[62] August 8, 1936.

[63] Athletes have also played a prominent role in the civil rights movement. Floyd Patterson and Jackie Robinson have raised funds to replace Negro churches burned down by racists in the South. Olympic gold medalists, John Woodruff and Andy Stanfield, took part in a "Freedom Run" from New York to Washington, D.C., to support the Selma, Alabama struggle for the right to vote in March, 1965.

Middle East to win friends for the United States abroad, to represent America at its best.

Miss Rudolph went to Mali and Senegal and taught teen-age African girls the rules of racing. Owens went to India, and Rafer Johnson to the Southeast Asian Peninsula Games in Burma in 1962. Whitfield, twice 800-meter Olympic champion, has gone to Africa five times as a physical education lecturer at the University of Nigeria. He told *Sports Illustrated:* "Sport is the best thing America has left with which to sell good will and democracy."

chapter 24

The Negro
and American Entertainment

Langston Hughes

"The Negro singers, as always, make opera credible. And, as always, they make music shine. They have a physical beauty of movement, natural distinction and grace. Musically they have rhythm, real resonance, excellent pitch, superb enunciation, and full understanding of the operatic convention. They never look bored or out-of-place on the stage or seem inappropriately cast for any musical style," so wrote in 1943 the distinguished composer and critic, Virgil Thompson, in commenting on the Broadway scene. Many before and since have confirmed his opinions.

The logs of slave ships crossing the Atlantic do not reveal African captives willingly singing for the pleasure of others during the long voyage under sail to the Americas. But in *A Journal of a Voyage Made in the Hannibal of London, Ann. 1693–1694* it is recorded, "We often at sea in the evenings would let the slaves come up into the sun to air themselves, and make them jump and dance for an hour or two to our bagpipes, harp, and fiddle, by which exercise to preserve them in health." And *An Account of the Slave Trade on the Coast of Africa* published in England in 1788 states concerning captives during the Middle Passage, "Exercise being deemed necessary for the preservation of their health, they are sometimes obliged to dance, when the weather will permit their coming on deck. . . . The poor wretches are frequently compelled to sing also; but when they do so, their songs are generally, as may naturally be expected, melancholy lamentations of their exile from their native country." Those Africans who revolted with Cinque aboard the *Amistad* off Cuba and themselves brought their ship to Northern waters, reported during their trial for murder and piracy in New Haven in 1839 that sometimes on the decks of that runaway slaver men in chains chanted songs of Africa and black mothers in shackles crooned to their children. On the shores of colonial America, very early records of life on the plantations and in the cities, as well, report whites as being entertained by the singing and dancing of their black chattels.

In the early eighteen hundreds in New Orleans on Sunday afternoons when the slaves were allowed a few hours of "freedom" to rest and play, the bamboula drums throbbed on Congo Square. There the whites often gathered to watch the blacks sing and dance in African fashion. Many of the newly imported slaves spoke neither French nor English, and their music was as yet uninfluenced by the European. There and then, say the chroniclers of jazz, the rhythms of Africa began to seep into America's musical heritage. Scarcely had the slaves set foot on our shores than their influence on American entertainment began.

Wealthy slave owners soon developed the habit of sending for their most musical slaves to sing and dance for them as they sat on their wide verandas of a summer evening. And some plantations permitted their more talented blacks to travel from plantation to plantation to entertain other wealthy masters and their guests. There were in these slave troups field hands who could crack jokes, others who shook the bones of spareribs or sheep in syncopated rhythms or played the comb or the banjo or the saw or the corn-stalk fiddle and could do the buck-and-wing or the *danse calinda.*

Slaves sometimes became name performers and their masters were in effect their booking agents. The following advertisement on behalf of Toler and Cook, appeared on June 27, 1853, in the *Richmond Daily Enquirer:* "FOR HIRE, either for the remainder of the year, or by the month, week, or job, the celebrated musician and fiddler, GEORGE WALKER. All persons desiring the services of George are notified that they must contract for them with us, and in no case pay to him or any other person the amount of his hire, without a written order from us. George Walker is admitted, by common consent, to be the best leader of a band in all eastern and middle Virginia." And in his slave memoirs of life on a Louisiana cotton plantation in the mid-eighteen fifties, Solomon Northrup wrote, "My master often received letters, sometimes from a distance of ten miles, requesting him to send me to play at a ball of festival of the whites. He received his compensation, and usually I also returned with many picayunes jingling in my pockets . . . and secured the loudest and heartiest welcome of them all at the Christmas dance."

The escaped slave, Frederick Douglass, in his *Life and Times,* wrote that on the plantations during the Christmas holidays, "fiddling, dancing, and jubilee beating was carried on in all directions. This latter performance was strictly Southern. It supplied the place of the violin or other musical instruments and was played so easily that almost every farm had its juba beater. The performer improvised as he beat the instrument, marking the words as he sang so as to have them fall pat with the movement of his hands. Once in a while among a mass of nonsense and wild frolic, a sharp hit was given to the meanness of the slaveholders. Take the following example:

We raise the wheat,
Dey gib us de corn,
We bake de bread,
Dey gib us de crust.
We sif de meal,
Dey gib us de huss.
We peel de meat,
Dey gib us de skin—
And dats de way
Dey take us in.

Thus were born, under the guise of entertainment, the first Negro protest songs. Others grew out of religious meetings and developed into such great ante-bellum spirituals as *Go Down, Moses, Oh, Freedom,* and *God's Gonna Cut You Down.* Using the spiritual as entertainment, seven singers born in slavery formed the major part of a group that comprised the Fisk Jubilee Singers who in 1871, eight years after Emancipation, began a concert tour of America and Europe that brought the spirituals to international attention. Since then these plantation songs have become world famous. The Negro as a factor in American entertainment stems from the plantation singer, dancer and jester who, in entertaining themselves, entertained their masters. Booker T. Washington in his *Up From Slavery* says that even after freedom came, when he went to Alabama in 1881 to found Tuskegee, the customs of slave Christmases still continued on the nearby plantations. Each night the field hands "usually had what they called a 'frolic.' "

At least one slave, Blind Tom, became nationally famous before Emancipation as a professional entertainer under the management of his master, Colonel Bethune. Tom became known as a concert headliner, booked as a moneymaking attraction long after slavery ended. Billed as the "MUSICAL PRODIGY—with wonder Powers as a Pianist," it was said that Tom could reproduce any piece of music, no matter how difficult, upon hearing it only once. It was also advertised that Tom could "perform with his back to the piano." Blind Tom had a highly successful run in New York City appearing in Irving Place both matinees and nights in the Spring of 1868 —and playing on a Steinway, no less.

Before the Civil War, as an outgrowth of the singing and dancing of plantation slaves, the nation's most popular form of entertainment, the all male blackface minstrels evolved. In these shows, white men imitated on stage the singing, dancing, speech and humor of the Southern blacks. Their sketches were often dramatized plantation stories. And popular American performers have been borrowing from Negroes ever since. It was in 1830 in

Cincinnati that the white minstrel, Dan Rice, saw a little black street urchin dancing to a ditty that went:

> Step first upon yo' heel
> An' den upon yo' toe,
> An' ebry time you turns around
> You jump Jim Crow.
> Next fall upon yo' knees
> Then jump up and bow low
> An' ebry time you turn around
> You jump Jim Crow.

Rice copied the song, learned the boy's dance steps, and made a fortune from them.

The Virginia Minstrels headed by Dan Emmett, composer of *Dixie*, was the first of such attractions to perform in New York. It opened on the Bowery in 1843. For more than 50 years thereafter minstrels were in vogue all over the country and in Europe. They played in theatres where the Negro whom the performers imitated could not even buy a ticket, and on whose stages black men were not allowed to perform. The earliest wide spread discrimination against the Negro in the American theatre, both as spectator and performer, began with the minstrels. This is an irony, if there ever was one, in that the minstrels derived their entertainment values solely from Negroes—Negro rhythms, Negro dance steps, plantation melodies, and a bold faced blackface imitation of Negro speech and humor.

The white minstrel performers developed so broad a burlesque of what the general public took to be "Negro life" that their shows created a stereotyped concept of colored Americans which continues to this day. The sooty burnt cork makeup, the exaggeratedly wide lips, the gold teeth, the gaudy clothing, the loud jokes, the fantastic dialect, the watermelon and razor props, and the dice that continue right down to *Porgy and Bess*, became so much a part of commercial theatre in the United States that black performers themselves, in order to be successful, felt impelled to imitate these blackface whites. As a result, Bert Williams made himself twelve shades darker than he really was and spoke, in the *Ziegfeld Follies*, a dialect he never heard except from white performers. Later Miller and Lyles imitated Moran and Mack so well that the white actors who played Amos and Andy in turn imitated Miller and Lyles. Then Rochester imitated all of them put together.

These performers as well as white Al Jolson and black Stephin Fetchit, white Eddie Cantor and black Mantan Moreland, all stemmed from the minstrel tradition. For a long time, most Negro comedians felt that in order to be funny, they had to work under cork. Strangest paradox of all was Pigmeat Markham, one of the funniest and most popular of Negro comedians. For years on stage his makeup was burnt cork. When changing times after the Second World War forced him to stop blacking himself up, his audiences were amazed to discover that in reality Pigmeat was himself darker than the burnt cork he had been using. For neither rhyme nor reason, some Negro performers continued to perpetuate the minstrel stereotype long after the minstrel era was over.

On the positive side, however, the white blackface minstrels introduced to the American public the entertainment values inherent in Negro material—before Negroes themselves could appear on Jim Crow stages. When genuine *Negro* minstrels did make their appearance, they had a public waiting for them, and in some cases were welcomed into theatres where Negroes had not formerly played. In 1865 a Negro, Charles Hicks, organized *The Georgia Minstrels* which later came under white management and toured America and Europe. In 1882 this troup became a part of *Callender's Consolidated Spectacular Colored Minstrels* and toured the United States, as did other Negro minstrel shows, the largest being the *Richards and Pringle Minstrels*. Comedians Sam Lucas and Billy Kersands, who could put a cup and saucer in his mouth, became famous Negro names in minstrelsy. But the Negro performer of those days whose work will live—because not only did he appear on stages at home and abroad but was a great song writer as well—is James Bland, composer of *In The Evening By The Moonlight* and *Carry Me Back To Old Virginny*, now the official song of the State of Virginia.

On the part of Negro performers, the first successful breakaway from all masculine blackface minstrels came in 1891 with the opening in Boston of *The Creole Show* which featured a singing and dancing chorus of sixteen beautiful girls. In 1893 this show played a full season at the Chicago World's Fair and toured for several years thereafter. During the Gay Nineties other successful Negro shows were *The South Before The War, The Octoroons,* and *Oriental America.* The latter was the first all-Negro company to appear on Broadway, the first to include operatic selections among its musical numbers and to feature in its cast trained musicians such as J. Rosamond Johnson. The success of these shows led at the turn of the century to the great era of Negro musical comedy in which not only performers but Negro composers and writers gained a foothold in the commercial theatre, and beauty became a part of the brownskin world of make believe.

Sissieretta Jones, a statuesque woman with a gorgeous voice, made such a hit in the Jubilee Spectacle at Madison Square Garden in the spring of

1892 that in the autumn she was invited to sing at the White House. Billed as Black Patti, Sissieretta Jones with her company of Troubadours toured for many years. Dora Dean, another beautiful woman of color, was such a gorgeous cakewalker that a song called *Dora Dean* was written about her and her dancing. Belle Davis, Ada Overton, Abbie Mitchell, all golden brown and talented, smartly dressed on stage and off, became the early leading ladies of the Negro theatre. Abbie Mitchell's career spanned more than a half century from star billing in turn of the century musicals to featured roles on Broadway in such contemporary dramas as Lillian Hellman's *The Little Foxes*. Still in her teens, Abbie Mitchell married the brilliant composer, Will Marion Cook, appeared in his *Clorindy*, the first ragtime musical, and later bore him a son, Mercer Cook, who became American ambassador to Senegal.

The Cakewalk was the first dance of Negro origin to sweep the country and become a ballroom favorite—as did other Negro steps much later—the Charleston, the Lindy Hop, the Jitterbug, and in our times the Twist. Derived from the plantation frolics, and popularized as a comic burlesque in the minstrels, the real charm of the Cakewalk with its high stepping grace did not reach the stage until Cook's *Clorindy: The Origin of the Cakewalk* (for that was its subtitle) was produced in 1898 at the Casino Roof in New York, with book and lyrics by Paul Laurence Dunbar. Performed by handsome couples, the women gorgeously gowned, and nobody in blackface, the dance was a joy. Williams and Walker first came to fame as exponents of the Cakewalk. And it was the Williams and Walker musicals that in the early nineteen hundreds had great success in the theatres. Their *Sons of Ham* played for two years. *In Dahomey* was a Broadway hit, repeated by a long run in London, with a command performance in 1903 at Buckingham Palace. In New York *Abyssinia* and *Bandana Land* followed, with Will Marion Cook and Will Vodery as composers, Alex Rogers, lyricist of *Nobody*, as librettist, and a largely all Negro staff in the production end of these popular musicals. In 1910 Bert Williams graduated to the *Ziegfeld Follies* and became Broadway's first Negro star in an otherwise all white show. His burnt cork comedy which stemmed from the minstrel tradition, and his droll songs kept him a star until his death in 1922. Williams and Walker, Cole and Johnson (*The Shoofly Regiment, Red Moon*) and Will Marion Cook were the musical pioneers who first opened the doors of Broadway to Negro entertainment.

But on the dramatic stage it took almost a hundred years for colored actors to attain success anywhere near that of the singers, dancers and comics. It was not for lack of trying. On Bleecker Street in New York City from 1821 to 1832 a group of free Negroes with James Hewlett as leading man, performed Shakespeare's *Othello, Richard the Third,* and other classics. The players were known as the African Company and their playhouse the African Grove—where, according to a chronical of the times, the breeze had "free access through the crevices of the boards." White hoodlums who came to laugh and jeer eventually forced this earliest of Negro dramatic theatres to close, but not before it had posted a sign which read: WHITE PEOPLE DO NOT KNOW HOW TO BEHAVE THEMSELVES AT ENTERTAINMENT DESIGNED FOR LADIES AND GENTLEMEN.

Before the African Grove closed, among its supers who helped create the illusion of a crowd on stage was a youngster from the nearby African Free School whose name was Ira Aldridge. His love for serious drama eventually made young Ira one of the greatest Shakespearean actors of his day—but *not* in the United States. He came to fame in Europe where, among other classic roles in London he played Othello to Edmund Keane's Iago, performed to acclaim in all the great capitals of the Continent, and never came home. When Theophile Gautier saw Ira Aldridge as King Lear in 1858 in a crowded Russian theatre, the French journalist wrote that so convincing was his performance in Caucasian makeup—silver locks, flowing white beard, sallow cheeks—that "Cordelia would never have suspected that her father was a Negro." After forty years of European successes, America's first international star of color died in Poland in 1867. Today at Stratford-on-Avon there is an Ira Aldridge Chair designated in his honor at the Shakespeare Memorial Theatre.

After the demise of the African Grove, it was over a half century before Negro dramatic actors had access to theatres of any permanency in which they might perform with regularity. In some sections of the country small stock companies sprang up which sometimes presented plays as well as musical entertainments. Such a company headed by Bob Cole became a permanent part of Worth's Museum in New York for several years, with a number of young Negro apprentices involved and, in the later days of the play's popularity, various companies of *Uncle Tom's Cabin* employed Negro actors, instead of whites blacked up, for the slave roles. But it was not until the formation by Lester Walton in 1914 of the Lafayette Stock Company in Harlem that the Negro performer found himself able to work for a full season in straight dramatic plays ranging from the classics to revivals of Broadway hits—sometimes tailored to the taste of colored audiences. From the Harlem productions of *Othello, Madame X, The Count of Monte Cristo,* and *On Trial* presented with all-colored casts, a number of talented players eventually reached Broadway and Hollywood—Charles Gilpin, Evelyn Ellis, Frank Wilson, Edna Thomas and Clarence Muse among others. Muse, a very dark young man from Baltimore, became a great favorite with Harlem audiences. At the Lafayette he pulled a complete switch from the days of the minstrels. Instead of appearing in blackface in such plays as *Within The Law,* Clarence Muse appeared in whiteface, complete with blond toupee. A quarter of a century later in *The Duchess of Malfi,* the late Canada Lee played the brother to Elizabeth Bergner on Broadway in white makeup. The Lincoln Theatre in Harlem, the Pekin Theatre in Chicago, the Standard in Philadelphia and the Howard in Washington also had, from time to time, stock companies, often borrowing stars from the Lafayette, whose production standards were high.

The Harlem chronicler, James Weldon Johnson, terms April 5, 1917, the most important date in the history of the Negro in the American theatre. On that evening at the Garden Theatre in downtown New York there opened a bill of three one-act plays, *The Rider of Dreams, Granny Maumee* and *Simon the Cyrenian,* by the poet Ridgeley Torrence. There was entr'acte music by a singing orchestra of Clef Club members conducted by J. Rosamond Johnson. The show was a great success and its presentation marked "the first time anywhere in the United States for Negro actors in the dramatic theatre to command the serious attention of the critics and the general press and public." Three years later at the Provincetown Theatre in the Village, Eugene O'Neill's first hit, *The Emperor Jones,* with Charles Gilpin in the title role, opened. Gilpin was acclaimed one of the ten best actors of the year, Eugene O'Neill began his ascent to fame, and from that time on the Negro performer in serious drama became an accepted part of the national scene.

Paul Green's earliest and greatest successes were also with plays cast largely with Negroes, among them *In Abraham's Bosom,* a Pulitzer Prize winner in 1926, in which Rose McClendon, Jules Bledsoe and Abbie Mitchell were featured. Commercially the most successful plays concerned with Negro life were then all written by whites, but a number of them furnished excellent vehicles for colored actors to achieve outstanding performances. Notable presentations included O'Neill's *All God's Chillun Got Wings* with Paul Robeson in 1924, David Belasco's production of *Lulu Belle* that same year, Laurence Stalling's *Deep River* in which Rose McClendon won nightly applause merely by her wordless descent of a winding staircase, Jim Tully's *Black Boy* with lovely Freddie Washington; and, finally the Theatre Guild's *Porgy* with Frank Wilson, Evelyn Ellis and Georgette Harvey. Rounding off a decade of almost continuous Broadway activity for Negroes came in 1930 *The Green Pastures* with Richard B. Harrison as De Lawd. This folk fantasy by Marc Connelly with a singing orchestra under Hall Johnson achieved one of the longest runs in Negro theatrical history. It opened at the end of a delightful decade of Harlem creativity in the arts known as the Negro Renaissance. But when the Depression came, things artistic went down-hill for Negroes. Their decade of popularity ended with *Green Pastures.* There came lean years both in the theatre and elsewhere for black men and women.

The Negro playwright hardly entered the picture during the rich decade of the Twenties although it was a good era for white playwrights and black actors. There were Negro playwrights then, but they seldom got a hearing. With little chance even to see plays in many parts of the country because of Jim Crow, and with almost no chance to gain any technical knowledge of theatre craft, the black playwright had a hard row to hoe. In the old days his scripts seldom got from the typed page to even the amateur stage, but perhaps a church might sponsor a reading. The earliest known American Negro playwright, William Wells Brown, gave one-man readings of his own plays in churches. In those days almost all plays had double titles. Wells' first play completed about 1856 was called *Experience or How to Give a Northern Man a Backbone;* his second was *The Escape, or a Leap for Freedom,* and the library rather than the stage was their fate.

It was fifty years before any other Negro playwright attracted any attention whatsoever when in 1903 the poet, Joseph S. Cotter, Sr., of Louisville published a drama, *Caleb, The Degenerate,* concerned with the racial theories of Booker T. Washington. Some ten years later, Angelina Grimke wrote *Rachel* which the NAACP produced at the Neighborhood Theatre in New York. But, other than functioning as sketch writers and occasional librettists for musical shows, Negroes attempted little creative writings for the theatre and they found no market for what little they did if it was of a serious nature. The commercial center of the theatre, Broadway, in all its history up to 1966 has displayed the work of less than a dozen Negro playwrights. When Wallace Thurman wrote the play *Harlem* which opened on Broadway in 1929, it seemed feasible for production purposes to accept the co-authorship of his agent, William Jordan Rapp—so the program credit reads, HARLEM by Wallace Thurman and William Jordan Rapp. Other Negro playwrights and many popular song writers and composers have accepted the co-authorship of whites on their creative work in order to achieve publication or production, but oftimes the Negro work is damaged rather than improved by what few white additions are added. The work may get published or produced though, which has often been a difficult thing for a Negro to achieve alone. It takes a great deal of black integrity to prefer anonymity to publication—even if with an unwelcome collaborator.

In the thirty-five years since Wallace Thurman's *Harlem* there have been ten Negro playwrights—only ten—produced on Broadway. In 1929 there was Garland Anderson's *Appearances;* in 1933 Hall Johnson's *Run, Little*

Chillun; the following year *Brother Mose* (retitled *Meek Mose*) by Frank Wilson; in 1935 *Mulatto* by Langston Hughes; in 1941 Richard Wright's *Native Son;* in 1947 Theodore Ward's *Our Lan';* in 1953 *Take A Giant Step* by Louis Peterson; in 1954 *Mrs. Patterson* by Charles Sebree; in 1957 *Simply Heavenly* by Langston Hughes; Lorraine Hansberry's *Raisin in the Sun* in 1959; *Purlie Victorious* by Ossie Davis in 1961; in 1963 *Tambourines to Glory* by Langston Hughes; *Blues For Mister Charlie* by James Baldwin, and Lorraine Hansberry's *The Sign In Sidney Brunstein's Window* in 1964. Only Lorraine Hansberry and Langston Hughes have had more than one production on Broadway. Their plays (*Mulatto* in the first instance, and *Raisin In The Sun* a quarter of a century later) enjoyed the longest runs of any vehicles by Negro authors, each playing for over a year in New York followed by extensive cross country tours. Both plays have also been translated and performed abroad, and *Raisin in the Sun* became a Hollywood picture.

Some of the most interesting work by Negro playwrights has been produced off-Broadway. The Federal Theatre of the Thirties in Harlem did Rudolph Fisher's *Conjur Man Dies, Turpentine* by J. A. Smith and Peter Morell, and in Chicago *Big White Fog* by Theodore Ward. The American Negro Theatre under Abram Hill's direction, sent its *Anna Lucasta* from Harlem to Broadway, and in its uptown productions such talented young actors as Sidney Poitier, Harry Belafonte, and Hilda Simms gained experience. The record run for any play in Harlem is that of the Suitcase Theatre's *Don't You Want To Be Free?* by Langston Hughes which had 135 performances. Ruth Jett's production of the Alice Childress *Just A Little Simple* had a considerable run at the Club Baron on Lenox Avenue in 1951, as did *A Medal for Willie* by William Branch. The most hospitable theatre in New York to the Negro playwright has been the Greenwich Mews under the direction of Stella Holt, dean of off-Broadway producers. In 1954, Miss Holt presented Branch's drama on John Brown and Frederick Douglass, *In Splendid Error;* in 1955 a hilarious comedy by Alice Childress, *Trouble in Mind;* and in 1956 Loften Mitchell's moving, *A Land Beyond The River* about integration in the South. In 1963 the Mews produced William Hairston's *Walk in Darkness;* and in 1964 *Jerico Jim Crow,* a freedom song-play by Langston Hughes, and in 1965 his *The Prodigal Son.*

Only the Karamu Theatre in Cleveland has been more active in presenting plays by or about Negroes than the Greenwich Mews. That is because Karamu, a settlement house project, has been at it for years. Founded by Russell and Rowena Jelliffe in 1916 and known then as the Gilpin Players, over the years Karamu has produced almost every play concerned with Negro life by a white or Negro author, including the world premieres of some, and the only performances to date of others. The plays of the young Nigerian Wole Soyinka, were first done in America by Karamu. And years ago the earliest comedies of Langston Hughes were presented by the Gilpin Players on a ramshackle stage before the erection of the present million dollar Karamu House which contains a proscenium theatre, an arena theatre, a concert hall and facilities for a children's theatre. Recognized as one of the most important of America's tributary theatres, Karamu has given to Broadway some excellent performers—Mildred Smith, Frank Marriott, Zelma George, Isabel Cooley, Clayton Corbin, Leesa Foster; and on its resident roster it has one of the masters of Negro humor, Nolan Bell, now a mature comedian who grew up from childhood with Karamu and has performed in many of its dramas and musicals.

If the Negro performer had had to depend entirely on Broadway for sustenance over the years, he would have fared badly indeed. Fortunately, between the First World War and the Second, there existed for about twenty years a booking agency for Southern Negro Theatres, known as the Theatre Owners Booking Association—the T. O. B. A.—or TOBY as performers called it. It booked some Northern theatres, too, the Lincoln in New York, the Monogram and the Grand in Chicago, the Gibson in Philadelphia, and its circuit supplied work for hundreds of Negro entertainers whose offerings ranged from blackface comedy and blues to one-act plays, opera arias, adagio dancing and magic—for the Negro performers' talents were many and varied. There have been tumblers like the Crackerjacks, ventriloquists like Wee Johnny Woods, magicians like the Great Gowongo, comics like Butterbeans and Susie, divas like Madame Fannie Wise, dancers like Eddie Rector, and of course great blues singers from Ma Rainey to Bessie Smith and the unforgettable Virginia Liston singing *The Titanic Blues*. Ethel Waters worked the T. O. B. A. circuit long before her name went up in lights at the Winter Garden in *As Thousands Cheer* or over the marquee of the Empire in *A Member of the Wedding*.

T. O. B. A. was essentially a vaudeville circuit, but it also booked entire companies such as Tutt's *Smarter Set*, S. J. Dudley and Company with his mule, and the famous Whitman Sisters. The Whitman Sisters, four singers and dancers who began as a church trio in Kansas, produced tabloid musicals of a very lively nature usually with two blackface comedians, a blues singer, a pretty leading lady and a high stepping chorus line. For several seasons their comedy team consisted of a tall lanky young man who did not wear burnt cork and a midget, Willie Bryant and Princess Wee Wee. T. O. B. A. was both a proving ground and a meal ticket for the Negro performer, as well as a source of living theatre to millions of Negroes barred from other playhouses. Touring Negro tent shows of a nature like that of Silas Green, the Florida Cotton Blossoms, and later Flournoy Miller's *The Smart Set* were profitable for many years—until television made its inroads on all live entertainment and black and white variety, indoors and out, went by the board. Popular favorites of big time vaudeville like the Mills Brothers, the Deep River Boys, and the Ink Spots turned almost entirely to night clubs, records, and spot appearances on radio or television for a livelihood, whereas Palace headliners like Bojangles, the late great dancer, and featured acts like Glenn and Jenkins, Moss and Frye and Hamtree Harrington sought refuge in revenues, cabarets, or foreign tours. Billy Banks went to Tokyo where he became a television favorite, the Nicolas Brothers to Mexico, South America, Paris, and Adelaide Hall to the London night clubs.

Night clubs from the Barbary Coast of San Francisco earthquake days to Harlem of the present have been lively showcases for Negro entertainers. By way of the Cotton Club (where she was a chorus girl) Lena Horne came to Broadway. By way of T. O. B. A. and the Harlem night clubs, Ethel Waters rose to fame. Duke Ellington, Cab Calloway, Fats Waller and Fletcher Henderson first attracted attention in Harlem cabarets before moving on to Broadway, Carnegie Hall and the world. During the Twenties, Smalls Paradise, Baron's, the Nest and later Minton's were midnight havens for Negro entertainers, a slew of Billies among them—Billie Holiday, Billie Daniels, Billie Eckstein, Billy Banks, Billy Mitchell. Minton's is credited as the birthplace of be-bop music. In more recent years, Smalls Paradise popularized the Madison and the Twist. For more than ten years the Club Baby Grand showcased Nipsey Russell, Harlem's favorite comedian and seemingly a permanent fixture there until his hilarious integration jokes caught the ear of downtown listeners and he moved on up a little higher to the Playboy Clubs and the national TV screens.

It is a long step from the dialect comedy of Bert Williams in grotesque makeup, oversized coat and funny shoes to the social satire of dapper young comics like Nipsey Russell or Dick Gregory, cool, well dressed and impudent. If the race problem got even a remote mention in the comedy routines of the T. O. B. A., vaudeville or night club performers in the old days, its mention would usually be in terms unintelligible to white listeners. Even at the Apollo Theatre in Harlem with a 90% Negro audience, race problems were seldom a part of the comedy monologue there. Jackie Moms Mabley alone of all the old comics, might slip in a racial wallop once in a while. Racial references, I think, were discouraged by the white owners and managers of most of the theatres and night clubs where Negroes performed. In changing this concept, Nipsey Russell and the Supreme Court were pioneers. The school desegregation decrees of 1954 and the subsequent front page explosions placed the race problem so squarely in the news that for even a night club comic to ignore it would be difficult. Nipsey Russell in his routines had never been ignoring it. At the Baby Grand he had long had free reign and just the right audience for his satire —an audience that would roar with laughter at the mention of the words *Little Rock* if uttered with proper recognition of their absurdity.

"You nine Negro boys and girls about to enter Little Rock High School for the first time," said Nipsey Russell impersonating a big race leader, "must uphold the honor of the Negro people when you go into that white school. I do not want you young people to go in there all belligerent and ignorant—like they expect Negroes to be. No! Don't go in that school carrying bricks, knives, razors or guns. Go in there *civilized*—throwing atom bombs!"

Jackie Moms Mabley, the grandmother of all Negro comediennes, who once performed in blackface but now contents herself with toothlessness and a red wig, has invented a great Cindy Ella story about the little colored girl who was invited by magic to the senior ball at the University of Mississippi—but at the stroke of midnight was changed back into her original little black self. Its telling and its denouement is one of the funniest and saddest bits to be heard on the American stage. Dick Gregory's entire night club act is composed of social material—something unheard of for a colored comedian a decade ago—and Godfrey Cambridge thoroughly ribs all forms of segregation in front of the most fashionable audiences in clubs where cover charges are high. The current crop of Negro comics, unlike Lenny Bruce and some other whites, have not as yet resorted to dirty words to add pungency to their comedy. Young Negro playwrights, in contrast to the comedians, are great users of graffiti. Perhaps influenced by *The Blacks* and the avant garde trend in Paris, London and New York, Adrienne Kennedy's *The Funny House of A Negro*, LeRoi Jones' *Dutchman*, *The Toilet*, *The Slave*, and James Baldwin's *Blues For Mister Charlie*—all 1964 productions—abound in what used to be called profanity. If a black Lenny Bruce appears on the scene as a social comic, the freedom movement can go no farther.

That the Negro has a great forte for comedy and music cannot be denied. The playbills for 100 years prove it so—from the minstrel comics of the eighteen sixties to Ozzie Davis and Pearl Bailey now; in song from Elizabeth Taylor Greenfield, known as the Black Swan in 1854 when she sang for Queen Victoria to Leontyne Price whose recordings are now in many a Royal record collection.

Some of the sweetest voices in the world today are Negro voices—the liquid voice of Camilla Williams, the mighty yet gentle baritone of William

Warfield, the cool fountain of sound of Mattiwilda Dobbs, of Adele Addison. (And there is always the memory of the incomparable Roland Hayes, still singing in concert at the age of 75; Marian Anderson announcing her farewell tour after a quarter of a century of great performances; and Dorothy Maynor whose *Depuis le Jour* was pure delight.) Younger singers of outstanding ability in concert and opera include Margaret Tynes, George Shirley, Grace Bumbry, Reri Grist, Betty Allen, Shirley Verrett, Martha Flowers, and Billie Lynn Daniels. La Scala, the Metropolitan and all the great opera houses of the world have opened their doors to American Negroes, beginning with the pioneers of the Twenties and Thirties, Lillian Evanti and Katerina Yarboro, divas who achieved success abroad.

The loudest singers in the world today in concert halls or out are gospel singers, products of the Negro church, and capable of raising at all times "a joyous noise unto the Lord." They are America's last uncontaminated source of pure folk singing. The most famous exponent of gospel singing is Mahalia Jackson. Not far behind are Clara Ward, the Davis Sisters, James Cleveland, Princess Stewart and the Caravans. Alex Bradford and Marion Williams have taken gospel singing from off-Broadway to the Philharmonic, to Europe, Asia, and around the world in the song-play, *Black Nativity* by Langston Hughes. They sang in 1963 in Coventry Cathedral in England, and their television film of *Black Nativity* received the Catholic Dove Award at Cannes. Since the advent of Josephine Baker and the *Revue Negre* in 1926, no group of American Negro artists received such opening night acclaim in Paris as did the *Black Nativity* company at the Champs Elysées, with the press hailing Marion Williams as a dynamic new star. It was in that same theatre that Josephine Baker made her Parisian debut some 35 years before.

Josephine Baker is the world's most famous international star. She has drawn capacity audiences in all the great cities of the world, singing as she does in several languages, and wearing the most expensively elegant wardrobes to be seen anywhere, especially designed for her by the great couturiers. That so beautiful and talented a woman happens to be colored, seems not to have affected her career adversely except for an interim period in her own homeland where, when she refused to accept segregation in New York or Miami Beach during appearances there, important columnists attacked her with false charges of radicalism—for which Miss Baker filed libel suits. Subsequent American appearances were highly successful, and Miss Baker's performance at 60 is as sparkling, as joyous and as heart warming as ever.

If one were to be asked to name the Twelve Great Personalities of the Negro entertainment field in the Twentieth Century regardless of categories, it would be impossible to omit Josephine Baker. Bert Williams, of course, would have to be included, as would Marian Anderson and Roland Hayes, Paul Robeson, Bojangles Bill Robinson, Rose McClendon, who could move an audience emotionally without saying a word, Jackie Moms Mabley who is one of the funniest women on earth, and Louis Armstrong, Sidney Poitier, Harry Belafonte, and Katherine Dunham. Certainly there are others that should be included. But a dozen is only 12. If a baker's dozen be allowed, the 13th would have to be Pearl Bailey. Or did somebody say Billie Holiday? Florence Mills? Bessie Smith? Ethel Waters? Canada Lee? Alvin Ailey? Lena Horne? Eartha Kitt? Except for Louis Armstrong as a singer, we are omitting entirely the field of jazz, pops, and folk—the great Ray Charles, Nina Simone, Lionel Hampton, Jackie Wilson, Chubby Checker, Odetta, Sonny Terry and Brownie McGhee—performing artists as well as jazzmen, personalities in the theatrical sense of the word as well as musicians—Duke Ellington, Charlie Mingus, Max Roach.

Creatively a most productive period for the Negro in the arts began in the Nineteen Twenties. It continued for a decade and was termed by literary commentators the Negro Renaissance, or the period of the New Negro. Its center was Harlem where poetry, prose and painting took a new lease on life, and in whose productivity the downtown white world vouched a more than passing interest. For a few years Harlem was in vogue, and the Negro in the arts was fashionable. This happy period began with the success in 1921 of an infectious musical called *Shuffle Along*. Intended for Negro audiences it opened at the Howard Theatre in Washington, moved on to Philadelphia, then ended up in a rather out of the way New York playhouse, the 63rd Street Theatre off Broadway, where it suddenly became the talk of the town and ran for nearly two years. It was the kind of joyous little show that people liked to see again and again. It sparkled. It exuded good nature. Its songs were catchy, its comedy easy-going, its girls prancingly pretty, and the overall effect one of happy syncopated fun. The book for *Shuffle Along* was by Miller and Lyles who performed the comedy routines. The songs were by Sissle and Blake who sang most of them. They produced the show themselves on a shoestring.

This ebullient musical had some wonderful people in it—most of them quite unknown at the time—Josephine Baker at the end of the chorus line, Hall Johnson and William Grant Still in the orchestra, the diva-to-be, Katerina Yaroboro among the singers, Trixie Smith shouting blues, and Florence Mills as the leading lady, substituting for Gertrude Saunders who after opening had gotten a better paying job in burlesque. Florence Mills became the star and *Shuffle Along* a milestone in Negro theatre. It created a vogue for Negro musicals that lasted until the Depression. By that time white writers had realized the profits inherent in Negro materials so they began to write shows especially for Negro casts. It then became difficult for colored writers to achieve commercial production. Lew Leslie's *Blackbirds* with a white score made Florence Mills—and in a later edition, *Ethel Waters* —Broadway headliners.

Following *Shuffle Along* came *Put and Take*, then *Liza*, then late in 1923 *Runnin' Wild* which introduced the Charleston, a foot-flinging hand-clapping dance that swept the world. Other lively all Negro shows within the next few years were *Africana, Dinah;* a second Miller and Lyles show, *Chocolate Dandies; Rang Tang, Hot Chocolates* with lyrics by Andy Razaf and music by Fats Waller; *Brown Buddies, Sugar Hill, Hot Rhythm, Fast and Furious* and *Rhapsody in Black* featuring Valaida Snow and the Berry Brothers. *The Plantation Revue* starred Florence Mills who then went to London in *From Dover to Dixie* (the same show renamed) and returned in *Dixie to Broadway*. At the time of her death in 1927, Florence Mills was one of the most beloved of Broadway performers. "I'm just a little black-bird looking for a bluebird" became her theme song and, as her funeral cortege went through Harlem an airplane overhead released a flock of bluebirds.

The big all-Negro musicals after the Thirties were for two decades almost all written by whites—Jimmy McHugh and Dorothy Fields, Vernon Duke, John LaTouche, Rogers and Hammerstein and others. Their shows included, besides various editions of *Blackbirds, Swinging The Blues, Swinging the Dream, The Hot Mikado, Cabin in the Sky, Carmen Jones,* and *The House of Flowers*. Then *Shinbone Alley* with Eartha Kitt, *Jamaica* with Lena Horne, *Mr. Wonderful* and later *Golden Boy* both starring Sammy Davis, and previously *No Strings* with Diahann Carroll began a trend away from all-Negro casts toward integrated shows built around Negro stars. Duke Ellington's *Beggar's Holiday* was an early integrated musical starring Alfred Drake, with sets by Broadway's lone Negro designer Perry Watkins. It marked the Negro composer's return to Broadway after a considerable absence. A Negro lyricist, Langston Hughes, in 1947 wrote the songs for what was termed the "first Broadway opera" *Street Scene*, with a score by Kurt Weill and book by Elmer Rice. Three years later, with a Hughes libretto and music by Jan Meyerowitz, *The Barrier* starring Lawrence Tibbett and Muriel Rahn, opened on Broadway.

In the integrated musical theatre, appearing with primarily white casts, Jules Bledsoe in New York and later Paul Robeson in London came to fame singing *Ole Man River* in *Show Boat*. Ethel Waters starred in *As Thousands Cheer*, and later in *At Home Abroad* with Bea Lillie. Juanita Hall sang the haunting *Bali Hai* in *South Pacific*, and was a leading performer in *Flower*

Drum Song. Todd Duncan was featured in *Lost in the Stars;* Thelma Carpenter in *The Seven Lively Arts;* Dooley Wilson and Richard Huey in *Bloomer Girl;* William Dillard in *My Darlin' Aida;* Pearl Bailey in *Arms and the Girl,* and Mae Barnes in *By the Beautiful Sea.* The all-Negro cast in the Harold Arlen-Johnny Mercer musical, *St. Louis Woman,* with a book by Arna Bontemps and Countee Cullen from the former's novel, *God Sends Sunday* again brought colored writers to Broadway, and gave Pearl Bailey her first big role. Another showcase for topnotch Negro talent was Virgil Thompson's *Four Saints in Three Acts* by Gertrude Stein, with Edward Matthews and a glorious group of singers. *Carmen Jones* first brought the current star of the Moral Rearmament movement, Muriel Smith, to fame. *Simply Heavenly* established Claudia McNeil. Negro performers had bit roles in *Finian's Rainbow* as well as being in the chorus. And from the late Nineteen Forties, Broadway musicals have increasingly included colored boys and girls in their singing and dancing choruses, and Negro musicians in the pit.

While musical integration was gaining a foothold on the Broadway scene, the dramatic stage only infrequently from time to time offered effective starring or featured roles to Negroes: Ethel Waters in *Mamba's Daughters* followed years later by *A Member of the Wedding;* Paul Robeson's triumphant *Othello;* Ruth Attaway in *You Can't Take It With You;* Canada Lee in *Native Son;* Jane White in *Strange Fruit* and later off-Broadway, *Once Upon A Mattress* and *The Trojan Women;* Gordon Heath in *Deep Are the Roots;* Ellen Holly in *Too Late the Phalarope;* Abbie Mitchell in *On Whitman Avenue;* Zelma Watson George in a powerful wheelchair revival of *The Medium;* Earl Hyman in *Mister Johnson;* Eartha Kitt in *Jolly's Progress;* Conchita Rivera and Reri Grist in *West Side Story;* Lawrence Winters in *The Long Dream;* Billy Dee Williams in *The Cool World,* and Claudia McNeil in *Tiger, Tiger Burning Bright.* Since World War II, more and more Negro performers have been able to gain professional experience, theatrical discipline, and even earn a living at their craft. For a professional actor, certainly the stage should be his bread basket.

The biggest single bread basket for the Negro in the history of the American stage has been *Porgy and Bess.* If ever colored performers erect a monument to a musician outside their race, it should be to George Gershwin, the composer of that melodic perennial based on the play, *Porgy,* dramatized from the DuBose Heyward novel of the same name concerning life in Catfish Row. The musical version has been performed all over the now known world. The moon is yet to see it, but it will in time. *Porgy and Bess* possesses great theatricality. It entertains. Commercially, it is a well-woven theatre basket, as durable as baskets come, and filled with a variegated kettle of fish. Its charms are many. Its songs, the melodies derived from the folk blues and spirituals of the Negro people are beautiful. There is prancing and dancing. Its argot is quaint. Its characters are color-ful and broadly drawn. There are children in the show, a goat, and a marching band. It has almost everything capable of drawing money into the box office. In other words, it is a good show. And it has fed, over long periods of time in many cities and many countries, a great many Negro performers.

If it were not for the racial complications in American life, one might forego any further discussion of *Porgy and Bess,* and accept it simply as an excellent theatre piece, and a helpful dinner basket. Unfortunately, its basket has been a trap, a steel-toothed trap leaving its marks upon the wrists of the Negro people who reached therein to touch its fish. And the fish themselves are tainted with racism. Art aside, it is an axiom in the American theatre that the cheapest shows to stage are Negro shows. Their cast budgets are always the lowest of any. If a Negro show is a hit, a great deal of money may be made. The bulk of this money does not go to Negroes. They are seldom if ever in the top echelons of management or production. Financially, the whites get the caviar, the Negroes get the porgies. A porgy is a fish, and *Porgy and Bess* concerns fishermen and their women. The character, Porgy, is a cripple, an almost emasculated man. His Bess is a whore. The denizens (as the critics term them) of Catfish Row are child-like ignorant blackamoors given to dice, razors, and singing at the drop of a hat. In other words, they are stereotypes in (to sensitive Negroes) the worst sense of the word. The long shadow of the blackface minstrel coarsens the charm of *Porgy* and darkens its grace notes. Those notes themselves are lifted from the Negro people. Borrowed is a more polite word; "derived from" an acceptable phrase.

Hall Johnson in *Opportunity,* the journal of the National Urban League, wrote in his review of the original production:

> The informing spirit of Negro music is not to be caught and understood merely by listening to the tunes, and Mr. Gershwin's much publicized visits to Charleston for local color do not amount even to a matriculation in the preparatory school that he needed for his work. Nothing can be more mis-leading, especially to an alien musician, than a few visits to Negro revivals and funerals. Here one encounters the "outside" at its most external. The obvious sights and sounds are only the foam, which has no meaning without the beer. And here let it be said that it is not the color nor the aloofness of the white investigator which keeps him on the outside. It is the powerful tang and thrill of the "foam" which excites him prematurely and makes him rush away too soon—to write books and music on a subject of which he has

not even begun to scratch the surface. . . . What we are to consider then is not a Negro opera by Gershwin, but Gershwin's idea of what a Negro opera should be. . . . Artistically, we darker Americans are in a most peculiar situation with regard to what we have to give the world. In our several hundred years of enforced isolation in this country we have had plenty of time and plenty of reason to sing each other songs and tell each other tales. These songs and stories have a hidden depth of meaning as well as a simple and sincere external beauty. But the same wall which forced them into existence has closed in tight upon their *meaning* and allows only their beauty to escape through the chinks. So that our folk culture is like the growth of some hardy yet exotic shrub whose fragrance never fails to delight discriminating nostrils even when there is no interest in the depths of its roots.

Following the long four year tour of *Porgy and Bess* throughout Europe and South America, initiated under State Department auspices, Paul Henry Lang in 1956 wrote in the *New York Herald Tribune:*

Foreign audiences are seldom aware that *Porgy* does not deal with the present. They do not know that the music is not genuine Negro art. . . . What they do believe is that this is the sad life of the oppressed Negro everywhere in America, a sordid life riddled with vice and crime in the black ghetto. While I was in Europe last summer, I had many heated discussions on the subject but could not explain away the "authenticity" of life as depicted in *Porgy.* . . . They cannot realize that the world of Catfish Row, created and set to music by white men, is a view from the outside focussed on the Negro only for their entertainment value and as a group apart rather than as members of society. *Porgy and Bess* is indeed an excellent show, but it is no American folk opera.

"Unfortunately, the people in other countries don't think they are acting. They think they are giving a realistic portrayal of actual Negro life," the composer, William Grant Still, said in *Tones and Overtones,* backing up his contention with quotations from overseas papers. A review in the Spanish music magazine *Ritmo* declared: "*Porgy* is a strong emotional document of the life of the Negro in North America depicting the humiliation and misery of his way of living, the violent sensuality and passion of his psychology, his crude and spontaneous reactions. All of this constitutes the substance and soul of the Negro, his character and his tragi-comic life amidst sordid surroundings." The *Australian Music News* called, "the whole libretto typically Negro." Which caused Mr. Still to ask, "Is that the impression we would like to have foreigners get of us, of our life here in America?"

"The ignorant, happy-foot, lust-loving, crap shooting clown—Porgy has them all," wrote Negro journalist, James Hicks. "The presentation of *Porgy* could not happen to any other race in America but the colored race. The Jewish People have their Anti-Defamation League which sees to it that the role of the 'Sheenie' no longer walks the American stage. Catholic groups each week police the theatres and movie houses and order death by boycott to any theatrical presentation which dares depict them in any other light but good."

In Negro America's largest newspaper, the *Pittsburgh Courier*, J. A. Rogers observed, "While this stereotype gives joy to whites, it is to thinking Negroes like the frogs in Aesop's fable. To the boys who were having so much fun throwing stones into a pond, the frogs said, "What is fun to you, is *death* to us."

When Samuel Goldwyn was casting the motion picture version of *Porgy and Bess* in 1957, Harlem's *Amsterdam News* ran a front page story to the effect that actor Sidney Poitier turned down a $75,000 offer to play the leading role. It quoted him as saying, "As a Negro I have a certain sensitiveness, and as an artist I have certain responsibilities. Certain things I will play, but they must be constructive to my life as a Negro. *Porgy and Bess* is always played within a restricted range for the actor. There is simply one crap game too many in it." Praising Poitier editorially, the *Amsterdam News* declared, "We think this is a ringing answer to those who say that Negroes are not willing to pay for their self-respect and freedom. . . . The Negro race has been dignified by his creed." But less than a month later, the wire services from Hollywood transmitted to the world Samuel Goldwyn's announcement of acceptance by Sidney Poitier of the role of Porgy. The *Amsterdam News* never informed Harlemites as to just what happened, so they were left wondering if Goldwyn's price went up, or Poitier's pride went down. Yet nobody faulted him much. Negroes are familiar with baskets that are also traps.

Backstage one cold day that winter at Harlem's Apollo Theatre, some of the actors were discussing another high salaried Negro artist of the female gender who had also accepted a part in the Goldwyn opus, but who felt impelled for the record to register a protest. After seeing the script she imperiously told Mr. Goldwyn, "I demands you remove them *dats* and *dis-es* from my role."

To which Mr. Goldwyn is said to have replied, "Why not, darling? Just talk like you are—and everything'll be all right."

So, "I loves you, Porgy" and "Bess, you is ma woman now—you *is*, you *is*, you *is!*" reached the screen intact, dialect and all, as did, "Oh, Lawd, I'm on ma way!" And a Todd-AO Technicolor wide screen million dollar production of *Porgy and Bess* went out to the whole wide world singing,

"I got plenty o' nuttin', an' nuttin's plenty fo' me." Fortunately, the junkie, Sporting Life, in the person of Sammy Davis, Jr., sang, "It ain't necessarily so."

RETURN OF A CLASSIC
Porgy and Bess Comes Home From Europe

headlined the *New York Times* in the lead article by Brooks Atkinson on the front page of its theatre section for March 15, 1953 when, after its tour abroad the Robert Breen production came home. "Now that *Porgy and Bess* has settled down in New York," wrote Mr. Atkinson, "the people who last September opposed the project of sending it abroad ought to feel ashamed of themselves. . . . In the realm of art, nothing matters so much as the quality of the art, which in the case of the Gershwin opera is magnificent. . . . The zeal for outward respectability is a sign of inner uncertainty, and it should not be resolved at the expense of people who know what they are doing." Brooks Atkinson could hardly be accused of ill will or insincerity. And zeal for outward respectability might well be a sign of inner uncertainty. But Mr. Atkinson himself would probably be filled with uncertainty had he been born colored, segregated most of his life, denied a job on the *Times* and even tickets to many American attractions, laughed at and ridiculed from minstrel days to the Ziegfeld Theatre, and then chided for not liking make-believe porgies in a Broadway basket— when you have had almost nothing but porgies all your life. Almost nothing but porgies—nothing but porgies, porgies, porgies.

Balance is what America has long needed in relation to the Negro and entertainment. There would be nothing greatly wrong with the U.S. State Department sponsoring *Porgy and Bess* abroad, if at the same time (or before or after) it also sent abroad other equally effective spectacles in which Negroes were not portrayed solely as childish darkies, crap shooters, dope addicts, ladies of little virtue, and quaint purveyors of "You *is*, you *is*, you *is*." From the days of the minstrels a hundred years ago, through the half century of Hollywood movies with their Stephin Fetchits and Butterfly McQueens and the Amos and Andys of radio and television, right up to *The Cool World* with its juvenile delinquents, the "you is" school has by and large prevailed in white versions of Negro theatrics. It has, with few exceptions, planted its concept of the Negro on the minds of the world. Always servants or clowns—and not just clowns or servants, but *burlesques* of clowns and servants. Certainly there are servants in the world so why should they not be portrayed in pictures? The late Hattie McDaniels once said, when attacked for her Hollywood roles as a domestic, "It is better getting $7,000 a week playing a servant, than $7.00 a week *being* one." Being an artist of ability, Miss McDaniels was capable of humanizing even the burlesque concepts of Hollywood directors.

A standard form of direction for Negro actors playing chauffeur's roles in Hollywood, so an old time performer told me, ran something like this. Upon opening the car door for one's white employer in any film, the director would command: "Jump to ground . . . Remove cap . . . Open car door . . . Step back and bow . . . Come up smiling . . . Now bow again . . . Now straighten up and grin."

The darkest actors with the widest mouths and the whitest teeth were the ones who until recent years got the best bit parts in Hollywood. There have been some decent, even charming films about Negroes—the early *Hallelujiah* and *Hearts in Dixie*, much later *Bright Road* based on Mary Elizabeth Vorman's lovely little story; Maidie Norman in *The Well;* James Edwards in *Home of the Brave;* the moving semi-documentary *The Quiet One;* Belafonte's *A Man Is Ten Feet Tall;* Sidney Poitier in *Lilies of the Fields;* and Bernie Hamilton in *One Potato, Two Potato* and also *Nothing But A Man.* And from Brazil via France came *Black Orpheus* with the beautiful American Negro star, Marpessa Dawn, who came to fame abroad.

In the theatre, one must note, ninety percent of the plays about Negroes drop their final curtain on defeat—usually death. A serious drama about Negroes simply cannot end happily it seems. From *Uncle Tom's Cabin* to *Blues for Mister Charlie* if every Negro who has died impotent and defeated on stage were to be buried end to end, their assembled corpses would reach around the world. Shakespeare started it with *Othello.* LeRoi Jones continues it with *Dutchman* where a white floozie stabs an Ivy Leaguish colored boy in the belly and has his body thrown between two subway cars. The stereotype of the Negro drama is the unhappy ending—spiritually and physicially defeated, lynched, dead—gotten rid of to the relief of the dramatist and the audience, in time for a late supper. O'Neill's *Emperor Jones*, stone cold dead in the jungle; *Mulatto*'s young hero a suicide; *Native Son* on his way to the electric chair; *Mandingo*, mortally cold cocked; the young African in *Mister Johnson* begging the white man to shoot him—rather than snatching the gun from the white man and firing a few shots himself; Fishbelly in Richard Wright's *The Long Dream* as dramatized by Ketti Frings should also have shot first—but no! Like the Indians in the old westerns, Fish bites the dust instead of his white enemy; likewise Richard Henry in *Blues for Mister Charlie*. Being such a bad, bad man, one would have thought the militant Negro in the Baldwin play might have shot first. But on Broadway Negro characters do *not* shoot first. They merely get shot.

A white dramatist once, when asked why the black hero in his play did not kill his white adversary, replied, "Why, that wouldn't be tragic!" Maybe his attitude explains why so many of the "serious" plays about Negroes ring hollow. Somebody's concept of tragedy is askew. Warren Miller's sociological study of Harlem delinquents reached the stage with all the nuances explaining how the delinquents got that way gone by the wayside. In a letter to the *New York Herald Tribune* Ellen Holly wrote, "The Cool World is about as concerned with sociology as an exposé magazine is concerned with morality. Such magazines leer endlessly through keyholes then tack on a sanctimonious conclusion in a pretense of respectability. To reiterate that a jungle produces animals tells us nothing new and brings us no closer to understanding. It is merely an excuse to ogle at that jungle." Ogling at the jungle, many Negroes feel, is about all Broadway drama in the past has been able to do in regard to Negro themes.

"The constant whine of knives being sharpened is the predominant sound of *The Cool World*. Indeed, by the end of the ninth scene at the Eugene O'Neill, what seems like the entire juvenile delinquent population of Harlem is hard at work honing machetes, switchblades and stolen kitchen utensils," wrote Walter Kerr in his review which termed it, a "distressingly dreary play about the street-corner jungle that turns schoolboys into heroin addicts, schoolgirls into dollar-and-a-half prostitutes, and a random assortment of the group into corpses."

"Somebody is trying to pin their own defeatism, their mind sickness and their death wishes on the Negro," wrote Arna Bontemps. "They haven't stopped to think that Negroes are too black and ugly for that stuff. Look at any of the Negro athletes on TV. They ain't fixin' to quit. Neither are those knotty-headed Africans around Lake Victoria and such places. Something *else* has got to give, not their skulls." In the U.S.A. if Negroes accepted defeat as fatalistically as their counterparts do on the Broadway stage, there would not be twenty million of them alive from Coast to Coast today. White Broadway by and large simply fails to reflect the Negro with any degree of basic truth no matter how famous the playwrights, how skilled the director, or who designs the sets.

Perhaps it is good that one hundred years after Emancipation integration is coming apace in the arts—that Leontyne Price now stars at the Metropolitan in Italian roles; that Lynn Hamilton plays the Queen in *Midsummer Night's Dream* in Manhattan parks; that Mabel Mercer is a favorite in East Side night spots; that Eartha Kitt not only performs in, but lives at the Plaza when she is in New York; that Frederick O'Neil is President of Actor's Equity; that Katherine Dunham choreographed *Aida* at the Met and *The Bible* in Rome; and Donald McKale and Talley Beatty direct non-Negro dances; that Anne Bancroft in Hollywood in full sight of 80 million television viewers, kissed Sidney Poitier when he received his Academy Award as the Best Actor of the Year; that Lorraine Hansberry's *Sign in Sidney Brunstein's Window* is cast with white actors; that Diana Sands plays a non-racial role as the leading lady in *The Owl and the Pussy Cat;* that Negro director Lloyd Richards is chosen to direct all-white casts; that white folk singers are singing colored gospel songs; that the great Martha Graham company, once all white, has three leading Negro dancers; and Arthur Mitchell is one of the stars of the New York City Ballet.

The formerly all Negro Alvin Ailey Dance Theater took a white ballerina and a Japanese one with its company to Paris. The ballet people sail happily through the international air with no regard whatsoever for racial problems or stereotypes. Such is the glory of the modern dance. May the Broadway theatre eventually acquire a similar glory. The American Negro has given great joy to the fields of light entertainment. He can add great understanding to the areas of serious make-believe as well. All he needs is playwrights, plays, and a reevaluation of what constitutes tragedy.

chapter 25

The Negro Contribution to American Letters

Arna Bontemps

Poetry

Early in the nineteenth century Americans of African descent, still some-what bewildered by the experience which had brought them into bondage in the New World, began to find a strangely satisfying expression for their thoughts and feelings in music. The songs which resulted, now known as Negro spirituals, have not only been a powerful musical influence on the nation as a whole but have been accepted with approval, even acclaim, throughout most of the world. It is well to remember, however, that the spirituals owe as much to their words as to their music. They mark a beginning of poetic expression as influential on subsequent poets as the music has been on later composers.

Actually, the lyrics of songs like "Roll, Jordan, Roll" and "Swing Low Sweet Chariot" were not the first attempts at verse by Negroes in the United States. An Indian raid on the little Massachusetts town of Deerfield in 1746 is commemorated in couplets by a semiliterate slave girl named Lucy Terry. She called her account "Bars Fight" and began it with these lines:

> August 'twas the twenty fifth
> Seventeen hundred forty-six
> The Indians did in ambush lay
> Some very valient men to slay
> The names of whom I'll not leave out.
> Samuel Allen like a hero fout
> And though he was so brave and bold
> His face no more shall we behold.

Though nothing more by her survives and no more is known of her interest in verse, Lucy Terry may have been still alive in Massachusetts when the child who became Phillis Wheatley was brought from Senegal in 1761 and when, a decade later, "A Poem by Phillis, A Negro Girl in Boston, on the Death of the Reverend George Whitefield" was published. Phillis was seventeen at the time, and this poem marked the beginning of a unique writing career.

Writing by slaves was not entirely an American phenomenon, as anyone familiar with the works of Terence, of Epictetus, in Rome and Greece respectively, may recall. Nor did all of them, despite their talents, succeed in winning freedom by their writing. Both Terence and Phillis Wheatley did, however, and when Phillis' health failed, she was advised by Boston doctors to take an ocean voyage. She embarked for England and there her *Poems on Various Subjects: Religious and Moral* was first published in 1773. The reception this volume received made her for a time, it has been said, the best-known of living American poets. Written in the spirit of John Calvin and in the manner of her English and American contemporaries, Phillis' poems were commended by George Washington and other prominent figures. But on the whole the poetry written in the American colonies in 1773, including that by Phillis, is of limited interest to poetry lovers in the twentieth century. This is equally true, perhaps a trifle more so, of the poetic composition by Jupiter Hammon which appeared as a broadside in 1760 under the title "An Evening Thought: Salvation by Christ, with Penitential Cries." A slave preacher on Long Island, Hammon appears to have been the first Negro American ever to see in print lines he had himself written.

Legal restrictions on the education of slaves were introduced in the American colonies after the period of Phillis Wheatley and Jupiter Hammon. The purpose was to keep from the slave news and propaganda likely to incite a lust for freedom. During the French Revolution and the Haitian Insurrections this was regarded as a serious matter, and slave uprisings in Virginia, South Carolina, and elsewhere added to the anxiety. Penalties were imposed on owners or other persons who violated the restrictions. Escaped slaves who later wrote autobiographies have left records of the mental anguish this deprivation caused them.

Denied the ABC's, slave poetry went underground, so to speak. Self-expression was obliged to become oral—as it had been for so many of their ancestors in Africa. Whether or not this was a blessing in disguise is a matter of opinion, but one fact is clear. The suppression of book learning by slaves coincided with the earliest musical and lyrical expression in the form which became known later as spirituals. The survival of "Roll, Jordan, Roll," for example, among the slaves from the United Sates isolated on a Caribbean island since 1824, would seem to place the beginnings of these songs very early in the nineteenth century or late in the eighteenth, allowing for the time it usually took such songs to develop and become generally known. Thus the elegies, commemorations, and devotional poems of Phillis Wheatley and Jupiter Hammon gave way to laments from the slave quarters such as:

> I know moonlight, I know starlight
>   I lay this body down
> I walk in the graveyard, I walk through the graveyard
>   To lay this body down.
>
> I lay in the grave and stretch out my arms,
>   I lay this body down,
> I go to the judgment in the evening of the day
>   When I lay this body down,
> And my soul and your soul will meet the day
>   I lay this body down.

or

> Bright sparkles in the churchyard
>   Give light unto the tomb;
> Bright summer, spring's lover—
>   Sweet flowers in their bloom.
>
> My mother once, my mother twice, my mother, she'll rejoice,
> In the Heaven once, in the Heaven twice, she'll rejoice.
> May the Lord, He will be glad of me
> In the Heaven, He'll rejoice.

This, then, was the kind of oral expression that replaced written poetry by Negro Americans during the Abolitionist campaign, the Civil War, and the Reconstruction after the war. Of course, there were minor exceptions and at least one that must considered major. Among the free men of color, as they were called in Louisiana, a strong French influence persisted and stimulated many broad cultural interests. Young colored men of talent were sent to Paris to be educated. Among them were poets like Armand Lanusse, Pierre Dalcour and most important, Victor Sejour who later became a successful French dramatist and moved in literary circles in which Alexandre Dumas was prominent. In their youth in New Orleans these three Louisiana poets with a group of their associates produced a collection called *Les Cenelles*, published in 1845, the first anthology of American Negro poetry. Included was "Epigram" by Lanusse which, as translated by Langston Hughes, shows how far the *Les Cenelles* poets and the free men of color of Louisiana were, culturally, from the slaves who created spirituals:

"Do you not wish to renounce the Devil!"
Asked a good priest of a woman of evil
Who had so many sins that every year
They cost her endless remorse and fear.

"I wish to renounce him forever," she said,
"But that I may lose every urge to be bad,
Before pure grace takes me in hand,
Shouldn't I show my daughter how to get a man?"

Meanwhile, however, George Moses Horton, a slave who had somehow become known to the editor of the *Raleigh Register* in North Carolina, published in 1829 a slender volume of verse under the title *Hope of Liberty*. Weston R. Gales, the editor, judged Horton to be about thirty-two at the time. Already, it seems, the slave poet had become a well-known figure among the college students at Chapel Hill, where he may have been employed, and found it possible to realize a bit of income from his verses. The nature of this writing can only be guessed, since none of it appears to have survived, but the circumstances would not lead one to think that it was passionate antislavery propaganda. Many of the students for whom Horton wrote and who evidently paid him were children of slaveholding families. Moreover, Horton retained in later life a noticeable capacity for humor, and it has been surmised that the poems with which he entertained the students at the University of North Carolina may have been in this vein.

As the title of his first collection indicates, Horton hoped to earn from the sale of his poetry enough money to buy his freedom. He did not succeed, and his attitude changed.

Alas! and am I born for this,
　　To wear this slavish chain?
Deprived of all created bliss,
　　Through hardship, toil, and pain?

How long have I in bondage lain,
　　And languished to be free?
Alas! and must I still complain,
　　Deprived of liberty?

In 1865, after the Union armies had won for him the emancipation his poems had failed to achieve, a second volume of Horton's verses was published in Raleigh under the title *Naked Genius*. By then, however, he was living in Philadelphia and not making a particularly good impression on the people who remembered him there more as a "character" than as a "natural-born" poet, as he impressed others. In any case, his second and last book contains stanzas which throw a certain light on his early reputation at Chapel Hill.

> My duck bill boots would look as bright,
> Had you in justice served me right;
> Like you, I then could step as light,
>   Before a flaunting maid.
> As nicely could I clear my throat,
> And to my tights my eyes devote;
> But I'd leave you bare, without the coat
>   For which you have not paid.

> Then boast and bear the crack,
> With the sheriff at your back,
> Huzzah for dandy Jack,
> My jolly fop, my Jo!

A contemporary of Horton's in Philadelphia was Frances Ellen (Watkins) Harper, whose *Poems on Miscellaneous Subjects* had been published in that city in 1854, when she was twenty-nine years old. Widely popular as an "elocutionist," Mrs. Harper's readings of her poems undoubtedly helped the sales of her book. Ten thousand copies were sold in the first five years, and it was reprinted three times thereafter before her second work, *Moses, a Story of the Nile*, appeared in 1869. Devoted to the cause of freedom, as most poets were inclined to be in the middle of the nineteenth century, as a Negro poet was practically obliged to be, she promptly came to grips with this theme:

> I ask no monument, proud and high,
> To arrest the gaze of the passer-by;
> All that my yearning spirit craves
> Is bury me not in a land of slaves.

Seven years after the publication of her first little volume, the war of liberation having begun and Mrs. Harper having established herself very favorably in the public eye as a "Negro" poet and a shining example (along with Frederick Douglass and other platform personalities) of what the Negro might become in freedom, she began to contemplate a provocative subject, about which she wrote to Thomas Hamilton, editor of the *Anglo-African,* a monthly magazine recently established: "If our talents are to be recognized we must write less of issues that are particular and more of feelings that are general. We are blessed with hearts and brains that compass more than ourselves in our present plight. . . . We must look to the future which, God willing, will be better than the present or the past, and delve into the heart of the world."

Where she had imbibed the notion that slavery was "particular" and not to be equated with the "general" craving of mankind for freedom is not indicated, but the point she raised has now been debated for more than a century and still remains crucial in any consideration of the place of the Negro in the arts, in American culture, as creator or as subject. It is therefore worth a moment to contemplate some of the themes Frances Ellen Harper favored when not writing about the specific problem that confronted her people. The evils of strong drink was one of these. Another was childhood, its innocence and blessedness. In "The Double Standard" she treats still another:

> Crime has no sex and yet today
>   I wear the brand of shame;
> Whilst he amid the gay and proud
>   Still bears an honest name.
>
>   . . . .
>
> Yes blame me for my downward course,
>   But Oh! remember well,
> Within your homes you press the hand
>   That led me down to hell.
>
>   . . . .
>
> No golden weights can turn the scale
>   Of Justice in His sight;
> And what is wrong in woman's life
>   In man's cannot be right.

Sketches of Southern Life, Mrs. Harper's third book, was published in 1873 and is notable for the language it put into the mouths of Negro characters. While avoiding dialect, as it was later to be used and popularized by Paul Laurence Dunbar, she nevertheless sought to suggest the flavor of Negro speech through characteristic patterns, phrases and nuances, a technique not unrelated to those used in the twentieth century by such writers as James Weldon Johnson and Langston Hughes.

Mrs. Harper was a frequent contributor to *Godey's Lady's Book* and other periodicals of the day. Understandably, she showed a fondness for the ballad in its most sentimental form, and it may be assumed that these pleased audiences who came to hear her public readings. Especially one such as "The Dying Bondman" which began:

> By his bedside stood the master
> Gazing on the dying one,

> Knowing by the dull gray shadows
> That life's sands were almost run.
>
> "Master," said the dying bondman,
> "Home and friends I soon shall see;
> But before I reach my country,
> Master write that I am free."

and ended some stanzas later with:

> Eagerly he grasped the writing;
> "I am free!" at last he said.
> Backward fell upon the pillow.
> He was free among the dead.

Her final collection of poems was *The Sparrow's Fall and Other Poems,* but she continued to write prose, though on the whole, less successfully.

Of her contemporaries and immediate successors among the Negro poets of the United States at least three are remembered. James Madison Bell's collected *Poetical Works* was published in 1904. John Wesley Holloway, a member of the famous Jubilee Singers of Fisk University and one of the first Negro schoolteachers in Georgia, anticipated Dunbar in the writing and publishing of poems in Negro dialect. George Marion McClellan, whose background was somewhat similar, appeared frequently in periodicals during the same period, though his volume *The Path of Dreams* was not collected until 1916. However, all told, more than thirty volumes of poetry by Negro Americans were published between Phillis Wheatley's collection and Dunbar's first.

The routine and format as well as the substance of minstrel show entertainment originated with Negro slaves in the United States around 1820. Constance Rourke noted in her *American Humor,* 1931, "Every plantation had its talented band that could crack jokes, and sing and dance to the accompaniment of banjo and bones." She added, significantly, "There is a record of at least one of these bands that became semiprofessional and travelled from plantation to plantation giving performances." After emancipation the steps from semiprofessionalism to professionalism were completed, with the results that are now familiar. Paul Laurence Dunbar's lyrics came at the high tide of minstrel popularity.

A son of former slaves, Paul Laurence Dunbar, greeted the twentieth century with *Lyrics of a Lowly Life,* 1896, a book which won for him a national reputation and enabled him to pursue a literary career for the rest of his life. Helped by the minstrel tradition, no doubt, his popularity was at first based mainly on poems written in the broad dialect of plantation folk.

In another sense his writing is in the tradition of Robert Burns, a poet fondly mentioned by literate Negroes who had themselves come out of plantation slavery. Dunbar's life was short, 1872 to 1906, and marred by declining health and personal problems. Other volumes of his verses preceded and followed the *Lyrics*. *Oak and Ivy*, his first, was privately printed in 1893 while he was employed as an elevator operator in Dayton, Ohio. Dunbar had graduated from high school in that city and written the class poem, but he had been unable to attend college. A second volume, *Majors and Minors*, followed in 1895. Neither of these attracted wide attention but they won enough approval to provoke a strong and influential introduction by William Dean Howells to *Lyrics of a Lowly Life*. His subsequent books of verse include *Lyrics of Love and Laughter*, 1903, *Lyrics of Sunshine and Shadow*, 1905, and *Complete Poems*, 1913. The latter has never been out of print, and it is found to contain, along with the dialect poems that made him famous, many poems in standard English, some of which provide the lyrics for songs which remain well known and loved. "Dawn" is an example:

> An angel, robed in spotless white.
> Bent down and kissed the sleeping Night.
> Night woke to blush; the sprite was gone.
> Men saw the blush and called it Dawn.

Another is "Who Knows?"

> Thou art the soul of a summer's day,
> Thou art the breath of the rose.
> > But the summer is fled
> > And the rose is dead
> Where are they gone, who knows,
> > who knows?
>
> Thou art the blood of my heart o' hearts,
> Thou art my soul's repose,
> > But my heart grows numb
> > And my soul is dumb.
> Where art thou, love, who knows,
> > who knows?
>
> Thou art the hope of my after years—
> Sun of my winter snows,
> > But the years go by
> > 'Neath a clouded sky.
> Where shall we meet, who knows,
> > who knows?

A contemporary of Dunbar's was James Weldon Johnson, but Johnson's first collection of poems was not published until eleven years after Dunbar's death. In the days when the two were acquainted, Johnson was known mainly by popular song lyrics, including one, "Lift Every Voice and Sing," which since its composition in 1900 has become a kind of national anthem for Negroes in the United States. His *Fifty Years and Other Poems*, 1917, ended what had begun to seem like a mournful silence by Negro poets in the wake of Dunbar's passing.

True, Fenton Johnson of Chicago contributed a few things to magazines like *Others* and *Poetry: A Magazine of Verse*, and the three women poets, Angelina W. Grimke, Anne Spencer and Georgia Douglas Johnson, were writing though not being published; but William Stanley Braithwaite, the only Negro to emerge as a poet in this period in the United States, was un-recognized as a Negro either in his book reviews for the *Boston Transcript*, his yearly anthologies of magazine verse, or his two early volumes of poetry, *Lyrics of Life and Love*, 1904, and *The House of Falling Leaves*, 1908.

James Weldon Johnson's "Fiftieth Anniversary Ode" on the emancipation in 1913 was seen by Braithwaite as the first move by a Negro poet to dis-engage their little tribe from whatever it was that had recently held them in thrall. The poem's reappearance in the volume *Fifty Years and Other Poems* was confirmation. While Braithwaite seems to have picked the right year for the first sign of the "disengagement," it is now possible to question his estimate of the influence of this particular book. Actually, Johnson's most significant poetic achievement was still a decade in the future, when his collection of folk sermons in verse was to be published as *God's Trombones* in 1927.

The year 1917 now stands out, where Negro poetry in the United States is concerned, as the year in which Claude McKay's poem "The Harlem Dancer" appeared in *The Seven Arts* magazine under the pen name of Eli Edwards. When this poem reappeared in McKay's *Harlem Shadows*, 1922, along with others so warm and fragrant they almost drugged the senses, things immediately began to happen. A chorus of new voices,* led by McKay, Jean Toomer, Langston Hughes, Countée Cullen and as many as half a dozen more, promptly began to make the Twenties a golden decade for poetry by American Negroes and to hear themselves referred to as heralds of a Negro Renaissance.

Interestingly, Braithwaite recognized McKay as the first of these to raise his voice, but he regarded him as "a genius meshed in [a] dilemma." It bothered Braithwaite that McKay seemed to "waver between the racial

---

* Among these most certainly must be added the name of Arna Bontemps himself, who won the *Crisis* poetry prize in 1926 with his poem "Nocturne at Bethesda."—J.P.D.

and the universal notes." At one time he seemed to be "contemplating life and nature with a wistful sympathetic passion." At another he was a "strident propagandist, using his poetic gifts to clothe arrogant and defiant thoughts." His "Spring in New Hampshire" and "The Harlem Dancer" were instances of the former, his "If We Must Die" of the latter. But a generation later it was "If We Must Die" that Winston Churchill quoted as climax and conclusion of his oration before the joint houses of the American Congress when he was seeking to draw this nation into the common effort in World War II. McKay had written it as the American Negro's defiant answer to lynching and mob violence in the Southern states. Churchill made it the voice of the embattled Allies as he read:

> If we must die—let it not be like hogs
> Hunted and penned in an inglorious spot,
> While round us bark the mad and hungry dogs,
> Making their mock at our accursed lot.
> If we must die—oh, let us nobly die,
> So that our precious blood may not be shed
> In vain; then even the monsters we defy
> Shall be constrained to honor us though dead!
> Oh, Kinsmen! We must meet the common foe;
> Though far outnumbered, let us show us brave,
> And for their thousand blows deal one deathblow!
> What though before us lies the open grave?
> Like men we'll face the murderous, cowardly pack,
> Pressed to the wall, dying, but fighting back!

Obviously neither Churchill nor McKay had at that time considered the possibilities of nonviolence. The poem does show, however, how a short span of years and certain historical events can alter the meaning of a literary work, as well as the risk involved in trying to separate too soon the local or special subject from the universal.

McKay had come to the United States from his native Jamaica, British West Indies, to study agriculture at Tuskegee Institute and later at Kansas State University. He had already published his first book *Songs of Jamaica*, 1911, mainly in the Jamaican dialect, while serving in the island constabulary, and followed it with another *Constab Ballads*, 1912. It took him less than three years to change his mind about agriculture as a career and head for New York and the literary life. In the course of a trip abroad he published in England in 1920 a small collection of lyrics under the title *Spring in New Hampshire*. On his return to America he became associate editor of the *Liberator* under Max Eastman. *Harlem Shadows*, 1922, was his first American publication. It contained most of the poems in the British collection as well as a number of new ones. For long periods thereafter McKay traveled and lived abroad, writing mostly prose. Not until his death in 1948 was another volume of his poems published, and this was the *Selected Poems*, 1953, bringing together the best of his early work and adding some poems written after his final homecoming to the United States and conversion to Roman Catholicism.

But the critic, Braithwaite who in his annual *Anthologies of Magazine Verse* had published Spoon River poems by Edgar Lee Masters, chants by Vachel Lindsey, free verse by Carl Sandburg and early work by many other important American poets before they appeared in other books, reserved his highest praise for Jean Toomer, among the poets of the Negro Renaissance. Of him he wrote:

> . . . In Jean Toomer, the author of *Cane*, we come upon the very first artist of the race, who with all an artist's passion and sympathy for life, its hurts, its sympathies, its desires, its joys, its defeats and strange yearnings, can write about the Negro without the surrender or compromise of the artist's vision. So objective is it, that we feel that it is a mere accident that birth or association has thrown him into contact with the life he has written about. He would write just as well, just as poignantly, just as transmutingly, about the peasants of Russia, or the peasants of Ireland, had experience brought him in touch with their existence. *Cane* is a book of gold and bronze, of dusk and flame, of ecstasy and pain, and Jean Toomer is a bright morning star of a new day of the race in literature.

Despite such reverberations, however, both Toomer and McKay were soon to be eclipsed by the twin stars of two even more infectious younger poets in the Harlem of the Twenties. Langston Hughes and Countée Cullen appeared almost simultaneously, where national recognition was concerned, in a time and place they helped to make significant.

Hughes' career as a writer may be said to have begun when he was a high school student in Cleveland, Ohio. His first poem in a national magazine appeared in *The Crisis* in 1921. It had been written the summer following his graduation, and he called it "The Negro Speaks of Rivers":

> I've known rivers:
> I've known rivers ancient as the world and
>   older than the flow of human blood in
>   human veins.
>
> My soul has grown deep like the rivers.
> I bathed in the Euphrates when dawns were young.
> I built my hut near the Congo and it lulled me to sleep.
> I looked upon the Nile and raised the pyramids above it.

I heard the singing of the Mississippi when
    Abe Lincoln went down to New Orleans,
    and I've seen its muddy bosom turn all
    golden in the sunset.

I've known rivers:
Ancient, dusky rivers.

My soul has grown deep like the rivers.

This poem by a recent high school graduate did more than launch a writing career. Among the poems written in the United States since 1921 there are certainly few, if any, that have been more widely read. It has been reprinted scores and scores of times and translated into so many languages the author has been unable to keep up with them. *The Weary Blues,* Hughes' first book of poems, appeared five years later, and many volumes have followed, all of them marked by an ease of expression and a naturalness of feeling that make them seem almost as if they had never been composed at all. Hughes' art can be likened to that of the creators of jazz. His sources are street music. His language is Harlemese. In his way he is an American original.

Countée Cullen was in many ways quite different. Educated in the public schools of New York City, he adopted the standard models for his poetry, from John Keats to E. A. Robinson. But if the forms were old, the ideas that went into Cullen's sonnets and quatrains were brand new in American poetry. This one, among his earliest, is an indication:

I doubt not God is good, well-meaning, kind,
And did He stoop to quibble could tell why
The little buried mole continues blind,
Why flesh that mirrors Him must someday die,
Make plain the reason tortured Tantalus
Is baited by the fickle fruit, declare
If merely brute caprice dooms Sisyphus
To struggle up a never-ending stair.
Inscrutable His ways are, and immune
To catechism by a mind too strewn
With petty cares to slightly understand
What awful brain compels His awful hand.
Yet do I marvel at this curious thing:
To make a poet black, and bid him sing!

He was a student at New York University when he wrote it, and *Color,* 1925, his first collection of poems, was published by Harper and Brothers in his senior year, after many individual poems had first appeared in leading American magazines. The book won him a Gold Award for literature from the Harmon Foundation as well as widespread critical approval. Cullen received a master's degree from Harvard the following year, and this coincided with a John Simon Guggenheim Fellowship for creative writing which then enabled him to spend two years in France. Meanwhile, in 1927, his *The Ballad of the Brown Girl* and *Copper Sun* were published. Returning to New York City, he became and remained a public school teacher for the rest of his life. Two books of prose and two more collections of his poems were issued before his death in 1946. A year later his own selections from all his poems (*The Black Christ,* 1929, and *The Medea and Other Poems,* 1935) were brought together posthumously in *On These I Stand.*

Frank Horne, Helene Johnson, Gwendolyn Bennett, Donald Jeffrey Hayes and Waring Cuney were among the contemporaries of Hughes and Cullen in the Harlem Renaissance whose poems continue to reappear in anthologies such as *American Negro Poetry* (Edited with an Introduction and Biographical Notes on the poets by Arna Bontemps, Hill and Wang, 1963), in schoolbooks and elsewhere. Sterling Brown's poetry began to appear in this period too, but it became better known in 1934 when his *Southern Road* was published. By then the renaissance was over in Harlem. Its poets had been scattered, and it was at once apparent that Brown's folk values, authentic and deeply felt, drew more from the rural environment surrounding the colleges in which he taught in those years than from the Harlem haunts that inspired Langston Hughes and Waring Cuney.

Since the Harlem period, Negro poets in the United States have appeared in procession rather than in groups, bands or clutches, but though thin, the line has been unbroken. Margaret Walker won the Yale University Younger Poets award in 1942 with her volume *For My People,* the title poem of which has become a favorite of Negro speakers and readers. Her "Molly Means" has been popular with verse choirs, but neither has received warmer critical approval than her "October Journey." Gwendolyn Brooks's first book was *A Street in Bronzeville,* 1945. Her *Annie Allen,* which followed in 1949, was awarded the Pulitzer Prize for Poetry, the first time this honor had been given to any Negro writer. A collection for children called *Bronzeville Boys and Girls,* 1956, was followed by a book of fiction and another book of poems *The Bean Eaters,* 1960, and these resulted in *Selected Poems* in 1963.

Meanwhile, Owen Dodson's poems were published in 1946 under the title *Powerful Long Ladder.* Despite the implication of the title, these showed clearly the influence of the New Poetry of our time on a Negro poet. The two books of Melvin B. Tolson's poetry also represent two attitudes toward his material. *Rendezvous with America,* 1944, shows the influence of Langston Hughes and Negro folklore. Tolson's *Libretto for the Republic of Liberia,* 1953, while treating a Negro theme, is an exercise in new poetics. Nevertheless, it won its author honors from the government of Liberia.

Among their successors, Robert Hayden (*A Ballad of Remembrance,* 1962), M. Carl Holman, Margaret Danner, Gloria C. Oden (*The Naked Frame,* 1952), Russell Atkins, James A. Emanuel, Samuel Allen, Conrad Kent Rivers and LeRoi Jones (*Preface to a Twenty-Volume Suicide Note* 1961) have continued to write and publish occasionally, as have a dozen or more even younger poets preoccupied with experimentation in verse as well as with a subject matter close to the heart of the Negro.

PROSE

Whatever else may be said of it, Negro writing in the United States has been from first to last, as Saunders Redding once observed, a "literature of necessity." In what sense and to what extent the same might be applied to all American writing need not detain us here. It is useful to recall, nevertheless, that the cause of the slave, his crying need for human freedom, became as intimate a part of the romantic movement as were the surge of democratic ideals in the nation as a whole and the growing assurance of the perfectibility of the individual.

Slave narratives, a most significant body of literature, offer a starting point and a key. Just as a kind of poetic tradition stemmed from the lyrics of spirituals, the work songs and playtime rhymes of slave folk, so a prose tradition influential on later Negro writers appears to have originated with the slave narrative. Two unpublished Ph. D. theses should be noted at this point: Marion Wilson Starling, *The Slave Narrative: Its Place in American Literary History,* New York University, 1946, and Charles H. Nichols, *A Study of the Slave Narrative,* Brown University, 1948. The subject has not been exhausted, however, and the emergence of Richard Wright, Ralph Ellison and James Baldwin and their attainment of stature have only served to pinpoint the relevance of this source of their power.

The first of the genre, *A Narrative of the Uncommon Sufferings and Surprising Deliverance of Briton Hammon, A Negro Man,* appeared in Boston in 1760. Another, a far more remarkable piece of writing, and still worth reading, was first published in London in 1789. Its author was Olaudah Equiano; its title, *The Interesting Narrative of the Life of Gustavus Vassa, the African.* Another edition, published in Leeds in 1814, was called *The Interesting Narrative of the Life of Olaudah Equiano, or Gustavus Vassa, The African, Written by Himself.*

Meanwhile, in the United States the slave's necessity provoked another expression. The slave-poet preacher Jupiter Hammon had published and circulated a prose writing called *An Address to the Negroes in the State of New York.* The point of view it reflected was in sharp contrast to the tenor of the slave narratives and may be read as a commentary on his own favored position as the literate slave of a Long Island master. In contrast to the "splendid folly," as Redding describes it, of the authors of the narratives who "burned themselves out in revolt," Jupiter Hammon was resigned to a life of servitude. These are his words:

> Respecting obedience to masters. Now whether it is right and lawful in the sight of God, for them to make slaves of us or not, I am certain that while we are slaves, it is our duty to obey our masters in all their lawful commands, and mind them. . . . As we depend upon our masters for what we eat and drink and wear, we cannot be happy unless we obey them.

Before he is condemned out of hand, it is necessary to remember that Hammon probably could not have gotten a stronger attack on slavery published, and he did add the following:

> Now I acknowledge that liberty is a great thing, and worth seeking for, if we can get it honestly; and by our good conduct prevail upon our masters to set us free: though for my own part I do not wish to be free, yet I should be glad if others, especially the young negroes, were to be free; for many of us who are grown up slaves, and have always had masters to take care of us, should hardly know how to take care of themselves. . . . That liberty is a great thing we may know from our own feelings, and we may likewise judge so from the conduct of the white people in the late war. How much money has been spent and how many lives have been lost to defend their liberty! I must say that I have hoped that God would open their eyes, when they were so engaged for liberty, to think of the state of the poor blacks, and to pity us.

Moreover, his "Address" does not belong to the great period of the flowering and fulfillment of the slave narrative. This coincided with the abolitionist campaign, 1830 to 1861.

Some of the Narratives were presented as autobiographies. *Scenes in the Life of Harriet Tubman,* 1869, and *Memoirs of Elleanor Eldridge,* 1838, belong in this category. Charles Ball's *Slavery in the United States,* 1836, and others like it have been regarded as fictionized truth, while still others like Emily Pierson's *The Fugitive* and Mattie Griffith's *Autobiography of a*

Female Slave are out-and-out fiction. Many were "told to" accounts, and these included *The Confession of Nat Turner*, 1831, *The Narrative of Solomon Northrup*, 1857, and *The Narrative of James Williams*, 1838, dictated to John Greenleaf Whittier. Interestingly, the Williams narrative was branded a fraud by the editor of the *Alabama Beacon*, whereupon the Antislavery Society, its publishers, suppressed it. Harriet Jacobs' *Incidents in the Life of a Slave Girl* was presented as edited and "arranged" by Lydia Maria Child.

Genuine slave narratives, however, authentic autobiographies recalling the bondage and freedom of gifted black men and mulattoes who happened to be born under the peculiar institution, are the ones that give significance to this body of writing and justify its place in American literary and cultural history. *Narrative of the Life of Frederick Douglass, an American Slave, Written by Himself*, Boston, 1845, is one of these. *Narrative of the Life of William W. Brown, a Fugitive Slave, Written by Himself*, Boston, 1848, is another. Still others include *The Fugitive Blacksmith, or Events in the History of James W. C. Pennington, Pastor of a Presbyterian Church, New York, Formerly a Slave in the State of Maryland, United States*, London, 1849, *Autobiography of a Fugitive Negro: His Anti-Slavery Labors in the United States, Canada, and England*, by Samuel Ringgold Ward, London, 1855; and *Running a Thousand Miles for Freedom: or The Escape of William and Ellen Craft from Slavery*, London, 1860.

A passage from the Douglass *Narrative* is perhaps enough to suggest the flavor and quality of this writing as well as the intellectual capacity of the runaways themselves. He wrote the book during the summer of 1844, less than five years after his escape, and the following is much of a piece with the writing as a whole:

> The heart-rending incidents, related in the foregoing chapter, led me, thus early, to inquire into the nature and history of slavery. *Why am I a slave? Why are some people slaves, and others masters? Was there ever a time when this was not so? How did the relation commence?* These were the perplexing questions which began now to claim my thoughts, and to exercise the weak powers of my mind, for I was still but a child, and knew less than children of the same age in the free states. As my questions concerning these things were only put to children a little older, and a little better informed than myself, I was not rapid in reaching a solid footing. By some means I learned from these inquiries, that *"God, up in the sky,"* made everybody; and that he made *white* people to be masters and mistresses, and *black* people to be slaves. This did not satisfy me, nor lessen my interest in the subject. I was told, too, that God was good, and that He knew what was best for me, and best for everybody. This was less satisfac-

tory than the first statement; because it came, point blank, against all my notions of goodness. It was not good to let old master cut the flesh off Esther, and make her cry so. Besides, how did people know that God made black people to be slaves? Did they go up in the sky and learn it? or, did He come down and tell them so. All was dark here. It was some relief to my hard notions of the goodness of God, that, although he made white men to be slaveholders, he did not make them to be *bad* slaveholders, and that, in due time, he would punish the bad slaveholders; that he would, when they died, send them to the bad place, where they would be "burned up." Nevertheless, I could not reconcile the relation of slavery with my crude notions of goodness.

Then, too, I found that there were puzzling exceptions to this theory of slavery on both sides, and in the middle. I knew of blacks who were *not* slaves; I knew of whites who were *not* slaveholders; and I knew of persons who were *nearly* white, who were slaves. *Color,* therefore, was a very unsatisfactory basis for slavery.

Once, however, engaged in the inquiry, I was not very long in finding out the true solution of the matter. It was not *color,* but *crime,* not *God,* but *man,* that afforded the true explanation of the existence of slavery; nor was I long in finding out another important truth, viz: what man can make, man can unmake. The appalling darkness faded away, and I was master of the subject.

A second and updated version of Douglass' *Narrative* was published ten years later under the title *My Bondage and My Freedom* and subdivided into Part I, *"Life as a Slave"* and Part II, *"Life as a Freeman."* In later years Douglass brought out a third version, again revised, updated and greatly expanded, and given a more standardized biographical title: *Life and Times of Frederick Douglass, Written by Himself,* 1882.

Special interest attaches to *The Life of Josiah Henson, Formerly a Slave Now an Inhabitant of Canada, as Narrated by Himself to Samuel Eliot,* Boston, 1849, because Henson came to be regarded as the original of Harriet Beecher Stowe's Uncle Tom. Both the American and the British editions of this narrative had satisfactory, if not spectacular, sales from the start, but a later version, 1858, with an introduction by Mrs. Stowe, and retitled *Truth Stranger than Fiction, Father Henson's Story of His Own Life,* had an advance sale of five thousand copies and did even better. The book was still going strong in 1879 when it came out again as *An Autobiography of the Rev. Josiah Henson (Mrs. Harriet Beecher Stowe's "Uncle Tom") from 1789–1879.* By then introductory notes by Wendell Phillips and John Greenleaf Whittier had been added to Mrs. Stowe's preface, and the publishers stated that 100,000 copies of the book had been sold previously.

There had been French and Dutch translations as well as the English-language editions.

As a matter of fact, good sales had become the rule for slave narratives. *Twelve Years a Slave: The Narrative of Solomon Northup*, 1853, for example, had sold 27,000 copies in its first two years. William Wells Brown's *Narrative* went through four editions in its first year. Frederick Douglass' achieved seven in this country alone, according to Ephraim Peabody, writing in the *Christian Examiner* of July, 1849. Meanwhile, earlier narratives, such as those by Gustavus Vessa and Moses Roper, continued to sell, reaching ten and eleven English-language editions respectively, not to mention translations, and the slave narrative had definitely caught on as a reading vogue. The number of them published ran into the hundreds.

Their popularity in the nineteenth century, all things considered, was not unlike the vogue of the Western story in the twentieth. The narratives evoked the setting and conditions of slavery, to be sure, but they also created a parable of the human condition, the fetters of mankind and the yearning for freedom. The perils of escape and the long journey toward the North Star did not grow stale with repetition until times changed and a new parable, or myth, the Western, replaced the earlier one.

The period in which the slave narrative flourished was, of course, the period in which the Negro spiritual reached its flowering. One was poetry, the other prose. Indeed, words from the spirituals are often quoted in the narratives. But the connection between the narratives and the subsequent literary expression they stimulated is more direct and immediate than that between the spirituals and the music they came eventually to influence.

William Wells Brown is the link. One of the three men who, in Saunders Redding's judgment, best reflected "the temper and opinion of the Negro in those years," Brown is elected as "the most representative Negro of the age." Of the other two, Charles Remond and Frederick Douglass, Remond's otherwise brilliant career as an antislavery exponent was marred by jealousy of Douglass, and Douglass seemed too exceptional to stand as "representative." All three devoted their lives to the cause of abolition, and only Remond did not leave an autobiography. All three could write effectively when the need arose, but only Brown's writing evolved into what might be called a literary career. Here his place among American Negroes is secure.

Like many Negroes before and since, indeed like many writers, Brown made maximum use of his personal history as literary material. Some of this can only lead to confusion if the truth is sought, because he gave at least three versions of his parentage and early childhood. In succcessive versions the details he gave became more exciting. Whether this reflects

burgeoning professionalism in letters or merely the shedding of early
reticence as he developed, the fact remains that contradictions exist.

First, he records that he was born of slave parents in Kentucky and grew
up as a slave child working in the fields and the house. His second account
introduces a bit of drama which reappears, interestingly, in all the
biographies of George Washington Carver. He speaks of being stolen by a
slave trader shortly after his birth. Then, in the second revised edition of his
Narrative, he really lets the chips fall. He was born, he states, here, of a
white father, scion of the family which owned his mulatto mother in Lexington, Kentucky. The father of his slave mother, "it was said, was the noted
Daniel Boon," according to this account.

The frequent references to white paternity in autobiographical narratives
like Brown's as well as in fictional stories of slaves in that period, have sometimes been branded as propaganda devices by abolitionists wishing to
stigmatize slavery by showing the demoralizing effect of the institution on
the master class. Photographic evidence, in Brown's case, as in many others,
would seem to support the disclosure at least to the extent of the mixed
parentage, and apparently no one offered to dispute it while he lived.

Brown got the name by which he became known and by which he is
remembered from the Quaker Wells Brown who first befriended him in Ohio
after his escape from slavery. Recaptured and passed from owner to owner,
he served in turn as cabin boy on riverboats, a slave trader's helper, and
eventually a printer's devil in the news office of Elijah P. Lovejoy. These
activities are not otherwise documented, but Brown's own story was that
he learned to read while working in the St. Louis print shop of the abolitionist journalist who was later mobbed and killed for supporting the cause of
freedom.

Constantly on the move as an escaped slave, he supported himself as he
could while applying most of his energies to study and made his way to
Canada. Later, he states, "I commenced lecturing as an agent of the western
New York Anti-Slavery Society, and have ever since devoted my time to the
cause of my enslaved countrymen." His antislavery work covered a period of
about fifteen years, including five between 1849 and 1854 which were spent
in England, and may have represented as many as three thousand public
speeches, judging by an estimate of the number he made abroad. Indications are that most, if not all, his speeches were extemporaneous and did not
survive the occasions on which they were delivered, but there is evidence
that writing of another kind had already become an even more serious
interest of his. William Wells Brown was the first creative prose writer of
importance produced by the Negro race in America.

In addition to three successful versions of the *Narrative of William Wells*

Brown his abolitionist years yielded also for the cause *Three Years in Europe: or, Places I Have Seen and People I Have Met,* London, 1852; *St. Domingo: Its Revolutions and Its Patriots,* Boston, 1855. But in this period he also wrote and published two novels and a play, the first pieces of fiction and the first drama by an American Negro. As such they may be read either as period pieces of literary Americana or as lineal antecedents of the works of Richard Wright and Lorraine Hansberry.

The first novel, when it appeared in London in 1853, was called *Clotelle; or, The President's Daughter.* Its heroine was a beautiful near-white girl, and there was an implication that it was based on truth, making a tie-in with gossip that was then current. This became a bit more restrained in the Boston edition published almost a decade later with a new subtitle: *A Tale of the Southern States.* According to Saunders Redding, "Brown was driven by the necessity for turning out propaganda in a cause that was too close to him for emotional objectivity and reasonable perspective. He had power without the artist's control, but in spite of this his successes are considerable and of great importance to the history of Negro creative literature. First novelist, first playwright, first historian: the list argues his place." [1]

A quotation from *Clotelle* suggests the mixture. Following a description of a Richmond slave market where a beautiful quadroon girl is offered to bidders, Brown summarizes:

> This was a Virginia slave-auction, at which the bones, sinews, blood and nerves of a young girl of eighteen were sold for $500: her moral character for $200; her superior intellect for $100; the benefits supposed to accrue from her having been sprinkled and immersed, together with a warranty of her devoted Christianity, for $300; her ability to make a good prayer, for $200; and her chastity for $700 more. This, too, in a city thronged with churches, whose tall spires look like so many signals pointing to heaven, but whose ministers preach that slavery is a God-ordained institution.

The second novel appears to have run in the New York *Anglo-African* as a serial, 1860–61. Its titles seem sufficiently descriptive: *Miralda or, The Beautiful Quadroon. A Romance of American Slavery. Founded on Fact.* Meanwhile, *The Escape: or, A Leap for Freedom, Drama in Five Acts,* was published in Boston in 1858. Brown's writings after the Civil War have been described as "more reasonable." With the campaign over and tensions relaxed, he settled down and began to produce histories and narrative essays that still do him credit, nearly a hundred years later. *The Negro in the American Rebellion,* 1868, *The Rising Son,* 1874, and *My Southern Home,* 1880, are representative.

[1] J. Saunders Redding, *To Make a Poet Black* (Chapel Hill, The University of North Carolina Press, 1939), p. 26.

Another first, possibly as significant as those he established in fiction, drama and historical writing, was also recorded by William Wells Brown. He was the first Negro in the United States to earn a living by his writing.

A novel by Martin R. Delany, a contemporary of Brown's and like him a stalwart of the antislavery campaign, was announced in the first issue of the *Anglo-African Magazine,* January, 1859, as "A Tale of the Mississippi Valley, the Southern United States and Cuba." The hero was described as "an educated West Indian black, who deprived of his liberty by fraud when young and brought to the United States, in maturer age, at the instance of of his wife being sold from him, sought revenge through the medium of a deep-laid secret organization." The title was *Blake; or, The Huts of America,* and the editorial note promised that the story would run to about eighty chapters or six hundred pages. It apparently didn't. Only seven installments followed in the *Anglo-African,* January to August, 1859, and decades were to elapse before Paul Laurence Dunbar and Charles Waddell Chesnutt broke the near-silence into which the writing of prose fiction by Negro Americans seemed to lapse.

Meanwhile, however, the tradition, or vogue, of the slave narrative did not end abruptly with the conclusion of the war of liberation. In addition to those which had established themselves as perennials and continued to be reissued (like Douglass' and Henson's), new ones continued to appear. Representative of these were *Incidents in the Life of a Slave Girl* by Harriet Jacobs, *Behind the Scenes by Elizabeth Keckley, Formerly a Slave, but More Recently Modiste and Friend to Mrs. Abraham Lincoln; or Thirty Years a Slave and Four Years in the White House,* 1868, *Scenes in the Life of Harriet Tubman, as told by Sarah Bradford,* 1869, *Harriet, the Moses of Her People,* by the same author, 1886, and finally *Up from Slavery, An Autobiography,* by Booker T. Washington, 1900.

Indeed a more perfect conclusion to the long sequence could scarcely have been imagined. *Up from Slavery* promptly established itself as a classic example of the American success story, but it was more than that. It was the last of the great slave narratives that had for more than a century disturbed the American conscience, while extending their influence by inspiring books like *Uncle Tom's Cabin* and plays like the *Octoroon.* With this genre out of its system, Negro writing was at last purged in a way that permitted a fresh start, a turn to other things. Dunbar and Chesnutt, both personal friends of Booker T. Washington, but neither sympathetic to his philosophy, were standing by—ready.

Dunbar's prose followed in the wake of his popularity as a poet. Many of his short stories and sketches make use of the same body of folk material. They appeared in the *Saturday Evening Post* and other magazines and subsequently in such collections as *Folks from Dixie*, 1898, *The Strength of Gideon*, 1900, *In Old Plantation Days*, 1903, and *The Heart of Happy Hollow*, 1904. The following sentences from the latter are a fair indication of the substance of all four:

> Wherever Negroes colonize in the cities or villages, North or South, wherever the hod-carrier, the porter, and the waiter are the society men of the town; wherever the picnic and the excursion are the chief summer diversion, and the revival the winter-time of repentance. . . . Wherever laughter and tears rub elbows by day, and the spirit of labour and laziness shake hands, there—there—is Happy Hollow.

At least one of the stories, however, stands out from the others. "The Trustfulness of Polly" is notable for at least three reasons. Dunbar handles the short story form with greater technical assurance here than elsewhere. He ventures into the lower strata of Negro life in New York for his material. In this, and in his dealing with the policy game, he anticipates by twenty-five years settings and subject matter that were later to fascinate nearly a whole generation of Negro writers in Harlem.

Three of the four novels Dunbar wrote, interestingly, differ from the stories and sketches about as the poems in standard English differ from the dialect verse. *The Uncalled*, 1898, *The Love of Landry*, 1900, and *The Fanatics*, 1901, were Negro novels only in the sense that their author was a Negro. Neither were they very good. But this does not prove what at first blush it might seem to prove. In *The Sport of the Gods*, 1902, when it would seem he was on surer ground, with Negro characters and a setting with which he was presumably more familiar, Dunbar was still not a very good novelist. At least one astute critic, Sterling Brown, has detected an improvement in the latter part of that novel over the first and suggested that had he lived longer and worked conscientiously at the art, Dunbar might eventually have mastered the fiction form.

Charles Waddell Chesnutt did work and did gain a certain mastery over his materials. While Dunbar's dialect stories were appearing in *The Saturday Evening Post* around the turn of the century, Chesnutt's were being published in the *Atlantic Monthly*. A cultivated man, practicing law in Cleveland, he attained an objectivity of vision in keeping with his technical skills, while at the same time facing up to the sociological realities. He has been called a pioneer of the color line, and in this his biographers have been supported by the critics who have studied his works.

The Wife of His Youth and Other Stories of the Color Line and *The Conjure Woman*, his two short story collections, were both published by Houghton-Mifflin in 1899. His first novel, *The House Behind the Cedars*, was published in 1900. *The Marrow of Tradition* came out the following year, all from the same publisher. His final novel, *The Colonel's Dream,* was published by Doubleday-Page in 1905.

While Chesnutt always wrote as a prose artist, mindful of aesthetic values, his novels must be regarded as problem novels, and the problems reappear in a good many of his stories. In each of these respects he was the first of his race to achieve clear-cut recognition.

Interestingly, from the point of view of his editors and readers, he was not at first recognized as a "Negro." This is mainly a commentary on the objectivity of his writing, but Chesnutt the man was similarly unrecognizable as a Negro. In this respect he was, like Jean Toomer and Walter White after him, what has sometimes been called a voluntary Negro. Only in America would he have been so classified, the actual racial mixture in his case being so preponderantly Caucasian, but if this was of any personal distress to him, he showed it only in his preoccupation with stories growing out of such relationships as this peculiar folkway can produce. Some aspect of this situation unfolds in each book of his fiction except *The Conjure Woman,* a collection of seven tales based on Negro superstition but departing sharply from the Uncle Remus and the Uncle Billy retelling of Negro folk stories. Chesnutt also wrote a short biography of Frederick Douglass.

Contemporary with Chesnutt, Dunbar and Booker T. Washington was a young Negro writer somewhat harder to classify in a purely literary context, but whose varied writings in that same period were to prove even more influential. Esteemed mainly as a brilliant scholar, William Edward Burkhardt Du Bois was the first Negro to earn a Ph.D. from Harvard, 1894. By 1897 he was contributing essays to *The Atlantic Monthly* and other American magazines that can still be read with amazement for their literary quality as well as their insights. These were collected, with others added, and published in 1903 as *The Souls of Black Folk,* a book which is still in print and which continues to hold its ground as the definitive response to *Up From Slavery* and equally as prologue (more than half a century earlier) and first projection of some of the most arresting ideas and angles of vision in the writings of such essayists and novelists as Ralph Ellison and James Baldwin.

Du Bois' writing took many turns after *The Souls of Black Folk,* much that was excellent going into *The Crisis,* a magazine he founded and edited from 1911 to 1933, and resulting in other collections of his short pieces, novels, histories, biographies and the autobiographical *Dusk of Dawn,* 1942. Due recognitions were sometimes tardy, but he lived long enough to reap and eventually enjoy them all.

Meanwhile, the first prose work of James Weldon Johnson was published anonymously in 1912, a novel titled *The Autobiography of an Ex-Coloured Man*. It did not make a great impression. In fact, it seemed to usher in a period of relative silence by Negro American writers in general. Fifteen years later, when it was rediscovered and reissued under his own name, it was as a part of the renaissance in Harlem, led by the poets Toomer, McKay, Hughes and Cullen. By then Johnson was serving the National Association for the Advancement of Colored People, but his prose writing as well as his poetry came into the picture.

By then, too, the body of prose writing by Negroes reached a point where some general observations could be allowed, though full-blown critical studies were still a generation away. What were the suitable subjects for Negro writers? Was it fitting to delve into "low" life? "Excepting now (and only quite recently) the Russian and the German, no group imposes upon its artists demands as great as does the Negro," Saunders Redding sighed with dismay. Should Negro writers use dialect? Should they concentrate on Negro characters or white? To all these questions the Harlem group formulated their own lively answers. In an article called "The Negro Artist and the Racial Mountain," published in *The Nation* in 1926, when the author of this chapter was still in his early twenties, he wrote:

> We younger Negro artists who create now intend to express our individual dark-skinned selves without fear or shame. If white people are pleased we are glad. If they are not, it doesn't matter. We know we are beautiful. And ugly too. The tom-tom cries and the tom-tom laughs. If colored people are pleased we are glad. If they are not, their displeasure doesn't matter either. We build our temples for tomorrow, strong as we know how, and we stand on top of the mountain free within ourselves.

The outburst of creative expression that occasioned this manifesto was called by Alain Locke and other participants or close observers a renaissance and a coming of age. According to Charles S. Johnson, sociologist and editor of the Urban League's influential *Opportunity: A Journal of Negro Life,* "A brief ten years have developed more confident self-expression, more widespread efforts in the direction of art than the long, dreary two centuries before" for the American Negro.

If the renaissance had done no more than rediscover and bring back into print a book like *The Autobiography of an Ex-Coloured Man* and inspired its author to project more Negro folk sermons as poetry for his book *God's Trombones*, it would have earned its name. Actually, however, a good many other positive results followed that happy awakening. Suddenly Roland Hayes was singing in Carnegie Hall, the first concert artist of his race to receive unqualified acceptance in the United States in his generation, perhaps ever. Duke Ellington began playing his indigos at the Cotton Club. Late at night and in small underground places the voices of Bessie Smith and Ethel Waters were heard. W. C. Handy arrived from Memphis, and presently the poets caught the beat.

Works of fiction took somewhat more time, and when they did appear, the first of them were greeted with almost embarrassing fanfare. In perspective the short stories by Jean Toomer collected with her early poems in *Cane,* 1923, do not seem to have been over praised. The four novels by Jessie Fauset and the two by Walter White, one suspects, belong exclusively to the period in which they were written. What such books as *There Is Confusion,* 1924, and *The Fire in the Flint,* 1924, contributed to the writing impulse among young Negroes in those years was not negligible, however. Claude McKay's *Home to Harlem,* 1928, became a bestseller. Eric Walrond's *Tropic Death,* 1926, seemed more than promising, as did Wallace Thurman's *The Blacker the Berry,* 1929. Rudolph Fisher showed talent in his short stories in the *Atlantic Monthly* and other magazines that was not quite sustained in his novel *The Walls of Jericho,* 1928. In 1930 the first novel by Langston Hughes was published. *Not Without Laughter* was followed four years later by a collection of his short stories, *The Ways of White Folks,* 1934. Both survived the period of the renaissance, as did his poetry.

The Great Depression scattered the Harlem group of writers. It was as if an earthquake had struck, and the effect was intensified when Thruman and Fisher, both under thirty, died about the same time, as if to pinpoint the ending of an era. Zora Neale Hurston, whose story telling had become a legend, returned to her native Florida and began turning out books like *Jonah's Gourd Vine,* 1934, *Men and Mules,* 1935, and *Their Eyes Were Watching God,* 1937. The author of the light-hearted novel *God Sends Sunday,* 1931, found a hiding place in Alabama and began writing, fearfully, *Black Thunder,* 1936, a tragic account of slave insurrection in another century.

Whatever else may be said of their achievements, the renaissance writers had by this time succeeded in putting an end to the novelty of the Negro as writer in the United States. Fiction by George Wylie Henderson, George W. Lee, Mercedes Gilbert, Waters Edward Turpin, William Attaway and Dorothy West, as well as subsequent work by the original Harlem group, appearing in the decade that followed, began to suffer the disadvantages of this necessary stage, as well as to profit by its advantages.

But the depression that sent the Harlem writers scurrying more than compensated for this damage by the opportunities it provided for the next wave of literary expression by Negroes. Into the Writers Projects of WPA wandered old defeated writers like the poet Fenton Johnson, to be sure, but the projects also drew the likes of Richard Wright, Ralph Ellison, Frank Yerby and Willard Motley, and began to create an environment in which the Negro writer could at last stretch himself full length. Wright ascended rapidly to major rank among American writers, without respect to race.

Here was a novelist powerful enough to break out of the narrow compartment previously occupied by Negro writers. For one thing, Wright was acutely aware of his prison, and it did not take him long to conclude, as some critics have done, that the novel as he knew it was and had been for generations a projection of the value system of the dominant class in the society. Taking advantage of the panic into which that society had been dumped by the depression, he allied himself with the critics of its basic assumptions and demanded that it hear him out. The consensus of intelligent readers was that he made sense, that he handled his themes with authority, expressed himself with power and eloquence, and was entitled to the place he had won in the literary firmament of the Depression years.

Uncle Tom's Children, the first in sequence of Wright's major works, was a collection of four short novels written while he was employed by the Illinois Writers Project. Drawn from memories of his Mississippi boyhood, the stories were almost unbearable evocations of cruel realities which the nation and the world had in the past been unable or unwilling to face. Wright's purpose, his determination as a prose writer was to force open closed eyes, to compel America to look at what it had done to the black peasantry into which he was born. In a competition offered by a publisher for the best fiction book submitted by a writer on WPA in 1938, *Uncle Tom's Children* was judged the winner. The critical reception was enthusiastic, and its author was launched.

The same critics were more than surprised, indeed they were bowled over when *Native Son* appeared two years later as a Book-of-the-Month Club selection and actually, as one of them said, "dwarfed" its powerful predecessor. From the Mississippi locale Wright had moved his setting to Chicago, and the narrative vigor which had impressed readers of the four novellas had been intensified by a deeper probing into the society that spawned the characters and produced the grim tragedy. The author had confirmed his own insights by a new acquaintance with the discipline of sociology.

That Wright's was the most impressive literary talent yet produced by Negro America was only rarely disputed in his time, and this estimate of his stature was concurred in by critics and readers abroad. Nearly fifty translations and foreign editions of his books followed in the next decade and a half as his writings became known in the major countries around the world. His name was bracketed with the small handful of America's foremost writers, and interest in him as a personality began to spread.

The latter development was aided, no doubt, by his third book, the autobiographical *Black Boy,* in 1945, which not only repeated the success of *Native Son* when it too became a Book-of-the-Month Club selection but also impressed a number of critics as being in some ways an even more remarkable accomplishment. Certainly *Black Boy* gave evidence that the range of its author, like his standing among his contemporaries, was still expanding. Relating Wright's personal history to the quests of his mind, the book showed the influence of another intellectual discovery. Where his first book had been sparked by Wright's conversion to Communism, his second by an embrace of sociology, *Black Boy* reflected Wright's encounter with the mysteries of psychoanalysis.

At this point Richard Wright moved his family to Paris and promptly became one of the most celebrated American expatriates in Europe. He did not publish another book for eight years, and when he did, *The Outsider,* his second full-length novel, 1953, showed him bringing to bear on his writing the attitudes of French existentialism of the post-World War II era. But *The Outsider* was not quite up to Wright's earlier books. Something was missing. Perhaps it was anger. His new French friends had made the suffering, alienated author feel at home. He had given them his love in return. The anguish and outrage that made his early books memorable faded in the fiction he wrote in the remaining years of his life. *The Long Dream,* 1956, was a dim echo of the Mississippi stories written while he was still bleeding. *Savage Holiday,* 1954, was a paperback potboiler. Some of the stories collected in the volume *Eight Men,* 1961, had been written years earlier and properly belong beside the novellas. *Lawd Today* was a fledgling work, apparently antedating *Uncle Tom's Children,* but salvaged posthumously in 1963 from Wright's unpublished manuscripts.

The Paris years that added nothing to Richard Wright's stature as a novelist stimulated considerable writing of another kind, however. In 1941, between *Native Son* and *Black Boy,* Wright had written a deeply-felt text for *Twelve Million Black Voices,* described as both a folk history of the Negro in the United States and "a broad picture of the processes of Negro life." *Black Power,* 1954, was also nonfiction but in another vein. Wright's account of his sojourn in West Africa was effective personal journalism. The formula was repeated in *The Color Curtain,* 1956, based on the author's attendance at the Bandung Conference of 1955 on the Island of Java, and again in *Pagan Spain,* 1957. *White Man, Listen,* 1957, brought together a series of lectures delivered in Europe under impressive auspices between

1950 and 1956, years when any statement by Richard Wright was likely to be regarded as important in France, Italy, Germany or Scandinavia. The papers show that he took his responsibilities as spokesman seriously.

Wright was singing the praises of young Ralph Ellison a number of years before the latter's *Invisible Man* was published in 1952. A painstaking worker, Ellison had evidently been chipping away at his sculptured novel for at least a decade, possibly more. No one who knew him was likely to doubt Ellison's seriousness or even, perhaps, his prospects, and Wright knew him well; the question was on his endurance. When the book finally appeared, it was hailed as a major contribution to American literature. Surprisingly, it bore little or no resemblance to the work of the man whom some had mistakingly assumed to have been its author's mentor.

Ellison's first novel was strikingly original. His aims as a story teller were as different from Richard Wright's as his methods. Where Wright had associated himself with the tradition in which Dostoievski and Dreiser wrote, Ellison had been influenced by T. S. Eliot and James Joyce. Complexity of form, layers of meaning, point and counterpoint could be seen as elements of Ellison's deliberate concern as well as possible explanation of his novel-a-decade rate of composition.

The American Booksellers gave their fiction award to *Invisible Man* in the year following its publication and seemed thereby to confirm the claims of its publishers that the book was not only a great triumph of storytelling and characterization but also a profound and uncompromising interpretation of the Negro's anomalous position in American society. The claim has not been withdrawn. Twelve years after publication the novel was still available in print in at least three different American editions, not to mention translations and other English-language editions abroad.

While Wright and Ellison made their direct assaults at winning a place in American literature with the kind of material they knew best, Yerby and Motley sought to "emancipate" themselves from what some have felt to be the limitations of Negro subjects and became the first "popular" writers among American Negroes. Together, it now seems fair to say, these four gave the Negro writer a new image, ushered in a new era.

Ann Petry, Chester Himes and Roi Ottley were among the first to profit by it. They have been followed by a young host. Such names as William Demby, Owen Dodson, Alden Bland, William Gardner Smith, Lloyd Brown and Willard Savoy appeared in publishers' lists as routinely as if novels by new Negro writers were to be expected. The emergence of Saunders Redding in this period was neither routine nor expected, but his essays and literary criticism link him uniquely with the writers of this period and their mood. No one has understood them better.

Redding's essays, however, despite their brilliance, did not strike fire when they first appeared in the way that James Baldwin's did a decade or more later. In between, the Negro rebellion—or revolution, if that is preferred—occurred in the United States, and young Negro writers were among the first beneficiaries, Baldwin most prominently.

After writing a good but unspectacular novel in *Go Tell It on the Mountain*, 1953, Baldwin began to produce personal essays so arresting as to convince some readers that he might succeed in reviving interest in what they had begun to think of as an old and possibly out-dated literary form. The first collection of his essays, as if to establish a link with Richard Wright, was published as *Notes of a Native Son*, 1955. The essays were provocative, and the title did no harm, but the reception was modest and remained within bounds. Another volume, subtitled *More Notes of a Native Son*, was published in 1961 as *Nobody Knows My Name*. This was followed in 1963 by *The Fire Next Time*, consisting of two pieces previously published in magazines: "Letter to My Nephew on the One Hundredth Anniversery of the Emancipation" (*The Progressive*) and "Letter from a Region in My Mind" (*The New Yorker*). The latter two volumes became national best-sellers, thanks in part, no doubt, to a favorable conjunction with the surge of the Negro protest movement in the United States. Astonishingly articulate on platform as well as printed page, calling on old skills in public address acquired as a boy preacher in storefront churches between the ages of fourteen and seventeen, Baldwin did not hesitate to speak out amid the storm. To nearly everyone's surprise, he was given rapt attention.

Meanwhile, his novels, treating subjects which previously might have been considered taboo, and certainly not in the mainstream of the Negro revolt, leaped to vast popularity. *Giovianni's Room* came out in 1956, *Another Country* in 1962. Baldwin's first published play was *Blues for Mister Charlie*, 1964.

Momentarily eclipsed by the Baldwin phenomenon, perhaps, the clutch of younger fiction writers which included Alston Anderson, Frank London Brown, William Melvin Kelley, John Oliver Killens, Paule Marshall, Julian Mayfield, Herbert Simmons and John A. Williams nevertheless look good by almost any comparison. More significantly, they arrive at a moment when middle-class culture is providing less and less of the subject matter for the serious novel of the contemporary scene. Whether or not this development will work to their advantage remains to be seen, but chances are they will have some responsibility for determining the outcome.

Index

An index is intended to help the reader find out if the book he has in hand has material about the subject in which he is interested. It should also help him to locate again something he remembers that he has already read in the book. The first purpose is the one that is usually most important in the indexes to reference books, because such books are not usually read through but are consulted for specific points instead. This book is intended for consecutive reading as well as for reference use, so that the index is doubly important in locating brief information quickly.

An index should offer as many ways of finding information in the text as possible. On the other hand, it should not be too bulky to use. Under each subject, it should give the reader some indication of the aspects of the subject which are treated in various places in the book, rather than an undifferentiated string of page references.

The indexers have made every effort to make the index to this book easy to use. It does, however, deal with a very broad and complex subject with as much compression as possible. The reader who plans to use the book intensively will save time and effort if he makes a brief study of the nature and peculiarities of the index. He will probably also find many references to topics of interest to him which he might otherwise have overlooked.

This index is a very full one. Even so, it has not been possible to give references to all persons, things, and concepts referred to in the text, since this would have made the index too large to be useful to the reader.

In most cases, the reader will find his subject without any difficulty. It is advisable to look first for the exact subject wanted. In seeking information on Dr. Charles Drew, for example, check first under "Drew, Dr. Charles" rather than looking under "Scientists" or "Physicians."

For almost every subject, a phrase or identifying note has been added to help pinpoint the exact information. While the general arrangement of the index is strictly alphabetical, word-by-word, first by the subject itself and then by the identifying phrase, some complex subjects are not in strict alphabetical order beyond the name of the subject itself. The entries under "Civil rights," "Education," and "Segregation" are examples of this. General references are usually given first, followed by chronological divisions, and then by other divisions, arranged in accordance with the nature of the subject. They are usually alphabetical by the most important term or aspect in the identifying phrase. The listings are arranged on the page so they can be easily scanned, and it is useful to scan all of the identifying phrases under the major subject.

Since the book is arranged by very broad topics, there are comparatively few very broad, inclusive page references in the index. These references are indicated by all the page references which appear after every modifier or identifying phrase for the appropriate subject. Tables as such are not usually covered by an index. The page references for the subject as discussed in the adjoining text will lead the reader to them.

The index has several special features, including a list of honors and awards won by Negroes, and lists of All-America team references, etc.

All abbreviations, whether they are usually written with periods ("A.M.E. Church") or without (CORE), are filed at the beginning of the letter section for the letter they begin with (CORE comes at the beginning of the C's). Entries proper, however, are usually under the full name rather than the abbreviation. United States government entries usually appear under "United States" ("United States Air Force," rather than "Air Force"). "Nonwhite" is sometimes filed as "Negro" in identifying phrases where the meaning of both terms is approximately the same.

This index was compiled in accordance with the standard for indexes issued by the American Standards Association. The chief indexer was Mrs. Jessica L. Harris, and the index was edited by Dr. Theodore C. Hines.

The compilers are most grateful to Mr. Davis for his generous assistance; their errors are their own, however.

Theodore C. Hines
Harold L. Roth
ROTHINES ASSOCIATES
74 South Munn Avenue
East Orange, New Jersey

A

AAU, see Amateur Athletics Union

ADC: see Aid for Dependent Children; Aid to Families with Dependent Children

AFDC, see Aid to Families with Dependent Children

AGCT, early 1940's, Negro scores, compared with white, 629-30

A.M.E. Review, periodical, 55

AME Church, see African Methodist Episcopal Church

AMEZ Church, see African Methodist Episcopal Zion Church

AMSAC, see American Society for African Culture

Aaron, Hank, National League Baseball records, 800

Abernathy, Ralph: arrested in Albany, Ga., 474; and Birmingham demonstrations, 1963, 475

Abolition: early favored by evangelical Christian groups, 398-99; Friends' work toward, colonial period, 362; resisted in Constitutional Convention, 1787, 22; resisted after Revolution, 22; William Wells Brown's work for, 868-69

Abolition bill in Massachusetts legislature, 1777, 22

Abolition movement, free Negro support, 35

Abolitionist societies organized, 18th century, 21

Aborigines Rights Protection Society, greets emigrants, 674

Abstractionism in Negro art, 773

Abyssinia, Williams and Walker musical, 831

Academy Award, Best Actor of the Year, to Sidney Poitier, 849

An Account of the Slave Trade on the Coast of Africa, 1788, on exercising of slaves by dancing, 826

Acreage allotments: effect on Negro farmers, 165, 167, 177-78; effect on tenant farmers, 175; cotton, 198; cotton, effect on Negro farmers, 167; tobacco, 198

Actors and actresses, Negro, 829-37, 841-49

Actor's Equity, Frederick O'Neil as president, 848

Adams, Abigail, on slavery, 1774, 19

Adams, John Quincy, defends *Amistad* slaves, 461

Addison, Adele, singer, 839

"An Address to the Negroes in the State of New York," by Jupiter Hammon, 864

Adjei, E. Ako, founder of *The African Interpreter,* 690

Africa: American Negro opportunity in, 695-96; American Negroes in, 664-73, 698; American Negroes in U.S. government positions in, 701-04; Negro missionary work in, 1787-1929, 667-73; poor image in America, 19th century, 663

"Africa for Africans": African Negro race consciousness increased by, 675-76; Universal Negro Improvement Association slogan, 675

"Africa Interest" of American Negroes, 666-67

Africa as national concern of U.S., 694-95

Africa Report, periodical, 694

Africa Today, periodical, 693

"African": as term for American Negroes, to 1800, 662; as term to describe American Negroes, before 1861, 700-01; as

find more opportunity in corporations, 333; gains in non-Negro market, 331; higher incomes in Negro market, 295-96; higher risks as factor reducing mortgage acquisition by Negro life insurance companies, 291, 321; non-white, incomes compared with non-white professionals, 1959, 296; as managers, small proportion, 1960, 322; marginal, 252; in personal services, 293; "Plans for Progress" improves opportunity, 323; promising fields for, 322; in retail trade, 293; nonwhite, run greater risk than general population, 296; strengthened in some fields, 1950-1960, 295

Butler, Benjamin F.: on equal pay for Negro Civil War soldiers, 607; frees slaves, 37-38; musters first Negro combat troops of Civil War, 1862, 602; sends Negro troops to most difficult sector of line at Newmarket Heights, to prove reliability, 612

Butler, Sol, athlete, Olympic Team member, 812-13

C

CIO, see Congress of Industrial Organizations

CME Church: see Christian Methodist Episcopal Church; Colored Methodist Episcopal Church

CORE, see Congress of Racial Equality

Cable, George Washington, opposed to segregation, 48

Cable, Theodore, athlete, 812

Caesar (slave), in Revolutionary navy, 595

Cakewalk, as Negro dance, 831

Caleb, The Degenerate, play by Joseph S. Cotter, Sr., 834

Calhoun, John C., allegations on Negro inferiority answered by James McCune Smith, 552

California Negro Convention, 1st, 1855, 463

California, University of, scholarship program for minority students, 389

Call Committee, of American Negro Leadership Conference on Africa, 700

Callaway, Marse, as Baltimore Republican Party boss, 429

Callender's Consolidated Spectacular Colored Minstrels, 830

Calloway, Cab, early career, 837

Calumet Wheelman (sports club), 797

Cambridge, Godfrey, comedian, 838

Cambridge, Md., demonstrations, 1963, 475

Campanella, Roy, baseball player; National League Most Valuable Player, 1951, 1953, 1955, 800

Campbell, Milton, Olympic champion, 1956, 821

Campbell, T. M., sponsored by Tuskegee Institute as first Negro demonstration specialist, 1906, 163

Camping, Negro, restricted by discrimination, 811

Canaan Academy, N.H., destroyed for admitting Negroes, 1831, 552

Cane, by Jean Toomer, 67, 860, 874

Caney, El (Battle), Negroes in, 615

Cantata, by Ulysses Kay, 754

Capon Springs Conference, 56

Caravans, gospel singing group, 839

Cardozo, Francis L.: educated at University of Glasgow and in London, 43, 422; as Principal of M Street High School, 1884-1896, 561; South Carolina Secretary of State, 1868-1872, 43, 422; South Carolina State Treasurer, 1872-1876, 43, 422

Cardozo, T. W., as Mississippi superintendent of education, 422

Carey, Archbishop J., as chairman of President's Committee on Government Employment Policy, 430

Carey, Lott: as emigrant, 1815, 675; missionary convention named for, 675

Carnegie Hall Concert of Negro Music, 1912, 738-39

Carolina slave laws, 1686-1722, 12

Carolinas, slavery in, 11-12

Carpenter, Thelma, in The Seven Lively Arts, 842

Carroll, Diahann: actress, 85; in No Strings, 841

Carroll, George D., elected mayor of Richmond, Calif., 1965, 425

"Carry Me Back to Old Virginny," composed by James Bland, 755, 830

early favored abolition, 398-99; efforts at slave conversion, 398-400; emotionalism as determinant of nature of Negro worship, 400; retreat from anti-slavery position, 399

Churches, Negro: as aid in group cohesion, 54; cooperation with white churches, 410; during Reconstruction, predominantly all-Negro, 402; civil rights work, 409; educational efforts, 409; interchurch cooperation, 410; members as officials of interracial church groups, 410; as members of National Council of the Churches of Christ, 410; as only Southern institution able to work for civil rights, 409; size, 1950, 72-73; spirituals as greatest contributions, 412; urban, 54

Churches: reintegration beginning, 73; slave, types, 401

—store-front: 407-08; as due to disinterest of established churches, 407-08; as due to interest in religion, 407-08; as providing group identification, 408; result of urbanization, 407; service to inner city, 407; usually sect-type, 407

—white: and Negro education, after 1863, 408; Negro membership, 406-07; Negroes in mixed congregations, 406-07; Negroes as officials, 406; Negroes in separate congregations, 406-07

Churchill, Sir Winston, quotes Claude McKay's "If We Must Die," 859

Cigarmakers' International Union, acceptance of Negroes by, 61

Cinque, leads revolt aboard slave ship Amistad, 460-61, 826

Cities, percentage of population Negro, 468

Cities with highest Negro population, 1960, 120

Citizens' League for Fair Play, organized by Rev. John H. Johnson, 1933, 68-69

Citizenship rights, Negro: as affected by Dred Scott decision, 1857, 485; guaranteed by 14th Amendment, 486

City councils: Negro members, 1920-1965, 425; Southern, Negro members, since 1945, 425

Civic clubs, Negro, work with Negro problems, 62

Civil rights:

—factors in improvement after World War II: African nations, 83; international opinion, 82-83

—government involvement after World War II, 85-86; legislation guaranteeing, 1866-1875, 487; lost after Reconstruction, 46; as Presidential campaign issue, 1964, 94; Presidential aid to, 452; and U.S. government, 479-81

Civil Rights Act:

—1866: 41-42; prohibits enforcement of restrictive covenants, 502; sections repealed, 1894, 58

—1870, guarantees right to be a witness in court, 518

—1875: 46; found unconstitutional, 1883, 46-47, 506; parts found unconstitutional, 487; guarantees right to jury service, 518; ignored, 423; not enforced, 1875-1883, 46; provisions, 423, 506

—1957: 86-87, 423, 480; effect on Southern Negro voter registration, to 1963, 434; strengthens voting rights, 490-91

—1960: 87, 423, 480; effect on Southern Negro voter registration, to 1963, 434; strengthens voting rights, 490-91

—1964: 93, 94, 423, 481; declared constitutional, 94, 496; effects desegregation, 94; as greatest achievement of sit-ins, 497; inability to change central city congestion quickly, 795-96; permits remedying discrimination in U.S. Department of Agriculture programs, 201-02; provides remedies for discrimination in employment, 513; provisions, 487-88, 496, 498; Robert S. McNamara on, 659-60; Southern senators call for obedience, 93; strengthens voting rights, 490-91

—1965, 423

Civil Rights Acts: 1866-1875, 487-88

—1957-1964, enacted under Presidents of both parties, 452

Civil rights cases, to Negro lawyers, 585-86

Civil Rights, Commission on, see Commission on Civil Rights

Civil rights: groups, changing with times, 459; laws, state, revival and strengthening, 1945-1964, 85-86; leaders enter-

35; first American Negro, 550; first Negro woman, 534-35
—Negro: families headed by, less likely to be female-headed, 542; increase in number, 1917-1940, 370; number, 1900, 676-77; number increasing faster than population, 341; female, 1900-1910, 535; female outnumber male, 535; male, 1900-1910, 535
College of New Jersey, early Negro students, 550
College students, Negro, female outnumber male, 535
College teachers, Negro, as percentage of all college teachers, 579
Colleges, Negro, established by churches, 1865-1870, 367
Colleges:
—land-grant, Negro: provided by 2nd Morrill Act, 1890, 368; improved financial support, 1917-1940, 370
—Negro: number, 1910, 535; Southern, growth, late 19th-early 20th centuries, 535
Colleges and universities, Negro: accredited, number, 1950, 384; advanced degrees awarded, 1920-1950, 382; church-related, 409; church-related, number of students, 409; emphasis on teacher education, 370; enrollment, 1900-1950, 382; faculty quality problems, 387; financial support problems, 387; football at, 805-06; former students receiving doctorates, 564-65; inadequate student preparation problems, 387; as main source of Negro college graduates, 381-82; number, 1900-1964, 382; number, 1950, 384; organized by white churches, after 1863, 408; prejudice problems, 387-88; problems, 386-88; providing undergraduate education for physicians, 575; reluctance to use Negro teachers, 553; reverse integration, 386; role in American education, 382; sororities, 543-44
Colleges and universities:
—non-Negro, opposition to employment of Negro teachers, 554
—Northern, attempts to attract Negro students, 388-89
—Southern: desegregated since 1954, 385-86; desegregated, 1964, 377

—white, Negroes on faculties, 1776-1861, 365
Collins, Leroy, as director of Community Relations Service, 93-94
The Colonel's Dream, by Charles Waddell Chestnutt, 872
Colonization: desire persistent among Negro masses, 675; Lincoln's attitude toward, 38; never undertaken on large scale, 105
Colonization movement: as means of disposing of freedmen, 669; rationale described, 669; as stimulator of missions, 669
Colonization societies, early 19th century, 662
Color, by Countée Cullen: 67; receives Harmon Foundation Gold Award, 861-62
Color and Democracy, by W.E.B. Du-Bois, 690
The Color Curtain, by Richard Wright, 876
"Colored," as term for American Negroes, 662
"Colored Archer," jockey (Isaac Murphy), 791-92, 794
Colored Men's Conventions, 1830-1953, 662
Colored Merchants Association, organized by National Negro Business League, 1929, 68
Colored Methodist Episcopal Church: 54, 405-06; name changed to Christian Methodist Episcopal Church, 1956, 405; separated from Methodist Episcopal Church, South, 1870, 405
Colored Women's League of Washington, founded, 542
Coltrane, John, jazz musician, 764
Comedians, Negro, 837-38
Commission on Civil Rights, see U.S. Commission on Civil Rights
Committee on Equality of Educational Opportunity, American Council on Education, 388
Committee on Government Contract Compliance, established 1951, 480
Committee for Improving Industrial Conditions of Negroes in New York City, organized 1905, 62, 469

Davis, Ossie: as actor, 85; as comedian, 838; *Purlie Victorious,* produced on Broadway, 1961, 835

Davis, Sammy, Jr., in *Mr. Wonderful* and *Golden Boy,* 841

Davis, Tommy, National League batting champion, 1962, 1963, 800

Davis Sisters, gospel singers, 839

Davis vs. County School Board, Prince Edward County, Va., school segregation case, 1954, 373

Davis vs. Schnell, 1949, 493

Dawn, Marpessa, actress, 847

"Dawn," by Paul Laurence Dunbar, 857

Dawson, William L.: as chairman of Government Operations Committee, U.S. House of Representatives, 424, 445; as Chicago alderman, 425; elected from predominantly Negro district, 444; political style, 448; political power, 445; as U.S. Congressman, 1942-, 84, 424, 443; as vice president of Democratic Party National Committee, 424

Dawson, William Levi: as composer, choir director, 749; as member of "Afro-American Five," 748; *Negro Symphony,* presented by Philadelphia Orchestra, 749

Day, Thomas, woodworker, 766

"The Deacon" (Tiger Flowers), 779, 787

Dean, Dora: actress, 831; song about (*Dora Dean*), 831

Death rates, see also Mortality rate

Death rates, Negro: 155-58; from infectious diseases as correlated with economic status, 157-58; related to economic status, 155, 157

DeBerry, Dr. W.N., 54

Declaration of Independence, preliminary draft, anti-slavery passage rejected by Southern delegation, 19

Declaration of Principles, Niagara Falls, Canada, Conference, 1905, 59

Dee, Ruby, actress, 85

Deep River, play by Laurence Stallings, 833

Deep River Boys, careers hurt by television, 837

Defeatism in drama about Negroes: 847-48; Arna Bontemps on, 848

Defendants, Negro, cases establish judicial principles, 519

DeGrasse, John V., as physician, 572

DeLaney, Beauford: Henry Miller on, 768-69; painter, 768-69

Delany, Martin R.: 39, 550, 552-53; as Civil War army surgeon, 609; graduates from Harvard University Medical School, 1852, 552; as justice of the peace, Charleston, S.C., 553; leads expedition to Nigeria, 552-53; as first Negro major in U.S. Army, 553; as member of international learned societies, 552; as physician, 550, 552, 572; *Blake; or, The Huts of America,* 870

de las Casas, Bartolomé, see Casas, Bartolomé de las

Delaware: extent of desegregation in schools, 1963, 378; slavery in, 14-15

Delta Sigma Theta, Negro sorority, formed, 1913, 543

Demby, William, author, 877

Democratic County Committee, New York County, J. Raymond Jones elected chairman, 1965, 425

Democratic Party: members added by voter registration drives, 451; Negro loyalty to, 1932-1964, strongest in lower class, 439; Negro preference for, 1936-1964, 438

—Negro shift to: 1932-1936, 438-39; 1936, fastest among middle class, 439

—Negroes attracted by New Deal, 429-30; Negroes first attracted by Alfred E. Smith, 429; Negroes given credit for carrying elections for, in urban areas, 430; rewards Negro support with important offices, 430; Southern Negro commitment less than Northern, 441; support by Negroes after 1928, 429-30

Dempsey, Jack, failure to fight Harry Wills, 786-87

Dennis, E. S., on bravery of Negro Civil War soldiers, 606

Dentists, Negro: see also Physicians, Negro; high proportion from "white collar" families, 581

Department of Agriculture, see U.S. Department of Agriculture

Dependent Children and Their Families, by U.S. Bureau of Family Services, report on families receiving ADC, 347-48

Depression: agricultural, as cause of migration north and west, 111; effect on

Dillard, William, in *My Darlin' Aida,* 842

Direct action in civil rights movement, 470-76

Discrimination: early 20th century, 59; as attempt to hold privilege, 724; as cause of apathy, 349; as cause of low Negro occupational status, 241, 243-44; as cause of migration north and west, 111; caused by assumed Negro inferiority, 47; economic costs, 271-74, 330; economic cost, 1946-63, 274; economic cost, 1949-1963, 271-74; economic gain from elimination, 282-83; economic, industrial, 61; economic opportunity limited by, 251; effect on learning ability, 341; effect on Negro consumption patterns, 275, 277; effect on nonwhite incomes, 259; elimination as producing attitude change, 707; influenced by economic factors, 727

—laws against: behavioral changes produced by enforcement of, 721; as reducing prejudice, 713

—may be eliminated without reducing prejudice, 726; may be positive or negative, 725; not coincident with prejudice, 719; as nationwide phenomenon, 475, 459; decrease in, as cause of improved Negro employment opportunity, 248; not fully explained by prejudice, 725; not present in all differentiated behavior, 726; not reduced by persuasion, 720-21; often not due to prejudice, 724; as producing race consciousness, 757; protects Negro insurance companies, 297; protects Negro life insurance companies, 309; Negro protest against, World War II, 77; protested by Thomas J. Bowers, 751; as reason for white-nonwhite income differential, 261; as reinforcement of prejudice, 707; reduced by laws, 720-21; restricts Negro access to goods and services, 251; self-esteem reduced by, 349; as shield for Negro life insurance companies, 332; sometimes stronger in speech than in action, 729; vested interests in, 728; and Negro colleges' problems in holding faculty, 387; defined, 725; distinguished from prejudice, 707, 725

—in Armed Forces, off-base: 656-60; official refusal to end, 656-58; prohibited, 1963, 658-60; World War I, 618

—in Armed Forces: World War I, 63; World War II, 77

—in baseball, 797-800; in basketball, 806-07; in camping facilities, 811; in civil liberties, 726; in civil protection, 726; in college football, 806; in courts as cause of family disorganization, 72; in courts, NAACP work against, 61

—in Department of Agriculture programs: 201-02; Commission on Civil Rights report on, 202

—in diversified agriculture, 168; in education, 725

—in employment: 61, 243-44, 725-26; prohibited, 1964, 488; prohibited by state laws, 1965, 511-12; Southern laws requiring, found unconstitutional, 511; in defense industries, FEPC established to end, 479; in Federal civil service, prohibited, 1949, 510; in state civil services, prohibited in some states, 510-11; as cause of family disorganization, 72; Federal measures against, 247; New York State law against, 1945, 720; as preventing Negroes from qualifying for business positions, 323-24

—in housing, 726; in jockey licensing, 793; in jury service, as grounds for reversal of Negro convictions, 518-19

—by labor unions: 61, 71, 468, 514-15; prohibited, 1964, 488

—in admission to medical schools: 19th century, 572; 1915-1947, 575; decreasing, 573

—against Negro officers in World War I, 618-20; in pay, Union Army, 40; in admission of physicians to hospital staffs and specialties, 579; in political rights, 726; in prizefighting, 1915-1935, 786-87; stopped by Joe Louis, 788-89; in public accommodation, 726; in public facilities, prohibition found unconstitutional, 1883, 488; in admission to public places, George Dixon's insistence on Negro admission to his New Orleans fight, 1892, 781; in public services, 726; in recreational facilities use, as factor in Negro failure to excel in some sports, 809; in rural areas easier, 199; against Negro soldiers in World War II, 77; in real estate sales, Southern rural, 196; in

U.S. Minister to Haiti, 427; biography by Charles Waddell Chestnutt, 872; William Branch's play, *In Splendid Error*, on, 835

Drake, Alfred, in *Beggar's Holiday*, 841

Drake, St. Clair, receives Ford Foundation Area Fellowship grant, 895

Drama: Negro, begun, 1821, 831-32; Negro difficulty in success in, 831-32; Negroes in, 832-34; about Negro life, most successful written by whites, 833

—about Negroes: defeat as theme of, 847-48; defeatism in, Arna Bontemps on, 848

Dramatists, see Playwrights

Dred Scott vs. Sandford, 1857, 484-86

Drew, Dr. Charles, and blood bank, 77

Drew, Howard P., as athlete, Olympic team member, 813

Driskell, David, painter, 772

Dropouts, school, see School dropouts

DuBois, W.E.B.: "Address to the Nations of the World," 681; African interest of, 679-85; at Atlanta University, 554; as *Atlantic Monthly* contributor, 872; as author, 67, 556-57, 690, 872; on cowardice charges against 92nd Division, World War I, 623-24; as founder, editor and contributor to *The Crisis*, 872; educated at Great Barrington High School, Mass., 560; becomes Ghanian citizen, 1962, 690; calls conference at Niagara Falls, Canada, 1905, 59; calls Pan-African Congress at Versailles Peace Conference, 685; "Close Ranks," July, 1918, 64; on color line, 56; conducts Atlanta University Conferences on the Negro Problem, 56; convenes 3rd and 4th Pan-African Congresses, 686; criticism of Booker T. Washington, 52; dies, 1963, 92, 690; as Envoy Extraordinary and Minister Plenipotentiary to Liberia, 686; as founder of Niagara Movement, 682; founds *Phylon*, 1940, 688; on Garvey Movement, 685-86; goes to Ghana to direct *Encyclopedia Africana*, 698; as Honorary Chairman of 5th Pan-African Congress, 1945, 691; influence on African nationalism, 678; interest in Africa, 677; in National Association for the Advancement of Colored People, 60; leaves NAACP, mid-1930's, 688; with

NAACP as adviser on African affairs, 1944, 690; leaves NAACP post, 690; organizes Niagara Movement, 1905, 464-65; at Pan Africa Conference, London, 1900, 680-81; receives Ph.D. from Harvard, 1896, 563; respected by Africans, 688; at 2nd Pan-African Congress, 1923, 685-86; as secretary of Pan-Africa Conference, London, 1900, 681; *The Souls of Black Folk*, criticizes Booker T. Washington, 464; *The Suppression of the African Slave Trade*, 26, 55; at Universal Races Congress, London, 1911, 683; opposes Booker T. Washington, 464

DuBois, William Edward Burghardt, see DuBois, W.E.B.

Dudley, Arthur, in combat, 651

Dudley, Edward, as Ambassador to Liberia, 1949-1953, 664

Dumas, Charles, athlete, 819

Dumas, Major F. E., 39

Dunbar, Paul Laurence: anticipates Harlem Renaissance, 871; as author and composer, 831; as lyricist for *Clorindy —The Origin of the Cake Walk*, 747; as poet, 55, 856-57; poetry praised by William Dean Howells, 55; as prose writer, 870-71; as *Saturday Evening Post* contributor, 870; use of dialect in poetry, 855

Dunbar High School, see M Street High School, Washington, D.C.

Duncan, John B., on District of Columbia Board of Commissioners, 84

Duncan, Todd, in *Lost in the Stars*, 842

Duncanson, Robert S.: painter, 767; invited by Tennyson to Isle of Wight, 767

Duncanson, William S., portrait of Daniel Payne's family, 771

Dunham, Katherine: as choreographer, 848; as entertainer, 840

Dunn, Oscar: as lieutenant governor of Louisiana, 582; sponsors Straight University law school's charter, 582

Dupree, James, athlete, 821

Dusk of Dawn, by W. E. B. DuBois, 872

Dutchman, play by LeRoi Jones: 838; defeatism in, 847

Dvořák, Anton, use of Negro themes, 749-50

South, illegal, 363; in white schools, 363; and slavery incompatible, 360
—Southern, unequal: Booker T. Washington's views used to support, 368; philanthropy used as support, 368
—urban: projects to help culturally deprived areas, 395; saturation programs described, 395
Educational: achievement, Negro, as affected by cultural deprivation, 393-95; expenditures, per capita, Southern, 1939-1940, Negro compared with white, 630; institutions, limited access by Negroes, 548; institutions, Negro, founded to provide African missionaries, 669;
—level: higher, as reducing stereotyping, 713; Negro: 1940-1962, 340-42; as cause of poor employment opportunity, 248; of Negro farmers, 188-89; of Negro farmers, a handicap, 189; as cause of low occupational status, 241; projected, 1985, 159
Edwards, James, in *Home of the Brave*, 847
Eight Men, by Richard Wright, 876
Eisenhower, Dwight D.: aids civil rights, 480; appoints Negroes, 84, 430, 446; refusal to give public support to Supreme Court school desegregation decision, 480; and troop integration, World War II, 646
Elaine, Ark., race riot, 61
El Caney (Battle), Negro participation, 615
Eldridge, Elleanor, *Memoirs of Elleanor Eldridge*, 864
Election, presidential, see Presidential election
Electoral college, favors cities, 432-33
Electrification, Negro: farm, 185; rural, 1940-1960, 198
Elective offices, important, none held by Negroes before Civil War, 418
Elijah Muhammad: leader of Black Muslims, 477-78; anticipated by Gabriel Prosser, 461; as race hero, 479
Eliot, John, teaches Negroes, 1674, 361
Ellerbe, Mozelle, athlete, 813
Ellington, Duke: as jazz band leader, 762, 840; as musician, 765, 874; early career, 837; *Beggar's Holiday*, 841; with Mahalia Jackson, 743

Ellis, Evelyn: actress, 832; in *Porgy and Bess*, 833
Ellison, Ralph: author, 863, 877; as American Booksellers Association fiction award winner, 1953, 877; in WPA Writers Project, 875; influenced by Richard Wright, 877
Emancipation: 37-39; Congressional action on, 38; as contributor to change of form in Negro music, 759-60; Lincoln's early attitude toward, 37; Union generals' attitude toward, 37-38; as war measure, 605
Emancipation Proclamation: issued January 1, 1863, 39; made ineffective by custom, 462-63; preliminary drafts, 38-39; provisional, 1862, 603; reaction to, 39
Emanuel, James A., as poet, 863
Emigration: see Migration, for movement within the United States
—movements: see also Colonization; Universal Negro Improvement Association; as arising from persistent idea, 674; favored by B.W. Arnett, 675; influenced by "Providential design" theory, 674; Martin R. Delany in, 552; rejected by Negro leadership, 675
Emmett, Dan, leader of *The Virginia Minstrels*, 829
The Emperor Jones, Charles Gilpin in title role, 833
Employment: see also Unemployment; of minority groups, 205-06
—Negro: 205-50, 342-44; compared with white: 234, 239; shorter job tenure, 239-40; shorter job tenure, related to migration, 241; and educational level, compared with white, 343; nonwhite, effect of business cycles on, 257-58;
—female: 213-14, 525-26; compared with white female: higher proportion, 526; higher proportion of married females, 526; higher unemployment rate, 526; more part-time, 526; as farm laborers, 526; professional, 1950-1960, 530; primarily unskilled, 525-26
—more often part-time than white, 343; primarily less skilled, 209-12; professional, 567-71; underemployment higher than white, 343; more wage earners per family than white, 343; in

surance to builders who discriminate in selling houses, 502

Executive Order 11114, 513

Exoduster movement, Kansas: 172, 174; decline, 174

Expenditure patterns, Negro, urban, 1960-1961, 352

Experience or How to Give a Northern Man a Backbone, play by William Wells Brown, 834

Explorers: French, accompanied by Negroes, 2
—Negro: 1-3; 15-16th centuries, 1-2
—Spanish, accompanied by Negroes, 2

Expressionism in Negro painting, 774

F

Farm workers, hired, Negro: 193; compared with tenant system, 194; concentrated in hand and stoop labor, 195; probable continuance of, 202-03; economic importance of, 194-95; households headed by women, 195; low incomes of, 195; number increasing, 193; proportion Negro and white, 1950-1960, 194; low status of, 193; tenants being replaced by, 194

Farmer, James: as Director of CORE, 92; as national director of CORE, 473; message to March on Washington, 92; as speaker in March on Washington, 1963, 476

Farmers, see also Agriculture

FEPC, see Fair Employment Practices Commission

FHA, discriminatory policies, to 1962, 502

Fahy Committee, report, 1950, 654-55

Fair Employment Practices Committee, 78-79

Fair Employment Practices Commission: established, 1941, 479; killed, 1945, by Congress, 479

Fair employment practices laws, state: 1945-1964, 86; 1965, 511-12; as creating climate for acceptance of non-discrimination, 512; inadequate, 247-48; seldom vigorously enforced, 512; and municipal, passed after expiration of FEPC, 1945, 479-80

Fair housing laws, state and local: 1965, 503; ineffective, 503

Families: broken, effect on children, 523-24
—Negro: headed by women: see also Matriarchy, Negro; Women, Negro, as heads of families; 1960, 537; causes, 540; effect on children, 538, 540-41, 542; smaller percentage among college-educated, 542
—impoverished, high proportion headed by women, 540; often broken, 536-37

Family: disorganization, Negro, contributing factors, 72
—Negro: approaching general American patterns, 337; characteristics compared with white, 1950-1960, 339-40; differences from white decreasing, 354; under slavery, 337; urban: 337-359; often broken, 349; effect of broken home, 349-50; father image lacking, 349-50; developing middle-class orientation, 352; and migration, 350; effects of overcrowding, 349; parent dominance, 350; problems, 351-52; and technological change, 353; urbanization, 337

The Fanatics, novel by Paul Laurence Dunbar, 871

Fanon, Franz, killed in Algerian Liberation movement, 679

Farad, Wali, see Wali Farad

Farm owners: Negro: age characteristics of, compared with white, 187-88; effect of boll weevil on, 164; effect of cotton-growing changes on, 167; effect of diversification on, 169; housing superior to tenants, 192-93; number declining, 1945-1959, 175; greater than white in certain localities, 175-76; New Deal encouragement of, 164-65; as "part owners," 175; productivity of, compared with tenants, 184-85
—as part owners, increasing, 196; small, effect of cotton picker on, 166

Farm ownership, Negro, decline, 1910-1960, 196

Farm Security Administration, refuses to permit discrimination, 70

Farmers: see also Farms; Tenant farmers; free Negro, outside South, 172
—Negro: 161-204; age characteristics of: compared with white, 187-88; effect on productivity, 188; areas where concentrated, 171-72; concentrated in former

462; colonial Georgia, 13; New England, 17; return provided in Constitution, 23

Fulbright scholarship, awarded to Ulysses Kay, 754

"Funk" in hard bop, 764

The Funny House of a Negro, by Adrienne Kennedy, 838

Future Farmers of America, Negro elected California chapter head, 174

Fortune, T. Thomas, as author, 55

G

Gaines, Lloyd: sues for admission to University of Missouri law school, 1938, 371; gains admission to Missouri Law School, 507

Gammon Theological Seminary: Congress on Africa, Atlanta, December 13-15, 1895, 680; Steward Foundation for Africa, 670

Gandy, Charles F.: awarded Silver Star, World War II, 639; receives promotion from General Clark, World War II, 639

Gans, Joe, prizefighter: world's lightweight champion, 1901-1908, 779, 780-81; in Boxing Hall of Fame, 780

Gantt, Harvey, secures admission to Clemson College, 507

Gardiner, Robert K., international civil servant, 688

Garnet, Henry Highland: as Minister to Liberia, 664; author, 35

Garretson, Freeborn, on sinfulness of slaveholding, 399

Garrison, William Lloyd: against Negro emigration, 663; supported by Negroes, 35

Garvey, Marcus: 675-76; dies, 1940, 476; emigrationist appeals, 69; lack of respect for African traditions, 676; as organizer of Universal Negro Improvement Association, 69; as Universal Negro Improvement Association leader, 476-77, 675

Garvey Movement, see Universal Negro Improvement Association

Gayle vs. Browder, 499

George, David, preacher, 400

George, William C.: diplomat, 664; appointed Vice Consul in Monrovia, Liberia, 1931, 664

George, Zelma Watson: as actress, 836; *Bibliographical Index to Negro Music,* 732; in *The Medium,* 842

George Gershwin Prize, won by Ulysses Kay, 754

George Peabody Fund, education of Negroes, 51

Georgetown University, Patrick Francis Healy as president, 563

Georgia: extent of desegregation in schools, 1964, 379; slave law, 1775, 13; slavery in, 13; slavery prohibited to 1750, 13

Georgia Council of Churches, Negro elected President, 1965, 410

Georgia Equal Rights League, 59

The Georgia Minstrels, organized, 1865, by Charles Hicks, 830

Germantown Quakers' Protest, 1688, 15

Gesell Committee, initial report, 1963, 658

Ghana, American Negroes encouraged to visit, 691-92

Gibson, Althea: as golfer, 809; as tennis player, 809-11

Gibson, Josh, baseball player, 799

Gilbert, Mercedes, author, 874

Gillem, Alvan C., studies Army racial policy, 1945, 653

Gilmore Medal, awarded to four Negro soldiers in Civil War, 40

Gilpin, Charles: actor, 832; in *The Emperor Jones,* 833

Gilpin Players, 835-36

Gini Index of income concentration, nonwhite and white, 1947-1960, 268-70

Giovanni's Room, by James Baldwin, 878

Globetrotters, Harlem, see Harlem Globetrotters

Go Tell It on the Mountain, by James Baldwin, 878

Goals, shared, as reducing prejudice, 716

God Sends Sunday: by Countée Cullen, 874; turned into musical, *St. Louis Woman,* 842

Godfrey, George, prizefighter, 789, 799

God's Trombones, by James Weldon Johnson, 67, 858, 873

Gold Coast, Negro missions to, 668

Goldwater, Barry, campaign affected by anti Civil Rights Act stand, 94

ment effect on scores, 394-95; in high school, as not predictive of Negro students' college success, 390

Interaction: effect on prejudice, 715-19; favorable, as reducing prejudice, 722-23; increased, as intensifying existing situation, 715

—situation characteristics favorable to reduced prejudice: common goals, 715-16; cooperative dependence, 715-17; equal status, 715-16; shared values, 716; support by authority, 715-17; effect on behavior, 719

Interdenominational Theological Center, Atlanta, Ga., formed by Methodist, AME, CME, and Baptist churches, 410

The Interesting Narrative of the Life of Gustavus Vassa, the African, by Olauda Equiano, 863-64

Intergroup Conflict and Cooperation: The Robbers Cave Experiment, by Muzafer Sherif, study of situational factors in prejudice, 722-23

Intergroup relations determined by differentiated groups, 724

International Conference on the Negro, Tuskegee, April 17-19, 1912: 683-84; poor African representation at, 683

International Council of Friends of Ethiopia, organized 1935, 75

International Ladies' Garment Workers Union, accepts Negroes, 71

International Statistical Congress, Martin R. Delaney as member, 552

Interstate Commerce Commission, rules against segregation in interstate transportation, 1961, 474

Inventors, Negro, 53

Investment policies of Negro life insurance companies, compared with all life insurance companies, 319-21, 324

Invisible Man, by Ralph Ellison: 877; as American Booksellers Association award winner, 1953, 877

Ira Aldridge Chair, Shakespeare Memorial Theatre, Stratford-on-Avon, 832

Isaacs, Harold, on Negro-African relations in Africa, 666

J

Jack, Beau, see Beau Jack

Jack, Hulan, elected borough president of Manhattan, 444

Jackson, Alexander, athlete, 812

Jackson, Andrew, on Negro troops in Battle of New Orleans, 599

Jackson, Levi, football player, 804

Jackson, Mahalia: gospel singer, 743, 839; in March on Washington, 92, 744

Jackson, Peter: Frederick Douglass on, 786; as heavyweight champion of Australia, 780; prizefight with Gene Corbett, 780; as prizefighter, 779

Jackson, William Tecumseh Sherman: football player, 775, 802; as football player and runner, 812

James I, King of England, African trade charter granted by, 1618, 4

James E. Sullivan Memorial Trophy awarded by AAU to Negroes in 1954, 1955, 1960, 1961, 824

Jay, John, as president of the New York Society for Promoting the Manumission of Slaves, 21

Jazz: see also Bebop; Blues; Boogie-woogie; Dixieland jazz; Hard bop; Ragtime; at its best outside mainstream of American culture, 765; as blues-derived instrumental music, 760; contribution of French quadrilles to, 761; cool, 763-64; early use of Caribbean music, 761; East Coast, 764

—free: removes white conventions from jazz, 764; as return to primitive blues, 764-65

—as influenced by gospel music, 744; interchange with gospel music, 743; Langston Hughes' art likened to, 861; as partially developed from Negro marching bands, 760; not begun in New Orleans, 761; as part of city blues, 743-44; as producer of equality, 756

—progressive: as reaction to bebop, 763; as white attempt to use European music in jazz context, 763

—publicly accepted, 739; role in democratization of taste, 756; seen as inferior, 765; Soul, as cool jazz, with gospel music influence, 744; spread by northward migrations, 761-62; use of African rhythms, 761

—bands: 738-39; first, on New York stage, 738; development as responsible for

Johnson, Leroy, as member of Georgia Senate, 423

Johnson, Lyndon B.: aids civil rights, 481; appoints Hobart Taylor assistant special counsel, 430; appoints Negroes to offices, 84-85; as chairman of President's Committee on Equal Employment Opportunity, 88; directs government agencies to recruit more Negroes into civil service, 430; Negro support, 1964, 94; strong civil rights position, 93

Johnson, Malvin Gray, painter, 768

Johnson, Mordecai W.: on Negro higher education expenditures in South, 1947, 384; as president of Howard University, 384

Johnson, Rafer: in Americans Abroad program, 824-25; as Olympic champion, 1960, 821; as winner of AAU James E. Sullivan Memorial Trophy, 1960, 824

Johnson, Robert, folk singer, 741-42

Johnson, Sargent: as abstractionist artist, 773; as sculptor, 770

Johnson, Stone, athlete, Olympic team member, 819

Johnson, William H.: as painter, 768-69; as primitive painter, 772-73

Johnson C. Smith University, established 1867, 367

Joint Committee on National Recovery, 72

Jonah's Gourd Vine, by Zora N. Hurston, 874

Jones, Absolom, as early African Methodist Episcopal Church leader, 24

Jones, Edward A.: as Episcopal priest in West Africa, 550; as first American Negro college graduate, 550

Jones, J. Raymond, elected chairman of N.Y. County Democratic Committee, 1965, 425

Jones, LeRoi: playwright, 838; *Dutchman*, defeatism in, 847; *Preface to a Twenty-Volume Suicide Note*, 863

Jones, Lois, painter, 772

Jones, Lou, athlete, Olympic team member, 1956, 818

Jones, Richard L., as Ambassador to Liberia, 1955-1956, 664

Jones, Sissieretta: 830-31; invited to sing at White House, 831

Jones, Thomas Jesse, 687

Jones-Quartey, K., as founder of *The African Interpreter*, 690

Jordan, L. G., report on missionary work of National Baptist Convention, 1912, 668

Joss, Addie, baseball player, 799

Journal of Negro Education: 74; founded, 1932, 370

Journal of Negro History: 74; published by Association for the Study of Negro Life and History, 677

"Juba Dance," music by R. Nathaniel Dett, 749

Jubilees, see Folk Music, Negro

Judges: Negro, 583; Negroes as, 426

Jugband revived by white performers, 742

The Juggler of Our Lady, opera by Ulysses Kay, 754

Julian, Colonel, pilot ("The Black Eagle"), 705

Julius Rosenwald Fund, grants for Negro school construction, 1913-1932, 369

Jumping, see Track and field athletics

Jury service: discrimination, as grounds for reversal of Negro convictions, 518-19; right guaranteed by 1875 Civil Rights Act, 518; right not enforced, to 1956, 518; by slaves, prohibited, 517

Just, Ernest E., education, 560

Just a Little Simple, by Alice Childress, 835

K

Kansas, refuses Negro suffrage, 1865-1868, 421

Karamu Theatre, Cleveland, presentation of Negro plays, 835-36

Katzenback vs. McClung, 496

Kay, Ulysses: as composer, 754; as Fulbright scholarship winner, 754; as George Gershwin Prize winner, Prix de Rome winner, 754; visits USSR, 1958, on cultural exchange program, 754

Kearsarge (Battleship), Negroes on, 610

Keene, Paul, abstractionist artist, 773

Keith, George, against slavery, 1693, 15

Kemble, Fanny, on free Negroes, 34

Kennedy, Adrienne, *The Funny House of a Negro,* 838

Little Stephen, explorer, 2

Livestock farming, Southern Negro: 1945-1959, 168; compared with white, 178

Liza, musical, 841

Lloyd, John Henry, baseball player, 799

Lloyd, Rupert: in diplomatic service in Liberia, 664; as Principal Officer of the United States Consulate in Tegucigalpa, Honduras, 664

Locke, Alain: educated at Central High School, Philadelphia, Pa., 560; in Howard University's fine arts program, 772; *The New Negro,* on Negro struggle for rights, 66-67; selection of representatives of "New Negro" in art, 773; on Carnegie Hall Concert of Negro Music, 1912, 738-39; on Will Marion Cook, 738-39; on Ford Dabney, 738-39; on Jim Europe, 738-39; on W. C. Handy, 738-39; criticism of Herskovitz' theory of African survivals in folk music, 735

Locke, John, on slavery, 12

Locker, Jesse D., as Ambassador to Liberia, 1953-1955, 664

Loendi Club (basketball team), 806

Logan, Rayford W.: *The Negro in American Life and Thought,* shows prejudice of American journals, 47-48; in World War I, 617

Lomax, Alan, on folk music, 740

London, Jack, on Jack Johnson, 782

The Long Dream, by Richard Wright: 876; defeatism in, 847

Longview, Texas, race riot, 1919, 65

"The Lotos-Eaters," painting by Robert S. Duncanson, 767

Lott Carey Baptist Foreign Missionary Convention, 673

Louis, Joe: prizefighter, 779, 787-89; breaks prizefighting color bar, 788-89; financial problems, 790; as race hero, 787-88; sportsmanship as helping Negro fighters, 789; in U.S. Army, 788; as world's heavyweight champion, June 22, 1937 to March 1, 1949, 788

Louisiana: disfranchises Negroes, 1898, 50; extent of desegregation in schools, 1964, 379-80; provision for Negro education after 1865, 365

Louisville Cubs (baseball club), 798

The Love of Landry, by Paul Laurence Dunbar, 871

Lovejoy, Elijah: abolitionist, 868; employs William Wells Brown, 868

Luca Family, musicians, 752

Lucas, Sam, comedian, 830

Lucy, Autherine, pioneer in school desegregation, 545

Lulu Belle, play by David Belasco, 833

Lunceford, Jimmie, jazz band, 762

Lynch, John R.: as U.S. Congressman, 43, 422; as speaker of Mississippi House, 43

Lynching: denounced by Franklin D. Roosevelt, 70; states with laws against, 517; number, 1882-1964, 516; 1900-1915, 467

Lyons, Jimmy, baseball player, 799

Lyrics of a Lowly Life, by Paul Laurence Dunbar, 55, 856-57

Lyrics of Life and Love, by William Braithwaite, 858

Lyrics of Love and Laughter, by Paul Laurence Dunbar, 857

Lyrics of Sunshine and Shadow, by Paul Laurence Dunbar, 857

M

M Street High School, Washington, D.C., preparation of Negro students for college study, 561-62

Mabley, Jackie Moms, comedienne, 837-38, 840

MacArthur, Douglas, willingness to use Negro troops, 637

"Magnolia Suite," music by R. Nathaniel Dett, 749

Maine, enfranchises Negroes on equal terms with whites, before 1865, 418

Majors and Minors, by Paul Laurence Dunbar, 857

Malcolm X: 479; announces intention to form national movement with immediate political objectives, 1964, 452; assassinated, 1965, 452, 479; entertained in UAR and Ghana, 699-700; as founder of Organization of Afro-American Unity, 1963, 479; as "race hero," 479

Manhattan, Borough of, President a Negro since 1950's, 425

Manumission Society, see New York Society for Promoting the Manumission of Slaves

"Outhouse" school of Negro printmakers, 771-73
The Outsider, by Richard Wright, 876
Overstreet, Joe, expressionist painter, 774
Overton, Ada, actress, 831
Overton, "Monk," jockey, 794
Overture, by Ulysses Kay, 754
Ovington, Mary White, and founding of National Negro Committee, 466
Owen, Chandler, receives jail sentence, 64
Owens, Jesse: as athlete, 813-19, 824; in Americans Abroad program, 824-25; as example to young people, 823; at 1936 Olympics, 822; as Olympic gold medalist, 822

P

Padmore, George: as Communist, 686; founds Pan-African Federation, 1936, 687; and 5th Pan-African Congress, 1945, 690-91; calls 6th Pan-African Congress, 1958, 692; *Pan-Africanism or Communism?,* 686; as publisher of *The Negro Workers,* 686; rejects Communism, 1936, 687
Pagan Spain, by Richard Wright, 876
Paige, Leroy "Satchel," baseball player, 799
Paine, Thomas, as member of Pennsylvania Abolition Society, 362
Painters, Negro: 771-74; abroad, 768-69; in Europe, 774; murals on Negro life, 769; primitive, 772-73; as teachers, 768
Painting, Negro: 766-69, 771-74; to 1800, 766-67; 1800-1865; 767-68; 1865-1890, 768; after 1890, 768-69; expressionist, 774
Pan-African Conference, London, 1900, 680-81
Pan-African Congress: 1st, February 19-21, 1919, 685; 2nd, 1923, 685; 3rd, convened by W. E. B. DuBois, 686; 4th, convened by W. E. B. DuBois, 686; 5th, 1945, 690-91; 6th, 1958, 692-93
Pan-African Congress movement, leadership passes to African leaders, 1945, 691
Pan-African Federation, London, founded 1936, by George Padmore, 687
Pan-Africanism: continental, emergence, 1958, 693

—racial: 673-79; in African-American Negro relations, 667, 673-79; in "Back to Africa" movements, 673-74; as based on fight against racism, 699-700; defined, 673; decline in interest after 1925, 686; emigrationist variety rejected by Negro leaderhip, 675; influence on African nationalists, 678; influence on Negro missionary movement, 673; as intellectual movement, 676-79; as joint effort of African, West Indian, and American Negroes, 679; originated by American Negroes, 678
Pan-Africanism or Communism?, by George Padmore, 686
Park, Robert E., and Congo Reform Association, 681
Parker, Charlie, jazz musician, 763-64, 765
Parker, Hattie, gospel singer, 743
Parker, John J., rejected from Supreme Court by Negro influence, 68
Parker, John P.: inventor of screw for tobacco presses, 53; manufacturer of tobacco presses, 53
Parks, Rosa, in Montgomery, Ala., bus boycott, 89, 470, 545
Parson, James B., on U.S. District Court, 84
Pastors, see Ministers
The Path of Dreams, by George Marion McClellan, 856
Patronage: controlled by Negro bosses, 429
—Federal: Negro Republican national committeemen accused of selling, 428; turnover hard on Negroes, early 20th century, 426-27
Patterson, Floyd: world's heavyweight champion, 789; in civil rights movement, 824
Patterson, Mary Jane: as first Negro woman college graduate, 1862, 534-35; as principal of M Street High School, Washington, D.C., 1870-1871, 1873-1874, 561
Paul Laurence Dunbar High School, Washington, D.C., see M Street High School, Washington, D.C.
Pay: see also Incomes
—equal: for Negro Civil War chaplains, granted, 609; to Negro musicians in

414; Negroes in, 84; Northern, Negro, 1865-1965, 423-26

Polk, L. B.: in Bureau of African Affairs, U.S. Department of State, 664; in diplomatic service in Liberia, 664

Poll tax: abolished, 1964, 436; abolition, 1964, small effect on voter registration, 436; Southern, after Reconstruction, 423; Southern, eliminated, 1963, by Constitutional amendment, 423; eliminated in Federal elections, 1964, 493

Pollard, Frederick Douglass, see Pollard, Fritz

Pollard, Fritz: football player, 796-97, 802-03, 804; All-American football player, 1916, 803

Pompey (slave), see Lamb, Pompey

Poole, Cecil, as U.S. Attorney, 84

Poole, Elijah, see Elijah Muhammed

Poor, Salem: in Battle of Bunker Hill, 19-20; commended by Mass. General Court for bravery, 593

Popular music, influenced by Negro music, 756

Population, free Negro: 1790-1860, 33; 1860, percentage of total Negro population, 559

Population, Negro: 96-160; Carolinas, 18th century, 12; Connecticut, 18th century, 16; Georgia, 18th century, 13; Massachusetts, 18th century, 16; New England, 18th century, 16; New Hampshirt, 18th century, 16; New Jersey, 18th century, 14-15; New York, 18th century, 14; Pennsylvania, 18th century, 15; Rhode Island, 18th century, 16; Virginia, 17th-18th centuries, 9; 1788, 23; 1790, 98; 1860, 98; 1866-1900, 46; 1900-1960, 556; 1940-1960, faster increase than white, 337; 1960, 98, 337, 522; 1962, 337; age distribution, 523; age characteristics of, farmer, 187-88; approaching white population in characteristics, 98; characteristics of as result of colonial patterns, 98; characteristics projected, 1985, 158; cities with highest, 1960, 118-20; as concentrated in few locations, 123; Congressional districts with high proportion, 1962, 433; decline expected after Civil War, 45; effect on attitudes of political representatives, 455-56

—female: 552; age distribution, 522-23; never married, percentage, 1960, 536; impoverished, 527; as proportion of total female population, 522; in proportion to Negro male population, 522-23; in proportion to Negro male population, effect on marriage, 522-23; in proportion to Negro male population, geographical distribution, 523; single, smaller than Negro male single, 536; 65, never married, percentage, 1960, 536; 65 and over, 525; 65 and over, mostly in South, 525

—foreign-born, 1900-1960, 109; impoverished, percentage, 529; male, never married, percentage, 1960, 536; median age lower than white, 523; Northern, proportion related to passage of state civil rights legislation, 452-53; percentage 19 or under, 523; proportion in farming, compared with white, 1965, 170-71; proportion of slave and free, 1790-1860, 100; proportion to white varied, 1630-1960, 102; proportional decline in South, 1860-1960, 105; proportional decline in South, 1860-1960, race relations related to, 105; by region, proportions, 1790-1960, 102, 468; rural, projected increase after 1970-1975, 204; rural farm, decrease, 1950-1960, 203; rural nonfarm, 1920-1960, 203; Northern due to migration, 108; Northern, origin of, 120; outside South, 1910-1962, 337; outside South, 1940-1960, 83-84; decline in South since 1910, 109; non-homogeneity in South, 105, 107-08; Southern, proportion of total Negro population, 1914, 467; Southern, proportion inversely related to voter registration, 437

—urban: see also Urbanization, Negro; 1860-1900, 57; 1910-1960, 115-36; 1910-1960, percentage compared to white, 118; 1940-1960, 83-84; 1950-1960, concentrated in central cities, 338-39; effect of increase on schools, 391-93; 1960 per cent, 432; increase of as partially due to high birth rate, 120; increase of a problem, 159; Southern, 1950-1960, decrease compared with white, 338

Population:

—nonwhite: 21 and over, 1960, 431;

ber, 1950-1960, 286; growth in number, 1950-1960, compared with white, 286; income increase, 1949-1959, 286-87; in Negro market, modest income gains, 1949-1959, 287

Saratoga (Battle), Negroes at, 20

"Sammy," sculpture by Sargent Johnson, 770

San Juan Hill (cavalry charge), Negroes in, 614-15

Sands, Diana, in *The Owl and the Pussy Cat*, 849

Santiago de Cuba (Battle), Negro participation, 614

St. Domingo: Its Revolutions and Its Patriots, by William Wells Brown, 869

Saperstein, Abe, as Harlem Globetrotters founder, 807-08

Saturation programs in education, described, 395

Saunders, Gertrude, actress, 840

Savage Holiday, by Richard Wright, 876

Savannah, Siege of: 1779, Negroes in, 20-21; 1779, St. Domingo legion at, 596; (Civil War), Negroes in, 40

Savings and loan associations, Negro, number, 1963, 297

Savings, nonwhite, increase if discrimination ended, 283

Savoy, Willard, author, 877

Scapegoating as factor in prejudice, 710-11

Scarborough, William S.: 557-58; as philologist, 557; slave-born, 557-58

Scenes in the Life of Harriet Tubman, by Harriet Tubman, 864

Scholar, defined, 548

Scholars, Negro: 548-89; contributions, 565-66; early, derived from upper class, 558-59; handicapped, 548-49, 566-67; as percentage of total scholars, 566; produced by unusual circumstances of literacy and economic security, 566-67

Scholarship, Negro: environment as factor, 558-59; racist explanation, 558

School: see also Education; age-grade retardation of Negro farm children in, 189

—average number of years completed: by Negroes, 144; by nonwhites, 1940-1962, compared with whites, 340; Negro Southern population compared with

white, 199; nonwhite farm population, compared with nonwhite urban population, 1960, 188; nonwhite farm population, compared with white urban population, 1960, 188; nonwhite, and income, compared with white, 260-62

—boards, Negro members, 425-26; boycotts, Chicago and New York, 93; districts, Southern, desegregated, 1961-1964, 357, 377; dropouts, Negro, 1961, 341-42; dropouts, Negro female, 533-34, 541; integration decision of Supreme Court, 1954, Southern opposition to, 82; Negro concentration in lower grades, 1920, 369; Negro enrollment, 1876-1895, increase compared with white, 368; Negro retardation, forces lack of self-esteem, 395; percentage of Negroes enrolled, 144; population, Negro, cities with over 50%, 391; proportion of nonwhites attending, 1960, compared with white, 340-41

Schools:

—desegregated: border states, number of Negro children attending, 1963, 375; former Confederate states, number of Negro children attending, 1963, 375; in South, 1964, 94; Southern, number of Negro children attending, 1963, 375

—elementary, Northern, urban, proportion nonwhite, 390-91; high, see high schools

—mission: 559-60; education of future physicians, 574; provision of academic background necessary to freedmen's advancement, 559-60

—Negro: inferior, 387; support in 1901, 51; urban, inferior, 394-95

—segregated, inadequate, 50

—urban: affected by population trends, 392; inadequate for present population density, 391-93; racially imbalanced, 391-93

"The Schooners," painting by Palmer Hayden, wins William E. Harmon Prize, 1928, 771

Schuyler, George, *Slaves Today*, 686

Scotia Seminary, established by Presbyterian Church, 367

Scott, Dred, 484

Scott, Dred vs. Sandford, 1857, 484-86

W